THE GOLD STANDARD

DAT BIOLOGY

Book I of IV

Gold Standard Contributors
• 4-Book GS DAT Set •

Brett Ferdinand BSc MD-CM
Karen Barbia BS Arch
Brigitte Bigras BSc MSc DMD
Ibrahima Diouf BSc MSc PhD
Amir Durmic BSc Eng
Adam Segal BSc MSc
Da Xiao BSc DMD
Naomi Epstein BEng
Lisa Ferdinand BA MA
Jeanne Tan Te
Kristin Finkenzeller BSc MD
Heaven Hodges BSc
Sean Pierre BSc MD
James Simenc BS (Math), BA Eng
Jeffrey Cheng BSc
Timothy Ruger MSc PhD
Petra Vernich BA
Alvin Vicente BS Arch

DMD Candidates

E. Jordan Blanche BS
[Harvard School of Dental Medicine]
Stephan Suksong Yoon BA
[Harvard School of Dental Medicine]

Gold Standard Illustrators
• 4-Book GS DAT Set •

Daphne McCormack
Nanjing Design
· Ren Yi, Huang Bin
· Sun Chan, Li Xin
Fabiana Magnosi
Harvie Gallatiera
Rebbe Jurilla BSc MBA

RuveneCo

The Gold Standard DAT was built for the US DAT.

The Gold Standard DAT is identical to Canadian DAT prep except QR and ORG.
Also, you must practice soap carving for the complete Canadian DAT.

The Gold Standard DAT is identical to OAT prep except PAT, which is replaced by OAT Physics; see our Gold Standard OAT book for Physics review and OAT practice test.

Be sure to register at www.DAT-prep.com by clicking on GS DAT Owners and following the directions for Gold Standard DAT Owners. Please Note: benefits are for 1 year from the date of online registration, for the original book owner only and are not transferable; unauthorized access and use outside the Terms of Use posted on DAT-prep.com may result in account deletion; if you are not the original owner, you can purchase your virtual access card separately at DAT-prep.com.

Visit The Gold Standard's Education Center at www.gold-standard.com.

ISBN 978-1-927338-09-4

Address all inquiries, comments, or suggestions to the publisher. For Terms of Use go to: www.DAT-prep.com

RuveneCo Inc
Gold Standard Multimedia Education
559-334 Cornelia St
Plattsburgh, NY 12901
E-mail: learn@gold-standard.com
Online at www.gold-standard.com

Table of Contents

EXAM SUMMARY

The Dental Admission Test (DAT) consists of 280 multiple-choice questions distributed across quite a diversity of question types in four tests. The DAT is a computer-based test (CBT). This exam requires approximately five hours to complete - including the optional tutorial, break, and post-test survey. The following are the four subtests of the Dental Admission Test:

1. Survey of the Natural Sciences (NS) – 100 questions; 90 min.
   - General Biology (BIO): 40 questions
   - General Chemistry (CHM): 30 questions
   - Organic Chemistry (ORG): 30 questions
2. Perceptual Ability Test (PAT) - 90 questions; 6 subsections; 60 min.
   - Apertures: 15 questions
   - Orthographic or View Recognition: 15 questions
   - Angle Discrimination: 15 questions
   - Paper Folding: 15 questions
   - Cube Counting: 15 questions
   - 3-D Form Development: 15 questions
3. Reading Comprehension (RC) – 50 questions; 3 reading passages; 60 min.
4. Quantitative Reasoning (QR) – 40 questions; 45 min.
   - Mathematics Problems: 30 questions
   - Applied Mathematics/Word Problems: 10 questions

You will get six scores from: (1) BIO (2) CHM (3) ORG (4) PAT (5) QR (6) RC.

You will get two additional scores which are summaries:
(7) Academic Average (AA) = BIO + CHM + ORG + QR + RC
(8) Total Science (TS) = BIO + CHM + ORG

Common Formula for Acceptance:

GPA + DAT score + Interview = Dental School Admissions*

*Note: In general, Dental School Admissions Committees will only examine the DAT score if the GPA is high enough; they will only admit or interview if the GPA + DAT score is high enough. Some programs also use autobiographical materials and/or references in the admissions process. Different dental schools may emphasize different aspects of your DAT score, for example: PAT, BIO, TS, AA. The average score for any section is approximately 17/30; the average AA for admissions is usually 18-20 depending on the dental school; the AA for admissions to Harvard is around 22-23; the 100th percentile is usually 25 meaning that virtually 100% of the approximately 13 000 students who take the DAT every year have an AA less than 25. Only a handful of students score 25/30. Our two student contributors scored 27/30 (AA).

PREFACE

The DAT is challenging, get organized.

dat-prep.com/dat-study-schedule

1. How to study:

1. Study the Gold Standard (GS) books and videos to learn
2. Do GS Chapter review practice questions
3. Consolidate: create and review your personal summaries (= Gold Notes) daily

2. Once you have completed your studies:

1. Full-length practice test
2. Review mistakes, all solutions
3. Consolidate: review all your Gold Notes and create more
4. Repeat until you get beyond the score you need for your targeted dental school

3. Full-length practice tests:

1. ADA practice exams
2. Gold Standard DAT exams
3. TopScore Pro exams
4. Other sources if needed

4. How much time do you need?

On average, 3-6 hours per day for 3-6 months

WARNING: Study more or study more efficiently. You choose. The Gold Standard has condensed the content that you require to excel at the DAT. We have had Ivy League dental students involved in the production of the Gold Standard series so that pre-dent students can feel that they have access to the content required to get a score satisfactory at any dental school in the country. To make the content easier to retain, you can also find aspects of the Gold Standard program in other formats such as:

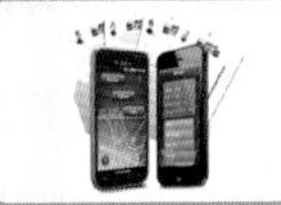

Is there something in the Gold Standard that you did not understand? Don't get frustrated, get online.

dat-prep.com/forum dat-prep.com/QRchanges-2015

Good luck with your studies!

Gold Standard Team

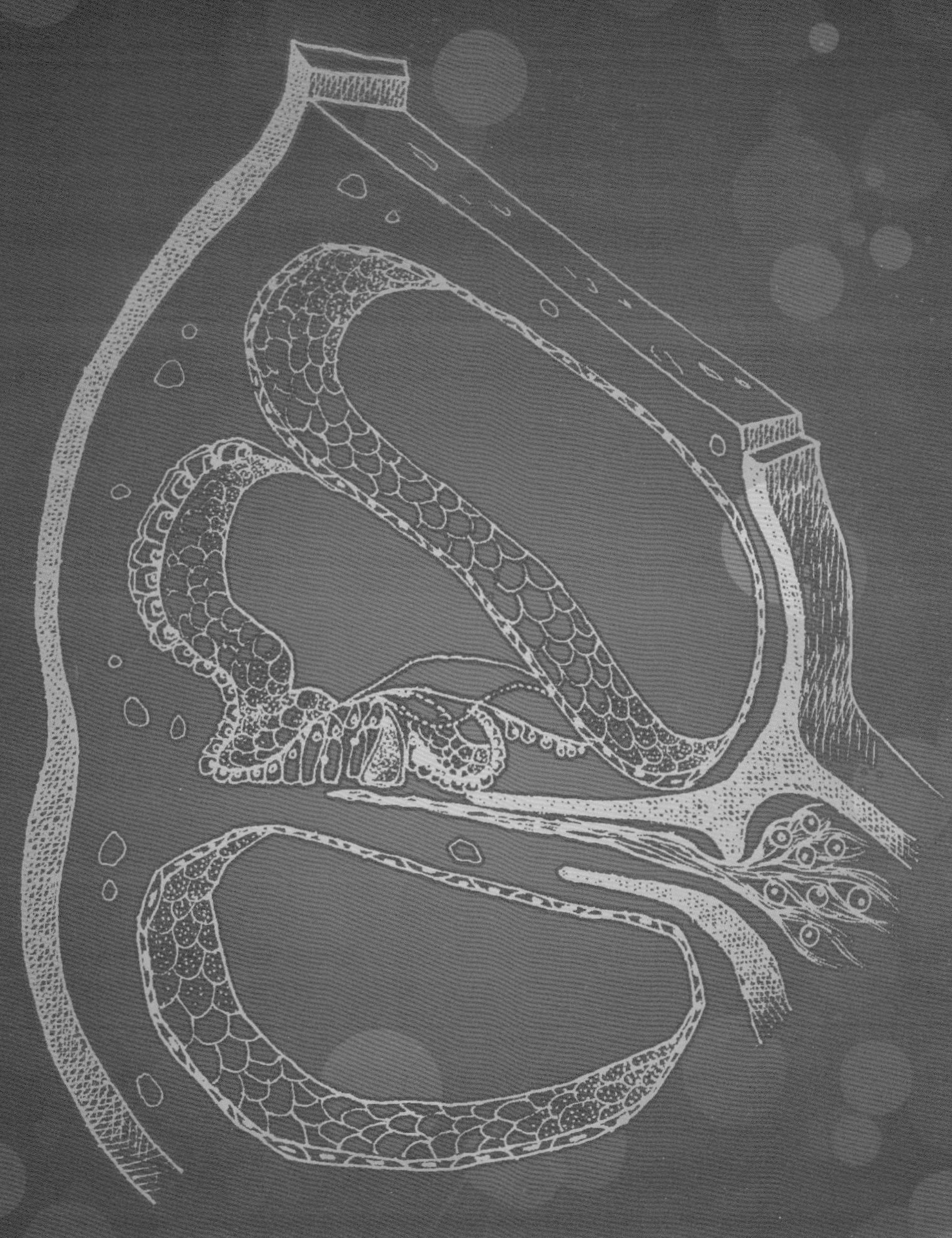

DAT-Prep.com

BIOLOGY

BIOLOGY

GENERALIZED EUKARYOTIC CELL
Chapter 1

Memorize

* Structure/function: cell/components
* Components and function: cytoskeleton
* DNA structure and function
* Transmission of genetic information
* Mitosis, events of the cell cycle
* Cell junctions, microscopy

Understand

* Membrane transport
* Hyper/hypotonic solutions
* Saturation kinetics: graphs
* Unique features of eukaryotes

Importance

2 to 5 out of the 40 Biology DAT questions are based on content in this chapter (in our estimation).

* Note that between 25% and 50% of the questions in DAT Biology are from 5 chapters: 1, 2, 14, 15, and 16.

DAT-Prep.com

Introduction

Cells are the basic organizational unit of living organisms. They are contained by a plasma membrane and/or cell wall. Eukaryotic cells (*eu* = true; *karyote* refers to nucleus) are cells with a true nucleus found in all multicellular and nonbacterial unicellular organisms including animal, fungal and plant cells. The nucleus contains genetic information, DNA, which can divide into 2 cells by mitosis. Please note: we will begin to explore characteristics specific to plant cells in Chapter 17.

Additional Resources

Free Online Q&A + Forum

Video: Online or DVD

Flashcards

Special Guest

1.1 Plasma Membrane: Structure and Functions

The plasma membrane is a semipermeable barrier that defines the outer perimeter of the cell. It is composed of lipids (fats) and protein. The membrane is dynamic, selective, active, and fluid. It contains phospholipids which are amphipathic molecules. They are amphipathic because their tail end contains fatty acids which are insoluble in water (*hydrophobic)*, the opposite end contains a charged phosphate head which is soluble in water (*hydrophilic*). The plasma membrane contains two layers or "leaflets" of phospholipids thus it is called a bilipid layer. Unlike eukaryotic membranes, prokaryotic membranes do not contain steroids such as cholesterol.

The Fluid Mosaic Model tells us that the hydrophilic heads project to the outside and the hydrophobic tails project towards the inside of the membrane. Further, these phospholipids are fluid - thus they move freely from place to place in the membrane. Fluidity of the membrane increases with increased temperature and with decreased saturation of fatty acyl tails. Fluidity of the membrane decreases with decreased temperature, increased saturation of fatty acyl tails and increase in the membrane's cholesterol content. The structures of these and other biological molecules are discussed in Chapter 20 of this book (= BIO 20).

Glycolipids are limited to the extracellular aspect of the membrane or outer leaflet. The carbohydrate portion of glycolipids extends from the outer leaflet into the extracellular space and forms part of the glycocalyx. "Glycocalyx" is the sugar coat on the outer surface of the outer leaflet of plasma membrane. It consists of oligosaccharide linked to

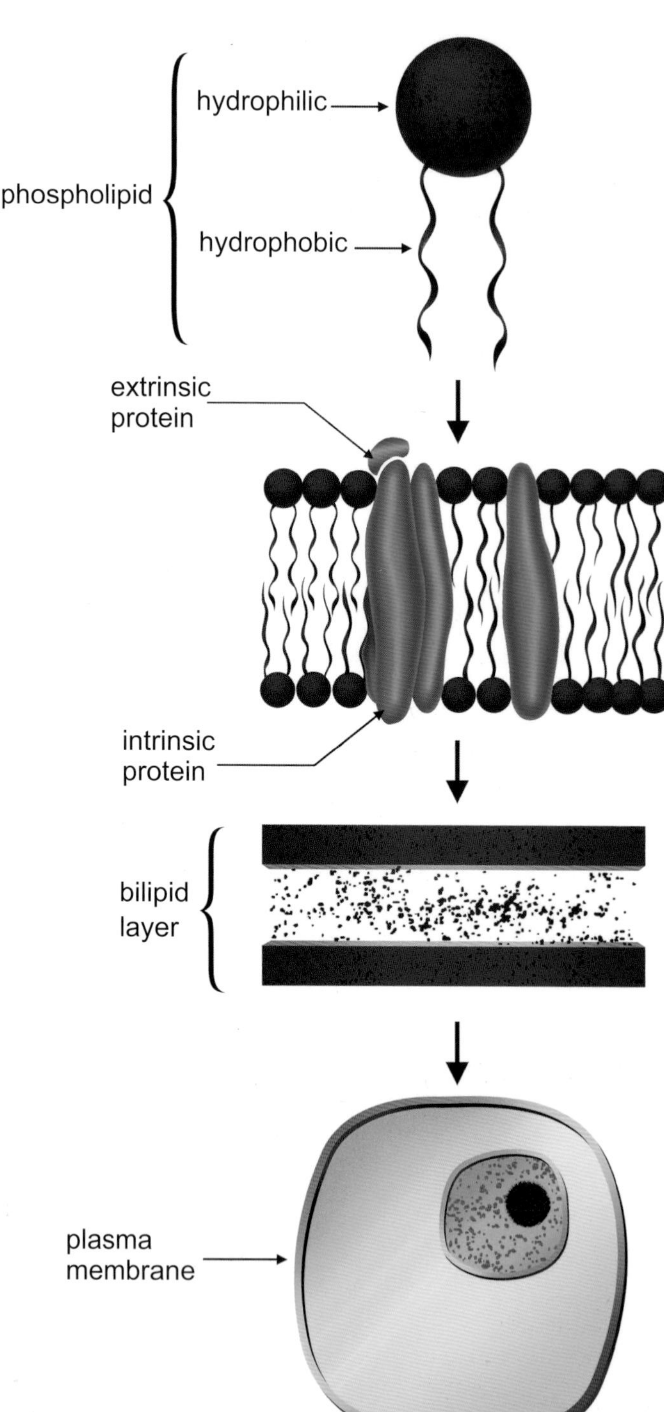

Figure IV.A.1.1: Structure of the plasma membrane. Note that: hydro = water, phobic = fearing, philic = loving

protein or lipids of the plasma membrane. The glycocalyx aids in attachment of some cells, facilitates cell recognition, helps bind antigen and antigen-presenting cells to the cell surface. Distributed throughout the membrane is a mosaic of proteins with limited mobility.

Proteins can be found associated with the outside of the membrane (extrinsic or peripheral) or may be found spanning the membrane (intrinsic or integral). Integral proteins are dissolved in the lipid bilayer. Transmembrane proteins contain hydrophilic and hydrophobic amino acids and cross the entire plasma membrane. Most transmembrane proteins are glycoproteins. They usually function as membrane receptors and transport proteins.

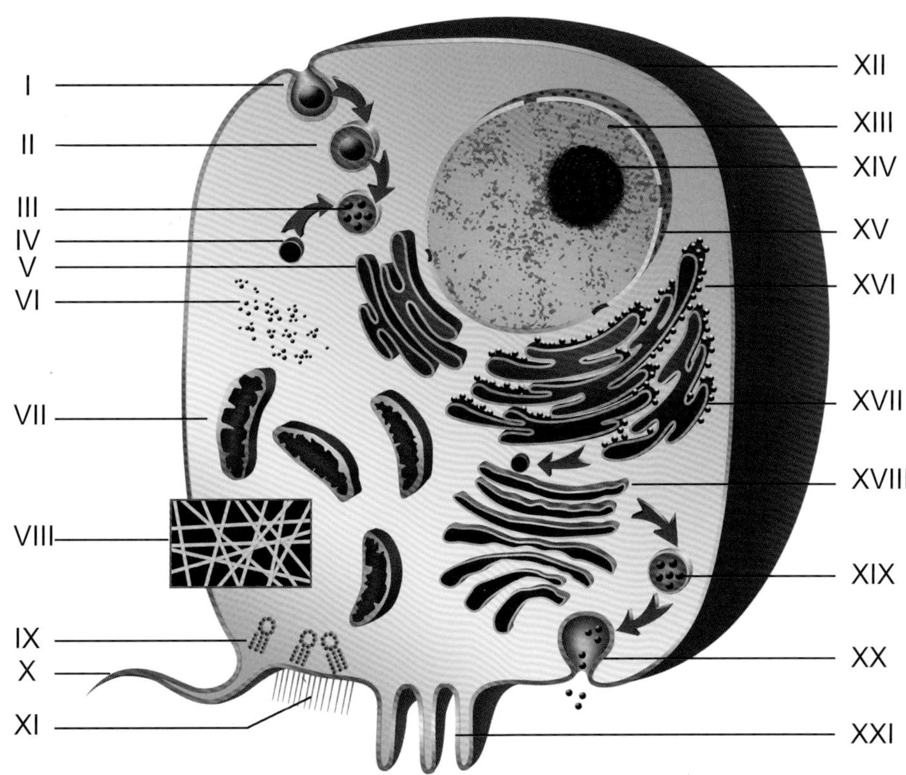

Figure IV.A.1.2: The generalized eukaryotic cell
To learn about the special characteristics of plant cells, see Chapter 17.

I	endocytosis	VIII	cytoskeleton (further magnified)	XV	nuclear envelope
II	endocytotic vesicle	IX	basal body (magnified)	XVI	cytosol
III	secondary lysosome	X	flagellum	XVII	rough endoplasmic reticulum
IV	primary lysosome	XI	cilia	XVIII	Golgi apparatus
V	smooth endoplasmic reticulum	XII	plasma membrane	XIX	exocytotic vesicle
VI	free ribosomes	XIII	nucleus	XX	exocytosis
VII	mitochondrion	XIV	nucleolus	XXI	microvillus

Peripheral proteins do not extend into the lipid bilayer but can temporarily adhere to either side of the plasma membrane. They bond to phospholipid groups or integral proteins of the membrane via noncovalent interactions. Common functions include regulatory protein subunits of ion channels or transmembrane receptors, associations with the cytoskeleton and extracellular matrix, and as part of the intracellular second messenger system.

The plasma membrane is semipermeable. In other words, it is permeable to small uncharged substances which can freely diffuse across the membrane (i.e. O_2, CO_2, urea). The eukaryotic plasma membrane does not have pores, as pores would destroy the barrier function. On the other hand, it is relatively impermeable to charged or large substances which may require transport proteins to cross the membrane (i.e. ions, amino acids, sugars) or cannot cross the membrane at all (i.e. protein hormones, intracellular enzymes). Substances which can cross the membrane may do so by simple diffusion, carrier-mediated transport, or by endo/exocytosis.

1.1.1 Simple Diffusion

Simple diffusion is the spontaneous spreading of a substance going from an area of higher concentration to an area of lower concentration (i.e. a concentration gradient exists). Gradients can be of a chemical or electrical nature. A chemical gradient arises as a result of an unequal distribution of molecules and is often called a concentration gradient. In a chemical (or concentration) gradient, there is a higher concentration of molecules in one area than there is in another area, and molecules tend to diffuse from areas of high concentration to areas of lower concentration.

Figure IV.A.1.2.1a: Isotonic Solution. The fluid bathing the cell (i.e. red blood cell or RBC in this case; see BIO 7.5) contains the same concentration of solute as the cell's inside or cytoplasm. When a cell is placed in an isotonic solution, the water diffuses into and out of the cell at the same rate.

An electrical gradient arises as a result of an unequal distribution of charge. In an electrical gradient, there is a higher concentration of charged molecules in one area than in another (this is independent of the concentration of all molecules in the area). Molecules tend to move from areas of higher concentration of charge to areas of lower concentration of charge.

Figure IV.A.1.2.1b: Hypertonic Solution. Here the fluid bathing the RBC contains a high concentration of solute relative to the cell's cytoplasm. When a cell is placed in a hypertonic solution, the water diffuses out of the cell, causing the cell to shrivel (crenation).

Figure IV.A.1.2.1c: Hypotonic Solution. Here the surrounding fluid has a low concentration of solute relative to the cell's cytoplasm. When a cell is placed in a hypotonic solution, the water diffuses into the cell, causing the cell to swell and possibly rupture (lyse).

Osmosis is the diffusion of water across a semipermeable membrane moving from an area of higher water concentration (i.e. lower solute concentration = hypotonic) to an area of lower water concentration (i.e. higher solute concentration = hypertonic). The hydrostatic pressure needed to oppose the movement of water is called the osmotic pressure. Thus, an isotonic solution (i.e. the concentration of solute on both sides of the membrane is equal), would have an osmotic pressure of zero.

{Memory guide: notice that the "O" in hyp-O-tonic looks like a swollen cell. The O is also a circle which makes you think of the word "around." So IF the environment is hypOtonic AROUND the cell, then fluid rushes in and the cell swells like the letter O}.

1.1.2 Carrier-mediated Transport

Amino acids, sugars and other solutes need to reversibly bind to proteins (carriers) in the membrane in order to get across. Because there are a limited amount of carriers, if the concentration of solute is too high, the carriers would be saturated, thus the rate of crossing the membrane would level off (= saturation kinetics).

The two carrier-mediated transport systems are:

(i) facilitated transport where the carrier helps a solute diffuse across a membrane it could not otherwise penetrate. Facilitated diffusion occurs via ion channels or carrier proteins and transport molecules down a concentration of electrochemical gradient. Ions and large molecules are therefore able to cross the membrane that would otherwise be impermeable to them.

ii) active transport where energy (i.e. ATP) is used to transport solutes against their

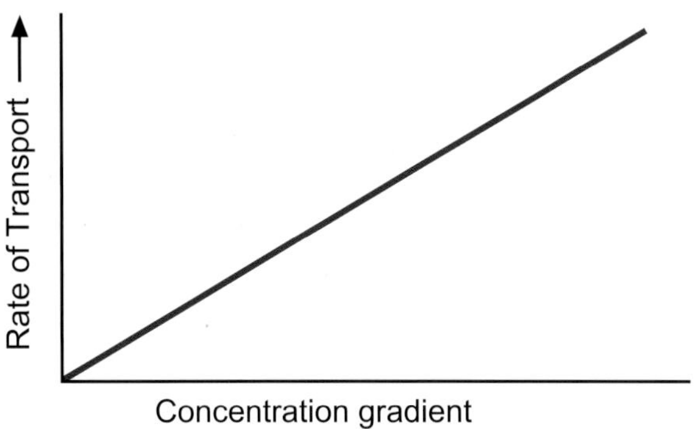

Simple Diffusion: the greater the concentration gradient, the greater the rate of transport across the plasma membrane.

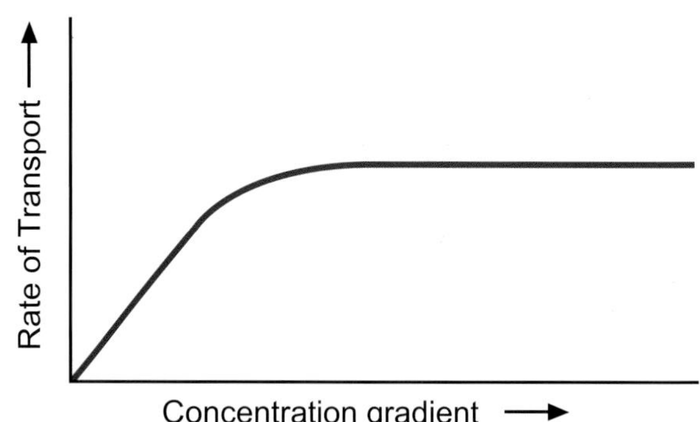

Carrier-mediated Transport: increasing the concentration gradient increases the rate of transport up to a maximum rate, at which point all membrane carriers are saturated.

Figure IV.A.1.3: Simple diffusion versus Carrier-mediated transport.

concentration gradients. The Na^+–K^+ exchange pump uses ATP to actively pump Na^+ to where its concentration is highest (outside the cell) and K^+ is brought within the cell where its concentration is highest (see Neural Cells and Tissues, BIO 5.1.1).

1.1.3 Endo/Exocytosis

Endocytosis is the process by which the cell membrane actually invaginates, pinches off and is released intracellularly (endocytotic vesicle). If a solid particle was ingested by the cell (i.e. a bacterium), it is called phagocytosis. If fluid was ingested, it is pinocytosis.

The receptor-mediated endocytosis of ligands (e.g. low density lipoprotein, transferrin, growth factors, antibodies, etc.) are mediated by clathrin-coated vesicles (CCVs). CCVs are found in virtually all cells and form areas in the plasma membrane termed clathrin-coated pits. Caveolae are the most common reported non-clathrin-coated plasma membrane buds, which exist on the surface of many, but not all cell types. They consist of the cholesterol-binding protein caveolin with a bilayer enriched in cholesterol and glycolipids.

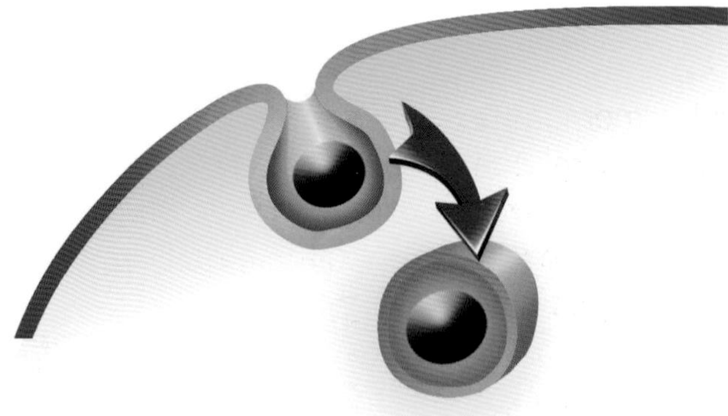

Figure IV.A.1.4: Endocytosis.

Exocytosis is, essentially, the reverse process. The cell directs an intracellular vesicle to fuse with the plasma membrane thus releasing its contents to the exterior (i.e. neurotransmitters, pancreatic enzymes, cell membrane proteins/lipids, etc.).

The transient vesicle fusion with the cell membrane forms a structure shaped like a pore (= *porosome*). Thus porosomes are cup-shaped structures where vesicles dock in the process of fusion and secretion. Porosomes contain many different types of protein including chloride and calcium channels, actin, and SNARE proteins that mediate the docking and fusion of vesicles with the cell membrane. The primary role of SNARE proteins is to mediate vesicle fusion through

Figure IV.A.1.5: Exocytosis.

full fusion exocytosis or open and close exocytosis. The former is where the vesicle collapses fully into the plasma membrane; in the latter, the vesicle docks transiently with the membrane (= “kiss-and-run”) and is recycled (i.e. in the synaptic terminal; BIO 1.5.1, 5.1).

1.2 The Interior of a Eukaryotic Cell

Cytoplasm is the interior of the cell. It refers to all cell components enclosed by the cell’s membrane which includes the cytosol, the cytoskeleton, and the membrane bound organelles. Transport within the cytoplasm occurs by cyclosis (circular motion of cytoplasm around the cell).

Cytosol is the solution which bathes the organelles and contains numerous solutes like amino acids, sugars, proteins, etc.

Cytoskeleton extends throughout the entire cell and has particular importance in shape and intracellular transportation. The cytoskeleton also makes extracellular complexes with other proteins forming a matrix so that cells can "stick" together. This is called cellular adhesion.

The components of the cytoskeleton in increasing order of size are: microfilaments, intermediate filaments, and microtubules. Microfilaments are important for cell movement and contraction (i.e. actin and myosin. See Contractile Cells and Tissues, BIO 5.2). Microfilaments, also known as actin filaments, are composed of actin monomer (G actin) linked into a double helix. They display polarity (= having distinct and opposite poles), with polymerization and depolymerization occuring preferentially at the barbed end [also called the plus (+) end which is where ATP is bound to G actin; BIO 5.2]. Microfilaments squeeze the membrane together in phagocytosis and cytokinesis. They are also important for muscle contraction and microvilli movement.

Intermediate filaments and microtubules extend along axons and dendrites of neurons acting like railroad tracks, so organelles or protein particles can shuttle to or from the cell body. Microtubules also form:

(i) the core of cilia and flagella (see the 9 doublet + 2 structure in BIO 1.5);
(ii) the mitotic spindles which we shall soon discuss; and
(iii) centrioles.

A flagellum is an organelle of locomotion found in sperm and bacteria. Eukaryotic flagella are made from microtubule configurations while prokaryotic flagella are thin strands of a single protein called flagellin. Thus, eukaryotic flagella move in a whip-like motion while prokaryotic flagella rotate. Cilia are hair-like vibrating organelles which can be used to move particles along the surface of the cell (e.g., in the fallopian tubes cilia can help the egg move toward the uterus). Microtubules are composed of tubulin subunits. They display polarity, with polymerization and depolymerization occuring preferentially at the plus end where GTP is bound to the tubulin subunit. Microtubules are involved in flagella and cilia construction, and the spindle apparatus. Centrioles are cylinder-shaped complexes of microtubules associated with the mitotic spindle (MTOC, see later). At the base of flagella and cilia, two centrioles can be found at right angles to each other: this is called a basal body.

Microvilli are regularly arranged finger-like projections with a core of cytoplasm (see BIO 9.5). They are commonly found in the small intestine where they help to increase the absorptive and digestive surfaces (= brush border).

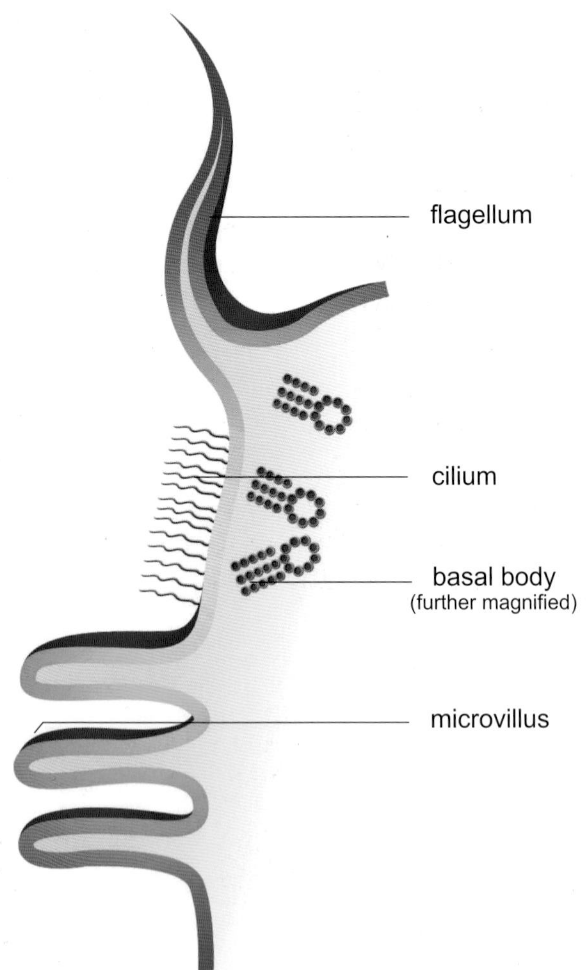

Figure IV.A.1.6: Cytoskeletal elements and the plasma membrane. The core of cilia and flagella is composed of 9 doublet or pairs of microtubules with another *doublet* in the center (= *axoneme*; see BIO 1.5).

1.2.1 Membrane Bound Organelles

Mitochondrion: The Power House

Mitochondria produce energy (i.e. ATP) for the cell through aerobic respiration (BIO 4.4). It is a double membraned organelle whose inner membrane has shelf-like folds which are called cristae. The matrix, the fluid within the inner membrane, contains the enzymes for the Krebs cycle and circular DNA. The latter is the only cellular DNA found outside of the nucleus with the exception of chloroplasts which will be discussed in Chapter 17. There are numerous mitochondria in muscle cells. Mitochondria synthesize ATP via the Krebs cycle via oxidation of glucose, amino acids or fatty acids.

Mitochondria have their own DNA and ribosomes and replicate independently from eukaryotic cells. However, most proteins used in mitochondria are coded by nuclear DNA, not mitochondrial DNA.

Figure IV.A.1.7: Mitochondria.

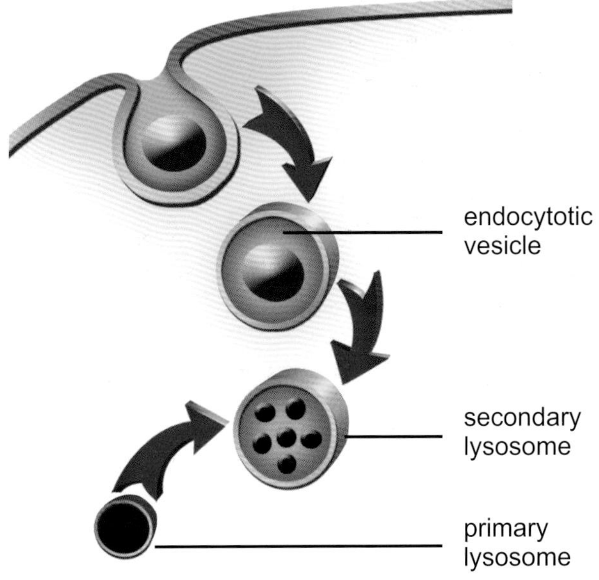

Figure IV.A.1.8: Heterolysis.

Lysosomes: Suicide Sacs

In a diseased cell, lysosomes may release their powerful acid hydrolases to digest away the cell (autolysis). In normal cells, a primary (normal) lysosome can fuse with an endocytotic vesicle to form a secondary lysosome where the phagocytosed particle (i.e. a bacterium) can be digested. This is called heterolysis. There are numerous lysosomes in phagocytic cells of the immune system (i.e. macrophages, neutrophils).

Endoplasmic Reticulum: Synthesis Center

The endoplasmic reticulum (ER) is an interconnected membraned system resembling flattened sacs and extends from the cell membrane to the nuclear membrane.

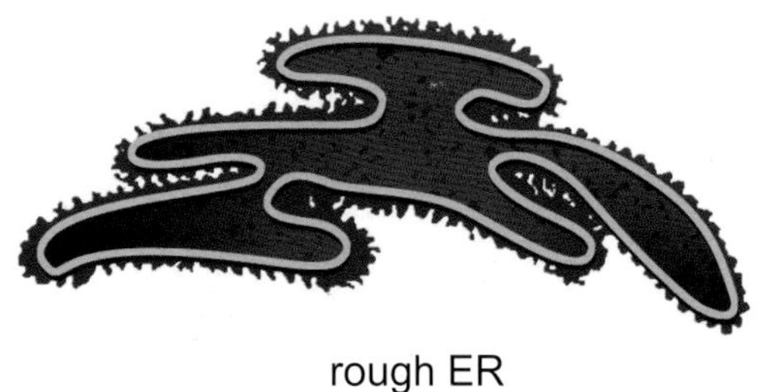

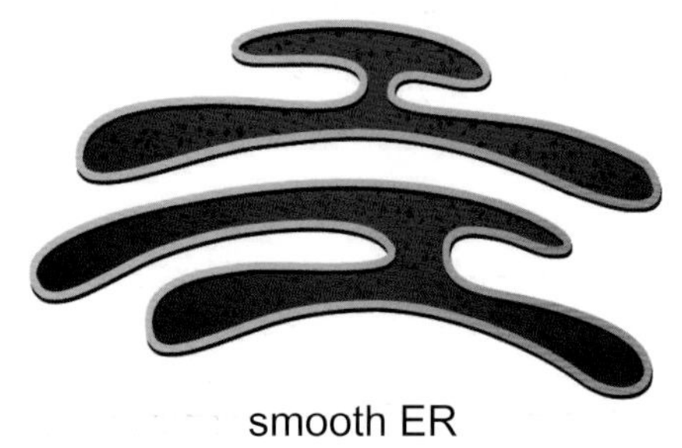

Figure IV.A.1.9: The endoplasmic reticulum.

There are two kinds: (i) dotted with ribosomes on its surface which is called rough ER and (ii) without ribosomes which is smooth ER.

The ribosomes are composed of ribosomal RNA (rRNA) and numerous proteins. It may exist freely in the cytosol or bound to the rough ER or outer nuclear membrane. The ribosome is a site where mRNA is translated into protein.

Rough ER is important in protein synthesis and is abundant in cells synthesizing secretory proteins. It is associated with the synthesis of secretory protein, plasma membrane protein, and lysosomal protein. Smooth ER is abundant in cells synthesizing steroids, triglycerides and cholesterol. It is associated with the synthesis and transport of lipids such as steroid hormone and detoxification of a variety of chemicals. It is also common in skeletal muscle cells involving muscle contraction and relaxation. It is a factor in phospholipid and fatty acid synthesis and metabolism.

Golgi Apparatus: The Export Department

The Golgi apparatus forms a stack of smooth membranous sacs or *cisternae* that function in protein modification, such as the addition of polysaccharides (i.e. glycosylation). The Golgi also packages secretory proteins in membrane bound vesicles which can be exocytosed.

The Golgi apparatus has a distinct polarity with one end being the "cis" face and the other being "trans". The cis face lies close to a separate vesicular-tubular cluster (VTC) also referred to as the ER-Golgi intermediate compartment (ERGIC) which is an organelle. The ERGIC mediates trafficking between the ER and Golgi complex, facilitating the sorting of 'cargo'. The medial (middle) compartment of the Golgi lies between the cis and trans faces. The trans face is oriented towards vacuoles

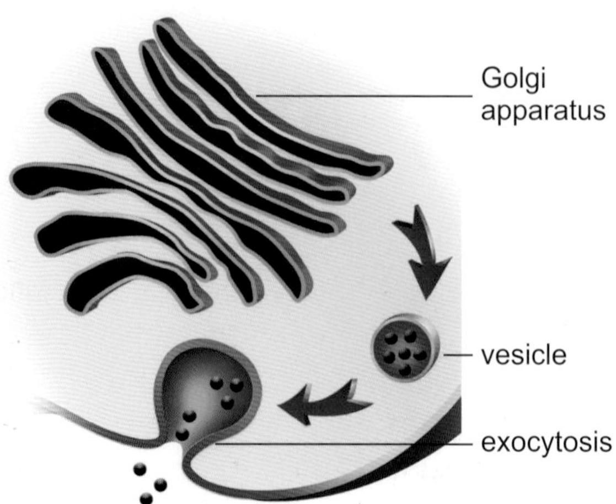

Figure IV.A.1.10: Golgi apparatus.

and secretory granules. The trans Golgi network separates from the trans face and sorts proteins for their final destination.

An abundant amount of rER and Golgi is found in cells which produce and secrete protein. For example, *B-cells* of the immune system which secrete antibodies, *acinar cells* in the pancreas which secrete digestive enzymes into the intestines, and *goblet cells* of the intestine which secrete mucus into the lumen.

Peroxisomes (Microbodies)

Peroxisomes are membrane bound organelles that contain enzymes whose functions include oxidative deamination of amino acids, oxidation of long chain fatty acids and synthesis of cholesterol.

The name "*perox*isome" comes from the fact that it is an organelle with enzymes that can transfer hydrogen from various substrates to oxygen, producing and then degrading hydrogen *perox*ide (H_2O_2).

The Nucleus

The nucleus is surrounded by a double membrane called the nuclear envelope. Throughout the membrane are nuclear pores which selectively allow the transportation of large particles to and from the nucleus. The nucleus is responsible for protein synthesis in the cytoplasm via ribosomal RNA (rRNA), messenger RNA (mRNA), and transfer RNA (tRNA).

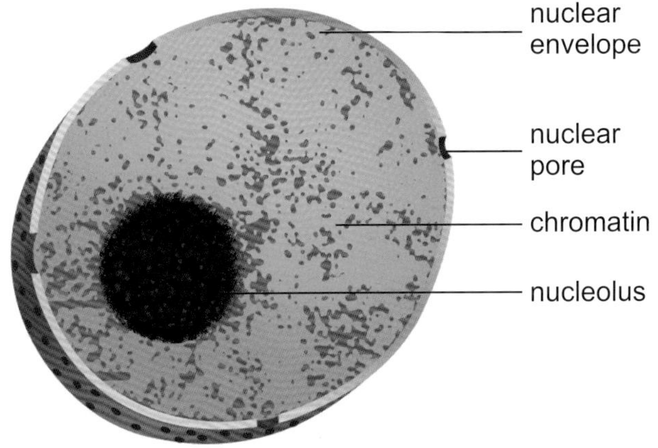

Figure IV.A.1.11: The nucleus.

DNA can be found within the nucleus as chromatin (DNA complexed to proteins like *histones*) or as chromosomes which are more clearly visible in a light microscope. The nucleolus is not membrane bound. It contains mostly ribosomal RNA and protein as well as the DNA necessary to synthesize ribosomal RNA.

The nucleolus is associated with the synthesis of ribosomal RNA (rRNA) and its assembly into ribosome precursors.

Chromosomes are basically extensively folded chromatin maintained by histone proteins. Each chromosome is composed of DNA and associated proteins, forming a nucleosome, the basic structural unit of chromatin. Chromatin exists as heterochromatin and euchromatin. Heterochromatin is a transcriptionally inactive form of chromatin while euchromatin is a transcriptionally active form of chromatin. Chromatin is responsible for RNA synthesis.

1.2.2 DNA: The Cell's Architect

Deoxyribonucleic Acid (DNA) and ribonucleic acid (RNA) are essential components in constructing the proteins which act as the cytoskeleton, enzymes, membrane channels, antibodies, etc. It is the DNA which contains the genetic information of the cell.

DNA and RNA are both important nucleic acids. Nucleotides are the subunits which attach in sequence or in other words polymerize via phosphodiester bonds to form nucleic acids. A nucleotide (also called a *nucleoside phosphate*) is composed of a five carbon sugar, a nitrogen base, and an inorganic phosphate.

The sugar in RNA is ribose but for DNA an oxygen atom is missing in the second position of the sugar thus it is 2-deoxyribose.

There are two categories of nitrogen bases: *purines* and *pyrimidines*. The purines have two rings and include adenine (A) and guanine (G). The pyrimidines contain one ring and include thymine (T), cytosine (C), and uracil (U).

DNA contains the following four bases: adenine, guanine, thymine, and cytosine. RNA contains the same bases except uracil is substituted for thymine.

Watson and Crick's model of DNA has allowed us to get insight into what takes shape as the nucleotides polymerize to form this special nucleic acid. The result is a double *helical* or *stranded* structure.

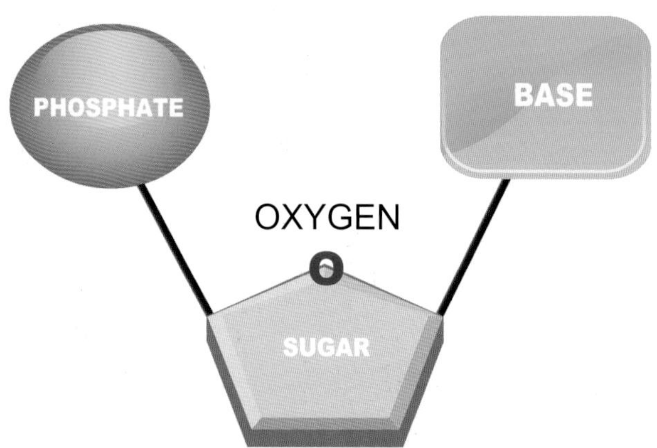

Figure IV.A.1.12: Nucleotide.

The DNA double helix is composed of two complementary and anti-parallel DNA strands held together by hydrogen bonds between base pairing A-T and G-C.

DNA is made from deoxyribose while RNA is made from ribose. DNA is double stranded while RNA is single stranded. DNA contains thymine while RNA contains uracil.

The backbone of each helix is the 2-deoxyribose phosphates. The nitrogen bases project to the center of the double helix in order to hydrogen bond with each other (imagine the double helix as a winding staircase: each stair would represent a pair of bases binding to keep the shape of the double helix intact).

There is specificity in the binding of the bases: one purine binds one pyrimidine. In fact, adenine only binds thymine (through two hydrogen bonds) and guanine only binds cytosine (through three hydrogen bonds).

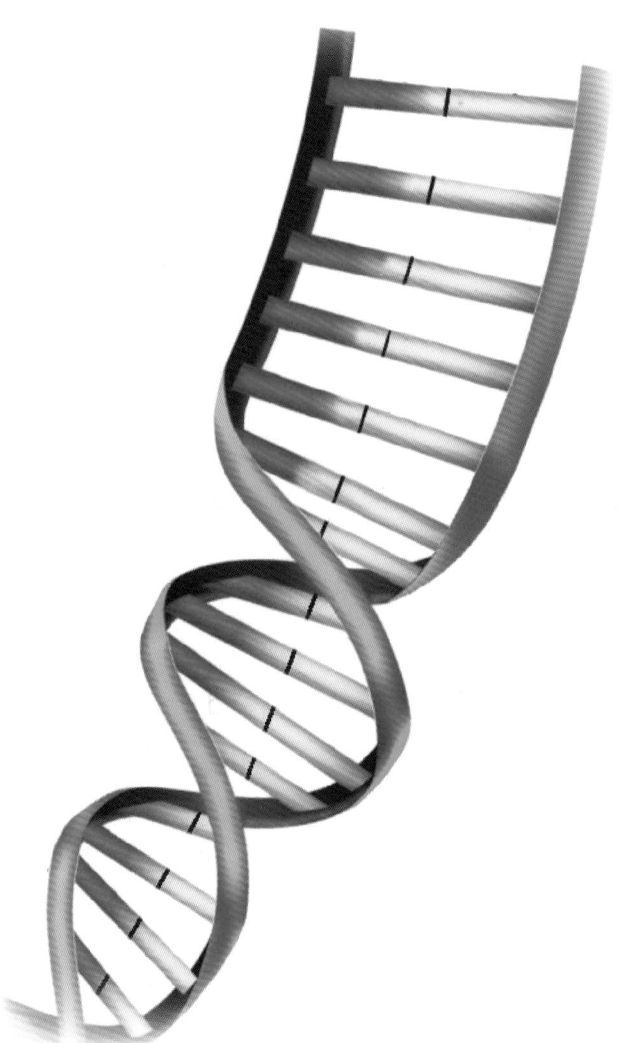

The more the H-bonds (i.e. the more G-C), the more stable the helix will be.

The *replication* (duplication) of DNA is semi-conservative: each strand of the double helix can serve as a template to generate a complementary strand. Thus for each double helix there is one parent strand (*old*) and one daughter strand (*new*). The latter is synthesized using one nucleotide at a time, enzymes including DNA polymerase, and the parent strand as a template. The preceding is termed "DNA Synthesis" and occurs in the S stage of interphase during the cell cycle.

Each nucleotide has a hydroxyl or phosphate group at the 3rd and 5th carbons designated the 3′ and 5′ positions (see BIO 20.3.2, 20.5). Phosphodiester bonds can be formed between a free 3′ hydroxyl group and a free 5′ phosphate group. Thus the DNA strand has *polarity* since one end of the molecule will have a free 3′ hydroxyl while the other terminal nucleotide will have a free 5′ phosphate group. Polymerization of the two strands occurs in opposite directions (= *antiparallel*). In other words, one strand runs in the 5′ - 3′ direction, while its partner runs in the 3′ - 5′ direction.

DNA replication is semi-discontinuous. DNA polymerase can only synthesize DNA in the 5′ to 3′ direction. As a result of the anti-parallel nature of DNA, the 5′ - 3′ strand is replicated continuously (the *leading strand*), while the 3′ - 5′ strand is replicated discontinuously (the *lagging strand*) in the reverse direction. The short, newly synthesized DNA fragments that are formed on the lagging strand are called *Okazaki fragments*. DNA synthesis begins at a specific site called the replication origin (*replicon*) and proceeds in both directions. Eukaryotic chromosomes contain multiple origins while prokaryotic chromosomes contain a single origin. The parental strand is always read in the 3′ - 5′ direction and the daughter strand is always synthesized in the 5′ - 3′ direction.

Previous knowledge of recombinant DNA techniques, restriction enzymes, hybridization, DNA repair mechanisms, etc., is not normally required for the DAT. However, because these topics do occasionally show up on the exam, they are discussed here and in BIO 2.2.1, 15.7 and the Appendix to Chapter 15. The following is an overview regarding DNA repair.

Because of environmental factors including chemicals and UV radiation, any one of the trillions of cells in our bodies may undergo as many as 1 million individual molecular "injuries" per day. Structural damage to DNA may result and could have many effects such as inducing mutation. Thus our DNA repair system is constantly active as it responds to damage in DNA structure.

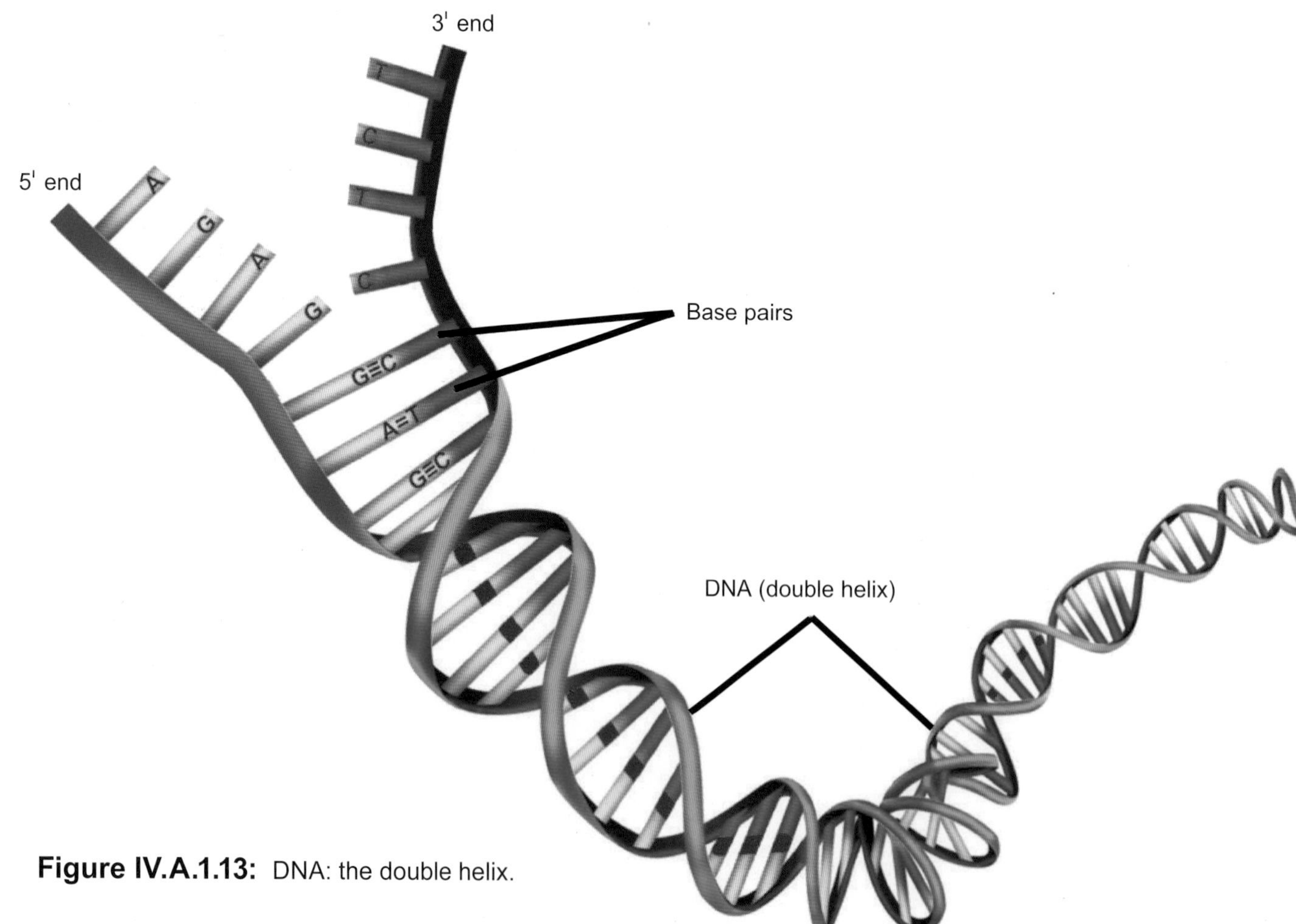

Figure IV.A.1.13: DNA: the double helix.

A cell that has accumulated a large amount of DNA damage, or one that no longer effectively repairs damage to its DNA, can: (1) become permanently dormant; (2) exhibit unregulated cell division which could lead to cancer; (3) succumb to cell suicide, also known as *apoptosis* or programmed cell death.

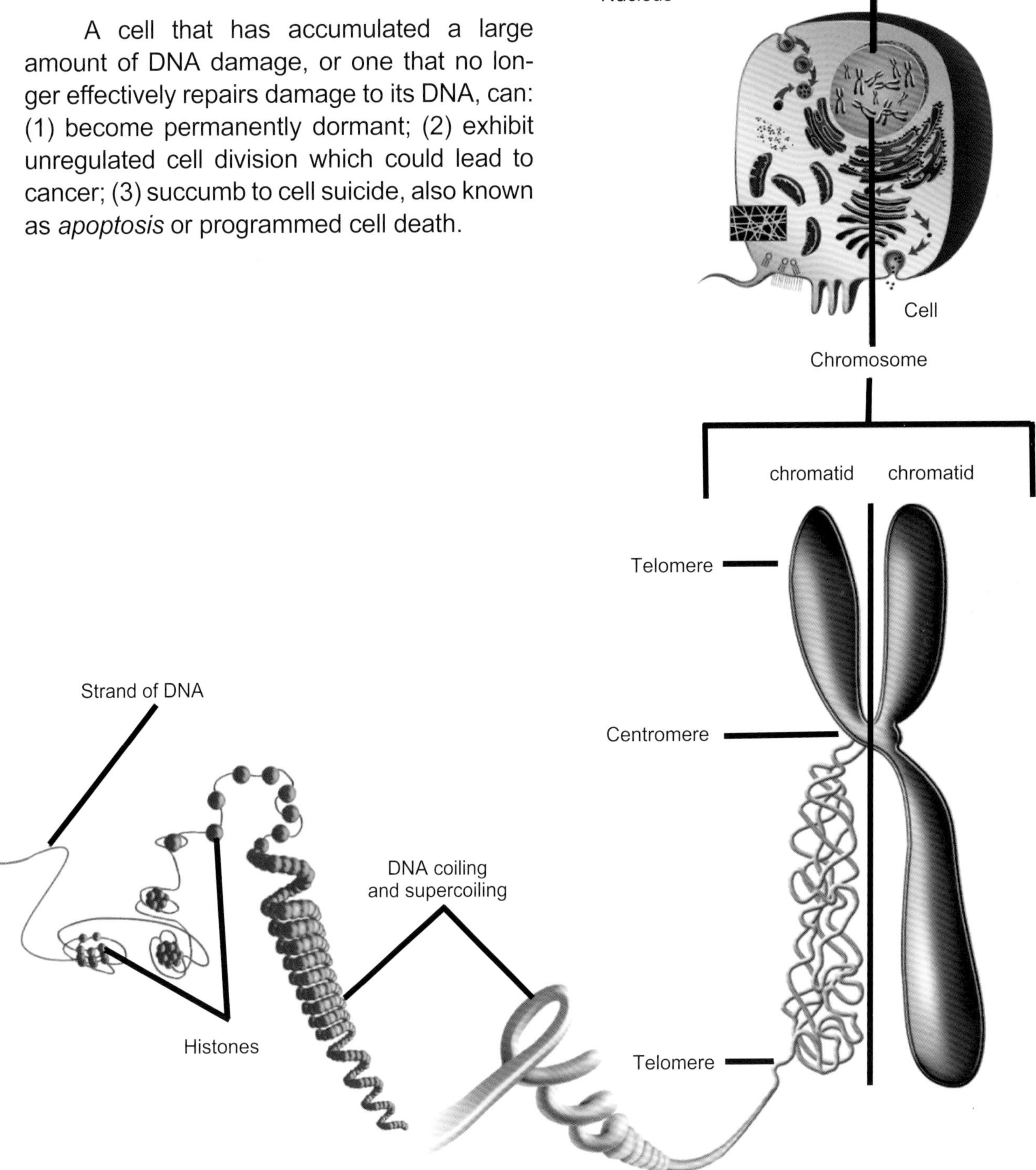

1.3 The Cell Cycle

The cell cycle is a period of approximately 18 - 22 hours during which the cell can synthesize new DNA and partition the DNA equally; thus the cell can divide. Mitosis involves nuclear division (*karyokinesis*) which is usually followed by cell division (*cytokinesis*). Mitosis and cytokinesis together define the mitotic (M) phase of the cell cycle - the division of the mother cell into two daughter cells, genetically identical to each other and to their parent cell. The cell cycle is divided into a number of phases: interphase (G_1, S, G_2) and mitosis (prophase, metaphase, anaphase and telophase).

The cell cycle is temporarily suspended in resting cells. These cells stay in the G_0 state but may reenter the cell cycle and start to divide again. The cell cycle is permanently suspended in non-dividing differentiated cells such as cardiac muscle cells.

Interphase occupies about 90% of the cell cycle. During interphase, the cell prepares for DNA synthesis (G_1), synthesizes or replicates DNA (S) resulting in duplication of chromosomes, and ultimately begins preparing for mitosis (G_2). During interphase, the DNA is not folded and the individual chromosomes are not visible. Also, centrioles grow to maturity, RNA and protein for mitosis are synthesized. Mitosis begins with prophase.

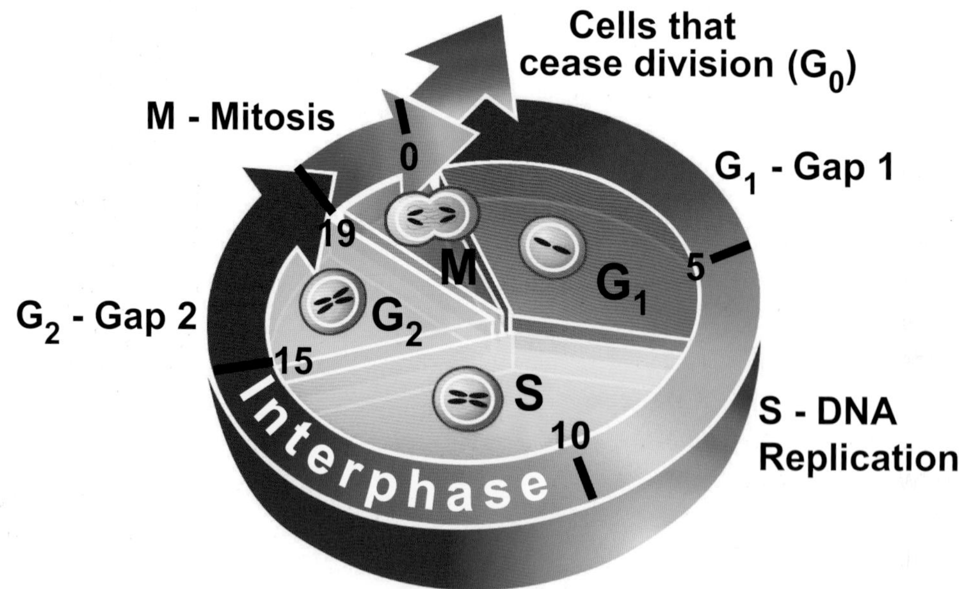

Figure IV.A.1.14: The cell cycle.
The numbers represent time in hours. Note how mitosis (M) represents the shortest period of the cycle.

Figure IV.A.1.15: Prophase.

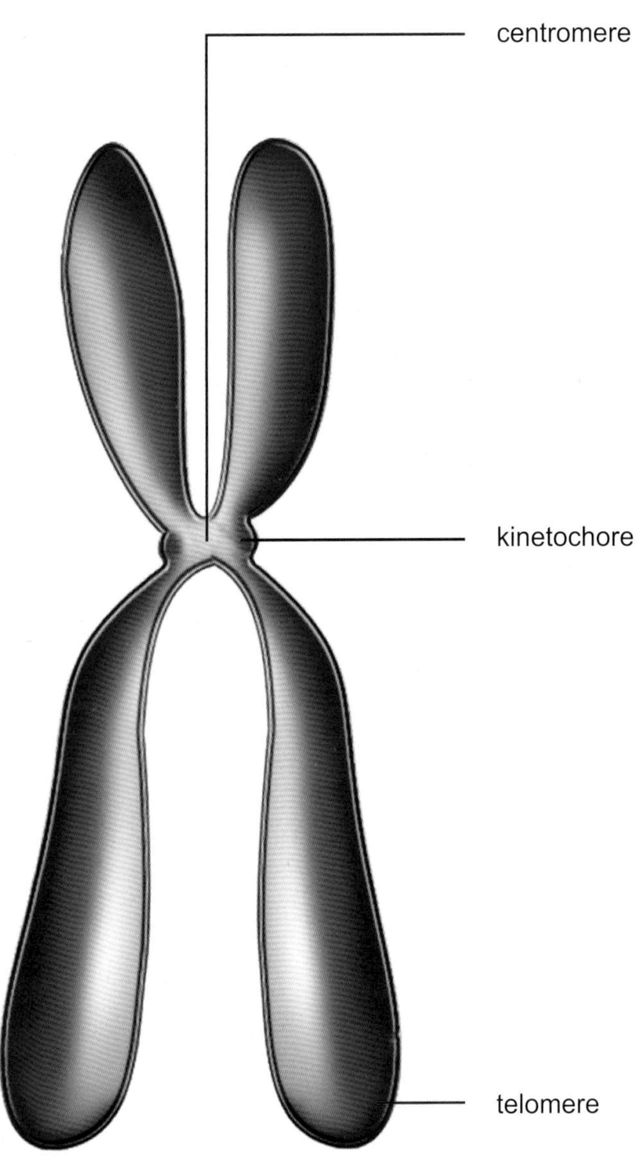

Figure IV.A.1.16: Chromosome Anatomy. Each chromosome has two arms separated by the centromere, labeled p (the shorter, named for 'petit' meaning 'small') and q (the longer of the two). The telomeres contain repetitive nucleotide sequences which protect the end of the chromosome. Over time, due to each cell division, the telomeres become shorter.

Prophase: pairs of centrioles migrate away from each other while microtubules appear in between forming a spindle. Other microtubules emanating from the centrioles give a radiating star-like appearance; thus they are called asters. Therefore, centrioles form the core of the Microtubule Organizing Centers (MTOC). The MTOC is a structure found in eukaryotic cells from which microtubules emerge and associated with the protein tubulin.

Simultaneously, the diffuse nuclear chromatin condenses into the visible chromosomes which consist of two sister chromatids - each being identical copies of each other. Each chromatid consists of a complete double stranded DNA helix. The area of constriction where the two chromatids are attached is the *centromere*. Kinetochores develop at the centromere region and function as MTOC. Just as centromere refers to the center, *telomere* refers to the ends of the chromosome (note: as cells divide and we age, telomeres progressively shorten). Ultimately, the nuclear envelope disappears at the end of prophase.

Figure IV.A.1.17: Metaphase.

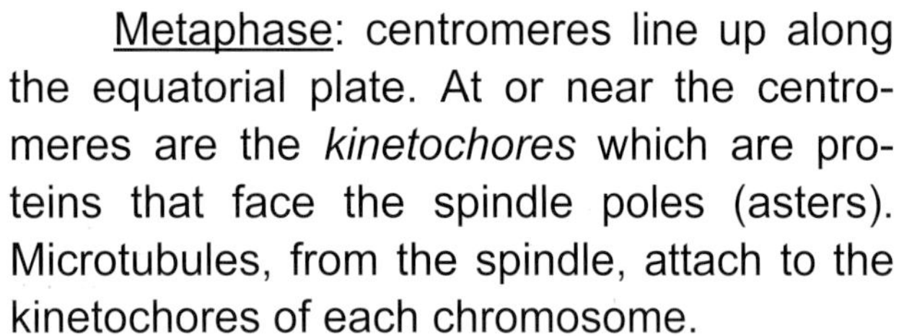

Metaphase: centromeres line up along the equatorial plate. At or near the centromeres are the *kinetochores* which are proteins that face the spindle poles (asters). Microtubules, from the spindle, attach to the kinetochores of each chromosome.

Anaphase: sister chromatids are pulled apart such that each migrates to opposite poles being guided by spindle microtubules. At the end of anaphase, a cleavage furrow forms around the cell due to contraction of actin filaments called the contractile ring.

Figure IV.A.1.18: Anaphase.

Figure IV.A.1.19: Telophase.

Telophase: new membranes form around the daughter nuclei; nucleoli reappear; the chromosomes uncoil and become less distinct (decondense). At the end of telophase, the cleavage furrow becomes deepened, facilitating the division of cytoplasm into two new daughter cells - each with a nucleus and organelles.

Finally, *cytokinesis* (cell separation) occurs. The cell cycle continues with the next interphase. {Mnemonic for the sequence of phases: P. MATI}

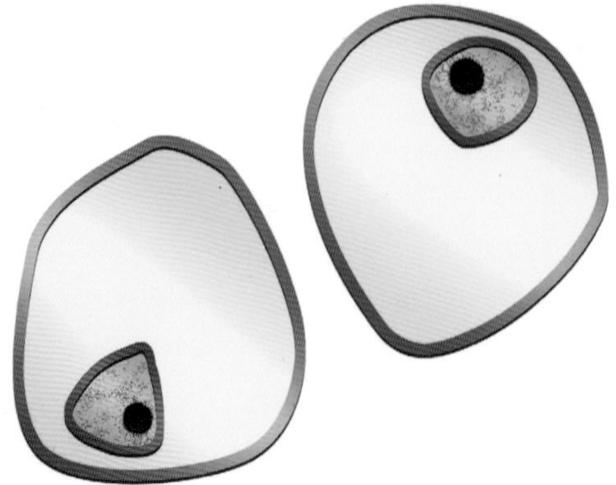

Figure IV.A.1.20: Interphase.

1.4 Cell Junctions

Multicellular organisms (i.e. animals) have cell junctions or intercellular bridges. They are especially abundant in epithelial tissues and serve as points of contact between cells and/or the extracellular matrix (BIO 4.3, 4.4). The multiprotein complex that comprise cell junctions can also build up the barrier around epithelial cells (*paracellular*) and control paracellular transport.

The molecules responsible for creating cell junctions include various cell adhesion molecules (CAMs). CAMs help cells stick to each other and to their surroundings. There are four main types: selectins, cadherins, integrins, and the immunoglobulin superfamily.

1.4.1 Types of Cell Junctions

There are three major types of cell junctions in vertebrates:

1. **Anchoring junctions**: (note: "adherens" means "to adhere to"): (i) Adherens junctions, AKA "belt desmosome" because they can appear as bands encircling the cell (= zonula adherens); they link to the actin cytoskeleton; (ii) desmosomes, AKA macula (= "spot") adherens analogous to spot welding. Desmosomes include cell adhesion proteins like cadherins which can bind intermediate filaments and provide mechanical support and stability; and (iii) hemidesmosomes ("hemi" = "half"), whereas desmosomes link two cells together, hemidesmosomes attach one cell to the extracellular matrix (usually anchoring the 'bottom' or basal aspect of the epithelial cell or keratinocyte to the basement membrane; see Fig. IV.A.1.21 and BIO 5.3).
2. **Communicating junctions**: Gap junctions which are narrow tunnels which allow the free passage of small molecules and ions. One gap junction channel is composed of two connexons (or hemichannels) which connect across the intercellular space.
3. **Occluding junctions**: Tight junctions, AKA zonula occludens, as suggested by the name, are a junctional complex that join together forming a virtually impermeable barrier to fluid. These associate with different peripheral membrane proteins located on the intracellular side of the plasma membrane which anchor the strands to the actin component of the cytoskeleton. Thus, tight junctions join together the cytoskeletons of adjacent cells. Often tight junctions form narrow belts that circumferentially surround the upper part of the lateral (i.e. "side") surfaces of adjacent epithelial cells.

Invertebrates have several other types of specific junctions; for example, the septate junction which is analogous to the tight junction in vertebrates.

In multicellular plants, the structural functions of cell junctions are instead provided for by cell walls. The analogues of communicating cell junctions in plants are called plasmodesmata (BIO 17.6.4).

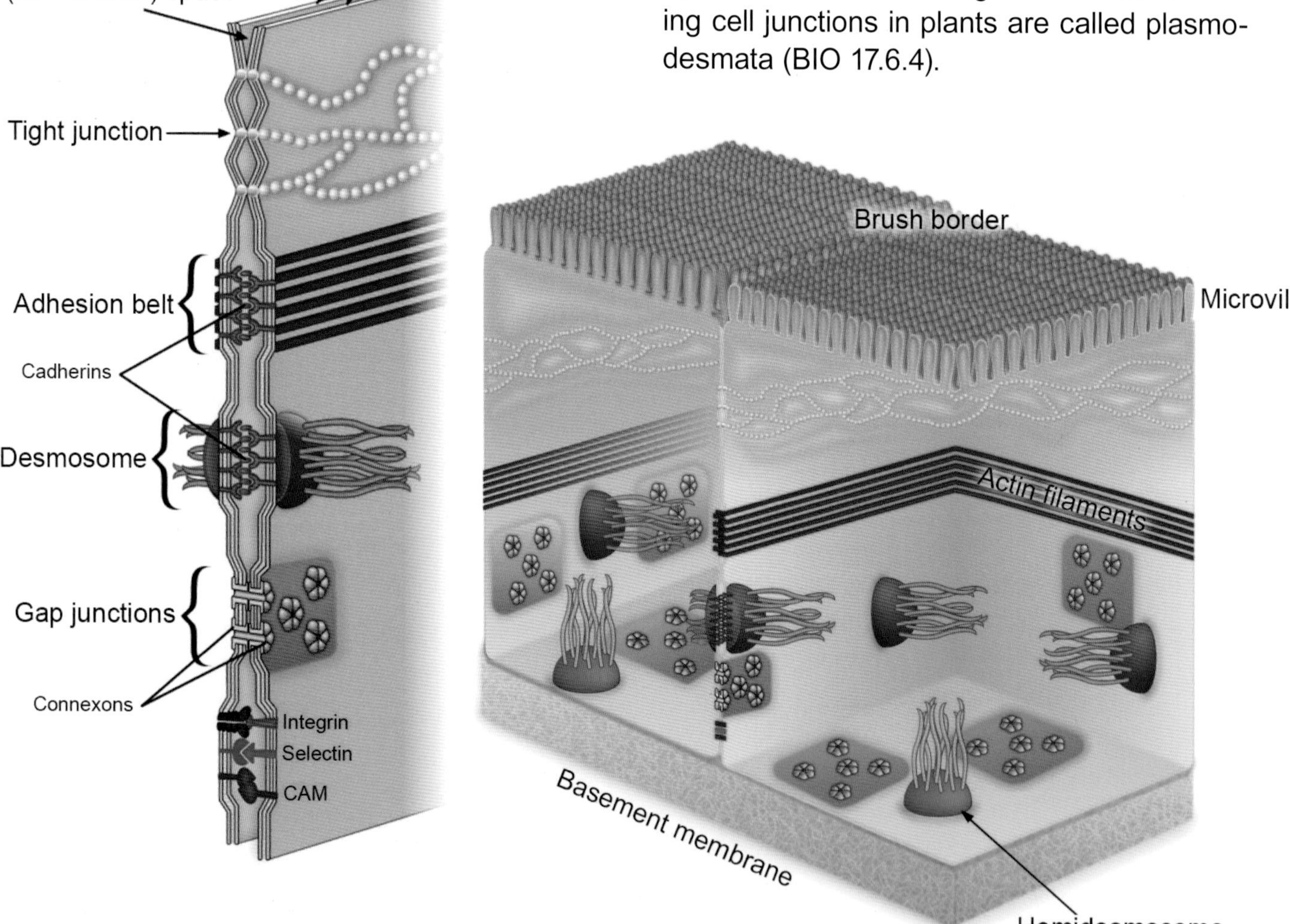

Figure IV.A.1.21: Various cell junctions in epithelia with microvilli at the surface (brush border, BIO 9.5).

1.5 Microscopy

A natural question about cells would be: if they are so small, how do we know what the inside of a cell really looks like? The story begins with the instrument used to produce magnified images of objects too small to be seen by the naked eye: the microscope.

Let us compare the basic principles of two popular methods of microscopy utilized by the vast majority of molecular biology research scientists: (1) the optical or light microscope; and (2) the electron microscope (the transmission electron microscope or TEM and the scanning electron microscope or SEM).

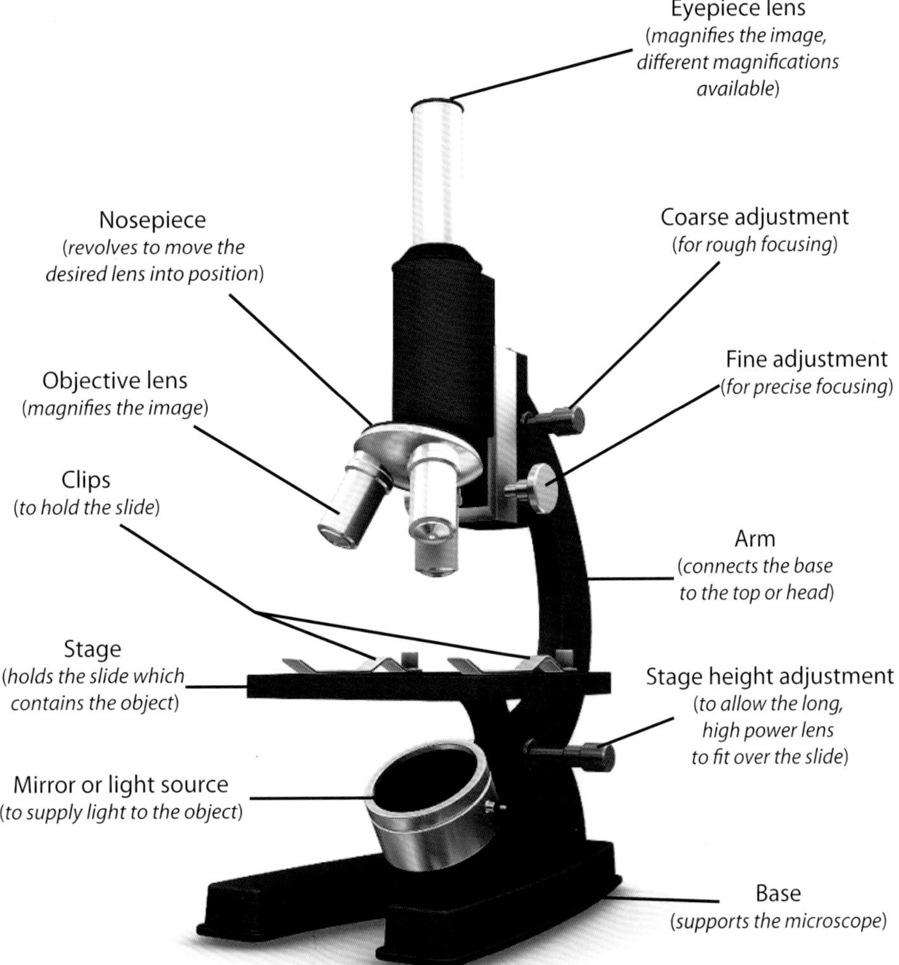

Figure IV.A.1.21: Compound light microscope. Typical magnification for the eyepiece is 10x and for the objective: 10x, 40x or 100x.

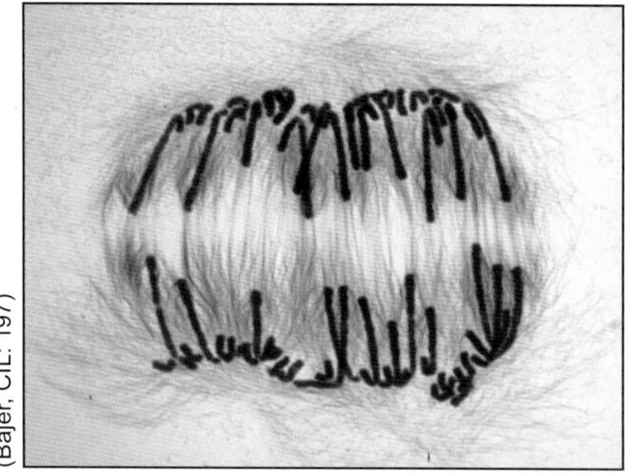
(Bajer, CIL: 197)

Figure IV.A.1.22: Light microscope image of a cell from the endosperm (BIO 17.2.1) of an African lily. Staining shows microtubules in red and chromosomes in blue during late anaphase (BIO 1.3).

Light microscopy involves the use of an external or internal light source. The light first passes through the *iris* which controls the amount of light reaching the specimen. The light then passes through a *condenser* which is a lens that focuses the light beam through the specimen before it ultimately meets the *objective lens* which magnifies the image depending on your chosen magnification factor. Two terms you should be familiar with are *magnification* (how much bigger the image appears) and *resolution* (the ability to distinguish between two points on an image).

Magnification is the ratio between the apparent size of an object (or its size in an image) and its true size, and thus it is a dimensionless number usually followed by the letter "x". A compound microscope uses multiple lenses to collect light from the sample or specimen (this lens is the objective with a magnification of up to 100x), and then a separate set of lenses to focus the light into the eye or camera (the eyepiece, magnification up to 10x). So the total magnification can be 100 x 10 = 1000 times the size of the specimen (1000x makes a 100 nanometer object visible).

Light microscopes enjoy their popularity thanks to their relative low cost and ease of use. A very important feature is that they can be used to view live specimens. Their shortfall is that the magnification is limited.

Common Units of Length in Biology

For details on units, see QR Chapter 3

- m = meter(s)
- cm = centimeter(s) (1 cm = 10^{-2} m)
- mm = millimeter(s) (1 mm = 10^{-3} m)
- μm = micrometer(s) (1 μm = 10^{-6} m)
  NOT micron or μ
- nm = nanometer(s) (1 nm = 10^{-9} m)
- Å = angstrom(s) (1 Å = 10^{-10} m)
- pm = picometer(s) (1 pm = 10^{-12} m)

The term "micron" is no longer in technical use.

Electron microscopy is less commonly used due to its high price and associated scarcity. It also cannot observe live organisms as a vacuum is required and the specimen is flooded with electrons. All images being produced are in black and white though color is sometimes added to the raw images. Its primary advantage lies in the fact that it is possible to achieve a magnification up to 10,000,000x and it is the obvious choice when a high level of detail is required using an extremely small specimen. In fact, an object as tiny as a small fraction of a nanometer becomes visible with an incredible 50 picometer resolution. TEM shows the interior of the cell while SEM shows the surface of the specimen.

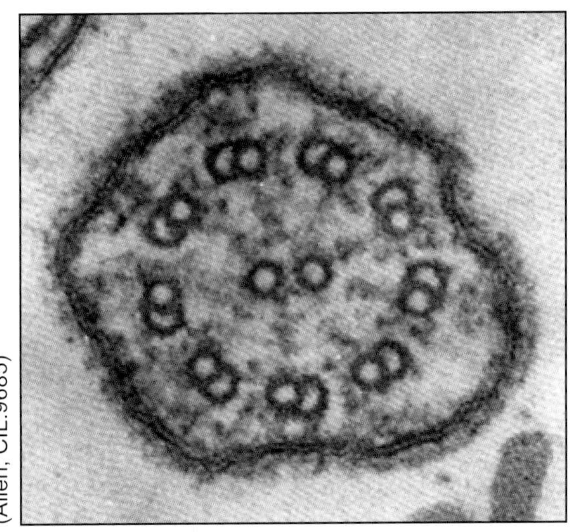

Figure IV.A.1.23: TEM of the cross section of a cilium (BIO 1.2) showing an axoneme consisting of 9 doublet and 2 central microtubules (= 9x2 + 2). Each doublet is composed of 2 subfibers: a complete A subfiber with dynein and an attached B subfiber. Eukaryotic flagella are also 9x2 + 2.

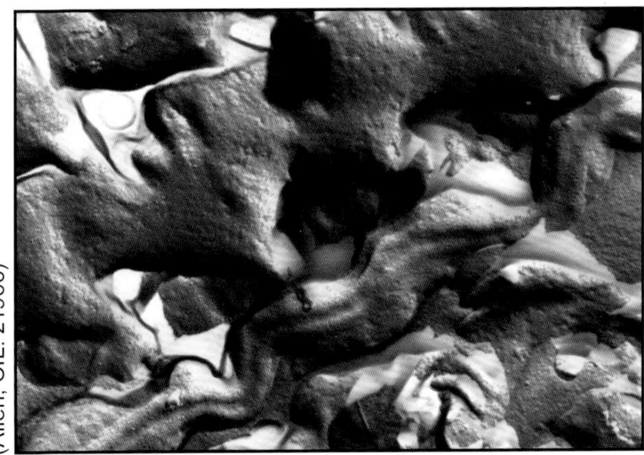

Figure IV.A.1.24: TEM freeze fracture of the plasma membrane which is cleaved between the acyl tails of membrane phospholipids (BIO 1.1, 20.4), leaving a monolayer on each half of the specimen. The "E" face is the inner face of the outer lipid monolayer. The complementary surface is the "P" face (the inner surface of the inner leaflet of the bilayer shown above). The 2 large ribbons are intrinsic proteins.

1.5.1 Fluorescent Microscopy and Immunofluorescence

Lastly, you should be familiar with fluorescent microscopy which is commonly used to identify cellular components (organelles, cytoskeleton, etc.) and microbes with a high degree of specificity and color. The fluorescent microscope makes use of a special filter that only permits certain radiation wavelengths that matches the fluorescing material being analyzed. It is an optical microscope and very similar to the light microscope except that a highly intensive light source is used to excite a fluorescent species in the sample of interest.

Immunofluorescence is a technique that uses the specificity of the antibody-antigen interaction (BIO 8.2) to target fluorescent dyes to specific molecules in a cell. Immunofluorescence can be used on tissue sections, cultured cell lines or individual cells. This can be called *immunostaining*, or specifically, *immunohistochemistry* where the location of the antibodies can be seen using fluorophores (= a fluorescent chemical that can re-emit light upon light excitation; CHM 11.5, 11.6).

There are two classes of immunofluorescence: direct (= primary) and indirect (= secondary).

Direct immunofluorescence uses a single antibody linked to a fluorophore. The antibody binds to the target molecule (antigen), and the fluorophore attached to the antibody can be detected with a microscope. This technique is cheaper, faster but less sensitive than indirect immunofluorescence.

Indirect immunofluorescence uses two antibodies: (1) the unlabeled first, or primary, antibody binds the antigen; and (2) the secondary antibody, which carries the fluorophore and recognizes the primary antibody and binds to it.

Photobleaching is the photochemical destruction of a dye or a fluorophore. Thus the fluorescent molecules are sometimes destroyed by the light exposure necessary to stimulate them into fluorescing. On the other hand, photobleaching can be fine tuned to improve the signal-to-noise ratio (like seeing the tree from the forest). Photobleaching can also be used to study the motion of molecules (i.e. FRAP).

Immunofluorescence samples can be seen through a simple fluorescent microscope (*epifluorescence*) or through the more complex *confocal* microscope.

A confocal microscope is a state-of-the-art fluorescent microscope which uses a laser as the light source. The confocal microscope is used in FRAP, fluorescence recovery after photobleaching, which is an optical technique used to "view" the movement of proteins or molecules. FRAP is capable of quantifying the 2D diffusion of a thin film of molecules containing fluorescently labeled probes, or to examine single cells. FRAP has had many uses including: studies of cell membrane diffusion and protein binding; determining if axonal transport is retrograde or anterograde, meaning towards or away from the neuron's cell body (soma), respectively.

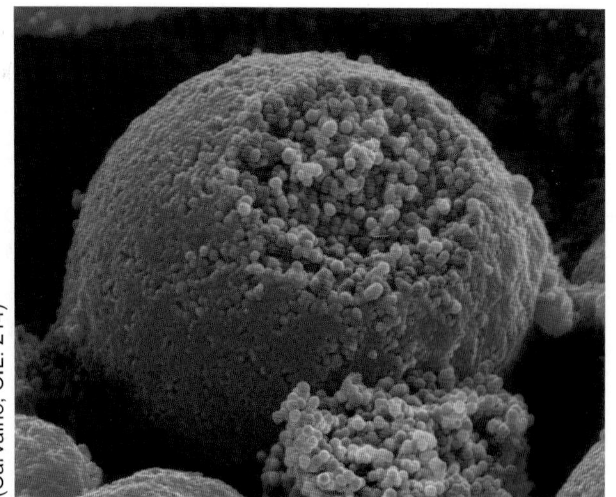

(Carvalho, CIL: 214)

Figure IV.A.1.25: SEM colorized image of a neuron's presynaptic terminal (BIO 5.1) that has been broken open to reveal the synaptic vesicles (orange and blue) beneath the cell membrane.

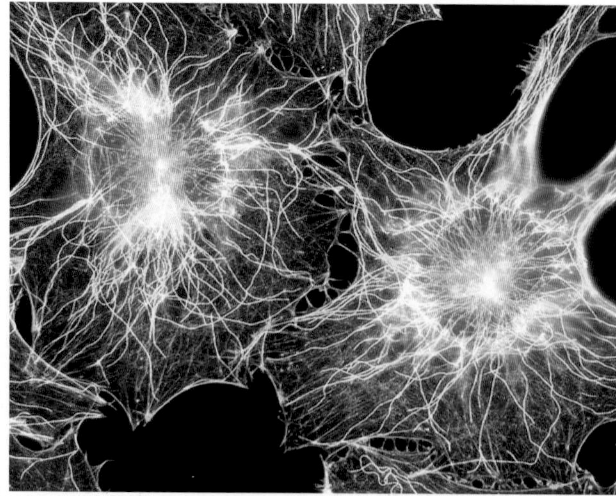

(Wittmann, CIL: 240)

Figure IV.A.1.26: Fluorescence microscopy of two interphase cells with immunofluorescence labeling of actin filaments (purple), microtubules (yellow), and nuclei (green).

GOLD STANDARD WARM-UP EXERCISES

CHAPTER 1: Generalized Eukaryotic Cell

1) Proteins in the plasma membrane can diffuse laterally, however, the specific orientations maintained by integral membrane proteins with respect to the bilayer suggest that rotation of these molecules through the plane of the bilayer very rarely occurs. The most likely reason for this is:

   A. the carbohydrate attachments to many of the proteins makes rotation impossible.
   B. rotation of these proteins would affect their ability to channel specific ions and molecules.
   C. rotation of these proteins would affect the permeability of the plasma membrane.
   D. since most integral proteins have some hydrophilic surface area, a transverse rotation would be energetically unfavorable.

2) Some peripheral proteins are bound to the membrane due to interactions with the integral membrane proteins. These interactions are likely:

   A. hydrophobic in nature.
   B. electrostatic in nature.
   C. covalent in nature.
   D. due to Van Der Waal's bonds.

3) Proteins are frequently adorned by straight/chain or branched oligosaccharides, in which case they are called glycoproteins. This type of modification can serve a variety of functions including to provide the protein with surface characteristics that facilitate its recognition. In which of the following cellular components would the greatest proportion of glycoproteins be expected?

   A. Lysosomes
   B. Microfilaments
   C. Mitochondria
   D. Phospholipid bilayer

4) Oligosaccharide modification most likely occurs in the:

   A. smooth endoplasmic reticulum.
   B. Golgi apparatus.
   C. lysosomes.
   D. cytosol.

5) Sweat is less concentrated than blood plasma and is secreted by the activity of sweat glands under the control of pseudomotor neurons. The transport of electrolytes in sweat from blood plasma to the sweat glands is best accounted for by which of the following processes?

   A. Osmosis
   B. Simple diffusion
   C. Active transport
   D. All of the above

6) Microfilaments and microtubules would have an important locomotive function in all but which of the following organelles?

   A. Flagella
   B. Endocytotic vesicles
   C. Lysosomes
   D. None of the above

7) All of the following are closely associated with microtubules EXCEPT:

   A. flagella.
   B. cilia.
   C. villi.
   D. centrioles.

8) Fas/APO-1 is a transmembrane receptor which, when stimulated, may activate intracellular mechanisms leading to cell death. Fas/APO-1 is likely:

A. a phospholipid.
B. a complex carbohydrate.
C. synthesized in the nucleus.
D. synthesized by rough endoplasmic reticulum.

9) The ATP-dependent dopamine transporter can be found at the presynaptic terminal of nerve cells. By which of the following mechanisms would the dopamine transporter most likely work?

A. Simple diffusion
B. Facilitated transport
C. Passive co-transport
D. Active transport

10) An effect of UV radiation on DNA is the formation of harmful covalent bonds among bases. For example, adjacent thymines form thymine dimers. Which of the following is most likely true of the bonds which create the dimers?

A. They consist of two carbon-carbon bonds between purines.
B. They consist of two carbon-carbon bonds between pyrimidines.
C. They consist of one carbon-carbon bond and one oxygen-sulfur bond between pyrimidines.
D. They consist of one carbon-carbon bond and one nitrogen-sulfur bond between pyrimidines.

11) Which of the following statements could be held LEAST accountable for DNA maintaining its helical structure?

A. Unwinding the helix would separate the base pairs enough for water molecules to enter between the bases, making the structure unstable.
B. The helix is stabilized by hydrogen bonds between bases.
C. The sugar phosphate backbone is held in place by hydrophilic interactions with the solvent.
D. C-G pairs have 3 hydrogen bonds between them but A-T pairs only have 2.

12) Apo-X is a drug which blocks prophase from occurring. When Apo-X is added to a tissue culture, in which phase of the cell cycle would most cells be arrested?

A. Mitosis
B. G_1
C. G_2
D. Synthesis

13) Evidence that DNA replication occurs in a bidirectional manner would be that shortly after initiation:

A. each gene in the E. coli genome would be represented only once.
B. each gene in the E. coli genome would be represented twice.
C. DNA duplication would begin on both sides of the origin of replication.
D. gene frequencies should be very high for regions symmetrically disposed about the origin.

14) If E. coli was allowed to replicate in the presence of ^{3}H-thymidine, during the second round of replication, what would an autoradiograph, which detects irradiation, show proving that the replication was semi-conservative?

A. A uniformly unlabeled structure
B. A uniformly labeled structure
C. One branch of the growing replication eye would be half as strongly labeled as the remainder of the chromosome
D. One branch of the growing replication eye would be twice as strongly labeled as the remainder of the chromosome

15) Colchicine is a plant alkaloid that inhibits normal mitosis by delaying the formation of daughter cells by inhibiting chromatid segregation. The advantage of colchicine treatment in this experiment is that in tissue so treated many cells become arrested in the state where the sister chromatids are paired. Colchicine might act by:

A. disrupting mitotic spindle formation.
B. inhibiting DNA synthesis.
C. inhibiting the replication of chromosomes.
D. preventing the degeneration of the nuclear envelope.

16) The Sanger method for sequencing DNA uses newly synthesized DNA that is randomly terminated. The method employs chain-terminating dideoxynucleotide triphosphates (ddXTPs) to produce a continuous series of fragments during catalyzed reactions. The ddXTPs act as terminators because while they can add to a growing chain during polymerization, they cannot be added onto because they must lack a:

A. hydroxyl group on their phosphoric acid component.
B. hydroxyl group on C1 of their ribose component.
C. hydroxyl group on C3 of their ribose component.
D. hydroxyl group on C5 of their ribose component.

17) When DNA is being sequenced, the appropriate enzymes are added to make a complementary copy of a primed single-stranded DNA fragment. Which of the following enzymes would have to be included in the Sanger method in order for it to work?

A. DNA gyrase
B. DNA polymerase
C. Reverse transcriptase
D. DNA helicase

18) The least likely of the following radioactive deoxynucleoside triphosphates to be used to label DNA fragments is:

A. dATP
B. dGTP
C. dUTP
D. dCTP

19) E. coli bacteriophages were added to E. coli cells in a medium containing inorganic ^{32}P-labelled phosphate and ^{35}S-labelled inorganic sulfate. After infection of the cells had occurred, examination of the progeny would show that:

A. the phosphorus had been incorporated into both the DNA and the protein components of the bacteriophages
B. the sulfur became incorporated into both the DNA and protein components of the bacteriophages.
C. the phosphorus became incorporated into the DNA component of the phages and the sulfur into their protein component.
D. the sulfur became incorporated into the DNA component of the phages and the phosforus into their protein component.

20) If increasing the concentration gradient across the plasma membrane increases the rate of transport until a maximum rate is reached, this would be convincing evidence for:

A. simple diffusion.
B. carrier-mediated transport.
C. osmosis.
D. the Fluid Mosaic model.

21. Receptor-mediated endocytosis is usually associated with:

A. clathrin.
B. selectin.
C. integrin.
D. tubulin.

22. In desmosomes, cadherins link to what aspect of an adjacent cell?

A. Intermediate filaments
B. Connexons
C. Actin
D. Integrins

23. Which of the following surrounds the cell like a belt and prevents the passage of substances between the cells?

A. Hemidesmosome
B. Tight junction
C. Desmosome
D. Gap junction

24. If the ocular of a light microscope is 10x and the objective is set at 40x, then what is the total magnification of the microscope?

A. 400x
B. 50x
C. 40x
D. 10x

25. A microscope used to visualize specific fluorophore-labeled proteins in a living cell is the:

A. compound light microscope.
B. transmission electron microscope (TEM).
C. scanning electron microscope (SEM).
D. confocal microscope.

GS ANSWER KEY

CHAPTER 1

#	Answer	Cross-Reference	#	Answer	Cross-Reference
1.	D	BIO 1.1, ORG 12.1.1	14.	D	BIO 1.2.2
2.	B	BIO 1.1, ORG 12.1-12.2.2, CHM 4.2	15.	A	BIO 1.2, 1.3
3.	D	BIO 1.1	16.	C	BIO 1.2.2, ORG 12.5
4.	B	BIO 1.2.1	17.	B	BIO 1.2.2
5.	B	BIO 1.1.1	18.	C	BIO 1.2.2
6.	D	BIO 1.2, 1.2.1, 7.5F	19.	C	BIO 1.2.2, ORG 12.2.2
7.	C	BIO 1.2	20.	B	BIO 1.2.2
8.	D	BIO 1.1, 1.2.1	21.	A	BIO 1.1.3
9.	D	BIO 1.2.2	22.	A	BIO 1.4.1
10.	B	BIO 1.2.2, ORG 12.2.2	23.	B	BIO 1.4.1
11.	A	BIO 1.2.2	24.	A	BIO 1.5
12.	C	BIO 1.3	25.	D	BIO 1.5, 1.5.1
13.	C	BIO 1.2.2, 3.0			

* Explanations can be found at the back of the book.

Go online to DAT-prep.com for additional chapter review Q&A and forum.

Go online to DAT-prep.com for additional chapter review Q&A and forum.

MICROBIOLOGY
Chapter 2

Memorize

* Structures, functions, life cycles
* Generalized viral life cycle
* Basic categories of bacteria
* Equation for bacterial doubling
* Differences, similtarities

Understand

* Eukaryotes vs. Prokaryotes
* General aspects of life cycles
* Gen. aspects of genetics/reproduction
* Calculation of exponential growth
* Scientific method

Importance

1 to 3 out of the 40 Biology
DAT questions are based on content in this chapter (in our estimation).
* Note that between 25% and 50% of the questions in DAT Biology are from 5 chapters: 1, 2, 14, 15, and 16.

Introduction 

Microbiology is the study of microscopic organisms including viruses, bacteria and fungi. It is important to be able to focus on the differences and similarities between these microorganisms and the generalized eukaryotic cell you have just studied. Classification of these microorganisms will be done in Chapter 16.

Additional Resources

Free Online Q&A + Forum

Video: Online or DVD

Flashcards

Special Guest

2.1 Viruses

Unlike cells, viruses are too small to be seen directly with a light microscope. Viruses infect all types of organisms, from animals and plants to bacteria and archaea (BIO 2.2). Only a very basic and general understanding of viruses is required for the DAT.

Viruses are obligate intracellular parasites; in other words, in order to replicate their genetic material and thus multiply, they must gain access to the inside of a cell. Replication of a virus takes place when the virus takes control of the host cell's synthetic machinery. Viruses are often considered non-living for several reasons:

(i) they do not grow by increasing in size

(ii) they cannot carry out independent metabolism

(iii) they do not respond to external stimuli

(iv) they have no cellular structure.

The genetic material for viruses may be either DNA or RNA, never both. Viruses do not have organelles or ribosomes. The nucleic acid core is encapsulated by a protein coat (capsid) which together forms the head region in some viruses. The tail region helps to anchor the virus to a cell. An extracellular viral particle is called a *virion*.

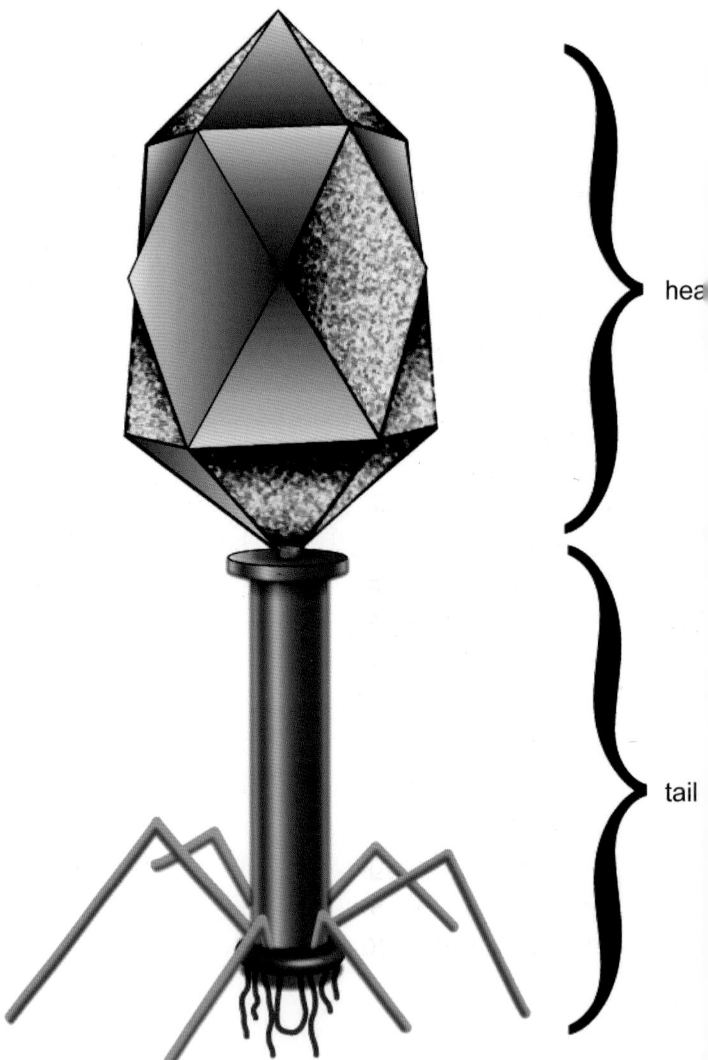

Figure IV.A.2.1: A virus.

Viruses are much smaller than prokaryotic cells (i.e. bacteria) which, in turn, are much smaller than eukaryotes (i.e. animal cells, fungi). A virus which infects bacteria is called a bacteriophage or simply a phage.

The life cycle of viruses has many variants; the following represents the main themes for DAT purposes. A virus attaches to a specific receptor on a cell. Some viruses may now enter the cell; others, as in the diagram, will simply inject their nucleic acid. Either way, viral molecules induce the metabolic machinery of the host cell to produce more viruses.

The new viral particles may now exit the cell by lysing (bursting). This is also a feature of many bacteria. The preceding is deemed lytic or virulent. Some virus lie latent for long periods of time without lysing the host and its genome becomes incorporated by genetic recombination into the host's chromosome. Therefore, whenever the host replicates, the viral genome is also replicated. These are called lysogenic or temperate viruses. Eventually, at some point, the virus may become activated and lyse the host cell.

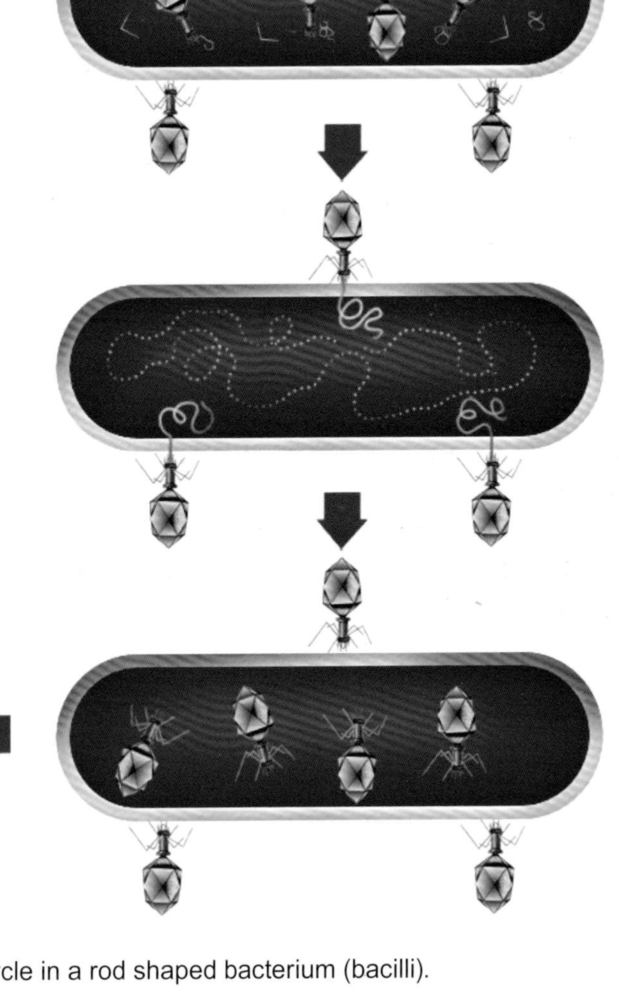

Figure IV.A.2.2: Lytic viral life cycle in a rod shaped bacterium (bacilli).

2.1.1 Retroviruses

A retrovirus uses RNA as its genetic material. It is called a retrovirus because of an enzyme (reverse transcriptase) that gives these viruses the unique ability of transcribing RNA (their RNA) into DNA (see Biology Chapter 3 for the central dogma regarding protein synthesis). The retroviral DNA can then integrate into the chromosomal DNA of the host cell to be expressed there. The human immunodeficiency virus (HIV), the cause of AIDS, is a retrovirus.

Retroviruses are used, in genetics, to deliver DNA to a cell (= a vector); in medicine, they are used for gene therapy.

2.2 Prokaryotes

Prokaryotes (= pre-nucleus) are organisms without a membrane bound nucleus which includes 2 types of organisms: bacteria (= Eubacteria) and archaea (= bacteria-like organisms that live in extreme environments). For the purposes of the DAT, we will focus on bacteria. They are haploid and have a long circular strand of DNA in a region called the nucleoid.

The nucleoid is a region in a bacterium that contains DNA but is not surrounded by a nuclear membrane. Because bacterial DNA is not surrounded by a nuclear membrane, transcription and translation can occur at the same time, that is, protein synthesis can begin while mRNA is being produced. Bacteria also have smaller circular DNA called plasmid, which is extra chromosomal genetic element that can replicate independently of the bacterial chromosome and helps to confer resistance to antibiotics.

Bacteria do not have mitochondria, Golgi apparatus, lysosomes, nor endoplasmic reticulum. Instead, metabolic processes can

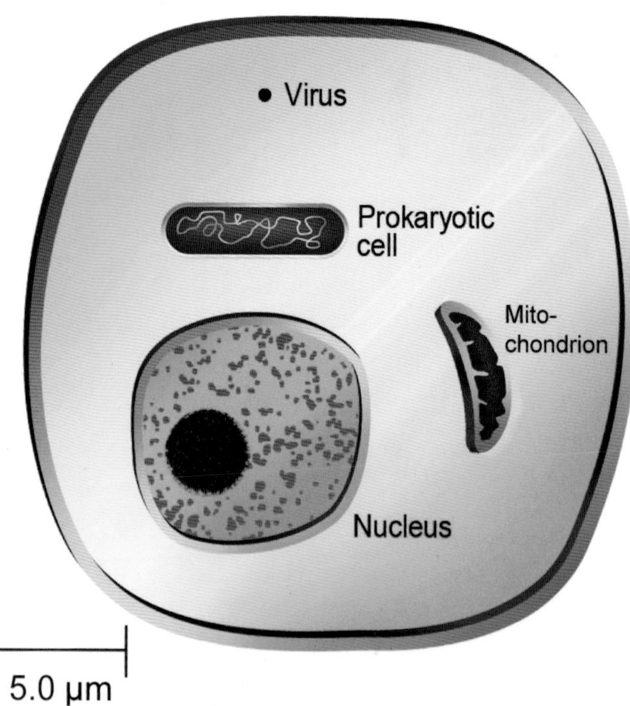

Figure IV.A.2.3
Comparing the size of a typical eukaryote, prokaryote and virus. Note that both the prokaryote and mitochondrion are similar in size and both contain circular DNA suggesting an evolutionary link.

be carried out in the cytoplasm or associated with bacterial membranes. Bacteria have ribosomes (smaller than eukaryotes), plasma membrane, and a cell wall. The cell wall, made of peptidoglycans, helps to prevent the hypertonic bacterium from bursting. Some bacteria have a slimy polysaccharide mucoid-like capsule on the outer surface for protection.

Bacteria can achieve movement with their flagella. Bacterial flagella are helical filaments, each with a rotary motor at its base which can turn clockwise or counterclockwise.

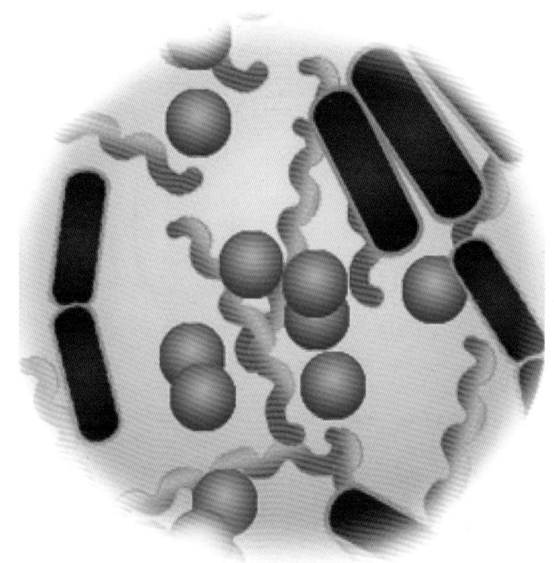

Figure IV.A.2.5
Schematic representation of bacteria colored for the purpose of identification: cocci (spherical, green), bacilli (cylindrical, purple) and spirilli (helical, orange).

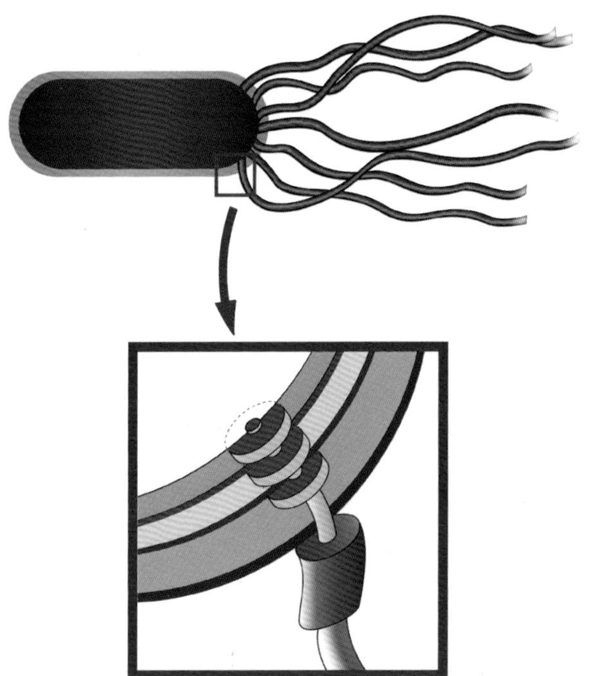

Figure IV.A.2.4
Schematic representation of the basis for flagellar propulsion. The flagellum, similar to a flexible hook, is anchored to the membrane and cell wall by a series of protein rings forming a motor. Powered by the flow of protons, the motor can rotate the flagellum more than 100 revolutions per second.

The form and rotary engine of flagella are maintained by proteins (i.e. flagellin) which interact with the plasma membrane and the basal body (BIO 1.2). Power is generated by a proton motive force similar to the proton pump in metabolism (Biology, Chapter 4).

Bacteria also have short, hairlike filaments called pili (also called fimbriae) arising from the bacterial cell wall. These pili are much shorter than flagella. Common pili can serve as adherence factors which promote binding of bacteria to host cells. Sex pili, encoded by a self-transmissible plasmid, are involved in transferring of DNA from one bacterium to another via conjugation.

Bacteria are partially classified according to their shapes: <u>cocci</u> which are spheri-

Prokaryotic Cells	Eukaryotic Cells
Small cells (1-10 μm)	Larger cells (10-100 μm)
Always unicellular	Often multicellular
No nuclei or any membrane-bound organelles, such as mitochondria	Always have nuclei and other membrane-bound organelles
DNA is circular, without proteins	DNA is linear and associated with proteins to form chromatin
Ribosomes are small (70S)	Ribosomes are large (80S)
No cytoskeleton	Always has a cytoskeleton
Motility by rigid rotating flagellum made of flagellin)	Motility by flexible waving cilia or flagellae (made of tubulin)
Cell division is by binary fission	Cell division is by mitosis or meiosis
Reproduction is always asexual	Reproduction is asexual or sexual
Great variety of metabolic pathways	Common metabolic pathways

Table IV.A.2.1: Summary of the differences between prokaryotic and eukaryotic cells.

cal or sometimes elliptical; bacilli which are rod shaped or cylindrical (Fig. IV.A.2.2 in BIO 2.1 showed phages attacking a bacillus bacterium); spirilli which are helical or spiral. They are also classified according to whether or not their cell wall reacts to a special dye called a Gram stain; thus they are gram-positive if they retain the stain and gram-negative if they do not.

Most bacteria engage in a form of asexual reproduction called binary fission. Two identical DNA molecules migrate to opposite ends of a cell as a transverse wall forms, dividing the cell in two. The cells can now separate and enlarge to the original size. Under ideal conditions, a bacterium can undergo fission every 10-20 minutes producing over 10^{30} progeny in a day and a half. If resources are unlimited, exponential growth would be expected. The doubling time of bacterial populations can be calculated as follows:

$$b = B \times 2^n$$

where b is the number of bacteria at the end of the time interval, B is the number of bacteria at the beginning of the time interval and n is the number of generations. Thus if we start with 2 bacteria and follow for 3 generations then we get:

$$b = B \times 2^n = 2 \times 2^3 = 2 \times 8 = 16$$

bacteria after 3 generations.

{Note: bacterial doubling time is a relatively popular question type.}

Bacteria do not produce gametes nor zygotes, nor do they undergo meiosis; however, four forms of genetic recombination do occur: transduction, transformation, conjugation and transposon insertion.

In transduction, fragments of bacterial chromosome accidentally become packaged into virus during a viral infection. These viruses may then infect another bacterium. A piece of bacterial DNA that the virus is accidentally carrying will be injected and incorporated into the host chromosome if there is homology between the newly injected piece of DNA and the recipient bacterial genome.

In transformation, a foreign chromosome fragment (plasmid) is released from one bacterium during cell lysis and enters into another bacterium. The DNA can then become incorporated into the recipient's genome if there is homology between the newly incorporated genome and the recipient one.

In conjugation, DNA is transferred directly by cell-to-cell contact formed by a conjugation bridge called the sex pilus. For conjugation to occur, one bacterium must have the sex factor called F plasmid. Bacteria that carry F plasmids are called F^+ cells. During conjugation, a F^+ cell replicates its F factor and will pass its F plasmid to an F^- cell, converting it to an F^+ cell. This type of exchange is the major mechanism for transfer of antibiotic resistance.

In transposon insertion, mobile genetic elements called transposons move from one position to another in a bacterial chromosome or between different molecules of DNA without having DNA homology.

Most bacteria cannot synthesize their own food and thus depend on other organisms for it; such a bacterium is heterotrophic. Most heterotrophic bacteria obtain their food from dead organic matter; this is called saprophytic. Some bacteria are autotrophic meaning they can synthesize organic compounds from simple inorganic substances. Thus some are photosynthetic producing carbohydrate and releasing oxygen, while others are chemoautotrophic obtaining energy via chemical reactions including the oxidation of iron, sulfur, nitrogen, or hydrogen gas.

Bacteria can be either aerobic or anaerobic. The former refers to metabolism in the presence of oxygen and the latter in the absence of oxygen (i.e. fermentation).

Based on variations in the oxygen requirement, bacteria are divided into four types:

1) Obligate aerobes: require oxygen for growth

2) Facultative anaerobes: are aerobic; however, can grow in the absence of oxygen by undergoing fermentation
3) Aerotolerant anaerobes: use fermentation for energy; however, can tolerate low amounts of oxygen
4) Obligate anaerobes: are anaerobic, can be damaged by oxygen

Symbiosis generally refers to close and often long term interactions between different biological species. Bacteria have various symbiotic relationships with, for example, humans. These include mutualism (both benefit: GI tract bacteria, BIO 9.5), parasitism (parasite benefits over the host: tuberculosis, appendicitis) and commensalism (one benefits and the other is not significantly harmed or benefited: some skin bacteria).

2.2.1 Operons

E. coli is a gram-negative, rod-shaped intestinal bacterium with DNA sequences called *operons* that direct biosynthetic pathways. Operons are composed of:

1. A repressor which can bind to an operator and prevent gene expression by blocking RNA polymerase. However, in the presence of an inducer, a repressor will be bound to the inducer instead, forming an inducer-repressor complex. This complex cannot bind to an operator and thus gene expression is permitted.
2. A promoter which is a sequence of DNA where RNA polymerase attaches to begin transcription.
3. Operators which can block the action of RNA polymerase if there is a repressor present.
4. A regulator which codes for the synthesis of a repressor that can bind to the operator and block gene transcription.
5. Structural genes that code for several related enzymes that are responsible for production of a specific end product.

The *lac operon* controls the breakdown of lactose and is the simplest way of illustrating how gene regulation in bacteria works. In the lac operon system there is an active repressor that binds to the operator. In this scenario RNA polymerase is unable to transcribe the structural genes necessary to control the uptake and subsequent breakdown of lactose. When the repressor is inactivated (in the presence of lactose) the RNA polymerase is now able to transcribe the genes that code for the required enzymes. These enzymes are said to be *inducible* as it is the lactose that is required to turn on the operon.

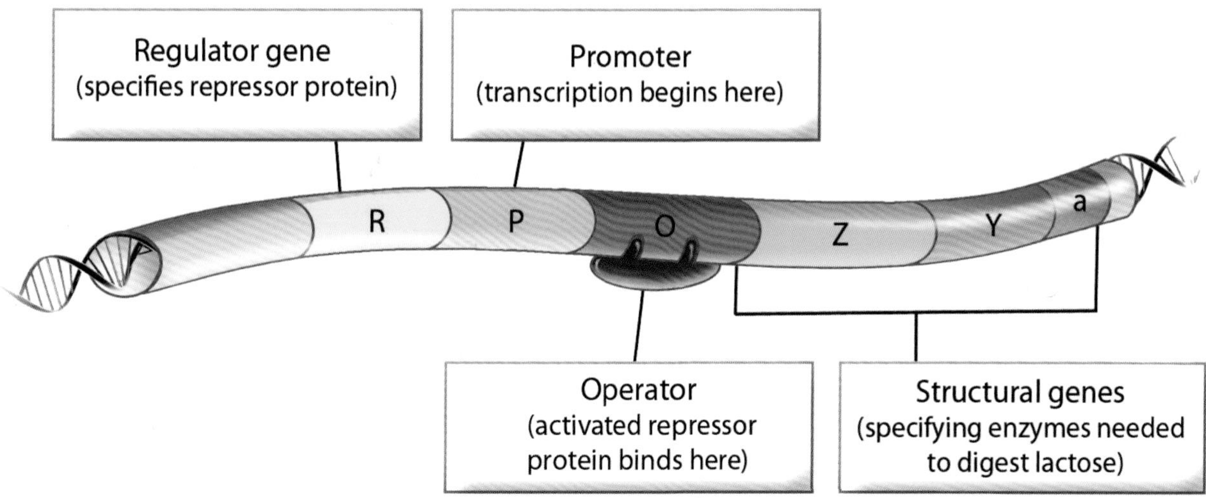

2.3 Fungi

Fungi are eukaryotic (= true nucleus) organisms which absorb their food through their chitinous cell walls. They may either be unicellular (i.e. yeast) or filamentous (i.e. mushrooms, molds) with individual filaments called hyphae which collectively form a mycelium. Fungal cell membranes contain ergosterol rather than cholesterol found in cell membranes of other eukaryotes.

Fungi often reproduce asexually. In molds, spores can be produced and then liberated from outside of a sporangium; or, as in yeast, a simple asexual budding process may be used. Sexual reproduction can involve the fusion of opposite mating types to produce asci (singular: ascus), basidia (singular: basidium), or zygotes. All of the three preceding diploid structures must undergo meiosis to produce haploid spores. If resources are unlimited, exponential growth would be expected.

Fungi are relatively important for humans as a source of disease and a decomposer of both food and dead organic matter. On the lighter side, they also serve as food (mushrooms, truffles), for alcohol and food production (cheese molds, bread yeast) and they have given us the breakthrough antibiotic, penicillin (from penicillium molds).

2.4 Vectors

A vector can be a person, animal or microorganism that carries and transmits an infectious organism (i.e. bacteria, viruses, etc.) into another living organism. Examples: the mosquito is a vector for malaria; bats are vectors for rabies and a SARS-like virus.

2.5 The Scientific Method

The scientific method could be used in conjunction with any DAT Biology experiment but microbiology is most common.

The point of the experiment is to test your ability to read scientific material, understand what is being tested, and determine if the hypothesis has been proved, refuted or neither. When a hypothesis survives rigorous testing, it graduates to a *theory*.

Observation, formulation of a theory, and testing of a theory by additional observation is called the scientific method. In biology, a key aspect to evaluate the validity of a trial or experiment is the presence of a *control group*. Generally, treatment is withheld from the control group but given to the *experimental group*.

First we will make an observation and then use deductive reasoning to create an appropriate hypothesis which will result in an experimental design. Consider the following: trees grow well in the sunlight. Hypothesis: exposure to light is directly related to tree growth. Experiment: two groups of trees are grown in similar conditions except one group (*experimental*) is exposed to light while the other group (*control*) is not exposed to light. Growth is carefully measured and the two groups are compared. Note that tree growth (*dependent variable*) is dependent on light (*independent variable*).

There are experiments where it is important to expose the control group to some factor different from the factor given to the experimental group (= *positive control*); as opposed to not giving the control group any exposure at all (= *negative control*). Exposure for a control group is used in medicine and dentistry because of the "Placebo Effect."

Experiments have shown that giving a person a pill that contains no biologically active material will cure many illnesses in up to 30% of individuals. Thus if Drug X is developed using a traditional control group, and the "efficacy" is estimated at 32%, it may be that the drug is no more effective than a sugar pill! In this case, the control group must be exposed to an unmedicated preparation to negate the Placebo Effect. To be believable the experiment must be well-grounded in evidence (= *valid*, based on the scientific method) and then one must be able to reproduce the results.

2.5.1 The Experiment

A lab in Boston reports 15% cell death when maximally stimulating the APO-1 receptor. In order to appropriately interpret the results, it must first be compared to:

A. data from other labs.
B. the attrition rate of other cell types.
C. the actual number of APO-1 cells dying in the tissue culture.
D. the rate of cell death without stimulation of APO-1.

- The experiment: stimulating a specific receptor on cells led to a 15% rate of cell death.
- Treatment is the stimulation of a receptor.
- The control (*group without treatment*): under the same conditions, do not stimulate the receptor (choice **D.**).

Choice **C.** does not answer the question. Choices **A.** and **B.** are most relevant if the initial data is shown to be significant. To prove that the data is significant or valid, one must first compare to a control group (choice **D.**).

GOLD STANDARD WARM-UP EXERCISES

CHAPTER 2: Microbiology

1) The blood of hepatitis B chronically infected people contains numerous particles of a harmless protein component of the virus called HBsAg. HBsAg is likely a component of:

   A. the capsid of the virus.
   B. the nucleic acid core of the virus.
   C. the tail of the virus.
   D. the slimy mucoid-like capsule on the outer surface of the virus.

2) Both bacteria and eukaryotic cells may share all of the following features EXCEPT:

   A. phospholipid bilayer.
   B. cell wall.
   C. ribosomes.
   D. nuclear membrane.

3) What features does the HIV virus share in common with all viruses?

   I. RNA as genetic material
   II. The ability to infect lymphocytes
   III. Obligate intracellular parasite

   A. I only
   B. III only
   C. II and III only
   D. I, II and III

4) Once teeth appear, the bacteria comprising the microbial flora of the tissues surrounding the teeth are mainly:

   A. gram-negative, aerobes.
   B. gram-positive, aerobes.
   C. gram-positive, facultative anaerobes.
   D. gram-negative, obligate anaerobes.

5) Streptococcus mutans is associated with the tooth surface and appears to be the major causative agent of dental caries, or tooth decay. Streptococcus mutans produces glucan, a sticky polymer of glucose that acts like a cement and binds the bacterial cells together and to the tooth surface. The enzyme which catalyzes the formation of glucan is likely located:

   A. in the cytosol of the cocci.
   B. in lysosomes within the cytoplasm of the cocci.
   C. in the nuclei of the cocci.
   D. on the cell surface membrane of the cocci.

6) The difference between the bacterium E. coli and the fungus Aspergillus is:

   A. Aspergillus contains ribosomes.
   B. E. coli has a cell wall.
   C. Aspergillus can undergo anaerobic metabolism.
   D. E. coli does not have a nucleus.

7) Streptococcus mutans and Lactobacillus are, respectively:

   A. spherical and helical.
   B. spherical and cylindrical.
   C. cylindrical and helical.
   D. helical and cylindrical.

8) The high number of bacteria in dental plaque result from the proliferation of bacteria by all of the following methods, EXCEPT:

   A. translocation.
   B. transduction.
   C. transformation.
   D. binary fission.

9) Given that the time for one TS type E. coli to divide at 30 °C is approximately 15 minutes, if 10 bacteria should begin dividing in ample culture media, approximately how many would be present 2 hours later?

A. 500
B. 1000
C. 2500
D. 5000

10) Given unlimited resources, which of the following graphs shows the population growth curve for the yeast Candida albicans once infection occurs?

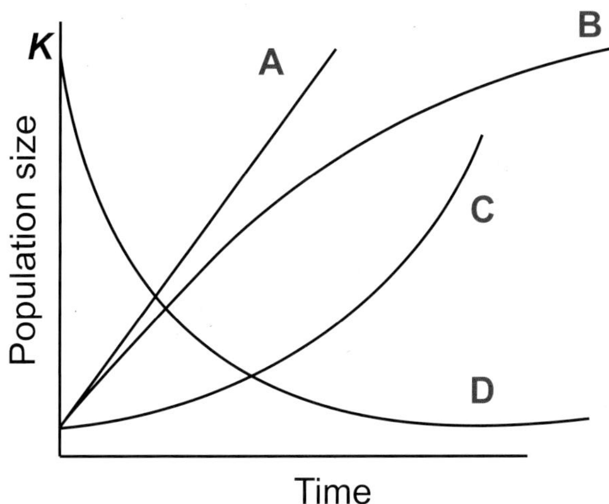

11) Yeast cells used for cloning the gene for HBsAg could be propagated by all but which of the following methods?

A. Budding
B. Transduction
C. Fusion
D. Meiotic division

12) Nitrogen fixation is accomplished by:

A. plants.
B. animals.
C. bacteria.
D. viruses.

GS ANSWER KEY

CHAPTER 2

#	Answer	Cross-Reference	#	Answer	Cross-Reference
1.	A	BIO 2.1	7.	B	BIO 2.2
2.	D	BIO 2.2	8.	A	BIO 2.2, 15.5
3.	B	BIO 2.1	9.	C	BIO 1.3, 2.2
4.	C	BIO 2.2, 4.5	10.	C	Ap A.4.2, BIO 2.3
5.	D	BIO 1.1, 2.2, 4.1	11.	B	BIO 2.3
6.	D	BIO 2.2-2.3	12.	C	BIO 2.2

* Explanations can be found at the back of the book.

Go online to DAT-prep.com for additional chapter review Q&A and forum.

APPENDIX

CHAPTER 2

Introduction to Advanced DAT-30 Topics

Most students will be accepted to dental school without coming near to a perfect score; and frankly, no student is going to obtain a perfect scaled score of 30/30. However, for students who have the time and the will to aim for a perfect score, we have added a number of advanced topics in the form of passages, followed by questions so that the material can be learned in an interactive way. As per usual, explanations are at the back of the book. You should decide if you wish to read these sections based on the requirements of the dental program(s) you wish to attend.

Advanced DAT-30 Topic: Chimeric Plasmid

Muscular dystrophy is one of the most frequently encountered genetic diseases, affecting one in every 4000 boys (but much less commonly girls) born in America. Muscular dystrophy results in the progressive degeneration of skeletal and cardiac muscle fibers, weakening the muscle and leading ultimately to death from respiratory or cardiac failure.

The gene responsible for a major form of muscular dystrophy has been identified. This gene codes for a protein known as dystrophin, which is absent or present in a nonfunctional form in patients with the disease. Dystrophin is located on the inner surface of the plasma membrane in normal muscle protein.

The cloning of a fragment of DNA allows indefinite amounts of dystrophin to be produced from even a single original molecule. An insertion generates a hybrid or chimeric plasmid or phage, consisting in part of the additional "foreign" sequences. These chimeric elements replicate in bacteria just like the original plasmid or phage and so can be obtained in large amounts. Copies of the original foreign fragment can be retrieved from the progeny. Since the properties of the chimeric species usually are unaffected by the particular foreign sequences that are involved, almost any sequence of DNA can be cloned in this way. Because the phage or plasmid is used to "carry" the foreign DNA as an inert part of the genome, it is often referred to as the cloning vector.

13) The functions of dystrophin likely include all of the following EXCEPT one. Which is the EXCEPTION?

- **A.** Recognition of protein hormones important to the functioning of the cells
- **B.** Maintenance of the structural integrity of the plasma membrane
- **C.** Keeping ion channels within the cells open
- **D.** Protection of elements within the membrane during contraction of the cells

14) In order for cloning of foreign DNA to take place:

A. plasmids must incorporate the foreign DNA into the DNA in their capsids.
B. there must be several sites at which DNA can be inserted.
C. bacteria must be able to resume their usual life cycle after additional sequences of DNA have been incorporated into their genomes.
D. bacteria must divide meiotically, so no two daughter cells are exactly alike.

15) Plasmid genomes are circular and a single cleavage converts the DNA into a linear molecule. The two ends can be joined to the ends of a linear foreign DNA to regenerate a circular chimeric plasmid. Which of the following rules would be most important in allowing this process to occur?

A. DNA replication occurs in a semi-conservative manner.
B. The genetic code is composed of triplets of bases which correspond to the 20 amino acids used in protein structure.
C. The stability of the DNA helix is dependent on the number of C-G bonds present.
D. Phosphodiester bonds must link the plasmid DNA to the foreign DNA.

16) One possible method of treating muscular dystrophy using cloning techniques would be to:

A. Splice the nonfunctional genes out of dystrophic muscle cells and clone them in bacterial plasmids.
B. Determine the amino acid sequence of dystrophin and introduce the protein into muscle cells artificially.
C. Clone the gene responsible for coding dystrophin and insert the normal gene into dystrophic muscle cells.
D. Prevent skeletal and cardiac muscle tissue degradation by cloning and inserting the genes for troponin and tropomyosin into dystrophic muscle cells.

17) If the gene which codes for troponin was absent from muscle cells, all of the following processes would be inhibited EXCEPT one. Which is the EXCEPTION?

A. The movement of tropomyosin to a new position on the actin molecules
B. The uncovering of the active sites for the attachment of actin to the cross bridges of myosin
C. The hydrolysis of ATP in the myosin head to produce ADP, P_i, and energy
D. The release of Ca^{2+} ions from the sarcoplasmic reticulum

ANSWER KEY

ADVANCED TOPICS - CHAPTER 2

		Cross-Reference
13.	A	P2, S3
14.	C	P3, S3, S5; BIO 2.2, BIO 15.7
15.	D	BIO 1.2.2, BIO 20.5, BIO 15.7
16.	C	deduce, BIO 15.7
17.	D	BIO 5.2

P = paragraph; *S* = sentence; *E* = equation; *T* = table; *F* = figure

Go online to DAT-prep.com for additional chapter review Q&A and forum.

PROTEIN SYNTHESIS
Chapter 3

Memorize

* The genetic code (triplet)
* Central Dogma: DNA ➡ RNA ➡ protein
* Definitions: mRNA, tRNA, rRNA
* Codon-anticodon relationship
* Initiation, elongation and termination

Understand

* Mechanism of transcription
* Mechanism of translation
* Roles of mRNA, tRNA, rRNA
* Role and structure of ribosomes

Importance

0 to 2 out of the 40 Biology
DAT questions are based on content in this chapter (in our estimation).
* Note that between 25% and 50% of the questions in DAT Biology are from 5 chapters: 1, 2, 14, 15, and 16.

DAT-Prep.com

Introduction 

Protein synthesis is the creation of proteins using DNA and RNA. Individual amino acids are connected to each other in peptide linkages in a specific order given by the sequence of nucleotides in DNA. Thus the process occurs through a precise interplay directed by the genetic code and involving mRNA, tRNA and amino acids - all in an environment provided by a ribosome.

Additional Resources

Free Online Q&A + Forum

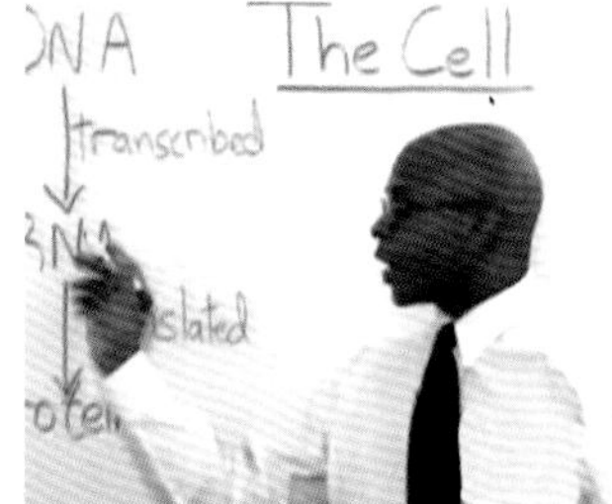

Video: Online or DVD

Flashcards

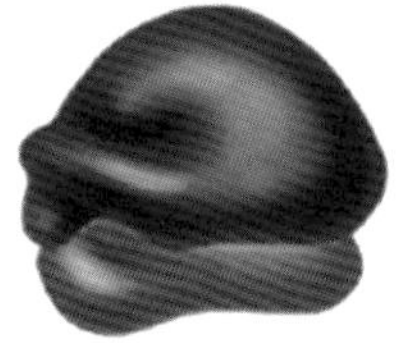

Special Guest

Building Proteins

Proteins (which comprise many hormones, enzymes, antibodies, etc.) are long chains formed by peptide bonds between combinations of twenty amino acid subunits. Each amino acid is encoded in a sequence of three nucleotides (a triplet code = the *genetic code*). A gene is a conglomeration of such codes and thus is a section of DNA which encodes for a protein (or a polypeptide which is exactly like a protein but much smaller).

DNA Transcription

The information in DNA is rewritten (transcribed) into a messenger composed of RNA (= mRNA); the reaction is catalyzed by the enzyme RNA polymerase. The newly synthesized mRNA is elongated in the 5′ to 3′ direction. It carries the complement of a DNA sequence.

Transcription can be summarized in 4 or 5 steps for prokaryotes or eukaryotes, respectively:

1. RNA polymerase moves the transcription bubble, a stretch of unpaired nucleotides, by breaking the hydrogen bonds between complementary nucleotides (see BIO 1.2.2 for nucleoside phosphates - nucleotides - and the binding of nitrogen bases).
2. RNA polymerase adds matching RNA nucleotides that are paired with complementary DNA bases.
3. The extension of the RNA sugar-phosphate backbone is catalyzed by RNA polymerase.
4. Hydrogen bonds of the untwisted RNA +

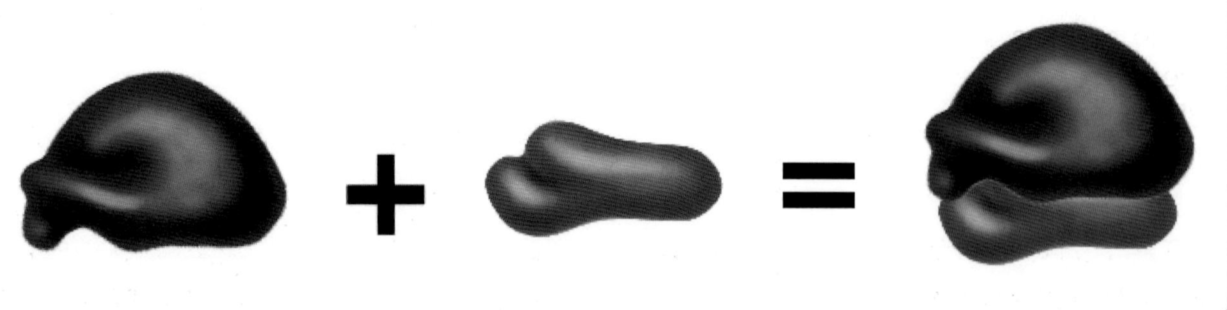

Figure IV.A.3.1: A ribosome provides the environment for protein synthesis. Ribosomes are composed of a large and a small subunit. The unit of measurement used is called the "Svedberg unit" (S) which is a measure of the rate of sedimentation in a centrifuge as opposed to a direct measurement of size. For this reason, fragment names do not add up (70S is made of 50S and 30S). Prokaryotes have 70S ribosomes, each comprised of a small (30S) and a large (50S) subunit. Eukaryotes have 80S ribosomes, each comprised of a small (40S) and large (60S) subunit. The ribosomes found in chloroplasts and mitochondria of eukaryotes also consist of large and small subunits bound together with proteins into one 70S ribosome. These organelles are believed to be descendants of bacteria ("Endosymbiotic theory") thus their ribosomes are similar to those of bacteria (see BIO 16.6.3).

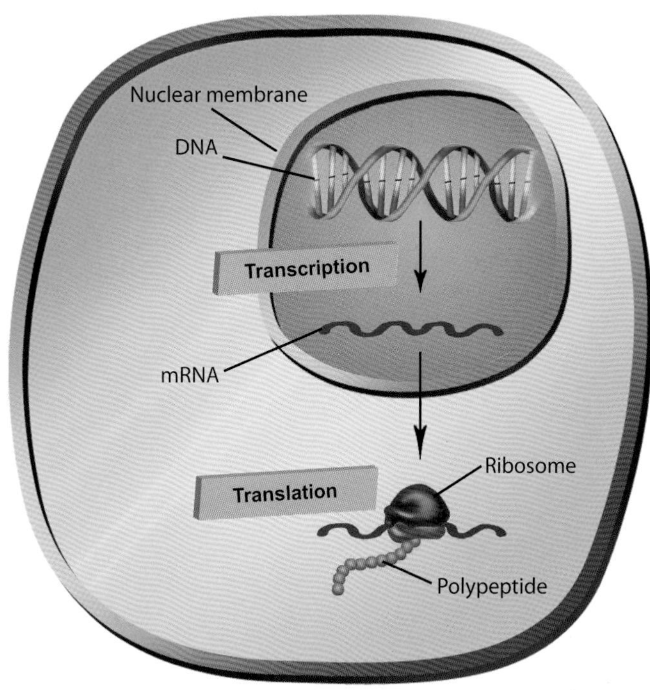

Figure IV.A.3.2: The central dogma of protein synthesis.

DNA helix break, freeing the newly synthesized RNA strand.

5. If the cell has a nucleus, the RNA is further processed [addition of a 5′ cap and a 3′ poly(A) tail] and then exits through the nuclear pore to the cytoplasm.

The mRNA synthesis in eukaryotes begins with the binding of RNA polymerase at a specific DNA sequence known as promoters. Elongation continues until the RNA polymerase reaches a termination signal. The initially formed primary mRNA transcript, also called pre-mRNA, contains regions called <u>introns</u> that are not expressed in the synthesized protein.The introns are removed and the regions that are <u>ex</u>pressed (<u>ex</u>ons) are spliced together to form the final functional mRNA molecule. {EXons EXpressed; INtrons IN the garbage!}

Post-transcriptional processing of mRNA occurs in the nucleus. Even before transcription is completed, a 7-methylguanosine cap is added to the 5′ end of the growing mRNA serving as attachment site for protein synthesis and protection against degradation. The 3′ end is added with a poly(A) tail consisting of 20 to 250 adenylate residues as protection. Of course, "A" refers to adenine and the nucleotide is thus adenosine monophosphate or AMP (BIO 1.2.2, ORG 12.5) which *poly*merizes to create the tail of residues. The mes-

Note the following summary of protein synthesis[1]:

DNA —TRANSCRIBED (in the nucleus)—> mRNA —TRANSLATED (in the cytosol)—> protein

[1] for eukaryotes; in prokaryotes, some of the above-mentioned events occur simultaneously since they contain no nucleus. In fact, in bacterial cells it is common to have several ribosomes working in parallel on a single mRNA, forming what is called polyribosomes or polysome.

senger then leaves the nucleus with the information necessary to make a protein.

RNA Translation

The mRNA is constantly produced and degraded, which is the main method through which cells regulate the amount of a particular protein they synthesize. It attaches to a small subunit of a ribosome which will then attach to a larger ribosomal subunit thus creating a full ribosome. A ribosome is composed of a complex of protein and ribosomal RNA (= rRNA). The rRNA is the most abundant of all RNA types.

Floating in the cytoplasm is yet another form of RNA; this RNA specializes in taking amino acids and transfering them onto other amino acids when contained within the environment of the ribosome. More specifically, this transfer RNA (tRNA) molecule can be charged with a specific amino acid by aminoacyl-tRNA synthetase enzyme, bring the amino acid to the environment of ribosome, recognize the triplet code (= codon) on mRNA via its own triplet code anticodon, which is a three nucleotide sequence on tRNA that recognizes the complementary codon in mRNA; and finally, tRNA can transfer its amino acid onto the preceding one thus elongating the polypeptide chain. In a way, tRNA translates the code that mRNA carries into a sequence of amino acids which can produce a protein.

Translation of mRNA into a protein involves three stages: initiation, elongation and termination. The direction of synthesis of the protein chain proceeds from the amino end/terminus to the carboxyl end/terminus. Synthesis begins when the ribosome scans the mRNA until it binds to a start codon (AUG), which specifies the amino acid methionine. During elongation, a peptide bond is formed between the existing amino acid in the protein chain and the incoming amino acid. Following peptide bond formation, the ribosome shifts by one codon in the 5′ to 3′ direction along mRNA and the uncharged tRNA is expelled and the peptidyl-tRNA grows by one amino acid. Protein synthesis terminates when the ribosome binds to one of the three mRNA termination codons (UAA, UAG or UGA; notice the similarity with the DNA stop codons in Table IV.A.3.1 except that U replaces T in this RNA molecule).

The 20 Amino Acids	The 64 DNA Codons
Alanine	GCT, GCC, GCA, GCG
Arginine	CGT, CGC, CGA, CGG, AGA, AGG
Asparagine	AAT, AAC
Aspartic acid	GAT, GAC
Cysteine	TGT, TGC
Glutamic acid	GAA, GAG
Glutamine	CAA, CAG
Glycine	GGT, GGC, GGA, GGG
Histidine	CAT, CAC
Isoleucine	ATT, ATC, ATA
Leucine	CTT, CTC, CTA, CTG, TTA, TTG
Lysine	AAA, AAG
Methionine	ATG
Phenylalanine	TTT, TTC
Proline	CCT, CCC, CCA, CCG
Serine	TCT, TCC, TCA, TCG, AGT, AGC
Threonine	ACT, ACC, ACA, ACG
Tyrosine	TAT, TAC
Tryptophan	TGG
Valine	GTT, GTC, GTA, GTG
Stop codons	TAA, TAG, TGA

Table IV.A.3.1: The 20 standard amino acids.

The 20 standard amino acids are encoded by the genetic code of 64 codons. Notice that since there are 4 bases (A, T, G, C), if there were only two bases per codon, then only 16 amino acids could be coded for ($4^2=16$). However, since at least 21 codes are required (20 amino acids plus a stop codon) and the next largest number of bases is three, then 4^3 gives 64 possible codons, meaning that some degeneracy exists.

Degeneracy is the redundancy of the genetic code. Degeneracy occurs because there are more codons than encodable amino acids. This makes the genetic code more tolerant to point mutations (BIO 15.5). For example, in theory, fourfold degenerate codons can tolerate any point mutation at the third position (see valine, alanine, glycine, etc. in Table IV.A.3.1 and notice that any 3rd base codes for the same amino acid). The structure of amino acids will be discussed in ORG 12.1.

A nonsense mutation is a point mutation (BIO 15.5) in a sequence of DNA that results in a premature stop codon (UAA, UAG, UGA), or a nonsense codon in the transcribed mRNA. Either way, an incomplete, and usually nonfunctional protein is the result. A missense mutation is a point mutation where a single nucleotide is changed to cause substitution of a different amino acid. Some genetic disorders (i.e. thalassemia) result from nonsense mutations.

Protein made on free ribosomes in the cytoplasm may be used for intracellular purposes (i.e. enzymes for glycolysis, etc.). Whereas proteins made on rER ribosomes are usually modified by both rER and the Golgi apparatus en route to the plasma membrane or exocytosis (i.e. antibodies, intestinal enzymes, etc.).

Key Points

Note the following: i) the various kinds of RNA are single stranded molecules which are produced using DNA as a template; ii) hormones can have a potent regulatory effect on protein synthesis (esp. enzymes); iii) allosteric enzymes (= proteins with two different configurations - each with different biological

DNA	Coding Strand (codons)	5′→ →------ T T C ------→ → 3′
	Template Strand (anticodons)	3′← ←------ A A G ------← ← 5′
mRNA	The Message (codons)	5′ → →------ U U C ------→ → 3′
tRNA	The Transfer (anticodons)	3′ ← ← A A G ← ← 5′
Protein	Amino Acid	**N-terminus** → → Phenylalanine → → **C-terminus**

Table IV.A.3.2. DNA, RNA and protein strands with directions of synthesis. For both DNA and RNA, strands are synthesized from the **5′** ends → → to the **3′** ends. Protein chains are synthesized from the **N-terminus** → → to the **C-terminus**. Color code: the **old** end is **cold blue**; the **new** end is **red hot** where new residues are added. As shown in the table, mRNA is synthesized complementary and antiparallel to the **template strand (anticodons)** of DNA, so the resulting mRNA consists of codons corresponding to those in the coding strand of DNA. The **anticodons of tRNA** read each three-base mRNA codon and thus transfers the corresponding **amino acid** to the growing **polypeptide chain** or **protein** according to the genetic code.

properties) are important regulators of transcription; iv) there are many protein factors which trigger specific events in the initiation (using a start codon, AUG), elongation and termination (using a stop codon) of the synthesis of a protein; v) one end of the protein has an amine group (-NH_2, which projects from the first amino acid), while the other end has a carboxylic acid group (-COOH, which projects from the last amino acid). {Amino acids and protein structure will be explored in ORG 12.1 and 12.2}

Note that the free amine group end, the start of the protein, is also referred to as: N-terminus, amino-terminus, NH_2-terminus, N-terminal end or amine-terminus. The free carboxylic acid end, which is the end of the protein, is also referred to as: C-terminus, carboxyl-terminus, carboxy-terminus, C-terminal tail, C-terminal end, or COOH-terminus.

Differences in translation between prokaryotes and eukaryotes:

1) Ribosomes: in prokaryotes it is 70S, in eukaryotes it is 80S

2) Start codon: the start codon AUG specifies formyl-methionine [f-Met] in prokaryotes, in eukaryotes it is methionine

3) Location of translation: in prokaryotes translation occurs at the same compartment and same time as transcription, in eukaryotes transcription occurs in the nucleus while translation occurs in the cytosol.

Because of the incredible variety of organisms that use the genetic code, it was thought to be a *truly* 'universal' code but that is not quite accurate. Variant codes have evolved. For example, protein synthesis in human mitochondria relies on a genetic code that differs from the standard genetic code.

Furthermore, not all genetic information is stored using the genetic code. DNA also has regulatory sequences, chromosomal structural areas and other non-coding DNA that can contribute greatly to phenotype. Such elements operate under sets of rules that are different from the codon-to-amino acid standard underlying the genetic code.

GOLD STANDARD WARM-UP EXERCISES

CHAPTER 3: Protein Synthesis

1) Which of the following enzymes is most important in RNA synthesis during transcription?

   A. DNA polymerase
   B. RNA replicase
   C. RNA polymerase
   D. Reverse transcriptase

2) The last step in translation, termination, in addition to the termination codon, requires release factors (RFs). Where would the RFs be expected to be found in the cell?

   A. Within the nuclear membrane
   B. Floating in the cytosol
   C. In the matrix of the mitochondria
   D. Within the lumen of the smooth endoplasmic reticulum

3) During the period of time that primary oocytes remain in prophase I of meiosis, they undergo an extended period of growth, including accelerated synthesis and accumulation of rRNA. The increased rate of rRNA synthesis is accompanied by:

   A. disassembly of ribosomes into their component parts.
   B. thickening of the nuclear membrane.
   C. an increase in the size and/or number of nucleoli.
   D. a decrease in nuclear chromatin material.

4) The 3 base pair sequence found on an mRNA strand is called which of the following?

   A. Codon
   B. Anticodon
   C. Genome
   D. Gene

5) A ribosome is:

   A. one of three binding sites for tRNA during translation.
   B. a sequence of nucleotides in DNA that marks the end of a gene and signals RNA polymerase to release the newly made RNA molecule and detach from the DNA.
   C. a noncoding, intervening sequence within a primary transcript that is removed from the transcript during RNA processing.
   D. a complex of rRNA and protein molecules that functions as a site of protein synthesis.

6) The triplet code of CAT in DNA is represented as ______ in mRNA and ______ in tRNA.

   A. GUA, CAU
   B. CAT, CAT
   C. GAA, CAT
   D. GTA, CAU

7) Transcription occurs along a ____ template forming an mRNA in the ____ direction.

   A. 3′ to 5′; 3′ to 5′
   B. 5′ to 3′; 3′ to 5′
   C. 5′ to 3′; 5′ to 3′
   D. 3′ to 5′; 5′ to 3′

8) What is the meaning of the degeneracy of the genetic code?

   A. A single codon may specify more than one amino acid.
   B. A single amino acid may have more than one codon.
   C. AUG is a single start codon.
   D. The first two bases specify the amino acid.

GS ANSWER KEY

CHAPTER 3

		Cross-Reference			*Cross-Reference*
1.	C	BIO 3.0	5.	D	BIO 3.0
2.	B	BIO 1.2.1, 3.0	6.	A	BIO 1.2.2, 3.0
3.	C	BIO 3.0, 1.2.1	7.	D	BIO 1.2.2, 3.0
4.	A	BIO 3.0	8.	B	BIO 3.0

* Explanations can be found at the back of the book.

Go online to DAT-prep.com for additional chapter review Q&A and forum.

APPENDIX

CHAPTER 3: Protein Synthesis

Advanced DAT-30 Topic: Release Factor Recognition

The last step in translation involves the cleavage of the ester bond that joins the complete peptide chain to the tRNA corresponding to its C-terminal amino acid. This process of termination, in addition to the termination codon, requires release factors (RFs). The freeing of the ribosome from mRNA during this step requires the participation of a protein called ribosome releasing factor (RRF).

Cells usually do not contain tRNAs that can recognize the three termination codons. In E. coli, when these codons arrive on the ribosome they are recognized by one of three release factors. RF-1 recognizes UAA and UAG, while RF-2 recognizes UAA and UGA. The third release factor, RF-3, does not itself recognize termination codons but stimulates the activity of the other two factors.

The consequence of release factor recognition of a termination codon is to alter the peptidyl transferase center on the large ribosomal subunit so that it can accept water as the attacking nucleophile rather than requiring the normal substrate, aminoacyl-tRNA.

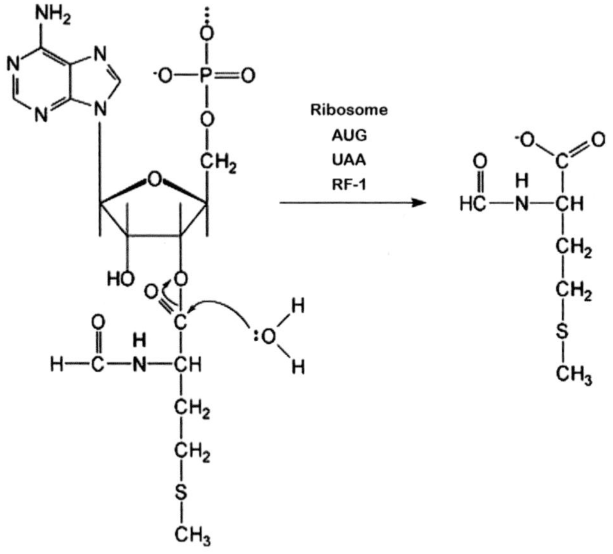

Ribosome
AUG
UAA
RF-1

Figure 1

9) The alteration to the peptidyl transferase center during the termination reaction serves to convert peptidyl transferase into a(n):

A. exonuclease
B. lyase.
C. esterase.
D. ligase.

10) Sparsomycin is an antibiotic that inhibits peptidyl transferase activity. The effect of adding this compound to an in vitro reaction in which E. coli ribosomes are combined with methionine aminoacyl-tRNA complex, RF-1 and the nucleotide triplets, AUG and UAA, would be to:

A. inhibit hydrolysis of the amino acid, allowing polypeptide chain extension.

B. inhibit peptide bond formation causing the amino acid to be released.

C. induce hydrolysis of the aminoacyl-tRNA complex.

D. inhibit both hydrolysis of the aminoacyl-tRNA complex and peptide bond formation.

11) If the water in the reaction in Fig. 1 was labeled with ^{18}O, which of the following molecules would contain ^{18}O at the end of the reaction?

A. The free amino acid

B. The phosphate group of the tRNA molecule

C. Oxygen-containing molecules in the cytoplasm.

D. The ribose moiety of the tRNA molecule

ANSWER KEY

ADVANCED TOPICS - CHAPTER 3

Cross-Reference

9.	C	P1; E; BIO 4.1, ORG 9.4
10.	D	P3; E; BIO 3.0, 4.2, 20.2.1
11.	A	BIO 20.2.1, ORG 8.1, 9.4

P = paragraph; *S* = sentence; *E* = equation; *T* = table; *F* = figure

ENZYMES AND CELLULAR METABOLISM
Chapter 4

Memorize

* Define: catabolism, anabolism, activation energy
* Define: metabolism, active/allosteric sites
* Substrates/products, especially: Acetyl CoA, pyruvate
* Enzymes: kinase, phosphatase

Understand

* Feedback, competitive, non-competitive inhibition
* Krebs cycle, electron transport chain: main features
* Oxidative phosphorylation, substrates and products, general features
* Metabolism: carbohydrates (glucose), fats and proteins

Importance

0 to 3 out of the 40 Biology DAT questions are based on content in this chapter (in our estimation).

* Note that between 25% and 50% of the questions in DAT Biology are from 5 chapters: 1, 2, 14, 15, and 16.

Introduction

Cells require energy to grow, reproduce, maintain structure, respond to the environment, etc. Biochemical reactions and other energy producing processes that occur in cells, including cellular metabolism, are regulated in part by enzymes. Pathways specific to plants will be discussed on Chapter 17.

Additional Resources

Free Online Q&A + Forum

Video: Online or DVD

Flashcards

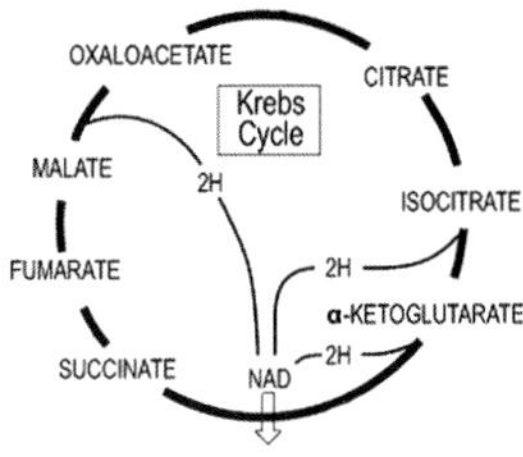

Special Guest

4.1 Overview

In an organism or an individual many biochemical reactions take place. All these biochemical reactions are collectively termed metabolism. In general, metabolism can be broadly divided into two main categories. They are:

(a) Catabolism which is the breakdown of macromolecules (larger molecules) such as glycogen to micromolecules (smaller molecules) such as glucose.

(b) Anabolism which is the building up of macromolecules such as protein using micromolecules such as amino acids.

As we all know, chemical reactions in general involve great energy exchanges when they occur. Similarly most catabolic and anabolic reactions would involve massive amounts of energy if they were to occur in vitro (outside the cell). However, all these reactions could be carried out within an environment of less free energy exchange, using molecules called enzymes.

What is an enzyme?

An enzyme is a protein catalyst. A protein is a large polypeptide made up of amino acid subunits. A catalyst is a substance that alters the rate of a chemical reaction without itself being permanently changed into another compound. A catalyst accelerates a reaction by decreasing the free energy of activation (see diagrams in CHM 9.5, 9.7).

Enzymes fall into two general categories:

(a) Simple proteins which contain only amino acids like the digestive enzymes ribonuclease, trypsin and chymotrypsin.

(b) Complex proteins which contain amino acids and a non-amino acid cofactor. Thus the complete enzyme is called a holoenzyme and it is made up of a protein portion (apoenzyme) and a cofactor.

Holoenzyme = Apoenzyme + Cofactor.

A metal may serve as a cofactor. Zinc, for example, is a cofactor for the enzymes carbonic anhydrase and carboxypeptidase. An organic molecule such as pyridoxal phosphate or biotin may serve as a cofactor. Cofactors such as biotin, which are covalently linked to the enzyme are called prosthetic groups or ligands.

In addition to their enormous catalytic power which accelerates reaction rates, enzymes exhibit exquisite specificity in the types of reactions that each catalyzes as well as specificity for the substrates upon which they act. Their specificity is linked to the concept of an active site. An active site is a cluster of amino acids within the tertiary (i.e. 3-dimensional) configuration of the enzyme where the actual catalytic event occurs. The active site is often similar to a pocket or groove with properties (chemical or structural) that accommodate the intended substrate with high specificity.

Examples of such specificity are as follows: Phosphofructokinase catalyzes a reaction between ATP and fructose-6-phosphate. The enzyme does not catalyze a reaction between other nucleoside triphosphates. It is worth mentioning the specificity of trypsin and chymotrypsin though both of them are proteolytic (i.e. they degrade or hydrolyse proteins). Trypsin catalyzes the hydrolysis of peptides and proteins only on the carboxyl side of polypeptidic amino acids lysine and arginine. Chymotrypsin catalyzes the hydrolysis of peptides and proteins on the carboxyl side of polypeptidic amino acids phenylalanine, tyrosine and tryptophan. The degree of specificity described in the previous examples originally led to the **Lock and Key Model** which has been generally replaced by the **Induced Fit Hypothesis**. While the former suggests that the spatial structure of the active site of an enzyme fits exactly that of the substrate, the latter is more widely accepted and describes a greater flexibility at the active site and a conformational change in the enzyme to strengthen binding to the substrate.

4.2 Enzyme Kinetics and Inhibition

There is an increase in reaction velocity (= reaction rate) with an increase in the concentration of substrate. At increasingly higher substrate concentrations the increase in activity is progressively smaller. From this, it could be inferred that enzymes exhibit saturation kinetics. The mechanism of the preceding lies largely with saturation of the enzyme's active sites. As substrate concentration increases, more and more enzymes are converted to the substrate bound enzyme complex until all the enzyme active sites are bound to substrate. After this point, further increase in substrate concentration will not increase reaction rate.

Enzyme inhibitors are classified as: competitive inhibitor, noncompetitive inhibitor and irreversible inhibitor. In competitive inhibition, the inhibitor and the substrate are analogues that compete for binding to the active site, forming an unreactive enzyme-inhibitor complex. However, at higher substrate concentration, the inhibition can be reversed. In noncompetitive inhibition, the inhibitor can bind to the enzyme at a site different from the active site where the substrate binds to, thus forming either an unreactive enzyme-inhibitor complex or enzyme-substrate-inhibitor complex. However, a higher substrate concentration does not reverse the inhibition. In irreversible inhibition, the inhibitor binds permanently to the enzyme and inactivates it (e.g. heavy metals, aspirin, organophosphates). The effects caused by irreversible inhibitors are only overcome by synthesis of new enzyme.

4.3 Regulation of Enzyme Activity

The activity of enzymes in the cell is subject to a variety of regulatory mechanisms. The amount of enzyme can be altered by increasing or decreasing its synthesis or degradation. Enzyme induction refers to an enhancement of its synthesis. Repression refers to a decrease in its biosynthesis.

Enzyme activity can also be altered by covalent modification. Phosphorylation of specific serine residues by protein kinases increases or decreases catalytic activity depending upon the enzyme. Proteolytic cleavage of proenzymes (e.g., chymotrypsinogen, trypsinogen, protease and clotting factors) converts an inactive form to an active form (e.g., chymotrypsin, trypsin, etc.).

Enzyme activity can be greatly influenced by its environment (esp. pH and temperature). For example, most enzymes exhibit optimal activity at a pH in the range 6.5 to 7.5. However, pepsin (an enzyme found in the stomach) has an optimum pH

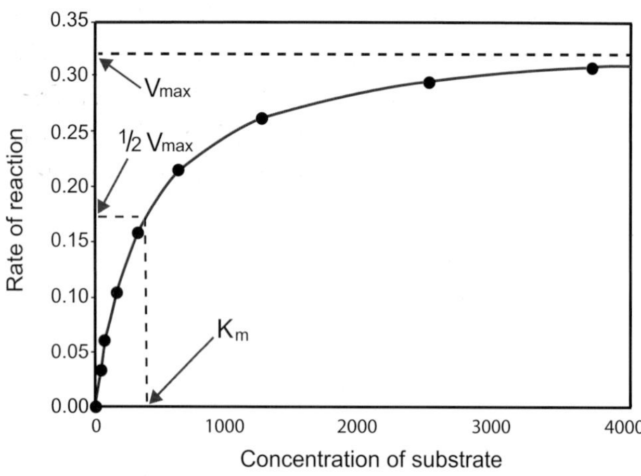

Michaelis-Menten Kinetics: Enzymes with single-substrate mechanisms usually follow the Michaelis-Menten model, in which the plot of velocity vs. substrate concentration [S] produces a rectangular hyperbola. Initially, the reaction rate [V] increases as substrate concentration [S] increases over a range of substrate concentration. However, as [S] gets higher, the enzyme becomes saturated with substrate and eventually the reaction rate [V] reaches maximum velocity V_{max} when the enzyme is fully saturated with substrate. Compare the diagram above with the curve of carrier-mediated transport (i.e. showing saturation kinetics) for solutes crossing the plasma membrane in BIO 1.1.2. The K_m is the substrate concentration at which an enzyme-catalyzed reaction occurs at half its maximal velocity, $V_{max}/2$. K_m is called the Michaelis constant. Each enzyme has a unique K_m value.

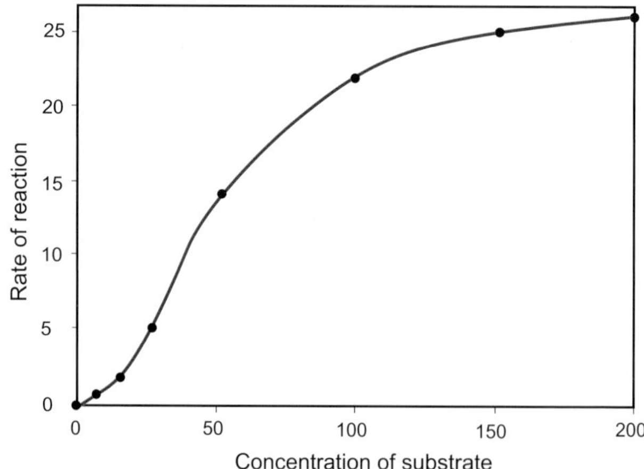

Non-Michaelis-Menten Kinetics: Some enzymes with multiple-substrate mechanisms exhibit the non-Michaelis-Menten model, in which the plot of velocity vs. substrate concentration [S] produces a sigmoid curve. This characterizes cooperative binding of substrate to the active site, which means that the binding of one substrate to one subunit affects the binding of subsequent substrate molecules to other subunits. This behavior is most common in multimeric enzymes with several active sites. Positive cooperativity occurs when binding of the first substrate increases the affinity of the other active sites for the following substrates. Negative cooperativity occurs when binding of the first substrate decreases the affinity of the other active site for the following substrates.

Fig. IV. A. 4.1 Enzyme Kinetic Curve Plot.

of ~ 2.0. Thus it cannot function adequately at a higher pH (i.e. in the small intestine). Likewise, enzymes function at an optimal temperature. When the temperature is lowered, kinetic energy decreases and thus the rate of reaction decreases. If the temperature is raised too much then the enzyme may become denatured and thus non-functional.

Enzyme activity can also be modified by an *allosteric* mechanism which involves binding to a site other than the active site. Isocitrate dehydrogenase is an enzyme in the Krebs Tricarboxylic Acid Cycle, which is activated by ADP. ADP is not a substrate or substrate analogue. It is postulated to bind a site *distinct* from the active site called the *allosteric site.* Positive effectors stabilize the more active form of enzyme and enhance enzyme activity while negative effectors stabilize the less active form of enzyme and inhibit enzyme activity.

Some enzymes fail to behave by simple saturation kinetics. In such cases a phenomenon called positive cooperativity is explained in which binding of one substrate or ligand shifts the enzyme from the less active form to the more active form and makes it easier for the second substrate to bind. Instead of a hyperbolic curve of velocity vs. substrate concentration [S] that many enzymes follow, sigmoid curve of velocity vs. [S] characterizes cooperativity (i.e. see the Enzyme Kinetic Curve Plot in this section as well as hemoglobin and myoglobin, BIO 7.5.1).

4.4 Bioenergetics

Biological species must transform energy into readily available sources in order to survive. ATP (adenosine triphosphate) is the body's most important short term energy storage molecule. It can be produced by the breakdown or oxidation of protein, lipids (i.e. fat) or carbohydrates (esp. glucose). If the body is no longer ingesting sources of energy it can access its own stores: glucose is stored in the liver as glycogen, lipids are stored throughout the body as fat, and ultimately, muscle can be catabolized to release protein (esp. amino acids).

We will be examining four key processes that can lead to the production of ATP: glycolysis, Krebs Citric Acid Cycle, the electron transport chain (ETC), and oxidative phosphorylation. Figure IV.A.4.2 is a schematic summary.

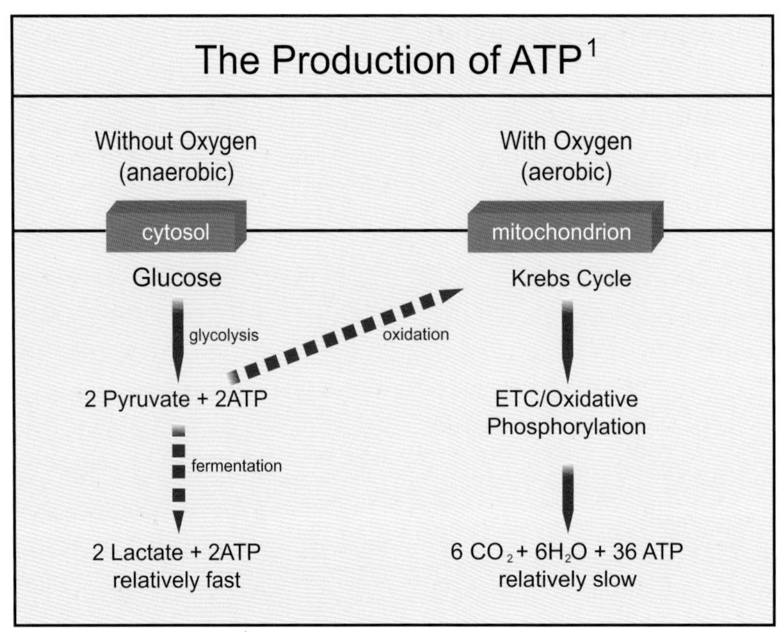

Figure IV.A.4.2: Summary of ATP production.

4.5 Glycolysis

The initial steps in the catabolism or *lysis* of D-glucose constitute the Embden - Meyerhof glyco*lytic* pathway. This pathway can occur in the absence of oxygen (anaerobic). The enzymes for glycolysis are present in all human cells and are located in the cytosol. The overall reaction can be depicted as follows (ADP: adenosine diphosphate, NAD: nicotinamide adenine dinucleotide, P_i: inorganic phosphate):

$$\text{Glucose} + 2\text{ADP} + 2\,\text{NAD}^+ + 2\text{P}_i \longrightarrow 2\text{Pyruvate} + 2\text{ATP} + 2\text{NADH} + 2\text{H}^+$$

The first step in glycolysis involves the phosphorylation of glucose by ATP. The enzyme that catalyzes this irreversible reaction is either hexokinase or glucokinase. Phosphohexose isomerase then catalyzes the conversion of glucose-6-phosphate to fructose-6-phosphate. Phosphofructokinase (PFK) catalyzes the second phosphorylation. It is an irreversible reaction. This reaction also utilizes 1 ATP. This step, which produces fructose-1,6-diphosphate, is said to be the rate limiting or pacemaker step in glycolysis. Aldolase then catalyzes the cleavage of fructose-1,6-diphosphate to glyceraldehyde-

3-phosphate and dihydroxyacetone phosphate (= 2 triose phosphates). Triose phosphate isomerase catalyzes the interconversion of the two preceding compounds. Glyceraldehyde-3-phosphate dehydrogenase mediates a reaction between the designated triose, NAD^+ and P_i to yield 1,3-diphosphoglycerate.

Next, phosphoglycerate kinase catalyzes the reaction of the latter, an energy rich compound, with ADP to yield ATP and phosphoglycerate. This reaction generates 2 ATP per glucose molecule. Phosphoglycerate mutase catalyzes the transfer of the phosphoryl group to carbon two to yield 2-phosphoglycerate. Enolase catalyzes a dehydration reaction to yield phosphoenolpyruvate and water. The enzyme enolase is inhibited by fluoride at high, nonphysiological concentrations. This is why blood samples that are drawn for estimation of glucose are added to fluoride to inhibit glycolysis. Phosphoenolpyruvate is then acted upon by pyruvate kinase to yield pyruvate which is a three carbon compound and 2 ATP.

NADH produced in glycolysis must regenerate NAD^+ so that glycolysis can continue. Under **aerobic** conditions (i.e. in the presence of oxygen) pyruvate is converted to Acetyl CoA which will enter the Krebs Cycle followed by oxidative phosphorylation producing a total of 38 ATP per molecule of glucose (i.e. 2 pyruvate). Electrons from NADH are transferred to the electron transfer chain located on the inside of the inner mitochondrial membrane and thus NADH produced during glycolysis in the cytosol is converted back to NAD^+.

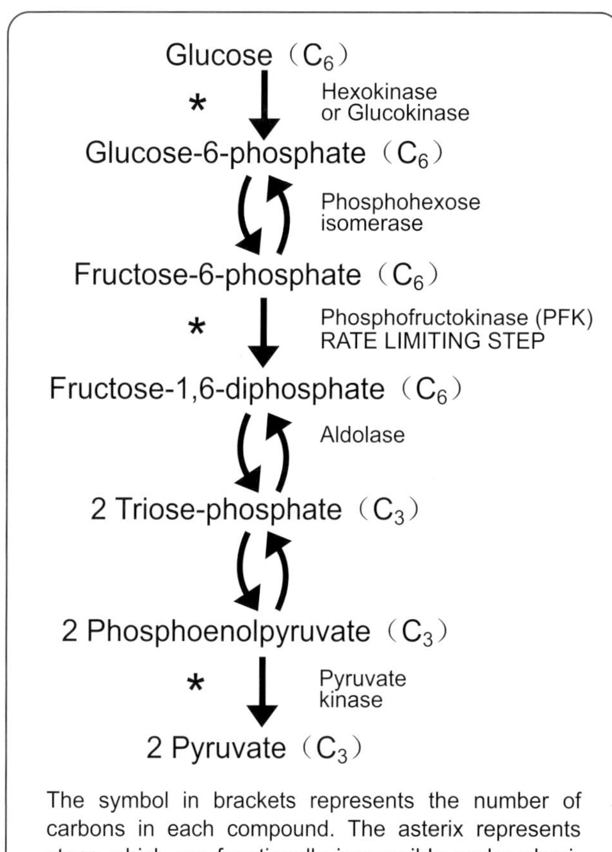

Figure IV.A.4.3: Summary of glycolysis.

Under **anaerobic conditions**, pyruvate is quickly reduced by NADH to lactic acid using the enzyme lactate dehydrogenase and NAD^+ is regenerated. A net of only 2 ATP is produced per molecule of glucose (this process is called *fermentation*).

Oxygen Debt: after running a 100m dash you may find yourself gasping for air even if you have completely ceased activity. This is because during the race you could not get an adequate amount of oxygen to your muscles and your muscles needed energy quickly; thus the anaerobic pathway was used. The lactic acid which built up during the race will require you to *pay back* a certain amount of oxygen in order to oxidize lactate to pyruvate and continue along the more energy efficient aerobic pathway.

4.6 Glycolysis: A Negative Perspective

An interesting way to summarize the main events of glycolysis is to follow the fate of the phosphate group which contains a negative charge. Note that *kinases* and *phosphatases* are enzymes that can add or subtract phosphate groups, respectively.

The first event in glycolysis is the phosphorylation of glucose. Thus glucose becomes negatively charged which prevents it from leaking out of the cell. Then glucose-6-phosphate becomes its isomer (= *same* molecular formula, *different* structure) fructose-6-phosphate which is further phosphorylated to fructose-1,6-diphosphate. Imagine that this six carbon sugar (*fructose*) now contains two large negatively charged ligands which repel each other! The six carbon sugar (*hexose*) sensibly breaks into two three-carbon compounds (*triose phosphates*).

A triose phosphate is ultimately converted to 1,3-diphosphoglycerate which is clearly an unstable compound (i.e. *two negative phosphate groups*). Thus it transfers a high energy phosphate group onto ADP to produce ATP. When ATP is produced from a substrate (i.e. 1,3-diphosphoglycerate), the reaction is called *substrate level phosphorylation*.

A closer look at ATP and glycolysis: from one molecule of glucose, 2 molecules of pyruvate are obtained. During the glycolytic reaction, 2 ATP are used (one used in the phosphorylation of glucose to glucose 6-phosphate and one used in the phosphorylation of fructose 6-phosphate to fructose 1,6-bisphosphate) and 4 ATP are generated (two in the conversion of 1,3-bisphophoglycerate to 3-phosphoglycerate and two in the conversion of phosphoenolpyruvate to pyruvate).

4.7 Krebs Citric Acid Cycle

Aerobic conditions: for further breakdown of pyruvate it has to enter the mitochondria where a series of reactions will cleave the molecule to water and carbon dioxide. All these reactions (which were discovered by Hans. A. Krebs) are collectively known as the Tricarboxylic Acid Cycle (TCA) or Krebs Citric Acid Cycle. Not only carbohydrates but also lipids and proteins use the TCA for channelling their metabolic pathways. This is why

TCA is often called the final common pathway of metabolism.

The glycolysis of glucose (C_6) produces 2 pyruvate (C_3) which in turn produces 2 CO_2 and 2 acetyl CoA (C_2). Pyruvate is oxidized to acetyl CoA and CO_2 by the pyruvate dehydrogenase complex (PDC). The PDC is a complex of 3 enzymes located in the mitochondria of eukaryotic cells (and of course, in the cytosol of prokaryotes). This step is also known as the *link reaction* or *transition step* since it links glycolysis and the TCA cycle.

The catabolism of both glucose and fatty acids yield acetyl CoA. Metabolism of amino acids yields acetyl CoA or actual intermediates of the TCA Cycle. The Citric Acid Cycle provides a pathway for the oxidation of acetyl CoA. The pathway includes eight discrete steps. Seven of the enzyme activities are found in the mitochondrial matrix; the eighth (succinate dehydrogenase) is associated with the Electron Transport Chain (ETC) within the inner mitochondrial membrane.

The following includes key points to remember about the TCA Cycle: i) glucose → 2 acetyl CoA → 2 turns around the TCA Cycle; ii) 2 CO_2 per turn is generated as a waste product which will eventually be blown off in the lungs; iii) one GTP (guanosine triphosphate) per turn is produced by substrate level phosphorylation; one GTP is equivalent to one ATP (*GTP + ADP → GDP + ATP*); iv) *reducing equivalents* are <u>hydrogens</u> which are carried by NAD^+ (→ NADH + H^+) three times per turn and FAD (→ $FADH_2$) once per turn; v) for each molecule of glucose, 2 pyruvates are produced and oxidized to acetyl CoA in the "fed" state (as opposed to the "fasting" state). The acetyl CoA then enters the TCA cycle, yielding 3 NADH, 1 $FADH_2$, and 1 GTP per acetyl CoA. These reducing equivalents will eventually be oxidized to produce ATP (*oxidative phosphorylation*) and eventually produce H_2O as a waste product (the last step in the ETC); vi) the hydrogens (*H*) which are reducing equivalents are not protons (H^+) - quite the contrary! Often the reducing equivalents are simply called electrons.

4.8 Oxidative Phosphorylation

The term oxidative phosphorylation refers to reactions associated with oxygen consumption and the phosphorylation of ADP to yield ATP. The synthesis of ATP is coupled to the flow of electrons from NADH and $FADH_2$ to O_2 in the electron transport chain. Oxidative phosphorylation is associated with an Electron Transport Chain or Respiratory Chain which is found in the inner mitochondrial membrane of eukaryotes. A similar process occurs within the plasma membrane of prokaryotes such as *E.coli*.

The importance of oxidative phosphorylation is that it accounts for the reoxidation of reducing equivalents generated in the reac-

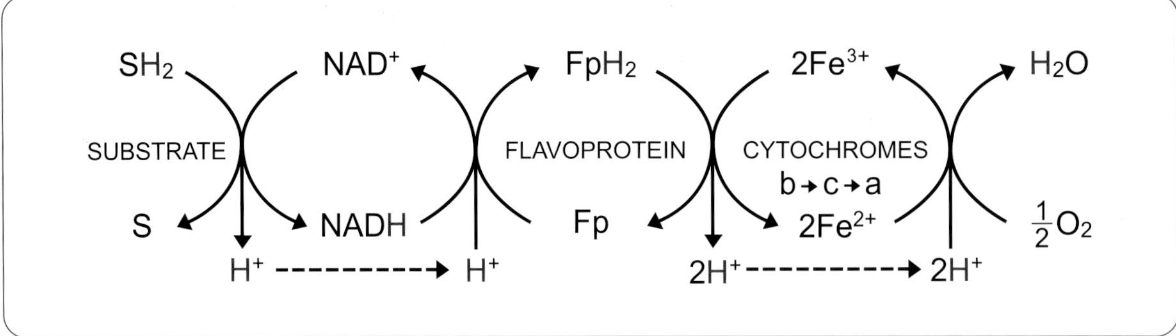

Figure IV.A.4.4: Transport of reducing equivalents through the respiratory chain. Examples of substrates (S) which provide reductants are isocitrate, malate, etc. Cytochromes contain iron (Fe).

tions of the Krebs Cycle as well as in glycolysis. This process accounts for the preponderance of ATP production in humans. The electron flow from NADH and $FADH_2$ to oxygen by a series of carrier molecules located in the inner mitochondrial membrane (IMM) provides energy to pump hydrogens from the mitochondrial matrix to the intermembrane space against the proton electrochemical gradient. The proton motive force then drives the movement of hydrogen back into the matrix thus providing the energy for ATP synthesis by ATP synthase. A schematic summary is in Figure IV.A.4.4.

The term *chemiosmosis* refers to the movement of protons across the IMM (a selectively permeable membrane) down their electrochemical gradient using the kinetic energy to phosphorylate ADP making ATP. The generation of ATP by chemiosmosis occurs in chloroplasts and mitochondria as well as in some bacteria.

4.9 Electron Transport Chain (ETC)

The following are the components of the ETC: iron - sulphur proteins, cytochromes c, b, a and coenzyme Q or *ubiquinone*. The respiratory chain proceeds from NAD specific dehydrogenases through flavoprotein, ubiquinone, then cytochromes and ultimately molecular oxygen. Reducing equivalents can enter the chain at two locations. Electrons from NADH are transferred to NADH dehydrogenase. In reactions involving iron - sulphur proteins electrons are transferred to coenzyme Q; protons are translocated from the mitochondrial matrix to the exterior of the inner membrane during this process. This creates a proton gradient, which is coupled to the production of ATP by ATP synthase.

Electrons entering from succinate dehydrogenase ($FADH_2$) are donated directly to coenzyme Q. Electrons are transported from reduced coenzyme Q to cytochrome b and then cytochrome c. Electrons are then carried by cytochrome c to cytochrome a. Cytochrome a is also known as *cytochrome oxidase*. It catalyzes the reaction of electrons and protons with molecular oxygen to produce water. Cyanide and carbon monoxide are powerful inhibitors of cytochrome oxidase.

4.10 Summary of Energy Production

Note the following: i) 1 NADH produces 3 ATP molecules while 1 $FADH_2$ produces only 2 ATP; ii) there is a cost of 2 ATP to get the two molecules of NADH generated in the cytoplasm (see the preceding point # 2.) to enter the mitochondrion, thus the *net yield for eukaryotes is 36 ATP.*

The efficiency of ATP production is far from 100%. Energy is lost from the system primarily in the form of heat. Under standard conditions, less than 40% of the energy generated from the complete oxidation of glucose is converted to the production of ATP. As a comparison, a gasoline engine fairs much worse with an efficiency rating generally less than 20%. Further inefficiencies reduce the net theoretical yield in the (non-DAT!) real world.

Process of reaction	ATP yield
1. Glycolysis (Glucose → 2 Pyruvate)	2
2. Glycolysis (2NADH from glyceraldehyde-3-phosphate dehydrogenase)	6
3. Pyruvate dehydrogenase (2NADH)	6
4. Isocitrate dehydrogenase (2NADH)	6
5. Alpha-ketoglutarate dehydrogenase (2NADH)	6
6. Succinate thiokinase (2GTP)	2
7. Succinate dehydrogenase (2$FADH_2$)	4
8. Malate dehydrogenase (2NADH)	6
TOTAL	38 ATP yield per hexose.

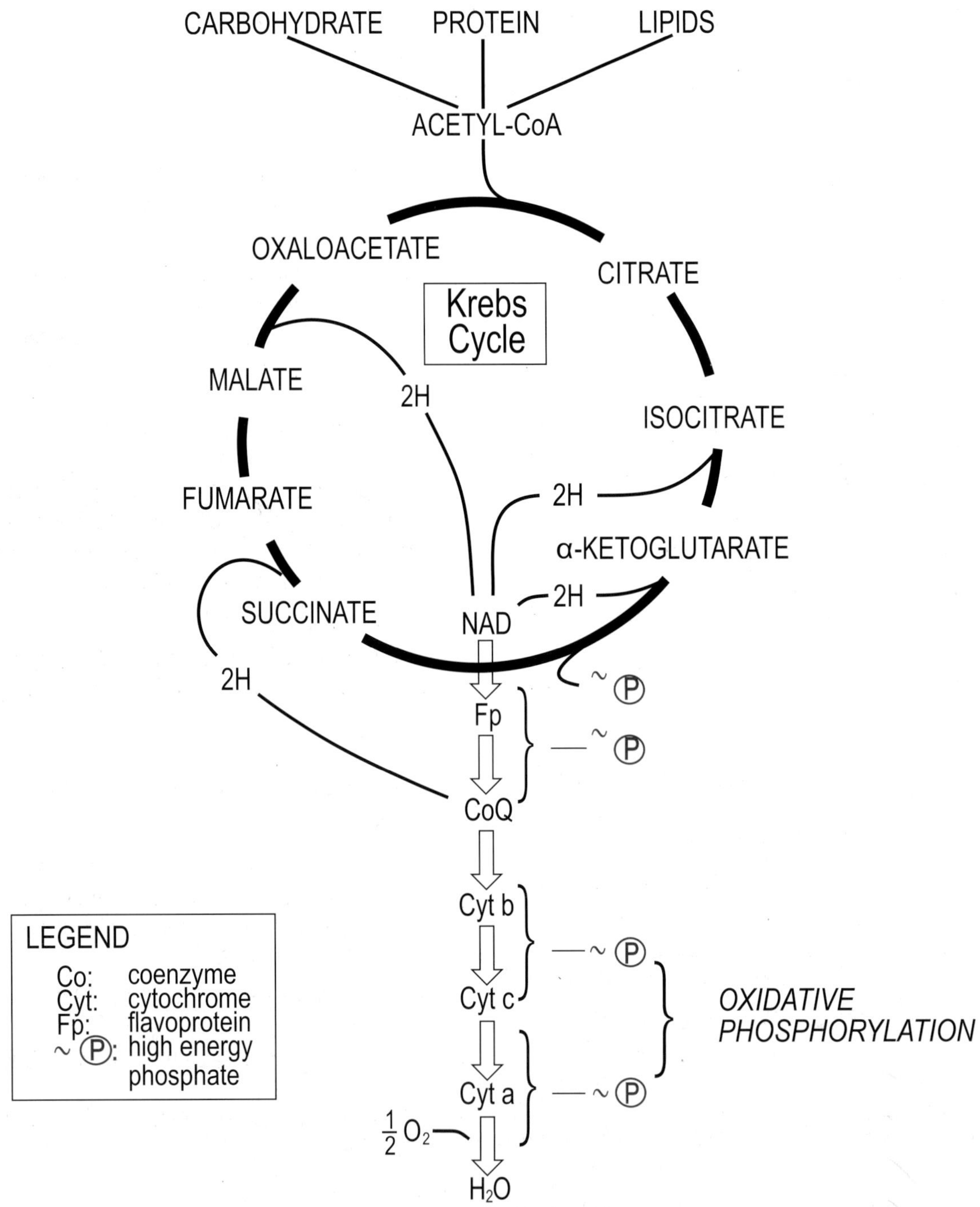

Figure IV.A.4.5: Summary of the Krebs Cycle and the Electron Transport Chain.

Note: Acetyl CoA can be the product of carbohydrate, protein, or lipid metabolism. Thick black arrows represent the Krebs Cycle while white arrows represent the Electron Transport Chain. High energy phosphate groups are transferred from ADP to produce ATP. Ultimately, oxygen accepts electrons and hydrogen from Cyt a to produce water.

GOLD STANDARD WARM-UP EXERCISES

CHAPTER 4: Enzymes and Cellular Metabolism

1) Oxidation of fats and carbohydrates within a cell would be an example of:

   A. biosynthesis.
   B. catabolism.
   C. anabolism.
   D. positive co-operativity.

2) If individuals with PKU disease lack the protein phenylalanine hydroxylase, what would best explain their being able to metabolize small amounts of phenylalanine?

   A. Non-specific enzymes cleave phenylalanine.
   B. Phenylalanine catalyzes reactions in the liver.
   C. Phenylalanine is broken down mechanically in the formation of chyme in the stomach.
   D. Phenylalanine is defecated from the body.

3) Phenylalanine hydroxylase most likely:

   A. cleaves a $-OCH_3$ group from phenylalanine.
   B. adds a $-OCH_3$ group to phenylalanine.
   C cleaves a $-OH_2$ group from phenylalanine.
   D. adds a -OH group to phenylalanine.

4) Prostaglandins are complex lipid molecules, some of which mediate the sensation of pain. Aspirin, a common pain reliever, likely works by:

   A. acting like a non-competitive reversible inhibitor and binding to the active site on the prostaglandin molecule.
   B. acting like a competitive inhibitor and binding to a site other than the active site on the prostaglandin molecule.
   C. acting like an allosteric inhibitor of the prostaglandin molecule.
   D. inhibiting the synthesis of the prostaglandin molecule.

5) The symmetry model describes a form of cooperative binding. Most enzymes do not engage in cooperative binding. The predicted shape of a graph representing the addition of substrate to most enzymes over a period of time would be expected to be:

   A. a hyperbola.
   B. a straight line with a positive slope.
   C. a straight line with a negative slope.
   D. sigmoidal.

6) Allosteric enzymes differ from other enzymes in that they:

   A. are not denatured at high temperatures.
   B. are regulated by compounds which are not their substrates and which do not bind to their active sites.
   C. they operate at an optimum pH of about 2.0.
   D. they are not specific to just one substrate.

7) What controls the steps in the respiration of glucose?

   A. Enzymes
   B. Rate of photosynthesis
   C. Amount of water present
   D. Absence of NAD

8) Which of the following is NOT a product of glycolysis?

A. A net 2 ATP
B. Acetyl-CoA
C. Pyruvate
D. Reducing equivalents

9) Most body heat, under normal conditions, is produced by:

A. the reduction of foods.
B. the oxidation of foods.
C. the breakdown of skeletal muscle.
D. the release of thyroid stimulating hormone.

10) What is the role of electron transfer in ATP synthesis?

A. Pump protons to create an electrochemical potential
B. Create a pH gradient
C. Create a concentration gradient
D. Create a chemical gradient

11) Why do you think the inner mitochondrial membrane (IMM) is impermeable to protons?

A. Because the IMM is positively charged.
B. Because the IMM is negatively charged.
C. Because the IMM is polar.
D. Because the IMM is highly selective due to its complex structure generating a gradient.

12) The highest amount of ATP per molecule of glucose would be generated as a result of:

A. glycolysis.
B. the Krebs cycle.
C. the hydrolysis of glycogen.
D. the transamination of amino acids.

GS ANSWER KEY

CHAPTER 4

		Cross-Reference			*Cross-Reference*
1.	B	BIO 4.1, 4.4	7.	A	BIO 4.5, 4.6
2.	A	BIO 4.1, 4.3	8.	B	BIO 4.5
3.	D	BIO 4.5-4.10	9.	B	BIO 4.4-4.10, 6.3.3
4.	D	BIO 4.2	10.	A	BIO 4.8, 4.9, 4.10
5.	A	Ap A.3.3, CHM 9.7F, BIO 4.1, 7.5.1	11.	D	BIO 4.8, 4.9, 4.10
6.	B	BIO 4.1, 4.3	12.	B	BIO 4.7, 4.10

* Explanations can be found at the back of the book.

Go online to DAT-prep.com for additional chapter review Q&A and forum.

APPENDIX

CHAPTER 4: Enzymes and Cellular Metabolism

Advanced DAT-30 Passage: The Symmetry Model (MWC Model)

Several models have been developed for relating changes in dissociation constants to changes in the tertiary and quaternary structures of oligomeric proteins. One model suggests that the protein's subunits can exist in either of two distinct conformations, R and T. At equilibrium, there are few R conformation molecules: 10 000 T to 1 R and it is an important feature of the enzyme that this ratio does not change. The substrate is assumed to bind more tightly to the R form than to the T form, which means that binding of the substrate favors the transition from the T conformation to R.

The conformational transitions of the individual subunits are assumed to be tightly linked, so that if one subunit flips from T to R the others must do the same. The binding of the first molecule of substrate thus promotes the binding of the second and if substrate is added continuously, all of the enzyme will be in the R form and act on the substrate. Because the concerted transition of all of the subunits from T to R or back, preserves the overall symmetry of the protein, this model is called the symmetry model (= the concerted model or MWC model, an acronym for Monod-Wyman-Changeux). The model further predicts that allosteric activating enzymes make the R conformation even more reactive with the substrate while allosteric inhibitors react with the T conformation so that most of the enzyme is held back in the T shape.

13) What assumption is made about the T and R conformations and the substrate?

- **A.** In the absence of any substrate, the T conformation predominates.
- **B.** In the absence of any substrate, the R conformation predominates.
- **C.** In the absence of any substrate, the T and R conformations are in equilibrium.
- **D.** In the absence of any substrate, the enzyme exists in another conformation, S.

14) The substrate binds more tightly to R because:

- **A.** T has a higher affinity for the substrate than R.
- **B.** R has a higher affinity for the substrate than T.
- **C.** there are 10 000 times more T conformation molecules than R conformation molecules.
- **D.** the value of the equilibrium constant does not change.

15) The symmetry model describes a form of cooperative binding. Most enzymes do not engage in cooperative binding. The predicted shape of a graph representing the addition of substrate to most enzymes over a period of time would be expected to be:

- **A.** a hyperbola.
- **B.** a straight line with a positive slope.
- **C.** a straight line with a negative slope.
- **D.** sigmoidal.

16) The symmetry model would NOT account for an enzyme:

A. with many different biologically active conformations.
B. which engages in positive cooperativity.
C. with a complex metal cofactor.
D. which is a catalyst for anabolic reactions.

17) Allosteric enzymes differ from other enzymes in that they:

A. are not denatured at high temperatures.
B. are regulated by compounds which are not their substrates and which do not bind to their active sites.
C. they operate at an optimum pH of about 2.0.
D. they are not specific to just one substrate.

ANSWER KEY

ADVANCED TOPICS - CHAPTER 4

		Cross-Reference
13.	A	P1
14.	B	BIO 4.1, 4.3
15.	A	BIO 4.3, 7.5.1
16.	A	Deduce; BIO 4.1, 4.2
17.	B	BIO 4.1, 4.3

P = paragraph; *S* = sentence; *E* = equation; *T* = table; *F* = figure

Go online to DAT-prep.com for additional chapter review Q&A and forum.

SPECIALIZED EUKARYOTIC CELLS AND TISSUES

Chapter 5

Memorize	Understand	Importance
* Neuron: basic structure and function * Reasons for the membrane potential * Structural characteristics of striated, smooth, and cardiac muscle * Basic structure/function: epithelial cells, sarcomeres, connective tissue cells	* Resting potential: electrochemical gradient/action potential, graph * Excitatory and inhibitory nerve fibers: summation, frequency of firing * Organization of contractile elements: actin and myosin filaments * Cross bridges, sliding filament model; calcium regulation of contraction	**0 to 2 out of the 40 Biology** DAT questions are based on content in this chapter (in our estimation). * Note that between 25% and 50% of the questions in DAT Biology are from 5 chapters: 1, 2, 14, 15, and 16.

DAT-Prep.com

Introduction

To build a living organism, with all the various tissues and organs, cells must specialize. Communication among cells and organs, movement, protection and support are achieved to a great degree by neurons, muscle cells, epithelial cells and the cells of connective tissue, respectively.

Additional Resources

Free Online Q&A + Forum

Video: Online or DVD

Flashcards

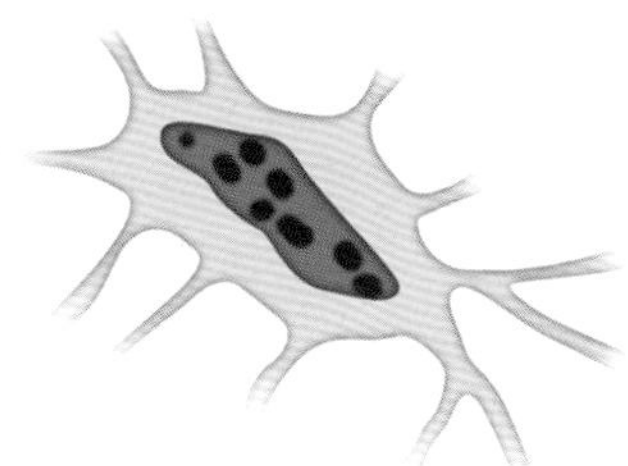

Special Guest

5.1 Neural Cells and Tissues

The brain, spinal cord and peripheral nervous system are composed of nerve tissue. The basic cell types of nerve tissue is the *neuron* and the *glial cell*. Glial cells support and protect neurons and participate in neural activity, nutrition and defense processes. Neurons (= nerve cells) represent the functional unit of the nervous system. They conduct and transmit nerve impulses.

Neurons can be classified based on the shape or *morphology*. Unipolar neurons possess a single process. Bipolar neurons possess a single axon and a single dendrite. Multipolar neurons possess a single axon and more than one dendrite and are the most common type. Pseudounipolar neurons possess a single process that subsequently branches out into an axon and dendrite (note that in biology "pseudo" means "false"). Neurons can also be classified based on function. Sensory neurons receive stimuli from the environment and conduct impulses to the CNS. Motor neurons conduct impulses from the CNS to other neurons, muscles or glands. Interneurons connect other neurons and regulate transmitting signal between neurons.

Each neuron consists of a nerve cell body (*perikaryon or soma*), and its processes, which usually include multiple *dendrites* and a single *axon*. The cell body of a typical neuron contains a nucleus, *Nissl* material which is rough endoplasmic reticulum, free ribosomes, Golgi apparatus, mitochondria, many neurotubules, neurofilaments and pigment inclusions. The cell processes of neurons occur as axons and dendrites.

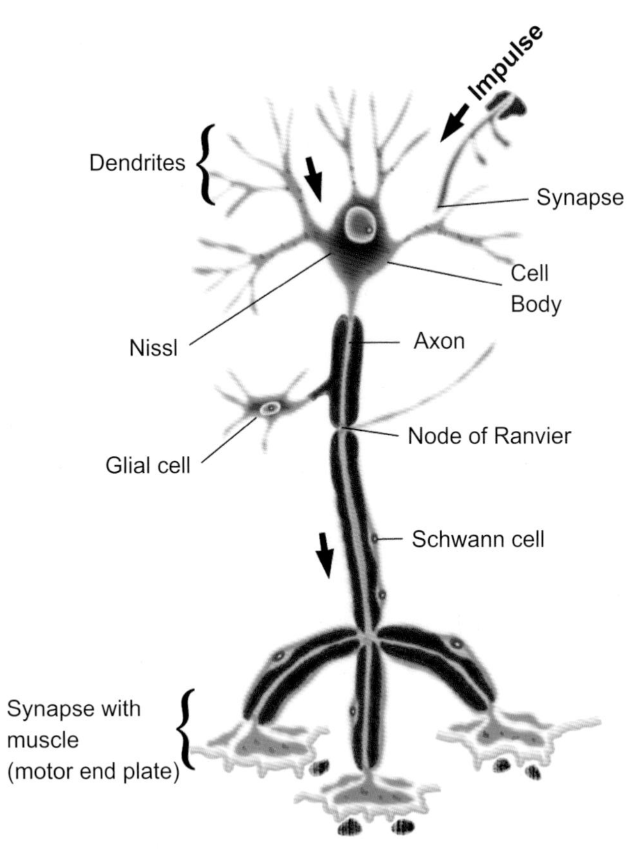

Figure IV.A.5.1: A neuron and other cells of nerve tissue, showing the neuromuscular junction, or motor end plate.

Dendrites contain most of the components of the cell, whereas axons contain major structures found in dendrites except for the Nissl material and Golgi apparatus. As a rule, dendrites receive stimuli from sensory cells, axons, or other neurons and conduct these impulses to the cell body of neurons and ultimately through to the axon. Axons are long cellular processes that conduct impulses away from the cell body of neurons. These originate from the axon hillock, a specialized region that contains many microtubules and neurofilaments. At the synaptic (terminal) ends of axons, the presynaptic process contains vesicles from which are elaborated excitatory or inhibitory substances.

Unmyelinated fibers in peripheral nerves lie in grooves on the surface of the neurolemma (= plasma membrane) of a type of glial cell (*Schwann cell*). **Myelinated** peripheral neurons are invested by numerous layers of plasma membrane of Schwann cells or oligodendrocytes that constitute a *myelin sheath*, which allows axons to conduct impulses faster. The myelin sheath is produced by oligodendrocytes in the CNS and by Schwann cells in the PNS. In junctional areas between adjacent Schwann cells or oligodendrocytes there is a lack of myelin. These junctional areas along the myelinated process constitute the nodes of Ranvier.

The neurons of the nervous system are arranged so that each neuron stimulates or inhibits other neurons and these in turn may stimulate or inhibit others until the functions of the nervous system are performed. The area between a neuron and the successive cell (i.e. another neuron, muscle fiber or gland) is called a *synapse*. Synapses can be classified as either a chemical synapse or an electrical synapse. A chemical synapse involves the release of a neurotransmitter by the presynaptic cell which then diffuses across the synapse and can act on the postsynaptic cell to generate an action potential. Signal transmission is delayed due to the time required for diffusion of the neurotransmitter across the synapse onto the membrane of the postsynaptic cell. An electrical synapse involves the movement of ions from one neuron to another via gap junctions (BIO 1.4.1). Signal transmission is immediate. Electrical synapses are often found in neural systems that require the fastest possible response, such as defensive reflexes.

When a neuron makes a synapse with muscle, it is called a *motor end plate* (see Fig. IV.A.5.1). The terminal endings of the nerve filament that synapse with the next cell are called presynaptic terminals, synaptic knobs, or more commonly - synaptic boutons. The postsynaptic terminal is the membrane part of another neuron or muscle or gland that is receiving the impulse. The synaptic cleft is the narrow space between the presynaptic and postsynaptic membrane.

At the synapse there is no physical contact between the two cells. The space between the dendrite of one neuron and the axon of another neuron is called the synaptic cleft and it measures about 200 - 300 angstroms (1 angstrom = 10^{-10} m) in a chemical synapse and about a tenth of that distance in an electrical synapse. The mediators in a chemical synapse, known as neurotransmitters, are housed in the presynaptic terminal and are exocytosed in response to an increase in intracellular Ca^{2+} concentration. The mediators or transmitters diffuse through the synaptic cleft when an impulse reaches the terminal and bind to receptors in the postsynaptic membrane. This transmitter substance may either excite the *postsynaptic* neuron or inhibit it. They are therefore called either excitatory or inhibitory transmitters (examples include *acetylcholine* and *GABA*, respectively).

5.1.1 The Membrane Potential

A membrane or resting potential (V_m) occurs across the plasma membranes of all cells. In large nerve and muscle cells this potential amounts to about 70 millivolts with positivity outside the cell membrane and negativity inside (V_m = -70 mV). The development of this potential occurs as follows: every cell membrane contains a Na^+ - K^+ ATPase that pumps each ion to where its concentration is highest. The concentration of K^+ is higher inside the neuron and the concentration of Na^+ is higher outside; therefore, Na^+ is pumped to the outside of the cell and K^+ to the inside. However, more Na^+ is pumped outward than K^+ inward (3Na^+ per 2K^+). Also, the membrane is relatively permeable to K^+ so that it can leak out of the cell with relative ease. Therefore, the net effect is a loss of positive charges from inside the membrane and a gain of positive charges on the outside. The resulting membrane potential is the basis of all conduction of impulses by nerve and muscle fibers.

5.1.2 Action Potential

The action potential is a sequence of changes in the electric potential that occurs within a small fraction of a second when a nerve or muscle membrane impulse spreads over the surface of the cell. An excitatory stimulus on a postsynaptic neuron depolarizes the membrane and makes the membrane potential less negative. Once the membrane potential reaches a critical threshold, the voltage-gated Na^+ channels become fully open, permitting the inward flow of Na^+ into the cell. The membrane potential is at the critical threshold when it is in a state where an action potential is inevitable. As a result, the positive sodium ions on the outside of the membrane now flow rapidly to the more negative interior. Therefore, the membrane potential suddenly becomes reversed with positivity on the inside and negativity on the outside. This state is called *depolarization* and is caused by an inward Na^+ current.

Depolarization also leads to the inactivation of the Na^+ channel and slowly opens the K^+ channel. The combined effect of the two preceding events repolarizes the membrane back to its resting potential. This is called *repolarization*. In fact, the neuron may shoot past the resting membrane potential and become even more negative, and this is called hyperpolarization. The depolarized nerve goes on depolarizing the adjacent nerve membrane in a wavy manner which is called an impulse. In other words, an impulse is a wave of depolarization. Different axons can propagate impulses at different speeds. The increasing diameter of a nerve fiber or degree of myelination results in a faster impulse. The impulse is fastest in myelinated fibers since the wave of depolarization "jumps" from node to node of Ranvier: this is called *saltatory* conduction because an action potential can be generated only at nodes of Ranvier.

Immediately following an action potential, the neuron will pass through three stages in the following order: a) it can no longer elicit

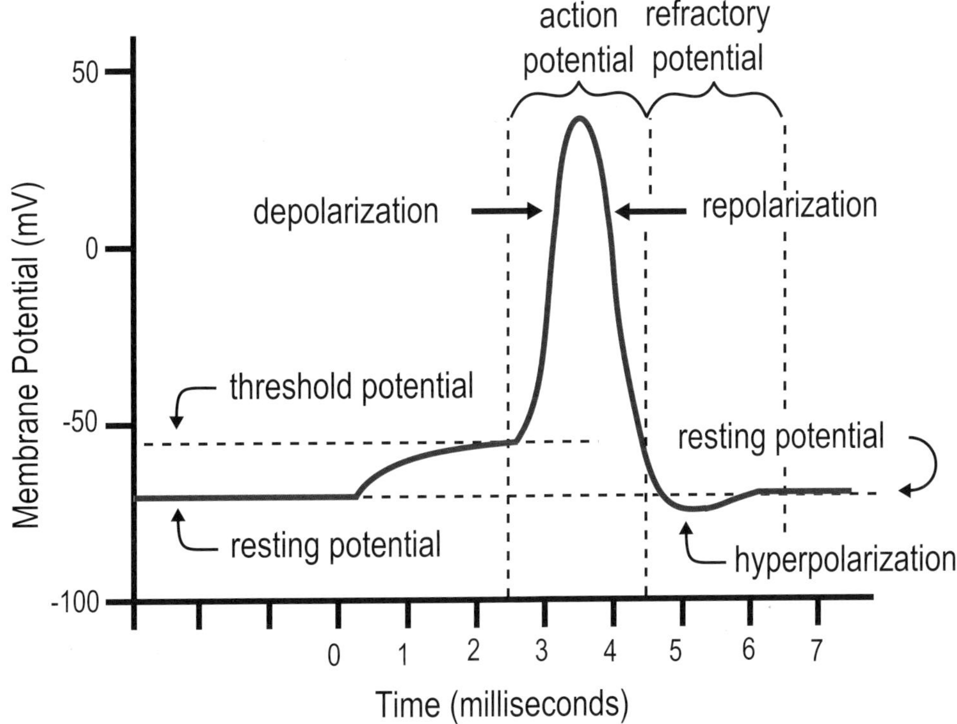

Figure IV.A.5.2: Action potential.

another action potential no matter how large the stimulus is = *absolute refractory period*; b) it can elicit another action potential only if a larger than usual stimulus is provided = *relative refractory period*; c) it returns to its original resting potential and thus can depolarize as easily as it originally did.

The action potential is an all-or-none event. The magnitude or strength of the action potential is not graded according to the strength of the stimulus. It occurs with the same magnitude each time it occurs, or it does not occur at all.

5.1.3 Action Potential: A Positive Perspective

To better understand the action potential it is useful to take a closer look at what occurs to the positive ions Na^+ and K^+. To begin with, there are protein channels in the plasma membrane that act like gates which guard the passage of specific ions. Some gates open or close in response to V_m and are thus called *voltage gated channels.*

Once a threshold potential is reached, the voltage gated Na^+ channels open allowing the permeability or *conductance* of Na^+ to increase. The Na^+ ions can now diffuse across their chemical gradient: from an area of high concentration (*outside the membrane*) to an area of low concentration (*inside the membrane*). The Na^+ ions will also diffuse across their electrical gradient: from an area of relative positivity (*outside the membrane*) to an area of relative negativity (*inside the membrane*). Thus the inside becomes positive and the membrane is depolarized. Repolarization occurs as the Na^+ channels close and the voltage gated K^+ channels open. As K^+ conductance increases to the outside (where K^+ concentration is lowest), the membrane repolarizes to once again become relatively negative on the inside.

5.2 Contractile Cells and Tissues

There are three types of muscle tissue: smooth, skeletal and cardiac. All three types are composed of muscle cells (fibers) that contain myofibrils possessing contractile filaments of actin and myosin.

Smooth muscle:- Smooth muscle cells are spindle shaped and are organized chiefly into sheets or bands of smooth muscle tissue. They contain a single nucleus and actively divide and regenerate. This tissue is found in blood vessels and other tubular visceral structures (i.e. intestines). Smooth muscles contain both actin and myosin filaments but actin predominates. The filaments are not organized into patterns that give cross striations as in cardiac and skeletal muscle. Filaments course obliquely in the cells and attach to the plasma membrane. Contraction of smooth muscle is involuntary and is innervated by the autonomic nervous system.

Skeletal muscle:- Skeletal muscle fibers are characterized by their peripherally located multiple nuclei and striated myofibrils. Myofibrils are longitudinally arranged bundles of thick and thin myofilaments. Myofilaments are composed of thick and thin filaments present in an alternating arrangement responsible for the cross-striation pattern. The striations in a sarcomere consists of an A-band (dark), which contains both thin and thick filaments. These are bordered toward the Z-lines by I-bands (light), which contain thin filaments only. The mid-region of the A-band contains an H-band (light), which contains thick filaments only and is bisected by an M-line. The Z lines are dense regions bisecting each I-band and anchor the thin filaments. The filaments interdigitate and are cross-bridged in the A-band with myosin filaments forming a hexagonal pattern of one myosin filament surrounded by six actin filaments. In the contraction of a muscle fiber,

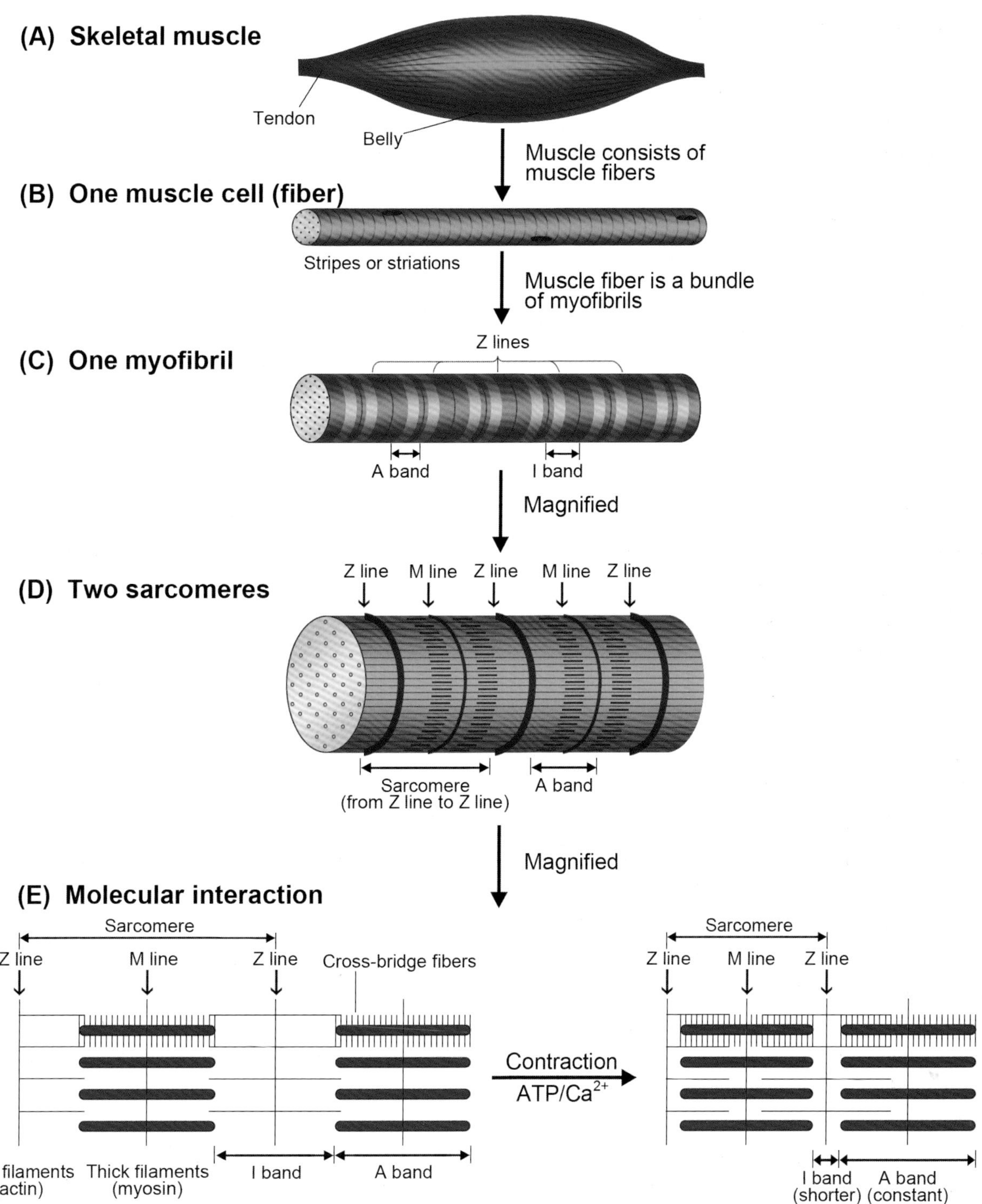

Figure IV.A.5.3: A schematic view of the molecular basis for muscle contraction. Note: the "H zone" is the central portion of an A band and is characterized by the presence of myosin filaments.

thick and thin filaments do not shorten but increase their overlap. The actin filaments of the I-bands move more deeply into the A-band, resulting in a shortening of the H-band and the I-bands as Z disks are brought closer. However, the A-band remains constant in length. {Mnemonic: "HI" bands shorten}

Each skeletal muscle fiber is invested with a sarcolemma (= plasmalemma = plasma membrane) that extends into the fiber as numerous small transverse tubes called T-tubules. These tubules ring the myofibrils at the A-I junction and are bounded on each side by terminal cisternae of the endoplasmic (sarcoplasmic) reticulum. The T-tubules, together with a pair of terminal cisternae form a triad. The triad helps to provide a uniform contraction throughout the muscle cell as it provides channels for ions to flow freely and helps to propagate action potentials. There are thousands of triads per skeletal muscle fiber.

The sarcoplasmic reticulum is a modified endoplasmic reticulum that regulates muscle contraction by either transporting Ca^{2+} into storage (muscle relaxation) or releasing Ca^{2+} during excitation-contraction coupling (muscle contraction).

The thick filaments within a myofibril are composed of about 250 myosin molecules arranged in an antiparallel fashion and some associated proteins. The myosin molecule is composed of two identical heavy chains and two pairs of light chain. The heavy chain consists of two "heads" and one "tail". The head contains an actin binding site which is involved in muscle contraction. The thin filaments within a myofibril are composed of actin and to a lesser degree two smaller proteins: *troponin and tropomyosin*. An action potential in the muscle cell membrane initiates depolarization of the T tubules, which causes the nearby sarcoplasmic reticulum to release its Ca^{2+} ions and thus an increase in intracellular [Ca^{2+}]. Calcium then attaches to a subunit of troponin resulting in the movement of tropomyosin and the uncovering of the active sites for the attachment of actin to the cross bridging heads of myosin. Due to this attachment, ATP in the myosin head hydrolyses, producing energy, Pi and ADP which results in a bending of the myosin head and a pulling of the actin filament into the A-band. These actin-myosin bridges detach again when myosin binds a new ATP molecule and attaches to a new site on actin toward the plus end as long as Ca^{2+} is bound to troponin. Finally, relaxation of muscle occurs when Ca^{2+} is sequestered by the sarcoplasmic reticulum. Thus calcium is pumped out of the cytoplasm and calcium levels return to normal, tropomyosin again binds to actin, preventing myosin from binding.

There are three interesting consequences to the preceding:

i) neither actin nor myosin change length during muscle contraction; rather, shortening of the muscle fiber occurs as the filaments slide over each other increasing the area of overlap.

ii) initially a dead person is very stiff (*rigor mortis*) since they can no longer produce the ATP necessary to detach the actin-myosin bridges thus their muscles remain locked in position.

iii) Ca^{2+} is a critical ion both for muscle contraction and for transmitter release from presynaptic neurons.

Cardiac muscle:- Cardiac muscle contains striations and myofibrils that are similar to those of skeletal muscle. Contraction of cardiac muscle is involuntary and is innervated by the autonomic nervous system. It differs from skeletal muscle in several major ways. Cardiac muscle fibers branch and contain centrally located nuclei (characteristically, one nucleus per cell) and large numbers of mitochondria. Individual cardiac muscle cells are attached to each other at their ends by *intercalated* disks. These disks contain several types of membrane junctional complexes, the most important of which is the *gap junction* (BIO 1.4.1). Cardiac muscle cells do not regenerate: injury to cardiac muscle is repaired by fibrous connective tissue.

The gap junction electrically couples one cell to its neighbor (= *syncytium*) so that electric depolarization is propagated throughout the heart by cell-to-cell contact rather than by nerve innervation to each cell. The sarcoplasmic reticulum - T-tubule system is arranged differently in cardiac muscle than in skeletal muscle. In cardiac muscle each T-tubule enters at the Z-line and forms a diad with only one terminal cisterna of sarcoplasmic reticulum.

5.3 Epithelial Cells and Tissues

Epithelia have the following characteristics:

1. they cover all body surfaces (i.e. skin, organs, etc.)
2. they are the principal tissues of glands
3. their cells are anchored by a nonliving layer (= the basement membrane)
4. they lack blood vessels and are thus nourished by diffusion.

Epithelial tissues are classified according to the characteristics of their cells. Tissues with elongated cells are called *columnar*, those with thin flattened cells are *squamous*, and those with cube-like cells are *cuboidal*. They are further classified as **simple** if they have a single layer of cells and **stratified** if they have multiple layers of cells. As examples of the classification, skin is composed of a stratified squamous epithelium while various glands (i.e. thyroid, salivary, etc.) contain a simple cuboidal epithelium. The former epithelium serves to protect against microorganisms, loss of water or heat, while the latter epithelium functions to secrete glandular products.

5.4 Connective Cells and Tissues

Connective tissue connects and joins other body tissue and parts. It also carries substances for processing, nutrition, and waste release. Connective tissue is characterized by the presence of relatively few cells surrounded by an extensive network of extracellular matrix, consisting of ground substance, extracellular fluid, and fibers.

The adult connective tissues are: connective tissue proper, cartilage, bone and blood (see *The Circulatory System*, section 7.5). Connective tissue proper is further classified into loose connective tissue, dense connective tissue, elastic tissue, reticular tissue and adipose tissue.

5.4.1 Loose Connective Tissue

Loose connective tissue is found in the superficial fascia. It is generally considered as the *packaging material* of the body, in part, because it frequently envelopes muscles. Fascia - usually a clear or white sheet (or band) of fibrous connective tissue - helps to bind skin to underlying organs, to fill spaces between muscles, etc. Loose connective tissue contains most of the cell types and all the fiber types found in the other connective tissues. The most common cell types are the fibroblast, macrophage, adipose cell, mast cell, plasma cell and wandering cells from the blood (which include several types of white blood cells).

Fibroblasts are the predominant cell type in connective tissue proper and have the capability to differentiate into other types of cells under certain conditions.

Macrophages are part of the *reticulo-endothelial system* (tissue which predominately destroys foreign particles). They are responsible for phagocytosing foreign bodies and assisting the immune response. They possess large lysosomes containing digestive enzymes which are necessary for the digestion of phagocytosed materials. Mast cells reside mostly along blood vessels and contain granules which include *heparin* and *histamine*. Heparin is a compound which prevents blood clotting and histamine is associated with allergic reactions. Mast cells mediate type I hypersensitivity.

Plasma cells are part of the immune system in that they produce circulatory antibodies (BIO 7.5, 8.2). They contain extensive amounts of rough endoplasmic reticulum (rER).

Adipose cells are found in varying quantities, when they predominate, the tissue is called adipose (fat) tissue.

Fibers are long protein polymers present in different types of connective tissue. Common types of fibers include collagen fiber, reticular fiber and elastic fiber.

Collagen fibers are usually found in bundles and provide **strength** to the tissue. Many different types of collagen fibers are identified on the basis of their molecular structure. Of the five most common types, collagen type I is the most abundant, being found in dermis, bone, dentine, tendons, organ capsules, fascia and sclera. Type II is located in hyaline and elastic cartilage. Type III is probably the collagenous component of reticular fibers. Type IV is found in a specific part (*the basal lamina*) of basement membranes. Type V is a component of placental basement membranes. **Reticular fibers** are smaller, more delicate fibers that form the basic framework of reticular connective tissue. **Elastic fibers** branch and provide elasticity and support to connective tissue.

Ground substance is the gelatinous material that fills most of the space between the cells and the fibers. It is composed of acid mucopolysaccharides and structural glycoproteins and its properties are important in determining the permeability and consistency of the connective tissue.

5.4.2 Dense Connective Tissue

Dense irregular connective tissue is found in the dermis, periosteum, perichondrium and capsules of some organs. All of the fiber types are present, but collagenous fibers predominate. Dense regular connective tissue occurs as aponeuroses, ligaments and tendons. In most ligaments and tendons collagenous fibers are most prevalent and are oriented parallel to each other. Fibroblasts are practically the only cell type present.

5.4.3 Cartilage

Cartilage is composed of chondrocytes (= cartilage cells) embedded in an intercellular (= extracellular) matrix, consisting of fibers and an amorphous firm ground substance. In cases of injury, cartilage repairs slowly since it has no direct blood supply. Three types of cartilage are distinguished on the basis of the amount of ground substance and the relative abundance of collagenous and elastic fibers. They are hyaline, elastic and fibrous cartilage.

Hyaline Cartilage is found as costal (rib) cartilage, articular cartilage and cartilage of the nose, larynx, trachea and bronchi. The extracellular matrix consists primarily of collagenous fibers and a ground substance rich in chondromucoprotein, a copolymer of a protein and chondroitin sulphates.

Elastic Cartilage is found in the pinna of the ear, auditory tube and epiglottis, and some laryngeal cartilage. Elastic fibers predominate and thus provide greater flexibility. Calcification of this type of cartilage is rare.

Fibrous Cartilage occurs in the anchorage of tendons and ligaments, in intervertebral disks, in the symphysis pubis, and in some interarticular disks and in some ligaments. Chondrocytes occur singly or in rows between large bundles of collagenous fibers. Compared with hyaline cartilage, only small amounts of hyaline matrix surround the chondrocytes of fibrous cartilage.

5.4.4 Bone

Bone tissue consists of three **cell types** and a calcified **extracellular matrix** that contains organic and inorganic components. The three cell types are: *osteoblasts* which synthesize the organic components of the matrix (osteoid) and become embedded in lacunae; *osteocytes* which are mature bone cells entrapped in their own lacunae within the matrix and maintain communication with each other via gap junctions; and *osteoclasts* which are large multinucleated cells functioning in resorption and remodeling of bone.

The organic matrix consists of dense collagenous fibers (primarily type I collagen) which is important in providing flexibility and tensile strength to bone. The inorganic component is responsible for the *rigidity* of the bone and is composed chiefly of calcium phosphate and calcium carbonate with small amounts of magnesium, fluoride, hydroxide, sulphate and hydroxyapatite.

Compact bone contains haversian systems (osteons), interstitial lamellae and circumferential lamellae. The Haversian system is the structural unit for bone and each osteon consists of a central Haversian canal surrounded by a number of concentric deposits of bony matrix called lamellae. Haversian systems consist of extensively branching haversian canals that are oriented chiefly longitudinally in long bones. Each canal contains blood vessels and is surrounded by 8 to 15 concentric lamellae and osteocytes.

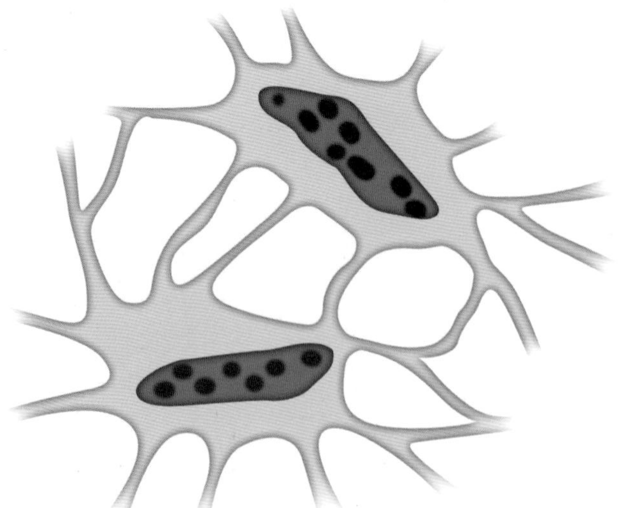

Figure IV.A.5.4: Osteocytes.

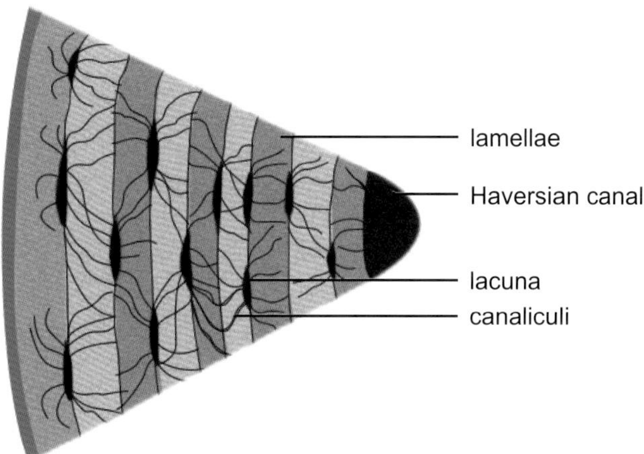

Figure IV.A.5.5: Schematic drawing of part of a haversian system.

Nutrients from blood vessels in the haversian canals pass through canaliculi and lacunae to reach all osteocytes in the system. Volkmann's canals traverse the bone transversely and interconnect the haversian systems. They enter through the outer circumferential lamellae and carry blood vessels and nerves which are continuous with those of the haversian canals and the periosteum. The periosteum is the connective tissue layer which envelopes bone. The endosteum is the connective tissue layer which lines the marrow cavities and supplies osteoprogenitor cells and osteoblasts for bone formation.

Figure IV.A.5.6
Schematic drawing of the wall of a long bone.

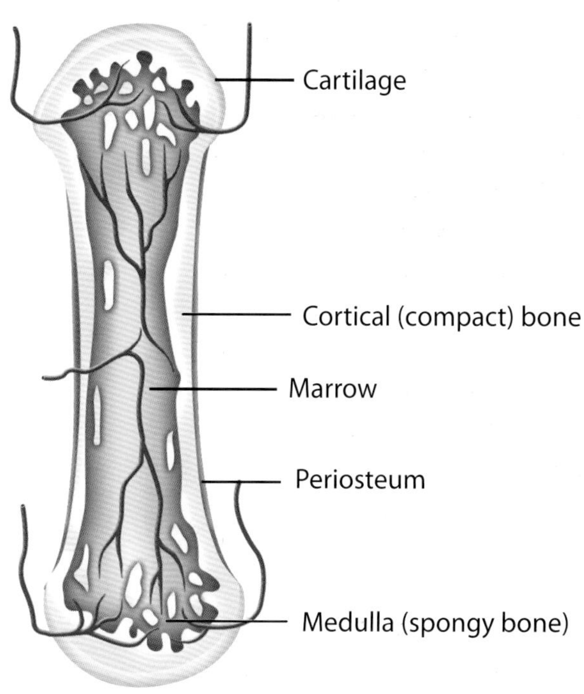

Figure IV.A.5.7
Schematic drawing of adult bone structure.

Bones are supplied by a loop of blood vessels that enter from the periosteal region, penetrate the cortical bone, and enter the medulla before returning to the periphery of the bone. Long bones are specifically supplied by arteries which pass to the marrow through diaphyseal, metaphyseal and epiphyseal arteries (for bone structure, see BIO 11.3.1).

Bone undergoes extensive remodelling, and harvesian systems may break down or be resorbed in order that calcium can be made available to other parts of the body. Bone resorption occurs by osteocytes engaging in osteolysis or by osteoclastic activity.

GOLD STANDARD WARM-UP EXERCISES

CHAPTER 5: Specialized Eukaryotic Cells and Tissues

1) Which of the following is NOT part of a neuron?

A. Synapse
B. Dendrite
C. Axon
D. Nissl bodies

2) The ATP-dependent dopamine transporter can be found at the presynaptic terminal of nerve cells. The dopamine transporter is most likely a:

A. protein in the neurolemma.
B. protein in the outer membrane of mitochondria.
C. protein in the neural nuclear membranes.
D. phospholipid in the plasma membrane.

3) Consider the following Table.

Table 1: Concentration of Na^+, K^+, and Cl^- inside and outside mammalian motor neurons.

Ion	Concentration (mmol/L H_2O)		Equilibrium potential (mV)
	Inside cell	Outside cell	
Na^+	15.0	150.0	+60
K^+	150.0	5.5	-90
Cl^-	9.0	125.0	-75
Resting membrane potential (V_m) = −70 mV			

At resting membrane potential, in what direction will K^+ ions move spontaneously in a cell?

A. From the cytosol to the nucleus
B. From the cytosol to the cell exterior
C. From the cell exterior to the cytosol
D. From the mitochondria to the cytosol

4) All of the following explain the ionic concentrations in Table 1 EXCEPT:

A. Na^+ and Cl^- ions passively diffuse more quickly into the extracellular fluid than K^+ ions.
B. Na^+ ions are actively pumped out of the intracellular fluid.
C. the negative charge of the cell contents repels Cl^- ions from the cell.
D. the cell membrane is more freely permeable to K^+ ions than to Na^+ and Cl^- ions.

5) At inhibitory synapses, a hyperpolarization of the membrane known as an inhibitory postsynaptic potential is produced rendering V_m more negative. This occurs as a result of (data from Table 1 can be considered):

A. an increase in the postsynaptic membrane's permeability to Na^+ and K^+ ions.
B. an increase in the permeability of the presynaptic membrane to Ca^{2+} ions.
C. the entry of Cl^- ions into the synaptic knob.
D. an increase in the permeability of the postsynaptic membrane to Cl^- ions.

6) Diisopropylfluorophosphate (DFP) acts as an irreversible inhibitor at the active site of acetylcholinesterase. This enzyme deactivates the chemical transmitter acetylcholine. The main effect of DFP would be to:

A. prevent the passage of nerve impulses along the postsynaptic neuron.
B. prevent the entry of Ca^{2+} into the synaptic knob.
C. initiate muscular tetany.
D. generate a very large action potential.

7) According to the following diagram, which ion channel opens and closes more quickly?

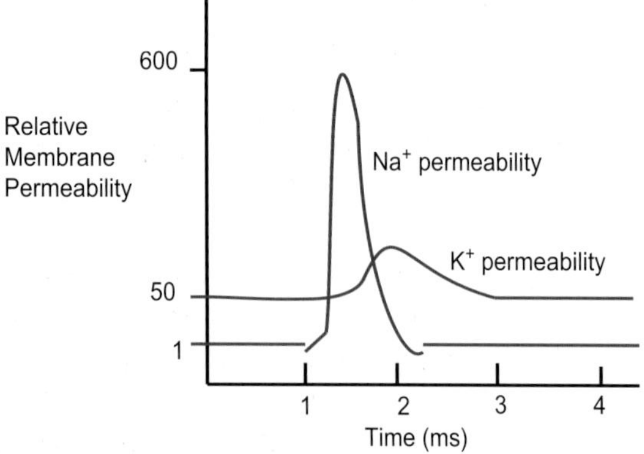

A. The K^+ channel because its relative membrane permeability is lower than for Na^+.
B. The Na^+ channel because its extracellular concentration is greater than for K^+.
C. The K^+ channel because it remains permeable for a longer period of time.
D. The Na^+ channel because its permeability increases and decreases at a faster rate.

8) An experiment is performed in which an inhibitor is applied to a single neuron. Upon stimulating the neuron and measuring both the intracellular and extracellular ion concentrations, it is found that the levels of K^+ and Na^+ have reached equilibrium. Based on these results, the inhibitor most likely inhibits the:

A. ATPase.
B. Cl^- channel.
C. K^+ channel.
D. Na^+ channel.

9) What would happen to the action potential in the previous diagram if K^+ channels were hindered but not completely blocked following depolarization?

A. The action potential would not repolarize.
B. The action potential would repolarize at a faster rate.
C. The duration of the action potential would be more than 1 ms.
D. The action potential would repolarize to less than -70 mV.

10) If cyanide was added to nerve cells, what would be expected to happen to the ionic composition of the cells?

A. Na^+ ions would be actively pumped into the cell and K^+ ions would be pumped out.
B. Intracellular Na^+ would increase since the sodium pump would stop functioning.
C. The potential of the cell membrane would not be reversed so that Cl^- ions would freely enter the cell.
D. The cell membrane would become freely permeable to Na^+ and Cl^- ions.

11) The temporary increase in the sarcolemma's permeability to Na^+ and K^+ ions that occurs at the motor end plate of a neuromuscular junction is immediately preceded by which of the following?

A. The release of acetylcholine from the motor neuron into the synaptic gap.
B. The release of adrenaline from the motor neuron into the synaptic gap.
C. The passage of a nerve impulse along the axon of a motor neuron.
D. The release of noradrenaline from a sensory neuron into the synaptic gap.

12) The overall reaction which takes place at the sodium pump is given by the equation:

$3Na^+_{(inside)} + 2K^+_{(outside)} + ATP^{4-} + H_2O \rightarrow$
$3Na^+_{(outside)} + 2K^+_{(inside)} + ADP^{3-} + P_i + H^+$

When a muscle is very active, at the end of glycolysis, pyruvate is converted to lactate by the addition of H^+ ions. During vigorous exercise, how many ions of K^+ could be pumped into a cell per molecule of glucose?

A. 2
B. 4
C. 8
D. 12

13) Stimulating electrodes were placed on a nerve and a recording electrode was placed near the motor end plate. First curare and then eserine were added to the solution bathing the muscle. The action potentials produced by stimulating the nerve were recorded and the results are shown.

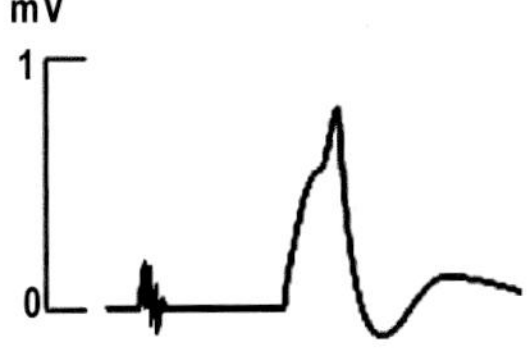

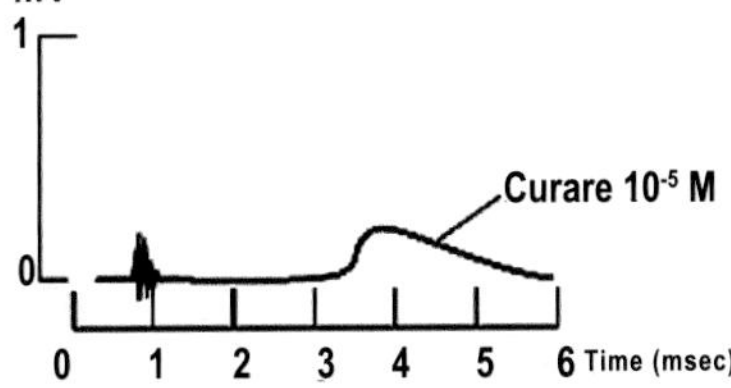

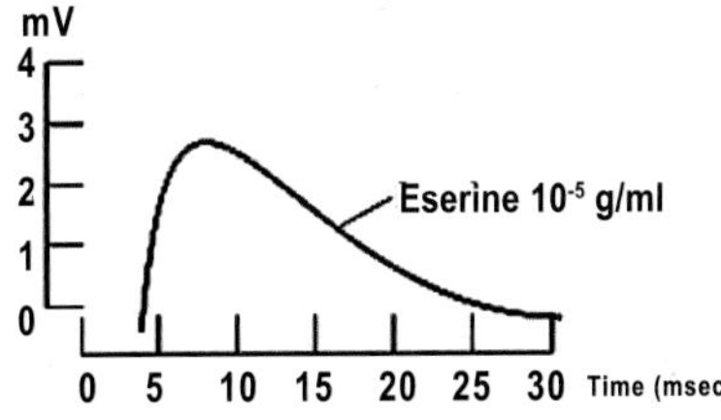

According to the results of the experiment, curare and eserine could act by, respectively:

A. blocking ion channels and binding to the receptors on ACh-activated channels.
B. blocking ion channels and preventing the hydrolysis of acetylcholinesterase.
C. initiating the entry of calcium ions into the synaptic knob and initiating the passage of a nerve impulse along the muscle cell.
D. binding to ACh receptor sites on the post-synaptic membrane and preventing the hydrolysis of acetylcholine.

14) In the control in the graph for the previous question, the part of the curve between 4 and 5 msec represents:

A. the absolute refractory period.
B. the relative refractory period.
C. the depolarization of the membrane.
D. saltatory conduction.

15) The depolarization across the muscle membrane triggers an all-or-none action potential in the muscle cell. This suggests that an increase in the amount of transmitter released at the neuromuscular junction would change:

A. the amplitude of the action potential.
B. the frequency of the nerve impulses.
C. the direction of the action potential.
D. the speed at which nerve impulses travel along the muscle cell.

16) Which of the following is true about muscle contraction?

A. Troponin and tropomyosin slide past one another allowing the muscle to shorten.
B. Decreased intracellular $[Ca^{++}]$ enhances the degree of muscular contraction.
C. Cardiac muscle fibers contain centrally located nuclei.
D. Neither actin nor myosin change length during muscle contraction.

17) In muscle cells, the actin filaments are:

A. thin and associated with the proteins troponin and collagen.
B. thin and associated with the proteins troponin and tropomyosin.
C. thick and associated with the proteins troponin and collagen.
D. thick and associated with the proteins troponin and tropomyosin.

18) If the gene which codes for troponin was absent from muscle cells, which of the following processes would NOT be inhibited?

A. The movement of tropomyosin to a new position on the actin molecules
B. The uncovering of the active sites for the attachment of actin to the cross bridges of myosin
C. The hydrolysis of ATP in the myosin head to produce ADP, P_i, and energy
D. The release of Ca^{2+} ions from the sarcoplasmic reticulum

19) Contraction of a muscle occurs when:

A. myosin binds and releases actin.
B. actin binds and releases myosin.
C. tropomyosin binds and releases actin.
D. actin binds and releases tropomyosin.

20) All of the following contain a phospholipid bilayer EXCEPT:

A. sarcolemma.
B. neurolemma.
C. basement membrane.
D. plasma membrane.

21) At the neuromuscular junction, the receptors on the acetylcholine-activated channels are likely located:

A. on the tubule of the T system.
B. in the sarcolemma.
C. on the muscle surface.
D. in the synaptic cleft.

22) Glycoproteins are found in all cellular compartments and are also secreted from the cell. Collagen, a secreted glycoprotein of the extracellular matrix, has simple carbohydrates - the disaccharide Glc beta (1,2) Gal linked to hydroxylysine. If a base mutation occurred in cells so that all the hydroxylysine residues were replaced by asparagine residues in the amino acid side chains, which of the following would result?

A. Glycoprotein formation would cease.
B. The strength of loose connective tissue might be affected.
C. Protein folding could not occur.
D. Protein recognition would be impossible.

23) What type of tissue is bone tissue?

A. Muscle
B. Epithelial
C. Connective
D. Nervous

24) Muscle is surrounded by what tough sheet of whitish connective tissue?

A. Tendon
B. Ligament
C. Marrow
D. Fascia

25) The organic portion of bone consists of which one of the following proteins?

A. Collagen
B. Fibrin
C. Actin
D. Myosin

GS ANSWER KEY

CHAPTER 5

		Cross-Reference			Cross-Reference
1.	A	BIO 5.1	14.	B	BIO 5.1.2
2.	A	BIO 5.1, 1.1, 1.1.3	15.	B	BIO 5.1.1-5.1.2
3.	B	BIO 5.1.1-5.1.3, deduce	16.	D	BIO 5.2
4.	A	BIO 1.2.2, 5.1.1-5.1.3, deduce	17.	B	BIO 5.2
5.	D	BIO 5.1.1-5.1.3, deduce	18.	D	BIO 5.2
6.	C	BIO 4.2, 5.1, 11.2	19.	A	BIO 5.2
7.	D	BIO 5.1.1-5.1.3, deduce	20.	C	BIO 1.1, 5.2-5.3
8.	A	BIO 4.2, 5.1.1-5.1.3, deduce	21.	B	BIO 1.1, 5.2 paragraph 4
9.	C	BIO 5.1.1, 5.1.2	22.	B	BIO 5.4.1
10.	B	BIO 4.4, 4.9, 5.1.1	23.	C	BIO 5.4
11.	A	BIO 5.1.1-5.1.3	24.	D	BIO 5.4.1, 5.4.2
12.	B	BIO 4.4, 5.1.1; CHM 1.5	25.	A	BIO 5.4.4
13.	D	BIO 5.1.2, deduce			

* Explanations can be found at the back of the book.

Go online to DAT-prep.com for additional chapter review Q&A and forum.

APPENDIX

CHAPTER 5: Specialized Eukaryotic Cells and Tissues

Advanced DAT-30 Passage: The Nernst Equation

When movement of ions is considered, two factors will influence the direction in which they diffuse: one is concentration, the other is electrical charge. An ion will usually diffuse from a region of its high concentration to a region of its low concentration. It will also generally be attracted towards a region of opposite charge, and move away from a region of similar charge. Thus ions are said to move down electrochemical gradients, which are the combined effects of both electrical and concentration gradients. Strictly speaking, active transport of ions is their movement against an electrochemical gradient powered by an energy source.

Consider the data in the following Table.

Table 1: Concentration of Na^+, K^+, and Cl^- inside and outside mammalian motor neurons. The sign of the potential (mV) is inside relative to the outside of the cell.

Ion	Concentration ($mmol/L\ H_2O$)		Equilibrium potential (mV)
	Inside cell	Outside cell	
Na^+	15.0	150.0	+60
K^+	150.0	5.5	-90
Cl^-	9.0	125.0	-75
Resting membrane potential (V_m) = -70 mV			

The value of the equilibrium potential for any ion depends upon the concentration gradient for that ion across the membrane. The equilibrium potential for any ion can be calculated using the Nernst equation.

$$E_{cell} = E^o_{cell} - (RT/nF)\ln Q$$

- E_{cell} = cell potential under nonstandard conditions (V); CHM 10.1
- E^o_{cell} = cell potential under standard conditions
- R = gas constant, which is 8.31 (volt-coulomb)/(mol-K); CHM 4.1.8
- T = temperature (K); CHM 4.1.1
- n = number of moles of electrons exchanged in the electrochemical reaction (mol)
- F = Faraday's constant (96,500 coulombs/mol); CHM 10.5
- Q = reaction quotient, which is the equilibrium expression with prevailing concentrations rather than, necessarilly, with equilibrium concentrations (= K_{eq}; CHM 9.8)
- ln = the natural logarithm which is log base e; CHM 6.5.1, QR Appendix

Once the relevant values have been

inserted, the Nernst equation can be simplified for specific ions. For example, the following is an approximation of the Nernst equation for the equilibrium potential for potassium (E_k in mV) at room temperature:

$$E_k = 60 \log_{10} \frac{[K^+]_o}{[K^+]_i}$$

- $[K^+]_o$ = extracellular K^+ concentration in mM
- $[K^+]_i$ = intracellular K^+ concentration in mM

The Goldman–Hodgkin–Katz voltage equation (= the Goldman equation) also determines the equilibrium potential across a cell's membrane. However, as opposed to the Nernst equation, the Goldman equation takes into account all of the ions that are permeant through that membrane.

26) If the concentration of potassium outside a mammalian motor neuron were changed to 0.55 mol/L, what would be the predicted change in the equilibrium potential for potassium?

A. 12 mV
B. 120 mV
C. 60 mV
D. 600 mV

27) A graph of E_k vs $\log_{10}[K^+]_o$ would be:

A. a straight line.
B. a logarithmic curve
C. an exponential curve.
D. a sigmoidal curve.

ANSWER KEY

ADVANCED TOPICS - CHAPTER 5

Cross-Reference

26. B E; T; CHM 6.5.1; QR Appendix
27. A E; QR Appendix

P = paragraph; *S* = sentence; *E* = equation; *T* = table; *F* = figure

Go online to DAT-prep.com for additional chapter review Q&A and forum.

NERVOUS AND ENDOCRINE SYSTEMS
Chapter 6

Memorize

Nervous system: basic structure, major functions
Basic sensory reception and processing
Basic ear, eye: structure and function
Define: endocrine gland, hormone
Major endocrine glands: names, locations, major hormones

Understand

* Organization of the nervous system; sensor and effector neurons
* Feedback loop, reflex arc: role of spinal cord, brain
* Endocrine system: specific chemical control at cell, tissue, and organ level
* Cellular mechanisms of hormone action, transport of hormones
* Integration with nervous system: feedback control

Importance

0 to 3 out of the 40 Biology

DAT questions are based on content in this chapter (in our estimation).
* Note that between 25% and 50% of the questions in DAT Biology are from 5 chapters: 1, 2, 14, 15, and 16.

Introduction 

The nervous and endocrine systems are composed of a network of highly specialized cells that can communicate information about an organism's surroundings and itself. Thus together, these two systems can process incoming information and then regulate and coordinate responses in other parts of the body.

Additional Resources

Free Online Q&A + Forum

Video: Online or DVD

Flashcards

Special Guest

6.1 Organisation of the Vertebrate Nervous System

The role of the nervous system is to control and coordinate body activities in a rapid and precise mode of action. The nervous system is composed of central and peripheral nervous systems.

The **central nervous system** (CNS) is enclosed within the cranium (skull) and vertebral (spinal) canal and consists respectively of the brain and spinal cord. The **peripheral nervous system** (PNS) is outside the bony encasement and is composed of peripheral nerves, which are branches or continuations of the spinal or cranial nerves. The PNS can be divided into the **somatic nervous system** and the **autonomic nervous system** which are *anatomically* a portion of both the central and peripheral nervous systems.

The somatic nervous system contains sensory fibers that bring information back to the CNS and motor fibers that innervate skeletal muscles. The autonomic nervous system (ANS) contains motor fibers that innervate smooth muscle, cardiac muscle and glands. The ANS is then divided into *sympathetic* and *parasympathetic* divisions, which generally act against each other. The sympathetic division acts to prepare the body for an emergency situation (fight or flight) while the parasympathetic division acts to conserve energy and restore the body to resting level (rest and digest).

As a rule, a collection of nerve cell bodies in the CNS is called a *nucleus* and outside the CNS it is called a *ganglion*. Neurons that carry information from the environment to the brain or spinal cord are called *afferent neurons*. Neurons that carry motor commands from the brain or spinal cord to the different parts of body are called *efferent neurons*. Neurons that connect sensory and motor neurons in neural pathways are called *interneurons*.

The spinal cord is a long cylindrical structure whose hollow core is called the *central canal*. The central canal is surrounded by a gray matter which is in turn surrounded by a white matter (the reverse is true for the brain: outer gray matter and inner white matter). Basically, the gray matter consists of the cell bodies of neurons whereas the white matter consists of the nerve fibers (axons and dendrites). There are 31 pairs of spinal nerves each leaving the spinal cord at various levels: 8 cervical (neck), 12 thoracic (chest), 5 lumbar (abdomen), 5 sacral and 1 coccygeal (these latter 6 are from the pelvic region). The lower end of the spinal cord is cone shaped and is called the *conus medullaris.*

The brain can be divided into three main regions: the forebrain which contains the telencephalon and the diencephalon; the midbrain; and the hindbrain which contains the cerebellum, the pons and the medulla. The **brain stem** includes the latter two structures and the midbrain.

The telencephalon is the **cerebral hemispheres** (cerebrum) which contain an outer surface (cortex) of gray matter. Its function is in higher order processes (i.e. learning, memory, emotions, voluntary motor activity, processing sensory input, etc.). For

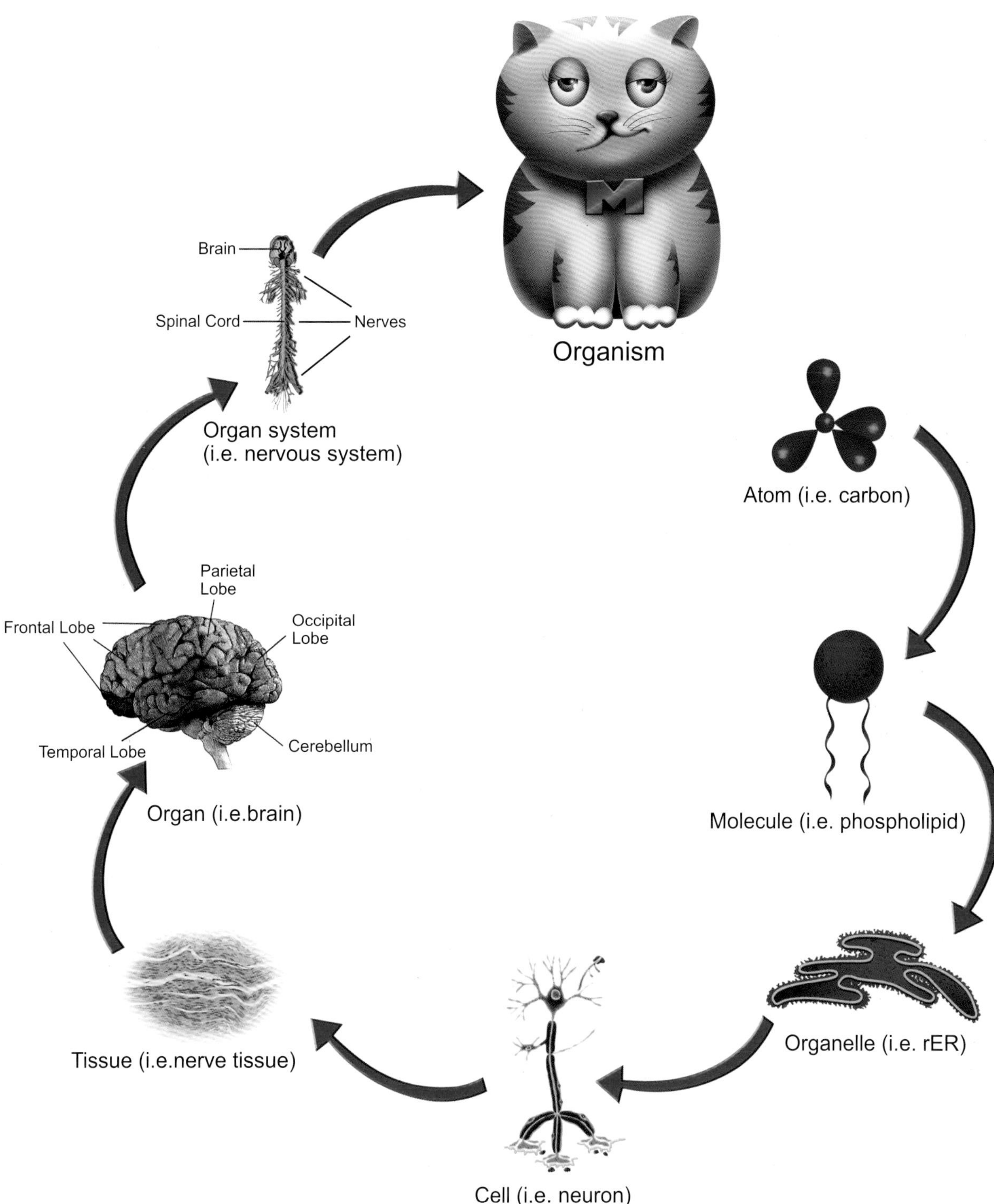

Figure IV.A.6.0: Levels of organization.

most people, the left hemisphere specializes in language, while the right hemisphere specializes in patterns and spatial relationships.

Each hemisphere is subdivided into four lobes: *occipital* which receives input from the optic nerve for vision; *temporal* which receives auditory signals for hearing; *parietal* which receives somatosensory information from the opposite side of the body (= heat, cold, touch, pain, and the sense of body movement); and *frontal* which is involved in problem solving and controls voluntary movements for the opposite side of the body.

The diencephalon contains the **thalamus** which is a relay center for sensory input, and the **hypothalamus** which is crucial for homeostatic controls (heart rate, body temperature, thirst, sex drive, hunger, etc.). Protruding from its base and greatly influenced by the hypothalamus is the **pituitary** which is an endocrine gland. The limbic system, which functions to produce emotions, is composed of the diencephalon and deep structures of the cerebrum (esp. basal ganglia).

The midbrain is a relay center for visual and auditory input and also regulated motor function.

The hindbrain consists of the cerebellum, the pons and the medulla. The cerebellum plays an important role in coordination and the control of muscle tone. The pons acts as a relay center between the cerebral cortex and the cerebellum. The medulla controls many vital functions such as breathing, heart rate, arteriole blood pressure, etc.

There are 12 pairs of cranial nerves which emerge from the base of the brain (esp. the brain stem): *olfactory* (I) for smell; *optic* (II) for vision; *oculomotor* (III), *trochlear* (IV) and *abducens* (VI) for eye movements; *trigeminal* (V) for motor (i.e. *mastication* which is chewing) and sensory activities (i.e. pain, temperature, and pressure for the head and face); *facial* (VII) for taste (sensory) and facial expression (motor); *vestibulo-cochlear* (VIII) for the senses of equilibrium (vestibular branch) and hearing (cochlear branch); *glosso-pharyngeal* (IX) for taste and swallowing; *vagus* (X) for speech, swallowing, slowing the heart rate, and many sensory and motor innervations to smooth muscles of the viscera (internal organs) of the thorax and abdomen; *accessory* (XI) for head rotation and shoulder movement; and *hypoglossal* (XII) for tongue movement.

Both the brain and the spinal cord are surrounded by three membranes (= meninges). The outermost covering is called the dura mater, the innermost is called the pia mater (which is in direct contact with nervous tissue), while the middle layer is called the arachnoid mater. {DAP = **d**ura - **a**rachnoid - **p**ia, repectively, from out to in}.

6.1.1 The Sensory Receptors

The sensory receptors include any type of nerve ending in the body that can be stimulated by some physical or chemical stimulus either outside or within the body. These receptors include the rods and cones of the eye, the cochlear nerve endings of the ear, the taste endings of the mouth, the olfactory endings in the nose, sensory nerve endings in the skin, etc. Afferent neurons carry sense signals to the central nervous system.

6.1.2 The Effector Receptors

These include every organ that can be stimulated by nerve impulses. An important effector system is skeletal muscle. Smooth muscles of the body and the glandular cells are among the important effector organs. Efferent neurons carry motor signals from the CNS to effector receptors. {The term "effector" in biology refers to an organ, cell or molecule that *acts* in response to a stimulus (cause-effect).}

6.1.3 Reflex Arc

One basic means by which the nervous system controls the functions in the body is the reflex arc, in which a stimulus excites a receptor, appropriate impulses are transmitted into the CNS where various nervous reactions take place, and then appropriate effector impulses are transmitted to an effector organ to cause a reflex effect (i.e. removal of one's hand from a hot object, the knee-jerk reflex, etc.). The preceding can be processed at the level of the spinal cord.

Example of knee-jerk reflex: tapping on the patellar tendon causes the thigh muscle (quadriceps) to stretch. The stretching of muscle stimulates the afferent fibers, which synapse on the motoneuron (= motor neuron; BIO 5.1) in the spinal cord. The activation of the motoneuron causes contraction of the muscle that was stretched. This contraction makes the lower leg extend.

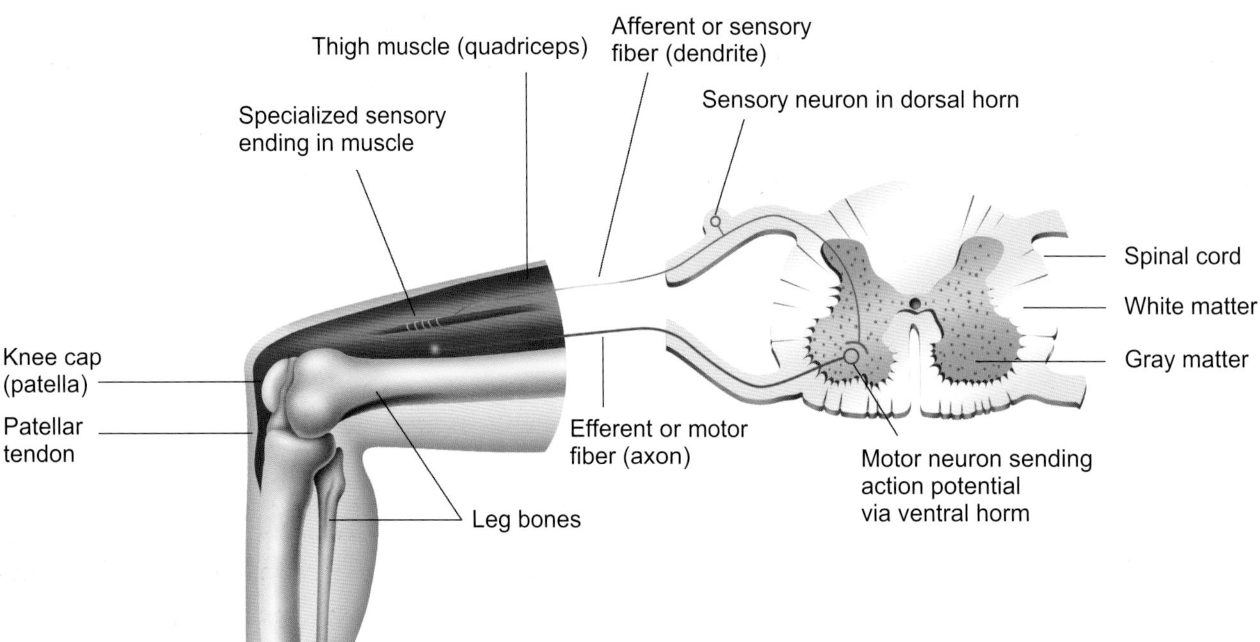

Figure IV.A.6.1: Schematic representation of the basis of the knee jerk reflex.

6.1.4 Autonomic Nervous System

While the Somatic Nervous System controls voluntary activities (i.e. innervates skeletal muscle), the Autonomic Nervous System (ANS) controls involuntary activities. The ANS consists of two components which often antagonize each other: the sympathetic and parasympathetic nervous systems.

The **Sympathetic Nervous System** originates in neurons located in the lateral horns of the gray matter of the spinal cord. Nerve fibers pass by way of anterior (ventral) nerve roots first into the spinal nerves and then immediately into the sympathetic chain. From here fiber pathways are transmitted to all portions of the body, especially to the different visceral organs and to the blood vessels.

The sympathetic nervous system uses norepinephrine as its primary neurotransmitter. This division of the nervous system is crucial in the "fight, fright or flight" responses (i.e. pupillary dilation, increase in breathing, blood pressure and heart rate, increase of blood flow to skeletal muscle, decrease of visceral function, etc.).

Parasympathetic Nervous System: The parasympathetic fibers pass mainly through the *vagus nerves*, though a few fibers pass through several of the other cranial nerves and through the anterior roots of the sacral segments of the spinal cord. Parasympathetic fibers do not spread as extensively through the body as do sympathetic fibers, but they do innervate some of the thoracic and abdominal organs, as well as the pupillary sphincter and ciliary muscles of the eye and the salivary glands.

The parasympathetic nervous system uses acetylcholine as its primary neurotransmitter. This division of the nervous system is crucial for vegetative responses (i.e. pupillary constriction, decrease in breathing, blood pressure and heart rate, increase in blood flow to the gastro-intestinal tract, etc.).

6.1.5 Autonomic Nerve Fibers

The nerve fibers from the ANS are primarily motor fibers. Unlike the motor pathways of the somatic nervous system, which usually include a single neuron between the CNS and an effector, those of the ANS involve *two* neurons. The first neuron has its cell body in the brain or spinal cord but its axon (= *preganglionic fiber*) extends outside of the CNS. The axon enters adjacent sympathetic chain ganglia, where they synapse with the cell body of a second neuron or travel up or down the chain to synapse with that of a remote second neuron (*recall: a ganglion is a collection of nerve cell bodies outside the CNS*). The axon of the second neuron (= *postganglionic fiber*) extends to a visceral effector.

The sympathetic ganglia form chains which, for example, may extend longitudinally along each side of the vertebral column. Conversely, the parasympathetic ganglia are located *near* or *within* various visceral organs (i.e. bladder, intestine, etc.) thus requiring relatively short postganglionic fibers. Therefore, sympathetic nerve fibers are characterized by short preganglionic fibers and long postganglionic fibers while parasympathetic nerve fibers are characterized by long preganglionic fibers and short postganglionic fibers.

Both divisions of the ANS secrete *acetylcholine* from their preganglionic fibers. Most sympathetic postganglionic fibers secrete *norepinephrine* (= nor**adren**alin), and for this reason they are called ***adren**ergic* fibers. The parasympathetic postganglionic fibers secrete acetyl**choline** and are called ***cholin**ergic fibers.*

There are two types of acetylcholine receptors (AChR) that bind acetylcholine and transmit its signal: muscarinic AChRs and nicotinic AChRs, which are named after the agonists muscarine and nicotine, respectively. The two receptors are functionally different, the muscarinic type is a G-protein coupled receptor that mediates a slow metabolic response via second messenger cascades (involving cAMP), while the nicotinic type is a ligand-gated ionotropic channel that mediates a fast synaptic transmission of the neurotransmitter (no use of second messengers).

6.2 Sensory Reception and Processing

Each modality of sensation is detected by a particular nerve ending. The most common nerve ending is the free nerve ending. Different types of free nerve endings result in different types of sensations such as pain, warmth, pressure, touch, etc. In addition to free nerve endings, skin contains a number of specialized endings that are adapted to respond to some specific type of physical stimulus.

Sensory endings deep in the body are capable of detecting proprioceptive sensations such as joint receptors, which detect the degree of angulation of a joint, Golgi tendon organs which detect the degree of tension in the tendons, and muscle spindles which detect the degree of stretch of a muscle fiber (see diagram of reflex with muscle spindle in BIO 6.1.2).

6.2.1 Olfaction

Olfaction (the sense of smell) is perceived by the brain following the stimulation of the olfactory epithelium located in the nostrils. The olfactory epithelium contain large numbers of neurons with chemoreceptors called olfactory cells which are responsible for the detection of different types of smell. Odorant molecules bind to the receptors located on the cilia of olfactory receptor neurons and produce a depolarizing receptor potential. Once the depolarization passes threshold, an action potential is generated and is conducted into CNS. It is believed that there might be seven or more primary sensations of smell which combine to give various types of smell that we perceive in life.

6.2.2 Taste

Taste buds in combination with olfaction give humans the taste sensation. Taste buds are primarily located on the surface of the tongue with smaller numbers found in the roof of the mouth and the walls of the pharynx (throat). Taste buds contain chemoreceptors which are activated once the chemical is dissolved in saliva which is secreted by the salivary glands. Contrary to olfactory receptor cells, taste receptors are not true neurons: they are chemical receptors only.

Four different types of taste buds are known to exist, each of these responding principally to saltiness, sweetness, sourness and bitterness.

When a stimulus is received by either a taste bud or an olfactory cell for the second time, the intensity of the response is diminished. This is called sensory *adaptation*.

6.2.3 Ears: Structure and Function

Ears function in both hearing and balance. It consists of three parts: the *external ear* which receives sound waves; the air-filled *middle ear* which transmits and amplifies sound waves; and the fluid-filled *inner ear* which transduces sound waves into nerve impulse. The vestibular organ, located in the inner ear, is responsible for equilibrium.

The external ear is composed of the external cartilaginous portion, the pinna or *auricle*, and the external auditory meatus or canal. The external auditory meatus connects the auricle and the middle ear or *tympanic cavity*. The tympanic cavity is bordered on the outside by the tympanic membrane, and inside the air-filled cavity are the auditory ossicles - the *malleus* (hammer), *incus* (anvil), and *stapes* (stirrup). The stapes is held by ligaments to a part of inner ear called the *oval window*. The auditory ossicles function in amplifying the sound vibration and transmitting it from the tympanic membrane to the oval window.

The inner ear or *labyrinth* consists of an osseous (= bony) labyrinth containing a membranous labyrinth. The bony labyrinth houses the semicircular canals, the cochlea and the vestibule. The semicircular canals contain the semicircular ducts of the membranous labyrinth, which can detect angular acceleration. The vestibule contains the saccule and utricle, which are sac-like thin connective tissue lined by vestibular hair cells which are responsible for the detection of linear acceleration. Together, the semicircular canals and the vestibule, known as the vestibular system,

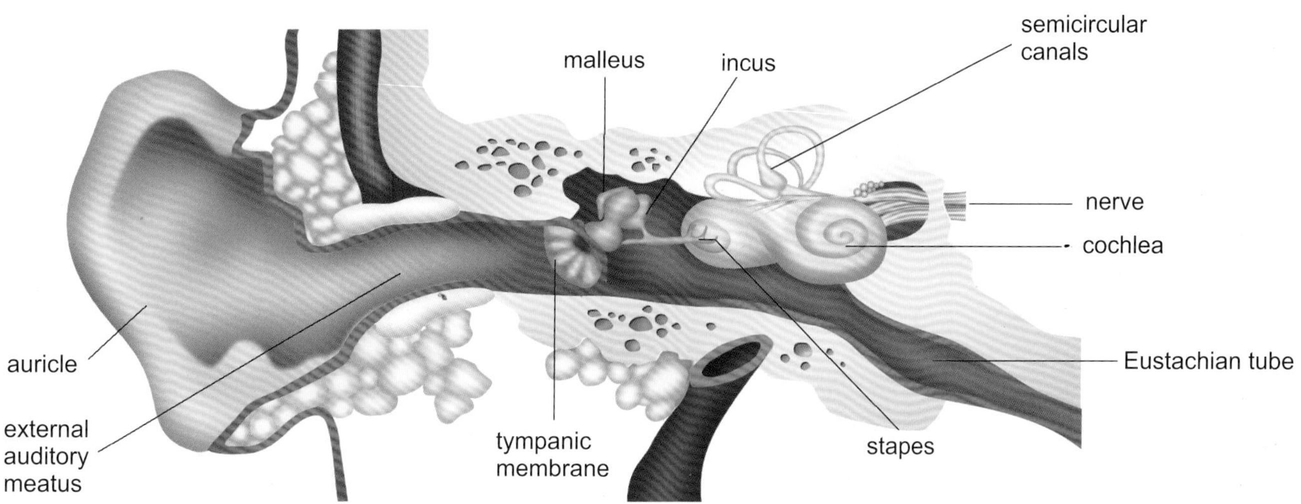

Figure IV.A.6.2: Structure of the external, middle and inner ear.

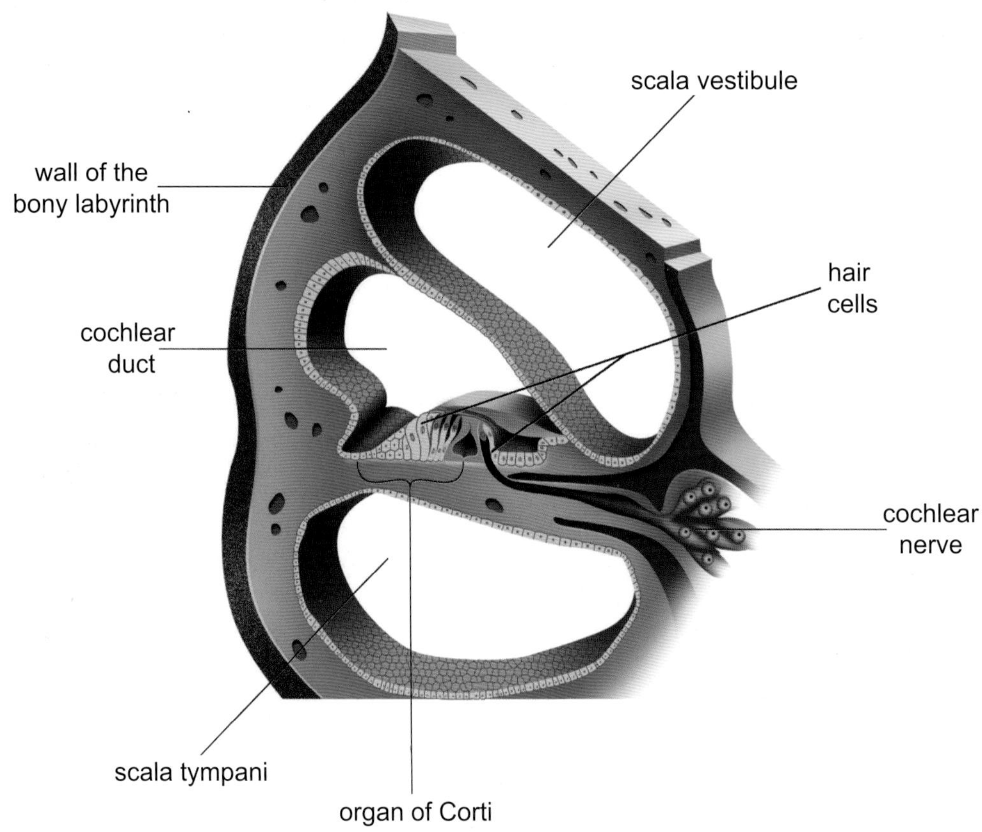

Figure IV.A.6.3: Cross-section of the cochlea.

are responsible for detection of linear and angular acceleration of the head. The cochlea is divided into three spaces: the scala vestibule, scala tympani and the scala media, or cochlear duct. The cochlear duct contains the spiral organ of Corti, which functions in the reception of sound and responds to different sound frequencies.

The eustachian tube connects the middle ear to the pharynx. This tube is important in maintaining equal pressure on both sides of the tympanic membrane. During ascent in an airplane, there is a decrease in cabin air pressure, leading to a relative increase in the pressure of the middle ear. Swallowing or yawning opens the eustachian tube allowing an equalization of pressure in the middle ear.

Mechanism of hearing: Sound is caused by the compression of waves that travel through the air. Each compression wave is funneled by the external ear to strike the tympanic membrane (ear drum). Thus the sound vibrations are transmitted through the osseous system which consists of three tiny bones (the malleus, incus, and stapes) into the cochlea at the oval window. Movement of the stapes at the oval window causes disturbance in the lymph of cochlea and stimulates the hair cells found in the basilar membrane which is called the *organ of Corti*. Bending of the hair cells causes depolarization of the basilar membrane. From here the auditory nerves carry the impulses to the auditory area of the brain (*temporal lobe*) where it is interpreted as sound.

6.2.4 Vision: Eye Structure and Function

The eyeball consists of three layers: i) an outer fibrous tunic composed of the sclera and cornea; ii) a vascular coat (uvea) of choroid, the ciliary body and iris; and iii) the retina formed of pigment and sensory (nervous) layers. The anterior chamber lies between the cornea anteriorly (in front) and the iris and pupil posteriorly (behind); the posterior chamber lies between the iris anteriorly and the ciliary processes and the lens posteriorly.

The transparent cornea constitutes the anterior one sixth of the eye and receives light from external environment. The sclera forms

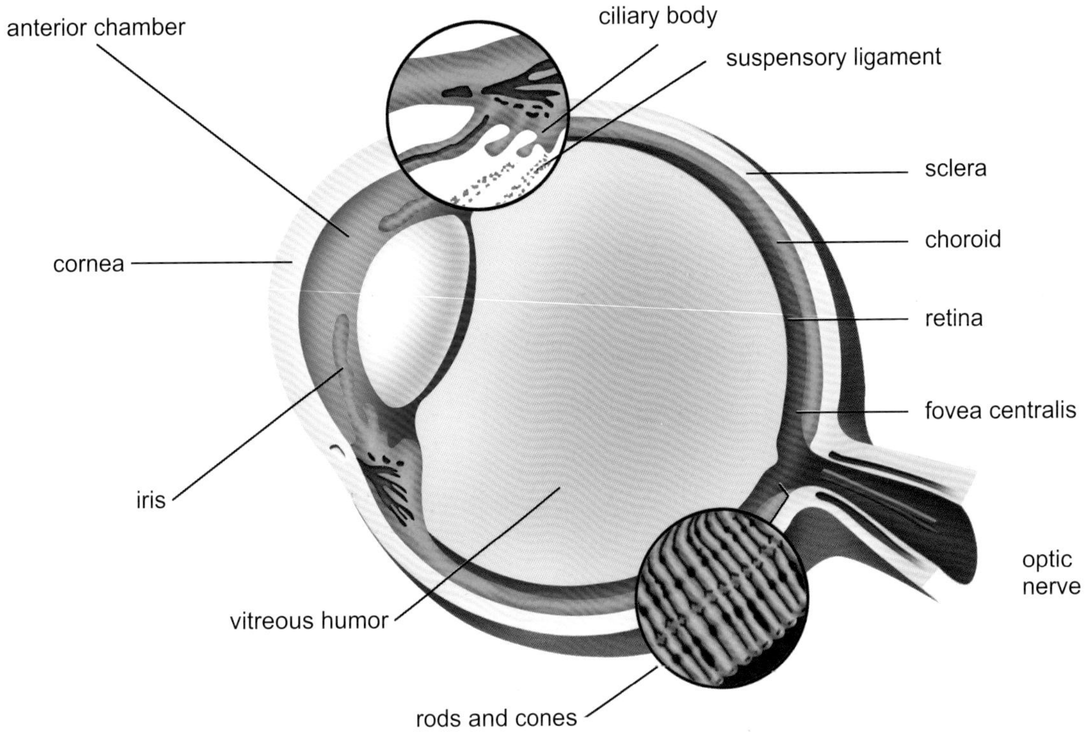

Figure IV.A.6.4: Structure of the eye.

the posterior five sixths of the fibrous tunic and is composed of dense fibrous connective tissue. The choroid layer consists of vascular loose connective tissue. The ciliary body is an anterior expansion of the choroid that encircles the lens. The lens can focus light on the retina by the contraction or relaxation of muscles in the ciliary body which transmit tension along suspensory ligaments to the lens.

Contraction of the ciliary muscle makes the lens become more convex, thereby allowing the eye to focus on nearby objects. Relaxation of the ciliary muscle allows the eye to focus on far objects. The iris separates the anterior and the posterior chamber and forms an aperture called the "pupil" whose diameter is continually adjusted by the pupillary muscles. This helps to control the intensity of light impinging on the retina.

The retina is divisible into ten layers. Layers two to five contain the rod and cone receptors of the light pathway.

Rods and Cones: The light sensitive receptors (*photoreceptors*) of the retina are millions of minute cells called rods and cones. The rods (*"night vision"*) distinguish only the black and white aspects of an image and are sensitive to light of low intensity (*"high sensitivity"*). The cones (*"day vision"*) are capable of distinguishing three colors: red, green and blue and are sensitive to light of high intensity (*"low sensitivity"*). From different combinations of these three colors, all colors can be seen.

Photoreceptors contain photosensitive pigments. For example, rods contain the membrane protein *rhodopsin* which is covalently linked to a form of vitamin A. Light causes an isomerization of *retinal* (an aldehyde form of vitamin A) which can affect Na^+ channels in a manner as to start an action potential.

The central portion of the retina which is called the fovea centralis has only cones, which allows this portion to have very sharp vision, while the peripheral areas, which contain progressively more and more rods, have progressively more diffuse vision. Since acuity and color vision are mediated by the same cells (cones), visual acuity is much better in bright light than dim light.

Each point of the retina connects with a discrete point in the visual cortex which is in the back of the brain (i.e. the occipital lobe). The image that is formed on the retina is upside down and reversed from left to right. This information leaves the eye via the optic nerve en route to the visual cortex which corrects the image.

Defects of vision

1. Myopia (short-sighted or nearsighted): In this condition, an image is formed in front of the retina because the lens converges light too much since the eyeballs are long. A diverging (concave) lens helps focus the image on the retina and it is used for the correction of myopia.

2. Hyperopia (long-sighted or farsighted): In this condition, an image is formed behind the retina since the eyeballs are too short. A converging (convex) lens helps focus the image on the retina.

3. Astigmatism: In this condition, the curvatures of either the cornea or the lens are different at different angles. A cylindrical lens helps to improve this condition.

4. Presbyopia: This condition is characterized by the inability to focus (especially objects which are closer). This condition, which is often seen in the elderly, is corrected by using a converging lens.

6.3 Endocrine Systems

The endocrine system is the set of glands, tissues and cells that secrete hormones directly into circulatory system (ductless). The hormones are transported by the blood system, sometimes bound to plasma proteins, en route to having an effect on the cells of a target organ. Thus hormones control many of the body's functions by acting - predominantly - in one of the following major ways:

1. By controlling transport of substances through cell membranes

2. By controlling the activity of some of the specific genes, which in turn determine the formation of specific enzymes

3. By controlling directly some metabolic systems of cells.

Steroid hormones can diffuse across the plasma membrane and bind to specific receptors in the cytosol or nucleus, thus forming a direct intracellular effect (i.e. on DNA; ORG 12.4.1). Non-steroid hormones do not diffuse across the membrane. They tend to bind plasma membrane receptors, which leads to the production of a second messenger.

Secondary messengers are a component of signal transduction cascades which amplify the strength of a signal (i.e. hormone, growth factors, neurotransmitter, etc.). Examples include cyclic AMP (cAMP), phosphoinositol, cyclic GMP and arachidonic acid systems.

In all four cases, a hormone (= the primary messenger or *agonist*) binds the receptor exposing a binding site for a G-protein (the *transducer*). The G-protein, named for its ability to exchange GDP on its alpha subunit for a GTP (BIO 4.4-4.10), is bound to the inner membrane. Once the exchange for GTP takes place, the alpha subunit of the G-protein transducer breaks free from the beta and gamma subunits, all parts remaining membrane-bound. The alpha subunit is now free to move along the inner membrane and eventually contacts another membrane-bound protein - the *primary effector*.

The primary effector has an action which creates a signal that can diffuse within the cell. This signal is the *secondary messenger*.

Calcium ions are important intracellular messengers which can regulate calmodulin and are responsible for many important physiological functions, such as in muscle contraction (BIO 5.2). The enzyme phospholipase C (primary effector) produces diacylglycerol and inositol trisphosphate (secondary messenger), which increases calcium ion (secondary effector) membrane permeability. Active G-protein can also open calcium channels. The other product of phospholipase C, diacylglycerol (secondary messenger), activates protein kinase C (secondary effector), which assists in the activation of cAMP (another second messenger).

The agonist epinephrine (hormone, BIO 6.1.3) can bind a receptor activating the transducer (G-protein) and using a primary effector (adenylyl cyclase) produces a secondary messenger (cAMP) which, in turn, brings about target cell responses that are recognized as the hormone's actions.

Of the following hormones, if there is no mention as to its chemical nature, then it is a non-steroidal hormone (i.e. protein, polypeptide, etc.).

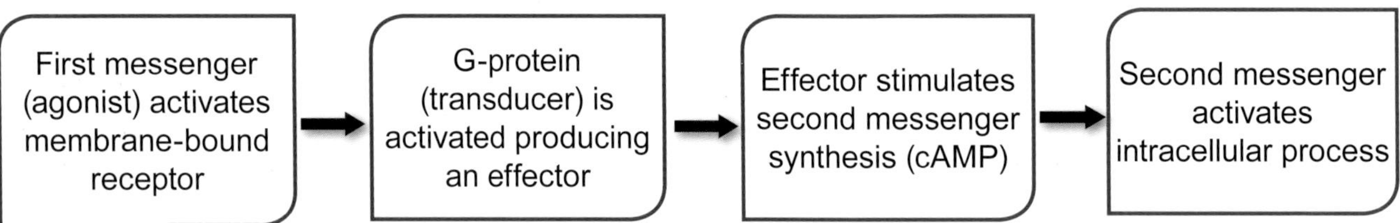

6.3.1 Pituitary Hormones

The **pituitary gland** secretes hormones that regulate a wide variety of functions in the body. This gland is divided into two major divisions: the anterior and the posterior pituitary gland. Six hormones are secreted by the anterior pituitary gland whereas two hormones are secreted by the posterior gland. The **hypothalamus** influences the secretion of hormones from both parts of the pituitary in different ways: i) it secretes specific *releasing factors* into special blood vessels (a *portal system* called hypothalamic-hypophysial portal system) which carries these factors (hormones) that affect the cells in the anterior pituitary by either stimulating or inhibiting the release of anterior pituitary hormones; ii) the hypothalamus contains neurosecretory cell bodies that synthesize, package and transport their products (esp. the two hormones oxytocin and ADH) down the axons directly into the posterior pituitary where they can be released into circulation.

The hormones secreted by the anterior pituitary gland are as follows:

1. Growth hormone (GH)
2. Thyroid Stimulating Hormone (TSH)
3. Adrenocorticotropic hormone (ACTH)
4. Prolactin
5. Follicle Stimulating Hormone (FSH) or Interstitial Cell Stimulating Hormone (ICSH)
6. Luteinizing Hormone (LH)

[N.B. these latter two hormones will be discussed in the section on Reproduction, see BIO 14.2, 14.3]

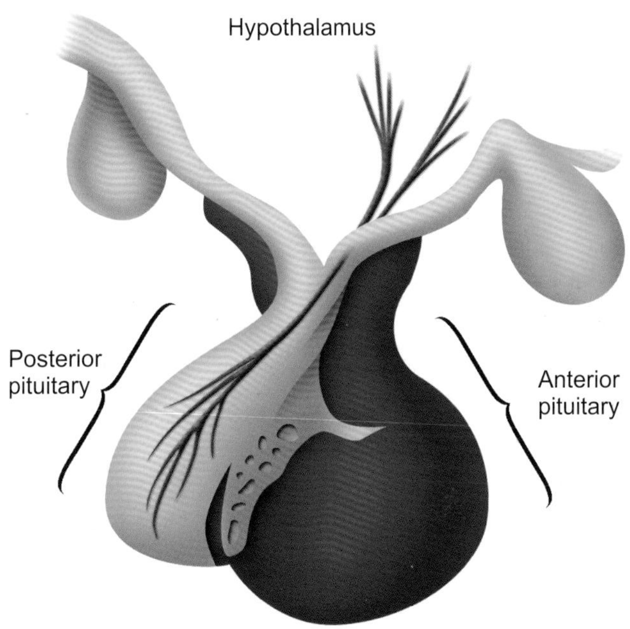

Figure IV.A.6.5: The pituitary gland.

Growth Hormone causes growth of the body. It causes enlargement and proliferation of cells in all parts of the body. Ultimately, the epiphyses of the long bones unite with the shaft of the bones (BIO 11.3.1). After adolescence, growth hormone continues to be secreted lower than the pre-adolescent rate. Though most of the growth in the body stops at this stage, the metabolic roles of the growth hormone continue such as the enhancement of protein synthesis and lean body mass, increasing blood glucose concentration, increasing lipolysis, etc.

Abnormal increase in the secretion of growth hormone at a young age results in a condition called gigantism, while a reduction in the production of growth hormone leads to dwarfism. Abnormal increase in the secretion of growth hormone in adults results in a condition called acromegaly, a disorder characterized by a disproportionate bone enlargement, especially in the face, hands and feet.

Thyroid Stimulating Hormone stimulates the thyroid gland. The hormones produced by the thyroid gland (*thyroxine:* T_4, *triiodothyronine:* T_3) contain four and three iodine atoms, respectively. They increase the basal metabolic rate of the body (BMR). Therefore, indirectly, TSH increases the overall rate of metabolism of the body.

Adrenocorticotropic hormone strongly stimulates the production of cortisol by the adrenal cortex, and it also stimulates the production of the other adrenocortical hormones, but to a lesser extent.

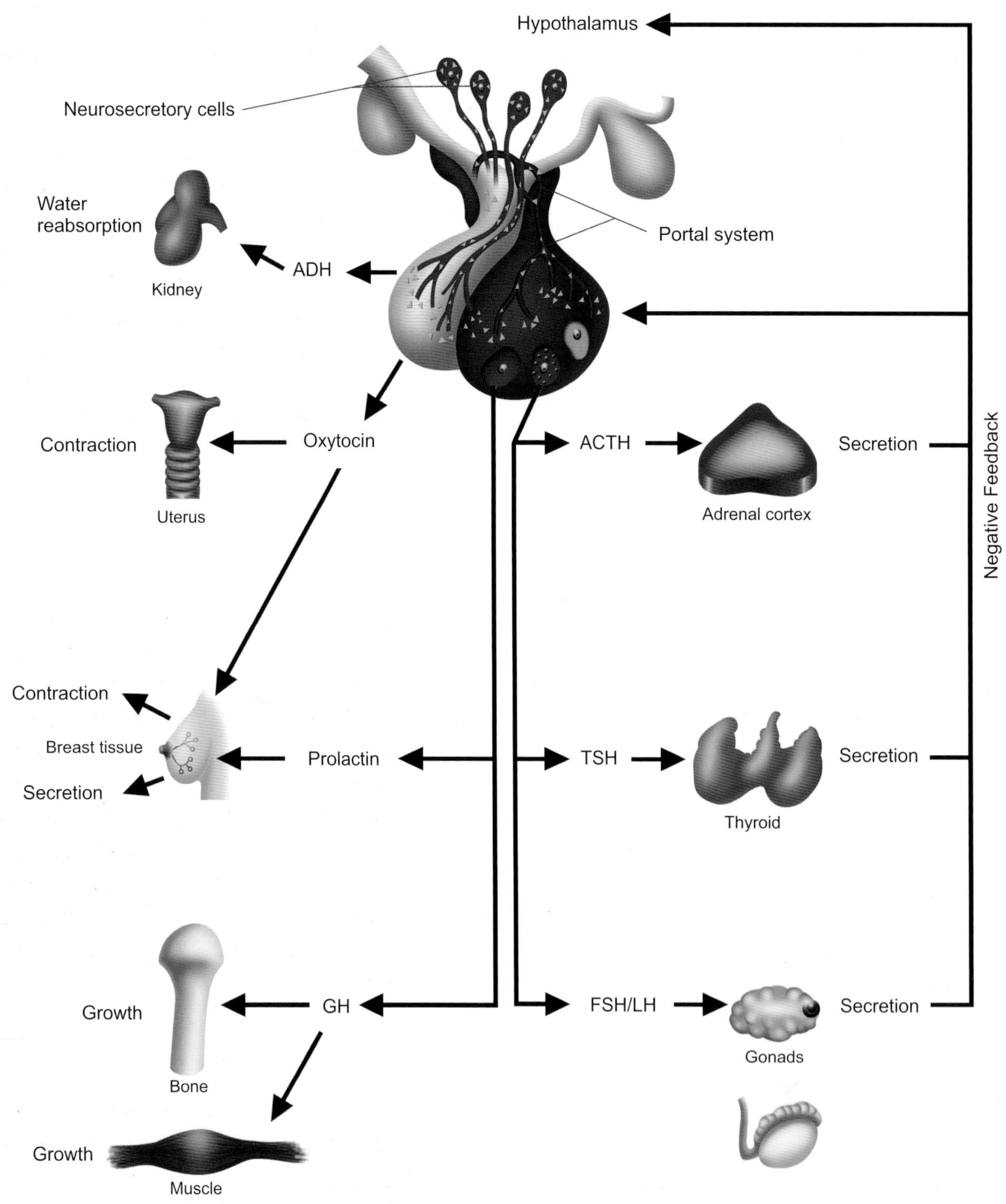

Figure IV.A.6.6: Pituitary hormones and their target organs.

Prolactin plays an important role in the development of the breast during pregnancy and promotes milk production in the breast. In addition, a high level of prolactin can inhibit ovulation.

Antidiuretic hormone (ADH) is synthesized by neurosecretory cells in the hypothalamus and then travels down the axons to the posterior pituitary for secretion. Antidiuretic hormone enhances the rate of water reabsorption from the renal tubules leading to the concentration of urine (BIO 10.3). ADH also constricts the arterioles and causes a rise in arterial pressure and hence it is also called *vasopressin*.

Similar to ADH, *oxytocin* originates in the hypothalamus and then travels down the axons to the posterior pituitary for secretion. Oxytocin causes contraction of the uterus and, to a lesser extent, the other smooth muscles of the body. It also stimulates the myoepithelial cells of the breast in a manner that makes the milk flow into the ducts. This is termed milk ejection or milk *let-down*.

6.3.2 Adrenocortical Hormones

On the top of each kidney lies an adrenal gland which contains an inner region (*medulla*) and an outer region (*cortex*). The adrenal cortex secretes three different types of steroid hormones that are similar chemically but vary widely in a physiological manner.

These are:

1. Mineralocorticoids - e.g., Aldosterone
2. Glucocorticoids - e.g., Cortisol, Cortisone
3. Sex Hormones e.g., Androgens, Estrogens

Mineralocorticoids - Aldosterone

The mineralocorticoids influence the electrolyte balance of the body. Aldosterone is a mineralocorticoid which is secreted and then enhances sodium transport from the renal tubules into the peritubular fluids, and at the same time enhances potassium transport from the peritubular fluids into the tubules. In other words, aldosterone causes conservation of sodium in the body and excretion of potassium in the urine. As a result of sodium retention, there is an increased passive reabsorption of chloride ions and water from the tubules. Overproduction of aldosterone will result in excessive retention of fluid, which leads to hypertension.

Glucocorticoids - Cortisol

Several different glucocorticoids are secreted by the adrenal cortex, but almost all of the glucocorticoid activity is caused by cortisol, also called hydrocortisone. Glucocorticoids affect the metabolism of carbohydrates, proteins and lipids. It causes an increase in the blood concentration of glucose by stimulation of gluconeogenesis (generation of glucose from non-carbohydrate carbon substrates). It causes degradation of proteins and causes increased use of fat for energy. Long term use of glucocorticoids suppresses the immune system. It also has an anti-inflammatory effect by inhibiting the release of inflammatory mediators.

Sex hormones

Androgens (i.e. testosterone) are the masculinizing hormones in the body. They are responsible for the development of the secondary sexual characteristics in a male (i.e. increased body hair). On the contrary estrogens have a feminizing effect in the body and they are responsible for the development of the secondary sexual characteristics in a female (i.e. breast development). The proceeding hormones supplement secretions from the gonads which will be discussed later (see "*Reproduction*"; BIO 14.2, 14.3).

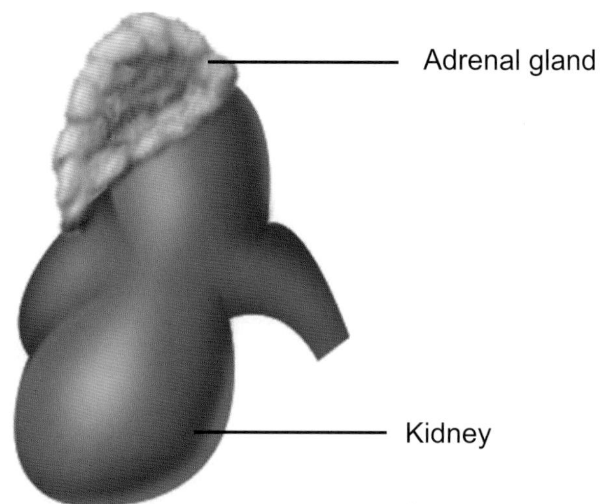

Figure IV.A.6.7: The adrenal gland sits on top of the kidney.

The Adrenal Medulla

The adrenal medulla synthesizes epinephrine (= *adrenaline*) and norepinephrine which: i) are non-steroidal stimulants of the sympathetic nervous system; ii) raise blood glucose concentrations; iii) increase heart rate and blood pressure; iv) increase blood supply to the brain, heart and skeletal muscle; and v) decrease blood supply to the skin, digestive system and renal system.

6.3.3 Thyroid Hormones

The thyroid gland is located anteriorly in the neck and is composed of follicles lined with thyroid glandular cells. These cells secrete a glycoprotein called thyroglobulin. The tyrosine residue of thyroglobulin then reacts with iodine forming mono-iodotyrosine (MIT) and di-iodotyrosine (DIT). When two molecules of DIT combine, thyroxine (T_4) is formed. When one molecule of DIT and one molecule of MIT combine, tri-iodothyronine (T_3) is formed. The rate of synthesis of thyroid hormone is influenced by TSH from the pituitary.

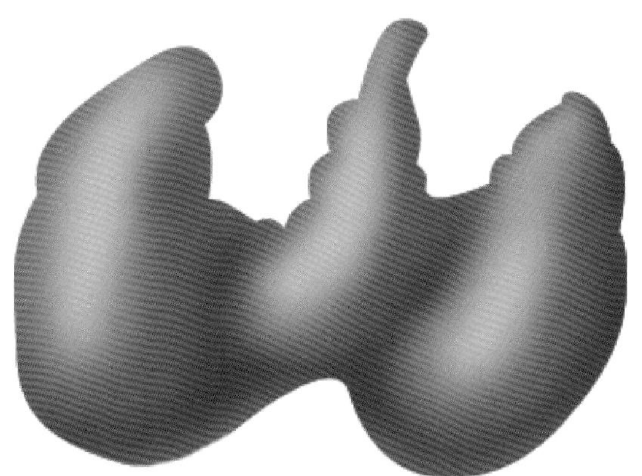

Figure IV.A.6.8: The thyroid gland.

Once thyroid hormones have been released into the blood stream they combine with several different plasma proteins. Then they are released into the cells from the blood stream. They play a vital role in maturation of CNS as thyroid hormone deficiency leads to irreversible mental retardation. They increase heart rate, ventilation rate and O_2 consumption. They also increase the size and numbers of mitochondria and these in turn increase the rate of production of ATP, which is a factor that promotes cellular metabolism; glycogenolysis and gluconeogenesis both increase; lipolysis increases; and protein synthesis also increases. The overall effect of thyroid hormone on metabolism is catabolic.

Hyperthyroidism is an excess of thyroid hormone secretion above that needed for normal function. Basically, an increased rate of metabolism throughout the body is observed. Other symptoms include fast heart rate and respiratory rate, weight loss, sweating, tremor, and protruding eyes.

Hypothyroidism is an inadequate amount of thyroid hormone secreted into the blood stream. Generally it slows down the metabolic rate and enhances the collection of mucinous fluid in the tissue spaces, creating an edematous (fluid filled) state called myxedema. Other symptoms include slowed heart rate and respiratory rate, weight gain, cold intolerance, fatigue, and mental slowness.

The thyroid and parathyroid glands affect blood calcium concentration in different ways. The thyroid produces *calcitonin* which inhibits osteoclast activity and stimulates osteoblasts to form bone tissue; thus blood [Ca^{2+}] decreases. The parathyroid glands produce parathormone (= parathyroid hormone = PTH), which stimulates osteoclasts to break down bone, thus raising [Ca^{2+}] and [PO_4^{3-}] in the blood (BIO 5.4.4).

6.3.4 Pancreatic Hormones

The pancreas contains clusters of cells (= *islets of Langerhans*) closely associated with blood vessels. The islets of Langerhans, which perform the endocrine function of the pancreas, contain alpha cells that secrete *glucagon* and beta cells that secrete *insulin*. Glucagon increases blood glucose concentration by promoting the following events in the liver: the conversion of glycogen to glucose (*glycogenolysis*) and the production of glucose from amino acids (*gluconeogenesis*). Insulin decreases blood glucose by increasing cellular uptake of glucose, promoting glycogen formation and decreasing gluconeogenesis. A deficiency in insulin or insensitivity to insulin results in *diabetes mellitus*.

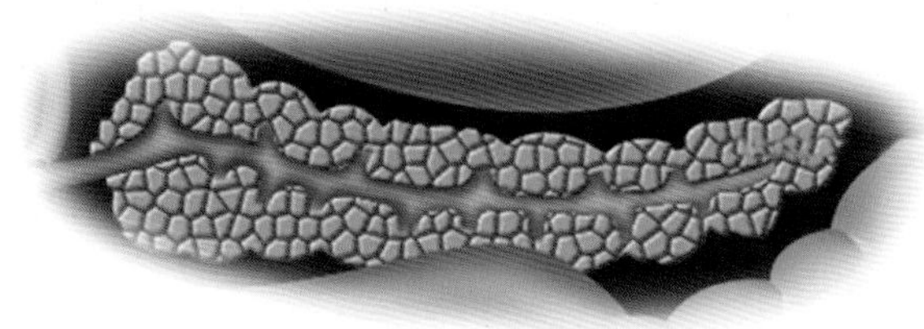

Figure IV.A.6.9: The pancreas.

6.3.5 Kidney Hormones

The kidney produces and secretes *renin*, *erythropoietin* and it helps in the activation of vitamin D. Renin is an enzyme that catalyzes the conversion of angiotensinogen to angiotensin I. Angiotensin I is then converted to angiotensin II by angiotensin-converting enzyme (ACE). Angiotensin II acts on the adrenal cortex to increase the synthesis and release of aldosterone, which increases Na^+ reabsorption, and causes vasoconstriction of arterioles leading to an increase in both blood volume and blood pressure. Erythropoietin increases the production of *erythrocytes* by acting on red bone marrow.

Vitamin D is a steroid which is critical for the proper absorption of calcium from the small intestine; thus it is essential for the normal growth and development of bone and teeth. Vitamin D can either be ingested or produced from a precursor by the activity of ultraviolet light on skin cells. It must be further activated in the liver and kidney by hydroxylation.

6.3.6 A Negative Feedback Loop

In order to maintain the internal environment of the body in equilibrium (= *homeostasis*), our hormones engage in various negative feedback loops. Negative feedback is self-limiting: a hormone produces biologic actions that, in turn, directly or indirectly inhibit further secretion of that hormone.

For example, if the body is exposed to extreme cold, the hypothalamus will activate systems to conserve heat (see *Skin as an Organ System*, BIO 13.1) and to produce heat. Heat production can be attained by increasing the basal metabolic rate. To achieve this, the hypothalamus secretes a releasing factor (thyrotropin releasing factor - TRF) which stimulates the anterior pituitary to secrete TSH. Thus the thyroid gland is stimulated to secrete the thyroid hormones.

Body temperature begins to return to normal. The high levels of circulating thyroid hormones begin to *inhibit* the production of TRF and TSH (= *negative feedback*) which in turn ensures the reduction in the levels of the thyroid hormones. Thus homeostasis is maintained.

6.3.7 A Positive Feedback Loop

As opposed to negative feedback, a positive feedback loop is where the body senses a change and activates mechanisms that accelerate or increase that change. Occasionally this may help homeostasis by working in conjunction with a larger negative feedback loop, but unfortunately it often produces the opposite effect and can be life-threatening.

An example of a beneficial positive feedback loop is seen in childbirth, where stretching of the uterus triggers the secretion of oxytocin (BIO 6.3.1), which stimulates uterine contractions and speeds up labor. Of course, once the baby is out of the mother's body, the loop is broken.

Often, however, positive feedback produces the very opposite of homeostasis: a rapid loss of internal stability with potentially fatal consequences. For example, most human deaths from SARS and the bird flu (H5N1) epidemic were caused by a "cytokine storm" which is a positive feedback loop between immune cells and cytokines (signalling molecules similar to hormones). Thus, in many cases, it is the body's exaggerated response to infection that is the cause of death rather than the direct action of the original infecting agent. Many diseases involve dangerous positive feedback loops.

GOLD STANDARD WARM-UP EXERCISES

CHAPTER 6: Nervous and Endocrine Systems

1) How many PAIRS of nerves leave the vertebrate brain?

A. 3
B. 6
C. 8
D. 12

2) The structure in the brain responsible for maintaining homeostasis (i.e. body temperature, heart rate, etc.) is the:

A. pituitary.
B. thalamus.
C. hypothalamus.
D. cerebellum.

3) Damage to which pair of nerves comprising the descending pathways, would likely cause persons with spinal-cord damage to have no control over the micturition process (i.e. urination)?

A. Vagus
B. Abducans
C. Trigeminal
D. Hypoglossal

4) Increased physical activity results in raising the heart rate and blood pressure. The nervous system specifically implicated is:

A. somatic.
B. peripheral.
C. parasympathetic.
D. sympathetic.

5) A collection of nerve cell bodies in the central nervous system is generally referred to as a:

A. nerve.
B. conus.
C. ganglion.
D. nucleus.

6) All of the following are correct concerning the autonomic nervous system EXCEPT:

A. nicotinic receptors operate through a second messenger system involving the regulation of cAMP.
B. both divisions of the ANS secrete acetylcholine from their preganglionic fibers.
C. the parasympathetic postganglionic fibers are cholinergic.
D. the sympathetic ganglia form chains which may extend longitudinally along each side of the vertebral column.

7) The vertebrate eyeball is bounded anteriorly by what convex, transparent tissue?

A. Sclera
B. Choroid
C. Cornea
D. Vitreous humor

8) What is the name given to the jelly-like substance filling the chamber behind the lens of the human eye?

A. Vitreous humor
B. Fovea centralis
C. Ciliary body
D. Choroid

9) All of the following are necessary for directing light onto the retina EXCEPT:

A. cornea.
B. iris.
C. lens.
D. aqueous humor.

10) The name of the ductless glands which secrete their products into the circulatory system are:

A. holocrine.
B. apocrine.
C. exocrine.
D. endocrine.

11) All of the following would be symptoms of hypothyroidism, EXCEPT:

A. hypothermia.
B. dry skin.
C. hyperactivity.
D. myxedema.

12) Which of the following endocrine glands would have the most direct antagonistic effect on the action of calcitonin?

A. Adrenal cortex
B. Thyroid
C. Pancreas
D. Parathyroid

13) Which of the following is the target organ of TRH?

A. Anterior pituitary
B. Posterior pituitary
C. Parathyroid
D. Thyroid

14) Increased levels of hormones in the adrenal gland would have which of the following effects?

A. Increased synthesis of proteins
B. Increased levels of sodium in the nephron
C. Increased metabolism of glycogen
D. Decreased blood volume

15) A certain compound has been found to strengthen bone by increasing calcium deposition in the bones. This compound would most likely stimulate which of the following?

A. Osteoclast activity
B. Calcitonin secretion
C. Parathyroid hormone secretion
D. Thyroxine secretion

16) The hypothalamus is best characterized as:

I. an endocrine gland.
II. a nexus of somatic receptor cells.
III. a producer of gonadotropin hormone.

A. I only
B. II only
C. II and III only
D. I, II, and III

17) This question refers to Fig. 1.

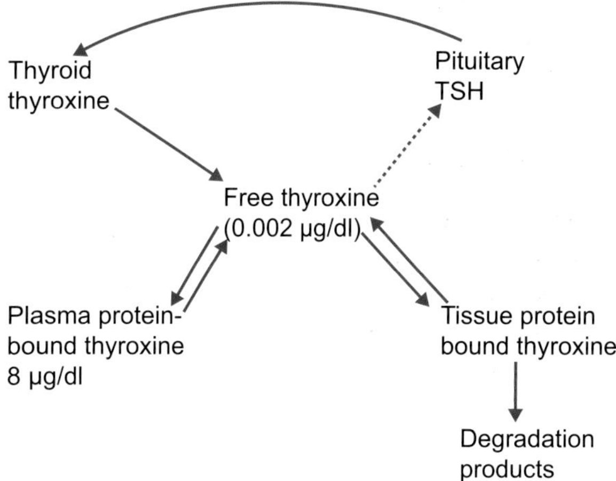

Figure 1

According to the equilibrium shown in Fig. 1, an elevation in the concentration of free thyroid hormone in the plasma is followed by:

A. an increase in tissue protein-bound thyroxine.
B. an increase in tissue protein-bound thyroxine and plasma protein-bound thyroxine.
C. an increase in the amount of TSH secreted from the pituitary gland.
D. an increase in both the amount of TSH secreted from the pituitary gland and the release of thyroxine from the thyroid gland.

18) Symptoms of hypothyroidism and hyperthyroidism, respectively, include:

A. a fine tremor and diminished concentration.
B. brittle nails and kidney stones.
C. rapid heart beat and increased irritability.
D. lethargy and nervous agitation.

19) Which of the following cell types would be expected to be maximally stimulated in a patient with hyperparathyroidism?

A. Osteoclasts
B. Osteoblasts
C. Fibroblasts
D. Chondrocytes

20) Parathormone influences calcium homeostasis by reducing tubular reabsorption of PO_4^{3-} in the kidneys. Which of the following, if true, would clarify the adaptive significance of this process?

A. PO_4^{3-} and Ca^{2+} feedback positively on each other.
B. Elevated levels of extracellular PO_4^{3-} result in calcification of bones and tissues.
C. Increased PO_4^{3-} levels cause an increase in parathormone secretion.
D. Decreased extracellular PO_4^{3-} levels cause a decrease in calcitonin production.

21) On a very hot day, the bladder would likely contain:

A. a large amount of urine hypertonic to blood plasma.
B. a large amount of urine hypotonic to blood plasma.
C. a small amount of urine hypertonic to blood plasma.
D. a small amount of urine hypotonic to blood plasma.

22) Which of the following best represents a possible series of physiological events following the detection by the hypothalamus of a cold environment?

A. heat promoting center → parasympathetic nerves → adrenal medulla → epinephrine production
B. heat promoting center → sympathetic nerves → sweat glands → stimulating local secretion
C. heat promoting center → sympathetic nerves → adrenal medulla → epinephrine production
D. heat promoting center → parasympathetic nerves → heart → dilated coronary vessels

23) Low blood pressure would normally result in which of the following?

A. Increased production of oxytocin in the hypothalamus.
B. Decreased levels of prolactin in the anterior pituitary.
C. Increased levels of parathyroid hormone.
D. Increased production of aldosterone in the adrenal cortex.

24) After radioactive iodine ^{131}I is injected into the vein of a patient, where would ^{131}I concentration be highest?

A. Liver
B. Parathyroid
C. Thyroid
D. Muscle cells

25) The hormone which exerts the most control on the concentration of the urine in the bladder is:

A. vasopressin.
B. oxytocin.
C. thyroxine.
D. prolactin.

26) Which of the following is an example of positive feedback?

A. An elevated body temperature of 101 °F causes a further increase.

B. Elevated TSH results in elevated thyroxine.

C. Calcitonin and parathromone regulate calcium levels.

D. Increased thyroid releasing factor (TRH) leads to increased TSH.

GS ANSWER KEY

CHAPTER 6

		Cross-Reference			*Cross-Reference*
1.	D	BIO 6.1	14.	C	BIO 6.3.1, 6.3.2
2.	C	BIO 6.1	15.	B	BIO 6.3.3
3.	A	BIO 6.1, 6.1.4	16.	A	BIO 6.3, 6.3.1
4.	D	BIO 6.1.4	17.	B	CHM 9.9, BIO 6.3.3, 6.3.6
5.	D	BIO 6.1	18.	D	BIO 6.3.3
6.	A	BIO 6.1.5	19.	A	BIO 5.4.4, 6.3.3
7.	C	BIO 6.2.4	20.	B	BIO 5.4.4, 6.3.3
8.	A	BIO 6.2.4	21.	C	BIO 1.1.1, 6.3.1 and F
9.	B	BIO 6.2.4	22.	C	BIO 6.1, 6.1.4, 6.3.2, 6.3.3
10.	D	BIO 6.3	23.	D	BIO 6.3.1, 6.3.2
11.	C	BIO 6.3.1, 6.3.3	24.	C	BIO 6.3.1
12.	D	BIO 6.3.3	25.	A	BIO 6.3, 6.3.1
13.	A	BIO 6.3.1, 6.3.3	26.	A	BIO 6.3.6, 6.3.7

* Explanations can be found at the back of the book.

Go online to DAT-prep.com for additional chapter review Q&A and forum.

Chapter 7

Memorize	Understand	Importance
* Circ. and lymphatic systems: basic structures and functions * Composition of blood, lymph, purpose of lymph nodes * RBC production and destruction; spleen, bone marrow * Basics: coagulation, clotting mechanisms * Equations for Q, EF, SV	* Circ: structure/function; 4 chambered heart: systolic/diastolic pressure * Oxygen transport; hemoglobin, oxygen content/affinity * Substances transported by blood, lymph * Source of lymph: diffusion from capillaries by differential pressure	**0 to 2 out of the 40 Biology** DAT questions are based on content in this chapter (in our estimation). * Note that between 25% and 50% of the questions in DAT Biology are from 5 chapters: 1, 2, 14, 15, and 16.

Introduction 

The circulatory system is concerned with the movement of nutrients, gases and wastes to and from cells. The circulatory or cardiovascular system (closed) distributes blood while the lymphatic system (open) distributes lymph.

Additional Resources

Free Online Q&A + Forum

Video: Online or DVD

Flashcards

Special Guest

7.1 Generalities

The circulatory system is composed of the heart, blood, and blood vessels. The heart (which acts like a pump) and its blood vessels (which act like a closed system of ducts) are called the *cardiovascular system* which moves the blood throughout the body.

The following represents some important functions of blood within the circulatory system.

* It transports:

- hormones from endocrine glands to target tissues
- molecules and cells which are components of the immune system
- nutrients from the digestive tract (usu. to the liver)
- oxygen from the respiratory system to body cells
- waste from the body cells to the respiratory and excretory systems.

* It aids in temperature control (*thermoregulation*) by:

- distributing heat from skeletal muscle and other active organs to the rest of the body
- being directed to or away from the skin depending on whether or not the body wants to release or conserve heat, respectively.

7.2 The Heart

The heart is a muscular, cone-shaped organ about the size of a fist. The heart is composed of connective tissue (BIO 5.4) and cardiac muscle (BIO 5.2) which includes a region that generates electrical signals (see BIO 11.2 for SA node). The heart contains four chambers: two thick muscular walled *ventricles* and two thinner walled *atria*. An inner wall or *septum* separates the heart (and therefore the preceding chambers) into left and right sides. The atria contract or *pump* blood more or less simultaneously and so do the ventricles.

Deoxygenated blood returning to the heart from all body tissues except the lungs (= *systemic circulation*) enters the right atrium through large veins (= *venae cavae*). The blood is then pumped into the right ventricle through the tricuspid valve (which is one of many one-way valves in the cardiovascular system). Next the blood is pumped to the lungs (= *pulmonary circulation*) through semilunar valves (pulmonary valves) and pulmonary arteries {remember: blood in arteries goes away from the heart}.

The blood loses CO_2 and is **oxygenated** in the lungs and returns through pulmonary veins to the left atrium. Now the blood is pumped through the mitral (= bicuspid) valve into the largest chamber of the heart: the left ventricle. This ventricle's task is to return

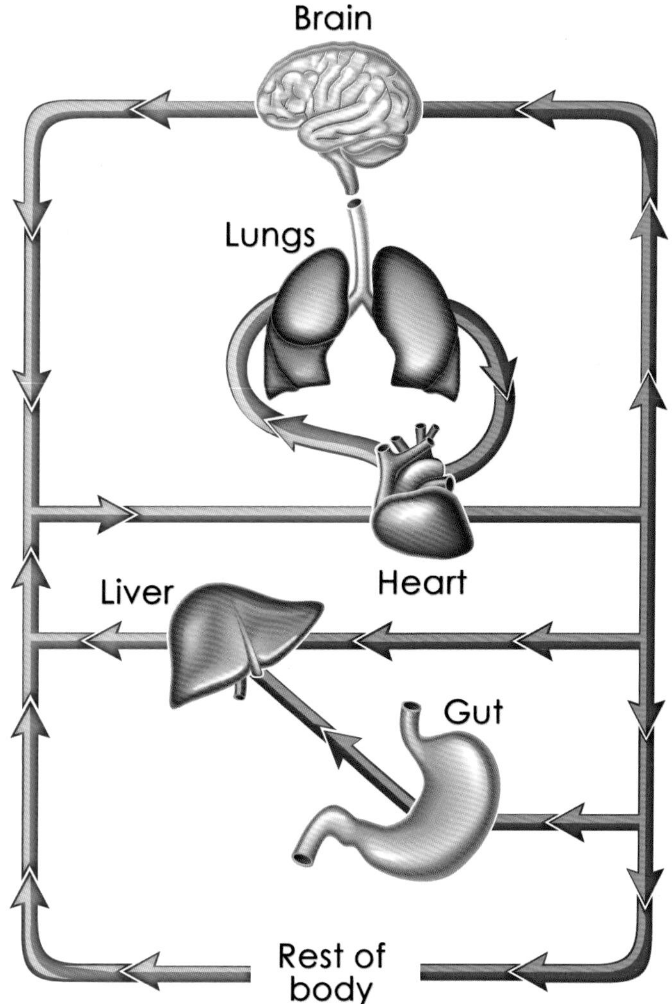

Figure IV.A.7.0: Overview of vascular anatomy.

The vascular anatomy of the human body or for an individual organ is comprised of both in-series and in-parallel vascular components. Blood leaves the heart through the aorta (high in oxygen, red in color) from which it is distributed to major organs by large arteries, each of which originates from the aorta. Therefore, these major distributing arteries are in parallel with each other. Thus the circulations of the head, arms, gastrointestinal systems, kidneys, and legs are all parallel circulations. There are some exceptions, notably the gastrointestinal (gut) and hepatic (liver) circulations, which are partly in series because the venous drainage from the intestines become the hepatic portal vein which supplies most of the blood flow to the liver. Vessels transporting from one capillary bed to another are called portal veins (besides the liver, note the portal system in the anterior pituitary, BIO 6.3.1).

blood into the systemic circulation by pumping into a huge artery: the *aorta* (its valve is the aortic valve).

The mitral (= bicuspid = 2 leaflets) and tricuspid (tri = 3 leaflets) valves are prevented from everting into the atria by strong fibrous cords (*chordae tendineae*) which are attached to small mounds of muscle (*papillary muscles*) in their respective ventricles. A major cause of heart murmurs is the inadequate functioning of these valves.

7.3 Blood Vessels

Blood vessels include arteries, arterioles, capillaries, venules and veins. Whereas arteries tend to have thick, smooth muscular walls and contain blood at high pressure, veins have thinner walls and low blood pressure. However, veins contain the highest proportion of blood in the cardiovascular system (about 2/3rds). The wall of a blood vessel is composed of an outer adventitia, an inner intima and a *m*iddle *m*uscle layer, the *media*.

Oxygenated blood entering the systemic circulation must get to all the body's tissues. The aorta must divide into smaller and smaller arteries (small artery = **arteriole**) in order to get to the level of the capillary which i) is the smallest blood vessel; ii) often forms branching networks called *capillary beds*; and iii) is the level at which the exchange of wastes and gases (i.e. O_2 and CO_2) occurs by diffusion.

In the next step in circulation, the newly deoxygenated blood enters very small veins (= **venules**) and then into larger and larger veins until the blood enters the venae cavae and then the right atrium. There are two venae cavae: one drains blood from the upper body while the other drains blood from the lower body (*superior* and *inferior* venae cavae, respectively).

Since the walls of veins are thin and somewhat floppy, they are often located in muscles. Thus movement of the leg squeezes the veins, which pushes the blood through 1-way bicuspid valves toward the heart. This is referred to as the *muscle pump*.

Coronary arteries branch off the aorta to supply the heart muscle.

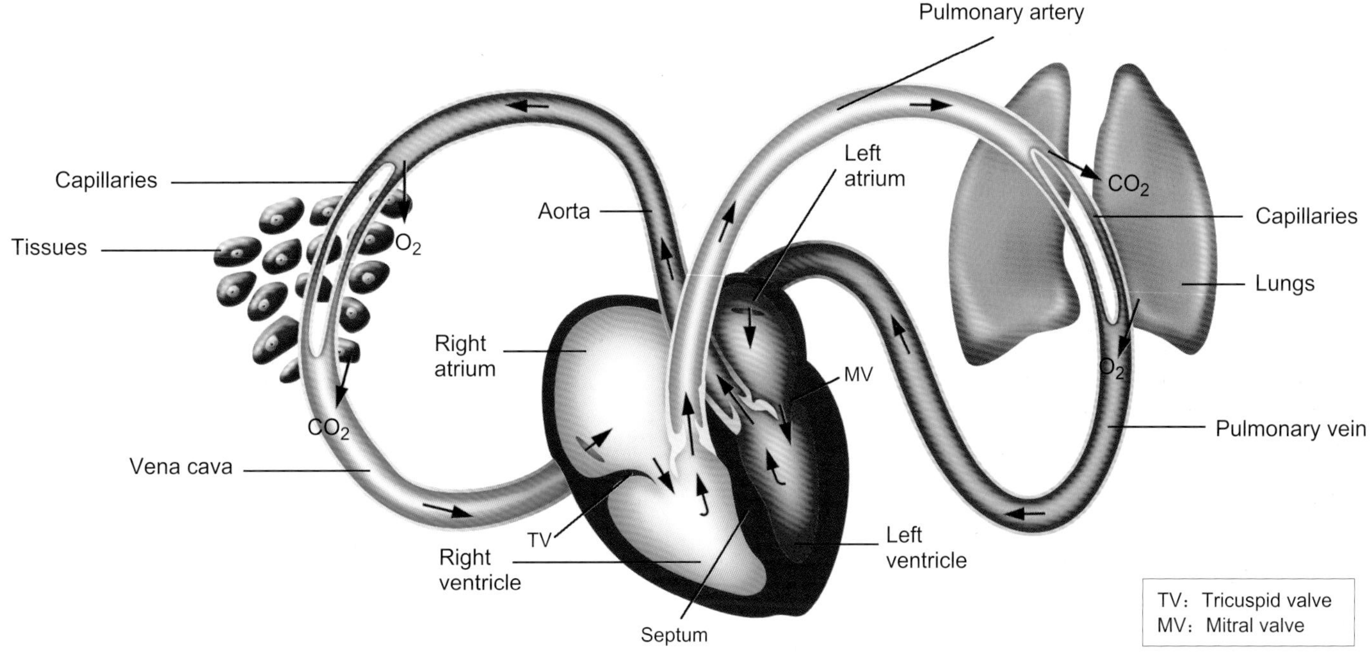

Figure IV.A.7.1: Schematic representation of the circulatory system.

Systemic circulation: transports blood from the left ventricle into the aorta then to all parts of the body and then returns to the right atrium from the superior and inferior venae cavae. *Pulmonary circulation:* transports blood from the right ventricle into pulmonary arteries to the lungs for exchange of oxygen and carbon dioxide and returns blood to the left atrium from pulmonary veins.

7.4 Blood Pressure

Blood pressure is the force exerted by the blood against the inner walls of blood vessels (esp. arteries). Maximum arterial pressure is measured when the ventricle contracts and blood is pumped into the arterial system (= *systolic pressure*). Minimal arterial pressure is measured when the ventricle is relaxed and blood is returned to the heart via veins (= *diastolic pressure*). Pulse pressure is the difference between the systolic pressure and the diastolic pressure. Blood pressure is usually measured in the brachial artery in the arm. A pressure of 120/80 signifies a systolic pressure of 120 mmHg and a diastolic pressure of 80 mmHg. The *pulse pressure* is the difference (i.e. 40 mmHg).

Peripheral resistance is essentially the result of arterioles and capillaries which resist the flow of blood from arteries to veins (the narrower the vessel, the higher the resistance). Arterioles are the site of the highest resistance in the cardiovascular system. An increase in peripheral resistance causes a rise in blood pressure. As blood travels down the systemic circulation, blood pressure decreases progressively due to the peripheral resistance to blood flow.

7.5 Blood Composition

Blood contains plasma (55%) and *formed elements* (45%). Plasma is a straw colored liquid which is mostly composed of water (92%), electrolytes, and the following plasma proteins:

* **Albumin** which is important in maintaining the osmotic pressure and helps to transport many substances in the blood

* **Globulins** which include both transport proteins and the proteins which form antibodies

* **Fibrinogen** which polymerizes to form the insoluble protein *fibrin* which is essential for normal blood clotting. If you take away fibrinogen and some other clotting factors from plasma you will be left with a fluid called *serum*.

The formed elements of the blood originate from precursors in the bone marrow which produce the following for the circulatory system: 99% red blood cells (= *erythrocytes*), then there are platelets (= *thrombocytes*), and white blood cells (= *leukocytes*). Red blood cells (RBCs) are biconcave cells without nuclei (*anucleate*) that circulate for 110-120 days before their components are recycled by macrophages. Interestingly, mature RBCs do not possess most organelles such as mitochondria, Golgi nor ER because RBCs are packed with hemoglobin. The primary function of hemoglobin is the transport of O_2 and CO_2 to and from tissue.

Platelets are cytoplasmic fragments of large bone marrow cells (*megakaryocytes*) which are involved in blood clotting by adhering to the collagen of injured vessels, releasing mediators which cause blood vessels to constrict (= *vasoconstriction*), etc.

Calcium ions (Ca^{2+}) are also important in blood clotting because they help in signaling platelets to aggregate.

White blood cells help in the defense against infection; they are divided into *granulocytes* and *agranulocytes* depending on whether or not the cell does or does not contain granules, respectively.

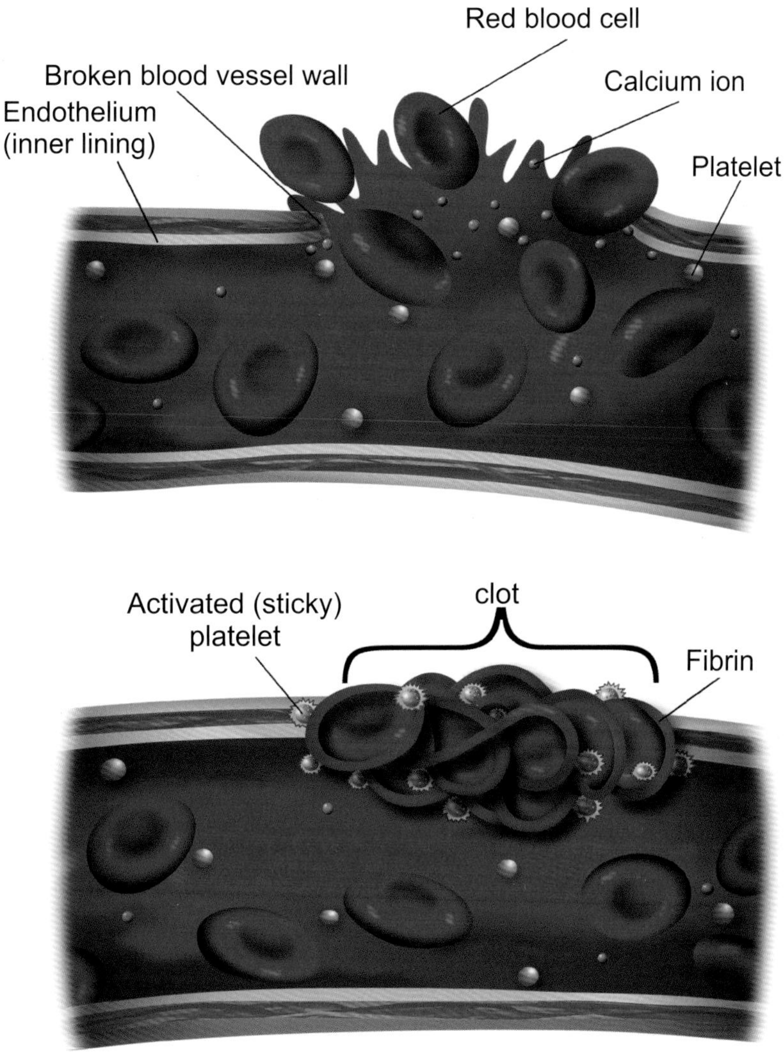

Figure IV.A.7.1.1: Schematic representation of blood clotting.

Granulocytes (= *polymorphonuclear leukocytes*) possess varying number of azurophilic (burgundy when stained) granules and are divided into: i) neutrophils which are the first white blood cells to respond to infection, they are important in controlling bacterial infection by phagocytosis - killing and digesting bacteria - and are the main cellular constituent of pus; ii) eosinophils which, like neutrophils, are phagocytic and also participate in allergic reactions and the destruction of parasites; iii) <u>basophils</u> which can release both anticoagulants (heparin) and substances important in hypersensitivity reactions (histamine).

Agranulocytes (= *mononuclear leukocytes*)) lack specific granules and are divided into: i) *lymphocytes* which are vital to the immune system (see *Immune System*, chapter 8); and monocytes (often called *phagocytes* or *macrophages* when they are outside of the circulatory system) which can phagocytose large particles.

The hematocrit measures how much space (volume) in the blood is occupied by red blood cells and is expressed as a percentage. Normal hematocrit in adults is about 45%.

{*See* BIO 15.2 *for ABO Blood Types*}

7.5.1 Hemoglobin

Each red blood cell carries hundreds of molecules of a substance which is responsible for their red color: **hemoglobin**. Hemoglobin (Hb) is a complex of *heme*, which is an iron-containing porphyrin ring, and *globin*, which is a tetrameric (= has 4 subunits) protein consisting of two α-subunits and two β-subunits. The iron from the heme group is normally in its reduced state (Fe^{2+}); however, in the presence of O_2, it can be oxidized to Fe^{3+}.

In the lungs, oxygen concentration or *partial pressure* is high, thus O_2 dissolves in the blood; oxygen can then quickly and reversibly combine with the iron in Hb forming bright red *oxyhemoglobin*. The binding of oxygen to hemoglobin is cooperative. In other words, each oxygen that binds to Hb facilitates the binding of the next oxygen. Consequently, the dissociation curve for oxyhemoglobin is sigmoidal as a result of the change in affinity of hemoglobin as each O_2 successively binds to the globin subunit (see BIO 4.3).

Examine Figure IV.A.7.2 carefully. Notice that at a PO_2 of 100 mmHg (e.g. arterial blood), the percentage of saturation of hemoglobin is almost 100%, which means all four heme groups on the four hemoglobin subunits are bound with O_2. At a PO_2 of 40 mmHg (e.g. venous blood), the percentage of saturation of hemoglobin is about 75%, which means three of the four heme groups on the four hemoglobin subunits are bound with O_2. At a PO_2 of 27 mmHg, the percentage of saturation of hemoglobin is only 50%, which means half of the four heme groups on the four hemoglobin subunits are bound with O_2. The partial pressure of oxygen (PO_2) at 50% saturation is called P50.

The curve can: (i) shift to the left which means that for a given PO_2 in the tissue capillary there is decreased unloading (release) of oxygen and that the affinity of hemoglobin for O_2 is increased; or (ii) shift to the right which means that for a given PO_2 in the tissue capillary there is increased

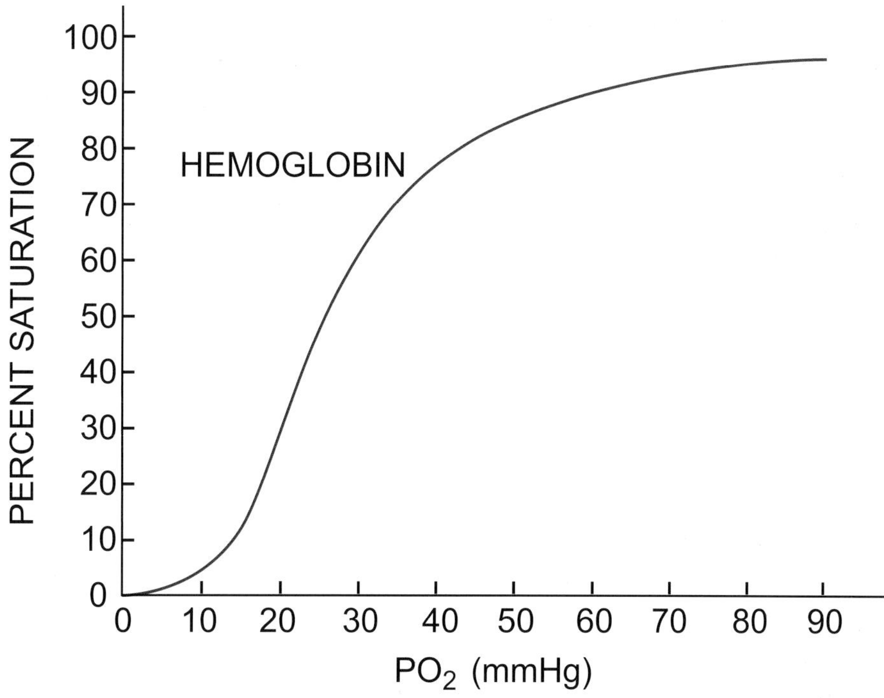

Figure IV.A.7.2: Oxygen dissociation curve: percent O_2 saturation versus O_2 partial pressure.

unloading of oxygen and that the affinity of hemoglobin for O_2 is decreased. The latter occurs when the tissue (i.e. muscle) is very active and thus requires more oxygen.

Thus a right shift occurs when the muscle is hot (↑ temperature during exercise), acid (↓ pH due to lactic acid produced in exercising muscle, see BIO 4.4. and 4.5), hypercarbic (↑CO_2 as during exercise, tissue produces more CO_2, see BIO 4.4. and 12.4.1), or contains high levels of organic phosphates (esp. increased synthesis of 2,3 DPG in red blood cells as a means to adapt to chronic hypoxemia).

In the body tissues where the partial pressure of O_2 is low and CO_2 is high, O_2 is released and CO_2 combines with the protein component of Hb forming the darker colored *carbaminohemoglobin* (also called: deoxyhemoglobin). The red color of muscle is due to a different heme-containing protein concentrated in muscle called myoglobin. Myoglobin is a monomeric protein containing one heme prosthetic group. The O_2 binding curve for myoglobin is hyperbolic, which means that it lacks cooperativity.

7.5.2 Capillaries: A Closer Look

Capillary fluid movement can occur as a result of two processes: diffusion (dominant role) and filtration (secondary role but critical for the proper function of organs, especially the kidney; BIO 10.3). Osmotic pressure (BIO 1.1.1, CHM 5.1.3) due to proteins in blood plasma is sometimes called colloid osmotic pressure or oncotic pressure. The Starling equation is an equation that describes the role of hydrostatic and oncotic forces (= Starling forces) in the movement of fluid across capillary membranes as a result of filtration.

When blood enters the arteriole end of a capillary, it is still under pressure produced by the contraction of the ventricle. As a result of this pressure, a substantial amount of water (hydrostatic) and some plasma proteins filter through the walls of the capillaries into the tissue space. This fluid, called interstitial fluid (BIO 7.6), is simply blood plasma minus most of the proteins.

Interstitial fluid bathes the cells in the tissue space and substances in it can enter the cells by diffusion (mostly) or active transport. Substances, like carbon dioxide, can diffuse out of cells and into the interstitial fluid.

Near the venous end of a capillary, the blood pressure is greatly reduced. Here another force comes into play. Although the composition of interstitial fluid is similar to that of blood plasma, it contains a smaller concentration of proteins than plasma and thus a somewhat greater concentration of water.

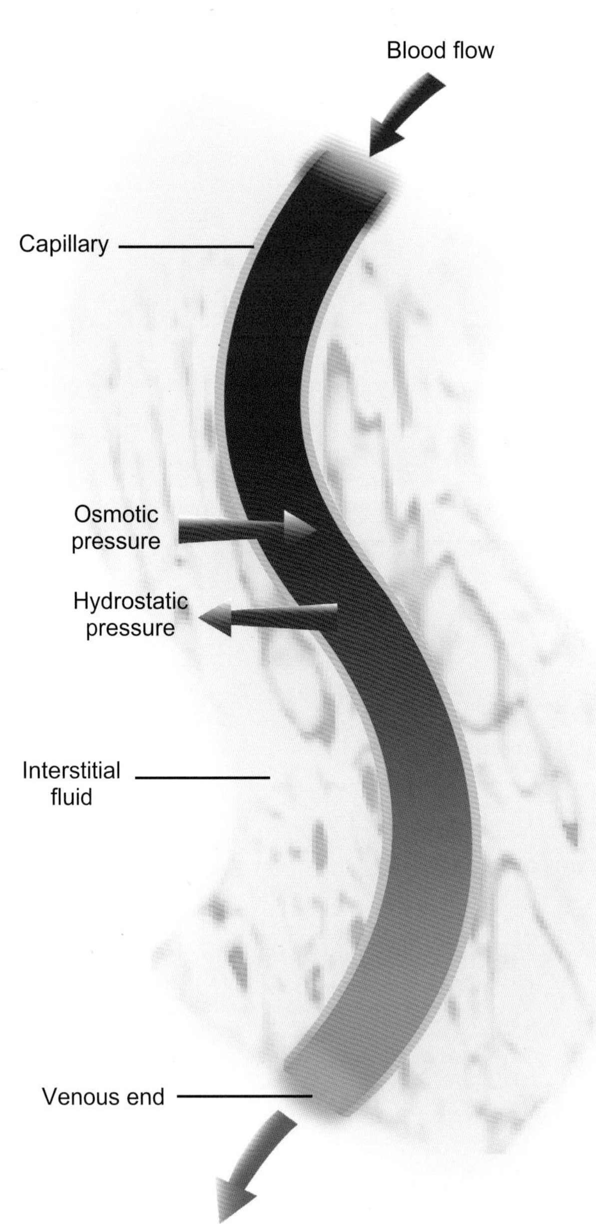

Figure IV.A.7.2b: Circulation at the level of the capillary. The exchange of water, oxygen, carbon dioxide, and many other nutrient and waste chemical substances between blood and surrounding tissues occurs at the level of the capillary.

This difference sets up an osmotic pressure. Although the osmotic pressure is small, it is greater than the blood pressure at the venous end of the capillary. Thus the fluid reenters the capillary here.

To summarize: when the blood pressure is greater than the osmotic pressure, filtration is favored and fluid tends to move out of the capillary; when the blood pressure is less than the osmotic pressure, reabsorption is favored and fluid tends to enter into the capillary.

7.6 The Lymphatic System

Body fluids can exist in blood vessels (intravascular), in cells (intracellular) or in a 3rd space which is intercellular (between cells) or extracellular (outside cells). Such fluids are called interstitial fluids. The **lymphatic system** is a network of vessels which can circulate fluid from the 3rd space to the cardiovascular system.

Aided by osmotic pressure, interstitial fluids enter the lymphatic system via small closed-ended tubes called *lymphatic capillaries* (in the small intestine they are called *lacteals*). Once the fluid enters it is called **lymph**. The lymph continues to flow into larger and larger vessels propelled by muscular contraction (esp. skeletal) and one-way valves. Then the lymph will usually pass through *lymph nodes* and then into a large vessel (esp. *the thoracic duct*) which drains into one of the large veins which eventually leads to the right atrium.

Lymph functions in important ways. Most protein molecules which leak out of blood capillaries are returned to the bloodstream by lymph. Also, microorganisms which invade tissue fluids are carried to lymph nodes by lymph. Lymph nodes contain *lymphocytes* and macrophages which are components of the immune system.

GOLD STANDARD WARM-UP EXERCISES

CHAPTER 7: The Circulatory System

1) In humans which of the following orders of blood circulation is correct?

   A. Vena cava → right atrium → right ventricle → pulmonary arteries → pulmonary veins → left atrium
   B. Vena cava → left atrium → left ventricle → pulmonary veins → pulmonary arteries → right ventricle
   C. Vena cava → right ventricle → left ventricle → pulmonary veins → pulmonary arteries → left atrium
   D. Vena cava → left atrium → left ventricle → pulmonary vein → pulmonary artery → right atrium

2) The rate of respiration is primarily dependent on the concentration of carbon dioxide in the blood. As carbon dioxide levels rise, chemoreceptors in blood vessels are stimulated to discharge neuronal impulses to the respiratory center in the medulla oblongata in the brain stem. These chemoreceptors are likely located in the:

   A. vena cava.
   B. pulmonary artery.
   C. femoral vein.
   D. aorta.

3) Veins tend to have ALL the following EXCEPT:

   A. very elastic walls.
   B. increasing size toward the heart.
   C. thin walls.
   D. valves for unidirectional flow.

4) Blood in the pulmonary veins is rich in:

   A. myoglobin.
   B. carbaminohemoglobin.
   C. oxyhemoglobin.
   D. lymph.

5) A biologically active agent, which completely diffuses through capillary beds, is injected into the brachiocephalic vein of the left arm. Which of the following would be most affected by the agent?

   A. Heart
   B. Lung
   C. Left arm
   D. Right arm

6) If the partial pressure of O_2 was increased to make up the total pressure of gas in blood which of the following would occur?

   A. There would be a decrease in HbO_2.
   B. There would be an increase in HbO_2.
   C. The concentrations of Hb would equal HbO_2.
   D. No answer can be determined from the information given.

7) Which of the following best explains why 97% of oxygen in blood is in the HbO_2 form?

   A. Oxygen binds irreversibly to the iron atoms in hemoglobin.
   B. Oxygen does not dissolve well in blood plasma.
   C. There are allosteric interactions between hemoglobin subunits
   D. Hemoglobin consists of four proteinacious subunits.

8) Which of the following graphs best represents the relationship between percent saturation of hemoglobin and pO_2 (mmHg) at different temperatures?

A.

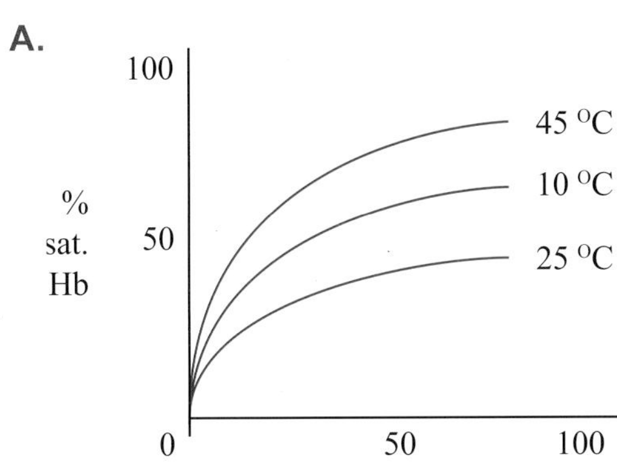

B.

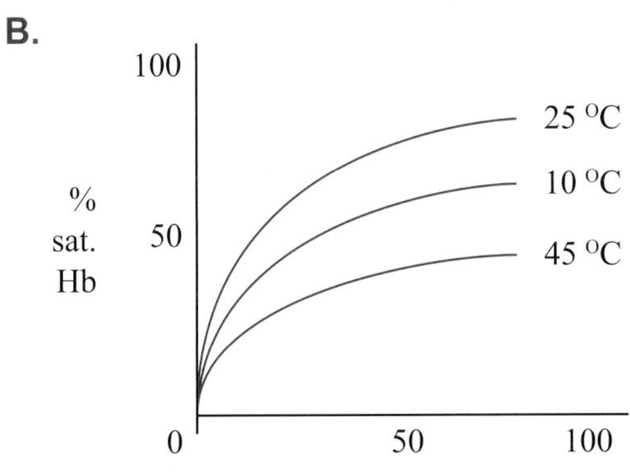

C.

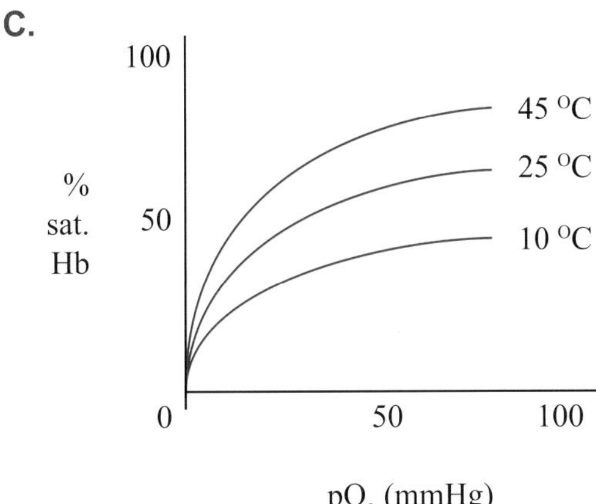

D.

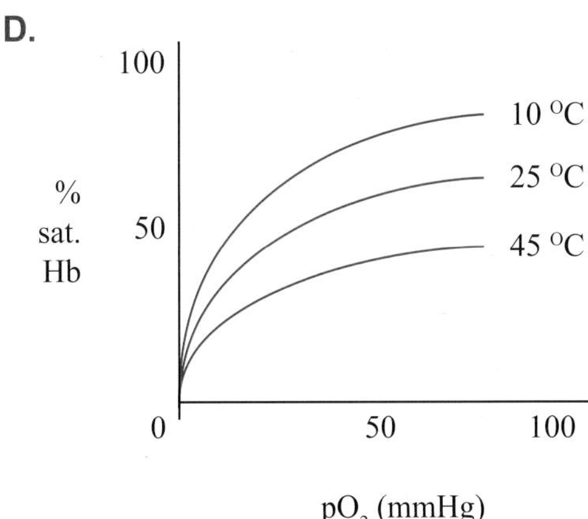

9) Which of the following body systems in humans is implicated in thermoregulation and transportation of components of the immune and endocrine systems?

A. The lymphatic system
B. Skin
C. The excretory system
D. The circulatory system

10) Once the erythrocytes enter the blood in humans, it is estimated that they have an average lifetime of how many days?

A. 75 days
B. 120 days
C. 220 days
D. 365 days

11) The net effect of the glycerate 2,3-biphosphate (GBP) is to shift the hemoglobin oxygen binding curve to higher oxygen tensions. Which of the following graphs represents the oxygen-binding curve in the presence of GBP?

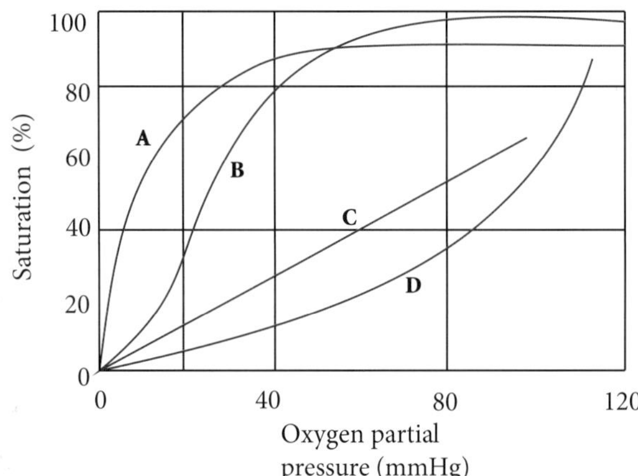

12) Glycerate 2,3-biphosphate functions to shift the oxygen binding curve by:

A. increasing the carbon carbon-dioxide concentration in the red blood cells.
B. altering the pH of the tissue fluid surrounding the red blood cells.
C. reducing the affinity between oxygen and hemoglobin at low oxygen concentrations.
D. forming a complex with oxygen at low oxygen concentrations.

13) Which of the following tissues most benefits from the shifts in the oxygen-binding curves caused by GBP and myoglobin?

A. Cardiac muscle tissue
B. Skeletal muscle tissue
C. Loose connective tissue
D. Intestinal wall tissue

14) In regions with an increased partial pressure of carbon dioxide, the oxygen dissociation curve is shifted to the right. This is known as the Bohr effect or shift. What is the physiological significance of this shift?

A. It counteracts the shift in the oxygen-binding curve caused by the presence of GBP.
B. It counteracts the shift in the oxygen-binding curve caused by the presence of myoglobin.
C. It increases the pH of actively respiring tissue.
D. It facilitates the delivery of increased quantities of oxygen from the blood to cells which produce energy.

15) Protons, like GBP, bind preferentially to deoxyhemoglobin. Thus, which of the following equations best explains the Bohr shift?

A. $CO_2 + H_2O \leftrightarrow H_2CO_3 \leftrightarrow H^+ + HCO_3^-$ (tissues)
B. $H^+ + HbO_2 \leftrightarrow HHb^+ + O_2$ (tissues)
C. $HCO_3^- + H^+ \leftrightarrow H_2CO_3 \leftrightarrow CO_2 + H_2O$ (lungs)
D. $HHb^+ + O_2 + HCO_3^- \leftrightarrow HbO_2 + CO_2 + H_2O$ (lungs)

16) Would the walls of the atria or ventricles expected to be thicker?

A. Atria, because blood ejection due to atrial contraction is high.
B. Atria, because blood ejection due to atrial contraction is low.
C. Ventricles, because ventricular stroke volume is high.
D. Ventricles, because ventricular stroke volume is low.

GS ANSWER KEY

CHAPTER 7

		Cross-Reference			Cross-Reference
1.	A	BIO 7.2, 7.3	9.	D	BIO 7.1
2.	D	BIO 7.3	10.	B	BIO 7.5
3.	A	BIO 7.3	11.	B	BIO 7.5.1
4.	C	BIO 7.2, 7.3, 7.5.1	12.	C	BIO 7.5.1
5.	B	BIO 7.3	13.	B	BIO 4.2, 11.2
6.	B	BIO 7.5.1	14.	D	BIO 4.4-4.5, 7.5.1, 12.4.1
7.	C	BIO 3.0, 4.3, 7.5.1	15.	B	BIO 7.5.1
8.	D	BIO 7.5.1	16.	C	BIO 7.2

* Explanations can be found at the back of the book.

Go online to DAT-prep.com for additional chapter review Q&A and forum.

APPENDIX

CHAPTER 7: The Circulatory System

Advanced DAT-30 Passage: The Cardiac Cycle

The cardiac cycle is the series of events comprising a complete contraction and relaxation of the heart's four chambers. The process of depolarization in the SA node (BIO 11.2) triggers the cardiac cycle which normally lasts about 0.22 seconds. The electronics of the cycle can be monitored by an electrocardiogram (EKG). The cycle is divided into two major phases, both named for events in the ventricle: the period of ventricular contraction and blood ejection, *systole*, followed by the period of ventricular relaxation and blood filling, *diastole*.

During the very first part of systole, the ventricles are contracting but all valves in the heart are closed thus no blood can be ejected. Once the rising pressure in the ventricles becomes great enough to open the aortic and pulmonary valves, the ventricular ejection or systole occurs. Blood is forced into the aorta and pulmonary trunk as the contracting ventricular muscle fibers shorten. The volume of blood ejected from a ventricle during systole is termed *stroke volume*. The total volume of blood pumped by the heart in one minute is the *cardiac output* (Q) and can be calculated as follows (<u>the equations in this section should be memorized</u>):

$$Q = \text{Stroke Volume} \times \text{Heart rate}$$

An average resting cardiac output would be 4.9 L/min for a human female and 5.6 L/min for a male.

During the very first part of diastole, the ventricles begin to relax, and the aortic and pulmonary valves close. No blood is entering or leaving the ventricles since once again all the valves are closed. Once ventricular pressure falls below atrial pressure, the atrioventricular (AV) valves open (i.e. mitral and tricuspid valves). Atrial contraction occurs towards the end of diastole, after most of the ventricular filling has taken place. The ventricle receives blood throughout most of diastole, not just when the atrium contracts. When the left ventricle is filled to capacity, it is known as End Diastolic Volume (EDV). Ejection fraction (EF) is the fraction of blood ejected by the left ventricle during systole and is usually given as a percentage:

$$EF = (\text{Stroke Volume})/(EDV) \times 100\%$$

17) Position P on the EKG of Fig. 1 probably correspond to:

A. atrial contraction.
B. ventricular contraction.
C. the beginning of ventricular systole.
D. the beginning of ventricular diastole.

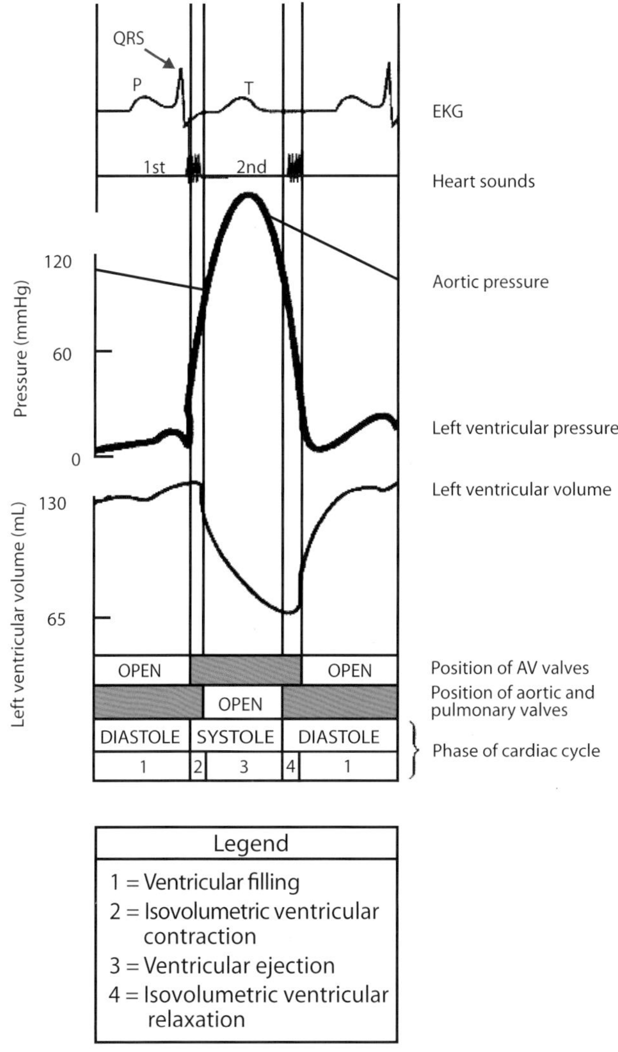

Figure 1: Electronic and pressure changes in the heart and aorta during the cardiac cycle.

18) The first heart sound represented in Fig. 1 is probably made when:

A. during ventricular systole, blood in the ventricle is forced against the closed atrioventricular valve.

B. during ventricular diastole, blood in the arteries is forced against the aortic and pulmonary artery pocket valves.

C. during ventricular diastole, blood in the ventricle is forced against the closed atrioventricular valve.

D. during ventricular systole, blood in the arteries is forced against the aortic and pulmonary artery pocket valves.

19) The graph below shows the effects on stroke volume of stimulating the sympathetic nerves to the heart.

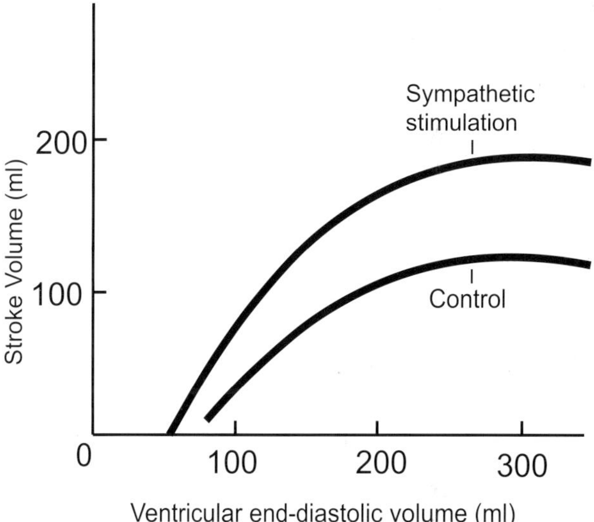

According to the graph, the net result of sympathetic stimulation on ejection fraction is to:

A. approximately double ejection fraction at any given end diastolic volume.

B. decrease ejection fraction at any given end diastolic volume.

C. increase ejection fraction at any given end diastolic volume.

D. leave ejection fraction relatively unchanged.

20) According to Fig. 1, the opening of the aortic and pulmonary valves is associated with all of the following EXCEPT one. Which one is the EXCEPTION?

- **A.** Ventricular systole
- **B.** A rise and fall in aortic pressure
- **C.** A drop and rise in left ventricular volume
- **D.** The third phase of the cardiac cycle

21) Stroke Volume / End Diastolic Volume is equal to which of the following?

- **A.** Cardiac output
- **B.** Ejection fraction
- **C.** Stroke volume
- **D.** End systolic volume

22) Which of the following correctly defines stroke volume (SV)?

- **A.** SV = cardiac output - end systolic volume
- **B.** SV = end diastolic volume - ejection fraction
- **C.** SV = end systolic volume - end diastolic volume
- **D.** SV = end diastolic volume - end systolic volume

ANSWER KEY

ADVANCED TOPICS - CHAPTER 7

		Cross-Reference
17.	A	F, BIO 7.2-7.4
18.	A	F, BIO 7.2-7.4
19.	C	F, BIO 6.1.4, 7.2-7.5
20.	C	F, BIO 7.2-7.4
21	B	Ch 12
22	D	**Appendix Ch 12, deduce**

P = paragraph; *S* = sentence; *E* = equation; *T* = table; *F* = figure

Go online to DAT-prep.com for additional chapter review Q&A and forum.

THE IMMUNE SYSTEM

Chapter 8

Memorize

* Roles in immunity: T-lymphocytes;
* B-lymphocytes
* Tissues in the immune system including bone marrow
* Spleen, thymus, lymph nodes

Understand

* Concepts of antigen, antibody, interaction
* Structure of antibody molecule
* Mechanism of stimulation by antigen

Importance

0 to 2 out of the 40 Biology

DAT questions are based on content in this chapter (in our estimation).

* Note that between 25% and 50% of the questions in DAT Biology are from 5 chapters: 1, 2, 14, 15, and 16.

Introduction

The immune system protects against disease. Many processes are used in order to identify and kill various microbes (see Microbiology, Chapter 2, for examples) as well as tumor cells. There are 2 acquired responses of the immune system: cell-mediated and humoral.

Additional Resources

Free Online Q&A + Forum

Video: Online or DVD

Flashcards

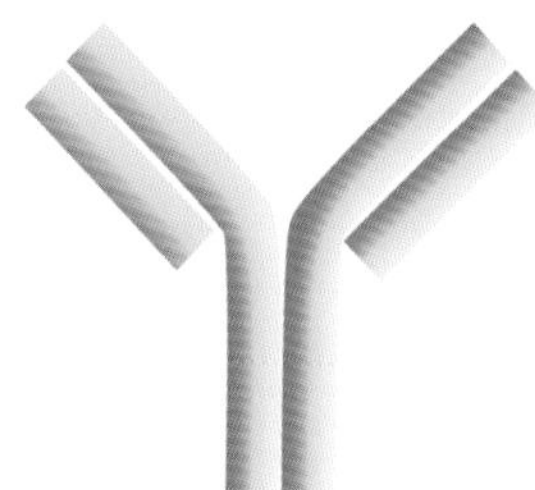

Special Guest

8.1 Overview

The immune system is composed of various cells and organs which defend the body against pathogens, toxins or any other foreign agents. Substances (usu. proteins) on the foreign agent causing an immune response are called **antigens**. There are two acquired responses to an antigen: (1) the **cell mediated response** where T-lymphocytes are the dominant force and act against microorganisms, tumors, and virus infected cells; and (2) the **humoral response** where B-lymphocytes are the dominant force and act against specific proteins present on foreign molecules.

8.2 Cells of the Immune System

B-lymphocytes originate in the bone marrow. Though T-lymphocytes also originate in the bone marrow, they go on to mature in the thymus gland. T-lymphocytes learn with the help of macrophages to recognize and attack only foreign substances (i.e. antigens) in a direct cell to cell manner (= *cell-mediated* or *cellular immunity*). T-lymphocytes have two major subtypes: T-helper cells and T-cytotoxic cells. Some T-cells (T_8, T_C, or T cytotoxic) mediate the apoptosis of foreign cells and virus-infected cells. Some T-cells (T_4, T_H or T *h*elper) mediate the cellular response by secreting substances to activate macrophages, other T-cells and even B-cells. {T_H-cells are specifically targeted and killed by the HIV virus in AIDS patients}

B-lymphocytes act indirectly against the foreign agent by producing and secreting antigen-specific proteins called **antibodies**, which are sometimes called immunoglobulins = *humoral immunity*). Antibodies are "designer" proteins which can specifically attack the antigen for which it was designed. The antibodies along with other proteins (i.e. complement proteins) can attack the antigen-bearing particle in many ways:

- **Lysis** by digesting the plasma membrane of the foreign cell

- **Opsonization** which is the altering of cell membranes so the foreign particle is more susceptible to phagocytosis by neutrophils and macrophages

- **Agglutination** which is the clumping of antigen-bearing cells

- **Chemotaxis** which is the attracting of other cells (i.e. phagocytes) to the area

- **Inflammation** which includes migration of cells, release of fluids and dilatation of blood vessels.

The activated antibody secreting B-lymphocyte is called a *plasma cell*. After the first or *primary* response to an antigen, both T- and B-cells produce *memory cells* which are formed during the initial response to an anti-

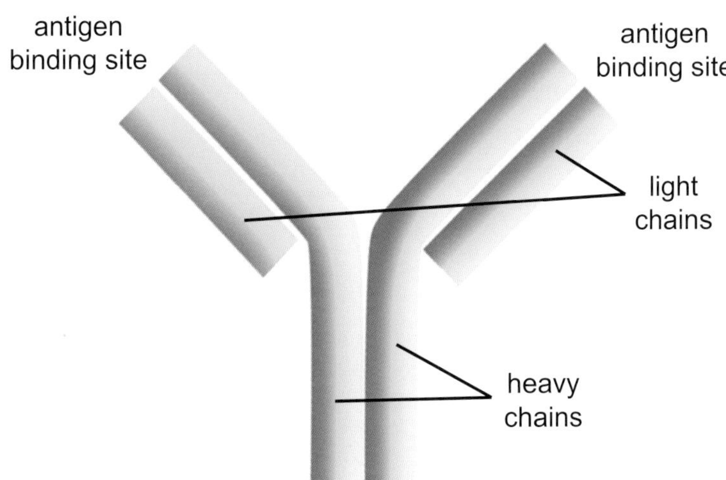

Figure IV.A.8.1: Schematic representation of an antibody. Antibodies are composed of disulfide bond-linked heavy and light chains. The unique part of the antigen recognized by an antibody is called the epitope. The antigen binding site on the antibody is extremely variable (= hypervariable).

Antibody (= Immunoglobulin = Ig)	**Description**
IgA	Found in saliva, tears and breast milk. Found in mucosal areas, such as the GI, respiratory and urogenital tracts thus prevents colonization by pathogens.
IgD	Functions mainly as an antigen receptor on B-cells that have not been exposed to antigens. Activates mast cells and basophils (BIO 7.5) to produce antimicrobial factors.
IgE	Binds to particles that induce allergic reactions (= allergens) and triggers histamine release from mast cells and basophils. Also protects against parasitic worms.
IgG	In its four forms, provides the majority of antibody-based immunity against invading germs or pathogens. The only antibody capable of crossing the placenta (BIO 14.6) to give passive immunity to the fetus.
IgM	Expressed on the surface of B-cells (monomer) and in a secreted form (pentamer = complex of 5 monomers). Eliminates pathogens in the early stages of B-cell mediated (humoral) immunity before there is sufficient IgG.

Table IV.A.8.1: Antibody isotypes of mammals. Antibodies are grouped into different "isotypes" based on which heavy chain they possess. The five different antibody isotypes known in mammals are displayed in the table.

genic challenge. These memory cells remain in the circulation and will make the next or secondary response much faster and much greater. {Note: though lymphocytes are vital to the immune system, it is the neutrophil which responds to injury first; BIO 7.5}

T-cells cannot recognise, and therefore react to, 'free' floating antigen. T-cells can only recognize an antigen that has been processed and presented by cells in association will a special cell surface molecule called the major histocompatibility complex (MHC). In fact, "antigen presenting cells", through the use of MHC, can teach both B-cells and T-cells which antigens are safe (*self*) and which are dangerous and should be attacked (*nonself*). MHC Class I molecules present to T_C cells while MHC Class II molecules present to T_H cells.

8.3 Tissues of the Immune System

The important tissues of the immune system are the bone marrow, and the lymphatic organs which include the thymus, the lymph nodes and the spleen. The roles of the bone marrow and the thymus have already been discussed. It is of value to add that the thymus secretes a hormone (= *thymosin*) which appears to help stimulate the activity of T-lymphocytes.

Lymph nodes are often the size of a pea and are found in groups or chains along the paths of the larger lymphatic vessels. Their functions can be broken down into three general categories: i) a non-specific filtration of bacteria and other particles from the lymph using the phagocytic activity of macrophages; ii) the storage and proliferation of T-cells, B-cells and antibody production; (iii) initiate immune response on the recognition of antigen.

The **spleen** is the largest lymphatic organ and is situated in the upper left part of the abdominal cavity. Within its lobules it has tissue called red and white pulp. The white pulp of the spleen contains all of the organ's lymphoid tissue (T-cells, B-cells, macrophages, and other antigen presenting cells) and is the site of active immune responses via the proliferation of T- and B-lymphocytes and the production of antibodies by plasma cells. The red pulp is composed of several types of blood cells including red blood cells, platelets and granulocytes. Its main function is to filter the blood of antigen and phagocytose damaged or aged red blood cells (the latter has a lifespan of approximately 110-120 days). In addition, the red pulp of the spleen is a site for red blood cell storage (i.e. a blood storage organ).

Autoimmunity!

Figure IV.A.8.2: Actually, "autoimmunity" refers to a disease process where the immune system attacks one's own cells and tissues as opposed to one's own car.

8.4 Advanced Topic: ELISA

ELISA, enzyme-linked-immunosorbent serologic assay, is a rapid test used to determine if a particular protein is in a sample and, if so, to quantify it (= assay). ELISA relies on an enzymatic conversion reaction and an antibody-antigen interaction which would lead to a detectable signal – usually a color change. Consequently, ELISA has no need of any radioisotope nor any radiation-counting apparatus.

There are 2 forms of ELISA: (1) direct ELISA uses monoclonal antibodies to detect antigen in a sample; (2) indirect ELISA is used to find a specific antibody in a sample (i.e. HIV antibodies in serum). {Notice the similarity with the concept of "direct" and "indirect" immunofluorescence, BIO 1.5.1}

GOLD STANDARD WARM-UP EXERCISES

CHAPTER 8: The Immune System

1) Helper T-cells are required to activate:

   A. hemoglobin and T lymphocytes.
   B. thrombocytes and B lymphocytes.
   C. B lymphocytes and T lymphocytes.
   D. erythrocytes and thrombocytes.

2) The retrovirus HIV infects primarily the helper T cells by making specific interactions with the cell's receptors. What must first occur in order for the retrovirus to infect the cell?

   A. The protein coat of the virus fuse with the helper T cell plasma membrane.
   B. The viral envelope must make contact and be recognized by helper T cell receptors.
   C. The viral RNA must be translated.
   D. The helper T cell must engulf the virus via phagocytosis.

3) Before being injected into humans as a vaccine, the hepatitis B virus (HBV) would first have to:

   A. be cloned in yeast cells to ensure that enough of the virus had been injected to elicit an immune response.
   B. have its protein coat removed.
   C. be purified.
   D. be inactivated.

4) The following graph shows the immune response for an initial injection of Hepatitis B Surface Antigen (HBsAg) and a subsequent injection of the HBV virus. Which of the following best explains the differences in the two responses?

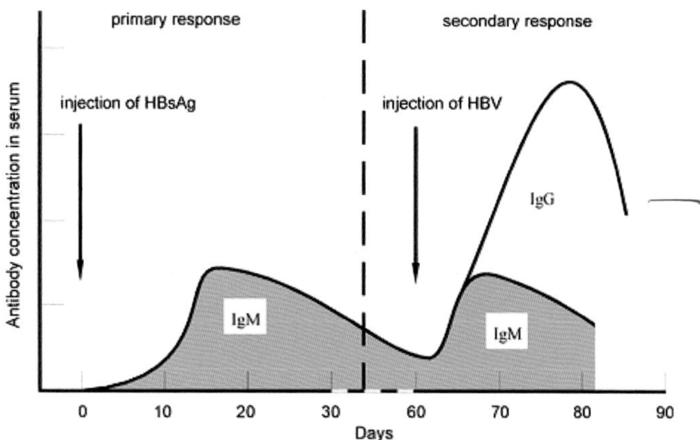

   A. During the initial response, the immune response was carried out primarily by macrophages and B-lymphocytes.
   B. During the secondary response, T-cells possessing membrane receptors, recognized and attacked the viral antigens.
   C. Memory cells produced by T- and B-cells during the first exposure made the second response faster and more intense.
   D. Memory cells produced by macrophages during the first infection recognized the viral antigens more quickly during the second infection, causing antibody production to be increased.

5) In terms of immunity, what is the major disadvantage of injecting monoclonal antibodies directly into the circulatory system instead of an inactivated form of the antigen?

A. Activated antigens can cause infection.
B. The immune response is faster when the inactivated antigen is injected.
C. The antibodies injected are often recognized as antigens by the immune system, thereby eliciting an immune response.
D. No memory cells are produced when the monoclonal antibody is directly injected into the circulatory system.

6) Which of the following biological processes would be inhibited by the removal of an adult human spleen?

A. The production of erythrocytes
B. The production of macrophages
C. The production of T-lymphocytes
D. The destruction of erythrocytes

7) Tissue transplantation is a technique which also can stimulate an immune response in recipients. Several methods are used to prevent rejection. These might include all but which of the following?

A. Exposure of the tissue to be transplanted to X-irradiation to prevent infection from occurring
B. Exposure of bone marrow and lymph tissues to X-irradiation
C. Immunosuppression
D. Tissue matching

8) Each antibody molecule is made up of how many PAIR of polypeptide chains joined together by disulfide bonds?

A. 1
B. 2
C. 3
D. 4

9) The immune system normally discriminates between which types of antigens?

A. Primary and secondary
B. Humoral and cell-mediated
C. B and T cells
D. Self and non-self

10) Surplus red blood cells, needed to meet an emergency, are MAINLY stored in what organ of the human body?

A. Spleen
B. Liver
C. Yellow marrow
D. Pancreas

GS ANSWER KEY

Chapter 8

		Cross-Reference			Cross-Reference
1.	C	BIO 8.2	6.	D	BIO 8.3
2.	B	BIO 2.1, 2.1.1, 8.2	7.	A	BIO 8.2, deduce
3.	D	BIO 2.1, 8.2	8.	B	BIO 8.2
4.	C	BIO 8.1, 8.2	9.	D	BIO 8.1, 8.2
5.	D	BIO 8.1, 8.2	10.	A	BIO 8.3

* Explanations can be found at the back of the book.

Go online to DAT-prep.com for additional chapter review Q&A and forum.

Go online to DAT-prep.com for additional chapter review Q&A and forum.

Chapter 9

Memorize	Understand	Importance
Basic anatomy of the upper GI and lower GI tracts Saliva as lubrication and enzyme source Stomach low pH, gastric juice, mucal protection against self-destruction Sites for production of digestive enzymes, sites of digestion Liver: nutrient metabolism, vitamin storage; blood glucose regulation, detoxification	* Basic function of the upper GI and lower GI tracts * Bile: storage in gallbladder, function * Pancreas: production of enzymes; transport of enzymes to small intestine * Small intestine: production of enzymes, site of digestion, neutralize stomach acid * Peristalsis; structure and function of villi, microvilli	**0 to 2 out of the 40 Biology** DAT questions are based on content in this chapter (in our estimation). * Note that between 25% and 50% of the questions in DAT Biology are from 5 chapters: 1, 2, 14, 15, and 16.

DAT-Prep.com

Introduction

The digestive system is involved in the mechanical and chemical break down of food into smaller components with the aim of absorption into, for example, blood or lymph. Thus digestion is a form of catabolism.

Additional Resources

Free Online Q&A + Forum

Video: Online or DVD

Flashcards

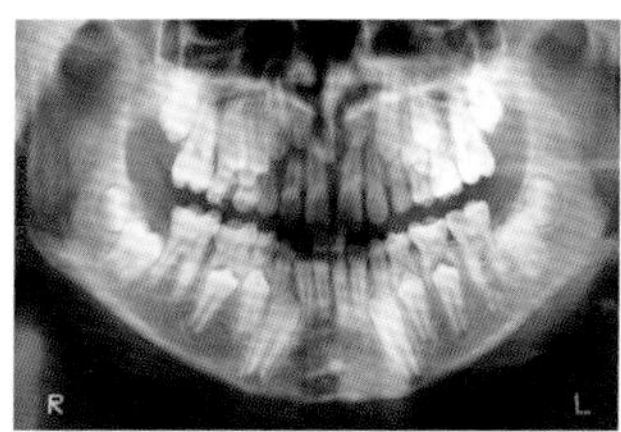

Special Guest

9.1 Overview

The digestive or *gastrointestinal* (= GI) system is principally concerned with the intake and reduction of food into subunits for absorption. These events occur in five main phases which are located in specific parts of the GI system: i) **ingestion** which is the taking of food or liquid into the mouth; ii) **fragmentation** which is when larger pieces of food are *mechanically* broken down; iii) **digestion** where macromolecules are *chemically* broken down into subunits which can be absorbed; iv) **absorption** through cell membranes; and v) **elimination** of the waste products. The GI system secretes enzymes and hormones that facilitate in the process of ingestion, digestion, absorption as well as elimination.

The GI tract (gut or *alimentary canal*) is a muscular tract about 9 meters long covered by a layer of mucosa which has definable characteristics in each area along the tract. The GI tract includes the oral cavity (mouth), pharynx, esophagus, stomach, small intestine, large intestine, and anus. The GI system includes the accessory organs which release secretions into the tract: the salivary glands, gallbladder, liver, and pancreas (*see Figure IV.A.9.1*).

9.2 The Oral Cavity and Esophagus

Ingestion, fragmentation and digestion begin in the oral cavity. Teeth are calcified, hard structures in the oral cavity used to fragment food (= *mastication*). Children have twenty teeth (= *deciduous*) and adults have thirty-two (= *permanent*). From front to back, each quadrant (= *quarter*) of the mouth contains: two incisors for cutting, one cuspid (= *canine*) for tearing, two bicuspids (= *premolars*) for crushing, and three molars for grinding.

Digestion of food begins in the oral cavity when the 3 pairs of salivary glands (*parotid*, *sublingual*, and *submandibular*) synthesize and secrete saliva. Saliva lubricates the oral cavity, assists in the process of deglutition, controls bacterial flora and initiates the process of digestion. Its production is unique in that it is increased by both sympathetic and parasympathetic innervation. Major components of saliva include salivary amylase, lysozyme, lingual lipase and mucus. Amylase is an enzyme which starts the initial digestion of carbohydrates by splitting starch and glycogen into disaccharide subunits. Lipase is an enzyme which starts the initial digestion of triglyceride (fats). The mucous helps to bind food particles together and lubricate it as it is swallowed.

Swallowing (= *deglutition*) occurs in a coordinated manner in which the tongue and pharyngeal muscles propel the bolus of food into the esophagus while at the same time the upper esophageal sphincter relaxes to permit food to enter. The epiglottis is a small flap of

Basic Dental Anatomy and Pathology

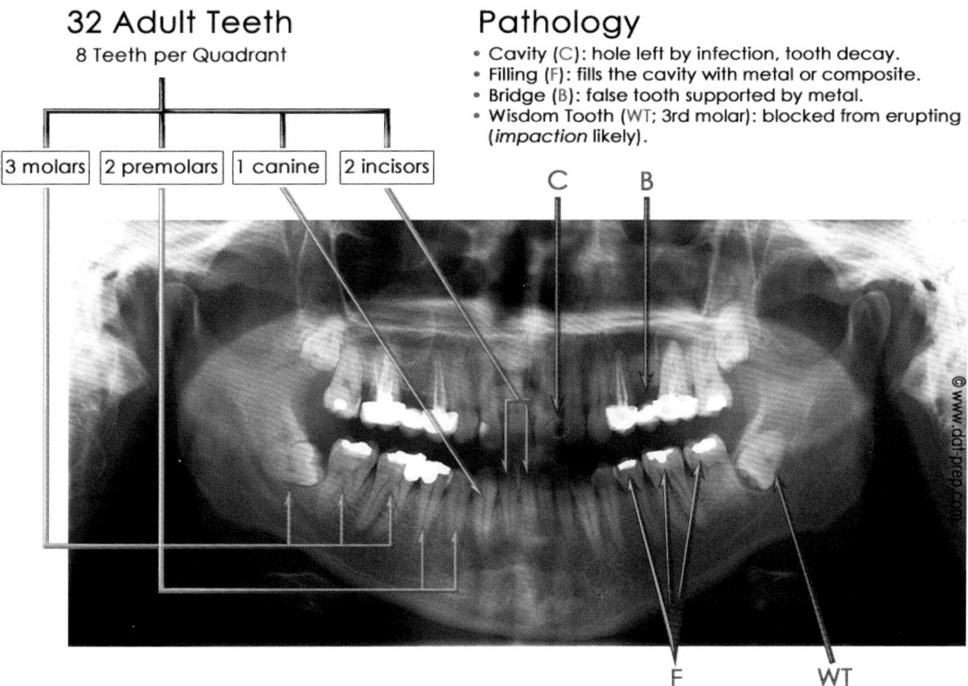

Figure IV.A.9.0a: Dental X-ray of an adult. The pathology of teeth is not prerequisite knowledge for the DAT and is only presented for your interest (and as a minor contribution to your future studies!).

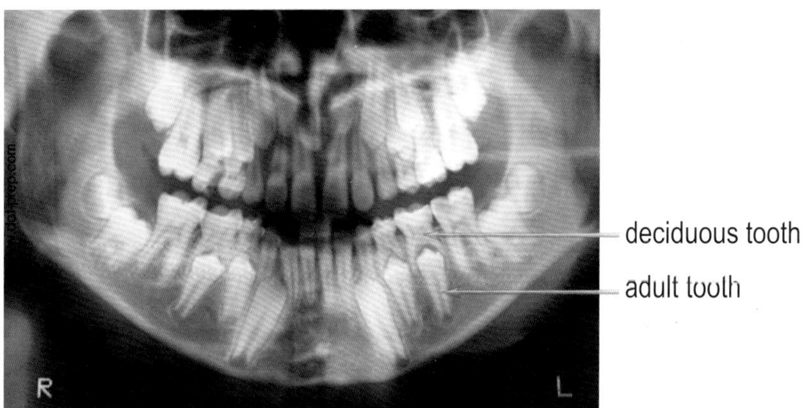

Figure IV.A.9.0b: Dental X-ray of a child showing deciduous (AKA: baby, primary, milk, temporary) teeth and emerging adult (permanent) teeth. Note the "R" on the X-ray indicates the right side of the patient who is facing the observer.

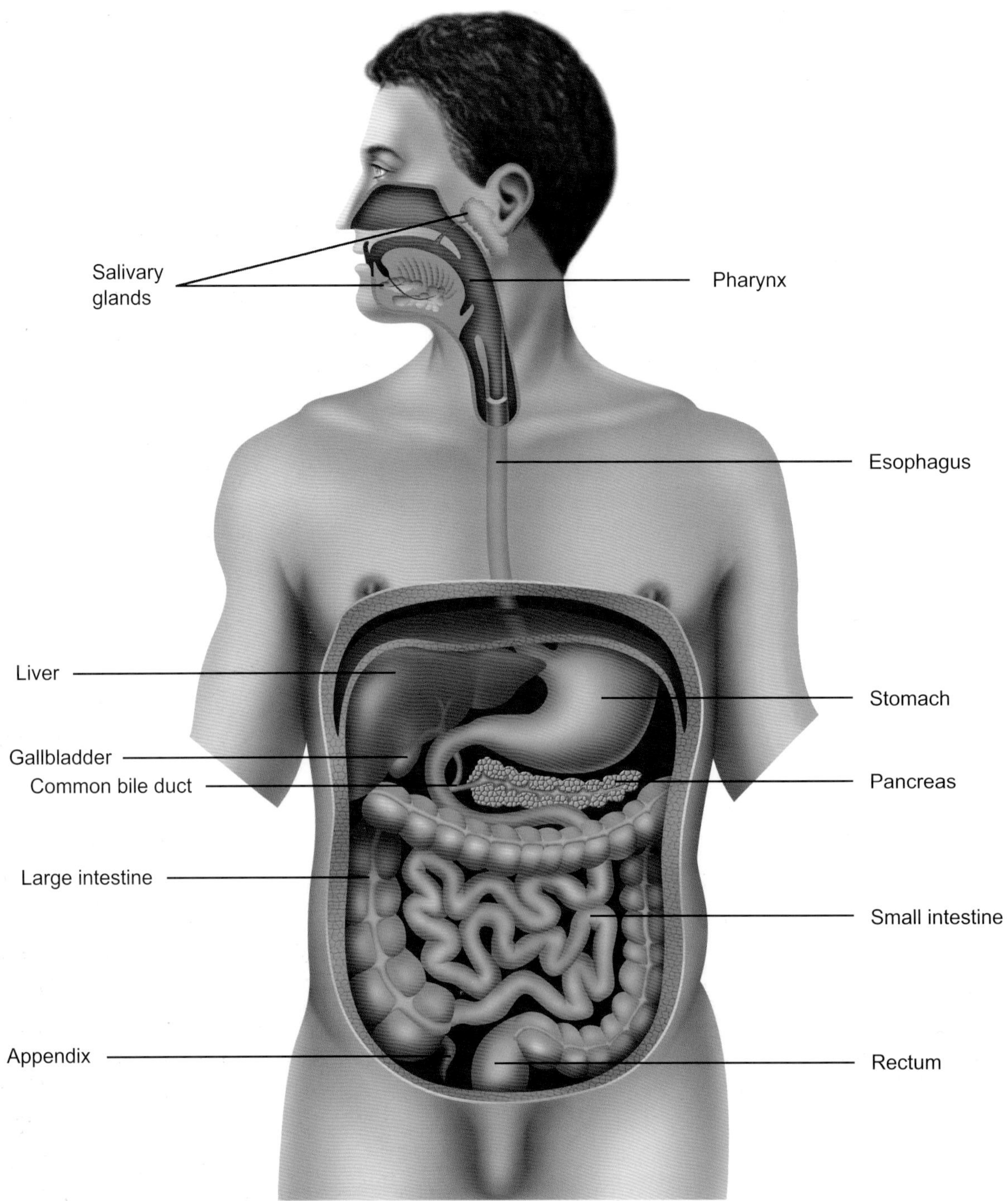

Figure IV.A.9.1: Schematic drawing of the major components of the digestive system.

tissue which covers the opening to the airway (= *glottis*) while swallowing. Gravity and peristalsis help bring the food through the esophagus to the stomach.

The GI system is supplied by both extrinsic innervation and intrinsic innervation. The extrinsic innervation includes the sympathetic and parasympathetic nervous system. The parasympathetic nervous system, mediated by the vagus and pelvic nerves, usually stimulates the functions of the GI tract while the sympathetic nervous system usually inhibits the functions of the GI tract. The intrinsic innervation located in the gut wall includes the *myenteric nerve plexus* and *submucosal nerve plexus* which control GI tract motility including peristalsis.

Peristalsis, which is largely the result of two muscle layers in the GI tract (i.e. the inner circular and outer longitudinal layers), is the sequential wave-like muscular contractions which propell food along the tract. The rate, strength and velocity of muscular contractions are modulated by the ANS.

9.3 The Stomach

The stomach continues in fragmenting and digesting the food with its strong muscular activity, its acidic gastric juice and various digestive enzymes present in the gastric juice. The walls of the stomach are lined by thick mucosa which contains goblet cells. These goblet cells of the GI tract protect the lumen from the acidic environment by secreting mucous.

The important components of gastric juice are: i) HCl which keeps the pH low (approximately = 2) to kill microorganisms, to aid in partial hydrolysis of proteins, and to provide the environment for ii) *pepsinogen*, an inactive form of enzyme (= *zymogen*) secreted by gastric chief cells, which is later converted to its active form *pepsin* in the presence of a low pH. Pepsin is involved in the breakdown of proteins. Both the hormone gastrin, which is produced in the stomach; and parasympathetic impulses can increase the production of gastric juice.

The preceding events turns food into a semi-digested fluid called chyme. Chyme is squirted through a muscular sphincter in the stomach, the *pyloric sphincter*, into the first part of the small intestine, the *duodenum*. Many secretions are produced by exocrine glands in the liver and pancreas and enter the duodenum via the *common bile duct*. Exocrine secretions eventually exit the body through ducts. For example, *goblet cells*, which are found in the stomach and throughout the intestine, are exocrine secretory cells which produce mucus which lines the epithelium of the gastrointestinal tract.

9.4 The Exocrine Roles of the Liver and Pancreas

9.4.1 The Liver

The liver occupies the upper right part of the abdominal cavity. It has many roles including: the conversion of glucose to glycogen; the synthesis of glucose from non-carbohydrates; the production of plasma proteins; the destruction of red blood cells; the deamination of amino acids and the formation of urea; the conversion of toxic ammonia to much less toxic urea (the urea cycle); the storage of iron and certain vitamins; the alteration of toxic substances and most medicinal products (*detoxification*); and its exocrine role - the production of **bile** by liver cells (= *hepatocytes*).

Bile is a yellowish - green fluid mainly composed of water, cholesterol, pigments (from the destruction of red blood cells) and salts. It is the **bile salts** which have a digestive function by the emulsification of fats. Emulsification is the dissolving of fat globules into tiny droplets called *micelles* which have hydrophobic interiors and hydrophilic exteriors (cf. Plasma Membrane, BIO 1.1). Bile salts orient themselves around those lipid droplets with their hydrophilic portions towards the aqueous environment and their hydrophobic portions towards the micelle interior and keep them dispersed. Emulsification also helps in the absorption of the fat soluble vitamins A, D, E, and K.

Thus bile is produced by the liver, stored and concentrated in a small muscular sac, the **gallbladder**, and then secreted into the duodenum via the common bile duct.

9.4.2 The Pancreas

The pancreas is close to the duodenum and extends behind the stomach. The pancreas has both endocrine (*see Endocrine Systems; BIO 6.3.4*) and exocrine functions. It secretes pancreatic juice, which consists of alkaline fluid and digestive enzymes, into the pancreatic duct that joins the common bile duct. Pancreatic juice is secreted both due to parasympathetic and hormonal stimuli. The hormones *secretin* and *CCK* are produced and released by the duodenum in response to the presence of chyme. Secretin acts on the pancreatic ductal cells to stimulate HCO_3^- secretion, whose purpose is to neutralize the acidic chyme. CCK acts on pancreatic acinar cells to stimulate the exocrine pancreatic secretion of digestive enzymes. These enzymes are secreted as enzymes or proenzymes (= *zymogens*; BIO 4.3) that must be activated in the intestinal lumen. The enzymes include pancreatic amylase, which can break down carbohydrates into monosaccharides; pancreatic lipase, which can break down fats into fatty acids and monoglycerides; and nuclease, which can break down nucleic acids. The protein enzymes (proteases) include trypsin, chymotrypsin, carboxypeptidase, which can break down proteins into amino acids, dipeptides or tripeptides.

9.5 The Intestines

The **small intestine** is divided into the duodenum, the jejunum, and the ileum, in that order. It is this part of the GI system that completes the digestion of chyme, absorbs the nutrients (i.e. monosaccharides, amino acids, nucleic acids, etc.), and passes the rest onto the large intestine. Peristalsis is the primary mode of transport. Contraction behind the bolus and simultaneous relaxation in front of the bolus propel chyme forward. Segmentation also aids in small intestine movement - it helps to mix the intestinal contents without any forward movement of chyme. Of course, parasympathetic impulses increase intestinal smooth muscle contraction while sympathetic impulses decrease intestinal smooth muscle contraction.

Absorption is aided by the great surface area involved including the finger-like projections **villi** and **microvilli** (*see the Generalized Eukaryotic Cell*, BIO 1.1F and 1.2). Intestinal villi, which increase the surface area ten-fold, are evaginations into the lumen of the small intestine and contain blood capillaries and a single lacteal (lymphatic capillary). Microvilli, which increase the surface area twenty-fold, contain a dense bundle of actin microfilaments cross-linked by proteins fimbrin and villin.

Absorption of carbohydrates, proteins and lipids is completed in the small intestine. Carbohydrates must be broken down into glucose, galactose and fructose for absorption to occur. In contrast, proteins can be absorbed as amino acids, dipeptides and tripeptides. Specific transporters are required for amino acids and peptides to facilitate the absorption across the luminal membrane. Lipids are absorbed in the form of fatty acids, monoglycerides and cholesterol. In the intestinal cells, they are re-esterified to triglycerides, cholesterol ester and phospholipids.

The lacteals absorb most fat products into the lymphatic system while the blood capillaries absorb the rest taking these nutrients to the liver for processing via a special vein - the *hepatic portal vein* [A portal vein carries blood from one capillary bed to another; BIO 7.3]. Goblet cells secrete a copious amount of mucus in order to lubricate the passage of material through the intestine and to protect the epithelium from abrasive chemicals (i.e. acids, enzymes, etc.).

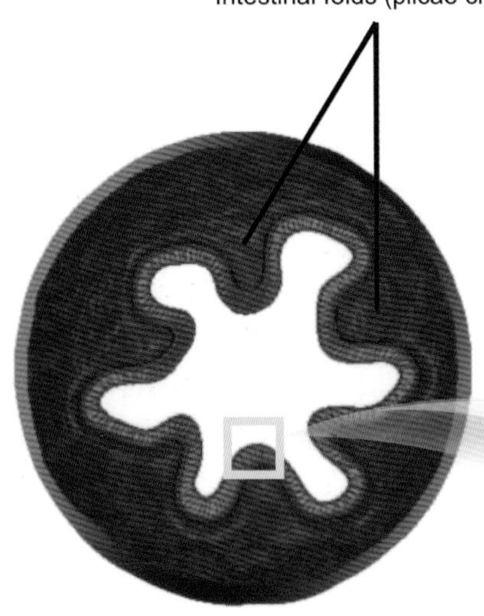

Cross-section of the small intestine.

4 intestinal villi.

Columnar cells (i.e. intestinal cells arranged in columns) with microvilli facing the lumen (brush border).

Figure IV.A.9.2: Levels of organization of the small intestine.

9.5.1 The Large Intestines

The large intestine is divided into: the cecum which connects to the ileum and projects a closed-ended tube - the appendix; the colon which is subdivided into ascending, transverse, descending, and sigmoid portions; the rectum which can store feces; and the anal canal which can expel feces (*defecation*) through the anus with the relaxation of the anal sphincter and the increase in abdominal pressure. The large intestine has little or no digestive functions. It absorbs water and electrolytes from the residual chyme and it forms feces. Feces is mostly water, undigested material, mucous, bile pigments (responsible for the characteristic color) and bacteria (= gut flora = 60% of the dry weight of feces).

Essentially, the relationship between the gut and bacteria is mutualistic and symbiotic (BIO 2.2). Though people can survive with no bacterial flora, these microorganisms perform a host of useful functions, such as fermenting unused energy substrates, training the immune system, preventing growth of harmful species, producing vitamins for the host (i.e. vitamin K), and bile pigments.

GOLD STANDARD WARM-UP EXERCISES

CHAPTER 9: The Digestive System

1) Cellulose is likely not broken down in the small intestine because:

   A. it is actively transported from the lumen of the intestine, across the epithelial lining, in the polysaccharide form.
   B. mastication, salivary amylase and enzymes in the upper part of the stomach completely break it down before it reaches the small intestine.
   C. humans do not possess the enzymes that break down cellulose.
   D. it is needed to propagate the necessary bacterial population in the large intestine.

2) In addition to starch, which of the following substances is also broken down by enzymes in the stomach?

   A. Glucose
   B. Fatty acids
   C. Protein
   D. Glycerol

3) After a meal rich in carbohydrates, monosaccharides are likely transported across the epithelium primarily by:

   A. diffusion.
   B. exocytosis.
   C. endocytosis.
   D. carrier mediated transport.

4) From the lumen of the small intestine, fat products are absorbed by and transported to:

   A. bile salts and the liver, respectively.
   B. bile salts and the lymphatic system, respectively.
   C. lacteals directly to the liver.
   D. lacteals and the lymphatic system, respectively.

5) Along with gastric acid, a zymogen exists in the stomach. The enzyme exists in this form in order to:

   A. prevent the enzyme's degradation while the stomach is empty.
   B. prevent the enzyme from neutralizing the gastric acid in the stomach.
   C. enhance the enzyme's activity.
   D. prevent the enzyme from digesting the cells which produce it.

6) A clogging of the bile duct interferes with the digestion of what category of food?

   A. Fats
   B. Fat soluble vitamins
   C. Triacyl glycerols
   D. All of the above

7) Extracts of the intestinal parasite Ascaris were found to contain irreversible non-competitive inhibitors of human enzymes. The enzymes were likely:

   A. HMG CoA synthetase and lyase.
   B. kinase and carboxypeptidase.
   C. trypsin and pepsin.
   D. hexokinase and vitamin D.

GS ANSWER KEY

CHAPTER 9

		Cross-Reference
1.	C	BIO 9.5; ORG 12.3.3; deduce
2.	C	BIO 9.3
3.	D	BIO 1.1.2
4.	D	BIO 9.5
5.	D	BIO 4.3, 9.3, 9.4
6.	D	BIO 9.4.1; ORG 12.4
7.	C	9.3, 9.4.2; cf BIO 4.1, 4.2

* Explanations can be found at the back of the book.

Go online to DAT-prep.com for additional chapter review Q&A and forum.

Go online to DAT-prep.com for additional chapter review Q&A and forum.

Chapter 10

Memorize	Understand	Importance
* Kidney structure: cortex, medulla * Nephron structure: glomerulus, Bowman's capsule, proximal tubule, etc. * Loop of Henle, distal tubule, collecting duct * Storage and elimination: ureter, bladder, urethra	* Roles of the excretory system in homeostasis * Blood pressure, osmoregulation, acid-base balance, N waste removal * Formation of urine: glomerular filtration, secretion and reabsorption of solutes * Concentration of urine; counter-current multiplier mechanism	**0 to 2 out of the 40 Biology** DAT questions are based on content in this chapter (in our estimation). * Note that between 25% and 50% of the questions in DAT Biology are from 5 chapters: 1, 2, 14, 15, and 16.

Introduction

The excretory system excretes waste. The focus of this chapter is to examine the kidney's role in excretion. This includes eliminating nitrogen waste products of metabolism such as urea.

Additional Resources

Free Online Q&A + Forum

Video: Online or DVD

Flashcards

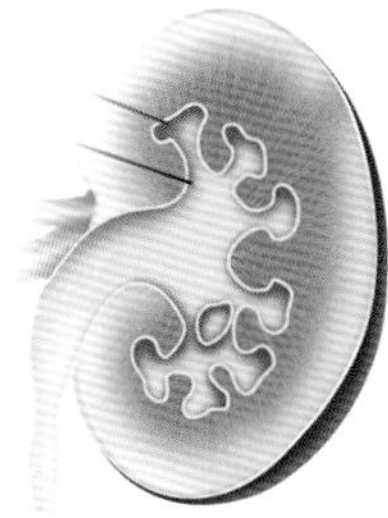

Special Guest

10.1 Overview

Excretion is the elimination of substances (usu. wastes) from the body. It begins at the level of the cell. Broken down red blood cells are excreted as bile pigments into the GI tract; CO_2, an end product of cellular aerobic respiration, is blown away in the lungs; urea and ammonia (NH_3), breakdown products of amino acid metabolism, creatinine, a product of muscle metabolism, and H_2O, a breakdown product of aerobic metabolism, are eliminated by the urinary system. In fact, the urinary system eliminates such a great quantity of waste it is often called the excretory system. It is composed of a pair of kidneys, a pair of ureters and one bladder and urethra.

The composition of body fluids remains within a fairly narrow range. The urinary system is the dominant organ system involved in electrolyte and water homeostasis (*osmoregulation*). It is also responsible for the excretion of toxic nitrogenous compounds (i.e. urea, uric acid, creatinine) and many drugs into the urine. The urine is produced in the kidneys (mostly by the filtration of blood) and is transported, with the help of peristaltic waves, down the tubular ureters to the muscular sack which can store urine, the bladder. Through the process of urination (= *micturition*), urine is expelled from the bladder to the outside via a tubular urethra.

The amount of volume within blood vessels (= *intravascular* or blood volume) and blood pressure are proportional to the rate the kidneys filter blood. Hormones act on the kidney to affect urine formation (see *Endocrine Systems*, BIO 6.3).

10.2 Kidney Structure

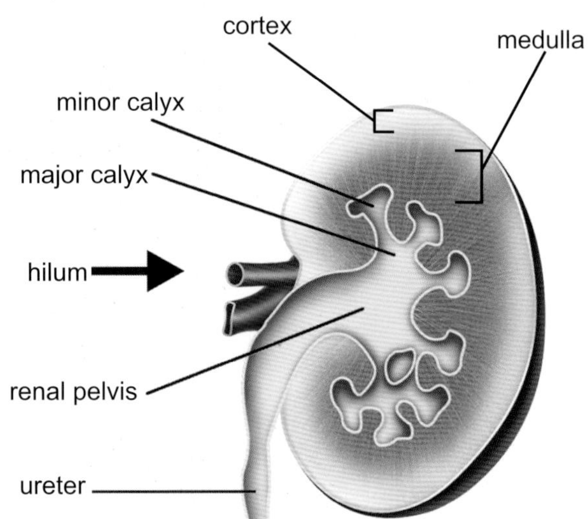

Figure IV.A.10.1: Kidney structure.

The kidney regulates the electrolyte levels in the extracellular fluid and maintains water homeostasis through the production and excretion of urine. The kidney resembles a bean with a concave border (= *the hilum*) where the ureter, nerves, and vessels (blood and lymph) attach. The kidney can be grossly divided into an outer granular-looking **cortex** and an inner dark striated **medulla**. The upper end of the ureter expands into the *renal pelvis* which can be divided into two or three *major calyces*. Each major calyx can be divided into several small branched *minor calyces*. The renal medulla lies deep to the cortex. It is composed of 10-18 medullary pyramids which consist mainly of loop of Henle and collecting tubules. The renal cortex is the superficial layer of the kidney right underneath the capsule. It is composed mainly of renal corpuscles and convoluted tubules.

The kidney is a *filtration-reabsorption-secretion* (excretion) organ. These events are clearly demonstrated at the level of the nephron.

10.3 The Nephron

The nephron is the functional unit of the kidney and consists of the **renal corpuscle** and the **renal tubule**. A renal corpuscle is responsible for the filtration of blood and is composed of a tangled ball of blood capillaries (= *the glomerulus*) and a sac-like structure which surrounds the glomerulus (= *Bowman's capsule*). *Afferent* and *efferent* arterioles lead towards and away from the glomerulus, respectively. The renal tubule is divided into *proximal* and *distal convoluted tubules* with a *loop of Henle* in between. The tube ends in a *collecting duct*.

Blood plasma is **filtered** by the glomerulus through three layers before entering Bowman's capsule. The first layer is formed by the *endothelial cells* of the capillary that possess small holes (= *fenestrae*); the second layer is the *glomerular basement membrane* (BIO 5.3); and the third layer is formed by the negatively charged cells (= *podocytes*) in Bowman's capsule which help repel proteins (most proteins are negatively charged).

The filtration barrier permits passage of water, ions, and small particles from the capillary into Bowman's capsule but prevents pas-

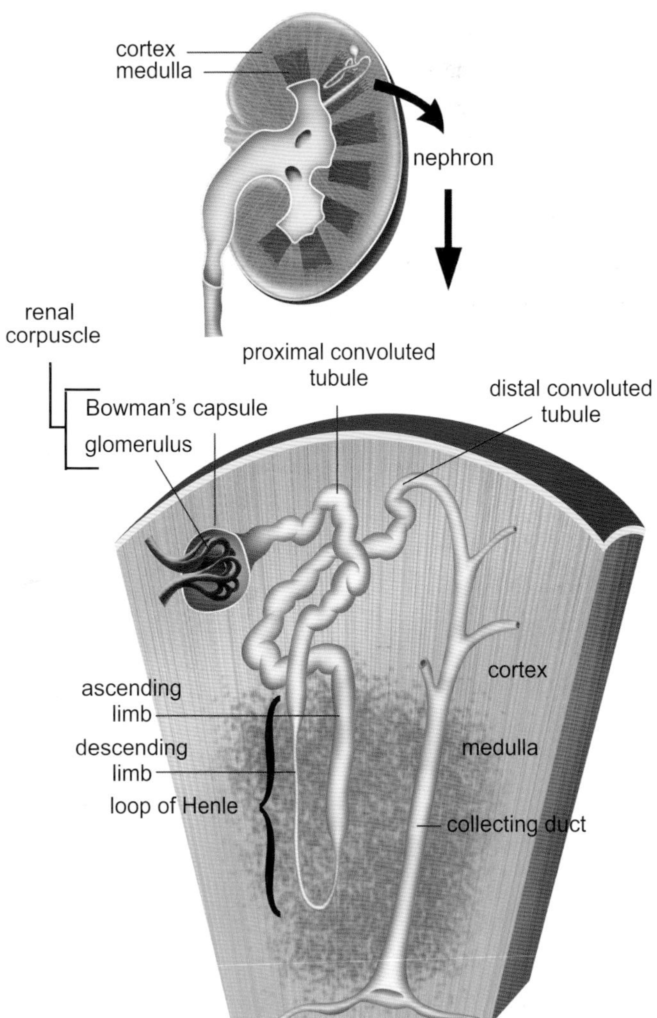

Figure IV.A.10.2: The kidney and its functional unit, the nephron.

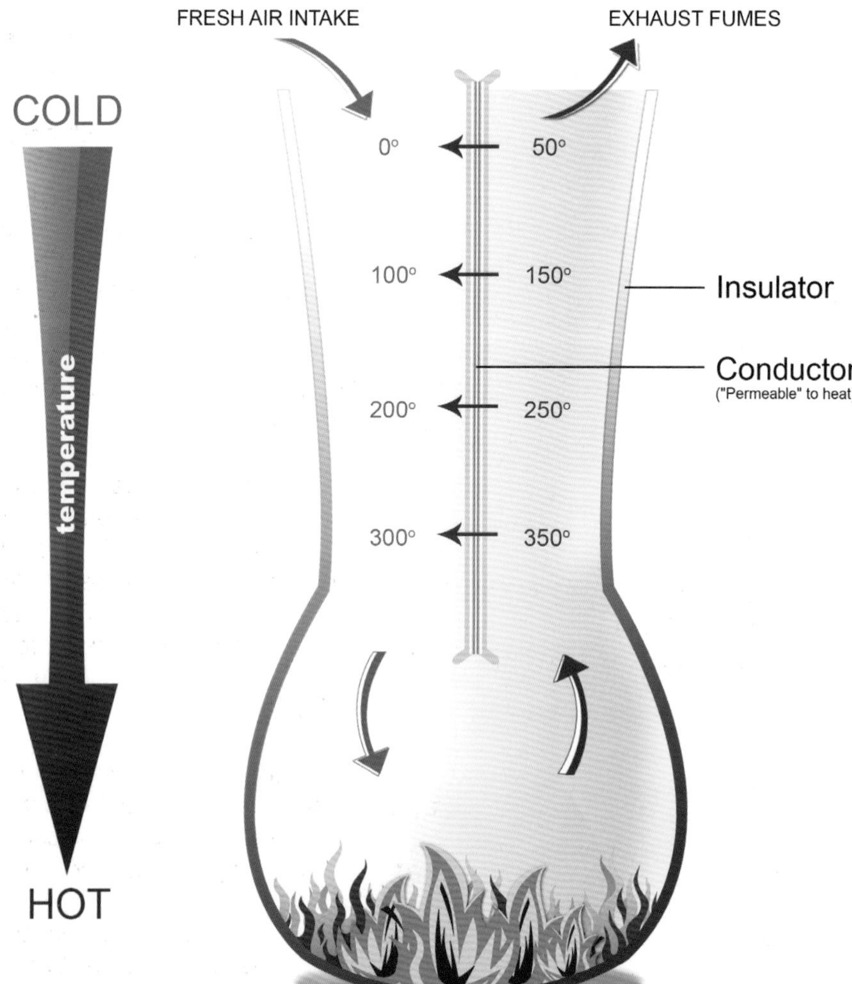

The countercurrent principle depends on a parallel flow arrangement moving in 2 different directions (countercurrent) in close proximity to each other. Our example is that of the air intake and exhaust pipe in this simplified schematic of a furnace.

Heat is transferred from the exhaust fumes to the incoming air.

The small horizontal temperature gradient of only 50° is multiplied longitudinally to a gradient of 300°. This conserves heath that would otherwise be lost.

Figure IV.A.10.3: The countercurrent principle (= counter-current mechanism) using a simplified furnace as an example.

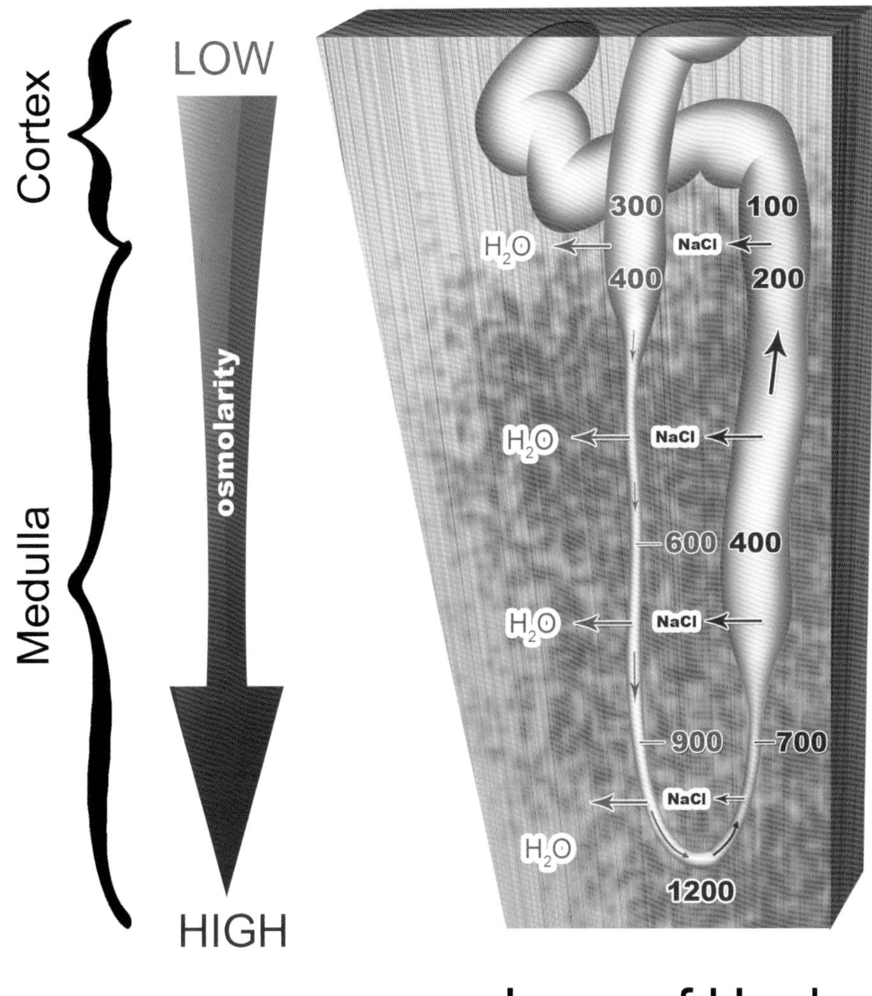

The countercurrent system involving the loop of Henle results in an osmotic gradient increasing from cortex to inner medulla (*juxtamedullary* nephrons). Solutes enter and exit at different segments of the nephron. The descending limb of the loop of Henle is highly permeable to water and relatively impermeable to NaCl (thus the filtrate becomes increasingly hypertonic). The ascending limb is impermeable to water but relatively (through active transport) permeable to NaCl.

Due to the increased osmolarity of the interstitial fluid, water moves out of the descending limb into the interstitial fluid by osmosis. Volume of the filtrate decreases as water leaves. Osmotic concentration of the filtrate increases (1200) as it rounds the hairpin turn of the loop of Henle.

Some of the NaCl leaving the ascending limb moves by diffusion into the descending limb from the interstitial fluid thus increasing the solute concentration in the descending limb. Also, new NaCl in the filtrate continuously enters the tubule inflow to be transported out of the ascending limb into the interstitial fluid. Thus this recycling multiplies NaCl concentration.

Figure IV.A.10.4: The countercurrent principle (= counter-current mechanism) in the loop of Henle.

10.3 The Nephron (cont'd)

sage of large/negatively charged particles (= *ultrafiltration*) and forms a filtrate in the Bowman's space. The rate of filtration is proportional to the net ultrafiltration pressure across the glomerular capillaries. This net pressure, which is usually positive and favors fluid filtration out of the capillary, can be derived from the difference between glomerular capillary hydrostatic pressure, which favors fluid out of the capillary, and the combined effect of glomerular capillary oncotic pressure and Bowman's space *hydrostatic* pressure, which favor fluid back into the capillary. {The oncotic pressure of Bowman's space is typically zero, so it is ignored here; keep in mind that 'oncotic pressure' is simply the osmotic pressure caused by proteins; see BIO 7.5.2}

The filtrate, which is similar to plasma but with minimal proteins, now passes into the proximal convoluted tubule (PCT). It is here that the body actively **reabsorbs** compounds that it needs (i.e. proteins, amino acids, and especially glucose); and over 75% of all ions and water are reabsorbed by *obligate* (= required) reabsorption from the PCT. To increase the surface area for absorption, the cells of the PCT have a lot of microvilli (= *brush border*, cf. BIO 1.2). Some substances like H^+, urea and penicillin are **secreted** into the PCT.

From the PCT the filtrate goes through the descending and ascending limbs of the loop of Henle which extend into the renal medulla. The purpose of the loop of Henle is to concentrate the filtrate by the transport of ions (Na^+ and Cl^-) into the medulla which produces an osmotic gradient (= *a countercurrent mechanism*). As a consequence of this system, the medulla of the kidney becomes concentrated with ions and tends to "pull" water out of the renal tubule by osmosis.

The filtrate now passes on to the distal convoluted tubule (DCT) which reabsorbs ions actively and water passively and secretes various ions (i.e. H^+). Hormones can modulate the reabsorption of substances from the DCT (= *facultative* reabsorption). Aldosterone acts at the DCT to absorb Na^+ which is coupled to the secretion of K^+ and the passive retention of H_2O.

Finally the filtrate, now called urine, passes into the collecting duct which drains into larger and larger ducts which lead to renal papillae, calyces, the renal pelvis, and then the ureter. ADH concentrates urine by increasing the permeability of the DCT and the collecting ducts allowing the medulla to draw water out by osmosis. Water returns to the circulation via a system of vessels called the *vasa recta*.

Renin is a hormone (BIO 6.3.5) which is secreted by cells that are "near the glomerulus" (= *juxtaglomerular cells*). At the beginning of the DCT is a region of modified tubular cells which can influence the secretion of renin (= *macula densa*). The juxtaglomerular cells and the macula densa are collectively known as the juxtaglomerular apparatus.

10.4 The Bladder

Urine flow through the ureters to the bladder is propelled by muscular contractions of the ureter wall - peristalsis. The urine is stored in the bladder and intermittently ejected during urination, termed micturition.

The bladder is a balloon-like chamber with walls of muscle collectively termed the detrusor muscle. The contraction of this muscle squeezes the urine into the lumen (= *space inside*) of the bladder to produce urination. That part of the detrusor muscle at the base of the bladder, where the urethra begins, functions as a sphincter - the internal urethral sphincter. Beyond the outlet of the urethra is the external urethral sphincter, the contraction of which can prevent urination even when the detrusor muscle contracts strongly.

The basic micturition reflex is a spinal reflex (BIO 6.1.3), which can be influenced by descending pathways from the brain. The bladder wall contains stretch receptors whose afferent fibers enter the spinal cord and stimulate the parasympathetic nerves that supply and stimulate the detrusor muscle. As the bladder fills with urine, the pressure within it increases and the stretch receptors are stimulated, thereby reflexively eliciting stimulation of the parasympathetic neurons and contractions of the detrusor muscle. When the bladder reaches a certain volume, the induced contraction of the detrusor muscle becomes strong enough to open the internal urethral sphincter. Simultaneously, the afferent input from the stretch receptors inhibits, within the spinal cord, the motor neurons that tonically stimulate the external urethral sphincter to contract. Both sphincters are now open and the contraction of the detrusor muscle is able to produce urination.

In summary:

- The internal sphincter is a continuation of the detrusor muscle and is thus composed of smooth muscle under involuntary or autonomic control. This is the primary muscle for preventing the release of urine.

- The external sphincter is made of skeletal muscle is thus under voluntary control of the somatic nervous system (BIO 6.1.4, 6.1.5, 11.2).

GOLD STANDARD WARM-UP EXERCISES

CHAPTER 10: The Excretory System

1) The functional unit of the kidney is the:
   A. renal corpuscle.
   B. Bowman's capsule.
   C. major calyx.
   D. nephron.

2) Through the process of micturition, urine is expelled from the bladder into the:
   A. urethra.
   B. ureter.
   C. major calyx.
   D. minor calyx.

3) In studies of the human body, which of the following terms is used to describe the first step in the production of urine?
   A. Minor calyces
   B. Glomerular filtration
   C. Tubular reabsorption
   D. Tubular secretion

4) In mammals, the primary function of the loop of Henle is:
   A. bicarbonate reabsorption.
   B. reabsorption of water.
   C. ammonia secretion.
   D. water secretion.

5) The internal urethral sphincter is:
   A. closed when the detrusor muscle is relaxed.
   B. open when the detrusor muscle is relaxed.
   C. not under the direct control of the detrusor muscle.
   D. innervated directly by motor neurons extending from the descending pathways.

6) Which of the following is the countercurrent multiplier in the kidney?
   A. Bowman's capsule around the glomerulus
   B. The proximal convoluted tubules
   C. The loop of Henle of a juxtamedullary nephron
   D. The vasa recta

7) Relative to the capillaries, the fluid in the descending limb of the loop of Henle is which of the following?
   A. Strongly hypotonic
   B. Weakly hypotonic
   C. Hypertonic
   D. Isotonic

8) Most tubular reabsorption occurs at the level of the:
   A. glomerulus.
   B. proximal convoluted tubule.
   C. loop of Henle.
   D. distal convoluted tubule.

9) The internal and external urethral sphincters consist of:
   A. skeletal and smooth muscle, respectively.
   B. skeletal muscle and connective tissue, respectively.
   C. smooth muscle and skeletal muscle, respectively.
   D. smooth muscle and connective tissue, respectively.

GS ANSWER KEY

CHAPTER 10

		Cross-Reference			Cross-Reference
1.	D	BIO 10.3	6.	C	BIO 10.3
2.	A	BIO 10.1	7.	C	BIO 10.3
3.	B	BIO 10.3	8.	B	BIO 10.3, 1.1.1, 7.5.2
4.	B	BIO 10.3	9.	C	BIO 10.4, 11.2
5.	A	BIO 10.4			

* Explanations can be found at the back of the book.

Go online to DAT-prep.com for additional chapter review Q&A and forum.

THE MUSCULOSKELETAL SYSTEM
Chapter 11

Memorize

- Structure of three basic muscle types: striated, smooth, cardiac
- Voluntary/involuntary muscles; sympathetic/parasympathetic innervation
- Basics: cartilage, ligaments, tendons
- Bone basics: structure, calcium/protein matrix, growth

Understand

* Muscle system, important functions
* Support, mobility, peripheral circulatory assistance, thermoregulation (shivering reflex)
* Control: motor neurons, neuromuscular junctions, motor end plates
* Skeletal system: structural rigidity/support, calcium storage, physical protection
* Skeletal structure: specialization of bone types, basic joint, endo/exoskeleton

Importance

0 to 2 out of the 40 Biology

DAT questions are based on content in this chapter (in our estimation).

* Note that between 25% and 50% of the questions in DAT Biology are from 5 chapters: 1, 2, 14, 15, and 16.

DAT-Prep.com

Introduction

The musculoskeletal system (= locomotor system) permits the movement of organisms with the use of muscle and bone. Other uses include providing form and stability for the organism; protection of vital organs (i.e. skull, rib cage); storage for calcium and phosphorous as well as containing a critical component to the production of blood cells (skeletal system).

Additional Resources

Free Online Q&A + Forum

Flashcards

Special Guest

11.1 Overview

The musculoskeletal system supports, protects and enables body parts to move. Muscles convert chemical energy (i.e. ATP, creatine phosphate) into mechanical energy (→ contraction). Thus body heat is produced, body fluids are moved (i.e. lymph), and body parts can move in accordance with lever systems of muscle and bone.

11.2 Muscle

There are many general features of muscle. A latent period is the lag between the stimulation of a muscle and its response. A twitch is a single contraction in response to a brief stimulus which lasts for a fraction of a second. Muscles can either *contract* or *relax* but they cannot actively expand. When muscles are stimulated frequently, they cannot fully relax - this is known as *summation*. Tetany is a sustained contraction (a summation of multiple contractions) that lacks even partial relaxation. If tetany is maintained, the muscle will eventually fatigue or tire. Muscle tone (*tonus*) occurs because even when a muscle appears to be at rest, some degree of sustained contraction is occurring.

The cellular characteristics of muscle have already been described (*see Contractile Cells and Tissues,* BIO 5.2). We will now examine the gross features of the three basic muscle types.

Cardiac muscle forms the walls of the heart and is responsible for the pumping action. Its contractions are continuous and are initiated by inherent mechanisms (i.e., they are myogenic) and modulated by the autonomic nervous system. Its activity is decreased by the parasympathetic nervous system and increased by the sympathetic nervous system. The sinoatrial node (SA node) or *pacemaker* contains specialized cardiac muscle cells in the right atrium which initiate the contraction of the heart (BIO 7.2). The electrical signal then progresses to the atrioventricular node (AV node) in the cardiac muscle (myocardium) - between the atria and ventricles - then through the bundle of His which splits and branches out to Purkinje fibers which can then stimulate the contraction of the ventricles (systole; BIO 7.2).

Smooth Muscle has two forms. One type occurs as separate fibers and can contract in response to motor nerve stimuli. These are found in the iris (*pupillary dilation or constriction*) and the walls of blood vessels (*vasodilation or constriction)*. The second and more dominant form occurs as sheets of muscle fibers and is sometimes called *visceral muscle*. It forms the walls of many hollow visceral organs like the stomach, intestines, uterus, and the urinary bladder. Like cardiac muscle, its contractions are inherent, involuntary, and rhythmic. Visceral muscle is responsible for peristalsis. Its contractility is usually slow and can be modulated by the autonomic nervous system, hormones, and local metabolites. The activity of visceral muscle is increased by the parasympathetic nervous system and decreased by the sympathetic nervous system.

Skeletal muscle is responsible for voluntary movements. This includes the skeleton and organs such as the tongue and the globe of the eye. Its cells can form a syncytium which is a mass of cells which merge and can function together. Thus skeletal muscle can contract and relax relatively rapidly (*see the Reflex Arc,* BIO 6.1.3).

It should be noted that there are 2 meanings of the word "syncytium" when describing muscle cells. A classic example is the formation of large multinucleated skeletal muscle cells produced from the fusion of thousands of individual muscle cells (= *myocytes*) as alluded to in the previous paragraph ("true syncytium"). However, "syncytium" can also refer to cells that are interconnected by gap junctions (BIO 1.4), as seen in cardiac muscle cells and certain smooth muscle cells, and are thus synchronized electrically during an action potential ("functional syncytium").

Most skeletal muscles act across joints. Each muscle has a movable end (= *the insertion*) and an immovable end (= *the origin*). When a muscle contracts its insertion is moved towards its origin. When the angle of the joint decreases it is called flexion, when it increases it is called extension. Abduction is movement away from the midline of the body and adduction is movement toward the midline. {Adduction is addicted to the middle (= midline)}

Muscles which assist each other are synergistic (for example: while the deltoid muscle abducts the arm, other muscles hold the shoulder steady). Muscles that can move a joint in opposite directions are antagonistic (for example: at the elbow the biceps can flex while the triceps can extend).

Control of skeletal muscle originates in the cerebral cortex. Skeletal muscle is innervated by the somatic nervous system. Motor (*efferent*) neurons carry nerve impulses from the CNS to synapse with muscle fibers at the *neuro-muscular junction.* The terminal end of the motor neuron (motor end plate) can secrete

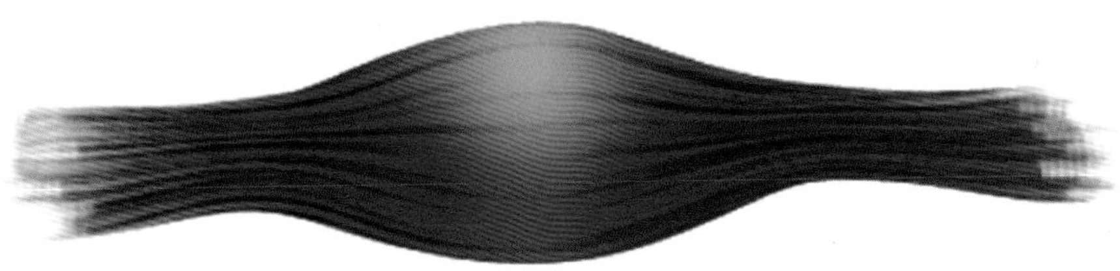

Skeletal muscle

acetylcholine which can depolarize the muscle fiber (BIO 5.1, 5.2). One motor neuron can depolarize many muscle fibers (= *a motor unit*).

The autonomic nervous system can supply skeletal muscle with more oxygenated blood in emergencies (sympathetic response) or redirect the blood to the viscera during relaxed states (parasympathetic response).

Skeletal muscle can be categorized as Type I or Type II. Type I fibers (= *cells*) appear red because of the oxygen-binding protein myoglobin (BIO 7.5.1). These fibers are suited for endurance and are slow to fatigue since they use oxidative metabolism to generate ATP (BIO 4.7-4.10). Type II fibers are white due to the absence of myoglobin and a reliance on glycolytic enzymes (BIO 4.5, 4.6). These fibers are efficient for short bursts of speed and power and use both oxidative metabolism and anaerobic metabolism depending on the particular sub-type. Type II myocytes are quicker to fatigue.

11.3 The Skeletal System

The microscopic features of bone and cartilage have already been described (*see Connective Cells and Tissues*, BIO 5.4.3/4). We will now examine the relevant gross features of the skeletal system.

The bones of the skeleton have many functions: i) acting like levers that aid in **body movement**; ii) the **storage** of inorganic salts like calcium and phosphorus (and to a lesser extent sodium and magnesium); iii) the production of blood cells (**= hematopoiesis**) in the metabolically active red marrow of the spongy parts of many bones. Bone also has a yellow marrow which contains fat storage cells.

11.3.1 Bone Structure and Development

Bone structure can be classified as follows: i) long bones which have a long shaft, the diaphysis, that is made up mostly of compact bone and expanded ends, like arm and leg bones; ii) short bones which are shaped like long bones but are smaller and have only a thin layer of compact bone surrounding a spongy bone interior; iii) flat bones which have broad surfaces like the skull, ribs, and the scapula and have two layers of compact bones with a layer of spongy bone in the middle; iv) irregular bones like the vertebrae and many facial bones and consist of a thin layer of compact bone covering a spongy bone

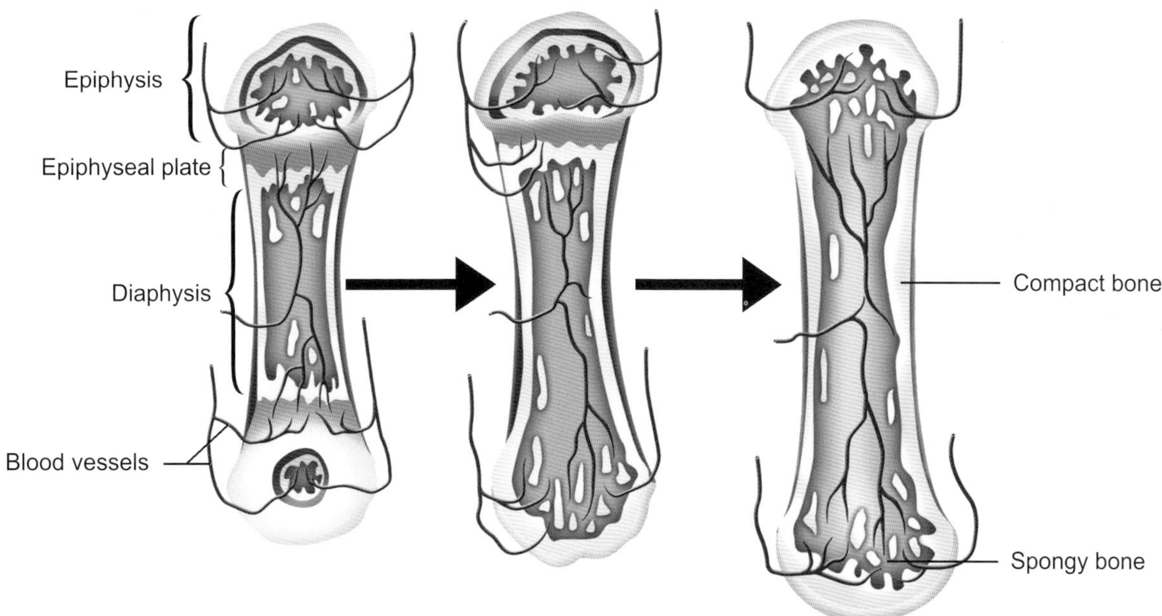

Figure IV.A.11.1: Bone structure and development.

interior. Bone structure can also be classified as: i) primary bone, also known as immature or woven bone, which contains many cells and has a low mineral content; ii) secondary bone, also known as mature or lamellar bone, which has a calcified matrix arranged in regular layers, or lamella.

The rounded expanded end of a long bone is called the *epiphysis* which contains spongy bone. The epiphysis is covered by fibrous tissue (*the periosteum*) and it forms a joint with another bone. Spongy bone contains bony plates called *trabeculae (= spicules)*. The shaft of the bone which connects the expanded ends is called the *diaphysis.* It is predominately composed of compact bone. This kind of bone is very strong and resistant to bending and has no trabeculae or bone marrow cavities.

Animals that fly have less dense, more light bones (spongy bone) in order to facilitate flying. Animals that swim do not need to have as strong bones as land animals as the buoyant force of the water takes away from the everyday stress on the bones. In the adult, yellow marrow is likely to be found in the diaphysis while red marrow is likely to be found in the epiphysis.

Bone growth occurs in two ways, intramembranous and endochondral bone formation. Both formations produce bones that are histologically identical. Intramembranous bone formation begins as layers of membranous connective tissue, which are later calcified by osteoblasts. Most of the flat bones are formed by this process. Endochondral bone formation is the process by which most of long bones are formed. It begins with hyaline cartilage that functions as a template for the bone to grow on.

Vascularizaton of the cartilage causes the transformation of cartilage cells to bone cells (osteoblasts), which later form a cartilage-calcified bone matrix. The osteoblasts continue to replace cartilage with bone and the osteoclasts create perforations to form bone marrow cavities. In children one can detect an **epiphyseal growth plate** on X-ray. This plate is a disk of cartilage between the epiphysis and diaphysis where bone is being actively deposited (= *ossification*).

11.3.2 Joint Structure

Articulations or joints are junctions between bones. They can be **immovable** like the dense connective tissue sutures which hold the flat bones of the skull together; **partly movable** like the hyaline and fibrocartilage joints on disks of the vertebrae; or **freely movable** like the synovial joints which are the most prominent joints in the skeletal system. Synovial joints contain a joint capsule composed of outer ligaments and an inner layer (= *the synovial membrane*) which secretes a lubricant (= *synovial fluid*).

Freely movable joints can be of many types. For example, ball and socket joints have a wide range of motion, like the shoulder and hip joints. On the other hand, hinge joints allow motion in only one plane like a hinged door (i.e. the knee, elbow, and interphalangeal joints).

11.3.3 Cartilage

The microscopic aspects of cartilage have already been discussed (*see Dense Connective Tissue*, BIO 5.4.2/3). Opposing and mobile surfaces of bone are covered by various forms of cartilage. As already mentioned, joints with hyaline or fibrocartilage allow little movement.

Ligaments attach bone to bone. They are formed by dense bands of fibrous connective tissue which reinforce the joint capsule and help to maintain bones in the proper anatomical arrangement.

Tendons connect muscle to bone. They are formed by the densest kind of fibrous connective tissue. Tendons allow muscular forces to be exerted even when the body (*or belly*) of the muscle is at some distance from the action.

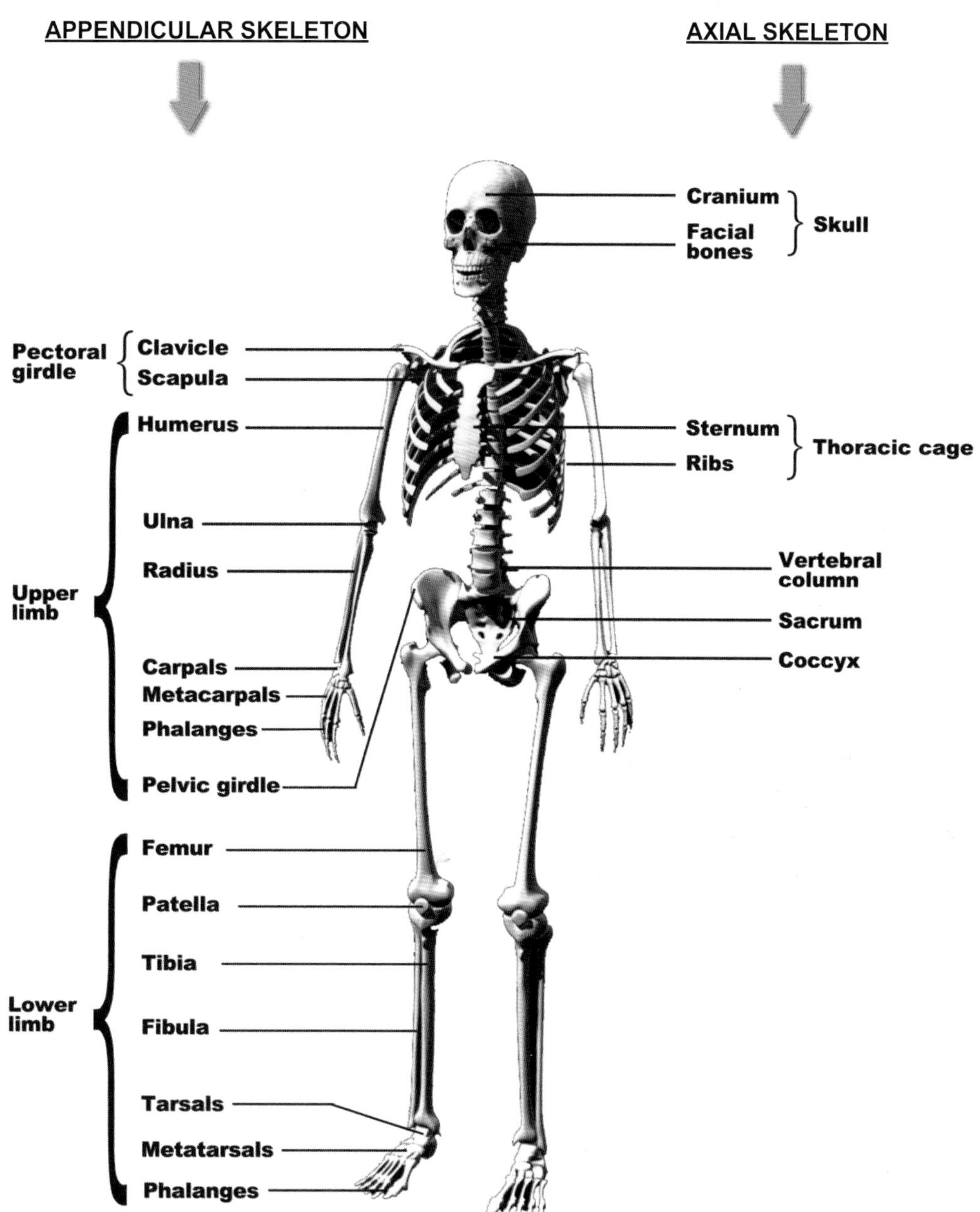

Figure IV.A.11.2: Skeletal structure. Note: in brackets some common relations - scapula (shoulder blade), clavicle (collarbone), carpals (wrist), metacarpals (palm), phalanges (fingers), tibia (shin), patella (kneecap), tarsals (ankle), metatarsals (foot), phalanges (toes), vertebral column (backbone). Note that the appendicular skeleton includes the bones of the appendages and the pectoral and pelvic girdles. The axial skeleton consists of the skull, vertebral column, and the rib cage.

GOLD STANDARD WARM-UP EXERCISES

CHAPTER 11: The Musculoskeletal System

1) As red muscle fibers go from a resting state to a rapidly contracting state, which of the following occurs?
   - A. Increased rate of consumption of oxygen
   - B. Decreased rate of production of carbon dioxide
   - C. Decreased rate of hydrolysis of ATP
   - D. Decreased rate of degradation of glucose

2) Suppose that the oxygen supply to continuously contracting red muscles fibers is abruptly cut off. Which of the following processes would occur in the muscles?
   - A. Increased rate of synthesis of muscle glycogen
   - B. Increased rate of production of ATP
   - C. Increased rate of production of carbon dioxide
   - D. Increased rate of production of lactic acid

3) Which of the following metabolic processes predominates in rapidly contracting white muscle fibers?
   - A. Oxidative phosphorylation
   - B. Alcoholic fermentation
   - C. Glycolysis
   - D. Krebs Citric Acid Cycle reaction

4) Cartilage is likely to be found in all the following adult tissues EXCEPT:
   - A. bronchus.
   - B. tendons and sternum.
   - C. pinna of the ear.
   - D. between the epiphysis and diaphysis of long bones.

5) Which of the following refers to a continuous partial contraction of a muscle?
   - A. Tetany
   - B. Tonus
   - C. Twitch
   - D. Pacemaker

6) Skeletal muscle is connected to bones by:
   - A. joints.
   - B. ligaments.
   - C. tendons.
   - D. loose connective tissue.

7) A joint that allows motion in only one plane (i.e. the knee, elbow) is called a:
   - A. ball and socket joint.
   - B. synovial joint.
   - C. hinged joint.
   - D. prominent joint.

8) Which of the following joints is formed by the articulation of the tibia, the malleolus of the fibula, and the tarsals?

A. Ankle
B. Knee
C. Hip
D. Wrist

9) Which of the following is NOT a component of the human axial skeleton?

A. Tarsals
B. Sternum
C. Vertebral column
D. Skull

10) Phalanges are found in the:

A. skull.
B. hip.
C. feet.
D. chest.

GS ANSWER KEY

CHAPTER 11

		Cross-Reference			Cross-Reference
1.	A	BIO 11.2, 4.5, 5.2	6.	C	BIO 11.3.3
2.	D	BIO 11.2, 4.5, 5.2	7.	C	BIO 11.3.2
3.	C	BIO 11.2, 4.5, 5.2	8.	A	BIO 11.3.2, 11.3.3
4.	D	BIO 5.4.3, 11.3.1	9.	A	BIO 11.3.3
5.	B	BIO 11.2	10.	C	BIO 11.3.3

* Explanations can be found at the back of the book.

Go online to DAT-prep.com for additional chapter review Q&A and forum.

Go online to DAT-prep.com for additional chapter review Q&A and forum.

Chapter 12

Memorize

* Basic anatomy and order

Understand

* Basic functions: gas exchange, thermoregulation, . . .
* Protection against disease, particulate matter
* Breathing mechanisms: diaphragm, rib cage, differential pressure
* Resiliency and surface tension effects
* The carbonic-acid-bicarbonate buffer

Importance

0 to 2 out of the 40 Biology DAT questions are based on content in this chapter (in our estimation).
* Note that between 25% and 50% of the questions in DAT Biology are from 5 chapters: 1, 2, 14, 15, and 16.

Introduction 

The respiratory system permits the exchange of gases with the organism's environment. This critical process occurs in the microscopic space between alveoli and capillaries. It is here where molecules of oxygen and carbon dioxide passively diffuse between the gaseous external environment and the blood.

Additional Resources

Free Online Q&A + Forum

Flashcards

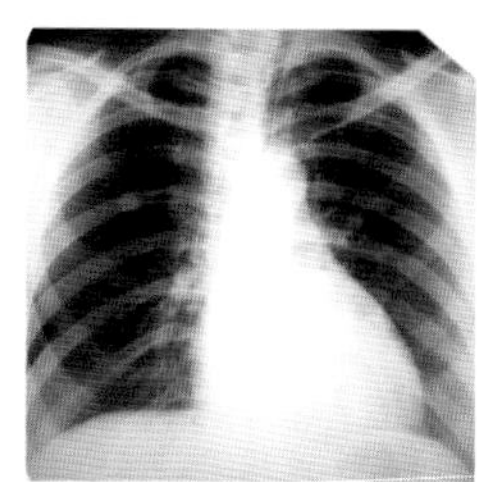

Special Guest

12.1 Overview

There are two forms of respiration: cellular respiration which refers to the oxidation of organic molecules (*see* BIO 4.4 - 4.10) and mechanical respiration where the gases related to cellular respiration are exchanged between the atmosphere and the circulatory system (O_2 in and CO_2 out).

The respiratory system, which is concerned with mechanical respiration, has the following principal functions:

- providing a conducting system for the exchange of gases
- the filtration of incoming particles
- to help control the water content and temperature (= *thermoregulation*) of the incoming air
- to assist in speech production, the sense of smell, and the regulation of pH.

The respiratory system is composed of the lungs and a series of airways that connect the lungs to the external environment, deliver air to the lungs and perform gas exchange.

12.2 The Upper Respiratory Tract

The respiratory system can be divided into an *upper* and *lower respiratory tract* which are separated by the pharynx. The **upper respiratory tract** is composed of the nose, the nasal cavity, the sinuses, and the nasopharynx. This portion of the respiratory system warms, moistens and filters the air before it reaches the lower respiratory system. The nose (*nares*) has receptors for the sense of smell. It is guarded by hair to entrap coarse particles. The nasal cavity, the hollow space behind the nose, contains a ciliated mucous membrane (= a form of *respiratory epithelium*) to entrap smaller particles and prevent infection (this arrangement is common throughout the respiratory tract; for cilia *see the Generalized Eukaryotic Cell*, BIO 1.2). The nasal cavity adjusts the humidity and temperature of incoming air. The nasopharynx helps to equilibrate pressure between the environment and the middle ear via the eustachian tube (BIO 6.2.3).

12.3 The Lower Respiratory Tract

The **lower respiratory tract** is composed of the larynx which contains the vocal cords, the trachea which divides into left and right main bronchi which continue to divide into smaller airways (→ 2° bronchi → 3° bronchi → bronchioles → terminal bronchioles). The terminal bronchioles are the most distal part of the conducting portion of the respira-

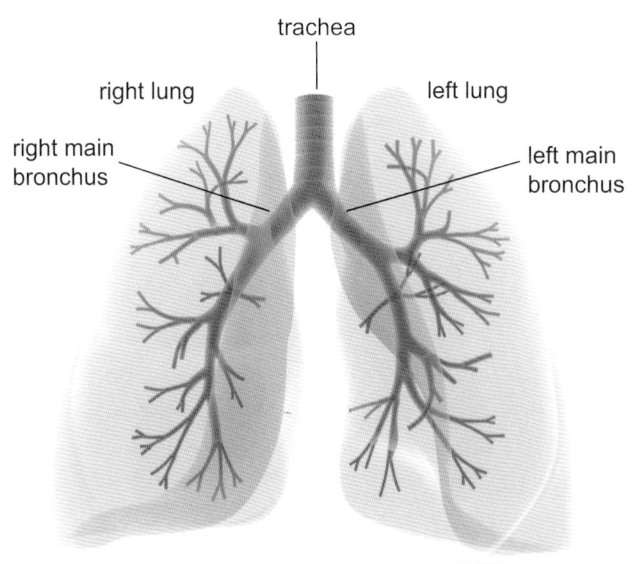

Figure IV.A.12.1: Illustration representing the lower respiratory tract including the dividing bronchial tree and grape-shaped alveoli with blood supply. Note that "right" refers to the patient's perspective which means the left side from your perspective.

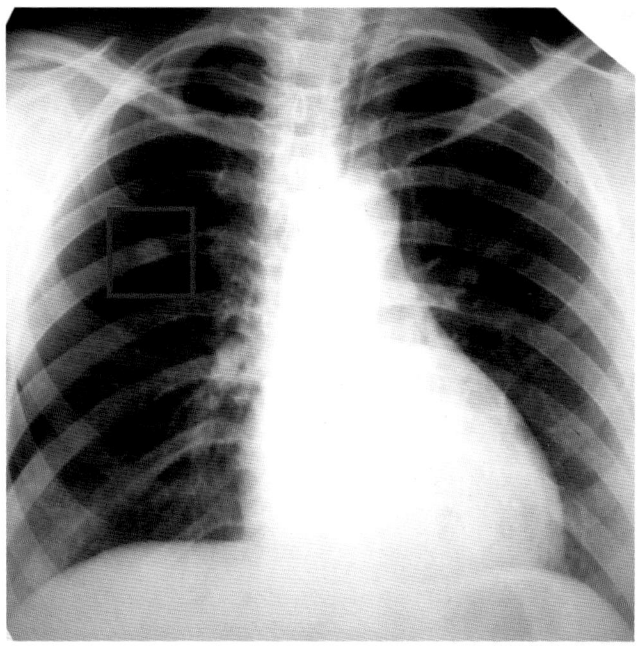

Figure IV.A.12.2: Chest x-ray of an adult male smoker. Notice the coin-shaped shadow in the right lung which presented with coughing blood. Further tests confirmed the presence of a right lung cancer. Cancer-causing chemicals (carcinogens) can irritate any of the cells lining the lower respiratory tract.

tory system. Starting from respiratory bronchioles → alveolar ducts → alveolar sacs until the level of the alveolus, these are considered the respiratory portion of respiratory system, where gas exchange takes place.

It is in these microscopic air sacs called *alveoli* that O_2 diffuses through the alveolar walls and enters the blood in nearby capillaries (where the concentration or *partial pressure* of O_2 is lowest and CO_2 is highest) and CO_2 diffuses from the blood through the walls to enter the alveoli (where the partial pressure of CO_2 is lowest and O_2 is highest). Gas exchange occurs by diffusion across the blood-gas barrier between the alveolar airspace and the capillary lumen. The blood-gas barrier is composed of three layers: type I pneumocyte cells, fused basal laminae and the endothelium of capillaries. *Alveolar macrophages* are phagocytes which help to engulf particles which reach the alveolus. A *surfactant* is secreted into alveoli by special lung cells (*pneumocytes type II*). The surfactant reduces surface tension and prevents the fragile alveoli from collapsing.

Sneezing and coughing, which are reflexes mediated by the medulla, can expel particles from the upper and lower respiratory tract, respectively.

The **lungs** are separated into left and right and are enclosed by the diaphragm and the thoracic cage. It is covered by a membrane (= *pleura*) which secretes a lubricant to reduce friction while breathing. The lungs contain the air passages, nerves, alveoli, blood and lymphatic vessels of the lower respiratory tract.

12.4 Breathing: Structures and Mechanisms

Inspiration is active and occurs according to the following main events: i) nerve impulses from the phrenic nerve cause the muscular diaphragm to contract; as the dome shaped diaphragm moves downward, the thoracic cavity increases; ii) simultaneously, the intercostal (= *between ribs*) muscles and/or certain neck muscles may contract further increasing the thoracic cavity (the muscles mentioned here are called *accessory respiratory muscles* and under normal circumstances the action of the diaphragm is much more important); iii) as the size of the thoracic cavity increases, its internal pressure decreases leaving it relatively negative; iv) the relatively positive atmospheric pressure forces air into the respiratory tract thus inflating the lungs.

Expiration is passive and occurs according to the following main events: i) the diaphragm and the accessory respiratory muscles relax and the chest wall pushed inward; ii) the elastic tissues of the lung, thoracic cage, and the abdominal organs recoil to their original position; iii) this recoil increases the pressure within the lungs (making the pressure relatively positive) thus forcing air out of the lungs and passageways.

12.4.1 Control of Breathing

Though voluntary breathing is possible (!), normally breathing is involuntary, rhythmic, and controlled by the *respiratory center* in the medulla of the brain stem. The respiratory center is sensitive to pH of the cerebrospinal fluid (CSF). An increase in blood CO_2 or consequently, decrease in pH of the CSF, acts on the respiratory center and stimulates breathing, returning the arterial PCO_2 back to normal. The increase in blood CO_2 and the decrease in pH are two interrelated events since CO_2 can be picked up by hemoglobin forming carbamino-hemoglobin (about 20%, BIO 7.5.1), but it can also be converted into carbonic acid by dissolving in blood plasma (about 5%) or by conversion in red blood cells by the enzyme *carbonic anhydrase* (about 75%). The reaction is summarized as follows:

$$CO_2 + H_2O \leftrightarrow \underset{\text{carbonic acid}}{H_2CO_3} \leftrightarrow \underset{\text{bicarbonate}}{HCO_3^-} + H^+$$

According to Henry's Law, the concentration of a gas dissolved in solution is directly proportional to its partial pressure. From the preceding you can see why the respiratory system, through the regulation of the partial pressure of CO_2 in blood, also helps in maintaining pH homeostasis (= a buffer). More generally, the carbonic-acid-bicarbonate buffer is the most important buffer for maintaining acid-base balance in the blood and helps to maintain pH around 7.4.

GOLD STANDARD WARM-UP EXERCISES

CHAPTER 12: The Respiratory System

1) All of the following are in the correct anatomic order EXCEPT:

   A. trachea --> larynx --> bronchus.
   B. bronchus --> bronchioles --> alveolar ducts.
   C. alveolar ducts --> alveolar sacs --> alveolus.
   D. nose --> nasal cavity --> nasopharynx.

2) The vocal cords form part of which of the following?

   A. Pharynx
   B. Larynx
   C. Trachea
   D. Bronchus

3) Which of the following can NOT engage in gas exchange?

   A. Alveolus
   B. Respiratory bronchiole
   C. Alveolar duct
   D. Terminal bronchiole

4) Which of the following secretes surfactant?

   A. Pneumocytes type I
   B. Pneumocytes type II
   C. Alveolar macrophage
   D. Alveolar adipocyte

5) Which of the following factors favors an increase in breathing rate?

   A. Increased blood carbon dioxide
   B. Decreased CSF acidity
   C. Increased CSF pH
   D. Increased blood oxygen

6) One of the the possible injuries during a high speed motor vehicle accident includes a traumatic hemothorax in which blood accumulates in the pleural cavity. With regards to a traumatic hemothorax, which of the following would be of greatest concern?

   A. High oxygenation due to spasms of the diaphragm
   B. Low oxygenation due to blood in the right bronchus
   C. High oxygenation due to hyperventilation
   D. Low oxygenation due to compression of the lung

7) The following are physiological systems which depend on stretch receptors EXCEPT:

   A. the circulatory system.
   B. the respiratory system.
   C. the endocrine system.
   D. the digestive system.

8) Active transport assumes particular importance in all but which of the following structures?

   A. Cells of the large intestine
   B. Alveoli
   C. Nerve and muscle cells
   D. Loop of Henle

GS ANSWER KEY

CHAPTER 12

		Cross-Reference
1.	A	BIO 12.2, 12.3
2.	B	BIO 12.3
3.	D	BIO 12.3
4.	B	BIO 12.3
5.	A	BIO 12.4.1
6.	D	BIO 12.3
7.	C	BIO 7.2-7.3, 9.1-9.3, 9.5, 12.3-12.4
8.	B	BIO 1.1.2, 12.3

* Explanations can be found at the back of the book.

Go online to DAT-prep.com for additional chapter review Q&A and forum.

APPENDIX

CHAPTER 12: The Respiratory System

Advanced DAT-30 Passage: Lung Function and Transpulmonary Pressure

The volume of air that flows into or out of an alveolus per unit time is directly proportional to the pressure difference between the atmosphere and alveolus and inversely proportional to the resistance to flow caused by the airways. During normal relaxed breathing, about 500 ml of air flows in and out of the lungs. This is the tidal volume. After expiration, approximately 2.5 liters of air remains in the lungs which is referred to as the functional residual capacity. A spirometer is an instrument for measuring air inhaled and exhaled; it provides a simple way of determining most of the lung volumes and capacities that are measured in pulmonary function tests. The

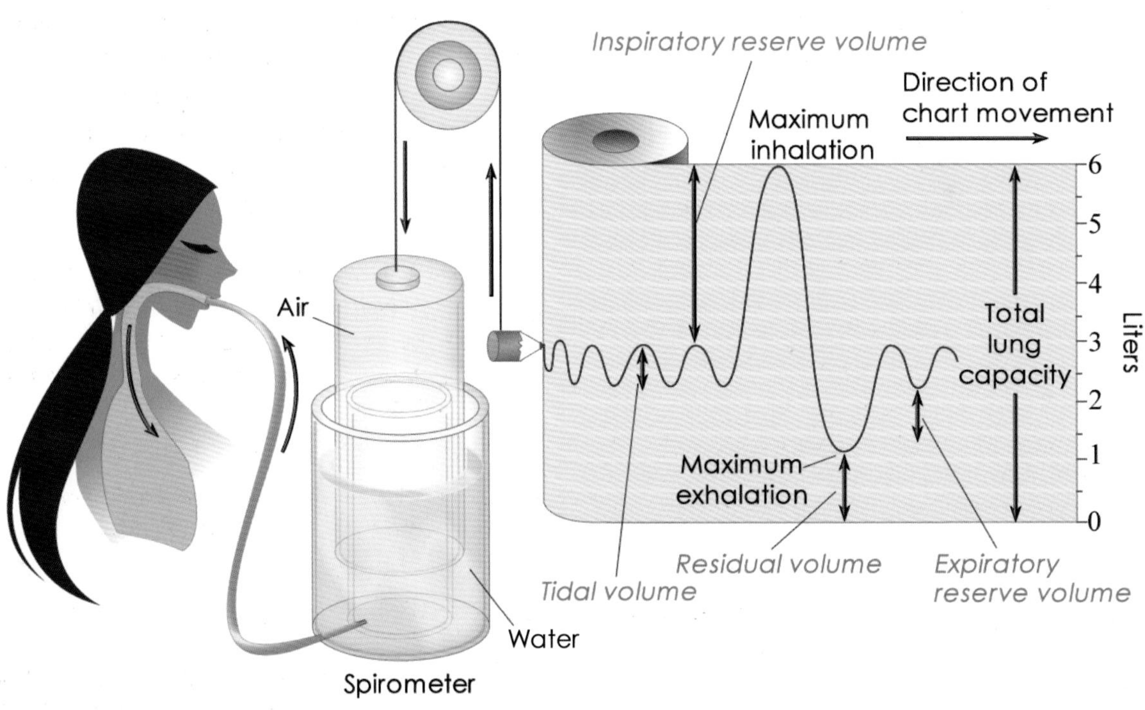

Figure IV.A.12.3: The four lung volumes measured by spirometer. Note that there are 4 key lung capacities: (1) the functional residual capacity which is the sum of the residual volume and the expiratory reserve volume (= ERV which is the maximum volume that can be exhaled following a normal quiet exhalation); (2) the vital capacity (VC) is the maximum volume that can be exhaled following a maximal inhalation; VC = inspiratory reserve volume (IRV) + tidal volume (VT) + ERV; (3) the inspiratory capacity (IC) is the maximum volume that can be inhaled following a normal quiet exhalation; IC = IRV + VT; (4) total lung capacity is the amount of air in the lung after maximal inhalation.

minute ventilation can be calculated as follows:

Minute ventilation =
Tidal volume x Respiratory rate

Airway resistance is: i) directly proportional to the magnitude of the viscosity between the flowing gas molecules; ii) directly proportional to the length of the airway; and iii) inversely proportional to the fourth power of the radius of the airway.

Resistance to air flow in the lung is normally small thus small pressure differences allow large volumes of air to flow. Physical, neural and chemical factors affect airway radii and therefore resistance. Transpulmonary pressure is a physical factor which exerts a distending force on the airways and alveoli. Such a force is critical to prevent small airways from collapsing.

The rate of respiration is primarily dependent on the concentration of carbon dioxide in the blood. As carbon dioxide levels rise, chemoreceptors in blood vessels are stimulated to discharge neuronal impulses to the respiratory center in the medulla oblongata in the brain stem. The respiratory center would then send impulses to the diaphragm causing an increase in the rate of contraction thus increasing the respiratory rate.

9) Given a resting respiratory rate of 12 breaths per minute, give an approximation of the minute ventilation.

A. 2.5 L/min
B. 5.0 L/min
C. 6.0 L/min
D. 3 0 L/min

10) Which of the following is consistent with the total lung capacity?

A. The amount of air inhaled and exhaled normally at rest
B. The sum of the residual volume and the expiratory reserve volume
C. The maximum volume that can be exhaled following a maximal inhalation
D. The maximum volume of air present in the lungs

11) During inspiration, transpulmonary pressure should:

A. increase, increasing airway radius and decreasing airway resistance.
B. increase, increasing airway radius and increasing airway resistance.
C. decrease, decreasing airway radius and decreasing airway resistance.
D. decrease, decreasing airway radius and increasing airway resistance.

12) Lateral traction refers to the process by which connective tissue fibers maintain airway patency by continuously pulling outward on the sides of the airways. As the lungs expand these fibers become stretched. Thus during inspiration lateral traction acts:

A. in the same direction as transpulmonary pressure, by increasing the viscosity of air.
B. in the opposite direction to transpulmonary pressure, by decreasing the viscosity of air.
C. in the same direction as transpulmonary pressure, by increasing the airway radius.
D. in the opposite direction to transpulmonary pressure, by increasing the airway radius.

13) The Heimlich Maneuver is used to aid individuals who are choking on matter caught in the upper respiratory tract through the application of a sudden abdominal pressure with an upward thrust. The procedure includes:

A. forcing the diaphragm downward, increasing thoracic size and causing a passive expiration.

B. forcing the diaphragm upward, increasing thoracic size and causing a forced expiration.

C. forcing the diaphragm upward, reducing thoracic size and causing a forced expiration.

D. forcing the diaphragm upward, increasing thoracic size and causing a passive expiration.

ANSWER KEY

ADVANCED TOPICS - CHAPTER 12

Cross-Reference

9.	C	Chap. 12 App.; P1, S3; dimensional analysis
10.	D	Chap. 12 App.
11.	A	BIO 12.4, Chap. 12 App. P2; P3, S2
12.	C	Chap. 12 App.; BIO 12.4
13.	B	BIO 12.4; deduce

P = paragraph; *S* = sentence; *E* = equation; *T* = table; *F* = figure

Go online to DAT-prep.com for additional chapter review Q&A and forum.

THE SKIN AS AN ORGAN SYSTEM

Chapter 13

Memorize	Understand	Importance
* Structure and function of skin, layer differentiation * Sweat glands, location in dermis	* Skin system: homeostasis and osmoregulation * Functions in thermoregulation: hair, erectile musculature, fat layer for insulation * Vasoconstriction and vasodilation in surface capillaries * Physical protection: nails, calluses, hair; protection against abrasion, disease organisms * Relative impermeability to water	**0 to 1 out of the 40 Biology** DAT questions are based on content in this chapter (in our estimation). * Note that between 25% and 50% of the questions in DAT Biology are from 5 chapters: 1, 2, 14, 15, and 16.

DAT-Prep.com

Introduction 

Skin is composed of layers of epithelial tissues which protect underlying muscle, bone, ligaments and internal organs. Thus skin has many roles including protecting the body from microbes, insulation, temperature regulation, sensation and synthesis of vitamin D.

Additional Resources

Free Online Q&A + Forum

Flashcards

Special Guest

13.1 Overview

The skin, or *integument*, is the body's largest organ. The following represents its major functions:

* **Physical protection:** The skin protects against the onslaught of the environment including uv light, chemical, thermal or even mechanical agents. It also serves as a barrier to the invasion of microorganisms.

* **Sensation:** The skin, being the body's largest sensory organ, contains a wide range of sensory receptors including those for pain, temperature, light touch, and pressure.

* **Metabolism:** Vitamin D synthesis can occur in the epidermis of skin (*see Endocrine Systems*, BIO 6.3). Also, energy is stored as fat in subcutaneous adipose tissue.

* **Thermoregulation and osmoregulation:** Skin is vital for the homeostatic mechanism of thermoregulation and to a lesser degree osmoregulation. Hair (*piloerection*, which can trap a layer of warm air against the skin's surface) and especially subcutaneous fat (*adipose tissue*) insulate the body against heat loss. Shivering, which allows muscle to generate heat, and decreasing blood flow to the skin (= *vasoconstriction*) are important in emergencies.

On the other hand, heat and water loss can be increased by increasing blood flow to the multitude of blood vessels (= *vasodilation*) in the dermis (cooling by radiation), the production of sweat, and the evaporation of sweat due to the heat at the surface of the skin; thus the skin cools. {Remember: the **hypothalamus** also regulates body temperature (*see The Nervous System*, BIO 6.1); it is like a thermostat which uses other organs as tools to maintain our body temperatures at about 37 °C (98.6 °F)}.

13.2 The Structure of Skin

Skin is divided into three layers: i) the outer **epidermis** which contains a stratified squamous keratinized epithelium; ii) the inner **dermis** which contains vessels, nerves, muscle, and connective tissues; iii) the innermost **subcutaneous layer**, known as hypodermis, which contains adipose and a loose connective tissue; this layer binds to any underlying organs.

The epidermis is divided into several different layers or *strata*. The deepest layer, *stratum basale*, contains actively dividing cells (keratinocytes) which are nourished by the vessels in the dermis. The mitotic activity of keratinocytes can keep regenerating epidermis approximately every 30 days. As these cells continue to divide, older epidermal cells are pushed towards the surface of the skin - *away from the nutrient providing dermal layer*; thus in time they die. Simultaneously, these cells are actively producing strands of a tough, fibrous, waterproof protein called keratin. This process is called *keratinization*. The two preceding events lead to the formation of an outermost layer (= *stratum corneum*) of keratin-filled dead cells which are devoid of organelles and are continuously shed by a process called *desquamation*.

Melanin is a dark pigment produced by cells (= *melanocytes*) whose cell bodies are usually found in the stratum basale. Melanin absorbs light thus protects against uv light induced cell damage (i.e. sunburns, skin cancer). Individuals have about the same number of melanocytes - regardless of race. Melanin production depends on genetic factors (i.e. race) and it can be stimulated by exposure to sunlight (i.e. tanning).

Langerhans cells have long processes and contain characteristic tennis-racket-shaped Birbeck granules. They function as antigen presenting cells in the immune response (BIO 8.2, 8.3).

Merkel cells are present in the richly innervated areas of stratum basale. They are responsible for receiving afferent nerve impulses and function as sensory mechanoreceptors (BIO 6.1.1).

The dermis is composed of dense irregular connective tissue including type I collagen fibers and a network of elastic fibers. It contains the blood vessels which nourish the various cells in the skin. It also contains motor fibers and many types of sensory nerve fibers such as fine touch receptors, pressure receptors and cold receptors.

13.3 Skin Appendages

The **appendages** of the skin include hair, sebaceous glands and sweat glands. Hair is a modified keratinized structure produced by a cylindrical downgrowth of epithelium (= *hair follicle*). The follicle extends into the dermis (sometimes the subcutaneous tissue as well). The arrector pili muscle attaches to the connective tissue surrounding a hair follicle. When this bundle of smooth muscle contracts (= *piloerection*), it elevates the hair and "goose bumps" are produced.

The sebaceous glands are lobular acinar glands that empty their ducts into the hair follicles. They are most abundant on the face, forehead and scalp. They release an oily/waxy secretion called sebum to lubricate and waterproof the skin.

Sweat glands can be classified as either eccrine sweat glands, which are simple tubular glands present in the skin throughout the body or apocrine sweat glands, which are large specialized glands located only in certain areas of the body (i.e. areola of the nipple, perianal area, axilla which is the "armpit") and will not function until puberty.

We have previously explored endocrine glands and saw how they secrete their products - without the use of a duct - directly into the bloodstream (BIO 6.3). Alternatively, endo-

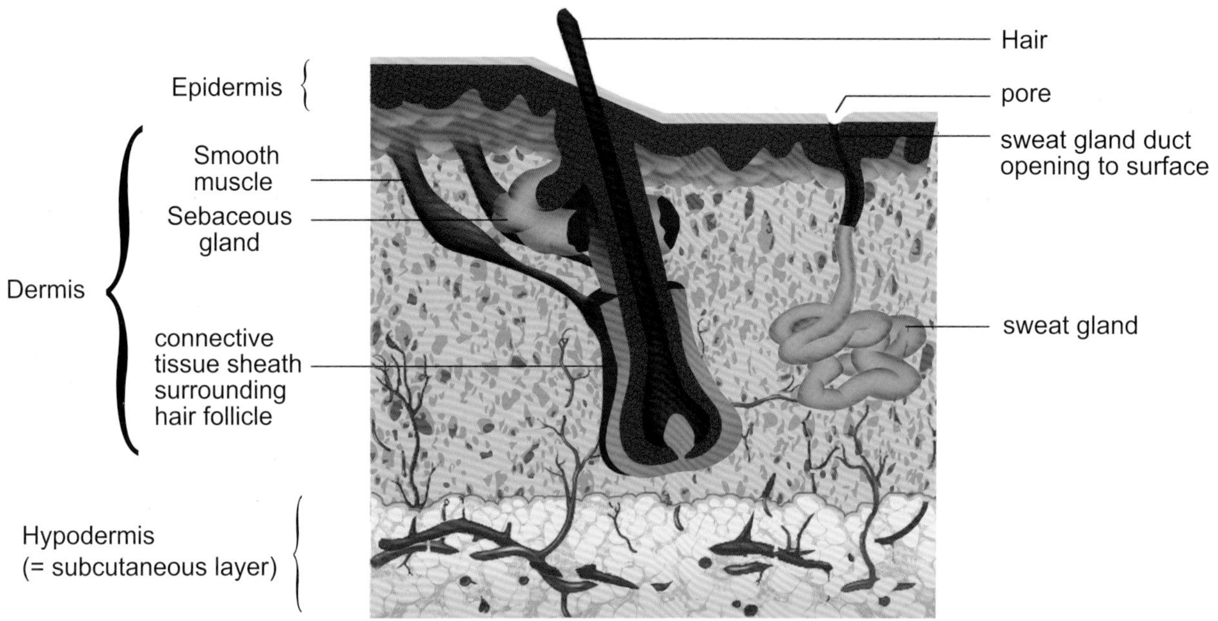

Figure IV.A.13.1: Skin structure with appendages.

crine products may diffuse into surrounding tissue (*paracrine signaling*) where they often affect only target cells near the release site.

An exocrine gland is distinguished by the fact that it excretes its product via a duct to some environment external to itself, either inside the body (BIO 9.3, 9.4) or on a surface of the body. Examples of exocrine glands include the sebaceous glands, sweat glands, salivary glands, mammary glands, pancreas and liver.

Holocrine (= *wholly secretory*) is a type of glandular secretion in which the entire secreting cell, along with its accumulated secretion, forms the secreted matter of the gland; for example, the sebaceous glands. Apocrine concentrates products at the free end of the secreting cell and are thrown off along with a portion of the cytoplasm (i.e. mammary gland, axilla). Eccrine, apocrine and holocrine are subdivisions of exocrine.

13.3.1 Nails, Calluses

Nails are flat, translucent, keratinized coverings near the tip of fingers and toes. They are useful for scratching and fine manipulation (including picking up dimes!).

A callus is a toughened, thickened area of skin. It is usually created in response to repeated friction or pressure thus they are normally found on the hands or feet.

GOLD STANDARD WARM-UP EXERCISES

CHAPTER 13: The Skin As An Organ

1) The skin, the body's largest organ, is divided into 3 layers including the epidermis. The latter contains a waterproof, tough protein called *keratin*. How then is it possible that humans can sweat freely in hot temperatures?
   - A. Specialized sweat glands can secrete their products into channels which pass through the epidermis.
   - B. Active and passive transport systems carry sweat across the epidermis.
   - C. Specialized sebaceous glands can secrete their products into channels which pass through the epidermis.
   - D. Osmotic pressure releases sweat across the epidermis.

2) Which of the following best describe why perspiring causes a reduction in body temperature?
   - A. Perspiration carries heated water to the surface.
   - B. Perspiration removes excess Na^+ and Cl^- ions from cells.
   - C. Perspiration evaporates and cools skin.
   - D. Perspiration causes vasoconstriction.

3) Which of the following is the best way to reduce body temperature?
   - A. Increase kidney function.
   - B. Constrict skeletal muscle.
   - C. Reduce insulin levels.
   - D. Relax smooth muscle of blood vessels.

4) Experiments have now confirmed that sweating only occurs as a result of a rise in core body temperature. Drinking iced water results in a lowering of core body temperature. Thus, exposing the skin to heat while drinking iced water would result in which of the following?
   - A. An increase in sweating
   - B. A decrease in sweating
   - C. An increase in sweating followed by a decrease in sweating
   - D. No change in sweat production

5) The name of the process by which oil glands in mammalian skins secrete oils is called:
   - A. osmosis.
   - B. active transport.
   - C. apocrine secretion.
   - D. holocrine secretion.

GS ANSWER KEY

CHAPTER 13

		Cross-Reference
1.	A	BIO 13.3
2.	C	BIO 13.1
3.	D	BIO 13.1, 7.3
4.	B	BIO 7.1, 13.1
5.	D	BIO 13.3

* Explanations can be found at the back of the book.

Go online to DAT-prep.com for additional chapter review Q&A and forum.

Go online to DAT-prep.com for additional chapter review Q&A and forum.

REPRODUCTION AND DEVELOPMENT

Chapter 14

Memorize	Understand	Importance
* Male and female reproductive structures, functions * Ovum, sperm: differences in formation, relative contribution to next generation * Reproductive sequence: fertilization; implantation; development * Major structures arising out of primary germ layers	* Gametogenesis by meiosis * Formation of primary germ layers: endoderm, mesoderm, ectoderm * Embryogenesis: stages of early development: order and general features of each * Cell specialization, communication in development, gene regulation in development * Programmed cell death; basic: the menstrual cycle	**1 to 3 out of the 40 Biology** DAT questions are based on content in this chapter (in our estimation). * Note that between 25% and 50% of the questions in DAT Biology are from 5 chapters: 1, 2, 14, 15, and 16.

DAT-Prep.com

Introduction

Reproduction refers to the process by which new organisms are produced. The process of development follows as the single celled zygote grows into a fully formed adult. These two processes are fundamental to life as we know it.

Additional Resources

Free Online Q&A + Forum

Video: Online or DVD

Flashcards

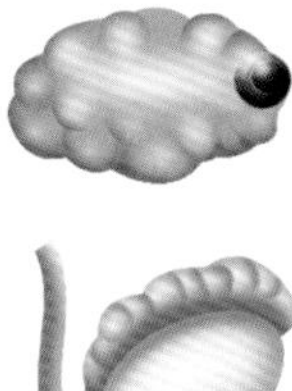

Special Guests

14.1 Organs of the Reproductive System

Gonads are the organs which produce gametes (= germ cells = reproductive cells). The female gonads are the two ovaries which lie in the pelvic cavity. Opening around the ovaries and connecting to the uterus are the Fallopian tubes (= *oviducts*) which conduct the egg (= *ovum*) from the ovary to the uterus. The uterus is a muscular organ. Part of the uterus (= the cervix) protrudes into the vagina or *birth canal*. The vagina leads to the external genitalia. The vulva includes the openings of the vagina, various glands, and folds of skin which are large (= labia majora) and small (= labia minora). The clitoris is found between the labia minora at the anterior end of the vulva. Like the glans penis, it is very sensitive as it is richly innervated. However, the clitoris is unique in being the only organ in the human body devoted solely to sensory pleasure.

The male gonads are the two testicles (= *testes*) which are suspended by spermatic cords in a sac-like scrotum outside the body cavity (this is because the optimal temperature for spermatogenesis is less than body temperature). Sperm (= *spermatozoa*) are produced in the seminiferous tubules in the testes and then continue along a system of ducts including: the epididymis where sperm complete their maturation and are collected and stored; the vas deferens which leads to the ejaculatory duct which in turn leads to the penile urethra which conducts to the exterior. The accessory organs include the seminal vesicles, the bulbourethral and prostate glands. They are exocrine glands whose secretions contribute greatly to the volume of the *ejaculate* (= semen = seminal fluid). The penis is composed of a body or shaft, which contains an erectile tissue which can be engorged by blood; a penile urethra which can conduct either urine or sperm; and a very sensitive head or glans penis which may be covered by foreskin (= *prepuce*, which is removed by circumcision).

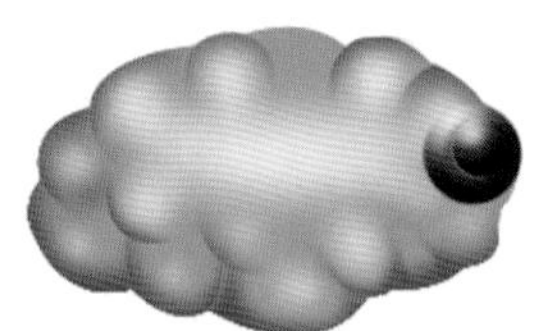
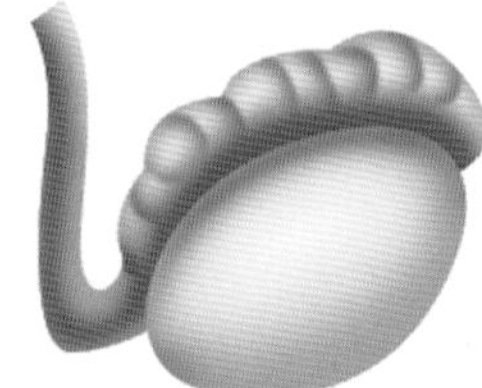

Figure IV.A.14.0: An ovulating ovary and a testicle with spermatic cord.

14.2 Gametogenesis

Gametogenesis refers to the production of gametes (eggs and sperm) which occurs by meiosis (*see Mitosis*, BIO 1.3, *for comparison*). Meiosis involves two successive divisions which can produce four cells from one parent cell. The first division, the reduction division, reduces the number of chromosomes from 2N (= *diploid*) to N (= *haploid*) where N = 23 for humans. This reduction division occurs as follows: i) in **prophase I** the chromosomes appear (= *condensed chromatin*), the nuclear membrane and nucleoli disappear and the spindle fibers become organized. Homologous paternal and maternal chromosomes pair[1] (= *synapsis*) forming a tetrad as each pair of homologous chromosomes consists of four chromatids. The exchange of genetic information (DNA) may occur by crossing over between homologous chromosomes at sites called *chiasmata*, therefore redistributing maternal and paternal genetic information ensuring variability; ii) **in metaphase I** the synaptic pairs of chromosomes line up midway between the poles of the developing spindle (= *the equatorial plate*). Thus each pair consists of 2 chromosomes (= 4 chromatids), each attached to a spindle fiber; iii) in **anaphase I** the homologous chromosomes migrate to opposite poles of the spindle, separating its paternal chromosomes from maternal ones. Thus, each daughter cell will have a unique mixture of paternal and maternal origin of chromosomes. In contrast to anaphase in mitosis, the two chromatids remain held together. Consequently, the centromeres do *not* divide; iv) in **telophase I** the parent cell divides into two daughter cells (= *cytokinesis*), the nuclear membranes and nucleoli reappear, and the spindle fibers are no longer visible. Each daughter cell now contains 23 chromosomes (1N).

The first meiotic division is followed by a short interphase I and then the second meiotic division which proceeds essentially the same as mitosis. Thus prophase II, metaphase II, anaphase II, and telophase II proceed like the corresponding mitotic phases.

Gametogenesis in males (= *spermatogenesis*) proceeds as follows: before the age of sexual maturity only a small number of primordial germ cells (= *spermatogonia*) are present in the testes. There are two types of spermatogonia, type A and type B. Type A spermatogonia (2N) are mitotically active and continuously provide a supply of type A or type B spermatogonia. Type B spermatogonia (2N) undergo meiosis and will give rise to primary spermatocytes. After sexual maturation these cells prolifically multiply throughout a male's life.

In the seminiferous tubules, the type B spermatogonia (2N) enter meiosis I and undergo chromosome replication forming primary spermatocytes with 2N chromosomes. Primary spermatocytes complete meiosis I producing two secondary spermatocytes with 1N chromosomes. Secondary spermatocytes quickly enter meiosis II without an intervening S phase to form four spermatids. Spermatids are haploid (1N) cells.

In summary, each primary spermatocyte results in the production of four spermatids. Spermatids undergo a post-meiotic cytodifferentiation whereby spermatids are transformed into **four** motile sperm (1N) through a process called *spermiogenesis*.

Sperm can be divided into: i) a *head* which is oval and contains the nucleus with its 23 chromosomes {since the nucleus carries either an X or Y sex chromosome, sperm determine the sex of the offspring}. The head is partly surrounded by the acrosome which contains enzymes (esp. hyaluronidase) which help the sperm penetrate the egg. The

[1]synapsing homologous chromosomes are often called *tetrads* or *bivalents*.

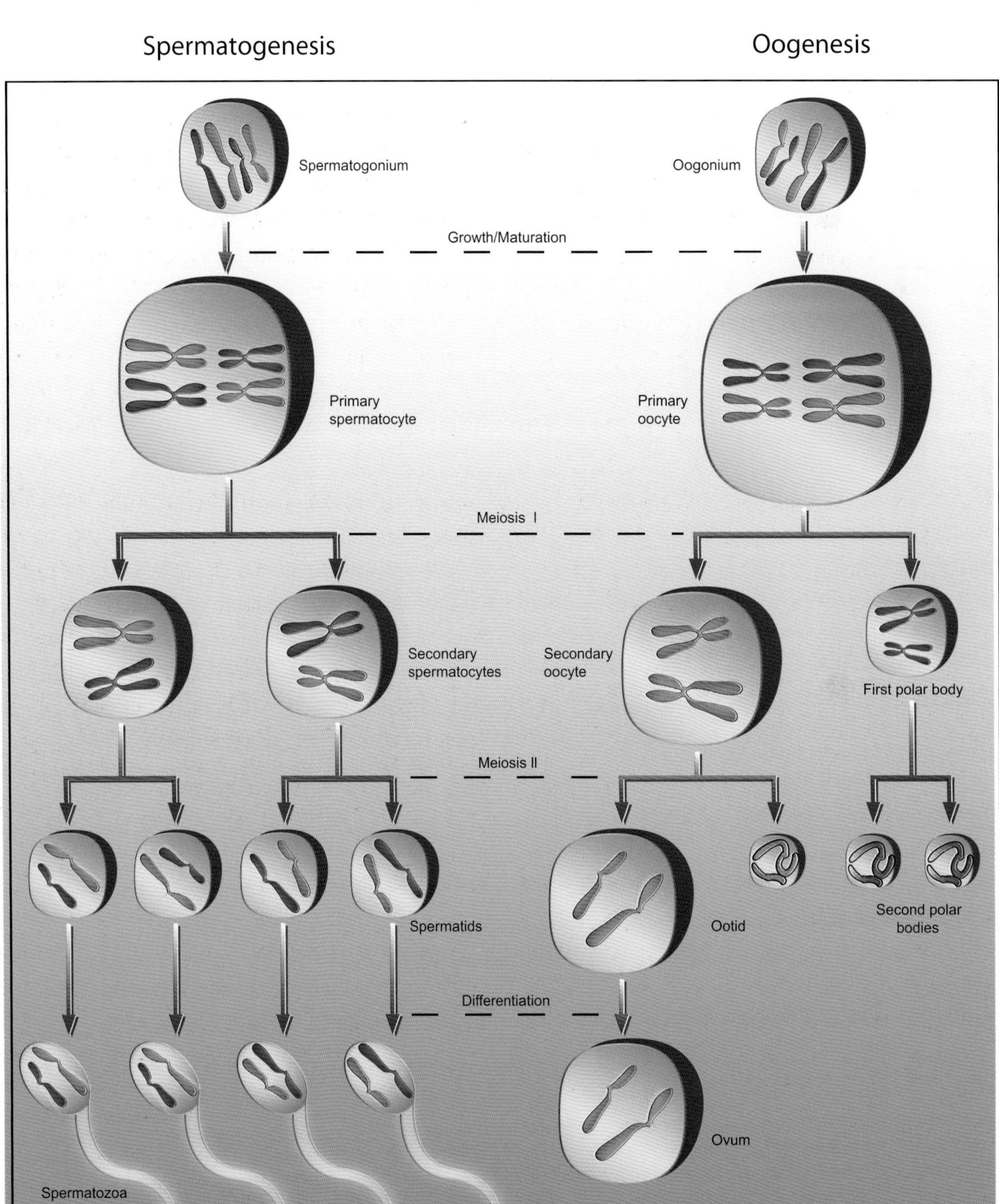

Figure IV.A.14.0a: Gametogenesis.

release of these enzymes is known as the acrosomal reaction; ii) the *body* of the sperm contains a central core surrounded by a large number of mitochondria for power; and iii) the *tail* constitutes a flagellum which is critical for the cell's locomotion. Newly formed sperm are incapable of fertilization until they undergo a process called capacitation, which happens in the female reproductive duct. After removal of its protein coating, the sperm becomes capable of fertilization. Also in the seminiferous tubules are Sertoli cells which support and nourish developing sperm and Leydig cells which produce and secrete testosterone. While LH stimulates the latter, FSH stimulates primary spermatocytes to undergo meiosis. {Remember: LH = Leydig, FSH = spermatogenesis}

Gametogenesis in females (= *oogenesis*) proceeds as follows: in fetal development, groups of cells (= *ovarian or primordial follicles*) develop from the germinal epithelium of the ovary) and differentiate into oogonia (2N). Oogonia (2N) enter meiosis I and undergo DNA replication producing primary oocytes (2N) which are surrounded by epithelia (= *follicular cells*) in the primordial follicle. The oocytes remain arrested in prophase I of meiosis until ovulation which occurs between the ages of about 13 (sexual maturity) and 50 (menopause). Thus, unlike males, all female germ cells are present at birth. Some follicles degenerate and are called *atretic*. During puberty, when the ovarian cycle begins, up to 20 primordial follicles may begin to differentiate to *Graafian follicles*. During this development, meiosis continues. In response to an LH surge from the pituitary gland, the primary oocyte (2N) completes meiosis I just prior to ovulation to form the secondary oocyte (1N) and the first polar body, which will probably degenerate. The secondary oocyte is surrounded by (from the inside out): a thick, tough membrane (= *the zona pellucida*), follicular cells (= *the corona radiata*), and estrogen-secreting thecal cells. It then enters meiosis II and remains arrested in metaphase of meiosis II until fertilization occurs.

Of the twenty or so maturing follicles, all the remaining secondary follicles will degenerate (= *atresia*) except for one which becomes the Graafian (mature) follicle. In response to the LH surge, the secondary oocyte leaves the ruptured Graafian follicle in the process called ovulation. This ovum, along with its zona pellucida and corona radiata, migrate to and through the Fallopian tube (oviduct) where a sperm may penetrate the secondary oocyte (= *fertilization*). If fertilization occurs then the second meiotic division proceeds, forming a mature oocyte, known as ovum, (1N) and a second polar body; if fertilization does not occur, then the ovum degenerates. Unlike in males, each primary germ cell (oocyte) produces one gamete and not four. This is a consequence of the production of *polar bodies* which are degenerated nuclear material. Up to three polar bodies can be formed: one from the division of the primary oocyte, one from the division of the secondary oocyte, and sometimes the first polar body divides.

14.3 The Menstrual Cycle

The "period" or menstrual cycle occurs in about 28 days and can be divided as follows: i) **Menses:** the first four days (days 1-4) of the cycle are notable for the menstrual blood flow. This occurs as a result of an estrogen and progesterone withdrawal which leads to vasoconstriction in the uterus causing the uterine lining (= *endometrium*) to disintegrate and slough away; ii) **Follicular** (ovary) or **Proliferative Phase** (days 5-14): FSH stimulates follicles to mature, and all but one of these follicles will stop growing, and the one dominant follicle in the ovary will continue to mature into a Graafian follicle, which in turn produces and secretes estrogen. Estrogen causes the uterine lining to thicken (= proliferate); iii) **Ovulation**: a very high concentration of estrogen is followed by an LH surge (estrogen-induced LH surge) at about day 15 (midcycle) which stimulates ovulation; iv) **Luteal** or **Secretory Phase** (days 15-28): the follicular cells degenerate into the corpus luteum which secretes estrogen *and* progesterone. Progesterone is responsible for a transient body temperature rise immediately after ovulation and it stimulates the uterine lining to become more vascular and glandular. Estrogen continues to stimulate uterine wall development and, along with progesterone, inhibits the secretion of LH and FSH (= negative feedback).

If the ovum is fertilized, the implanted embryo would produce the hormone *human chorionic gonadotropin* (= hCG) which would stimulate the corpus luteum to continue the secretion of estrogen and progesterone {hCG is the basis for most pregnancy tests}. If there is no fertilization, the corpus luteum degenerates causing a withdrawal of estrogen and progesterone thus the cycle continues [*see* i) *above*].

14.4 The Reproductive Sequence

During sexual stimulation parasympathetic impulses in the male lead to the dilatation of penile arteries combined with restricted flow in the veins resulting in the engorgement of the penis with blood (= *an erection*). In the female, the preceding occurs in a similar manner to the clitoris, along with the expansion and increase in secretions in the vagina. Intercourse or copulation may lead to orgasm which includes many responses from the sympathetic nervous system. In the male, the ejaculation of semen accompanies orgasm. In the female, orgasm is accompanied by many reflexes including an increase in muscular activity of the uterus and the Fallopian tubes. The latter may help in the transport of the already motile sperm to reach the tubes where the egg might be.

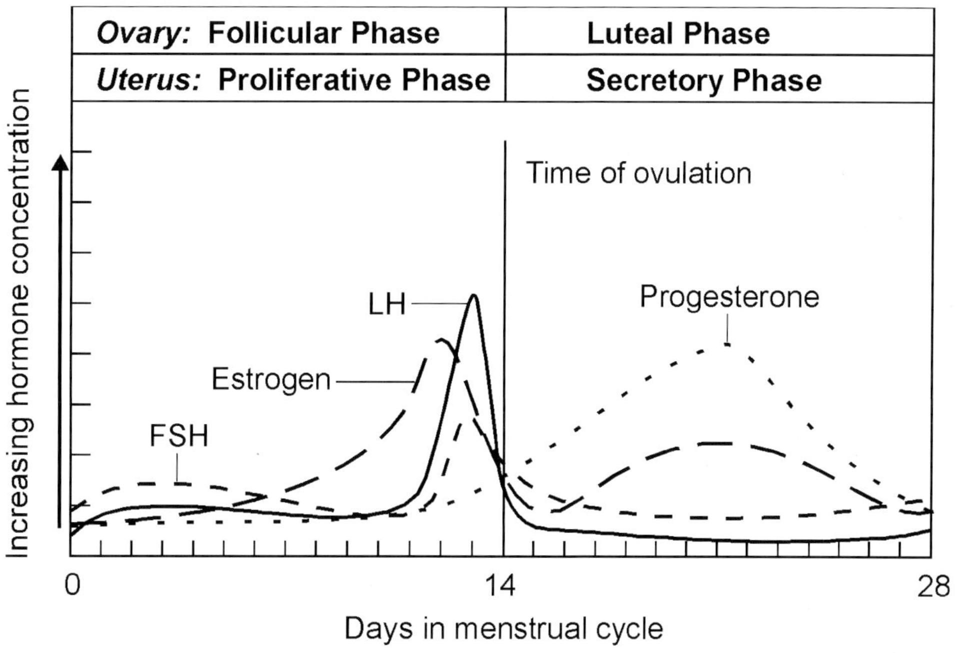

Figure IV.A.14.1: Changing hormone concentration during the menstrual cycle.

14.5 Embryogenesis

The formation of the embryo or *embryogenesis* occurs in a number of steps within two weeks of fertilization. Many parts of the developing embryo take shape during this period (= *morphogenesis*).

Penetration of the zona pellucida leads to the *cortical reaction*, in which the secondary oocyte is no longer permeable to other sperm.

Fertilization is a sequence of events which include: the sperm penetrating the corona radiata and the zona pellucidum due to the release of lytic enzymes from the acrosome known as the acrosome reaction; the fusion of the plasma membranes of the sperm and egg; the egg, which is really a secondary oocyte, becomes a mature ovum by completing the second meiotic division; the nuclei of the ovum and sperm are now called *pronuclei*; the male and female pronuclei fuse forming a zygote (2N). Fertilization, which normally occurs in the Fallopian tubes, is completed within 24 hours of ovulation.

Cleavage consists of rapid, repeated mitotic divisions beginning with the zygote.

Because the resultant daughter cells or blastomeres are still contained within the zona pellucidum, the cytoplasmic mass remains constant. Thus the increasing number of cells requires that each daughter cell be smaller than its parent cell. A morula is a solid ball of about 16 blastomeres which enters the uterus.

Blastulation is the process by which the morula develops a fluid filled cavity (= *blastocoel*) thus converting it to a blastocyst. Since the zona pellucidum degenerates at this point, the blastocyst is free to implant in the uterine lining or endometrium. The blastocyst contains some centrally located cells (= *the inner cell mass*) called the embryoblast which develops into the embryo. The outer cell mass called the trophoblast becomes part of the placenta.

Implantation. The zona pellucida must degenerate before the blastocyst can implant into the endometrium of the uterus. Once implantation is completed, the blastocyst becomes surrounded by layers of cells that further invade the endometrium.

Gastrulation is the process by which the blastula invaginates, and the inner cell mass is converted into a three layered (= *trilaminar*) disk. The trilaminar disk includes the **three primary germ layers**: an outer ectoderm, a middle mesoderm, and an inner endoderm. The ectoderm will develop into the epidermis and the nervous system; the mesoderm will become muscle, connective tissue (incl. blood, bone), and circulatory, reproductive and excretory organs; the endoderm will become the epithelial linings of the respiratory tract, and digestive tract, including the glands of the accessory organs (i.e. the liver and pancreas). During this stage the embryo may be called a gastrula.

Neurulation is the process by which the neural plate and neural folds form and close to produce the neural tube. The neural plate is formed by the thickening of ectoderm which is induced by the developing *notochord*. The notochord is a cellular rod that defines the axis of the embryo and provides some rigidity. Days later, the neural plate invaginates along its central axis producing a central neural groove with neural folds on each side. The neural folds come together and fuse thus converting the neural plate into a neural tube which separates from the surface ectoderm. Special cells on the crest of the neural folds (= *neural crest cells*) migrate to either side of the developing neural tube to a region called the neural crest.

As a consequence, we are left with **three** regions: the surface ectoderm which will become the epidermis; the neural tube which will become the central nervous system (CNS); and the neural crest which will become cranial and spinal ganglia and nerves and the medulla of the adrenal gland. During this stage the embryo may be called a *neurula*.

14.5.1 Mechanisms of Development

Though this is a subject which is still poorly understood, it seems clear that morphogenesis relies on the coordinated interaction of genetic and environmental factors. When the zygote passes through its first few divisions, the blastomeres remain indeterminate or uncommitted to a specific fate. As development proceeds the cells become increasingly committed to a specific outcome (i.e. neural tube cells → CNS). This is called **determination**.

In order for a cell to specialize it must differentiate into a committed or determined cell. Since essentially all cells in a person's body have the same amount of genetic information, differentiation relies on the *difference* in the way these genes are *activated*. For example, though brain cells (neurons) have the same genes as osteoblasts, neurons do not activate such genes (otherwise we would have bone forming in our brains!). The general mechanism by which cells differentiate is called **induction**.

Induction can occur by many means. If two cells divide unevenly, the cell with more cytoplasm might have the necessary amount of a substance which could *induce* its chromosomes to activate cell-specific genes. Furthermore, sometimes a cell, through contact (i.e. *contact inhibition*) or the release of a chemical mediator, can influence the development of nearby cells (*recall that the notochord induces the development of the neural plate*). The physical environment (pH, temperature, etc.) may also influence the development of certain cells. Irrespective of what form of induction is used, the signal must be translated into an intracellular message which influences the genetic activity of the responding cells.

Programmed cell-death (PCD = apoptosis) is death of a cell in any form, which is controlled by an intracellular program. PCD is carried out in a regulated process directed by DNA which normally confers advantage during an organism's life-cycle. PCD serves fundamental functions during tissue development. For example, the development of the spaces between your fingers requires cells to undergo PCD.

Thus cells specialize and develop into organ systems (morphogenesis). The embryo develops from the second to the ninth week, followed by the fetus which develops from the ninth week to birth (*parturition*).

14.6 The Placenta

The **placenta** is a complex vascular structure formed by part of the maternal endometrium (= *the decidua basalis*) and cells of embryonic origin (= *the chorion*). The placenta begins to form when the blastocyst implants in the endometrium. A cell layer from the embryo invades the endometrium with fingerlike bumps (= *chorionic villi*) which project into intervillous spaces which contain maternal blood. Maternal spiral arteries enter the intervillous spaces allowing blood to circulate.

The placenta has three main functions: i) the **transfer** of substances necessary for the development of the embryo or fetus from the mother (O_2, H_2O, carbohydrates, amino acids, IgG antibodies - BIO 8.2, vitamins, etc.) and the **transfer** of wastes from the embryo or fetus to the mother (CO_2, urea, uric acid, etc.); ii) the placenta can synthesize substances (i.e. glycogen, fatty acids) to use as an energy source for itself and the embryo or fetus; iii) the placenta produces and secretes a number of hormones including human chorionic gonadotropin (hCG), estrogen and progesterone. The hCG rescues the corpus luteum from regression and stimulates its production of progesterone.

14.7 Fetal Circulation

Consider the following: the fetus has lungs but does not breathe O_2. In fact, the placenta is, metaphorically, the "fetal lung." Oxygenated and nutrient-rich blood returns to the fetus from the placenta via the left umbilical vein. Most of the blood is directed to the inferior vena cava through the ductus venosus. From there, blood joins the deoxygenated and nutrient-poor blood from the superior vena cava and empties into the right atrium. However, most of the blood is diverted from the pulmonary circulation (bypassing the right ventricle) to the left atrium via a hole in the atrial septum: the patent foramen ovale (for adult circulation and anatomy, see chapter 7). Blood then enters the left ventricle and is distributed through the body (systemic circulation) via the aorta.

Some blood in the right atrium enters into the right ventricle and then proceeds into the pulmonary trunk. However, resistance in the collapsed lung is high and the pulmonary artery pressure is higher than it is in the aorta. Consequently, most of the blood bypasses the lung via the ductus arteriosus back to the aorta.

Blood circulates through the body and is sent back to the placenta via right and left umbilical arteries. The placenta re-oxygenates this deoxygenated and nutrient-poor blood and returns it to the fetus through the umbilical vein and the cardiovascular cycle repeats. Notice that in the fetus, oxygenated and nutrient-rich blood can be carried by veins to the right chambers of the heart which cannot occur in normal adult circulation.

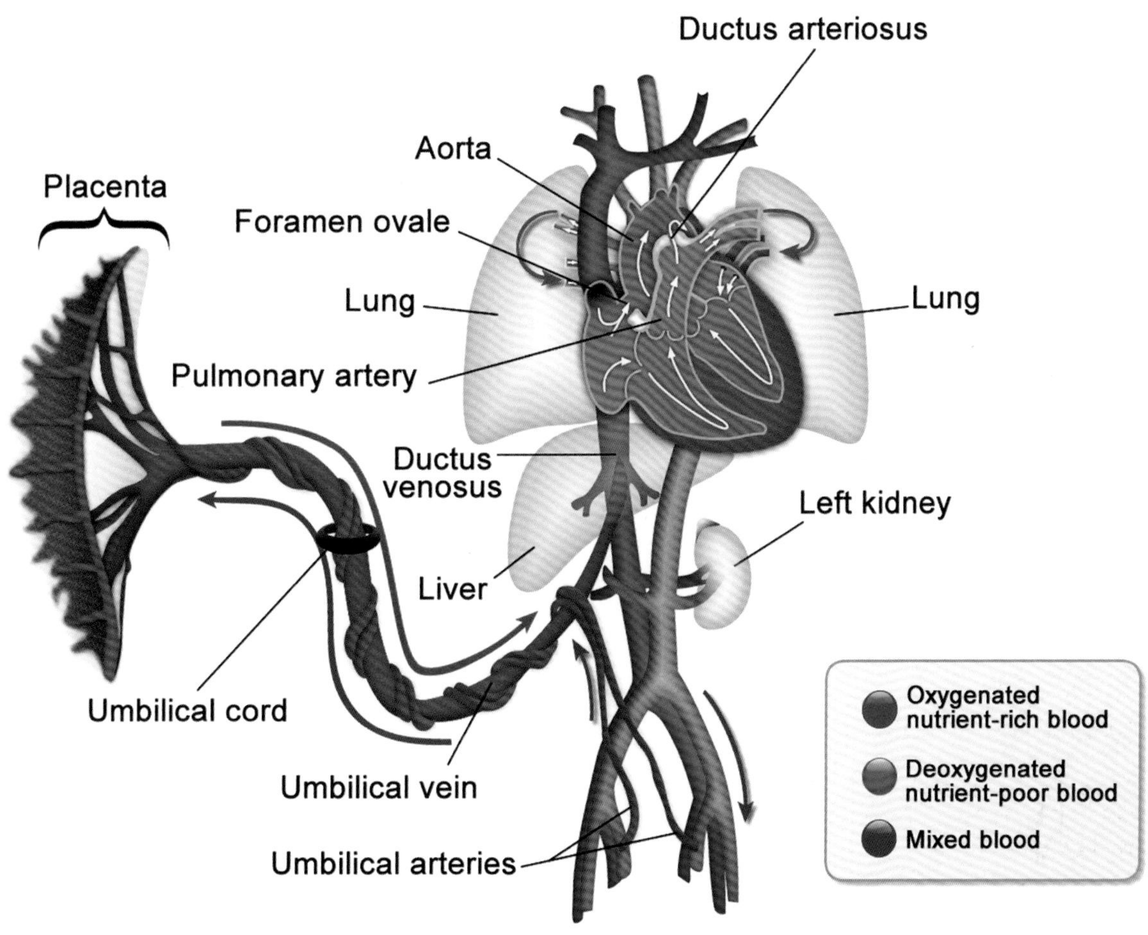

Fig.IV.A.14.2: Fetal circulation.

14.8 Fetal Sexual Development

The normal sexual development of the fetus depends on the genotype (XX female, XY male), the morphology of the internal organs and gonads, and the phenotype or external genitalia. Later, these many factors combine to influence the individual's self-perception along with the development of secondary sexual characteristics (i.e. breast development in females, hair growth and lower pitched voice in males).

Every fetus, regardless of genotype, has the capacity to become a normally formed individual of either sex. Development naturally proceeds towards "female" unless there is a Y chromosome factor present. Thus the XX genotype leads to the maturation of the Müllerian ducts into the uterus, fallopian tubes, and part of the vagina. The primitive gonad will develop into a testis only if the Y chromosome is present and encodes the appropriate factor and eventually the secretion of testosterone. Thus the XY genotype leads to the involution of the Müllerian ducts and the maturation of the Wolffian ducts into the vas deferens, seminiferous tubules and prostate.

Reproductive biology is the only science where multiplication and division mean the same thing. :)

GOLD STANDARD WARM-UP EXERCISES

CHAPTER 14: Reproduction and Development

1) Fertilization of the ovum by the sperm usually occurs in the:

A. vagina.
B. uterus.
C. oviduct.
D. ovary.

2) Sperm can travel through each of the following EXCEPT one. Which one is the EXCEPTION?

A. Ureter
B. Urethra
C. Vas deferens
D. Epididymis

3) Which of the following does NOT follow the normal anatomic sequence?

I. gametogenesis → seminal vesicles → seminiferous tubules
II. seminiferous tubules → epididymis → vas deferens
III. vas deferens → ejaculatory duct → urethra

A. I only
B. II only
C. I and II only
D. II and III only

4) Which of the following can initiate a second meiotic division?

A. FSH
B. LH
C. Estrogen and progesterone
D. Fertilization

5) The corpus luteum secretes:

A. FSH.
B. LH.
C. progesterone.
D. HCG.

6) The hormone causing growth of the endometrium is:

A. oxytocin.
B. estrogen.
C. luteinizing hormone.
D. prolactin.

7) In the human menstrual cycle, which hormone is preferentially secreted in the follicular phase by the ovary?

A. Estrogen
B. FSH
C. LH
D. Progesterone

8) Which of the following hormones leads to the expulsion of the egg from the ovaries?

A. LH
B. FSH
C. Estrogen
D. Progesterone

9) In vitro fertilization begins by injecting a woman with medications which stimulate multiple egg production in the ovary. Drugs that stimulate multiple egg production probably contain, or increase the production of, which of the following hormones?

I. LH
II. FSH
III. ACTH
IV. Estrogen

A. I only
B. IV only
C. I, II and IV only
D. I, II, III and IV

10) After fertilization, the zygote will develop into a female if:

A. the zygote possesses an X chromosome.
B. the primary oocyte possesses an X chromosome.
C. the egg possesses an X chromosome.
D. the sperm possesses an X chromosome.

11) Damage to the ectoderm during gastrulation will result in an embryo with an underdeveloped:

A. reproductive system.
B. nervous system.
C. excretory system.
D. digestive system.

12) The blastula develops into which of the following?

A. The morula
B. The blastula
C. The gastrula
D. The neurula

13) The developing fetus has a blood vessel called the ductus arteriosus which connects the pulmonary artery to the aorta. When a baby is born, the ductus arteriosus closes permanently. Which is the dominant feature found in a newborn whose ductus arteriosus failed to obliterate?

A. Increased O_2 partial pressure in pulmonary arteries
B. Decreased CO_2 partial pressure in pulmonary arteries
C. Increased O_2 partial pressure in systemic arteries
D. Decreased O_2 partial pressure in systemic arteries

14) The placenta in humans is derived from the:

A. embryo only.
B. uterus only.
C. endometrium and embryo.
D. uterus and fallopian tube.

15) Synapsis and crossing over of chromosomes occurs is which phase of meiosis?

A. Prophase I
B. Prophase II
C. Metaphase I
D. Metaphase II

GS ANSWER KEY

CHAPTER 14

		Cross-Reference			Cross-Reference
1.	C	BIO 14.1, 14.5	9.	C	BIO 14.3
2.	A	BIO 14.1, 10.1, 10.2	10.	D	BIO 14.2, 14.8
3.	A	BIO 14.1	11.	B	BIO 14.5
4.	D	BIO 14.2	12.	C	BIO 14.5
5.	C	BIO 3.0	13.	D	BIO 7.2, 7.3, 14.7
6.	B	BIO 14.3	14.	C	BIO 14.6
7.	A	BIO 6.3.1F, 14.3	15.	C	BIO 14.2
8.	A	BIO 14.3			

* Explanations can be found at the back of the book.

Go online to DAT-prep.com for additional chapter review Q&A and forum.

Go online to DAT-prep.com for additional chapter review Q&A and forum.

GENETICS

Chapter 15

Memorize

* Define: phenotype, genotype, gene, locus, allele: single and multiple
* Homo/heterozygosity, wild type, recessiveness, complete/co-dominance
* Incomplete dominance, gene pool
* Sex-linked characteristics, sex determination
* Types of mutations: random, translation error, transcription error, base subs., etc.

Understand

* Importance of meiosis; compare/contrast with mitosis; segregation of genes, assortment, linkage, recombination
* Single/double crossovers; relationship of mutagens to carcinogens
* Hardy-Weinberg Principle, inborn errors of metabolism
* Test cross: back cross, concepts of parental, F1 and F2 generations
* DNA recombination and genetic technology

Importance

3 to 7 out of the 40 Biology

DAT questions are based on content in this chapter (in our estimation).

* Note that between 25% and 50% of the questions in DAT Biology are from 5 chapters: 1, 2, 14, 15, and 16.

DAT-Prep.com

Introduction 

Genetics is the study of heredity and variation in organisms. The observations of Gregor Mendel in the mid-nineteenth century gave birth to the science which would reveal the physical basis for his conclusions, DNA, about 100 years later.

Additional Resources

Free Online Q&A + Forum

Video: Online or DVD

Flashcards

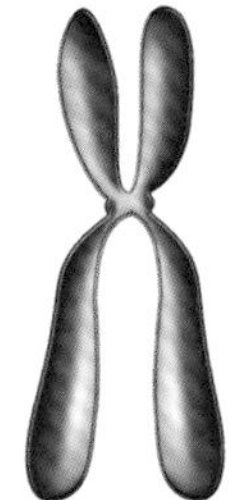

Special Guest

15.1 Background Information

Genetics is a branch of biology which deals with the principles and mechanics of heredity; in other words, the *means* by which *traits* are passed from parents to offspring. To begin, we will first examine some relevant definitions - a few of which we have already discussed.

Chromosomes are a complex of DNA and proteins (incl. histones; BIO 1.2.2). A gene is that sequence of DNA that codes for a protein or polypeptide. A locus is the *position* of the gene on the DNA molecule. Recall that humans inherit 46 chromosomes - 23 from maternal origin and 23 from paternal origin (BIO 14.2). A given chromosome from maternal origin has a counterpart from paternal origin which codes for the same products. This is called a **homologous pair** of chromosomes.

Any homologous pair of chromosomes have a pair of genes which codes for the same product (i.e. hair color). Such pairs of genes are called **alleles**. Thus for one gene product, a nucleus contains one allele from maternal origin and one allele from paternal origin. If both alleles are identical (i.e. they code for the same hair color), then the individual is called **homozygous** for that trait. If the two alleles differ (i.e. one codes for dark hair while the other codes for light hair), then the individual is called **heterozygous** for that trait.

The set of genes possessed by a particular organism is its genotype. The appearance or phenotype of an individual is expressed as a consequence of the genotype and the environment. Consider a heterozygote that expressed one gene (dark hair) but not the other (light hair). The expressed gene would be called dominant while the other unexpressed allele would be called recessive. The individual would have dark hair as their phenotype, yet their genotype would be heterozygous for that trait. The dominant allele is expressed in the phenotype. This is known as Mendel's Law of Dominance.

It is common to symbolize dominant genes with capital letters (A) and recessive genes with small letters (a). From the preceding paragraphs, we can conclude that with two alleles, three genotypes are possible: homozygous dominant (AA), heterozygous (Aa), and homozygous recessive (aa). Note that this only results in two phenotypes since both AA and Aa express the dominant gene, while only aa expresses the recessive gene.

Each individual carries **two** alleles while populations may have many or **multiple alleles**. Sometimes these genes are not strictly dominant or recessive. There may be degrees of blending (= *incomplete dominance*) or sometimes two alleles may be equally dominant (= *codominance*). ABO blood types are an important example of multiple alleles with codominance.

Incomplete dominance occurs when the phenotype of the heterozygote is an intermediate of the phenotypes of the homozygotes. A classic example is flower color in snapdragon: the snapdragon flower color is red for homozygous dominant and white for homozygous recessive. When the red homozygous flower is crossed with the white homozygous flower, the result yields a 100% pink snapdragon flower. The pink snapdragon is the result of the combined effect of both dominant and recessive genes.

15.2 ABO Blood Types

Codominance occurs when multiple alleles exist for a particular gene and more than one is dominant. When a dominant allele is combined with a recessive allele, the phenotype of the recessive allele is completely masked. But when two dominant alleles are present, the contributions of both alleles do not overpower each other and the phenotype is the result of the expression of both alleles. A classic example of codominance is the ABO blood type in humans.

Red blood cells can have various antigens or *agglutinogens* on their plasma membranes which aid in blood typing. The important two are antigens A and B. If the red blood cells have only antigen A, the blood type is A; if they have only antigen B, then the blood type is B; if they have both antigens, the blood type is AB; if neither antigen is present, the blood type is O. There are three allelic genes in the population (I^A, I^B, i^O). Two are codominant (I^A, I^B) and one is recessive (i^O). Thus in a given population, there are six possible genotypes which result in four possible phenotypes:

Genotype	*Phenotype*
I^AI^A, I^Ai^O	blood type A
I^BI^B, I^Bi^O	blood type B
I^AI^B	blood type AB
i^Oi^O	blood type O

Blood typing is critical before doing a blood transfusion. This is because people with blood type A have anti-B antibodies, those with type B have anti-A, those with type AB have neither antibody, while type O has both anti-A and anti-B antibodies. If a person with type O blood is given types A, B, or AB, the clumping of the red blood cells will occur (= *agglutination*). Though type O can only receive from type O, it can give to the other blood types since its red blood cells have no antigens {type O = universal donor}. Type AB has neither antibody to react against A or B antigens so it can receive blood from all blood types {type AB = universal recipient}.

The only other antigens which have some importance are the Rh factors which are coded by different genes at different loci from the A and B antigens. Rh factors are either there (Rh^+) or they are not there (Rh^-). 85% of the population are Rh^+. The problem occurs when a woman is Rh^- and has been exposed to Rh^+ blood and then forms anti-Rh^+ antibodies (note: unlike the previous case, exposure is necessary to produce these antibodies). If this woman is pregnant with an Rh^+ fetus her antibodies may cross the placenta and cause the fetus' red blood cells to agglutinate (*erythroblastosis fetalis*). This condition is fatal if left untreated.

15.3 Mendelian Genetics

Recall that in gametogenesis homologous chromosomes separate during the first meiotic division. Thus alleles that code for the same trait are segregated: this is **Mendel's First Law of Segregation. Mendel's Second Law of Independent Assortment** states that different chromosomes (*or factors which carry different traits*) separate independently of each other. For example, consider a primary spermatocyte (2N) undergoing its first meiotic division. It is not the case that all 23 chromosomes of paternal origin will end up in one secondary spermatocyte while the other 23 chromosomes of maternal origin ends up in the other. Rather, each chromosome in a homologous pair separates *independently* of any other chromosome in other homologous pairs.

However, it has been noted experimentally that sometimes traits on the same chromosome assort independently! This non-Mendelian concept is a result of *crossing over* (recall that this is when homologous chromosomes exchange parts, BIO 14.2). In fact, it has been shown that two traits located far apart on a chromosome are more likely to cross over and thus assort independently, as compared to two traits that are close. The propensity for some traits to refrain from assorting independently is called linkage. Double crossovers occur when two crossovers happen in a chromosomal region being studied.

Another exception to Mendel's laws involves **sex linkage**. Mendel's laws would predict that the results of a genetic cross should be the same regardless of which parent introduces the allele. However, it can be shown that some traits follow the inheritance of the sex chromosomes. Humans have one pair of sex chromosomes (XX = female, XY = male), and the remaining 22 pairs of homologous chromosomes are called **autosomes**.

Since females have two X chromosomes and males have only one, a single recessive allele carried on an X chromosome could be expressed in a male since there is no second allele present to mask it. When males inherit one copy of the recessive allele from an X chromosome, they will express the trait. In contrast, females must inherit two copies to express the trait. Therefore, an X-linked recessive phenotype is much more frequently found in males than females. In fact, a typical pattern of sex linkage is when a mother passes her phenotype to all her sons but **none** of her daughters. Her daughters become *carriers* for the recessive allele. Certain forms of hemophilia, colorblindness, and one kind of muscular dystrophy are well-known recessive sex-linked traits. {In what was once known as Lyon's Hypothesis, it has been shown that every female has a condensed, inactivated X chromosome in her body or somatic cells called a Barr body.}

Let us examine the predictions of Mendel's First Law. Consider two parents, one homozygous dominant (AA) and the other homozygous recessive (aa). Each parent can only form one type of gamete with respect to that trait (*either* A *or* a, *respectively*). The next generation (*called first filial or* $\mathbf{F_1}$) must then be uniformly heterozygotes or *hybrids* (Aa). Now the F_1 hybrids can produce gametes that can be either A half the time or a half the time. When the F_1 generation is self-crossed, i.e. Aa X Aa, the F_2 generation will be more genotypically and phenotypically diverse and we can predict the outcome in the next generation (F_2) using a Punnett square:

	1/2 A	1/2 a
1/2 A	1/4 AA	1/4 Aa
1/2 a	1/4 Aa	1/4 aa

Here is an example as to how you derive the information within the square: when you cross A with A you get AA (i.e. 1/2 A × 1/2 A = 1/4 AA). Thus by doing a simple *mono*hybrid cross (Aa × Aa) with random mating, the Punnett square indicates that in the F_2 generation, 1/4 of the population would be AA, 1/2 would be Aa (1/4 + 1/4), and 1/4 would be aa. In other words the *genotypic* ratio of homozygous dominant to heterozygous to homozygous recessive is 1:2:1. However, since AA and Aa demonstrate the same *phenotype* (i.e. dominant) the ratio of dominant phenotype to recessive phenotype is 3:1.

Now we will consider the predictions of Mendel's Second Law. To examine independent assortment, we will have to consider a case with two traits (usu. on different chromosomes) or a *di*hybrid cross. Imagine a parent which is homozygous dominant for two traits (AABB) while the other is homozygous recessive (aabb). Each parent can only form one type of gamete with respect to those traits (*either* AB *or* ab, *respectively*). The F_1 generation will be uniform for the dominant trait (i.e. *the genotypes would all be* AaBb). In the gametes of the F_1 generation, the alleles will assort independently.

Consequently, an equal amount of all the possible gametes will form: 1/4 AB, 1/4 Ab, 1/4 aB, and 1/4 ab. When the F_1 generation is self-crossed, i.e. AaBb X AaBb, we can predict the outcome in the F_2 generation using the Punnett square:

	1/4 AB	1/4 Ab	1/4 aB	1/4 ab
1/4 AB	1/16 AABB	1/16 AABb	1/16 AaBB	1/16 AaBb
1/4 Ab	1/16 AABb	1/16 AAbb	1/16 AaBb	1/16 Aabb
1/4 aB	1/16 AaBB	1/16 AaBb	1/16 aaBB	1/16 aaBb
1/4 ab	1/16 AaBb	1/16 Aabb	1/16 aaBb	1/16 aabb

Thus by doing a dihybrid cross with random mating, the Punnett square indicates that there are nine possible genotypes (*the frequency is given in brackets*): AABB (1), AABb (2), AaBb (4), AaBB (2), Aabb (2), aaBb (2), AAbb (1), aaBB (1), and aabb (1). Since A and B are dominant, there are only four phenotypic classes in the ratio 9:3:3:1 which are: the expression of both traits (AABB + AABb + AaBb + AaBB = 9), the expression of only the first trait (AAbb + Aabb = 3), the expression of only the second trait (aaBB + aaBb = 3), and the expression of neither trait (aabb = 1). Now we know, for example, that 9/16 represents that fraction of the population which will have the phenotype of both dominant traits.

15.3.1 A Word about Probability

If you were to flip a quarter, the probability of getting "heads" is 50% (p = 0.5). If you flipped the quarter ten times and each time it came up heads, the probability of getting heads on the next trial is still 50%. After all, previous trials have no effect on the next trial.

Since chance events, such as fertilization of a particular kind of egg by a particular kind of sperm, occur independently, the genotype of one child has no effect on the genotypes of other children produced by a set of parents. Thus in the previous example of the dihybrid cross, the chance of producing the genotype AaBb is 4/16 (25%) irrespective of the genotypes which have already been produced.

15.4 The Hardy-Weinberg Law

The Hardy-Weinberg Law deals with population genetics. A **population** includes all the members of a species which occupy a more or less well defined geographical area and have demonstrated the ability to reproduce from generation to generation. A **gene pool** is the sum of all the unique alleles for a given population. A central component to evolution is the changing of alleles in a gene pool from one generation to the next.

Evolution can be viewed as a changing of gene frequencies within a population over successive generations. The Hardy-Weinberg Law or *equilibrium* predicts the outcome of a randomly mating population of sexually reproducing diploid organisms who are not undergoing evolution.

For the Hardy-Weinberg Law to be applied, the idealized population must meet the following conditions: i) **random mating**: the members of the population must have no mating preferences; ii) **no mutations**: there must be no errors in replication nor similar event resulting in a change in the genome; iii) **isolation**: there must be no exchange of genes between the population being considered and any other population; iv) **large population**: since the law is based on statistical probabilities, to avoid sampling errors, the population cannot be small; v) **no selection pressures**: there must be no reproductive advantage of one allele over the other.

To illustrate a use of the law, consider an idealized population that abides by the preceding conditions and have a gene locus occupied by either A or a. Let p = the frequency of allele A in the population and let q = the frequency of allele a. Since they are the only alleles, $p + q = 1$. Squaring both sides we get:

$$(p + q)^2 = (1)^2$$

OR

$$p^2 + 2pq + q^2 = 1$$

The preceding equation (= *the Hardy-Weinberg equation*) can be used to calculate genotype frequencies once the allelic frequencies are given. This can be summarized by the following:

	pA	qa
pA	p^2AA	pqAa
qa	pqAa	q^2aa

The Punnett square illustrates the expected frequencies of the three genotypes in the next generation: AA = p^2, Aa = 2pq, and aa= q_2.

For example, let us calculate the percentage of heterozygous individuals in a population where the recessive allele q has a frequency of 0.2. Since p + q = 1, then p = 0.8. Using the Hardy-Weinberg equation and squaring p and q we get:

$$0.64 + 2pq + 0.04 = 1$$

$$2pq = 1 - 0.68 = 0.32$$

Thus the percentage of heterozygous (2pq) individuals is 32%.

A practical application of the Hardy-Weinberg equation is the prediction of how many people in a generation are carriers for a particular recessive allele. The values would have to be recalculated for every generation since humans do not abide by all the conditions of the Hardy-Weinberg Law (i.e. *humans continually evolve*).

15.4.1 Back Cross, Test Cross

A back cross is the cross of an individual (F_1) with one of its parents (P) or an organism with the same genotype as a parent. Back crosses can be used to help identify the genotypes of the individual in a specific type of back cross called a test cross. A test cross is a cross between an organism whose genotype for a certain trait is unknown and an organism that is homozygous recessive for that trait so the unknown genotype can be determined from that of the offspring. For example, for P: AA x aa and F_1: Aa, we get:

Backcross #1: Aa x AA
Progeny #1: 1/2 Aa and 1/2 AA

Backcross #2: Aa x aa
Progeny #2: 1/2 Aa and 1/2 aa

15.5 Genetic Variability

Meiosis and mutations are sources of genetic variability. During meiosis I, crossing over occurs between the parental and maternal genes which leads to a recombination of parental genes yielding unique haploid gametes. Thus recombination can result in alleles of linked traits separating into different gametes. However, the closer two traits are on a chromosome, the more likely they will be linked and thus remain together, and vice versa.

Further recombination occurs during the random fusion of gametes during fertilization.

Consequently, taking Mendel's two laws and recombination together, we can predict that parents can give their offspring combinations of alleles which the parents never had. This leads to **genetic variability**.

Mutations are rare, inheritable, random changes in the genetic material (DNA) of a cell. Mutations are much more likely to be either neutral (esp. *silent mutations*) or negative (i.e. cancer) than positive for an organism's survival. Nonetheless, such a change in the genome increases genetic variability. Only mutations of gametes, and not somatic cells, are passed on to offspring.

The following are some forms of mutations:

- **Point mutation** is a change affecting a single base pair in a gene
- **Deletion** is the removal of a sequence of DNA, the regions on either side being joined together
- **Inversion** is the reversal of a segment of DNA
- **Translocation** is when one chromosome breaks and attaches to another
- **Duplication** is when a sequence of DNA is repeated.
- **Frame shift mutations** occur when bases are added or deleted in numbers other than multiples of three. Such deletions or additions cause the rest of the sequence to be shifted such that each triplet reading frame is altered.

A mutagen is any substance or agent that can cause a mutation. A mutagen is not the same as a carcinogen. Carcinogens are agents that cause cancer. While many mutagens are carcinogens as well, many others are not. The Ames test is a widely used test to screen chemicals used in foods or medications for mutagenic potential.

Mutations can produce many types of genetic diseases including inborn errors of metabolism. These disorders in normal metabolism are usually due to defects of a single gene that codes for one enzyme.

15.6 Genetics and Heredity: A Closer Look

The rest of this chapter begins to push into more advanced topics in genetics. However, these topics continue to represent legitimate exam material.

Epistasis occurs when one gene masks the phenotype of a second gene. This is often the case in pigmentation where one gene turns on (or off) the production of pigment, while a second gene controls the amount of pigment produced. Such is the case in mice fur where one gene codes for the presence or absence of pigmentation and the other codes for the color. If C and c represent the alleles for the presence or absence of color and B and b represent black and brown then a phenotype of CCbb and Ccbb would both correspond to a brown phenotype. Whenever cc is inherited the fur will be white.

Pleiotropy occurs when a single gene has more than one phenotypic expression. This is often seen in pea plants where the gene that expresses round or wrinkled texture of seeds also influences the expression of starch metabolism. For example, in wrinkled seeds there is more unconverted glucose which leads to an increase of the osmotic gradient. These seeds will subsequently contain more water than round seeds. When they mature they will dehydrate and produce the wrinkled appearance.

Polygenic inheritance refers to traits that cannot be expressed in just a few types but rather as a range of varieties. The most popular example would be human height which ranges from very short to very tall. This phenomenon (many genes shaping one phenotype) is the opposite of pleiotropy.

Penetrance refers to the proportion of individuals carrying a particular variant of a gene (allele or genotype) that also express the associated phenotype. Alleles which are highly penetrant are more likely to be noticed. Penetrance only considers whether individuals express the trait or not. *Expressivity* refers to the variation in the degree of expression of a given trait.

Nondisjunction occurs when the chromosomes do not separate properly and do not migrate to opposite poles as in normal anaphase of meiosis (BIO 14.2). This could arise from a failure of homologous chromosomes to separate in meiosis I, or the failure of sister chromatids to separate during meiosis II or mitosis. Most of the time, gametes produced after nondisjunction are sterile; however, certain imbalances can be fertile and lead to genetic defects. Down Syndrome (Trisomy 21 = 3 copies of chromosome 21 due to its nondisjunction, thus the person has an extra chromosome making a total of 47 chromosomes); Turner and Klinefelter Syndrome (nondisjunction of sex chromosomes); and Cri du Chat (deletion in chromosome 5) are well known genetic disorders. Hemophilia and red-green color blindness are common sex-linked disorders and are recessive.

Phenylketonuria, sickle-cell anemia and Tay-Sachs disease are common autosomal recessive disorders.

Gene linkage refers to genes that reside on the same chromosome and are unable to display independent assortment because they are physically connected (BIO 15.3). The further away the two genes are on the chromosome the higher probability there is that they will crossover during synapsis. In these cases recombination frequencies are used to provide a linkage map where the arrangement of the genes can be ascertained. For example, say you have a fly with genotype BBTTYY and the crossover frequency between B and T is 26%, between Y and T is 18% and between B and Y is 8%. Greater recombination frequencies mean greater distances so you know that B and T are the furthest apart. This corresponds to a gene order of B-Y-T and since frequencies are a direct measure of distance you know exactly how far apart each allele is and can easily calculate the map distances.

15.6.1 Mitochondrial DNA

Mitochondrial DNA (mtDNA or mDNA) has become increasingly popular as a tool to determine how closely populations are related as well as to clarify the evolutionary relationships among species (= phylogenetics). Mitochondrial DNA is circular (BIO 1.2.2, 16.6.3) and can be regarded as the smallest chromosome. In most species, including humans, mtDNA is inherited solely from the mother. The DNA sequence of mtDNA has been determined from a large number of organisms and individuals (including some organisms that are extinct).

15.7 DNA Recombination and Genetic Technology

DNA recombination involves DNA that contains segments or genes from different sources. The foreign DNA can come from another DNA molecule, a chromosome or from a complete organism. Most DNA transferred is done artificially using DNA recombination techniques which use restriction enzymes to cut pieces of DNA. These enzymes originate from bacteria and are extremely specific because they only cut DNA at specific recognition sequences along the strand. These recognition sites correspond to different nucleotide sequences and produce sticky and blunt ends when a double stranded DNA segment is cut.

The sticky end is the unpaired part of the DNA that is ready to bind with a complementary codon (sequence of three adjacent nucleotides; BIO 3.0). These cut pieces or **restriction fragments** are often inserted into plasmids (circular piece of DNA that is able to replicate independently of the chromosomal DNA) which are then able to be introduced into the bacteria via transformation (see BIO 2.2).

Treating the plasmid, or replicon, with the same restriction enzymes used on the original fragment produces the same sticky ends in both pieces allowing base pairing to occur when they are mixed together. This attachment is stabilized by DNA ligase. After the ends are joined and the recombinant plasmid is incorporated into bacteria, the bacteria become capable of producing copious amounts of a

Bacterium and Vector Plasmid

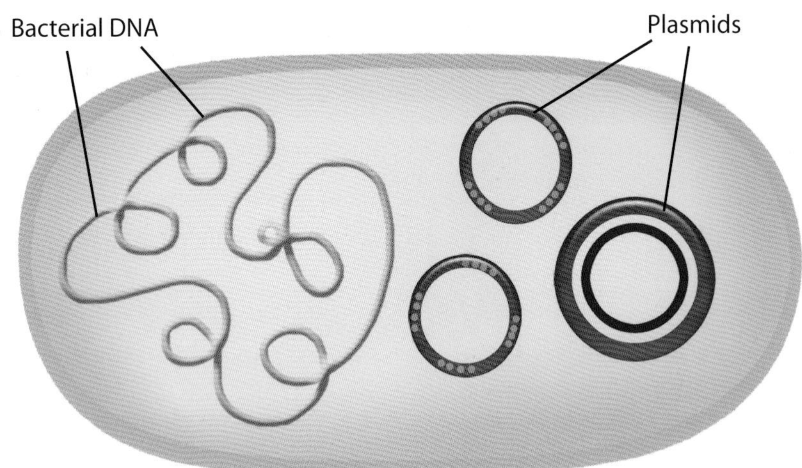

specific protein that was not native to its species (i.e. bacteria with recombinant DNA producing insulin to treat diabetes).

Gel electrophoresis is a method of separating restriction fragments of differing lengths based on their size (as described in the previous section, a restriction fragment is a fragment of DNA cleaved by a restriction enzyme). The DNA fragments are passed through a gel which is under the influence of an electric field. Since DNA is negatively charged it will move towards the cathode (positive electrode). The shorter fragments move faster than the longer ones and can be visualized as a banding pattern using autoradiography techniques.

SDS-PAGE, sodium dodecyl sulfate polyacrylamide gel electrophoresis (ORG 13), also separates proteins according to their electrophoretic mobility. SDS is an anionic detergent (i.e. negatively charged) which has the following effect: (1) linearize proteins and (2) give an additional negative charge to the linearized proteins. In most proteins, the binding of SDS to the polypeptide chain gives an even distribution of charge per unit mass, thus fractionation will approximate size during electrophoresis (i.e. not dependent on charge).

Restriction fragment length polymorphisms or RFLP is a technique that exploits variations in restriction fragments from one individual to another that differ in length due to polymorphisms, or slight differences in DNA sequences. The process involves digesting DNA sequences with different restriction enzymes, detecting the resulting restriction fragments by gel electrophoresis, and comparing their lengths. In DNA fingerprinting, commonly used to analyze DNA left at crime scenes, RFLP's are produced and compared to RFLP's of known suspects in order to catch the perpetrator.

Sometimes it is necessary to obtain the DNA fragment bearing the required gene directly from the mRNA that codes for the polypeptide in question. This is due to the presence of introns (non-coding regions on a DNA molecule; BIO 3.0) which prevent transcription of foreign genes in the genome of bacteria, a common problem in recombinant technology. To carry this out one can use reverse transcriptase producing complementary DNA (cDNA) which lack the problematic introns.

Rather than using a bacterium to clone DNA fragments, sometimes DNA is copied directly using the polymerase chain reaction (PCR). This method allows us to rapidly amplify the DNA content using synthetic primers that initiate replication at specific nucleotide sequences. This method relies on thermal cycling (repeated heating and cooling) of the DNA primers and can lead to thousands and even millions of copies in relatively short periods of time.

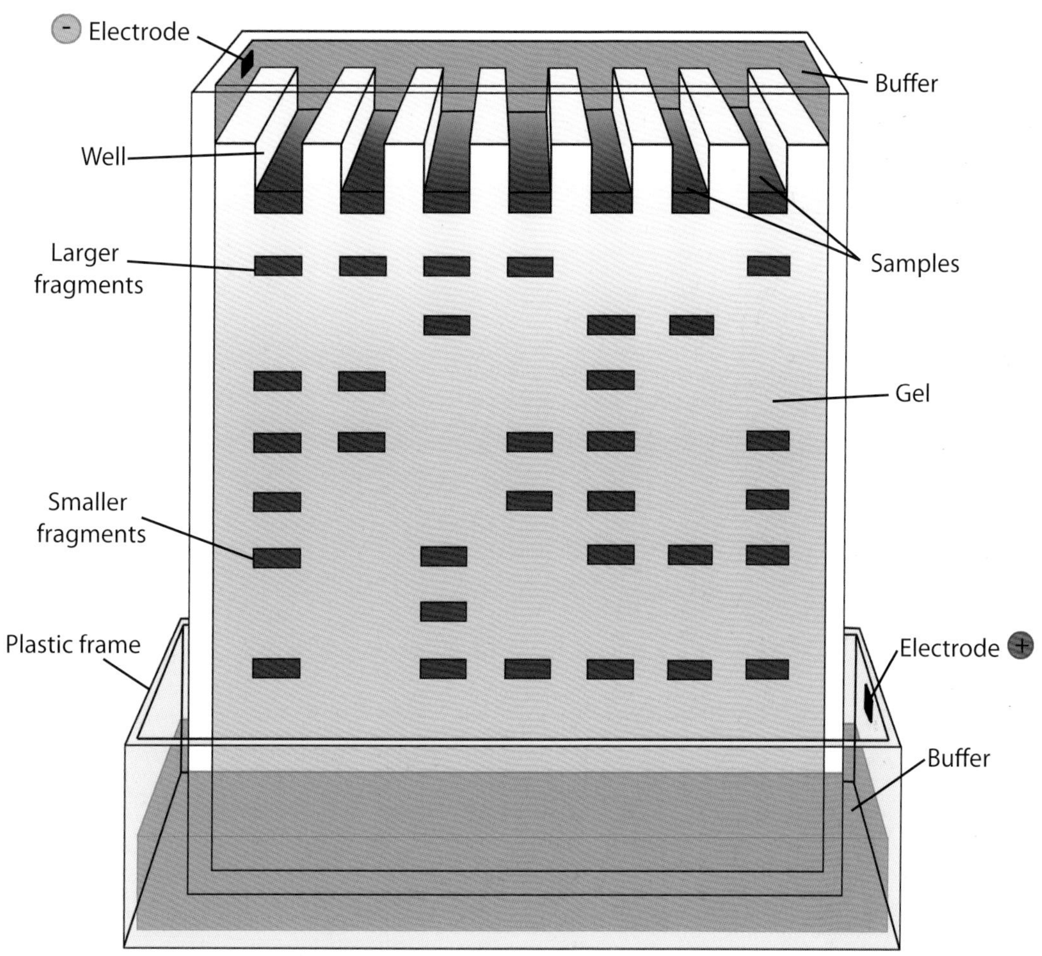

Figure IV.A.15.1: Gel Electrophoresis.

Southern blotting, named after Dr. E. Southern, is the process of transferring DNA fragments from the electrophoresis agarose gel onto filter paper where they are identified with probes. The procedure begins by digesting DNA in a mixture with *restriction endonucleases* to cut out specific pieces of DNA. The DNA fragments are then subjected to gel electrophoresis. The now separated fragments are bathed in an alkaline solution where they immediately begin to denature. These fragments are then placed (or blotted) onto nitrocellulose paper and then incubated with a specific probe whose location can be visualized with autoradiography.

Northern blotting is adapted from the Southern blot to detect specific sequences of RNA by hybridization with cDNA. Similarly, *Western blotting* is used to identify specific amino-acid sequences in proteins. Some students prefer to remember the blotting techniques with the mnemonic SNOW DROP.

SNOW	DROP
Southern	**D**NA
Northern	**R**NA
O	**O**
Western	**P**rotein

DNA microarray technology (= DNA chip or biochip or "laboratory-on-a-chip") helps to determine which genes are active and which are inactive in different cell types. This technology evolved from Southern blotting and can also be used to genotype multiple regions of a genome. DNA microarrays are created by robotic machines that arrange incredibly small amounts of hundreds or thousands of gene sequences on a single microscope slide. These sequences can be a short section of a gene or other DNA element that is used to hybridize a cDNA or cRNA (also called antisense RNA) sample. The hybridization is usually observed and quantified by the detection of fluorescent tag.

NB: The molecular biology techniques of FRAP (BIO 1.5) and ELISA (BIO 8.4) were described earlier in this book. Basic lab techniques and equipment are presented in General Chemistry Chapter 12. Electrophoresis and chromatography are discussed in Organic Chemistry Chapter 13.

GOLD STANDARD WARM-UP EXERCISES

CHAPTER 15: Genetics

1) Which of the following is the LEAST likely reason for the phenotype of PKU disease lacking phenylalanine hydroxylase?
   A. An added nucleotide in the genetic code results in an altered sequence of nucleotides which gets translated into an altered sequence of amino acids.
   B. A deletion in the genetic code results in an altered sequence of nucleotides which gets translated into an altered sequence of amino acids.
   C. The stereochemistry of the chromosome becomes altered.
   D. A deletion in the genetic code creates a stop codon in the nucleotide sequence.

2) In general terms, what is the primary genetic difference between a hepatocyte (a liver cell) and a muscle cell?
   A. The amount of DNA
   B. The number of chromosomes
   C. The number of genes
   D. The expression of genes

3) Over 10 million North Americans are treated for thyroid diseases and, overwhelmingly, women are much more likely than men to succumb to these conditions. Is it reasonable to conclude that thyroid disease is sex-linked?
   A. No, because thyroid disease appears to be caused by a defect of the immune system and not a defective DNA sequence.
   B. No, because if the disease was sex-linked, there would be a high incidence in the male, rather than the female, population.
   C. Yes, because the high incidence of the disease in women suggests that a gene found on the X chromosome codes for the disease.
   D. Yes, because the same factor increases the risk of women getting the disease, regardless of familial background.

4) Although the cloned sheep Dolly contains the exact DNA as her genetic mother, there are a few visible and behavioral differences in Dolly. This is most probably due to:
   A. the sheep in which the embryo was implanted.
   B. the induction of specific genes not expressed in the mother.
   C. mutations caused by incubation in the nutrient-deficient solution.
   D. environmental factors.

5) In fruit flies, males have XY sex chromosomes, females have XX, and white eye color is sex linked. If red-eyed (heterozygous) females are crossed with white-eyed males, what would be the expected eye colors and sexes of the progeny?
   A. ¾ white-eyed female and ¼ red-eyed male.
   B. ½ red-eyed female and ½ white-eyed male.
   C. All red eyed, half male and half female.
   D. ¼ red-eyed female, ¼ white-eyed female, ¼ red-eyed male and ¼ white-eyed male.

6) The members of a homologous pair of genes are separated during meiosis of reproductive cells so that each gamete contains one of the alleles. The preceding is an expression of which of the following laws?

A. The law of segregation
B. The law of sorting
C. The law of independent assortment
D. The law of gene isolation

7) Which of the following refers to a cross in which traits are considered simultaneously?

A. Filial cross
B. Double cross
C. Dihybrid cross
D. Punnett cross

8) Which of the following terms refers to the frequency with which a gene is expressed in a detectable way?

A. Penetrance
B. Polygenetics
C. Codominance
D. Allelism

9) Which of the following terms refers to the collection of all alleles of every gene present in the members of a population?

A. Genetic assortment
B. Population
C. Gene diversity
D. Gene pool

10) Although there is some evidence that pronounced differences in DNA content can interfere with chromosome pairing between species, the effect is surprisingly slight; hybrids between related species of grasses that differ by as much as 50 percent in DNA content have virtually normal chromosome pairing, chiasma formation and segregation. Which of the following processes likely occurs to allow the normal chromosome pairing observed in grass species?

A. The interstitial repetitive sequences in one homologous chromosome would loop so that pairing could occur.
B. The unpaired sequences in the homologous chromosome without the interstitial repetitive sequences would duplicate so that pairing could occur.
C. The homologous chromosome with the interstitial repetitive sequence would undergo a translocation so that pairing could occur.
D. The homologous chromosome with the interstitial repetitive sequence would undergo a deletion so that pairing could occur.

11) Von Willebrand's disease is an autosomal dominant bleeding disorder. A man who does not have the disease has two children with a woman who is heterozygous for the condition. If the first child expresses the bleeding disorder, what is the probability that the second child will have the disease?

A. 0.25
B. 0.50
C. 0.75
D. 1.00

12) A transfusion of red blood cells is being considered. Which of the following donors would NOT elicit and immune response in a recipient who is type B and Rh-negative?

A. One who was type A and Rh-negative.
B. One who was type AB and Rh-negative, but had been previously exposed to Rh-positive blood.
C. One who was type B and Rh-negative, but had been previously exposed to Rh-positive blood.
D. One who was type B and Rh-positive.

13) Given that the ABO system elicits a much stronger immune response (i.e. more immunogenic) than the Rh-factor, an Rh-negative type O mother carrying an Rh-positive child will most likely manufacture anti-Rh antibodies if fetal cells enter the maternal circulation if the child is:

A. type A.
B. type B.
C. type O.
D. type AB.

14) The risk of hemolytic disease of the newborn increases with each Rh-positive pregnancy that an Rh-negative woman has. The main reason for this is that:

A. the probability of the fetus being Rh-positive increases with every pregnancy.
B. Rh-negative antibodies in the maternal circulation can cross the placental barrier to attack and hemolyse the erythrocytes of the fetus.
C. anti-Rh antibodies in the maternal circulation can cross the placental barrier to attack and hemolyse the erythrocytes of the fetus.
D. anti-Rh agglutins are not strongly expressed in the fetal circulation.

15) Nonsense mutations and frame shift mutations would most likely originate during which of the following?

A. DNA replication
B. Transcription
C. Translation
D. Splicing

16) Consider the following crossover frequencies:

Crossover	*Genes Frequency*
B and *D*	2%
C and *A*	7%
A and *B*	15%
C and *B*	20%
C and *D*	25%

Which of the following represents the relative positions of the four genes A, B, C and D, on the chromosome?

A. *ADCB*
B. *CABD*
C. *DBCA*
D. *ABCD*

17) From which grandparent or grandparents did you inherit your mitochondria?

A. Paternal grandfather
B. Maternal grandmother
C. Mother's parents
D. Grandmothers

How can you distinguish the sex chromosomes? Pull down their genes! :)

GS ANSWER KEY

CHAPTER 15

		Cross-Reference			Cross-Reference
1.	C	BIO 15.1, 15.5	10.	A	BIO 15.5, 14.2, deduce
2.	D	BIO 15.1, 14.5.1	11.	B	BIO 15.3
3.	B	BIO 15.3	12.	C	BIO 15.2
4.	D	BIO 15.1	13.	C	BIO 15.2
5.	D	BIO 15.1, 15.3	14.	C	BIO 15.2, 15.3.1, 8.2
6.	A	BIO 15.3	15.	A	BIO 15.5, 1.2.2, 14.2
7.	C	BIO 15.3	16.	C	BIO 1.2.2, ORG 12.5
8.	A	BIO 15.6	17.	B	BIO 1.2.2
9.	D	BIO 15.4			

* Explanations can be found at the back of the book.

Go online to DAT-prep.com for additional chapter review Q&A and forum.

APPENDIX

CHAPTER 15: Genetics

Advanced DAT-30 Passage: Polymerase Chain Reaction

The polymerase chain reaction (PCR) is a powerful biological tool that allows the rapid amplification of any fragment of DNA without purification. In PCR, RNA primers are made to flank the specific DNA sequence to be amplified. These RNA primers are then extended to the end of the DNA molecule with the use of a heat-resistant DNA polymerase. The newly synthesized DNA strand is then used as the template to undergo another round of replication.

The 1st step in PCR is the melting of the target DNA into 2 single strands by heating the reaction mixture to approximately 94 °C, and then rapidly cooling the mixture to allow annealing of the RNA primers to their specific locations (note: annealing is the sticking together of complementary single strands which, of course, involves the formation of hydrogen bonds between the base pairs; BIO 1.2.2). Once the primer has annealed, the temperature is elevated to 72 °C to allow optimal activity of the DNA polymerase. The polymerase will continue to add nucleotides until the entire complimentary strand of the template is completed at which point the cycle is repeated (Figure 1).

One of the uses of PCR is sex determination, which requires amplification of intron 1 of the amelogenin gene. This gene found on the X-Y homologous chromosomes has a 184 base pair deletion on the Y homologue. Therefore, by amplifying intron 1, females can be distinguished from males by the fact that males will have 2 different sizes of the amplified DNA while females will only have 1 unique fragment size.

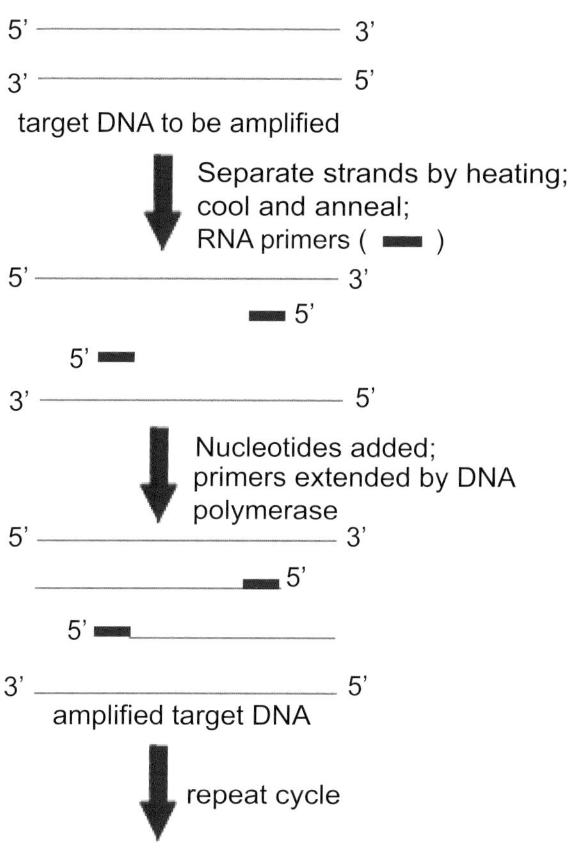

Figure 1

18) The polymerase chain reaction resembles which of the following cellular process?

A. Transcription of DNA
B. Protein synthesis
C. DNA replication
D. Translation

19) Why is a heat resistant DNA polymerase required for successive replication in the polymerase chain reaction, rather than simply a human DNA polymerase?

A. The high temperatures required to melt the DNA double strand may denature a normal human cellular DNA polymerase.
B. The high temperatures required to melt the DNA would cause human DNA polymerase to remain bound to the DNA strand.
C. Heat resistant DNA polymerase increases the rate of the polymerase chain reaction at high temperatures whereas human DNA polymerase lowers the rate.
D. Heat resistant DNA polymerase recognizes RNA primers whereas human DNA polymerase does not.

20) The use of PCR for sex determination relies on the fact that:

A. the amelogenin gene is responsible for an autosomal recessive trait.
B. the X and Y homologous chromosomes have different sizes of intron 1 of the amelogenin gene.
C. females have an X and Y chromosome and males have two X chromosomes.
D. intron 1 has a different nucleotide length than intron 2.

21) What would PCR amplification of an individual's intron 1 of the amelogenin gene reveal if the individual were male?

A. One type of intron 1 since the individual has one X chromosome and one Y chromosome.
B. Two types of intron 1 since the individual has only one X chromosome.
C. One type of intron 1 since the individual has only one X chromosome.
D. Two types of intron 1 since the individual has one X chromosome and one Y chromosome.

22) The technique that utilizes probes to detect specific DNA sequences is known as which of the following?

A. Southern blot
B. RFLP
C. Western blot
D. PCR

ANSWER KEY

ADVANCED TOPICS - CHAPTER 15

Cross-Reference

18.	C	BIO 1.2.2
19.	A	BIO 1.2.2, BIO 4.3, deduce
20.	B	BIO 15.3, Chap 15 Appendix
21.	D	BIO 15.3, Chap 15 Appendix
22	A	BIO 15.7, Chap 15 Appendix

P = paragraph; *S* = sentence; *E* = equation; *T* = table; *F* = figure

Go online to DAT-prep.com for additional chapter review Q&A and forum.

EVOLUTION
Chapter 16

Memorize

* Define: species, genetic drift
* The Six-Kingdom System: taxonomy, features of its members including structure and function

Understand

* Natural selection, speciation
* Genetic drift
* Basics: origin of life
* Basics: comparative anatomy
* Basics: eukaryotic, prokaryotic evolution

Importance

2 to 5 out of the 40 Biology DAT questions are based on content in this chapter (in our estimation).

* Note that between 25% and 50% of the questions in DAT Biology are from 5 chapters: 1, 2, 14, 15, and 16.

Introduction 

Evolution is, quite simply, the change in the inherited traits of a population of organisms from one generation to another. This change over time can be traced to 3 main processes: variation, reproduction and selection. The major mechanisms that drive evolution are natural selection and genetic drift. Chemical evolution led to cellular evolution and, ultimately, to the enormous diversity within 3 Domains and 6 Kingdoms.

Additional Resources

Free Online Q&A + Forum

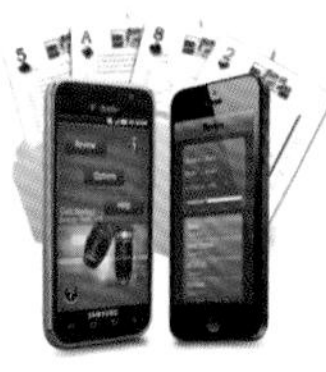

Flashcards

Special Guest

16.1 Overview

Evolution is the change in frequency of one or more alleles in a population's gene pool from one generation to the next. The evidence for evolution lies in the fossil record, biogeography, embryology, comparative anatomy, and experiments from artificial selection. The most important mechanism of evolution is the **selection** of certain phenotypes provided by the **genetic variability** of a population.

16.2 Natural Selection

Natural selection is the non-random differential survival and reproduction from one generation to the next. Natural selection contains the following premises: i) genetic and phenotypic variability exist in populations: offspring show variations compared to parents; ii) more individuals are produced than live to grow up and reproduce; iii) the population competes to survive; iv) individuals with some genes are more likely to survive (greater fitness) than those with other genes; v) individuals that are more likely to survive transmit these favorable variations (genes) to their offspring so that these genes become more dominant in the gene pool.

It is not necessarily true that natural selection leads to the the Darwin-era expression "survival of the fittest"; rather it is the genes, and not necessarily the individual, which are likely to survive.

Evolution goes against the foundations of the Hardy-Weinberg Law. For example, natural selection leads to non-random mating due to phenotypic differences. Evolution occurs when those phenotypic changes depend on an underlying genotype; thus non-random mating can lead to changes in allelic frequencies. Consider an example: if female peacocks decide to only mate with a male with long feathers, then there will be a selection pressure against any male with a genotype which is expressed as short feathers. Because of this differential reproduction, the alleles which are expressed as short feathers will be eliminated from the population. Thus this population evolves.

The three forms of natural selection are: i) **stabilizing selection** in which genetic diversity decreases as the population stabilizes on an average phenotype (*phenotypes have a "bell curve" distribution*). This is the most common form of natural selection. It is basically the opposite of disruptive selection, instead of favoring individuals with extreme phenotypes, it favors the intermediate phenotype; ii) **directional selection** when an extreme phenotype has a selective advantage over the average phenotype causing the allele frequency continually shifting in one direction (*thus the curve can become skewed to the left or right*). It occurs most often when populations migrate to new areas with environmental pressures; iii) **disruptive selection** where both extremes

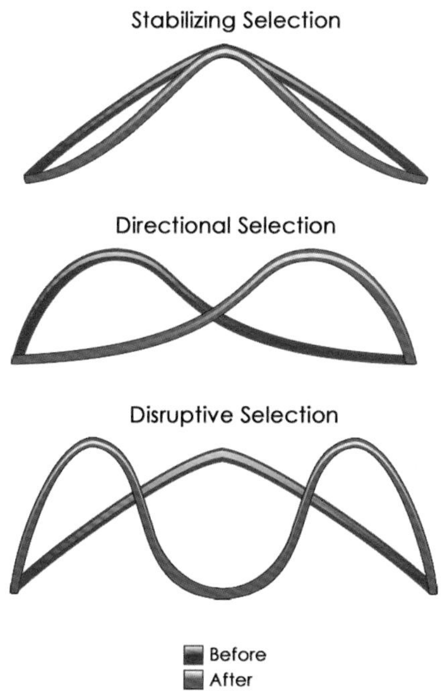

are selected over the average phenotype; this would produce a split down the middle of the "bell curve" such that two new and separate "bell curves" would result. For example, if a bird only ate medium sized seeds and left the large and small ones alone, two new populations or groups of seeds would have a reproductive advantage. Thus by selecting against the group of medium sized seeds, two new groups of large and small seeds will result. This is an example of group selection causing *disruptive selection*.

16.3 Species and Speciation

Species can be defined as the members of populations that interbreed or can interbreed under natural conditions. There are great variations within species. A **cline** is a gradient of variation in a species across a geographical area. **Speciation** is the evolution of new species by the isolation of gene pools of related populations. The isolation of gene pools is typically geographic. An ocean, a glacier, a river or any other physical barrier can isolate a population and prevent it from mating with other populations of the same species. The two populations may begin to differ because their mutations may be different, or, there may be different selection pressures from the two different environments, or, *genetic drift* may play a role.

Genetic drift is the random change in frequencies of alleles or genotypes in a population (recall that this is antagonistic to the Hardy-Weinberg Law). Genetic drift normally occurs when a small population is isolated from a large population. Since the allelic frequencies in the small population may be different from the large population (*sampling error*), the two populations may evolve in different directions.

Populations or species can be sympatric, in which speciation occurs after ecological, genetic or behavioral barriers arise within the same geographical boundary of a single population, or allopatric, in which speciation occurs through geographical isolation of groups from the parent population {Sympatric = live together, Allopatric = live apart}. Mechanisms involved in allopatric speciation are represented in the two preceding paragraphs.

The following represents some isolating mechanisms that prevent sympatric populations of different species from breeding together: i) habitat differences; ii) different breeding times or seasons; iii) mechanical differences (i.e. different anatomy of the genitalia); iv) behavioral specificity (i.e. different courtship behavior); v) gametic isolation (= fertilization cannot occur); vi) hybrid inviability (i.e. the hybrid zygote dies before reaching the age of sexual maturity); vii) hybrid sterility; viii) hybrid breakdown: the hybrid offspring is fertile but produces a next generation (F_2) which is infertile or inviable.

16.4 Origin of Life

Evidence suggests that the primitive earth had a reducing atmosphere with gases such as H_2 and the reduced compounds H_2O (vapor), $NH_{3(g)}$ (ammonia) and $CH_{4(g)}$ (methane). Such an atmosphere has been shown (i.e. Miller, Fox) to be conducive to the formation and stabilization of organic compounds. Such compounds can sometimes polymerize (*possibly due to autocatalysis*) and evolve into living systems with metabolism, reproduction, digestion, excretion, etc.

Critical in the early history of the earth was the evolution of: (1) the reducing atmosphere powered with energy (e.g. lightening, UV radiation, outgassing volcanoes) converting reduced compounds (water, ammonia, methane) into simple organic molecules (the 'primordial soup'); (2) self-replicating molecules surrounded by membranes forming protocells (very primitive microspheres, coacervates assembling into the precursor of prokaryotic cells: protobionts); (3) chemosynthetic bacteria which are anaerobes that used chemicals in the environment to produce energy; (4) photosynthesis which releases O_2 and thus converted the atmosphere into an oxidizing one; (5) respiration, which could use the O_2 to efficiently produce ATP; and (6) the development of membrane bound organelles (*a subset of prokaryotes which evolved into eukaryotes,* BIO 16.6.3) which allowed eukaryotes to develop meiosis, sexual reproduction, and fertilization.

It is important to recognize that throughout the evolution of the earth, organisms and the environment have and will continue to shape each other.

16.5 Comparative Anatomy

Anatomical features of organisms can be compared in order to derive information about their evolutionary histories. Structures which originate from the same part of the embryo are called homologous. **Homologous** structures may have similar anatomical features shared by two different species as a result of a common ancestor but with a late divergent evolutionary pattern in response to different evolutionary forces. Such structures may or may not serve different functions. **Analogous** structures have similar functions in two different species but arise from different evolutionary origins and entirely different developmental patterns (see Figure IV.A.16.1).

Vestigial structures represent further evidence for evolution since they are organs which are useless in their present owners, but are homologous with organs which are important in other species. For example, the appendix in humans is a vestige of an organ that had digestive functions in ancestral species. However, it continues to assist in the digestion of cellulose in herbivores.

Taxonomy is the branch of biology which deals with the classification of organisms. Humans are classified as follows:

Kingdom	Animalia
Phylum (= Division)	Chordata
Subdivision	Vertebrata
Class	Mammalia
Order	Primates
Family	Hominidae
Genus	*Homo*
Species	*Homo sapiens*

{Mnemonic for remembering the taxonomic categories: King Philip came over for great soup}

The subphyla Vertebrata and Invertebrata are subdivisions of the phylum Chordata. Acorn worms, tunicates, sea squirts and amphioxus are invertebrates. Humans, birds, frogs, fish, and crocodiles are vertebrates. We will examine features of both the chordates and the vertebrates.

Chordates have the following characteristics at some stage of their development: i) a notochord; ii) pharyngeal gill slits which lead from the pharynx to the exterior; iii) a hollow dorsal nerve cord. Other features which are less defining but are nonetheless present in chordates are: i) a more or less segmented anatomy; ii) an internal skeleton (= *endoskeleton*); iii) a tail at some point in their development.

Vertebrates have all the characteristics of chordates. In addition, vertebrates have: i) a vertebral column; ii) well developed sensory and nervous systems; iii) a ventral heart with a closed vascular system; iv) some sort of a liver, endocrine organs, and kidneys; and v) cephalization which is the concentration of sense organs and nerves to the front end of the body producing an obvious head.

16.6 Patterns of Evolution

The evolution of a species can be divided into four main patterns:

1. Divergent evolution – Two or more species originate from a common ancestor.
2. Convergent evolution – Two unrelated species become more alike as they evolve due to similar ecological conditions. The traits that resemble one another are called analogous traits. Similarity in species of different ancestry as a result of convergent evolution is homoplasty. For example, flying insects, birds and bats have evolved wings independently.
3. Parallel evolution – This describes two related species that have evolved similarly after their divergence from a common ancestor. For example, the appearance of similarly shaped leaves in many genera of plant species.
4. Coevolution – This is the evolution of one species in response to adaptations gained by another species. This most often occurs in predator/prey relationships where an adaptation in the prey species that makes them less vulnerable leads to new adaptations in the predator species to help them catch their prey (BIO 19.2, 19.4).

16.6.1 Macroevolution

Macroevolution describes patterns of evolution for groups of species rather than individual species. There are two main theories:

1. **Phyletic gradualism** – This theory argues that evolution occurs through gradual accumulation of small changes. They point to fossil evidence as proof that major changes in speciation occur over long periods of geological time and state that the incompleteness of the fossil record is the reason why some intermediate changes are not evidenced.
2. **Punctuated equilibrium** – This theory states that evolutionary history is marked

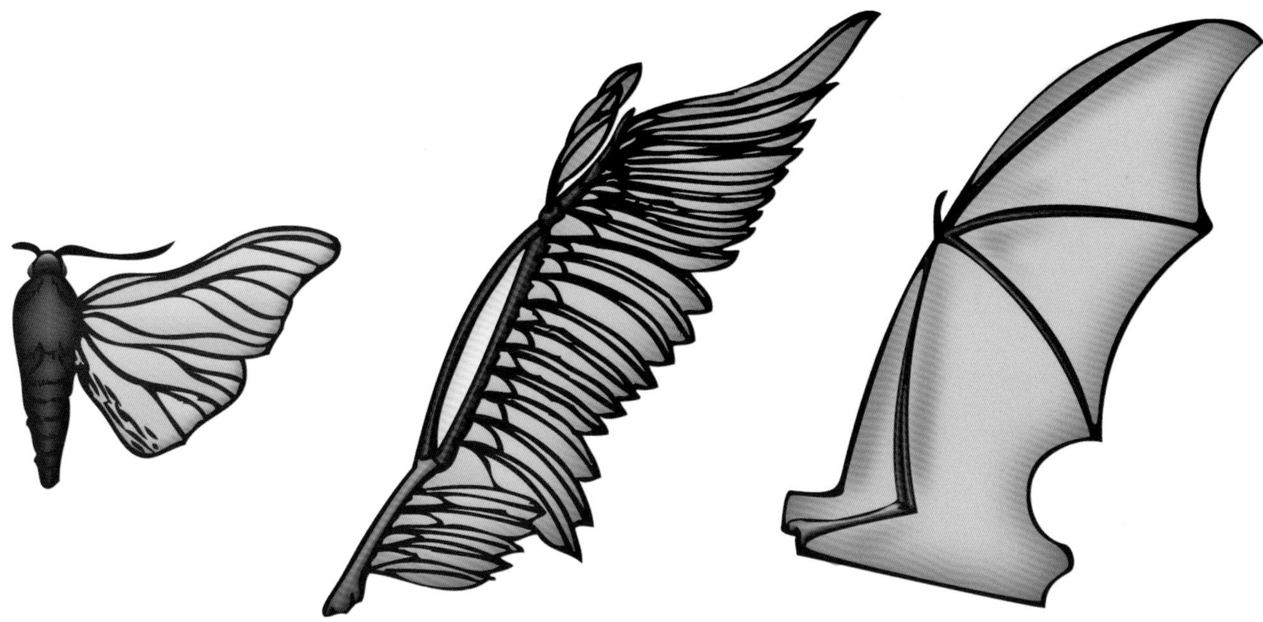

Figure IV.A.16.1: Analogous and homologous structures. The light blue wings represent analogous structures between different species: a flying insect, a bird and a bat, respectively. The bones are homologous structures. For example, green represents the humerus, purple represents the radius and ulna, red represents metacarpals and phalanges. Of course, insects have no bones. See the skeleton in BIO 11.3 to remind yourself of the meaning of some of these bony structures homologous in humans.

by sudden bursts of rapid evolution with long periods of inactivity in between. Punctuated equilibrium theorists point to the absence of fossils showing intermediate change as proof that evolution occurred in short time periods.

16.6.2 Basic Patterns for Changes in Macroevolution

1. Phyletic change (anagenesis): gradual change in an entire population that results in an eventual replacement of ancestral species by novel species and ancestral populations can be considered extinct.
2. Cladogenesis: one lineage gives rise to two or more lineages each forming a "clad". It leads to the development of a variety of sister species and often occurs when it is introduced to a new, distant environment.
3. Adaptive radiation: a formation of a number of lineages from a single ancestral species. A single species can diverge into a number of different species, which are able to exploit new environments.
4. Extinction: more than 99.9% of all species are no longer present.

16.6.3 Eukaryotic Evolution

Eukaryotes evolved from primitive heterotrophic prokaryotes in the following manner:

1. Heterotrophs first formed in the primordial soup (mixture of organic material) present in the early Earth (BIO 16.4). As the cells reproduced, competition increased and natural selection favored those heterotrophs who were best suited to obtain food.
2. Heterotrophs evolved into autotrophs (capable of making own food) via mutation. The first autotrophs were highly successful because they were able to manufacture their own food supply using light energy or energy from inorganic substrates (i.e. cyanobacteria).
3. As a by-product of the photosynthetic activity of autotrophs, oxygen was released into the atmosphere. This lead to formation of the ozone layer which prevented UV light from reaching the earth's surface. The interference of this major autotrophic resource was caused by the increased blockage of light rays.
4. Mitochondria, chloroplasts, and possibly other organelles of eukaryotic cells, originate through the symbiosis between multiple microorganisms. According to this theory, certain organelles originated as free-living bacteria that were taken inside another cell as endosymbionts. Thus mitochondria developed from proteobacteria and chloroplasts from cyanobacteria. This is the belief of the endosymbiotic theory which counts the following as evidence that it bodes true:
   - **A.** Mitochondria and chloroplasts possess their own unique DNA which is very similar to the DNA of prokaryotes (circular). Their ribosomes also resemble one another with respect to size and sequence.
   - **B.** Mitochondria and chloroplasts reproduce independently of their eukaryotic host cell.
   - **C.** The thylakoid membranes of chloroplasts resemble the photosynthetic membranes of cyanobacteria.

16.6.4 The Six-Kingdom, Three-Domain System

Organisms are classified into categories called *taxa* whereas species receive a name followed by a *genus*. Closely related animals are grouped in the same genus. Genera that share related features are grouped in a family which is then grouped into orders. Orders become grouped into classes, phyla and finally kingdoms (BIO 16.5).

The following is an example of how a dog is classified:

Kingdom > Animalia
Phylum > Chordata
Class > Mammalia
Order > Carnivora
Family > Canidae
Genus > Canis
Species > Canis familiaris

Five vs. Six Kingdoms

Over generations, taxonomists have developed several systems for the classification of organisms. From the model based on Linnaeus' hierarchical system grouping organisms based on common physical characteristics (1735), the 'classic' Five-Kingdom system evolved (1969): Monera, Protista, Fungi, Plantae, and Animalia.

Genetic sequencing has given researchers tools to group organisms based on molecular differences (primarily ribosomal RNA structure). By 1990, Woese's Three-Domain System was established. The domains are Archaea, Bacteria, and Eukarya.

Under this system, there are six kingdoms: Archaebacteria (ancient bacteria), Eubacteria (true bacteria), Protista, Fungi, Plantae, and Animalia. The Archaea and Bacteria domains contain prokaryotic organisms. Eubacteria are classified under the Bacteria domain and archaebacteria are classified as Archaeans.

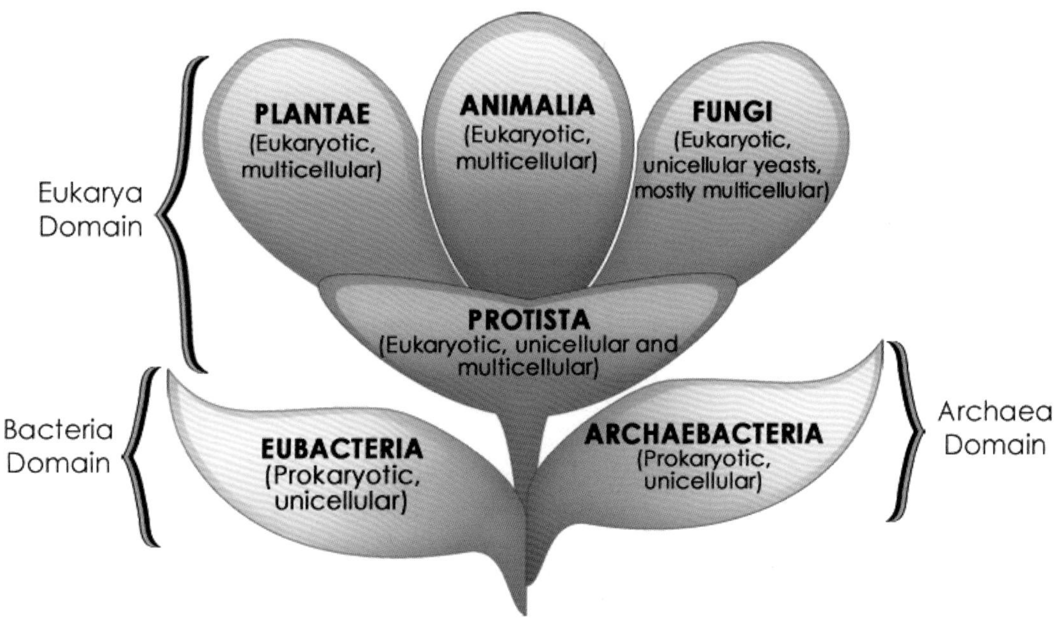

Figure IV.A.16.2: The Six-Kingdom, Three-Domain System.

The Eukarya domain includes eukaryotes and is subdivided into the kingdoms Protista, Fungi, Plantae, and Animalia.

Three-Domain System

- Archaea Domain
  Kingdom Archaebacteria
- Bacteria Domain
  Kingdom Eubacteria
- Eukarya Domain
  Kingdom Protista
  Kingdom Fungi
  Kingdom Plantae
  Kingdom Animalia

Kingdom Archaebacteria and Kingdom Eubacteria

The old designation of these 2 kingdoms was "Kingdom Monera". Every organism in this kingdom is a prokaryote which lack nuclei and various cellular organelles. Cell walls of most prokaryotes contain peptidoglycans. Many prokaryotes are categorized by their mode of nutrition. Autotrophs manufacture their own food and consist of photoautotrophs (use light energy) and chemoautotrophs (use inorganic sources). Various examples of inorganic substances used are H_2S, NH_3 and NO. Heterotrophs on the other hand must obtain their energy by consuming organic substances produced by autotrophs. Parasites prey on living tissues from a host while saprobes feed on decaying organic matter.

Prokaryotes are further divided based on their ability to survive with or without oxygen. Obligate aerobes require oxygen while obligate anaerobes can only survive in the absence of oxygen (see BIO 2.2).

Archaebacteria – The archaebacteria are classified by cell walls which lack peptidoglycan, ribosomes that resemble eukaryotic ribosomes and plasma membranes that differ in their lipid content. Examples of archaebacteria are methanogens, halophiles (salt lovers) and thermoacidophiles that can only live in hot, acidic environments such as springs or volcanic vents.

Eubacteria – Eubacteria (BIO 2.2) are mainly categorized by their mode of nutrition and by their means of motility (flagella or gliding). They are classified into three main shapes; cocci (spherical), bacilli (rod shaped) and spirilla (spiral). Finally, they are divided into either gram negative or gram positive. Bacteria that stain positive with the gram stain technique have a thick peptidoglycan wall while gram negative bacteria have a thin wall with very little peptidoglycan. Examples of eubacteria are cyanobacteria, chemosynthetic bacteria, nitrogen-fixing bacteria and spirochetes.

Kingdom Protista

Organisms in this kingdom can be algae-like, animal-like, fungus-like, unicellular or multicellular and do not generally possess strong evolutionary ties. The algae-like protists, such as phytoplankton which are important sources of food for marine organisms, all obtain their

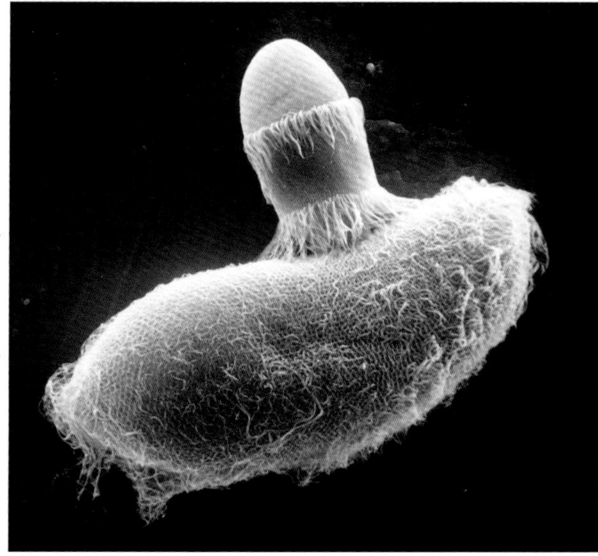

Figure IV.A.16.3: David and Golliath: Two animal-like unicellular, ciliated protists in an epic struggle. The larger of the two carnivores, Paramecium, is attacked from above by the smaller Didinium. In this case, the organisms were preserved for this SEM micrograph before the outcome could be determined. Like other ciliates (ciliaphora), they can reproduce asexually (binary fission) or sexually (conjugation); osmoregulation is via contractile vacuoles; and, they are also visible using a light microscope.

energy via photosynthesis and possess chlorophyll pigments. They are further characterized by the form of carbohydrate in which they use to store energy, the number of flagella present and the composition of their cells walls. Various examples of algae-like protists are euglenophyta, dinoflagellata, chlorophyta (green algae with both chlorophyll a and b and cellulose in their cell walls) and rhodophyta. The animal-like protists are all heterotrophic and include rhizopoda (amoebas), sporozoa, ciliophora and zoomastigophora. Fungus-like protists resemble fungi by forming spore-bearing bodies and include acrasiomycota (cellular slime molds), myxomycota (plasmodial slime molds) and oomycota (water molds). They exist in alternative forms between an aggregate form and an individual cell. The aggregate form consists of a large mass of cytoplasm (protoplasm) with many nuclei. It is not truly multicellular and such an arrangement is called coenocytic (many nuclei).

Kingdom Fungi

Fungi grow as a mass of hyphae called a *mycelium*. With the exception of yeast, fungi are multicellular (yeast are unicellular). Some fungi have septa which divide the hyphae into separate compartments containing individual nuclei. The fungi cell walls consist of chitin and they are either parasites or saprobes. Fungi are predominantly haploid and can reproduce sexually or asexually. The sexual reproduction involves temporary diploid structures while the asexual method of reproduction occurs through budding, fragmentation or asexual spores (sporangiospores and conidia). All fungi are heterotrophs. They may be parasitic or saprophytic (= saprobe; see detritivores, BIO 19.6). In either case, they absorb rather than ingest their food from the environment by secreting digestive enzymes outside their bodies.

Examples of fungi include *zygomycota* (lack septa and reproduce sexually by fusion of their hyphae with different strains of other neighboring hyphae), *ascomycota* (have septa and reproduce sexually by producing haploid ascospores), *basidiomycota* (have septa and reproduce sexually through haploid basidiospores), *deuteromycota* (no sexual reproduction observed, i.e. penicillin) and *lichens* (mutualistic associations between fungi and algae). See BIO 2.3 for an introduction to fungi.

Kingdom Plantae

The major adaptation for plants in order to survive the transition from water to land was evolving increasingly efficient methods of water conservation. Besides being vital for growth, water also played a major role in reproduction by providing a medium for the delivery of flagellated sperm to eggs. Plants also became much more susceptible to ultraviolet radiation. In order to combat these new problems plants have evolved several methods for survival on land:

1. Except for bryophytes (mosses) all plants have a diploid sporophyte as the dominant generation in their sexual reproduction. Diploid (2N) is more likely to survive radiation damage because of the presence of two alleles which allows recessive mutations to be masked. Plants undergo an alteration of generations with a sexual haploid stage (gametophyte) followed by an asexual diploid stage (sporophyte).
2. A waxy cuticle that limits desiccation (being dried out).
3. The development of a vascular system which eliminated the need for close proximity to water. Two groups of vascular tissues evolved, xylem and phloem, specializing in water transport and food transport, respectively.
4. Sperm became packaged as pollen allowing distribution via wind or animals; in advanced divisions of plants such as the anthophyta, the gametophytes are enclosed within an ovary.

The following is a list of the major plant divisions. All plants are multicellular, nonmotile, photosynthetic autotrophs. Notice how each division shows an increasingly greater adaptation to survival on land:

1. **Bryophyta** – The Bryophyta consist of the mosses, liverworts and hornworts. They are characterized by still being dependent on water for sexual reproduction and a lack of organized vascular tissue. Therefore, most bryophytes must live in moist places. Bryophytes undergo alteration of generations. The dominant life cycle stage is the haploid gametophyte, which is large and nutritionally independent. The sporophyte is small, short-lived and nutritionally dependent on the gametophyte for survival.
2. **Tracheophyta** – These divisions all contain vascular tissue xylem (water conducting) and phloem (food conducting) and are informally classified as tracheophytes. In contrast to Bryophytes, the sporophyte generation is dominant in Tracheophytes. The gametophyte is short-lived and nutritionally dependent.
3. **Coniferophyta** – The conifers include pines, firs, cedars and redwoods and are part of the gymnosperm group. Conifers produce seeds that contain a

partially developed sporophyte that has been arrested in its development. The gametophyte stage is short-lived. The male microsporangia meiotically produce many haploid microspores, which mature into the pollen grains (male gametophyte). As pollen grains can be carried by wind, the requirement of a water environment is eliminated for conifers. The pollen grain grows into a tube and provides a path for the sperm to reach the egg through an opening called the micropyle. The female macrosporangia produce haploid cells. Three of the four degenerate and the fourth one survives to become the megaspore (female gametophyte). The ovule is the final result.

4. **Angiosperms** – These are the flowering plants and consist of some major parts, including the pistil which is the female reproductive structure and consists of the ovary, style and stigma. The ovary develops into the fruit. The stamen is the male counterpart and consists of a pollen-bearing anther and a filament stalk. The petals attract the pollinators (= biotic vectors that move pollen from the male anthers to the female stigma for fertilization like bees or other insects). The anther of the male stamen produces microspores and the ovary of the female pistil produces megaspores. Fertilization occurs when pollen lands on the sticky stigma and a pollen tube grows down the style towards the ovule. One sperm cell fertilizes the egg forming a diploid zygote while the other sperm cell fuses with polar nuclei forming the triploid endosperm (3N) which is the food source for the growing embryo. This is collectively referred to as double fertilization. {Note: Plants will be further explored in Chapter 17; see BIO 1.5 to see an endosperm cell in mitosis.}

Kingdom Animalia

All members of Kingdom Animalia are multicellular, heterotrophic, display motility, have a dominant diploid generation in their life cycle and undergo a period of embryonic development with two or three germ layers (BIO 14.5). The coelomate can also be divided into two branches: deuterostomes and protostomes. There is however tremendous diversity which is evidenced in the following characteristics:

1. **Tissue complexity** – Most animals are part of the eumetazoa (true tissues) group and are diploblastic (possessing two germ layers) or triploblastic (three layers). However, the parazoan cells are not organized into true tissues and no organs develop.
2. **Body symmetry** – Animals are either radial or bilateral. Radial symmetry features a top and bottom but no front nor back; bilateral symmetry features top, bottom, front and back. Radial symmetry animals consist of two phyla: cnidaria and ctenophore, which are diploblastic. All the rest belong to bilateral symmetry, which are triploblastic (possessing a third germ layer, the mesoderm) and can be further divided into acoelomate (lack

of coelom), pseudocoelomate (incomplete lining of coelom) and true coelom.

3. **Cephalization** – A progressively greater increase in nerve tissue towards the head.
4. **Coelom** – A fluid filled *coelom* (= body cavity) cushions the internal organs and its presence correlates with body size. An acoelomate lacks a coelom (platyhelminthes and rhynchocoela) while a pseudocoelomate possesses a cavity that is not completely lined by mesoderm (rotifera and nematoda). A true coelom consists of a fluid filled cavity within the mesoderm, which is completely lined by epithelium (annelida, mollusca, arthropoda, echinoderm and chordates).
5. **Protostomes and deuterostomes** – The coelomates can also be divided into two branches: deuterostomes and protostomes. This has to do with the type of cleavage, or cell division that takes place during the development of the zygote. Protostomes features spiral cleavage and the archenteron (infolding of the gut during embryogenesis) develops into the mouth followed by anus formation. Deuterostomes display radial cleavage and the archenteron forms the anus followed by mouth formation. Major protostome phyla include platyhelminthes, nematoda, mollusca, annelida and arthropoda. Major deuterostome phyla include echinodermata and chordates.
6. **Differentiation of tissue and organs** – Animals exhibit variant degrees of differentiation. Simple animals develop few systems (i.e. reproductive system, digestive system) to support life. Advanced animals present with higher degrees of differentiation (i.e. digestive system, reproductive system, nervous system, circulatory system, etc.). For example, regarding the circulatory system: (1) Porifera, Cnidaria, Platyhelminthes and Nematoda have none; (2) the open circulatory system is common to molluscs and arthropods and other invertebrates. "Blood" (= *hemolymph*) is pumped by a heart into a body cavity (= *hemocoel*) where tissues are bathed so they can access oxygen and nutrients by diffusion. The blood moves slowly and the animal must move its muscles to move the blood within the cavities (compare with the human lymphatic system: BIO 7.6); (3) the closed circulatory system is present in all vertebrates (i.e. humans; see BIO 7.1-7.5) and a few invertebrates (i.e. annelids, cephalopods). Closed circulatory systems have the blood within vessels at higher pressure and moving at greater speeds. In this type of system, blood is pumped by a heart through vessels, and does not normally fill body cavities. Birds and mammals (also crocodilians) have a four-chambered heart which acts as two separate pumps (BIO 7.2, 7.3).
7. **Locomotion** – All animals exhibit some form of locomotion, in contrast to plants, which are considered non-motile. Animals can have a support structure for muscle that is external (exoskeleton, i.e. Mollusca, Arthropoda) or internal (endoskeleton, i.e. Porifera, Echinodermata,

Chordata). A hydrostatic skeleton, composed of fluid under pressure in closed compartments, is used by soft bodied animals like Cnidaria, Nematoda, Annelida, Echinodermata, etc.

There are ten major phyla:

1. **Porifera** – Sponges are classified with the parazoa because they do not display true tissues. They feed via a filtering mechanism ("suspension feeders") where food is drawn in by flagellated cells called choanocytes (also called "collar cell" because there is a collar of cytoplasm surrounding the flagellum), through a cavity (= *spongocoel*) and out through an opening (= *osculum*). The body is two layered: an outer epidermis layer and an inner sheet consisting of choanocytes. Their spongy wall contains spicules made from $CaCO_3$. Most sponges are *hermaphrodites* which means that each individual functions as both male and female.
2. **Cnidaria** – Hydrozoans, jellyfish and corals. Cnidarians are also composed of two layers: the ectoderm and the endoderm and contain a digestive sac that is sealed at one end. A single opening functions as both mouth and anus. They display radial symmetry and feature two body types: the medusa (floating umbrella shaped structure) and the sessile (= *attached*) polyp (cylindrical in shape and elongated at the axis of the body). Cnidarians are *carnivores* (BIO 19.3) and their specialized features include: a nerve net and tentacles armed with *cnidocytes* which are cells with organelles (= *nematocysts*) that eject a stinging thread. This is responsible for the stings delivered by jellyfish.
3. **Platyhelminthes** – Flatworms (planarians, flukes and tapeworms) that are bilaterally symmetrical and develop from three germ layers and are thus known as triploblastic. They do not have digestive tracts (acoelomates) or circulatory systems. Many flatworms have evolved adaptations to suit their parasitic nature; for example, tapeworms feature hooks and suckers near the "head" (= *scolex*) which help them attach to the digestive tracts of humans. The bodies of platyhelminthes are divided into segments (*proglottids*) which contain the male and female reproductive structures, so each segment can reproduce independently.
4. **Nematoda** –Roundworms with locomotion by peristalsis and possess pseudocoelomate bodies with complete digestive tracts. However, they lack circulatory systems. Some species of nematodes are important parasites of plants and animals.
5. **Rotifera** – Rotifers with complete digestive tracts and that are mostly filter feeders (through action of their cilia).
6. **Mollusca** – Snails, oysters, clams, squids and octopuses. Most possess shells and are coelomates with complete digestive tracts. They secrete a calcium carbonate substance which is later incorporated into their exoskeleton

(= external skeleton; i.e. shell). They breathe by gills and contain an open circulatory system, except for the cephalopods, and a highly developed nervous system. The class Cephalopoda (squids, octopuses, cuttlefish) are carnivores with beak-like jaws surrounded by tentacles.

7. **Annelida** – Earthworms and leeches that all display segmentation. Annelida have true coeloms (true body cavity completely lined with epithelium). They have well defined systems including nervous, digestive and closed circulatory systems. Earthworms have *setae* (tiny bristles) on their bodies which help them move around in the soil while leeches possess suckers at opposite ends of their bodies that are used for attachment and movement. Leeches suck blood and can secrete a chemical (= *hirudin*) to prevent blood from clotting.

8. **Arthropoda** – Spiders, insects and crustaceans (= crabs, lobsters, shrimp, etc.). All have jointed appendages, well developed nervous systems, specialization of body segments and an exoskeleton (= shell or *cuticle*) made of layers of protein and the polysaccharide chitin (BIO 20.3.3). When an arthropod grows, it sheds its exoskeleton (= *molting*) through a process called *ecdysis*. Arthropods have an open circulatory system and are true coelomates. They are the most successful of the invertebrates with respect to the numbers of species.

9. **Echinodermata** – Sea stars ("starfish"), urchins and sand dollars. Unlike the previous phyla, the echinodermata are deuterostomes that most closely resemble the next and final phyla, the chordates. Evolutionary evidence suggests a link between echinoderms and chordates. Echinoderms are radially symmetrical as adults (with multiples of 5, like traditional starfish) and bilaterally symmetrical as larvae or embryos. They possess true coeloms. Most echinoderms, including starfish, are slow-moving or sessile marine animals. They have a thin epidermis covering an endoskeleton of hard calcareous plates. They have a unique water vascular system which is a network of hydraulic canals branching into tube feet that aid in locomotion and feeding. Males and females are usually separate. Starfish can regrow lost arms.

10. **Chordata** – These are deuterostomes and include invertebrates (tunicates and lancelets) or vertebrates (sharks, fish, amphibians, birds and humans). All possess four principle features:
    - **A** A notochord during development
    - **B** A dorsal hollow nerve cord that forms the basis of the nervous system
    - **C** Pharyngeal gill slits in adulthood or at some early stage of embryonic development
    - **D** A muscular tail at some stage

Humans are, of course, vertebrates. Details of the various body systems of humans have already been reviewed in Chapters 6 to 14.

Taxonomy is not being truly respected when the word "invertebrates" is being used.

You might have already noticed that the term "invertebrate" covers several phyla: Porifera, Cnidaria, Echinodermata, Platyhelminthes, etc., and, of course, the subphylum Invertebrata! In fact, it would be easier to state the reverse: all Animalia are invertebrates and thus do not develop a vertebral column, except for 3% of all animals which are in the subphylum Vertebrata. Although the preceding states a fact, it is an imperfect and, almost random, way to divide the immense Kingdom Animalia.

GOLD STANDARD WARM-UP EXERCISES

CHAPTER 16: Evolution

1) All of the following can provide evidence for evolution EXCEPT one. Which is the EXCEPTION?

   A. Fossil record
   B. Embryology
   C. Spontaneous generation
   D. Comparative anatomy

2) Which one of the following would cause the Hardy-Weinberg principle to be inaccurate?

   A. Individuals mate with each other at random.
   B. There is no source of new copies of alleles from outside the population.
   C. The size of the population is very large.
   D. Natural selection is present.

3) Which statement most accurately reflects what geneticists refer to as “fitness”?

   A. Fitness reflects the number of mates each individual of the population reproduces with.
   B. Fitness is a measure of the contribution of a genotype to the gene pool of the next generation.
   C. Fitness refers to the relative health of a population as a whole.
   D. Fitness is the measure of the relative health of individuals within a population.

4) The increasing occurrence over time of very colorful male birds with a reduction in moderately colorful male birds is an example of:

   A. directional selection.
   B. stabilizing selection.
   C. disruptive selection.
   D. the bell curve.

5) Which one of the following populations would most quickly lead to two groups with few shared traits?

   A. A population with stabilizing selection
   B. A population with disruptive selection
   C. A population with no selection
   D. A population with directional selection

6) The random loss of alleles in a population is called:

   A. natural selection.
   B. mutation.
   C. genetic drift.
   D. nondisjunction.

7) Which of the following molecules is thought to have been absent from the primitive reducing atmosphere?

   A. Ammonia (NH_3)
   B. Water vapor (H_2O)
   C. Oxygen (O_2)
   D. Hydrogen (H_2)

8) All of the following is true about a protocell EXCEPT one. Which is the EXCEPTION?

A. It would have contained a biochemical pathway for energy metabolism and self-replicating molecules.
B. It would have been present before the development of a true cell.
C. It might have been like a coacervate droplet in which a semipermeable boundary allows some materials to be absorbed from the surrounding environment.
D. It did not contain a nucleus but had a cell wall and circular DNA.

9) The appearance of photosynthetic cyanobacteria and aerobic bacteria in the early history of the Earth:

A. eliminated the conditions that originally led to the first life on Earth.
B. resulted in the development of an oxidizing atmosphere on Earth.
C. led to the production of the ozone layer and thus reduced the amount of UV light reaching the Earth.
D. All of the above.

10) A taxon consisting of the most closely related species is called a(n):

A. genus.
B. family.
C. order.
D. class.

11) The structural similarities between the flippers of whales and the arms of humans are used to show that:

A. humans and whales have a common ancestry.
B. humans began life in water.
C. whales evolved from humans.
D. whales can swim but humans are not meant to swim.

12) All chordates possess a:

A. hollow dorsal nerve cord.
B. vertebral column.
C. closed vascular system.
D. tail in the adult form.

13) The theory that evolutionary change is slow and continuous is known as:

A. punctuated equilibrium.
B. geographic isolation.
C. gradualism.
D. speciation.

14) Unicellular eukaryotes could be found in:

A. Fungi and Eubacteria.
B. Fungi and Protista.
C. Fungi, Protista and Eubacteria.
D. only Protista.

15) Sponges are included in which of the following phyla?

A. Annelida
B. Cnidaria
C. Porifera
D. Rotifera

16) The most successful of the invertebrate groups with respect to the numbers of species is:

A. Mollusca.
B. Echinodermata.
C. Arthropoda.
D. Annelida.

17) Which of the following groups is characterized by radially symmetrical members?

A. Annelids
B. Cnidaria
C. Mollusks
D. Arthropods

18) A flatworm lacks:

A. a true coelom.
B. bilateral symmetry.
C. bilateral symmetry and a true coelom.
D. bilateral symmetry, a true coelom, and mesodermal tissue.

19) Which of the following has a gut with two openings, a mouth and an anus?

A. Annelids
B. Cnidarians
C. Tapeworms
D. Flatworms

20) Exoskeletons are characteristic of which of the following?

A. Echinoderms
B. Mollusks
C. Arthropods
D. B and C

GS ANSWER KEY

Chapter 16

		Cross-Reference			Cross-Reference
1.	C	BIO 16.1	11.	A	BIO 16.5
2.	D	BIO 15.4, 16.2	12.	A	BIO 16.5, 16.6.4
3.	B	BIO 16.2	13.	C	BIO 16.6.1
4.	A	BIO 16.2	14.	B	BIO 16.6.4
5.	B	BIO 16.2	15.	C	BIO 16.6.4
6.	C	BIO 16.3	16.	C	BIO 16.6.4
7.	C	BIO 16.4, 16.6.3	17.	B	BIO 16.6.4
8.	D	BIO 16.4	18.	A	BIO 16.6.4
9.	D	BIO 16.4, 16.6.3, 16.6.4	19.	A	BIO 16.6.4
10.	A	BIO 16.5	20.	D	BIO 16.6.4

* Explanations can be found at the back of the book.

Go online to DAT-prep.com for additional chapter review Q&A and forum.

Go online to DAT-prep.com for additional chapter review Q&A and forum.

PLANTS
Chapter 17

Memorize

* Kingdom Plantae: basic taxonomy, biochemistry, structures and function

Understand

* Monocots vs. dicots
* Seeds, tissues, roots, leaves
* Sap transportation
* Plant hormones, responses to stimuli
* Photosynthesis: light/dark, C3/C4/CAM

Importance

0 to 2 out of the 40 Biology

DAT questions are based on content in this chapter (in our estimation).

* Note that between 25% and 50% of the questions in DAT Biology are from 5 chapters: 1, 2, 14, 15, and 16.

DAT-Prep.com

Introduction 

Plants are eukaryotes with cell walls with cellulose and obtain most of their energy from sunlight via photosynthesis using chlorophyll contained in chloroplasts, which gives them their green color. Plants provide most of the world's free oxygen and basic foods. We have already explored the basic features of Kingdom Plantae in BIO 16.6.4.

Additional Resources

Free Online Q&A + Forum

Flashcards

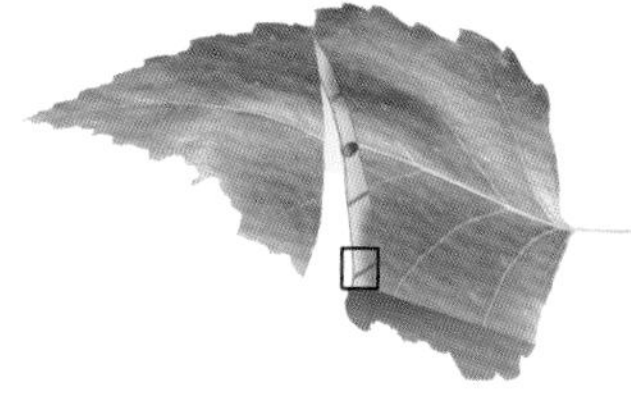

Special Guest

17.1 Plants: Monocots vs. Dicots

A major distinction in plants lies within the angiosperms (see BIO 16.6.4 for an overview of Kingdom Plantae). The angiosperms, along with the gymnosperms comprise the seed plants. Angiosperms, however, can be divided into *monocots* and *dicots*. The differences are as follows:

1. Monocots have only one cotyledon (nutritive tissue for developing seedling) where as dicots have two.
2. Monocots have a parallel pattern of veins in their leaves while dicots display a netted pattern.
3. Monocot petals come in multiples of three while dicots are multiples of four or five.
4. The vascular bundle (xylem and phloem tissue) is scattered in monocots and ring-patterned in dicots.
5. Monocots have fibrous roots and dicots have taproots (large single root).

17.2 Plant Tissues

There are three major groups of plant tissue:

1. **Ground tissue** – This includes the parenchyma cells (most common type, can be specialized in gas exchange, storage and photosynthesis or can remain totipotent and be able to divide to produce new populations of undifferentiated cells), the collenchyma (thick walls, function in mechanical support and meanwhile offer flexibility, therefore also known as "plastic support" cells) and schlerenchyma (similar to collenchyma but with thicker walls, provide load-bearing support). The hypodermis can be found below (= *hypo*) the epidermis and includes some ground tissue. Two groups of sclerenchyma cells exist: fibers and sclereids. Their walls consist of cellulose, hemicellulose and lignin.
2. **Dermal tissue** – Epidermal portion of the plants, covered by a waxy cuticle in the aerial parts and consists of guard cells that surround the stomata, glandular cells and epidermal hair cells.
3. **Vascular tissue** – Consists of the xylem and phloem which together form vascular bundles. The xylem cells are often located toward the center of the vascular bundle. Their thick cell walls provide mechanical support and are made up of dead cells. Its primary function is to conduct water and minerals up the plant. There are two types of xylem cells: trancheids and vessel elements.

The water passes through tracheids, specialized types of xylem cells, which are long and tapered. They also travel through vessel members which have small perforations in them to make the movement of water more efficient. Phloem are located toward the outside of the vascular bundle and are made up of sieve-tube members that form tubes. Unlike xylem, the phloem is comprised of living tissue even though they lack nuclei. Cambium cells are a type of actively dividing, undifferentiated cell known as meristem lying between the phloem and xylem. They provide for lateral growth of plants by adding to phloem or xylem. The vascular cambium is the source of both the secondary xylem (cambium located near the xylem) and the secondary phloem (cambium located near the phloem). Their primary function is to transport nutrients (i.e. carbohydrates) down the stem.

17.2.1 Seeds

The formation of a seed after fertilization completes the process of reproduction in seed plants. The seed itself consists of an embryo, a seed coat and endosperm which surrounds the embryo and provides nutrition in the form of starch, though it can also contain oils and protein. The zygote divides mitotically to form a mass of cells (= embryo), which is an immature plant that will develop into a new plant under proper conditions.

An embryo is composed of different parts, the epicotyl which forms the shoot (stems, flowering stems and leaves), the hypocotyl which connects the epicotyl, the radicle which develops into the primary root, the cotyledons which form the seed leaves, the endosperm which stores nutrition, and the seed coat which develops from integument of the ovule and forms the outer covering of the seed.

In monocotyledonous plants, a protective sheath (= coleoptile) is present to protect emerging shoots. Germination is a process in which metabolic pathways in a seed embryo are reactivated leading to growth and the emergence of a seedling above the soil surface. It occurs when the seed receives an environmental cue (most likely water). In order for the seed coat to split, the embryo soaks up water during the water imbibition phase. The seed coat cracks and the hypocotyl begins to elongate forming the early shoot. Primary growth now begins at the tips called the *apical meristems* which contain actively dividing meristematic (undifferentiated) cells, much like stem cells in humans. The root grows via a zone of cell

Dicot Seed

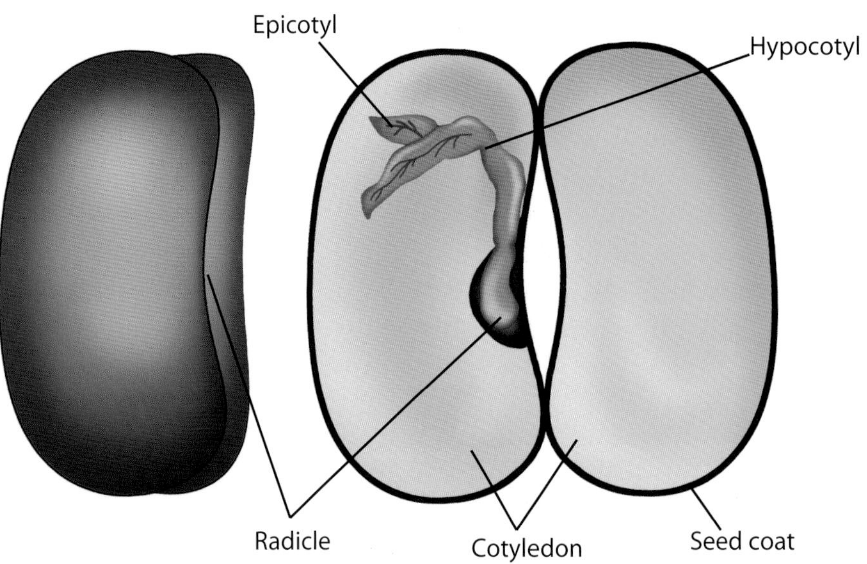

division located in the apical meristem. The cells now elongate in the zone of elongation and are followed by the zone of maturation where cells differentiate into xylem, phloem or epidermal tissues.

17.2.2 Roots

Roots consist of the following specialized tissues:

1. **Epidermis** – Lines the outside of the root and feature root hairs which increase the surface area for better absorption.
2. **Cortex** – The cortex, composed mostly of undifferentiated cells, makes up the bulk of the root and functions in storage and transportation of materials into the center of the root through diffusion.
3. **Endodermis** – Found at the innermost portion of the cortex. Contains suberin that creates a water-impenetrable barrier called the <u>Casparian strip</u>. All water is forced to pass through the endodermal cells and not between them. Therefore, water moving into or out of the xylem through the diffusional space outside the plasma membranes can be regulated by endodermal cells to control the degree of movement of water and the uptake of ions or molecules.

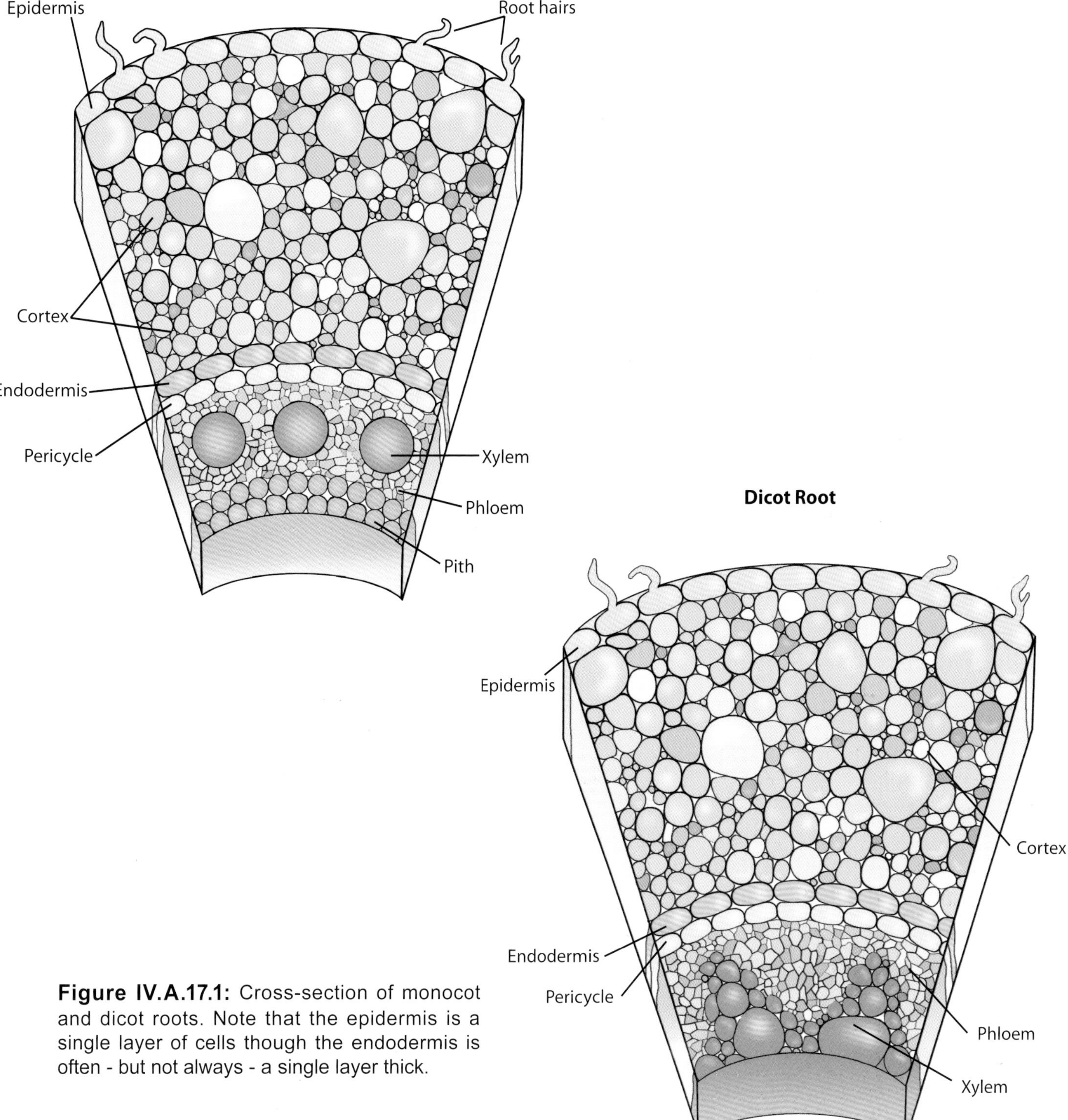

Figure IV.A.17.1: Cross-section of monocot and dicot roots. Note that the epidermis is a single layer of cells though the endodermis is often - but not always - a single layer thick.

4. **Stele** – The stele makes up the tissues inside the endodermis and consists of the pericycle from which the lateral roots arise, xylem found in the center and phloem cells which occupy the regions between the xylem lobes. In monocot roots, there is a pith, or medulla, which is surrounded by the xylem and phloem. The pith is composed of soft, spongy parenchyma cells, which store and transport nutrients throughout the plant. Observe the illustrations and BIO 17.2.4 for the differences between monocots and dicots.

17.2.3 Leaves

Leaves display the following structures:

1. **Epidermis** – Covered by a waxy, acellular cuticle which reduces transpiration (loss of water through evaporation). The epidermis serves several functions: protection against water loss through transpiration, regulation of gas exchange and absorption of water.
2. **Palisade mesophyll** – tightly packed cells directly under the epidermis. This layer contains many more chloroplasts than the spongy layer below. The regular arrangement of these cells allows maximal absorption of sunlight for photosynthesis to occur.
3. **Spongy mesophyll** – Consists of loosely arranged parenchyma cells with the intercellular air spaces acting as chambers that provide CO_2 to photosynthesizing cells.
4. **Guard cells** – Flank the stomata and function as specialized cells that control opening and closing allowing gas exchange.
5. **Vascular bundles** – Consist of xylem, phloem and bundle sheath cells that surround the vascular bundles.

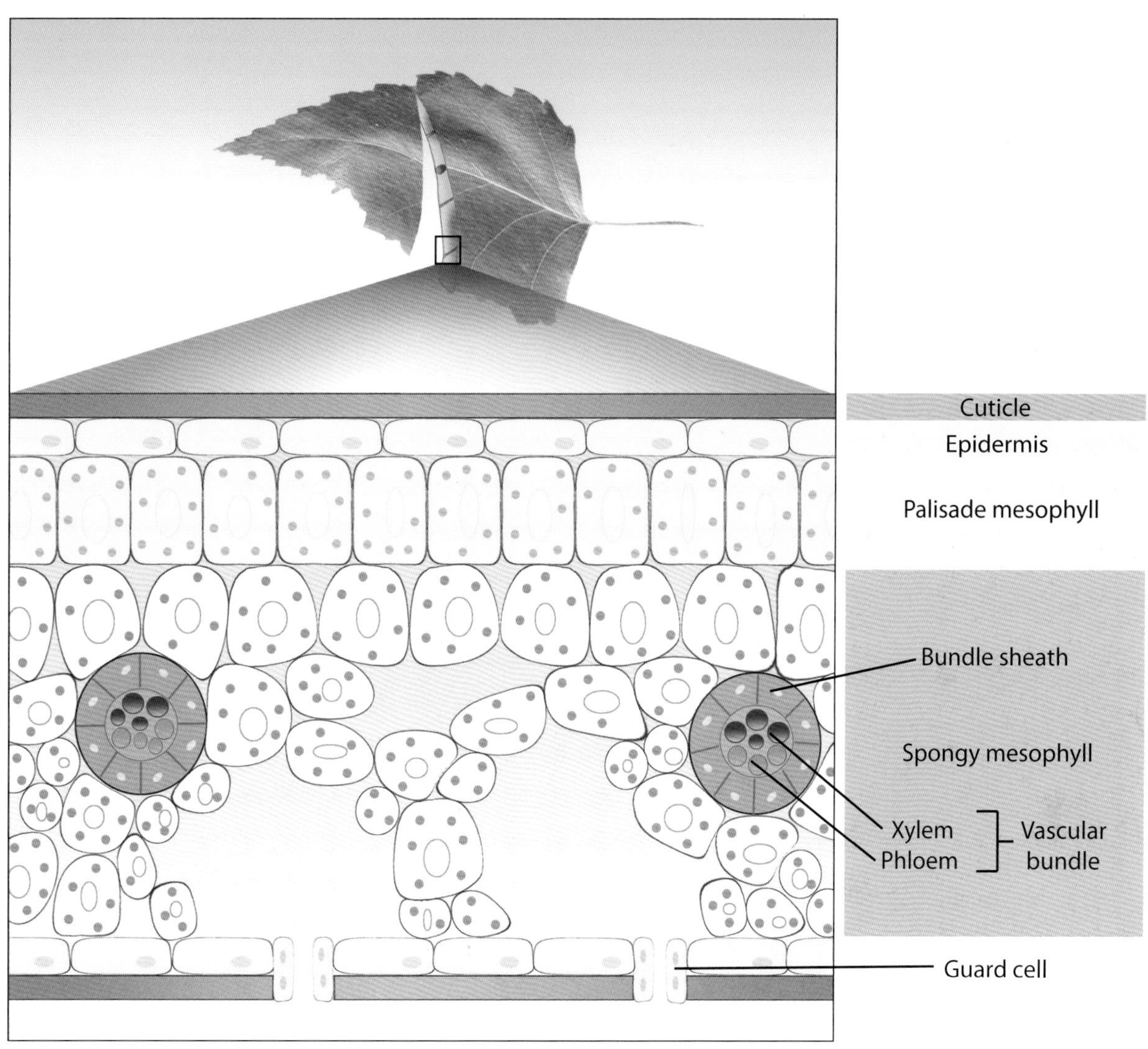

Figure IV.A.17.2: Cross-section of a leaf.

17.2.4 Monocot vs. Dicot Revisited: Additional DAT-30 Content

Now that we have reviewed many features of plants, we can summarize previous and additional characteristics that help to distinguish monocots and dicots.

	Monocots	Dicots
Embryo	Single cotyledon	Two cotyledons
Seeds	One-piece (i.e. corn)	Two-piece (i.e. beans)
Petals of flower	Multiples of 3	Multiples of 4 or 5
Leaf veins	Mostly parallel each other	Branch out from a central vein (= net pattern = reticulated)
Root systems	mostly branch out equally from base (fibrous roots)	mostly have one major root from which smaller ones grow (taproot)
Stems	• Do not grow in ring pattern • Herbaceous, never woody • Hypodermis: sclerenchyma	• Sometimes grow in ring pattern • Herbaceous, sometimes woody • Hypodermis: collenchyma
Vascular bundles	• Form ring pattern in roots • Scattered in stems • Conjoint, collateral and closed in stems	• In middle of root • Can form ring in stems • Conjoint, collateral and open in stems
Pollen	Single furrow or pore	Three furrows or pores
Secondary growth	Rare (i.e. palm tree)	Often present (i.e. secondary xylem is commercially important as wood)
Examples	Grains (wheat, corn, millet, rice), grasses, lilies, daffodils, sugar cane, ginger, onions, bamboo, palm tree, banana tree	Legumes (pea, beans, lentils, peanuts), daisies, mint, grass, lettuce, tomato, oak tree, cacti

Table IV.A.17.1: Summary of monocots vs. dicots. When xylem and phloem elements are found in the same line, the arrangement is called conjoint; if phloem is only external to xylem it is called collateral (i.e. in many stems); if xylem and phloem alternate with each other as in roots, it is called radial. Cambium is the cellular plant tissue from which phloem, xylem, or cork grow by division, resulting in secondary thickening (= woody plants). Open vascular bundles have cambium and the possibility of further xylem and phloem. There is no cambium in closed vascular bundles. {Note: "closed" does NOT mean that the vascular bundles are blocked at the ends.}

17.3 Transport of Water and Sugar

Sap is a fluid transported in xylem cells (tracheids or vessel elements) or phloem sieve tube elements.

Xylem sap is mostly water, with some hormones, mineral elements and other nutrients in aqueous form. It flows from the roots towards the leaves - best explained by the cohesion-tension theory.

Phloem sap is mostly water, with some sugars, hormones, and mineral elements in aqueous form. It flows from where carbohydrates are produced or stored to where they are used - best explained by the pressure flow hypothesis.

Note: Glucose is known as the principle carbohydrate. Glucose is one of the main products of photosynthesis (BIO 17.6) and the primary fuel for cellular respiration (BIO 4.4-4.10).

Sucrose (a disaccharide of fructose and glucose) is the *translocatable* carbohydrate (i.e. *moves* within the phloem of the plant). Starch is called the storage carbohydrate and cellulose is the structural carbohydrate (for more about carbohydrates: BIO 20.3).

17.3.1 Transportation in Xylem

As mentioned before, water is transported through the plant via dead, hardened tracheids found in xylem tissue (BIO 17.2). The water initially enters by osmosis and can move in either the *symplast* or the *apoplast* pathway. Apoplast is a diffusional space outside the plasma membrane formed by the continuum of cell walls of adjacent cells. In the apoplast pathway, water moves through this space without ever entering the cells.

In the symplast pathway, the plasmodesmata (small tubes that connect the cytoplasm of adjacent cells; see BIO 1.4) allow direct cytoplasm-to-cytoplasm flow of water and other nutrients between cells along concentration gradients. In particular, it is used in root systems to bring in nutrients. The apoplast pathway is eventually blocked by the Casparian strip (BIO 17.2.2) and the water can only enter the stele via the symplast pathway. There are three main mechanisms in the movement of water in plants:

1. **Osmosis** – A concentration gradient is maintained between the soil and the root via the higher mineral concentration inside the stele. As a result, water moves from the soil and into the root where it can reach the xylem.

2. **Capillary action** – Results from the forces of adhesion and causes the water to move up the xylem towards the apical region.

3. **Cohesion-tension theory** – Accounts for most movement of water in the xylem and is based on transpiration (a negative pressure within the leaves that builds up due to evaporative loss of water), cohesion (a result of hydrogen bonding in water which allows it to behave as a single column) and bulk flow (occurs when water molecules evaporate from the leaf surface causing the drawing up of another column).

17.3.2 Transportation in Phloem

The Pressure Flow Hypothesis (= Mass Flow Hypothesis) is the best-supported theory to explain the movement of food through the phloem (mnemonic: PFFP – **P**ressure **F**low **F**ood **P**hloem). Movement occurs by bulk flow (mass flow) by means of turgor pressure, also described as hydrostatic pressure.

Sucrose is the primary translocatable carbohydrate (= *sugar that moves within the plant*) in the great majority of plants. Translocation of sugars is accomplished through phloem cells and begins at a source and ends at a sink. The sink refers to the site where the carbohydrates are utilized by the plant. The sugar enters sieve-tube members through active transport and causes the concentration of solutes to be much higher in the source than in the sink. Water now enters by osmosis and the pressure builds due to the inability of the rigid cell wall to expand. The sugars now move upwards via bulk flow towards the sink where the carbohydrates are used. Some sugars are stored as starch which is insoluble in water allowing any cell to act as a sink when the soluble sugars are converted to starch.

17.4 Plant Hormones

Much like in human physiology, plant hormones also function in affecting the division, growth or differentiation of their target cells. They are signal chemicals only required in very small quantities and their effects depend on the particular hormone, its concentration and the presence or absence of other hormones.

There are five main classes of plant hormones:

1. **Auxin or IAA (indolacetic acid)** – Auxins promote plant growth by loosening cellulose fibers inside the cells which raises turgor pressure causing the cell

wall to expand. It is most often found at the tips of shoots and roots where it plays a role in influencing a plant's response to light and gravity (discussed later). They stimulate the production of new xylem cells by the cambium. Auxins inhibit development of lateral buds. They also promote lateral root development while inhibit root elongation.

2. **Gibberellins** – Also promote cell growth and are synthesized in young leaves and seeds. In contrast to auxins which stimulate production of new xylem cells, gibberellins stimulate the production of new phloem cells by the cambium. They also reverse the dormancy of seeds. In addition, they reverse the inhibition of shoot growth induced by inhibitors such as abscisic acid.
3. **Cytokinins** – Stimulate cell division and are produced in roots. They also stimulate the growth of lateral buds, weakening apical dominance (dominant growth of the apical meristem) and delay senescence (aging). Cytokinins (= kinins) work synergistically with auxins, and the ratio of these two groups of plant hormones is important in affecting major growth periods and the timing of differentiation of a plant.
4. **Ethylene** – This hormone is a gas that promotes fruit ripening and the production of flowers. They also, in concert with auxins, inhibit the elongation of roots and stems, counteracting the effect of gibberellins.
5. **Abscisic acid** – A chief growth inhibitor, it serves to maintain dormancy in seeds which is eventually broken by the presence of gibberellins or by environmental cues such as water or light. At the beginning of a plants' life, there is high abscisic acid (ABA) levels. Just before the seed germinates, ABA levels decrease and growth commences. As plants become more mature with fully functional shoots and leaves, ABA levels increase again, slowing down the cellular growth.

17.5 Plant Responses to Stimuli

Rather than change their location, plants alter their growth patterns in response to an environmental stimulus. This is referred to as a tropism and there are three main forms:

1. **Phototropism** – This is a plant's response to light and is governed by auxin. When there is an equal amount of light hitting all sides of the plant, the growth of the stem is uniform and proceeds straight upward. In the event that one side does not receive as much light as the other the auxin concentrates on the shady side of the stem and causes differential growth with the shady side growing more than the sunny side, causing the stem to bend towards the light.

2. **Gravitropism** – A plant responds to gravity in the following manner: If the stem is horizontal the auxins will concentrate on the lower side stimulating the lower side to elongate faster than the upper and thus causing the stem to bend upwards as it grows. This is known as negative geotropism. If a root is horizontal the auxins will again concentrate on the lower side, however the effect on the root cells is the opposite. In roots auxins inhibit growth due to a large presence of auxins already found in the roots, allowing the upper side to elongate faster than the lower and thus causing the root to bend downwards as it grows. And this is known as positive geotropism.
3. **Thigmotropism** – This is a plant's response to touch. Its mechanism is not well understood.

Photoperiodism is a plant's response to changes in the length of day and night. They are able to detect shorter days or shorter nights due to the presence of an endogenous clock (keeps track of time even in the absence of external cues) which allows them to maintain a circadian rhythm (= an intrinsic oscillation of about 24 hours). External cues in this case would be dawn or dusk.

A protein called phytocrome plays a role in maintaining this rhythm and comes in two forms: red (P_r) or far-red (P_{fr}). The far-red form resets the clock while the red form is what is synthesized in plant cells. Flashes of red or far-red light during the night resets the clock; however, flashes of darkness during the day do nothing. This leads to the conclusion that night length is responsible for resetting the circadian rhythm.

Flowering plants can either be long-day (only flower when daylight is increasing such as in the early summer), short-day (flower when daylight is less than a critical length or when night exceeds a critical length) or day-neutral (do not flower in response to daylight changes). A hormone called *florigen* is believed to play a major role in the initiation of flowering when the photoperiod allows for it.

17.6 Photosynthesis

17.6.1 Overview

Photosynthesis is the process of converting light energy into energy stored within chemical bonds that plants can access to meet their metabolic demands. A typical plant can convert sunlight into chemical energy (i.e. carbohydrates such as glucose and other sugars, cellulose, lignin) with an efficiency of approximately 1%. In plants, photosynthesis takes place in a specialized organelle - the chloroplast (BIO 17.6.4). Some bacteria lack chloroplasts but may have membranes that function in a similar manner. The equation breaks down as follows:

$$Light + 6H_2O + 6CO_2 \rightarrow C_6H_{12}O_6 + 6O_2$$

The process begins when light is captured by one of the three main photosynthetic pigments: *chlorophyll a*, *chlorophyll b* and the *carotenoids*. Each is capable of absorbing light at a specific wavelength allowing them to optimize energy absorption. The chlorophylls are both green while the carotenoids show a red/orange or yellow color. When light hits one of these pigments the electrons associated with the atoms of the molecule become excited and immediately re-emit the absorbed energy due to their instability. This process continues until the energy is ultimately absorbed by either *chlorophyll a* or *chlorophyll b*. Chlorophyll a and b are part of the two photosystems, photosystem I and II. A photosystem is composed of chlorophyll molecules coupled to other proteins and is the functional and structural unit of protein complexes that carry out the absorption of light and the transfer of energy and electrons. Each photosystem can be identified by the wavelength of light to which it is most reactive. Photosystem I (PS I) contains the chlorophyll a molecule that absorbs best at 700 nm and uses ferredoxin iron sulfur protein as the terminal electron acceptor. Photosystem II (PS II) contains the chlorophyll dimer molecule that absorbs best at 680 nm and uses quinine as the terminal electron acceptor.

Photosynthesis involves the conversion of CO_2 to carbohydrate accompanied by the release of oxygen using the energy from sunlight. The net reaction is as follows:

$$6CO_2 + 12H_2O + \text{light energy} \rightarrow C_6H_{12}O_6 + 6O_2 + 6H_2O$$

Photosynthesis occurs in two distinct stages and both take place in the chloroplast. In the first stage, the light-dependent stage, energy of the sunlight is captured and converted into chemical energy in the form of ATP and NADPH. In the second stage, the light-independent stage, the former ATP and NADPH drive the conversion of CO_2 into sugars in a process called carbon fixation. Therefore, this process is also called reduction synthesis. Although the light-independent stage is also called the dark reaction, it is not completely independent of light as it is coupled to the light-dependent reaction for an energy source.

Photophosphorylation begins with PS II and is the process of making ATP from ADP and inorganic phosphate P_i using light energy. Electrons trapped by P_{680} are energized by light and are passed to the primary electron acceptor. Next, the electrons pass through the electron transport chain (ETC), which consists of proteins whose job it is to pass electrons from one carrier protein to the next (i.e. ferredoxin and cytochrome). The electrons lose energy as they move down the ETC and terminate at P_{700} (PS I). The energy lost is used to phosphorylate 1.5 ATP molecules. Once they reach PS I, the electrons are re-energized by sunlight and passed to a different primary electron acceptor. Two elec-

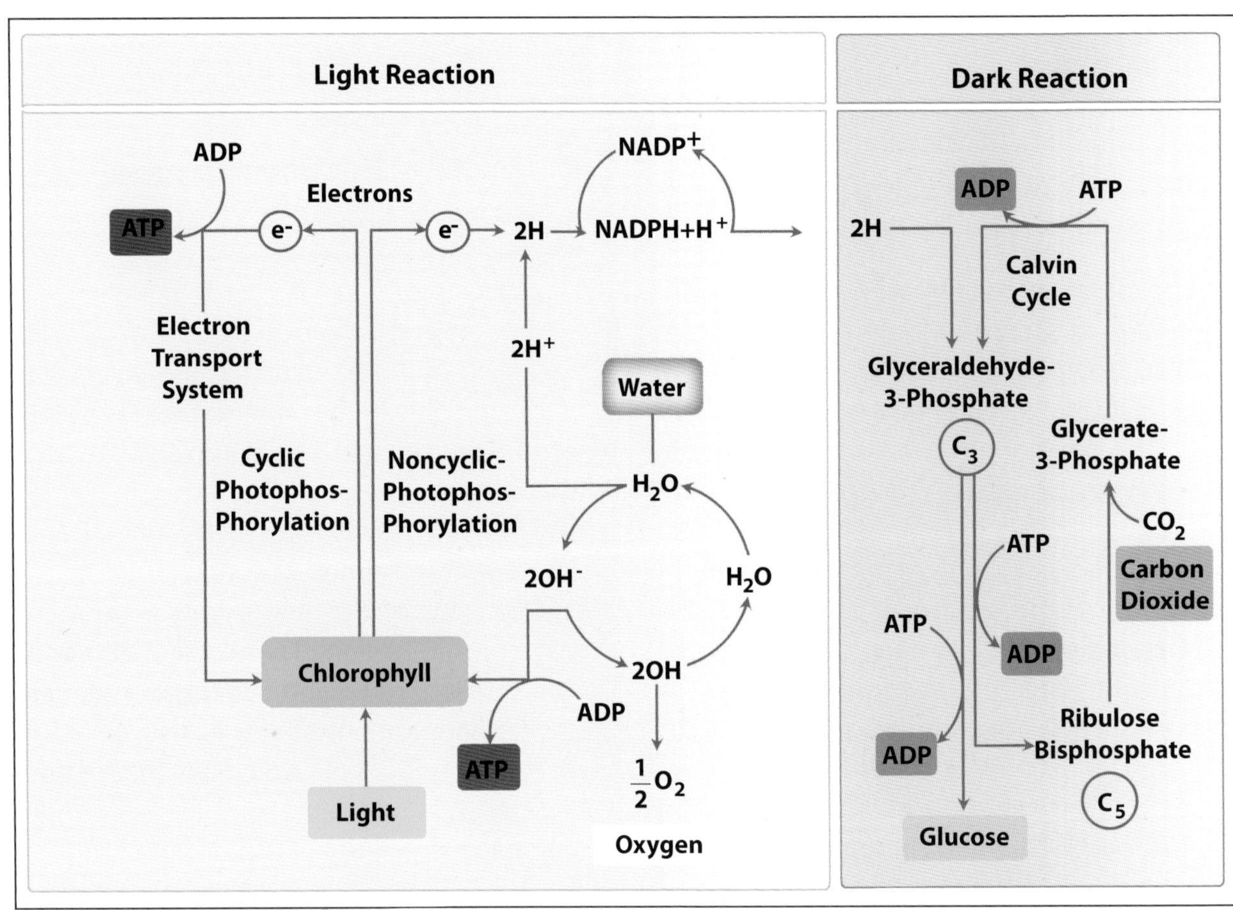

trons pass through another shorter ETC and combine with $NADP^+$ and H^+ to form NADPH which is an important energy-rich coenzyme. The two electrons that have now been incorporated into NADPH and were originally lost from PS II, are replaced when H_2O is split into $2H^+$ and $\frac{1}{2}O_2$. The remaining H^+ provides the H in NADPH. This process is called photolysis and is catalyzed by a manganese containing protein complex.

Cyclic photophosphorylation is very similar to noncyclic except that here the electrons energized in PS I are recycled and eventually return to PS I instead of being incorporated into NADPH. It is considered a primitive form of photosynthesis.

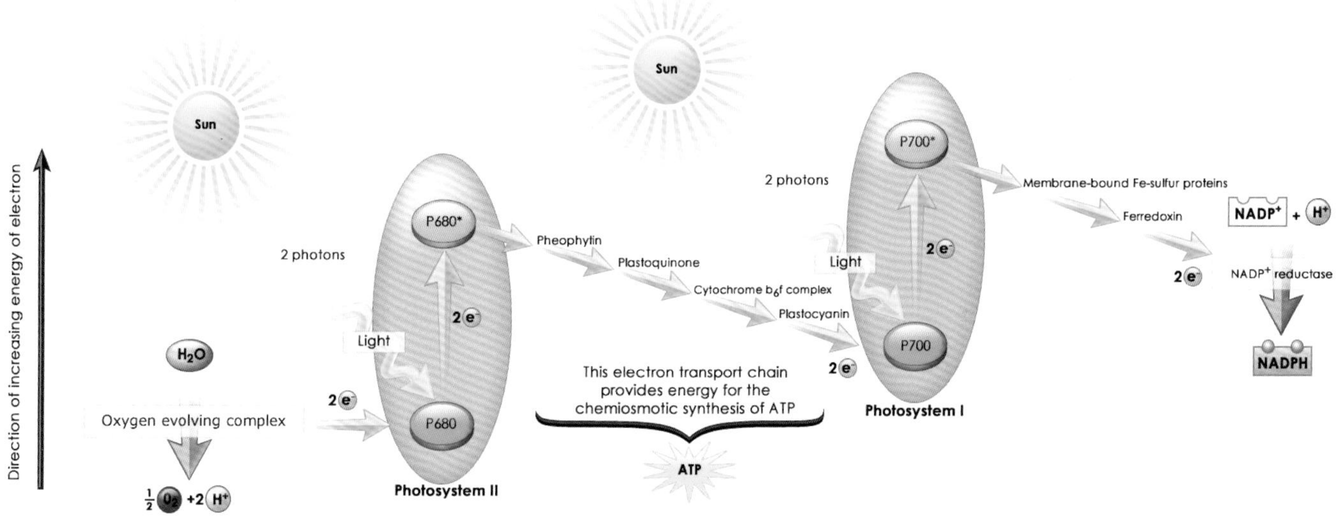

Figure IV.A.17.3: The first stage of photosynthesis: Light-dependent reactions (photoreduction) in which light energy is converted to chemical energy ATP and NADPH on the thylakoid membranes of chloroplasts.

17.6.2 The Light-Dependent Reactions: A Closer Look

The light-dependent reactions, or *photoreduction*, is the first stage of photosynthesis, and has two forms: cyclic electron flow and non-cyclic electron flow. In the non-cyclic form, the chlorophyll molecule within photosystem II (P_{680}) absorbs photons and the light energy excites electrons to a higher energy level. These high energy electrons are then shuttled through an electron transport chain (ETC), whose job is to pass electrons from one carrier protein to the next (i.e. ferredoxin and cytochrome) and to generate an electrochemical proton gradient across the membrane. The proton gradient across the thylakoid membrane creates a proton-motive force, which is used by ATP synthase to form ATP (= *chemiosmosis* which is the same process used in mitochondria).

The electrons lose energy as they move down the ETC and terminate at photosystem I (P_{700}). Once they reach P_{700}, the electrons are re-energized by photons and passed to a different electron acceptor, which again is passed down lowering energies of electron acceptors. Instead of returning to P_{700} along the carrier chain, the electrons are transferred to NADP to form NADPH. The electron hole that P_{700} is left with will be filled by electrons coming from P_{680} and the electron hole that P_{680} is left with will be filled by electrons coming from photolysis of water. Therefore, the net result of the non-cyclic reaction is the production of NADPH and ATP and the photolysis of water.

The cyclic form is similar to that of the non-cyclic form, but differs in that it generates only ATP but no NADPH. The cyclic reaction takes place only at photosystem I (P_{700}). The electron energized in photosystem I is displaced and passed down the electron acceptor molecules and returns to photosystem I, from where it is emitted, hence the name cyclic reaction.

17.6.3 The Light-Independent Reactions: A Closer Look

The next step of photosynthesis involves the Calvin-Benson cycle which fixes CO_2 in the sense that it takes the inert, inorganic CO_2 and incorporates it into a usable form capable of integration into biological systems. The end result is the formation of a single molecule of glucose which takes six complete turns of the Calvin cycle and consumes six CO_2 molecules.

It begins with the enzyme *rubisco* (= ribulose-1,5-bisphosphate carboxylase oxygenase = RuBisCO) which catalyzes the merging of CO_2 and ribulose biphosphate. The CO_2 that is incorporated into ribulose-1,5-bisphosphate (RuBP) produces a six-carbon intermediate that immediately splits in half forming two molecules of 3-phosphoglycerate (PGA), and is the reason why the Calvin cycle is referred to as C3 photosynthesis (12 PGA are made from 6 CO_2 and 6 RuBP).

What follows is that in the presence of ATP and NADPH, 3-phosphoglycerate is reduced to phosphoglyceraldehyde (PGAL). For every six cycles, 12 ATP and 12 NADPH are used to convert 12 PGA into 12 PGAL. Five out of every 6 molecules of the PGAL produced is used to regenerate RuBP to keep the process continuing. However, the 1 out of every 6 molecules of the PGAL that is not recycled will be combined with another PGAL to form hexose phosphates, which ultimately yield sugar compounds. Next, the 6 RuBP originally used to combine with 6 CO_2 are regenerated (6 ATP are used to convert 10 PGAL or G3P to 6 RuBP). Lastly, the remaining 2 PGAL are used to form glucose.

Since no light is directly involved with this reaction, the Calvin cycle can also be referred to as the *dark reaction* even though it cannot proceed in the dark. This is because

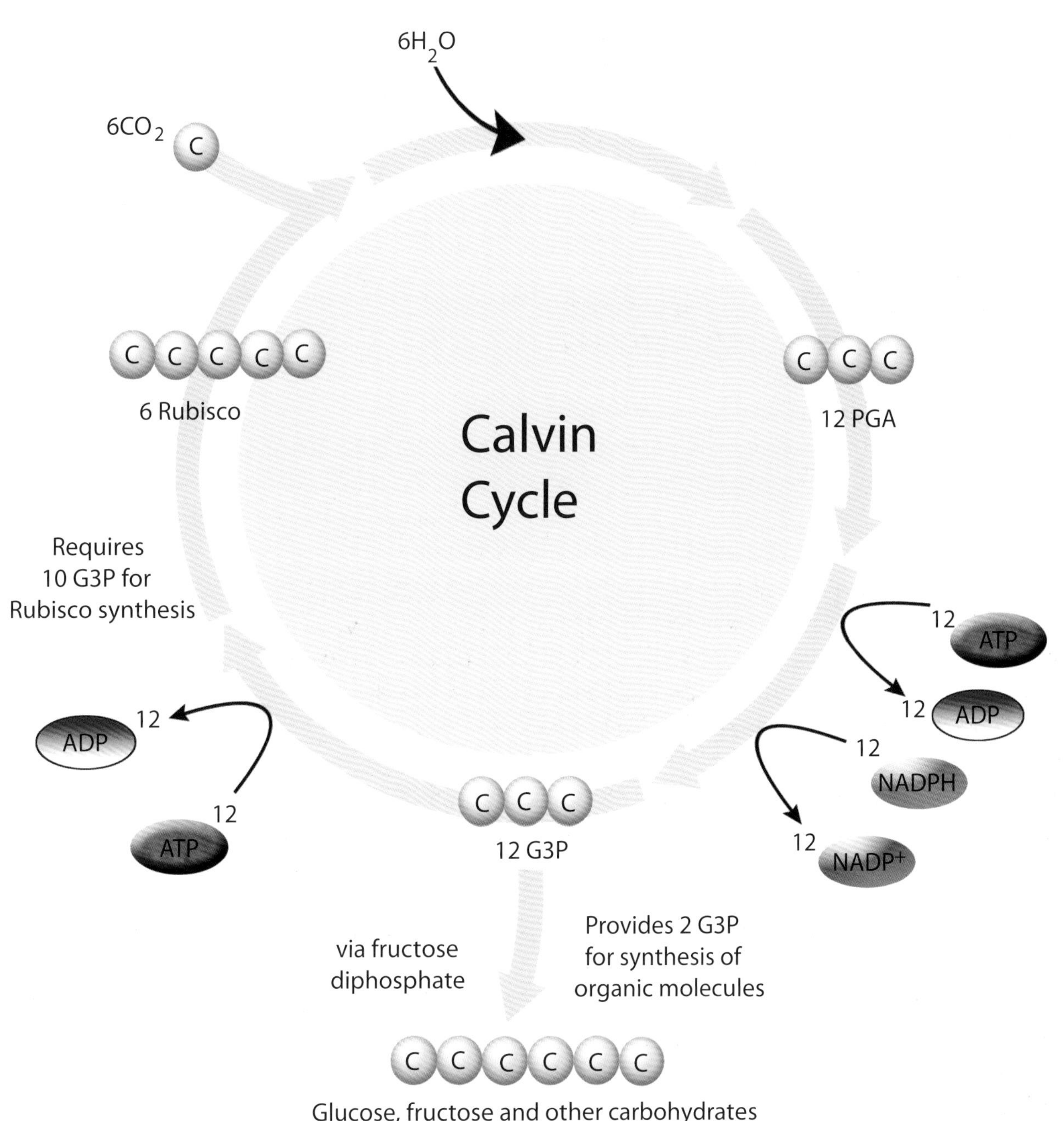

Figure IV.A.17.4: The Calvin Cycle (C3).

it is dependent on energy from NADPH and ATP, formed during the light reactions of photosynthesis. Keep in mind that none of these reactions occur spontaneously. Each one is dependent on a coenzyme or metal cofactor.

The sum of reactions in the Calvin cycle is the following (P_i = inorganic phosphate):

$$3\ CO_2 + 6\ NADPH + 5\ H_2O + 9\ ATP \rightarrow \text{glyceraldehyde-3-phosphate (G3P)} + 2\ H^+ + 6\ NADP^+ + 9\ ADP + 8\ P_i$$

17.6.4 Characteristic Features of Plant Cells

In Chapter 1, we explored many features of the generalized eukaryotic cell. We will now take a closer look at 3 characteristic - though *not* necessarily unique - features of plant cells: the cell wall, vacuoles and plastids.

The cell wall: Imagine that a cell is like a floppy water balloon. Well, the cell wall is like putting the balloon in a box. The cell wall is a fairly rigid layer that lies outside of the cell's plasma membrane. The cell wall provides structural support and acts as a pressure vessel, preventing overexpansion when water enters the cell.

There are specialized pores through the wall called plasmodesmata that provide a cytoplasmic connection between adjacent plant cells (BIO 17.3.1; compare with gap junctions, BIO 1.5). The cytoplasm of a plant is, therefore, more or less contiguous throughout the entire plant.

Cell walls are made of carbohydrates (BIO 20.3) and are found in plants (cellulose, hemicellulose and the 'glue' that binds cell walls together - pectin); bacteria (peptidoglycan; BIO 2.2); fungi (chitin; BIO 2.3, 16.6.4); algae (glycoproteins and polysaccharides); and some archaea (glycoproteins and polysaccharides). Animals and protozoa do not have cell walls.

Vacuoles: Membrane-bound organelles present in all plant and fungal cells, and some protist, animal and bacterial cells. Vacuoles are filled with water and some inorganic and organic molecules including enzymes in solution, and rarely engulfed solids.

Plant cells can have one large central vacuole instrumental in maintaining internal hydrostatic pressure and pushing the plasma membrane against the cell wall (= *turgor pressure*). Incredibly, the vacuole may occupy from 20% to up to 80-90% of the cell's volume.

Plastids: All arise from a common precursor: *proplastid*. Plastids are all surrounded by a double plasma membrane and contain their own double stranded DNA molecule (see endosymbiotic theory; BIO 16.6.3). However, similar to mitochondria, most plastid proteins are coded by nuclear DNA. Plastids can be found in plants and other eukaryotes (protists; BIO 16.6.4).

Here are some common plastids:

- Amyloplasts – store starch
- Chromoplasts – contain colorful pigments
- Chloroplasts – photosynthesis which we will continue to examine.

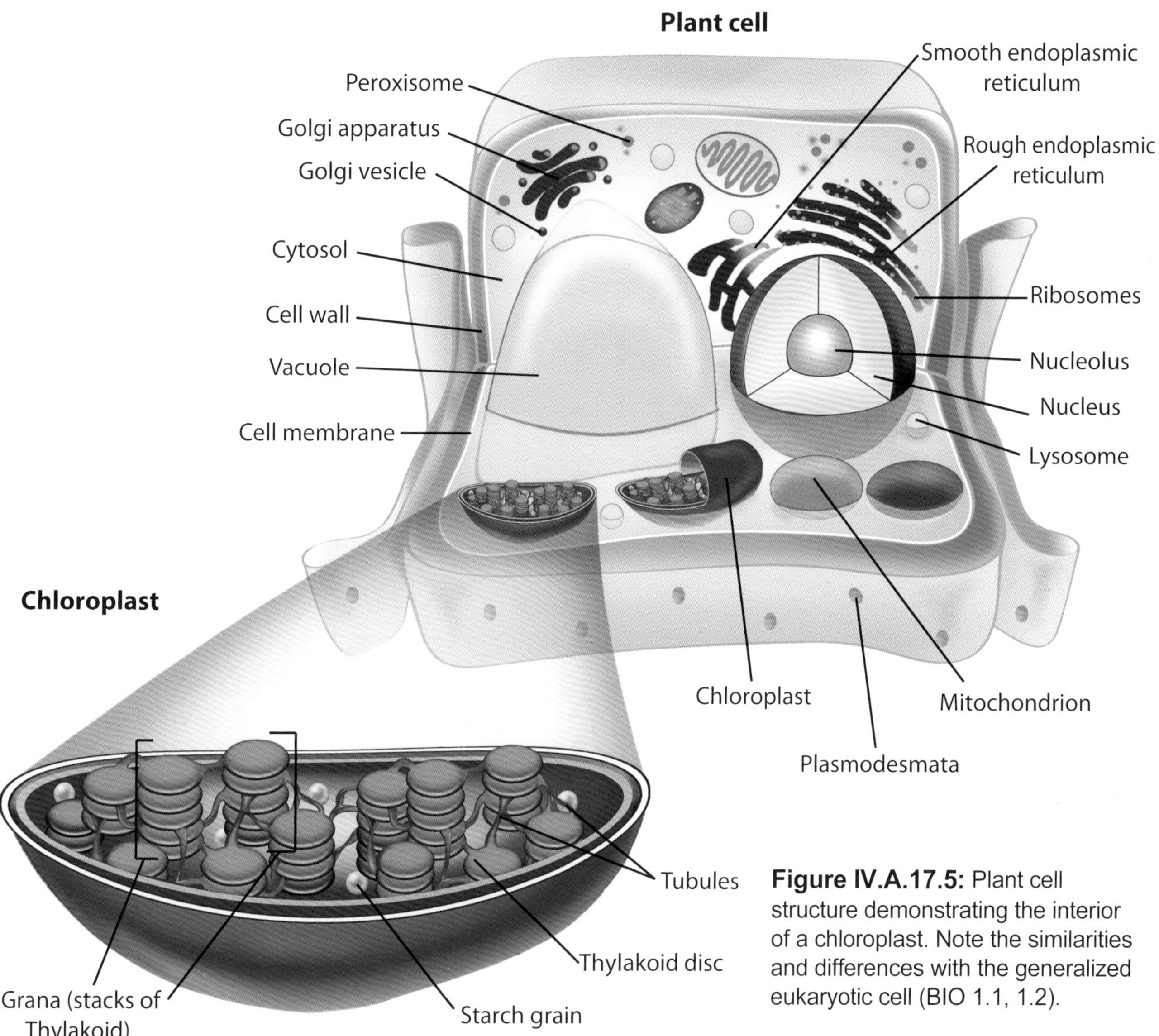

Figure IV.A.17.5: Plant cell structure demonstrating the interior of a chloroplast. Note the similarities and differences with the generalized eukaryotic cell (BIO 1.1, 1.2).

Both the light and dark reactions occur in chloroplasts. Within the inner membrane, in the region called the *stroma*, there is a system of interconnecting flattened membrane compartments, called the *thylakoids*, which stacked collectively form a granum (plural: *grana*). Chlorophyll resides within the thylakoid membranes. It is within the thylakoids where the machinery and pigments for the light-dependent reactions are found. The light independent reaction, or the dark reactions, occur in the stroma.

17.6.5 Photorespiration

Photorespiration is the biosynthetic pathway that leads to the fixation of oxygen. This occurs because rubisco is capable of fixing both CO_2 and O_2. This is undesirable as the products formed when rubisco fixes O_2 are not of any use to the plant. Peroxisomes, a specialized organelle, are found near chloroplasts and break down the wasteful products of photorespiration (BIO 1.2.1).

17.6.6 Other Photosynthetic Pathways

Some plants have managed to evolve more efficient ways of photosynthesis. The C4 pathway and CAM method are the two main modifications to the original C3 photosynthesis and they overcome the tendency of the enzyme rubisco to fix oxygen rather than carbon dioxide thus avoiding the production of undesirable products of photorespiration. In C4 photosynthesis the CO_2 combines with PEP (phosphoenolpyruvate) rather than rubisco and forms OAA (oxaloacetate). OAA has 4 carbons and is immediately converted to malate which is then shuttled to the bundle sheath cells (see BIO 17.2.3). There the malate is converted to pyruvate and CO_2. The pyruvate is converted back to PEP, which is transported back to the mesophyll cell and CO_2 now enters the Calvin cycle.

The process repeats with the ultimate goal being the movement of CO_2 from mesophyll cells to the bundle sheath cells. This is key as the bundle sheath cells are more or less isolated from O_2 and the C3 pathway can now proceed as normal, minimizing photorespiration. The C4 pathway is usually found in arid, hot climates. Stomata must be open in order to allow CO_2 to enter. However, when these stomata are open the plant loses water. C4 plants are extremely efficient at photosynthesis and this allows them to minimize the time in which they have their stomata open, reducing H_2O loss.

CAM photosynthesis is very similar to C4 except that in CAM the OAA is converted to malic acid instead of malate and is shuttled to the vacuole of the cell rather than the bundle

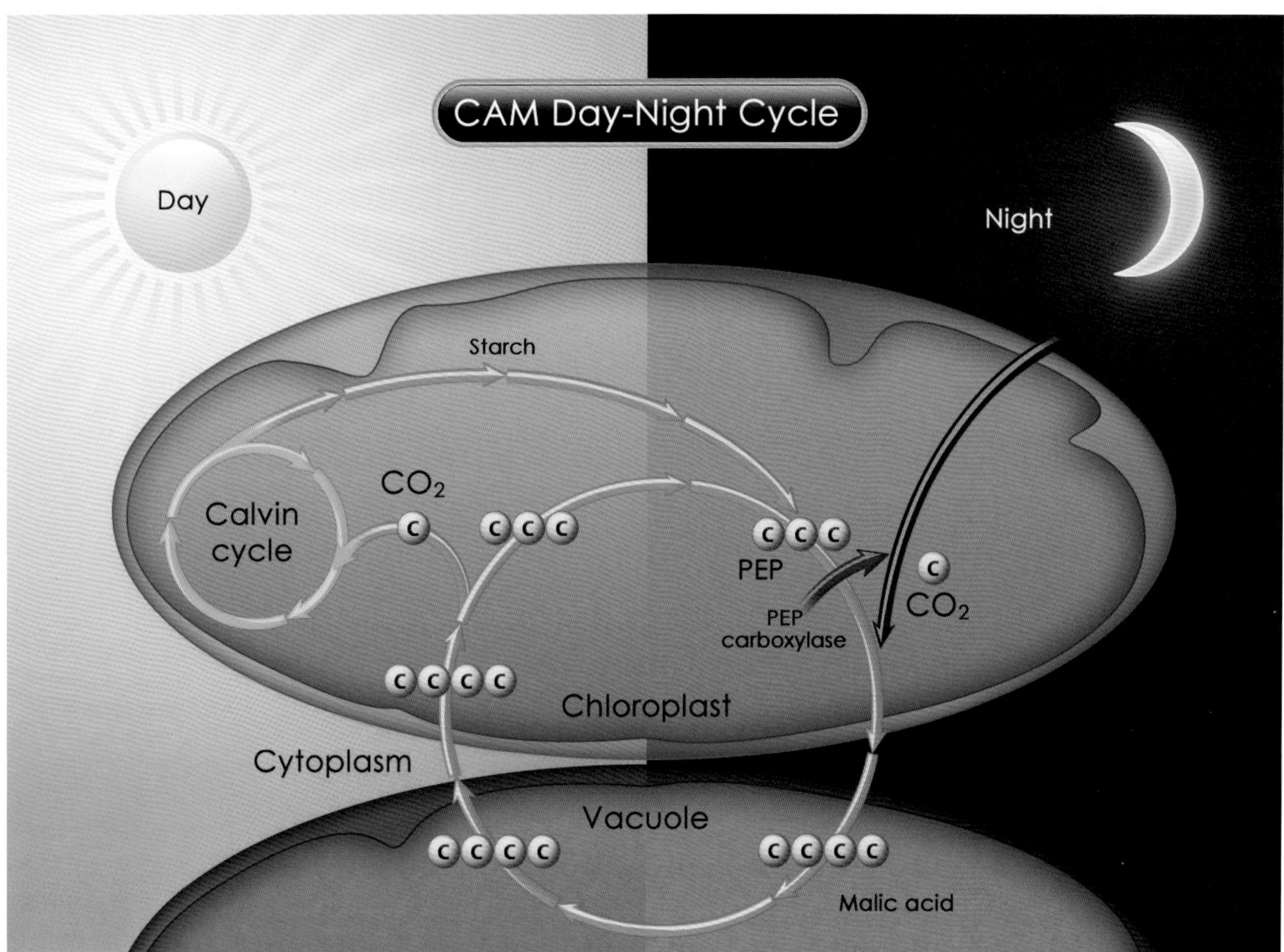

Figure IV.A.17.6: The CAM Day-Night Cycle. In CAM plants the photosynthesis and initial carbon fixation occur at night and a 4-carbon acid is stored in the cell's vacuole. During the day, the Calvin cycle operates in the same chloroplasts.

sheath cells. Stomata remain open at night where PEP carboxylase is active and the malic acid accumulates in the vacuoles. However, instead of being immediately passed on to the Calvin cycle, the malic acid is stored for later use. During the day the stomata are closed which is the reverse of most other plants. During this time the CO_2 is fixed by rubisco and the Calvin cycle proceeds. Being able to keep stomata closed during the day minimizes the loss of water through evaporation, allowing plants that utilize the CAM method to grow in environments that would otherwise be too dry for C3 plants. Therefore, CAM plants are also found in hot, dry climates with cool nights.

GOLD STANDARD WARM-UP EXERCISES

CHAPTER 17: Plants

NOTE: these Warm-up Questions refer to this chapter on Plants as well as content covering Kingdom Plantae from Chapter 16.

1) The ovary of a flowering plant can develop into a:

A. cone.
B. seed.
C. fruit.
D. spore.

2) The part of the flower that is adapted to catch pollen is the:

A. stigma.
B. anther.
C. ovule.
D. style.

3) The part of a stamen containing the pollen sacs in flowers is known as the:

A. style.
B. filament.
C. pistil.
D. anther.

4) The ancestors of land plants were aquatic algae. All of the following are evolutionary adaptations to life on land EXCEPT one. Which is the EXCEPTION?

A. Xylem and phloem
B. A waxy cuticle
C. Sperm packaged as pollen
D. The Calvin cycle

5) Which of the following nourishes a developing seed?

A. Endosperm
B. Nectar
C. Zygote
D. Pollen tube

6) Match the following:

I. Epidermal tissue	i. Storage and photo-synthesis
II. Parenchyma	ii. Mechanical support
III. Collenchyma	iii. Stomata
IV. Sclerenchyma	iv. Actively dividing
V. Meristem	v. Sclereid cells

A. I-iv, II-v, III-iii, IV-ii, V-i
B. I-iii, II-i, III-ii, IV-v, V-iv
C. I-ii, II-iv, III-v, IV-i, V-iii
D. I-i, II-iii, III-v, IV-ii, V-iv

7) In a plant, the layer of persistently meristematic tissue, giving rise to secondary tissues, resulting in growth in diameter is which of the following?

A. Pores
B. Bark
C. Cambium
D. Capsule

8) Which of the following describes the loss of water vapor by plants?

A. Transpiration
B. Perspiration
C. Respiration
D. Absorption

9) An important function of root hairs is that they:

A. anchor a plant in the soil.
B. increase the surface area for absorption.
C. store and transport starches.
D. provide a niche for bacteria.

10) Which of the following is correct regarding the Casparian strip in plant roots?

A. It ensures that all water must pass through a cell membrane before entering the stele.
B. It provides increased surface area for the absorption of water.
C. It is located between the epidermis and the cortex.
D. It supplies ATP for the active transport of minerals into the stele from the cortex.

11) All of the following form part of a plant's apoplast EXCEPT one. Which one is the EXCEPTION?

A. The lumen of a sieve tube
B. The lumen of a xylem vessel
C. The cell wall of a root hair
D. The cell wall of a mesophyll cell

12) What regulates the flow of water through xylem?

A. Active transport by tracheids and vessel elements
B. Passive transport by the endodermis
C. Active transport by sieve tube members
D. The evaporation of water from the leaves

13) What is theorized to be the driving force for the transport of sap in phloem?

A. Water transpiration
B. Root pressure
C. Gravity
D. Hydrostatic pressure

14) Which of the following plant hormones are produced in roots and stimulate cell division?

A. Cytokinins
B. Ethylene
C. Abscisic acid
D. Gibberellins

15) The tendency of a plant to grow toward light is called:

A. phototropism.
B. photosynthesis.
C. photorespiration.
D. photoinduction.

16) In the first stage of photosynthesis, light energy is used to:

A. produce carbohydrates.
B. move water molecules.
C. denature chlorophyll.
D. split water.

17) What percent of the total radiant energy received by a plant is converted to chemical energy?

A. Less than 2%
B. 10%
C. 30%
D. 50%

18) Molecular oxygen formed during plant photosynthesis is derived exclusively from:

A. carbohydrates.
B. proteins.
C. water.
D. CO_2.

19) During the light phase of photosynthesis, choose the molecule that is oxidized and the molecule that is reduced, respectively.

A. Water and NADP
B. Water and CO_2
C. NADPH and CO_2
D. CO_2 and Water

20) The oxygen molecule in glucose formed during photosynthesis comes from:

A. fructose.
B. water.
C. NADP.
D. CO_2.

21) The light-dependent reactions of photosynthesis result in the formation of which of the following?

A. ATP
B. O_2
C. NADPH + H^+
D. All of the above

22) All of the following are true EXCEPT one. Which one is the EXCEPTION?

A. In C3 plants, the light and dark reactions can take place at the same time.
B. In C4 plants, the light and dark reactions can take place at the same time.
C. CAM and C3 plants are adapted to arid environments but C4 plants are not.
D. CAM plants keep their stomata closed during the day to reduce the loss of water.

23) What directly powers the light-independent reactions?

A. Carbon dioxide
B. Sunlight
C. ADP and $NADP^+$ produced by the light-dependent reactions
D. ATP and NADPH produced by the light-dependent reactions

GS ANSWER KEY

CHAPTER 17

		Cross-Reference			Cross-Reference
1.	C	BIO 16.6.4 (Kingdom Plantae)	13.	D	BIO 17.3, 17.3.2
2.	A	BIO 16.6.4 (Kingdom Plantae)	14.	A	BIO 17.4
3.	D	BIO 16.6.4 (Kingdom Plantae)	15.	A	BIO 17.5
4.	D	BIO 16.6.4 (Kingdom Plantae); BIO 17.6.3	16.	D	BIO 17.6.1, 17.6.2
5.	A	BIO 17.1, 17.2.1	17.	A	BIO 17.6.1
6.	B	BIO 17.2, 17.2.2	18.	C	BIO 17.6.1
7.	C	BIO 17.2, 17.2.4	19.	A	BIO 4.7-4.9, 17.6.1, 17.6.2; CHM 1.5.1, 1.6, 10.1, 10.2
8.	A	BIO 17.2.3, 17.3	20.	D	BIO 17.6.1
9.	B	BIO 17.2.2	21.	D	BIO 17.6.1
10.	A	BIO 17.2.2	22.	C	BIO 17.6
11.	A	BIO 17.2.3, 17.3, 17.3.1	23.	D	BIO 17.6.3
12.	D	BIO 17.3, 17.3.1			

* Explanations can be found at the back of the book.

Go online to DAT-prep.com for additional chapter review Q&A and forum.

ANIMAL BEHAVIOR
Chapter 18

Memorize	Understand	Importance
* Animal movement	* Different forms of behavior * Chemical communication * Social behavior	**0 to 1 out of the 40 Biology** DAT questions are based on content in this chapter (in our estimation). * Note that between 25% and 50% of the questions in DAT Biology are from 5 chapters: 1, 2, 14, 15, and 16.

DAT-Prep.com

Introduction 

Behavior is what an animal does. Nature and nurture shape the behavior of animals. Nature is innate, described as "instinct" where genes determine the behavior. Nurture is learned, described as "experience" where learning influences behavior. The two extremes are not mutually exclusive and both nature and nurture are deeply influenced by evolution.

Additional Resources

Free Online Q&A + Forum

Flashcards

18.1 Introduction to Animal Behavior

Most behavior exhibited by animals is molded by natural selection and evolutionary forces. It can also be inherited through genes (innate). There are six main forms of behavior:

1. **Instinct** – This type of behavior is inherited (= innate, i.e. a mother caring for her offspring).
2. **Fixed action pattern** – This pattern is also innate and is initiated by a specific stimulus. It is always carried out to completion (i.e. mating dance with the female acting as the stimulus or cows herding). Because this pattern is innate, it is less likely to be modified by learning. In addition, an animal has a limited ability to develop any new fixed-action patterns.
3. **Imprinting** – An irreversible behavior that is acquired during a critical period via an appropriate stimulus (i.e. Konrad Lenz's famous gosling experiment where he discovered that during the first two days of life the goslings will recognize any moving object as their mother. Lenz himself swam with the goslings during this critical period and was accepted as their mother). If the proper environmental pattern or object is not presented during this critical period, the behavior pattern will not develop properly.
4. **Associative learning** – Occurs when an animal learns that two or more events are connected. Classical conditioning is an example of this behavior as is seen in Ivan Pavlov's legendary experiment where he discovered that dogs would salivate in response to a ringing bell even when food did not immediately follow as was normally the case. The dogs associated the bell (substitute stimulus) with the food (normal stimulus) and the bell itself was able to elicit the salivary response. This type of conditioning involves the association of an autonomic response with an environmental stimulus. In Pavlov's experiment the normal stimulus, known as unconditioned stimulus as it elicits response naturally, is replaced by a neutral stimulus (substitute stimulus) chosen by the experimenter that will not elicit a response by itself. During conditioning, the neutral stimulus (substitute stimulus) and the unconditioned stimulus are linked together and eventually, the neutral stimulus is able to elicit a response without the presence of the unconditioned stimulus and it becomes the conditioned stimulus.
5. **Trial and error learning** – A second form of associative learning where an animal connects its own behavior with a particular environmental response. The response can be positive or negative, thereby encouraging or discouraging the animal's likeliness in repeating the behavior (i.e. B.F. Skinner's rat experiment where he trained them to push levers to obtain food pellets or avoid mild electrical shocks). This type of behavior is also known as operant or instrumental conditioning. Under certain conditions, random activities are directed into a behavior pattern with the use of reward or reinforcement. Conversely, lack of certain activities is directed into a

behavior pattern with the use of punishment. The loss of an acquired behavior is called extinction as would be the case if the rats stopped receiving food after pushing on the lever.

6. **Habituation** – A learned behavior that allows an animal to decrease their response to a certain stimulus after they have seen it many times before. This is seen in virtually every organism on the planet. However, if a stimulus is removed, the response tends to recover and this is called spontaneous recovery.

18.2 Animal Movement

Three kinds of movement are commonly found in animals:

1. **Kinesis** – An undirected, random change in speed in an animal's movement in response to a certain stimulus. It will slow down in a favorable situation and speed up in unfavorable ones (i.e. woodlice becoming sluggish as humidity increases).
2. **Taxis** – A directed movement in response to a stimulus. Can be either toward or away from the stimulus (i.e. moths move towards the light at night).
3. **Migration** – The long distance, seasonal movement of animals (i.e. many species of birds migrate south for the winter).

18.3 Chemical Communication

Animals use pheromones in order to communicate on the chemical level. Pheromones are secreted or excreted chemical factors, usually in minute quantities, that trigger a social response in members of the same species. Releaser pheromones cause immediate and reversible behavioral changes in the recipient. For example, releaser pheromones can be secreted as an alarm substance. Primer pheromones cause long term, physiological changes in the recipient. For example, primer pheromones can play a role in the regulation of reproductive capacities of animals. Bombykol was the first known pheromone and is released by the female silkworm in order to attract mates.

18.4 Social Behavior

Most social behaviors have evolved in order to optimize individual fitness. All animals must at some point communicate with others in order to reproduce. There are four main types:

1. **Agonistic behavior** – Aggressive displays of behavior that usually originate from competition for a particular resource, most often food or mates.
2. **Dominance hierarchies** – Established in order to maintain power and status relationships between individuals within a group. This is referred to as a pecking order in chickens.
3. **Territoriality** – Involves the defense of one's territory and ensures adequate food supplies and ample room to rear young. Territoriality functions in distributing members of species to minimize intraspecific aggressions. Therefore, the larger the population the smaller the territories can be. Overt fighting is usually avoided by some form of clear display, which can be visual (i.e. the red breast of the robin), auditory (i.e. bird song) or olfactory, through scent marking (i.e. urination, defecation or through the smearing of excretions from scent glands).
4. **Altruistic behavior** – An unselfish, sacrificing behavior that reduces the overall fitness of the individual. This type of behavior is seen when animals risk their safety by defending a friend or family member or when they sacrifice their reproduction to help another individual (always of the same species). Altruism is, in part, correlated with the "coefficient of relatedness" which is the ratio of identical genes in two individuals. The interaction between related individuals can affect gene frequencies (*kin selection*).

GOLD STANDARD WARM-UP EXERCISES

CHAPTER 18: Animal Behavior

1) Which of the following is consistent with associative learning?

   A. Operant conditioning
   B. Classical conditioning
   C. Pavlovian conditioning
   D. All of the above

2) Fish in aquariums tend to swim to the water's surface when a person approaches. Their behavior has likely formed through:

   A. insight.
   B. instinct.
   C. classical conditioning.
   D. imprinting.

3) After a young duck imprints on a plastic mechanical toy, the young duck will:

   A. follow only that plastic mechanical toy.
   B. follow all plastic mechanical toys .
   C. then imprint on any real adult duck.
   D. then imprint on its mother.

4) You want to train a puppy to "sit". You give the dog a treat every time he does as you ask. You are applying:

   A. habituation.
   B. imprinting.
   C. classical conditioning.
   D. operant conditioning.

5) Animals that help other animals are expected to be:

   A. carrying the most "fit" genes.
   B. carrying the least "fit" genes.
   C. related to the animals they help.
   D. stronger than other animals.

GS ANSWER KEY

CHAPTER 18

		Cross-Reference
1.	D	BIO 18.1
2.	C	BIO 18.1
3.	A	BIO 18.1
4.	D	BIO 18.1
5.	C	BIO 18.1

* Explanations can be found at the back of the book.

Go online to DAT-prep.com for additional chapter review Q&A and forum.

Go online to DAT-prep.com for additional chapter review Q&A and forum.

ECOLOGY
Chapter 19

Memorize	Understand	Importance
* Basic ecology nomenclature, graphs and interactions * Population growth equation * Pyramids, percentage transfer * Biomes	* Population, community ecology * Coevolution, ecosystems * Biomes	**0 to 2 out of the 40 Biology** DAT questions are based on content in this chapter (in our estimation). * Note that between 25% and 50% of the questions in DAT Biology are from 5 chapters: 1, 2, 14, 15, and 16.

Introduction

Ecology is the study of the relationships that living organisms have with each other and with their natural environment. Areas of interest include the distribution, number, total amount (biomass), composition, and changing states of organisms within and among ecosystems. Biodiversity is the variety of species in ecosystems and the genetic variations they contain.

Additional Resources

Free Online Q&A + Forum

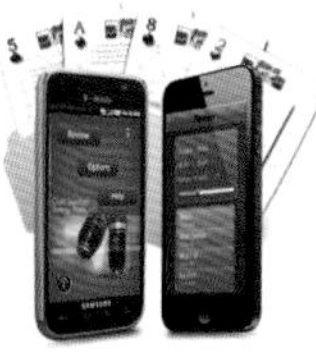

Flashcards

Special Guest

19.1 Ecology: An Overview

The studying of ecology encompasses both the biotic (living) and abiotic (non living) environment as it involves the interaction of species with other organisms as well as with their physical surroundings. There are six key terms that must be defined before we go any further:

1. **Population** – A group of individuals of the same species living in the same area.
2. **Community** – A group of populations of different species interacting with each other in the same area.
3. **Ecosystem** – The interaction between organisms in a community and their physical environment.
4. **Biosphere** – Comprises all regions of the earth that contain living things.
5. **Habitat** – The specific place where an organism dwells.
6. **Niche** – The unique role an organism plays in the biotic and abiotic environment, focusing on all the resources used by that particular animal. Organisms occupying the same niche compete for the same resources; therefore, no two species can occupy the same niche: the competition will drive either extinction of one of the species or divergent evolution leading to two species with greater differences. A niche is such a specific segment of ecospace that a species can be identified by the niche it occupies.

19.2 Population Ecology

The first major subtopic of ecology is population ecology, specifically the study of the growth and distribution of populations. It is described by its size, density, dispersion (they can be either random, clumped or uniformly distributed), age structure and the type of survivorship curve. There are three types of survivorship curves:

(a) **Type I** – Species who generally are able to survive until middle age, at which point mortality rates are high when you pass this midpoint (i.e. humans).

(b) **Type II** – Species who display a random pattern of survivorship (i.e. rodents).

(c) **Type III** – Species where most individuals die young. Typical of many insects, oysters and any other species that produces free swimming larvae.

Population growth is characterized by the biotic potential, the carrying capacity and any limiting factors that prevent said population from reaching its full potential. *Biotic potential* is the maximum growth rate of a population under ideal circumstances. Such a scenario is rarely achieved as any number of resource or growth restriction problems can negatively affect the rate and limit growth. The *carrying capacity* refers to the maximum

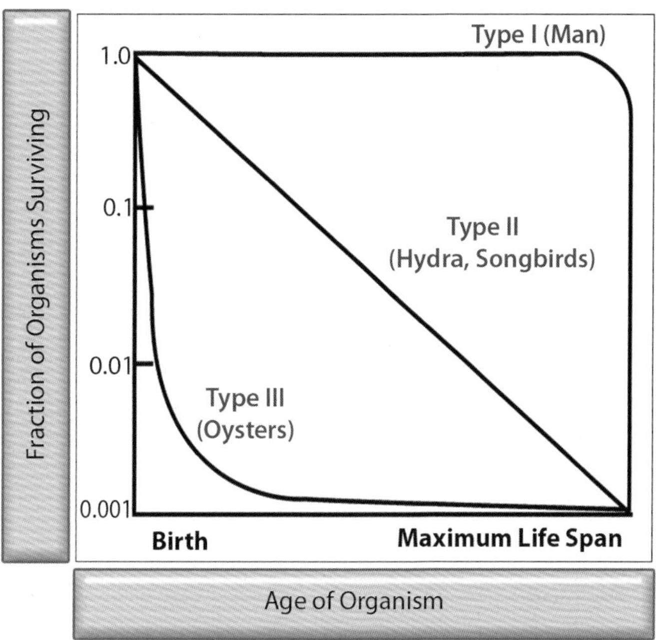

Scaled to maximum life span for each species.

number of individuals of a certain population that can be sustained in a particular habitat. Limiting factors can be density-dependent (become important when population size increases and resources become scarce) or density-independent (factors that occur independently of population density such as natural disasters or climate changes).

The growth of a population can be described by the following equation:

$$r = (\text{births} - \text{deaths})/N$$

r = growth rate
N = population size
numerator = the net increase in individuals

When births exceed deaths, r will be positive and the population will increase. If births and deaths are equal, then the population size remains constant. When deaths exceed births, r will be negative and the population will decrease.

There are two general patterns of population growth:

1. **Exponential growth** – Occurs whenever the reproductive rate is greater than zero. Forms a J shaped curve.
2. **Logistic growth** – Occurs when limiting factors keep the population in check. Produces an S shaped curve. The point at which the growth rate levels off is the <u>carrying capacity</u>. Once growth is reduced below the carrying capacity,

resources become more readily available and the population is often able to recover. This is not always the case. Sometimes the population may crash into extinction or in milder cases it will establish a new lower carrying capacity.

Exponential and logistic growth drives evolution in one of two types of life-history strategies: r- or K-selection.

1. **r-selected species (unstable environment)** – In unstable environments, r selection predominates and exhibits the ability to reproduce many offspring, each of which has a relatively low probability to survive to adulthood. Other characteristics of r-selection include small body size of individuals, early maturity, little parent care requirement, high fertility, and short generation time.
2. **K-selected species (stable environment)** – In stable environments, K-selection predominates and exhibits the ability to compete successfully for limited resources. In contrast to r-selected populations, which can vary significantly, K-selected population size remains constant and is close to the maximum that the environment can allow (close to the carrying capacity). A small number of offspring is produced that require extensive parental care until they mature. Other characteristics of K-selection include large body size of individuals and longer life expectancy.

One key example of a population cycle seen in nature is the relationship between a predator and its prey. This type of association tends to fluctuate (when the predator population decreases the prey population increases and vice versa). However; it is not always a given that changes in one predator population directly lead to changes in the prey population. Food or seasonal factors may also affect the relationship.

19.3 Community Ecology

Community ecology deals with the interaction of populations. Interspecific competition refers to competition between different species while intraspecific competition is between members of the same species. There are three ways that organisms can go about reducing competiton:

1. **Competitive exclusion (Gause's principle)** – Gause's principle states that no two species can occupy the same niche and coexist. Species occupying the same niche compete for at least one resource in common. What inevitably occurs is that one species outcom-

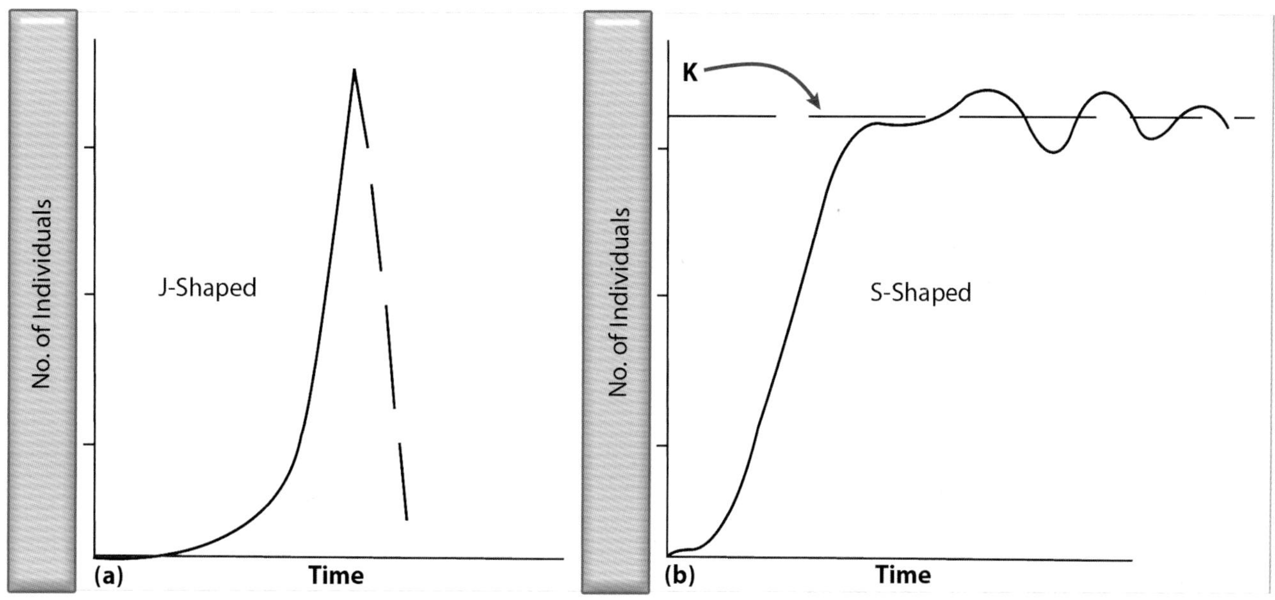

Population Growth Forms: (a) J-shaped; (b) S-shaped - K represents the carrying capacity.

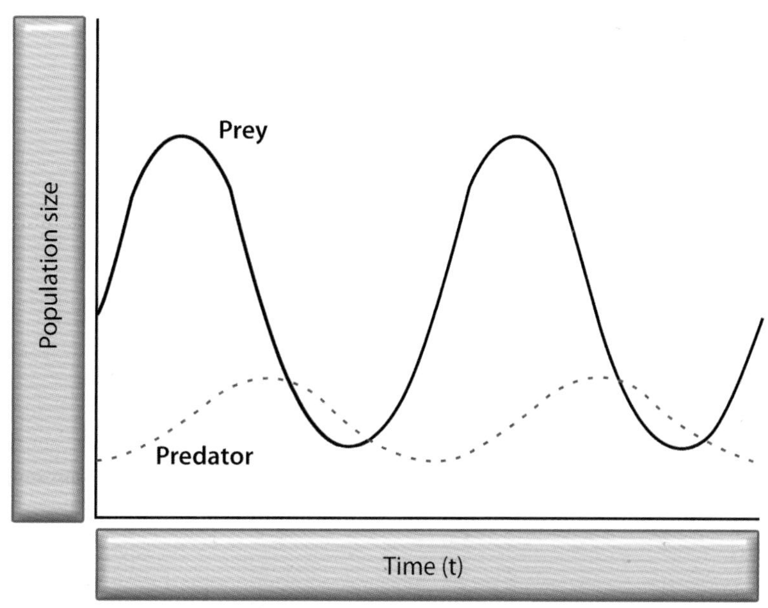

petes the other leading to the extinction of the weaker, less adaptable species.

2. **Resource partitioning** – When species adapt to occupy slightly different niches in order to coexist.
3. **Niche shift** – Selection of characteristics that enable one species to better obtain resources leads to an eventual niche shift and leads to divergence of features or character displacement.

A community is an integrated system of species living within the same area. The major types of interspecific interactions include symbiosis, predation, saprophytism and scavengers.

1. **Symbiosis** is a term that applies to two species living in close proximity with each other, which may or may not benefit both sides. There are four main types of symbiotic relationships: mutualism, commensalism, parasitism and amensalism.
   a) **Mutualism** – Any relationship between individuals of different species where both individuals derive some benefit. An example of mutual symbiosis can be seen in lichens, a very close association between fungus and algae. The algae supply sugars obtained via photosynthesis for itself and the fungus, while the fungus provides carbon dioxide and nitrogenous wastes for the algae to use for photosynthesis and protein synthesis. Another example is between legumes and symbiotic nitrogen-fixing bacteria that live together. The bacteria grow on the roots of legumes to form root nodules. In the nodule, the legume provides nutrients for itself and the bacteria while the bacteria fixes nitrogen, making it useable for the legume.
   b) **Commensalism** – Any relationship between two living organisms where one benefits and the other is not significantly affected. An example is between a remora (a 'suckerfish') and a shark, where the remora attaches itself to the shark and uses it for transportation (wide geographic dispersal) and for protection. The shark is completely unaffected.
   c) **Parasitism** – Any relationship where one member of the association, the parasite, benefits at the expense of the other, the host. Parasitic symbioses take many forms, from endoparasites that live within the host to ectoparasites that live on the exterior surface of the host. In addition, parasites may even have parasites of their own. For example, an animal may have a parasitic worm, which in turn is parasitized by bacteria. A classic example of parasitism is between a virus and the host cell. All viruses are parasites (BIO 2.1). Once they enter into the host, the viruses take over the host cell function and use it for their own.
   d) **Amensalism** – Any relationship between two living organisms where one is completely obliterated (harmed) and the other is unaffected (not benefited). A common example is between the bread mold penicillium and bacteria. Penicillium secretes penicillin which kills

bacteria. Throughout the process the penicillium is unaffected.

2. **Predation** is a term that describes an interspecific interaction where a predator feeds on other living organisms. This definition includes carnivores (diet: mainly or exclusively animal tissue), herbivores (diet: plant based) and omnivores (diet can include plants, animals, algae and fungi). A key characteristic of the predator-prey relationship is the predator's direct impact in controlling the prey's population but not so as to threaten its existence.

3. **Saprophytism** is a term that describes the process of chemical decomposition of dead or decayed organic matter extracellularly through which nutrients are later absorbed. They play a vital role in the ecosystem by completing the cycling of organic matter within the system.

4. **Scavenger** is a term that can be applied to both carnivorous and herbivorous in which the scavengers consume dead animal or plants or decaying matter. They play a vital role in the ecosystem by contributing to the decomposition of dead or decaying matter.

19.4 Coevolution

Coevolution is the evolution of one species in response to new adaptations found in another species. Organisms need to be able to coexist. This is paramount to the continued viability of the ecosystem and the planet as a whole. Important examples of coevolution include camouflage (an animal blending in with its surroundings to avoid predation), secondary compounds (toxic chemicals produced in plants to discourage herbivores), aposematic coloration (conspicuous colorations or patterns found on the body of an organism that warn predators of their defense mechanisms) and mimicry (two or more species resemble one another in appearance). There are two specific types:

1. **Mullerian mimicry** – Occurs when several harmful species, may or may not be closely related, share the same warning signals. This helps protect all species involved by making their coloration/patterns better known to their shared predators (i.e. bees, wasps and hornets).

2. **Batesian mimicry** – In contrast to Mullerian mimicry where both parties are harmful, this type of mimicry occurs when a harmless species, known as the mimic, mimics the warning signals of a harmful species, known as the model (i.e. a harmless fly adopting a yellow/black pattern to resemble bees).

19.5 Ecological Succession

The concept of ecological succession is seen when one community with a certain species inhabiting it is gradually replaced by another community consisting of a different species until a climax community is established. As succession progresses species diversity and biomass (total mass of all living organisms) increases. The final stage, or *sere*, is called the climax community where the combination of species and their habitat remains the same until it is destroyed by some sort of catastrophic event such as a forest fire or earthquake. Some of the factors that change over time before the climax stage is reached include substrate texture, soil pH, light availability and crowding.

The plants and animals that are the first to colonize a new habitat are called the pioneer species (most often r-selected species that grow quickly and produce many offspring). The pioneer species are eventually replaced by K-selected species which are more stable and live longer.

There are two types of succession:

1. **Primary succession** – Occurs on substrates that never previously supported living things such as volcanic islands. In this scenario succession often begins with the establishment of lichens followed by many species of bacteria, mosses, insects and other arthropods. Grasses, herbs and plants appear next when the soil becomes arable. More r-selected species follow and are eventually replaced by K-selected ones.
2. **Secondary succession** – Begins in habitats where there has been prior colonization by various communities of organisms. Areas damaged by fires, floods or insect devastation are prime candidates. This occurs faster than primary succession because conditions are already in place to support life.

19.6 Ecosystems

The study of ecosystems focuses on the production and utilization of energy and organizes different plant and animal groups into trophic (= feeding/nutrition) levels that are each associated with a particular energy source. There are five types:

1. **Primary producers** – Autotrophs such as plants and chemotrophs such as oxidizing bacteria that utilize light energy or simple raw materials, respectively, to synthesize all the necessary organic compounds.
2. **Primary consumers** – Herbivores that eat the primary producers.
3. **Secondary consumers** – Primary carnivores that eat the primary consumers.

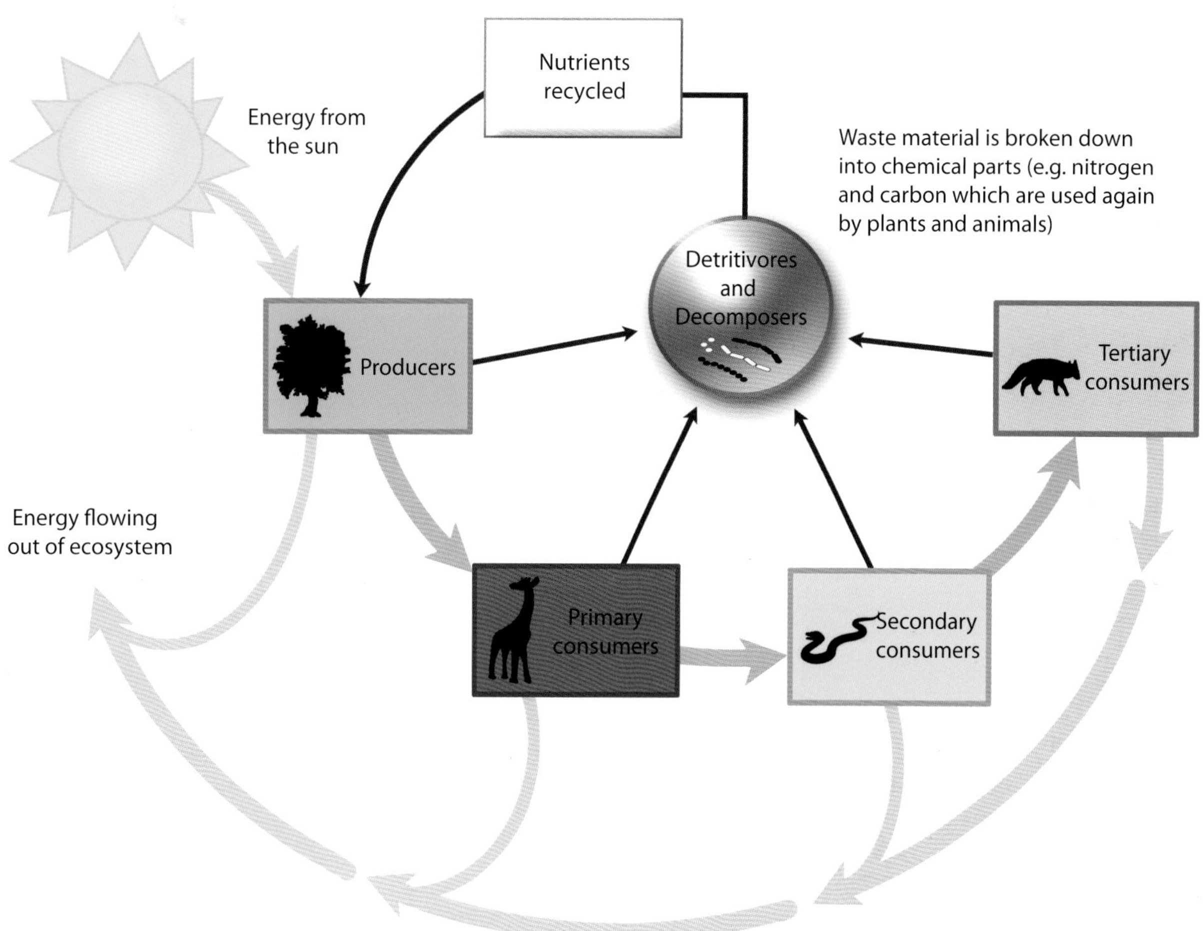

4. **Tertiary consumers** – Secondary carnivores that eat the secondary consumers.
5. **Detritivores** – Consumers that obtain their energy from dead plants and animals.

Ecological pyramids are used to show the relationship between the different trophic levels. The horizontal bars represent the sizes and the order of the levels represents how energy is transferred. There are three main types of pyramids:

1. **Pyramid of energy:** The producer at the base of the pyramid contains the most amount of energy. Less energy becomes available for primary consumers and even less for secondary or tertiary consumers. The least amount of energy is present at the top of the pyramid.

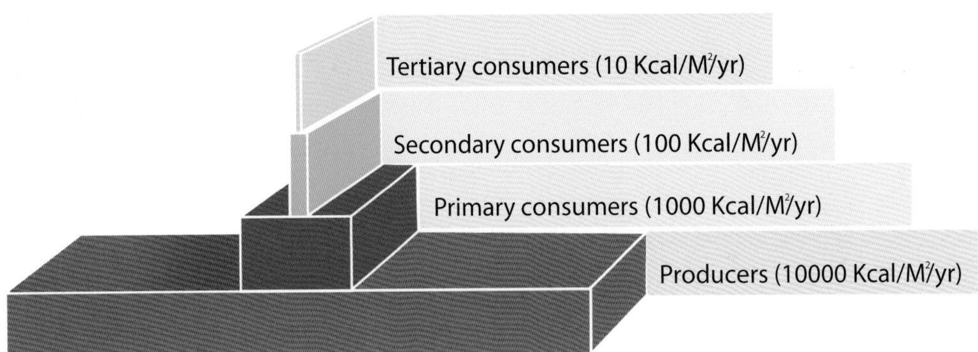

2. **Pyramid of numbers:** The producer at the base of the pyramid contains the greatest number of organisms. As the pyramid is ascended, there is a smaller number of organisms. The least number of organisms is present at the top of the pyramid.

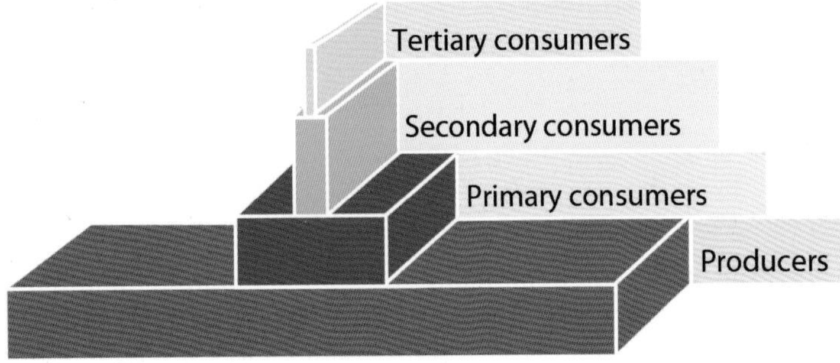

3. **Pyramid of biomass:** The producer at the base of the pyramid contains the most amount of mass since organisms from upper levels of the pyramid derive their food from lower levels. The least amount of biomass is present at the top of the pyramid.

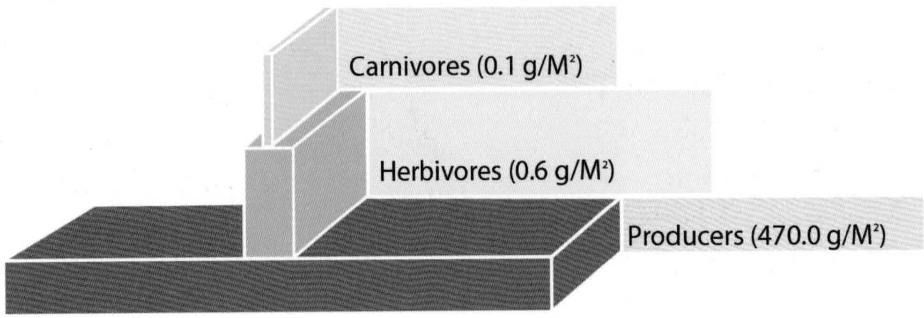

The concept of ecological efficiency relates to the pyramids by describing the proportion of energy in one trophic level that is transferred to the next level. Large horizontal bars represent energy that is transferred with high efficiency while the narrower bars are indicative of decreased efficacy. On average, only about 10% of the energy produced at one trophic level is transferred to the next. The remaining 90% is consumed by metabolic demand of the plant or animal found in that level. Food chains (linear flow charts of who eats whom) and food webs (more complete version of the food chain) diagram the flow of energy between organisms.

19.7 Biomes

Biomes are occupied by unique communities of plants and animals that possess adaptations tailored to the conditions of their collective habitat. Each biome is a component of the biosphere (BIO 19.1):

1. **Tropical rain forest** – Characterized by high temperatures, heavy rainfall, lush vegetation and many different types of species (monkeys, lizards and snakes). Little plant growth occurs on the floor due to lack of sunlight, a direct result of the tall trees that form a canopy and shade the surface. Epiphytes are commonly found in rain forests and are small plants that grow on the branches of the larger trees, further shading the ground surface.
2. **Savannas** – Grasslands with scattered plant life that receive less water than the rain forests. As suggested by its name, "grasslands" are areas where the vegetation is dominated by grasses and other non-woody (= herbaceous) plants.
3. **Temperate grasslands** – Receive even less water than the savannas and are subject to lower temperatures (i.e. North American prairie).
4. **Temperate deciduous forests** - Occupy regions which have warm summers, cold winters and moderate precipitation.
5. **Alpine** - Upper altitudes of mountains, where cooler climates give rise to communities which resemble (but do not duplicate) the taiga, tundra and frozen biomes.
6. **Deserts** – Arid and hot with little precipitation. Feature cacti and species of animal that have tremendous water conservation adaptations (i.e. camels and kangaroo rats).
7. **Taigas** – Coniferous forests with cold winters and snow. Pines and firs occupy this region. Taiga is also knows as boreal forest. {"Coniferous" refers to trees or shrubs that bear cones and

evergreen leaves (see Kingdom Plantae, BIO 16.6.4).}

8. **Tundra** – Extremely harsh winters with little if any vegetation. Animals living in the tundra have adaptations to the cold and cannot survive in moderate biomes (i.e. polar bears and penguins). Tundra has short growing seasons, a large variation in annual temperatures and usually has permafrost (= a thick layer of soil that remains frozen). The ecological boundary (= ecotone) between the forest and tundra is called the tree line (= timberline). Depending on the classification system, Tundra is sometimes referred to as Arctic, Antarctic or Frozen. The latter two cannot support vegetation because it is too cold and dry.

GOLD STANDARD WARM-UP EXERCISES

CHAPTER 19: Ecology

1) A certain plant requires light, moisture, oxygen, carbon dioxide and minerals in order to survive. The preceding information is consistent with the idea that the plant depends on:
   A. symbiotic relationships.
   B. amensalism.
   C. biotic factors.
   D. abiotic factors.

2) Which of the following graphs best describes logistic growth?
   A. J shaped curve
   B. S shaped curve
   C. K-selected species
   D. r-selected curve

3) The idea that two different species cannot occupy the same niche for long is consistent with the:
   A. Competitive Exclusion Principle.
   B. Principle of Ecology.
   C. Hardy-Weinberg Law.
   D. Theory of Natural Selection.

4) Certain bacteria living in the human colon help to produce vitamin K is an example of:
   A. mutualism.
   B. commensalism.
   C. amensalism.
   D. parasitism.

5) The trophic structure of an ecosystem can be represented as a pyramid of:
   A. biomass.
   B. numbers.
   C. energy.
   D. all of the above.

6) Which of the following is a producer?
   A. A silkworm
   B. A mushroom
   C. A pregnant lioness
   D. An oak tree

7) Organisms that use inorganic nutrients and an outside energy source to produce sugars and other organic nutrients for themselves and other members of the community are:
   A. autotrophs.
   B. producers.
   C. heterotrophs.
   D. both A and B.

8) An example of a detritus feeder is a(n):
   A. cow.
   B. dog.
   C. earthworm.
   D. photosynthetic bacterium.

9) Tertiary consumers feed on:
   A. producers.
   B. chemoautotrophs.
   C. primary consumers.
   D. secondary consumers.

10) Solar energy is first transformed by which of the following when it enters an ecosystem?

A. Chemoautotrophs
B. Detritivores
C. Producers
D. Primary consumers

11) As nutrients cycle through an ecosystem, the inorganic nutrients are returned to autotrophs by:

A. detritivores.
B. producers.
C. chemoautotrophs.
D. primary consumers.

12) The main difference between a tropical rainforest and a savanna is the difference in:

A. precipitation.
B. temperature.
C. animals.
D. hemisphere.

13) On the Arctic tundra, only the topmost layer of earth thaws but the layer beneath is referred to as:

A. subsoil.
B. permafrost.
C. temperate earth.
D. arctic vegetation.

14) Which of the following is (are) treeless?

A. Desert
B. Tundra
C. Grasslands
D. All of the above

15) Which of the following is consistent with a coniferous forest?

A. Deciduous forest
B. Temperate Forest
C. Boreal Forest
D. Tropical Rainforest

GS ANSWER KEY

CHAPTER 19

		Cross-Reference			Cross-Reference
1.	D	BIO 19.1	9.	D	BIO 19.6
2.	B	BIO 19.2, 19.3	10.	C	BIO 19.6
3.	A	BIO 16.2, 19.3	11.	A	BIO 19.6
4.	A	BIO 2.2, 9.5, 19.3	12.	A	BIO 19.7
5.	D	BIO 19.6	13.	B	BIO 19.7
6.	D	BIO 16.6.4, 19.6	14.	D	BIO 19.7
7.	D	BIO 2.2, 19.6	15.	C	BIO 19.7
8.	C	BIO 16.6.4, 19.6			

* Explanations can be found at the back of the book.

Go online to DAT-prep.com for additional chapter review Q&A and forum.

APPENDIX

CHAPTER 19: Ecology

Advanced DAT-30 Passage: Coevolution: A Closer Look

Much of the study of evolution of interspecific interactions had focused on the results rather than the process of coevolution. In only a few cases has the genetic bases of interspecific interactions been explored. One of the most intriguing results has been the description of "gene-for-gene" systems governing the interaction between certain parasites and their hosts. In several crop plants, dominant alleles at a number of loci have been described that confer resistance to a pathogenic fungus; for each such gene, the fungus appears to have a recessive allele for "virulence" that enables the fungus to attack the otherwise resistant host. Cases of <u>character displacement</u> - the evolutionary divergence of similar traits among competing sympatric species - are among the best evidence that interspecific interactions can result in genetic change.

Assuming that parasites and their hosts coevolve in an "arms race," we might deduce that the parasite is "ahead" if local populations are more capable of attacking the host population with which they are associated than other populations. Whereas the host may be "ahead" if local populations are more resistant to the local parasite than to other populations of the parasite.

Several studies have been done to evaluate coevolutionary interactions between parasites and hosts, or predators and prey. In one, the fluctuations in populations of houseflies and of a wasp that parasitized them were recorded. The results of the experiment are shown in Fig. 1.

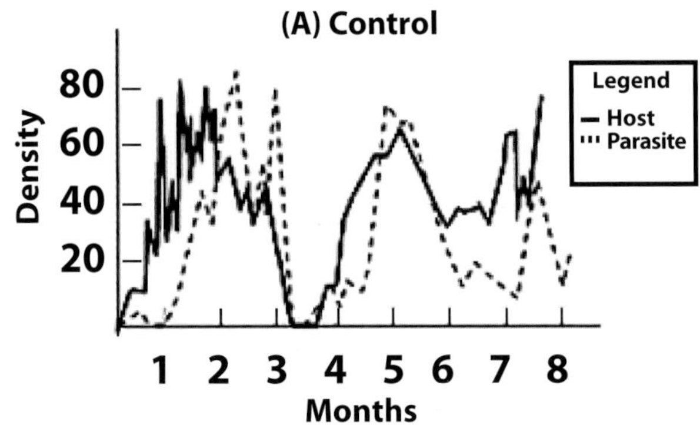

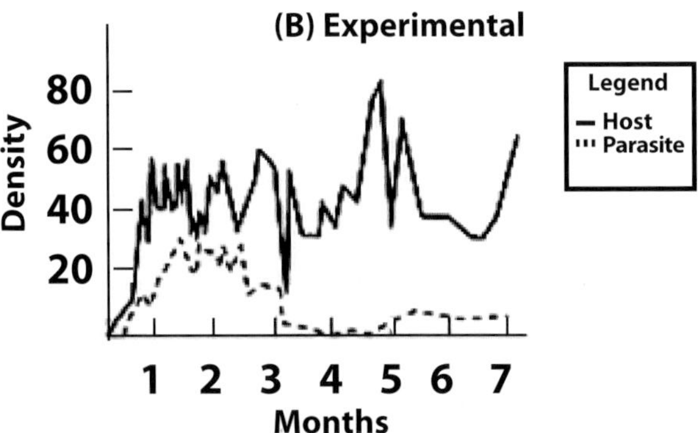

Figure 1

16) A pathogenic fungus is more capable of growth and reproduction on its native population of its sole host, the wild hog peanut, than on plants from other populations of the same species. It is reasonable to conclude that:

A. the fungus, in this instance, was capable of more rapid adaptation to its host than vice versa.

B. the fungus, in this instance, was capable of more rapid adaptation to all populations of the host species than vice versa.

C. the host, in this instance, was capable of more rapid adaptation to the fungus than vice versa.

D. all populations of the host species were capable of more rapid adaptation to the fungus than vice versa.

17) According to Fig. 1, the experiment showed that over time:

A. coevolution caused a decrease in both the host and parasite populations.

B. coevolution caused both a decrease in fluctuation of the host and parasite populations, and a lowered density of the parasite population.

C. coevolution caused a marked increase in the fluctuation of only the host population, and lowered the density of the parasite population.

D. coevolution caused a decrease in the population density of the parasite population but caused a marked increase in the density of the host population.

18) The control in the experiment likely consisted of:

A. members from different populations of the host and parasite species used in the experimental group, that had a short history of exposure to one another.

B. members of the host and parasite species used in the experimental group, that had a long history of exposure to one another.

C. members of the host and parasite species used in the experimental group that had no history of exposure to one another.

D. members from different populations of the host and parasite species used in the experimental group, that had a long history of exposure to one another.

19) Which of the following is the least likely explanation of the results obtained for the control group in Fig. 1?

A. A low parasite population results in a lowered host population by the sheer virulence of the parasite.

B. A very low host population can increase a parasite population by forcing the parasite to seek an alternate source for food.

C. A high parasite population destroys the host population resulting in a lowered host population.

D. A high host population creates a breeding ground for parasites thus increasing the parasite population.

20) Penicillin is an antibiotic which destroys bacteria by interfering with cell wall production. Could the development of bacterial resistance to Penicillin be considered similar to coevolution?

A. Yes, a spontaneous mutation is likely to confer resistance to Penicillin.

B. No, an organism can only evolve in response to another organism.

C. Yes, as antibiotics continue to change there will be a selective pressure for bacterial genes which confer resistance.

D. No, bacteria have plasma membranes and can survive without cell walls.

ANSWER KEY

Advanced Topics - Chapter 19

Cross-Reference

16.	A	BIO 2.1, 2.3, 16.2, 16.6, 19.2, 19.3, 19.4
17.	B	BIO 16.2, 16.3, 16.6, 19.2, 19.3, 19.4
18.	C	BIO 2.5, 2.5.1, 16.6, 19.2, 19.3, 19.4
19.	A	BIO 2.5, 2.5.1, 16.3, 16.6, 19.2, 19.3, 19.4
20.	C	BIO 16.3, 16.6, 19.2, 19.3, 19.4

P = paragraph; ***S*** = sentence; ***E*** = equation; ***T*** = table; ***F*** = figure

Go online to DAT-prep.com for additional chapter review Q&A and forum.

BIOCHEMISTRY
Chapter 20

Memorize

Nomenclature and structures of common molecules
Isoelectric point equation
Define: amphoteric, zwitterions

Understand

* Effect of H, S, hydrophobic bonds
* Basic mechanisms of reactions
* Effect of pH, isoelectric point
* Protein structure
* Basics: carbohydrates, lipids, steroids, phosphorus
* Biological buffers

Importance

0 to 2 out of the 40 Biology DAT questions are based on content in this chapter (in our estimation).
* Note that between 25% and 50% of the questions in DAT Biology are from 5 chapters: 1, 2, 14, 15, and 16.

DAT-Prep.com

Introduction 

Biological molecules truly involve the chemistry of life. Such molecules include amino acids and proteins, carbohydrates (glucose, disaccharides, polysaccharides), lipids (triglycerides, steroids) and nucleic acids (DNA, RNA).

Additional Resources

Free Online Q&A + Forum

Video: Online or DVD

Flashcards

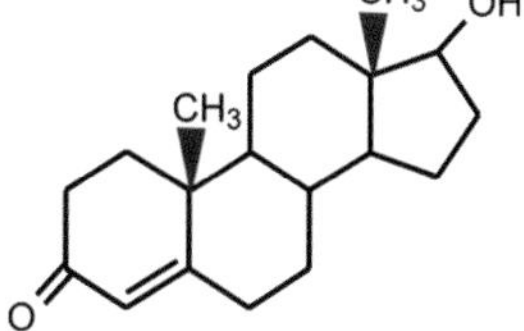

Special Guest

20.0 Prelude to Biochemistry

If Biochemistry is not your favorite subject, here is the good news: most biochemistry has been covered in previous chapters including our review of DNA, RNA and protein (chapters 1 and 3), enzymes and cellular metabolism (chapters 4 and 17), etc. Thermodynamics, enthalpy, thermochemistry, and rate processes in chemical reactions are reviewed in GS DAT General Chemistry (chapters 7, 8 and 9).

In this chapter, we will only review those aspects of biochemistry that could be asked in DAT Biology but not reviewed elsewhere in the GS series of DAT books. This chapter overlaps GS DAT Organic Chemistry Chapter 12 (Biological Molecules) which has more details regarding stereochemistry, reactions and mechanisms.

20.1 Amino Acids

Amino acids are molecules that contain a side chain (*R*), a carboxylic acid, and an amino group at the α carbon. Thus the general structure of α-amino acids is:

H_2N—C(COOH)(R)—H: L - amino acid

H—C(COOH)(R)—NH_2: D - amino acid

Amino acids may be named systematically as substituted carboxylic acids, however, there are 20 important α-amino acids that are known by common names. These are naturally occurring and they form the building blocks of most proteins found in humans. The following are a few examples of α-amino acids:

NH_2—CH_2—C(=O)—OH: Glycine

H_2N—C(COOH)(CH_3)—H: Alanine

H_2N—C(COOH)(CH_2OH)—H: Serine

H_2N—C(COOH)(CH_2COOH)—H: Aspartic acid

Note that all amino acids have the same relative configuration, the L-configuration. However, the absolute configuration depends on the priority assigned to the side group (*see ORG 2.3.1 for rules*). In the preceding amino acids, the S-configuration prevails.

20.1.1 Hydrophilic vs. Hydrophobic

Different types of amino acids tend to be found in different areas of the proteins that they make up. Amino acids which are ionic and/or polar are hydrophilic, and tend to be found on the exterior of proteins (i.e. *exposed to water*). These include aspartic acid and its amide, glutamic acid and its amide, lysine, arginine and histidine. Certain other polar amino acids are found on either the interior or exterior of proteins. These include serine, threonine, and tyrosine. Hydrophobic amino acids which may be found on the interior of proteins include methionine, leucine, tryptophan, valine and phenylalanine. Hydrophobic molecules tend to cluster in aqueous solutions (= *hydrophobic bonding*). Alanine is a nonpolar amino acid which is unusual because it is less hydrophobic than most nonpolar amino acids. This is because its nonpolar side chain is very short.

Glycine is the smallest amino acid, and the only one that is not optically active. It is often found at the 'corners' of proteins. Alanine is small and, although hydrophobic, is found on the surface of proteins.

20.1.2 Acidic vs. Basic

Amino acids have both an acid and basic components (= *amphoteric*). The amino acids with the R group containing an amino ($-NH_2$) group, are basic. The two basic amino acids are lysine and arginine. Amino acids with an R group containing a carboxyl (–COOH) group are acidic. The two acidic amino acids are aspartic acid and glutamic acid. One amino acid, histidine, may act as either an acid or a base, depending upon the pH of the resident solution. This makes histidine a very good physiologic buffer. The rest of the amino acids are considered to be neutral.

The basic $-NH_2$ group in the amino acid is present as an ammonium ion, $-NH_3^+$. The acidic carboxyl –COOH group is present as a carboxylate ion, $-COO^-$. As a result, amino acids are dipolar ions, or *zwitterions*. In an aqueous solution, there is an equilibrium present between the dipolar, the anionic, and the cationic forms of the amino acid:

$$\underset{\text{Acidic}}{H_3\overset{+}{N}-\underset{\substack{|\\CH_3}}{CH}-CO_2H} \underset{H_3O^+}{\rightleftharpoons} \underset{\text{Neutral}}{H_3\overset{+}{N}-\underset{\substack{|\\CH_3}}{CH}-CO_2^-} \underset{H_3O^+}{\rightleftharpoons} \underset{\text{Basic}}{H_2N-\underset{\substack{|\\CH_3}}{CH}-CO_2^-}$$

Therefore the charge on the amino acid will vary with the pH of the solution, and with the isoelectric point. This point is the pH where a given amino acid will be neutral (i.e. have no net charge). This isoelectric point is the average of the two pK_a values of an amino acid (*depending on the dissociated group*):

$$\text{isoelectric point} = pI = (pK_{a1} + pK_{a2})/2$$

As this is a common exam question, let's further summarize for the average amino acid: When in a relatively acidic solution, the amino acid is fully protonated and exists as a cation, that is, it has two protons available for dissociation, one from the carboxyl group and one from the amino group. When in a relatively basic solution, the amino acid is fully deprotonated and exists as an anion, that is, it has two proton accepting groups, the carboxyl group and the amino group. At the isoelectric point, the amino acid exists as a neutral, dipolar zwitterion, which means that the carboxyl group is deprotonated while the amino group is protonated.

20.1.3 The 20 Alpha-Amino Acids

Approximately 500 amino acids are known - of these, only 22 are proteinogenic ("protein building") amino acids. Of these, 20 amino acids are known as "standard" and are found in human beings and other eukaryotes, and are encoded directly by the universal genetic code (BIO 3). The 2 exceptions are the "non-standard" pyrrolysine — found only in some methanogenic organisms but not humans — and selenocysteine which is present in humans and a wide range of other organisms.

Of the 20 standard amino acids, 9 are called "essential" for humans because they cannot be created from other compounds by the human body, and so must be taken in as food.

The following summarizes the categories of amino acids based on side chains, pK_a and charges at physiological pH:

1. Nonpolar amino acids: R groups are hydrophobic and thus decrease solubility. These amino acids are usually found within the interior of the protein molecule.

2. Polar amino acids: R groups are hydrophilic and thus increase the solubility. These amino acids are usually found on the protein's surface.

3. Acidic amino acids: R groups contain an additional carboxyl group. These amino acids have a negative charge at physiological pH.

4. Basic amino acids: R groups contain an additional amine group. These amino acids have a positive charge at physiological pH. Note that asparagine and glutamine have amide side chains and are thus not considered basic (see ORG 9.3).

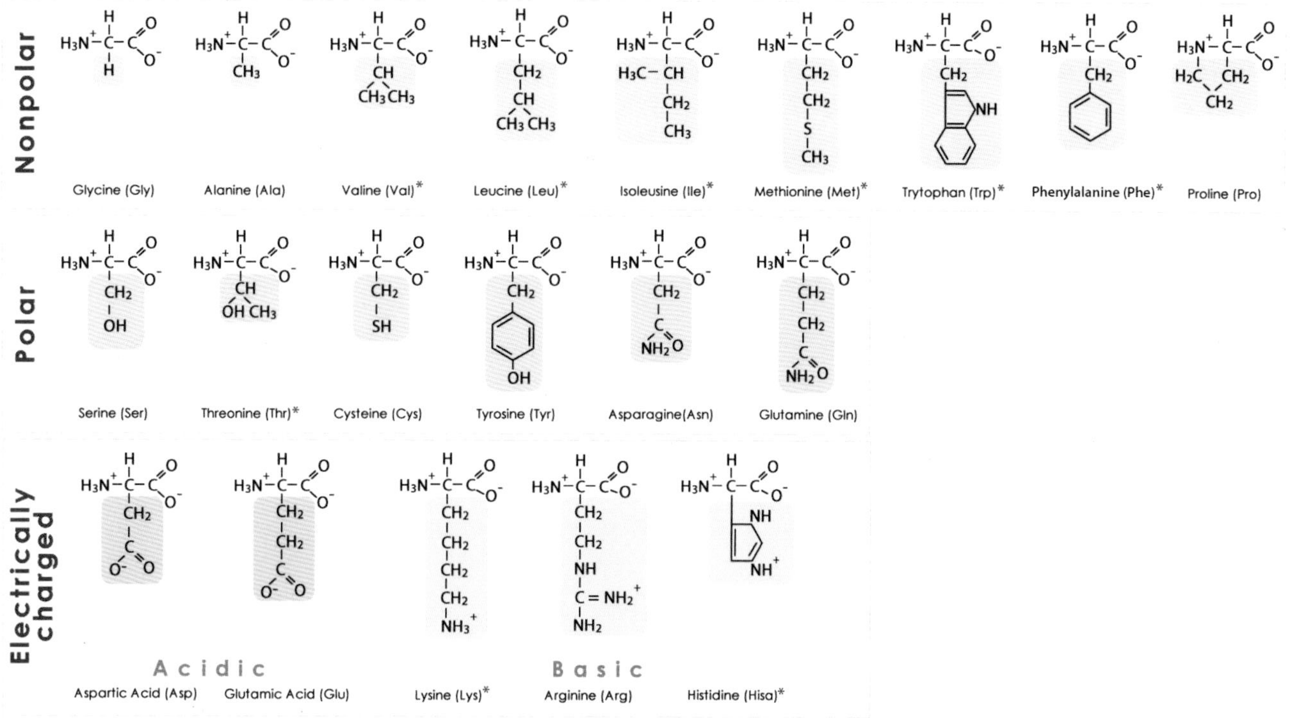

Nonpolar

Glycine (Gly) Alanine (Ala) Valine (Val)* Leucine (Leu)* Isoleusine (Ile)* Methionine (Met)* Trytophan (Trp)* Phenylalanine (Phe)* Proline (Pro)

Polar

Serine (Ser) Threonine (Thr)* Cysteine (Cys) Tyrosine (Tyr) Asparagine(Asn) Glutamine (Gln)

Electrically charged

Acidic

Aspartic Acid (Asp) Glutamic Acid (Glu)

Lysine (Lys)*

Basic

Arginine (Arg) Histidine (Hisa)*

Figure IV.A.20.1: The 20 Standard Amino Acids. A red asterix * is used to indicate the 9 essential amino acids.

20.2 Proteins

20.2.1 General Principles

An oligopeptide consists of between 2 and 20 amino acids joined together by amide *(peptide)* bonds. Oligopeptides include dipeptides (2 amino acids), tripeptides (3), tetrapeptides (4), pentapeptides (5), etc. Polypeptides - generally regarded to be between the size of oligopeptides and proteins - are polymers of up to 100 or even 1000 α-amino acids (depending on the molecule and the reference). Proteins are long chain polypeptides which often form higher order structures. These peptide bonds are derived from the amino group of one amino acid, and the acid group of another. When a peptide bond is formed, a molecule of water is released (*condensation* = *dehydration*). The bond can be broken by adding water (*hydrolysis*).

Since proteins are polymers of amino acids, they also have isoelectric points. Classification as to the acidity or basicity of a protein depends on the numbers of acidic and basic amino acids it contains. If there is an excess of acidic amino acids, the isoelectric point will be at a pH of less than 7. At pH = 7, these proteins will have a net negative charge. Similarly, those with an excess of basic amino acids will have an isoelectric point at a pH of greater than 7. Therefore, at pH = 7, these proteins will have a net positive charge. Proteins can be separated according to their isoelectric point on a polyacrylamide gel (*electrophoresis*; BIO 15.7; ORG 13).

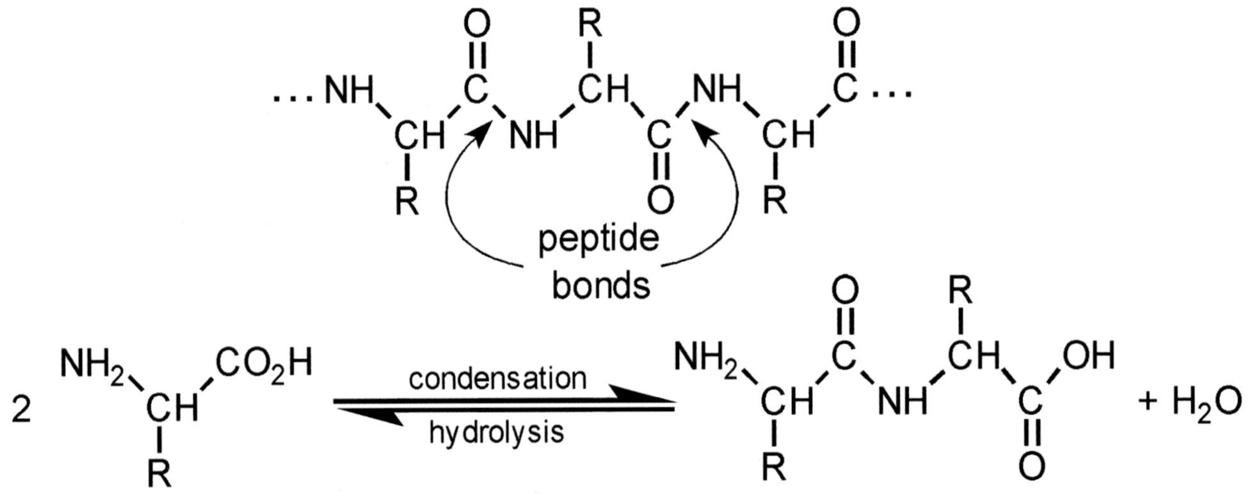

peptide bonds

condensation

hydrolysis

20.2.2 Protein Structure

Protein structure may be divided into primary, secondary, tertiary and quaternary structures. The primary structure is the sequence of amino acids as determined by the DNA and the location of covalent bonds (*including disulfide bonds*). This structure determines the higher order structures.

The secondary structure is the orderly inter- or intramolecular *hydrogen bonding* of the protein chain. The resultant structure may be the more stable α-helix (e.g. keratin), or a β-pleated sheet (e.g. silk). Proline is an amino acid which cannot participate in the regular array of H-bonding in an α-helix. Proline disrupts the α-helix, thus it is usually found at the beginning or end of a molecule (i.e. hemoglobin).

The tertiary structure is the further folding of the protein molecule onto itself. This structure is maintained by *noncovalent bonds* like hydrogen bonding, Van der Waals forces,

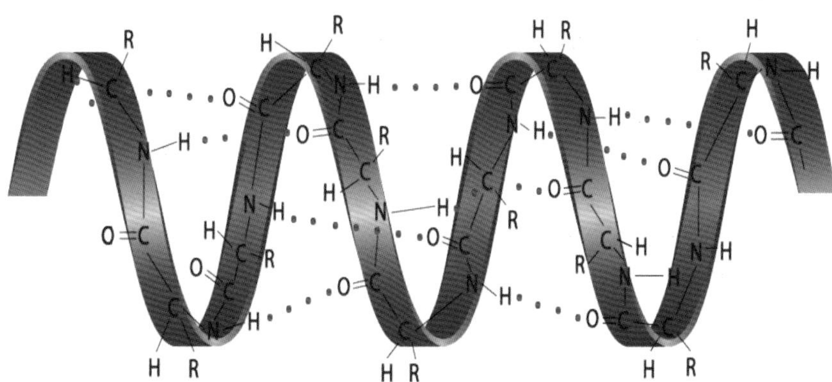

Figure IV.A.20.2: Secondary Structure: α-helix. This is a structure in which the peptide chain is coiled into a helical structure around a central axis. This helix is stabilized by hydrogen bonding between the N-H group and C=O group four residues away. A typical example with this secondary structure is keratin.

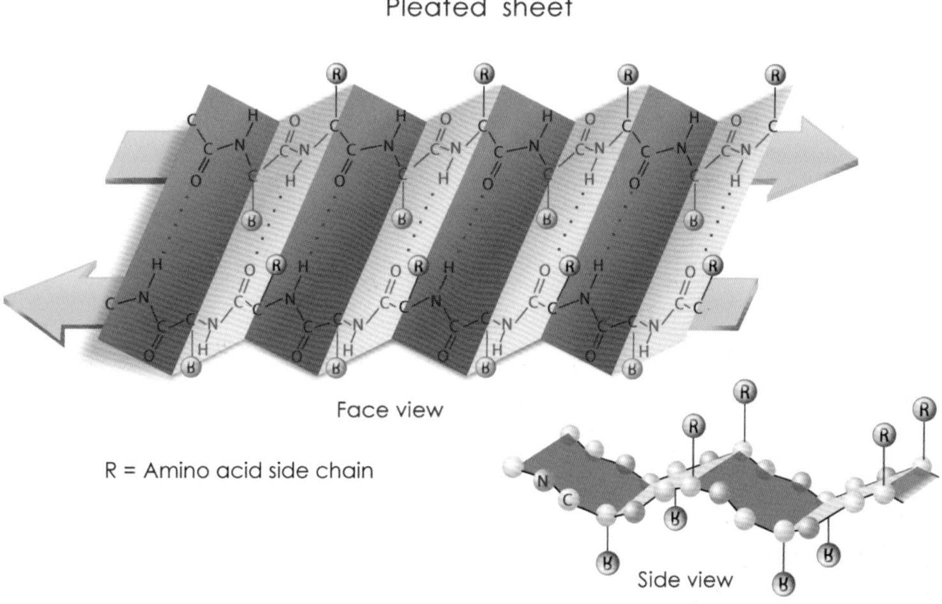

Figure IV.A.20.3: Secondary Structure: β-pleated sheet. Peptide chains lie alongside each other in a parallel manner. This structure is stabilized by hydrogen bonding between the N-H group on one peptide chain and C=O group on another. A typical example with this secondary structure is produced by some insect larvae: the protein fiber "silk" which is mostly composed of fibroin.

hydrophobic bonding and electrostatic bonding (CHM 4.2). The resultant structure is a globular protein with a hydrophobic interior and hydrophilic exterior. Enzymes are classical examples of such a structure. In fact, enzyme activity often depends on tertiary structure.

The covalent bonding of cysteine (*disulfide bonds or bridge*) helps to stabilize the tertiary structure of proteins. Cysteine will form sulfur-sulfur covalent bonds with itself, producing *cystine*.

$$2H_2N-\underset{\underset{\text{cysteine}}{CH_2SH}}{\overset{}{CH}}-CO_2H \xrightarrow{-H_2} H_2N-\underset{}{\overset{CO_2H}{CH}}(CH_2-S-S-CH_2)\overset{CO_2H}{CH}-NH_2$$

cystine

The quaternary structure is when there are two or more protein chains bonded together by noncovalent bonds. For example, hemoglobin consists of four polypeptide subunits (*globin*) held together by hydrophobic bonds forming a globular almost tetrahedryl arrangement.

20.3 Carbohydrates

20.3.1 Description and Nomenclature

Carbohydrates are sugars and their derivatives. Formally they are 'carbon hydrates,' that is, they have the general formula $C_m(H_2O)_n$. Usually they are defined as polyhydroxy aldehydes and ketones, or substances that hydrolyze to yield polyhydroxy aldehydes and ketones. The basic units of carbohydrates are monosaccharides (sugars).

There are two ways to classify sugars. One way is to classify the molecule based on the type of carbonyl group it contains: one with an aldehyde carbonyl group is an *aldose*; one with a ketone carbonyl group is a *ketose*. The second method of classification depends on the number of carbons in the molecule: those with 6 carbons are *hexoses*, with 5 carbons are *pentoses*, with 4 carbons are *tetroses*, and with 3 carbons are *trioses*. Sugars may exist in either the ring form, as hemiacetals, or in the straight chain form, as polyhydroxy aldehydes. *Pyranoses* are 6 carbon sugars in the ring form; *furanoses* are 5 carbon sugars in the ring form.

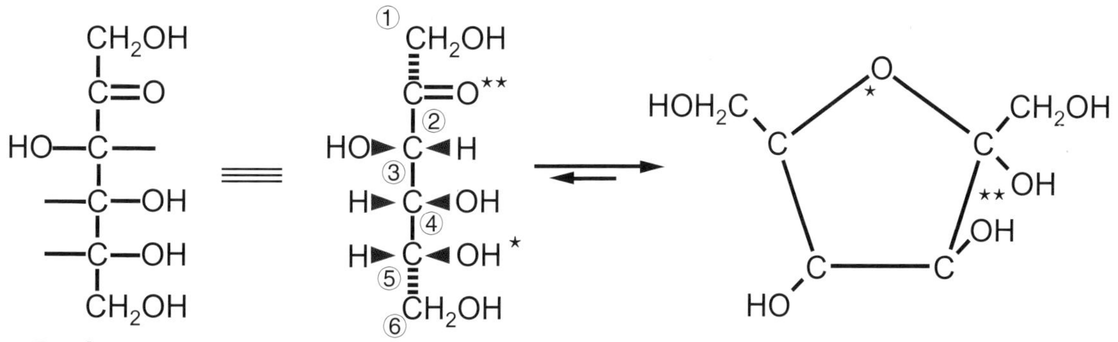

D - fructose

α - D - fructose
(a furanose)

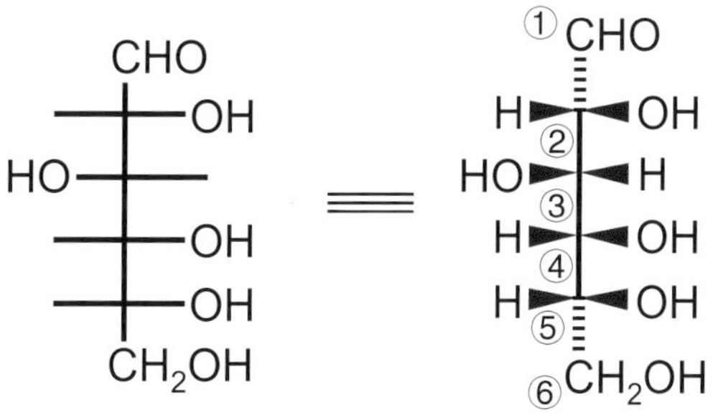

D - Glucose
(an aldose hexose)

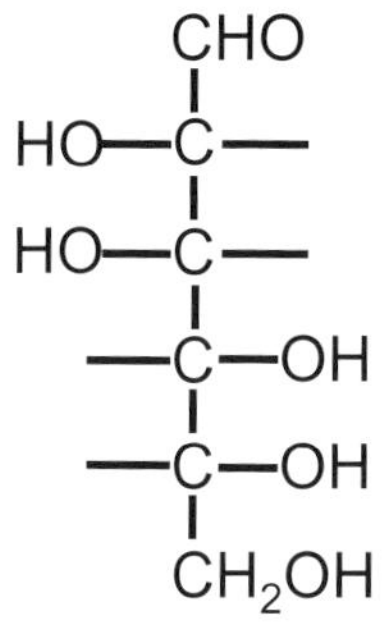

D - Mannose
(C_2 epimer
of glucose)

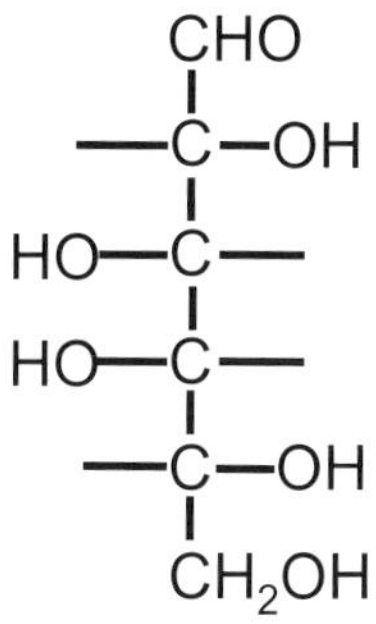

D - Galactose
(C_4 epimer
of glucose)

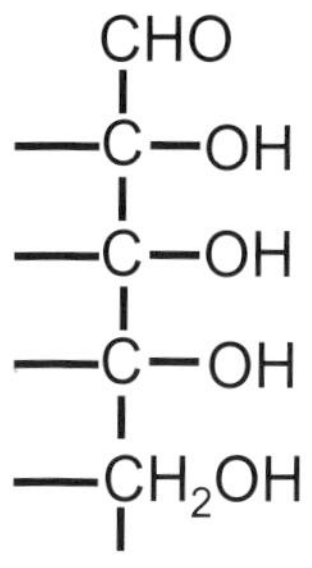

D - Ribose
(in RNA)

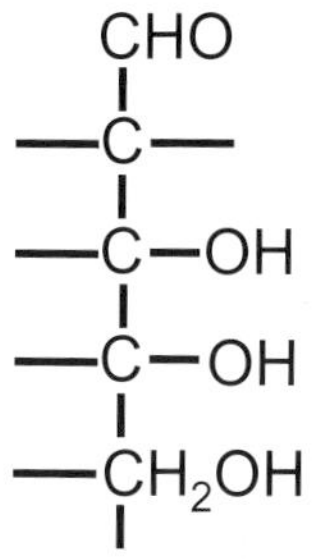

2 - Deoxy - D - ribose
(in DNA)

Figure IV.A.20.4: Names, structures and configurations of common sugars.

In the ring form, there is the possibility of α or β *anomers*. Anomers occur when 2 cyclic forms of the molecule differ in conformation only at the hemiacetal carbon (carbon 1). Generally, pyranoses take the 'chair' conformation, as it is very stable, with all (usually) hydroxyl groups at the equatorial position. *Epimers* are diastereomers that differ in the configuration of only one stereogenic center. For carbohydrates, epimers are 2 monosaccharides which differ in the conformation of one hydroxyl group.

Most but not all of the naturally occurring aldoses have the D-configuration. Thus they have the same *relative* configuration as D-glyceraldehyde.

The names and structures of some common sugars are shown in Figure IV.A.20.4.

20.3.2 Important Reactions of Carbohydrates

A disaccharide is a molecule made up of two monosaccharides, joined by a *glycosidic bond* between the hemiacetal carbon of one molecule, and the hydroxyl group of another. The glycosidic bond forms an α-1,4-glycosidic linkage if the reactant is an α anomer. A β-1,4-glycosidic linkage is formed if the reactant is a β anomer. When the bond is formed, one molecule of water is released (condensation). In order to break the bond, water must be added (hydrolysis):

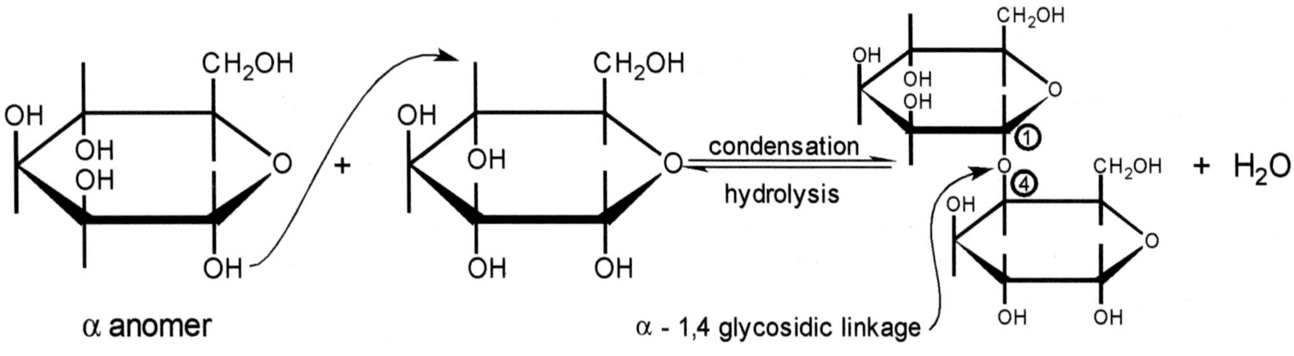

- Sucrose (common sugar) = glucose + fructose
- Lactose (milk sugar) = glucose + galactose
- Maltose (α-1,4 bond) = glucose + glucose
- Cellobiose (β-1,4 bond) = glucose + glucose

20.3.3 Polysaccharides

Polymers of many monosaccharides are called polysaccharides. As in disaccharides, they are joined by glycosidic linkages. They may be straight chains, or branched chains. Some common polysaccharides are:

- Starch (plant energy storage; BIO 17.3)
- Cellulose (plant structural component; BIO 17.3)
- Glycocalyx (associated with the plasma membrane; BIO 1.1)
- Glycogen (animal energy storage in the form of glucose; BIO 4.1, 4.4, 9.4.1)
- Chitin (structural component found in shells or arthropods; BIO 16.6.4: Fungi and Arthropoda)

Carbohydrates are the most abundant organic constituents of plants. They are the source of chemical energy in living organisms, and, in plants, they are used in making the support structures. Cellulose consists of β(1→4) linked D-glucose. Starch and glycogen are mostly α(1→4) glycosidic linkages of D-glucose.

20.4 Lipids

Lipids are a class of organic molecules containing many different types of substances, such as fatty acids, fats, waxes, triacyl glycerols, terpenes and steroids.

Triacyl glycerols are oils and fats of either animal or plant origin. In general, fats are solid at room temperature, and oils are liquid at room temperature.

Triacyl glycerols are also commonly referred to as triglycerides (= triacylglycerides) and are, by definition, fatty acid triesters of the trihydroxy alcohol glycerol.

Glycerol + 3 Fatty acids = Triglyceride

The general structure of a triacyl glycerol is:

$$\begin{array}{l} CH_2O-\overset{\displaystyle O}{\overset{\|}{C}}-R \\ | \\ CH_2O-\overset{\displaystyle O}{\overset{\|}{C}}-R' \\ | \\ CH_2O-\overset{\displaystyle O}{\overset{\|}{C}}-R'' \end{array}$$

The R groups may be the same or different, and are usually long chain alkyl groups.

Upon hydrolysis of a triacyl glycerol, the products are three fatty acids and glycerol (*see* ORG 9.4.1). The fatty acids may be saturated (= no multiple bonds, i.e. *palmitic acid*) or unsaturated (= containing double or triple bonds, i.e. *oleic acid*). Unsaturated fatty acids are usually in the cis configuration. Saturated fatty acids have a higher melting point than unsaturated fatty acids. Some common fatty acids are:

$$CH_3(CH_2)_{14}COOH$$
palmitic acid

$$CH_3(CH_2)_{16}COOH$$
stearic acid

$$CH_3(CH_2)_7CH=CH(CH_2)_7CO_2H$$
oleic acid (cis: both H on the same side of C=C)

"<u>Essential</u>" fatty acids are fatty acids that humans - and other animals - must ingest because the body requires them but cannot synthesize them. Only two are known in humans: alpha-linolenic acid and linoleic acid. Because they have multiple double bonds that begin near the methyl end, they are both known as polyunsaturated omega fatty acids.

<u>Soap</u> is a mixture of salts of long chain fatty acids formed by the hydrolysis of fat. This process is called <u>saponification</u>. Soap possesses both a nonpolar hydrocarbon tail and a

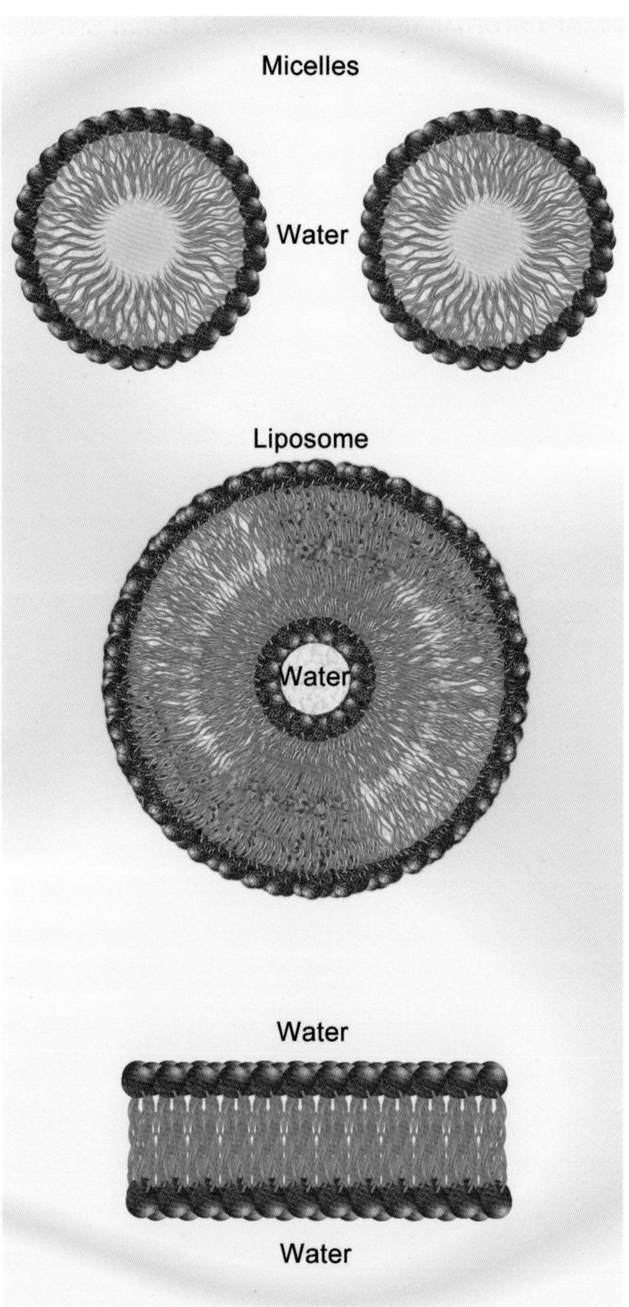

Figure IV.A.20.5. Amphipathic molecules arranged in micelles, a liposome and a bilipid layer.

polar carboxylate head. When soaps are dispersed in aqueous solution, the long nonpolar tails are inside the sphere while the polar heads face outward. Recall that a sphere is the shape that minimizes surface tension (i.e. the smallest surface area relative to volume; CHM 4.2).

Soaps are <u>surfactants</u> (BIO 12.3). They are compounds that lower the surface tension of a liquid because of their amphipathic nature (i.e. they contain both hydrophobic tails and hydrophilic heads; see BIO 1.1).

Of course, the cellular membrane is a lipid bilayer (Biology Chapter 1). The polar heads of the lipids align towards the aqueous environment, while the hydrophobic tails minimize their contact with water and tend to cluster together. Depending on the concentration of the lipid, this interaction may result in micelles (spherical), liposomes (spherical) or other lipid bilayers.

<u>Micelles</u> are closed lipid monolayers with a fatty acid core and polar surface. The main function of bile (BIO 9.4.1) is to facilitate the formation of micelles, which promotes the processing or emulsification of dietary fat and fat-soluble vitamins.

<u>Liposomes</u> are composed of a lipid bilayer separating an aqueous internal compartment from the bulk aqueous environment. Liposomes can be used as a vehicle for the administration of nutrients or pharmaceutical drugs.

20.4.1 Steroids

Steroids are derivatives of the basic ring structure:

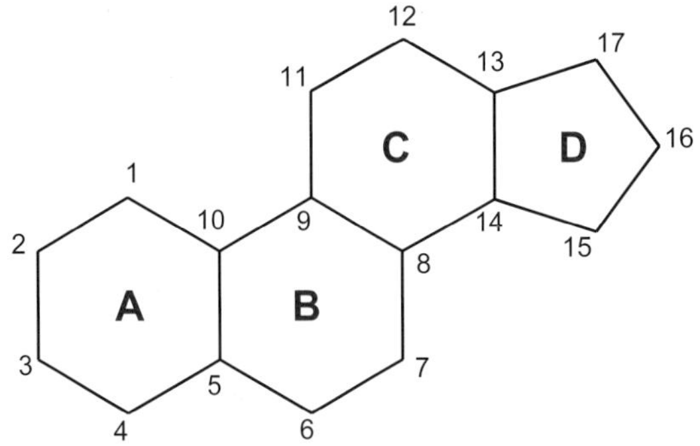

The IUPAC-recommended ring-lettering and the carbon atoms are numbered as shown. Many important substances are steroids, some examples include: cholesterol, D vitamins, bile acids, adrenocortical hormones, and male and female sex hormones.

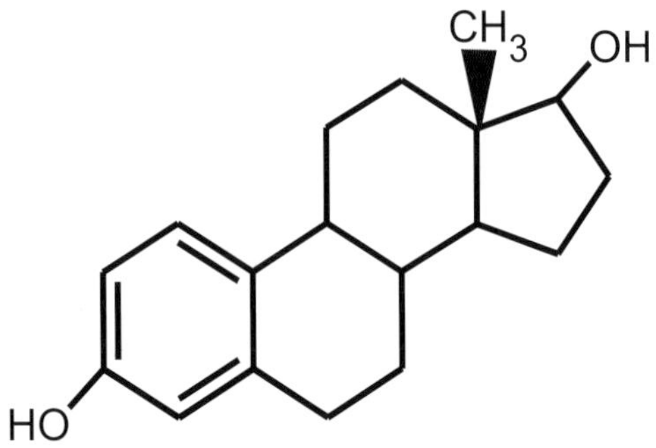

Estradiol
(an estrogen)

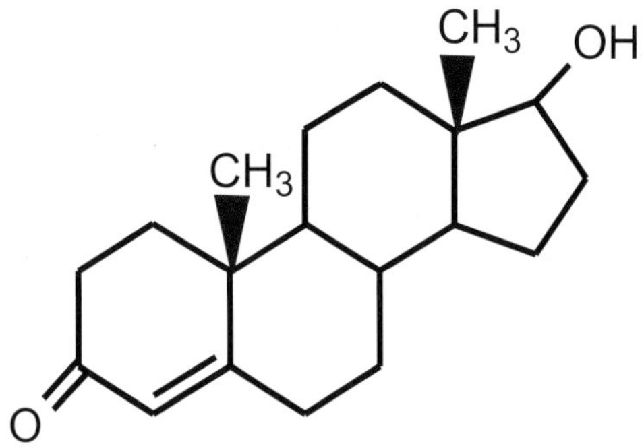

The rate limiting step in the production of steroids (= *steroidogenesis*) in humans is the conversion of cholesterol to pregnenolone, which is in the same family as progesterone. This occurs inside of mitochondria and serves as the precursor for all human steroids.

Testosterone
(an androgen)

Since such a significant portion of a steroid contains hydrocarbons, which are hydrophobic, steroids can dissolve through the hydrophobic interior of a cell's plasma membrane (BIO 1.1, 6.3). Furthermore, steroid hormones contain polar side groups which allow the hormone to easily dissolve in water. Thus steroid hormones are well designed to be transported through the vascular space, to cross the plasma membranes of cells, and to have an effect either in the cell's cytosol or, as is usually the case, in the nucleus.

20.5 Phosphorous in Biological Molecules

Phosphorous is an essential component of various biological molecules including adenosine triphosphate (ATP), phospholipids in cell membranes (BIO 1.1), and the nucleic acids which form DNA (BIO 1.2.2). Phosphorus can also form phosphoric acid and several phosphate esters:

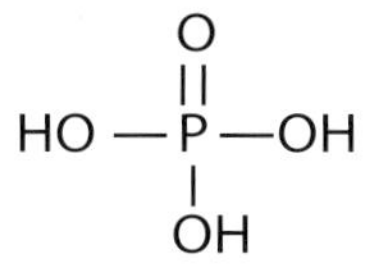

O
||
HO —P—OH
|
OH
phosphoric acid

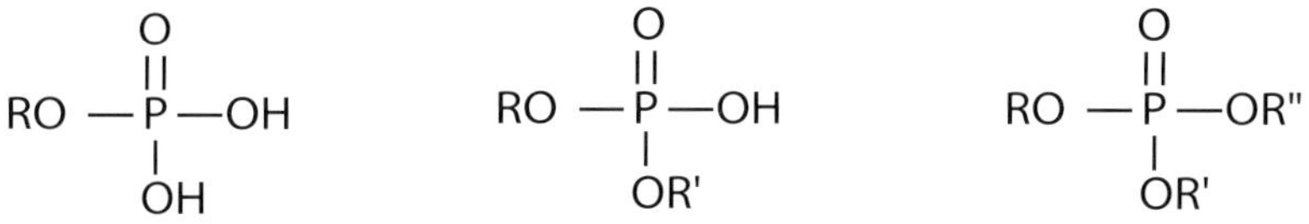

O
||
RO —P—OH
|
OH

O
||
RO —P—OH
|
OR'

O
||
RO —P—OR"
|
OR'
phosphate esters

A phospholipid is produced from three ester linkages to glycerol. Phosphoric acid is ester linked to the terminal hydroxyl group and two fatty acids are ester linked to the two remaining hydroxyl groups of glycerol (*see Biology Section 1.1 for a schematic view of a phospholipid*).

In DNA, the phosphate groups engage in two ester linkages creating phosphodiester bonds. It is the 5' phosphorylated position of one pentose ring which is linked to the 3' position of the next pentose ring (*see* BIO 1.2.2):

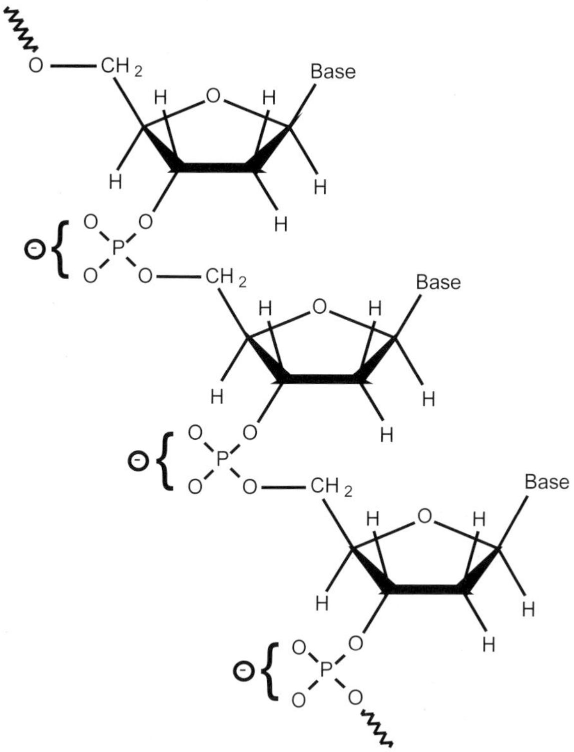

O — CH_2 Base H O H H H H
O O P O O — CH_2 Base H O H H H H
O O P O O — CH_2 Base H O H H H H
O O P O O

In Biology Chapter 4, the production of ATP was discussed. In each case, the components ADP and P_i (= *inorganic phosphate*) combined using the energy generated from a coupled reaction to produce ATP. The linkage between the phosphate groups are via *anhydride bonds*:

$$\text{adenine—ribose—O—}\underset{\text{O}^-}{\overset{\text{O}}{\overset{\|}{\text{P}}}}\text{—O—}\underset{\text{O}^-}{\overset{\text{O}}{\overset{\|}{\text{P}}}}\text{—OH}$$

adenosine diphosphate

$$+ \ \text{HO—}\underset{\text{O}^-}{\overset{\text{O}}{\overset{\|}{\text{P}}}}\text{—O}^- \xrightarrow[\text{energy}]{}$$

inorganic phosphate

$$\text{A—O—}\underset{\text{O}^-}{\overset{\text{O}}{\overset{\|}{\text{P}}}}\text{—O—}\underset{\text{O}^-}{\overset{\text{O}}{\overset{\|}{\text{P}}}}\text{—O—}\underset{\text{O}^-}{\overset{\text{O}}{\overset{\|}{\text{P}}}}\text{—O}^- + H_2O$$

adenosine triphosphate

20.6 Biological pH Buffers

A pH buffer is like a molecular sponge for protons. They are molecules which have the ability to minimize changes in pH when an acid - or base - is added to it.

Plasma pH is normally maintained at 7.4. A pH less than 7.35 is acidosis, whereas a pH of greater than 7.45 is alkalosis. Either condition can be a result of either respiratory or metabolic changes.

It is expected for the DAT that you have an understanding of the chemistry of buffers including equilibrium constants, pH, pK_a, titration and the Henderson-Hasselbalch Equation (GS DAT General Chemistry Chapter

6). These fundamental concepts will not be reviewed here.

It should be noted that the major buffer system in extracellular fluids is the CO_2-bicarbonate buffer system mediated by the enzyme carbonic anhydrase (BIO 12.4.1). This is responsible for about 75% of extracellular buffering. Protein and phosphate buffers dominate the intracellular space. Other buffer systems, though important, have a lesser impact and include ammonia (urine), calcium carbonate (bone), hemoglobin (red blood cells), and many others.

The amino acid histidine is a very good physiologic buffer (mentioned in BIO 20.1.2). Among the reasons is that its pK_a of 6.5 is not far from plasma pH and when protonated, it is resonance stabilized. Histidine is one of the building blocks of carbonic anhydrase, hemoglobin and many other proteins.

Major Buffer Systems of the Human Body

Bicarbonate buffer	$CO_2 + H_2O \rightleftharpoons H_2CO_3 \rightleftharpoons H^+ + HCO_3^-$	In blood plasma, interstitial fluids
Hemoglobin	$Hb\text{-}H \rightleftharpoons Hb^- + H^+$	Interior of red blood cells
Phosphate buffer	$H_2PO_4^- \rightleftharpoons H^+ + HPO_4^{2-}$	Most important in urine but also intracellular fluid
Protein	$Pr\text{–}H \rightleftharpoons Pr^- + H^+$	Most important in intracellular fluid with a relatively minor effect in blood

GOLD STANDARD WARM-UP EXERCISES

CHAPTER 20: Biochemistry

1) The functional groups of the amino acids located in the interior of the enzyme phenylalanine hydroxylase are mostly likely:

A. basic.
B. acidic.
C. hydrophilic.
D. hydrophobic.

2) A student is synthesizing tripeptides using three different amino acids. How many distinct molecules can she create?

A. 3
B. 4
C. 6
D. 9

3) Which of the following best describes the primary structure of proteins?

A. The arrangement of different protein subunits in a multiprotein complex.
B. The order in which amino acids are linked together in a protein.
C. Regions of ordered structure within a protein.
D. The overall three dimensional shape of a protein.

4) It has been found that proinsulin, the precursor molecule to insulin, contains a portion that is held together by disulfide bonds. This information provides data most characteristic to what level of protein structure?

A. Primary structure
B. Secondary structure
C. Tertiary structure
D. Quaternary structure

5) Which of the following best identifies the following organic compound?

$$HOCH_2-\overset{\overset{\large O}{\|}}{C}-\underset{OH}{\underset{|}{CH}}-\underset{OH}{\underset{|}{CH}}-\underset{OH}{\underset{|}{CH}}CH_2OH$$

A. Aldehyde
B. Triacyl glyceride
C. Protein
D. Carbohydrate

6) Streptococcus mutans produces glucan, a sticky polymer of glucose that acts like a cement and binds the bacterial cells together and to the tooth surface. Glucan is formed only in the presence of the disaccharide sucrose (the type of sugar found in sweets), through a process catalyzed by an enzyme of the cocci. The enzyme links glucose molecules together to form glucan, while fructose molecules are fermented by the streptococci into lactic acid. Lactic acid can etch the surface of the teeth, enhancing microbial adherence.

Given the preceding, the enzyme produced by Streptococcus mutans likely initially acts by:

A. catalyzing the formation of glycosidic bonds between glucose molecules.
B. splitting sucrose into fructose and glucose.
C. catalyzing the formation of glycosidic bonds between fructose molecules.
D. catalyzing the fermentation of fructose.

7) Fructose and glucose are:
   - A. isotopes.
   - B. monosaccharides.
   - C. six-carbon sugars.
   - D. both B and C.

8) Cholesterol, cortisone and cortisol are best identified as:
   - A. cholesterols.
   - B. corticosteroids.
   - C. bile acids.
   - D. steroids.

9) ATP is considered an "energy rich" compound because of what kind of bonds?
   - A. Phosphoanhydride
   - B. Phosphodiester
   - C. Phosphoglycosidic
   - D. Adenosine

10) The three most important buffer systems in body fluids include the bicarbonate buffer system, the phosphate buffer system, and which of the following?
   - A. Hemoglobin
   - B. Protein
   - C. Sodium benzoate
   - D. Calcium carbonate

11) What is the most effective intracellular inorganic buffer?
   - A. Phosphate
   - B. Protein
   - C. Hemoglobin
   - D. Bicarbonate

12) What is the normal pH of blood?
   - A. 7.3-7.4
   - B. 7.25-7.35
   - C. 7-8
   - D. 7.35-7.45

GS ANSWER KEY

CHAPTER 20

#	Answer	*Cross-Reference*	#	Answer	*Cross-Reference*
1.	D	BIO 20.1.1	7.	D	BIO 20.3.1, 20.3.2
2.	C	BIO 20.2.1; QR 7	8.	D	BIO 6.3, 6.3.2, 20.4.1
3.	B	BIO 20.2.2	9.	A	BIO 4.4-4.10, 20.5
4.	C	BIO 20.2.2	10.	B	BIO 20.6
5.	D	BIO BIO 20.3.1	11.	A	BIO 20.6
6.	B	BIO BIO 20.3.2	12.	D	BIO 20.6.1

* Explanations can be found at the back of the book.

Go online to DAT-prep.com for additional chapter review Q&A and forum.

APPENDIX

CHAPTER 20: Biochemistry

Advanced DAT-30 Passage: Acidosis and Alkalosis

Although buffers in the body fluids help resist changes in pH, the respiratory system and the kidneys regulate the pH of the body fluids. Malfunctions of either the respiratory system or renal system can result in acidosis or alkalosis which may be beyond the capacity of the buffers to repair without the intervention of one of these organ systems.

Respiratory acidosis occurs with an increase in concentration (= *partial pressure*) of carbon dioxide (i.e. impaired breathing or ventilation as seen in COPD, chronic obstructive pulmonary disease which includes chronic bronchitis and emphysema). The result is a lowered ratio of bicarbonate to pCO_2 resulting in a decrease in pH (acidosis; see BIO 12.4.1). The acidosis is reversed gradually when kidneys increase the rate at which they secrete hydrogen ions into the filtrate and increase the absorption of bicarbonate.

Metabolic acidosis can result from the loss of bicarbonate ions (i.e. severe diarrhea) or the accumulation of metabolic acids (i.e. lactic acid, keto acids). This can lead to severe metabolic complications warranting intravenous bicarbonate therapy. The reduced pH stimulates the respiratory center which causes hyperventilation. During hyperventilation, carbon dioxide is eliminated at a greater rate.

Respiratory alkalosis occurs during hyperventilation, when excessive carbon dioxide is eliminated from the system (which lowers pCO_2), the pH of the blood increases, resulting in alkalosis. This can be seen in conditions such as hysteria, stroke and hepatic failure. The kidneys help to compensate for respiratory alkalosis by decreasing the rate of hydrogen ions secretion into the urine and the rate of bicarbonate ion reabsorption.

Metabolic alkalosis generally results when bicarbonate levels are higher in the blood. This can be observed, for example, after sustained vomiting of acidic gastric juices. Kidneys compensate for alkalosis by increasing the excretion of bicarbonate ions. The increased pH inhibits respiration. Reduced respiration allows carbon dioxide to accumulate in the body fluids.

13) Diabetic ketoacidosis is an example of which of the following imbalances?

- **A.** Respiratory acidosis
- **B.** Respiratory alkalosis
- **C.** Metabolic acidosis
- **D.** Metabolic alkalosis

14) All of the following can be seen as a consequence of vomiting EXCEPT one. Which one is the EXCEPTION?

- **A.** Metabolic alkalosis
- **B.** Dehydration
- **C.** Metabolic acidosis
- **D.** Respiratory alkalosis

15) Normal pCO_2 is 40 mmHg with the normal range being 35-45 mmHg. If a patient's pH is 7.3 and pCO_2 is 50 mmHg, the patient must have:

A. respiratory acidosis.
B. respiratory alkalosis.
C. metabolic acidosis.
D. metabolic alkalosis.

Don't forget to create your own Gold Notes and review them frequently. Please visit our Forum at dat-prep.com/forum and let us know how we can improve. Good luck with your studies!

- The Gold Standard Team

ANSWER KEY

ADVANCED TOPICS - CHAPTER 20

Cross-Reference

13. C BIO 20 App.
14. D BIO 9.4.2, BIO 20 App.
15. A BIO 12.4.1, BIO 20 App.

P = paragraph; *S* = sentence; *E* = equation; *T* = table; *F* = figure

Chapter Review Solutions

Question 1 D

See: BIO 1.1, ORG 12.1.1

Proteins spanning the plasma membrane contain hydrophobic regions (mostly uncharged, neutral molecules), which tend to associate with the hydrophobic lipid bilayer, and hydrophilic regions (mostly charged or polar molecules), which tend to associate with the inside or outside hydrophilic environment of the cell. In order for a protein to rotate through the plane of the bilayer, hydrophilic regions would have to traverse the hydrophobic bilayer. As a rule, interactions of this nature (hydrophobic-hydrophilic) are energetically unfavorable.

Question 2 B

See: BIO 1.1, ORG 12.1-12.2.2, CHM 4.2

It is unlikely that weak forces, such as Van Der Waal's, would provide the stable protein-protein interaction needed to anchor a protein to the plasma membrane. On the other hand, covalent bonds occur intramolecularly as opposed to intermolecularly, eliminating answer choice *C*. We would not expect a peripheral protein or the portion of an integral protein facing the extracellular fluid to be hydrophobic, because of the hydrophilic nature of the fluid. This leaves us with answer choice *B*.; the interactions are likely to occur between a charged (hydrophilic) portion of the integral protein with the charged portion of the peripheral protein. The interaction in electrostatic charges is based on 'opposite charges attract'.

Question 3 D

See: BIO 1.1

The question gives a function of glycoproteins. The question asks which of the cellular components has characteristics that would suit the special functions of a glycoprotein. A phospholipid bilayer is a membrane, and one of the functions of the oligosaccharide attached to a protein is to anchor the protein to a membrane and facilitate recognition.

Question 4 B

See: BIO 1.2.1

To answer this question basic knowledge of the function of various cell components is necessary. The Golgi apparatus functions in protein modification like glycosylation (the addition of poly/oligosaccharides).

Question 5 B

See: BIO 1.1.1

The question states that sweat is less concentrated (with electrolytes) than blood plasma. The question asks how electrolytes would be transported *from* blood plasma (high concentration) *to* sweat (low concentration). Osmosis is the mechanism by which water, not electrolytes, is transported across membranes. Active transport is used to move molecules *against* their concentration gradient. Simple diffusion is the movement of molecules in the direction in which they naturally tend to move: from areas of high concentration to areas of low concentration, as in this case.

Question 6 D

See: BIO 1.2, 1.2.1, 7.5F

Microfilaments are important in phagocytosis and locomotion. All the choices provided are involved directly or indirectly in both processes. Flagella are used by sperm for locomotion; endocytotic vesicles are formed during phagocytosis at which point they can fuse with primary lysosomes to form secondary lysosomes; granulocytes are phagocytic cells of the immune system. Thus the only difference is that all are organelles except granulocytes which are cells. *Note:* an organelle is simply a cellular structure that has specialized functions. That includes flagella, cilia, vesicles, etc., and of course the ones that you are used to reading about (mitochondria, lysosomes, etc).

Ref: http://en.wikipedia.org/wiki/Organelle

Question 7 C

See: BIO 1.2

You must be familiar with cellular structures to answer this question.

Question 8 D

See: BIO 1.1, 1.2.1

Membrane receptors are proteins which are usually produced by rough endoplasmic reticulum (as opposed to free ribosomes).

Question 9 D

See: BIO 1.2.2

The question identifies the transporter (protein carrier) as ATP-dependent. Only active transport is a carrier-mediated transport system that requires energy in the form of ATP.

Question 10 B

See: BIO 1.2.2, ORG 12.2.2

You can solve this problem by knowing 2 basic facts: (1) thymine is a pyrimidine; and (2) sulfur is not a component of nitrogen bases. Note: sulfur is a component of the amino acid cysteine which can make disulfide bonds with itself creating cystine which stabilizes the tertiary structure of proteins.

Question 11 A

See: BIO 1.2.2

Option *D*. is an accurate description of how the nitrogenous bases bind together to form the helical structure. Option *C*. is also a feature of the molecule which aids in maintaining the shape. The hydrophobic bases are kept in the center of the helix while the hydrophillic backbone interacts with the outside environment. Option *B*. is similar to option *D*. in that it describes the bonds which give the helical molecule its strength. Option *A*. is a description of a negative consequence of DNA not holding its helical structure. It is not a process or interaction by which DNA maintains its shape.

Question 12 C

See: BIO 1.3

The order of events in the cell cycle is: G_1, S (*synthesis*), G_2, Prophase, Metaphase, Anaphase, Telophase. If a drug prevents prophase from occurring, most cells will be arrested at the stage immediately prior to prophase, G_2.

Question 13 C

See: BIO 1.2.2, 3.0

Bidirectional replication suggests that replication will occur in two directions. The only option consistent with this is option *C.* which states that DNA replication will begin on both sides of the origin.

Question 14 D

See: BIO 1.2.2

Drawing a diagram would be helpful for you to visualize the circular replication of the chromosome. In the first replication a uniformly normal circular chromosome would replicate producing two molecules that are half normal and half labelled (one parent strand, one new ^{3}H-thymidine labelled daughter strand). The preceding is the essence of semi-conservative replication. When this molecule replicates (the second round of replication), the parent strand will be the template on one branch of the replication fork and the labelled strand will be the template on the other branch of the replication fork. The parent (normal) strand will produce another half normal, half labelled molecule. The labelled strand will produce a new molecule in which both strands are labelled (e.g. has twice as much labelled portion as the other daughter molecule).

Question 15 A

See: BIO 1.2, 1.3

The question indicates that colchicine inhibits segregation of the daughter cells during mitosis. Segregation is accomplished in anaphase, whereby the spindle microtubules guide the sister chromatids to opposing sides of the cell. Based on this information, we would expect colchicine to disrupt spindle formation. Note that answer choices *B.* and *C.* both refer to the same cell process (DNA replication), and therefore, can be eliminated on this basis alone.

Question 16 C

See: BIO 1.2.2, ORG 12.5

You must be familiar with the method by which DNA is linked together. You should know that the chain is made by additions to the hydroxyl group of the third carbon in the sugar. Thus if the nucleotide will not accept a bond (= *phosphodiester*; ORG 12.5), then the hydroxyl group at C3 must be missing.

Question 17 B

See: BIO 1.2.2

DNA polymerase is the only enzyme listed that functions to build the new chain of complementary DNA.

Question 18 C

See: BIO 1.2.2

Note the word *deoxy*nucleoside. This should alert you to the fact that you are dealing with DNA and not RNA. The only option listed that is used in RNA but not DNA is *C.*, dUTP (A = adenosine; G = guanosine; C = cytosine; U = uracil).

Question 19 C

See: BIO 1.2.2, ORG 12.2.2

The DNA double helix is composed of a sugar-*phosphate* backbone from which bases extend towards the center of the helix. Although amino acids in proteins do not contain phosphate, there are 2 amino acids whose side chains contain the sulfur atom. Therefore, if the bacteriophage enter the bacterial cell to replicate (= form progeny) in a medium containing labelled sulfur and phosphate molecules, we would expect the phosphate and sulfur atoms to be incorporated into DNA and protein components, respectively.

Question 20 B

See: BIO 1.2.2

Carrier-mediated transport is the only option listed that has a maximum rate at which molecules can be helped to cross the membrane. At this point all of the carrier molecules are operating at their maximum rate and increasing the concentration gradient will have no effect. If the method of transport was simple diffusion, more and more molecules would diffuse as the concentration gradient increased (see the classic curves: BIO 1.1.2F). Osmosis is the diffusion of water, and it would increase as the concentration gradient also increased.

Question 21 A

See: BIO 1.1.3

The receptor-mediated endocytosis of ligands (e.g. low density lipoprotein, transferrin, growth factors, antibodies, etc.) are mediated by clathrin-coated vesicles which are found in virtually all cells.

Question 22 A

See: BIO 1.4.1

Desmosomes include cell adhesion proteins like cadherins which can bind intermediate filaments and provide mechanical support and stability. Tight junctions anchor to the actin component of the cytoskeleton.

Question 23 B

See: BIO 1.4.1

A tight junction surrounds a cell like a belt, preventing substances from passing between cells (occlusion). Note that an adherens junctions, AKA "belt desmosome", are anchoring not occluding junctions.

Question 24 A

See: BIO 1.5

The total magnification is calculated by multiplying the ocular magnification by the objective magnification so 10 x 40 = 400 times magnification of the specimen size. An excellent light microscope can comfortably magnify up to 1000 times.

Question 25 D

See: BIO 1.5, 1.5.1

Electron microscopy (TEM and SEM) cannot observe live organisms as a vacuum is required and the specimen is flooded with electrons. The most specific answer is a confocal microscope which is a state-of-the-art fluorescent microscope that can visualize the fluorophore labeling on a molecule, using, for example, a technique like FRAP.

Question 1 A

See: BIO 2.1

You should know the basic structure of a virus. HBsAg is described as a protein. A virus is very simple in structure and the protein outer coating is called the *capsid*. Viruses do not have 'slimy mucoid-like' capsules around them like some bacteria.

Question 2 D

See: BIO 2.2

Prokaryotes (bacteria) have no nuclei thus no nuclear membrane. The do have both plasma membranes and cell walls. If you chose answer choice B then you may have forgotten that some eukaryotes also have cell walls: fungi, plants.

Question 3 B

See: BIO 2.1

All viruses require cells to replicate: obligate intracellular parasites. However, some viruses use DNA as genetic material and viruses may infect numerous cell types including bacteria (phage). Specific knowledge of HIV is irrelevant.

Question 4 C

See: BIO 2.2, 4.5

To begin with, the issue of gram positive or gram negative is irrelevant and should not distract you. This question actually reduces to the following simple concepts: your mouth is sometimes open (*exposed to oxygen*) and sometimes closed (*little or no oxygen*). Thus in order to survive in your mouth, a bacterium would need to be able to produce energy in the presence or absence of oxygen (= *facultative anaerobe*).

Question 5 D

See: BIO 1.1, 2.2, 4.1

From the description in the question it is clear that glucan is formed outside of the bacteria. It adheres to the teeth and is present between bacteria. Therefore, the enzyme which catalyzes the formation of glucan must be located on an external surface of the bacteria.

Question 6 D

See: BIO 2.2-2.3

The question is asking for a difference between a bacterium and a fungus. Options *A.*, *B.* and *C.* may very well be correct attributes of the organism stated, but for it to be the correct answer it must be a characteristic that the other organism does not also possess. Bacteria are prokaryotes and therefore do not have a nucleus. Fungi, on the other hand, are eukaryotes and therefore contain a nucleus, so this is the difference between the two organisms. Note that both fungi and bacteria have cell walls, ribosomes and can undergo anaerobic metabolism.

Question 7 B

See: BIO 2.2

The suffix 'coccus' refers to the shape and means sphere. The suffix 'bacillus' also refers to the shape and means cylindrical. {*P.S.: never let the mere size of a word or molecule intimidate you!*}

Question 8 A

See: BIO 2.2, 15.5

Answer choices *B.*, *C.* and *D.* are processes by which bacteria multiply or by which they change their genetic makeup thereby enhancing their chances of survival (which contributes to their proliferation). Answer choice *A.* sounds very similar to these bacterial processes, but is not associated with an increase in viability or with multiplication.

Question 9 C

See: BIO 1.3, 2.2

In the span of two hours, the bacteria will have divided eight times (8 x 15 min = 120 min = 2 hours). You can think about it like this: in 15 min (#1 = 1st doubling time), the 10 bacteria will all have duplicated, making 20. After another 15 min (#2 = 2nd doubling time), all of those 20 bacteria will have duplicated, making 40. This doubling goes on and on a total of 8 times: #3 = 80, #4 = 160, #5 = 320, #6 = 640, #7 = 1280, #8 = 2560.

Alternatively, there are equations for doubling time and half-lives, and you should be familiar with how to use them. For doubling time, $X \times 2^n$, where X is the number originally present and n is the number of doubling times. Thus we get:

$$X \times 2^n = 10 \times 2^8 = 10 \times 256 = 2560.$$

For half-lives, $X \times (1/2)^n$, where X is the number originally present and n is the number of half-lives. {*see* CHM 11}

Question 10 C

See: Ap A.4.2, BIO 2.3

An exponential curve describes the growth of an organism reproducing by budding or cell fission. In this graph, curve C is representative of exponential growth.

Question 11 B

See: BIO 2.3

You must understand the basic processes involved in the reproduction of fungi to answer this question. Budding is a common process in plants and fungi (includes unicellular yeast like Candida). It also occurs in certain animals, particularly the Hydra (sponges). In fungi the bud stays for a while, and then detaches to grow fully as a new individual. Budding is a form of asexual reproduction since the process results in the formation of new individual but is a clone of the primary organism.

Question 12 C

See: BIO 2.2

Nitrogen fixation is the conversion by certain soil microorganisms of atmospheric nitrogen into compounds that plants and other organisms can assimilate. Some bacteria are photosynthetic and others are chemoautotrophic obtaining energy via chemical reactions including the oxidation of nitrogen, iron, sulfur and hydrogen gas.

Question 13 A

See: P2, S3

The passage clearly states that the protein dystrophin is located on the inner surface of the plasma membrane (P2, S3). All that is required for this question is that you recall that protein hormones (answer choice *A.*) do not diffuse across the plasma membrane (BIO 1.1, 6.3) and thus have their effect on the outer surface of the membrane (cf. steroid hormones). This recognition is then transduced into an intracellular message using intermediates like intrinsic proteins which span the membrane and cyclic AMP.

Question 14 C

See: P3, S3, S5; BIO 2.2, BIO 15.7

To clone a piece of DNA, large quantities of DNA must be produced (P3). The method by which this is done is through the use of bacterial plasmids. The foreign DNA is inserted into plasmid DNA (not capsid, as in option A.). The bacterial plasmid is replicated through the normal life cycle of bacteria, which is short enough to allow rapid replication of the foreign sequence. For cloning to take place sites must exist where foreign DNA can be inserted. However, inserting the DNA is of no use unless the bacteria can complete its usual life cycle after being altered in such a way.

Question 15 D

See: BIO 1.2.2, ORG 12.5, BIO 15.7

Let's translate the question into more basic language: if you have a DNA molecule (*plasmid*) and you want to add another DNA molecule (*foreign DNA*), how can this be done? The answer is that a DNA molecule is elongated via phosphodiester bonds (answer choice D.). DNA *replication* is a completely different mechanism as it refers to the duplication of DNA strands *within* a DNA molecule which is related to appropriate base pairing (cf. answer choice *C.*) and occurs in a semi-conservative manner (answer choice *A.*). Answer choice *B.* is irrelevant.

Question 16 C

See: deduce, BIO 15.7

Answer choice *A.* is false because we are looking for a functional gene for dystrophin! Answer choice *B.* is false since it does not refer to any cloning techniques as requested in the question. Answer choice *D.* is false since it is known that dystrophin (P2) and not troponin or tropomyosin is responsible for muscular dystrophy. Answer choice *C.* presents a possible method to treat the disease by: (a) using a cloning technique and (b) inserting the needed gene into diseased cells which would then make them capable of producing dystrophin. {Incidental: this type of research is currently being done on humans using special viruses to insert the missing gene into the cells of the patient}

Question 17 D

See: BIO 5.2

You must understand the structures and processes involved in muscle contraction to answer this question. If you do not remember, it's OK, we'll review the details in Chapter 5!

CHAPTER REVIEW SOLUTIONS — CHAPTER 3

Question 1 C

See: BIO 3.0

You should be familiar with the names of different enzymes involved in the replication, transcription and translation of DNA. Even if you don't know, it is easy to make a good guess just by looking at the names. You are asked for an enzyme that will help synthesize a chain of RNA. You can then narrow it down to a choice which includes the word RNA. The two choices are either replicase or polymerase. In producing a strand of RNA, nothing is being replicated. A chain (polymer) of RNA is being made which is complementary but not identical to the strand of DNA. It is easy to conclude that RNA polymerase must be involved (BIO 3.0).

Question 2 B

See: BIO 1.2.1, 3.0

Releasing factors need to be located near ribosomes engaging in protein synthesis. You should know that such ribosomes are located in the cytosol (answer choice *B.*) or associated with *rough* endoplasmic reticulum, not within the nucleus, nor *smooth* endoplasmic reticulum, nor mitochondria.

Question 3 C

See: BIO 3.0, 1.2.1

rRNA is synthesised from a DNA template in the nucleolus.

Question 4 A

See: BIO 3.0

The codon is on mRNA and the anti-codon is on tRNA.

Question 5 D

See: BIO 3.0

Also, a ribosome consists of a large and a small subunit. In eukaryotic cells, each subunit is assembled in the nucleolus where we find a relatively high density of rRNA.

Question 6 A

See: BIO 1.2.2, 3.0

CAT in DNA becomes GUA in mRNA because C pairs with G, A pairs with U and T pairs with A. Then GUA in mRNA is paired with CAU in tRNA. There is no thymine in RNA.

Question 7 D

See: BIO 1.2.2, 3.0

In BIO 3.0, see Table IV.A.3.2.

Question 8 B

See: BIO 3.0

Degeneracy is the redundancy of the genetic code. Degeneracy occurs because there are more codons than encodable amino acids. The consequence is that a single amino acid can have multiple codons.

Question 9 C

See: P1; E; BIO 4.1, ORG 9.4

The name of an enzyme is usually related to its function. In termination, cleavage of an ester bond is required (P1). Therefore, esterase is the most appropriate name.

Question 10 D

See: P3; E; BIO 3.0, 4.2, 20.2.1

Peptidyl transferase is involved in making the peptide bonds in the forming amino acid (P3). In termination, the activity of peptidyl transferase is altered by releasing factors so that a molecule of water may be added (= hydrolysis) instead of another aminoacyl tRNA (P3; E). So, if peptidyl transferase activity is inhibited, both of these processes are inhibited.

Background: enzymes often let you know their activity by their name. Peptidyl transferase transfers one amino acid to another thus creating a peptide bond: the continuation of this process creates and elongates a protein.

Read P3 again.

Translation of all the above: peptidyl transferase is important for 2 things: (1) peptide bonds and (2) when modified, peptidyl transferase can permit water to attack. So both (1) and (2) will not occur if peptidyl transferase activity is inhibited.

Question 11 A

See: BIO 20.2.1, ORG 8.1, 9.4

Attack of the carbon shown in Figure 1 by water will cause the oxygen that is already attached to the sugar to leave the amino acid (see arrow in Figure 1). The oxygen of the water will become part of the amino acid as it loses its hydrogens.

CHAPTER REVIEW SOLUTIONS — CHAPTER 4

Question 1 B

See: 4.1, 4.4

Catabolism is the breakdown of macromolecules into smaller molecules.

Question 2 A

See: BIO 4.1, 4.3

Proteins can undergo cleavage by non-specific enzymes. The cleaved products are then used as metabolites by the body.

Question 3 D

See: BIO 3.0, 1.2.1

OH is a hydroxyl group and an enzyme named *hydroxylase* would be expected to affect the hydroxyl group.

Question 4 D

See: BIO 4.2

Aspirin inhibits the synthesis of prostaglandins. This answer is best reached through elimination. Answer choices *A.*, *B.* and *C.* can be discounted because they describe various types of inhibition of the prostaglandin molecule by aspirin, however, prostaglandins are not enzymes and consequently, are unaffected by inhibitors (*Note:* the question states that prostaglandins are lipids but enzymes are proteins).

Question 5 A

See: Ap A.3.3, CHM 9.7F, BIO 4.1, 7.5.1

The graph described would have time along the horizontal axis and the amount of substrate-enzyme complex (amount of substrate added to enzyme) along the vertical axis. The amount of substrate-enzyme complex would increase steadily as more substrate is added until a point at which all enzymes are involved in a substrate-enzyme complex, and any more substrate added will have no effect. The graph would show a steadily increasing line of positive slope which reaches a point at which it levels off into a horizontal line. This curve is called a hyperbola. A sigmoidal shape would be expected in cooperative binding (i.e. the symmetry model or hemoglobin, BIO 7.5.1).

Question 6 B

See: BIO 4.1, 4.3

You must be familiar with how enzyme function is regulated to answer this question. An allosteric enzyme has a site other than the one for the substrate at which a molecule (not the substrate) that directs the function of the enzyme can bind.

Question 7 A

See: BIO 4.5, 4.6

DNA is only able to control the activities of a cell through the expression of proteins which includes enzymes.

Question 8 B

See: BIO 4.5

Glycolysis is the process by which glucose is broken down into two molecules of pyruvate. At this point the lysis of glucose (glyco-lysis) is finished. The following step of converting the pyruvate molecules into acetyl-CoA is not a part of glycolysis.

Question 9 B

See: BIO 4.4-4.10, 6.3.3

Mammals oxidize food (answer choice *B*), but NOT reduction (answer choice *A*). Clearly mammals do not break down muscle under normal circumstances to maintain heat (answer choice *C*). Though TSH (thyroid stimulating hormone from the anterior pituitary) increases metabolism indirectly through the activity of hormones from the thyroid gland, it is secreted, like other homeostatic hormones, when higher metabolism is required. In other words, it is not secreted to be the main source of normal baseline body heat. Oxidation of foods creates ATP but the process is not 100% efficient. Most of the waste goes to the creation of heat energy.

Question 10 A

See: BIO 4.8, 4.9, 4.10

The function of the electron transport chain is to produce a transmembrane proton electrochemical gradient as a result of the redox reactions. If protons flow back through the membrane, they enable mechanical work, such as rotating bacterial flagella. ATP synthase converts this mechanical into chemical energy by producing ATP. A small amount of ATP is available from substrate-level phosphorylation, for example, in glycolysis. In most organisms the majority of ATP is generated in electron transport chains, while only some obtain ATP by fermentation.

Question 11 D

See: BIO 4.8, 4.9, 4.10

Because the phospholipid bilayer is impermeable to ions, protons are able to cross the membrane only through a protein channel. This restriction allows the energy in the electrochemical gradient to be harnessed and converted to ATP as a result of the action of a complex involved in oxidative phosphorylation, ATP synthase.

If the inner mitochondrial membrane was permeable to the diffusion of ions, the electrochemical gradient would be destroyed.

Question 12 B

See: BIO 4.7, 4.10

In animal cells, one mole of glucose initially produces a total of *8* ATPs [2 net ATP directly 2 NADH (recall that 1 NADH => 3 ATPs during oxidative phosphorylation)]. In turn, the conversion of pyruvate to Acetyl-CoA produces *6* ATP (via 2 NADH) and finally the Krebs cycle produces the remaining *24* ATPs [2 GTP 2 FADH (recall that 1 FADH => 2 ATPs during oxidative phosphorylation) 6 NADH], <u>for a total of *38* ATPs per mole of glucose</u> (net = 36 ATP; the actual number is less due to inefficiencies in the system). Therefore, the Krebs cycle produces the most ATP (indirectly). The hydrolysis of glycogen (a polymer of glucose-phosphate) produces mainly glucose-phosphate monomers and the (leftover) glycogen polymer. Transamination consists of interconversions involving keto acids and amino acids; this reaction does not involve the net production of ATP.

Question 13 A

See: P1

Information concerning the relative amounts of T and R conformations present before substrate is added is given in the passage.

Question 14 B

See: BIO 4.1, 4.3

If a molecule has a high affinity for something, it is likely to be associated with it maximally. The substrate binds more tightly to the R conformation even though the R conformation is present in small amounts because R has a higher affinity for the substrate than T.

Question 15 A

See: BIO 4.3, 7.5.1

The graph described would have time along the horizontal axis and the amount of substrate-enzyme complex (amount of substrate added to enzyme) along the vertical axis. The amount of substrate-enzyme complex would increase steadily as more substrate is added until a point at which all enzymes are involved in a substrate-enzyme complex, and any more substrate added will have no effect. The graph would show a steadily increasing line of positive slope which reaches a point at which it levels off into a horizontal line. This curve is called a hyperbola. A sigmoidal shape would be expected in cooperative binding (i.e. the symmetry model as described in the passage or hemoglobin; see diagrams in BIO 4.3 and 7.5.1).

Question 16 A

See: Deduce; BIO 4.1, 4.2

The symmetry model describes an instance of something which may be described as positive cooperativity (P2). The model does not exclude the enzyme from having cofactors, and places no restriction on what the enzyme's function will be. However, the symmetry model does not account for the existence of any other conformations than the two described (P2).

Question 17 B

See: BIO 4.1, 4.3

You must be familiar with how enzyme function is regulated to answer this question. An allosteric enzyme has a site other than the one for the substrate at which a molecule (not the substrate) that directs the function of the enzyme can bind.

Question 1 A

See: BIO 5.1

The area or space between the terminal ending of a neuron and a successive cell is called a synapse.

Question 2 A

See: BIO 5.1, 1.1, 1.1.3

The presynaptic terminal contains vesicles and is enveloped by the plasma membrane of the nerve cell (= neurolemma). Proteins are the carriers or transporters in plasma membranes.

Question 3 B

See: BIO 5.1.1-5.1.3, deduce

In order to answer this question, you can go by memory or look at Table 1. The table indicates that the intracellular K^+ concentration is much larger (30 times) than the extracellular concentration. Consequently, by simple diffusion the ions will move from inside the cell to the outside. In other words, K^+ will move from the cytosol to the cell exterior.

Question 4 A

See: BIO 1.2.2, 5.1.1-5.1.3, deduce

Answer choice *A.* is a false statement making it the correct answer! Table 1 shows us that the inside of the membrane is negatively charged (V_m = -70 mV), yet there are 10 times the number of sodium cations *outside* the membrane as compared to inside. The question suggests that there should be a strong gradient for positively charged sodium to diffuse into the *intracellular* fluid (recall opposite *charges attract*). Also, since Table 1 shows that the ionic concentration of sodium outside the cell is so much greater than inside, then this would be another reason that sodium should diffuse into the cell. Thus the only way for sodium to be driven against its charge and concentration (= *electrochemical*) gradient is by *active transport* not diffusion.

Question 5 D

See: BIO 5.1.1-5.1.3, deduce

Let's begin by translating the question: *how do we make the membrane potential (V_m) more negative*? The easy way to answer is simply by looking at the equilibrium potentials of the ions in Table 1. Only chloride and potassium have equilibrium potentials more negative than V_m. If the permeability of either of the two ions could be increased then V_m would become more negative (i.e. the value would become closer to that of the ion whose permeability increased). Thus answer choice *D.* is the only possible answer. In reality the membrane is always very permeable to potassium and that is an important reason resting V_m is negative. Thus increasing the already very high potassium permeability is not an important factor in membrane hyperpolarization. Imagine what would happen if the permeability to sodium suddenly increased: Vm would tend towards the equilibrium potential of sodium which is positive (= *depolarization*).

Question 6 C

See: BIO 4.2, 5.1, 11.2

At the neuromuscular junction, a depolarization of the cell due to an action potential causes the opening of Ca^{2+} channels in the presynaptic terminal. An increase in intracellular calcium leads to the fusion of acetylcholine-filled vesicles to the membrane. Acetylcholine (Ach) diffuses into the synapse where it binds to receptors on the post-synaptic membrane, leading to the activation of muscle fibers. The enzyme acetylcholinesterase, also present in the junction, terminates the signal by deactivating Ach. The deactivation of the enzyme by DFP will lead to a relative increase in Ach in the synapse and consequently, the Ach signal will be amplified, leading to muscle tetany (= successive activation of a muscle fiber over a short period of time such that the muscle does not have time to recover from an action potential, and it is in a constant state of activation). Note that an action potential is referred to as an "all-or-none" phenomenon; once the minimal threshold has been reached for a particular cell, the action potential has a characteristic magnitude and duration, which cannot be altered by an increase in stimulus. Therefore, an increase in Ach binding as a result of DFP deactivation will lead to an increase in frequency of activation of the action potential in the post-synaptic membrane as opposed to an increase in the magnitude of the action potential (as stated by answer choice *D.*).

Question 7 D

See: BIO 5.1.1-5.1.3, deduce

The figure provided illustrates the membrane permeability of both Na^+ and K^+. The permeability is dependent upon how long the respective channels remain open. As can be seen in the graph, the permeability for Na^+ increases sharply and decreases within 1 ms, whereas the peak for K^+ is much lower and decreases within approximately 2 ms. As a result, the Na^+ channel opens and closes more quickly (turnover rate) because its permeability increases and decreases at a faster rate.

Question 8 A

See: BIO 4.2, 5.1.1-5.1.3, deduce

Maintenance of a negative membrane potential following depolarization is due in part to the ATPase. During an action potential, K^+ and Na^+ channels open to allow the ions to move down their concentration gradient. However, in order to keep the intracellular and extracellular levels of the ions, energy must be used to move the ions back against their concentration gradients. That is, in order to repolarize the cell, K^+ must be brought into the cell while Na+ is brought out. This is accomplished by the Na^+ /K^+ ATPase which uses ATP to move 3 Na^+ ions out of the cell in exchange for 2 K^+ ions into the cell. This net movement will provide a negative resting membrane potential. Consequently, inhibiting the ATPase will simply cause both the ions to reach equilibrium since they will only be able to move down their concentration gradient.

Question 9 C

See: BIO 5.1.1, 5.1.2

During an action potential, repolarization of the membrane is due in part to the increased permeability of the K+ channels which allows the ions to move out of the cell. If the K+ channels were only partly blocked, repolarization would occur at a much slower rate resulting in a longer action potential beyond 1ms as is shown in the previous diagram. This would have detrimental effects on an organism since the transmission of information via nerve impulses relies on rapid action potentials.

Question 10 B

See: BIO 4.4, 4.9, 5.1.1

The sodium-potassium pump uses energy to transport these molecules against their concentration gradients. Cyanide is an inhibitor of an essential enzyme of the electron transport chain (cytochrome oxidase), which is a major source of ATP (*energy*) for the cell. If cyanide is added to the cells, considerably less energy will be produced, and the sodium potassium pump will be unable to function.

Question 11 A

See: BIO 5.1.1-5.1.3

To answer this question you must know that acetylcholine is an excitatory neurotransmitter that is important in motor neurons. Acetylcholine must cause an action potential in the following cell to continue the signal to the appropriate muscle. Action potentials start with the membrane becoming temporarily more permeable to sodium ions, causing depolarization of the membrane. Therefore, the post-synaptic membrane (*motor end plate*; BIO 5.1F) will become more permeable to the positive ions immediately following acetylcholine being released from the pre-synaptic membrane and reaching receptors on the post-synaptic membrane by diffusion.

Question 12 B

See: BIO 4.4, 5.1.1; CHM 1.5

Since the exercise is "vigorous," mostly anaerobic conditions prevail. Therefore, one molecule of glucose produces 2 molecules of ATP. Since we have 2 ATP, now you can multiply the given equation (in this question) through by 2. Thus the coefficient for potassium becomes 4.

Question 13 D

See: BIO 5.1.2, deduce

We can see three graphs. The first (A) is the "control" which is actually a classic tracing of an action potential. The next curve (B) demonstrates that adding curare drastically *reduces the depolarization*. The final curve (C) demonstrates that the addition of eserine greatly *increases the depolarization* [*notice that the x and y-axis for (C) is several times greater than (A) or (B)*]. Thus curare (B), which reduces depolarization, may block (bind) acetylcholine (ACh) receptors on the muscle cell (*= postsynaptic membrane*) preventing ACh from engaging in depolarization. And eserine (C), which increases depolarization, may prevent the hydrolysis of acetylcholine thus prolonging and increasing its depolarization capability.

Note: experiments are not common DAT questions but since they sometimes come up on exams, we have sprinkled some in the chapter review questions and in the GS practice tests.

Question 14 B

See: BIO 5.1.2

You need to examine the figure carefully to determine that between four and five msec the membrane potential is in the process of returning to its resting potential [note that (A) and (B) are drawn to the same scale]. The lowest point in the curve has just been passed at four msec. The period between the highest point of the curve and the lowest point corresponds to the absolute refractory period in which another action potential cannot be generated. In the process of returning from the lowest point to the resting potential, action potentials may be generated but with difficulty. This corresponds to the relative refractory period.

Question 15 B

See: BIO 5.1.1-5.1.2

We are told that the muscle cell engages in an "all-or-none" action potential. In other words, either the action potential occurs (100%) or it does not occur (0%), but there is nothing in between. Another way of considering the concept "all-or-none" is graphically. The Figure in BIO 5.1.2 is a classic action potential curve which occurs under natural conditions. Thus in nature, either the curve occurs essentially as drawn or it does not (i.e. no action potential), but the action potential curve does not occur in a graded fashion (all-or-none). Thus answer choice *A.* is false.

Question 16 D

See: BIO 5.2

This is a classic DAT and college/university-type question. The process of muscle contraction must be well understood to answer this question. Option *C.* contains a correct statement, however it does not answer the question as it is not related to muscle contraction.

Question 17 B

See: BIO 5.2

This answer should be committed to memory, as it is the subject of regular DAT questions. The thin actin filaments in the myofibrils of muscle cells are attached to troponin and tropomyosin.

Question 18 D

See: BIO 5.2

You must understand the structures and processes involved in muscle contraction to answer this question.

Question 19 A

See: BIO 5.2

Tropomyosin is an actin-binding protein that regulates actin mechanics. In resting muscle, tropomyosin overlays the myosin binding sites on actin. Upon release of calcium from the sarcoplasmic reticulum calcium binds to troponin which "unlocks" tropomyosin from actin, allowing it to move away from the binding groove. Myosin heads can now access binding sites and thus bind to actin. Once one myosin head binds, this fully displaces tropomyosin and allows additional myosin heads to bind, initiating muscle shortening and contraction involving the hydrolysis of ATP. Once calcium is pumped out of the cytoplasm and calcium levels return to normal, tropomyosin again binds to actin, preventing myosin from binding which, along with the gain of ATP, assures that myosin releases actin.

Question 20 C

See: BIO 1.1, 5.2-5.3

The sarcolemma and the neurolemma are specialized plasma membranes located in muscle cells and neurons, respectively. Recall that the plasma membrane consists of a lipid bilayer, in accordance with the Fluid Mosaic Model. The basement membrane, formed from a homogenous noncellular material lies at the base of the epithelial cells of the body.

Question 21 B

See: BIO 1.1, 5.2 paragraph 4

The synaptic terminal faces the muscle and the acetylcholine released must reach receptors on the muscle. These receptors should logically be located on the surface of the muscle with which the neurotransmitter will first come into contact (*motor end plate*, BIO 5.1F). However, it should be known from the biology review that muscle fibers are covered by a plasma membrane, or sarcolemma (BIO 5.2). This will be the first surface the neurotransmitter comes into contact with, so it should contain receptors (BIO 1.1).

Question 22 B

See: BIO 5.4.1

From the question it is found that collagen involves a disaccharide linked to hydroxylysine. If all hydroxylysine residues are replaced by asparagine, the function of collagen is sure to be affected. It is necessary to know from the biology review that collagen is an important component of the loose connective tissue in order to correctly answer the question. It is possible, however, to narrow down the options. One function of the oligosaccharide part of the glycoprotein is to aid in recognition. Since only the protein part of the glycoprotein is changed, protein recognition should remain possible. This rules out option *D*.

Question 23 C

See: BIO 5.4

Adult connective tissue includes blood, bone and cartilage.

Question 24 D

See: BIO 5.4.1, 5.4.2

Fascia is considered to be the 'packaging material' of the body as it a sheet of fibrous connective tissue enveloping, separating, or binding together muscles or other soft structures of the body.

Question 25 A

See: BIO 5.4.1, 5.4.4

Collagen is the main structural protein (= organic) found in animals and thus it is an important constituent of bone, cartilage, tendon, and other connective tissue.

Question 26 B

See: E; T; CHM 6.5.1; QR Appendix

If $[K^+]_o$ = 0.55 mol/L = 550 mmol/L then this is 100 times the value of $[K^+]_o$ in Table 1 which is only 5.5 mmol/L. Thus 60log(100) = 60log 10^2 = 120 mV.

Note: the DAT does not permit the use of calculators in Natural Sciences (you are permitted during the QR test). So if you happen to get one of these advanced questions requiring the use of logs, you must be quick and efficient. If you are aiming for a perfect score then you should review the sections cross-referenced.

Now let's pretend that you did not notice how the problem could be solved easily and you had 2 other things that you won't have for the DAT: lots of time and a scientific calculator. If you did, then you would do the long calculation using the approximation of the Nernst equation given in the passage, using the data in Table 1 where $[K^+]_o$ = 0.55 mol/L and $[K^+]_i$ = 150 mol/L and your scientific calculator would estimate E_k to be -86 (not far from the real value of -90 in Table 1). If you then used $[K^+]_o$ = 0.55 mol/L = 550 mmol/L in the same equation, your calculator would suggest about +34. And so, the difference would be 34 – (-86) = 120 mV, success! But, there would not be enough time to do the other questions!

Question 27 A

See: E; QR Appendix

The purpose of logarithms is to mathematically convert a curve that is increasing exponentially into a straight line. Logarithms are used frequently in Biology (Nernst, Goldman, exponential growth) and General Chemistry (pH, pK, kinetics/rate of reaction).

Chapter Review Solutions — Chapter 6

Question 1 D

See: BIO 6.1

12 pairs of cranial nerves leave the brain stem.

Question 2 C

See: BIO 6.1

The hypothalamus is crucial for homeostatic controls including heart rate, blood temperature, thirst, sex drive and hunger.

Question 3 A

See: BIO 6.1, 6.1.4

This question requires that you know the functions of the cranial nerves. The most important one to be familiar with, the vagus nerve, innervates smooth muscles of internal organs (i.e. the bladder). Micturition is urination.

Question 4 D

See: BIO 6.1.4

The sympathetic nervous system is involved in 'fight or flight' reactions. These reactions include many of the same effects that are caused by increasing physical activity.

Question 5 D

See: BIO 6.1

Only two of the answer choices should seem possible: the ganglion and the nucleus. A ganglion is a cluster of nerve cell bodies in the *peripheral* nervous system, while a nucleus is a cluster of nerve cell bodies in the *central* nervous system.

Question 6 A

See: BIO 6.1.5

The muscarinic type is a G-protein coupled receptor that mediates a slow metabolic response via second messenger cascades (involving cAMP), while the nicotinic type is a ligand-gated ionotropic channel that mediates a fast synaptic transmission of the neurotransmitter (no use of second messengers).

Question 7 C

See: BIO 6.2.4

The transparent cornea constitutes the anterior 1/6th of the eye.

Question 8 A

See: BIO 6.2.4

The vitreous humor is a transparent jelly-like tissue filling the eyeball behind the lens.

Question 9 B

See: BIO 6.2.4

The iris helps to control the intensity of light impinging on the retina by alternating the diameter of the pupil; however, the iris does not stand between light and the retina as the other 3 tissues do.

Question 10 D

See: BIO 6.3

Endocrine secretes into the circulatory system; exocrine secretes through ducts to the epithelium ('outside' of the body); apocrine concentrates products at the free end of the secreting cell and are thrown off along with a portion of the cytoplasm (i.e. mammary gland); holocrine: the entire secreting cell, along with its accumulated secretion, forms the secreted matter of the gland (sebaceous glands, BIO 13.3). Apocrine and holocrine are subdivisions of exocrine.

Question 11 C

See: BIO 6.3.1, 6.3.3

Hypothyroidism causes a depression in metabolism, growth, and muscular activity.

Question 12 D

See: BIO 6.3.3

The parathyroid produces parathyroid hormone which increases blood calcium levels.

Question 13 A

See: BIO 6.3.1, 6.3.3

The anterior pituitary is induced by TRH to release TSH which stimulates the thyroid to release thyroid hormones.

Question 14 C

See: BIO 6.3.1, 6.3.2

Adrenal hormones such as glucocorticoids and catecholamines function to convert glycogen to glucose for energy use. The main hormones of the adrenal cortex: glucocorticoids (cortisol), aldosterone, androgens. Catecholamines like epinephrine and norepinephrine are made by the adrenal medulla. Aldosterone causes water to be retained to increase blood volume. Sodium is also retained (and ends up in the extracellular fluid, not in the nephron). Potassium is excreted into the urine. Glucocorticoids function to increase blood glucose. They do this by stimulation of gluconeogenesis (forming new glucose from amino acids/lipids) and decreasing glucose storage, by preventing it from going into the muscle and fat cells. They do not cause glycogen metabolism. The breakdown of glycogen from stores in the muscle and liver for quick energy is stimulated by epinephrine (made by the adrenal medulla) and glucagon (from the pancreas).

Question 15 B

See: BIO 6.3.3

This question simply asks what is responsible for increasing calcium in the bones. Of the 4 possible choices, only calcitonin would have such an effect. Calcitonin, which is secreted by the thyroid gland, stimulates osteoblast activity while inhibiting osteoclasts activity, thereby increasing calcium levels in the bones. Parathyroid hormone and osteoclast activity both have opposite effects.

Question 16 A

See: BIO 6.3, 6.3.1

The hypothalamus is an important part of the brain involved in homeostatic control and important endocrine regulation. In terms of the endocrine function, the hypothalamus both secretes releasing factors which controls hormone secretion from the anterior pituitary AND produces/secretes hormones directly into the posterior pituitary. Gonadotropins (FSH, LH) are secreted by the anterior pituitary.

Question 17 B

See: CHM 9.9, BIO 6.3.3, 6.3.6

According to Figure 1, free thyroxine (thyroid hormone) is involved in an equilibrium reaction with both tissue protein-bound thyroxine and plasma protein-bound thyroxine. By Le Chatelier's principle, a change in the system (increasing free thyroxine) will cause the system to evolve in such a way as to minimize the change. So adding more free thyroid hormone will cause both equilibria to shift to the product side, producing more tissue and plasma protein-bound thyroxine.

Still not clear? OK, let's look at it this way: there are a couple of ways that you could have properly interpreted Figure 1: (a) a true equilibrium has double arrows (arrows in both directions between reactants/products); notice that the answers follow this rule; or (b) notice that the single direction arrow leading to the TSH is a broken arrow. The fact that the arrow is broken (not like the others) should have made you question the meaning of that arrow. Then, on reflection, you would remember that increases in thyroxine leads to decreased TSH due to a negative feedback loop.

Question 18 D

See: BIO 6.3.3

The prefix 'hypo' tends to refer to things that are low or slowed down in some way (lethargy). The prefix 'hyper' tends to refer to things that are elevated or overactive (i.e. your kid brother!).

Question 19 A

See: BIO 5.4.4, 6.3.3

Hyperparathyroidism refers to an overactive parathyroid gland. This condition leads to an increase in the level of calcium in plasma and tissues. This calcium comes from the breaking down of bone by *osteoclasts*, which are stimulated by parathyroid hormone.

Question 20 B

See: BIO 5.4.4, 6.3.3

If it is true that elevated levels of extracellular phosphate results in the calcification of bones and tissues (answer choice *B.*), then circulating calcium must be *lowered* in order to participate in the calcification process. However, parathormone *increases* circulating calcium. Thus in would be logical that parathormone finds ways to reduce extracellular phosphate in order to avoid the calcification process.

Question 21 C

See: BIO 1.1.1, 6.3.1 and F

On a hot day, the body would tend to conserve all the water it can. Thus the bladder would contain less urine than usual. Since the body is trying to resorb water not electrolytes (i.e. ADH, BIO 6.3.1, 6.3.1F) the urine the bladder contains would be more concentrated with solutes (less water present). This corresponds to a small amount of hypertonic urine. {*For the definitions of hypertonic and hypotonic, see* BIO 1.1.1}

Question 22 C

See: BIO 6.1, 6.1.4, 6.3.2, 6.3.3

By process of elimination: answer choice A suggests that the parasympathetic nervous system could stimulate adrenaline (= epinephrine) which is actually the hallmark product of the *sympathetic* nervous system; answer choice C). Answer choice B suggests that the body's response to cold is sweating which is incorrect. Answer choice D is wrong for suggesting that the parasympathetic system would be involved in a process like shivering AND that dilating blood vessels of the heart would be relevant to the body's response to a cold environment.

Question 23 D

See: BIO 6.3.1, 6.3.2

Aldosterone increases intravascular salt which leads to passive reabsorption of water from the renal tubules; thus more water in blood vessels means higher pressure.

Question 24 C

See: BIO 6.3.1

The thyroid gland incorporates iodine into two compounds, triiodothyronine or T_3 (contains 3 iodine atoms per molecule) and thyroxine or T_4 (contains 4 iodine atoms per molecule), which are responsible for the increase in basal metabolic rate seen upon thyroid stimulation by TSH.

Question 25 A

See: BIO 6.3, 6.3.1

You should know about the excretory system and the hormones which affect it, which would allow you to choose the correct answer immediately. As well, you should also know the functions of different hormones, which would allow you to eliminate those that do not affect the urine.

Question 26 A

See: BIO 6.3.6, 6.3.7

Many endocrine glands are linked to neural control centers by homeostatic feedback mechanisms. The two types of feedback mechanisms are negative feedback and positive feedback. Negative feedback decreases the deviation from an ideal normal value, and is important in maintaining homeostasis. Most endocrine glands are under the control of negative feedback mechanisms.

Negative feedback mechanisms act like a thermostat in the home. As the temperature rises (deviation from the ideal normal value), the thermostat detects the change and triggers the air-conditioning to turn on and cool the house. Once the temperature reaches its thermostat setting (ideal normal value), the air conditioning turns off.

Positive feedback mechanisms control self-perpetuating events that can be out of control and do not require continuous adjustment. In positive feedback mechanisms, the original stimulus is promoted rather than negated. Positive feedback increases the deviation from an ideal normal value. Unlike negative feedback that maintains hormone levels within narrow ranges, positive feedback is rarely used to maintain homeostatic functions.

If calcium decreases, the parathyroid glands sense the decrease and secrete more parathyroid hormone. The parathyroid hormone stimulates calcium release from the bones and increases the calcium uptake into the bloodstream from the collecting tubules in the kidneys. Conversely, if blood calcium increases too much, the parathyroid glands reduce parathyroid hormone production. Both responses are examples of negative feedback because in both cases the effects are negative (opposite) to the stimulus.

However, if the body temperature is elevated and that abnormality only makes the body temperature rise even more, then this is positive feedback.

CHAPTER REVIEW SOLUTIONS — CHAPTER 7

Question 1 A

See: BIO 7.2, 7.3

The answer to this question represents basic facts about the circulatory system.

Question 2 D

See: BIO 7.3

This is a classic DAT/Sesame Street type of question: "one of these things is not like the other . . ." The vena cava, the pulmonary artery and the femoral *vein* all carry deoxygenated blood to the lungs. Among our choices, only the aorta carries blood away from the lungs. Thus the aorta would be a perfect place to have receptors which would indicate whether the carbon dioxide exchange in the lung required an increase or decrease in respiratory rate in order to improve the quality of the blood supply to the rest of the body's organs.

Question 3 A

See: BIO 7.3

Arteries are well know for having a relatively large number of collagen and elastin which gives them the ability to stretch in response to each pulse or heart beat (relatively high pressure). Veins do not have as many elastic fibers as arteries as the pressure in veins is relatively low.

Question 4 C

See: BIO 7.2, 7.3, 7.5.1

Deoxygenated blood coming from the systemic circulation is pumped through the right ventricle, to the pulmonary artery and finally, toward the lungs. From the lungs, the *oxygenated* blood, containing oxyhemoglobin (= hemoglobin bound to oxygen) travels through the pulmonary vein toward the left side of the heart. Note that the pulmonary *vein* consisting of *oxygenated* blood is the exception to the rule; in most cases, *oxygenated* blood is located in the *arteries* while *deoxygenated* blood is in the *veins* of the circulation.

Question 5 B

See: BIO 7.3

vein --> lung cap.

This question can be translated thus: if something enters a vein in your arm, where is the *first* capillary bed which will be encountered? The following is simply part of the basic cardiovascular anatomy you need to know: vein in arm (= *upper body*) --> larger veins --> *superior* vena cava --> right atrium of the heart --> right ventricle of the heart --> pulmonary artery --> smaller arteries in the lung --> arterioles in the lung --> *capillary beds in the lung* --> venules in the lung --> veins in the lung --> pulmonary veins --> left atrium of the heart --> left ventricle of the heart --> aorta --> many different arteries --> many different arterioles --> many different *capillary beds of the body system* including those that supply the heart muscle, the arms, the kidneys, the brain, the liver, etc. --> venules --> veins, and the story repeats itself.

Question 6 B

See: BIO 7.5.1

$Hb + O_2 <=> HbO_2$

Clearly if you increase oxygen in the equation provided (which you should be able to derive), the equation must shift to the right (Le Chatelier's Principle).

Question 7 C

See: BIO 3.0, 4.3, 7.5.1

$Hb + O_2 <=> HbO_2$

Answer choice *A* is impossible because oxygen must bind reversibly so that when it reaches relatively deoxygenated cells, it can exit the red blood cell to provide oxygen to the tissues. Answer choice *B* is incorrect because in order for oxygen to go from the interior of an alveolus in the lung to the interior of a red blood cell in a capillary, essentially all oxygen must dissolve in plasma. Answer choice *D* is a true statement which does not answer the question. Allosteric proteins have different configurations (BIO 3.0, 4.3). Hemoglobin has cooperative binding which means that each oxygen facilitates the binding of the next oxygen (BIO 7.5.1) which occurs as a result of changes in the molecule's configuration.

Question 8 D

See: BIO 7.5.1

When you consider the human body, think about what would most urgently require oxygen to be off loaded from hemoglobin: a very active muscle. And what are the features of an active muscle? It is hot, acidic (lactic acid), hypercarbic (high carbon dioxide), high in phosphates (like 2,3-DPG which is high in glycolysis), etc. Thus all the preceding features of an active muscle, including increased temperature, would lead to oxygen leaving Hb (ie. low % Hb oxygen saturation) and going to the oxygen starved overworked tissue.

Question 9 D

See: BIO 7.1

The circulatory system is involved in thermoregulation via constriction/relaxation of the arterioles that allow changes in blood flow to the surface of the skin, where radiation occurs. In addition, the blood contains components of the immune (e.g. white blood cells) and endocrine systems (e.g. hormones) which are circulated throughout the body.

Question 10 B

See: BIO 7.5

In humans, mature red blood cells are flexible biconcave disks. They lack a cell nucleus and most organelles in order to accommodate maximum space for hemoglobin. RBCs develop in the bone marrow and circulate for about 120 days in the body before their components are recycled by macrophages.

Question 11 B

See: BIO 7.5.1

The question states that "the net effect of GBP is to shift the oxygen-binding curve . . .", thus the curve may move in one direction or the other but there is no suggestion that the shape of the curve is altered. Therefore, to answer this question, we only need to identify a curve with the same shape as the oxygen-binding curve (= oxygen dissociation curve) which is sigmoidal.

Question 12 C

See: BIO 7.5.1

The effect of GBP is to cause a greater release of oxygen at areas of lower oxygen tension, without affecting the ability of hemoglobin to pick up oxygen at high pressures (i.e. in the lungs). To release oxygen to the cells, the affinity of hemoglobin for oxygen must be low, but only at those points at which oxygen is needed (where oxygen concentration is low).

Question 13 B

See: BIO 4.2, 7.5.1, 11.2

Body tissues other than lung, in other words parts of the body with relatively low oxygen concentrations, both myoglobin and hemoglobin with GBP begin to release oxygen at a tremendous rate. The question can be translated thus: which of the following tissues can deplete its oxygen reserves quickest and thus would benefit most from a molecule which is used to delivering oxygen to oxygen-starved tissue? Oxygen debt can be most pronounced in skeletal muscle. Voluntary or *skeletal* muscle can deplete its oxygen stores so quickly that it switches to anaerobic respiration thus incurring an oxygen debt. The oxygen tension (= *partial pressure = concentration*) in this tissue is extremely low and will therefore benefit most from an influx of oxygen. {*Note that myoglobin like myosin implies muscle*}

Question 14 D

See: BIO 4.4-4.5, 7.5.1, 12.4.1

This question reveals an interesting physiology lesson. Here is a statement you can easily deduce or should be memorized (!): *an exercising muscle is acidic, hot and has a high partial pressure of carbon dioxide; an exercising muscle requires increased quantities of oxygen* (= answer choice *D*.).

For your interest, we will examine the details: an exercising muscle is acidic because of (i) the accumulation of lactic *acid* and (ii) the high partial pressure of carbon dioxide which results in an increase carbonic *acid*. An exercising muscle is hot because of the increased metabolic rate and blood flow. Carbon dioxide is in high concentration in an exercising muscle since it is a product of aerobic respiration. If you were to draw a sigmoidal shaped oxygen-binding curve to the right of answer choice *B*. in Q11, you will notice that for a given partial pressure of oxygen, the curve shows a greater tendency to unload oxygen (= *a lower oxygen saturation*). Thus the exercising muscle gets increasing oxygen delivery as the curve shifts to the right.

Question 15 B

See: BIO 7.5.1

This question boils down to the following: as described in the answer for the previous question, if the tissue is acidic then it needs increased oxygen delivery to those tissues. Only answer choice *B*. delivers oxygen to the tissues.

Question 16 C

See: BIO 7.2

Thicker walls in a particular part of the heart would indicate that it is more muscular, and therefore is more efficient or forceful during its contraction. This immediately rules out answer choices *B*. and *D*., as they suggest that the thicker walled chamber would be less efficient or forceful. It should be known from the biology review (BIO 7.2) that the ventricles are more muscular (thicker-walled), but in the event that this is not initially known, information regarding the function of both the atria and the ventricles can be derived. First, systole, the period of contraction, refers to the period of contraction of the ventricles not the atria. This would indicate that the contraction of the ventricles might be more relevant in some way. Second, during diastole, atrial contraction occurs after most of the ventricle is already filled and serves to push the small amount of blood necessary to complete the filling into the ventricles. Since the atrial contraction does not need to move a large amount of blood (the ventricle is already mostly full), it does not need to be as muscular.

Question 17 A

See: F, BIO 7.2-7.4

Following vertically down from position P in Figure 1, note that it occurs during a period of diastole. The last paragraph of the passage gives information concerning the actions of the heart during diastole which would lead to answer choice *A*. In P1, S2 diastole is described as a period of ventricular relaxation, ruling out answer choice *B*. Position P in Figure 1 occurs during a period of diastole and it occurs at a point about halfway through that period, ruling out answer choices *C*. and *D*. Alternatively, the answer can be deduced through information in the passage and figure.

Question 18 A

See: F, BIO 7.2-7.4

This question indicates that we should be looking at the graph representing "Heart sounds" in Figure 1. The graph for heart sounds can be described thus: a horizontal line is followed by a narrow burst of spikes or activity; prior to the spikes is the label "1st" implying that the spikes represent the 1st heart sound. The first heart sound begins immediately after the first long vertical line. By following this vertical line downwards, we can note any other events which may initiate or occur at the time as the first heart sound: beginning near the bottom of Figure 1, note that the first heart sound occurs (i) in phase 2 of the cardiac cycle; (ii) at the beginning of ventricular SYSTOLE; (iii) during a period that the aortic and pulmonary valves are not opened (i.e. closed); and (iv) the first heart sound begins exactly when the position of the AV valves *just become closed*. Therefore, strictly according to the figure, during ventricular systole the AV valves suddenly close just as the first heart sound is created. Thus answer choice *A*. is the only plausible answer.

Question 19 C

See: F, BIO 6.1.4, 7.2-7.5

This question is easily answered by reading the graph and remembering the direct relation between ejection fraction and stroke volume. Compared to the curve labeled 'control', the curve labeled 'sympathetic stimulation' is always at a higher stroke volume for a given end-diastolic volume. However, by looking at stroke volume values for both curves at any end-diastolic volume value (i.e. 200), it is clear that the stroke volume for sympathetic stimulation is always less than twice the control (i.e. 160 vs. 100), thus eliminating answer choice *A*. Thus we are left with answer choice *C*.

Question 20 C

See: F, BIO 7.2-7.4

Close analysis of Figure 1 (*compare to* previous questions) reveals that during the period that the aortic and pulmonary valves are OPEN, the curve for left ventricular volume drops (= *decreases*) but does not rise (= *increase*).

Question 21 B

See: Appendix Ch 12

Memorize: Ejection Fraction (EF) = stroke volume / end diastolic volume

It is usually given as a percentage but can be given as a fraction. The importance is to know the relationship between the variables.

Question 22 D

See: Appendix Ch 12

Recall that the volume of blood ejected from a ventricle during systole is termed stroke volume. So the amount of blood that remained in the ventricle (was not ejected) would be the end systolic volume. As described in the passage, the ventricle would be 'full' at the end of diastole. So the maximum volume (end diastolic) minus the blood remaining (end systolic) would equal the blood ejected (stroke volume).

Memorize: SV = end diastolic volume - end systolic volume

Question 1 C

See: BIO 8.2

Helper T-cells belong to the group of T lymphocytes and are required for the activation of other T lymphocytes (such as cytotoxic T cells) as well as B lymphocytes. Activation of B lymphocytes will lead to the production of specific antibodies which will recognize invading foreign organisms, whereas the activation of cytotoxic T cells will cause the direct elimination of these microbes.

Question 2 B

See: BIO 2.1, 2.1.1, 8.2

In order for any virus to infect a cell, the first step must be to specifically recognize the host cell. This is accomplished when the viral capsid makes contact with specific receptors on the target cell. Since different cell types will have different cell surface receptors, depending on the virus' protein envelope each virus will be very selective as to the cells it infects. Hence, in order for the HIV to infect the cell the viral envelope must first make contact and be recognized by helper T cell receptors.

Question 3 D

See: BIO 2.1, 8.2

In order to be effective, the vaccine must elicit an immune response without giving the person the full-blown disease. Before injecting the virus it must be cloned, but it cannot simply be injected in its natural harmful form. Also, the protein coat is how the immune system will initially identify the virus in order to produce antibodies against it. For this reason, the protein coat should not be destroyed. The most important thing is to ensure that the virus will be unable to cause harm (inactivated), yet will still elicit the appropriate immune response.

Question 4 C

See: BIO 8.1, 8.2

Basic knowledge of the immune response would be helpful here; nonetheless, certain options can be ruled out. The question has asked for an explanation of why the first immune response differs from the second. An appropriate answer should include some information about both responses to show the difference. Options *A.* and *B.* contain one statement concerning only one of the two immune responses. This is not useful in explaining why the two are different. You should also know that macrophages do not produce memory cells, and this rules out option *D.* By carefully examining the graph it is clear that the antibody concentration in serum is higher (*more intense*) and faster in the secondary response. This is consistent with option *C.* and information from the biology review.

Question 5 D

See: BIO 8.1, 8.2

By injecting a person with an inactivated form of an antigen, an immune response is elicited in which antibodies are produced and memory cells are made that will react quickly in the event of a subsequent infection. This is the process by which vaccines work (= "active" immunity). The antigen is inactivated so as to activate the immune system *without* risking the development of the disease or infection. Injecting the person with the antibody itself may help the person if they have been infected by something displaying the corresponding antigen (= "passive" immunity), but it will not induce the body to produce its own antibodies nor memory cells, so it offers no future protection against a subsequent infection.

Question 6 D

See: BIO 8.3

You should be familiar with the function of the spleen from the biology review. The spleen does not produce blood cells in the adult.

Question 7 A

See: BIO 8.2, deduce

Rejection will occur when the recipient produces antibodies against foreign antigens present in the tissue of the donor. Tissue matching, which would ensure that the antigens present in the tissue match those of the recipient would decrease the likelihood of an immune response (this is analogous to matching blood types for donation). A second method would consist of decreasing the immune response by suppression of the system. This is accomplished with medications or by X-irradiation of the B-cells, which produce the antibodies, located mainly in the bone marrow and lymph tissues. Answer choice A. would damage the tissues to be transplanted, which would not decrease the chances of rejection.

Question 8 B

See: BIO 8.2

An antibody is composed of a pair of heavy and a pair of light polypeptide chains, and the generic term 'immunoglobulin' is used for all such proteins.

Question 9 D

See: BIO 8.1, 8.2

The immune system attacks antigens which are usually proteins on a foreign agent ("non-self") that activate an immune response. One's immune system does not normally attack one's own cells ("self").

Question 10 A

See: BIO 8.3

The spleen has many functions, among which, it is considered to be a blood storage organ because of the activity of its red pulp.

Question 1 C

See: BIO 9.5; ORG 12.3.3; deduce

Cellulose is passed through the mouth, stomach and small intestine unchanged. It is only because of bacteria in the large intestine that cellulose gets broken down at all. This would indicate that humans do not possess enzymes to break down this particular polysaccharide. Because of the preceding, cellulose is often referred to as "dietary fiber".

Question 2 C

See:BIO 9.3

The components of gastric juice in the stomach should be known from the biology review. One of these, pepsinogen, converts to its active form in low pH to become pepsin. Pepsin acts to break down proteins in the stomach. However, the great majority of digestion is completed in the small intestine.

Question 3 D

See: BIO 1.1.2

Membranes are usually semipermeable. Small neutral molecules can pass relatively freely by diffusion. Monosaccharides, however, are large polar molecules thus require some assistance in crossing the hydrophobic interior of plasma membranes. Exocytosis and endocytosis are found most commonly in the context of releasing proteins or ingesting large particles (i.e. viruses, bacteria). Therefore, carrier mediated transport is most likely.

Question 4 D

See: BIO 9.5

From the biology review it should be clear that bile salts do not *absorb* fat, they *emulsify* fat. This immediately rules out options *A*. and *B*. Most products of digestion are absorbed and processed in the liver, but fat products are an exception. Fats are absorbed into the lymphatic system via lacteals, giving answer *D*.

Question 5 D

See: BIO BIO 4.3, 9.3, 9.4

The question is asking why an enzyme exists in the stomach which is present in an inactive form until conditions exist in which it is converted into its active form (e.g. a zymogen). You should be able to recognize that the question is referring to pepsinogen and should be familiar with its function. Nothing exists in the stomach which would break down pepsin should it remain in its active form. As well, pepsinogen converts to its active form, pepsin, in the presence of low pH. It would not make sense that the active enzyme would neutralize the acid, as this would cause the enzyme to be converted back to its inactive form. The inactive form offers no enhancement of activity, but suggests some form of protection, either for the enzyme itself or for surrounding cells. Option *D*. makes sense because if the enzyme remained active even when not needed, perhaps it could continue to function on molecules it was not meant to break down.

Question 6 D

See: BIO 9.4.1; ORG 12.4

Bile helps to emulsify fats (i.e. lipids including triacyl glycerol) for digestion as well as the absorption of fat soluble vitamins A, D, E and K.

Question 7 C

See: BIO 9.3, 9.4.2; cf BIO 4.1, 4.2

This question is asking: which of the following enzymes are present in the gastro-intestinal tract? Among the answer choices, carboxypeptidase, trypsin and pepsin are correct.

{Note: in order for a parasite to have gained access to the intestines, it must have passed through the stomach.}

{Aiming for a perfect exam score? Do you remember the name of the antibody that attacks intestinal (parasitic) worms? See the table in BIO 8.2}

CHAPTER REVIEW SOLUTIONS CHAPTER 10

Question 1 D

See: BIO 10.3

The nephron is the functional unit of the kidney and contains Bowman's capsule and the renal corpuscle.

Question 2 A

See: BIO 10.1

You should be familiar with the structures involved in the excretory system from the biology review.

Question 3 B

See: BIO 10.3

The kidney is a filtration-reabsorption-secretion (excretion) organ thus the first step is filtration which occurs at the level of the glomerulus.

Question 4 B

See: BIO 10.3

The countercurrent multiplier system uses electrolyte pumps so that the loop of Henle can create an area of high urine concentration in the medulla. Water present in the filtrate in the DCT and collecting duct flows passively down its concentration gradient. This process reabsorbs water and creates a concentrated urine for excretion. Some desert animals have disproportionately extensive loops of Henle because of their vital need to preserve water.

Question 5 A

See: BIO 10.4

When the detrusor muscles contract, the internal sphincter opens, or conversely, the internal sphincter is closed when the detrusor muscles relax.

Question 6 C

See: BIO 10.3

The loop of Henle of juxtamedullary (= "at the edge" of the medulla) nephrons form the countercurrent multiplier in the kidney.

Question 7 C

See: BIO 10.3

The fluid in the descending limb is relatively hypertonic (see the illustrations regarding the countercurrent principle, BIO 10.3) while the ascending limb is becomes relatively hypotonic.

Question 8 B

See: BIO 10.3, 1.1.1, 7.5.2

Over 75% of the water and dissolved substances lost through the Bowman's capsule is reabsorbed (obligate) back into the blood at the proximal convoluted tubule level.

Question 9 C

See: BIO 10.4, 11.2

You should be familiar with the different types of muscles and where they are likely to be found. Smooth muscles often form the lining of organs such as the stomach which can be filled with some substance and contracts in an involuntary manner. Skeletal muscles are involved in voluntary movements. We know that the detrusor muscles (and thus the internal urethral sphincter) are controlled in part by parasympathetic neurons, which would indicate a degree of involuntary action (BIO 10.4). The external urethral sphincter can be contracted even when the detrusor muscle is strongly contracting, indicating some sort of voluntary control. These descriptions fit the functions of the smooth and skeletal muscles for internal and external urethral sphincters, respectively.

Chapter Review Solutions — Chapter 11

Question 1 A

See: BIO 11.2, 4.5, 5.2

When aerobic respiration, increased use of energy (ATP) requires more oxygen, more glucose, more hydrolysis of ATP and more CO_2 is produced.

Question 2 D

See: BIO 11.2, 4.5, 5.2

Conversion to anaerobic respiration means less efficiency, less ATP, increased lactic acid (fermentation), more need for glucose which means more breakdown of glycogen and reduced production of the waste products of aerobic respiration; $CO_2 + H_2O$.

Question 3 C

See: BIO 11.2, 4.5, 5.2

Glycolysis is much faster (though less efficient) than aerobic respiration. Note that fermentation in vertebrates produces lactate not alcohol (BIO 4.4, 4.5).

Question 4 D

See: BIO 5.4.3, 11.3.1

Cartilage can exist in all of the listed tissues. However, the question asks about cartilage in adult tissues. In children who are still growing, a disc of cartilage exists between the epiphysis and diaphysis of long bones, but in adults, this cartilage has been replaced by bone. The other tissues listed will remain as cartilage even in adults.

Question 5 B

See: BIO 11.2

The difference between tetanus and tonus is that the former is a sustained contraction, lacking any relaxation, while the latter describes the state of partial contraction of all muscles.

Question 6 C

See: BIO 11.3.3

Tendons are composed of dense connective tissue and they connect muscle to bones.

Question 7 C

See: BIO 11.3.2

Motion of a joint in one plane gets its name from a hinged door which has a similar limitation in motion.

Question 8 A

See: BIO 11.3.2, 11.3.3

See the diagram of the skeleton in section 11.3.

Question 9 A

See: BIO 11.3.3

The axial skeleton includes the skull, thoracic cage (sternum + ribs), vertebral column, sacrum and coccyx.

Question 10 C

See: BIO 11.3.3

Phalanges are the bones of the fingers and toes.

Chapter Review Solutions — Chapter 12

Question 1 A

See: BIO 12.2, 12.3

You must be familiar with the structures of the upper and lower respiratory tracts to answer this question. The larynx comes before the trachea.

Question 2 B

See: BIO 12.3

The vocal cords are twin infoldings stretched horizontally across the larynx.

Question 3 D

See: BIO 12.3

The terminal bronchiole forms part of the conducting portion of the respiratory system.

Question 4 B

See: BIO 12.3

Surfactant is secreted into alveoli by pneumocytes type II. The surfactant reduces surface tension and prevents the fragile alveoli from collapsing.

Question 5 A

See: BIO 12.4.1

The factors that stimulate breathing are high carbon dioxide, low pH, high acidity, and low oxygen levels in the blood.

Question 6 D

See: BIO 12.3

The lung is covered by a membrane (= the pleura). Lungs reside in the thoracic cage which includes the ribs, sternum and the muscles between the ribs (intercostal muscles). If blood accumulates in the space outside the lungs (the pleural space or cavity), since the thoracic cage is firm, the blood will apply pressure on the pliant lung thus reducing the size of the lung (reducing the surface area for the exchange of oxygen and carbon dioxide). Thus blood oxygen levels can become dangerously low.

Question 7 C

See: BIO 7.2-7.3, 9.1-9.3, 9.5, 12.3-12.4

You should know enough about each of the systems listed so that this question should seem easy. The circulatory system has vessels which are elastic and muscular, indicating that stretching may occur. The respiratory system also involves muscles and stretching. The digestive system includes the stomach, and anyone who has ever eaten too much knows that there is some stretching going on (BIO 9.1/2/3/5)! The endocrine system, however, includes glands which secrete different substances into the circulatory system. Its function does not seem to rely on stretch receptors.

Question 8 B

See: BIO 1.1.2, 12.3

Active transport moves molecules against a gradient and requires energy. Blood returning to the lungs from the rest of the body is deoxygenated and comes into contact with a high concentration of O_2 in the lungs. Clearly O_2 does not need to be actively transported and, rather, will readily diffuse. The alveoli of the lungs require such fast and efficient transport of O_2 into the body and CO_2 out of the body that only the rapid process of diffusion will do.

Question 9 C

See: Chap. 12 App.; P1, S3; dimensional analysis

Minute ventilation = tidal volume x respiratory rate

Minute ventilation = 500 ml/breath x 12 breaths/minute x (1 L)/(1000 ml) = 6.0 L/minute

Incidentally, the average total lung capacity of an adult human male is about 6 L of air.

Question 10 D

See: Chap. 12 App.

The following are the definitions of the answer choices in order from A to D: Tidal volume is the amount of air inhaled and exhaled normally at rest. The functional residual capacity is the sum of the residual volume and the expiratory reserve volume. The vital capacity is the maximum volume that can be exhaled following a maximal inhalation. Total lung capacity is the maximum volume of air present in the lungs.

Incidentally (in case you did not read this in the previous solution!), the average total lung capacity of an adult human male is about 6 L of air.

Question 11 A

See: BIO 12.4, Chap. 12 App. P2; P3, S2

By various mechanisms (BIO 12.4), inspiration increases the size of your chest, or more precisely, your thoracic cavity. The increased amount of air in the chest in combination with the chest's desire to return to its initial position (= recoil) leads to an increased pressure in the lungs (= transpulmonary). Airway radius is inversely proportional to airway resistance (P2).

Question 12 C

See: Chap. 12 App.; BIO 12.4

The passage explains that there exists fibers which *pull* on the airways and become *stretched* during inspiration. The preceding implies that the radius of the airway is increased by the stretching of the fibers. Thus both transpulmonary pressure (compare with the previous question) and lateral traction result in an increase in airway radius.

Question 13 B

See: BIO 12.4; deduce

Clearly if food is stuck, for example, in the trachea then inspiration may pull the food into the lung (= *not good!*), but expiration could expel the food from the body (= *much better!*). The events in expiration normally include decreasing the size of the thoracic cavity and relaxation or raising of the diaphragm (BIO 12.4). The fact that the Heimlich Maneuver includes an upward abdominal *thrust* means that it is a *forcible* maneuver which suddenly increases the size and pressure in the thoracic cavity thus dislodging the food.

If you were to try applying upward pressure to your abdominal cavity (not too much pressure!). You will notice that your chest (thoracic) size increases. Of course, your thoracic volume is decreasing due to the abdominal contents entering the chest cavity.

Question 1 A

See: BIO 13.3

Sweat glands are exocrine glands which secrete their products to the outside of the human body.

Question 2 C

See: BIO 13.1

The answer is a basic fact about the skin as an organ system.

Question 3 D

See: BIO 13.1, 7.3

Body heat and water loss are increased by increasing blood flow in the dermis of the skin which occurs by relaxation of the smooth muscle (= media, BIO 7.3) of blood vessels in the skin (vasodilation). The result is cooling by radiation, the production of sweat, and evaporation of sweat due to heat at the surface of the skin causing cooling.

Question 4 B

See: BIO 7.1, 13.1

The effect of two changes to the temperature of the body on sweating is being questioned here. One change, exposing the skin to heat, affects the outer parts of the body. The other, drinking iced water, affects the inner core of the body. The question clearly states that sweating only occurs as a result of a rise in core body temperature. Therefore, heating the skin will not affect sweating. Since we now know that it is the iced water which will affect sweating it is a question of exactly what effect the iced water will have. A rise in core body temperature causes an increase in sweating, so it stands to reason that a decrease in core body temperature (caused by the iced water) will cause a decrease in sweating.

Question 5 D

See: BIO 13.3

Holocrine (= wholly secretory) is a type of glandular secretion in which the entire secreting cell, along with its accumulated secretion, forms the secreted matter of the gland; for example, the sebaceous glands which secrete oils. Apocrine concentrates products at the free end of the secreting cell and are thrown off along with a portion of the cytoplasm (i.e. mammary gland). Apocrine and holocrine are subdivisions of exocrine.

Question 1 C

See: BIO 14.1, 14.5

Fertilization normally occurs in the Fallopian tubes (oviduct).

Question 2 A

See: BIO 14.1, 10.1, 10.2

The ureter connects the kidney with the bladder (BIO 10.1, 10.2) and is not directly related to the male gonads.

Question 3 A

See: BIO 14.1

The structures and processes of the male reproductive system should be understood from the biology review.

Question 4 D

See: BIO 14.2

You must understand the process of gametogenesis in females to answer this question.

Question 5 C

See: BIO 14.3

The corpus luteum in the ovary secretes estrogen and progesterone in the luteal phase.

Question 6 B

See: BIO 14.3

Estrogen causes proliferation of the uterine lining (endometrium).

Question 7 A

See: BIO 6.3.1F, 14.3

You must be familiar with the menstrual cycle to answer this question. If you know which hormones the pituitary gland secretes (FSH, LH), you can narrow down the choices since the question asks which hormone the ovary secretes. One of the hallmarks of the follicular phase is that estrogen causes thickening (*proliferation*) of the uterine lining (*endometrium*).

Question 8 A

See: BIO 14.3

The expulsion of the egg from the ovaries is referred to as ovulation. Ovulation, which occurs at approximately day 14 of the menstrual cycle, is induced by an LH surge. Thus, LH is responsible for ovulation.

Question 9 C

See: BIO 14.3

The hormonal cycle of women is relatively complex and involves all four sex hormones (LH, FSH, estrogen and progesterone), at one point or another. Following the menses, caused by a low concentration of estrogen in the blood, the cycle continues in the follicular or proliferative phase in which FSH (= follicle stimulating hormone) stimulates the production of estrogen and the maturation of the follicles in the ovary. At midcycle, a surge of concentration stimulates ovulation (i.e. egg production).

Question 10 D

See: BIO 14.2, 14.8

The nucleus of sperm carries either an X or Y sex chromosome which determines the sex of the offspring.

Question 11 B

See: BIO 14.5

The ectoderm will develop into the epidermis and the nervous system.

Question 12 C

See: BIO 14.5

The 3 primary germ layers (ectoderm, mesoderm, endoderm) are first seen in the gastrula after the invagination of the blastula.

Question 13 D

See: BIO 7.2, 7.3, 14.7

You can only understand fetal circulation if you understand normal adult circulation. The *ductus arteriosus* connects the pulmonary artery to the aorta. If the ductus arteriosus remains open or patent after birth, some of the deoxygenated blood from the pulmonary artery will flow through the ductus into the aorta which contains fresh oxygenated blood from the newborn's lungs. Thus the mixing causes a decrease in oxygen and an increase in carbon dioxide partial pressures in the aorta. The aorta leads the blood into systemic arteries and circulation.

Question 14 C

See: BIO 14.6

The placenta is derived from the maternal endometrium and the embryonic chorion.

Question 15 C

See: BIO 14.2

Crossing over occurs with synapsing homologous pairs of chromosomes (tetrads or bivalents) appear in prophase I. There are no tetrads in prophase II (there are only sister chromatids).

CHAPTER REVIEW SOLUTIONS — CHAPTER 15

Question 1 C

See: BIO 15.1, 15.5

An inability to produce phenylalanine hydroxylase would least likely be accounted for by the altering of the stereochemistry of the chromosome because such an alteration is too general of a cause for specific mutation.

Question 2 D

See: BIO 15.1, 14.5.1

1It is important to understand that all cells in the body have the same genetic information, that is, they all have the same DNA content. What differentiates between one cell type and another is the induction of the various genes within the cell's genome. For instance, only the genes in a hepatocyte that are relevant to its function will be turned on. Although these same genes are also found in a muscle cell, they will not be expressed in the muscle cell (BIO 14.5.1). Hence, answer choice *D.* is the correct answer.

Question 3 B

See: BIO 15.3

You should be familiar with the reasoning behind sex-linked diseases. The disease in question cannot be sex-linked because it occurs more often in women. If the gene for this disease were located on sex chromosomes, the male would get the disease more often.

Question 4 D

See: BIO 15.1

The process of morphogenesis (alteration of physical and behavioral characteristics) from one generation to the next relies on both genetic and environmental factors). Although 2 organisms may have the same DNA, certain external factors including peers and family, and location of upbringing will affect the disposition of an individual. It is for this same reason that although 2 identical twins may look the same, their attitudes and character may be completely different.

Question 5 D

See: BIO 15.1, 15.3

Sex linked means that the gene in question is present on the X chromosome. Let E = red eye which is dominant and e = white eyed which is recessive. We are crossing heterozygous females X^EX^e with white eyed males X^eY.

	X^E	X^e
X^e	X^EX^e	X^eX^e
Y	X^EY	X^eY

Question 6 A

See:BIO 15.3

By definition.

Question 7 C

See: BIO 15.3

To consider the law of independent assortment, one should consider a case with 2 traits (usually on different chromosomes) which is called a dihybrid cross (as opposed to a monohybrid cross such as Aa x Aa).

Question 8 A

See: BIO 15.6

By definition.

Question 9 D

See: BIO 15.4

A gene pool is the sum of all the genes in a population.

Question 10 A

See: BIO 15.5, 14.2, deduce

Option *B.* suggests that sequences in the chromosome will duplicate themselves and then pairing could occur with the repetitive sequences in the homologous chromosome, which is not possible since duplication is a random mutation {*note that the suggestion that "unpaired sequences . . . duplicate" (i.e. mutation) is not the same as replication/duplication using the repetitive sequences as templates*}. Option *C.* suggests a translocation of the unmatched genetic material to allow pairing. However, translocation occurs randomly and could not guarantee that the correct sequence is moved each time. Option *D.* suggests that the chromosome with the unmatched sequence will undergo a deletion. Like translocation and duplication, deletion would occur randomly. Secondarily, a deletion would rarely be so large as to delete an entire repetitive sequence. The only reasonable option is answer choice *A.* in which the unmatched sequence can be temporarily moved out of the way (looped).

Question 11 B

See: BIO 15.3

We are told that Von Willebrand's is an autosomal dominant disease. Let V be the allele for the disease while v is the absence of the allele for the disease. Thus the father is vv and the mother who is heterozygous is Vv. The Punnett square reveals the following:

	V	**v**
v	Vv	vv
v	Vv	vv

Thus the frequency of Vv is 0.50 (= 2/4) and that of vv is also 0.50 (= 2/4). Since the gene is dominant all heterozygotes (Vv) will have the disease. The chance that the next child expresses the disease is not dependent on what happened to the parent's previous children.

Question 12 C

See: BIO 15.2

Type B blood cells contain B antigens and anti-A antibodies; consequently, any blood type with A antigens (i.e. type A and/or type AB) would trigger an immune response (antibody-antigen response). Type O can be donated to any blood type without triggering an immune response (this is why Type O is referred to as the universal donor) but it is not an option. We now know that type B must be in our answer.

The presence of the Rh antigen would elicit an immune response in a person who is Rh-negative. Thus answer choice D. is incorrect. Note that if a person has had previous exposure to Rh-positive blood, their serum would contain antibodies but their blood cells remain Rh-negative.

Question 13 C

See: BIO 15.2

According to the question, antigens of the ABO system are more inclined to elicit an immune response than those of the Rh system. Therefore, to unmask the presence of the less immunogenic Rh factor, the immune response would be maximal if antigens of the ABO system did not interfere (i.e. same blood type).

Question 14 C

See: BIO 15.2, 15.3.1, 8.2

An Rh-negative woman carrying an Rh-positive fetus will produce antibodies (called anti-Rh antibodies) against the Rh antigen of the fetal cells usually at delivery, when the fetal erythrocytes cross the placental barrier. Therefore, anti-Rh antibodies should not affect the first Rh-positive newborn; however, their presence in maternal circulation will substantially increase the risk of hemolytic disease for the next Rh-positive fetus, in accordance with answer choice C. Since the presence of the Rh factor is determined by the parents' genes, the probability of the fetus being Rh-positive will be the same for every pregnancy of any two given parents (eliminating answer choice A.). Answer choice B. is incorrect because antibodies are not characterized as Rh-positive or Rh-negative, but are simply referred to as anti-Rh antibodies.

Question 15 A

See: BIO 15.5, 1.2.2, 14.2

By definition, mutations are rare, inheritable, random changes in the genetic material of the cell. Consequently, in order to alter the genetic material one must alter the DNA sequence of a cell. Whether it is a nonsense mutation or a frame shift mutation, in order to alter the DNA base pairing requires an error in a process that involves DNA. This mode of thought leaves either answer choices A. or B.. During DNA replication the double helical strand becomes separated as DNA polymerase uses each strand as a template to form a new strand. During transcription, the DNA strand acts as a template to produce an mRNA strand. Comparing both processes, it is most likely that genetic mutations occur during DNA replication, since in this process an error can occur as the polymerase adds an incorrect base pair to DNA. Such an error will be amplified in the following generations as the cell divides. An error by RNA polymerase during transcription will only alter the mRNA sequence and leave the DNA sequence intact. Hence, answer choice A. is the best answer.

Question 16 B

See: BIO 15.6

The further away the two genes are on the chromosome the higher probability there is that they will crossover during synapsis. Thus *C* and *D* are furthest apart, *C* and *B* are next furthest apart (*B* and *D* are very close) and *C* is least far from *A*. Thus there is only one choice.

Question 17 B

See: BIO 15.6

In most species, including humans, mitochondrial DNA is inherited solely from the mother; and so, the mother of your mother is your maternal grandmother.

Question 18 C

See: BIO 1.2.2

As described in the passage, the polymerase chain reaction utilizes RNA primers that anneal to the DNA template. DNA polymerase then extends the RNA primers in an effort to replicate the DNA strand. These steps are identical to those of DNA replication in a cell (BIO 1.2). However, in a cell, the cycle occurs once per cellular division.

Question 19 A

See: BIO 1.2.2, BIO 4.3, deduce

Since mammalian cells function at 37 °C, this is also the optimal temperature for enzyme activity. The temperatures used in PCR, which are well above 70 °C, would easily denature human DNA polymerase which is why a heat resistant DNA polymerase is required (BIO 4.3). Using human DNA polymerase would require new enzyme after each cycle, and therefore would not be very efficient.

Question 20 B

See: BIO 15.3, Chap 15 Appendix

According to the passage, sex determination can be determined by amplifying intron 1 of the amelogenin gene which is found on the sex chromosomes. Due to a deletion, intron 1 on the Y sex homologue is shorter than intron 1 on the X sex homolog. This difference in size can be used to distinguish between males and females because males have one X and one Y chromosome while females have two X chromosomes. Therefore, females will have only one uniform size of intron 1 which does not bear the deletion. In contrast, males will have 2 different sizes of intron 1 following its amplification. Hence, B. is the correct answer choice.

Question 21 D

See: BIO 15.3, Chap 15 Appendix

A male individual, which contains one X and one Y chromosome, should have 2 types of intron 1. The passage states that intron 1 on the Y chromosome has a deletion which renders it smaller in length than the corresponding allele on the X chromosome, thereby providing males with 2 different size fragments. Females which have 2 X chromosomes will then have only 1 type of intron 1 of uniform size.

Question 22 A

See: BIO 15.7, Chap 15 Appendix

A Southern blot is routinely used in molecular biology for detection of a specific DNA sequence in DNA samples. Southern blotting combines techniques including the transfer of electrophoresis-separated DNA fragments to a filter membrane and subsequent fragment detection by probe hybridization.

CHAPTER REVIEW SOLUTIONS — CHAPTER 16

Question 1 C

See: BIO 16.1

The other 3 answer choices are enumerated as evidence for evolution (BIO 16.1). Spontaneous generation is an obsolete concept regarding the ordinary formation of living organisms without descent from similar organisms. For example, the idea was that certain organisms such as fleas could arise from inanimate matter such as dust, or that maggots could arise from dead flesh.

Question 2 D

See: BIO 15.4, 16.2

Evolution goes against the foundations of the Hardy-Weinberg Law. For example, natural selection leads to non-random mating due to phenotypic differences.

Question 3 B

See: BIO 16.2

One way to define fitness, is to describe it as the probability that the line of descent from an individual with a specific trait will not die out. Notice the focus is the gene. Note that is not necessarily true that natural selection leads to the "survival of the fittest"; rather it is the genes, and not necessarily the individual, which are likely to survive.

Question 4 A

See: BIO 16.2

Directional selection is when extreme phenotypes have a selective advantage.

Question 5 B

See: BIO 16.2

In disruptive selection, selection pressures act against individuals in the middle of the trait distribution. The result is a bimodal, or two-peaked, curve in which the two extremes of the curve create their own smaller curves. Such a population, in which multiple distinct forms or morphs exist (= polymorphic) would share fewer traits than other forms of selection.

Question 6 C

See: BIO 16.3

Genetic drift is the random change in frequencies of alleles or genotypes in a population (= antagonistic to the Hardy-Weinberg Law).

Question 7 C

See: BIO 16.4, 16.6.3

Photosynthesis, which releases oxygen, converted the primitive atmosphere from a reducing one into an oxidizing one. Note that the most abundant gases in our current atmosphere is nitrogen (78%), followed by oxygen (21%; CHM 1.1).

Question 8 D

See: BIO 16.4

All the answer choices seem reasonable except D. which describes prokaryotes whereas protocells are the precursors of true cells, and specifically, prokaryotes.

A coacervate is a tiny spherical droplet of assorted organic molecules (i.e. lipid molecules) which is held together by hydrophobic forces from a surrounding liquid.

Question 9 D

See: BIO 16.4, 16.6.3, 16.6.4

As a by-product of the photosynthetic activity of autotrophs, oxygen was released into the atmosphere. This lead to the formation of the ozone layer which prevented UV light from reaching the earth's surface. The termination of the major autotrophic source resulted from the blockage of light rays.

Question 10 A

See: BIO 16.5

Singular taxon, plural taxa, the study is taxonomy; species are grouped into genera (a genus).

Question 11 A

See: BIO 16.5

The study of homologous structures in mature organisms provides evidence for the evolutionary relationships among certain groups of organisms. This field of study, comparing structural similarities, is called comparative anatomy. The more similar the structures of 2 different species, the closer the evolutionary link, and the more recently they would have shared a common ancestor.

Question 12 A

See: BIO 16.5, 16.6.4

You must be familiar with characteristics of the phylum Chordate and the subphylum Vertebrate. While vertebrates share many characteristics of chordates, they are somewhat more complex in that they have vertebral columns and closed vascular systems. Chordates have a tail at some point in development, but not necessarily in the adult form. The only option that applies only to chordates is the hollow dorsal nerve cord.certain groups of organisms. This field of study, comparing structural similarities, is called comparative anatomy. The more similar the structures of 2 different species, the closer the evolutionary link, and the more recently they would have shared a common ancestor.

Question 13 C

See: BIO 16.6.1

Phyletic gradualism is a model of evolution in which species evolve gradually, slowly and uniformly. Punctuated equilibrium is where species remain stable for long periods of time and then, due to a large environmental change, change rapidly in response. Both theories are supported by the fossil record.

Question 14 B

See: BIO 16.6.4

Eubacteria are prokaryotes. Yeast are unicellular fungi which are eukaryotes. Protista are eukaryotes that can be algae-like, animal-like, fungus-like, unicellular or multicellular.

Question 15 C

See: BIO 16.6.4

Sponges are classified in Porifera, they do not display true tissues and they feed via a filtering mechanism where food is drawn in by flagellated cells called choanocytes.

Question 16 C

See: BIO 16.6.4

The phylum Arthropoda includes spiders, insects and crustaceans. They have an open circulatory system and are the most numerous of the invertebrate species.

Question 17 B

See: BIO 16.6.4

Phylum Cnidaria includes hydrozoans, jellyfish and corals. Cnidarians are composed of two layers: the ectoderm and the endoderm and contain a digestive sac that is sealed at one end. They display radial symmetry.

Question 18 A

See: BIO 16.6.4

Phylum Platyhelminthes includes flatworms (planarians, flukes and tapeworms) that are bilaterally symmetrical and possess three layers of cells known as triploblastic (all 3 germ layers: ectoderm, endoderm, mesoderm). They do not have digestive tracts (acoelomates) nor a circulatory system.

Question 19 A

See: BIO 16.6.4

Phylum Annelida includes earthworms and leeches that all display segmentation. Annelida are true coeloms (true body cavity completely lined with epithelium). They have well-defined systems including nervous, digestive and closed circulatory systems.

Question 20 D

See: BIO 16.6.4

An exoskeleton is an external skeleton that protects and supports an animal's body. Phylum Arthropoda includes spiders, insects and crustaceans. All have jointed appendages, well-developed nervous systems, specialization of body segments and an exoskeleton made of chitin. Phylum Mollusca includes snails, squids and octopuses. Most possess shells which are exoskeletons and are secreted as a calcium carbonate substance.

Question 1 C

See: BIO 16.6.4 (Kingdom Plantae)

Angiosperms are the flowering plants and possess a "pistil" which is the female reproductive structure and composed of the ovary, style and stigma. The ovary develops into the fruit.

Question 2 A

See: BBIO 16.6.4 (Kingdom Plantae)

Fertilization occurs when pollen lands on the sticky stigma and a pollen tube grows down the style towards the ovule.

Question 3 D

See: BIO 16.6.4 (Kingdom Plantae)

The stamen is the male counterpart and consists of a pollen-bearing anther and a filament stalk. The anther of the male stamen produces microspores and the ovary of the female pistil produces megaspores.

Question 4 D

See: BIO 16.6.4 (Kingdom Plantae); BIO 17.6.3

The Calvin cycle is referred to as C3 photosynthesis; it is one of the light-independent (dark) reactions used for carbon fixation. Photosynthesis takes place in autotrophs which includes plants and organism that live in the oceans: algae and cyanobacteria thus C3 photosynthesis is not an adaptation for life on land.

Question 5 A

See: BIO 17.1, 17.2.1

Endosperm is the tissue produced inside the seeds of most flowering plants around the time of fertilization. It surrounds the embryo and provides nutrition in the form of starch, though it can also contain oils and protein.

Question 6 B

See: BIO 17.2, 17.2.2

A stoma is a pore, found in the leaf and stem epidermis that functions for gaseous exchange. The pore is bordered by a pair of specialized guard cells that are responsible for regulating the size of the opening. Ground tissue includes the parenchyma cells which can be specialized in gas exchange, storage and photosynthesis or can remain totipotent and be able to divide to produce new populations of undifferentiated cells. Collenchyma have thick walls and function in mechanical support and offer flexibility. Two groups of sclerenchyma cells exist: fibers and sclereids. Cambium cells are a type of actively dividing, undifferentiated cell known as meristem lying between the phloem and xylem.

Question 7 C

See: BIO 17.2, 17.2.4

Cambium cells are a type of actively dividing, undifferentiated cell known as meristem lying between the phloem and xylem. Cambium is the cellular plant tissue from which phloem, xylem, or cork grows by division, resulting in secondary thickening (= woody plants; BIO 17.2.4 caption).

Question 8 A

See: BIO 17.2.3, 17.3

The epidermis is covered by a cuticle which reduces transpiration (= loss of water through evaporation).

Question 9 B

See: BIO 17.2.2

Roots have an epidermis which lines their exterior and feature root hairs which increase the surface area for better absorption.

Question 10 A

See: BIO 17.2.2

The endodermis is the innermost portion of the cortex and contains suberin that creates a water-impenetrable barrier called the Casparian strip. All water is forced to pass through the endodermal cells and not between them.

Question 11 A

See: BIO 17.2.3, 17.3, 17.3.1

Xylem: Apoplast is a diffusional space outside the plasma membrane formed by the continuum of cell walls of adjacent cells. In the apoplast pathway, water moves through this space without ever entering the cells.

Phloem: Translocation of sugars is accomplished through phloem cells and begins at a source and ends at a sink. The sugar enters sieve-tube members through active transport and causes the concentration of solutes to be much higher in the source than in the sink.

Question 12 D

See: BIO 17.3, 17.3.1

Cohesion-tension theory – Accounts for most movement of water in the xylem and is based on transpiration (a negative pressure within the leaves builds up due to evaporative loss of water), cohesion (a result of hydrogen bonding in water which allows it to behave as a single column) and bulk flow (occurs when water molecules evaporate from the leaf surface causing the drawing up of another column).

Question 13 D

See: BIO 17.3, 17.3.2

The Pressure Flow Hypothesis (= Mass Flow Hypothesis) is the best-supported theory to explain the movement of food through the phloem. Movement occurs by bulk flow (mass flow) by means of turgor pressure, also described as hydrostatic pressure.

Translocation of sugars is accomplished through phloem cells and begins at a source and ends at a sink. The sink refers to the site where the carbohydrates are utilized by the plant. The sugar enters sieve-tube members through active transport and causes the concentration of solutes to be much higher in the source than in the sink.

Question 14 A

See: BIO 17.4

Cytokinins – Stimulate cell division and are produced in roots. They also stimulate the growth of lateral buds and delay senescence (aging).

Question 15 A

See: BIO 17.5

Phototropism – This is a plant's response to light and is governed by auxin. When there is an equal amount of light hitting all sides of the plant, the growth of the stem is uniform and proceeds straight upward. In the event that one side does not receive as much light as the other the auxin concentrates on the shady side of the stem and causes differential growth with the shady side growing more than the sunny side, causing the stem to bend towards the light.

Question 16 D

See: BIO 17.6.1, 17.6.2

The net result of non-cyclic reaction in photosynthesis is the production of NADPH and ATP and photolysis of water ("photo" refers to light and "lysis" in biology refers to splitting). See the diagrams in BIO 17.6.1 and 17.6.2.

Question 17 A

See: BIO 17.6.1

A typical plant can convert sunlight into chemical energy (i.e. carbohydrates such as glucose and other sugars, cellulose, lignin) with an efficiency of approximately 1%. An aside: Lignin or lignen is derived from wood and is an integral part of the secondary cell walls of plants.

Question 18 C

See: BIO 17.6.1

During photosynthesis, H_2O is split into $2H^+$ and $\frac{1}{2}O_2$. The remaining H^+ provides the H in NADPH. This process is called photolysis ("photo" refers to light and "lysis" in biology refers to splitting). See the diagram in BIO 17.6.1.

Question 19 A

See: BIO 4.7-4.9, 17.6.1, 17.6.2; CHM 1.5.1, 1.6, 10.1, 10.2

During light phase, water is oxidized and the released hydrogen is accepted by NADP, thus it is reduced to NADPH.

Note: Reduction reactions can be defined as the gain of hydrogen ions, the gain of electrons, or the loss of O_2, while oxidation reactions are the opposite: the loss of hydrogen ions, the loss of electrons, or the gain of O_2.

Question 20 D

See: BIO 17.6.1

Since glucose is formed from CO_2 and hydrogen released from water, therefore oxygen comes from CO_2.

Question 21 D

See: BIO 17.6.1, 17.6.2

During the light phase, ATP and NADPH are products and oxygen is the by-product. See the diagram in BIO 17.6.1.

Question 22 C

See: BIO 17.6

CAM plants are different from C3 and C4 plants because they have temporal division of the light and dark reactions of photosynthesis. CAM plants keep their stomata closed during the day to reduce the loss of water. The rate of evaporation is highest during the day. The light reactions do not require carbon dioxide, so the light reactions can take place when the stomata are closed. At night, when the evaporation rates are lower the stomata are open to allow the intake of carbon dioxide so the dark reactions can take place. In C3 plants the reactions can take place at the same time. In C4 plants, the reactions can also take place at the same time due to a special enzyme which helps the plant produce carbon dioxide and access carbon dioxide so that the dark reactions can take place when the stomata are closed. Therefore, C4 plants are also adapted to arid environments.

Question 23 D

See: BIO 17.6.3

Since no light is directly involved with the light-independent reactions, the Calvin cycle can also be referred to as the dark reactions - even though it cannot proceed in the dark. This is because it is dependent on energy from NADPH and ATP, formed during the light reactions of photosynthesis.

CHAPTER REVIEW SOLUTIONS — CHAPTER 18

Question 1 D

See: BIO 18.1

Associative learning – Occurs when an animal learns that two or more events are connected. Pavlov's classical conditioning and Skinner's operant conditioning are examples.

Question 2 C

See: BIO 18.1

Classical conditioning is a type of associative learning in which an otherwise meaningless stimulus is associated with a reward or a punishment.

Question 3 A

See: BIO 18.1

Imprinting is a rapid learning process where a newborn or very young animal establishes a behavior pattern of recognition and attraction to another animal of its own kind or to a substitute or an object identified as the "parent". It is an irreversible behavior.

Question 4 D

See: BIO 18.1

Operant conditioning is a type of associative learning that is the basis for most animal training. The trainer encourages a behavior by rewarding the animal. Eventually, the animal will perform the behavior without necessarily receiving a reward.

Question 5 C

See: BIO 18.1

Animals that help other animals are engaging in altruistic behavior. It is an unselfish, sacrificing behavior that reduces the overall fitness of the individual. This type of behavior is seen when animals risk their safety by defending a friend or family member or when they sacrifice their reproduction to help another individual (always of the same species). This is not a matter of strength or fitness.

CHAPTER REVIEW SOLUTIONS — CHAPTER 19

Question 1 D

See: BIO 19.1

Abiotic factors are nonliving factors in an ecosystem and includes light, water, minerals, gases, pH, temperature, etc. These are climatic conditions that control what plants can live that environment.

Question 2 B

See: BIO 19.2, 19.3

The "J" shape is the classic shape of an exponential curve. Logistic growth occurs when limiting factors keep the population in check and produces an S shaped curve. The point at which the growth rate levels off is the carrying capacity. K-selected species can be the result but it can not be described as a graph.

Question 3 A

See: BIO 16.2, 19.3

Gause's competitive exclusion principle is described by this question.

Question 4 A

See: BIO 2.2, 9.5, 19.3

When both species benefit, the relationship is mutualism. Humans get vitamin K and the bacteria get a place to live. Commensalism is when one organism benefits and the other is not affected. Parasitism is when one organism benefits at the other organism's expense. Amensalism is where one is completely obliterated (harmed) and the other is unaffected (not benefited).

Question 5 D

See: BIO 19.6

"Trophic" relates to the feeding habits or food relationship of different organisms in a food chain as described by all 3 pyramids among the answer choices.

Question 6 D

See: BIO 16.6.4, 19.6

Producers include autotrophs and chemotrophs. Plants and cyanobacteria are examples of primary producers. Mushrooms are members of the Kingdom Fungi (BIO 16.6.4). All fungi are heterotrophs. They may be parasitic or saprophytic and thus they are detritivores and decomposers.

Question 7 D

See: BIO 2.2, 19.6

"Trophic" relates to the feeding habits or food. "Auto" means operating independently and without needing help. Autotrophic organisms can synthesize their own food (organic compounds) from the sun (photosynthetic) or from simple inorganic chemicals (chemoautotrophs). Producers include autotrophs and chemotrophs.

Question 8 C

See: BIO 16.6.4, 19.6

Detritus feeders (= detritivores = detritophages) are heterotrophs that obtain their energy from dead plants and animals. Common worms or earthworms (Phylum Annelida, BIO 16.6.4) are a good example of soil-dwelling detritivores.

Question 9 D

See: BIO 19.6

Tertiary consumers are secondary carnivores who feed off of secondary consumers.

Question 10 C

See: BIO 19.6

Plants and cyanobacteria are autotrophs as well as examples of primary producers.

Question 11 A

See: BIO 19.6

An autotroph is a producer that produces complex organic compounds (such as carbohydrates, fats, and proteins) from simple substances present in its surroundings - generally using energy from light (by photosynthesis) or inorganic chemical reactions (chemosynthesis). Detritus feeders (= detritivores = detritophages) are heterotrophs that obtain their energy from dead plants and animals. Thus they contribute to decomposition and nutrient cycles (i.e. the nitrogen cycle). See the diagram in BIO 19.6.

Question 12 A

See: BIO 19.7

An autotroph is a producer that produces complex organic compounds (such as carbohydrates, fats, and proteins) from simple substances present in its surroundings - generally using energy from light (by photosynthesis) or inorganic chemical reactions (chemosynthesis). Detritus feeders (= detritivores = detritophages) are heterotrophs that obtain their energy from dead plants and animals. Thus they contribute to decomposition and nutrient cycles (i.e. the nitrogen cycle). See the diagram in BIO 19.6.

Question 13 B

See: BIO 19.7

Permafrost is a thick subsurface layer of soil that remains frozen throughout the year, mostly in polar regions.

Question 14 D

See: BIO 19.7

All the answer choices represent biomes that do not support the growth of trees.

Question 15 C

See: BIO 19.7

The taiga biome (boreal forest) is a coniferous forest (cones and evergreens; see also Kingdom Plantae, BIO 16.6.4) with cold winters and snow.

Question 16 A

See: BIO 2.1, 2.3, 16.2, 16.6, 19.2, 19.3, 19.4

The fungus is better adapted to live on one population of the host species than another. In this case the fungus displays more rapid adaptation than the host since the fungus is better able to live on this host than others. The fungus did not display more rapid adaptation with respect to all host populations, as its ability to grow and reproduce on other populations of hosts is limited.

Question 17 B

See: BIO 16.2, 16.3, 16.6, 19.2, 19.3, 19.4

By looking at the experimental results (*B*) in Figure 1, you can see that over time the parasite population noticeably declines. The fluctuation (frequency of oscillation of the curve) of both populations is also somewhat reduced compared to the control (*A*).

Question 18 C

See: BIO 2.5, 2.5.1, 16.6, 19.2, 19.3, 19.4

The passage suggests (= *hypothesis*) that evolution occurs between two different species, a parasite and a host, which have had prolonged exposure to each other [= *experimental group*; Fig.1 (*B*)]. To prove that the preceding is true and significant, the result must first be compared to a control which is not exposed to the "treatment" (i.e. *members of the parasite and host species which have no prior exposure to each other*). In this manner, we can attribute the *difference* in the two graphs to the only factor which changed - the exposure to each other which is the basis for coevolution. You may want to review the section on experiments (BIO 2.5, 2.5.1) or coevolution (BIO 19.2, 19.3, 19.4).

Question 19 A

See: BIO 2.5, 2.5.1, 16.3, 16.6, 19.2, 19.3, 19.4

You need to identify what the trend is in the graph for the control group in order to identify possible explanations for these events. As the host population increases [Fig. 1 (A)], the parasite population also increases until a point at which the host population declines, probably as a result of too many parasites. The parasite population quickly drops off in response to this decline (i.e. too few hosts to infect). The host population starts to increase again, followed shortly after by the parasite population. Options *C.* and *D.* are adequate explanations of the events occurring in the populations. Option *B.* is less likely, as eliminating the parasite's source of food is not likely to increase that population but it does appear to happen in Fig. 1 when the host population is at its lowest. A very low decrease in the host population is followed shortly after by an increase in parasite population and in this way option *B.* provides a possible explanation of events that actually do occur. Option *A.* is illogical as the virulence of the parasites when the population is low is unlikely to have a large enough effect to decrease the host population significantly. Also, this option explains an event which does not occur on the graph. In no place does the parasite population lower first, followed by a lowering of the host population. Logically, the opposite should occur. You may want to review the section on experiments (BIO 2.5, 2.5.1) or coevolution (BIO 19.2, 19.3, 19.4).

Question 20 C

See: BIO 16.3, 16.6, 19.2, 19.3, 19.4

Knowledge of bacteria or even current affairs should tell you that it is definitely possible for a bacterium to develop resistance to a drug. Those bacteria which happen to be able to survive in the presence of the drug (because of mutations or other reasons) will be the ones that will reproduce, likely passing this resistance on to the new bacteria (selective pressure) which are similar to the mechanisms described in this chapter regarding coevolution.

Chapter Review Solutions — Chapter 20

Question 1 D

See: BIO 20.1.1

Hydrophobic portions (R-groups) of the enzyme are on the interior of an enzyme because the external portion of the molecule is in an aqueous medium and the internal portion protects the hydrophobic R groups.

Question 2 C

See: BIO 20.2.1; QR 7

This question is essentially a mathematics problem. It is asking how many different ways a certain number of things can be ordered (permutations). There are three different amino acids and they can be arranged in 3! different ways to create six different molecules (QR Chap. 7):

$$n! = 3! = 3 \times 2 \times 1 = 6.$$

If you did not know the math, you can use your note board and do it the long way: ABC, ACB, BAC, BCA, CAB, CBA. Recall that the tripeptides A-B-C and C-B-A are different since one end has an amino group and the other has a carboxylic acid group.

Question 3 B

See: BIO 20.2.2

Primary structure of a protein is defined as the order or sequence of the amino acids in the protein. Secondary structure indicates regions of ordered structure, and tertiary structure is the overall structure of the protein. Quaternary structure refers to the structure of a multiprotein complex.

Question 4 C

See: BIO 20.2.2

Technically, disulfide bonds influence all levels of protein structure but it most characteristic of one level in particular. Disulfide bonds are sulfur-sulfur covalent bonds that help to stabilize the tertiary structure of proteins. Primary structures involve the amino acid sequence with the amino acids held together by amide bonds. Secondary structures involve the conformation of the polypeptide backbone through hydrogen bonds. Tertiary structures pertain to the 3 dimensional folding of one polypeptide chain involving both covalent (sulfur bridges) and non-covalent bonds, whereas quaternary structures involve the 3 dimensional folding of more than one polypeptide.

Question 5 D

See: BIO 20.3.1

Carbohydrates are polyhydroxy ketones or polyhydroxy aldehydes.

Question 6 B

See: BIO 20.3.2

We are told that glucan is formed only in the presence of sucrose, which is a disaccharide made up of fructose and glucose. The enzyme acts on glucose molecules to form glucan and fructose molecules to form lactic acid. However, the question asks how the enzyme acts initially. To get the glucose and fructose which the enzyme will ultimately change, the enzyme first needs to split its starting product, sucrose, into those constituent sugars.

Long questions are not typical for the DAT but it happens from time to time so it's best to be prepared!

Question 7 D

See: BIO 20.3.1, 20.3.2

The six-carbon monosaccharides fructose + glucose form the disaccharide sucrose.

Question 8 D

See: BIO 6.3, 6.3.2, 20.4.1

All these compounds have the basic structure of steroids. It is important to understand that the dietary fat cholesterol is a steroid but all steroids are not cholesterols. "Steroidogenesis" is the process by which steroids are generated from cholesterol and transformed into other steroids.

Question 9 A

See: BIO 4.4-4.10, 20.5

Adenosine triphosphate (ATP) has energy stored in its bonds which is released when ATP breaks down into ADP and Pi (= *inorganic phosphate*). The linkage which breaks between the phosphate groups are *anhydride bonds*. In DNA, the phosphate groups engage in two ester linkages creating phosphodiester bonds.

Question 10 B

See: BIO 20.6

The bicarbonate system dominates the extracellular space and the phosphate and, particularly, the protein buffer system (because of the molecular structure of contributing amino acids) dominate the intracellular space as buffers.

Question 11 A

See: BIO 20.6

Hemoglobin and proteins are organic. Bicarbonate is the most effective extracellular buffer. Phosphate is the most effective intracellular inorganic buffer.

Question 12 D

See: BIO 20.6.1

Plasma pH is normally maintained at 7.4. A pH less than 7.35 is acidosis, whereas a pH of greater than 7.45 is alkalosis.

Question 13 C

See: BIO 20 App.

On the Surface: If there is an acidosis OR alkalosis that is NOT because of the respiratory system then we know that it must be metabolic and not respiratory. Thus only one answer is possible: metabolic acidosis.

Going Deeper: Keto acids contain a ketone group (= keto) and a carboxylic acid group (= acid). Keto acids are involved in the Krebs cycle and glycolysis (pyruvic acid, oxaloacetic acid).

When ingested carbohydrate levels are low, stored fats and proteins become the primary source of ATP production. Fats can be used to form ketone bodies. Amino acids can be deaminated to produce alpha keto acids and ketone bodies.

Diabetic ketoacidosis (DKA) is potentially life-threatening and results from a shortage of insulin; since the body can't bring the glucose into cells for use, the body switches to burning fatty acids and producing acidic ketone bodies that can cause symptoms and complications.

Question 14 D

See: BIO 9.4.2, BIO 20 App.

On the Surface: "Respiratory" means that the origin of the problem is the lungs (hyperventilation vs. hypoventilation) which is not consistent with the act of vomiting, thus D must be the exception.

Going Deeper: Vomiting results in loss of fluids (dehydration, B) and the loss of gastric acid (BIO 9.3) leaving the body relatively basic (metabolic alkalosis, A). However, prolonged vomiting may lead to the vomiting of intestinal contents including bile and pancreatic juice (which is high in bicarbonate to neutralize acid from the stomach; BIO 9.4.2). This could lead to metabolic alkalosis (A). It would be very rare to have a question this challenging on the DAT.

Question 15 A

See: BIO 12.4.1, BIO 20 App.

Acidosis is a pH of < 7.35 so only answers A and C are possible; "respiratory" means that the source of the problem is ventilation (breathing). Hypoventilation reduces the lungs ability to 'blow off' carbon dioxide so CO_2 accumulates in the blood which increases hydrogen ion concentration (pH decreases = acidosis; see BIO 12.4.1). So the answer must be A, respiratory acidosis.

Biology Index

D

E

F

G

H

I

J

K

L

M

N

O

P

R

S

T

U

V

W

Y

Z

$v = \sqrt{600} = \sqrt{6(100)} =$

THE GOLD STANDARD

DAT CHEM

General Chemistry [CHM]
and Organic Chemistry [ORG]

Book II of IV

Gold Standard Contributors
• 4-Book GS DAT Set •

Brett Ferdinand BSc MD-CM
Karen Barbia BS Arch
Brigitte Bigras BSc MSc DMD
Ibrahima Diouf BSc MSc PhD
Amir Durmic BSc Eng
Adam Segal BSc MSc
Da Xiao BSc DMD
Naomi Epstein BEng
Lisa Ferdinand BA MA
Jeanne Tan Te
Kristin Finkenzeller BSc MD
Heaven Hodges BSc
Sean Pierre BSc MD
James Simenc BS (Math), BA Eng
Jeffrey Cheng BSc
Timothy Ruger MSc PhD
Petra Vernich BA
Alvin Vicente BS Arch

DMD Candidates

E. Jordan Blanche BS
[Harvard School of Dental Medicine]
Stephan Suksong Yoon BA
[Harvard School of Dental Medicine]

$ET = Ek + Ep = 1/2mv2 + mgh$

glutamate recept
floating bridges
epithelial-mesenc
subatomic partic

Gold Standard Illustrators
• 4-Book GS DAT Set •

Daphne McCormack
Nanjing Design
· Ren Yi, Huang Bin
· Sun Chan, Li Xin
Fabiana Magnosi
Harvie Gallatiera
Rebbe Jurilla BSc MBA

floating bridges
subatomic particles
brain functions
receptors Helico bacteria

RuveneCo

The Gold Standard DAT was built for the US DAT.

The Gold Standard DAT is identical to Canadian DAT prep except QR and ORG. Also, you must practice soap carving for the complete Canadian DAT.

The Gold Standard DAT is identical to OAT prep except PAT, which is replaced by OAT Physics; see our Gold Standard OAT book for Physics review and OAT practice test.

Be sure to register at www.DAT-prep.com by clicking on GS DAT Owners and following the directions for Gold Standard DAT Owners. Please Note: benefits are for 1 year from the date of online registration, for the original book owner only and are not transferable; unauthorized access and use outside the Terms of Use posted on DAT-prep.com may result in account deletion; if you are not the original owner, you can purchase your virtual access card separately at DAT-prep.com.

Visit The Gold Standard's Education Center at www.gold-standard.com.

ISBN 978-1-927338-10-0

Address all inquiries, comments, or suggestions to the publisher. For Terms of Use go to: www.DAT-prep.com

RuveneCo Inc
Gold Standard Multimedia Education
559-334 Cornelia St
Plattsburgh, NY 12901
E-mail: learn@gold-standard.com
Online at www.gold-standard.com

Table of Contents

EXAM SUMMARY

The Dental Admission Test (DAT) consists of 280 multiple-choice questions distributed across quite a diversity of question types in four tests. The DAT is a computer-based test (CBT). This exam requires approximately five hours to complete - including the optional tutorial, break, and post-test survey. The following are the four subtests of the Dental Admission Test:

1. Survey of the Natural Sciences (NS) – 100 questions; 90 min.
    - General Biology (BIO): 40 questions
    - General Chemistry (CHM): 30 questions
    - Organic Chemistry (ORG): 30 questions
2. Perceptual Ability Test (PAT) - 90 questions; 6 subsections; 60 min.
    - Apertures: 15 questions
    - Orthographic or View Recognition: 15 questions
    - Angle Discrimination: 15 questions
    - Paper Folding: 15 questions
    - Cube Counting: 15 questions
    - 3-D Form Development: 15 questions
3. Reading Comprehension (RC) – 50 questions; 3 reading passages; 60 min.
4. Quantitative Reasoning (QR) – 40 questions; 45 min.
    - Mathematics Problems: 30 questions
    - Applied Mathematics/Word Problems: 10 questions

You will get six scores from: (1) BIO (2) CHM (3) ORG (4) PAT (5) QR (6) RC.

You will get two additional scores which are summaries:
(7) Academic Average (AA) = BIO + CHM + ORG + QR + RC
(8) Total Science (TS) = BIO + CHM + ORG

Common Formula for Acceptance:

GPA + DAT score + Interview = Dental School Admissions*

*Note: In general, Dental School Admissions Committees will only examine the DAT score if the GPA is high enough; they will only admit or interview if the GPA + DAT score is high enough. Some programs also use autobiographical materials and/or references in the admissions process. Different dental schools may emphasize different aspects of your DAT score, for example: PAT, BIO, TS, AA. The average score for any section is approximately 17/30; the average AA for admissions is usually 18-20 depending on the dental school; the AA for admissions to Harvard is around 22-23; the 100th percentile is usually 25 meaning that virtually 100% of the approximately 13 000 students who take the DAT every year have an AA less than 25. Only a handful of students score 25/30. Our two student contributors scored 27/30 (AA).

PREFACE

The DAT is challenging, get organized.

dat-prep.com/dat-study-schedule

1. How to study:

1. Study the Gold Standard (GS) books and videos to learn
2. Do GS Chapter review practice questions
3. Consolidate: create and review your personal summaries (= Gold Notes) daily

2. Once you have completed your studies:

1. Full-length practice test
2. Review mistakes, all solutions
3. Consolidate: review all your Gold Notes and create more
4. Repeat until you get beyond the score you need for your targeted dental school

3. Full-length practice tests:

1. ADA practice exams
2. Gold Standard DAT exams
3. TopScore Pro exams
4. Other sources if needed

4. How much time do you need?

On average, 3-6 hours per day for 3-6 months

WARNING: Study more or study more efficiently. You choose. The Gold Standard has condensed the content that you require to excel at the DAT. We have had Ivy League dental students involved in the production of the Gold Standard series so that pre-dent students can feel that they have access to the content required to get a score satisfactory at any dental school in the country. To make the content easier to retain, you can also find aspects of the Gold Standard program in other formats such as:

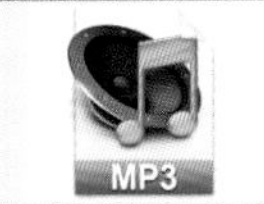

Is there something in the Gold Standard that you did not understand? Don't get frustrated, get online.

dat-prep.com/forum   dat-prep.com/QRchanges-2015

Good luck with your studies!

Gold Standard Team

DAT-Prep.com

GENERAL CHEMISTRY

STOICHIOMETRY

Chapter 1

Memorize	Understand	Importance
* Define: molecular weight * Define: empirical/molecular formula * Rules for oxidation numbers * Common redox agents	* Composition by % mass * Mole concept, limiting reactants * Avogadro's number * Calculate theoretical yield * Basic types of reactions * Calculation of ox. numbers * Stoichiometric coefficients, balancing equations, reaction types	**2 to 4 out of the 30 Gen CHM** DAT questions are based on content in this chapter (in our estimation). * Note that between 50% and 85% of the questions in DAT General Chemistry are from 6 chapters: 1, 2, 4, 5, 6 and 9.

DAT-Prep.com

Introduction

Stoichiometry is simply the math behind the chemistry involving products and reactants. The math is quite simple, in part, because of the law of conservation of mass that states that the mass of a closed system will remain constant throughout a chemical reaction.

Additional Resources

Free Online Forum

Video: Online or DVD

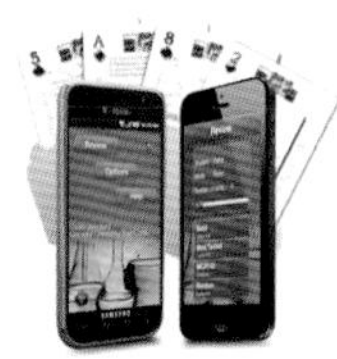

Flashcards

1.1 Generalities

Most substances known to us are mixtures of pure compounds. Air, for instance, contains the pure compounds nitrogen (~78%), oxygen (~21%), water vapor and many other gases (~1%). The compositional ratio of air or any other mixture may vary from one location to another. Each pure compound is made up of molecules which are composed of smaller units: the *atoms*. Atoms combine in very specific ratios to form molecules. A molecule is the smallest unit of a compound presenting the properties of that compound. During a chemical reaction molecules break down into individual atoms which then recombine to form new compounds. Stoichiometry establishes relationships between the above-mentioned specific ratios for individual molecules (or moles) or for molecules involved in a given chemical reaction.

1.2 Empirical Formula vs. Molecular Formula

The molecules of oxygen (O_2) are made up of two atoms of the same element. Water molecules on the other hand are composed of two different elements: hydrogen and oxygen in the specific ratio 2:1. Note that water is not a mixture of hydrogen and oxygen since this ratio is specific and does not vary with the location or the experimental conditions. The *empirical formula* of a pure compound is the simplest whole number ratio between the numbers of atoms of the different elements making up the compound. For instance, the empirical formula of water is H_2O (2:1 ratio) while the empirical formula of hydrogen peroxide is HO (1:1 ratio). The *molecular formula* of a given molecule states the exact number of the different atoms that make up this molecule. The empirical formula of water is identical to its molecular formula, i.e. H_2O; however, the molecular formula of hydrogen peroxide, H_2O_2, is different from its empirical formula (both correspond to a 1:1 ratio).

1.3 Mole - Atomic and Molecular Weights

Because of the small size of atoms and molecules chemists have to consider collections of a large number of these particles to bring chemical problems to our macroscopic scale. Collections of tens or dozens of atoms are still too small to achieve this practical purpose. For various reasons the number 6.02×10^{23} (Avogadro's number:N_A) was chosen. It is the number of atoms in 12 grams of the most abundant *isotope* of carbon (isotopes are elements which are identical chemically since the number of protons are the same; their masses differ slightly since the number of neutrons differ). A mole of atoms or molecules (or in fact any particles in general) contains an Avogadro number of these particles. The weight in grams of a mole of atoms of a given element is the gram-atomic weight, GAW, of that element (sometimes weight is measured in atomic mass units - *see CHM 11.2, 11.3*). Along the same lines, the weight in grams of a mole of molecules of a given compound is its gram-molecular weight, GMW. Here are some equations relating these concepts in a way that will help you solve some of the stoichiometry problems:

For an element:

$$\text{moles} = \frac{\text{weight of sample in grams}}{\text{GAW}}$$

For a compound:

$$\text{moles} = \frac{\text{weight of sample in grams}}{\text{GMW}}$$

The GAW of a given element is not to be confused with the mass of a single atom of this element. For instance the mass of a single atom of carbon-12 (GAW = 12 g) is $12/N_A = 1.993 \times 10^{-23}$ grams. Atomic weights are dimensionless numbers based on carbon-12 as the reference standard isotope and are defined as follows:

$$\frac{\text{mass of an atom of X}}{\text{mass of an atom of Y}} = \frac{\text{atomic weight of element X}}{\text{atomic weight of element Y}}$$

Clearly if the reference element Y is chosen to be carbon-12 (which is the case in standard periodic tables) the GAW of any element X is numerically equal to its atomic weight. In the table of atomic weights, all the elements then have values in which are relative to the carbon-12 isotope. The molecular weight of a given molecule is equal to the sum of the atomic weights of the atoms that make up the molecule. For example, the molecular weight of H_2O is equal to 18.0 amu/molecule (H = 1.008 and O = 16.00). The molar weight (or molar mass) of H_2O is numerically equal to the molecular weight (18.0) however, the units are in grams/mol as the molar weight is based on a mole amount of substance. Thus, molecular weight and molar weight are numerically equivalent however, molecular weight is the weight (amu) per molecule and molar weight is based on the weight (grams) per mole (1 mol = 6.02×10^{23} molecules).

1.4 Composition of a Compound by Percent Mass

The percentage composition of a compound is the percent of the total mass of a given element in that compound. For instance, the chemical analysis of a 100 g sample of pure vitamin C demontrates that there are 40.9 g of carbon, 4.58 g of hydrogen and 54.5 g of oxygen. The percentage composition of pure vitamin C is:

$$\%C = 40.9;\ \%H = 4.58;\ \%O = 54.5$$

The composition of a compound by percent mass is closely related to its empirical formula. For instance, in the case of vitamin

C, the determination of the number of moles of atoms of C, H or O in a 100 g of vitamin C is rather straightforward:

moles of atoms of C in a 100 g of vitamin C = 40.9/12.0 = 3.41

moles of atoms of H in a 100 g of vitamin C = 4.58/1.01= 4.53

moles of atoms of O in a 100 g of vitamin C = 54.5/16.0 = 3.41

[GAW can be determined from the periodic table in Chapter 2]

To deduce the smallest ratio between the numbers above, one follows the simple procedure:

(i) divide each one of the previously obtained numbers of moles by the smallest one of them (3.41 in our case):

for C: 3.41 mol/3.41 mol = 1.00
for H: 4.53 mol/3.41 mol = 1.33
for O: 3.41 mol/ 3.41 mol = 1.00

(ii) multiply the numbers obtained in the previous step by a small number to obtain a whole number ratio. In our case we need to multiply by 3 (in most cases this factor is between 1 and 5) so that :

for C: $1.00 \times 3 = 3$
for H: $1.33 \times 3 = 4$ and
for O: $1.00 \times 3 = 3$

Therefore, in this example, the simplest whole number ratio is 3C:4H:3O and we conclude that the empirical formula for vitamin C is: $C_3H_4O_3$.

In the previous example, instead of giving the composition of vitamin C by percent weight we could have provided the raw chemical analysis data and asked for the determination of that composition.

For instance, this data would be that the burning of a 4.00 mg sample of pure vitamin C yields 6.00 mg of CO_2 and 1.632 mg of H_2O. Since there are 12.0 g of carbon in 44.0 g of CO_2 the number of milligrams of carbon in 6.00 mg of CO_2 (which corresponds to the number of mg of carbon in 4.00 mg of vitamin C) is simply:

6.00 mg $\times$ (12.0 g C/44.0 g CO_2) = 1.636 mg of C in 6.00 mg of CO_2 or 4.00 mg of vitamin C for further clarification.

To convert this number into a percent mass is then trivial. Similarly, the percent mass of hydrogen is obtained from the previous data and bearing in mind that there are 2.02 g of hydrogen (and not 1.01 g) in 18.0 g of water.

Incidentally, "burning" means <u>combustion</u> (CHM 1.5.1, ORG 3.2.1) which takes place in the presence of excess oxygen and results in the production of heat (exothermic), the conversion of the chemical species (new products), and light can be produced (glowing or a flame).

1.5 Description of Reactions by Chemical Equations

The convention for writing chemical equations is as follows: compounds which initially combine or react in a chemical reaction are called *reactants*; they are always written on the left-hand side of the chemical equation. The compounds which are produced during the same process are referred to as the *products* of the chemical reaction; they always appear on the right-hand side of the chemical equation. In the chemical equation:

$$2\ BiCl_3 + 3\ H_2O \rightarrow Bi_2O_3 + 6\ HCl$$

the coefficients represent the relative number of moles of reactants that combine to form the corresponding relative number of moles of products: they are the stoichiometric coefficients of the balanced chemical equation. The law of conservation of mass requires that the number of atoms of a given element remains constant during the process of a chemical reaction.

Balancing a chemical equation is putting this general principle into practice. Chemical equations must be balanced so that there are equal numbers of atoms of each element on both sides of the equation. Many equations are balanced by trial and error however, caution must be practiced when balancing a chemical equation. It is always easier to balance elements that appear only in one compound on each side of the equation; therefore, as a general rule, always balance those elements first and then deal with those which appear in more than one compound last. Thus, a general suggestive procedure for balancing equations would be as follows: (1) count and compare the atoms on both sides of the chemical equation, (2) balance each element one at a time by placing whole number coefficients in front of the formulas resulting in the same number of atoms of each element on each side of the equation. Remember that a coefficient in front of a formula multiplies every atom in the formula (i.e., $2BiCl_3 = 2Bi + 6Cl$). It is best to leave pure elements or metals until the end. Therefore, balance the carbon atoms in both the reactant and product side first. (3) Balance hydrogens in both the reactant and products; and (4) finally, check if all elements are balanced with the smallest possible set of whole number coefficients.

Given the preceding chemical reaction, if H_2O is present in excessive quantity, then $BiCl_3$ would be considered the **limiting reactant.** In other words, since the amount of $BiCl_3$ is relatively small, it is the $BiCl_3$ which determines how much product will be formed. Thus if you were given 316 grams of $BiCl_3$ in *excess* H_2O and you needed to determine the quantity of HCl produced (theoretical yield), you would proceed as follows:

- Determine the number of moles of $BiCl_3$ (*see* CHM 1.3) given Bi = 209 g/mol and Cl = 35.5 g/mol, thus $BiCl_3 = (1 \times 209) + (3 \times 35.5) = 315.5$ or approximately 316 g/mol:

$$\#\ \text{moles}\ BiCl_3 = (316\ \text{g})/(316\ \text{g/mol}) = 1.0\ \text{mole of}\ BiCl_3.$$

- From the stoichiometric coefficients of the balanced equation:

2 moles of $BiCl_3$: 6 moles of HCl; therefore, 1 mole of $BiCl_3$: 3 moles of HCl

- Given H = 1.00 g/mol, thus HCl = 36.5 g/mol, we get:

3 moles × 36.5 g/mol = 110 g of HCl (approx.).

Please note: The theoretical yield is the calculated amount of product that can be predicted from a balanced chemical reaction and is seldom obtained in the laboratory. The actual yield is the actual amount of product produced and recovered in the laboratory. The Percentage yield = Actual yield/Theoretical Yield × 100%.

1.5.1 Categories of Chemical Reactions

Throughout the chapters in General Chemistry we will explore many different types of chemicals and some of their associated reactions. The various chemical reactions may be classified generally as either a redox type (see section 1.6) or as a non-redox type reaction.

The following chart represents a general overview of the chemical reaction classifications or categories followed by a brief description of each of the reaction categories.

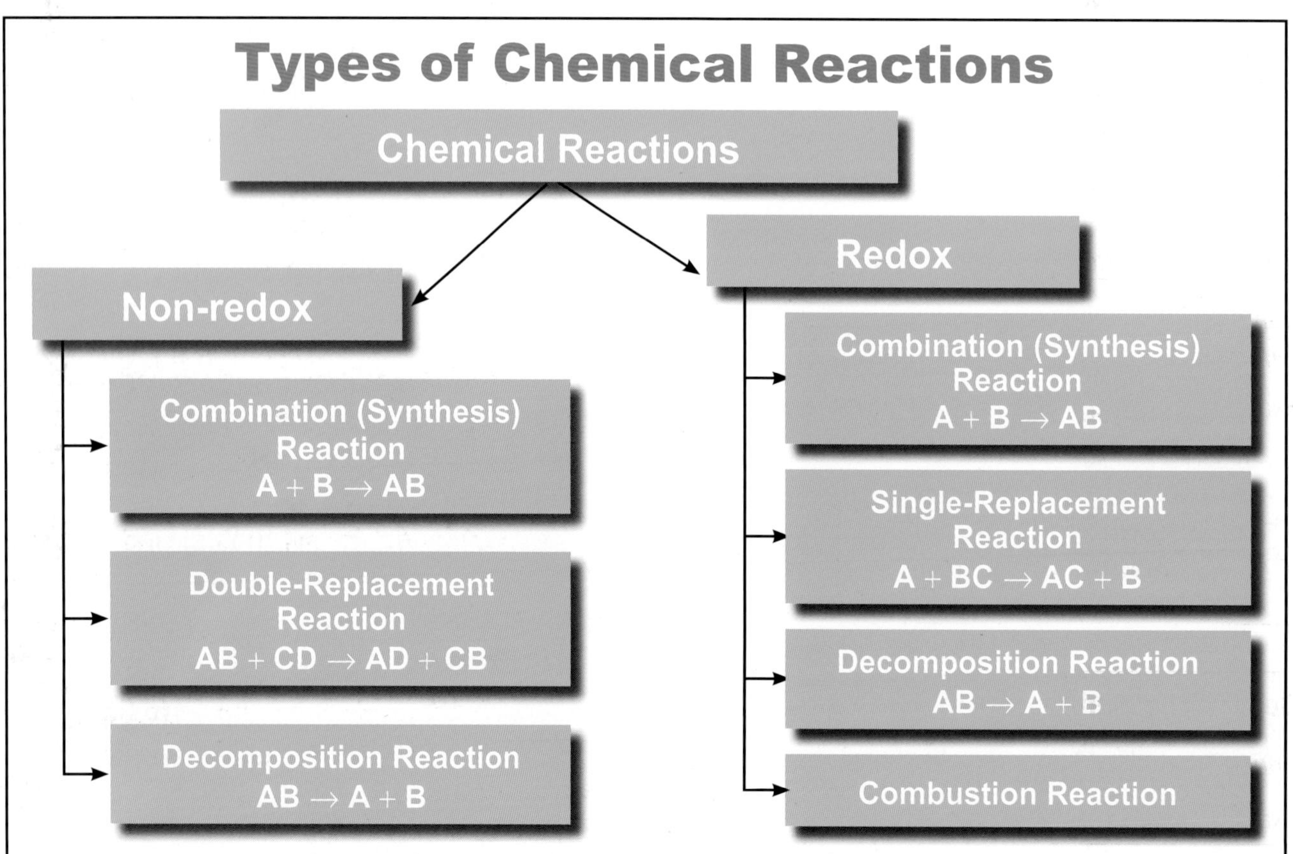

Non-redox

Combination (Synthesis) Reaction

General equation: $A + B \rightarrow AB$

Example: $SO_2(g) + H_2O(l) \rightarrow H_2SO_3\ (aq)$

Double-Replacement Reaction (or Metathesis Reaction)

(a) Precipitation Type

General equation: $AB + CD \rightarrow AD + CB$

Example: $CaCl_2(aq) + Na_2CO_3(aq)$
$\rightarrow CaCO_3(s) + 2NaCl(aq)$

(b) Acid-Base Neutralization Type

General equation: $HA + BOH \rightarrow H_2O + BA$
(HA = any H^+ acid & BOH = any OH^- Base)

Example:
$2HCl(l) + Ba(OH)_2(aq) \rightarrow H_2O(l) + BaCl_2(aq)$

(c) Gas Evolution Type Reaction

General equation: $HA + B \rightarrow H_2O + BA$
(HA = H^+ acid & B = special base salt $NaHCO_3$)

Example: $HCl(aq) + NaHCO_3(aq)$
$\rightarrow H_2CO_3(aq)^* + NaCl(aq)$
$\rightarrow H_2O(l) + CO_2(g) + NaCl(aq)$
(*H_2CO_3 is carbonic acid, the "fizz" in sodas, which degrades to $CO_2(g)$ and $H_2O(l)$)

Decomposition Reaction (CHM 4.3.1)

General equation: $AB \rightarrow A + B$

Example: $H_2CO_3(aq) \rightarrow H_2O(l) + CO_2(g)$

Redox

Combination (Synthesis) Reaction

General equation: $A + B \rightarrow AB$

Example: $SO_3(g) + H_2O(l) \rightarrow H_2SO_4(aq)$

Single-Replacement Reaction

General equation: $A + BC \rightarrow AC + B$

Example:
$Zn(s) + CuSO_4(aq) \rightarrow Cu(s) + ZnSO_4(aq)$

Decomposition Reaction

General equation: $AB \rightarrow A + B$

Example: $2NaCl(s) \rightarrow 2Na(l) + Cl_2(g)$
(electrolysis reaction)

Combustion Reaction

Example: $CH_4(g) + 2O_2(g) \rightarrow CO_2(g) + 2H_2O(g)$

Note that compounds in the preceding chart are identified as solid (s), liquid (l), gas (g) or solubilized in water which is an aqueous (aq) solution.

Combination (or synthesis) and decomposition type reactions are classified as both redox and non-redox reactions. Single replacement and combustion type reactions are classified as only redox type reactions; as the oxidation state of at least one atom species changes through electron transfer (oxidation/reduction) on either side of the chemical equation.

The double-replacement type reactions are basically known as precipitation (or solid forming) type reactions or acid-base (neutralization) type reactions. A double replacement type reaction involves ions (CHM 5.2) which exchange partners and may or may not form precipitates depending on the water solubility of the products formed (CHM 5.3). In acid-base (neutralization) type reactions, the usual products formed are both water and a salt (CHM 6.7). Certain acid-base type reactions however are known to form gas products otherwise known as "Gas Evolution type reactions" due to the instability of an intermediate salt product formed as a result of the acid-base reaction (see preceding chart).

When replacement reactions occur, often there are ions known as "spectator ions" that do not undergo any changes and remain ionized in aqueous solutions. These ions can be left out of the end equation known as a "net ionic equation" because it does away with the spectator ions that are consequential to the reaction. Net ionic equations are used to show the actual chemical reaction that occurs during a single or double-replacement type reaction. Thus, it is essential to recognize and familiarize oneself to the various categories of reactions to enable one to further understand chemical reactivity.

1.6 Oxidation Numbers, Redox Reactions, Oxidizing vs. Reducing Agents

A special class of reactions known as *redox* reactions are better balanced using the concept of oxidation state. In a redox reaction, oxidation and reduction must occur simultaneously. Oxidation is defined as either an increase in oxidation number or a loss of one or more electrons and reduction is defined as a decrease in oxidation number or a gain of one or more electrons. This section deals with these reactions in which electrons are transferred from one atom (or a group of atoms) to another.

First of all, it is very important to understand the difference between the ionic charge and the oxidation state of an element. For this let us consider the two compounds sodium chloride (NaCl) and water (H_2O). NaCl is made up of the charged species or ions: Na^+ and Cl^-. During the formation of this ionic compound, one electron is transferred from the Na atom to the Cl atom. It is possible to verify this fact experimentally and determine that the charge of sodium in NaCl is indeed +1 and that the one for chlorine is −1. The elements in the periodic table tend to lose (oxidation) or gain (reduction) electrons to different extents. Therefore, even in non-ionic compounds electrons are always transferred, to different degrees, from one atom to another during the formation of a molecule of the compound. The actual partial charges that result from these partial transfers of electrons can also be determined experimentally. The oxidation state is not equal to such partial charges. It is rather an artificial concept that is used to perform some kind of "electron bookkeeping."

In a molecule like H_2O, since oxygen tends to attract electrons more than hydrogen, one can predict that the electrons that allow bonding to occur between hydrogen and oxygen will be displaced towards the oxygen atom. For the sake of "electron bookkeeping" we assign these electrons to the oxygen atom. The charge that the oxygen atom would have in this artificial process would be −2: this defines the oxidation state of oxygen in the H_2O molecule. In the same line of reasoning one defines the oxidation state of hydrogen in the water molecule as +1. The actual partial charges of hydrogen and oxygen are in fact smaller; but, as we will see later, the concept of oxidation state is very useful in stoichiometry.

Here are the general rules one needs to follow to assign oxidation numbers (or oxidation states) to different elements in different compounds:

1. In elementary substances, the oxidation number of an uncombined element regardless of whether it is monatomic (1 atom), diatomic (2 atoms) or polyatomic (multiple atoms), is zero. This is, for instance, the case for N in N_2 or Na in sodium element, O in O_2, or S in S_8.

2. In monatomic ions the oxidation number of the element that make up this ion is equal to the charge of the ion. This is the case for Na in Na^+ (+1) or Cl in Cl^- (−1) or Fe in Fe^{3+} (+3). Clearly, monatomic ions are the only species for which atomic charges and oxidation numbers coincide.

3. In a neutral molecule the sum of the oxidation numbers of all the elements that make up the molecule is zero. In a polyatomic ion (e.g. SO_4^{2-}) the sum of the oxidation numbers of the elements that make up this ion is equal to the charge of the ion.

4. Some useful oxidation numbers to memorize:

For H: +1, except in metal hydrides (general formula XH where X is from the first two columns of the periodic table) where it is equal to −1.

For O: −2 in most compounds. In peroxides (e.g. in H_2O_2) the oxidation number for O is −1, it is +2 in OF_2 and −1/2 in superoxides (e.g. potassium superoxide: KO_2 which contains the O_2^- ion as opposed to the O^{2-} ion).

For alkali metals (first column in the periodic table): +1.

For alkaline earth metals (second column): +2.

Aluminium always has an oxidation number of +3 in all its compounds. (i.e. chlorides $AlCl_3$, nitrites $Al(NO_2)_3$, etc.)

The oxidation number of each Group VIIA element is −1; however, when it is combined with an element of higher electronegativity, the oxidation number is +1. For example, the oxidation number of Cl is −1 in HCl and the oxidation number of Cl is +1 in HClO.

An element is said to have been *reduced* during a reaction if its oxidation number decreased during this reaction, it is said to have been oxidized if its *oxidation* number increased. A simple example is:

	$Zn(s)$	+	$CuSO_4(aq)$	⟶
Oxid.#:	0		+2	
	$ZnSO_4(aq)$	+	$Cu(s)$	
Oxid.#:	+2		0	

During this reaction Cu is reduced (oxidation number decreases from +2 to 0) while Zn is oxidized (oxidation number increases from 0 to +2). Since, in a sense, Cu is reduced by Zn, Zn can be referred to as the reducing agent. Similarly, Cu is the oxidizing agent.

The redox titrations will be dealt with in the section on titrations (CHM 6.10). Many of the redox agents in the table below will be explored in the chapters on Organic Chemistry.

Common Redox Agents

Reducing Agents	Oxidizing Agents
* Lithium aluminium hydride ($LiAlH_4$) * Sodium borohydride ($NaBH_4$) * Metals * Ferrous ion (Fe^{2+})	* Iodine (I_2) and other halogens * Permanganate (MnO_4) salts * Peroxide compounds (i.e. H_2O_2) * Ozone (O_3); osmium tetroxide (OsO_4) * Nitric acid (HNO_3); nitrous oxide (N_2O)

1.7 Mixtures

In many stoichiometry problems, it can be assumed that the liquids and solids in the reaction mixtures are pure. Of course, the real world is more complicated since substances are often part of a mixture. A mixture is a material system made up of two or more different substances which are mixed but are not combined chemically. Thus mixtures can be the blending of elements or compounds, without chemical bonding or other chemical change, so that each ingredient substance retains its own chemical properties.

A mixture can be homogeneous (uniform in composition) or heterogeneous (lacks uniformity). In chemistry, a homogeneous mixture means that when dividing the volume in half, the same amount of material is suspended in both halves of the substance. An example of a homogeneous mixture is air. Technically, air can be described as a gaseous solution (oxygen and other gases dissolved in the major component, nitrogen).

Examples of mixtures include alloys, solutions, colloids, and suspensions (coarse dispersion). The following table shows the main properties of three types of mixtures.

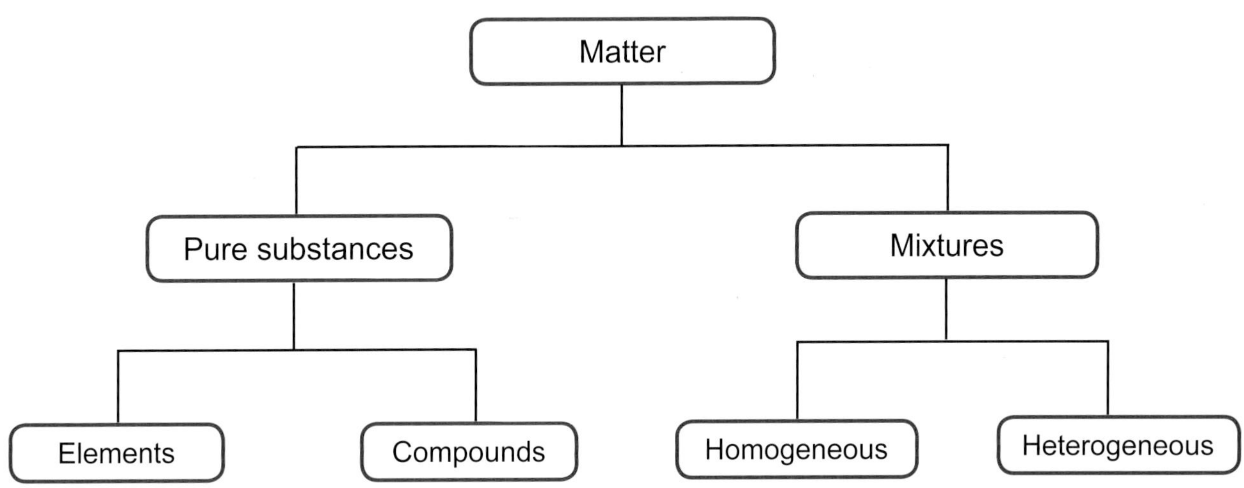

	Solution	**Colloid**	**Suspension**
Mixture homogeneity	Homogeneous	Visually homogeneous but microscopically heterogeneous	Heterogeneous
Particle size	< 1 nm	between 1 nm and 1 micrometer	> 1 micrometer
Physical stability	Yes	Yes	No: needs stabilizing agents
Separates in a centrifuge	No	Yes	–
Separates by decantation	No	No	Yes

Decantation is normally performed by pouring off the upper clear portion of a fluid (supernatant) gently, leaving the sediment in the vessel.

An emulsion is a mixture of two or more liquids that are normally immiscible (nonmixable or unblendable). Emulsions are a type of colloid. Vinaigrettes are emulsions.

An alloy is a mixture of two or more metals, or of a metal or metals with a nonmetal. The following are examples:

- steel is an alloy of iron with carbon and, usually, small amounts of a number of other elements;
- stainless steel alloys are a combination of iron, chromium and nickel frequently modified by the presence of other elements. This family of alloys is particularly resistant to corrosion, in contrast to the rusting that can consume ordinary steel;
- pewter is an alloy of tin with minor amounts of copper;
- copper with some zinc makes brass;
- copper with tin forms bronze;
- 18-carat gold is 75% gold, with the balance usually made up of nickel, copper and zinc.

GOLD STANDARD WARM-UP EXERCISES

CHAPTER 1: Stoichiometry

Note: Use the periodic table from the end of Chapter 2 when needed for any Gold Standard Warm-Up Exercises. You will have access to a periodic table for the DAT. Calculators are not permitted for the Natural Sciences.

1) In the manufacture of HCl, 10 grams of chlorine gas were used. If the reaction went to completion and the hydrogen gas was in excess, how many grams of HCl were obtained?

$$H_2 + Cl_2 \rightarrow 2HCl$$

A. 2.5
B. 5.1
C. 10.3
D. 20.0

2) Pig iron consists of iron with about 5% manganese. Which of the following most accurately describes pig iron?

A. It is a colloid.
B. It is a solid solution.
C. It is a complex molecule.
D. It is an alloy.

3) Assume that the composition by volume of air is 80% N_2 and 20% O_2. Which of the following gases are denser than air assuming they are at the same temperature and pressure?

$$CH_4, Cl_2, CO_2, NH_3, NO_2, O_3, SO_2$$

A. CH_4, CO_2, Cl_2, SO_2
B. CO_2, Cl_2, SO_2, NH_3, O_3
C. Cl_2, CO_2, NH_3, NO_2, O_3, SO_2
D. Cl_2, CO_2, NO_2, O_3, SO_2

4) Two moles of a diatomic gas P_2 were mixed with four moles of another diatomic gas Q_2 in a closed vessel. All of the P_2 and Q_2 molecules reacted to yield one triatomic product. Which of the following shows the net reaction between P and Q?

A. $2P_2 + 4Q_2 \rightarrow P_4Q_8$
B. $P_2 + 2Q_2 \rightarrow 2PQ_2$
C. $2P + 4Q \rightarrow P_2Q_4$
D. $P_2 + Q_4 \rightarrow P_2Q_4$

5) What is the oxidation state of the halogen (Hal) in the halate ($HalO_3^-$) molecule?

A. –1
B. –5
C. 1
D. 5

6) What is the oxidation state of chromium in $Cr_2O_7^{2-}$?

A. 6
B. 7
C. 8
D. 12

7) What is the oxidation state of nitrogen in each of the two products in the following reaction, respectively?

$$H_2O + 3NO_2(g) \rightarrow 2HNO_3(aq) + NO(g)$$

A. –5, +2
B. +5, +2
C. +2, +2
D. –2, +2

8) What type of reaction is the following?

$2MnO_4^- + 16H^+ + 10Cl^- \rightarrow 2Mn^{2+} + 5Cl_2(g) + 8H_2O$

A. Lewis acid – Lewis base
B. Double replacement
C. Oxidation–reduction
D. Dissociation

9) When the following equation is balanced, how many moles of water will be produced for each mole of calcium phosphate?

$\_Ca(OH)_2 + \_H_3PO_4 \rightarrow \_H_2O + \_Ca_3(PO_4)_2$

A. 2
B. 3
C. 4
D. 6

10) What would be the approximate ratio between the mass of manganese in the steel sample and the mass of chlorine gas produced?

$2MnO_4^- + 16H^+ + 10Cl^- \rightarrow 2Mn^{2+} + 5Cl_2(g) + 8H_2O$

A. 2:5
B. 3:2
C. 3:4
D. 1:3

GS ANSWER KEY

CHAPTER 1

		Cross-Reference			Cross-Reference
1.	**C**	**CHM 1.3, 1.5**	**6.**	**A**	**CHM 1.6**
2.	**D**	**CHM 1.7**	**7.**	**B**	**CHM 1.6**
3.	**D**	**CHM 1.3**	**8.**	**C**	**CHM 1.6**
4.	**B**	**CHM 1.5**	**9.**	**D**	**CHM 1.5**
5.	**D**	**CHM 1.6**	**10.**	**D**	**CHM 1.3, 1.5**

* Explanations can be found at the back of the book.

Go online to DAT-prep.com for additional chapter review Q&A and forum.

GOLD NOTES

ELECTRONIC STRUCTURE AND THE PERIODIC TABLE
Chapter 2

Memorize

* Definitions of quantum numbers
* Shapes of s, p orbitals
* Order for filling atomic orbitals

Understand

* Conventional notation, Pauli, Hund's
* Box diagrams, IP, electronegativity
* Valence, EA
* Variation in shells, atomic size
*Trends in the periodic table

Importance

2 to 4 out of the 30 Gen CHM

DAT questions are based on content in this chapter (in our estimation).

* Note that between 50% and 85% of the questions in DAT General Chemistry are from 6 chapters: 1, 2, 4, 5, 6 and 9.

Introduction

The periodic table of the elements provides data and abbreviations for the names of elements in a tabular layout. The purpose of the table is to illustrate recurring (periodic) trends and to classify and compare the different types of chemical behavior. To do so, we must first better understand the atom. Please note: more advanced aspects of nuclear (atomic) chemistry will be explored in Chapter 11.

Additional Resources

Free Online Forum

Video: Online or DVD

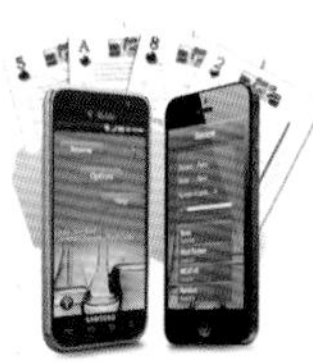

Flashcards

Special Guest

2.1 Electronic Structure of an Atom

The modern view of the structure of atoms is based on a series of discoveries and complicated theories that were put forth at the turn of the twentieth century. The atom represents the smallest unit of a chemical element. It is composed of subatomic particles: protons, neutrons and electrons. At the center of the atom is the nucleus composed of protons and neutrons surrounded by electrons forming an electron cloud.

The protons and neutrons have nearly identical masses of approximately 1 amu whereas electrons, by contrast, have an almost negligible mass. Protons and electrons both have electrical charges equal in magnitude but opposite in sign. Protons consist of a single positive (+1) charge, electrons consist of a single negative charge (−1) and neutrons have no charge.

Atoms have equal numbers of protons and electrons unless ionization occurs in which ions are formed. Ions are defined as atoms with either a positive charge (cation) due to loss of one or more valence electrons or negative charge (anion) as a result of a gain in electron(s). An atom's valence electrons are electrons furthest from the nucleus and are responsible for an element's chemical properties and are instrumental in chemical bonding (See CHM 2.2 and 2.3 and Chapter 3).

Atoms of a given element all have an equal number of protons however, may vary in the number of neutrons. Atoms that differ only by neutron number are known as isotopes. Isotopes have the same atomic number but differ in atomic mass due to the differences in their neutron numbers. As they have the same atomic number, isotopes therefore exhibit the same chemical properties.

In the following paragraphs, we will only present the main ideas behind the findings that shaped our understanding of atomic structure. The first important idea is that electrons (as well as any subatomic particles) are in fact waves as well as particles; this concept is often referred to in textbooks as the "dual nature of matter".

Contrary to classical mechanics, in this modern view of matter information on particles is not derived from the knowledge of their position and momentum at a given time but by the knowledge of the wave function (mathematical expression of the above-mentioned wave) and their energy. Mathematically, such information can be derived, in principle, by solving the master equation of quantum mechanics known as the Schrödinger equation. Moreover, the mathematical derivation of atomic orbitals and respective energies comes from solving the equation which includes the total energy profiles for the electrons as well as the wave function describing the wavelike nature of the electrons. Thus, the various solutions to the Schrödinger equation describes the atomic orbitals as complicated wave functions which may alternatively be graphically represented (See Figure III.A.2.1 and Figure III.A.2.2).

In the case of the hydrogen atom, this equation can be solved exactly. It yields the possible states of energy in which the electron can be found within the hydrogen atom and the wave functions associated with these states. The square of the wave function associated with a given state of energy gives the probability to find the electron, which is in that same state of energy, at any given point in space at any given time. These wave functions as well as their geometrical representations are referred to as the *atomic orbitals*. We shall explain further below the significance of these geometrical representations.

Atoms of any element tend to exist toward a minimal energy level (= ground state) unless subjected to an external environmental change. Even for a hydrogen atom there is a large number of possible states in which its single electron can be found (when it is subjected to different external perturbations). A labeling of these states is necessary. This is done using the quantum numbers. Hence, any orbital may be completely described by four quantum numbers; n, *l*, m_l and m_s. The position and energy of an electron and each of the orbitals are therefore described by its quantum number or energy state. The four quantum numbers are thus described as follows:

(i) n: *the principal quantum number*. This number takes the integer values 1, 2, 3, 4, 5... The higher the value of n the higher the energy of the state labelled by this n. This number defines the atomic shells K (n = 1), L (n = 2), M (n = 3) etc... or the size of an orbital.

(ii) *l*: *the angular momentum quantum number*. It defines the shape of the atomic orbital in a way which we will discuss further below. For a given electronic state of energy defined by n, *l* takes all possible integer values between 0 and n – 1. For instance for a state with n = 0 there is only one possible shape of orbital, it is defined by *l* = 0. For a state defined by n = 3 there are 3 possible orbital shapes with *l* = 0, 1 and 2.

All orbitals with *l* = 0 are called "s"-shaped, all with *l* = 1 are "p"-shaped, those with *l* = 2 or 3 are "d" or "f"-shaped orbitals respectively. The important shapes to remember are: i) s = spherical, and ii) p = 2 lobes or "dumbbell" (*see the following diagrams*). For values of *l* larger than 3, which occur with an n greater or equal to 4, the corresponding

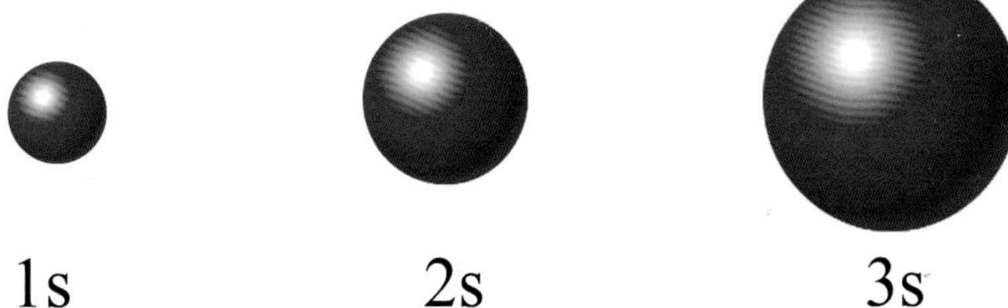

Figure III.A.2.1: Atomic orbitals where *l* = 0. Notice that the orbitals do not reveal the precise location (position) or momentum of the fast moving electron at any point in time (Heisenberg's Uncertainty Principle). Instead, we are left with a 90% chance of finding the electron somewhere within the shapes described as orbitals.

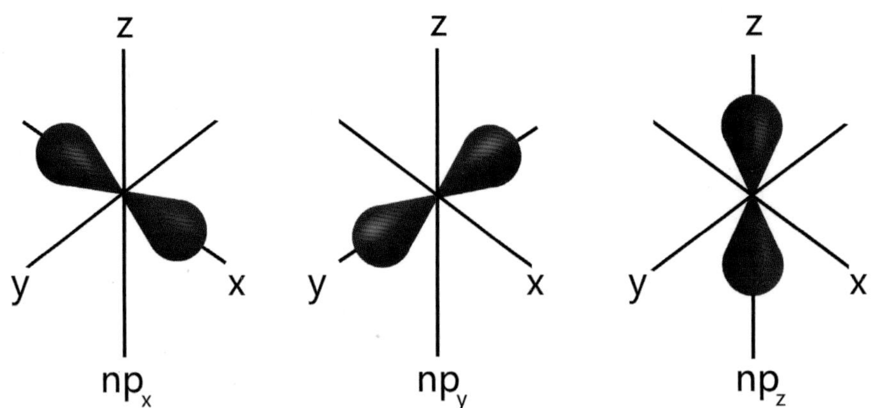

Figure III.A.2.2: Atomic orbitals where $l = 1$.

series of atomic orbitals follows the alphabetical order h, i, j, etc...

(iii) m_l: *the magnetic quantum number.* It defines the orientation of the orbital of a given shape. For a given value of l (given shape), m_l can take any of the $2l + 1$ integer values between $-l$ and $+l$. For instance for a state with $n = 3$ and $l = 1$ (3p orbital in notation explained in the previous paragraph) there are three possible values for m_l: -1, 0 and 1. These 3 orbitals are oriented along x, y or the z axis of a coordinate system with its origin on the nucleus of the atom: they are denoted as $3p_x$, $3p_y$ and $3p_z$. Figure III.A.2.2 shows the representation of an orbital corresponding to an electron in a state ns, np_x, np_y, and np_z. These are the 3D volumes where there is 90% chance to find an electron which is in a state ns, np_x, np_y, or np_z, respectively. This type of diagram constitutes the most common geometrical representation of the atomic orbitals (besides looking at the diagrams, consider watching one of the videos if you are having trouble visualizing these facts).

(iv) m_s: *the spin quantum number.* This number takes the values $+1/2$ or $-1/2$ for the electron. Some textbooks present the intuitive, albeit wrong, explanation that the spin angular momentum arises from the spinning of the electron around itself, the opposite signs for the spin quantum number would correspond to the two opposite rotational directions. We do have to resort to such an intuitive presentation because the spin angular moment has, in fact, no classical equivalent and, as a result, the physics behind the correct approach is too complex to be dealt with in introductory courses.

A node is where the probability of finding an electron is zero (the concept behind nodes comes from wave theory which is Physics and not specifically required for the DAT). Nonetheless, the number of nodes is related to the frequency of a wave and therefore its energy. The greater the number of nodes, the greater the energy of the system. In general, with respect to the shapes and the angular or radial nodes of the s, p and d-orbitals, note the following:

s-orbital

The number of radial nodes increases with the principal quantum number n, i.e. 1s orbital has 0 nodes, 2s has 1 node, and 3s has 2 nodes. The s orbital can hold two electrons (n = 1,2,3, $l = 0$, $m_l = 0$, $m_s = +1/2, -1/2$).

p-orbital

p orbital starts at the 2nd shell or principal level. The angular momentum quantum number for p orbitals is 1; therefore each orbital has 1 angular node. There are three different magnetic quantum numbers, which give rise to three different orientations of the p orbital. Since each orbital holds two electrons, the three p orbitals hold a total of 6 electrons (n = 2,3,4, $l = 1$, $m_l = -1,0,+1$, $m_s = +1/2, -1/2$).

d-orbital

d orbital starts at a principal level of 3 or the 3rd shell. The angular momentum quantum number for d orbitals is 2; therefore each orbital has 2 angular nodes. There are five different magnetic quantum numbers, which give rise to five different orientations of the d orbital. Since each orbital holds two electrons, the three d orbitals hold a total of 10 electrons (n = 3,4,5, $l = 2$, $m_l = -2,-1,0,+1,+2$, $m_s = +1/2, -1/2$).

To summarize: the energy of the atom is determined by the number of nodes which is related to the principal quantum number n by: nodes = n–1.

The number of angular nodes is labelled by a letter (s, p, d, f, g, h, i, ...)

- s: no angular nodes
- p: one angular node
- d: two angular nodes
- f: three angular nodes, etc...

Note: The number of radial nodes is the total number of nodes minus the number of angular nodes.

2.2 Conventional Notation for Electronic Structure

As described in the previous section, the state of an electron in an atom is completely defined by a set of four quantum numbers (n, l, m_l, m_s). If two electrons in an atom share the same n, l and m_l numbers their m_s have to be of opposite signs: this is known as the Pauli's exclusion principle which states that no two electrons in an atom can have the same four quantum numbers. This principle along with a rule known as Hund's rule which states that electrons fill orbital's singly first until all orbitals of the same energy are filled, constitutes the basis for the procedure that one needs to follow to assign the possible (n, l, m_l, m_s) quantum states to the electrons of a polyelectronic atom. Orbitals are "filled" in sequence, according to an example shown below. When filling a set of orbitals with the same n and l (e.g. the three 2p orbitals: $2p_x$, $2p_y$ and $2p_z$ which differ by their m_l's) electrons are assigned to orbitals with different m_l's first with parallel spins (same sign for their m_s), until each orbital of the given group is filled with one electron, then, electrons are paired in the same orbital with antiparallel spins (opposite signs for m_s). This procedure is illustrated in an example which follows. The electronic configuration which results from orbitals filled in accordance with the previous set of rules corresponds to the atom being in its lowest overall state of energy. This state of lowest energy is referred to as the ground state of the atom.

The restrictions related to the previous set of rules lead to the fact that only a certain number of electrons is allowed for each quantum number:

for a given n (given shell): the maximum number of electrons allowed is $2n^2$. The greater the value of n, the greater the energy level of the shell.

for a given *l* (s, p, d, f...): this number is $4l + 2$.

for a given m_l (given orbital orientation): a maximum of 2 electrons is allowed.

There is a **conventional notation** for the electronic structure of an atom:

(i) orbitals are listed in the order they are filled (See Figure III.A.2.3)

(ii) generally, in this conventional notation, no distinction is made between electrons in states defined by the same n and l but which do not share the same m_l.

For instance the ground state electronic configuration of oxygen is written as:

$$1s^2\ 2s^2\ 2p^4$$

When writing the electronic configuration of a polyelectronic atom orbitals are filled (with electrons denoted as the superscripts of the configurations) in order of increasing energy: 1s 2s 2p 3s 3p 4s 3d ... according to the following figure:

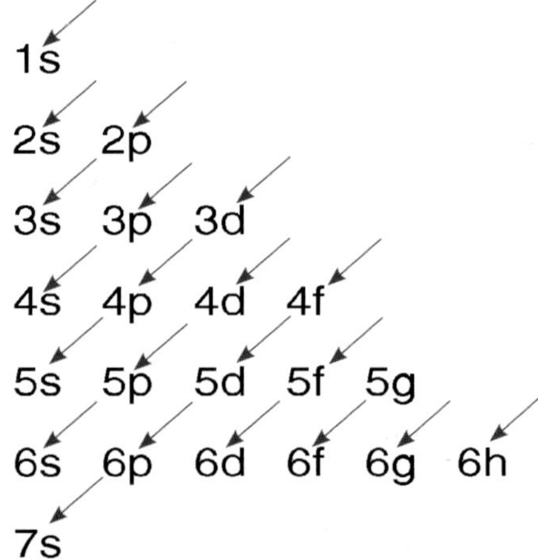

follow the direction of successive arrows moving from top to bottom

Figure III.A.2.3: The order for filling atomic orbitals.

Thus, the electronic configuration or the pattern of orbital filling of an atom generally abides by the following rules or principles:

1. Always fill the lowest energy (or ground state) orbitals first (Aufbau principle)

2. No two electrons in a single atom can have the same four quantum numbers; if n, *l*, and m_l are the same, m_s must be different such that the electrons have opposite spins. (Pauli exclusion principle) and

3. Degenerate orbitals of the subshell are each occupied singly with electrons of parallel spin before double occupation of the orbitals occurs (Hund's rule).

An alternative way to write the aforementioned electronic configuration is based on the avoidance in writing out the inner core electrons. Moreover, this is an abbreviation of the previous longer configuration or otherwise known as a short hand electronic configuration. Here, the core electrons are represented by a prior noble gas elemental symbol within brackets. As an example, calcium may be written in its expanded form or more commonly as a short hand notation represented as [Ar]$4s^2$ shown with the prior noble gas symbol for argon [Ar] written within brackets.

Another illustrative notation is also often used. In this alternate notation orbitals are represented by boxes (hence the referring to this representation as "box diagrams"). Orbitals with the same *l* are grouped together and electrons are represented by vertical ascending or descending arrows (for the two opposite signs of m_s).

For instance for the series H, He, Li, Be, B, C we have the following electronic configurations:

H: $1s^1$ box diagram: [↑]

He: $1s^2$ box diagram: [↑↓] and not [↑↑] (rejected by Pauli's exclusion principle)

Li: $1s^2$ $2s^1$
[↑↓] [↑]

Be: $1s^2$ $2s^2$
[↑↓] [↑↓]

B: $1s^2$ $2s^2$ $2p^1$
[↑↓] [↑↓] [↑][ ][ ]

C: $1s^2$ $2s^2$ $2p^2$
[↑↓] [↑↓] [↑][↑][ ]

(to satisfy Hund's rule of maximum spin)

To satisfy Hund's rule the next electron is put into a separate 2p "box". The 4th 2p electron (for oxygen) is then put into the first box with an opposite spin.

O: [↑↓] [↑↓] [↑↓][↑][↑]
$1s^2$ $2s^2$ $2p^4$

Within a given subshell l, orbitals are filled in such a way to maximize the number of half-filled orbitals with parallel spins. An unpaired electron generates a magnetic field due to its spin. Consequently, when a material is composed of atoms with unpaired electrons, it is said to be *paramagnetic* as it will be attracted to an applied external magnetic field (i.e. Li, Na, Cs). Alternatively, when the material's atoms have paired electrons, it is weakly repelled by an external magnetic field and it is said to be *diamagnetic* (i.e. Cu, molecular carbon, H_2, H_2O). Non-chemists simply call diamagnetic materials "not magnetic". The strongest form of magnetism is a permanent feature of materials like Fe, Ni and their alloys and is said to be *ferromagnetic* (i.e. a fridge magnet).

For the main group elements, the valence electrons of an atom are those that are involved in chemical bonding and are in the outermost principal energy level or shell. For example, for Group IA and Group IIA elements, only electrons from the s subshell are valence electrons. For Group IIIA through Group VIIIA elements, electrons from s and p subshell are valence electrons. Under certain circumstances, elements from Group IIIA through Group VIIA may accept electrons into its d subshell, leading to more than 8 valence electrons.

Finally, as previously mentioned, we should point out that electrons can be promoted to higher unoccupied (or partially occupied) orbitals when the atom is subjected to some external perturbation which inputs energy into the atom. The resulting electronic configuration is then called an excited state configuration (this concept will be explored further in CHM 11.5, 11.6).

2.3 Elements, Chemical Properties and The Periodic Table

Since most chemical properties of the atom are related to their outermost electrons (valence electrons), it is the orbital occupation of these electrons which is most relevant in the complete electronic configuration. The periodic table (there is one at the end of this chapter with a summary of trends) can be used to derive such information in the following way:

(i) the row or period number gives the "n" of the valence electrons of any given element of the period.

(ii) the first two columns or groups and helium (He) are referred to as the "s" block. The valence electrons of elements in these groups are "s" electrons.

(iii) groups 3A to 8A (13th to 18th columns) are the "p" group. Elements belonging to these groups have their ground state electronic configurations ending with "p" electrons.

(iv) Elements in groups 3B to 2B (columns 3 to 12) are called transition elements. Their electronic configurations end with $ns^2(n-1)d^x$ where n is the period number and x = 1 for column 3, 2 for column 4, 3 for column 5, etc… Note that these elements sometimes have unexpected or unusual valence shell electronic configurations.

This set of rules should make the writing of the ground-state valence shell electronic configuration very easy. For instance: Sc being an element of the "d" group on the 4th period should have a ground-state valence shell electronic configuration of the form: $4s^23d^x$. Since it belongs to group 3B (column 3) x = 1; therefore, the actual configuration is simply: $4s^23d^1$. However, half-filled (i.e. Cr) and filled (i.e. Cu, Ag, Au) d orbitals have remarkable stability. This stability behavior is essentially related to the closely spaced 3d and 4s energy levels with the stability associated with a half-filled (as in Cr) or completely filled (as in Cu) sublevel. Hence, this stability makes for unusual configurations (i.e. by the rules Cr = $4s^23d^4$, but in reality Cr = $4s^13d^5$ creating a half-filled d orbital). It can be noted that Cr therefore has an electronic configuration of $[Ar]4s^13d^5$, although four d electrons would be expected to be seen instead of five. This is because one electron from a s subshell jumps into the d orbital, giving the atom a half filled d subshell. As for Cu, it would have an electronic configuration of $[Ar]4s^23d^9$ by the rules. However, the Cu d shell is just one electron away from stability, and therefore, one electron from the s shell jumps into the d shell to convert it into $[Ar]4s^13d^{10}$.

Some metal ions form colored solutions due to the transition energies of the d-electrons.

A number of physical and chemical properties of the elements are periodic, i.e. they vary in a regular fashion with atomic numbers. We will define some of these properties and explain their trends:

(A) Ionization Energy

(i) The ionization energy (IE) is defined as the energy required to remove an electron from a gaseous atom or ion. The first ionization energy or potential (1st IE or IP) is the energy required to remove one of the outermost valence electrons from an atom in its gaseous state. The ionization potential increases from left to right within a period and decreases from the top to the bottom of a group or column of the periodic chart. The 1st IP drops sharply when we move from the last element of a period (inert gas) to the first element of the next period. These are general trends, elements located after an element with a half-filled shell, for instance, have a lower 1st IP than expected by these trends.

(ii) The second ionization is the energy or potential (2nd IE or IP) required to remove a second valence electron from the ion to form a divalent ion: the previous trends can be used if one remembers the relationship between 1st and 2nd ionization processes of an atom of element X:

$$X + \text{energy} \rightarrow X^{+} + 1e^{-}$$
1st ionization of X
$$X^{+} + \text{energy} \rightarrow X^{2+} + 1e^{-}$$
2nd ionization of X

The second ionization process of X can be viewed as the 1st ionization of X^+. With this in mind it is very easy to predict trends of 2nd IP's. For instance, let us compare the 2nd IP's of the elements Na and Al. This is equivalent to comparing the 1st IP's of Na^+ and Al^+. These, in turn, have the same valence shell electronic configurations as Ne and Mg, respectively. Applying the previous general principles on Ne and Mg we arrive at the following conclusions:

- the 1st IP of Ne is greater than the 1st IP of Mg
- the 1st IP of Na^+ is therefore expected to be greater than the 1st IP of Al^+
- the latter statement is equivalent to the final conclusion that the 2nd IP of Na is greater than the 2nd IP of Al.

(B) Electron Affinity

(iii) Electron affinity (EA) is the energy change that accompanies the following process for an atom of element X:

$$X(gas) + 1e^{-} \rightarrow X^{-}(gas)$$

This property measures the ability of an atom to accept an electron. The stronger the attraction of a nucleus for electrons, the greater the electron affinity (EA) will be. The electron affinity becomes more negative for non-metals than metals. Thus, halogen atoms (F, Cl, Br...) have a very negative EA because they have a great tendency to form negative ions. On the other hand, alkaline earth metals which tend to form positive rather than negative ions have very large positive EA's. The overall tendency is that EA's become more negative as we move from left to right across a period, they are more negative (less positive) for non-metals than for metals and they do not change considerably within a group or column.

(C) Atomic Radii

(iv) The atomic radius generally decreases from left to right across a period since the effective nuclear charge increases as the number of protons within an atom increases. The effective nuclear charge is the net charge experienced by the valence electrons as a result of the nucleus (ie, protons) and core electrons. Additionally, the atomic radius increases when we move down a group due to the shielding effect of the additional core electrons and the presence of another electron shell.

(D) Electronegativity

(v) Electronegativity is a parameter that measures the ability of an atom, when engaged in a molecular bond, to pull or repel the bond electrons. This parameter is determined from the 1st IE and the EA of a given atom. Electronegativity follows the same general trends as the 1st IE. The greater the electronegativity of an atom, the greater its attraction for bonding electrons. In general, electronegativity is inversely related to atomic size. Moreover, the larger the atom, the less the ability for it to attract electrons to itself in chemical bonding.

In conclusion, as one moves to the right across a row in the periodic table, the atomic radii decreases, the ionization energy (IE) increases and the electronegativity increases. As one moves down along a column within the periodic table, the atomic radii increases, the ionization energy (IE) decreases and electronegativity decreases.

2.3.1 Bond Strength

When there is a big difference in electronegativity between two atoms sharing a covalent bond then the bond is generally weaker as compared to two atoms with little electronegativity difference. This is because in the latter case, the bond is shared more equally and is thus more stable.

Bond strength is inversely proportional to bond length. Thus, all things being equal, a stronger bond would be shorter. Bonds and bond strength is further discussed in ORG 1.3-1.5.1.

2.4 Metals, Nonmetals and Metalloids

The elements of the periodic table belong in three basic categories: metals, nonmetals and metalloids (or semimetals).

Metals – high melting points and densities characterize metals. They are excellent conductors of heat and electricity due to their valence electrons being able to move freely. This fact also accounts for the major characteristic properties of metals: large atomic radius, low ionization energy, high electron affinities and low electronegativity. Groups IA and IIA are the most reactive of all metal species.

Of course, metals tend to be shiny and solid (with the exception of mercury, Hg, a liquid at STP). They are also *ductile* (they can be drawn into thin wires) and *malleable* (they can be easily hammered into very thin sheets).

Nonmetals – Nonmetals have high ionization energies and electronegativities. As opposed to metals, they do not conduct heat or electricity. They tend to gain electrons easily contrarily to metals that readily lose electrons when forming bonds.

Metalloids – The metalloids share properties with both metals and nonmetals. Their densities, boiling points and melting points do not follow any specific trends and are very unpredictable. Ionization energy and electronegativity values vary and can be found in between those of metals and nonmetals. Examples of metalloids are boron, silicon, germanium, arsenic, antimony and tellurium.

Table III A.2.1

*General characteristics of metals, nonmetals and metalloids		
Metals	**Nonmetals**	**Metalloids**
• Hard and Shiny	• Gases or dull, brittle solids	• Appearence will vary
• 3 or less valence electrons	• 5 or more valence electrons	• 3 to 7 valence electrons
• Form + ions by losing e^-	• Form – ions by gaining e^-	• Form + and/or – ions
• Good conductors of heat and electricity	• Poor conductors of heat and electricity	• Conduct better than nonmetals but not as well as metals

*These are general characteristics. There are exceptions beyond the scope of the exam.

2.4.1 The Chemistry of Groups

Alkali metals – The alkali metals are found in Group IA and are different than other metals in that they only have one loosely bound electron in their outermost shell. This gives them the largest ionic radius of all the elements in their respective periods. They are also highly reactive (especially with halogens) due to their low ionization energies and low electronegativity and the relative ease with which they lose their valence electron.

Alkaline Earth metals – The alkaline earth metals are found in Group IIA and also tend to lose electrons quite readily. They have two electrons in their outer shell and experience a stronger effective nuclear charge than alkali metals. This gives them a smaller atomic radius as well as low electronegativity values.

Halogens – The halogens are found in Group VIIA and are highly reactive nonmetals with seven valence electrons in their outer shell. This gives them extremely high electronegativity values and makes them reactive towards alkali metals and alkaline earth metals that seek to donate electrons to form a complete octet. Some halogens are gaseous at Standard Temperature and Pressure (STP; CHM 4.1.1) (F_2 and Cl_2) while others are liquid (Br_2) or solid (I_2).

Noble gases – The noble gases, also called the inert gases, are found in Group VIII and are characterized by being a mostly nonreactive species due to their complete valence shell. This energetically favorable configuration of electrons gives them high ionization energies, low boiling points and no real electronegativities. They are all gaseous at room temperature.

Transition Elements – The transition elements are found in Groups IB to VIIIB and are characterized by high melting points and boiling points. Their key chemical characteristic is their ability to exist in a variety of different oxidation states. For the transition elements, the 4s shell gets filled prior to the 3d shell according to the Aufbau rule. However, electrons are lost from the 4s shell before the 3d shell. Thus, as the d electrons are held only loosely, this contributes to the high electrical conductivity and malleability of transition elements. This is because transition elements can lose electrons from both their s and d orbitals of their valence shell; the d electrons are held more loosely than the s electrons. They display low ionization energies and high electrical conductivities.

PERIODIC TABLE OF THE ELEMENTS

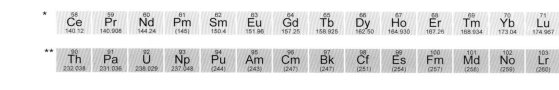

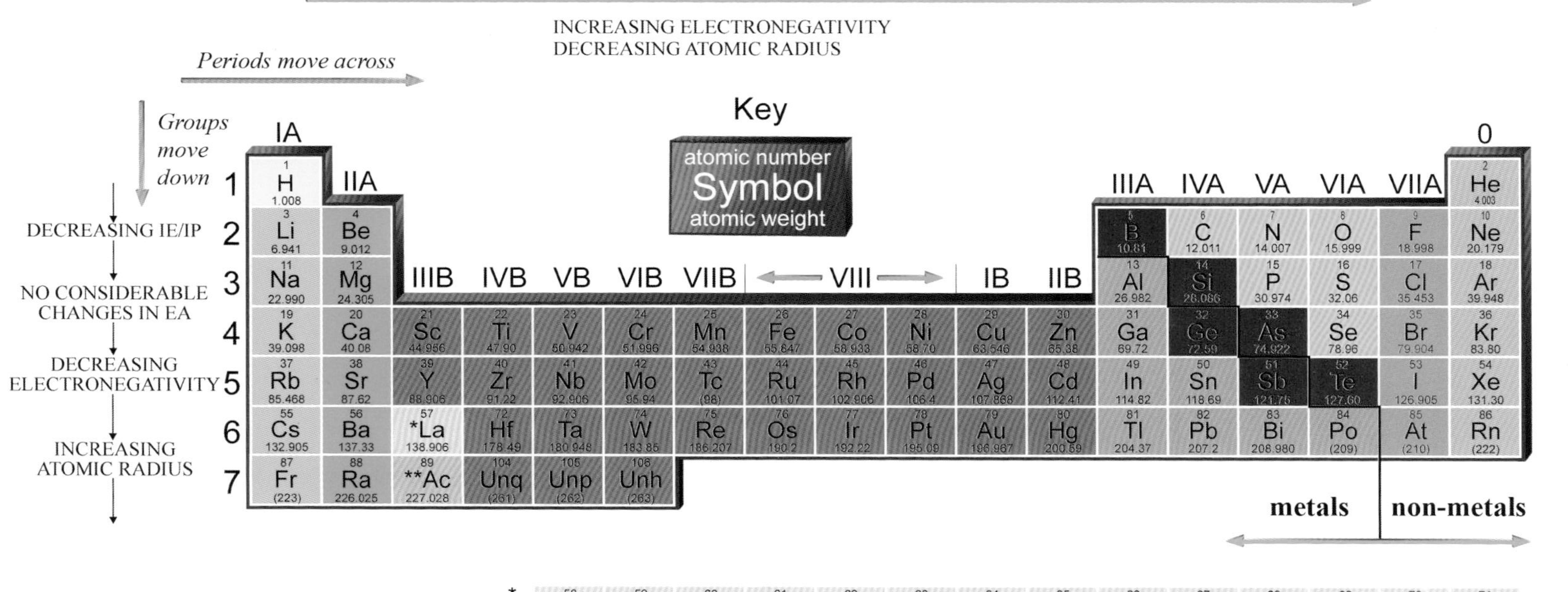

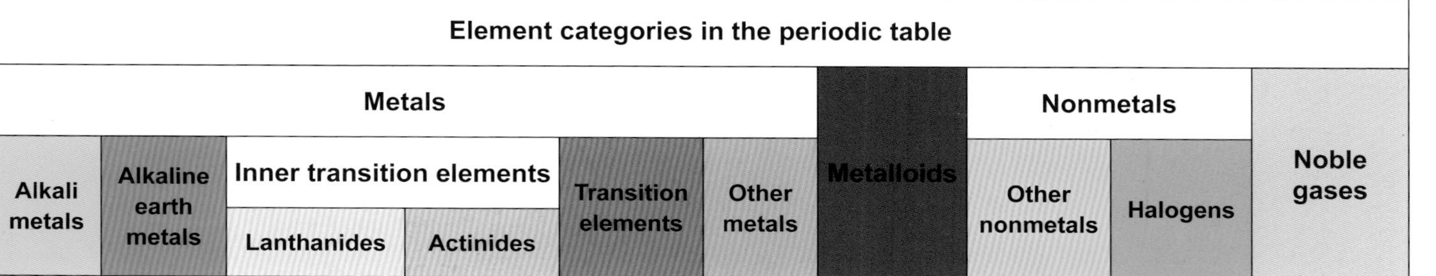

Element	Symbol	Atomic Number
Actinium	Ac	89
Aluminum	Al	13
Americium	Am	95
Antimony	Sb	51
Argon	Ar	18
Arsenic	As	33
Astatine	At	85
Barium	Ba	56
Berkelium	Bk	97
Beryllium	Be	4
Bismuth	Bi	83
Boron	B	5
Bromine	Br	35
Cadmium	Cd	48
Calcium	Ca	20
Californium	Cf	98
Carbon	C	6
Cerium	Ce	58
Cesium	Cs	55
Chlorine	Cl	17
Chromium	Cr	24
Cobalt	Co	27
Copper	Cu	29
Curium	Cm	96
Dysprosium	Dy	66
Einsteinium	Es	99
Erbium	Er	68

Element	Symbol	Atomic Number
Europium	Eu	63
Fermium	Fm	100
Fluorine	F	9
Francium	Fr	87
Gadolinium	Gd	64
Gallium	Ga	31
Germanium	Ge	32
Gold	Au	79
Hafnium	Hf	72
Helium	He	2
Holmium	Ho	67
Hydrogen	H	1
Indium	In	49
Iodine	I	53
Iridium	Ir	77
Iron	Fe	26
Krypton	Kr	36
Lanthanum	La	57
Lawrencium	Lr	103
Lead	Pb	82
Lithium	Li	3
Lutetium	Lu	71
Magnesium	Mg	12
Manganese	Mn	25
Mendelevium	Md	101
Mercury	Hg	80
Molybdenum	Mo	42

Element	Symbol	Atomic Number
Neodymium	Nd	60
Neon	Ne	10
Neptunium	Np	93
Nickel	Ni	28
Niobium	Nb	41
Nitrogen	N	7
Nobelium	No	102
Osmium	Os	76
Oxygen	O	8
Palladium	Pd	46
Phosphorous	P	15
Platinum	Pt	78
Plutonium	Pu	94
Polonium	Po	84
Potassium	K	19
Praseodymium	Pr	59
Promethium	Pm	61
Protactinium	Pa	91
Radium	Ra	88
Radon	Rn	86
Rhenium	Re	75
Rhodium	Rh	45
Rubidium	Rb	37
Ruthenium	Ru	44
Samarium	Sm	62
Scandium	Sc	21

Element	Symbol	Atomic Number
Selenium	Se	34
Silicon	Si	14
Silver	Ag	47
Sodium	Na	11
Strontium	Sr	38
Sulfur	S	16
Tantalum	Ta	73
Technetium	Tc	43
Tellurium	Te	52
Terbium	Tb	65
Thallium	Tl	81
Thorium	Th	90
Thulium	Tm	69
Tin	Sn	50
Titanium	Ti	22
Tungsten	W	74
(Unnilhexium)	(Unh)	106
(Unnilpentium)	(Unp)	105
(Unnilquadium)	(Unq)	104
Uranium	U	92
Vanadium	V	23
Xenon	Xe	54
Ytterbium	Yb	70
Yttrium	Y	39
Zinc	Zn	30
Zirconium	Zr	40

GOLD STANDARD WARM-UP EXERCISES

CHAPTER 2: Electronic Structure and the Periodic Table

1) Which groups of the periodic table comprise the s–block elements?
   - A. Groups I, II and III
   - B. Groups I and III
   - C. Groups II and III
   - D. Groups I and II

2) Why do chlorine atoms form anions more easily than they form cations?
   - A. The valence electron shell of chlorine contains seven electrons.
   - B. Attractive forces between halogen nuclei and valence electrons are weak.
   - C. The valence electron shell of chlorine is vacant.
   - D. Attractive forces between the valence electrons and the nuclei in halogens are strong.

3) The ability of silver ions to form complexes of many different colors identifies it as being a:
   - A. univalent metal.
   - B. Group IB element.
   - C. Period V element.
   - D. transition metal.

4) Why does potassium possess a higher first electron affinity than first ionization energy?
   - A. Its valence shells are only partially filled.
   - B. The attractive forces between the nucleus and the valence electrons are strong.
   - C. It possesses very few inner electron shells.
   - D. Its valence electron shell contains only one electron.

5) Carbon is in Group IV of the periodic table, along with such elements as silicon. However, compared with silicon, carbon forms more stable covalent bonds with itself. Why is a C–C bond stronger than a Si–Si bond?
   - A. Because carbon is not as good an electrical conductor.
   - B. Because carbon has a smaller atomic number.
   - C. Because carbon has a smaller atomic radius.
   - D. Because carbon has a smaller relative atomic mass.

6) Which of the following energy sublevels can contain the most electrons?
   - A. $n = 4, l = 0$
   - B. $n = 5, l = 2$
   - C. $n = 6, l = 3, m_l = 1$
   - D. $n = 4, l = 3$

7) Which of the following electronic configurations is an accurate representation of the electron distribution in a chromium atom?
   - A. $1s^2, 2s^2, 2p^6, 3s^2, 3p^6, 3d^6, 4s^0$
   - B. $1s^2, 2s^2, 2p^6, 3s^2, 3p^6, 3d^5, 4s^1$
   - C. $1s^2, 2s^2, 2p^6, 3s^2, 3p^6, 3d^4, 4s^2$
   - D. $1s^2, 2s^2, 2p^6, 3s^2, 3p^6, 3d^3, 4s^2, 4p^1$

8) Which of the following typically has a low melting point?
   - A. Metals
   - B. Metalloids
   - C. Non–metals
   - D. Transition metals

9) A researcher tries to determine the ionization energy of iron (Fe) by irradiating the metal with X rays of known energy (E) and then measuring the kinetic energy (K_e) of the emitted electrons. How will she compute the ionization energy from the data obtained?
   - A. $E - K_e$
   - B. $K_e - E$
   - C. $(E)(K_e)$
   - D. $(K_e)/(E)$

GS ANSWER KEY

Chapter 2

		Cross-Reference			Cross-Reference
1.	D	CHM 2.3	6.	D	CHM 2.1, 2.2
2.	D	CHM 2.3	7.	B	CHM 2.3
3.	D	CHM 2.3	8.	C	CHM 2.3
4.	D	CHM 2.3	9.	A	CHM 2.3, 11
5.	C	CHM 2.3, 2.3.1			

* Explanations can be found at the back of the book.

Go online to DAT-prep.com for additional chapter review Q&A and forum.

BONDING

Chapter 3

Memorize	Understand	Importance
* Hybrid orbitals, shapes * Define Lewis: structure, acid, base * Define: octet rule, formal charge	* Ionic, covalent bonds * VSEPR, Resonance * Dipole, covalent polar bonds * Trends in the periodic table	**1 to 3 out of the 30 Gen CHM** DAT questions are based on content in this chapter (in our estimation). * Note that between 50% and 85% of the questions in DAT General Chemistry are from 6 chapters: 1, 2, 4, 5, 6 and 9.

DAT-Prep.com

Introduction

Attractive interactions between atoms and within molecules involve a physical process called chemical bonding. In general, strong chemical bonding is associated with the sharing or transfer of electrons between atoms. Molecules, crystals and diatomic gases are held together by chemical bonds which makes up most of the matter around us.

Additional Resources

Free Online Forum

Video: Online or DVD

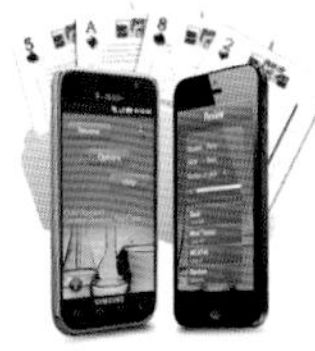

Flashcards

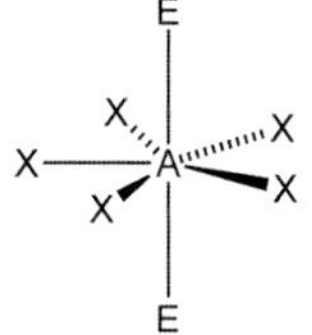

Special Guest

3.1 Generalities

Chemical bonds can form between atoms of the same element or between atoms of different elements. Chemical bonds are classified into three groups: ionic, covalent and metallic.

To summarize, if the electronegativity values of two atoms are:

- significantly different...
  - Ionic bonds are formed.
- similar...
  - Metallic bonds form between two metal atoms.
  - Covalent bonds form between two nonmetal atoms (or between metal and nonmetal atoms).
    - Non-polar covalent bonds form when the electronegativity values are very similar.
    - Polar covalent bonds form when the electronegativity values are somewhat further apart.

We will also see in this chapter that many bonds are formed according to the octet rule, which states that an atom tends to form bonds with other atoms until the bonding atoms obtain a stable electron configuration of eight valence electrons in their outermost shells, similar to that of Group VIIIA (noble gas) elements. There are certain exceptions to the octet rule such as, hydrogen forming bonds with two valence electrons; beryllium, which can bond to attain four valence electrons; boron, which can bond to attain six; and elements such as phosphorus and sulfur, which can incorporate d orbital electrons to attain more than eight valence electrons.

3.1.1 The Ionic Bond

Ionic bonds form when there is a complete transfer of one or more electrons between a metal and a nonmetal atom. When an element X with a low ionization potential is combined with an element Y with a large negative electron affinity, one or more electrons are transferred from the atoms of X to the atoms of Y. This leads to the formation of cations X^{n+} and anions Y^{m-}. These ions of opposite charges are then attracted to each other through electrostatic forces which then aggregate to form large stable spatial arrangements of ions: crystalline solids. The bonds that hold these ions together are called ionic bonds.

There exists a large difference in electronegativity between ionically bonded atoms. Electronegativity is defined as the ability of an atom to attract electrons towards its nucleus in bonding and each atomic element is assigned a numerical electronegativity value with a greatest value of 4.0 assigned to the most electronegative element, fluorine. Ionic compounds are known to have high melting and boiling points and high electrical conductivity. In our general example, note that to maintain electrical neutrality the empirical formula of this ionic compound has to be of the general form: X_mY_n (the total positive charge: $n \times m$ is equal to the total negative charge: $m \times n$ in a unit formula).

For instance, since aluminium tends to form the cation Al^{3+} and oxygen the anion O^{2-} the empirical formula for aluminium oxide is Al_2O_3. Thus, the empirical or simplest formula is written for each of the formula units (Al_2O_3) which are part of a larger crystalline solid. The actual ionic solid lattice formed however, consists of a large and equal number of ions packed together in a manner to allow maximal attraction of all the oppositely charged ions.

H	2.1												
Li	1.0	Be	1.5	B	2.0	C	2.5	N	3.0	O	3.5	F	4.0
Na	0.9	Mg	1.2	Al	1.5	Si	1.8	P	2.1	S	2.5	Cl	3.0
K	0.8	Ca	1.0	Ga	1.6	Ge	1.8	As	2.0	Se	2.4	Br	2.8
Rb	0.8	Sr	1.0	In	1.7	Sn	1.8	Sb	1.9	Te	2.1	I	2.5
Cs	0.7	Ba	0.9	Tl	1.8	Pb	1.9	Bi	1.9	Po	2.0	At	2.2

Table III.A.3.0: Pauling's values for the electronegativity of some important elements. Note that elements in the upper right hand corner of the periodic table have high electronegativities and those in the bottom left hand corner of the table have low electronegativities (CHM 2.3, 2.4.1). Note that Pauling's electronegativity is dimensionless since it measures electron attracting ability on a relative scale.

3.2 The Covalent Bond

Atoms are held together in non-ionic molecules by covalent bonds. In this type of bonding two valence electrons are shared between two atoms. Two atoms sharing one, two or three electron pairs form single, double or triple covalent bonds, respectively. As the number of shared electron pairs increases, the two atoms are pulled closer together, leading to a decrease in bond length and a simultaneous increase in bond strength. As opposed to ionic bonds, atoms in covalent bonds have similar electronegativity. Ionic and covalent bonding are thus considered as the two extremes in bonding types. Covalent bonding is further categorized into the following subclasses; non-polar, polar and coordinate types of covalent bonding.

Non-polar covalent bonding occurs when two bonding atoms have either equal or similar electronegativities or a calculated electronegativity difference of less than 0.4.

Polar covalent bonding occurs when there is a small difference in electronegativity between atoms in the range of approximately 0.4 up to 2.0. When the difference in electronegativity is greater than 2.0, ionic bonding is then known to occur between two atoms. The more electronegative atom will attract the bonding electrons to a larger extent. As a result, the more electronegative atom acquires a partial negative charge and the less electronegative atom acquires a partial positive charge.

Coordinate covalent bonding occurs when the shared electron pair comes from the lone pair of electrons of one of the atoms in the bonding component. Typically coordinate bonds form between Lewis acids (electron acceptors) and Lewis bases (electron donors) as shown below.

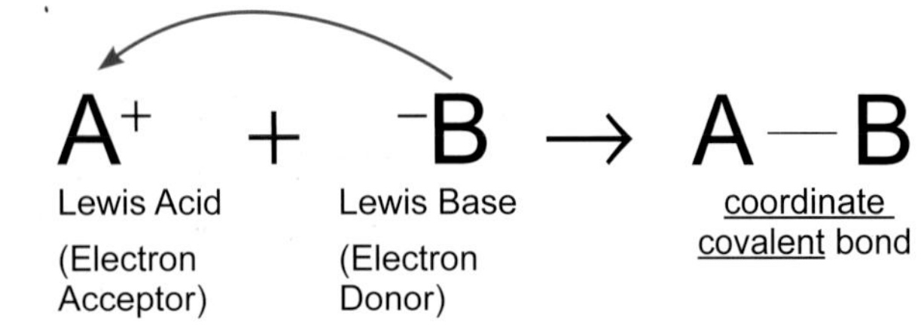

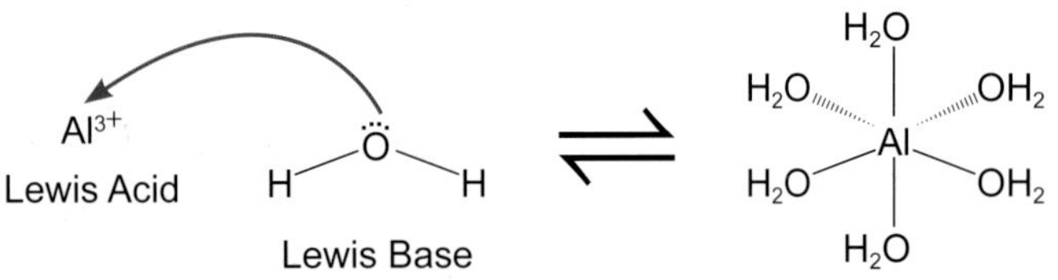

$$A^+ + {}^-B \rightarrow A—B$$

Lewis Acid (Electron Acceptor) | Lewis Base (Electron Donor) | coordinate covalent bond

Al^{3+} Lewis Acid + $H—\ddot{O}—H$ Lewis Base $\rightleftharpoons$ $Al(H_2O)_3(OH_2)_3$

A Lewis structure is a representation of covalent bonding in which shared electrons are shown either as lines or as pairs of dots between two atoms. For instance, let us consider the H_2O molecule. The valence shell electronic configurations of the atoms that constitute this molecule are:

O: $2s^2 2p^4$
H: $1s^1$

Since hydrogen has only one electron to share with oxygen there is only one possible covalent bond that can be formed between the oxygen atom and each of the hydrogen atoms. Four of the valence electrons of the oxygen atom do not participate in this covalent bonding, these are called non-bonding electrons or lone pairs. The Lewis structure of the water molecule is:

H:Ö:H or H-Ö-H

Lewis formulated the following general rule known as the octet rule concerning these representations: atoms tend to form covalent bonds until they are surrounded by 8 electrons (with few exceptions such as for hydrogen which can be surrounded by a maximum of only 2 electrons; see CHM 3.1). To satisfy this rule (and if there is a sufficient number of valence electrons), two atoms may share more than one pair of electrons thus forming more than one covalent bond at a time. In such instances the bond between these atoms is referred to as a double or a triple bond depending on whether there are two or three pairs of shared electrons, respectively.

Some molecules cannot fully be described by a single Lewis structure. For instance, for the carbonate ion: CO_3^{2-}, the octet rule is satisfied for the central carbon atom if one of the C...O bonds is double (see the following diagrams). While this leads us to thinking that the three C...O bonds are not equivalent, every piece of experimental evidence concerning this molecule shows that the three bonds are in fact the same (same length, same polarity, etc...). This suggests that in such instances a molecule cannot be described fully by a single Lewis structure. However, a molecule may in fact be represented by two or more valid Lewis structures. Indeed, since there is no particular reason to choose one oxygen atom over another we can write three equivalent Lewis structures for the carbonate ion. These three structures are called resonance structures represented with a double-headed arrow between each resonance structure. The carbonate ion (CO_3^{2-}) actually exists as a hybrid of the three equivalent structures. It is the full set of resonance structures that describe such a molecule. In this picture, the C…O bonds are neither double nor single, they are intermediate and have both a single and a double bonded character (see the following diagrams).

CO_3^{2-}

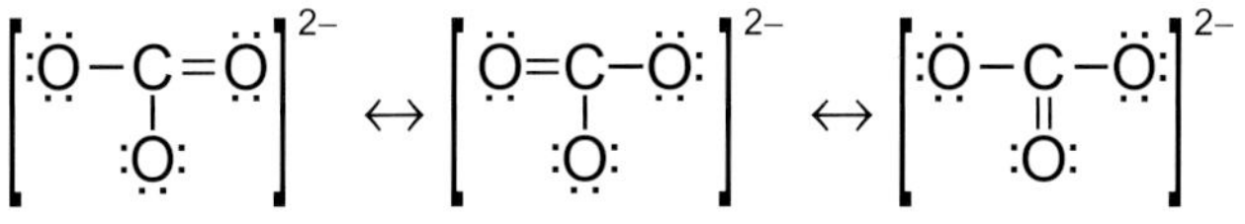

The actual structure of the carbonate ion is therefore one which is intermediate between the three resonance structures and is known as a resonance hybrid as shown:

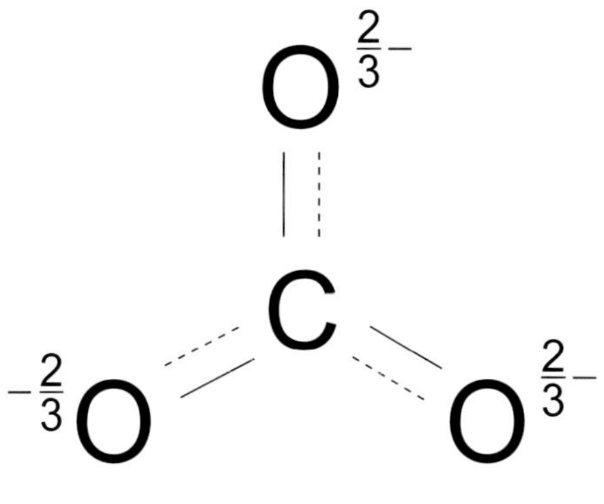

In many molecular structures, all of the respective resonance structures contribute equally to the hybridized representation. However, for some, resonance structures may not all contribute equally. Moreover, the more stable the resonance structure, the more contribution of that structure to the true hybrid structure based on formal charges.

Thus, based on their stabilities, non-equivalent resonance structures may contribute differently to the true overall hybridized structure representation of a molecule.

It is often interesting to compare the number of valence electrons that an atom possesses when it is isolated and when it is engaged in a covalent bond within a given molecule. This is often quantitatively described by the concept of formal charge.

Generally, a formal charge is a calculated conjured charge assigned to each individual atom within a Lewis structure allowing one to distinguish amongst various possible Lewis structures. The formal charge on any individual atom is calculated based on the difference between the atom's actual number of valence electrons and the number of electrons the atom possesses as part of a Lewis structure.

Moreover, the number of electrons attributed to an atom within a Lewis structure (covalently bonded) is not necessarily the same as the number of valence electrons that would be isolated within that free atom, and the difference is thus referred to as the "formal charge" of that atom. This concept is defined as follows:

Formal charge (of atom X) = Total number of valence electrons in a free atom (V) – [(total number of nonbonding electrons

(N) + ½ total number of bonding electrons (B) in a Lewis structure)].

Where, V is the number of valence electrons of the atom in isolation (atom in ground state); N is the number of non-bonding valence electrons on this atom in the molecule; and B is the total number of bonding electrons shared in covalent bonds with other atoms in the molecule (see structure of CO_3^{2-} in the previous illustrations).

Let us apply this definition to the two previous examples: H_2O and CO_3^{2-}. This process is fairly straightforward in the case of the water molecule:

total # of valence e^-'s in free O:	6
– total # of non-bonding e^-'s on O in H_2O:	4
– 1/2 (total # of bonding e^-'s) on O in H_2O:	2
Formal charge of O in $H_2O = 0$	

In the case of the CO_3^{2-} ion, it is not as obvious. If we consider one of the three equivalent resonance forms, that of the oxygen with a double bond to carbon we have:

total # of valence e^-'s in free O:	6
- total # of non-bonding e^-'s on O in the ion:	4
- 1/2 (total # of bonding e^-) on O in the ion:	2
Formal charge of O of C=O in the ion = 0	

Similarly, the calculation of the formal charge for one of the two singly bonded oxygen's of C–O in the same ion leads to the following: $6 - 6 - 1/2(2) = -1$. Considering that CO_3^{2-} is represented by three resonance forms, the actual formal charge of the oxygen atom is $1/3\ (-1 - 1 + 0) = -2/3$. This value formally reflects the idea that the oxygen atoms are equivalent and that any one of them has a –1 charge in 2 out of three of the resonance forms of this ion. Here are some simple rules to remember about formal charges:

(i) For neutral molecules, the formal charges of all the atoms should add up to zero.

(ii) For an ion, the sum of the formal charges must equal the ion's charge.

The following rules should help you select a plausible Lewis structure:

(i) If you can write more than one Lewis structure for a given neutral molecule; the most plausible one is the one in which the formal charges of the individual atoms are zero.

(ii) Lewis structures with the smallest formal charges on each individual atom are more plausible than the ones that involve large formal charges.

(iii) Out of a range of possible Lewis structures for a given molecule, the most plausible ones are the ones in which negative formal charges are found on the most electronegative atoms and positive charges on the most electropositive ones.

In addition to these rules, remember that some elements have a tendency to form molecules that do not satisfy the octet rule:

(i) When sulfur is the central atom in a molecule or a polyatomic ion, it almost invariably does not fulfill the octet rule.

(ii) The number of electrons around S in these compounds is usually 12 (e.g. SF_6, SO_4^{2-}). This situation (expanded octets) also occurs in other elements in and beyond the third period.

(iii) Molecules that have an element from the 3A group (B, Al, etc...) as their central atom do not generally obey the octet rule. In these molecules there are less than 8 electrons around the central atom (e.g. AlI_3 and BF_3).

(iv) Some molecules with an odd number of electrons can clearly not obey the octet rule (e.g. NO and NO_2).

3.3 Partial Ionic Character

Except for homonuclear molecules (molecules made of atoms of the same element, e.g. H_2, O_3, etc...), bonding electrons are not equally shared by the bonded atoms. Thus a diatomic (= *two atoms*) compound like Cl_2 shares its bonding electrons equally; whereas, a binary (= *two* different *elements*) compound like CaO (calcium oxide) or NaCl (sodium chloride) does not. Indeed, for the great majority of molecules, one of the two atoms between which the covalent bond occurs is necessarily more electronegative than the other. This atom will attract the bonding electrons to a larger extent (see CHM 3.2). Although this phenomenon does not lead to the formation of two separate ionic species, it does result in a molecule in which there are partial charges on these particular atoms: the corresponding covalent bond is said to possess partial ionic character. This polar bond will also have a dipole moment given by:

$$D = q \cdot d$$

where q is the absolute value of the partial charge on the most electronegative or the most electropositive bonded atom and d is the distance between these two atoms. To obtain the total dipole moment of a molecule one must add the individual dipole moment vectors present on each one of its bonds. Since this is a vector addition (see ORG 1.5), the overall result may be zero even if the individual dipole moment vectors are very large.

Non-polar bonds are generally stronger than polar covalent and ionic bonds, with ionic bonds being the weakest. However, in compounds with ionic bonding, there is generally a large number of bonds between molecules and this makes the compound as a whole very strong. For instance, although the ionic bonds in one compound are weaker than the non-polar covalent bonds in another compound, the ionic compound's melting point will be higher than the melting point of the covalent compound. Polar covalent bonds have a partially ionic character, and thus the bond strength is usually intermediate between that of ionic and that of non-polar covalent bonds. The strength of bonds generally decreases with increasing ionic character.

3.4 Lewis Acids and Lewis Bases

The Lewis model of acids and bases focuses on the transfer of an electron pair. Generally, a Lewis acid is defined as any substance that may accept an electron pair to form a covalent bond, while a Lewis base, is defined as any substance that donates an electron pair to form a respective covalent bond. Hence, as per the Lewis definition of an acid or base, a substance need not contain a hydrogen as defined by either Arrhenius or Bronsted-Lowry to be an acid, nor is a hydroxyl group (OH^-) needed to be a base (see CHM 6.1). A Lewis acid therefore generally has an empty electronic orbital that can accept an electron pair whereas a Lewis base will contain a full electronic orbital or lone pair of electrons ready to be donated.

In CHM 3.2, we pointed out some exceptions to the Lewis' octet rule. Among these were molecules that had a deficiency of electrons around the central atom as described previously (e.g. BF_3). When such a molecule is put into contact with a molecule with lone pairs (e.g. NH_3) a reaction occurs. Such a reaction can be interpreted as a donation of a pair of electrons from the second type of molecule (Lewis base) to the first type of molecule (Lewis acid), or alternately by an acceptance of a pair of electrons by the first type of molecule. Thus, as previously shown, molecules such as BF_3 are referred to as <u>Lewis acids</u> while molecules such as NH_3 are known as <u>Lewis bases</u>. Thus some examples of Lewis acids are: BF_3, H^+, Cu^{2+}, and Cr^{3+} and Lewis bases are: NH_3, OH^-, and H_2O. {l**E**wis **A**cids: **E**lectron pair **A**cceptors}.

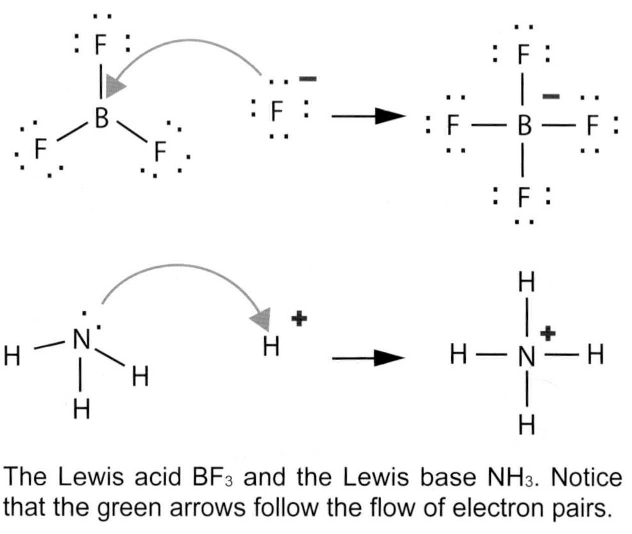

The Lewis acid BF_3 and the Lewis base NH_3. Notice that the green arrows follow the flow of electron pairs.

3.5 Valence Shell Electronic Pair Repulsions (VSEPR Models)

One of the shortcomings of Lewis structures is that they cannot be used to predict molecular geometries. In this context a model known as the valence-shell electronic pair repulsion or VSEPR model is very useful. In this model, the geometrical arrangement of atoms or groups of atoms bound to a central atom A is determined by the number of pairs of valence electrons around A. VSEPR procedure is based on the principle that these electronic pairs around the central atom are arranged in such a way that the repulsions between them are minimized. The general VSEPR procedure starts with the determination of the number of electronic pairs around A:

  # of valence electrons in a free atom of A
+ # of sigma (or single) bonds involving A
− # of pi (or double) bonds involving A

= (total # of electrons around A)

The division of this total number by 2 yields the total number of electron pairs around A. Note the following important points:

(i) A single bond counts for 1 sigma bond, a double bond for 1 sigma bond and 1 pi bond and a triple bond for 1 sigma and two pi bonds.

(ii) The general calculation that we have presented is performed for the purposes of VSEPR modeling; its result can be quite different from the one obtained in the corresponding Lewis structure.

(iii) For all practical purposes, one always assigns a double bond (i.e. 1 sigma bond and one pi bond) to a terminal oxygen (an oxygen which is not a central atom and is not attached to any other atom besides the central atom).

(iv) A terminal halogen is always assigned a single bond.

Once the number of pairs around the central atom is determined, the next step is to use Figure III.A.3.1 to predict the geometrical arrangement of these pairs around the central atom.

The next step is to consider the previous arrangement of the electronic pairs and place the atoms or groups of atoms that are attached to the central atom in accordance with such an arrangement. The pairs of electrons which are not involved in the bonding between these atoms and the central atom are known as lone pairs. If we subtract the number of lone pairs from the total number of pairs of electrons, we readily obtain the number of bonding electron pairs. It is the number of bonding electron pairs which ultimately determines the molecular geometry in the VSEPR model according to Table III.A.3.1.

On the other hand, as for the *electronic* geometrical arrangement of a molecule, one is also to consider the free lone pair(s) of electrons. Consequently, a simple molecule such as SO_2 (see Table III.A.3.1) will have a trigonal planar electronic geometry with a bent molecular geometry with the respective differences in geometrical arrangement based solely on the lone pair of the central sulfur atom. Thus, the electron and molecular geometry of a molecule may be different. (Note: electron geometry is based on the geometrical arrangement of electron pairs around a central atom, whereas, molecular geometry is based on the geometrical arrangement of the atoms surrounding a central atom). Let us consider three examples: CH_4, H_2O and CO_2.

1 – CH_4:

	# of valence electrons on C:	4
+	# of sigma bonds:	+ 4
–	# of pi bonds:	– 0
		= 8/2 = 4 pairs

According to Figure III.A.3.1 CH_4 corresponds to a tetrahedral arrangement. Each of these four pairs of electrons corresponds to a H atom bonded each to the central atom of carbon. Therefore, all 4 pairs of electrons are bonding pairs with a tetrahedral molecular and electronic geometry, respectively (due to a lack in lone pairs).

2 – H_2O:

	# of valence electrons on O:	6
+	# of sigma bonds on the central O:	+ 2
-	# of pi bonds on the central O:	– 0
		= 8/2 = 4 pairs

For the H_2O geometry, it also corresponds to a tetrahedral arrangement (i.e. 4 pairs). However, due to lone pairs surrounding each of the oxygen atoms, the molecular geometry is of a bent geometrical shape with a tetrahedral electronic geometrical configuration.

3 – CO_2:

	# of valence electrons on C:	4
+	# of sigma bonds for terminal O's:	+ 2
-	# of pi bonds for terminal O's:	– 2
		= 4/2 = 2 pairs

This total number of pairs corresponds to a linear arrangement. Since both of these electron pairs are used to connect the central C atom to the terminal O's there are no lone pairs left on C. Therefore, the number of bonding pairs is also 2 and both the molecular and electronic geometries are also linear.

Here are some additional rules when applying the VSEPR model:

(i) When dealing with a cation (positive ion) subtract the charge of the ion from the total number of electrons.

(ii) When dealing with an anion (negative ion) add the charge of the ion to the total number of electrons.

(iii) A lone pair repels another lone pair or a bonding pair very strongly. This causes some deformation in bond angles. For instance, the H–O–H angle is smaller than 109.5°.

Table III.A.3.1: Geometry of simple molecules in which the central atom A has one or more lone pairs of electrons (= e^-).

Total number of e^- pairs	Number of lone pairs	Number of bonding pairs	Electron Geometry, Arrangement of e^- pairs	Molecular Geometry (Hybridization State)	Examples
3	1	2	Trigonal planar	Bent (sp^2)	SO_2
4	1	3	Tetrahedral	Trigonal pyramidal (sp^3)	NH_3
4	2	2	Tetrahedral	Bent (sp^3)	H_2O
5	1	4	Trigonal bipyramidal	Seesaw (sp^3d)	SF_4
5	2	3	Trigonal bipyramidal	T-shaped (sp^3d)	ClF_3

Note: dotted lines only represent the overall molecular shape and not molecular bonds. In brackets under "Molecular Geometry" is the hybridization, to be discussed in ORG 1.2.

(iv) The previous rule also holds for a double bond. Note that in one of our previous examples (CO_2), the angle is still 180° since there are two double bonds and no lone pairs. Indeed, in this geometry, the strong repulsions between the two double bonds are symmetrical.

(v) The VSEPR model can be applied to polyatomic molecules. The procedure is the same as above except that one can only determine the arrangements of groups of atoms around one given central atom at a time. For instance, you could apply the VSEPR model to determine the geometrical arrangements of atoms around C or around O in methanol (CH_3OH). In the first case the molecule is treated as $CH_3 - X$ (where –X is –OH) and in the second it is treated as HO–Y (where –Y is $-CH_3$). The geometrical arrangement is tetrahedral in the first case which gives HCX or HCH

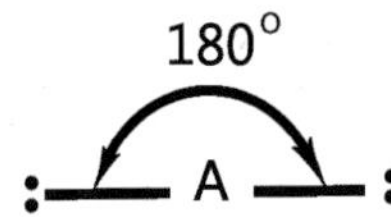

linear arrangement of 2 electron pairs around central atom A

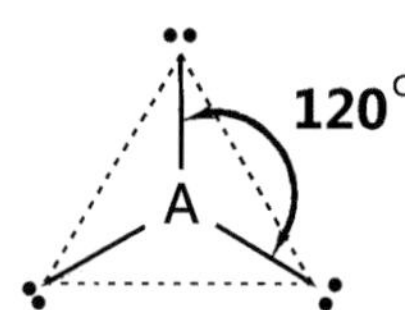

trigonal planar arrangement of 3 electron pairs around central atom A

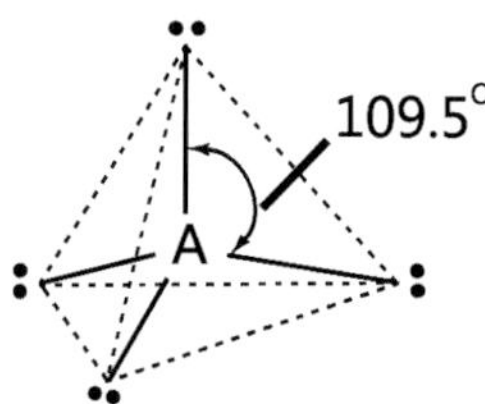

tetrahedral arrangement of 4 electron pairs around central atom A

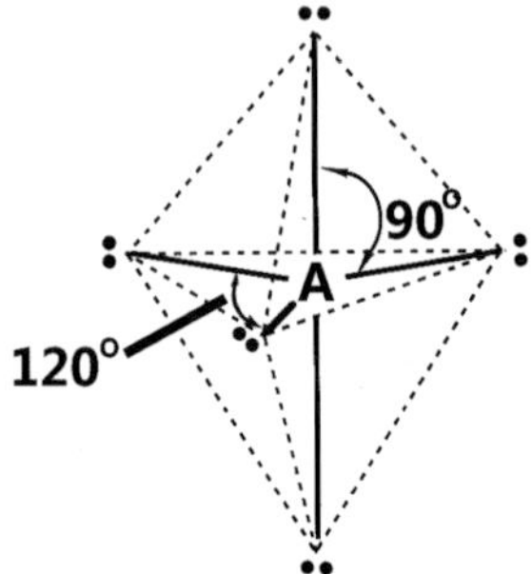

trigonal bipyramidal arrangement of 5 electron pairs around central atom A

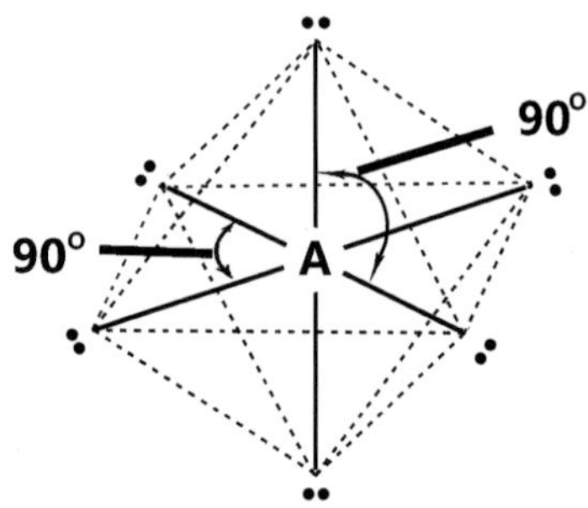

octahedral arrangement of 6 electron pairs around central atom A

Figure III.A.3.1: Molecular arrangement of electron pairs around a central atom A. Dotted lines only represent the overall molecular shape and not molecular bonds.

angles close to 109°. The second case corresponds to a bent arrangement (with two lone pairs on the oxygen) and gives an HOY angle close to 109° as well.This also corresponds to a tetrahedral arrangement, however only two of these pairs are bonding pairs (connecting the H atoms to the central oxygen atom); therefore, the actual geometry according to Table III.A.3.1 is bent or V-shape geometry.

3.5.1 The AXE Method

The "AXE method" of electron counting can be used when applying the VSEPR model. As we have seen in the previous section, the A signifies the central atom. The X represents the number of sigma bonds between the central atom and outside atoms (see "B" in Table III.A.3.1). Multiple covalent bonds (double, triple, etc.) count as one X. The E is the number of lone pair electrons surrounding A. The sum of X and E, known as the steric number, is also associated with the total number of hybridized orbitals (ORG 1.2). Based on the steric number and the distribution of X's and E's, the VSEPR model makes the predictions in Table III.A.3.2.

Table III.A.3.2: Using the AXE method to determine molecular geometry.

Steric No.	BASIC GEOMETRY			
	0 lone pair	**1 lone pair**	**2 lone pairs**	**3 lone pairs**
2	X—A—X Linear (CO_2)			
3	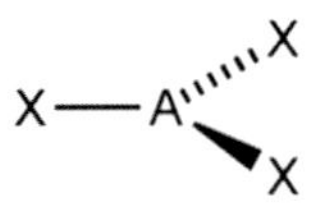 Trigonal planar (BCl_3)	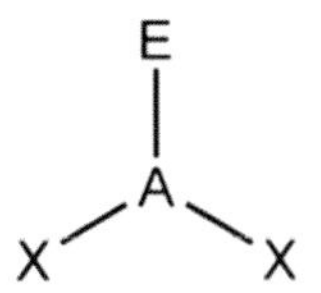 Bent (SO_2)		
4	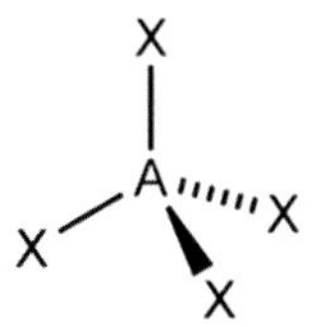 Tetrahedral (CH_4)	 Trigonal pyramidal (NH_3)	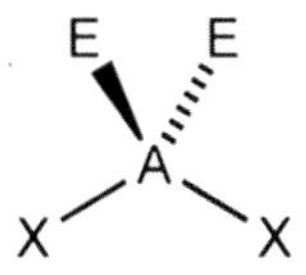 Bent (H_2O)	

Table III.A.3.2: *(continued)*

Steric No.	BASIC GEOMETRY			
	0 lone pair	**1 lone pair**	**2 lone pairs**	**3 lone pairs**
5	 Trigonal bipyramidal (PCl_5)	 Seesaw (SF_4)	 T-shaped (ClF_3)	 Linear (I_3^-)
6	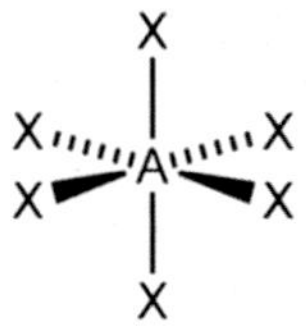 Octahedral (SF_6)	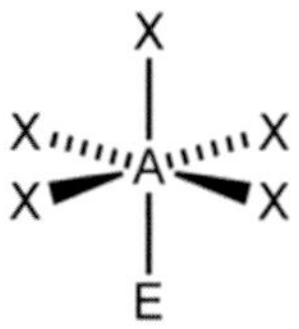 Square pyramidal (BrF_5)	 Square planar (XeF_4)	
7	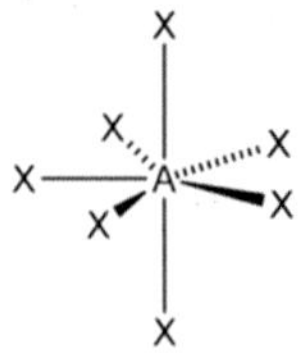 Pentagonal bipyramidal (IF_7)	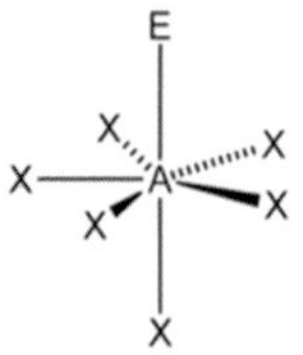 Pentagonal pyramidal ($XeOF_5^-$)	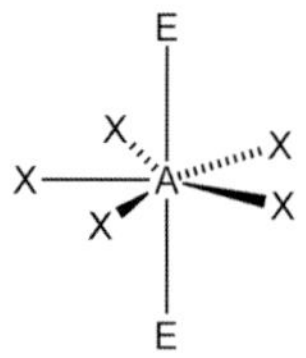 Pentagonal planar (XeF_5^-)	

PLEASE NOTE: Intermolecular bonds is discussed in CHM 4.2.

GOLD STANDARD WARM-UP EXERCISES

CHAPTER 3: Bonding

1) What is the formal charge on the carbon atom in the carbonate ion?
   A. 0
   B. 1
   C. 2
   D. –2

2) Diamond consists of tetrahedral arrangements of carbon atoms, with each atom covalently bound to four others to yield a giant molecular structure. What is the hybridization state of carbon in diamond?
   A. It is not hybridized.
   B. sp
   C. sp^2
   D. sp^3

3) Which of the following describes the orbital geometry of an sp^2 hybridized atom?
   A. Trigonal planar
   B. Linear
   C. Tetrahedral
   D. Octahedral

4) In the hypothetical molecule PQ_2, the atom P possesses a lone pair of electrons, what would be the expected shape of the product molecule?
   A. Linear
   B. Bent
   C. Trigonal pyramidal
   D. Tetrahedral

5) Aniline ($C_6H_5NH_2$) acts as a Lewis base because aniline:

   $$C_6H_5NH_2 + H_2O \leftrightarrow C_6H_5NH_3^+ + OH^-$$

   A. exhibits hydrogen bonding.
   B. has a lone pair of electrons on its nitrogen atom.
   C. is an electron pair acceptor.
   D. produces OH^- when in solution.

6) Which of the following best summarizes VSEPR?
   A. Hybridized bonds are the key to molecular stability.
   B. The repulsion between bonds helps determine the shapes of covalent molecules.
   C. The repulsion of atomic nuclei helps determine the shapes of covalent molecules.
   D. The repulsion between electrons helps determine the shapes of covalent molecules.

7) Using the VSEPR theory, the shape of PCl_5 is:
   A. pentagonal planar.
   B. octahedral.
   C. trigonal bipyramidal.
   D. square pyramidal.

8) Using the VSEPR theory, the shape of SF_6 is:
   A. octahedral.
   B. tetrahedral.
   C. trigonal bipyramidal.
   D. square pyramidal.

9) Using the VSEPR theory, the shape of ClF_3 is:
   A. trigonal planar.
   B. tetrahedral.
   C. trigonal pyramidal.
   D. T-shaped.

10) Which pair of atoms would most likely form an ionic compound when bonded to each other?
   A. Silicon and nitrogen
   B. Calcium and fluorine
   C. Two sulfur atoms
   D. Carbon and silicon

GS ANSWER KEY

CHAPTER 3

		Cross-Reference			Cross-Reference
1.	**A**	**CHM 3.2, 3.5**	**6.**	**D**	**CHM 3.5**
2.	**D**	**CHM 3.5**	**7.**	**C**	**CHM 3.5**
3.	**A**	**CHM 3.5, ORG 1.2**	**8.**	**A**	**CHM 3.5**
4.	**B**	**CHM 3.2-3.5**	**9.**	**D**	**CHM 3.5**
5.	**B**	**CHM 3.4**	**10.**	**B**	**CHM 2.3, 3.1.1**

* Explanations can be found at the back of the book.

Go online to DAT-prep.com for additional chapter review Q&A and forum.

PHASES AND PHASE EQUILIBRIA
Chapter 4

Memorize	Understand	Importance
* Define: temp. (C, K), gas P and weight * Define: STP, ideal gas, deviation * Define: H bonds, dipole forces	* Kinetic molecular theory of gases * Maxwell distribution plot, H bonds, dipole F. * Deviation from ideal gas behavior * Equations: ideal gas/Charles'/Boyle's * Partial Press., mole fraction, Dalton's * Intermolecular forces, phase change/ diagrams	**4 to 6 out of the 30 Gen CHM** DAT questions are based on content in this chapter (in our estimation). * Note that between 50% and 85% of the questions in DAT General Chemistry are from 6 chapters: 1, 2, 4, 5, 6 and 9.

Introduction

A phase, or state of matter, is a uniform, distinct and usually separable region of material. For example, for a glass of water: the ice cubes are one phase (solid), the water is a second phase (liquid), and the humid air over the water is the third phase (gas = vapor). The temperature and pressure at which all 3 phases of a substance can coexist is called the triple point.

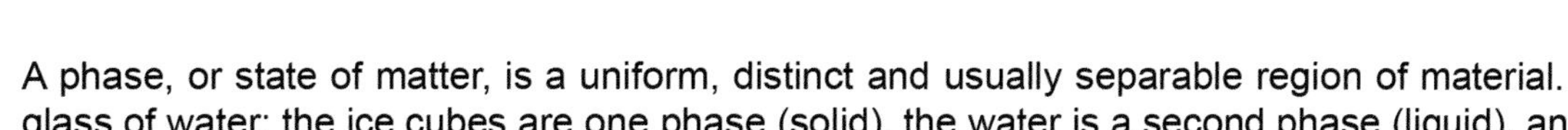

Additional Resources

Free Online Forum

Video: Online or DVD

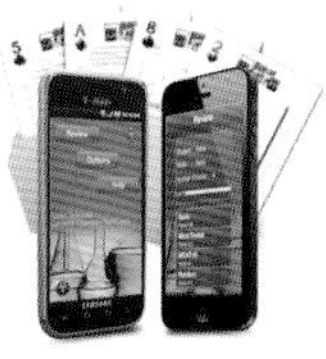

Flashcards

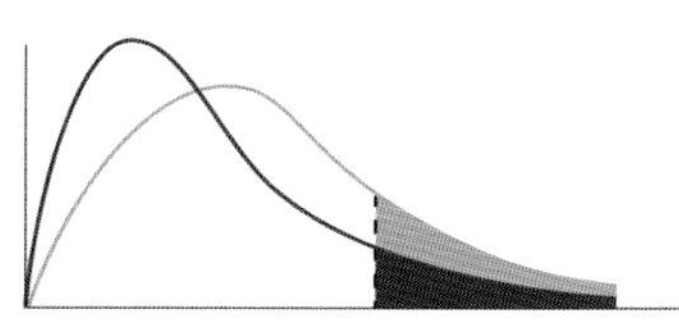

Special Guest

Elements and compounds exist in one of three states: the gaseous state, the liquid state or the solid state.

4.1 The Gas Phase

A substance in the gaseous state has neither fixed volume nor fixed shape: it spreads itself uniformly throughout any container in which it is placed.

4.1.1 Standard Temperature and Pressure, Standard Molar Volume

Any given gas can be described in terms of four fundamental properties: mass, volume, temperature and pressure. To simplify comparisons, the volume of a gas is normally reported at 0°C (273.15 K) and 1.00 atm (101.33 kPa = 760 mmHg = 760 torr); these conditions are known as the standard temperature and pressure (STP). {Note: the SI unit of pressure is the pascal (Pa) and the old-fashioned Imperial unit is the pound per square inch because pressure is defined as force per unit area}

The volume occupied by one mole of any gas at STP is referred to as the standard molar volume and is equal to 22.4 L.

4.1.2 Kinetic Molecular Theory of Gases (A Model for Gases)

The kinetic molecular theory of gases describes the particulate behavior of matter in the gaseous state. A gas that fits this theory exactly is called an ideal gas. The essential points of the theory are as follows:

1. Gases are composed of extremely small particles (either molecules or atoms depending on the gas) separated by distances that are relatively large in comparison with the diameters of the particles.
2. Particles of gas are in constant motion, except when they collide with one another.
3. Particles of an ideal gas exert no attractive or repulsive force on one another.
4. The collisions experienced by gas particles do not, on the average, slow them down; rather, they cause a change in the direction in which the particles are moving. If one particle loses energy as a result of a collision, the energy is gained by the particle with which it collides. Collisions of the particles of an ideal gas with the walls of the container result in no loss of energy.

5. The average kinetic energy of the particles (KE = 1/2 mv^2) increases in direct proportion to the temperature of the gas (KE = 3/2 kT) when the temperature is measured on an absolute scale (i.e. the Kelvin scale) and k is a constant (the Boltzmann constant). The typical speed of a gas particle is directly proportional to the square root of the absolute temperature.

The plot of the distribution of collision energies of gases is similar to that of liquids. However, molecules in liquids require a minimum escape kinetic energy in order to enter the vapor phase (see Figure III.A.4.1 in CHM 4.1.2).

The properties of gases can be explained in terms of the kinetic molecular theory of ideal gases.

Experimentally, we can measure four properties of a gas:

1. The weight of the gas, from which we can calculate the number (N) of molecules or atoms of the gas present;

2. The pressure (P), exerted by the gas on the walls of the container in which this gas is placed (N.B.: a vacuum is completely devoid of particles and thus has *no* pressure);

3. The volume (V), occupied by the gas;

4. The temperature (T) of the gas.

In fact, if we know any three of these properties, we can calculate the fourth. So the minimum number of these properties required to fully describe the state of an ideal gas is three.

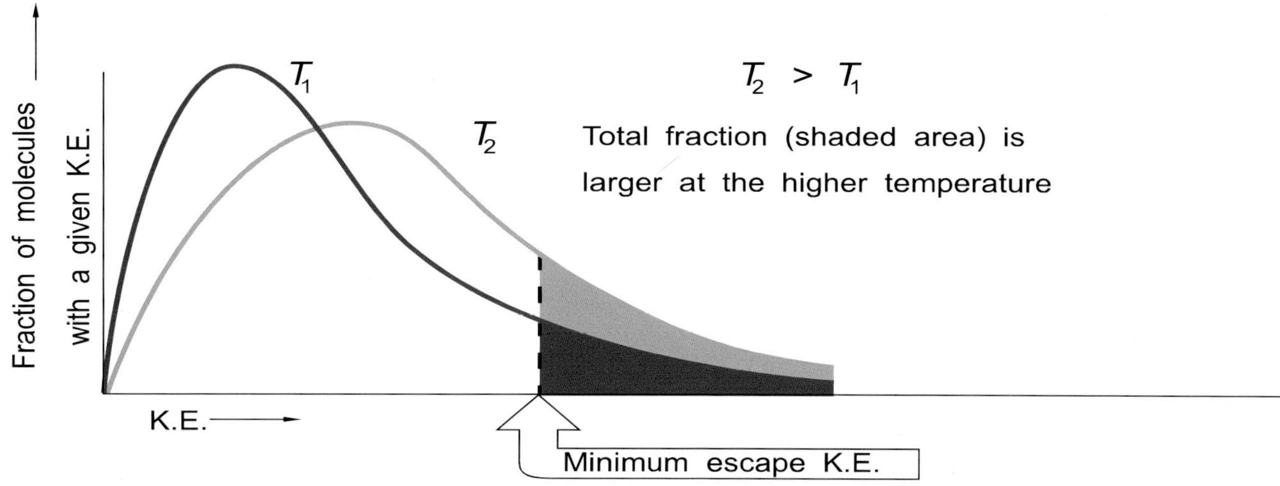

Figure III.A.4.1: The Maxwell Distribution Plot. At a higher temperature T_2, the curve peak is flattened, which means that gas particles within the sample are travelling at a wider range of velocities. Additionally, the larger shaded area at a temperature T_2 means that a greater proportion of molecules will possess the minimum escaping kinetic energy (KE) required to evaporate.

4.1.3 Graham's Law (Diffusion and Effusion of Gases)

Graham's law describes the mean (average) free path of any typical gas particle taken per unit volume. The process taken by such gas particles is known as *diffusion* and its related process *effusion* which are defined as follows:

Diffusion is the flow of gas particles spreading out evenly through random motion. Gas particles diffuse from regions of high concentration to regions of low concentration. The rate at which a gas diffuses is inversely proportional to the square root of its molar mass. The ratio of the diffusion rates of two different gases is inversely proportional to the square root of their respective molar masses. $Rate_1/Rate_2$ and M_1/M_2 represents diffusion rates of gases 1 and 2 and the molar mass of gases 1 and 2. Lighter particles diffuse quicker than heavier particles.

Effusion is the movement of a gas through a small hole or pore into another gaseous region or into a vacuum. If the hole is large enough, the process may be considered diffusion instead of effusion. The rates at which two gases effuse are inversely proportional to the square root of their molar masses, the same as that for diffusion:

$$\frac{Rate_1}{Rate_2} = \sqrt{\frac{M_2}{M_1}}$$

4.1.4 Charles' Law

The volume (V) of a gas is directly proportional to the absolute temperature (expressed in Kelvins) when P and N are kept constant.

$$V = \text{Constant} \times T \quad \text{or} \quad V_1/V_2 = T_1/T_2$$

NOTE: For Charles' Law and all subsequent laws, the subscripts 1 and 2 refer to both initial and final values of all variables for the gas in question.

4.1.5 Boyle's Law

The volume (V) of a fixed weight of gas held at constant temperature (T) varies inversely with the pressure (P).

$$V = \text{Constant} \times 1/P \quad \text{or} \quad P_1V_1 = P_2V_2$$

4.1.6 Avogadro's Law

The volume (V) of a gas at constant temperature and pressure is directly proportional to the number of particles or moles (n) of the gas present.

$$V/n = \text{Constant} \quad \text{or} \quad V_1/n_1 = V_2/n_2$$

4.1.7 Combined Gas Law

For a given constant mass of any gas the product of its pressure and volume divided by its Kelvin temperature is equal to a constant (k). Therefore, by using the combined gas law, one may calculate any of the three variables of a gas exposed to two separate conditions as follows:

$$\frac{P_1V_1}{T_1} = k = \frac{P_2V_2}{T_2} \quad \text{(at constant mass)}$$

This relationship depicts how a change in pressure, volume, and/or temperature of any gas (at constant mass) will be affected as a function of the other quantities (P_2, V_2 or T_2).

4.1.8 Ideal Gas Law

The combination of Boyle's law, Charles' law and Avogadro's law yields the "ideal gas law":

$$PV = nRT$$

where R is the universal gas constant and n is the number of moles of gas particles.

$$R = 0.0821 \text{ L-atm/K-mole}$$
$$= 8.31 \text{ kPa-dm}^3\text{/K-mole}$$

A typical ideal gas problem is as follows: an ideal gas at 27 °C and 380 torr occupies a volume of 492 cm^3. What is the number of moles of gas?

Ideal Gas Law problems often amount to mere exercises of unit conversions. The easiest way to do them is to convert the units of the values given to the units of the R gas constant.

$$P = 380 \text{ torr} = \frac{380 \text{ torr}}{(760 \text{ torr/atm})} = 0.500 \text{ atm}$$

$$T = 27\,°\text{C} = 273 + 27°\text{C} = 300 \text{ K}$$

$$V = 492 \text{ cm}^3 = 492 \text{ cm}^3 \times (1 \text{ liter}/1000\text{cm}^3)$$
$$= 0.492 \text{ liter}$$

$$PV = n\text{RT}$$

$$n = \text{PV/RT}$$

$$n = \frac{(0.500 \text{ atm} \times 0.492 \text{ L})}{(0.0821 \text{ L-atm/K-mole} \times 300 \text{ K})}$$

$$n = 0.0100 \text{ mole}$$

Also note that the ideal gas law could be used in the following alternate ways (Mwt = molecular weight):

(i) since n = (mass m of gas sample)/(Mwt M of the gas)

$$PV = (m/M)\text{R}T$$

(ii) since m/V is the density (d) of the gas:

$$P = \frac{d\text{RT}}{M}$$

4.1.9 Partial Pressure and Dalton's Law

In a mixture of unreactive gases, each gas distributes evenly throughout the container. All particles exert the same pressure on the walls of the container with equal force. If we consider a mixture of gases occupying a total volume (V) at a temperature (T) the term partial pressure is used to refer to the pressure exerted by one component of the gas mixture if it were occupying the entire volume (V) at the temperature (T).

Dalton's law states that the total pressure observed for a mixture of gases is equal to the sum of the pressures that each individual component would exert were it alone in the container.

$$P_T = P_1 + P_2 + \ldots + P_i$$

where P_T is the total pressure and P_i is the partial pressure of any component (i).

The mole fraction (X_i) of any one gas present in a mixture is defined as follows:

$$X_i = n_i/n_{(total)}$$

where n_i = moles of that gas present in the mixture and $n_{(total)}$ = sum of the moles of all gases present in the mixture (see CHM 5.3.1).

Of course, the sum of all mole fractions in a mixture must equal one:

$$\Sigma X_i = 1$$

The partial pressure (P_i) of a component of a gas mixture is equal to:

$$P_i = X_i P_T$$

The ideal gas law applies to any component of the mixture:

$$P_i V = n_i R T$$

4.1.10 Deviation of Real Gas Behavior from the Ideal Gas Law

The particles of an ideal gas have zero volume and no intermolecular forces. It obeys the ideal gas law. Its particles behave as though they were moving points exerting no attraction on one another and occupying no space. Real gases deviate from ideal gas behavior particularly when the gas particles are forced into close proximity under high pressure and low temperature, as follows:

1. They do not obey $PV = nRT$. We can calculate n, P, V and T for a real gas on the assumption that it behaves like an ideal gas but the calculated values will not agree with the observed values.

2. Their particles are subject to intermolecular forces (i.e. forces of attraction between different molecules like Van der Waal forces; CHM 4.2) which are themselves independent of temperature. But the deviations they cause are more pronounced at low temperatures because they are less effectively opposed by the slower motion of particles at lower temperatures. Similarly, an increase in pressure at constant temperature will crowd the particles closer together and reduce the average distance between them. This will increase the attractive force between the particles and the stronger these forces, the more the behavior of the real gas will deviate from that of an ideal gas. Thus, a real gas will act less like an ideal gas at higher pressures than at lower pressures. {Mnemonic: an ideal Plow and Thigh = an ideal gas exists when **P**ressure is **low** and **T**emperature is **high**}

3. The particles (i.e. molecules or atoms) occupy space. When a real gas is subjected to high pressures at ordinary temperatures, the fraction of the total volume occupied by the particles increases. At moderately high pressure, gas particles are pushed closer together and intermolecular attraction causes the gas to have a smaller volume than would be predicted by the ideal gas law. At extremely high pressure, gas particles are pushed even closer in such a way that the distance between them are becoming insignificant

compared to the size of the particles, therefore causing the gas to take up a smaller volume than would be predicted by the ideal gas law. Under these conditions, the real gas deviates appreciably from ideal gas behavior.

4. Their size and mass also affect the speed at which they move. At constant temperature, the kinetic energy (KE = 1/2 mv^2) of all particles – light or heavy – is nearly the same. This means that the heavier particles must be moving more slowly than the lighter ones and that the attractive forces between the heavier particles must be exercising a greater influence on their behavior. The greater speed of light particles, however, tends to counteract the attractive forces between them, thus producing a slight deviation from ideal gas behavior. Thus, a heavier particle (molecule or atom) will deviate more widely from ideal gas behavior than a lighter particle. At low temperature, the average velocity of gas particles decreases and the intermolecular attraction becomes increasingly significant, causing the gas to have a smaller volume than would be predicted by the ideal gas law. {The preceding is given by Graham's law, where the rate of movement of a gas (*diffusion* or streaming through a fine hole – *effusion*) is inversely proportional to the square root of the molecular weight of the gas (see CHM 4.1.3)}

4.2 Liquid Phase (Intra- and Intermolecular Forces)

Liquids have the ability to mix with one another and with other phases to form solutions. The degree to which two liquids can mix is called their miscibility. Liquids have definite volume, but no definite shape. As we will discuss, molecules of liquids can be attracted to each other (*cohesion*) as they can be attracted to their surroundings (*adhesion*). The most striking properties of a liquid are its viscosity and surface tension (see CHM 4.2.1, 4.2.2). Liquids also distinguish themselves from gases in that they are relatively incompressible. The molecules of a liquid are also subject to forces strong enough to hold them together. These forces are intermolecular and they are weak attractive forces that is, they are effective over short distances only. Molecules like methane (CH_4) are non-polar and so they are held together by weak intermolecular forces also known as Van der Waal forces (these include forces that are dipole-dipole, dipole-induced dipole and London forces). Whereas, molecules like water have much stronger intermolecular attractive forces because of the hydrogen bonding amongst the molecules. Hence, the most important forces are:

1. Dipole-dipole forces which depend on the orientation as well as on the distance between the molecules; they are inversely proportional to the fourth power of the distance. In addition to the forces between permanent dipoles, a dipolar molecule induces in a neighboring mol-

ecule an electron distribution that results in another attractive force, the dipole-induced dipole force, which is inversely proportional to the seventh power of the distance and which is relatively independent of orientation.

2. London forces (or Dispersive forces) are attractive forces acting between nonpolar molecules. They are due to the unsymmetrical instantaneous electron distribution which induces a dipole in neighboring molecules with a resultant attractive force. This instantaneous unsymmetrical distribution of electrons causes rapid polarization of the electrons and formation of short-lived dipoles. These dipoles then interact with neighboring molecules, inducing the formation of more dipoles. Dispersion forces are thus responsible for the liquefaction of noble gases to form liquids at low temperatures (and high pressures).

3. Hydrogen bonds occur whenever hydrogen is covalently bonded to an atom such as O, N or F that attract electrons strongly. Because of the differences in electronegativity between H and O or N or F, the electrons that constitute the covalent bond are closer to the O, N or F nucleus than to the H nucleus leaving

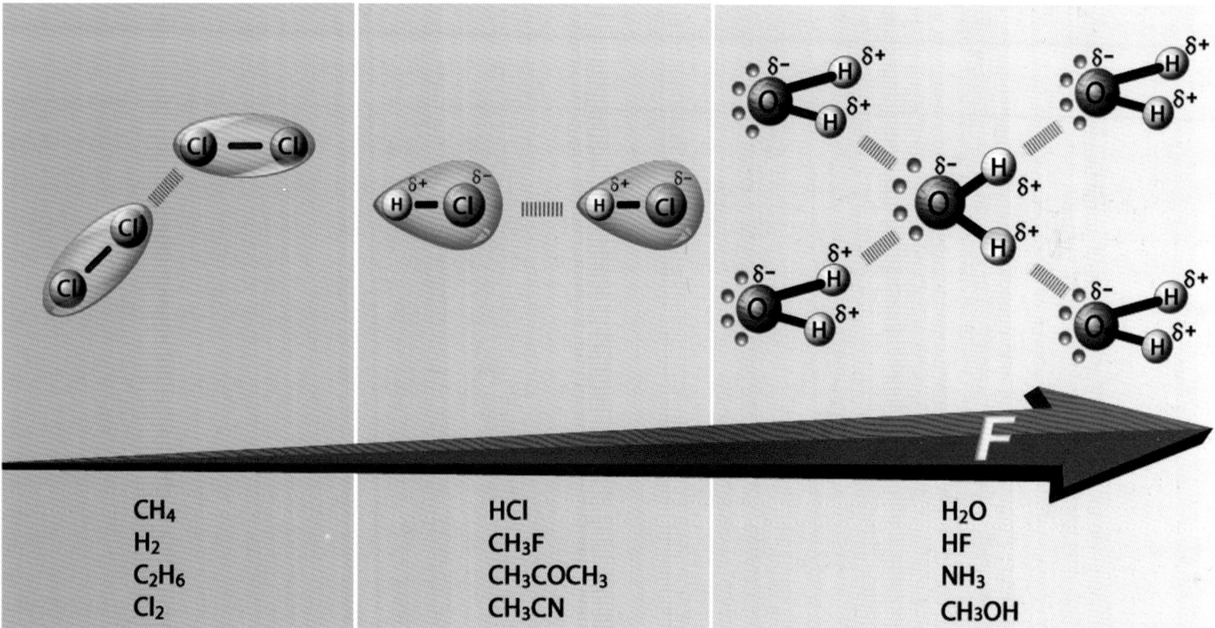

Table III.A.4.1: Van Der Waal's forces (weak) and hydrogen bonding (strong). London forces between Cl_2 molecules, dipole-dipole forces between HCl molecules and H-bonding between H_2O molecules. Note that a partial negative charge on an atom is indicated by δ^- (delta negative), while a partial positive charge is indicated by δ^+ (delta positive). Notice that one H_2O molecule can potentially form 4 H-bonds with surrounding molecules which is highly efficient. The preceding is one key reason that the boiling point of water is higher than that of ammonia, hydrogen fluoride or methanol.

the latter relatively unshielded. The unshielded proton is strongly attracted to the O, N or F atoms of neighboring molecules since these form the negative end of a strong dipole.

The slightly positive charge of the hydrogen atom will then be strongly attracted to the more electronegative atoms of nearby molecules. These forces are weaker than intramolecular bonds, but are much stronger than the other two types of intermolecular forces. Hydrogen bonding is a special case of dipole-dipole interaction. Hydrogen bonds are characterized by unusually strong interactions and high boiling points due to the vast amount of energy required (relative to other intermolecular forces) to break the hydrogen bonds. {Though the H-bonding atoms are often remembered by the mnemonic "Hydrogen is FON!", sulfur is also known to H-bond though far weaker than the more electronegative FON atoms.}

4.2.1 Viscosity

Viscosity is analogous to friction between moving solids. It may, therefore be viewed as the resistance to flow of layers of fluid or liquid past each other. This also means that viscosity, as in friction, results in dissipation of mechanical energy. As one layer flows over another, its motion is transmitted to the second layer and causes this layer to be set in motion. Since a mass m of the second layer is set in motion and some of the energy of the first layer is lost, there is a transfer of momentum between the layers.

The greater the transfer of this momentum from one layer to another, the more energy that is lost and the slower the layers move.

The viscosity (η) is the measure of the efficiency of transfer of this momentum. Therefore the higher the viscosity coefficient, the greater the transfer of momentum and loss of mechanical energy, and thus loss of velocity. The reverse situation holds for a low viscosity coefficient.

Consequently, a high viscosity coefficient substance flows slowly (e.g. molasses), and a low viscosity coefficient substance flows relatively fast (e.g. water). Note that the transfer of momentum to adjacent layers is in essence, the exertion of a force upon these layers to set them in motion.

4.2.2 Surface Tension

Molecules of a liquid exert attractive forces toward each other (cohesive forces), and exert attractive forces toward the surface they touch (adhesive forces). If a liquid is in a gravity free space without a surface, it will form a sphere (smallest area relative to volume).

If the liquid is lining an object, the liquid surface will contract (due to cohesive forces) to the lowest possible surface area. The forces between the molecules on this surface will create a membrane-like effect. Due to the contraction, a potential energy (PE) will present in the surface.

This PE is directly proportional to the surface area (A). An exact relation is formed as follows:

$$PE = \gamma A$$

γ = *surface tension* = *PE/A* = *joules/m*^{2}

An alternative formulation for the surface tension (γ) is:

$$\gamma = F/l$$

F = force of contraction of surface
l = length along surface

Because of the contraction, a small object which would ordinarily sink in the liquid may float on the surface membrane. For example, a small insect like a "water strider."

The liquid will rise or fall on a wall or in a capillary tube if the adhesive forces are greater than cohesive or vice versa (*see* Figure III.A.4.1b).

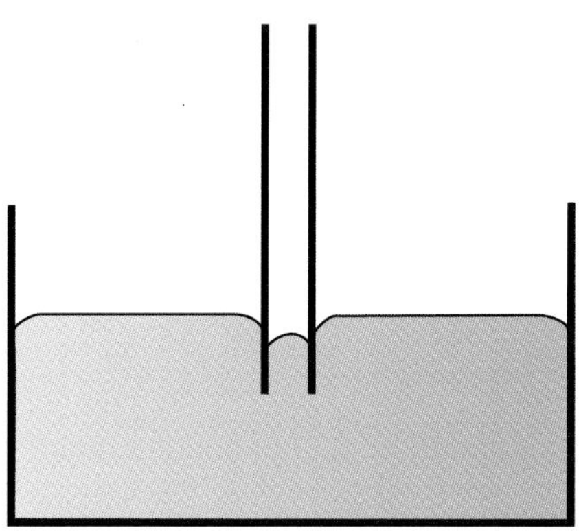

(a) cohesive > adhesive

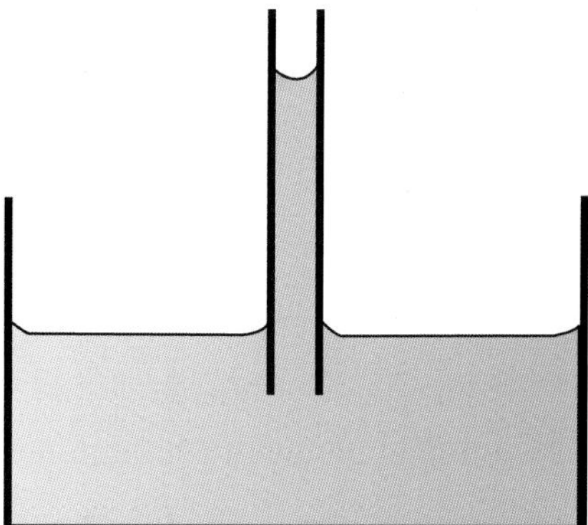

(b) adhesive > cohesive

Figure III.A.4.1b: Effects of adhesive and cohesive forces. The distance the liquid rises or falls in the tube is directly proportional to the surface tension γ and inversely proportional to the liquid density and radius of the tube. Examples of 2 liquids consistent with the illustrations include: (a) mercury; (b) water.

4.3 Solid Phase

Solids have definite volume and shape and are incompressible under pressure. Intermolecular forces between molecules of molecular solids and electrostatic (i.e. coulombic or "opposite charges attract") interactive forces between ions of ionic solids are strong enough to hold them into a relatively rigid structure. A solid may be crystalline (ordered) or amorphous (disordered). A crystalline solid, such as table salt (NaCl) has a structure with an ordered geometric shape. Its atoms are arranged geometrically with a repeating pattern. It has a specific melting point. An amorphous solid, such as glass, has a molecular structure with no specific shape. It melts over a wide range of temperatures since the molecules require different amounts of energies to break bonds between them.

4.4 Phase Equilibria (Solids, Liquids and Gases)

4.4.1 Phase Changes

Elements and compounds can undergo transitions between the solid, liquid and gaseous states. They can exist in different phases and undergo phase changes which need not involve chemical reactions. Phase changes are reversible with an equilibrium existing between each of the phases. A phase is a homogeneous, physically distinct and mechanically separable part of a system. Each phase is separated from other phases by a physical boundary.

A few examples:

1. Ice/liquid water/water vapor (3 phases)
2. Any number of gases mix in all proportions and therefore constitute just one phase.
3. The system $CaCO_3(s) \rightarrow CaO(s) + CO_2(g)$ (2 phases, i.e. 2 solids: $CaCO_3$ and CaO and a gas: CO_2)
4. A saturated salt solution (3 phases: solution, undissolved salt, vapor)

An example of phase change is the vaporization of water into its vapor state. A system is considered homogeneous when it is uniform throughout its volume so that its properties are the same in all parts. This does not imply a single molecular species: a solution of sodium chloride is homogeneous provided its concentration is the same throughout.

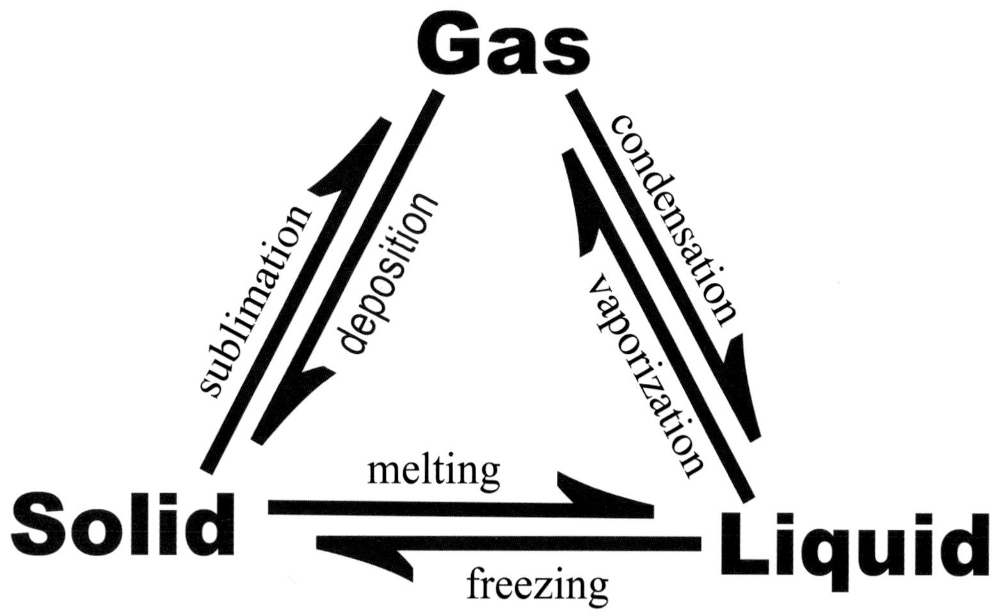

Figure III.A.4.2: Phase Changes

4.4.2 Freezing Point, Melting Point, Boiling Point

The conversion of a liquid to a gas is called vaporization. We can increase the rate of vaporization of a liquid by (i) increasing the temperature (ii) reducing the pressure, or (iii) both. Molecules escape from a liquid because, even though their average kinetic energy is constant, not all of them move at the same speed (*see Figure III.A.4.1*). A fast moving molecule can break away from the attraction of the others and pass into the vapor state. When a tight lid is placed on a vessel containing a liquid, the vapor molecules cannot escape and some revert back to the liquid state. The number of molecules leaving the liquid at any given time equals the number of molecules returning. Equilibrium is reached and the number of molecules in the fixed volume above the liquid remains constant. These molecules exert a constant pressure at a fixed temperature which is called the vapor pressure of the liquid. The vapor pressure is the partial pressure exerted by the gas molecules over the liquid formed by evaporation, when it is in equilibrium with the gas phase condensing back into the liquid phase. The vapor pressure of any liquid is dependent on the intermolecular forces that are present within the liquid and the temperature. Weak intermolecular forces result in volatile substances whereas strong intermolecular forces result in nonvolatile substances.

Boiling and evaporation are similar processes but they differ as follows: the vapor from a boiling liquid escapes with sufficient pressure to push back any other gas present, rather than diffusing through it. Vapor pressure increases as the temperature increases, as more molecules have sufficient energy to break the attraction between each other to escape into the gas phase. The boiling point is therefore the temperature at which the vapor pressure of the liquid equals to the opposing external pressure. Under a lower pressure, the boiling point is reached at a lower temperature. Increased intermolecular interactions (i.e. H_2O see CHM 4.2, alcohol see ORG 6.1, etc.) will decrease the vapor pressure thus raising the boiling point. Other factors being equal, as a molecule becomes heavier (increasing molecular weight), it becomes more difficult to push the molecule into the atmosphere thus the boiling point increases (i.e. alkanes see ORG 3.1.1).

The freezing point of a liquid is the temperature at which the vapor pressure of the solid equals the vapor pressure of the liquid. Increases in the prevailing atmospheric pressure decreases the melting point and increases the boiling point.

When a solid is heated, the kinetic energy of the components increases steadily. Finally, the kinetic energy becomes great enough to overcome the forces holding the components together and the solid changes to a liquid. For pure crystalline solids, there is a fixed temperature at which this transition from solid to liquid occurs. This temperature is called the melting point. Pure solids melt completely at one temperature. Impure solids begin to melt at one temperature but become completely liquid at a higher temperature.

4.4.3 Phase Diagrams

Figure III.A.4.3 shows the temperature of ice as heat is added. Temperature increases linearly with heat until the melting point is reached. At this point, the heat energy added does not change the temperature. Instead, it is used to break intermolecular bonds and convert ice into water. There is a mixture of both ice and water at the melting point. After all of the complete conversion of ice into water, the temperature rises again linearly with heat addition. At the boiling point, the heat added does not change the temperature because the energy is again used to break the intermolecular bonds. After complete conversion of water into gas, the temperature will rise linearly again with heat addition.

Thus, during a phase change, there is no change in temperature. The energy that is added into the system is being used to weaken/break intermolecular forces; in other words, there is an increase in the potential energy of molecules rather than an increase in the average kinetic energy of molecules. The amount of energy to change one mole of substance from solid to liquid or from liquid to gas is called the molar *heat of fusion* and the molar *heat of vaporization* (CHM 8.7) Each

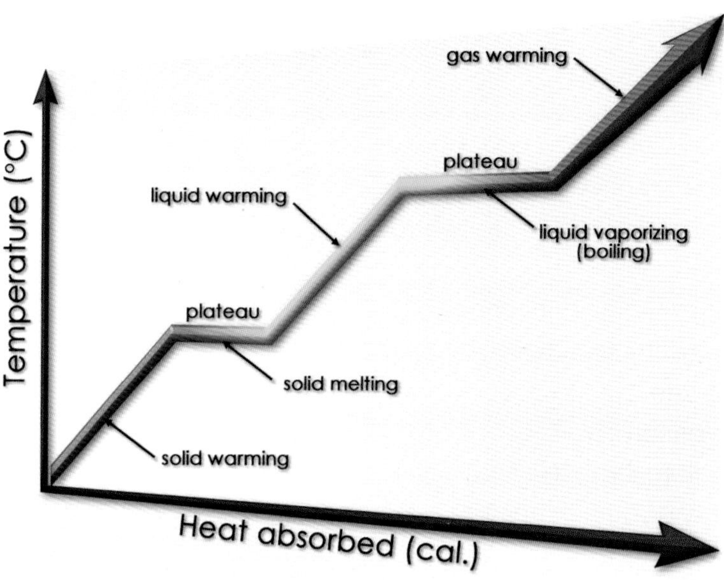

Figure III.A.4.3 Heating curve for H_2O

phase has its own specific heat. Enthalpy of vaporization is greater than that of fusion because more energy is required to break intermolecular bonds (from liquid phase to gas phase) than just to weaken intermolecular bonds (from solid phase to liquid phase).

The temperatures at which phase transitions occur are functions of the pressure of the system. The behavior of a given substance over a wide range of temperature and pressure can be summarized in a phase diagram, such as the one shown for the water system (Fig.III.A.4.4). The diagram is divided into three areas labeled **solid** (ice), **liquid** (water) and **vapor** in each of which only one phase exists. In these areas, *P* and *T* can be independently varied without a second phase appearing. These areas are bounded by curves AC, AD and AB. Line AB represents sublimation/deposition (sublimation curve). Line AC represents evaporation/condensation (vaporization curve) and Line AD represents melting/freezing (fusion curve). At triple point A, all three phases are known to coexist. At any point on these curves, two phases are in equilibrium. Thus on AC, at a given T, the saturated vapor pressure of water has a fixed value. The boiling point of water (N) can be found on this curve, 100 °C at 760 mmHg pressure. The curve only extends as far as C, the critical point, where the vapor and liquid are indistinguishable. In general, the gas phase is found at high temperature and low pressure; the solid phase is found at low temperatures and high pressure; and the liquid phase is found at high temperatures and high pressure. The temperature at which a substance boils when the pressure is 1 atm is called the normal boiling point.

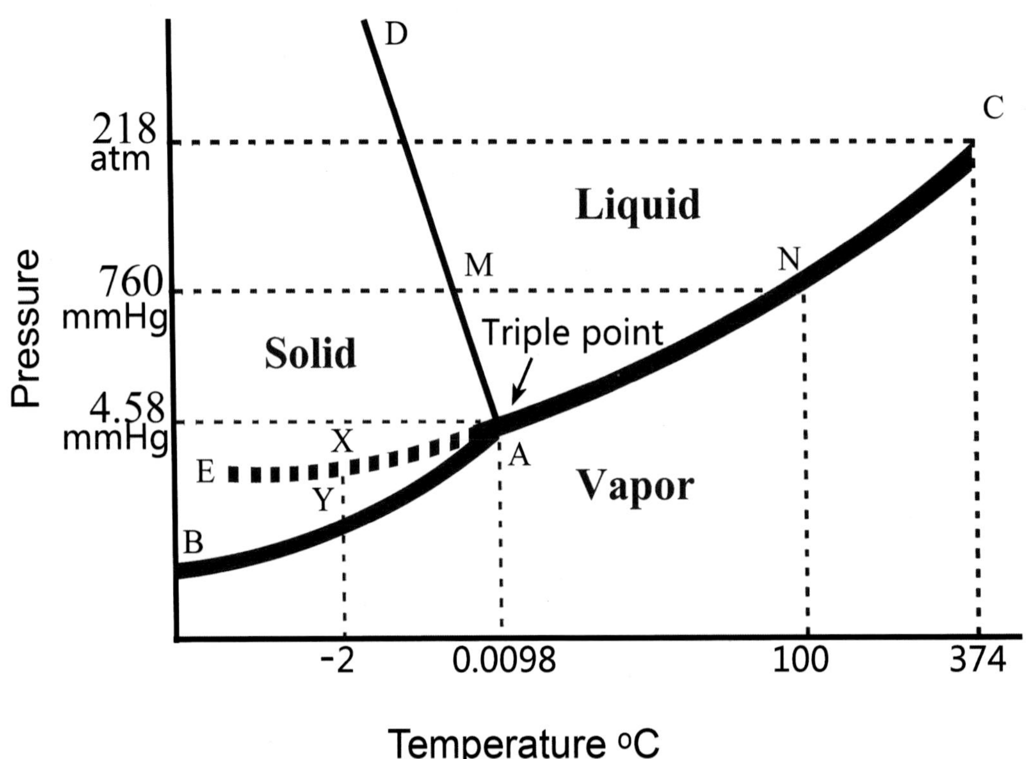

Figure III.A.4.4: Phase diagram for H_2O.

The extension of the curve CA to E represents the metastable equilibrium (*meta* = beyond) between supercooled water and its vapor. If the temperature is slightly raised at point X, a little of the liquid will vaporize until a new equilibrium is established at that higher temperature. Curve AB is the vapor pressure curve for ice. Its equilibria are of lower energy than those of AE and thus more stable.

The slope of line AD shows that an increase in P will lower the melting point of ice. This property is almost unique to water. Because of the negative slope of line AD, an isothermal increase in pressure will compress the solid (ice) into liquid (water). Thus H_2O is unique in that its liquid form is denser than its solid form. The high density of liquid water is due mainly to the cohesive nature of the hydrogen-bonded network of water molecules (see Table III.A.4.1 in CHM 4.2).

Most substances *increase* their melting points with increased pressure. Thus the line AD slants to the right for almost all substances. Point M represents the true melting point of ice, 0.0023 °C at 760 mmHg of pressure. (The 0 °C standard refers to the freezing point of water saturated with air at 760 mmHg). At point A, solid, liquid and vapor are in equilibrium. At this one temperature, ice and water have the same fixed vapor pressure. This is the triple point, 0.0098 °C at 4.58 mmHg pressure.

GOLD STANDARD WARM-UP EXERCISES

CHAPTER 4: Phases and Phase Equilibria

1) Under what conditions would the ideal gas equation be valid?

   A. Volume unknown, pressure high
   B. Average pressure, average volume
   C. Low pressure, high temperature
   D. Normal volume, low temperature

2) If a gas behaved ideally, which of the following would be expected on cooling the gas to 1 K?

   A. It would remain a gas.
   B. It would liquify.
   C. It would solidify.
   D. Cannot be determined from the information given.

3) Reaction I is usually carried out at atmospheric pressure. During the reaction, before equilibrium was reached, the mole fractions of SO_2 (g) and SO_3 (g) were 1/2 and 1/6 respectively. What was the partial pressure of O_2 (g)?

Reaction I

$2SO_2(g) + O_2(g) \leftrightarrow 2SO_3(g) \qquad \Delta H = -197 \text{ kJ mol}^{-1}$

   A. 0.66 atm
   B. 0.16 atm
   C. 0.50 atm
   D. 0.33 atm

4) Assuming ideal conditions, how many liters of oxygen are required to react with 48 liters of ammonia in the reaction below?

$$4NH_3(g) + 5O_2 \rightarrow 4NO(g) + 6H_2O(g)$$

   A. 48 L
   B. 60 L
   C. 72 L
   D. The answer cannot be determined without knowing the precise densities of the gases.

5) Which of the following is a correct representation of the phase diagram for carbon dioxide?

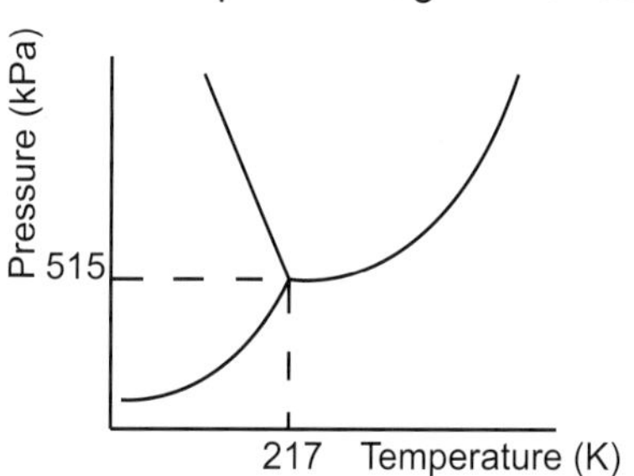

A.

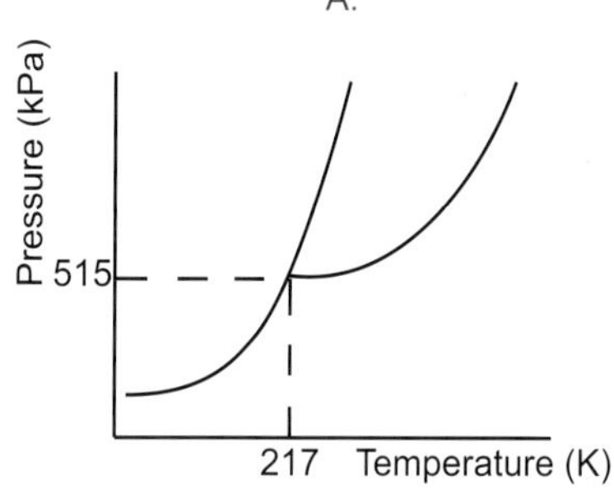

B.

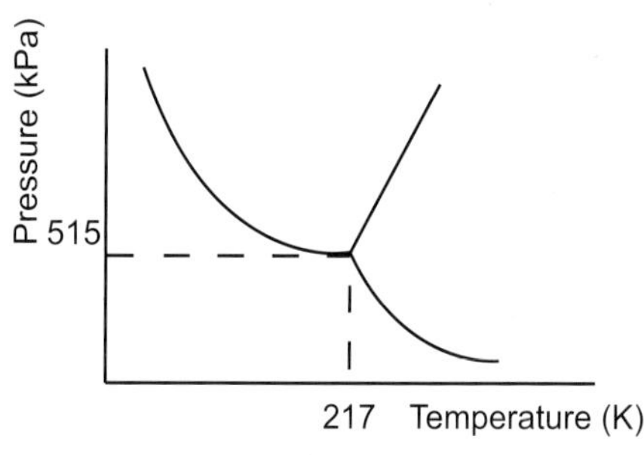

C.

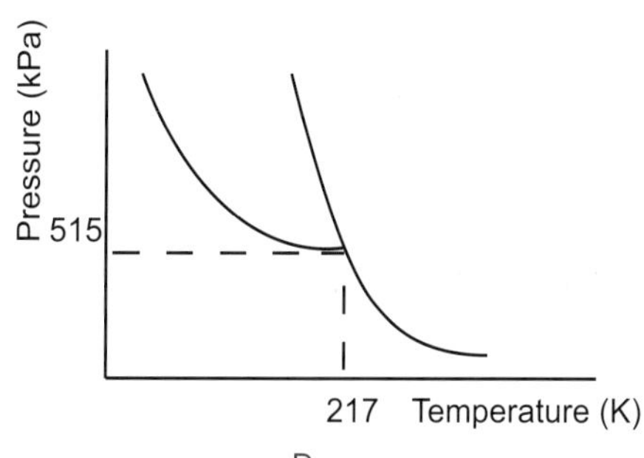

D.

6) Consider the diagram below. The diagram illustrates the effect on the temperature of Substance T–34 undergoing simple transitions from solid to liquid to gas states as heat is added. Which segment of the graph represents fusion of Substance T–34?

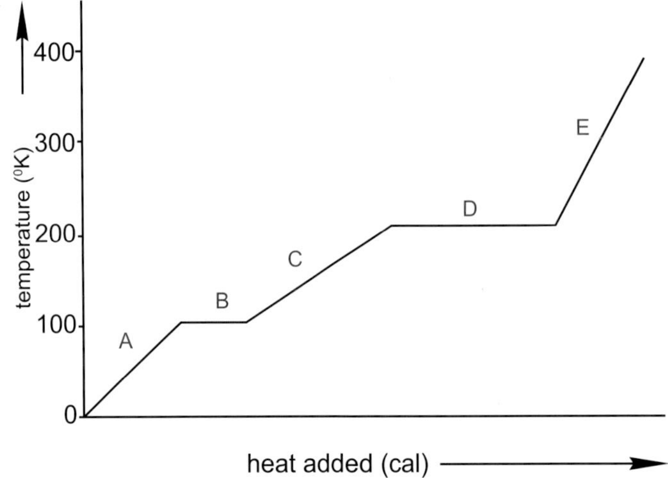

7) Why does "solid" water (ice) float on "liquid" water?

A. Because it is less dense.
B. Because it occupies less volume.
C. Because it exists at lower temperatures.
D. Because it is a solid.

8) Two identical evacuated flasks are filled with different gases to the same pressure and temperature. The first is filled with hydrogen and the second with propane. The molecular weight of propane is 44 g/mol. Compared with the first flask, the flask filled with propane weighs:

A. 11 times more.
B. 22 times more.
C. the same.
D. 44 times more.

9) A soccer ball with initial pressure P and initial volume V is inflated with air until the pressure becomes 2P and the volume becomes 1.1V. The temperature being kept constant, the weight of air in the ball has increased by a factor of:

A. 2.2
B. 1.1
C. 1.0
D. 2.0

10) The density of an unknown gas is determined to be 1.97 g/L at STP. If the gas is known to be one of the following substances, which is most likely?

A. C_3H_8
B. HCHO
C. C_2H_2
D. CH_3CH_3

11) If the anesthetic mixture is inspired at the rate of 1000 mL/min, what mass of halothane ($CHClBrCF_3$, MW = 197.4) is inspired in one minute if the partial pressure of halothane is 7.6 torr and the temperature is 21 °C? {R = 0.0821 L-atm/K-mole}

A. 0.08 g
B. 0.80 g
C. 1.80 g
D. 3.36 g

12) A 50–50 (by weight) mixture of He and H_2 exerts a pressure of 600 torr. Approximately what is the partial pressure due to H_2?

A. 200 torr
B. 300 torr
C. 400 torr
D. 450 torr

GS ANSWER KEY

CHAPTER 4

		Cross-Reference			Cross-Reference
1.	C	CHM 4.1.10 (4.1.8)	7.	A	CHM 4
2.	A	CHM 4.1.2	8.	B	CHM 4.1.8
3.	D	CHM 4.1.9	9.	A	CHM 4.1.8
4.	B	CHM 4.1.6, 4.1.7, 4.1.8, 4.1.9	10.	A	CHM 4.1.1
5.	B	CHM 4.3.3	11.	A	CHM 4.1.6
6.	B	CHM 4.3, 8.7	12.	C	CHM 4.1.9

* Explanations can be found at the back of the book.

Go online to DAT-prep.com for additional chapter review Q&A and forum.

SOLUTION CHEMISTRY

Chapter 5

Memorize	Understand	Importance
* Define saturated, supersatured, nonvolatile * Common anions and cations in solution * Units of concentration * Define electrolytes with examples	* Colligative properties, Raoult's law * Phase diagram change due to colligative properties * Bp elevation, fp depression * Osmotic pressure equation * Solubility product, common-ion effect	**2 to 4 out of the 30 Gen CHM** DAT questions are based on content in this chapter (in our estimation). * Note that between 50% and 85% of the questions in DAT General Chemistry are based on content from 6 chapters: 1, 2, 4, 5, 6 and 9.

Introduction

A solution is a homogeneous mixture composed of two or more substances. For example, a solute (salt) dissolved in a solvent (water) making a solution (salt water). In addition, solutions can involve liquids in liquids (i.e. ethanol in water), gases in liquids (i.e. oxygen in water), gases in gases (i.e. nitrogen in air) or even solids in solids (i.e. alloys). Two substances are immiscible if they can't mix to make a solution. Solutions can be distinguished from non-homogeneous mixtures like colloids and suspensions (the differences were discussed in CHM 1.7).

Additional Resources

Free Online Forum

Video: Online or DVD

Flashcards

5.1 Solutions and Colligative Properties

Water (H_2O) is a universal solvent known as a pure substance or a one component system. Pure substances are often mixed together to form solutions. A solution is a sample of matter that is homogeneous but, unlike a pure substance, the composition of a solution can vary within relatively wide limits. Ethanol and water are each pure substances and each have a fixed composition, C_2H_5OH and H_2O, but mixtures of the two can vary continuously in composition from almost 100% ethanol to almost 100% water. Solutions of sucrose in water, however, are limited to a maximum percentage of sucrose - the solubility - which is 67% at 20°C, thus the solution is saturated. If the solution is heated, a higher concentration of sucrose can be achieved (i.e. 70%). Slowly cooling down to 20°C creates a supersaturated solution which may precipitate with any perturbation.

Intermolecular forces (see CHM 4.2) amongst various other parameters may either promote or may prevent the formation of a solution. The formation of solutions primarily involves the breaking of intermolecular forces between solutes and between solvents and the subsequent reformation of new intermolecular interactions amongst the solute and solvent. The initial step in solution formation (i.e. breakage of intermolecular forces amongst the solutes and solvent separately) is endothermic and the second step (i.e. reformation of intermolecular interactions between solute-solvent) is exothermic. If an overall reaction in solution formation is exothermic, the new intermolecular bonds between solute and solvent are more stable and a solution is formed. {Note: "endothermic" - absorbs heat, "exothermic" - releases heat; "enthalpy" is a measure of the total energy; see CHM chapters 7 and 8 for details}

In the energetic requirements of solution formation, the formation of a solution may result in either an increase or a decrease in the enthalpy of solution dependant on the magnitude of interactions between the solute and solvent. Hence, energy changes do occur when a solution forms (i.e exothermic or endothermic). An increase in enthalpy, a positive heat of solution, results in more energy in a system i.e. less stable and weaker bonds. Whereas a decrease in enthalpy, a negative heat of solution, results in less energy in a system i.e. more stable and stronger bonds and thus the respective drive to the formation of a solution.

Lastly, the formation of a solution always results in an increase in entropy or disorder due to the insidious tendency for energy to disperse.

Generally the component of a solution that is stable in the same phase as the solution is called the solvent. If two components of a solution are in the same phase, the component present in the larger amount is called the solvent and the other is called the solute. Many properties of solutions are dependent only on the relative number of molecules (or ions) of the solute and of the solvent. Properties that depend **only** on the number of particles present and not the kind of particles are called colligative properties. For all colligative properties, a factor known as the Van't Hoff factor (i) is essentially required and defined as, the ratio of moles of particles or ions in a solution to the moles of all undissociated formula units (or molecules) within a solution. The factor (i) is therefore incorporated as a multiple of all the colligative properties equations, respectively (see below). Thus, for non-ionic solutions, the factor (i) is essentially equal to 1 as the particles are undissociated such as for sugar solutions. However, for ionic solutions, the factor (i) is dependent on the number of ions dissociated in solution (i.e., $NaCl = 2$, $CaCl_2 = 3$, etc.). Hence, the most important colligative properties can be found in the following sections.

5.1.1 Vapor-Pressure Lowering (Raoult's Law)

The vapor pressure of the components of an ideal solution behaves as follows:

$$p_i = X_i\,(p_i)_{pure}$$

where p_i = vapor pressure of component i in equilibrium with the solution
$(p_i)_{pure}$ = vapor pressure of pure component i at the same T
X_i = mole fraction of component i in the liquid.

Thus the vapor pressure of any component of a mixture is lowered by the presence of the other components. Experimentally, it can be observed that when dissolving a solute which cannot evaporate (= *nonvolatile*) into a solvent, the vapor pressure of the resulting solution is lower than that of the pure solvent. The extent to which the vapor pressure is lowered is determined by the mole fraction of the solvent in solution ($X_{solvent}$):

$$P = P^{\circ}X_{solvent}$$

where P = vapor pressure of solution
P° = vapor pressure of pure solvent (at the same temperature as P).

When rearranged this way, the vapor pressure of a solution is quantified by Raoult's law which states that the lowering of the vapor pressure of the solvent is proportional to the mole fraction of solvent and independent of the chemical nature of the solute.

Hence, to show by how much a solution's vapor pressure is lowered by a solute, we can therefore define the vapor pressure lowering (ΔP) by the following equation; $\Delta P = X_{solute}\,P^{\circ}_{solvent}$. Where, $\Delta P = P^{\circ}_{solvent} - P_{solution}$ and rearranging the differences between the solvent and solution vapor pressures and substituting the solvent mole fraction ($X_{solvent}$) with the solute mole fraction as $X_{solvent} = 1 - X_{solute}$, results in Raoult's law which indicates that the lowering of the vapor pressure is directly proportional to the solute mole fraction as stated previously.

5.1.2 Boiling-Point Elevation and Freezing-Point Depression

When the vapor-pressure curve of a dilute solution and the vapor-pressure curve of the pure solvent are plotted on a phase diagram (see Figure III.A.5.1), it can be seen that a vapor pressure lowering of a solution occurs at all temperatures and that the freezing point and boiling point of a solution must therefore be different from those of the pure liquid.

The freezing point of a pure solvent (water) is lowered or depressed with the addition of another substance; meaning that a solution (solvent + solute) has a lower freezing point than a pure solvent, and this phenomenon is called a "freezing point depression". Alternatively, the boiling point of a pure solvent (water) is elevated when another substance is added; meaning that a solution

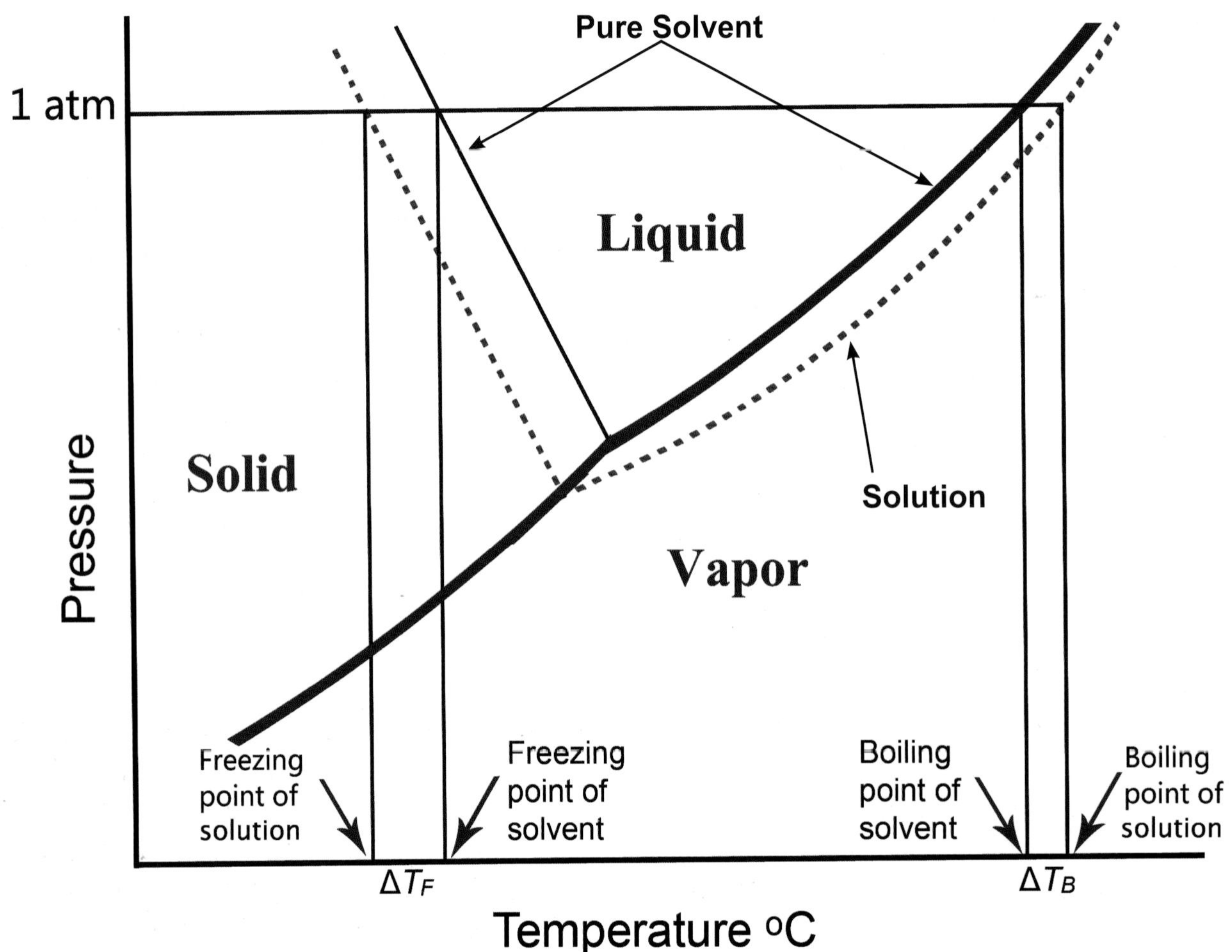

Figure III.A.5.1: Phase diagram of water demonstrating the effect of the addition of a solute.

has a higher boiling point than a pure solvent, and this phenomenon is called "boiling point elevation". The boiling point is therefore higher for the solution than for the pure liquid and the freezing point is lower for the solution than for the pure liquid. Since the decrease in vapor pressure is proportional to the mole fraction (see CHM 5.3.1) of solute, the boiling point elevation (ΔT_B) is also proportional to the mole fraction of solute and:

$$\Delta T_B = i\, K_B' X_B = i\, K_B m$$

where K_B' = boiling point elevation constant for the solvent
X_B = mole fraction of solute
m = *molality* (moles solute per kilogram of solvent; CHM 5.3.1)
i = Van't Hoff factor

K_B is related to K_B' through a change of units.

Similarly, for the freezing point depression (ΔT_F):

$$\Delta T_F = i\, K_F' X_B = i\, K_F m$$

where K_F' = freezing point depression constant for the solvent.

If K_F or K_B is known, it is then possible to determine the molality of a dilute solution simply by measuring the freezing point or the boiling point. These constants can be determined by measuring the freezing point and boiling point of a solution of known molality. If the mass concentration of a solute (in kg solute per kg of solvent) is known and the molality is determined from the freezing point of the solution, the mass of 1 mole of solute can be calculated.

It is important to recall that for a strong electrolyte solution such as NaCl which dissociates to positive and negative ions, the right hand side of the equation is multiplied by the Van't Hoff factor (i) equal to the number of ionic species generated per mole of solute. For NaCl n = 2 but for $MgCl_2$ n = 3. {Remember: colligative properties depend on the **number** of particles present}

5.1.3 Osmotic Pressure

The osmotic pressure (Π) of a solution describes the equilibrium distribution of solvent across semipermeable membranes separated by two compartments. When a solvent and solution are separated by a membrane permeable only to molecules of solvent (a <u>semipermeable</u> membrane), the solvent spontaneously migrates into the solution. The semipermeable membrane allows the solvent to pass but not the solute. Since pure solute cannot pass through the semipermeable membrane into the pure solvent side to equalize the concentrations, the pure solvent begins to then move into the solution side containing the solute. As it does so, the solution level rises and the pressure increases. Eventually a balance is achieved and the increased pressure difference on the solution side is the osmotic pressure. The solvent therefore migrates into the solution across the membrane until a sufficient hydrostatic pressure develops to prevent further migration of solvent. The pressure required to prevent migration of the solvent is therefore the osmotic pressure of the solution and is equal to:

$$\Pi = iMRT$$

where R = gas constant per mole
T = temperature in degrees K and
M = concentration of solute (mole/liter)
i = Van't Hoff factor

Note: molarity (M) is used in the osmotic pressure formulation in place of molality as is used for the other respective colligative properties as molarity is temperature dependent and molality is not temperature dependent.

Osmosis and osmotic pressure are also discussed in the context of biology in the following sections: BIO 1.1.1 and 7.5.2.

5.2 Ions in Solution

An important area of solution chemistry involves aqueous solutions. Water has a particular property that causes many substances to split apart into charged species, that is, to dissociate and form ions. Ions that are positively charged are called cations and negatively charged ions are called anions. {Mnemonic: anions are negative ions} As a rule, highly charged species (i.e. $AlPO_4$, Al^{3+}/PO_4^{3-}) have a greater force of attraction thus are much less soluble in water than species with little charge (i.e. NaCl, Na^+/Cl^-). The word "aqueous" simply means containing or dissolved in water. All the following ions can form in water.

Common Anions					
F^-	Fluoride	OH^-	Hydroxide	ClO^-	Hypochlorite
Cl^-	Chloride	NO_3^-	Nitrate	ClO_2^-	Chlorite
Br^-	Bromide	NO_2^-	Nitrite	ClO_3^-	Chlorate
I^-	Iodide	CO_3^{2-}	Carbonate	ClO_4^-	Perchlorate
O^{2-}	Oxide	SO_4^{2-}	Sulfate	SO_3^{2-}	Sulfite
S^{2-}	Sulfide	PO_4^{3-}	Phosphate	CN^-	Cyanide
N^{3-}	Nitride	$CH_3CO_2^-$	Acetate	MnO_4^-	Permanganate

Common Cations			
Na^+	Sodium	H^+	Hydrogen
Li^+	Lithium	Ca^{2+}	Calcium
K^+	Potassium	Mg^{2+}	Magnesium
NH_4^+	Ammonium	Fe^{2+}	Iron (II)
H_3O^+	Hydronium	Fe^{3+}	Iron (III)

Table III.A.5.1: Common Anions and Cations.

The DAT does not normally ask Inorganic Chemistry nomenclature (= *naming*) questions but it may be useful to know the International Union of Pure and Applied Chemistry (IUPAC) standard suffixes: (1) Single atom anions are named with an *-ide suffix* (i.e. fluoride); (2) Oxyanions (*polyatomic* or "many atom" anions containing oxygen) are named with *-ite* or *-ate*, for a lesser or greater quantity of oxygen. For example, NO_2^- is nitrite, while NO_3^- is nitrate. The hypo- and per- prefixes can also indicate less oxygen and more oxygen, respectively (see hypochlorite and perchlorate among the Common Anions in Table III.A.5.1). (3) -ium is a very common ending of atoms in the periodic table (CHM 2.3) and it is also common among cations; (4) Compounds with cations: The name of the compound is simply the cation's name (usually the same as the element's), followed by the anion. For example, NaCl is *sodium chloride* and Ca_3N_2 is *calcium nitride*.

5.3 Solubility

The solubility of any substance is generally defined as the amount of the substance (solute) known to dissolve into a particular amount of solvent at a given temperature.. The solubility of a solute into a solvent is dependent on the entropy change of solubilization as well as the types of intermolecular forces involved (see CHM 4.2 and 5.1). Solvation or dissolution is the process of interaction between solute and solvent molecules. This process occurs when the intermolecular forces between solute and solvent are stronger than those between solute particles themselves. Generally, ionic and polar solutes are soluble in polar solvents and nonpolar solutes are soluble in nonpolar solvents. Consequently, the expression “like dissolves like” is often used for predicting solubility.

In the following section, the definitions of the various solution concentration units are given with examples.

5.3.1 Units of Concentration

There are a number of ways in which solution concentrations may be expressed.

Molarity (*M*): A one-molar solution is defined as one mole of substance in each liter of solution: M = moles of solute/liter of solution (solution = solute + solvent).

For example: If 55.0g of $CaCl_2$ is mixed with water to make 500.0 ml (0.5 L) of solution, what is the molarity (*M*) of the solution?

55.0g of $CaCl_2$ = 55.0 g/110.0 g/mol
= 0.500 mol of $CaCl_2$

Therefore, the Molarity = 0.500 mol $CaCl_2$/0.5L = 1.00 mol $CaCl_2$/L solution

Normality (*N*): A one-normal solution contains one equivalent per liter. An equivalent is a mole multiplied by the number of reacting units for each molecule or atom; the equivalent weight is the formula weight divided by the number of reacting units.

# of Equiv. = mass (in g)/eq. wt. (in g/equiv.)
= Normality (in equiv./liter) × Volume (in liters)

For example, sulfuric acid, H_2SO_4, has two reacting units of protons, that is, there are two equivalents of protons in each mole. Thus:

eq. wt. = 98.08 g/mole/2 equiv./mole
= 49.04 g/equiv.

and the normality of a sulfuric acid solution is twice its molarity. Generally speaking:

$$N = n\,M$$

where *N* is the normality,
M the molarity,
n the number of equivalents per unit formula.

Thus for 1.2 M H_2SO_4:

1.2 moles/L × 2 eq/mole = 2.4 eq/L = 2.4 N.

Molality (*m*): A one-molal solution contains one mole/1000g of solvent.

m = moles of solute/kg of solvent.

For example: If 20.0g of NaOH is mixed into 500.0g (0.50 kg) of water, what is the molality of the solution?

20.0g of NaOH = 20.0 g/40.0 g/mol
= 0.500 mol of NaOH

Therefore, the Molality = 0.500 mol NaOH/0.50 kg water = 1.0 mol NaOH/kg water

Molal concentrations are not temperature-dependent as molar and normal concentrations are (since the solvent volume is temperature-dependent).

Density (ρ): Mass per unit volume at the specified temperature, usually g/ml or g/cm³ at 20°C.

Osmole (*Osm*): The number of moles of particles (molecules or ions) that contribute to the osmotic pressure of a solution.

Osmolarity: A one-osmolar solution is defined as one osmole in each liter of solution. Osmolarity is measured in osmoles/liter of solution (Osm/L).

For example, a 0.001 *M* solution of sodium chloride has an osmolarity of 0.002 Osm/L (twice the molarity), because each NaCl molecule ionizes in water to form two ions (Na^+ and Cl^-) that both contribute to the osmotic pressure.

Osmolality: A one-osmolal solution is defined as one osmole in each kilogram of solution. Osmolality is measured in osmoles/kilogram of solution (Osm/kg).

For example, the osmolality of a 0.01 molal solution of Na_2SO_4 is 0.03 Osm/kg because each molecule of Na_2SO_4 ionizes in water to give three ions (2 Na^+ and 1 SO_4^{2-}) that contribute to the osmotic pressure.

Mole Fraction: Is expressed as a mole ratio as the amount of solute (in moles) divided by the total amount of solvent and solute (in moles).

For example: If 110.0g of $CaCl_2$ is mixed with 72.0g water, what are the mole fractions of the two components?

72.0g of H_2O = 72.0g/18.0 g/mol
= 4 mol H_2O

110.0g of $CaCl_2$ = 110.0g/110 g/mol
= 1 mol $CaCl_2$

Total mol = 4 mol H_2O + 1 mol $CaCl_2$
= 5 mol (H_2O and $CaCl_2$)

Therefore,
X($CaCl_2$) = 1mol $CaCl_2$/5 mol $CaCl_2$ + H_2O = 0.2
and
X(water) = 4 mol H_2O/5 mol H_2O + $CaCl_2$ = 0.8

Dilution: When solvent is added to a solution containing a certain concentration of solute it becomes diluted to produce a solution of a lower solute concentration. The equation representing this is:

$$M_iV_i = M_fV_f$$

Where *M* = molarity and
V = volume with the initial (*i*) and final (*f*) concentrations being measured.

For example: How many ml of a 10.0 mol/L NaOH solution is needed to prepare 500 ml of a 2.00 mol/L NaOH solution?

Given: $M_iV_i = M_fV_f$, where M_i = 10.0 mol/L, M_f = 2.00 mol/L and V_f = 500 ml. Therefore, rearranging the equation gives $V_i = M_f \times V_f/Mi$ and so V_i = (2.00 mol/L)(0.5 L)/(10.0 moL) = 100 mL.

5.3.2 Solubility Product Constant, the Equilibrium Expression

Any solute that dissolves in water to give a solution that contains ions, and thus can conduct electricity, is an *electrolyte*. The solid (s) that dissociates into separate ions surrounded by water is hydrated, thus the ions are aqueous (*aq*).

If dissociation is extensive and irreversible, we have a strong electrolyte:

$$NaCl\ (s) \rightarrow Na^+\ (aq) + Cl^-\ (aq)$$

If dissociation is incomplete and reversible, we have a weak electrolyte:

$$CH_3COOH\ (aq) \rightleftharpoons CH_3COO^-\ (aq) + H^+\ (aq)$$

If dissociation does not occur, we have a nonelectrolyte:

$C_6H_{12}O_6$ (aq) or glucose sugar does NOT dissociate.

Strong electrolytes: salts (NaCl), strong acids (HCl), strong bases (NaOH).

Weak electrolytes: weak acids (CH_3COOH), weak bases (NH_3), complexes ($Fe[CN]_6$), tap water, certain soluble organic compounds, highly charged species (CHM 5.2; $AlPO_4$, $BaSO_4$, exception: AgCl as it is a precipitate in aqueous solutions).

Nonelectrolytes: deionized water, soluble organic compounds (sugars).

The solubility of a solute substance is the maximum amount of solute that can be dissolved in an appropriate solvent at a particular temperature. It can be expressed in units of concentration such as molarity, molality and so on (see CHM 5.3.1). When a maximum amount of solute has been dissolved, the solution is in equilibrium and is said to be saturated. As temperature increases, the solubility of most salts generally increases. However, it is the opposite for gases, as the solubility of gases is known to generally decrease as temperature increases.

When substances have limited solubility and their solubility is exceeded, the ions of the dissolved portion exist in equilibrium with the solid material. When a compound is referred to as insoluble, it is not completely insoluble, but is slightly soluble.

For example, if solid AgCl is added to water, a small portion will dissolve:

$$AgCl\ (s) \rightleftharpoons Ag^+\ (aq) + Cl^-\ (aq)$$

The precipitate will have a definite solubility (i.e. a definite amount in g/liter) or molar solubility (in moles/ liter) that will dissolve at a given temperature.

An overall equilibrium constant can be written for the preceding equilibrium, called the solubility product, K_{sp}, given by the following equilibrium expression:

$$K_{sp} = [Ag^+][Cl^-]$$

The preceding relationship holds regardless of the presence of any undissociated intermediate. In general, each concentration must be raised to the power of that ion's coefficient in the dissolving equation (in our example = 1). A different example would be Ag_2S which would have the following solubility product expression: $K_{sp} = [Ag^+]^2[S^{2-}]$. The calculation of molar solubility s in mol/L for AgCl would simply be: $K_{sp} = [s][s] = s^2$. On the other hand, the expression for Ag_2S would become: $K_{sp} = [2s]^2[s] = 4s^3$.

Knowing K_{sp} at a specified temperature, the molar solubility of compounds can be calculated under various conditions. The amount of slightly soluble salt that dissolves does not depend on the amount of the solid in equilibrium with the solution, as long as there is enough to saturate the solution. Rather, it depends on the volume of solvent. {Note: a low K_{sp} value means little product therefore low solubility and vice-versa}.

The following are examples of problems on solubility product constant and solubility calculations given one or the other.

Another example: The molar solubility of $PbCl_2$ in an aqueous solution is 0.0159 M. What is the K_{sp} for $PbCl_2$?

$$PbCl_2(s) \rightleftharpoons Pb^{2+}(aq) + 2Cl^-(aq)$$

$$K_{sp} = [Pb^{2+}][Cl^-]^2$$

For every mol of $PbCl_2$ that dissociates, one mol of Pb^{2+} and two mol of Cl^- are produced. Since the molar solubility is 0.0159M, $[Pb^{2+}] = 0.0159M$ and $[Cl^-] = 0.0159 \times 2 = 0.0318M$

Therefore,

$$K_{sp} = [0.0159][0.0318]^2 = 1.61 \times 10^{-5}$$

Another example: What are the concentrations of each of the ions in a saturated solution of Ag_2CrO_4 given that solubility product constant K_{sp} is 1.1×10^{-12}?

$$Ag_2CrO_4(s) \rightleftharpoons 2Ag^+(aq) + CrO_4^{2-}(aq)$$

$$K_{sp} = [Ag^+]^2 [CrO_4^{2-}]$$

For every Ag_2CrO_4 that dissociates, two mol of Ag^+ ion and one mol of CrO_4^{2-} ion are produced.

Let x = concentration of CrO_4^{2-}, then 2x = concentration of Ag^+

Therefore,

$$K_{sp} = [2x]^2 [x]$$

$$1.1 \times 10^{-12} = [2x]^2 [x]$$

solving for x gives; $x = 6.50 \times 10^{-5}$ M

so,

$$[Ag^+] = 1.3 \times 10^{-4} \text{ M and}$$

$$[CrO_4^{2-}] = 6.5 \times 10^{-5} \text{ M}$$

5.3.3 Common-ion Effect on Solubility

If there is an excess of one ion over the other, the concentration of the other is suppressed. This is called the common ion effect. The solubility of the precipitate is decreased and the concentration can still be calculated from the K_{sp}.

For example, Cl^- ion can be precipitated out of a solution of AgCl by adding a slight excess of $AgNO_3$. If a stoichiometric amount of $AgNO_3$ is added, $[Ag^+] = [Cl^-]$. If excess $AgNO_3$ is added, $[Ag^+] > [Cl^-]$ but K_{sp} remains constant. Therefore, $[Cl^-]$ decreases if $[Ag^+]$ is increased. Because the K_{sp} product always holds, precipitation will not take place unless the product of $[Ag^+]$ and $[Cl^-]$ exceeds the K_{sp}. If the product is just equal to K_{sp}, all the Ag^+ and Cl^- ions would remain in solution. Thus, the solubility of an ionic compound in solution containing a common ion is decreased in comparison to the same compound's solubility in water. As another example, the solubility of CaF_2 in water at 25°C would be much larger in comparison to the solubility of the same CaF_2 compound in a solution containing a common ion such as NaF. This decrease in solubility of CaF_2 in a solution containing NaF would be due to the common fluoride (F^-) ion effect on the solubility of CaF_2.

5.3.4 Solubility Product Constant (K_{sp}) vs. Reaction Quotient (Q_{sp})

Solubility product constants are used to describe saturated solutions of ionic compounds of relatively low solubility. A saturated solution is in a state of dynamic equilibrium described by the equilibrium constant (K_{sp}).

$$M_xA_y(s) \leftrightarrow x\,M^{y+}(aq) + y\,A^{x-}(aq)$$

The solubility product constant $K_{sp} = [M^{y+}]^x[A^{x-}]^y$ in a solution at equilibrium (saturated solution). Note that "M" is meant to symbolize the metal and "A" represents the anion.

A reaction quotient is defined by the same formula: $Q_{sp} = [M^{y+}]^x\,[A^{x-}]^y$ in a solution at any point, not just equilibrium.

K_{sp} therefore represents the ion product at equilibrium while Q_{sp} represents the ion product at any point, not just at equilibrium; and in fact, equilibrium is just a special case of the reaction coefficient as we will see below:

If $Q_{sp} < K_{sp}$, the solution is unsaturated and no precipitate will form.

If $Q_{sp} = K_{sp}$, the solution is saturated and at equilibrium.

If $Q_{sp} > K_{sp}$, the solution is supersaturated and unstable. A solid salt will precipitate until ion product once again equals to K_{sp}.

5.3.5 Solubility Rules

The chemistry of aqueous solutions is such that solubility rules can be established:

1. All salts of alkali metals are soluble.

2. All salts of the ammonium ion are soluble.

3. All chlorides, bromides and iodides are water soluble, with the exception of Ag^{+}, Pb^{2+}, and Hg_2^{2+}.

4. All salts of the sulfate ion (SO_4^{2-}) are water soluble with the exception of Ca^{2+}, Sr^{2+}, Ba^{2+}, and Pb^{2+}.

5. All metal oxides are insoluble with the exception of the alkali metals and CaO, SrO and BaO.

6. All hydroxides are insoluble with the exception of the alkali metals and Ca^{2+}, Sr^{2+}, Ba^{2+}

7. All carbonates (CO_3^{2-}), phosphates (PO_4^{3-}), sulfides (S^{2-}) and sulfites (SO_3^{2-}) are insoluble, with the exception of the alkali metals and ammonium.

GOLD STANDARD WARM-UP EXERCISES

CHAPTER 5: Solution Chemistry

1) Consider the diagram below. At constant temperature, what is the effect of an increase in pressure on a liquid–gas equilibrium mixture?

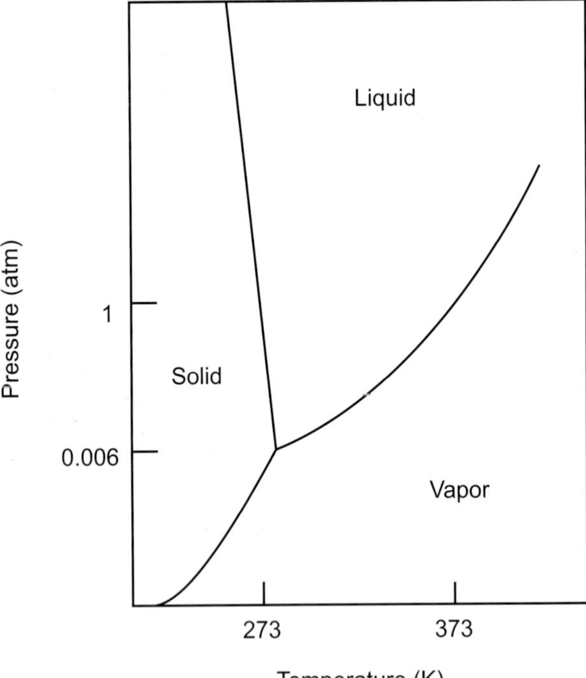

A. Change in the slope of the solid–liquid equilibrium
B. Increase in amount of vapor present
C. Increase in amount of solid present
D. Increase in amount of liquid present

2) What was the concentration of sodium sulfate in solution if the sodium ion concentration happens to be 0.02 M?

A. 0.02 M
B. 0.01 M
C. 0.04 M
D. 0.03 M

3) Two moles of sodium chloride, magnesium chloride and aluminium chloride were added to one liter of water in different beakers. Which solution will have the greatest osmolarity assuming that all of the salts are soluble in water?

A. All the solutions will have the same osmolarity.
B. The sodium chloride solution.
C. The magnesium chloride solution.
D. The aluminium chloride solution.

4) The molarity of a dilute solution is approximately equal to its molality when which of the following is true?

A. Under any circumstance
B. When the volume of the solvent in cm^{-3} is equal to its mass in grams
C. When the temperature of the solute is 300 K (i.e. room temperature)
D. When the number of moles of solute in solution is less than one

5) A solution of the sparingly soluble salt $SrCO_3$ in water boils at a higher temperature than pure water. Why is this?

A. $SrCO_3$ increases the density of water.
B. $SrCO_3$ decreases the vapor pressure of the water.
C. $SrCO_3$ has a low solubility in water.
D. $SrCO_3$ decreases the surface tension of the water.

6) What do you expect to happen to the melting point of solid water (ice) if an increased external pressure is applied to the system?

A. The melting point would increase.
B. The melting point would decrease.
C. The melting point would remain at the same value.
D. The direction of change in the value of the

melting point depends on the magnitude of the applied pressure.

7) What is the K_{sp} expression for PbS?

A. $[Pb^{2+}]/[S^{2-}]$
B. $[Pb^{2+}]^2/[S^{2-}]$
C. $[Pb^{2+}][S^{2-}]$
D. $[Pb^{2+}]^2[S^{2-}]$

8) The K_{sp} expression for Bi_2S_3 is:

A. $[Bi_2^{3+}][S_3^{2-}]$
B. $[Bi^{3+}][S^{2-}]$
C. $[Bi^{3+}]^2[S^{2-}]^3$
D. $[2Bi^{3+}]^3[3S^{2-}]^2$

9) Given the solubility of $MgCO_3$ (1.30×10^{-3} mol L^{-1} in H_2O), calculate the solubility product.

A. 1.3×10^{-4}
B. 2.6×10^{-4}
C. 1.7×10^{-6}
D. 6.7×10^{-8}

10) $Ca(OH)_2$ has approximately the same K_{sp} as $CaSO_4$. Which of them has the greater solubility in terms of mol L^{-1}?

A. They both have the same solubility.
B. $Ca(OH)_2$
C. $CaSO_4$
D. It depends on the temperature at the time.

11) A beaker contains equal concentrations of Mn^{2+} and Ni^{2+} ions. It is found that NiS can be selectively precipitated by adding a certain quantity of K_2S to the beaker. If the K_{sp} of NiS is 3.2×10^{-19}, the K_{sp} of MnS must be:

A. less than 3.2×10^{-19}.
B. greater than 3.2×10^{-19}.
C. equal to 3.2×10^{-19}.
D. cannot be determined with the information provided.

12) MgF_2(s) is added to a beaker of water until there is an amount at the bottom that will not dissolve. What is the concentration of F^-?

(The K_{sp} of MgF_2 is 6.5×10^{-9})

A. 2.4×10^{-3}M
B. 1.6×10^{-9}M
C. 2.4×10^{-4}M
D. 1.2×10^{-3}M

13) What is the concentration of F^- in the solution of the preceding question if $MgCl_2$ is added to the solution such that the final concentration of Mg^{2+} becomes 0.1 M?

A. 0.05 M
B. 5.0×10^{-4} M
C. 5.0×10^{-3} M
D. 2.5×10^{-4} M

14) A student adds magnesium sulfate to a solution that is 10^{-4} M in each of the ions F^- and CO_3^{2-} until the Mg^{2+} concentration is also 10^{-4} M. Which of the following salts will precipitate from the final mixture?

(Data: K_{sp} $MgF_2 = 10^{-8}$; K_{sp} $MgCO_3 = 10^{-5}$)

A. MgF_2 only
B. $MgCO_3$ only
C. Neither MgF_2 nor $MgCO_3$
D. Both MgF_2 and $MgCO_3$

15) Capillaries are much more permeable than most semipermeable membranes. The only plasma constituents they do not allow through them are proteins. Given that the concentration of protein in plasma is roughly 1.5 mmol/L and the concentration of all solutes in plasma is roughly 290 mmol/L, what is the oncotic pressure (i.e. osmotic pressure exerted by proteins) of plasma at 37 °C as far as capillaries are concerned? (Assume the gas constant is 60 L-torr/K-mol.)

A. 43 mmHg
B. 35 mmHg
C. 5400 mmHg
D. 28 mmHg

16) How much ethylene glycol ($C_2H_6O_2$) must be added to 1 kg of water to depress the freezing point to –40 °C?

Assume the K_f of water is 1.9 K/m.

A. 0.9 kg
B. 0.87 kg
C. 130 g
D. 1.3 kg

GS ANSWER KEY

Chapter 5

#	Answer	*Cross-Reference*	#	Answer	*Cross-Reference*
1.	**D**	**CHM 4.3.3, 5.1.2**	**9.**	**C**	**CHM 5.3.2**
2.	**B**	**CHM 1.5, 5.2**	**10.**	**B**	**CHM 5.3.2**
3.	**D**	**CHM 3.1, 5.2**	**11.**	**B**	**CHM 5.3.2, 5.3.3**
4.	**B**	**CHM 5.3.1**	**12.**	**A**	**CHM 5.3.2, 5.3.3**
5.	**B**	**CHM 5.1.1/2**	**13.**	**D**	**CHM 5.3.2, 5.3.3**
6.	**B**	**CHM 5.1.2**	**14.**	**C**	**CHM 5.3.2, 5.3.3**
7.	**C**	**CHM 5.3.2**	**15.**	**D**	**CHM 5.1.3**
8.	**C**	**CHM 5.3.2**	**16.**	**D**	**CHM 5.1.2**

* Explanations can be found at the back of the book.

Go online to DAT-prep.com for additional chapter review Q&A and forum.

ACIDS AND BASES

Chapter 6

Memorize	Understand	Importance
* Define: Bronsted acid, base, pH * Examples of strong/weak acids/bases * K_w at STP, neutral H_2O pH, conjugate acid/base, zwitterions * Equations: K_a, K_b, pK_a, pK_b, K_w, pH, pOH * Equivalence point, indicator, rules of logarithms	* Calculation of K_a, K_b, pK_a, pK_b, K_w, pH, pOH * Calculations involving strong/weak acids/bases * Salts of weak acids/bases, buffers; indicators * Acid-Base titration/curve, redox titration	**2 to 4 out of the 30 Gen CHM** DAT questions are based on content in this chapter (in our estimation). * Note that between 50% and 85% of the questions in DAT General Chemistry are based on content from 6 chapters: 1, 2, 4, 5, 6 and 9.

DAT-Prep.com

Introduction

Acids are compounds that, when dissolved in water, give a solution with a hydrogen ion concentration greater than that of pure water. Acids turn litmus paper (an indicator) red. Examples include acetic acid (in vinegar) and sulfuric acid (in car batteries). Bases may have $[H^+]$ less than pure water and turn litmus blue. Examples include sodium hydroxide (= lye, caustic soda) and ammonia (used in many cleaning products).

Additional Resources

Free Online Forum

Video: Online or DVD

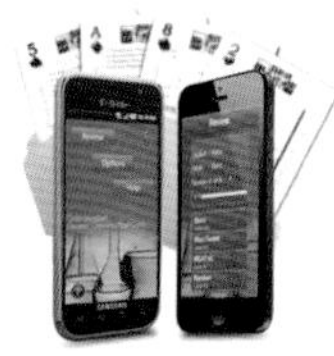

Flashcards

6.1 Acids

A useful definition is given by Bronsted and Lowry: an acid is a proton (i.e. hydrogen ion) donor (cf. Lewis acids and bases, *see* CHM 3.4). A substance such as HF is an acid because it can donate a proton to a substance capable of accepting it. In aqueous solution, water is always available as a proton acceptor, so that the ionization of an acid, HA, can be written as:

$$HA + H_2O \rightleftharpoons H_3O^+ + A^-$$

or:

$$HA \rightleftharpoons H^+ + A^-$$

The equilibrium constant is:

$$K_a = [H^+][A^-]/[HA]$$

Examples of ionization of acids are:

$$HCl \rightleftharpoons H^+ + Cl^- \qquad K_a = \text{infinity}$$

$$HF \rightleftharpoons H^+ + F^- \qquad K_a = 6.7 \times 10^{-4}$$

$$HCN \rightleftharpoons H^+ + CN^- \qquad K_a = 7.2 \times 10^{-10}$$

Acids are generally divided into two categories known as binary acids and oxyacids. The first category is that of acids composed of hydrogen and a nonmetal such as chlorine (HCl). For the halogen containing binary acids, the acid strength increases as a function of the halogen size. Moreover, as the halogen size increases, its bond length increases while its bond strength decreases and as such, its acidity increases. Thus, the acidity of HI > HBr > HCl > HF.

The second category of acids form from oxyanions (anions containing a nonmetal and oxygen such as the hydroxide or nitrate ions, see CHM 5.2) are known as the oxyacids. The oxyacids contain a hydrogen atom covalently bonded to an oxygen atom which is bonded to another central atom X (H-O-X-etc). The more oxygen atoms that are bounded to the central atom, the more acidic the oxyacids. Some examples of oxyacids are listed in Table III.A.6.1.

Note: a diprotic acid (*two protons*, i.e. H_2SO_4) would have K_a values for each of its two ionizable protons: K_{a1} for the first and K_{a2} for the second. Diprotic or any polyprotic acids are known to ionize in successive steps in which each of the steps contain their own dissociation or ionization acid constant, K_a. The first ionization constant (K_{a1}) is typically much larger than the subsequent ionization constants ($K_{a1} > K_{a2} > K_{a3}$, etc...).

Table III.A.6.1: Examples of strong and weak acids.

STRONG	WEAK	STRONG	WEAK
Perchloric $HClO_4$ Chloric $HClO_3$ Nitric HNO_3 Hydrochloric HCl	Hydrocyanic HCN Hypochlorous HClO Nitrous HNO_2 Hydrofluoric HF	Sulfuric H_2SO_4 Hydrobromic HBr Hydriodic HI Hydronium Ion H_3O^+	Sulfurous H_2SO_3 Hydrogen Sulfide H_2S Phosphoric H_3PO_4 Benzoic, Acetic and other Carboxylic acids

6.2 Bases

A base is defined as a proton acceptor. In aqueous solution, water is always available to donate a proton to a base, so the ionization of a base B, can be written as:

$$B + H_2O \rightleftharpoons HB^+ + OH^-$$

The equilibrium constant is:

$$K_b = [HB^+][OH^-]/[B]$$

Examples of ionization of bases are:

$$CN^- + H_2O \rightleftharpoons HCN + OH^- \quad K_b = 1.4 \times 10^{-5}$$

$$NH_3 + H_2O \rightleftharpoons NH_4^+ + OH^- \quad K_b = 1.8 \times 10^{-5}$$

$$F^- + H_2O \rightleftharpoons HF + OH^- \quad K_b = 1.5 \times 10^{-11}$$

Strong bases include any hydroxide of the group 1A metals. The most common weak bases are ammonia and any organic amine.

6.3 Conjugate Acid-Base Pairs

The strength of an acid or base is related to the extent that the dissociation proceeds to the right, or to the magnitude of K_a or K_b; the larger the dissociation constant, the stronger the acid or the base. From the preceding K_a values, we see that HCl is the strongest acid (almost 100% ionized), followed by HF and HCN. From the K_b's given, NH_3 is the strongest base listed, followed by CN^- and F^-. Clearly, when an acid ionizes, it produces a base. The acid, HA, and the base produced when it ionizes, A^-, are called a conjugate acid-base pair, so that the couples HF/F^- and HCN/CN^- are conjugate acids and bases.

Thus, an acid that has donated a proton becomes a conjugate base and a base that has accepted a proton becomes a conjugate acid of that base. For example, HCO_3^-/CO_3^{2-} are a conjugate acid/base pair, wherein HCO_3^- is the acid and CO_3^{2-} is the conjugate base. Both dissociate partially in water and reach equilibrium.

A strong acid (HCl) has a weak conjugate base (Cl^-) and a strong base (NaOH) has a weak conjugate acid (OH^-). Whereas, a weak acid (CH_3COOH) has a strong conjugate base (CH_3COO^-) and a weak base (NH_3) has a related strong conjugate acid (NH_4^+).

Another example of conjugate acid-base pairs is amino acids. Amino acids bear at least 2 ionizable weak acid groups, a carboxyl (–COOH) and an amino ($-NH_3^+$) which act as follows:

$$R\text{–}COOH \rightleftharpoons R\text{–}COO^- + H^+$$

$$R\text{–}NH_3^+ \rightleftharpoons R\text{–}NH_2 + H^+$$

R–COO⁻ and R–NH₂ are the conjugate bases (i.e. proton acceptors) of the corresponding acids. The carboxyl group is thousands of times more acidic than the amino group. Thus in blood plasma (pH ≈ 7.4) the predominant forms are the carboxylate anions (R–COO⁻) and the protonated amino group ($R–NH_3^+$). This form is called a *zwitterion* as demonstrated by the amino acid alanine at a pH near 7:

CH_3-CH-COO^- (with NH_3^+ on the CH)

Alanine

The zwitterion bears no net charge.

6.4 Water Dissociation

Water itself can ionize:

$$H_2O + H_2O \rightleftharpoons H_3O^+ + OH^-$$

or:

$$H_2O \rightleftharpoons H^+ + OH^-$$

At STP, $K_w = [H^+][OH^-] = 1.0 \times 10^{-14}$ = ion product constant for water. It increases with temperature and in a neutral solution, $[H^+] = [OH^-] = 10^{-7}$ M. Note that $[H_2O]$ is not included in the equilibrium expression because it is a pure liquid and it is a large constant ($[H_2O]$ is incorporated in K_w).

6.5 The pH Scale

The pH of a solution is a convenient way of expressing the concentration of hydrogen ions [H⁺] in solution, to avoid the use of large negative powers of 10. It is defined as:

$$pH = -\log_{10}[H^+]$$

Thus, the pH of a neutral solution of pure water where $[H^+] = 10^{-7}$ is 7.

A similar definition is used for the hydroxyl ion concentration:

$$pOH = -\log_{10}[OH^-]$$

Since, $K_w = [H^+][OH^-]$

And so, $1.0 \times 10^{-14} = [H^+][OH^-]$

And taking the –log of both sides gives $-\log[1.0 \times 10^{-14}] = -\log[H^+][OH^-]$

So, $14.0 = -\log[H^+] + -\log[OH^-]$

Therefore, 14.0 = pH + pOH

Finally, at 25°C, pH + pOH = 14.0

A pH of 7 is neutral. Values of pH that are greater than 7 are alkaline (basic) and values that are lower are acidic. The pH can be measured precisely with a pH meter (quantitative) or globally with an indicator which will have a different color over different pH ranges (qualitative). For example, *litmus paper* (very common) becomes blue in basic solutions and red in acidic solutions; whereas, *phenolphthalein* is colorless in acid and pink in base.

We will see in CHM 6.9 that a weak acid or base can serve as a visual (qualitative) indicator of a pH range. Usually, only a small quantity (i.e. drops) of the indicator is added to the solution as to minimize the risk of any side reactions.

6.5.1 Properties of Logarithms

Many DAT problems every year rely on a basic understanding of logarithms for pH problems, rate law (CHM 9.10) or a 'random' Nernst equation question (BIO 5 Appendix). Here are the rules you must know:

1) $\log_a a = 1$
2) $\log_a M^k = k \log_a M$
3) $\log_a(MN) = \log_a M + \log_a N$
4) $\log_a(M/N) = \log_a M - \log_a N$
5) $10^{\log_{10} M} = M$

For example, let us calculate the pH of 0.001 M HCl. Since HCl is a strong acid, it will completely dissociate into H^+ and Cl^-, thus :

$$[H^+] = 0.001$$
$$-\log[H^+] = -\log(0.001)$$
$$pH = -\log(10^{-3})$$
$$pH = 3 \log 10 \quad \text{(rule \#2)}$$
$$pH = 3 \quad \text{(rule \#1, a = 10)}$$

6.6 Weak Acids and Bases

Weak acids (HA) and bases (B) partially dissociate in aqueous solutions reaching equilibrium following their dissociation. The following is the generic reaction of any weak acid (HA) dissociation in an aqueous solution.

$$HA + H_2O \rightleftharpoons A^- + H_3O^+$$

Now let us begin by taking a closer look at the development of the acid and base equilibrium constants. Like all equilibrium, acid/base dissociation will have a particular equilibrium constant (K_a or K_b) which will determine the extent of the dissociation (CHM 6.3). Thus, from the preceding equation for any generic acid (HA), the acid dissociation constant $K = [H_3O^+][A^-]/[H_2O][HA]$.

Very little water actually reacts and thus the concentration of water during the reaction is constant and can therefore be excluded from the expression for K. Therefore, this gives rise to the acid dissociation constant known as K_a.

Where, $K_a = K[H_2O] = [H_3O^+][A^-]/[HA]$

Likewise for a weak base dissociation in equilibrium,

$$B + H_2O \rightleftharpoons OH^- + BH^+$$

This gives rise to the base dissociation constant known as K_b.

Where, $K_b = K[H_2O] = [OH^-][BH^+]/[B]$

Weak acids and bases are only partially ionized. The ionization constant can be used to calculate the amount ionized, and from this, the pH.

Since weak acids are not completely dissociated, one needs to find the $[H^+]$ from the acid dissociation and then use a method known in most textbooks as the "ICE method". ICE is an acronym used in which, I = Initial acid $[H^+]$ concentration, C = Change in acid $[H^+]$ concentration and E = acid $[H^+]$ concentration at equilibrium. Thus, the acid concentration $[H^+]$ also represented as (x) at equilibrium is then used to calculate the pH. NOTE: the equilibrium concentration x is usually very small as the acid (or base) is weak and partially dissociated (or ionized). The following is an example of the application of the ICE method in solving for the $[H^+] = x$ at equilibrium and subsequently determining the pH of a weak acid solution.

Example: Calculate the pH and pOH of a 10^{-2} M solution of acetic acid (HOAc). K_a of acetic acid at 25°C = 1.75×10^{-5}.

$$HOAc \rightleftharpoons H^+ + OAc^-$$

The concentrations are:

	[HOAc]	$[H^+]$	$[OAc^-]$
Initial	10^{-2}	0	0
Change	$-x$	$+x$	$+x$
Equilibrium	$10^{-2} - x$	x	x

$$K_a = [H^+][OAc^-]/[HOAc] = 1.75 \times 10^{-5}$$
$$= (x)(x)/(10^{-2} - x)$$

The solution is a quadratic equation which may be simplified if less than 5% of the acid is ionized by neglecting x compared to the concentration (10^{-2} M in this case). We then have:

$$x^2/10^{-2} = 1.75 \times 10^{-5}$$
$$x = 4.18 \times 10^{-4} = [H^+]$$

And $\quad pH = -\log(4.18 \times 10^{-4}) = 3.38$

$$pOH = 14.00 - 3.38 = 10.62$$

To confirm the 5% criterion one needs to calculate as follows: $(4.18 \times 10^{-4})/(1.00 \times 10^{-2}) \times 100 = 4.18\%$ which is less than 5% and therefore justifies the usage of the 5% criterion.

Similar calculations hold for weak bases. Note that all the preceding can be estimated without a calculator once you know the squares of all numbers between 1 and 15. The root of 1.69 (a fair estimate of 1.75) is thus 1.3 (also *see* CHM 6.6.1 to see how to estimate an answer without a calculator).

6.6.1 Determining pH with the Quadratic Formula

If you need to calculate pH on the DAT, it is very unlikely that you would need to use the quadratic equation; however, you are expected to be familiar with the different ways to calculate pH and that is why it is presented here.

The solutions of the quadratic equation

$$ax^2 + bx + c = 0$$

are given by the formula (QR 4.6, 4.6.2)

$$x = [-b \pm (b^2 - 4ac)^{1/2}]/2a$$

The problem in CHM 6.6 can be reduced to

$$K_a = (x)(x)/(10^{-2} - x) = 1.75 \times 10^{-5}$$

or

$$x^2 + (1.75 \times 10^{-5})X + (-1.75 \times 10^{-7}) = 0$$

Using the quadratic equation where $a = 1$, $b = 1.75 \times 10^{-5}$ and $c = -1.75 \times 10^{-7}$, and doing the appropriate multiplications we get:

$$X = [-1.75 \times 10^{-5} \pm (3.06 \times 10^{-10} + 7.0 \times 10^{-7})^{1/2}]/2$$

Thus $x = [-1.75 \times 10^{-5} \pm (7.00 \times 10^{-7})^{1/2}]/2$
$= [-1.75 \times 10^{-5} \pm 8.37 \times 10^{-4}]/2$

Hence the two possible solutions are

$$X = [-1.75 \times 10^{-5} - 8.37 \times 10^{-4}]/2 = -4.27 \times 10^{-4}$$

Or

$$X = = [-1.75 \times 10^{-5} + 8.37 \times 10^{-4}]/2$$
$$= 4.10 \times 10^{-4}$$

The first solution is a negative number which is physically impossible for $[H^+]$, therefore $pH = -\log(4.10 \times 10^{-4}) = 3.39$

Our estimate in CHM 6.6 (pH = 3.38) was valid as it is less than 1% different from the more precise calculation using the quadratic formula.

Given a multiple choice question with the following choices: 2.5, 3.4, 4.3 and 6.8 – the answer can be easily deduced.

$$-\log (4.10 \times 10^{-4}) = -\log 4.10 - \log 10^{-4}$$
$$= 4 - \log 4.10$$

however

$$0 = \log 10^0 = \log 1 < \log 4.10 << \log 10 = 1$$

Thus a number slightly greater than 0 but significantly less than 1 is substracted from 4. The answer could only be 3.4.

6.7 Salts of Weak Acids and Bases

A *salt* is an ionic compound in which the anion is not OH^- or O^{2-} and the cation is not H^+.

Acids and bases react with each other, forming a salt and water in a reaction known as a neutralization reaction. Salts are compounds composed of both a cation and anion (i.e. Na_2SO_4). As salts contain both a cation and anion, salts may therefore form acidic, basic or neutral solutions when dissolved into water. Hence, a salt can react with water to give back an acid or base in a reaction known as salt hydrolysis and thus affect the solution's pH. Moreover, a salt composed of an anion from a weak acid (CH_3COO^-) and a cation from a strong base (Na^+) dissociates and reacts in water to give rise to OH^- ions (a basic solution). Whereas, a salt composed of an anion from a strong acid (Cl^-) and a cation from a weak base (NH_4^+) dissociates and reacts in water to give rise to H^+ (an acidic solution).

Examples:

NaClO dissociates in water:

$$ClO^- + H_2O \rightleftharpoons HClO + OH^- \text{ (Basic)}$$

NH_4NO_3 dissociates in water:

$$NH_4^+ + H_2O \rightleftharpoons H_3O^+ + NH_3 \text{ (Acidic)}$$

The salt of a weak acid is a Bronsted base, which will accept protons. For example,

$$Na^+ OAc^- + H_2O \rightleftharpoons HOAc + Na^+ OH^-$$

The HOAc here is undissociated and therefore does not contribute to the pH. Because it hydrolyzes, sodium acetate is a weak base (the conjugate base of acetic acid). The ionization constant is equal to the basicity constant of the salt. The weaker the conjugate acid, the stronger the conjugate base, that is, the more strongly the salt will combine with a proton.

$$K_H = K_b = [HOAc][OH^-]/[OAc^-]$$

K_H is the hydrolysis constant of the salt. The product of K_a of any weak acid and K_b of its conjugate base is always equal to K_w.

$$K_a \times K_b = K_w$$

For any salt of a weak acid, HA, that ionizes in water:

$$A^- + H_2O \rightleftharpoons HA + OH^-$$
$$[HA][OH^-]/[A^-] = K_w/K_a.$$

The pH of such a salt is calculated in the same manner as for any other weak base.

Similar equations are derived for the salts of weak bases. They hydrolyze in water as follows:

$$BH^+ + H_2O \rightleftharpoons B + H_3O^+$$

B is undissociated and does not contribute to the pH.

$$K_H = K_a = [B][H_3O^+]/[BH^+]$$

And

$$[B][H_3O^+]/[BH^+] = K_w/K_b.$$

In conclusion, there are four types of salts formed based on the reacting acid and base strengths as follows:

(1) Strong acid + strong base:

$$HCl(aq) + NaOH(aq) \rightleftharpoons NaCl(aq) + H_2O(l)$$

Salts in which the cation and anion are both conjugates of a strong base and a strong acid form neutral solutions.

(2) Strong acid + weak base:

$$HCl(aq) + NH_3(aq) \rightleftharpoons NH_4Cl\ (aq)$$

Salts that are formed based on a strong acid reacting with a weak base form acidic solutions.

(3) Weak acid + strong base:

$$HOAc(aq) + NaOH(aq) \rightleftharpoons NaOAc(aq) + H_2O(l)$$

(note: HOAc = acetic acid = CH_3COOH)

A salt in which the cation is the counterion of a strong base and the anion is the conjugate base of a weak acid results in the formation of basic solutions.

(4) Weak acid + weak base:

$$HOAc(aq) + NH_3(aq) \rightleftharpoons NH_4OAc(aq)$$

A salt in which the cation is a conjugate acid of a weak base and the anion is the anion of a weak acid will form a solution in which the pH will be dependent on the relative strengths of the acid and base.

6.8 Buffers

A buffer is defined as a solution that resists change in pH when a small amount of an acid or base is added or when a solution is diluted. A buffer solution consists of a mixture of a weak acid and its salt or of a weak base and its salt.

For example, consider the acetic acid-acetate buffer. The acid equilibrium that governs this system is:

$$HOAc \rightleftharpoons H^+ + OAc^-$$

Along with the acid equilibrium component of the buffer solution as shown above, the buffer solution must also contain a significant amount of the conjugate base of the acid as a salt. The following equation depicts the conjugate base salt dissociation of the acetic acid-acetate buffer solution:

$$NaOAc \rightarrow Na^+ + OAc^-.$$

Thus, the buffer is made up of two components (1) a weak acid (HOAc) and (2) the conjugate base of the weak acid as a salt (NaAOc) so that both components are part of the buffer system in apt concentrations to make for a fully functional buffer.

When a small amount of NaOH base is added to the acetic acid/acetate buffer solution, the OH^- ions from the base will react with the free H^+ ions present in the buffer solution from the acetic acid dissociation. This will shift the equilibrium of the buffer toward the right which means more dissociation of the acid (HOAc). Thus, an increase in $[OH^-]$ from the addition of base to the buffer solution does not change pH significantly due to the reaction of the basic OH^- ions with the free protons (H^+) in solution.

The resistance to pH change is also noted with the addition of an acid (H^+) to the acetic acid/acetate buffer solution. The addition of acidic H^+ from the acid will react with the acetate ions ($HOAc^-$) from the salt dissociation of the buffer and this will also allow for the buffering capacity of the solution. Thus, due to the presence of both a weak acid and a conjugate base from the salt (or common ion), the buffer solution thus is known to maintain a pH within a certain range known as the buffering capacity.

Buffers must contain a significant amount of both a weak acid or weak base and its conjugate salts. A strong acid or strong base would not have any buffering capacity or effect within a buffer system as the dissociation would be irreversible and so the buffer capacity would not be present. In addition, a weak acid or base in itself would also not be able to work as a buffer system regardless of the fact that there is the presence of their conjugates as the concentrations of the conjugate acid or base from the weak acids or bases would not be sufficient to neutralize the addition of acids (H^+) or bases (OH^-). Thus, buffers require the addition of a conjugate acid or base as a salt to the weak acid or base component so to increase the salt concentration of the buffer solution.

If we were to add acetate ions into the system (i.e. from the salt), the H^+ ion concentration is no longer equal to the acetate ion concentration. The hydrogen ion concentration is:

$$[H^+] = K_a\ ([HOAc]/[OAc^-])$$

Taking the negative logarithm of each side, where $-\log K_a = pK_a$, yields:

$$pH = pK_a - \log\ ([HOAc]/[OAc^-])$$

or

$$pH = pK_a + \log([OAc^-]/[HOAc])$$

This equation is referred to as the Henderson-Hasselbach equation. It is useful for calculating the pH of a weak acid solution containing its salt. A general form can be written for a weak acid, HA, that dissociates into its salt, A^- and H^+:

$$HA \rightleftharpoons H^+ + A^-$$

$$pH = pK_a + \log([salt]/[acid])$$

The buffering capacity of the solution is determined by the concentrations of HA and A^-. The higher their concentrations, the more acid or base the solution can tolerate. The buffering capacity is also governed by the ratios of HA to A^-. It is maximum when the ratio is equal to 1, i.e. when $pH = pK_a$.

Similar calculations can be made for mixtures of a weak base and its salt:

$$B + H_2O \rightleftharpoons BH^+ + OH^-$$

And

$$pOH = pK_b + \log([salt]/[base])$$

Many biological reactions of interest occur between pH 6 and 8. One useful series of buffers is that of phosphate buffers (see BIO 20.5, 20.6). By choosing appropriate mixtures of $H_3PO_4/H_2PO_4^-$, $H_2PO_4^-/HPO_4^{2-}$ or HPO_4^{2-}/PO_4^{3-}, buffer solutions covering a wide pH range can be prepared. Another useful clinical buffer is the one prepared from tris(hydroxymethyl) aminomethane and its conjugate acid, abbreviated Tris buffer.

Amphoteric Species: Some substances such as water can act as either an acid or a base (i.e. a dual property). These types of substances are known as amphoteric substances. Water behaves as an acid when reacted with a base (OH^-) and alternatively, water behaves as a base when reacted with an acid (H^+). Many metal oxides and hydroxides are also known to be amphoteric substances. Furthermore, molecules that contain both acidic and basic groups such as amino acids are considered to be amphoteric in nature as well (ORG 12.1.2). The following are examples of the amphoteric nature of HCO_3^- reacting with an acid and a base and water (H_2O) reacting with an acid and base.

In acids: $HCO_3^- + H_3O^+ \rightarrow H_2CO_3 + H_2O$
In bases: $HCO_3^- + OH^- \rightarrow CO_3^{2-} + H_2O$
In acids: $H_2O + HCl \rightarrow H_3O^+ + Cl^-$
In bases: $H_2O + NH_3 \rightarrow NH_4^+ + OH^-$

6.9 Acid-base Titrations

The purpose of a titration is usually the determination of concentration of a given sample of acid or base (the analyte) which is reacted with an equivalent amount of a strong base or acid of known concentration (the titrant). The end point or equivalence point is reached when a stoichiometric amount of titrant has been added. This end point is usually detected with the use of an indicator which changes color when this point is reached. Note: the end point is not exactly the same as the equivalence point. The equivalence point is where a reaction is theoretically complete whereas an end point is where a physical change in solution such as a color change is determined by indicators. Regardless, the volume difference between an end point and an equivalence point can usually be ignored.

The end point is determined precisely by measuring the pH at different points of the titration. The curve pH = f(V) where V is the volume of titrant added is called a titration curve. While a strong acid/strong base titration will have an equivalence point at a neutralization pH of 7, the equivalence point of other titrations do not necessarily occur at pH 7. In fact, a weak acid/strong base titration will result in an equivalence point of a pH > 7 and a strong acid/weak base titration results in an equivalence point of a pH < 7. The differential pH effects at the relative equivalence points are due to the conjugate acids and/or bases formed. An indicator for an acid-base titration is a weak acid or base.

The weak acid and its conjugate base should have two different colors in solution. Most indicators require a pH transition range during the titration of about two pH units. An indicator is chosen so that its pK_a is close to the pH of the equivalence point.

6.9.1 Strong Acid versus Strong Base

In the case of a strong acid versus a strong base, both the titrant and the analyte are completely ionized. For example, the titration of hydrochloric acid with sodium hydroxide:

$$H^+ + Cl^- + Na^+ + OH^- \rightarrow H_2O + Na^+ + Cl^-$$

The H^+ and OH^- combine to form H_2O and the other ions remain unchanged, so the net result is the conversion of the HCl to a neutral solution of NaCl. A typical strong-acid-strong base titration curve is shown in Fig. III.A.6.1 (case where the titrant is a base).

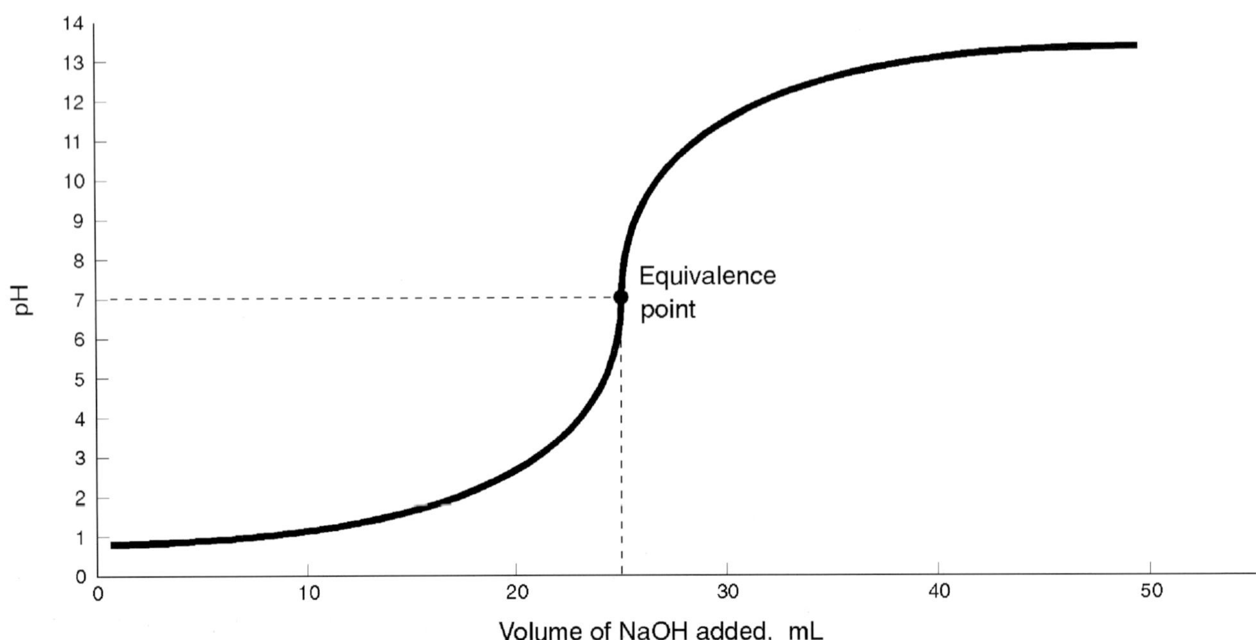

Figure III.A.6.1: The titration curve for a strong acid-strong base is a relatively smooth S-shaped curve with a very steep inclination close to the equivalence point. A small addition in titrant volume near the equivalence point will result in a large change in pH.

If the analyte is an acid, the pH is initially acidic and increases very slowly. When the equivalent volume is reached the pH sharply increases. Midway between this transition jump is the equivalence point. In the case of strong acid-strong base titration the equivalence point corresponds to a neutral pH (because the salt formed does not react with water). If more titrant is added the pH increases and corresponds to the pH of a solution of gradually increasing concentration of the titrant base. This curve is simply reversed if the titrant is an acid.

6.9.2 Weak Acid versus Strong Base

The titration of acetic acid with sodium hydroxide involves the following reaction:

$$HOAc + Na^+ + OH^- \rightarrow H_2O + Na^+ + OAc^-$$

The acetic acid is only a few percent ionized. It is neutralized to water and an equivalent amount of the salt, sodium acetate. Before the titration is started, the pH is calculated as described for weak acids. As soon

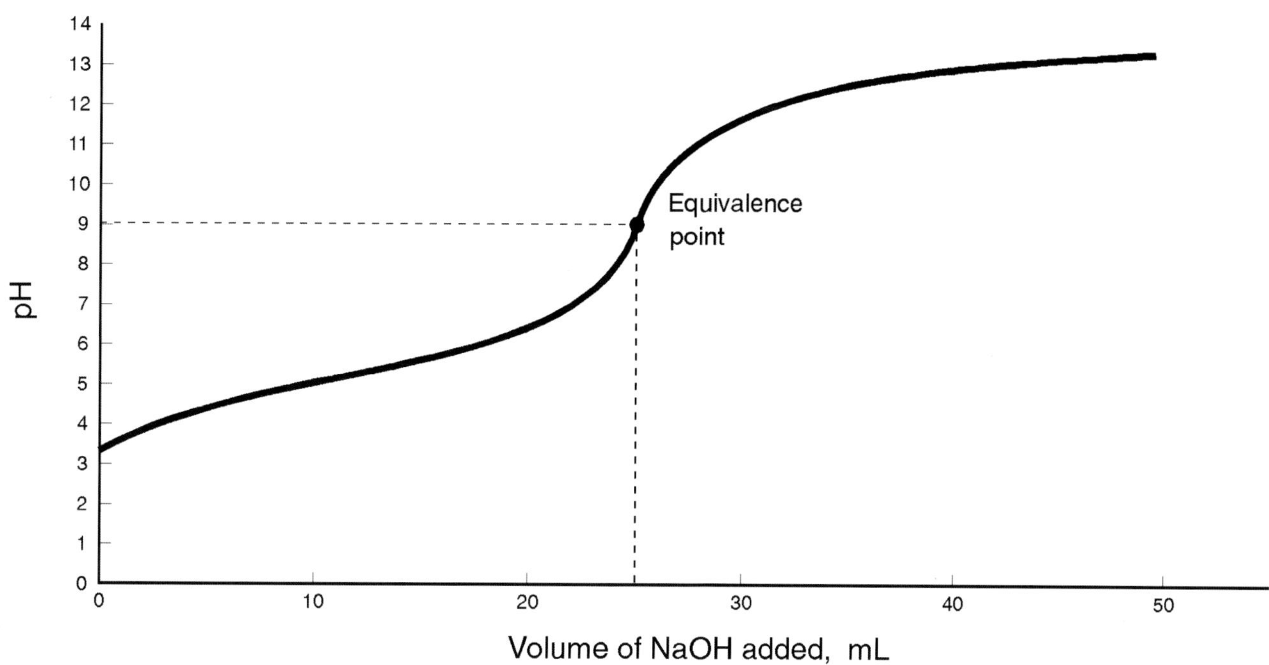

Figure III.A.6.2: The titration curve for a weak acid-strong base or alternatively a strong acid-weak base is somewhat irregular. The pH at the start of the titration prior to base addition is greater than that of a strong acid as the acid is a weak acid. The inclination close to the equivalence point is less significant due to the buffering effect of the solution prior to the equivalence point. A small addition in titrant volume near the equivalence point will therefore result in a small change in pH.

as the titration is started, some of the HOAc is converted to NaOAc and a buffer system is set up. As the titration proceeds, the pH slowly increases as the ratio $[OAc^-]/[HOAc]$ changes. Halfway towards the equivalence point, $[OAC^-] = [HOAC]$ and the pH is equal to pK_a. At the equivalence point, we have a solution of NaOAc. Since it hydrolyzes, the pH at the equivalence point will be alkaline. The pH will depend on the concentration of NaOAc. The greater the concentration, the higher the pH. As excess NaOH is added, the ionization of the base, OAc^-, is suppressed and the pH is determined only by the concentration of excess OH^-. Therefore, the titration curve beyond the equivalence point follows that for the titration of a strong acid. The typical titration curve in this case is illustrated in Figure III.A.6.2.

6.9.3 Weak Base versus Strong Acid

The titration of a weak base with a strong acid is analogous to the previous case except that the pH is initially basic and gradually decreases as the acid is added (curve in preceding diagram is reversed). Consider ammonia titrated with hydrochloric acid:

$$NH_3 + H^+ + Cl^- \rightarrow NH_4^+ + Cl^-$$

At the beginning, we have NH_3 and the pH is calculated as for weak bases. As soon as some acid is added, some of the NH_3 is converted to NH_4^+ and we are in the buffer region. At the midpoint of the titration, $[NH_4^+] = [NH_3]$ and the pH is equal to $(14 - pK_b)$. At the equivalence point, we have a solution of NH_4Cl, a weak acid which hydrolyzes to give an acid solution. Again, the pH will depend on concentration: the greater the concentration, the lower the pH. Beyond the equivalence point, the free H^+ suppresses the ionization and the pH is determined by the concentration of H^+ added in excess. Therefore, the titration curve beyond the equivalence point will be similar to that of the titration of a strong base. {The midpoint of the titration is the equivalence point of the titration curve}

6.10 Redox Titrations

Redox titrations are based on a redox reaction or reduction-oxidation type reaction between an analyte (or sample) and a titrant. More specifically, redox titrations involve the reaction between an oxidizing agent, which accepts one or more electrons, and a reducing agent, which reduces the other substance by donating one or more electrons (CHM 1.6).

The most useful oxidizing agent for titrations is potassium permanganate - $KMnO_4$. Solutions of this salt are colorful since they contain the purple MnO_4^- ion. On the other hand, the more reduced form, Mn^{++}, is nearly colorless. So here is how this redox titration works: $KMnO_4$ is added to a reaction mixture with a reducing agent (i.e. Fe^{++}). MnO_4^- is quickly reduced to Mn^{++} so the color fades immediately. This will continue until there is no more reducing agent in the mixture. When the last bit of reducing agent has been oxidized (i.e. all the Fe^{++} is converted to Fe^{+3}), the next drop of $KMnO_4$ will make the solution colorful since the MnO_4^- will have nothing with which to react. Thus if the amount of reducing agent was unknown, it can be calculated using stoichiometry guided by the amount of potassium permanganate used in the reaction.

GOLD STANDARD WARM-UP EXERCISES

CHAPTER 6: Acids and Bases

1) Sulfuric acid, H_2SO_4, is a polyprotic acid. Consider the following solutions of sulfuric acid and/or its sodium salts.

   Solution I: 0.5 M H_2SO_4

   Solution II: 0.5 M $NaHSO_4$

   Solution III: 0.5 M Na_2SO_4

   Solution IV: A mix of equal volumes of I and II

   Which solution has the highest pH?

   A. Solution I
   B. Solution II
   C. Solution III
   D. Solution IV

2) The first proton of sulfurous acid (H_2SO_3) ionizes as if from a strong acid while the second ionizes as if from a weak acid ($K_{a2} = 5.0 \times 10^{-6}$). What is the pH of 0.01 M H_2SO_3?

   A. 1.0
   B. 2.0
   C. 3.0
   D. 4.0

3) An indicator is usually:

   A. a weak acid or base which can form two distinct colors.
   B. a weak acid or base which can form one distinct color.
   C. a strong acid or base which can form two distinct colors.
   D. a strong acid or base which can form one distinct color.

4) A 20.00 mL aliquot of aniline ($C_6H_5NH_2$) was titrated with 0.01 M HCl and a few of the values of the titration are shown in Table 1.

Table 1

Volume of HCl added (mL)	pH
0.0	8.8
15.0	4.6
30.0	2.8

Which of the following graphs accurately depicts the change in pH for the titration of aniline with increasing volumes of hydrochloric acid?

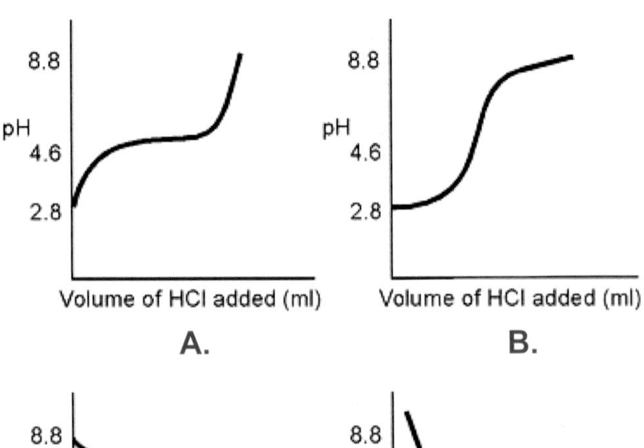

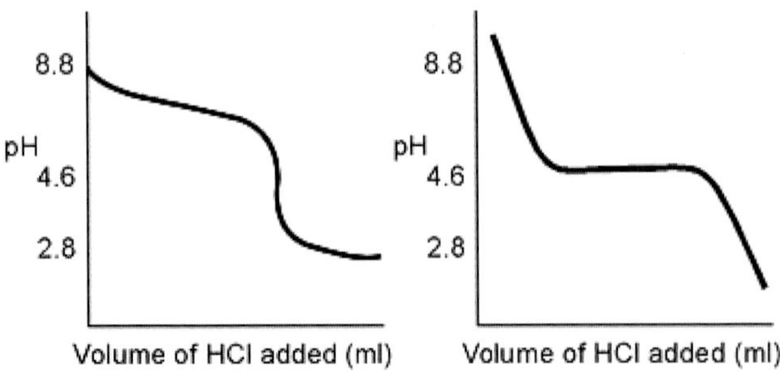

5) The most suitable acid/base indicator for the determination of the end point of the titration in the previous question would probably have a pH range of:

A. 2.1–3.2.
B. 3.0–5.0.
C. 4.8–6.4.
D. 6.2–7.4.

6) In the aniline-HCl titration, the pH of the reaction mixture drops sharply near the equivalence point of the titration because:

A. the concentration of $C_6H_5NH_2$ decreases sharply.
B. the concentration of $C_6H_5NH_3^+$ decreases sharply.
C. the concentration of H^+ increases sharply.
D. the concentration of H^+ decreases sharply.

7) Usually, the color change of an indicator occurs over a range of about two pH units. Hydrogen ion concentration must change by at least what factor for the indicator in solution to change color?

A. 2
B. 10
C. 100
D. 200

8) The conjugate base of sulfuric acid is:

A. $H_3SO_4^+$
B. HSO_4^-
C. HSO_3^-
D. $H_2SO_3^-$

9) What would the pH of a 0.10 M solution of HCOOH be? $K_a = 1.8 \times 10^{-4}$

A. 1.0
B. 2.4
C. 4.7
D. 7.0

10) A 0.10 M solution of formic acid (CH_2O_2) has a pH of 2.38. What is the K_a of formic acid?

A. 1.8×10^{-3}
B. 1.8×10^{-4}
C. 1.8×10^{-5}
D. 1.8×10^{-6}

11) What is the pH of a 0.1 M solution of NH_4Cl?

(K_b of NH_3 is 1.8×10^{-5})

A. 3.4
B. 5.5
C. 7.0
D. 9.7

12) H_2SO_4 has $K_{a1} = 1.0 \times 10^3$ and $K_{a2} = 1.2 \times 10^{-2}$. What is the approximate hydrogen ion concentration of 1.0 M H_2SO_4?

A. 1.00 M
B. 1.01 M
C. 1.05 M
D. 1.10 M

GS ANSWER KEY

CHAPTER 6

		Cross-Reference			*Cross-Reference*
1.	**C**	**CHM 6.1, 6.5**	**7.**	**C**	**CHM 6.5, 6.5.1, 6.9**
2.	**B**	**CHM 6.5, 6.6**	**8.**	**B**	**CHM 6.9, 6.9.1/2**
3.	**A**	**CHM 6.5, 6.9**	**9.**	**B**	**CHM 6.5, 6.5.1, 6.6**
4.	**C**	**CHM 6.9.3**	**10.**	**B**	**CHM 6.5, 6.5.1**
5.	**B**	**CHM 6.5, 6.9**	**11.**	**B**	**CHM 6.2, 6.5**
6.	**C**	**CHM 6.9.3**	**12.**	**B**	**CHM 6.1**

* Explanations can be found at the back of the book.

Go online to DAT-prep.com for additional chapter review Q&A and forum.

Memorize

* Define: state function
* Conversion: thermal to mechanical E.

Understand

* System vs. surroundings
* Law of conservation of energy
* Heat transfer
* Conduction, convection, radiation

Importance

0 to 2 out of the 30 Gen CHM

DAT questions are based on content in this chapter (in our estimation).

* Note that between 50% and 85% of the questions in DAT General Chemistry are based on content from 6 chapters: 1, 2, 4, 5, 6 and 9.

Introduction

Thermodynamics, in chemistry, refers to the relationship of heat with chemical reactions or with the physical state. Thermodynamic processes can be analyzed by studying energy and topics we will review in the next chapter including entropy, volume, temperature and pressure.

Additional Resources

Free Online Forum

Video: Online or DVD

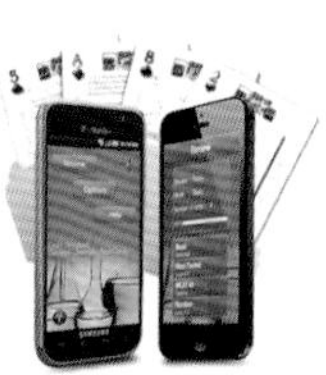

Flashcards

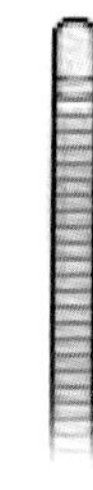

Special Guest

7.1 Generalities

Thermodynamics deals with fundamental questions concerning energy transfers. One difficulty you will have to overcome is the terminology used. For instance, remember that heat and temperature have more specific meanings than the ones attributed to them in every day life.

A thermodynamic transformation can be as simple as a gas leaking out of a tank or a piece of metal melting at high temperature or as complicated as the synthesis of proteins by a biological cell. To solve some problems in thermodynamics we need to define a "system" and its "surroundings." The system is simply the object experiencing the thermodynamic transformation. The gas would be considered as the system in the first example of transformations. Once the system is defined any part of the universe in direct contact with the system is considered as its surroundings. For instance, if the piece of metal is melted in a high temperature oven: the system is the piece of metal and the oven constitutes its surroundings.

In other instances, the limit between the system and its surroundings is more arbitrary, for example if one considers the energy exchanges when an ice cube melts in a thermos bottle filled with orange juice; the inside walls of the thermos bottle could be considered as part of "the system" or as part of the surroundings. In the first case one would carry out all calculations as though the entire system (ice cube + orange juice + inside walls) is isolated from its surroundings (rest of the universe) and all the energy exchanges take place within the system. In the second case the system (ice cube + orange juice) is not isolated from the surroundings (walls) unless we consider that the heat exchanges with the walls are negligible. There is also no need to include any other part of the universe in the latter case since all exchanges take place within the system or between the system and the inside walls of the thermos bottle.

Some systems may exchange both matter and energy with the surroundings. This is called an "open system". Alternatively, some systems may exchange energy only but not matter with the surroundings. This is called a "closed system". Finally, some systems do not exchange matter or energy with their surroundings. This is called an "isolated system". An isolated system therefore does not interact with its surroundings in any way.

7.2 The First Law of Thermodynamics

Heat, internal energy and work are the first concepts introduced in thermodynamics. Heat is thermal energy (a dynamic property defined during a transformation only), it is not to be confused with temperature (a static property defined for each state of the system). Internal energy is basically the average total mechanical energy (kinetic + potential) of the particles that make up the system. The first law of thermodynamics is often expressed as follows: when a system absorbs an amount of heat Q from the surroundings and does a quantity of work W on the same surroundings its internal energy changes by the amount:

$$\Delta E = Q - W$$

This law is basically the law of conservation of energy for an isolated system. Indeed, it states that if a system does not exchange any energy with its surroundings, its internal energy should not vary. If on the other hand a system does exchange energy with its surroundings, its internal energy should change by an amount corresponding to the energy it takes in from the surroundings.

The sign convention related to the previous mathematical expression of the first law of thermodynamics is:

- heat absorbed by the system: $Q > 0$
- heat released by the system: $Q < 0$
- work done by the system on its surroundings: $W > 0$
- work done by the surroundings on the system: $W < 0$

Caution: Some textbooks prefer a different sign convention: any energy (Q or W) flowing from the system to the surroundings (lost by the system) is negative and any energy flowing from the surroundings to the system (gained by the system) is positive. Within such a sign convention the first law is expressed as:

$$\Delta E = Q + W$$

i.e. the negative sign in the previous equation is incorporated in W.

7.3 Equivalence of Mechanical, Chemical and Thermal Energy Units

The previous equation does more than express mathematically the law of conservation of energy, it establishes a relationship between thermal energy and mechanical energy. Historically thermal energy was always expressed in calories (abbreviated as cal.) defined as the amount of thermal energy required to raise the temperature of 1 g of water by 1 degree Celcius. The standard unit used for mechanical work is the "Joule" (J). This unit eventually became the standard unit for any form of energy. The conversion factor between the two units is:

$$1 \text{ cal} = 4.184 \text{ J}$$

Chemists often refer to the amount of energies exchanged between the system and its surroundings to the mole, i.e., quantities of energy are expressed in J/mol or cal/mol. To obtain the energy per particle (atom or molecule), you should divide the energy expressed in J or cal by Avogadro's number.

7.4 Temperature Scales

There are three temperature scales in use in science textbooks: the Celsius scale, the absolute temperature or Kelvin scale, and the Farenheit scale. In the Celsius scale the freezing point and the boiling point of water are arbitrarily defined as 0 °C and 100 °C, respectively. The scale is then divided into equal 1/100th intervals to define the degree Celsius or centigrade (from latin centi = 100). The absolute temperature or Kelvin scale is derived from the centigrade scale, i.e., an interval of 1 degree Celsius is equal to an interval of 1 degree Kelvin. The difference between the two scales is in their definitions of the zero point:

$$0\ K = -273.13\ °C.$$

Theoretically, this temperature can be approached but never achieved, it corresponds to the point where all motion is frozen and matter is destroyed. The Farenheit scale used in English speaking countries has the disadvantage of not being divided into 100 degrees between its two reference points: the freezing point of water is 32 °F and its boiling point is 212 °F. To convert Farenheit degrees into Celsius degrees you have to perform the following transformation:

$$(X\ °F - 32) \times 5/9 = Y\ °C$$

or

$$°F = 9/5\ °C + 32.$$

7.5 Heat Transfer

There are three ways in which heat can be transferred between the system and its surroundings:

(a) heat transfer by conduction

(b) heat transfer by convection

(c) heat transfer by radiation

In the first case (a) there is an intimate contact between the system and its surroundings and heat propagates through the entire system from the heated part to the unheated parts. A good example is the heating of a metal rod on a flame. Heat is initially transmitted directly from the flame to one end of the rod through the contact between the metal and the flame. When carrying out such an experiment you would notice at some point that the part of the rod which is not in direct contact with the flame becomes hot as well (please do not attempt!).

In the second case (b), heat is transferred to the entire system by the circulation of a hot liquid or a gas through it. The difference between this mode of transfer and the previous one, is that the entire system or a major part of it is heated up directly by the surroundings and not by propagation of the thermal energy from the parts of the system which are in direct contact with the heating source and the parts which are not.

In the third case (c) there is no contact between the heating source and the system. Heat is transported by radiation. The perfect example is the microwave oven where the water inside the food is heated by the microwave source. Most heat transfers are carried out by at least two of the above processes at the same time.

Note that when a metal is heated it expands at a rate which is proportional to the change in temperature it experiences. {For a definition of the coefficient of expansion, OAT students can see PHY 6.3; DAT students can happily ignore that statement since there is no physics on the DAT!}

7.6 State Functions

As previously mentioned, the first law of thermodynamics introduces three fundamental energy functions, i.e., the internal energy E, heat Q, and work W. Let us consider a transformation that takes the system from an initial state (I) to a final state (F) (which can differ by a number of variables such as temperature, pressure and volume). The change in the internal energy during this transformation depends only on the properties of the initial state (I) and the final state (F). In other words, suppose that to go from (I) to (F) the system is first subjected to an intermediate transformation that temporarily takes it from state (I) to an intermediate state (Int.) and then to another transformation that brings it from (Int.) to (F), the change in internal energy between the initial state (I) and the final state (F) are independent of the properties of the intermediate state (Int.). The internal energy is said to be a path-independent function or a state function. This is not the case for W and Q. In fact, this is quite conceivable since the amount of W or Q can be imposed by the external operator who subjects the system to a given transformation from (I) to (F). For instance, Q can be fixed at zero if the operator uses an appropriate thermal insulator between the system and its surroundings. In which case the change in the internal energy is due entirely to the work w ($\Delta E = -w$). It is easy to understand that the same result [transformation from (I) to (F)] could be achieved by supplying a small quantity of heat q while letting the system do more work W on the surroundings so that q – W is equal to –w. In which case we have:

	Work	Heat	Change in internal energy
1st transf.	w	0	$-w$
2nd transf.	$W = w + q$	q	$-w$

and yet in both cases the system is going from (I) to (F).

W and *Q* are not state functions. They depend on the path taken to go from (I) to (F). If you remember the exact definition of the internal energy you will understand that a system changes its internal energy to respond to an input of *Q* and *W*. In other words, contrary to *Q* and *W*, the internal energy cannot be directly imposed on the system.

The fact that the internal energy is a state function can be used in three other equivalent ways:

(i) If the changes in the internal energy during the intermediate transformation are known, they can be used to calculate the change for the entire process from (I) to (F): the latter is equal to the sum of the changes in the internal energy for all the intermediate steps.

(ii) If the change in the internal energy to go from a state (I) to a state (F) is $E_{I \to F}$ the change in the internal energy for an opposite transformation that would take the system from (F) to (I) is:

$$\Delta E_{F \to I} = -\Delta E_{I \to F}$$

(iii) If we start from (I) and go back to (I) through a series of intermediate transformations the change in the internal energy for the entire process is zero.

<u>*W* can be determined experimentally by calculating the area under a pressure-volume curve</u>. The mathematical relation is presented in CHM 8.1.

GOLD STANDARD WARM-UP EXERCISES

CHAPTER 7: Thermodynamics

1) Beaker A has a 100 g sample of water maintained at 25 °C and 1 atm for 24 hours. Beaker B has 100 g of water that was heated to 100 °C from 0 °C over 23 hours and then cooled to 25 °C at 1 atm by the 24th hour. Which of the following is true?
   A. Beaker A has more internal energy than Beaker B.
   B. Beaker B has less internal energy than Beaker A.
   C. Both beakers have the same internal energy.
   D. None of the above.

2) If a system loses 25 kJ of heat at the same time that it is doing 50 kJ of work, what is the change in the internal energy of the system?
   A. –25 kJ
   B. +25 kJ
   C. –75 kJ
   D. +75 kJ

3) Metal foil would aid in preventing heat gain via which of the following processes?
   A. Reflecting radiant energy
   B. Conduction
   C. Convection
   D. Radiation and conduction

4) Hess's law is valid because enthalpy is a state function. Which of the following is not a state function?
   A. Volume
   B. Internal energy
   C. Work
   D. Entropy

5) Down-filled winter clothing reduces heat losses by incorporating pockets of air into the material. Which type of heat transfer process do the air pockets limit?
   A. Radiation
   B. Conduction
   C. Convection
   D. Conduction and convection

GS ANSWER KEY

CHAPTER 7

		Cross-Reference			Cross-Reference
1.	C	CHM 7.6	4.	C	CHM 7.6
2.	C	CHM 7.5	5.	B	CHM 7.5
3.	A	CHM 7.5			

* Explanations can be found at the back of the book.

Go online to DAT-prep.com for additional chapter review Q&A and forum.

GOLD NOTES

ENTHALPY AND THERMOCHEMISTRY
Chapter 8

Memorize	Understand	Importance
* Define: endo/exothermic	* Area under curve: PV diagram * Equations for enthalpy, Hess's law, free E. * Calculation: Hess, calorimetry, Bond diss. E. * 2nd law of thermodynamics * Entropy, free E. and spontaneity	**0 to 3 out of the 30 Gen CHM** DAT questions are based on content in this chapter (in our estimation). * Note that between 50% and 85% of the questions in DAT General Chemistry are based on content from 6 chapters: 1, 2, 4, 5, 6 and 9.

DAT-Prep.com

Introduction

Thermochemistry is the study of energy absorbed or released in chemical reactions or in any physical transformation (i.e. phase change like melting and boiling). Thermochemistry for the DAT includes understanding and/or calculating quantities such as enthalpy, heat capacity, heat of combustion, heat of formation, and free energy.

Additional Resources

Free Online Forum

Video: Online or DVD

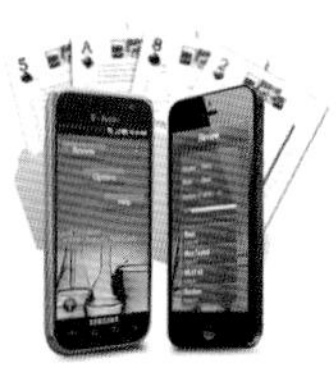

Flashcards

8.1 Enthalpy as a Measure of Heat

The application of the general laws of thermodynamics to chemistry lead to some simplifications and adaptations because of the specificities of the problems that are dealt with in this field. For instance, in chemistry it is critical, if only for safety reasons, to know in advance what amounts of heat are going to be generated or absorbed during a reaction. In contrast, chemists are generally not interested in generating mechanical work and carry out most of their chemical reactions at constant pressure. For these reasons, although internal energy is a fundamental function its use is not very adequate in thermochemistry. Instead, chemists prefer to use another function derived from the internal energy: the enthalpy (*H*). This function is mathematically defined as:

$$\Delta H = \Delta E + P \times (\Delta V)$$

where *P* and *V* are respectively the pressure and the volume of the system. Hence, the enthalpy change (ΔH) of any system is the sum of the change in its internal energy (ΔE) and the product of its pressure (P) and volume change (ΔV). As the three components, internal energy, pressure and volume are all state functions, the enthalpy (H) or enthalpy change (ΔH) of a system is therefore also a state function. Thus, enthalpy change depends only on the enthalpies of the initial and final states (ΔH) and not on the path and therefore it is an example of a state function itself. The enthalpy change of a reaction is defined by the following equation $\Delta H = H_{final} - H_{initial}$; where ΔH is the enthalpy change, H_{final} is the enthalpy of the products of a reaction, and $H_{initial}$ is the enthalpy of the reactants of a reaction. A positive enthalpy change ($+\Delta H$) would indicate the flow of heat into a system as a reaction occurs and is called an "endothermic reaction". A cold pack added over an arm swelling would provide for a good example of an <u>endothermic reaction</u>. A negative enthalpy change ($-\Delta H$) would be called an "exothermic reaction" which essentially gives heat energy off from a system into its surroundings. A bunsen burner flame (CHM 12.4.5) would be an appropriate example of an <u>exothermic reaction</u>.

You may wonder about the use of artificially introducing another energy function when internal energy is well defined and directly related to kinetic and potential energy of the particles that make up the system. To answer this legitimate question you need to consider the case of the majority of the chemical reactions where P is constant and where the only type of work that can possibly be done by the system is of a mechanical nature. In this case, since a change in internal energy (ΔE) occurring during a chemical reaction is basically a measure of all the systems energy as heat and work (Q + W) exchange with the system's surroundings, therefore, $\Delta E = Q + W$ and since, $W = -P\Delta V$, then, the change in enthalpy during a chemical reaction reduces to: $\Delta H = \Delta E + P \times V = (Q + W) + P \times V = Q + W - W = Q$ In other words, the change in enthalpy during a chemical reaction reduces to:

$$\Delta H = \Delta E + P \times V = (Q + W) + P \times V = Q$$

In other words, the change of enthalpy is a direct measure of the heat that evolves or is absorbed during a reaction carried out at constant pressure.

8.1.1 The Standard Enthalpy of Formation or Standard Heat of Formation ($\Delta H_f°$):

The standard enthalpy of formation, $\Delta H_f°$, is defined as the change of enthalpy that would occur when one mole of a substance is formed from its constituent elements in a standard state reaction. All elements in their standard states (oxygen gas, solid carbon as graphite, etc., at 1 atm and 25°C) have a standard enthalpy of formation of zero, as there is no change involved in their formation. The calculated standard enthalpy of various compounds can then be used to find the standard enthalpy of a reaction. For example, the standard enthalpy of formation for methane (CH_4) gas at 25°C would be the enthalpy of the following reaction:

$$C(s,graphite) + 2H_2(g) \rightarrow CH_4(g),$$

where $\Delta H_f° = -74.6$ KJ/mol. Thus, the chemical equation for the enthalpy of formation of any compound is always written with respect to the formation of 1 mole of the studied compound.

The standard enthalpy change for a reaction denoted as $\Delta H°_{rxn}$, is the change of enthalpy that would occur if one mole of matter is transformed by a chemical reaction with all reactants and products under standard state. It can be expressed as follows:

$$\Delta H°_{rxn} = (\text{sum of } n_f \Delta H°_f \text{ of products}) - (\text{sum of } n_r \Delta H°_f \text{ of reactants}),$$

where n_r represents the stoichiometric coefficients of the reactants and n_f the stoichiometric coefficients of the products. The $\Delta H°_f$ represents the standard enthalpies of formation.

8.2 Heat of Reaction: Basic Principles

As discussed, a reaction during which heat is released is said to be *exothermic* (ΔH is negative). If a reaction requires the supply of a certain amount of heat it is *endothermic* (ΔH is positive).

Besides the basic principle behind the introduction of enthalpy there is a more fundamental advantage for the use of this function in thermochemistry: it is a state function. This is a very practical property. For instance, consider two chemical reactions related in the following way:

reaction 1: $A + B \rightarrow C$
reaction 2: $C \rightarrow D$

If these two reactions are carried out consecutively they lead to the same result as the following reaction:

overall reaction: $A + B \rightarrow D$

Because H is a state function we can apply the same arguments here as the ones we previously used for E. The initial state (I) corresponding to $A + B$, the intermediate state (Int.) to C, and the final state (F) to the final product D. If we know the changes in the enthalpy of the system for reactions 1 and 2, the change in the enthalpy during the overall reaction is:

$$\Delta H_{OVERALL} = \Delta H_1 + \Delta H_2$$

This is known as Hess's law. Remember that Hess's law is a simple application of the fact that H is a state function.

Thus, since the enthalpy change of a reaction is dependant only on the initial and final states, and not on the pathway that a reaction may follow, the sum of all the reaction step enthalpy changes must therefore be equivalent to the overall reaction enthalpy change (ΔH). The enthalpy change for a reaction can then be calculated without any direct measurement by using previously determined enthalpies of formation values for each reaction step of an overall equation. Consequently, if the overall enthalpy change is determined to be negative ($\Delta H_{net} < 0$), the reaction is exothermic and is most likely to be of a spontaneous type of reaction and a positive ΔH value would correspond to an endothermic reaction. Thus, Hess's law claims that enthalpy changes are additive and thus the ΔH for any single reaction can be calculated from the difference between the heat of formation of the products and the heat of formation of the reactants as follows:

$$\Delta H^\circ_{reaction} = \Sigma\Delta H_f^\circ{}_{(products)} - \Sigma\Delta H_f^\circ{}_{(reactants)}$$

where the $^\circ$ superscript indicates standard state values.

8.3 Hess's Law

Hess's law can be applied in several equivalent ways which we will illustrate with several examples:

Example: assume that we know the following enthalpy changes:

$$2H_2(g) + O_2(g) \rightarrow 2H_2O(l) \qquad \Delta H_1 = -136.6 \text{ kcal : R1}$$

$$Ca(OH)_2(s) \rightarrow CaO(s) + H_2O(l) \qquad \Delta H_2 = 15.3 \text{ kcal : R2}$$

$$2CaO(s) \rightarrow 2\,Ca(s) + O_2(g) \qquad \Delta H_3 = +303.6 \text{ kcal : R3}$$

and are asked to compute the enthalpy change for the following reaction:

$$Ca(s) + H_2(g) + O_2(g) \rightarrow Ca(OH)_2(s) : R$$

It is easy to see that reaction (R) can be obtained by the combination of reactions (R_1), (R_2) and (R_3) in the following way:

$$\begin{array}{lll} - & 1/2\ (R3): & Ca(s) + 1/2\ O_2(g) \rightarrow CaO(s) \\ + & 1/2\ (R1): & H_2(g) + 1/2\ O_2(g) \rightarrow H_2O(l) \\ - & (R2): & CaO(s) + H_2O(l) \rightarrow Ca(OH)_2(s) \\ \hline & & Ca(s) + H_2(g) + O_2(g) \rightarrow Ca(OH)_2(s) \end{array}$$

As we previously explained, since H is a state function the enthalpy change for (R) will be given by:

$$\Delta H = -1/2\Delta H_3 + 1/2\Delta H_1 - \Delta H_2$$

Example: assume that we have the following enthalpy changes as shown below:

R1: $B_2O_3\ (s) + 3H_2O\ (g) \rightarrow 3O_2\ (g) + B_2H_6\ (g)$ ($\Delta H_1 = 2035$ kJ/mol)

R2: $H_2O\ (l) \rightarrow H_2O\ (g)$ ($\Delta H_2 = 44$ kJ/mol)

R3: $H_2\ (g) + (1/2)O_2\ (g) \rightarrow H_2O\ (l)$ ($\Delta H_3 = -286$ kJ/mol)

R4: $2B\ (s) + 3H_2\ (g) \rightarrow B_2H_6\ (g)$ ($\Delta H_4 = 36$ kJ/mol)

and are then asked to find the enthalpy change or ΔH_f of the following reaction (R):

R: $2B\ (s) + (3/2)O_2\ (g) \rightarrow B_2O_3\ (s)$ ($\Delta H_f = ?$)

After the required multiplication and rearrangements of all step equations (and their respective enthalpy changes), the result is as follows:

$(-1) \times$ (R1) $B_2H_6\ (g) + 3O_2\ (g) \rightarrow B_2O_3\ (s) + 3H_2O\ (g)$ ($\Delta H_1 = -2035$ kJ/mol)

$(-3) \times$ (R2) $3H_2O\ (g) \rightarrow 3H_2O\ (l)$ ($\Delta H_2 = -132$ kJ/mol)

$(-3) \times$ (R3) $3H_2O\ (l) \rightarrow 3H_2\ (g) + (3/2)O_2\ (g)$ ($\Delta H_3 = 858$ kJ/mol)

$(+1) \times$ (R4) $2B\ (s) + 3H_2\ (g) \rightarrow B_2H_6\ (g)$ ($\Delta H_4 = 36$ kJ/mol)

adding the equations while canceling out all common terms, we finally obtain:

$2B\ (s) + (3/2)O_2\ (g) \rightarrow B_2O_3\ (s)$ ($\Delta H_f = -1273$ kJ/mol)

As noted in the initial example, it is shown that the enthalpy change (ΔH_f) for the final reaction is given by the following:

$$\Delta H_f = (-1)\Delta H_1 + (-3)\Delta H_2 + (-3)\Delta H_3 + (1)\Delta H_4$$

There are no general rules that would allow you to determine which reaction to use first and by what factor it needs to be multiplied. It is important to proceed systematically and follow some simple ground rules:

(i) For instance, you could start by writing the overall reaction that you want to obtain through a series of reaction additions.

(ii) Number all your reactions.

(iii) Keep in mind as you go along that the reactants of the overall reaction should always appear on the left-hand side and that the products should always appear on the right-hand side.

(iv) Circle or underline the first reactant of the overall reaction. Find a reaction in your list that involves this reactant (as a reactant or a product). Use that reaction first and write it in such a way that this reactant appears on the left-hand side with the appropriate stoichiometric coefficient (i.e., if this reactant appears as a product of a reaction on your list you should reverse the reaction).

(v) Suppose that in (iv) you had to use the second reaction on your list and that you had to reverse and multiply this reaction by a factor of 3 to satisfy the preceding rule. In your addition, next to this reaction or on top of the arrow write $-3 \times \Delta H_2$.

(vi) Repeat the process for the other reactants and products of the overall reaction until your addition yields the overall reaction. As you continue this process, make sure to cross out the compounds that appear on the right and left-hand sides at the same time.

8.4 Standard Enthalpies

Hess's law has a very practical use in chemistry. Indeed, the enthalpy change for a given chemical reaction can be computed from simple combinations of known enthalpy changes of other reactions. Because enthalpy changes depend on the conditions under which reactions are carried out it is important to define standard conditions:

(i) Standard pressure: 1 atmosphere pressure (approx. = 1 bar).

(ii) Standard temperature for the purposes of the calculation of the standard enthalpy change: generally 25 °C. The convention is that if the temperature of the standard state is not mentioned then it is assumed to be 25 °C, the standard temperature needs to be specified in all other instances.

(iii) Standard physical state of an element: it is defined as the "natural" physical state of an element under the above standard pressure and temperature. For instance, the standard physical state of water under the standard temperature and pressure of 1 atm and 25 °C is the liquid state. Under the same conditions oxygen is a gas.

Naturally, the standard enthalpy change (notation: ΔH°) for a given reaction is defined as the enthalpy change that accompanies the reaction when it is carried out under standard pressure and temperature with all reactants and products in their standard physical state.

Note that the standard temperature defined here is different from the standard temperature for an ideal gas which is: 0 °C.

8.5 Enthalpies of Formation

The enthalpy of formation of a given compound is defined as the enthalpy change that accompanies the formation of the compound from its constituting elements. For instance, the enthalpy of formation of water is the ΔH_f° for the following reaction:

$$H_2 + 1/2\ O_2 \rightarrow H_2O$$

To be more specific the standard enthalpy of formation of water ΔH_f° is the enthalpy change during the reaction:

$$H_2(g) + 1/2O_2(g) \xrightarrow[1\text{ atm}]{25^\circ C} H_2O(l)$$

where the reactants are in their natural physical state under standard temperature and pressure.

Note that according to these definitions, several of the reactions considered in the previous sections were in fact examples of reactions of formation. For instance, in section 8.3 on Hess's law, reaction (R1) is the reaction of formation of two moles of water, if reversed reaction (R3) would be the reaction of formation of two moles of CaO and the overall reaction (R) is the reaction of formation of 1 mole $Ca(OH)_2$. Also note that although one could use the reverse of reaction (R2) to form $Ca(OH)_2$, this reaction, even reversed, is not the reaction of formation of $Ca(OH)_2$. The reason is that the constitutive elements of this molecule are: calcium (Ca), hydrogen (H_2) and oxygen (O_2) and not CaO and H_2O. Enthalpies of formation are also referred to as heats of formation. As previously explained, if the reaction of formation is carried out at constant pressure, the change in the enthalpy represents the amount of heat released or absorbed during the reaction.

8.6 Bond Dissociation Energies and Heats of Formation

The bond dissociation energy, also known as the bond dissociation enthalpy, is a measure of bond strength within a particular molecule defined as a standard enthalpy change in the *homolytic* cleavage (= 2 free radicals formed; CHM 9.4) of any studied chemical bond. An example of bond dissociation energies would be the successive homolytic cleavage of each of the C-H bonds of methane (CH_4) to give, $CH_3\bullet + \bullet H$, $CH_2\bullet + \bullet H$, $CH\bullet + \bullet H$ and finally $C\bullet + \bullet H$. The bond dissociation energies for each of the homolytic CH bond cleavage of methane are determined to be as follows: 435 KJ/mol, 444 KJ/mol, 444 KJ/mol and 339 KJ/mol, respectively. The average of these four individual bond dissociation energies is known as the bond energy of the CH bond and is 414 KJ/mol. Thus, with the exception of all diatomic molecules where only one chemical bond is involved so that bond energy and bond dissociation energy are in this case equivalent, the bond dissociation energy is not exactly the same as bond energy. Bond energy is more appropriately defined as the energy required to sever 1 mole of a chemical bond in a gas and not necessarily the measure of a chemical bond strength within a particular molecule. Bond energy is therefore a measure of bond strength. Moreover as just described, bond energy may be considered as an average energy calculated from the sum of bond dissociation energies of all bonds within a particular compound. Bond energies are always positive values as it always takes energy to break bonds apart.

The difficulty in defining bond dissociation energies in polyatomic molecules is that the amounts of energy required to break a given bond (say an O–H bond) in two different polyatomic molecules (H_2O and CH_3OH, for instance) are different. Bond dissociation energies in polyatomic molecules are approximated to an average value for molecules of the same nature. Within the framework of this commonly made approximation we can calculate the enthalpy change of any reaction using the *sum* of bond energies of the reactants and the products in the following way:

$$\Delta H^{\circ}_{(reaction)} = \Sigma BE_{(reactants)} - \Sigma BE_{(products)}$$

where BE stands for bond energies.

Standard enthalpy changes of chemical reactions can also be computed using enthalpies of formation in the following way:

$$\Delta H^{\circ}_{(reaction)} = \Sigma\Delta H_{(bonds\ broken)} + \Sigma\Delta H_{(bonds\ formed)}$$
$$= \Sigma BE_{(reactants)} - \Sigma BE_{(products)}$$

Note how this equation is similar but not identical to the one making use of bond energies. This comes from the fact that a bond energy is defined as the energy required to break (and not to form) a given bond. Also note that the standard enthalpy of formation of a mole of any **element** is zero.

8.7 Calorimetry

Measurements of changes of temperature within a reaction mixture allow the experimental determination of heat absorbed or released during the corresponding chemical reaction. Indeed the amount of heat required to change the temperature of any substance X from T_1 to T_2 is proportional to $(T_2 - T_1)$ and the quantity of X:

$$Q = mC(T_2 - T_1)$$

or

$$Q = nc(T_2 - T_1)$$

where m is the mass of X, n the number of moles. The constant C or c is called the heat capacity. The standard units for C and c are, respectively, the $Jkg^{-1}K^{-1}$ and the $Jmol^{-1}K^{-1}$. C which is the heat capacity per unit mass is also referred to as the specific heat capacity. If you refer back to the definition of the calorie (see CHM 7.3) you will understand that the specific heat of water is necessarily: 1 cal g^{-1} $°C^{-1}$.

Note that heat can be absorbed or released without a change in temperature (CHM 4.3.3). In fact, this situation occurs whenever a phase change takes place for a pure compound. For instance, ice melts at a constant temperature of 0 °C in order to break the forces that keep the water molecules in a crystal of ice we need to supply an amount of heat of 6.01 kJ/mol. There is no direct way of calculating the heat corresponding to a phase change.

Heats of phase changes (heat of fusion, heat of vaporization, heat of sublimation) are generally tabulated and indirectly determined in calorimetric experiments. For instance, if a block of ice is allowed to melt in a bucket of warm water, we can determine the heat of fusion of ice by measuring the temperature drop in the bucket of water and applying the law of conservation of energy. The relevant equation is:

$$Q = m\,L$$

where L is the latent heat which is a constant.

Calorimetry is the science of measuring the heat evolved or exchanged due to a chemical reaction. The thermal energy of a reaction (defined as the system) is measured as a function of its surroundings by observing a temperature change (ΔT) on the surroundings due to the system. The magnitude in temperature change is essentially a measure of a system's or sample's energy content which is measured either while keeping a volume constant (bomb calorimetry) or while keeping a pressure constant (coffee-cup calorimetry).

In a constant volume calorimetry measurement, the bomb calorimeter is kept at a constant volume and there is essentially no heat exchange between the calorimeter and the surroundings and thus, the net heat exchange for the system is zero. The heat exchange for the reaction is then compensated for by the heat change for the water and bomb calorimeter material steel (or surroundings). Thus, $\Delta q_{system} = \Delta q_{reaction} + \Delta q_{water} + \Delta q_{steel} = 0$ in bomb calorimetry, and so $q_{cal} = -q_{reaction}$ in which the temperature change is related to the heat absorbed by the calorimeter (q_{cal}) and if no heat escapes the constant volume calorimeter, the amount of heat gained by the calorimeter then equals that released by the system and so, $q_{cal} = -q_{reaction}$ as stated previously. Note that since $Q = mc\Delta T$ as previously defined, and $q_{reaction} = -(q_{water} + q_{steel})$ therefore, $q_{reaction} = -(m_{water})(c_{water})\Delta T + (m_{steel})(c_{steel})\Delta T$.

For aqueous solutions, a coffee-cup calorimeter is usually used to measure the enthalpy change of the system. This is simply a polystyrene (Styrofoam) cup with a lid and a thermometer. The cup is partially filled with a known volume of water. When a chemical reaction occurs in the coffee-cup calorimeter, the heat of the reaction is absorbed by the water. The change in water temperature is used to calculate the amount of heat that has been absorbed (used to make products, so water temperature decreases) or evolved (lost to the water, so its temperature increases) in the reaction.

8.8 The Second Law of Thermodynamics

The first law of thermodynamics allows us to calculate energy transfers during a given transformation of the system. It does not allow us to predict whether a transformation can or cannot occur spontaneously. Yet our daily observations tell us that certain transformations always occur in a given direction. For instance, heat flows from a hot source to a cold source. We cannot spontaneously transfer heat in the other direction to make the hot source hotter and the cold source colder. The second law of thermodynamics states that entropy (S) of an isolated system will never decrease. In order for a reaction to proceed, the entropy of the system must increase. For any spontaneous process, the entropy of the universe increases which results in a greater dispersal or randomization of the energy ($\Delta S > 0$). The second law of thermodynamics allows the determination of the preferred direction of a given transformation. Transformations which require the smallest amount of energy and lead to the largest disorder of the system are the most spontaneous.

8.9 Entropy

Entropy is regarded as the main driving force behind all the chemical and physical changes known within the universe. All natural processes tend toward an increase in energy dispersal or, in other words, an entropy increase within our universe. Thus, a chemical system or reaction proceeds in a direction of universal entropy increase.

Entropy S is the state function which measures the degree of "disorder" in a system. For instance, the entropy of ice is lower than the entropy of liquid water since ice corresponds to an organized crystalline structure (virtually no disorder). In fact, generally speaking, the entropy increases as we go from a solid to a liquid to a gas. For similar reasons, the entropy decreases when an elastic band is stretched. Indeed, in the "unstretched" elastic band the molecules of the rubber polymer are coiled up and form a disorganized structure. As the rubber is stretched these molecules will tend to line up with each other and adopt a more organized structure.

Entropy has the dimension of energy as a function of temperature as J/K or cal/K. Entropy can therefore be related to temperature and is thus a measure of energy dispersal (in joules) per unit of temperature (in kelvins).

The second law of thermodynamics can be expressed in the alternative form: a spontaneous transformation corresponds to an increase of the entropy of the system plus its surroundings. Hence, a chemical system is known to proceed in a direction that increases the entropy of the universe. As a result, ΔS must be incorporated in an expression that includes both the system and its surroundings so that, $\Delta S_{universe} = \Delta S_{surroundings} + \Delta S_{system} > 0$. When a system reaches a certain temperature equilibrium, it then also reaches its maximal entropy and so, $\Delta S_{universe} = \Delta S_{surroundings} + \Delta S_{system} = 0$. The entropy of the thermodynamic system is therefore a measure of how far the equalization has progressed.

Entropy, like enthalpy, is a state function and is therefore path independent. Hence, a change in entropy depends only on the initial and final states ($\Delta S = S_{final} - S_{initial}$) and not on how the system arrived at that state. Under standard conditions, for any process or reaction, the entropy change for that reaction will be the difference between the entropies of products and reactants as follows:

$$\Delta S^{\circ}_{reaction} = \Delta S^{\circ}_{products} - \Delta S^{\circ}_{reactants}$$

8.10 Free Energy

The Gibbs free energy G is another state function which can be used as a criterion for spontaneity. This function is defined as:

$$G = H - T \cdot S$$

where: H is the enthalpy of the system in a given state,

T is the temperature,

and S is the entropy of the system.

Consequently, Gibbs Free Energy (G) also determines the direction of a spontaneous change for a chemical system. The derivation for the formulation thus incorporates both the entropy and enthalpy parameters studied in the previous sections. Following various manipulations and derivations, one can then note that Gibbs Free Energy is an alternative form of both enthalpy and the entropy changes of a chemical process.

The standard Gibbs Free Energy of a reaction (ΔG°_{rxn}), is determined at 25°C and a pressure of 1 atm. For a reaction carried out at constant temperature we can write that the change in the Gibbs free energy is:

$$\Delta G = \Delta H - T\Delta S$$

A reaction carried out at constant pressure is spontaneous if

$$\Delta G < 0$$

It is not spontaneous if:

$$\Delta G > 0$$

and it is in a state of equilibrium (reaction spontaneous in both directions) if:

$$\Delta G = 0.$$

As noted in the previous chapter, the study of thermodynamics generally describes the spontaneity or the direction and extent to which a reaction will proceed. It therefore enables one to predict if a reaction will occur spontaneously or not. Note that non spontaneous processes may turn into spontaneous processes if coupled to another spontaneous process or more specifically by the addition of some external energy.

Thermochemistry then can be used to essentially calculate how much work a system can do or require. Thermodynamics basically then deals with the relative potentials of both the reactants and products of a chemical system. The next chapter will describe the actual rate (or chemical kinetics or speed) of a chemical reaction. In chemical kinetics, the chemical potential of intermediate states of a chemical reaction may also be described and thus enabling one to determine why a reaction may be slow or fast.

GOLD STANDARD WARM-UP EXERCISES

CHAPTER 8: Enthalpy and Thermochemistry

1) If a chemical reaction is at equilibrium, which of the following is true?
   A. The change in entropy is zero.
   B. The number of reacting molecules is zero.
   C. The change in enthalpy is zero.
   D. The change in free energy is zero.

2) In the reaction $N_2(g) + 3H_2(g) \leftrightarrow 2NH_3(g)$, the entropy among the molecules involved:
   A. increases.
   B. remains the same.
   C. decreases.
   D. cannot be determined with the information given.

3) When the reaction $N_2(g) + 3H_2(g) \leftrightarrow 2NH_3(g)$ is at equilibrium, it is "far to the right." The forward reaction must be:
   A. ectoplasmic.
   B. exothermic.
   C. endothermic.
   D. endergonic.

4) A student observes the melting of an ice cube. She concludes that the overall observed process has led to:
   A. the completion of real work.
   B. an increase in the efficiency of the universe.
   C. an increase in the entropy of the universe.
   D. an increase in the total energy of the universe.

5) What would be the expected change in the solubility of a gas when a solution containing the gas is heated and when a solution containing the gas has the pressure over the solution decreased, respectively?
   A. Increase, increase
   B. Increase, decrease
   C. Decrease, increase
   D. Decrease, decrease

6) A phase diagram is a graph showing the thermodynamic conditions of a substance – solid, liquid, gas - at different pressures and temperatures. Which of the following statements is consistent with the triple point of a substance?
   A. The absolute temperature dominates the effect on Gibbs free energy.
   B. The reaction is spontaneous, Gibbs free energy is negative.
   C. The enthalpy change is equal to the effect of the entropy change.
   D. The entropy change is negative because there is more disorder overall.

7) Consider the following data:

$$CH_4(g) + 2O_2(g) \rightarrow CO_2(g) + 2H_2O(l) \quad \Delta H^\circ = -890 \text{ kJ/mol}$$

$$H_2O(l) \rightarrow H_2O(g) \quad \Delta H^\circ = 44 \text{ kJ/mol}$$

Calculate the enthalpy (ΔH°) of the following reaction:

$$CH_4 + 2O_2(g) \rightarrow CO_2(g) + 2H_2O(g)$$

   A. +846 kJ/mol
   B. –846 kJ/mol
   C. +802 kJ/mol
   D. –802 kJ/mol

8) The standard enthalpies of formation of SO_2 and SO_3 are –297 and –396 kJ/mol, respectively. Calculate the standard enthalpy of reaction for the following:

$$SO_2 + {}^1/_2O_2 \rightarrow SO_3.$$

A. –99 kJ
B. +99 kJ
C. –396 kJ
D. +396 kJ

9) How much heat is needed to convert a 10-gram ice cube at 0 °C to steam at 100 °C?

Heat of fusion = 80 kcal/kg

Heat of vaporization = 540 kcal/kg

A. 620 cal
B. 1000 cal
C. 1620 cal
D. 7200 cal

10) The total area of the Hubble telescope exposed to the sun is 70 000 m^2. The rate of solar energy incident on the telescope is 120 Wm^{-2}. If a channel covering the entire exposed surface contains water and the temperature of the water must rise by at least 10 °C in order to keep the telescope cool, at what approximate rate must the water be made to flow assuming that energy transfer is instantaneous?

Specific heat capacity of water = 4.2 J g^{-1} $°C^{-1}$

Density of water = 1000 kg m^{-3}

A. 200 L s^{-1}
B. 3150 L s^{-1}
C. 2.0×10^5 L s^{-1}
D. 3.1×10^6 L s^{-1}

GS ANSWER KEY

CHAPTER 8

		Cross-Reference			Cross-Reference
1.	D	CHM 8.10	6.	C	CHM 4.3.3, 8.10
2.	C	CHM 8.9	7.	D	CHM 8.5
3.	B	CHM 8.2, 8.9, 8.10, 9.10	8.	A	CHM 8.5
4.	C	CHM 8.8, 8.9	9.	D	CHM 8.7
5.	D	CHM 5.3, 8.10, 9.10	10.	A	CHM 8.7

* Explanations can be found at the back of the book.

RATE PROCESSES IN CHEMICAL REACTIONS
Chapter 9

Memorize

Reaction order
Define: rate determining step
Generalized potential energy diagrams
Define: activation energy, catalysis
Define: saturation kinetics, substrate

Understand

* Reaction rates, rate law, determine exponents
* Reaction mechanism for free radicals
* Rate constant equation; apply Le Chatelier's
* Kinetic vs. thermodynamic control
* Law of mass action, equations for Gibbs free E., saturation kinetics, Keq

Importance

2 to 4 out of the 30 Gen CHM

DAT questions are based on content in this chapter (in our estimation).
* Note that between 50% and 85% of the questions in DAT General Chemistry are based on content from 6 chapters: 1, 2, 4, 5, 6 and 9.

Introduction

Rate processes (or chemical kinetics) involve the study of the velocity (speed) and mechanisms of chemical reactions. **Reaction rate** (= *velocity*) tells us how fast the concentrations of reactants change with time. **Reaction mechanisms** show the sequence of steps to get to the overall change. Experiments show that 4 important factors generally influence reaction rates: (1) the nature of the reactants, (2) their concentration, (3) temperature, and (4) catalysis.

Additional Resources

Free Online Forum

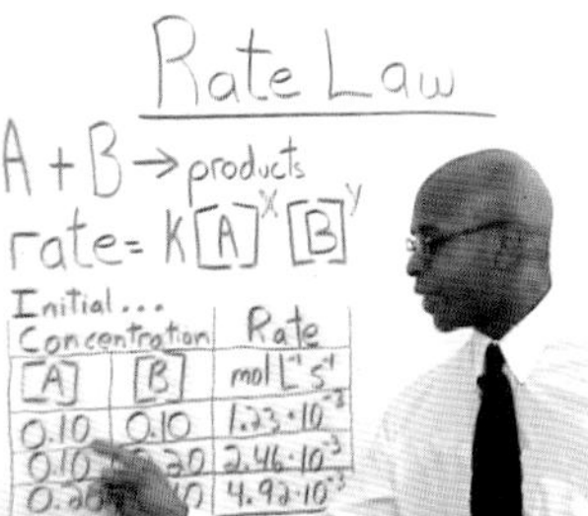

Video: Online or DVD

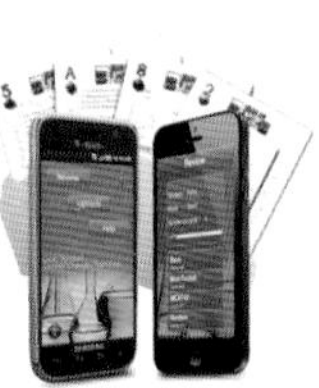

Flashcards

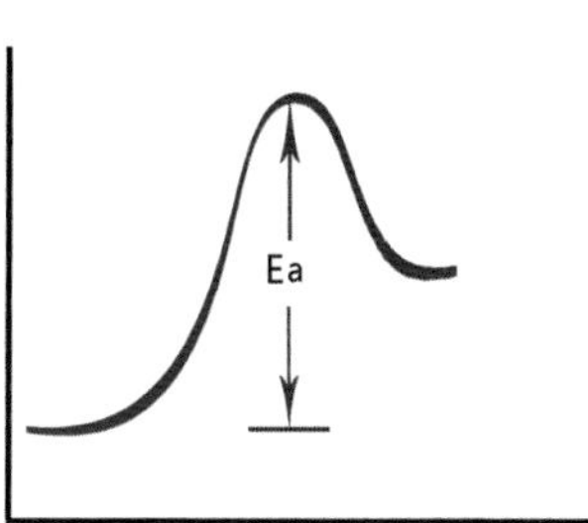

Special Guest

9.1 Reaction Rate

Consider a general reaction

$$2\,A + 3\,B \rightarrow C + D$$

The rate or the velocity at which this reaction proceeds can be expressed by one of the following:

(i) rate of disappearance of A: $-\Delta[A]/\Delta t$

(ii) rate of disappearance of B: $-\Delta[B]/\Delta t$

(iii) rate of appearance or formation of C: $\Delta[C]/\Delta t$

(iv) rate of appearance or formation of D: $\Delta[D]/\Delta t$

Where [ ] denotes the concentration of a reactant or a product in moles/liter. Thus, the reaction rate measure is usually expressed as a change in reactant or product concentration ($\Delta_{conc.}$) per unit change in time (Δt).

Since A and B are disappearing in this reaction, [*A*] and [*B*] are decreasing with time, i.e. $\Delta[A]/\Delta t$ and $\Delta[B]/\Delta t$ are negative quantities. On the other hand, the quantities $\Delta[C]/\Delta t$ and $\Delta[D]/\Delta t$ are positive since both C and D are being formed during the process of this reaction. By convention: rates of reactions are expressed as positive numbers; as a result, a negative sign is necessary in the first two expressions.

Suppose that A disappears at a rate of 6 (moles/liter)/s. In the same time interval (1s), in a total volume of 1L we have:

(3 mol B/2 mol A) × 6 mol A
= 9 moles of B disappearing
(1 mol C/2 mol A) × 6 mol A
= 3 moles of C being formed
(1 mol D/2 mol A) × 6 mol A
= 3 moles of D being formed

Therefore individual rates of formation or disappearance are not convenient ways to express the rate of a reaction. Indeed, depending on the reactant or product considered the rate will be given by a different numerical value unless the stoichiometric coefficients are equal (e.g. for C and D in our case).

A more convenient expression of the rate of a reaction is the overall rate. This rate is simply obtained by dividing the rate of formation or disappearance of a given reactant or product by the corresponding stoichiometric coefficient, i.e.:

$$\text{overall rate} = -(1/2)\,\Delta[A]/\Delta t, \text{ or } -(1/3)\,\Delta[B]/\Delta t,$$

$$\text{or } \Delta[C]/\Delta t, \text{ or } \Delta[D]/\Delta t.$$

A simple verification on our example will show you that these expressions all lead to the same numerical value for the overall rate: 3 (moles/L)/s. Therefore for a generic equation such as, $aA + bB \rightarrow cC + dD$, a generalization of the overall reaction rate would be as follows:

$$\text{Rate} = \frac{-1}{a}\frac{\Delta[A]}{\Delta t} = \frac{-1}{b}\frac{\Delta[B]}{\Delta t} = \frac{+1}{c}\frac{\Delta[C]}{\Delta t} = \frac{+1}{d}\frac{\Delta[D]}{\Delta t}$$

It can be seen from the preceding overall rate relationship that the rate is the same whether we use one of the reactants or one of the products to calculate the rates. Generally, one can see that knowing the rate of change in the concentration of any one reactant or product at a certain time point allows one to invariably determine the rate of change in the concentration of any other reactant or product at the same time point using the stoichiometrically balanced equation.

Whenever the term "rate" is used (with no other specification) it refers to the "overall rate" unless individual and overall rates are equal.

9.2 Dependence of Reaction Rates on Concentration of Reactants

The rate of a reaction (given in moles per liter per second) can be expressed as a function of the concentration of the reactants. In the previous chemical reaction we would have:

$$\text{rate} = k\,[A]^m\,[B]^n$$

where [ ] is the concentration of the corresponding reactant in moles per liter

k is referred to as the rate constant
m is the order of the reaction with respect to A
n is the order of the reaction with respect to B
m+n is the overall reaction order.

The rate constant k is reaction specific. It is directly proportional to the rate of a reaction. It increases with increasing temperature since the proportion of molecules with energies greater than the activation energy E_a of a reaction increases with higher temperatures.

According to the rate law above, the reaction is said to be an (m + n)*th* order reaction, or, an m*th* order reaction with respect to A, or, an nth order reaction with respect to B.

The value of the m or n*th* rate orders of the reaction describes how the rate of the reaction depends on the concentration of the reactant(s).

For example, a zero rate order for reactant A (where m = 0), would indicate that the rate of the reaction is independent of the concentration of reactant A and therefore has a constant reaction rate (this is also applicable to reactant B). The rate equation can therefore be expressed as a rate constant k or the rate = k. The rate probably depends on temperature or other factors excluding concentration.

A first rate order for reactant A (where m = 1) would indicate that the rate of the reaction is directly proportional to the concentration of the reactant A (or B, where n = 1). Thus, the rate equation can be expressed as follows: rate = $k[A]^1$ or rate = $k[B]^1$.

A second rate order for reactant A (m = 2) would indicate that the rate is proportional to the square of the reactant concentration. The rate equation can thus be expressed as follows: rate = $k[A]^2$.

Hence, the rate orders or exponents in the rate law equation can be integers, fractions, or zeros and are not necessarily equal to the stoichiometric coefficients in the given reaction except when a reaction is the rate-determining step (or elementary step). Consequently, although there are other orders, including both higher and mixed orders or fractions that are possible as described, the three described orders (0, 1st and 2nd), are amongst the most common orders studied.

As shown by the graphical representation below, for the zero order reactant, as the concentration of reactant A decreases over time, the slope of the line is constant and thus the rate is constant. Moreover, the rate does not change regardless of the decrease in reactant A concentration over time and thus the zero order rate order. For the first order, the decrease in reactant A concentration is shown to affect the rate of reaction in direct proportion. Thus, as the concentration decreases, the rate decreases proportionally. Lastly, for the second order, the rate of the reaction is shown to decrease proportionally to the square of the reactant A concentration. In fact, the curves for 1st and 2nd order reactions resemble exponential decay.

Reactant Concentration versus Time

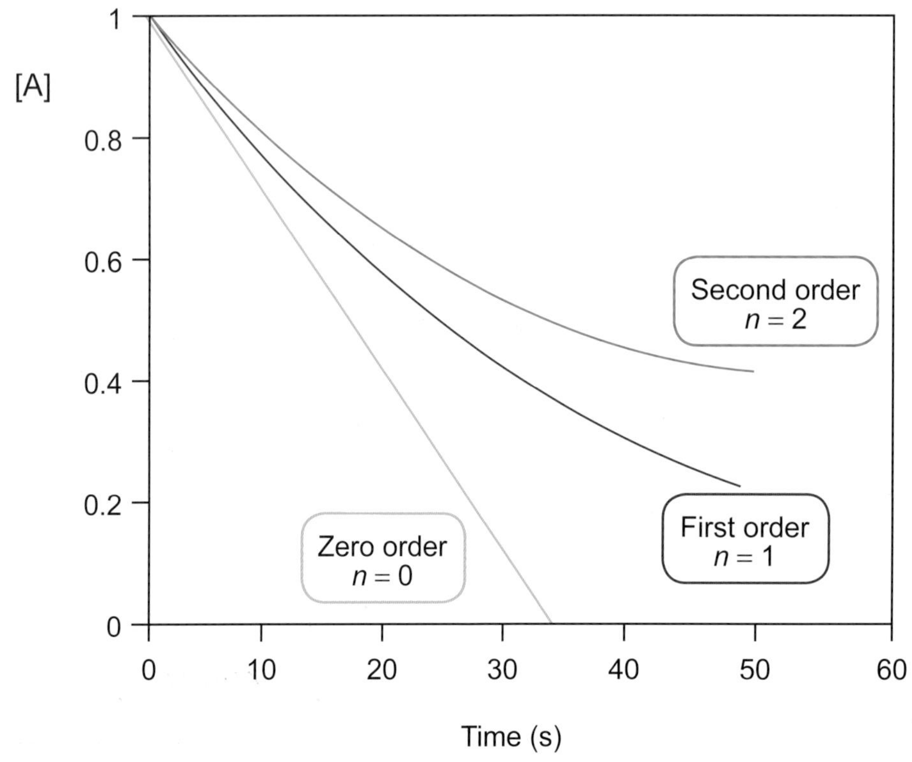

9.2.1 Differential Rate Law vs. Integrated Rate Law (Advanced DAT-30 Topic)

Rate laws may be expressed as differential equations or as integrated rate laws. As differential equations, the relationship is shown between the rate of a reaction and the concentration of a reactant. Alternatively, the integrated rate law expresses a rate as a function of concentration of a reactant or reactants and time.

For example, for a zero order rate, Rate $= k[A]^0 = k$ and since Rate $= -\Delta[A]/\Delta t$, then $-\Delta[A]/\Delta t = k$ and following the integration of the differential function, the following zero-order integrated rate law is obtained: $[A]_t = -kt + [A]_o$, where $[A]_t$ = is the concentration of A at a particular time point t and $[A]_0$ is the initial concentration of A and k is the rate constant.

The following table summarizes the main rate laws of the 0,1st and 2nd rate orders and their respective relationships.

Table 9.2.1

Rate Law Summary

Reaction Order	Rate Law	Units of *k*	Integrated Rate Law	Straight-Line Plot	Half-Life Equation
0	Rate $= k[A]^0$	$M \cdot s^{-1}$	$[A]_t = -kt + [A]_0$	[A] vs. Time *t*; *y*-intercept = $[A]_0$; slope = $-k$	$t_{1/2} = \frac{[A]_0}{2k} = \frac{1}{k}\frac{[A]_0}{2}$
1	Rate $= k[A]^1$	s^{-1}	$\ln[A]_t = -kt + \ln[A]_0$ $\ln\frac{[A]_t}{[A]_0} = -kt$	ln[A] vs. Time *t*; *y*-intercept = $\ln[A]_0$; slope = $-k$	$t_{1/2} = \frac{0.693}{k} = \frac{1}{k}(0.693)$
2	Rate $= k[A]^2$	$M^{-1} \cdot s^{-1}$	$\frac{1}{[A]_t} = kt + \frac{1}{[A]_0}$	1/[A] vs. Time *t*; slope = k; *y*-intercept = $1/[A]_0$	$t_{1/2} = \frac{1}{k[A]_0} = \frac{1}{k}\frac{1}{[A]_0}$

As depicted by the table, the first and second order rate laws are also derived in a similar manner as the zero order rate law.

Included within the table is also the half-life's of the three described rate laws. The half-life of a reaction is defined as the time needed to decrease the concentration of the reactant to one-half of the original starting concentration (CHM 11.4). Note that each rate order has its own respective half-life.

The rate order of a reactant may be determined experimentally by either the isolation or initial rates method as described in the following section or by plotting concentration, or some function of concentration such as ln[ ] or 1/[ ] of reactant as a function of time. A linear relationship between the dependent concentration variable of reactant and the independent time variable will then delineate the actual order of the reactant. Moreover, if a linear curve is obtained when plotting [reactant] versus time, the order would be zero whereas, if a linear relationship is noted when plotting ln [reactant] versus time, this would be first order and second order would be for a linear relationship between 1/[reactant] versus time.

Therefore, the rate law of a reaction with a multi-step mechanism cannot be deduced from the stoichiometric coefficients of the overall reaction; it must be determined experimentally for a given reaction at a given temperature as will be described in the following section.

9.3 Determining Exponents of the Rate Law

The only way to determine the exponents with certainty is via experimentation. The rate law for any reaction must therefore always be determined by experimentation, often by a method known as the "initial rates method or the isolation method".

In the initial rates method, if there are two or more reactants involved in the reaction, the reactant concentrations are usually varied independent of each other so that, for example, in a two reactant reaction, if one reactant concentration is altered the other reactant concentration would be kept constant and the effect on the initial rate of the reaction would be measured. Consider the following five experiments varying the concentrations of reactants A and B with resulting initial rates of reaction:

$$A + B \rightarrow \text{products}$$

In the first three experiments the concentration of A changes but B remains the same. Thus the resultant changes in rate only depend on the concentration of A. Note that when [A] doubles (Exp. 1, 2) the reaction rate doubles, and when [A] triples (Exp. 1, 3) the reaction

Exp. #	Initial Concentration		Initial Rate ($mol\ L^{-1}\ s^{-1}$)
	[A]	[B]	
1	0.10	0.10	0.20
2	0.20	0.10	0.40
3	0.30	0.10	0.60
4	0.30	0.20	2.40
5	0.30	0.30	5.40

rate triples. Because it is directly proportional, the exponent of [A] must be 1. Thus the rate of reaction is first order with respect to A.

In the final three sets of experiments, [B] changes while [A] remains the same. When [B] doubles (Exp. 3, 4) the rate increases by a factor of 4 (= 2^2). When [B] triples (Exp. 3, 5) the rate increases by a factor of 9 (= 3^2). Thus the relation is exponential where the exponent of [B] is 2. The rate of reaction is second order with respect to B.

$$\text{initial rate} = k[A]^1[B]^2$$

The overall rate of reaction (n+m) is third order. The value of the rate constant k can be easily calculated by substituting the results from any of the five experiments. For example, using experiment #1:

$$k = \frac{\text{initial rate}}{[A]^1\ [B]^2}$$

$$k = \frac{0.20\ mol\ L^{-1}\ s^{-1}}{(0.10\ mol\ L^{-1})\ (0.10\ mol\ L^{-1})^2}$$

$$= 2.0 \times 10^2\ L^2mol^{-2}s^{-1}$$

k is the rate constant for the reaction which includes all five experiments.

Note: The units of the resultant rate constant "k" will differ depending on the overall rate order of a reaction.

9.4 Reaction Mechanism - Rate-determining Step

Chemical equations fail to describe the detailed process through which the reactants are transformed into the products. For instance, consider the reaction of formation of hydrogen chloride from hydrogen and chlorine:

$$Cl_2(g) + H_2(g) \rightarrow 2\ HCl(g)$$

The equation above fails to mention that in fact this reaction is the result of a chain of reactions proceeding in three steps:

Initiation step: formation of free chlorine radicals by photon irradiation or introduction of heat (= *radicals*, the mechanism will be discussed in organic chemistry):

$$1/2\ Cl_2 \rightleftharpoons Cl\cdot$$

The double arrow indicates that in fact some of the Cl free radicals recombine to form chlorine molecules, the whole process eventually reaches a state of equilibrium where the following ratio is constant:

$$K = [Cl\cdot]/[Cl_2]^{1/2}$$

The determination of such a constant will be dealt with in the sub-section on "equilibrium constants."

Propagation step: formation of reactive hydrogen free radicals and reaction between hydrogen free radicals and chlorine molecules:

$$Cl\cdot + H_2 \rightarrow HCl + H\cdot$$

$$H\cdot + Cl_2 \rightarrow HCl + Cl\cdot$$

Termination step: Formation of hydrogen chloride by reaction between hydrogen free radicals and chlorine free radicals.

$$H\cdot + Cl\cdot \rightarrow HCl$$

The detailed chain reaction process above is called the mechanism of the reaction. Each individual step in a detailed mechanism is called an elementary step. Any reaction proceeds through some mechanism which is generally impossible to predict from its chemical equation. Such mechanisms are usually determined through an experimental procedure. Generally speaking each step proceeds at its own rate.

The rate of the overall reaction is naturally limited by the slowest step; therefore, the rate-determining step in the mechanism of a reaction is the slowest step. In other words, the overall rate law of a reaction is basically equal to the rate law of the slowest step. The faster processes have an indirect influence on the rate: they regulate the concentrations of the reactants and products. The chemical equation of an elementary step reflects the exact molecular process that transforms its reactants into its products. For this reason its rate law can be predicted from its chemical equation: in an elementary process, the orders with respect to the reactants are equal to the corresponding stoichiometric coefficients.

In our example, experiments show that the rate-determining step is the reaction between chlorine radicals and hydrogen molecules, all the other steps are much faster. According to the principles stated, the rate law of the overall reaction is equal to the rate law of this rate-determining step. Therefore, the rate of the overall reaction is proportional to the concentration of hydrogen molecules and chlorine radicals but is not directly proportional to the concentration of chlorine molecules. However, since the ratio of concentrations of Cl and Cl_2 is regulated by the initiation step concentration, it can be shown that according to the mechanism provided the rate law is:

$$\text{rate} = k[H_2] \cdot [Cl_2]^{1/2}$$

It is important to note that the individual orders of a reaction are generally not equal to the stoichiometric coefficients.

9.5 Dependence of Reaction Rates upon Temperature

Rates of chemical reactions are generally very sensitive to temperature fluctuations. In particular, many reactions are known to slow down by decreasing the temperature or vise versa. How does one therefore explain the temperature dependence on reaction rates? The rate of a reaction is essentially equal to the reactant concentration raised to a reaction order (n) times the rate constant k or rate $= k[A]^x$. From the collision theory of chemical kinetics it was established that the rate constant of a reaction can be expressed as follows:

$$k = A\,e^{-Ea/RT}$$

- A is a constant referred to as the "Arrhenius constant" or the frequency factor which includes two separate components known as, the orientation factor (p) and the collision frequency (z). More specifically, the collision frequency (z) is defined as the number of collisions that molecules acquire per unit time and the orientation factor (p) is defined as the proper orientation reactant molecules require for product formation. Thus, the Arrhenius constant, A, is related to both the frequency of collisions (z) and the proper orientation (p) of the molecular collisions required for final product formation and so A = pz.
- e is the base of natural logarithms,
- E_a is the activation energy, it is the energy required to get a reaction started. For reactants to transform into products, the reactants must go through a high energy state or "transition state" which is the minimum energy (activation energy) required for reactants to transform into products. If two molecules of reactants collide with proper orientation and sufficient energy

or force in such a way that the molecules acquire a total energy content surpassing the activation energy, E_a, the collisions will result in a complete chemical reaction and the formation of products. Note: only a fraction of colliding reactant molecules will have sufficient kinetic energy to exceed an activation energy barrier.

- R is the ideal gas constant (1.99 cal mol^{-1} K^{-1})
- *T* is the absolute temperature.

It can therefore be seen that the rate constant, k, contains the temperature component as an exponent and thus, temperature affects a reaction rate by affecting the actual rate constant k. Note: A rate constant remains constant only when temperature remains constant. The rate constant equation otherwise known as the "Arrhenius equation" thus describes the relationship between the rate constant (k) and temperature.

Either an increase in temperature or decrease in activation energy will result in an increase in the reaction constant k and thus an increase in the reaction rate. The species formed during an efficient collision, before the reactants transform into the final product(s) is called the activated complex or the transition state.

Within the framework of this theory, when a single step reaction proceeds, the potential energy of the system varies according to Figure III.A.9.1.

The change in enthalpy (ΔH) during the reaction is the difference between the total energy of the products and the reactants.

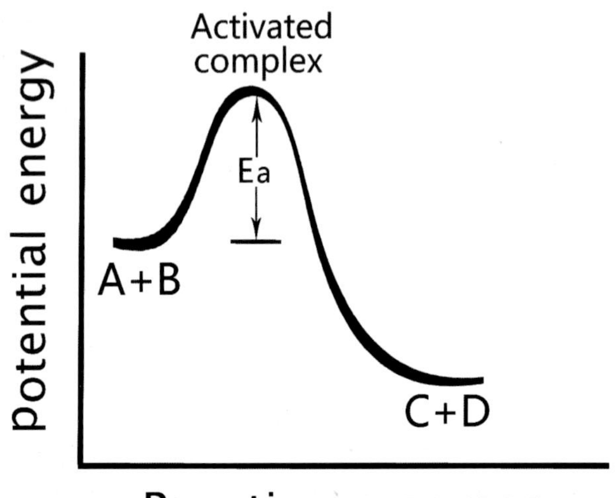

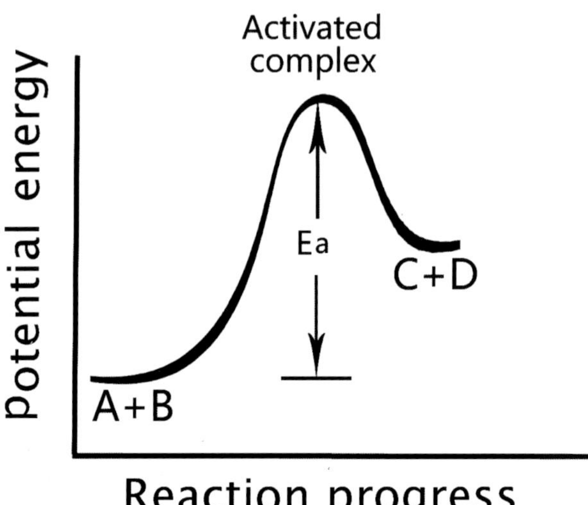

Figure III.A.9.1: Potential energy diagrams: exothermic vs. endothermic reactions.

The left curve of Figure III.A.9.1 shows that the total energy of the reactants is higher than the total energy of the products: this is obviously the case for an exothermic reaction. The right curve of Figure III.A.9.1, shows the profile of an endothermic reaction. A negative enthalpy change indicates an exothermic reaction and a positive enthalpy change depicts an endothermic reaction. The difference in potential energy between the reactant(s) and the activated complex is the activation energy of the forward reaction and the difference between the product(s) and the activated complex is the activation energy of the reverse reaction. Also note that the bigger the difference between the total energy of the reactants and the activated complex, i.e. the activation energy E_a, the slower the reaction.

If a reaction proceeds through several steps one can construct a diagram for each step and combine the single-step diagrams to obtain the energy profile of the overall reaction.

9.6 Kinetic Control vs. Thermodynamic Control

Consider the case where two molecules A and B can react to form either products C or D. Suppose that C has the lowest Gibbs free energy (i.e. the most thermodynamically stable product). Also suppose that product D requires the smallest activation energy and is therefore formed faster than C. If it is product C which is exclusively observed when the reaction is actually performed, the reaction is said to be thermodynamically controlled (i.e. out of a list of possible pathways the reactants choose the one leading to the most stable product). If on the other hand the reactants choose the pathway leading to the product which is produced more quickly it is said to be kinetically controlled.

9.7 Catalysis

A catalyst is a compound that does not directly participate in a reaction (the initial number of moles of this compound in the reaction mixture is equal to the number of moles of this compound once the reaction is completed). Catalysts work by providing an alternative mechanism for a reaction that involves a different transition state, one in which a lower activation energy occurs at the rate-determining step. Catalysts help lower the activation energy of a reaction and help the reaction to proceed. Enzymes are the typical biological catalysts. They are protein molecules with very large molar masses containing one or more active sites (BIO 4.1-4.4). Enzymes are very specialized catalysts. They are generally specific and operate only on certain biological reactants called substrates. They also generally increase the rate of reactions by large factors. The general mechanism of operation of enzymes is as follows:

Enzyme (E) + Substrate (S) $\rightarrow$ ES (complex)

ES $\rightarrow$ Product (P) + Enzyme (E)

If we were to compare the energy profile of a reaction performed in the absence of an enzyme to that of the same reaction performed with the addition of an enzyme we would obtain Figure III.A.9.2.

As you can see from Figure III.A.9.2, the reaction from the substrate to the product is facilitated by the presence of the enzyme because the reaction proceeds in two fast steps (low E_a's). Generally, catalysts (or enzymes) stabilize the transition state of a reaction by lowering the energy barrier between reactants and the transition state. Catalysts (or enzymes) do not change the energy difference between reactants and products. Therefore, catalysts do not alter the extent of a reaction or the chemical equilibrium itself. Generally, the rate of an enzyme-catalysed reaction is :

$$\text{rate} = k[ES]$$

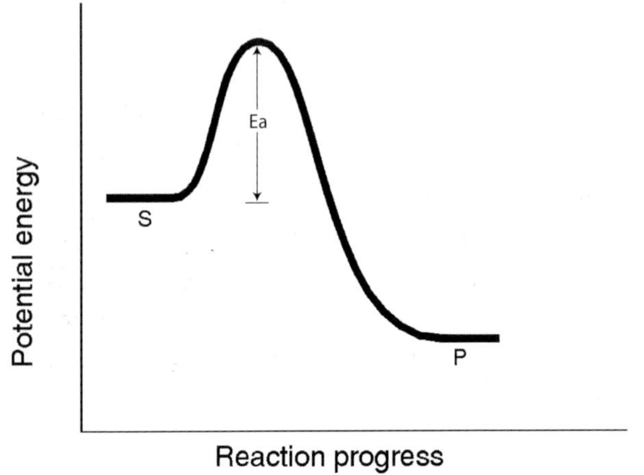

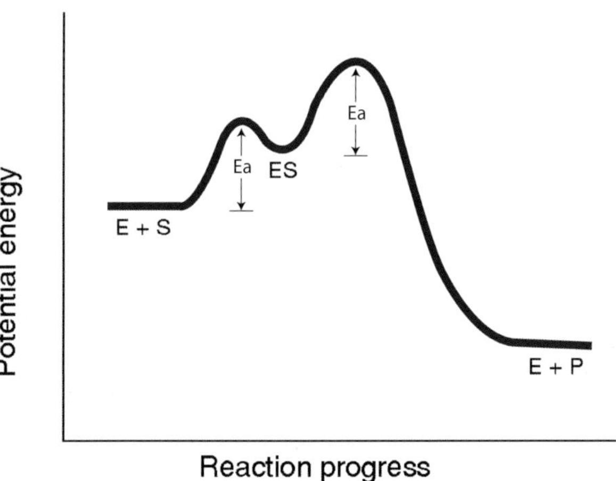

Figure III.A.9.2: Potential energy diagrams: without and with a catalyst.

The rate of formation of the product $\Delta[P]/\Delta t$ vs. the concentration of the substrate $[S]$ yields a plot as in Figure III.A.9.3.

When the concentration of the substrate is large enough for the substrate to occupy all the available active sites on the enzyme, any further increase would have no effect on the rate of the reaction. This is called *saturation kinetics* (BIO 1.1.2).

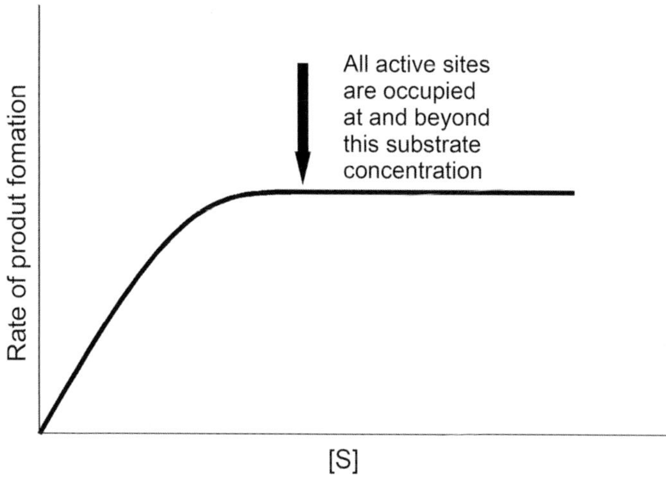

Figure III.A.9.3: Saturation kinetics.

9.8 Equilibrium in Reversible Chemical Reactions

In most chemical reactions once the product is formed, it reacts in such a way to yield back the initial reactants. Eventually, the system reaches a state where there are as many molecules of products being formed as there are molecules of reactants being generated through the reverse reaction. At equilibrium, the concentrations of reactants and products will not necessarily be equal, however, the concentrations remain the same. Hence, the relative concentrations of all components of the forward and reverse reactions become constant at equilibrium. This is called a state of "dynamic equilibrium". It is characterized by a constant K:

$$aA + bB \rightleftharpoons cC + dD$$

where a, b, c and d are the corresponding stoichiometric coefficients:

$$K = \frac{[C]^c\,[D]^d}{[A]^a\,[B]^b}$$

The equilibrium constant K (sometimes symbolized as K_{eq}) has a given value at a given temperature. If the temperature changes the value of K changes. At a given temperature, if we change the concentration of A, B, C or D, the system evolves in such a way as to re-establish the value of K. This is called the law of mass action. {Note: catalysts speed up the rate of reaction without affecting K_{eq}}

The following is an example of how an equilibrium constant K is calculated based on a chemical reaction at equilibrium. Remember that the equilibrium constant K can be directly calculated only when the equilibrium concentrations of reactants and products are known or obtained.

As an example, suppose that initially, 5 moles of reactant X are mixed with 12 moles of Y and both are added into an empty 1 liter container. Following their reaction, the system eventually reaches equilibrium with 4 moles of Z formed according to the following reaction:

$$X\ (g) + 2Y\ (g) \rightleftharpoons Z\ (g)$$

For this gaseous, homogeneous mixture (CHM 1.7), what is the value of the equilibrium constant K?

At equilibrium, 4 moles of Z are formed and therefore, 4 moles of X and 8 moles of Y are consumed based on the mole:mole ratio of the balanced equation. Since 5 moles X and 12 moles Y were initially available prior to equilibrium, at equilibrium following the reaction, there remains 1 mol X and 4 moles Y. Since all of the reaction takes place in a 1 L volume, the equilibrium concentrations are therefore, 1 mol/L for X, 4 mol/L for Y and Z, respectively.

Thus, the equilibrium constant can then be calculated as follows:

$$K = [Z]/[X][Y]^2 = [4]/[1][4]^2 = 0.25.$$

The K value is an indication of where the equilibrium point of a reaction actually lies, either far to the right or far to the left or somewhere in between. The following is a summary of the significance of the magnitude of an equilibrium constant K and its meaning:

1. If $K > 1$, this means that the forward reaction is favored and thus, the reaction favors product formation. If K is very large, the equilibrium mixture will then contain very little reactant compared to product.

2. If $K < 1$, the reverse reaction is favored and so the reaction does not proceed very far towards product formation and thus very little product is formed.

3. If $K = 1$, neither forward nor reverse directions are favored.

Note: Pure solids and pure liquids do not appear in the equilibrium constant. Thus in heterogeneous equilibria, since the liquid and solid phases are not sensitive to pressure, their "concentrations" remain constant throughout the reaction and so, mathematically, their values are denoted as 1.

Naturally, H_2O is one of the most common liquids dealt with in reactions. Remember to set its activity equal to 1 when it is a liquid but, if H_2O is written as a gas, then its concentration must be considered.

9.8.1 The Reaction Quotient Q to Predict Reaction Direction

The reaction quotient Q is the same ratio as the equilibrium constant K. Q defines all reaction progresses including the K value. In other words, the equilibrium constant K is a special case of the reaction quotient Q.

Thus, the Q ratio has many values dependent on where the reaction lies prior to or subsequent to the concentrations at equilibrium. One may therefore determine if a reaction is going towards an equilibrium by making more products or, alternatively, if a reaction is moving towards equilibrium by making more reactants. The following is a summary of what Q means in relation to K.

Consider the following reaction:

$$aA + bB \rightleftharpoons cC + dD,$$

$$Q = [C]^c[D]^d/[A]^a[B]^b$$

The reaction quotient Q relative to the equilibrium constant K is essentially a mea-

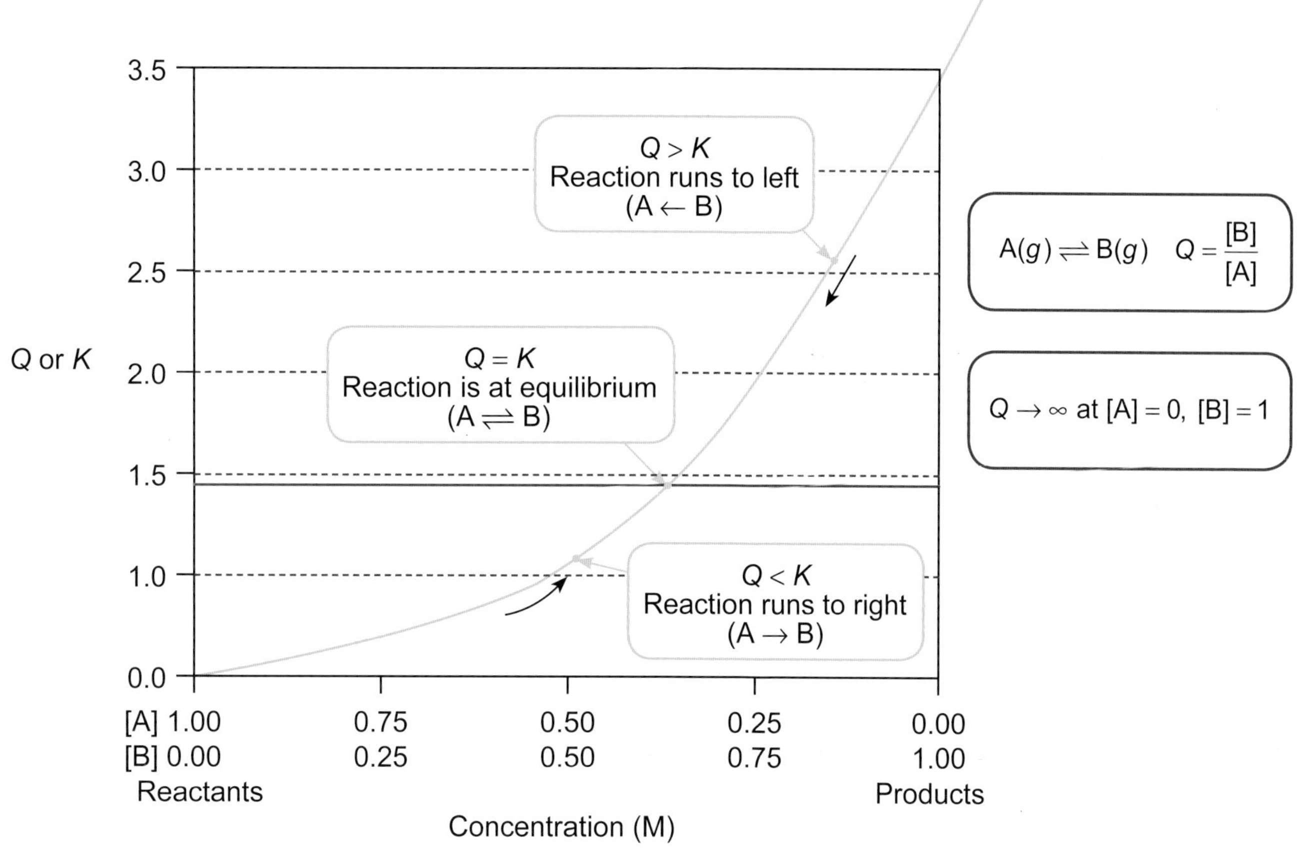

sure of the progress of a reaction toward equilibrium. The reaction quotient Q has many different values and changes continuously as a reaction progresses and depends on the current state of a reaction mixture. However, once all equilibrium concentrations have been reached, $Q = K$.

If $Q = K$, the reaction is at equilibrium and all concentrations are at equilibrium. If $Q > K$, there are more products initially than there are reactants so the reaction proceeds in reverse direction towards a decrease in product concentrations and a simultaneous increase in reactant concentrations until equilibrium is reached. If $Q < K$, there are more reactants then products and so the reaction proceeds forward towards product formation until equilibrium is reached.

9.9 Le Chatelier's Principle

Le Chatelier's principle states that whenever a perturbation is applied to a system at equilibrium, the system evolves in such a way as to compensate for the applied perturbation. For instance, consider the following equilibrium:

$$N_2 + 3H_2 \rightleftharpoons 2NH_3$$

If we introduce some more hydrogen in the reaction mixture at equilibrium, i.e. if we increase the concentration of hydrogen, the system will evolve in the direction that will decrease the concentration of hydrogen (from left to right). If more ammonia is introduced, the equilibrium shifts from the right-hand side to the left-hand side, while the removal of ammonia from the reaction vessel would do the opposite (i.e. shifts equilibrium from the left-hand side to the right-hand side).

In a similar fashion, an increase in total pressure (decrease in volume) favors the direction which decreases the total number of compressible (i.e. gases) moles (from the left-hand side where there are 4 moles to the right-hand side where there are 2 moles). It can also be said that when there are different forms of a gaseous substance, an increase in total pressure (decrease in volume) favors the form with the greatest density, and a decrease in total pressure (increase in volume) favors the form with the lowest density.

Finally, if the temperature of a reaction mixture at equilibrium is increased, the equilibrium evolves in the direction of the endothermic (heat-absorbing) reaction. For instance, the forward reaction of the equilibrium:

$$N_2O_4(g) \rightleftharpoons 2NO_2(g)$$

is endothermic; therefore, an increase in temperature favors the forward reaction over the backward reaction. In other words, the dissociation of N_2O_4 increases with temperature.

9.10 Relationship between the Equilibrium Constant and the Change in the Gibbs Free Energy

In the "thermodynamics" section we defined the Gibbs free energy. The *standard* Gibbs free energy ($G°$) is determined at 25 °C (298 K) and 1 atm. The change in the standard Gibbs free energy for a given reaction can be calculated from the change in the standard enthalpy and entropy of the reaction using:

$$\Delta G° = \Delta H - T\,\Delta S°$$

where T is the temperature at which the reaction is carried out. If this reaction happens to be the forward reaction of an equilibrium, the equilibrium constant associated with this equilibrium is simply given by:

$$\Delta G° = -\mathrm{R}\,T\,ln\,K_{eq}$$

where R is the ideal gas constant (1.99 cal mol^{-1} K^{-1}) and ln is the natural logarithm (i.e. log to the base *e*; see QR Appendix).

It is important to remember the sign for Gibbs free energy when the reaction is not spontaneous, spontaneous and at equilibrium (CHM 8.10).

GOLD STANDARD WARM-UP EXERCISES

CHAPTER 9: Rate Processes in Chemical Reactions

1) The reaction P + 3Q ↔ R was studied and the data in Table 1 were collected.

Table 1

Exp.	[P] in M	[Q] in M	Initial rate of reaction
A	0.30	0.90	5.0×10^{-6}
B	0.30	1.80	1.0×10^{-5}
C	0.90	0.90	4.5×10^{-5}

The rate determining step in this reaction probably involves:

A. two molecules of P and two molecules of Q.
B. three molecules of P and one molecule of Q.
C. one molecule of P and three molecules of Q.
D. two molecules of P and one molecule of Q.

2) This reaction is shifted to the right on the application of heat:

$$3HalO^- \leftrightarrow 2Hal^- + HalO_3^-$$

The ΔH_{rxn} for the reaction is probably:

A. zero.
B. positive.
C. negative.
D. dependent on the temperature at which the reaction occurs.

3) If no catalyst was used in Reaction I, which of the following would experience a change in its partial pressure when the same system reaches equilibrium?

Reaction I

$2SO_2(g) + O_2(g) \leftrightarrow 2SO_3(g) \qquad \Delta H = -197$ kJ mol^{-1}

A. There will be no change in the partial pressure of any of the reactants.
B. SO_3 (g)
C. SO_2 (g)
D. O_2 (g)

4) If the temperature was decreased in Reaction I of the previous question, which of the following would experience an increase in its partial pressure when the same system reaches equilibrium?

A. There will be no change in the partial pressure of any of the reactants.
B. SO_3 (g)
C. SO_2 (g)
D. O_2 (g) and SO_2 (g)

5) In an experiment carried out at 25 °C, P_2 and Q_2 molecules reacted to yield one triatomic product. This took place spontaneously and was associated with an increase in the temperature of the reaction vessel. If the reaction is an equilibrium type reaction, what does Le Chatelier's Principle predict for a decrease in temperature?

A. Reaction shifts to the right to yield more products
B. Reaction shifts to the left to yield more reactants
C. Reaction equilibrium position is unaffected
D. Depends on whether or not the reaction vessel is connected to a water manometer

6) Which of the following represents the general shape of the potential energy diagram for the following reaction?

$2NO(g) + O_2(g) \rightarrow 2NO_2(g) \qquad \Delta H^\circ = -116.2\text{ kJ}$

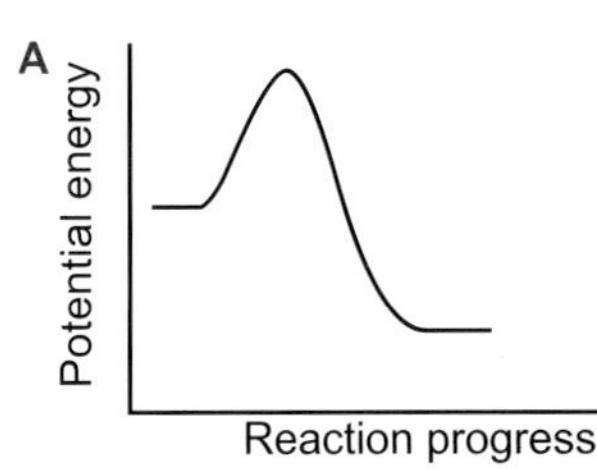

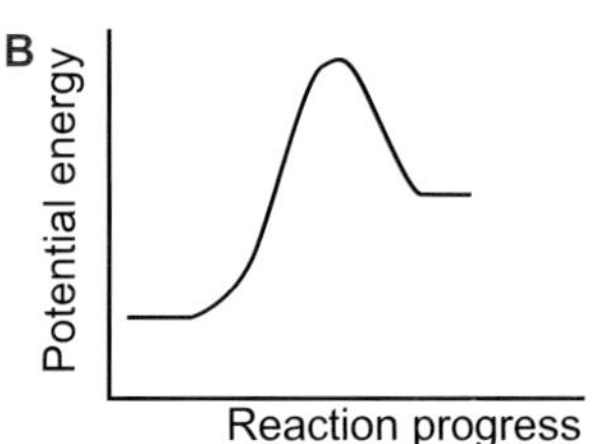

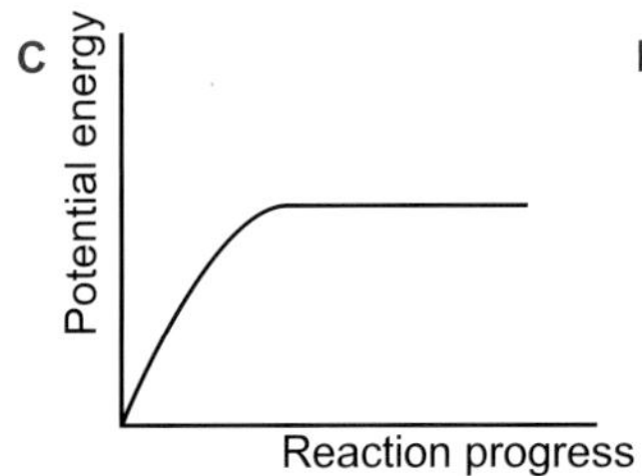

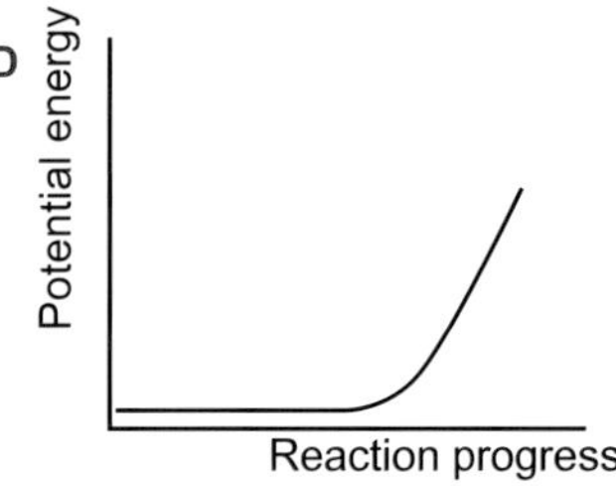

7) The equilibrium shown below was established within the confines of a closed system.

Reaction I

$$4NH_3(g) + 5O_2(g) \rightleftharpoons 4NO(g) + 6H_2O(g)$$

$$\Delta H_{rxn} = -1100\text{ kJ mol}^{-}1$$

What effect will increasing the pressure have on this system?

A. The equilibrium will shift to the left.
B. The equilibrium will shift to the right.
C. The equilibrium position will remain the same.
D. The equilibrium position will depend on whether a catalyst is present or not.

8) Given that $K_{a1}(H_2S) = 9.1 \times 10^{-8}$ and $K_{a2}(H_2S) = 1.2 \times 10^{-15}$, what would be the effect on Reaction I if protons were added to the reaction mixture at equilibrium?
(note: the effect of protons on CN^- is relatively negligible).

Reaction I

$$Ag_2S + 4CN^- \leftrightarrow 2[Ag(CN)_2]^- + S^{2-}$$

A. The equilibrium would shift to the left.
B. The equilibrium would shift to the right.
C. There would be no change in the equilibrium position of the reaction.
D. The change in the equilibrium position cannot be determined from the information given.

9) Consider the following gas phase reaction at equilibrium:

$$H_2 + I_2 \leftrightarrow 2HI$$

ΔH for the forward reaction (production of HI) is negative. Raising the ambient temperature of the reaction would cause:

A. a decrease in entropy.
B. a decrease in pressure.
C. an increase in the concentration of H_2 and I_2.
D. no change in the equilibrium concentrations of reactants and products.

10) Consider the data in Table 1, which pertain to the following reaction:

$$A + B \rightarrow C$$

The equation above may or may not be balanced.

Table 1

Experiment	[A]	[B]	Initial rate of reaction
1	0.10	0.10	4.0×10^{-5}
2	0.10	0.20	4.0×10^{-5}
3	0.20	0.10	16×10^{-5}

The rate law for the reaction is:

A. Rate = k[A][B].
B. Rate = $k[A]^2[B]$.
C. Rate = $k[A]^2$.
D. Rate = $k[A][B]^2$.

11) Based on Table 1 in the previous question, the rate constant, k, is:

A. $4.0 \times 10^{-3}\ M^{-1}s^{-1}$
B. $4.0 \times 10^{-3}\ Ms^{-1}$
C. $4.0 \times 10^{-5}\ M^{-1}s^{-1}$
D. $4.0 \times 10^{-5}\ Ms^{-1}$

12) The mechanism of the reaction described in Table 1 from the previous questions most likely involves:

A. a termolecular rate (3 molecules)–determining step.
B. a bimolecular rate–determining step involving two molecules of A, followed by a fast step involving a molecule of B.
C. a fast step involving a molecule of A and a molecule of B, followed by a bimolecular rate-determining step involving another molecule of A.
D. a bimolecular rate–determining step involving a molecule of A and a molecule of B, followed by a fast step involving another molecule of A.

13) Which of the following statements is/are true?

I. k increases with activation energy.
II. k increases with temperature.
III. k decreases with increasing concentrations of products.

A. Only II
B. I and II
C. II and III
D. I, II and III

14) When sucrose is digested, it is hydrolyzed to form glucose and fructose. The following data in Table 1 are collected for the hydrolysis of sucrose in 0.100 M HCl at 35 °C.

Table 1

Concentration of Sucrose (M)	Initial Rate (M/min)
0.500	1.80×10^{-3}
0.400	1.46×10^{-3}
0.200	7.32×10^{-4}

Which of the following might be the rate law for the hydrolysis of sucrose under these conditions?

A. rate = $(1.46 \times 10^{-4}\ min^{-1})$[sucrose]
B. rate = $(1.46 \times 10^{-3}\ min^{-1}M^{-1})$[sucrose]^2
C. rate = $(3.66 \times 10^{-3}\ min^{-1})$[sucrose]
D. rate = $(3.66 \times 10^{-4}\ min^{-1}M^{-1})$[sucrose]^2

15) The graph below represents the exothermic energy changes of the following reaction:

$$A + B \rightarrow C$$

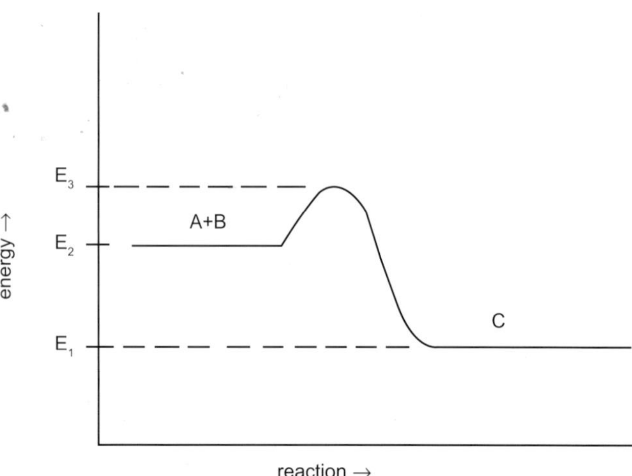

What is the activation energy of this reaction?

A. $E_3 - E_1$
B. $E_2 - E_1$
C. $E_3 - E_2$
D. None of the above

GS ANSWER KEY

Chapter 9

		Cross-Reference			*Cross-Reference*
1.	D	CHM 9.3, 9.4	9.	C	CHM 9.9
2.	B	CHM 8.2, 9.9	10.	C	CHM 9.2, 9.3
3.	A	CHM 9.7, 9.8	11.	A	CHM 9.2, 9.3
4.	B	CHM 9.9	12.	B	CHM 9.2, 9.3
5.	A	CHM 9.9	13.	A	CHM 9.2, 9.3
6.	A	CHM 9.5	14.	C	CHM 9.3
7.	A	CHM 9.9	15.	C	CHM 9.5
8.	B	CHM 5.3.3, 9.9			

* Explanations can be found at the back of the book.

Go online to DAT-prep.com for additional chapter review Q&A and forum.

ELECTROCHEMISTRY

Chapter 10

Memorize

- Define: anode, cathode, anion, cation
- Define: standard half-cell potentials
- Define: strong/weak oxidizing/reducing agents

Understand

* Electrolytic cell, electrolysis
* Calculation involving Faraday's law
* Galvanic (voltaic) cell, purpose of salt bridge
* Half reaction, reduction potentials
* Direction of electron flow

Importance

1 to 3 out of the 30 Gen CHM

DAT questions are based on content in this chapter (in our estimation).
* Note that between 50% and 85% of the questions in DAT General Chemistry are based on content from 6 chapters: 1, 2, 4, 5, 6 and 9.

DAT-Prep.com

Introduction 

Electrochemistry links chemistry with electricity (the movement of electrons through a conductor). If a chemical reaction produces electricity (i.e. a battery or galvanic/voltaic cell) then it is an **electrochemical cell**. If electricity is applied externally to drive the chemical reaction then it is **electrolysis**. In general, oxidation/reduction reactions occur and are separated in space or time, connected by an external circuit.

Additional Resources

Free Online Forum

Video: Online or DVD

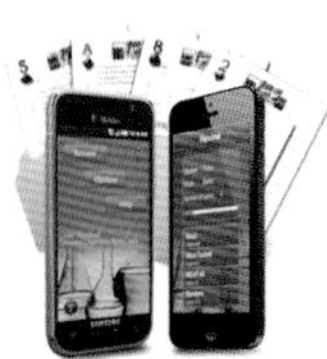

Flashcards

10.1 Generalities

Electrochemistry is based on oxidation-reduction or redox reactions in which one or more electrons are transferred from one ionic species to another. Recall that oxidation is defined as the loss of one or more electrons and reduction is defined as the gain in electron(s). In a redox reaction, reduction and oxidation must occur simultaneously. Before you read this section you should review the rules that allow the determination of the oxidation state of an element in a polyatomic molecule or ion and the definition of oxidation and reduction processes. We had previously applied the rules for the determination of oxidation numbers in the case of the following overall reaction (see CHM 1.6):

$$CuSO_4(aq) + Zn(s) \rightleftharpoons$$
Oxid.#: +2 0
$$Cu(s) + ZnSO_4(aq)$$
Oxid.#: 0 +2

The reduction and oxidation half-reactions of the forward process are:

reduction half-reaction:
$Cu^{2+}(aq) + 2e^- \rightarrow Cu(s)$

oxidation half-reaction:
$Zn(s) \rightarrow Zn^{2+}(aq) + 2e^-$

A half reaction does not occur on its own merit. Any reduction half reaction must be accompanied by an associated oxidation half reaction or vise versa, as electrons need to be transferred accordingly from one reactant to another. To determine the number and the side on which to put the electrons one follows the simple rules:

(i) The electrons are always on the left-hand side of a reduction half-reaction.

(ii) The electrons are always on the right-hand side of an oxidation half-reaction.

(iii) For a reduction half-reaction:

# of electrons required = initial oxidation # – final oxidation #

(iv) For an oxidation half-reaction:
# of electrons required = final oxidation # – initial oxidation #

The next step is to balance each half-reaction, i.e. the charges and the number of atoms of all the elements involved have to be equal on both sides. The preceding example is very simple since the number of electrons required in the two half-reactions is the same. Consider the following more complicated example:

reduction: $Sn^{2+}(aq) + 2e^- \rightarrow Sn(s)$
oxidation: $Al(s) \rightarrow Al^{3+}(aq) + 3e^-$

to balance the overall reaction you need to multiply the first half-reaction by a factor of 3 and the second by a factor of 2.

Balancing redox reactions in aqueous solutions may not always be as straight forward as balancing other types of chemical reactions. For redox type reactions, both the mass and the charge must be balanced. In addition, when looking at redox reactions occurring in aqueous solutions one must also consider at times if the solution is acidic or basic. The procedure used to balance redox reactions in acidic versus basic solutions is slightly different. Generally, the recommended steps used in balancing redox reactions is as follows and the method used is called the "*half-reaction method of balancing*":

1) Identify all the oxidation states of all elements within the redox reaction.

2) Identify the elements being oxidized and those being reduced.

3) Separate the overall redox reaction into its corresponding oxidation and reduction half reactions.

4) Balance all elements for each half reaction excluding hydrogen and oxygen.

5) Balance oxygen by the addition of water to the side missing the oxygen and balance the oxygen atoms by adding the appropriate coefficients in front of water.

6) Balance hydrogen by the addition of H^+ ion to the side missing the hydrogen atoms until hydrogen is balanced with the appropriate coefficients added. Note that the difference in balancing redox reactions in acidic versus basic aqueous solutions is at this step. In basic solutions, an additional step is required to neutralize the H^+ ions with the addition of OH^- ions so that both may then combine to form water.

7) Balance the half reactions with respect to charge by the addition of electrons on the appropriate side.

8) Balance the number of electrons for each half reaction by multiplying each of the half reactions (if required) with the appropriate coefficient.

9) Add the two half reactions making sure that all electrons are cancelled.

10) Finally, as a check: you should always verify that all elements and charges are balanced on both sides of the overall reaction and that the final overall reaction *never contains any free electrons.*

Example: In acidic solution, balance the following redox reaction:

$Fe^{2+}(aq) + MnO_4^-(aq) \rightarrow Fe^{3+}(aq) + Mn^{2+}(aq)$

Step 1: +2   +7 −2   +3   +2

Step 2: Fe is oxidized (+2 to +3)
Mn in MnO_4^- is reduced to Mn^{2+}
(+7 to +2, oxygen will be balanced with water)

Step 3: Oxidation: $Fe^{2+}(aq) \rightarrow Fe^{3+}(aq)$
Reduction: $MnO_4^-(aq) \rightarrow Mn^{2+}(aq)$

Step 4, 5 and 6: Oxidation: $Fe^{2+}(aq) \rightarrow Fe^{3+}(aq)$
Reduction: $8H^+(aq) + MnO_4^-(aq) \rightarrow Mn^{2+}(aq) + 4H_2O(l)$

Step 7: Oxidation: $Fe^{2+}(aq) \rightarrow Fe^{3+}(aq) + 1e^-$
Reduction: $5e^- + 8H^+(aq) + MnO_4^-(aq) \rightarrow Mn^{2+}(aq) + 4H_2O(l)$

Step 8: Oxidation: $5[Fe^{2+}(aq) \rightarrow Fe^{3+}(aq) + 1e^-]$
$5Fe^{2+}(aq) \rightarrow 5Fe^{3+}(aq) + 5e^-$
Reduction: $5e^- + 8H^+(aq) + MnO_4^-(aq) \rightarrow Mn^{2+}(aq) + 4H_2O(l)$

Step 9: Overall: $5Fe^{2+}(aq) + 8H^+(aq) + MnO_4^-(aq) \rightarrow 5Fe^{3+}(aq) + Mn^{2+}(aq) + 4H_2O(l)$

Step 10: Check if all is balanced.

The oxidation/reduction capabilities of substances are measured by their standard reduction half reaction potentials E°(V). The reduction potential E°(V) is a measure of the tendency of a chemical species to acquire electrons and thereby be reduced. The more positive the reduction potential, the more likely the species is to be reduced. Thus, the species would be regarded as a strong oxidizing agent. These potentials are relative. The reference half-cell electrode chosen to measure the relative potential of all other half cells is known as the **s**tandard **h**ydrogen **e**lectrode or SHE and it corresponds to the following half-reaction:

$$2H^+(1\ \text{molar}) + 2e^- \rightarrow H_2(1\ \text{atm}) \quad E° = 0.00\ (V).$$

As the reference SHE cell potential is defined as 0.00 V, any half-cell system that accepts electrons from a SHE cell is reduced and therefore defined by a positive redox potential. Alternatively, any half-cell that donates electrons to a SHE cell is defined by a negative redox potential. Thus, the larger the reduction potential value of a half-cell, the greater the tendency for that half-cell to gain electrons and become reduced. Standard half-cell potentials for other half-reactions have been tabulated and you will see examples to follow, and more in the chapter review Warm-Up Exercises. They are defined for standard conditions, i.e., concentration of all ionic species equal to 1 molar and pressure of all gases involved, if any, equal to 1 atm. The standard temperature is taken as 25 °C. In the case of the Cu^{2+}/Zn reaction the relevant data is tabulated as reduction potentials as follows:

$$Zn^{2+}(aq) + 2e^- \rightarrow Zn(s) \quad E° = -0.76\ \text{volts}$$
$$Cu^{2+}(aq) + 2e^- \rightarrow Cu(s) \quad E° = +0.34\ \text{volts}$$

As shown, it can be seen that the Cu/Cu^{2+} electrode is positive relative to the SHE and that the Zn/Zn^{2+} is negative relative to the SHE. The more positive the E° value, the more likely the reaction will occur spontaneously as written. The strongest reducing agents have large negative E° values. The strongest oxidizing agents have large positive E° values. Therefore, in our example Cu^{2+} is a stronger oxidizing agent than Zn^{2+}. This conclusion can be expressed in the following practical terms:

(i) If you put Zn in contact with a solution containing Cu^{2+} ions a spontaneous redox reaction will occur.

$$Zn(s) \rightarrow Zn^{2+}(aq) + 2e^-; \quad E°(V) = +0.76$$
$$Cu^{2+}(aq) + 2e^- \rightarrow Cu(s); \quad E°(V) = +0.34$$
$$E°_{cell} = E°_{red} + E°_{ox} = +0.34 + 0.76 = +1.10\ V.$$

(ii) If you put Cu directly in contact with a solution containing Zn^{2+} ions, no reaction takes place spontaneously.

$$Cu(s) \rightarrow Cu^{2+}(aq) + 2e^-; \quad E°(V) = -0.34$$
$$Zn^{2+}(aq) + 2e^- \rightarrow Zn(s); \ E°(V) = -0.76$$
$$E°_{cell} = E°_{red} + E°_{ox} = -0.76 + (-0.34) = -1.10\ V.$$

Thus for the spontaneous reaction:

(1) $E° = E°_{red} - E°_{ox}$

$$E° = E°_{red} - E°_{ox} = +0.34 - (-0.76) = 1.10\ V.$$

or **(2)** $E°_{cell} = E°_{red} + E°_{ox} = +0.34 + 0.76 = 1.10\ V.$

The positive value confirms the spontaneous nature of the reaction. {The theme of many exam questions: the oxidizing agent is *reduced*; the reducing agent is *oxidized*}

For a cell potential (E°) calculation, if one is to calculate it using the formula **(1)** should use the tabulated reduction potentials for both half cell reduction reactions. Alternatively, if one were to calculate the cell potential using the second formula **(2)**, the half cell potential that has the lower potential value or the oxidized half cell (more negative value), needs to be reversed to have it in an oxidized format and therefore the electromotive (E°) potential sign itself is also inverted accordingly and the sum of the two half cells is then calculated. Also, note that the stoichiometric factors are not used if one is simply calculating the E° of the cell (because the concentrations are, of course, standard at 1 M).

10.2 Galvanic Cells

As a result of a redox reaction, one may harvest a substantial amount of energy and the energy generated is usually carried out in what is known as an electrochemical cell. There are two types of electrochemical cells: a galvanic (or voltaic) cell and an electrolytic cell. A galvanic cell produces electrical energy from a spontaneous chemical reaction that takes place within an electrochemical cell. On the other hand, an electrolytic cell induces a nonspontaneous chemical reaction within an electrochemical cell by the consumption of electrical energy.

Batteries are self-contained galvanic cells. A galvanic cell uses a spontaneous redox reaction to produce electricity. For instance, one can design a galvanic cell based on the spontaneous reaction:

$$Zn(s) + CuSO_4(aq) \rightarrow Cu(s) + ZnSO_4(aq)$$

An actual view of a galvanic cell is depicted in Figure III.A.10.1a. In addition, Figure III.A.10.1b shows a sketch of a line diagram of the same galvanic cell outlining all the different parts. Note that in Figure III.A.10.1b, Zn is not in direct contact with the Cu^{2+} solution; otherwise electrons will be directly transferred from Zn to Cu^{2+} and no electricity will be produced to an external circuit.

The half-reaction occurring in the left-hand (anode) compartment is the oxidation:

$$Zn(s) \rightarrow Zn^{2+}(aq) + 2e^-$$

The half-reaction occurring in the right-hand (cathode) compartment is the reduction:

$$Cu^{2+}(aq) + 2e^- \rightarrow Cu(s)$$

Therefore, electrons flow out of the compartment where the oxidation occurs to the compartment where the reduction takes place.

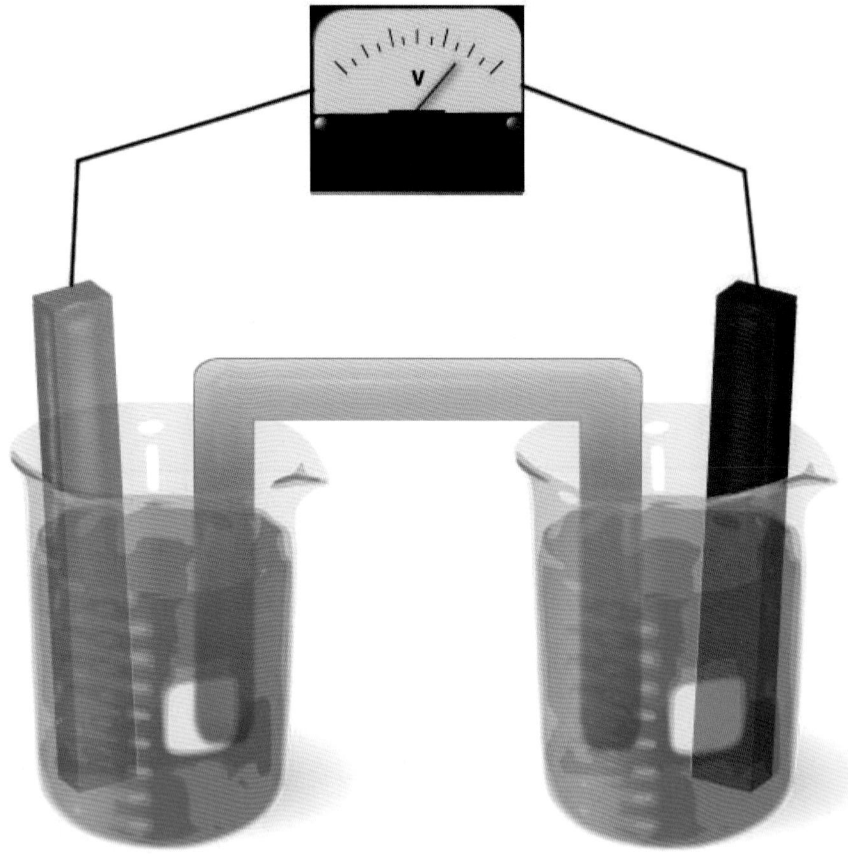

Figure III.A.10.1a: A galvanic (electrochemical) cell. As shown by the displacement in voltage via the voltmeter, the energy of a spontaneous redox reaction is essentially captured within the galvanic cell. A galvanic cell consists mainly of the following parts: **1)** Two separate half cells; **2)** Two solid element electrodes with differing redox potentials; **3)** Two opposing aqueous solutions each in contact with opposing solid electrodes; **4)** One salt bridge with an embedded salt solution; **5)** One ammeter or voltmeter and; **6)** An electrical solid element or wire to allow conductivity of electrons from anode to cathode.

The metallic parts (Cu(*s*) and Zn(*s*) in our example) of the galvanic cell which allow its connection to an external circuit are called electrodes. The electrode out of which electrons flow is the anode, the electrode receiving these electrons is the cathode. In a galvanic cell the oxidation occurs in the anodic compartment and the reduction in the cathodic compartment. The voltage difference between the two electrodes is called the electromotive force (*emf*) of the cell. The voltage is measured by the voltmeter.

All of the participants belonging to each of the half cells are included within their respective half cell. Consequently, one half of the electrochemical cell consists of an appropriate metal (Zn) immersed within a solution containing the ionic form of the same metal ($ZnSO_4$). The other half then contains the complemen-

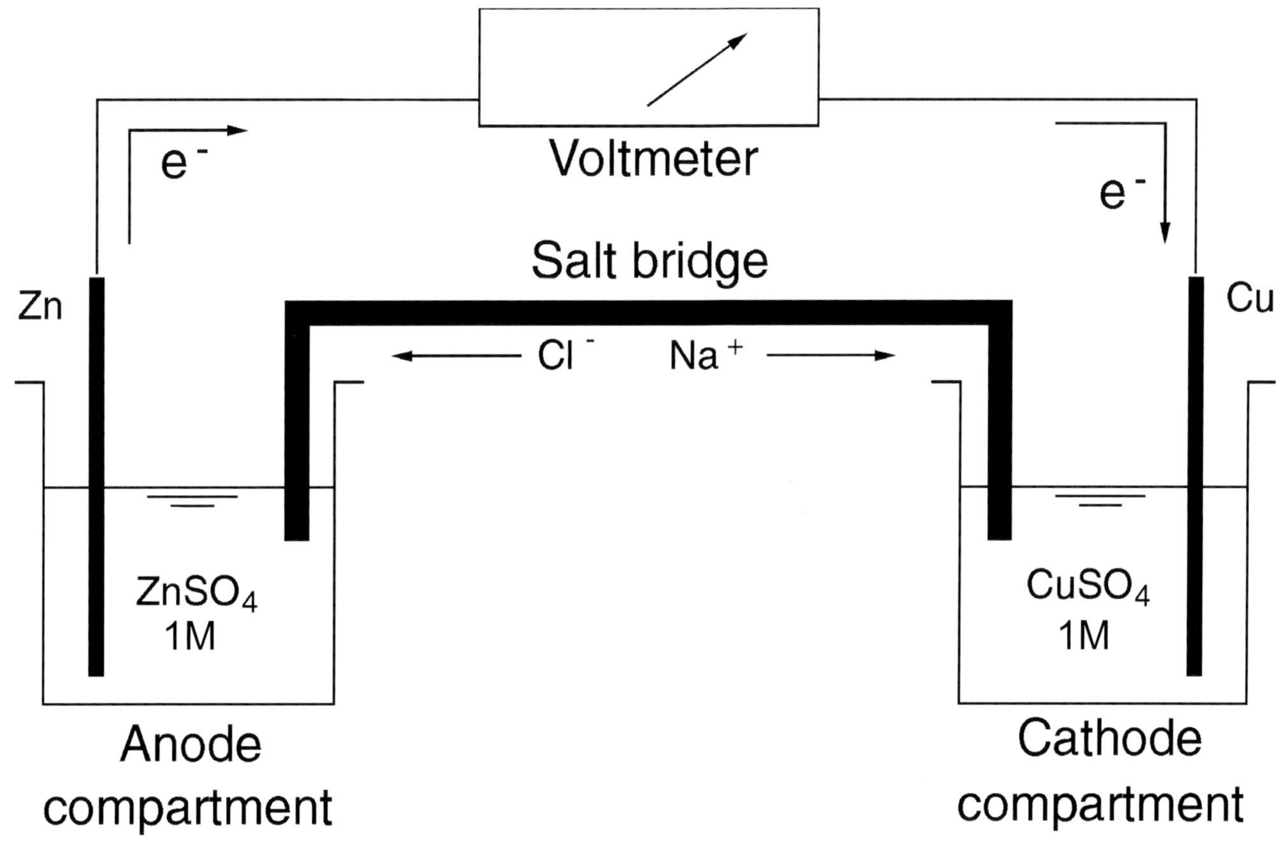

Figure III.A.10.1b: Line diagram of a galvanic (electrochemical) cell.

tary metal (Cu) immersed into an aqueous solution consisting of its metal ion ($CuSO_4$) (Figure III.A.10.1b).

In certain cells, however, the participants involved in the reduction half reaction may all be part of the aqueous solution; in such a case, an inert electrode would replace the respective metal electrode. The inert electrode such as graphite or platinum would act as a conductive surface for electron transfer. An example of such a half-cell would be one where the reduction of manganese (Mn^{7+}) as MnO_4^- occurs in a solution which also contains manganese as ions (Mn^{2+}). To complete the electrochemical circuit, the two half-cells are then connected with a conducting wire which provides a means for electron flow. Electrons always flow from the anode (oxidation half-cell) to the cathode (reduction half-cell). The electrical energy from the flow of electrons may then be harvested and transformed into some alternative form of energy or mechanical work (as required). In order to prevent an excessive charge build up within each of the half-cell solutions as a result of oxidation and reduction reactions at the anode and cathode, a salt bridge is constructed and used to connect both half-cell solutions.

Mnemonic: LEO is A GERC
- Lose Electrons Oxidation is Anode
- Gain Electrons Reduction at Cathode

Electrochemical cells are usually represented as a cell diagram or a compact notation denoting all the parts of the cell. For example, the cell diagram of the cell that was previously discussed in which Zn is oxidized and Cu reduced would be represented as follows:

$$Zn(s) \mid Zn^{2+}(aq) \parallel Cu^{2+}(aq) \mid Cu(s).$$

The oxidation half reaction is on the left and the reduction half reaction is on the right side of the cell diagram. The single vertical lines represent the substances of each half-cell in different phases (solid and aqueous) and the double vertical line represents the salt bridge.

10.2.1 The Salt Bridge

A salt bridge is a U-shaped tube with a strong electrolyte suspended in a gel allowing the flow of the ions into the half-cell solutions. The salt bridge connects the two compartments chemically (for example, with Na^+ and Cl^-). It has two important functions:

1) Maintenance of Neutrality: As Zn(*s*) becomes Zn^{2+}(*aq*), the net charge in the anode compartment becomes positive. To maintain neutrality, Cl^- ions migrate to the anode compartment. The reverse occurs in the cathode compartment: positive ions are lost (Cu^{2+}), therefore positive ions must be gained (Na^+).

2) Completing the Circuit: Imagine the galvanic cell as a circuit. Negative charge leaves the anode compartment via *electrons* in a wire and then returns via *chemicals* (i.e. Cl^-) in the salt bridge. Thus the galvanic cell is an *electrochemical* cell.

As an alternative to a salt bridge, the solutions (i.e. $ZnSO_4$ and $CuSO_4$) can be placed in one container separated by a porous material which allows certain ions to cross (i.e. SO_4^{2-}, Zn^{2-}). Thus it would serve the same functions as the salt bridge.

10.3 Concentration Cell

If the concentration of the ions in one of the compartments of a galvanic cell is not 1 molar, the half-cell potential E is either higher or lower than E°. Therefore, in principle one could use the same substance in both compartments but with different concentrations to produce electricity.

Thus, one may construct a galvanic cell in which both half-cell reactions are the same however, the difference in concentration is the driving force for the flow of current. The emf is equal in this case to the difference between the two potentials E. Such a cell is called a concentration cell.

To determine the direction of electron flow the same rules as previously described are used. The cathodic compartment, in which the reduction takes place is the one corresponding to the largest positive (smallest negative) E.

The electromotive force varies with the differences in concentration of solutions in the half-cells. When the concentration of solution is not equal to 1M, the emf or E_{cell} can be determined by the use of the Nernst equation (BIO Appendix 5) as follows:

$$E_{cell} = E^{\circ}_{cell} - (RT/nF)(\ln Q)$$

or

$$E_{cell} = E^{\circ}_{cell} - 0.0592V/n\ (\log Q)$$

where; E°_{cell} is the standard electromotive force, R is the gas constant 8.314J/Kmol, T is the absolute temperature in K, F is the Faraday's constant (CHM 10.5), n is the number of moles of electrons exchanged or transferred in the redox reaction, and Q is the reaction quotient (CHM 9.8.1).

Under standard conditions, $Q = 1.00$ as all concentrations are at 1.00 M and since $\log 1 = 0$, $E_{cell} = E^{\circ}_{cell}$.

10.4 Electrolytic Cell

There is a fundamental difference between a galvanic cell or a concentration cell and an electrolytic cell: in the first type of electrochemical cell a spontaneous redox reaction is used to produce a current, in the second type a current is actually imposed on the system to drive a non-spontaneous redox reaction. A cathode is defined as the electrode to which cations flow to and an anode is defined as the electrode to which anions flow. Thus, a similarity between the two cells is that the cathode attracts cations, whereas the anode attracts anions. In both the galvanic cell and the electrolytic cell, reduction occurs always at the cathode and oxidation always occurs at the anode.

Remember the following key concepts:

(i) generally a battery is used to produce a current which is imposed on the electrolytic cell.

(ii) the battery acts as an electron pump: electrons flow into the electrolytic cell at the cathode and flow out of it at the anode.

(iii) the half-reaction occurring at the cathode is a reduction since it requires electrons.

(iv) the half-reaction occurring at the anode is an oxidation since it produces electrons.

In galvanic cells, a spontaneous oxidation reaction takes place at the cell's anode creating a source of electrons. For this reason, the anode is considered the negative electrode. However, in electrolytic cells, a non-spontaneous reduction reaction takes place at the cell's cathode using an external electrical energy as the source of electrons such as a battery. For this reason, the cathode is considered the negative electrode.

An electrolytic cell is composed of three parts: an electrolyte solution and two electrodes made from an inert material (i.e. platinum). The oxidation and reduction half reactions are usually placed in one container.

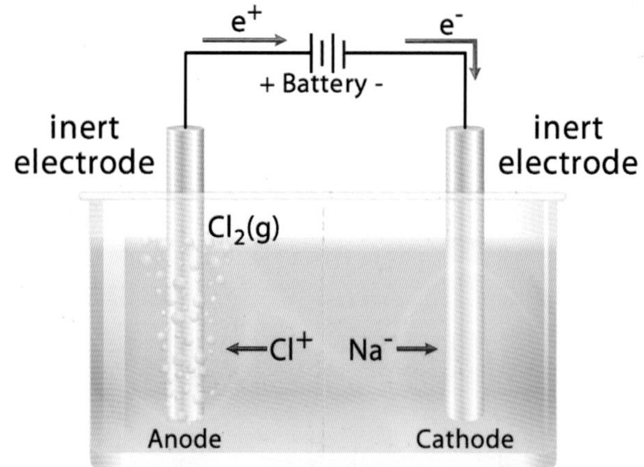

The diagram is a depiction of the electrolysis of molten NaCl. As such, the Na^+ and Cl^- ions are the only species that are present in the electrolytic cell. Thus, the chloride anion (Cl^-) cannot be reduced any further and so it is oxidized at the anode and the sodium cation (Na^+) is therefore reduced. The final products are sodium solid formation at the cathode and chlorine (Cl_2) gas formation at the anode.

Note: the flow of electrons is still from anode to cathode as is for galvanic cells.

10.5 Faraday's Law

Faraday's law relates the amount of elements deposited or gas liberated at an electrode due to current.

We have seen that in a galvanic cell $Cu^{2+}(aq)$ can accept electrons to become Cu(*s*) which will actually plate onto the electrode. Faraday's Law allows us to calculate the amount of Cu(*s*). In fact, the law states that the weight of product formed at an electrode is proportional to the amount of electricity transferred at the electrode and to the equivalent weight of the material. Thus we can conclude that 1 mole of $Cu^{2+}(aq)$ + 2 moles of electrons will leave 1 mole of Cu(*s*) at the electrode. One mole (= Avogadro's number) of electrons is called a *faraday* ($\mathfrak{F}$). A faraday is equivalent to 96 500 coulombs. A coulomb is the amount of electricity that is transferred when a current of one ampere flows for one second ($1C = 1A \cdot S$).

10.5.1 Electrolysis Problem

How many grams of copper would be deposited on the cathode of an electrolytic cell if, for a period of 20 minutes, a current of 2.0 amperes is run through a solution of $CuSO_4$? {The molecular weight of copper is 63.5.}

Calculate the number of coulombs:

$$Q = It = 2.0\text{ A} \times 20\text{ min} \times 60\text{ sec/min} = 2400\text{ C}$$

Thus

$$\text{Faradays} = 2400\text{ C} \times 1\mathfrak{F}/96\,500\text{ C} = 0.025\mathfrak{F}$$

Faradays can be related to moles of copper since

$$Cu^{2+} + 2e^- \rightarrow Cu$$

Since 1 mol Cu: 2 mol e^- we can write

$$0.025\mathfrak{F} \times (1\text{ mol Cu}/2\mathfrak{F}) \times (63.5\text{g Cu/mol Cu}) = 0.79\text{g Cu}$$

Electrolysis would deposit 0.79 g of copper at the cathode.

To do the previous problem, you must know the definition of current and charge (CHM 10.5) but the value of the constant (a Faraday) would be given on the exam. You should be able to perform the preceding calculation quickly and efficiently because it involves dimensional analysis.

GOLD STANDARD WARM-UP EXERCISES

CHAPTER 10: Electrochemistry

1) What should happen when a piece of copper is placed in 1M HCl?

Table 1 below shows some Standard State Reduction Potentials.

Reaction	Standard reduction potential (E°)
$Cu^{2+} + 2e^- \leftrightarrow Cu$	0.34 V
$2H^+ + 2e^- \leftrightarrow H_2$	0.00 V

A. The copper is completely dissolved by the acid.
B. The copper is dissolved by the acid with the release of hydrogen gas.
C. The copper bursts into greenish flames.
D. Nothing happens.

2) What should happen when a piece of lead is placed in 1M HCl?

Reaction	Standard reduction potential (E°)
$2H^+ + 2e^- \leftrightarrow H_2$	0.00 V
$Pb^{2+} + 2e^- \leftrightarrow Pb$	−0.13 V

A. The lead is completely dissolved by the acid.
B. The lead begins to dissolve with the release of hydrogen gas.
C. The lead bursts into flames.
D. Nothing happens.

3) A voltaic cell is set up with F_2/F^- as one half-cell and Br_2/Br^- as the other. What is the voltage of this cell at standard state?

Reaction	Standard reduction potential (E°)
$F_2 + 2e^- \leftrightarrow 2F^-$	2.87 V
$Br_2 + 2e^- \leftrightarrow 2Br^-$	1.09 V

A. 3.96 V
B. 1.78 V
C. 1.09 V
D. 1.87 V

4) What is the standard cell potential for the galvanic cell formed using the Cl_2/Cl^- and MnO_4^-/Mn^{2+} half cells given the following?

$$Cl_2 + 2e^- \rightarrow 2Cl^- \qquad E^\circ = +1.36\ V$$

$$MnO_4^- + 8H^+ + 5e^- \leftrightarrow Mn^{2+} + 4H_2O \qquad E^\circ = +1.51\ V$$

A. +0.15 V
B. +0.83 V
C. +2.87 V
D. +5.29 V

5) If a current was passed through a solution of sulfate ions and one mole of sulfur dioxide was obtained, how many moles of chromium metal would be obtained if the same current was passed through a solution of chromium (III) ions in solution?

Table 1

Reaction	Standard reduction potential (E°)
$SO_4^{2-} + 4H^+ + 2e \leftrightarrow 2H_2O + SO_2$	+0.17 V
$Cr^{3+} + 3e \leftrightarrow Cr$	−0.74 V

A. 0.33 moles
B. 0.67 moles
C. 1.00 moles
D. 2.00 moles

6) Assume that the standard reduction potential for the reaction

$$A^{3+} + e^- \rightarrow A^{2+}$$

is E°A, and the standard reduction potential for the reaction

$$B^+ + e^- \rightarrow B$$

is E°B. A solution initially containing 1.0 M A^{3+}, 1.0 M A^{2+} and 1.0 M B^+ is agitated with excess solid B metal. When equilibrium is attained, the solution contains 0.7 M of A^{3+}, 1.3 M of A^{2+} and 1.3 M of B^+. Which of the following can we conclude?

A. $E°A = E°B$
B. $E°A > E°B$
C. $E°A < E°B$
D. $E°A + E°B = 0$

7) In the context of electrochemistry, “standard state” implies that:

A. All solutions are 1 M; all gases have a partial pressure of 1 MPa; the temperature is 273 K.
B. All solutions are 0.1 M; all gases have a partial pressure of 0.1 MPa; temperature is 273 K.
C. All solutions are 0.1 M; all gases have a partial pressure of 0.1 MPa.
D. All solutions are 1 M; all gases have a partial pressure of 0.1 MPa.

8) Which of the halogens will oxidize water to oxygen?

Reactions	Standard reduction potential (E°)
$Cl_2 + 2e^- \rightarrow 2Cl^-$	+1.36 V
$ClO_3^- + 6H^+ + 5e^- \rightarrow (½)Cl_2 + 3H_2O$	+1.47 V
$HClO^- + H^+ + e^- \rightarrow (½)Cl_2 + H_2O$	+1.63 V
$BrO_3^- + 6H^+ + 5e^- \rightarrow (½)Br_2 + 3H_2O$	+1.52 V
$F_2 + 2H^+ + 2e^- \rightarrow 2HF$	+3.06 V
$O_2 + 4H^+ + 4e^- \rightarrow 2H_2O$	+1.23 V
$O_3 + 2H^+ + 2e^- \rightarrow O_2 + H_2O$	+2.07 V
$Br_2 + 2e^- \rightarrow 2Br^-$	+1.07 V
$I_2 + 2e^- \rightarrow 2I^-$	+0.62 V

A. All of them
B. fluorine and chlorine
C. fluorine and bromine
D. fluorine, chlorine and bromine

9) The following reaction is spontaneous:

$$Ag^+ + Fe^{2+} \rightarrow Ag + Fe^{3+}$$

If a voltaic cell has one half cell as Ag^+/Ag and the other half cell as Fe^{2+}/Fe^{3+}, the silver electrode will be:

A. the anode and negative.
B. the anode and positive.
C. the cathode and positive.
D. the cathode and negative.

10) For an oxidation–reduction reaction, which of the following is a consistent set of relations?

A. $\Delta G° < 0$, $\Delta E° > 0$, $K_{eq} < 1$
B. $\Delta G° > 0$, $\Delta E° < 0$, $K_{eq} < 1$
C. $\Delta G° < 0$, $\Delta E° < 0$, $K_{eq} < 1$
D. $\Delta G° < 0$, $\Delta E° < 0$, $K_{eq} > 1$

11) A sample of iron was placed in a beaker of water and exposed to the atmosphere for one hour. After this, the iron that remained was removed from the beaker and a current of 0.2 A passed through the beaker which contained only Fe^{2+} in solution. After one hour and twenty minutes, all the iron present had been deposited on the cathode. Given that the Faraday constant F = 96000 C, what was the rate of rusting in grams per hour?

A. 0.209
B. 0.279
C. 0.140
D. 0.450

GS ANSWER KEY

Chapter 10

		Cross-Reference			Cross-Reference
1.	D	CHM 10.1, 10.2, 10.4, 6.1	7.	D	CHM 4.1.1, 10.1
2.	B	CHM 10.1, 10.2, 10.4, 6.1	8.	B	CHM 10.1
3.	B	CHM 10.1, 10.2, 10.4	9.	C	CHM 10.1
4.	A	CHM 10.1, 10.2	10.	B	CHM 1.6, 8.10, 9.10, 10.1
5.	B	CHM 10.5	11.	B	CHM 10.5.1
6.	B	CHM 10			

* Explanations can be found at the back of the book.

Go online to DAT-prep.com for additional chapter review Q&A and forum.

GOLD NOTES

NUCLEAR CHEMISTRY

Chapter 11

Memorize

- Equation relating energy and mass; half-life
- Alpha, beta, gamma particles
- Equation for maximum number of electrons in a shell
- Equation relating energy to frequency
- Equation for the total energy of the electrons in an atom

Understand

* Basic atomic structure, amu
* Fission, fusion; the Bohr model of the atom
* Problem solving for half-life
* Quantized energy levels for electrons
* Fluorescence

Importance

1 to 3 out of the 30 Gen CHM

DAT questions are based on content in this chapter (in our estimation).

* Note that between 50% and 85% of the questions in DAT General Chemistry are based on content from 6 chapters: 1, 2, 4, 5, 6 and 9.

Introduction

Atomic structure can be summarized as a nucleus orbited by electrons in different energy levels. Transition of electrons between energy levels and nuclear structure (i.e. protons, neutrons) are important characteristics of the atom.

Additional Resources

Free Online Forum

Video: Online or DVD

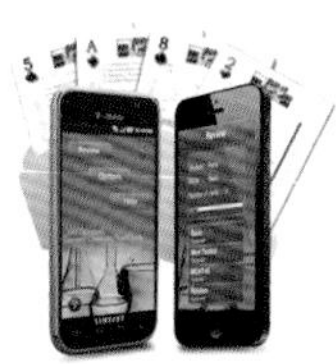

Flashcards

11.1 Protons, Neutrons, Electrons

Only recently, with high resolution electron microscopes, have large atoms been visualized. However, for years their existence and properties have been inferred by experiments. Experimental work on gas discharge effects suggested that an atom is not a single entity but is itself composed of smaller particles. These were termed elementary particles. The atom appears as a small solar system with a heavy nucleus composed of positive particles and neutral particles: *protons* and *neutrons*. Around this nucleus, there are clouds of negatively charged particles, called *electrons*. The mass of a neutron is slightly more than that of a proton (both $\approx 1.7 \times 10^{-24}$ g); the mass of the electron is considerably less (9.1×10^{-28} g).

Since an atom is electrically neutral, the negative charge carried by the electrons must be equal in magnitude (but opposite in sign) to the positive charge carried by the protons.

Experiments with electrostatic charges have shown that opposite charges attract, so it can be considered that electrostatic forces hold an atom together. The difference between various atoms is therefore determined by their *composition*.

A hydrogen atom consists of one proton and one electron; a helium atom of two protons, two neutrons and two electrons. They are shown in diagram form in Figure III.A.11.1.

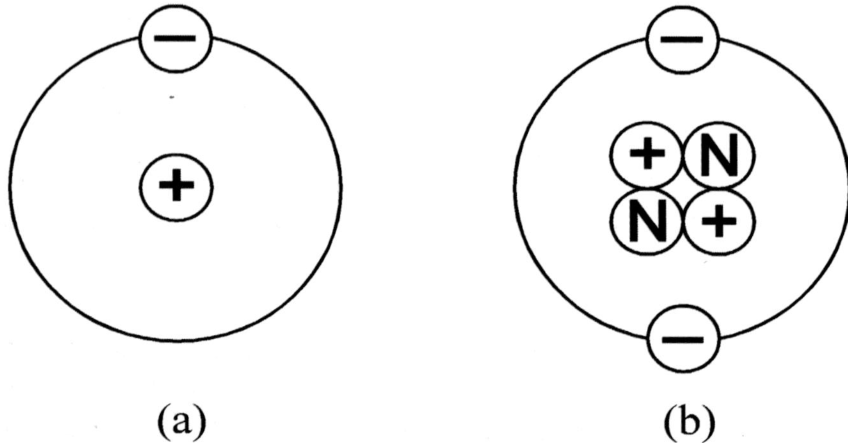

Figure III.A.11.1: Atomic structure simplified: (a) hydrogen atom; (b) helium atom.

11.2 Isotopes, Atomic Number, Atomic Weight

A proton has a mass of 1 a.m.u. (*atomic mass unit*) and a charge of +1, whereas, a neutron has a mass of 1 a.m.u. and no charge. The *atomic number* (*AN*) of an atom is the number of protons in the nucleus. In an atom of neutral charge, the atomic number (AN) is also equal to the number of electrons.

The atomic number is conventionally represented by the letter "Z". Each of the chemical elements has a unique number of protons which is identified by its own atomic number "Z". As an example, for the hydrogen H element, Z = 1 and for Na, Z = 11.

An *element* is a group of atoms with the same AN. *Isotopes* are elements which have the same atomic number (Z) but different number of neutrons and hence a different mass number (MN). As an example, the three carbon isotopes differ only in the number of neutrons and therefore have the same number of protons and electrons but differ in mass and are usually represented as follows: C-12, C-13 and C-14 or more specifically as follows: $^{12}_{6}C$, $^{13}_{6}C$ and $^{14}_{6}C$. It is therefore the number of protons that distinguishes elements from each other. The *weighted average* follows the natural abundance of the various isotopic compositions of an element.

The *mass number* (*MN*) of an atom is the number of protons and neutrons in an atom. The *atomic weight* (*AW*) is the weighted average of all naturally occurring isotopes of an element.

For example: Silicon is known to exist naturally as a mixture of three isotopes (Si-28, Si-29 and Si-30). The relative amount of each of the three different silicon isotopes is found to be 92.2297% with a mass of 27.97693, 4.6832% with a mass of 28.97649 and the remaining 3.0872% with a mass of 29.97377. The atomic weight of silicon is then determined as the weighted average of each of the isotopes as follows:

$$\begin{aligned}\text{Si mass} &= (27.97693 \times 0.922297) \\ &\quad + (28.97649 \times 0.046832) \\ &\quad + (29.97377 \times 0.030872) \\ &= 28.0854 \text{ g/mol.}\end{aligned}$$

It is also important to note that as the number of protons distinguishes *elements* from each other, it is their electronic configuration (CHM 2.1, 2.2, 2.3) that determines their *reactivity*.

The mass of a nucleus is always smaller than the combined mass of its constituent protons and neutrons. The difference in mass is converted to energy (E) which holds protons and neutrons together within the nuclear core.

11.3 Nuclear Forces, Nuclear Binding Energy, Stability, Radioactivity

Coulomb repulsive force (between protons) in the nuclei are overcome by nuclear forces. The nuclear force is a non-electrical type of force that binds nuclei together and is equal for protons and neutrons. The nuclear binding energy (E_b) is a result of the relation between energy and mass changes associated with nuclear reactions,

$$\Delta E = \Delta mc^2$$

in ergs in the CGS system, i.e. m = grams and c = cm/sec; ΔE = energy released or absorbed; Δm = mass lost or gained, respectively; c = velocity of light = 3.0×10^{10} cm/sec.

Conversions:
1 *gram* = 9×10^{20} *ergs*
1 *a.m.u.* = 931.4 *MeV* (*Mev* = 10^6 electron volts)
1 *a.m.u.* = 1/12 the mass of ${}_6C^{12}$.

The preceding equation is a statement of the law of conservation of mass and energy. The value of E_b depends upon the mass number (MN) as follows, (*see Figure III.A.11.2*):

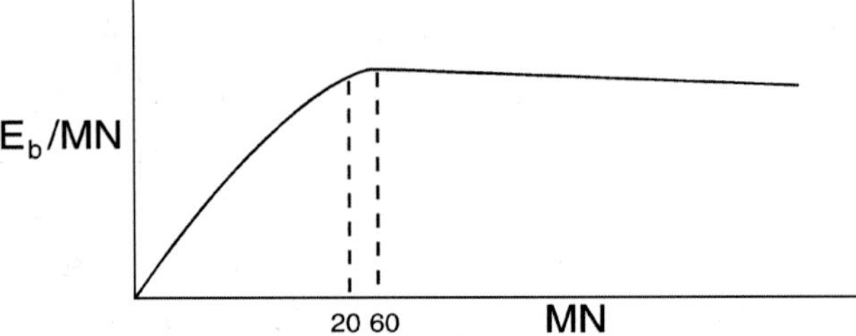

Figure III.A.11.2: Binding Energy per Nucleus. *E_b/MN = binding energy per nucleus; this is the energy released by the formation of a nucleus.*

The peak E_b/MN is at MN = 60. Also, E_b/MN is relatively constant after MN = 20. Fission is when a nucleus splits into smaller nuclei. Fusion is when smaller nuclei combine to form a larger nucleus. Energy is released from a nuclear reaction when nuclei with MN >> 60 undergo fission or nuclei with MN << 60 undergo fusion. Both fusion and fission release energy because the mass difference between the initial and the final nuclear states is converted into energy.

Not all combinations of protons are stable. The most stable nuclei are those with an even number of protons and an even number of neutrons. The least stable nuclei are those with an odd number of protons and an odd number of neutrons. Also, as the atomic number (AN) increases, there are more neutrons (N) needed for the nuclei to be stable.

According to the *Baryon number conservation*, the total number of protons and neutrons remains the same in a nuclear reaction even with the inter-conversions occurring between protons and neutrons.

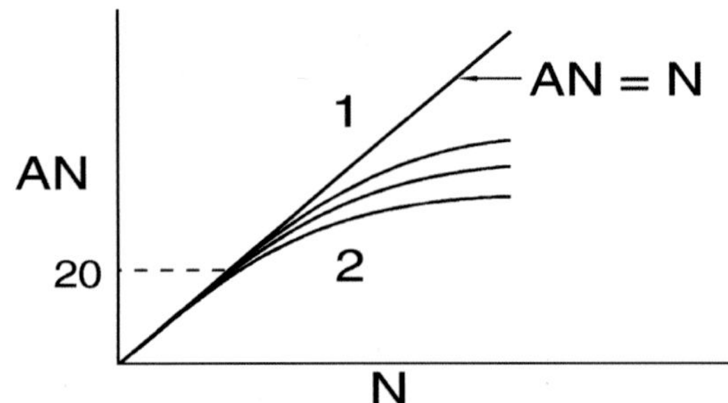

Figure III.A.11.3: Stability of Atoms. AN = atomic number and N = number of neutrons.

Up to AN = 20 (Calcium) the number of protons is equal to the number of neutrons, after this there are more neutrons. If an atom is in region #1 in Figure III.A.11.3, it has too many protons or too few neutrons and must decrease its protons or increase its neutrons to become stable. The reverse is true for region #2. All nuclei after AN = 84 (Polonium) are unstable.

Unstable nuclei become stable by fission to smaller nuclei or by absorption or emission of small particles. Spontaneous fission is rare. Spontaneous radioactivity (emission of particles) is common. The common particles are:

(1) alpha (α) particle = ${}_2He^4$ (helium nucleus);

(2) beta (β) particle = ${}_{-1}e^0$ (an electron);

(3) a positron ${}_{+1}e^0$ (same mass as an electron but opposite charge);

(4) gamma (γ) ray = no mass and no charge, just electromagnetic energy;

(5) orbital electron capture - nucleus takes electrons from K shell and converts a proton to a neutron. If there is a flux of particles such as neutrons (${}_0n^1$), the nucleus can absorb these also.

A neutron walks into a bar and asks the bartender: "How much for a beer?"
The bartender answers: "For you, no charge." :)

11.4 Nuclear Reaction, Radioactive Decay, Half-Life

Nuclear reactions are reactions in which changes in nuclear composition occur. An example of a nuclear reaction which involves uranium and hydrogen:

$${}_{92}U^{238} + {}_1H^2 \rightarrow {}_{93}Np^{238} + 2{}_0n^1$$

for ${}_{92}U^{238}$: 238 = mass number, 92 = atomic number. The sum of the lower (or higher) numbers on one side of the equation equals the sum of the lower (or higher) numbers on the other side of the equation. Another way of writing the preceding reaction is: ${}_{92}U^{238}({}_1H^2, 2{}_0n^1){}_{93}Np^{238}$. {# neutrons (i.e. ${}_{92}U^{238}$) = superscript (238) – subscript (92) = 146}

Radioactive decay is a naturally occurring spontaneous process in which the atomic nucleus of an unstable atom loses energy by the emission of ionizing particles. Such unstable nuclei are known to spontaneously decompose and emit minute atomic sections to essentially gain some stability. The radioactive decay fragments are categorized into alpha, beta and gamma-ray decays. The radioactive decay can result in a nuclear change (*transmutation*) in which the parent and daughter nuclei are of different elements. For example, a C-14 atom may undergo an alpha decay and emit radiation and as a result, transform into a N-14 daughter nucleus. It is also possible that radioactive decay does not result in transmutation but only decreases the energy of the parent nucleus. As an example, a Ni-28 atom undergoing a gamma decay will emit radiation and then transform to a lower energy Ni-28 nucleus. The following is a brief description of the three known types of radioactive decay.

(1) **Alpha (α) decay:** Alpha decay is a type of radioactive decay in which an atomic nucleus emits an alpha particle. An alpha particle is composed of two protons and two neutrons which is identical to a helium-4 nucleus. An alpha particle is the most massive of all radioactive particles. Because of its relatively large mass, alpha particles tend to have the most potential to interact with other atoms and/or molecules and ionize them as well as lose energy. As such, these particles have the lowest penetrating power. If an atomic nucleus of an element undergoes alpha decay, this leads to a transmutation of that element into another element as shown below for the transmutation of Uranium-238 to Thorium-234:

$$^{238}_{92}U \rightarrow {}^{234}_{90}Th + {}^{4}_{2}He^{2+}$$
$$^{238}U \rightarrow {}^{234}Th + \alpha$$

(2) **Beta (β) decay:** Beta decay is a type of decay in which an unstable nucleus emits an electron or a positron. A positron is the antiparticle of an electron and has the same mass as an electron but opposite in charge. The electron from a beta decay forms when a neutron of an unstable nuclei changes into a proton and in the process, an electron is then emitted. The electron in this case is referred to as a beta minus particle or β^-. In beta decays producing positron emissions, it is referred to as beta plus or β^+. For an atomic nucleus undergoing beta decay, the process leads to the transmutation of that element into another as shown for the transmutation of Cesium-137 for beta minus and Na-22 for beta plus emissions:

$$^{137}_{55}Cs \rightarrow {}^{137}_{56}Ba + \beta^-$$
$$^{22}_{11}Na \rightarrow {}^{22}_{10}Ne + \beta^+$$

(3) **Gamma (γ) decay:** Gamma decay is different from the other two types of decays. Gamma decay emits a form of electromagnetic radiation. Gamma rays are high energy photons known to penetrate matter very well and are symbolized by the Greek letter gamma (γ). A source of gamma decay could be a case in which an excited daughter nucleus - following an alpha or beta decay - lowers its energy state further by gamma-ray emission without a change in mass number or atomic number. The following is an example:

$$^{60}Co \rightarrow {}^{60}Ni^* + \beta^-$$

Co-60 decays to an excited Ni*-60 via beta decay and subsequently, the excited Ni*-

60 drops to ground state and emits gamma (γ) rays as follows:

$$^{60}Ni^* \rightarrow {}^{60}Ni + \gamma$$

To summarize, a gamma ray has no charge and no mass since it is a form of electromagnetic radiation. As shown, gamma rays are usually emitted in conjunction with other radiation emissions.

Spontaneous radioactive decay is a first order process. This means that the rate of decay is *directly* proportional to the amount of material present:

$$\Delta m/\Delta t = \text{rate of decay}$$

where Δm = change in mass, Δt = change in time.

The preceding relation is equalized by adding a proportionality constant called the decay constant (k) as follows,

$$\Delta m/\Delta t = -km.$$

The minus sign indicates that the mass is decreasing. Also, $k = -(\Delta m/m)/\Delta t$ = fraction of the mass that decays with time.

The *half-life* ($T_{1/2}$) of a radioactive atom is the time required for one half of it to disintegrate. The half-life is related to k as follows,

$$T_{1/2} = 0.693/k.$$

If the number of half-lifes n are known we can calculate the percentage of a pure radioactive sample left after undergoing decay since the fraction remaining = $(1/2)^n$.

For example, given a pure radioactive substance X with $T_{1/2} = 9$ years, calculating the percentage of substance X after 27 years is quite simple,

$$27 = 3 \times 9 = 3\ T_{1/2}$$

Thus

$$n = 3,\ (1/2)^n = (1/2)^3 = 1/8 \text{ or } 13\%.$$

After 27 years of disintegration, 13% of pure substance X remains. {Similarly, note that *doubling time* is given by $(2)^n$; see BIO 2.2}

Table III.A.11.1: Modes of Radioactive Decay

Decay Mode	Participating particles	Change in (A, Z)	Daughter Nucleus
Alpha decay	α	A = –4, Z = –2	(A – 4, Z – 2)
Beta decay	β^-	A = 0, Z = +1	(A, Z + 1)
Gamma decay	γ	A = 0, Z = 0	(A, Z)
Positron emission	β^+	A = 0, Z = –1	(A, Z – 1)

11.5 Quantized Energy Levels For Electrons, Emission Spectrum

Work by Bohr and others in the early part of the last century demonstrated that the electron orbits are arranged in shells, and that each shell has a defined maximum number of electrons it can contain.

For example, the first shell can contain two electrons, the second eight electrons (see CHM 2.1, 2.2). The maximum number of electrons in each shell is given by:

$$N_{electrons} = 2n^2$$

$N_{electrons}$ designates the number of electrons in shell n.

The state of each electron is determined by the four quantum numbers:

- *principal quantum number n* determines the number of shells, possible values are: 1 (K), 2 (L), 3 (M), etc...
- *angular momentum quantum number l*, determines the subshell, possible values are: 0 (s), 1 (p), 2 (d), 3 (f), n-1, etc...
- *magnetic momentum quantum number* m_l, possible values are: $\pm l, \ldots, 0$
- *spin quantum number* m_s, determines the direction of rotation of the electron, possible values are: ±1/2.

Chemical reactions and electrical effects are all concerned with the behavior of electrons in the outer shell of any particular atom. If a shell is full, for example, the atom is unlikely to react with any other atom and is, in fact, one of the noble (inert) gases such as helium.

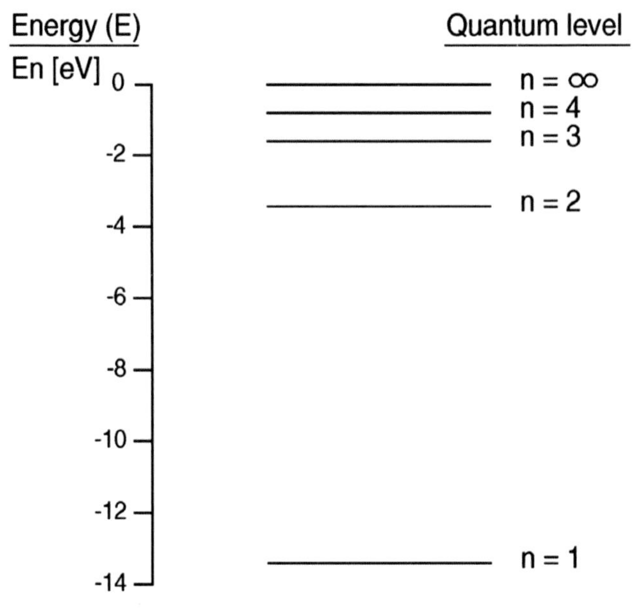

Figure III.A.11.4: Energy levels. The energy E_n in each shell n is measured in electron volts.

The energy that an electron contains is not continuous over the entire range of possible energy. Rather, electrons in a atom may contain only discrete energies as they occupy certain orbits or shells. Electrons of each atom are restricted to these discrete energy levels. These levels have an energy below zero.

This means energy is released when an electron moves from infinity into these energy levels.

If there is one electron in an atom, its ground state is n = 1, the lowest energy level available. Any other energy level, n = 2, n = 3, etc., is considered an excited state for that electron. The difference in energy (*E*) between the levels gives the absorbed (or emitted) energy when an electron moves to a higher orbit (or lower orbit, respectively) and therefore, the frequency (*f*) of light necessary to cause excitation.

$$E_2 - E_1 = hf$$

where E_1 = energy level one, E_2 = energy level two, h = planck's constant, and f = the frequency of light absorbed or emitted.

Therefore, if light is passed through a substance (e.g., gas), certain wavelengths will be absorbed, which correspond to the energy needed for the electron transition. An *absorption* spectrum will result that has dark lines against a light background. Multiple lines result because there are possible transitions from all quantum levels occupied by electrons to any unoccupied levels.

An *emission* spectrum results when an electron is excited to a higher level by another particle or by an electric discharge, for example. Then, as the electron falls from the excited state to lower states, light is emitted that has a wavelength (which is related to frequency) corresponding to the energy difference between the levels since: $E_1 - E_2 = hf$.

The resulting spectrum will have light lines against a dark background. The absorption and emission spectrums should have the same number of lines but often will not. This is because in the absorption spectrum, there is a rapid radiation of the absorbed light in all directions, and transitions are generally from the ground state initially.

These factors result in fewer lines in the absorption than in the emission spectrum.

The total energy of the electrons in an atom, where KE is the kinetic energy, can be given by:

$$E_{total} = E_{emission}\ (\text{or } E_{ionization}) + KE$$

11.6 Fluorescence

Fluorescence is an emission process that occurs after light absorption excites electrons to higher electronic and vibrational levels. The electrons spontaneously lose excited vibrational energy to the electronic states. There are certain molecular types that possess this property, e.g., some amino acids (tryptophan).

The fluorescence process is as follows:

- **Step 1** - absorption of light;

• **Step 2** - spontaneous deactivation of vibrational levels to zero vibrational level for electronic state;

• **Step 3** - fluorescence with light emission (longer wavelength than absorption).

Figure III.A.11.5 shows diagrammatically the steps described above. Step 2 which is not shown in the figure is the intermediate step between light absorption and light emission. See BIO 1.5.1 for fluorescence as applied to microscopy.

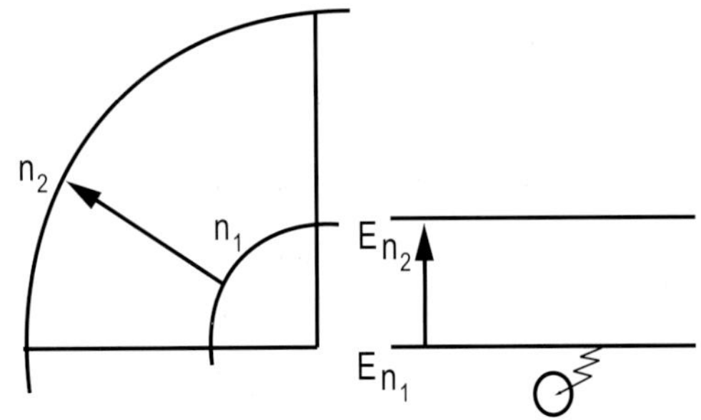

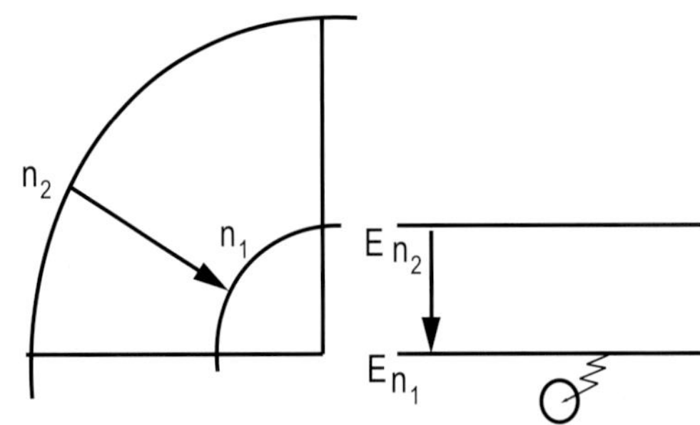

Figure III.A.11.5: The fluorescence process. Represented is an atom with shells n1, n2 and their respective energy levels En.

GOLD STANDARD WARM-UP EXERCISES

CHAPTER 11: Nuclear Chemistry

1) How do gamma rays behave in an electric field?
   A. They are not deflected in any direction.
   B. They are deflected toward the positive plate.
   C. They are deflected toward the negative plate.
   D. They oscillate between plates, that is, they are attracted to one plate and then the other.

2) Why would a neutron be preferred to a proton for bombarding atomic nuclei?
   A. It is smaller than a proton.
   B. It weighs less than a proton.
   C. It has no charge.
   D. It can be obtained from a nucleus.

3) A sample of radioactive substance has a half–life of six months. What percentage of the sample is left undecayed after one year?
   A. 0%
   B. 25%
   C. 50%
   D. 75%

4) Astatine is the last member of Group VII and is radioactive with a half–life of 8 hours. The transport of an astatine sample took 20 hours. What proportion of the sample had undergone radioactive decay?
   A. 0.58
   B. 0.18
   C. 0.82
   D. 0.42

5) Which of the following types of radioactive emissions involves the emission of a helium nucleus?
   A. alpha decay
   B. beta decay
   C. gamma ray
   D. None of the above

6) Given the following reactions, identify X.

$$^{1}_{0}n + ^{238}_{92}U \rightarrow ^{239}_{92}U + X$$
$$^{239}_{92}U \rightarrow ^{239}_{93}Np + ^{0}_{-1}e$$
$$^{239}_{93}Np \rightarrow ^{239}_{94}Pu + ^{0}_{-1}e$$

   A. α – particle
   B. β – particle
   C. γ – ray
   D. proton

7) In a hypothetical radioactive series, Tl–210 undergoes 3 beta decay processes, 1 alpha decay process and 1 gamma ray emission to yield a stable product. What is the product?
   A. $^{214}_{76}Os$
   B. $^{214}_{84}Po$
   C. $^{206}_{86}Rn$
   D. $^{206}_{82}Pb$

8) $^{230}_{90}Th$ undergoes a series of radioactive decay processes, resulting in ^{214}Bi being the final product. What was the sequence of the processes that occurred?
   A. alpha, alpha, alpha, gamma, beta
   B. alpha, alpha, alpha, alpha, beta
   C. alpha, alpha, beta, beta
   D. alpha, beta, beta, beta, gamma

9) Which of the following represents the relative penetrating power of the three types of radioactive emissions in decreasing order?

A. beta > alpha > gamma
B. beta > gamma > alpha
C. gamma > alpha > beta
D. gamma > beta > alpha

10) The beta decay of carbon–14 results in the production of nitrogen, a beta particle and a gamma ray as follows:

$$^{14}_{6}C \rightarrow {}^{X}_{7}N + \beta^{-} + \gamma$$

The value for X in the formula for nitrogen is equal to:

A. 15.
B. 14.
C. 13.
D. 12.

11) How would you expect a positron will react in an electric field?

A. It would retain its original flight direction.
B. It would be attracted to the positive plate.
C. It would be attracted to the negative plate.
D. It would be attracted to the plate with the greater charge density.

12) A living organism has a C-14 to C-12 ratio of 1/20 during lifetime. Its remains now has a C-14 to C-12 ratio of 1/80. Approximately how old is this organism? Take the half-life of C-14 to be 6000 years.

A. It is 6000 years old.
B. It is 12000 years old.
C. It is 18000 years old.
D. It is 24000 years old.

13) The half-life of one isotope of radium is about 1600 years. In a given sample of this isotope, 15/16 of the radium atoms will decay in a time most nearly equal to:

A. 1500.
B. 3200.
C. 6400.
D. 12800.

14) Tl decays by the emission of beta particles (half-life = 3.1 mins). As a result, Pb is produced. After 9.3 mins, an initially pure sample of Tl contains 7 g of Pb. What was the approximate mass of the original sample?

A. 7 g
B. 8 g
C. 28 g
D. 32 g

15) A radioactive form of phosphorus undergoes β - decay. What would the radioactivity level (R) versus time graph for the decay process look like?

A.
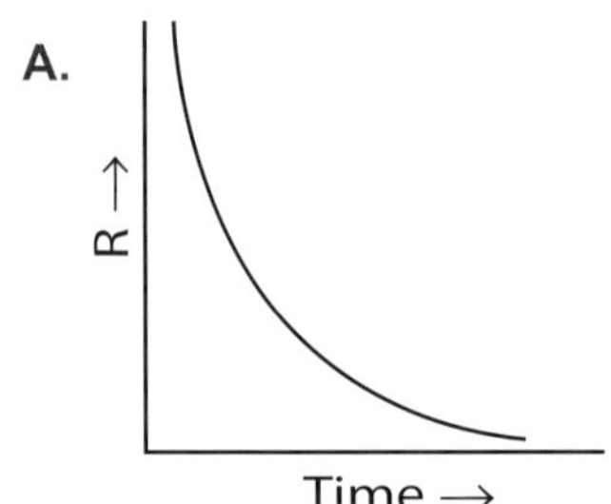

B.
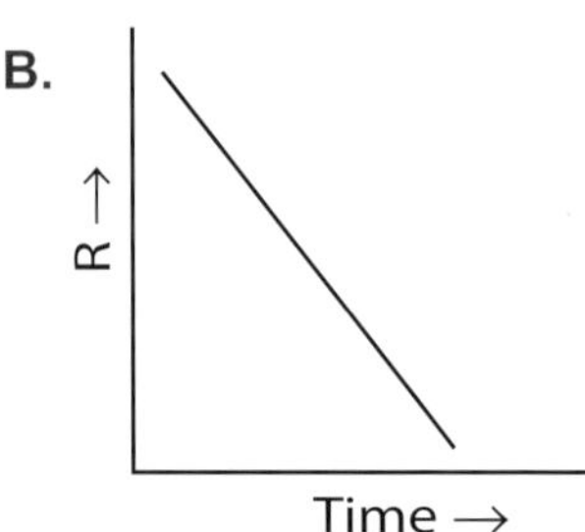

C.
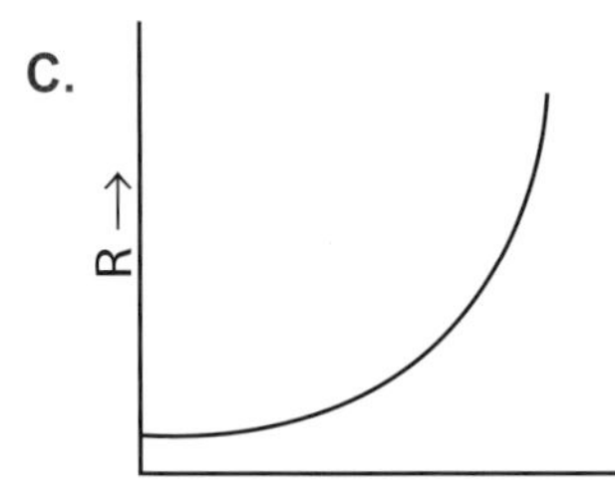

D.
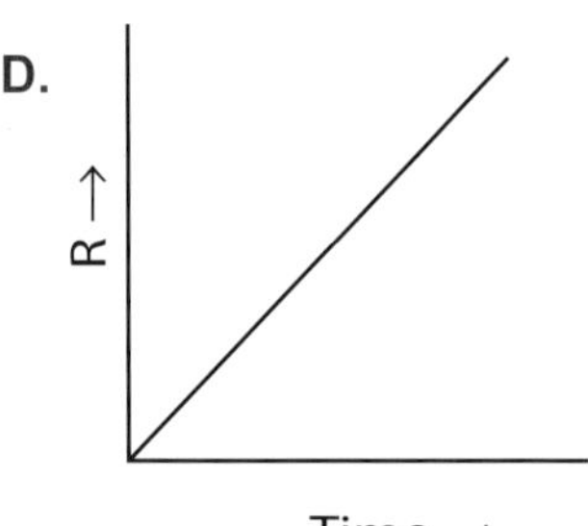

GS ANSWER KEY

Chapter 11

		Cross-Reference			Cross-Reference
1.	A	CHM 11	9.	D	CHM 11.3, 11.4
2.	C	CHM 11.1	10.	B	CHM 11.3, 11.4
3.	B	CHM 11.4	11.	C	CHM 11.3
4.	C	CHM 11.4	12.	B	CHM 11.4
5.	A	CHM 11.3	13.	C	CHM 11.4
6.	C	CHM 11.3, 11.4	14.	B	CHM 11.4
7.	D	CHM 11.3, 11.4	15.	A	CHM 11.4
8.	B	CHM 11.3, 11.4			

* Explanations can be found at the back of the book.

Go online to DAT-prep.com for additional chapter review Q&A and forum.

LABORATORY

Chapter 12

Memorize	Understand	Importance
Glassware, basic equipment	* Safety * Basic techniques * Equipment: especially glassware * Error and data analysis	**0 to 2 out of the 30 Gen CHM** DAT questions are based on content in this chapter (in our estimation). * Note that between 50% and 85% of the questions in DAT General Chemistry are based on content from 6 chapters: 1, 2, 4, 5, 6 and 9.

Introduction

The laboratory (or lab) is where scientific research and development is conducted and analyses performed. Some students see a lab as a sterile, boring environment with lots of rules. Others recognize that it is the controlled, uniform environment of a lab - with its many different techniques, instruments and procedures - that has helped produce countless discoveries in chemistry, pharmacy, biotechnology including the human genome project, nanotechnology and much more to come.

Additional Resources

Free Online Forum

Video: Online or DVD

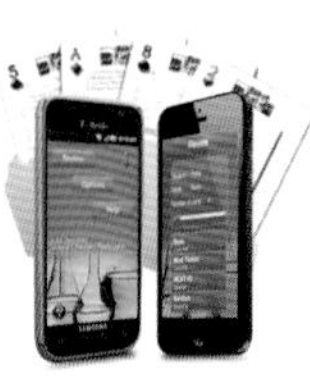

Flashcards

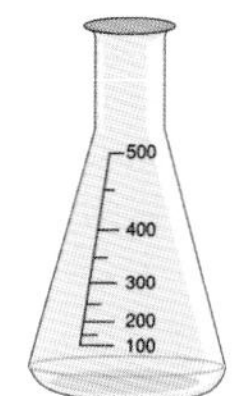

Special Guest

12.1 Introduction

The laboratory is a place in which one may have the opportunity to apply the principles and theories of chemistry. An understanding of laboratory basics is mandatory for anyone studying chemical sciences, biological sciences or the DAT! Despite its potential dangers, the laboratory may be regarded as one of the safest environments.

Good science requires the collection of reliable, accurate and reproducible data. The scientist and/or experimenter must have a working knowledge of applied laboratory techniques as well as an understanding of the equipment used to acquire such data.

12.2 Laboratory Safety

One must be aware of all dangers that may occur in the laboratory and more importantly, one must always take precautionary measures when working in a chemistry laboratory. While in the laboratory, you are not only responsible for your own safety but for the safety of others working with you.

Laboratory Rules and Safety Procedures:

1. Always wear protective eye goggles or glasses. These glasses should be safety grade and made to wrap around the eyes so that no liquids or solids may splash into your eyes.
2. Contact lenses are NEVER to be worn.
3. Always wear a protective lab coat or apron and shoes must completely cover your feet and skin must NEVER be exposed.
4. One must always be made aware of all pertinent safety locations and the proper usage of all available safety equipment such as (amongst others): fire extinguishers, eye wash, safety showers, fire blankets, and all other available equipment.
5. Always tie your hair if worn long and do not wear loose clothing or jewelry while performing any lab work.
6. Your bench top should always be clean and clear of all objects as you perform your lab work. Personal belongings should always be kept away from your work area.
7. One must always keep all stock solutions and solids in a well ventilated and appropriate storage area.
8. Always keep balances and the surrounding area as clean as possible to avoid contamination.
9. Appropriately label all reagent bottles as well as working solutions and all respective materials used should always be appropriately labeled and dated.
10. Always be aware and knowledgeable of all solids, solvents and solutions you are to work with.
11. Never return unused solvents or chemicals back into an initial stock solution or any reagent bottles. This is a major

source of contamination of the entire stock and/or initial solutions.

12. Always dispose of all chemicals and waste as advised by the appropriate and/or responsible party.

13. Always report all accidents no matter how minor it may seem.

14. Never perform experiments that have not been authorized.

15. Always have some other colleague in the lab working with you and so never be alone in a lab while performing experimental work.

12.3 Laboratory Techniques

12.3.1 Glassware

Chemical glassware forms a staple of basic laboratory equipment in chemistry and is thus a regular question on real DAT tests. It is advisable that you memorize the following types of lab glassware and equipment and know when they are appropriate.

Some items have volumetric graduation or are *graduated for volume* which means, in practical terms, one can measure the volume of the liquid in the container (usually in ml).

A well equipped laboratory generally has various pieces of glassware designed to measure liquid volumes. In the following table, you will find a list of some of the most common glassware in order from least to the most accurate piece of equipment.

A major problem encountered by many when measuring the level of a liquid in a tube is the fact that the surface is not flat due to adhesive forces or cohesive forces (see CHM 4.2.2). This curved surface is known as a meniscus. Read the level at the midpoint of the meniscus. This point is the bottom for aqueous solutions where the meniscus is curved downwards (concave due to adhesive forces; see image of graduated cylinder); whereas, the midpoint is the top in mercury where the meniscus is curved upwards (convex due to cohesive forces; CHM 4.2.2). In certain instances (highly colored solutions), the meniscus is not clearly defined and this may causes a decrease in accuracy. When

Least accurate	Droppers
	Beakers and Erlenmeyer flasks
	Graduated cylinders
Most accurate	Glass Pipettes, burettes and volumetric flasks

reading a liquid level, the eye must be on the same level as the meniscus in order to accurately read the bottom of the curve and avoid making a *parallax* error.

When discussing glassware, "graduated" means that there are marked intervals on the glass for use in measurement.

Glassware is generally marked to indicate the temperature at which the apparatus was calibrated (usually 20 °C), and marked to indicate if it is calibrated to measure either the amount of liquid it may contain (= TC = "to contain") or the amount of liquid that it may deliver (= TD = "to deliver"). There is no real one volume marking that may measure both of these quantities. As suggested by their names, TD, used on burettes and pipets and some graduated cylinders, means that the apparatus is calibrated to accurately deliver or transfer the stated volume to another container. TC, used on volumetric flasks and most graduated cylinders, means that the markings give an accurate measure of the volume contained, but that pouring the liquid into another container will not necessarily deliver the indicated volume.

The following is a short description of each of the major types of glassware:

Droppers, Beakers and Erlenmeyer Flasks

These types of glassware are used for the approximate measurements of volume. The dropper is generally used for volumes of less than or equal to 5 mL. Droppers are known to vary in the volume they deliver (1 mL = 15–20 drops) and contain a high level of uncertainty of approximately ± 10%. Various beakers and Erlenmeyer flasks have approximate volume markings on the outside of the glass with values of ~5% accuracy. When performing precise work, it is not recommended to use any of these glassware pieces.

Graduated Cylinders (TC)

Graduated cylinders contain volume markings used to measure the amount of liquid held by the cylinder with an accuracy of approximately ± 2%. They normally range in size from 10 ml to 1000 ml.

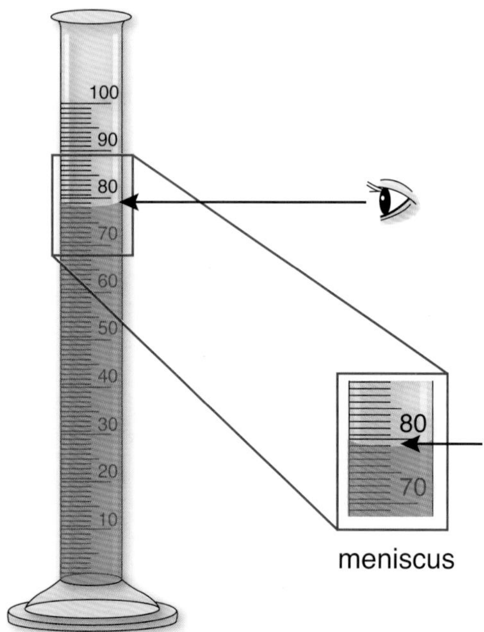

Graduated cylinder

Glass Pipette (also Pipet)

Pipettes are used to deliver measured volumes with an inherent uncertainty of about ± 0.2% and are used mainly for high accuracy work. Generally, there are two types of glass pipettes, volumetric pipettes with one volume mark and graduated pipettes with several markings. In addition to these classes of pipettes, there are also Eppendorf micropipettes and multichannel pipettes that are used for very small volumes ranging from 1.00 μL up to 1000 μL (1 mL). Pipetting requires skill and can be done with a pump or a bulb.

Volumetric flasks (TC)

Volumetric flasks are used to prepare stock solutions of known molar concentrations and for dilutions of measured volumes. Volumetric flasks are known to be precise to approximately ± 0.2%. They are characterized by a flat bottomed bulb and a long neck with a single line for measuring a specified volume.

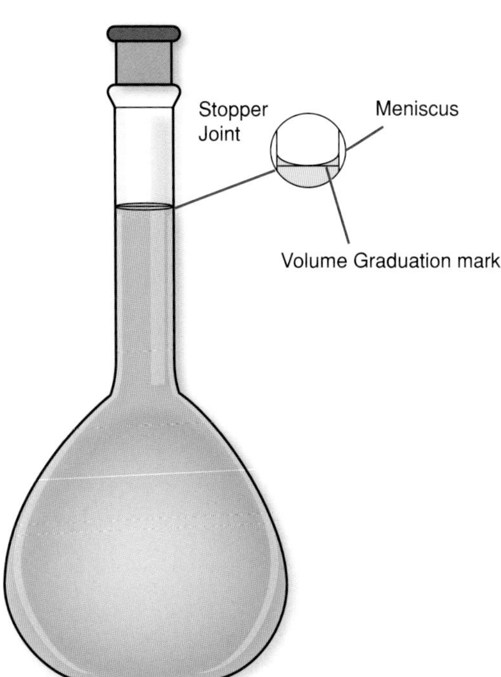

Volumetric flask

Burette (also Buret)

Burettes are calibrated to measure the volume of liquid delivered. The volume in a burette should be always read to the second decimal place. Burettes can dispense a small measured volume of a liquid, such as in a titration, with extreme precision with volumetric graduation and a stopcock at the bottom. As opposed to most glassware, burettes measure from the top since the liquid is dispensed from the bottom. To properly read a buret, your line of sight should still be level with the bottom of the meniscus.

A typical titration (CHM 6.9) begins with a beaker or Erlenmeyer flask containing a precise volume of the titrand (= the chemical being analyzed) and a small amount of indicator placed underneath a calibrated burette containing the titrant (= titrator reagent prepared as a standard solution).

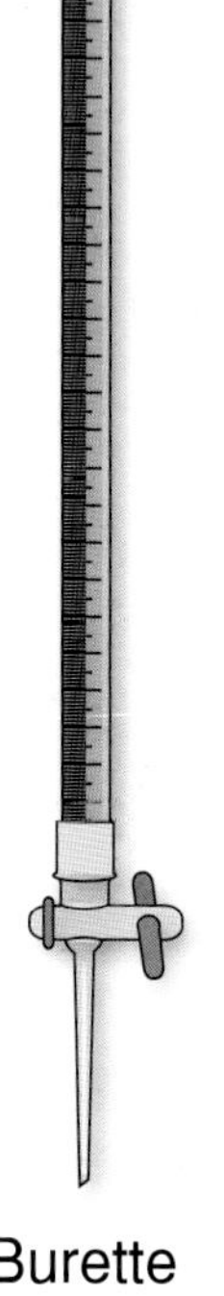

Burette

Beaker

Beakers are used to create reactions (i.e. precipitation, electrolysis) and to measure approximate amounts of liquids. It is a graduated container with a spout for pouring.

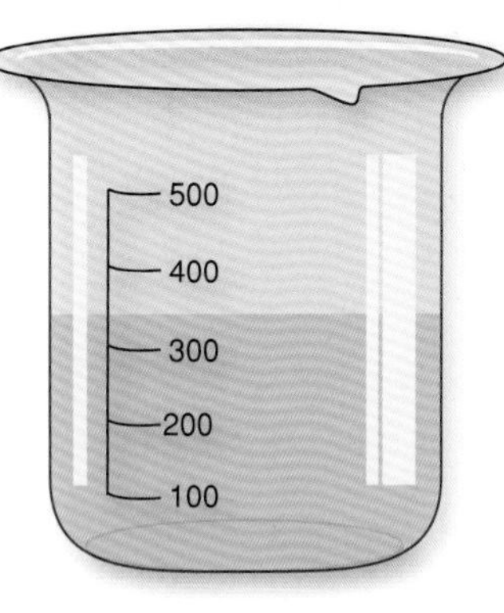

Beaker

Test tube

The most common of all lab supplies. Holds liquids but does not allow for accurate measurement.

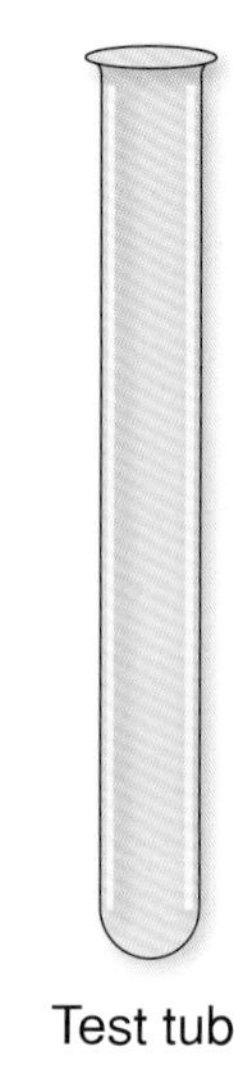

Test tube

Erlenmeyer flask

Used to measure, mix and store liquids. Note that it is a graduated cone-shaped container that usually holds 250 ml or 500 ml of liquid.

Erlenmeyer Flask

Wash bottle

Used especially for cleaning equipment (i.e. pipettes, test tubes). It is normally a flexible plastic (not 'glassware') and it is squeezed lightly to squirt liquid.

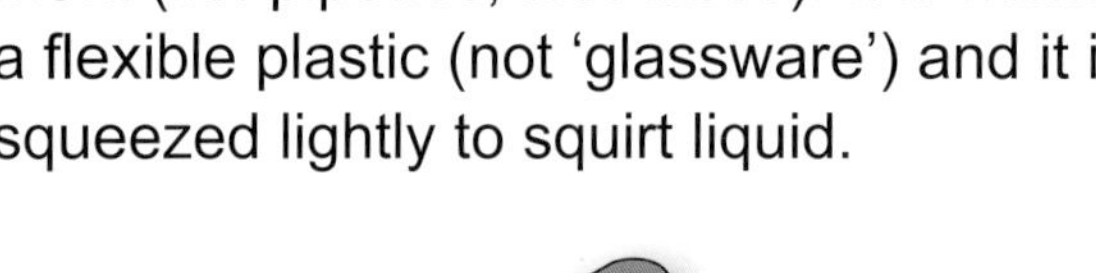

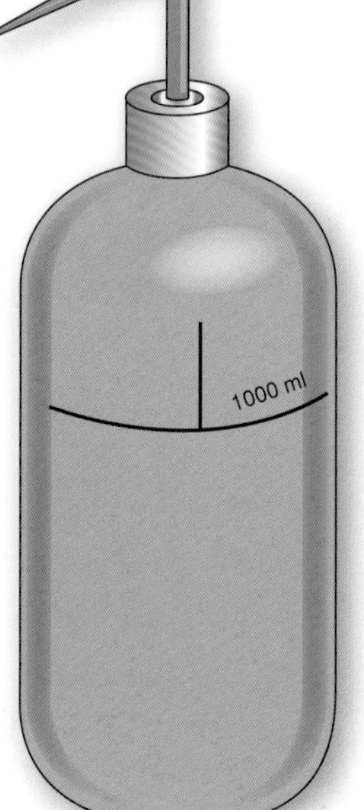

Wash bottle

Florence flask

Used mainly for boiling liquids and often as part of a distillation apparatus. Also known as "boiling flask" or "round bottom flask".

Florence Flask

Soxhlet extractor

Used to extract a compound (usually lipids within solids) that has limited solubility in a extracting solvent. Similar to the standard distillation apparatus (CHM 12.7). This setup requires a round-bottom flask at one end and a condenser at the other. In between is the Soxhlet extractor (sections 3, 4, 5, 6 and 7) which is designed to direct the solvent back down via the syphon arms to the round-bottom flask.

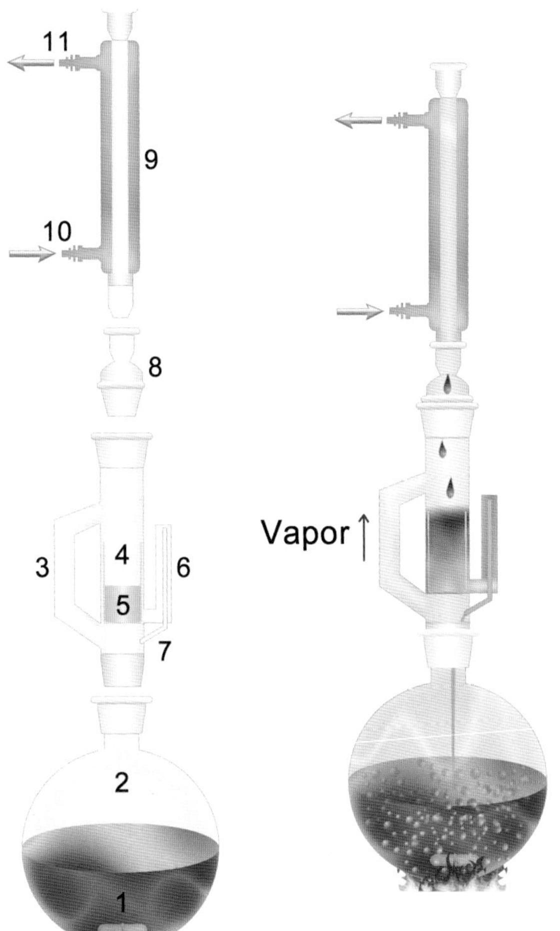

1: Stir bar (or flea, a magnetic bar used to stir liquid) or boiling chip (= boiling stone, anti-bumping granules, ebulliator; ORG 13)
2: Round bottom flask - should not be over-filled with solvent.
3: Distillation path
4: Soxhlet thimble to hold the solid sample for solvent extraction
5: Extraction solid (residue solid) usually to extract lipids
6: Syphon arm inlet
7: Syphon arm outlet
8: Reduction adapter
9: Condenser (also see the diagram in CHM 12.4.4)
10: Cooling water in from the bottom
11: Cooling water out from the top

Flaming can be done using a Bunsen burner or alcohol lamp for sterilization. This is commonly used for small metal or glassware. A variation is to dip the object in 70% ethanol (or a higher concentration) and then touch the object briefly to the Bunsen burner flame. The ethanol will ignite and burn off in a few seconds.

Before starting a titration, the pipette, burette and any required flask are rinsed with deionised water, rather than tap water. Tap water contains ions that may affect the titration result.

12.3.2 Mass Measurements

Along with the requirements of proper glassware, a well equipped laboratory must also contain the appropriate devices for mass measurements of solids as well as liquids (if densities are to be measured). A sample is generally "massed" in one of two ways. The sample may be added to a clean and dry container and the mass of the container and sample together are then taken and the mass of the two are subsequently subtracted. The second alternative, and more frequently used today, is that in which a container or weighing paper is zeroed (or *tarred*) and the sample is then placed onto the tarred container. For this second method, modern electronic balances are mainly used with a tarring capability.

There are different balances with varying degrees of sensitivities. Laboratory grade range from a "triple-beam balance" which was traditionally used with a sensitivity of approximately ± 0.01g, to the electronic top-loading balance with a sensitivity of ± 0.001g, and finally, to the electronic analytical balance used in most modern laboratories today with a very high sensitivity of approximately ± 0.0001g (= one tenth of a milligram or one ten-thousanth of a gram).

1) Triple beam balance

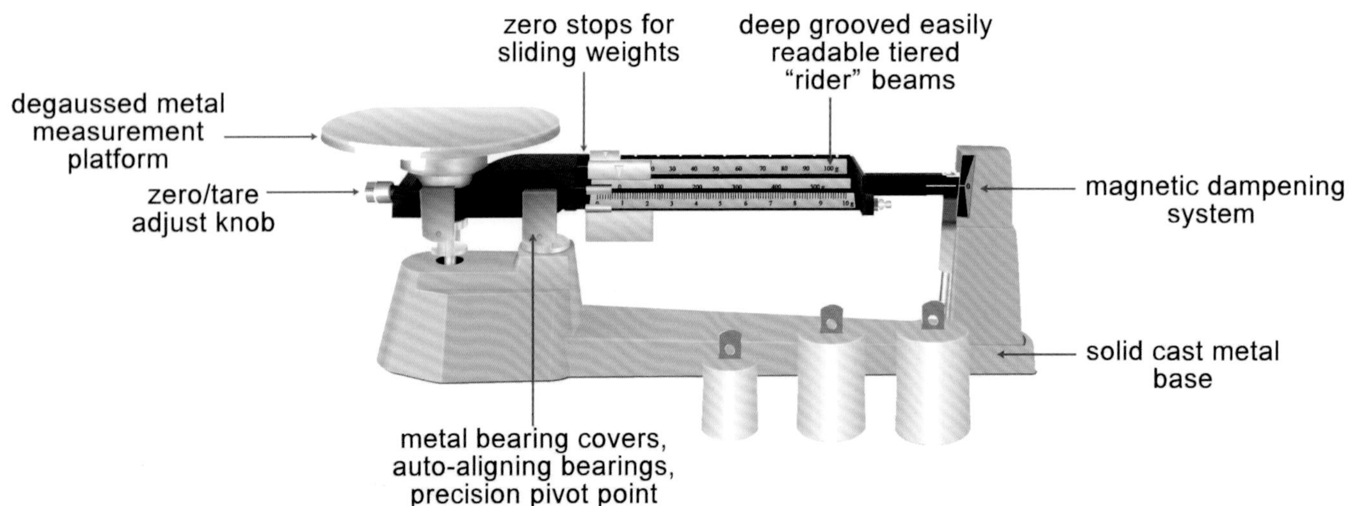

2) Top loading electronic balance

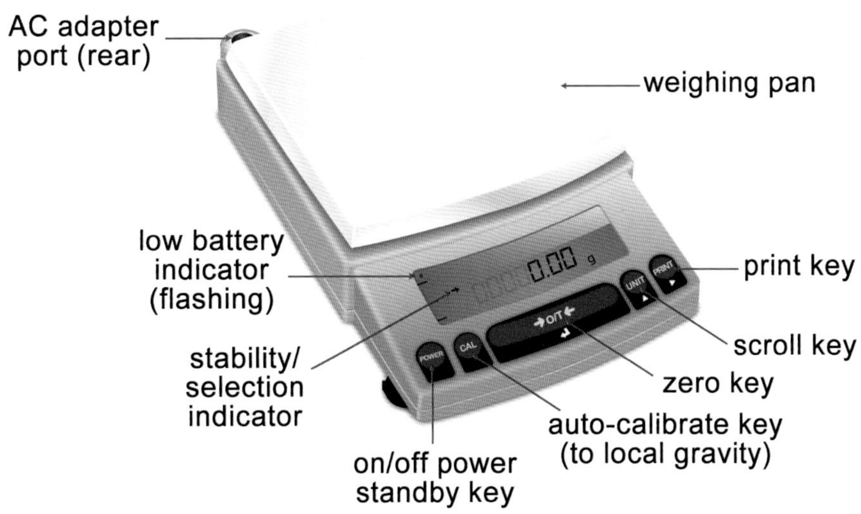

3) Electronic analytical balance

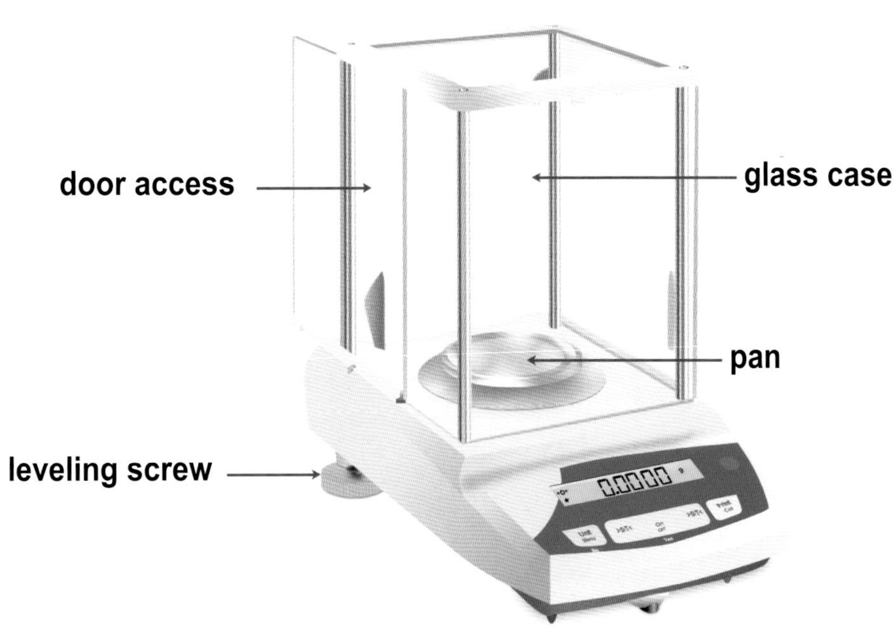

12.4 Data Analysis and Basic Lab Techniques

12.4.1 Scientific Notation

If you have already studied for QR, or if you are already comfortable with math, then you may not need to review this section nor CHM 12.4.2.

Numbers with many zeroes on either side of a decimal can be written in *scientific notation.* For example, a number which is an integer power of ten, the number of zeroes equals the exponent; thus $10^0 = 1$, $10^1 = 10$, $10^2 = 10 \cdot 10 = 100$, $10^3 = 10 \cdot 10 \cdot 10 = 1000$, and so on.

Conversely, the negative exponent corresponds to the number of places to the right of the decimal point; thus $10^{-1} = 1/10 = 0.1$, $10^{-2} = 1/(10 \cdot 10) = 0.01$, $10^{-3} = 1/(10 \cdot 10 \cdot 10) = 0.001$, and so on.

Scientific notation allows us to express a number as a product of a power of ten and a number between 1 and 10. For example, the number 5,478,000 can be expressed as 5.478×10^6; 0.0000723 can be expressed as 7.23×10^{-5}.

12.4.2 Error Analysis

If we divide 2 by 3 on a calculator, the answer on the display would be 0.6666666667. The leftmost digit is the *most significant digit* and the rightmost digit is the *least significant digit*. The number of digits which are really significant depends on the accuracy with which the values 2 and 3 are known.

For example, suppose we wish to find the sum of two numbers *a* and *b* with experimental errors (or *uncertainties*) Δa and Δb, respectively. The uncertainty of the sum c can be determined as follows:

$$c \pm \Delta c = (a \pm \Delta a) + (b \pm \Delta b) = a + b \pm (\Delta a + \Delta b)$$

thus

$$\Delta c = \Delta a + \Delta b.$$

The sign of the uncertainties are not correlated, so the same rule applies to subtraction. Therefore, *the uncertainty of either the sum or difference is the sum of the uncertainties.*

Now we will apply the preceding to significant digits. The number 3.7 has an implicit uncertainty. Any number between 3.65000... and 3.74999... rounds off to 3.7, thus 3.7 really means 3.7 ± 0.05. Similarly, 68.21 really means 68.21 ± 0.005. Adding the two values and their uncertainties we get: $(3.7 \pm 0.05) + (68.21 \pm 0.005) = 71.91 \pm 0.055$. The error is large enough to affect the first digit to the right of the decimal point; therefore, the last digit to the right is not significant. The answer is thus 71.9.

The rule for signiifcant digits states that *the sum or difference of two numbers carries the same number of significant digits to the right of the decimal as the number with the least significant digits to the right of the decimal.* For example, 105.64 − 3.092 = 102.55.

Multiplication and division is somewhat different. Through algebraic manipulation, the uncertainty or experimental error can be determined:

$$c \pm \Delta c = (a \pm \Delta a)(b \pm \Delta b)$$

after some manipulation we get

$$\Delta c/c = \Delta a/a + \Delta b/b.$$

The preceding result also holds true for division. Thus for (10 ± 0.5)/(20 ± 1), the fractional error in the quotient is:

$$\Delta c/c = \Delta a/a + \Delta b/b = 0.5/10 + 1/20 = 0.1 \text{ (10\% error)}$$

Thus the quotient including its absolute error is $c \pm \Delta c = 0.5(1 \pm 0.1) = 0.5 \pm 0.05$.

The rule for significant digits can be derived from the preceding and it states that *the product or quotient of two numbers has the same number of significant digits as the number with the least number of significant digits.*

12.4.3 Analyzing the Data

When quantitative data is to be properly reported, the data collected as a result of experimentation must reflect the reliability of all equipment and instruments used to make such measurements. It is therefore extremely important to report such data to the correct number of significant figures (also known as significant digits, and often shortened to sig figs or sf) as well as reporting all calculated results to the correct number of significant figures. Significant figures are used to clearly express the precision of such measurements. The number of significant figures obtained as a result of a measurement is equivalent to the number of certain figures in a made measurement plus an additional last figure denoting the uncertainty of the number.

The uncertain figure of a measurement is the last significant figure of the measurement.

Numbers that are known as conversion factors or numbers that define some entity are known as “Exact Numbers”. Examples of exact numbers are relationships such as 1 dozen = 12 or 1 foot = 12 inches. Exact numbers have an infinite number of significant figures. Table 12.1 demonstrates how one may distinguish significant figures from non-significant figures.

Table 12.1: Examples of significant figures versus non-significant figures.

Significant	Examples	Non-Significant
Non-zero integers	1.234 (4 sf)	
Zeros between non-zero integers*	1.004 (4 sf)	
Zeros to the right of decimal place AND integers*	1.2000 (5 sf) 0.0041 (2 sf)	Zeros to the right of decimal place BUT to the left of integers
	430 (2 sf)	Zeros to the left of decimal place BUT to the right of integers
	013.2 (3 sf)	Zeros to the left of decimal place AND integers

* Zeros in any number is used to convey either accuracy or magnitude. If a zero is to convey accuracy, then it is known as a significant value and if the zero is used to convey magnitude, then it is non-significant.

When performing mathematical operations on data with a fixed number of significant figures, it is critical to have the correct number of significant figures in the final answer, based upon the number of significant figures in the starting data. The following are examples of such operations:

For Addition and Subtraction:

The answer is limited by the data with the least number of significant figures after the decimal place.

e.g. $23.84 - 1.7 = 22.1$
(2 sf) (1 sf) (1 sf) after decimal place

For Multiplication and Division:

The answer is limited by the data with the least number of significant figures in total.

e.g. $250.00/5.00 = 50.0$
(5 sf) (3 sf) (3 sf)

12.4.4 Basic Lab Techniques

Distillation is the process by which compounds are separated based on differences in boiling points. A classic example of simple distillation is the separation of salt from water. The solution is heated. Water will boil and vaporize at a far lower temperature than salt. Hence the water boils away leaving salt behind. Water vapor can now be condensed into pure liquid water (*distilled water*). As long as one compound is more volatile, the distillation process is quite simple. If the difference between the two boiling points is low, it will be more difficult to separate the compounds by this method. Instead, fractional distillation can

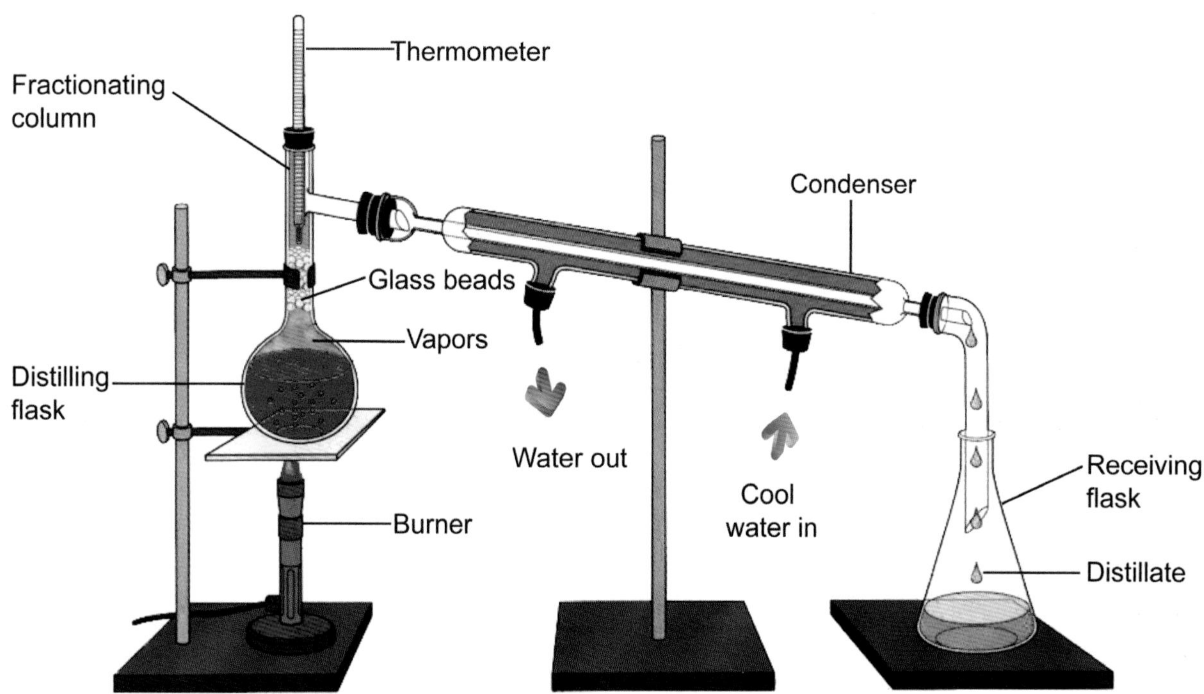

Figure III.A.12.: Standard fractional distillation apparatus

be used in which, for example, a column is filled with glass beads which is placed between the distillation flask and the condenser. The glass beads increase the surface area over which the less volatile compound can condense and drip back down to the distillation flask below. The more volatile compound boils away and condenses in the condenser. Thus the two compounds are separated.

The efficiency of the distillation process in producing a pure product is improved by repeating the distillation process, or, in the case of fractional distillation, increasing the length of the column and avoiding overheating. Overheating may destroy the pure compounds or increase the percent of impurities. Some of the methods which are used to prevent overheating include boiling slowly, the use of boiling chips (= *ebulliator*, which makes bubbles) and the use of a vacuum which decreases the vapor pressure and thus the boiling point.

Extraction is the process by which a solute is transferred (*extracted*) from one solvent and placed in another. This procedure is possible if the two solvents used cannot mix (= *immiscible*) and if the solute is more soluble in the solvent used for the extraction.

For example, consider the extraction of solute A which is dissolved in solvent X. We choose solvent Y for the extraction since solute A is highly soluble in it and because solvent Y is immiscible with solvent X. We now add solvent Y to the solution involving solute A and solvent X. The container is agitated. Solute A begins to dissolve in the solvent where it is most soluble, solvent Y. The container is left to stand, thus the two immiscible solvents separate. The phase containing solute A can now be removed.

In practice, solvent Y would be chosen such that it would be sufficiently easy to evaporate (= *volatile*) after the extraction so solute A can be easily recovered. Also, it is more efficient to perform several extractions using a small amount of solvent each time, rather than one extraction using a large amount of solvent.

<u>Chromatography</u> is the separation of a mixture of compounds by their distribution between two phases: one stationary and one moving. Molecules are separated based on differences in polarity and molecular weight.

In <u>gas-liquid chromatography</u>, the *stationary phase* is a liquid absorbed to an inert solid. The liquid can be polyethylene glycol, squalene, or others, depending on the polarity of the substances being separated.

The mobile phase is a gas (i.e. He, N_2) which is unreactive both to the stationary phase and to the substances being separated. The sample being analyzed can be injected in the direction of gas flow into one end of a column packed with the stationary phase. As the sample migrates through the column certain molecules will move faster than others. As mentioned the separation of the different types of molecules is dependent on size (*molecular weight*) and charge (*polarity*). Once the molecules reach the end of the column special detectors signal their arrival.

If you are studying for the US DAT or the OAT, then we suggest that you complete your Gold Notes followed by the Warm-Up Exercises in the book and online, and then update your notes and continue to your Organic Chemistry review. It is very important that you review your notes from the beginning on a regular basis. If you are studying for the Canadian DAT, where Organic Chemistry is not required, we suggest that you still review ORG 1.1 to 1.5 because it overlaps General Chemistry, and also review Organic Chemistry Chapter 13 which overlaps this chapter as well as Electrophoresis which is only partly covered at the end of Biology Chapter 15.

Perhaps this is a fair quote to end General Chemistry: “A diamond is merely a lump of coal that did well under pressure.” Good luck!

GOLD STANDARD WARM-UP EXERCISES

CHAPTER 12: Laboratory

1) In a titration, a burette is used to:

   A. measure the concentration of the unknown sample.
   B. measure the mass of the unknown sample.
   C. accurately add the indicator.
   D. accurately add the standard reagent.

2) Flaming is a technique used to:

   A. sterilize glassware before use.
   B. colorize a titration.
   C. clean hands after working with bacteria.
   D. clean instruments after use.

3) A student weighs out 0.0127 mol of pure, dry HCl in order to prepare a 0.127 M HCl solution. Of the following pieces of laboratory equipment, which would be most important for preparing the solution?

   A. 100 mL volumetric flask
   B. 100 mL graduated beaker
   C. 100 mL Erlenmeyer flask
   D. 50 mL volumetric pipette

4) The number 0.086030 has how many significant figures?

   A. 4
   B. 5
   C. 6
   D. 7

5) The weight of a metal is 24.7 grams and its volume is 3.3 cm^3. Considering the significant figures in your calculation, the value of the density, in g/cm^3, should be reported as:

   A. 7
   B. 7.5
   C. 7.4
   D. 7.48

GS ANSWER KEY

CHAPTER 12

		Cross-Reference			*Cross-Reference*
1.	**D**	**CHM 6.9, 12.3.1**	**4.**	**B**	**CHM 12.4.2, 12.4.3**
2.	**A**	**CHM 12.3.1**	**5.**	**B**	**CHM 12.4.2, 12.4.3**
3.	**A**	**CHM 12.3.1**			

* Explanations can be found at the back of the book.

Go online to DAT-prep.com for additional chapter review Q&A and forum.

CHAPTER REVIEW SOLUTIONS

Question 1 C

See: CHM 1.3, 1.5

Reaction I shows us that the stoichiometric ratio between Cl_2 and HCl is 1:2.

Using Number of moles Cl_2
= (Mass used)/(relative molecular mass Cl_2)

Number of moles Cl_2 = 10 g/[(35.5 × 2) g mol^{-1}]
= 10 g/(71.0 g mol^{-1})

From the ratio above, number of moles HCl produced
= 2 × number of moles Cl_2

Number of moles HCl = 2 × 10 g/(71.0 g mol^{-1})

Using Number of grams HCl
= Number of moles HCl × Relative molecular mass of HCl

Number of grams HCl = 2 × 10 g/(71.0 g mol^{-1})
× (1 + 35.5 g mol^{-1}) approx.
= 2 × 10 g × 1/2 = 10 g

Question 2 D

See: CHM 1.7

A solid mixture of two or more metals is referred to as an *alloy.*

Question 3 D

See: CHM 1.3

Molecular weight of N_2 = 28
Molecular weight of O_2 = 32
Average molecular weight of air
= (80% × 28) + (20% × 32)
= 28.8

Gases denser than air will have a molecular weight greater than 28.8.

CH_4: Mw = 16
Cl_2: Mw = 71
CO_2: Mw = 44
NH_3: Mw = 17
NO_2: Mw = 46
O_3: Mw = 48
SO_2: Mw = 64

Thus, Cl_2, CO_2, NO_2, O_3, and SO_2 are denser than air.

Question 4 B

See: CHM 1.5

The question indicates that there are 2 moles of P_2 gas and 4 moles of Q_2 gas in the vessel. Next, we learn that all the molecules have reacted to produce a *tri*atomic product. Thus the product must have three (*tri*) atoms. Only one answer has a product with three atoms, answer choice B. We know that the product must have a structure P_mQ_n (since both gases have reacted), where m + n = 3. Because there are twice as many Q atoms as P atoms, the overall reaction must be:

$$2P_2 + 4Q_2 \rightarrow 4PQ_2 \quad \text{or} \quad P_2 + 2Q_2 \rightarrow 2PQ_2$$

Question 5 D

See: CHM 1.6

This question is relatively easy. We know that each of the three oxygens has a charge of -2 (total charge -6) and that the overall charge on the molecule is -1. Letting X represent the oxidation state of the halogen, we have:

$$X + (-6) = -1$$
$$X = +5.$$

Question 6 A

See: CHM 1.6

The oxidation state of oxygen is usually -2. Therefore, the total oxidation state due to oxygen = 7 × -2 = -14. The overall charge on the molecule is -2. There are 2 Cr atoms per $Cr_2O_7^{2-}$ molecule, thus:

2 × oxidation state of Cr + (-14) = -2
2 × oxidation state of Cr = 12
Oxidation state of Cr = 12/2 = 6

Question 7 B

See: CHM 1.6

Looking at our answer choices, the oxidation state of N in NO is obviously +2, which makes sense because the oxidation state of oxygen is -2 and the overall charge of NO = 0. For nitric acid, where the charge of H = +1, the charge of O = -2 and the overall charge of the molecule = 0, we obtain:

$$(1 \times H) + (1 \times N) + (3 \times O) = 0 \rightarrow (+1) + (N) + (3 \times -2) = 0$$
$$(+1) + (N) + (-6) = 0 \rightarrow N - 5 = 0 \rightarrow N = +5.$$

Question 8 C

See: CHM 1.6

The oxidation state of oxygen is -2; therefore, the total oxidation state of the oxygens in MnO_4^- = -2 × 4 = -8. Since the net charge on the ion is -1,

Oxidation state of Mn + (-8) = -1, thus Mn = -1 + 8 = +7

Since the oxidation state of Mn in Mn^{2+} is +2, there has been a decrease in the oxidation state, that is, a reduction has occurred. {GERC = gain electrons reduction...CHM 10.2}

The oxidation state of Cl in Cl^- is -1 and is 0 in Cl_2 (the oxidation state of an element in naturally occurring form = 0) so an increase in the oxidation state, that is, an oxidation has occurred. {LEO = loss of electrons is oxidation...}

Question 9 D

See: CHM 1.5

Scanning the equation, you should be drawn to Ca in $Ca_3(PO_4)_2$ and you would conclude that you need at least $3Ca(OH)_2$ and thus $2H_3PO_4$ which gives $6H_2O$s.

$$3Ca(OH)_2 + 2H_3PO_4 \rightarrow 6H_2O + Ca_3(PO_4)_2$$

Question 10 D

See: CHM 1.3, 1.5

From the Reaction I, mole ratio between Mn and Cl_2 = 2:5
Relative atomic mass of Mn = 55 approximately (*see the periodic table)*

Relative molecular mass of Cl_2 = 35.5 × 2 = 71.0

Therefore, the mass ratio between Mn and Cl_2
= (2 × 55):(5 × 71.0)
= 110:355 = 11:35.5 = 1:3 approximately

Question 1 D
See: CHM 2.3
The s-block elements are those whose s-orbital is the valent orbital.

Question 2 D
See: CHM 2.3
Because the attractive forces between the nuclei and the valence electrons are strong, there is less tendency for electrons to be lost and hence a greater tendency for an electron to be gained in order to attain the more stable noble gas configuration.

Question 3 D
See: CHM 2.3
Colored complexes are a well-known characteristic of most transition metals.

Question 4 D
See: CHM 2.3
Since potassium only has one electron in its outer shell, it is easily removed (i.e. low first ionization potential/energy), thus leaving potassium with the more stable noble gas-like configuration (i.e. Ar). On the other hand, adding an electron to neutral potassium would require much energy (i.e. high first electron affinity) which would leave potassium with two valence electrons which would not be stable.

Noble gases are the most stable elements in the periodic table.

Question 5 C
See: CHM 2.3, 2.3.1
The smaller the atomic radii of the two atoms, the shorter the bond length. Bond **strength** is inversely related to bond **length**. Carbon has the *smaller* atomic radius thus it has the *greater* bond strength. {*This force of attraction is analogous to Coulomb's Law* (a physics principle but the basis for 'opposites attract' in general and organic chemistry) *where the positive nucleus is attracted to the bond which contains negative electrons*}

Question 6 D
See: CHM 2.1, 2.2
n is the principal quantum number and is irrelevant for this question since each of the choices is broken down to l or m quantum numbers.

l gives the shape of the orbital. 0 indicates s, 1 indicates p, 2 indicates d, 3 indicates f, etc. The maximum number of electrons in each of these is 2, 6, 10, 14, etc., respectively (it is given by the equation 4l + 2 but most students just memorize the preceding 4 maximum numbers). m gives the spatial orientation of an orbital. At most, only 2 electrons can occupy a single m orbital. Thus:

	Max. no. of electrons
n = 4, l = 0	2
n = 5, l = 2	10
n = 6, l = 3, l_m = +1	2
n = 4, l = 3	14
Therefore, the answer is D.	

Question 7 B
See: CHM 2.3
In the periodic table, chromium has an atomic number of 24, which means the Cr atom has 24 protons and 24 electrons. To do this problem, refer to CHM 2.2, Figure III.A.2.3, where the arrows show the order for filling atomic orbitals from top to bottom. The diagram shows that the orbital 4s is of lower energy than 3d; however, recall that a half-filled 3d orbital creates a more stable atom [CHM 2.3 (iv)] thus answer choice B. is correct.

Question 8 C
See: CHM 2.3
When you consider non-metals, think of examples: Noble gases, oxygen, nitrogen, etc. They are all gases at room temperature.

Question 9 A
See: CHM 2.3, 11
Ionization energy (or *potential*) is the energy required to remove the least tightly bound electron from an atom. If at the end of the process, that electron has some additional energy (ie. K_e) then that is clearly over and above just the energy required to remove the electron. Thus we can write:

$$\text{Total Energy } E = IE + K_e$$
$$IE = E - K_e$$

Question 1 A
See: CHM 3.2, 3.5
Formal charge is found by dividing the electrons in each bond between the atoms, and then comparing the number of electrons assigned to each atom with the number of electrons on a neutral atom of the element.
In a carbonate ion, we can assign 4 electrons to the C atom, and since C has 4 valence electrons, its formal charge is 0.
Going deeper: note that two of the O's each have a formal charge of -1, and the third O has a formal charge of 0. Thus, the carbonate ion has an overall charge of -2. Or, since each O is equivalent, the charge on each can be considered to be -2/3.

Question 2 D
See: CHM 3.5
The rule is that an atom which exhibits tetrahedral geometry is sp^3 hybridized.

Question 3 A
See: CHM 3.5, ORG 1.2
As in ethene and SO_2, the sp^2 hybridized atom has a trigonal planar orientation.

Question 4 B

See: CHM 3.2-3.5

The question describes a triatomic molecule (PQ_2). The central atom P is thus bonded twice to Q and, according to the question, P also has a lone pair of electrons. Thus P is surrounded by 3 electron pairs (minimum) which is a trigonal planar arrangement leaving a bent molecule (CHM 3.5T).

Question 5 B

See: CHM 3.4

The lone pair of electrons on the nitrogen atom allows it to **donate** a pair of electrons which is the definition of a Lewis base.

Question 6 D

See: CHM 3.5

Valence shell electron pair repulsion (VSEPR) rules predict the shape of individual molecules based on the extent of electron-pair repulsion. Valence electron pairs surrounding an atom repel each other, and thus make an arrangement that minimizes this repulsion producing the molecule's geometry.

Question 7 C

See: CHM 3.5

PCl_5 has 5 valence shell electron pairs. These will arrange themselves in a trigonal bipyramidal shape.

Question 8 A

See: CHM 3.5

SF_6 has 6 valence shell electron pairs. These will arrange themselves in an octahedral shape.

Question 9 D

See: CHM 3.5

ClF_3 has 5 valence shell electron pairs. These would normally arrange themselves in an trigonal bipyramidal fashion. However, since two of the electron pairs are lone pairs, the molecule is consequently T-shaped.

Question 10 B

See: CHM 2.3, 3.1.1

The larger the difference in electronegativity between two atoms involved in a bond, the more ionic (polar) the bond is. Scanning the periodic table, you will notice that Ca is to the far left and F (the most electronegative atom on the periodic table) is to the far right making a great situation for ionic bonding.

Chapter Review Solutions — Chapter 4

Question 1 C

See: CHM 4.1.10 (4.1.8)

The ideal gas equation assumes that (1) the volume occupied by the particles of gas is negligible compared to the overall volume of the gas and (2) there are no intermolecular interactions. To closely approximate these assumptions, low pressure is used so that the overall volume of the gas is large (because pressure and volume are inversely related) and high temperature minimizes intermolecular interactions.

{Remember: an ideal Plow and Thigh! (CHM 4.1.10)}

Question 2 A

See: CHM 4.1.2

If a gas is ideal, its particles have absolutely no attractive forces between them. Therefore, it should remain as a gas at all temperatures since liquefaction and solidification are based on mutual electrostatic forces of attraction between particles.

Question 3 D

See: CHM 4.1.9

The sum of the mole fractions of each species present must be unity (=1). Therefore, the partial pressure of O_2 is 1 - (1/6 + 1/2) = 1/3. The partial pressure of a species is given by the product of its mole fraction and the total pressure of the system. Therefore, the answer is given by 1/3 × 1 atm = 0.33 atm, approximately.

Question 4 B

See: CHM 4.1.6, 4.1.7, 4.1.8, 4.1.9

In Reaction 1, 4 moles of NH_3 react with 5 moles of O_2. We are told to assume ideal conditions so that we are dealing with ideality thus the ideal gas equation applies:

$$PV = nRT$$

If P and T are constant (i.e. at the time the two reactants are exposed to each other) thus:

$$V = n\ (RT/P) \text{ thus } V = n\ (\text{constant}).$$

{This concept is the basis for molar volume at S.T.P. (CHM 4.1.1); in fact, you can skip the steps above and directly apply Avogadro's Law (CHM 4.1.6)}

$$\text{Since } V_1/n_1 = \text{constant} = V_2/n_2 \text{ then:}$$

$$48/4 = V(O_2)/5 \text{ thus } 12 = V(O_2)/5$$

Thus

$$V(O_2) = 60 \text{ L}.$$

Question 5 B

See: CHM 4.3.3

Answer choice **B.** is a typical phase diagram for a substance. The exceptions to this rule include substances which exhibit larger intermolecular forces than usual, for example hydrogen bonding. These include water and ammonia, which would yield a phase diagram such as that in answer choice **A.** See the last paragraphs of CHM 4.3.3}

Question 6 B

See: CHM 4.3, 8.7

The latent heat, whether in fusion (solid to liquid transformation) or in vaporization (liquid/vapor transformation), takes place at constant temperature (either B or D). Clearly, fusion must occur at the lower temperature(B).

Question 7 A

See: CHM 4

Less dense solids or liquids float on denser liquids.

Question 8 B

See: CHM 4.1.8

Rearranging the ideal gas equation, we get:

$$n = PV/RT.$$

Since P, V, and T are the same for both gas samples, n is also the same. However, propane has a molecular weight of 44, while H_2 has a molecular weight of 2. Therefore, a molecule of propane weighs 22 times more than a molecule of hydrogen. Consequently, the sample of propane weighs 22 times more than the sample of hydrogen.

Question 9 A

See: CHM 4.1.8

Using n = PV/RT,

$$n_{final} = (2P \times 1.1V)/RT = 2.2 \times n_{initial}.$$

Therefore, the weight of air in the ball is also 2.2 times heavier than initially.

Question 10 A

See: CHM 4.1.1

Molar volume at STP is 22.4 L (CHM 4.1.1).
Use given values and estimate: (2 g/L)(22 L/mol) = 44 g/mol. Taking atomic weights from the periodic table, we find the molecular weight of C_3H_8: $(3 \times 12) + (8 \times 1) = 44$ g/mol.

Question 11 A

See: CHM 4.1.6

PV = nRT, n = PV/RT.
P = (7.6 torr.)(1 atm/760 torr.) = 0.01 atm.
R = 0.08 L * atm/K * mol.
V = (1000 mL/min)(1 min) = 1L.
T = 293 K (approximately 300 K).
n = (.01)(1)/(.08)(300) = 1/2400 mol.

mass = (200 g/mol) (1/2400 moles) = 1/12 = 0.08 grams. (Note: the MW was estimated at 200 instead of 197,4). Remember: check the answers, if they are very close (ie. 0.08, 0.082, 0.083, etc) then clearly you cannot round off figures (estimate). But the answers in this problem are multiples of each other so estimating within reason is logical.

Question 12 C

See: CHM 4.1.9

The partial pressure (pp) is based on the mole fraction (CHM. 4.1.9) not the weight. We must convert the weight into mole fraction, using the atomic weight from the periodic table. Given an arbitrary 200 g of mixture, there is:

H_2: (100 g)/(2 g/mol) = 50 mol of H_2,
He: (100 g)/(4 g/mol) = 25 mol of He.

Mole fraction of H_2: 50/(50 + 25) = 2/3.

Thus, pp of H_2 = 600 (2/3) = 400 torr.

Chapter Review Solutions — Chapter 5

Question 1 D

See: CHM 4.3.3, 5.1.2

Simply look at the graph, choose any temperature and then watch what happens as you increase the pressure to infinity: liquid!

Question 2 B

See: CHM 1.5, 5.2

Sodium sulfate dissociates in solution according to the following equation:

$$Na_2(SO_4) \rightarrow 2\ Na^+ + SO_4^{2-}$$

One mole of sodium sulfate dissociates into 2 moles of the sodium ion. Therefore, if the $[Na^+]$ = 0.02 M then the $[Na_2(SO_4)]$ is 0.02/2 = 0.01 M.

Question 3 D

See: CHM 3.1, 5.2

Osmolarity, a colligative property (depends on the number of particles, not the nature of the particles; CHM 5.1), is a measure of the amount of solute ions or molecules in solution. Since the three choices in the question are strong electrolytes (i.e. salts), we assume they will dissociate completely into ions according to the following equations:

1. $NaCl \rightarrow Na^+ + Cl^-$ = 2 ions in solution/mole of salt dissolved
2. $MgCl_2 \rightarrow Mg^{+2} + 2Cl^-$ = 3 ions in solution/mole of salt dissolved
3. $AlCl_3 \rightarrow Al^{+3} + 3Cl^-$ = 4 ions in solution/mole of salt dissolved

Since aluminum chloride will dissolve into the most particles, the $AlCl_3$ solution will have the highest osmolarity.

Question 4 B

See: CHM 5.3.1

Molarity = Number of moles per liter [= mol/(1000cm^3)]
Molality = Number of moles per 1000 g of solvent [= mol/(1000 g)]

Then, if 1000 cm^3 = 1000 g,
Molarity = Molality

Question 5 B

See: CHM 5.1.1/2

A non-volatile solute causes a lowering of the vapor pressure of the solvent and hence an elevation of the boiling point. The preceding is a colligative property.

Question 6 B

See: CHM 5.1.2

The negative slope of the solid liquid equilibrium curve in the phase diagram depicts that increasing the pressure causes a decrease in the melting point.

Going Deeper:

(1) ideally, you would recognize the shape of the Phase Diagram for Water with its classic features. One of which is the triple point: the point at which solid, liquid and gas exist at equilibrium. The pressure at the triple point is indicated in the graph but the temperature is not. However, you are expected to know that the temperature should be approximately 0 °C (after all, triple point means ice, liquid water and vapor; this is a simplified approximation; details at CHM 5.1.2).

Knowing that the triple point is about 0 °C, now examine the negative slope (upper left part of the graph) which represents the line where solid and liquid exist and equilibrium (melting point). As the pressure P increases, the negative slope demonstrates a decrease in temperature (below 0 °C).

(2) an interesting example: you can't skate on ice! If you have ever skated, you will know about this example. Ice is not very slippery; however, water on ice is VERY slippery. A skate is designed to put a lot of pressure (the weight of the individual) funneled to a very narrow blade. This narrow metal blade literally melts ice by the extreme pressure as the person's skate hits the surface allowing the metal to slide gracefully over the more slippery thin film of water on the ice surface. If the temperature becomes too low for the pressure to have a significant effect, skating becomes too difficult (too much resistance).

Question 7 C

See: CHM 5.3.2

To figure out the K_{sp} expression, it is wise to write the dissociation equation:

$$PbS \leftrightarrow Pb^{2+} + S^{2-}.$$

The K_{sp} is the product of the concentration of each ion raised to the power of the stochiometric coefficient in the equation. In this case,

$$K_{sp} = [Pb^{2+}][S^{2-}].$$

Question 8 C

See: CHM 5.3.2

$$Bi_2S_3 \leftrightarrow 2Bi^{3+} + 3S^{2-}$$

$$K_{sp} = [Bi^{3+}]^2[S^{2-}]^3$$

Question 9 C

See: CHM 5.3.2

Since $MgCO_3 \leftrightarrow Mg^{2+} + CO_3^{2-}$, $K_{sp} = [Mg^{2+}][CO_3^{2-}] = s \times s = s^2$ where s is the solubility. From the information provided, $s = 1.30 \times 10^{-3}$ mol L^{-1}. Thus $K_{sp} = [Mg^{2+}][CO_3^{2-}] = s^2 = (1.30 \times 10^{-3})^2 = 1.69 \times 10^{-6} \approx 1.7 \times 10^{-6}$. {Mathfax: $(13)^2 = 169$ therefore $(1.3)^2 = 1.69$; also, to increase speed you should at least be able to recognize the squares of numbers between 1-15, i.e. $(12)^2 = 144$; rules of exponents: see QR; of course, you will have a calculator at your disposal but recognizing patterns can make you faster.}

Question 10 B

See: CHM 5.3.2

Consider these two equations:

(i) $CaSO_4 \leftrightarrow Ca^{2+} + SO_4^{2-}$
(ii) $Ca(OH)_2 \leftrightarrow Ca^{2+} + 2OH^-$

On the Surface: for the same K_{sp}, the more ions produced means the more soluble ($Ca(OH)_2$ produces 3 ions as opposed to just 2). Though temperature is indeed related to solubility, it would affect both compounds in a similar way so having 3 ions will still mean that it is more soluble than just 2 ions.

Going Deeper: If $[Ca^{2+}] = s$ = solubility of salt, then:
For (i): $s^2 = K_{sp}$, therefore s = square root of K_{sp} (cf. with previous question/answer)

For (ii): $(2s)^2 \times s = K_{sp}$, therefore s = cube root of $(1/4 \times K_{sp})$

Since K_{sp} is always *less* than 1 for sparingly soluble salts, the value for *s* obtained in (ii) *necessarily* is greater than that obtained in (i). {*For fun(!), work out values for 's' in* (i) *and* (ii) *using any value for* K_{sp} *less than* 1}

Question 11 B

See: CHM 5.3.2, 5.3.3

By adding K_2S, we are essentially adding sulfide anions, which first combine with Ni^{2+} ions to form a NiS precipitate. Since MnS has not yet precipitated, it must be more soluble than NiS. And since both cations (Ni^{2+} and Mn^{2+}) have a charge of +2, their coefficients in their respective dissolution equations must be the same. Thus, MnS must have a higher K_{sp} than NiS; in fact, the K_{sp} of MnS is 3.0×10^{-13}.

Question 12 A

See: CHM 5.3.2, 5.3.3

The balanced equation for the dissolution of $MgF_2(s)$ is:

$$MgF_2(s) \leftrightarrow Mg^{2+}(aq) + 2F^-(aq).$$

$$K_{sp} = [Mg^{2+}][F^-]^2 = 6.5 \times 10^{-9}$$

For convenience, let us denote $[Mg^{2+}]$ as X. Thus:

$$6.5 \times 10^{-9} = X(2X)^2 = X(4X^2) = 4X^3$$

$$X = \text{cube root of } \{(6.5 \times 10^{-9})/4\} = 1.18 \times 10^{-3}$$

Finally, $[F^-] = 2X = 2.35 \times 10^{-3}$.

Question 13 D

See: CHM 5.3.2, 5.3.3

$$K_{sp} = [Mg^{2+}]\,[F^-]^2 = 6.5 \times 10^{-9} = 0.1\,[F^-]^2$$

Thus:

$$[F^-] = \text{sq root } (6.5 \times 10^{-9} \times 10) = 2.5 \times 10^{-4}\text{ M}$$

Question 14 C

See: CHM 5.3.2, 5.3.3

$$MgF_2 \rightarrow Mg^{2+} + 2F^-$$

$$Ksp = [Mg^{2+}][F^-]^2 = 10^{-8}$$

Given Ksp = $[10^{-4}][10^{-4}]^2 = 10^{-12}$

Our calculated Ksp (10^{-12}) is much less than the value above which a precipitate is formed (10^{-8}),

$$MgCO_3 \rightarrow Mg^{2+} + CO_3^{2-}$$

$$Ksp = [Mg^{2+}][CO_3^{2-}] = 10^{-5}$$

Given Ksp = $[10^{-4}][10^{-4}] = 10^{-8}$

Again the calculated value is far below the value needed to precipitate (10^{-5}).

Question 15 D

See: CHM 5.1.3

First we should define "osmotic pressure": Osmotic pressure is the hydrostatic (ie. water) pressure produced by a solution in a space divided by a semipermeable membrane (the capillary wall) due to a differential in the concentrations of solute (because we are told that the capillary wall is permeable to everything except proteins then only the proteins constitute the differential concentrations of solute).

$$\Pi = (n/V)RT$$
$$= 0.0015 \times 60 \times 310$$
$$= 27.9 \text{ mmHg or Torr}$$

(The term "oncotic pressure" refers to the osmotic pressure exerted by colloids only (see CHM 1.7). Colloids include proteins and starches in solution.)

Question 16 D

See: CHM 5.1.2

The freezing point of water is 0 °C.

To depress the freezing point to -40 °C,

$$\text{molality of solution} = \Delta T/K_f$$
$$= 40/1.9$$
$$= 21 \text{ m or } 21 \text{ moles/kg of water}$$

Molecular weight of ethylene glycol = 62

Therefore, mass of ethylene glycol = moles × mw

= 21 × 62

= 1300 g

= 1.3 kg

Question 1 C

See: CHM 6.1, 6.5

$pH = -\log_{10}[H^+]$

The highest pH has the lowest $[H^+]$. Clearly, Na_2SO_4 is the only choice that does not even have dissociable H^+!

Question 2 B

See: CHM 6.5, 6.6

Reaction I

$$H_2SO_3 + H_2O \rightarrow H_3O^+ + HSO_3^- \qquad K_{a1} = \text{very high}$$

Reaction II

$$HSO_3^- + H_2O \leftrightarrow H_3O^+ + SO_3^{2-} \qquad K_{a2} = 5.0 \times 10^{-6}$$

Since we are told to consider the first ionization of H_2SO_3 as if from a strong acid, we assume that the first proton completely dissociates. However, the second proton ionizes as if from a very weak acid. After all, a $K_a \approx 10^{-6}$ means that the product of the reactants is about 1 000 000 (one million!) times greater than the product of the products (which includes the second proton; for K_a see CHM 6.1). The preceding fact combined with the imprecision of the available multiple choice answers means that our answer can be estimated by assuming that H_2SO_3 acts as a strong monoprotic acid like HCl.

Therefore, one proton completely dissociates while the second proton's concentration is relatively negligible; thus $[H^+] = 0.01$ mol dm-3 ($1\ dm^{-3} = 1\ L^{-1}$, see QR). The pH is equal to the negative logarithm of $[H^+] = -\log(0.01) = -\log(10^{-2}) = 2$.

Question 3 A

See: CHM 6.5, 6.9

An indicator is added to titration solutions to detect the pH change associated with the endpoint of a titration. The solution is titrated until a color *change* is observed (eliminating answer choices B. and D.) when a stoichiometric amount of titrant has been added. The indicator consists of a weak acid or base whose undissociated state is a different color than its dissociated (conjugate) state. The indicator chosen should have its pK_a close to the expected pH of the equivalence point.

Question 4 C

See: CHM 6.9.3

HCl is an acid, so one would expect the pH of the reaction mixture to decrease (that is, become more acidic) as increasing volumes of HCl are added. Thus only C. and D. are possible answers. Answer choice D. is wrong because there should be two "plateaus" (*that is, where the slope of a curve approximates 0 in that region*) in this type of graph, there are just regions where the slope approaches infinity (*that is, the slope is almost vertical which is not logical for a titration curve; furthermore, consider the data in Table 1 for pH = 8.8*).

Question 5 B

See: CHM 6.5, 6.9

The range of the indicator should include the range where the graph depicts an almost vertical slope, that is, it should include the *equivalence point* in the middle of that region. This is approximately 4.6 in this instance (*see previous question* C.). Even if you did not know which titration curve was correct in the previous question, all answer choices change the direction of the curve (in math, this is called the point of inflection) around 4.6 which indicates the equivalence point.

Question 6 C

See: CHM 6.9.3

Once the $C_6H_5NH_2$ is depleted (*producing* $C_6H_5NH_3^+$), additional protons from the HCl can no longer be neutralized. Thus the $[H^+]$ increases dramatically, leading to a decrease in pH.

Question 7 C

See: CHM 6.5, 6.5.1, 6.9

Two pH units are equivalent to a 100 fold $[H^+]$ difference as shown below.

$$pH = -\log(x) = 2$$
$$x = 10^2 = 100$$

The proper interpretation of the answer is: if the pH goes down by 2 units, we have 100 times more hydrogen ion concentration, and if the pH goes up by 2 units, we would have 1/100th of the original hydrogen ion concentration: either an increase or decrease of 100x.

Question 8 B

See: CHM 6.9, 6.9.1/2

Answer choices **A** and **C** are characteristics of a neutral solution, which may not necessarily exist at the equivalence point of a titration.

Question 9 B

See: CHM 6.5, 6.5.1, 6.6

Since formic acid is considered a weak acid (*see* K_a) it will dissociate according to the following equation:

$$HCOOH \leftrightarrow H^+ + HCOO^-$$

The K_a of the reaction must be used to calculate the concentration of protons and the pH:

$$K_a = [H^+][HCOO^-]/[HCOOH]$$

After dissociation, an equal amount X of $[H^+]$ and $[HCOO^-]$ will be in solution with a certain concentration of acid left undissociated (0.10 M - X). Substituting these values, we get:

$$K_a = (X)(X)/(0.10\text{ M} - X) = X^2/(0.10\text{ M} - X).$$

Since we expect that $X<<0.10$, we can approximate the denominator to be 0.10 M (*see* CHM 6.6). Substituting the value of K_a, we can calculate the concentration of protons:

$$1.8 \times 10^{-4} = X^2/0.10$$
$$X^2 = 1.8 \times 10^{-5}$$
$$X = (16 \times 10^{-6})^{1/2} = 4 \times 10^{-3} \text{ approx.}$$

Using:

$$pH = -\log[H^+]$$
$$pH = -\log(4 \times 10^{-3}) = -\log(10^{\text{between 0 and 1}} \times 10^{-3})$$
$$= -(\text{between 0 and 1}) + 3 = \text{a pH between 2 and 3.}$$

Question 10 B

See: CHM 6.5, 6.5.1

$$pH = -\log_{10}[H^+]$$
$$[H^+] = [CHO_2^-]$$
$$= 10^{-pH} = 10^{-2.38}$$
$$Ka = [H^+][CHO_2^-]/[CH_2O_2]$$
$$= (10^{-2.38})^2/0.1$$
$$= 10^{-4.76}/0.1$$
$$= 10^{-3.76} \text{ (now check A, B, C, D)}$$
$$= \text{(approximately) } 1.8 \times 10^{-4}$$

Question 11 B

See: CHM 6.2, 6.5

Since K_b of NH_3 is 1.8×10^{-5}, K_a of conjugate acid (NH_4^+) is:

$$10^{-14}/1.8 \times 10^{-5} = \text{(approximately) } 10^{-10}.$$

Now, K_a of $NH_4^+ = [H^+][NH_3]/[NH_4^+]$,
where $[NH_4^+] = 0.1$ M and $[H^+] = [NH_3]$.
Therefore:

$$[H^+] = \text{sq rt } (K_a\,[NH_4^+])$$
$$= \text{sq rt } (10^{-10} \times 0.1)$$
$$= \text{sp rt } 10^{-11}$$
$$= 10^{-5.5}$$
$$pH = -\log_{10}[H^+]$$
$$= 5.5$$

Question 12 B

See: CHM 6.1

First, consider:

$$K_{a1} = [H^+][HSO_4^-]/[H_2SO_4] = 10^3$$
$$[H^+] = [HSO_4^-] = \text{approximately } 1.0\text{ M},$$

since K_{a1} is so high and the solution is 1 M H_2SO_4. However, HSO_4^- is also an acid and will dissociate with:

$$K_{a2} = [H^+][SO_4^{2-}]/[HSO_4^-] = 1.2 \times 10^{-2}.$$

Since $[HSO_4^-] = 1.0$ M from the first reaction,

$$[SO_4^{2-}] = K_{a2}$$
$$= 1.2 \times 10^{-2} = 0.012\text{ M}.$$

Thus:

$[H^+]$ generated from the second reaction = $[SO_4^{2-}]$ = 0.012 M.

Finally, $[H^+]_{total} = 1 + 0.012 = 1.012$ M.

CHAPTER REVIEW SOLUTIONS — CHAPTER 7

Question 1 C

See: CHM 7.6

The internal energy of the water is a state function and does not depend on the history of the sample.

Question 2 C

See: CHM 7.5

The system is doing work on the surroundings so the work "w" must have a negative sign since you must always look at the problem from the point of view of the system - not the surroundings. The system is also losing heat to the surroundings so the sign for the heat "q" will also be negative. The energy is the sum of q + w = -25 - 50 = -75

Question 3 A

See: CHM 7.5

Light colors tend to reflect incident electromagnetic radiation including infrared rays, the main type of electromagnetic radiation associated with heat. The answer is easily deduced since there is only one answer which refers to the *reflective* property of the metal foil.

Question 4 C

See: CHM 7.6

A state function is one that depends only on the present state of a system and not the path used to get to the present state. A system's volume, internal energy, and entropy do not depend on how the system arrived at the current state. However, the work done does depend on the path taken, e.g.: the work done could be as large as we want by taking a path as long as we want.

Question 5 B

See: CHM 7.5

Air is a poor *conductor* of heat. Both radiation and convection typically need air, or some other fluid, as a medium to transmit energy/heat.

Question 1 D

See: CHM 8.10

Answer choice **D** is true for all equilibria.

Question 2 C

See: CHM 8.9

In this reaction, four molecules react to form two molecules, thus increasing the order and decreasing the entropy.

Of course, this is true because we are only examining this one reaction; in truth, there must be some other process driving this reduction in entropy and thus, overall, if we were to include that other process, the entropy of the universe increases.

Example? Put liquid water in your freezer and, indeed, the disorder in the liquid becomes organized water crystals known as ice! Clearly, from the water's point of view, entropy decreased. But, if you were to touch the back of your freezer (we are NOT recommending this!), you will see that it is hot, lots of used and wasted energy creating increased randomness in the universe just to make a few ice cubes!

Question 3 B

See: CHM 8.2, 8.9, 8.10, 9.10

$$\Delta G = \Delta H - T(\Delta S)$$

Since the reaction is spontaneous, $\Delta G < 0$.

Since $\Delta S < 0$, $-T(\Delta S) > 0$.

Thus, for ΔG to be strictly less than zero, ΔH must be strictly less than zero, which means that the reaction is exothermic.

Question 4 C

See: CHM 8.8, 8.9

Moving from an organized crystalline solid (ice cube) to liquid water is clearly an increase in randomness of water molecules. The Second Law of Thermodynamics suggests that the total entropy (randomness or disorder) increases in any real system.

Question 5 D

See: CHM 5.3, 8.10, 9.10

This is an application of Henry's law. Consider what happens when you open a can of Coke: the carbon dioxide bubbles out of the solution - at times, faster than we want it to - because the pressure within the can is higher than atmospheric pressure. Thus the solubility of the gas decreased as the pressure over the solution was decreased.

The concept that the solubility of a dissolved gas will decrease when the solution is heated sounds a bit backwards since we usually heat up a solvent in order to dissolve something. The can be explained by discussing the overall energy of a system (Gibbs free energy) which is dependent on enthalpy and entropy (CHM 8.10, 9.10). Temperature is associated with entropy or randomness. If you heat up a solution of a gas and the gas escapes, the system becomes more random therefore it is favorable to have a decrease in solubility. Back to the can of Coke: heating up the can before opening it will result in a very rapid escape of gas (please do NOT try this!).

Question 6 C

See: CHM 4.3.3, 8.10

The triple point is where solid, liquid and gas exist at equilibrium and, by definition, ΔG is zero.

$$\Delta G = \Delta H - T\Delta S$$
$$0 = \Delta H - T\Delta S$$
$$\Delta H = T\Delta S$$

Thus the enthalpy change is equal to the effect of the entropy change. One could argue for answer choice A if indeed $\Delta H < T\Delta S$ which is not the case. Note that answer choice B does not apply because the reaction is at equilibrium. Regarding answer choice D, the reverse is theoretically true: an increase in disorder creates a positive change in entropy.

Question 7 D

See: CHM 8.5

Add the two equations to give the third one keeping in mind that the 2nd equation needs to be multiplied through by 2 so that we can cancel $2H_2O(l)$ which is not needed in the final reaction.

$$CH_4(g) + 2O_2(g) \rightarrow CO_2(g) + 2H_2O(l) \quad \Delta H° = -890 \text{ kJ/mol}$$
$$2H_2O(l) \rightarrow 2H_2O(g) \quad \Delta H° = 88 \text{ kJ/mol}$$

Add the equations (note that $2H_2O(l)$ cancels from both sides of the equation) and their enthalpies.

$$CH_4 + 2O_2(l) \rightarrow CO_2(g) + 2H_2O(g) \quad \Delta H° = -802 \text{ kJ/mol}$$

Question 8 A

See: CHM 8.5

Write the equations according to the data given (note the sign of ΔH is reversed because the direction of the equation is reversed; this is done so that when we add the equations, cancellations can occur to produce the desired final reaction):

$$SO_2(g) \rightarrow S(s) + O_2(g) \qquad \Delta H = 297 \text{ kJ}$$

$$S(s) + {}^3/_2O_2 \rightarrow SO_3 \qquad \Delta H = -396 \text{ kJ}$$

Add the two equations to give

$$SO_2(g) + {}^1/_2O_2 \rightarrow SO_3 \qquad \Delta H = -99 \text{ kJ}$$

Question 9 D

See: CHM 8.7

The definition of a calorie is the amount of thermal energy required to raise the temperature of water by 1 degree Celcius (CHM 7.3). Thus it would be normal for you to know that the specific heat "c" of liquid water is 1 cal g^{-1} °C^{-1} (i.e. 1 kcal/kg °C has the same meaning because of dimensional analysis).

1. Heat required to convert 10 grams of ice to 10 grams of water at 0 °C; L = latent heat of fusion.

   $$Q = mL = (10)(80) = 800 \text{ cal}$$

2. Heat required to convert 10 grams of water at 0 °C to 10 grams of water at 100 °C.

   $$Q = mc\Delta T = 10(1)100 = 1000 \text{ cal}$$

3. Heat required to convert 10 grams of water at 100 °C to 10 grams of steam at 100 °C; L = latent heat of vaporization.

   $$Q = mL = (10)(540) = 5400 \text{ cal}$$

   ADD (1) + (2) + (3) = 7200 cal

Question 10 A

See: CHM 8.7

This problem is solved by giving special attention to units (i.e. 1 W = 1 J per s):

Rate of incident solar energy

$$= 70\ 000 \text{ m}^2 \times 120 \text{ J s}^{-1} \text{ m}^{-2} = 8\ 400\ 000 \text{ J s}^{-1}$$

From Quantity of heat (Q)

= Mass (m) × Specific heat capacity (c)

× temperature change (T)

Thus in one second:

$$Q = 8\ 400\ 000 \text{ J} = m \times (4.2 \text{ J g}^{-1} \text{ °C}^{-1}) \times (10 \text{ °C})$$

$$42 \times m = 8\ 400\ 000; \quad \text{thus } m = 200\ 000 \text{ g} = 200 \text{ kg}$$

Using Density = (Mass)/(Volume)

Volume = (Mass)/(Density) = 200 kg/1000 kg m^{-3}

= 0.2 m^3 = 0.2 m^3 × 1000 dm^3/m^3

Volume = 200 dm^3 = 200 L in one second

Time for a break!

Question 1 D

See: CHM 9.3, 9.4

When [P] is increased by a factor of 3 (Exp A and C, [Q] *is constant*), the initial rate of reaction is increased by a factor of 9 (= 32). Thus the order of reaction with respect to P is 2. When [Q] is increased by a factor of 2 (Exp A and B, [P] *is constant*), the initial rate of reaction is also increased by a factor of 2 (= 21). Therefore, the order of reaction with respect to Q is 1. The order of reaction with respect to a certain component tells you how many molecules of that component are involved in the rate determining step of the reaction which may not be equivalent to the stoichiometric coefficients.

Question 2 B

See: CHM 8.2, 9.9

The question stem indicates that addition of heat to the reaction would shift the reaction to the right. According to Le Chatelier's principle, the addition of a reactant will shift a reaction to the right while the addition of a product has the reverse effect. In this example, we can consider heat as a reactant, which means that the reaction is endothermic and the enthalpy has a positive value.

Question 3 A

See: CHM 9.7, 9.8

Catalysts only affect the rate at which equilibrium is achieved, not the equilibrium position itself.

Question 4 B

See: CHM 9.9

Reaction I is exothermic (ΔH is negative therefore heat is released). The reaction could be written as:

$$2SO_2(g) + O_2(g) \leftrightarrow 2SO_3(g) + \text{Heat}$$

Adding heat (increasing the temperature) adds to the right hand side of the equilibrium forcing a shift to the left in order to compensate. The reverse occurs by decreasing the temperature thus creating a shift to the right which would produce more $SO_3(g)$ and more heat is released. {Note: an increase in pressure would also lead to a right shift; see Le Chatelier's Principle, CHM 9.9}.

Question 5 A

See: CHM 9.9

An easy way to figure out questions involving Le Chatelier's Principle applied to temperature changes is to write out "heat" in the equation as a reactant or a product. In this example, heat is released from the reaction (shown by the temperature rise in the reaction vessel) so it can be considered a product:

$$P_2 + 2Q_2 \rightarrow 2PQ_2 + \text{heat}$$

If we decrease the temperature of the vessel, then we are decreasing the product on the right of the equation and the equilibrium of the reaction will shift towards the right to counteract this, in accordance with Le Chatelier's Principle.

Question 6 A

See: CHM 9.5

As with any potential energy curve of a reaction, we are looking for the shape of a hill because the transition state of the reaction, as a rule, has higher energy than the reactants and the products, eliminating answer choices C. and D. The negative enthalpy of the reaction means that the reaction is exothermic and that the energy of the products (on the right side of the hill) will be lower than the energy of the reactants (on the left side of the hill), as represented by answer choice A.

Question 7 A

See: CHM 9.9

Less particles are on the left side of the equation (9 moles versus 10). Therefore, the increase in pressure favors a shift in the equilibrium position to the left as the reactants occupy less volume (*Le Chatelier's principle*).

Question 8 B

See: CHM 5.3.3, 9.9

Because the acidity constants are small, the undissociated form of the acid tends to predominate in solution, that is, the equilibria $H_2S \leftrightarrow HS^- + H^+$ ($K_{a1} \approx 10^{-7}$) and $HS^- \leftrightarrow H^+ + S^{2-}$ ($K_{a2} \approx 10^{-15}$) both are heavily shifted to the left. According to Le Chatelier's principle, this would lead to Reaction I shifting to the right to counteract the effects of the loss of sulfide anions caused by the addition of protons (H^+).

Question 9 C

See: CHM 9.9

A negative ΔH signifies an exothermic reaction, which means heat (energy) is released.

Thus: $$H_2 + I_2 \leftrightarrow 2\ HI + heat$$

If you increase the heat (i.e. temperature), the excess heat causes the reverse reaction to occur until equilibrium is again reached (CHM 9.9).

Question 10 C

See: CHM 9.2, 9.3

From the data, it can be seen that changing [B] while holding [A] constant has no effect on the rate. So B should not be a variable in the rate law. Also, it can be seen that doubling [A] leads to the rate quadrupling. So the rate is proportional to $[A]^2$. Thus, the rate law for the reaction is:

$$Rate = k[A]^2.$$

Question 11 A

See: CHM 9.2, 9.3

Let's look at Experiment 1 in Table 1 (this choice is arbitrary).

$$Rate = k[A]^2$$
$$4.0 \times 10^{-5} = k \times 0.1^2$$
$$k = 4.0 \times 10^{-5}/0.01$$
$$= 4.0 \times 10^{-3}$$

Now let's look at the units.

$$Rate = k[A]^2$$
$$M/s = [k] \times M^2$$
$$[k] = (M/s)/M^2$$
$$= M^{-1}s^{-1}$$

Thus, $$k = 4.0 \times 10^{-3}\ M^{-1}s^{-1}.$$

Question 12 B

See: CHM 9.2, 9.3

For choice A to be correct, the rate law would have to be one of the following, since three molecules would be involved in the rate-determining step.

$$Rate = k[A]^3$$
$$Rate = k[A]^2[B]$$
$$Rate = k[A][B]^2$$
$$Rate = k[B]^3$$

Incidentally, termolecular reactions are extremely rare because of the high improbability of having 3 molecules colliding at their reactive sites simultaneously.

For choice C to be correct, the rate law would have to be:

$$rate = k[A]^2[B].$$

The reason is the following: A and B first quickly react to form, say, AB. AB then reacts slowly with free A to form C. So:

$$rate = k[AB][A].$$

But [AB] is equal to [A][B], therefore:

$$rate = k[A][B][A] = k[A]^2[B].$$

(Note: k is just an arbitrary (nondescript) constant.)

For choice D to be correct, the rate law would have to be:

$$Rate = k[A][B].$$

The actual rate law (rate = $k[A]^2$) tells us however that the rate determining step involves two molecules of A -not one of A and another of B, nor a single one of A, etc. Thus, answer choice B is correct.

Question 13 A

See: CHM 9.2, 9.3

I. k would decrease if the activation energy were higher since fewer molecules would have the necessary kinetic energy to proceed with the reaction.

II. k does increase with increasing temperature since more molecules would have the necessary kinetic energy to proceed with the reaction.

III. k is unaffected by the concentrations of reactants.

Thus, only statement II is correct.

Question 14 C

See: CHM 9.3

When the concentration of sucrose doubles (i.e. from 0.200 to 0.400M), the rate also doubles (from 7.32×10^{-4} to 1.46×10^{-3}). Therefore:

$$Rate = K\ [sucrose]$$

Now plug in any pair of values, for example:

$$1.80 \times 10^{-3} = K(0.500)$$

Multiply through by 2:

$$3.60 \times 10^{-3} = K$$

Thus: rate = (3.6×10^{-3})[sucrose]

Question 15 C

See: CHM 9.5

The activation energy is the difference between the total energy of the reactants (E_2) and the activated complex (E_3).

Question 1 D

See: CHM 10.1, 10.2, 10.4, 6.1

The relevant reaction is $Cu + 2H^+ \rightarrow Cu^{2+} + H_2$
Using the data provided, E = -0.34 + 0.00 = -0.34 V
Since E < 0, the reaction is not spontaneous.

Question 2 B

See: CHM 10.1, 10.2, 10.4, 6.1

The relevant reaction is $Pb + 2H^+ \rightarrow Pb^{2+} + H_2$
Using the data provided, E = 0.00 - (-0.13) = 0.13 V
Since E > 0, the reaction is spontaneous.

Question 3 B

See: CHM 10.1, 10.2, 10.4

Voltage = 2.87 - 1.09 = 1.78 V

Question 4 A

See: CHM 10.1, 10.2

Galvanic cells use spontaneous redox reactions to produce electricity. Recall that E° = E(reduction) - E(oxidation), and that a positive value of E° means that the reaction is spontaneous. The E° of the reaction for the Cl_2/Cl^- half cell given by the 1st reaction of Table 1 is 1.36 compared to an E° value of 1.51 for Reaction III. In order for the redox reaction to be spontaneous, Reaction III (with the higher E°) will proceed as a reduction (as written) while Cl^- will be oxidized to Cl_2. The overall Eo can be calculated as follows:

$$E° = E° \text{ red} - E° \text{ ox} = 1.51 - 1.36 = 0.15 \text{ V}.$$

You should always double check that your overall Eo value is positive for a spontaneous reaction.

Question 5 B

See: CHM 10.5

From Table 1 we can see that each mole of sulfate ions requires *two* moles of electrons for reduction to one mole of sulfur dioxide, but each mole of chromium (III) cations requires *three* moles of electrons for reduction to one mole of chromium metal. Hence, the ratio of the number of moles of electrons available to produce the chromium metal will be 2: 3 producing 0.67 moles of the metal.

Question 6 B

See: CHM 10

Since $[A^{3+}]$ decreases and $[A^{2+}]$ and $[B^+]$ increase, the reaction can be written as:

$$A^{3+} + B \rightarrow A^{2+} + B^+.$$

Clearly, A^{3+} gains an electron from B and is therefore reduced. B loses an electron and is therefore oxidized. A^{3+} is more readily reduced than B^+, therefore:

$$E°A > E°B.$$

Question 7 D

See: CHM 4.1.1, 10.1

1 M is a "nice round number" and 0.1 MPa is approximately the atmospheric pressure (1 atm = 101.3 kPa = 0.101 MPa; conversions in CHM 4.1.1). Note that temperature is sometimes excluded from the definition of standard state. However, for fluids, standard temperature is 25 °C (298 K). When reduction potentials are stated, the temperature is usually cited as well.

Question 8 B

See: CHM 10.1

Table 1 gives us the standard reduction potentials (E°) for the halogens. When comparing 2 reactions, the equation with the highest (E°) will proceed as written (as a reduction) while the reaction with the lowest (E°) will proceed from right to left (as an oxidation reaction). Recall that in a redox reaction, one species is reduced by gaining electrons while the other is oxidized by losing electrons (CHM 1.6, 10.1). In this example, the halogen reactions that have a higher E° than the oxygen/water reaction (the 6th reaction in Table 1) will oxidize water. From Table 1, we see that the relative values of E° are: $Br_2 < O_2 < C_{12} < F_2$ (1.07 < 1.23 < 1.36 < 3.06). Therefore, the reactions involving fluorine and chlorine will proceed as written when coupled to the oxygen reaction, which will proceed from right to left (i.e. water → oxygen).

Question 9 C

See: CHM 10.1

Since silver gains an electron, it is reduced. By convention, reduction is always at the cathode. Also, since silver gains an electron, electrons must flow through the wire into the Ag^+/Ag half cell. By convention, current flows in the opposite direction to electron flow, so current is flowing from the Ag^+/Ag half cell to the Fe^{2+}/Fe^{3+} half cell.

Thus, also by convention, the silver electrode is *positive.*

Question 10 B

See: CHM 1.6, 8.10, 9.10, 10.1

For a spontaneous redox reaction,

$$\Delta G° < 0$$
$$\Delta E° > 0$$
$$K_{eq} > 1$$

This means that for the reverse reaction, $\Delta G° > 0$, $\Delta E° < 0$, $K_{eq} < 1$
Reminder: Electrolysis is non-spontaneous and as such is viewed as the opposite of galvanic cells (batteries).

Question 11 B

See: CHM 10.5.1

Using Quantity of electricity (Q) = Current(I) × Time(t)

$$Q = 0.2 \text{ A} \times (80 \text{ min} \times 60 \text{ s min}^{-1}) = 960 \text{ C}$$

Number of faradays required to add 2 moles of electrons to one mole of Fe^{2+} (*to obtain one mole of Fe*) = 2 × F = 2 × 96000 C.

Using Number of moles Fe obtained = Q/(Number of Faradays required to produce 1 mole Fe)

Number of moles Fe = 960 C/(2 × 96000 C) = 1/(100 × 2) = 1/200 mol

Using Number of grams Fe = Number of moles Fe × Relative atomic mass Fe
Number of grams Fe = 1/200 mol × 55.8 g mol^{-1}
Number of grams Fe = (1/200 × 56) g approximately = 7/25 g = 28/100 g = 0.28 g in one hour
{*Nice math!*}

Question 1 A

See: CHM 11

Since gamma rays are uncharged electromagnetic rays, they are not deflected in magnetic or electric fields under normal conditions.

Question 2 C

See: CHM 11.1

Since a neutron has no charge, it would not be impeded in its motion by the positively charged nucleus, unlike the similarly charged proton. {*Note: answer choices* A. *and* B. *are false; answer choice* D. *is true for both a neutron and a proton and is thus an inappropriate answer*}

Question 3 B

See: CHM 11.4

Beware, an entire radioactive sample does not completely decay in two half-lives. Theoretically, it takes forever for every atom of the sample to decay.

Question 4 C

See: CHM 11.4

A half-life of 8 hours means that every 8 hours, half of the sample will undergo radioactive decay. The total number of half-lives undergone by the sample is: 20 hours/(8 hours/half-life) = 5/2 = 2.5. The percentage of the sample leftover after radioactive decay is given by: $(1/2)^n$ where n = number of half lives. After 20 hours, the amount of our sample remaining is: $(1/2)^{2.5} = (1/2)^3$ = 1/8 (approx.). Therefore, the proportion of the sample that has undergone radioactive decay is: 1 - 1/8 = 7/8 = 0.88. Note that the real answer is slightly lower than this value if you take our approximation into account. We could have deduced the answer without the equation by realizing that after 8 hours, 50% (half) of the sample has undergone radiation and after 16 hours, 75 % (half of the half remaining) of the sample has undergone radiation. Thus after 20 hours, the amount must be somewhat more than 75 % leaving only one possible answer (answer choice C.).

Question 5 A

See: CHM 11.3

An alpha particle is defined as a (*doubly positively charged*) helium nucleus.

Question 6 C

See: CHM 11.3, 11.4

The sum of the atomic numbers (*bottom figures or subscripts*) and mass numbers (*top figures or superscripts*) must be the same on both sides of the arrow since matter cannot be destroyed or created (*at least not in DAT Chemistry!*). From this, it is seen that "X" must be (essentially) massless and without charge. Gamma rays fit this description.

Question 7 D

See: CHM 11.3, 11.4

$$^{210}_{81}Th \rightarrow {}^{x}_{y}Z + 3\,{}^{0}_{-1}e^{-} + {}^{4}_{2}He^{2+} + \text{gamma ray}$$

Since the sum of the atomic numbers and mass numbers on either side of the equation must be equal (matter cannot be created or destroyed), we get:

$$210 = x + (3 \times 0) + 4 + 0\ ;\ x = 206$$
$$81 = y + (3 \times -1) + 2 + 0\ ;\ y = 82$$

You can stop at this point or examine the periodic table for the name of the correct element (answer choice D.). Note that the atomic number and mass number of gamma rays are both zero.

Question 8 B

See: CHM 11.3, 11.4

$$^{230}_{90}Th \rightarrow {}^{214}_{83}Bi + x\,{}^{0}_{-1}e^{-} + y\,{}^{4}_{2}He + z\ (\textit{gamma ray})$$

Since the sum of the atomic numbers and mass numbers on either side of the equation must be equal (matter cannot be created or destroyed), we get:

$$90 = 83 - x + 2y \qquad \text{Equation (i)}$$
$$230 = 214 + 4y; \qquad y = 4\ (\text{i.e. } \textit{4 alpha decay reactions})$$

Substituting for y in Equation (i)

$$90 = 83 - x + 8;\ x = 1 \qquad (\text{i.e. } \textit{1 beta decay reaction})$$

The order of the reactions is irrelevant (i.e. alpha, beta,..). Since gamma rays have no atomic number or mass number, the value of z does not affect this particular calculation.

Question 9 D

See: CHM 11.3, 11.4

Alpha radiation consists of the largest particles (*helium nuclei* with a mass number of 4 thus the greatest inertia) and are the slowest (about 1/3 times the speed of light). Beta radiation consists of smaller (*electrons*, 1/1370 times lighter than a proton), faster particles (about 4/5 times the speed of light). Gamma radiation consists of the smallest particles (*photons*, no mass) which travel at the greatest speed (at the speed of light).

Question 10 B

See: CHM 11.3, 11.4

On the Surface: In radioactive decay, we must have overall conservation of charge and mass. Recall that a $beta^-$ particle consists of an electron (charge = -1, mass = negligible) and a gamma (γ) ray is electromagnetic energy (mass = 0, charge = 0). In the equation, the atomic mass on the left of the equation = 14, so the atomic masses on the right must also = 14 to conserve mass: 14 (mass of 14C) = X (mass of xN) + 0 (mass of β^-) + 0 (mass of γ) → 14 = X.

Going Deeper: In beta decay, a neutron decays into a proton and an electron (β^-). Thus on the left-hand side of the equation, there are 8 neutrons and 6 protons. The right-hand side of the equation has 7 neutrons and 7 protons. Thus X must be 14 (to calculate # protons, neutrons).

Question 11 C

See: CHM 11.3

It would be attracted to the plate of opposite charge, negative, since a positron is positively charged.

Question 12 B

See: CHM 11.4

The present amount of C14 to the past amount or C14 is 1/4, corresponding to two half-lives.

Question 13 C

See: CHM 11.4

The amount undecayed is 1/16 = $(1/2)^4$ of the original sample, which corresponds to four half-lives: 6400 years.

Question 14 B

See: CHM 11.4

3 half-lives have elapsed (9.3 mins/3.1 mins).
Since the emission of a beta particle results in a neutron turning into a proton, the atomic masses of the Pb and Tl are the same.

If there were initially X g of Tl, after 3.1 mins X/2 g of Pb are formed, after the next 3.1 mins X/4 g of Pb are formed, and after the next 3.1 mins X/8g of Pb are formed. Therefore,

$$X/2\ X/4\ X/8 = 7 \text{ g of Pb or, } 4X/8\ 2X/8\ X/8 = 7X/8 = 7$$

Thus, X = 8 g

Question 15 A

See: CHM 11.4

This is the shape of the graph for all natural radioactive decay processes (and all first order reactions). If you did not know that then you should at least deduce as follows: (1) radioactivity decreases over time (thus only 2 choices because only 2 graphs have values decreasing over time); and (2) radioactive decay is exponential (so the graph cannot be linear). For fun (!!), compare with the curves and descriptions in CHM 9.2.

Chapter Review Solutions

Chapter 12

Question 1 D

See: CHM 6.9, 12.3.1

A typical titration (CHM 6.9) begins with a beaker or Erlenmeyer flask containing a precise volume of the titrand (= the chemical being analyzed) and a small amount of indicator placed underneath a calibrated burette containing the titrant (= titrator reagent prepared as a standard solution). Thus the burette adds the standard reagent.

Question 2 A

See: CHM 12.3.1

Flaming sterilizes glassware using a Bunsen burner or alcohol lamp for sterilization.

Question 3 A

See: CHM 12.3.1

0.0127 mol NaCl x 1 L/0.127 mol = 0.1 L (100 mL)
The most accurate way to measure 0.1 L of solution is to use a volumetric flask. Volumetric flasks are known to be precise to approximately $\pm$0.2%.

Question 4 B

See: 12.4.2, 12.4.3

Do not count any zeros to the left of the first non zero integer and then you will be left with 5 digits: 8, 6, 0, 3, 0. If that last 0 to the right was not truly significant then it should not have been reported.

Question 5 B

See: 12.4.2, 12.4.3

The density would be 24.7/3.3 = 7.4848 g/cm^3. For multiplication and division: the number of significant figures is limited by the data with the least number of significant figures in total. Since the volume only has 2 sig figs, the answer must be rounded off to 2 sig figs so 7.4848 becomes 7.5.

General Chemistry Equation List and Tables

CHAPTER 1: Stoichiometry

1.3 Mole - Atomic and Molecular Weights

For an element:

$$\text{moles} = \frac{\text{weight of sample in grams}}{\text{GAW}}$$

1 mol = 6.02×10^{23} atoms

For a compound:

$$\text{moles} = \frac{\text{weight of sample in grams}}{\text{GMW}}$$

1 mol = 6.02×10^{23} molecules

1.5.1 Categories of Chemical Reactions

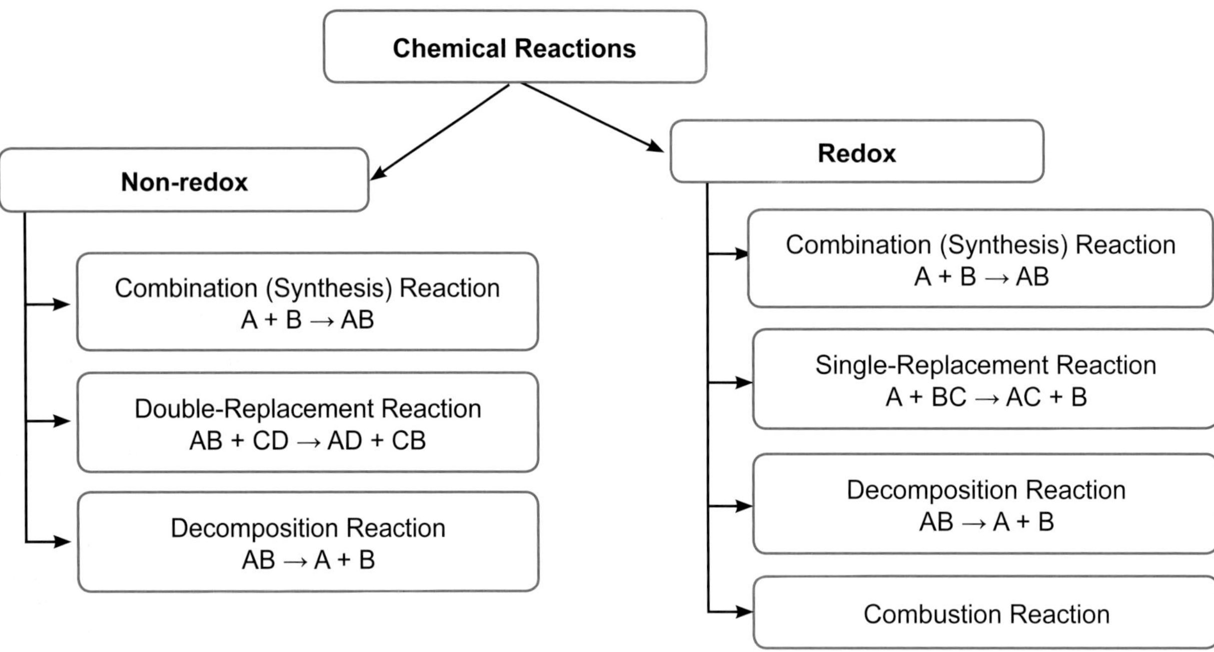

1.6 Oxidation Numbers, Redox Reactions, Oxidizing vs. Reducing Agents

Here are the general rules:

1. In elementary substances, the oxidation number of an uncombined element is zero.
2. In monatomic ions the oxidation number of the element that make up this ion is equal to the charge of the ion.
3. In a neutral molecule the sum of the oxidation numbers of all the elements that make up the molecule is zero.
4. Some useful oxidation numbers to memorize:

   For H: +1, except in metal hydrides where it is equal to -1.

   For O: -2 in most compounds. In peroxides (e.g. in H_2O_2) the oxidation number for O is -1, it is +2 in OF_2 and -1/2 in superoxides.

   For alkali metals +1.

   For alkaline earth metals +2.

   Aluminium always has an oxidation number of +3 in all its compounds.

Common Redox Agents	
Reducing Agents	**Oxidizing Agents**
* Lithium aluminium hydride ($LiAlH_4$) * Sodium borohydride ($NaBH_4$) * Metals * Ferrous ion (Fe^{2+})	* Iodine (I_2) and other halogens * Permanganate (MnO_4) salts * Peroxide compounds (i.e. H_2O_2) * Ozone (O_3); osmium tetroxide (OsO_4) * Nitric acid (HNO_3); nitrous oxide (N_2O)

1.7 Mixtures

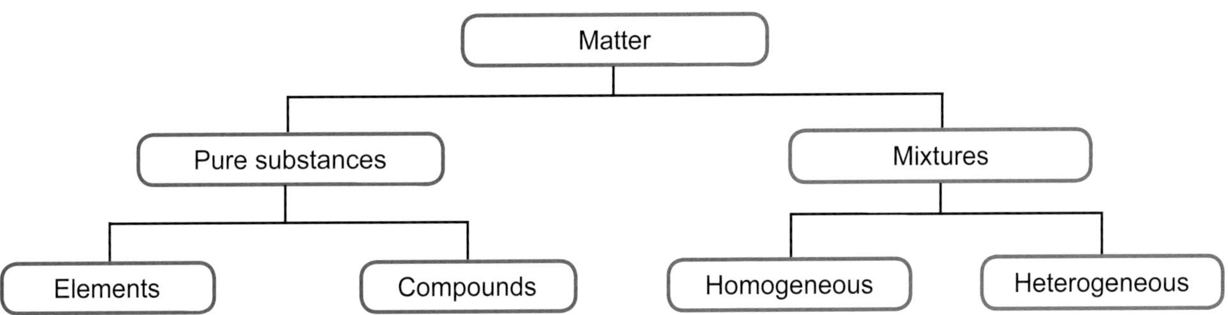

CHAPTER 2: Electronic Structure and the Periodic Table

2.2 Conventional Notation for Electronic Structure

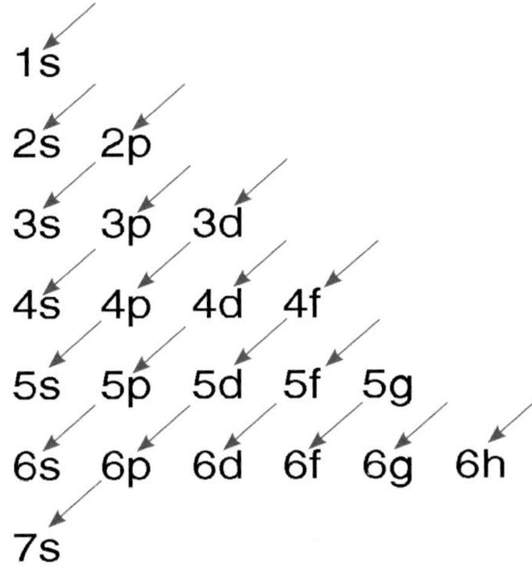

follow the direction of successive arrows moving from top to bottom

Figure III.A.2.3: The order for filling atomic orbitals.

2.4 Metals, Nonmetals and Metalloids

Table III A.2.1

*General characteristics of metals, nonmetals and metalloids		
Metals	**Nonmetals**	**Metalloids**
• Hard and Shiny	• Gases or dull, brittle solids	• Appearence will vary
• 3 or less valence electrons	• 5 or more valence electrons	• 3 to 7 valence electrons
• Form + ions by losing e^-	• Form – ions by gaining e^-	• Form + and/or – ions
• Good conductors of heat and electricity	• Poor conductors of heat and electricity	• Conduct better than nonmetals but not as well as metals

*These are general characteristics. There are exceptions beyond the scope of the exam.

CHAPTER 3: Bonding

3.3 Partial Ionic Character

This polar bond will also have a dipole moment given by:

$$D = q \cdot d$$

where q is the charge and d is the distance between these two atoms.

3.4 Lewis Acids and Lewis Bases

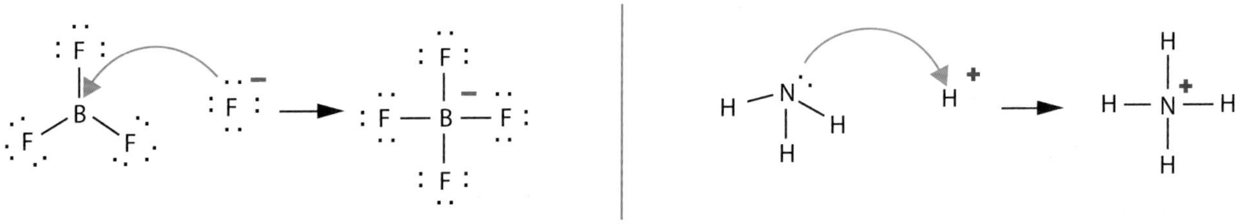

The Lewis acid BF_3 and the Lewis base NH_3. Notice that the green arrows follow the flow of electron pairs.

3.5 Valence Shell Electronic Pair Repulsions (VSEPR Models)

Table III.A.3.1a: Geometry of simple molecules in which the central atom A has one or more lone pairs of electrons (= e^-).

Total number of e^- pairs	Number of lone pairs	Number of bonding pairs	Electron Geometry, Arrangement of e^- pairs	Molecular Geometry (Hybridization State)	Examples
3	1	2	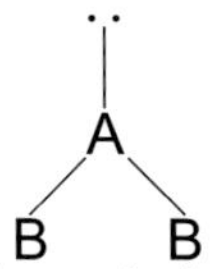 Trigonal planar	Bent (sp^2)	SO_2
4	1	3	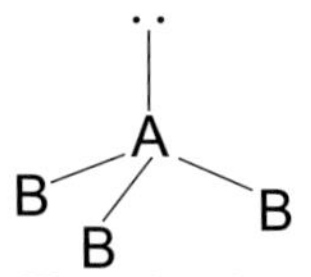 Tetrahedral	Trigonal pyramidal (sp^3)	NH_3
4	2	2	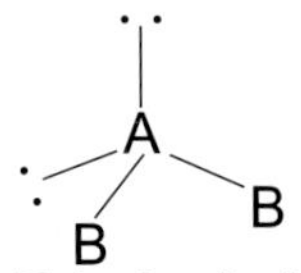 Tetrahedral	Bent (sp^3)	H_2O
5	1	4	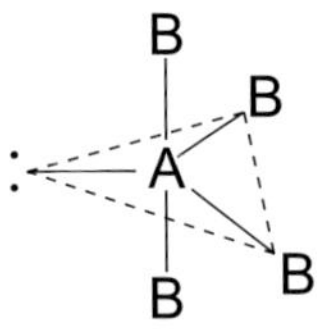 Trigonal bipyramidal	Seesaw (sp^3d)	SF_4
5	2	3	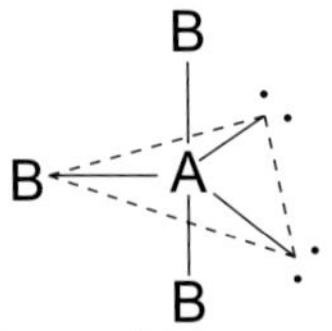 Trigonal bipyramidal	T-shaped (sp^3d)	ClF_3

Note: dotted lines only represent the overall molecular shape and not molecular bonds. In brackets under "Molecular Geometry" is the hybridization, to be discussed in ORG 1.2.

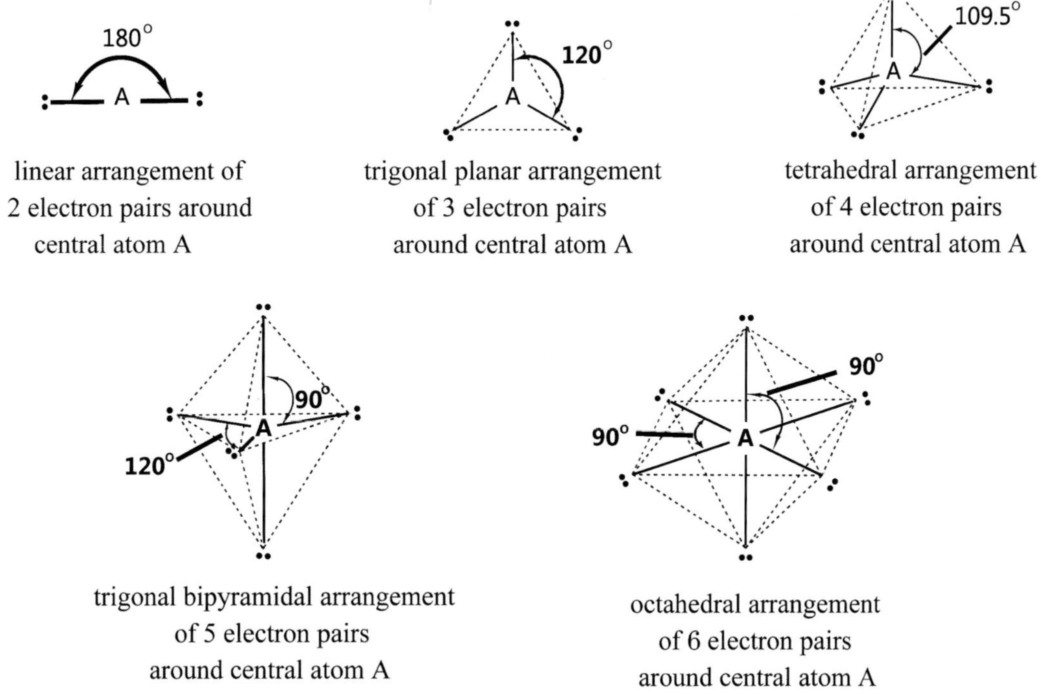

Figure III.A.3.1: Molecular arrangement of electron pairs around a central atom A. Dotted lines only represent the overall molecular shape and not molecular bonds.

CHAPTER 4: Phases and Phase Equilibria

4.1.1 Standard Temperature and Pressure, Standard Molar Volume

0°C (273.15 K) and 1.00 atm (101.33 kPa = 760 mmHg = 760 torr); these conditions are known as the standard temperature and pressure (STP). {Note: the SI unit of pressure is the pascal (Pa).

The volume occupied by one mole of any gas at STP is referred to as the standard molar volume and is equal to 22.4 L.

4.1.2 Kinetic Molecular Theory of Gases (A Model for Gases)

The average kinetic energy of the particles (KE = 1/2 mv^2) increases in direct proportion to the temperature of the gas (KE = 3/2 kT) when the temperature is measured on an absolute scale (i.e. the Kelvin scale) and k is a constant (the Boltzmann constant).

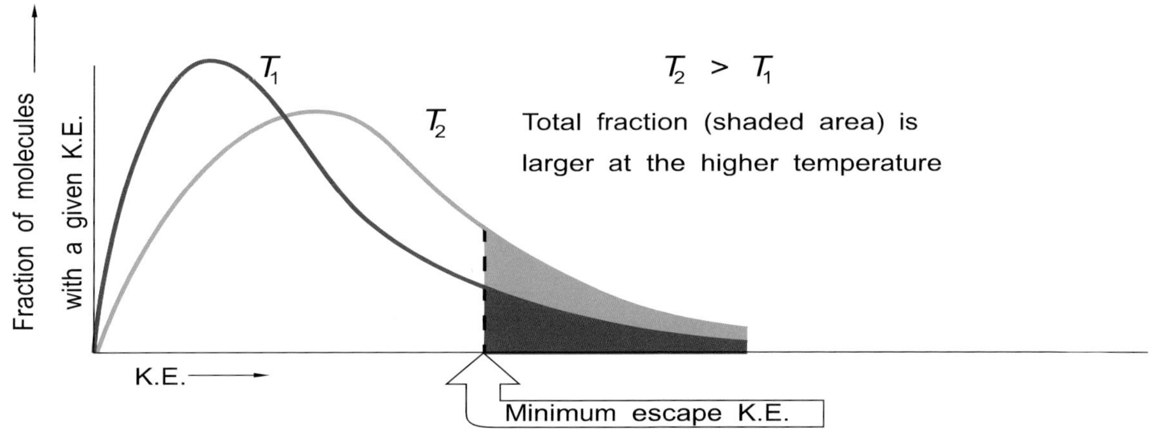

Figure III.A.4.1: The Maxwell Distribution Plot.

4.1.3 Graham's Law (Diffusion and Effusion of Gases)

$$\frac{\text{Rate}_1}{\text{Rate}_2} = \sqrt{\frac{M_2}{M_1}}$$

4.1.4 Charles' Law

$$V = \text{Constant} \times T \quad \text{or} \quad V_1/V_2 = T_1/T_2$$

4.1.5 Boyle's Law

$$V = \text{Constant} \times 1/P \quad \text{or} \quad P_1V_1 = P_2V_2$$

4.1.6 Avogadro's Law

$$\text{V/n} = \text{Constant} \quad \text{or} \quad \text{V}_1/\text{n}_1 = \text{V}_2/\text{n}_2$$

4.1.7 Combined Gas Law

$$\frac{P_1V_1}{T_1} = \text{k} = \frac{P_2V_2}{T_2} \quad \text{(at constant mass)}$$

4.1.8 Ideal Gas Law

$$PV = \text{n}RT$$

since m/V is the density (d) of the gas:

$$P = \frac{d\text{RT}}{M}$$

4.1.9 Partial Pressure and Dalton's Law

$$P_T = P_1 + P_2 + \ldots + P_i$$

Of course, the sum of all mole fractions in a mixture must equal one:

$$\Sigma X_i = 1$$

The partial pressure (P_i) of a component of a gas mixture is equal to:

$$P_i = X_i P_T$$

4.2 Liquid Phase (Intra- and Intermolecular Forces)

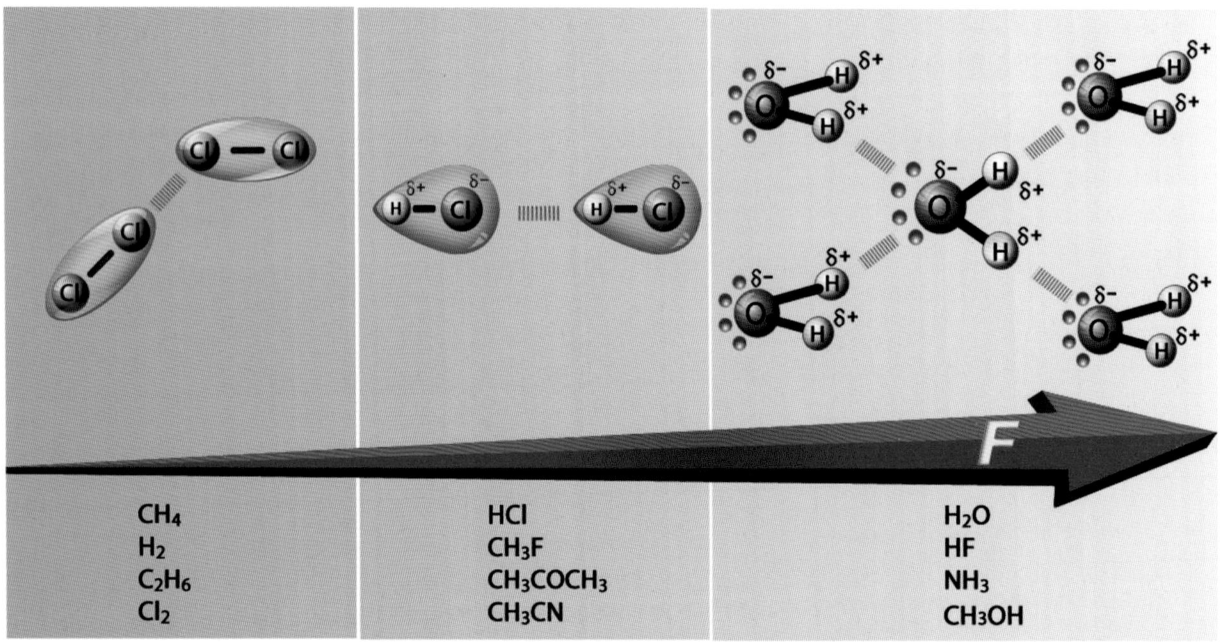

Table III.A.4.1: Van Der Waal's forces (weak) and hydrogen bonding (strong). London forces between Cl_2 molecules, dipole-dipole forces between HCl molecules and H-bonding between H_2O molecules. Note that a partial negative charge on an atom is indicated by δ^- (delta negative), while a partial positive charge is indicated by δ^+ (delta positive). Notice that one H_2O molecule can potentially form 4 H-bonds with surrounding molecules which is highly efficient. The preceding is one key reason that the boiling point of water is higher than that of ammonia, hydrogen fluoride or methanol.

4.2.2 Surface Tension

PE is directly proportional to the surface area (A).

$$PE = \gamma A$$
$$\gamma = \textit{surface tension}$$

$$\gamma = F/l$$
$$F = \textit{force of contraction of surface}$$
$$l = \textit{length along surface}$$

(a) cohesive > adhesive (b) adhesive > cohesive

4.4.1 Phase Changes

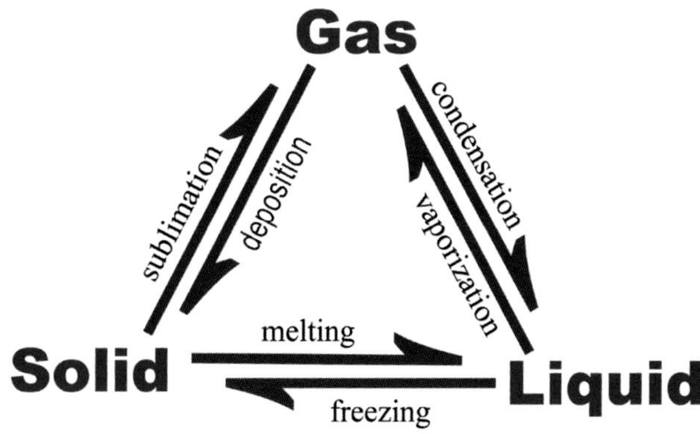

Figure III.A.4.2: Phase Changes

4.4.3 Phase Diagrams

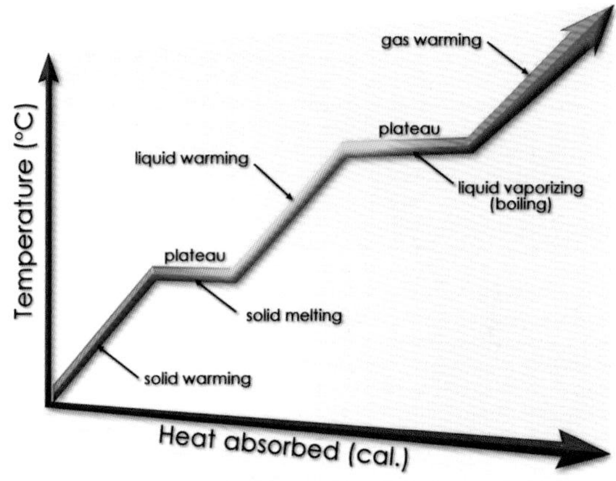

Figure III.A.4.3 Heating curve

CHAPTER 5: Solution Chemistry

5.1.1 Vapor-Pressure Lowering (Raoult's Law)

$$P = P^{\circ} X_{solvent}$$

where P = vapor pressure of solution
P° = vapor pressure of pure solvent (at the same temperature as P).

5.1.3 Osmotic Pressure

$$\Pi = i\,MRT$$

where R = gas constant per mole
T = temperature in degrees K and
M = concentration of solute (mole/liter)
i = Van't Hoff factor

5.1.2 Boiling-Point Elevation and Freezing-Point Depression

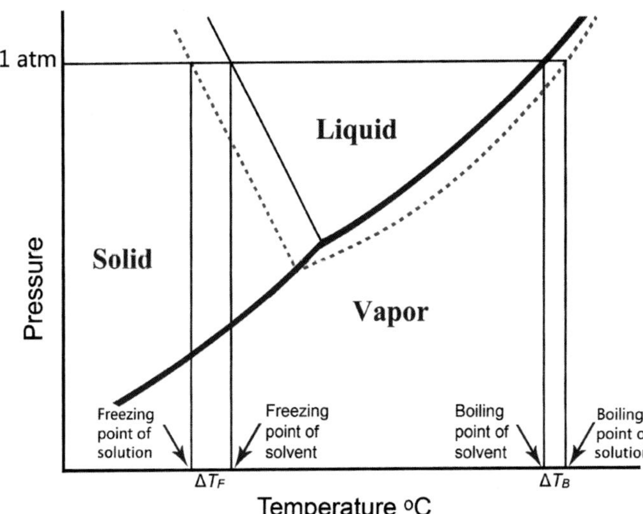

Figure III.A.5.1: Phase diagram of water demonstrating the effect of the addition of a solute.

$$\Delta T_B = i\,K_B m$$
$$\Delta T_F = i\,K_F m$$

5.2 Ions in Solution

Ions that are positively charged are called cations and negatively charged ions are called anions. {Mnemonic: anions are negative ions}

The word "aqueous" simply means containing or dissolved in water.

Common Anions					
F^-	Fluoride	OH^-	Hydroxide	ClO^-	Hypochlorite
Cl^-	Chloride	NO_3^-	Nitrate	ClO_2^-	Chlorite
Br^-	Bromide	NO_2^-	Nitrite	ClO_3^-	Chlorate
I^-	Iodide	CO_3^{2-}	Carbonate	ClO_4^-	Perchlorate
O^{2-}	Oxide	SO_4^{2-}	Sulfate	SO_3^{2-}	Sulfite
S^{2-}	Sulfide	PO_4^{3-}	Phosphate	CN^-	Cyanide
N^{3-}	Nitride	$CH_3CO_2^-$	Acetate	MnO_4^-	Permanganate

Common Cations			
Na^+	Sodium	H^+	Hydrogen
Li^+	Lithium	Ca^{2+}	Calcium
K^+	Potassium	Mg^{2+}	Magnesium
NH_4^+	Ammonium	Fe^{2+}	Iron (II)
H_3O^+	Hydronium	Fe^{3+}	Iron (III)

Table III.A.5.1: Common Anions and Cations.

5.3.1 Units of Concentration

Molarity (M): moles of solute/liter of solution (solution = solute + solvent).

Normality (N): one equivalent per liter.

Molality (m): one mole/1000g of solvent. Molal concentrations are not temperature-dependent as molar and normal concentrations are.

Density (ρ): Mass per unit volume at the specified temperature.

Osmole (*Osm*): The number of moles of particles (molecules or ions) that contribute to the osmotic pressure of a solution.

Osmolarity: osmoles/liter of solution.

Osmolality: osmoles/kilogram of solution.

Mole Fraction: amount of solute (in moles) divided by the total amount of solvent and solute (in moles).

Dilution: $M_iV_i = M_fV_f$

5.3.2 Solubility Product Constant, the Equilibrium Expression

$$AgCl\ (s) \rightleftharpoons Ag^+\ (aq) + Cl^-\ (aq)$$

$$K_{sp} = [Ag^+][Cl^-]$$

Because the K_{sp} product always holds, precipitation will not take place unless the product of $[Ag^+]$ and $[Cl^-]$ exceeds the K_{sp}.

5.3.5 Solubility Rules

1. All salts of alkali metals are soluble.
2. All salts of the ammonium ion are soluble.
3. All chlorides, bromides and iodides are water soluble, with the exception of Ag^+, Pb^{2+}, and Hg_2^{2+}.
4. All salts of the sulfate ion (SO_4^{2-}) are water soluble with the exception of Ca^{2+}, Sr^{2+}, Ba^{2+}, and Pb^{2+}.
5. All metal oxides are insoluble with the exception of the alkali metals and CaO, SrO and BaO.
6. All hydroxides are insoluble with the exception of the alkali metals and Ca^{2+}, Sr^{2+}, Ba^{2+}
7. All carbonates (CO_3^{2-}), phosphates (PO_4^{3-}), sulfides (S^{2-}) and sulfites (SO_3^{2-}) are insoluble, with the exception of the alkali metals and ammonium.

CHAPTER 6: Acids and Bases

6.1 Acids

$$K_a = [H^+][A^-]/[HA]$$

Table III.A.6.1: Examples of strong and weak acids.

STRONG	WEAK	STRONG	WEAK
Perchloric $HClO_4$ Chloric $HClO_3$ Nitric HNO_3 Hydrochloric HCl	Hydrocyanic HCN Hypochlorous HClO Nitrous HNO_2 Hydrofluoric HF	Sulfuric H_2SO_4 Hydrobromic HBr Hydriodic HI Hydronium Ion H_3O^+	Sulfurous H_2SO_3 Hydrogen Sulfide H_2S Phosphoric H_3PO_4 Benzoic, Acetic and other Carboxylic acids

6.2 Bases

$$K_b = [HB^+][OH^-]/[B]$$

Strong bases include any hydroxide of the group 1A metals. The most common weak bases are ammonia and any organic amine.

6.3 Conjugate Acid-Base Pairs

The acid, HA, and the base produced when it ionizes, A^-, are called a conjugate acid-base pair.

6.4 Water Dissociation

$$K_w = [H^+][OH^-] = 1.0 \times 10^{-14}$$

6.5 The pH Scale

$$pH = -\log_{10}[H^+]$$

$$pOH = -\log_{10}[OH^-]$$

at 25°C, pH + pOH = 14.0

6.5.1 Properties of Logarithms

1) $\log_a a = 1$
2) $\log_a M^k = k \log_a M$
3) $\log_a(MN) = \log_a M + \log_a N$
4) $\log_a(M/N) = \log_a M - \log_a N$
5) $10^{\log_{10} M} = M$

6.7 Salts of Weak Acids and Bases

$$K_a \times K_b = K_w$$

6.8 Buffers

$$pH = pK_a + \log([salt]/[acid])$$

$$pOH = pK_b + \log([salt]/[base])$$

CHAPTER 7: Thermodynamics

7.2 The First Law of Thermodynamics

$$\Delta E = Q - W$$

- heat absorbed by the system: $Q > 0$
- heat released by the system: $Q < 0$
- work done by the system on its surroundings: $W > 0$
- work done by the surroundings on the system: $W < 0$

7.4 Temperature Scales

$$0\ K = -273.13\ °C.$$

$$(X\ °F - 32) \times 5/9 = Y\ °C$$

7.6 State Functions

	Work	Heat	Change in internal energy
1st transf.	w	0	$-w$
2nd transf.	$W = w + q$	q	$-w$

W can be determined experimentally by calculating the area under a pressure-volume curve.

CHAPTER 8: Enthalpy and Thermochemistry

8.2 Heat of Reaction: Basic Principles

A reaction during which heat is released is said to be *exothermic* (ΔH is negative). If a reaction requires the supply of a certain amount of heat it is *endothermic* (ΔH is positive).

$$\Delta H_{OVERALL} = \Delta H_1 + \Delta H_2$$

$$\Delta H°_{reaction} = \Sigma\Delta H_f°_{(products)} - \Sigma\Delta H_f°_{(reactants)}$$

8.6 Bond Dissociation Energies and Heats of Formation

$$\Delta H^\circ_{(reaction)} = \Sigma\Delta H_{(bonds\ broken)} + \Sigma\Delta H_{(bonds\ formed)} = \Sigma BE_{(reactants)} - \Sigma BE_{(products)}$$

8.7 Calorimetry

$$Q = mC(T_2 - T_1)$$

$$Q = mL$$

8.8 The Second Law of Thermodynamics

For any spontaneous process, the entropy of the universe increases which results in a greater dispersal or randomization of the energy ($\Delta S > 0$).

8.9 Entropy

$$\Delta S^\circ_{reaction} = \Delta S^\circ_{products} - \Delta S^\circ_{reactants}$$

8.10 Free Energy

$$\Delta G = \Delta H - T\Delta S$$

A reaction carried out at constant pressure is spontaneous if

$$\Delta G < 0$$

It is not spontaneous if:

$$\Delta G > 0$$

and it is in a state of equilibrium (reaction spontaneous in both directions) if:

$$\Delta G = 0.$$

CHAPTER 9: Rate Processes in Chemical Reactions

9.2 Dependence of Reaction Rates on Concentration of Reactants

$$\text{rate} = k\,[A]^m\,[B]^n$$

where [ ] is the concentration of the corresponding reactant in moles per liter
k is referred to as the rate constant
m is the order of the reaction with respect to A
n is the order of the reaction with respect to B
m+n is the overall reaction order.

9.2.1 Differential Rate Law vs. Integrated Rate Law (Advanced DAT-30 Topic)

Table 9.2.1

Rate Law Summary					
Reaction Order	**Rate Law**	**Units of k**	**Integrated Rate Law**	**Straight-Line Plot**	**Half-Life Equation**
0	Rate = $k[A]^0$	$M \cdot s^{-1}$	$[A]_t = -kt + [A]_0$	[A] vs. Time t; y-intercept = $[A]_0$; slope = $-k$	$t_{1/2} = \frac{[A]_0}{2k} = \frac{1}{k}\frac{[A]_0}{2}$
1	Rate = $k[A]^1$	s^{-1}	$\ln[A]_t = -kt + \ln[A]_0$ $\ln\frac{[A]_t}{[A]_0} = -kt$	ln[A] vs. Time t; y-intercept = $\ln[A]_0$; slope = $-k$	$t_{1/2} = \frac{0.693}{k} = \frac{1}{k}(0.693)$
2	Rate = $k[A]^2$	$M^{-1} \cdot s^{-1}$	$\frac{1}{[A]_t} = kt + \frac{1}{[A]_0}$	1/[A] vs. Time t; slope = k; y-intercept = $1/[A]_0$	$t_{1/2} = \frac{1}{k[A]_0} = \frac{1}{k}\frac{1}{[A]_0}$

9.5 Dependence of Reaction Rates upon Temperature

$$k = A\,e^{-Ea/RT}$$

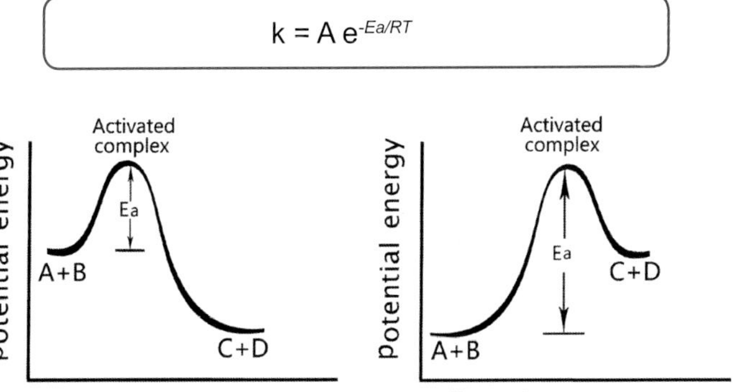

Figure III.A.9.1: Potential energy diagrams: exothermic vs. endothermic reactions.

9.7 Catalysis

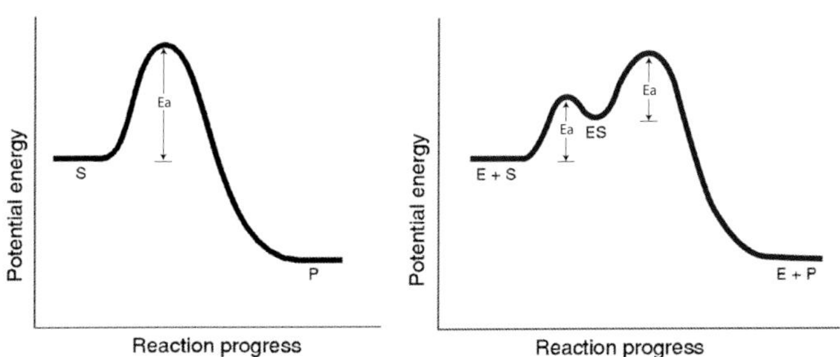

Figure III.A.9.2: Potential energy diagrams: without and with a catalyst.

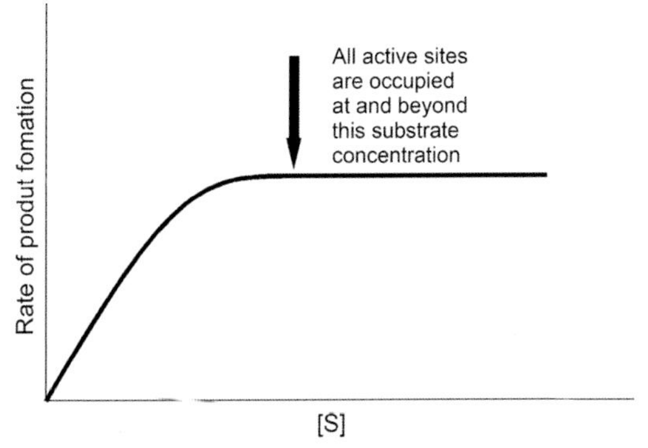

Figure III.A.9.3: Saturation kinetics.

9.8 Equilibrium in Reversible Chemical Reactions

$$aA + bB \rightleftharpoons cC + dD$$

$$K = \frac{[C]^c\,[D]^d}{[A]^a\,[B]^b}$$

{Note: catalysts speed up the rate of reaction without affecting Keq}

9.8.1 The Reaction Quotient Q to Predict Reaction Direction

$$Q = [C]^c[D]^d/[A]^a[B]^b$$

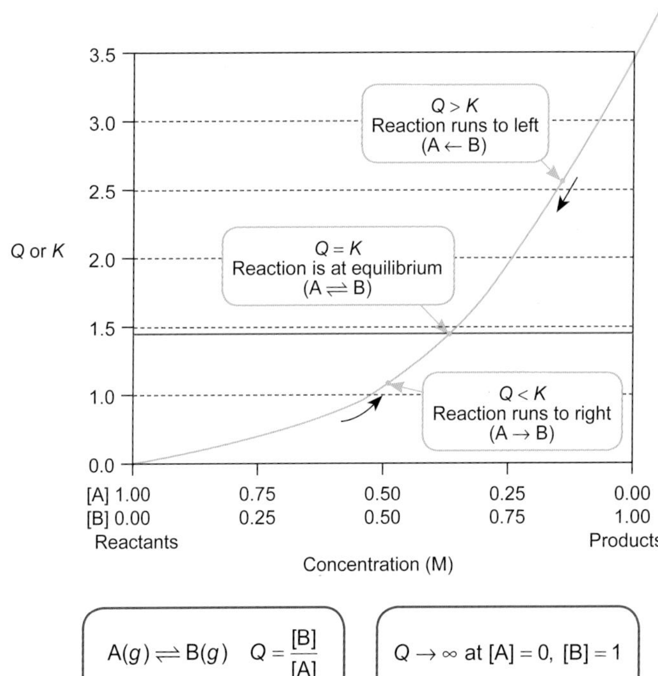

$A(g) \rightleftharpoons B(g) \quad Q = \frac{[B]}{[A]}$

$Q \rightarrow \infty$ at $[A] = 0,\ [B] = 1$

9.9 Le Chatelier's Principle

Le Chatelier's principle states that whenever a perturbation is applied to a system at equilibrium, the system evolves in such a way as to compensate for the applied perturbation.

9.10 Relationship between the Equilibrium Constant and the Change in the Gibbs Free Energy

$$\Delta G° = -R\,T\,ln\,K_{eq}$$

CHAPTER 10: Electrochemistry

10.1 Generalities

The more positive the E° value, the more likely the reaction will occur spontaneously as written. The strongest reducing agents have large negative E° values. The strongest oxidizing agents have large positive E° values. The oxidizing agent is *reduced*; the reducing agent is *oxidized*.

10.2 Galvanic Cells

Mnemonic: LEO is A GERC

- Lose Electrons Oxidation is Anode
- Gain Electrons Reduction at Cathode

10.3 Concentration Cell

Nernst equation

$$E_{cell} = E°_{cell} - (RT/nF)(\ln Q)$$

CHAPTER 11: Nuclear Chemistry

11.3 Nuclear Forces, Nuclear Binding Energy, Stability, Radioactivity

$$\Delta E = \Delta mc^2$$

The common particles are:

(1) alpha (α) particle = $_2He^4$ (helium nucleus);
(2) beta (β) particle = $_{-1}e^0$ (an electron);
(3) a positron $_{+1}e^0$ (same mass as an electron but opposite charge); and
(4) gamma (γ) ray = no mass and no charge, just electromagnetic energy.

11.4 Nuclear Reaction, Radioactive Decay, Half-Life

neutrons (i.e. $_{92}U^{238}$)
= superscript (238) – subscript (92)
= 146

$$T_{1/2} = 0.693/k.$$

If the number of half-lifes n are known we can calculate the percentage of a pure radioactive sample left after undergoing decay since the fraction remaining = $(1/2)^n$.

Table III.A.11.1: Modes of Radioactive Decay

Decay Mode	Participating particles	Change in (A, Z)	Daughter Nucleus
Alpha decay	α	A = –4, Z = –2	(A – 4, Z – 2)
Beta decay	β^-	A = 0, Z = +1	(A, Z + 1)
Gamma decay	γ	A = 0, Z = 0	(A, Z)
Positron emission	β^+	A = 0, Z = –1	(A, Z – 1)

10.5 Faraday's Law

Faraday's law relates the amount of elements deposited or gas liberated at an electrode due to current.

One mole (= Avogadro's number) of electrons is called a *faraday* ($\mathfrak{F}$). A faraday is equivalent to 96 500 coulombs. A coulomb is the amount of electricity that is transferred when a current of one ampere flows for one second (1C = 1A . S).

11.5 Quantized Energy Levels For Electrons, Emission Spectrum

The maximum number of electrons in each shell is given by:

$$N_{electrons} = 2n^2$$

$N_{electrons}$ designates the number of electrons in shell n.

The state of each electron is determined by the four quantum numbers:

- *principal quantum number n* determines the number of shells, possible values are: 1 (K), 2 (L), 3 (M), etc...
- *angular momentum quantum number l*, determines the subshell, possible values are: 0 (s), 1 (p), 2 (d), 3 (f), n-1, etc...
- *magnetic momentum quantum number m_l*, possible values are: ±*l*, ... , 0
- *spin quantum number m_s*, determines the direction of rotation of the electron, possible values are: ±1/2.

$$E_2 - E_1 = hf$$

where E_1 = energy level one, E_2 = energy level two, h = planck's constant, and f = the frequency of light absorbed or emitted.

The total energy of the electrons in an atom, where KE is the kinetic energy, can be given by:

$$E_{total} = E_{emission}\ (\text{or } E_{ionization}) + KE$$

CHAPTER 12: Laboratory

12.3.1 Glassware

Least accurate	Droppers Beakers and Erlenmeyer flasks Graduated cylinders
Most accurate	Glass Pipettes, burettes and volumetric flasks

12.4.3 Analyzing the Data

The uncertain figure of a measurement is the last significant figure of the measurement.

Table 12.1: Examples of significant figures versus non-significant figures.

Significant	Examples	Non-Significant
Non-zero integers	1.234 (4 sf)	
Zeros between non-zero integers*	1.004 (4 sf)	
Zeros to the right of decimal place AND integers*	1.2000 (5 sf) 0.0041 (2 sf)	Zeros to the right of decimal place BUT to the left of integers
	430 (2 sf)	Zeros to the left of decimal place BUT to the right of integers
	013.2 (3 sf)	Zeros to the left of decimal place AND integers

* Zeros in any number is used to convey either accuracy or magnitude. If a zero is to convey accuracy, then it is known as a significant value and if the zero is used to convey magnitude, then it is non-significant.

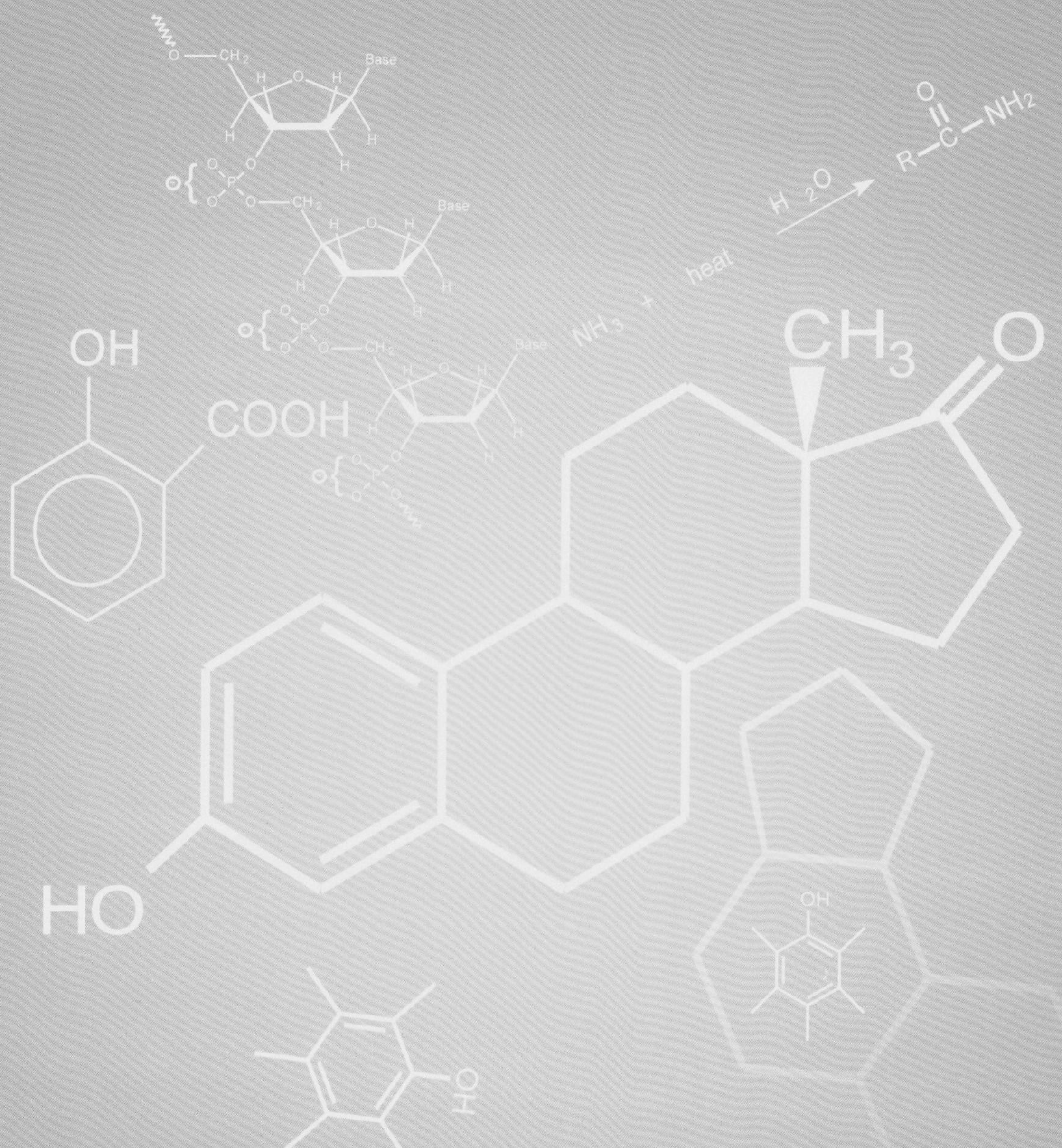

DAT-prep.com

ORGANIC CHEMISTRY

ORGANIC
CHEMISTRY

MOLECULAR STRUCTURE OF ORGANIC COMPOUNDS
Chapter 1

Memorize

* Hybrid orbitals and geometries
* Periodic table trends
* Define: Lewis, dipole moments
* Ground rules for reaction mechanisms

Understand

* Delocalized electrons and resonance
* Multiple bonds, length, energies
* Basic stereochemistry
* Principles for reaction mechanisms

Importance

2 to 4 out of the 30 ORG

DAT questions are based on content in this chapter (in our estimation).
* Note that between 30% and 60% of the questions in DAT Organic Chemistry are based on content from 4 chapters: 1, 2, 5 and 6.

Introduction

Organic chemistry is the study of the structure, properties, composition, reactions, and preparation (i.e. synthesis) of chemical compounds containing carbon. Such compounds may contain hydrogen, nitrogen, oxygen, the halogens as well as phosphorus, silicon and sulfur. If you master the basic rules in this chapter, you will be able to conquer DAT mechanisms with little or no further memorization.

Additional Resources

Free Online Q&A + Forum

Video: Online or DVD

Flashcards

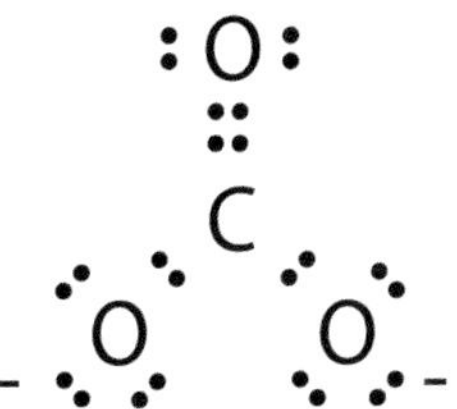

Special Guest

1.1 Overview: The Atoms of Organic Chemistry

Organic chemistry may be defined as the chemistry of the compounds of carbon. Organic chemistry is very important, as living systems are composed mainly of water and organic compounds. Other important organic molecules form essential components of fuels, plastics and other petroleum derivatives.

Carbon (C), hydrogen (H), oxygen (O), nitrogen (N) and the halides (i.e. fluorine – F, chlorine – Cl, bromine – Br, etc.) are the most common atoms found in organic compounds. The atoms in most organic compounds are held together by covalent bonds (*the sharing of an electron pair between two atoms*). Some ionic bonding (*the transfer of electrons from one atom to another*) does exist. Common to both types of chemical bonds is the fact that the atoms bond such that they can achieve the electron configuration of the nearest noble gas, usually eight electrons. This is known as the *octet rule*.

A **carbon** atom has one s and three p orbitals in its outermost shell, allowing it to form 4 single bonds. As well, a carbon atom may be involved in a double bond, where two electron pairs are shared, or a triple bond, where three electron pairs are shared. An **oxygen** atom may form 2 single bonds, or one double bond. It has 2 unshared (lone) electron pairs. A **hydrogen** atom will form only one single bond. A **nitrogen** atom may form 3 single bonds. As well, it is capable of double and triple bonds. It has one unshared electron pair. The **halides** are all able to form only one (single) bond. Halides all have three unshared electron pairs.

Throughout the following chapters we will be examining the structural formulas of molecules involving H, C, N, O, halides and phosphorus (P). However it should be noted that less common atoms often have similar structural formulas within molecules as compared to common atoms. For example, silicon (Si) is found in the same group as carbon in the periodic table; thus they have similar properties. In fact, Si can also form 4 single bonds leading to a tetrahedral structure (i.e. SiH_4, SiO_4). Likewise sulfur (S) is found in the same group as oxygen. Though it can be found as a solid (S_8), it still has many properties similar to those of oxygen. For example, like O in H_2O, sulfur can form a bent, polar molecule which can hydrogen bond (H_2S). We will later see that sulfur is an important component in the amino acid cysteine. {*To learn more about molecular structure, hybrid orbitals, polarity and bonding, review General Chemistry chapters 2 and 3*}

Mnemonic: HONC

H requires 1 more electron in its outer shell to become stable
O requires 2
N requires 3
C requires 4

1.2 Hybrid Orbitals

In organic molecules, the orbitals of the atoms are combined to form **hybrid orbitals**, consisting of a mixture of the s and p orbitals. In a carbon atom, if the one s and three p orbitals are mixed, the result is four hybrid sp^3 orbitals. Three hybridized sp^2 orbitals result from the mixing of one s and two p orbitals, and two hybridized sp orbitals result from the mixing of one s and one p. The geometry of the hybridized orbitals is shown in Figure IV.B.1.1.

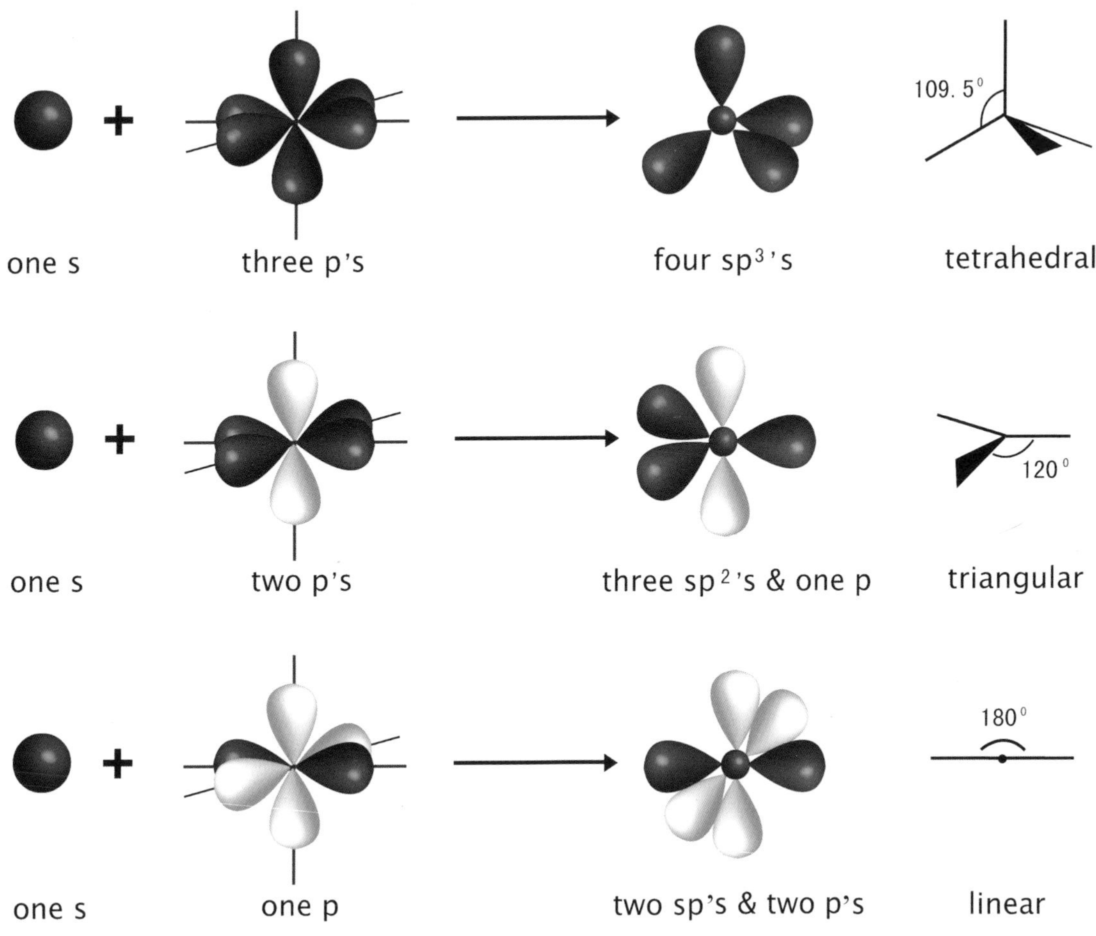

Figure IV.B.1.1: Hybrid orbital geometry

NOTE: For details regarding atomic structure and orbitals, see General Chemistry (CHM) sections 2.1, 2.2. For more details regarding hybridized bonds and bond angles (especially for carbon, nitrogen, oxygen and sulfur), see CHM 3.5.

1.3 Bonding

Sigma (or single) bonds are those in which the electron density is between the nuclei. They are symmetric about the axis, can freely rotate, and are formed when orbitals (regular or hybridized) overlap directly. They are characterized by the fact that they are circular when a cross section is taken and the bond is viewed along the bond axis. The electron density in pi bonds overlaps both above and below the plane of the atoms. A single bond is a sigma bond; a double bond is one sigma and one pi bond; a triple bond is one sigma (σ) and two pi (π) bonds.

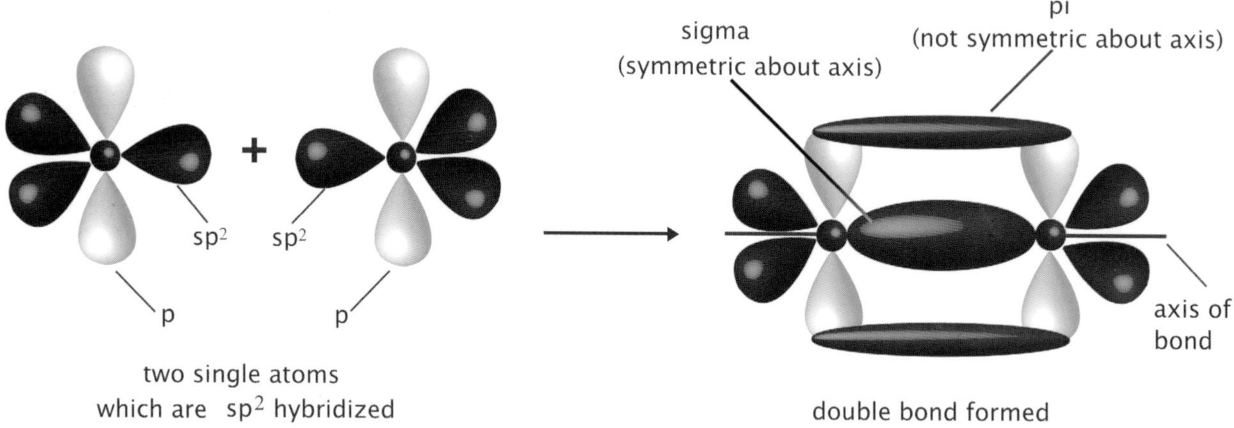

Figure IV.B.1.2: Sigma and pi bonds. The sp^2 hybrids overlap between the nuclei to form a σ bond; the p orbitals overlap above and below the axis between the nuclei to form a π bond.

1.3.1 The Effects of Multiple Bonds

The pi bonds in doubly and triply bonded molecules create a barrier to free rotation about the axis of the bond. Thus multiple bonds create molecules which are much more rigid than a molecule with only a single bond which can freely rotate about its axis.

As a rule, the length of a bond decreases with multiple bonds. For example, the carbon-carbon triple bond is shorter than the carbon-carbon double bond which is shorter than the carbon-carbon single bond.

Bond strength and thus the amount of energy required to break a bond (= *BE, the bond dissociation energy*) varies with the number of bonds. One σ bond has a BE ≈ 110 kcal/mole and one π bond has a BE ≈ 60 kcal/mole. Thus a single bond (one σ) has a BE ≈ 110 kcal/mole while a double bond (one σ + one π) has a BE ≈ 170 kcal/mole. Hence multiple bonds have greater bond strength than single bonds.

1.4 Delocalized Electrons and Resonance

Delocalization of charges in the pi bonds is possible when there are hybridized orbitals in adjacent atoms. This delocalization may be represented in two different ways, the molecular orbital (MO) approach or the resonance (*valence bond*) approach. The differences are found in Figure IV.B.1.3.

The MO approach takes a linear combination of atomic orbitals to form molecular orbitals, in which electrons form the bonds. These molecular orbitals cover the whole molecule, and thus the delocalization of electrons is depicted. In the resonance approach, there is a linear combination of different structures with localized pi bonds and electrons, which together depict the true molecule, or **resonance hybrid**. There is no single structure that represents the molecule.

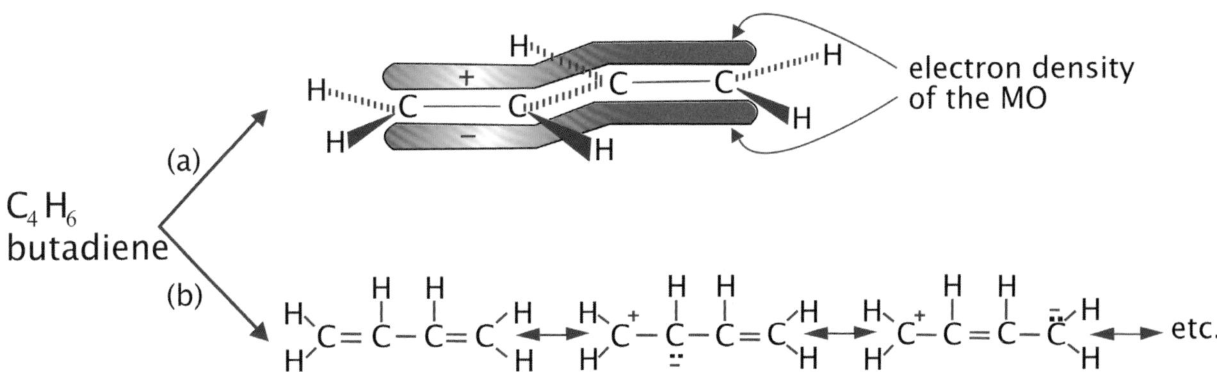

Figure IV.B.1.3: A comparison of MO and resonance approaches. (a) The electron density of the MO covers the entire molecule such that π bonds and p orbitals are not distinguishable. (b) No singular resonance structure accurately portrays butadiene; rather, the true molecule is a composite of all of its resonance structures.

1.5 Lewis Structures, Charge Separation and Dipole Moments

The outer shell (or **valence**) electrons are those that form chemical bonds. **Lewis dot structures** are a method of showing the valence electrons and how they form bonds. These electrons, along with the octet rule (*which states that a maximum of eight electrons are allowed in the outermost shell of an atom*) holds only for the elements in the second row of the periodic table (C,N,O,F). The elements of the third row (Si, P, S, Cl) use d orbitals, and thus can have more than eight electrons in their outer shell.

Let us use CO_2 as an example. Carbon has four valence electrons and oxygen has six. By covalently bonding, electrons are shared and the octet rule is followed,

·C· + 2 :O: ⟶

O :: C :: O or O = C = O

Carbon and oxygen can form resonance structures in the molecule CO_3^{-2}. The –2 denotes two extra electrons to place in the molecule. Once again the octet rule is followed,

In the final structure, each element counts one half of the electrons in a bond as its own, and any unpaired electrons are counted as its own. The sum of these two quantities should equal the number of valence electrons that were originally around the atom.

If the chemical bond is made up of atoms of different electronegativity, there is a **charge separation:**

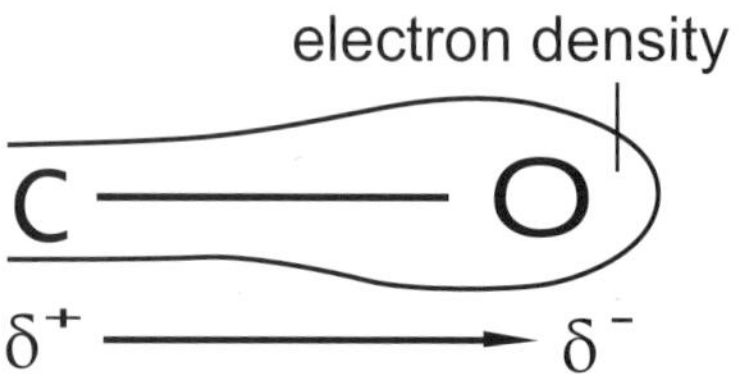

There is a slight pulling of electron density by the more electronegative atom (oxygen in the preceding example) from the less electronegative atom (carbon in the preceding example). This results in the C–O bond having **partial ionic character** (i.e. *a polar bond; see* CHM 3.3). The charge separation also causes an <u>electrical dipole</u> to be set up in the direction of the arrow. A dipole has a positive end (carbon) and a negative end (oxygen). A dipole will line up in an electric field.

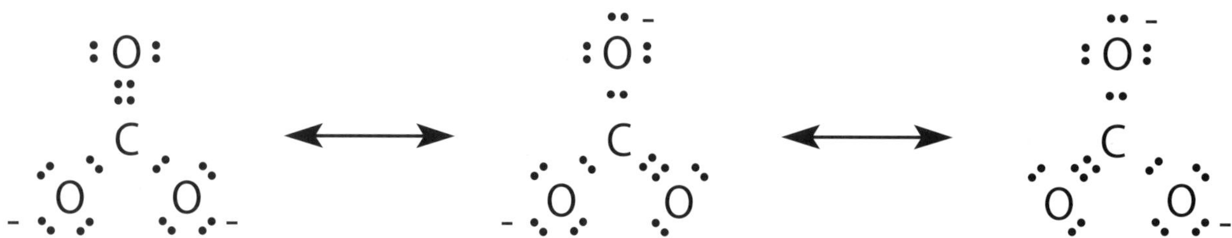

The most electronegative elements (in order, with electronegativities in brackets) are fluorine (4.0), oxygen (3.5), nitrogen (3.0), and chlorine (3.0) [To examine trends, see the periodic table in CHM 2.3]. These elements will often be paired with hydrogen (2.1) and carbon (2.5), resulting in bonds with partial ionic character. The **dipole moment** is a measure of the charge separation and thus, the electronegativities of the elements that make up the bond; the larger the dipole moment, the larger the charge separation.

No dipole moment is found in molecules with no charge separation between atoms (i.e. Cl_2, Br_2), or, when the charge separation is symmetric resulting in a cancellation of bond polarity like vector addition in physics (i.e. CH_4, CO_2).

A molecule where the charge separation between atoms is not symmetric will have a non-zero dipole moment (i.e. CH_3F, H_2O, NH_3 - *see* ORG 11.1.2). It is important to note that lone pair electrons make large contributions to the overall dipole moment of a molecule.

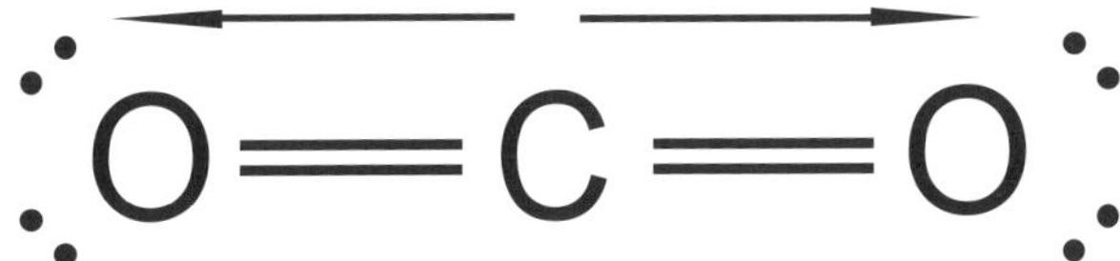

Figure IV.B.1.4: CO_2 - polar bonds but overall it is a non-polar molecule; therefore, CO_2 has a zero dipole moment.

1.5.1 Strength of Polar vs. Non-Polar Bonds

Non-polar bonds are generally stronger than polar covalent and ionic bonds, with ionic bonds being the weakest. However, in compounds with ionic bonding, there is generally a large number of bonds between molecules and this makes the compound as a whole very strong. For instance, although the ionic bonds in one compound are weaker than the non-polar covalent bonds in another compound, the ionic compound's melting point will be higher than the melting point of the covalent compound. Polar covalent bonds have a partially ionic character, and thus the bond strength is usually intermediate between that of ionic and that of non-polar covalent bonds. The strength of bonds generally decreases with increasing ionic character.

1.6 Ground Rules

Opposites attract. Like charges repel. Such simple statements are fundamental in solving over 90% of mechanisms in organic chemistry. Once you are comfortable with the basics - electronegativity, polarity and resonance - you will not need to memorize the grand majority of outcomes of given reactions. You will be capable of quickly deducing the answer even when new scenarios are presented.

A substance which has a formal positive charge ($^+$) or a partial positive charge ("delta$^+$" or δ^+) is attracted to a substance with a formal negative charge ($^-$) or a partial negative charge (δ^-). In general, a substance with a formal charge would have a greater force of attraction than one with a partial charge when faced with an oppositely charged species. There is an important exception: spectator ions. Ions formed by elements in the first two groups of the periodic table (i.e. Na^+, K^+, Ca^{++}) do not actively engage in reactions in organic chemistry. They simply watch the reaction occur then at the very end they associate with the negatively charged product.

In most carbon-based compounds the carbon atom is bonded to a more electronegative atom. For example, in a carbon-oxygen bond the oxygen is δ^- resulting in a δ^+ carbon (*see* ORG 1.5). Because opposites attract, a δ^- carbon (which is unusual) could create a carbon-carbon bond with a δ^+ carbon (which is common). There are two important categories of compounds which can create a carbon-carbon bond; a) alkyl lithiums (RLi) and b) Grignard reagents (RMgBr), because they each have a δ^- carbon. Note that the carbon is δ^- since lithium is to the left of carbon on the periodic table (for electronegativity trends *see* CHM 2.3).

The expressions "like charges repel" and "opposites attract" are the basic rules of electrostatics. "Opposites attract" is translated in Organic Chemistry to mean "nucleophile attacks electrophile". The nucleophile is "nucleus loving" and so it is negatively charged or partially negative, and we follow its electrons using arrows in reaction mechanisms as it attacks the "electron loving" electrophile which is positively charged or partially positively charged. Sometimes we will use color, or an asterix*, or a "prime" symbol on the letter R (i.e. R vs R' vs R'' vs R'''), during reaction mechanisms to help you follow the movement of atoms. You will better understand the meaning in the pages to follow.

For nucleophiles, the general trend is that the stronger the nucleophile, the stronger the base it is. For example:

$$RO^- > HO^- >> RCOO^- > ROH > H_2O$$

For information on the quality of leaving groups, see ORG 6.2.4.

Chapter review questions are available online for free. Doing practice questions will help clarify concepts and ensure that you study in a targeted way. We also have an IUPAC nomenclature program that you can use for free.

First, register at DAT-prep.com, then login and click on DAT Textbook Owners in the right column. Your online access continues for one full year from your online registration.

Chapter 2

Memorize	Understand	Importance
* Categories of stereoisomers * Define enantiomers, diastereomers * Define ligand, chiral, racemic mixture * IUPAC nomenclature	* Rules for stereochemistry * Identify meso compounds * Assign R/S/E/Z * Fischer projections	2 to 4 out of the 30 ORG DAT questions are based on content in this chapter (in our estimation). * Note that between 30% and 60% of the questions in DAT Organic Chemistry are based on content from 4 chapters: 1, 2, 5 and 6.

DAT-Prep.com

Introduction

Stereochemistry is the study of the relative spatial (3 D) arrangement of atoms within molecules. An important branch of stereochemistry, and very relevant to the DAT, is the study of chiral molecules.

Additional Resources

Free Online Q&A + Forum

Video: Online or DVD

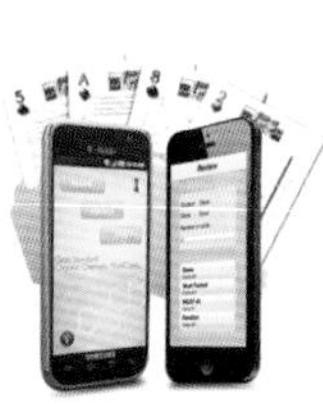

Flashcards

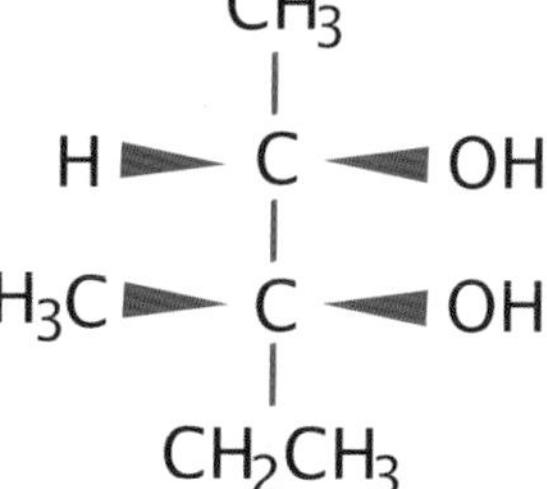

Special Guest

2.1 Isomers

Stereochemistry is the study of the arrangement of atoms in a molecule, in three dimensions. Two *different molecules* with the same number and type of atoms (= *the same molecular formula)* are called isomers. Isomers fall into two main categories: *structural* (constitutional) isomers and *stereoisomers* (spatial isomers). Structural isomers differ by the way their atoms are connected and stereoisomers differ in the way their atoms are arranged in space (enantiomers and diastereomers; see Figure IV.B.2.1.1).

2.1.1 Structural (Constitutional) Isomers

Structural isomers have different atoms and/or bonding patterns in relation to each other like the following *chain* or *skeletal* isomers:

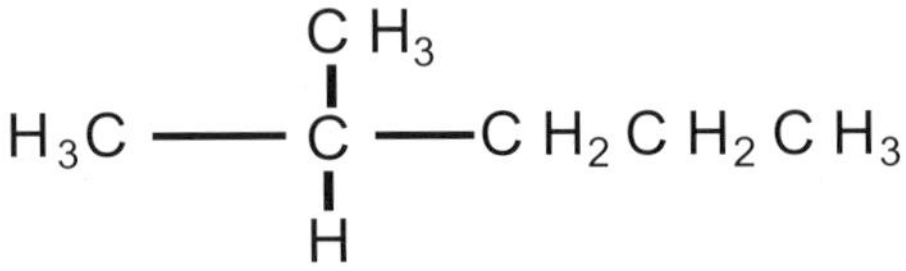

$$H_3C-CH(CH_3)-CH_2CH_2CH_3 \quad \text{and} \quad H_3C-CH(CH_2CH_3)-CH_2CH_3$$

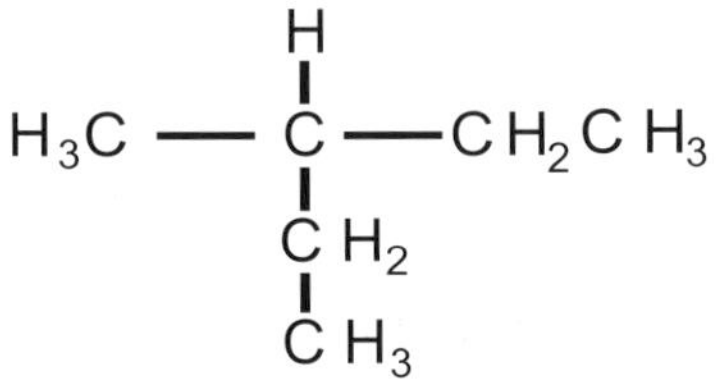

Functional isomers are structural isomers that have the same molecular formula but have different functional groups or *moieties*. For example, the following alcohol (ORG 6.1) and ether (ORG 10.1):

butan-1-ol
(n-butanol)

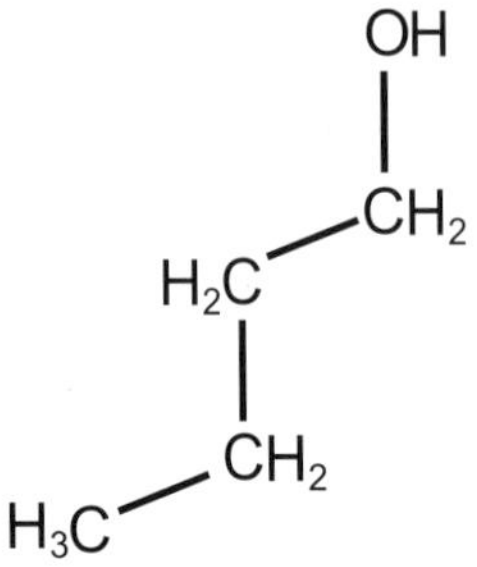

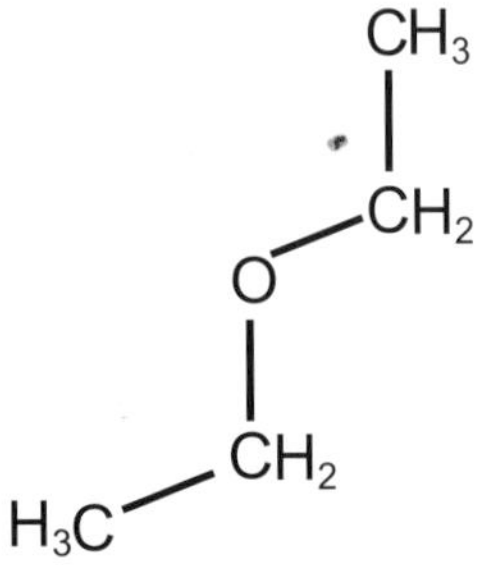

$$H_3C-CH_2-CH_2-CH_2-OH$$

$$H_3C-CH_2-O-CH_2-CH_3$$

ethoxyethane
(diethyl ether)

Positional or regioisomers are structural isomers where the functional group changes position on the parent structure. For example, the hydroxyl group (-OH) occupying 3 different positions on the n-pentane (= normal, non-branched alkane with 5 carbons) chain resulting in 3 different compounds:

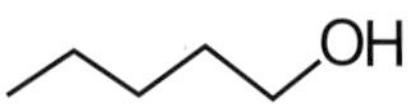

pentan-1-ol
(1-pentanol)

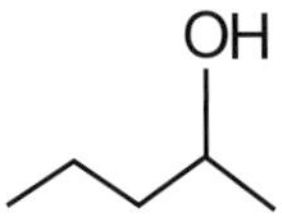

2-pentanol

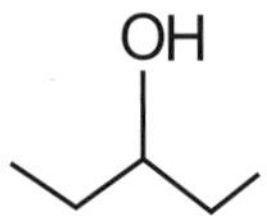

3-pentanol

2.2 Spatial/Stereoisomers

2.2.1 Geometric Isomers *cis/trans*, E/Z

Geometric isomers occur because carbons that are in a ring or double bond structure are *unable* to freely rotate (see conformation of cycloalkane; ORG 3.3, 3.3.1). This results in *cis* and *trans* compounds. When the substituents (i.e. Br) are on the same side of the ring or double bond, it is designated cis. When they are on opposite sides, it is designated trans. The *trans* isomer is more stable since the substituents are further apart, thus electron shell repulsion is minimized.

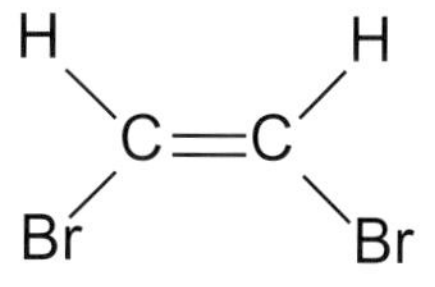

H, H / C=C / Br, Br and H, Br / C=C / Br, H

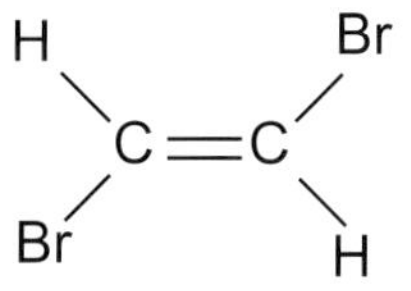

cis-dibromoethene *trans*-dibromoethene

In general, structural and geometric isomers have different reactivity, spectra and physical properties (i.e. boiling points, melting points, etc.). Geometric isomers may have different physical properties but, in general, tend to have similar chemical reactivity.

The E, Z notation is the IUPAC preferred method for designating the stereochemistry of double bonds. E, Z is particularly used for isomeric compounds with 4 different substituent groups bonded to the two *ethenyl* or *vinyl* carbons (i.e. C=C which are sp^2 hybridized carbon atoms). We have just reviewed how to use *cis/trans*. The E, Z notation is used on more complex molecules and, as described, on situations were 4 different substituents are present.

To begin with, each substituent at the double bond is assigned a priority (see 2.3.1 for rules). If the two groups of higher priority are on opposite sides of the double bond, the bond is assigned the configuration E, (from *entgegen*, the German word for "opposite"). If the two groups of higher priority are on the same side of the double bond, the bond is assigned the configuration Z, (from *zusammen,* the German word for "together"). {Generally speaking, learning German is NOT required for the DAT!}

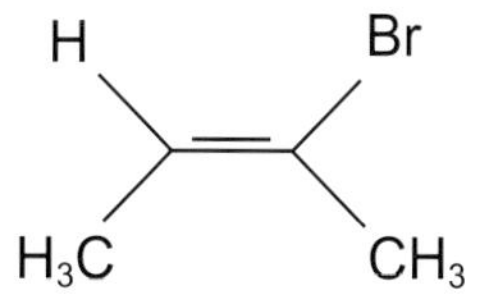

H, Br / H_3C, CH_3

cis-2-bromobut-2-ene
(2 methyl groups on same side)

BUT

(*E*)-2-bromobut-2-ene
(Br is higher priority than methyl)

Mnemonic: Z = Zame Zide; E = Epposites.

2.2.2 Enantiomers and Diastereomers

Stereoisomers are different compounds with the same structure, differing only in the spatial orientation of the atoms (= *configuration*). Stereoisomers may be further divided into enantiomers and diastereomers. Enantiomers must have opposite absolute configurations at each and every chiral carbon.

We will soon highlight the easy way to remember the meaning of a *chiral molecule*, however, the formal definition of chirality is of an object that is not identical with its mirror image and thus exists in two enantiomeric forms. A molecule cannot be chiral if it contains a plane of symmetry. A molecule that has a plane of symmetry must be superimposable on its mirror image and thus must be *achiral.* The most common chirality encountered in organic chemistry is when the carbon atom is bonded to four different groups. Such a carbon lacks a plane of symmetry and is referred to as a *chiral center.* When a carbon atom has only three different substituents, such as the central carbon in methylcyclohexane, it has a plane of symmetry and is therefore achiral.

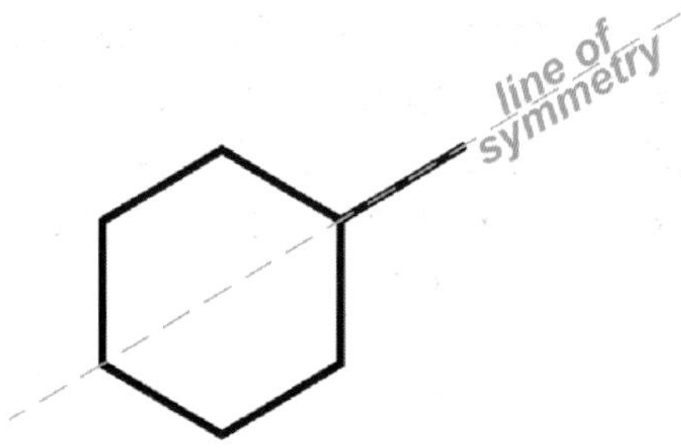

methylcyclohexane

A stereocenter (= stereogenic center) is an atom bearing attachments such that interchanging any two groups produces a stereoisomer. If a molecule has n stereocenters, then it can have up to 2^n different non-superimposable (non-superposable) structures (= enantiomers).

Enantiomers come in pairs. They are two non-superimposable molecules, which are mirror images of each other. In order to have an enantiomer, a molecule must be chiral. Chiral molecules contain at least one chiral carbon which is a carbon atom that has four different substituents attached. For the purposes of the DAT, the concepts of a chiral carbon, asymmetric carbon and stereocenter are interchangeable.

Enantiomers have the same chemical and physical properties. The only difference is with their interactions with other chiral molecules, and their rotation of plane polarized light.

Conversely, diastereomers are any pair of stereoisomers that are not enantiomers. Diastereomers are both chemically and physically different from each other.

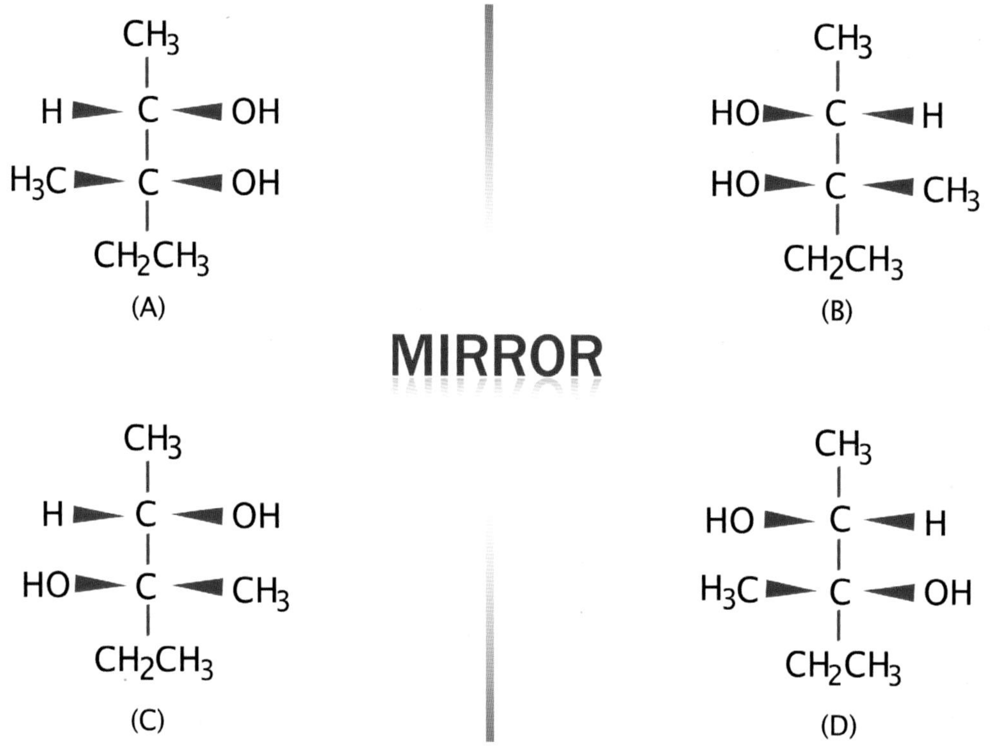

CH_3 | H ◄ C ► OH | H_3C ◄ C ► OH | CH_2CH_3

(A)

CH_3 | HO ◄ C ► H | HO ◄ C ► CH_3 | CH_2CH_3

(B)

MIRROR

CH_3 | H ◄ C ► OH | HO ◄ C ► CH_3 | CH_2CH_3

(C)

CH_3 | HO ◄ C ► H | H_3C ◄ C ► OH | CH_2CH_3

(D)

Figure IV.B.2.1: Enantiomers and diastereomers. The enantiomers are A & B, C & D. The diastereomers are A & C, A & D, B & D, B & C. Thus there are 2 pairs of enantiomers. This is consistent with the 2^n equation since each of the structures above have exactly 2 chiral carbons (stereocenters) and thus $2^2 = 4$ enantiomers.

2.3 Absolute and Relative Configuration

Absolute configuration uses the R, S system of naming compounds (*nomenclature;* ORG 2.3.1) and relative configuration uses the D, L system (ORG 2.3.2).

Before 1951, the absolute three dimensional arrangement or configuration of chiral molecules was not known. Instead chiral molecules were compared to an arbitrary standard (*glyceraldehyde*). Thus the *relative* configuration could be determined. Once the actual spatial arrangements of groups in molecules were finally determined, the *absolute* configuration could be known.

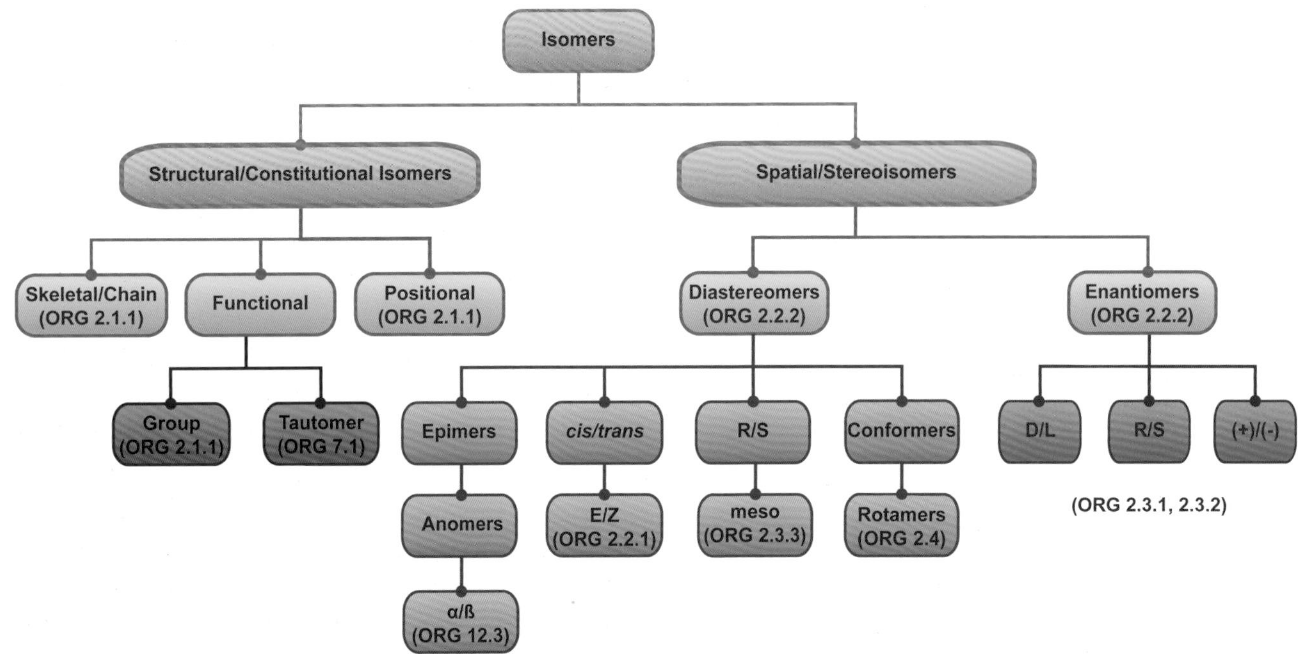

Figure IV.B.2.1.1: Categories of isomers.

2.3.1 The R, S System and Fischer Projections

One consequence of the existence of enantiomers, is a special system of nomenclature: the R, S system. This system provides information about the absolute configuration of a molecule. This is done by assigning a stereochemical configuration at each asymmetric (*chiral*) carbon in the molecule by using the following steps:

1. Identify an asymmetric carbon, and the four attached groups.

2. Assign priorities to the four groups, using the following rules:

   i. Atoms of higher atomic number have higher priority.
   ii. An isotope of higher atomic mass receives higher priority.
   iii. The higher priority is assigned to the group with the atom of higher atomic number or mass at the first point of difference.
   iv. If the difference between the two groups is due to the number of otherwise identical atoms, the higher priority is assigned to the group with the greater number of atoms of higher atomic number or mass.

v. To assign priority of double or triple bonded groups, multiple-bonded atoms are considered as equivalent number of single bonded atoms:

–CH=CH is taken as –CH–CH with a C attached to each CH

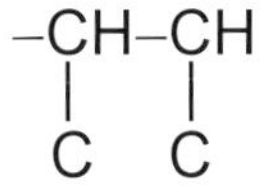

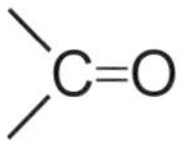

>C=O is taken as >C(–O)(–O–C)

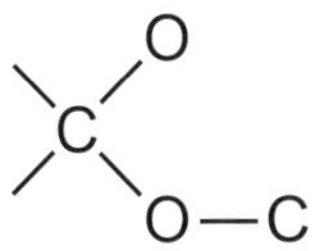

–CH≡CH is taken as –C–CH with two C attached to each of the C and the CH

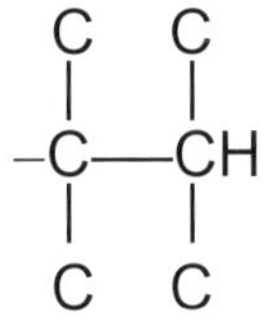

3. In other words, you must re-orient the molecule in space so that the group of lowest priority is pointing directly back, away from you. The remaining three substituents with higher priority should radiate from the asymmetric carbon atom like the spoke on a steering wheel.

4. Consider the clockwise or counterclockwise order of the priorities of the remaining groups. If they increase in a clockwise direction, the asymmetric carbon is said to have the R configuration. If they decrease in a clockwise direction, the asymmetric carbon is said to have the S configuration {Mnemonic: Clockwise means that when you get to the top of the molecule, you must turn to the Right = R}.

A stereoisomer is named by indicating the configurations of each of the asymmetric carbons.

A Fischer projection is a 2-D way of looking at 3-D structures. All horizontal bonds project toward the viewer, while vertical bonds project away from the viewer. In organic chemistry, Fischer projections are used mostly for carbohydrates (*see* ORG 12.3.1, 12.3.2). To determine if 2 Fischer projections are superimposable, you can: (1) rotate one projection 180° or (2) keep one substituent in a fixed position and then you can rotate the other 3 groups either clockwise or counterclockwise. Using either technique preserves the 3-D configuration of the molecule.

Assigning R, S configurations to Fischer projections:

1. Assign priorities to the four substituents.

2. If the lowest priority group is on the vertical axis, determine the direction of rotation by going from priority 1 to 2 to 3, and then assign R or S configuration.

3. If the lowest priority group is on the horizontal axis, determine the direction of rotation by going from priority 1 to 2 to 3, obtain the R or S configuration, now the TRUE configuration will be the <u>opposite</u> of what you have just obtained.

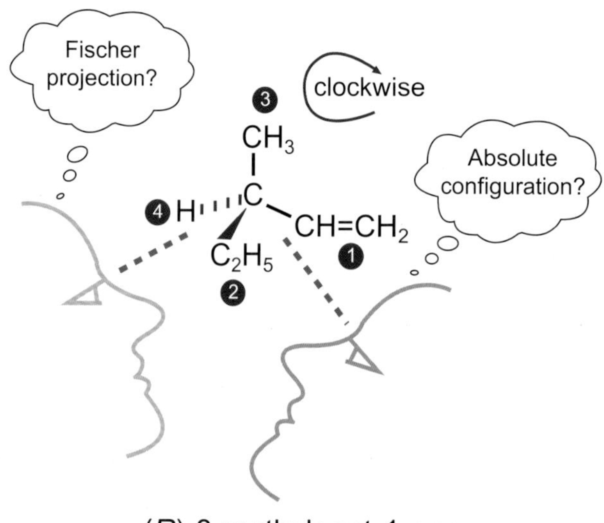

(*R*)-3-methylpent-1-ene

Figure IV.B.2.2(a): Assigning Absolute Configuration. In organic chemistry, the directions of the bonds are symbolized as follows: a broken line extends away from the viewer (i.e. INTO the page), a solid triangle projects towards the viewer, and a straight line extends in the plane of the paper. According to rule #3, we must imagine that the lowest priority group (H) points away from the viewer.

Fischer Projection

Figure IV.B.2.2(b): Creating the Fischer projection of (*R*)-3-methyl-1-pentene. Notice that the perspective of the viewer in the image is the identical perspective of the viewer on the left of Figure IV.B.2.2(a). In either case, a perspective is chosen so that the horizontal groups project towards the viewer.

2.3.2 Optical Isomers and the D, L System

Optical isomers are enantiomers and thus are stereoisomers that differ by different spatial orientations about a chiral carbon atom. Light is an electromagnetic wave that contains oscillating fields. In ordinary light, the electric field oscillates in all directions. However, it is possible to obtain light with an electric field that oscillates in only one plane. This type of light is known as **plane polarized light**. When plane polarized light is passed through a sample of a chiral substance, it will emerge vibrating in a different plane than it started. Optical isomers differ only in this rotation. If the light is rotated in a clockwise direction, the compound is dextrorotary, and is designated by a D or (+). If the light is rotated in a counterclockwise direction, the compound is levrorotary, and is designated by an L or (–). All L compounds have the same relative configuration as L-glyceraldehyde.

A racemic mixture will show no rotation of plane polarized light. This is a consequence of the fact that a racemate is a mixture with equal amounts of the D and L forms of a substance.

Specific rotation (α) is an inherent physical property of a molecule. It is defined as follows:

$$\alpha = \frac{\text{Observed rotation in degrees}}{(\text{tube length in dm})\ (\text{concentration in g/ml})}$$

The observed rotation is the rotation of the light passed through the substance. The tube length is the length of the tube that contains the sample in question. The specific rotation is dependent on the solvent used,

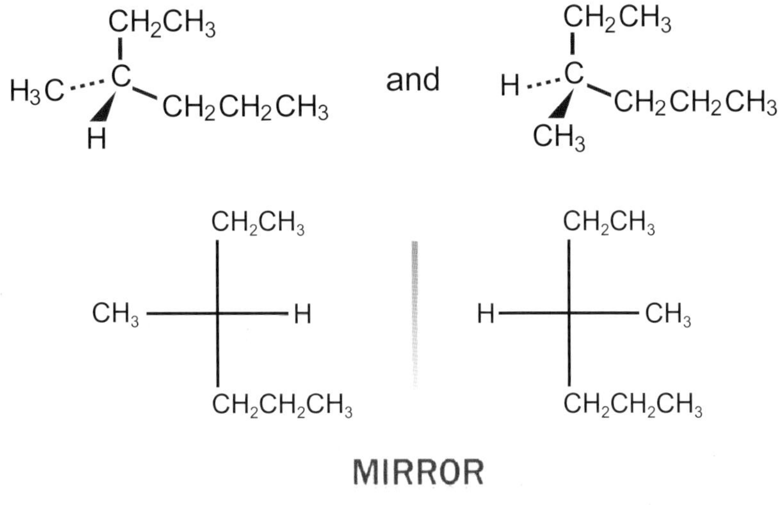

Figure IV.B.2.3: Optical isomers and their Fischer projections. To prove to yourself that the 2 molecules are non-superimposable mirror images (enantiomers), review the rules for Fischer projections (ORG 2.3.1) and compare.

the temperature of the sample, and the wavelength of the light.

It should be noted that there is no clear correlation between the absolute configuration (i.e. R, S) and the direction of rotation of plane polarized light, designated by D/(+) or L (-). Therefore, the direction of optical rotation cannot be determined from the structure of a molecule and must be determined experimentally.

2.3.3 Meso Compounds

Tartaric acid (= 2,3-dihydroxybutanedioic acid which, in the chapters to come, is a compound that you will be able to name systematically = using IUPAC rules) has two chiral centers that have the same four substituents and are equivalent. As a result, two of the four possible stereoisomers of this compound are identical due to a plane of symmetry. Thus there are only three stereoisomeric tartaric acids. Two of these stereoisomers are enantiomers and the third is an achiral diastereomer, called a meso compound. Meso compounds are achiral (optically inactive) diastereomers of chiral stereoisomers.

In a *meso compound*, an internal plane of symmetry exists by drawing a line that will cut the molecule in half. For example, notice that in *meso*-tartaric acid, you can draw a line perpendicular to the vertical carbon chain creating 2 symmetric halves {**M**e**S**o = **M**irror of **S**ymmetry}.

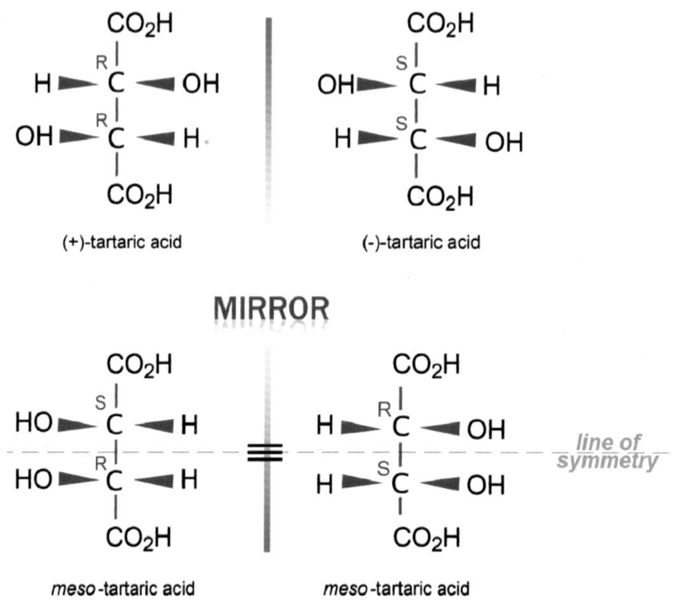

(+)-tartaric acid

(-)-tartaric acid

MIRROR

line of symmetry

meso-tartaric acid

meso-tartaric acid

2.4 Conformational Isomers

Conformational isomers are isomers which differ only by the rotation about single bonds. As a result, substituents (= *ligands* = *attached atoms or groups*) can be maximally close (*eclipsed conformation*), maximally apart (*anti or staggered conformation*) or anywhere in between (i.e. *gauche conformation*). Though all conformations occur at room temperature, anti is most stable since it minimizes electron shell repulsion. Conformational isomers are not true isomers. Conformers are different spatial orientations of the same molecules.

Different conformations can be seen when a molecule is depicted from above and from the right, sawhorse projection, or where the line of sight extends along a carbon-carbon bond axis, a Newman projection. The different conformations occur as the molecule is rotated about its axis.

Example 1: Ethane

The lowest energy, most stable conformation, of ethane is the one in which all six carbon-hydrogen bonds are as far away from each other as possible: *staggered*. The reason, of course, is that atoms are surrounded by an outer shell of negatively charged electrons and, the basic rule of electrostatics is that, like charges repel (= electron shell repulsion = **ESR**). The highest energy, or least stable conformation, of ethane is the one in which all six carbon-hydrogen bonds are as close as possible: *eclipsed*. In between these two extremes are an infinite number of possibilities. As we have previously reviewed, when carbon is bonded to four different atoms (i.e. ethane), its bonds are sp^3 hybridized and the carbon atom sits in the center of a tetrahedron (ORG 1.2, CHM 3.5).

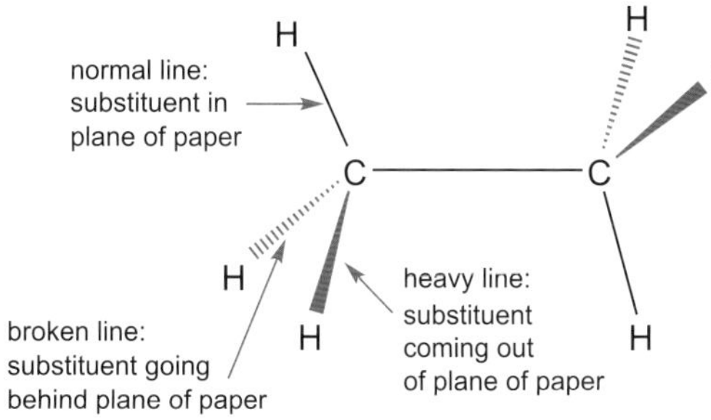

normal line: substituent in plane of paper

broken line: substituent going behind plane of paper

heavy line: substituent coming out of plane of paper

skeletal formula (structure)

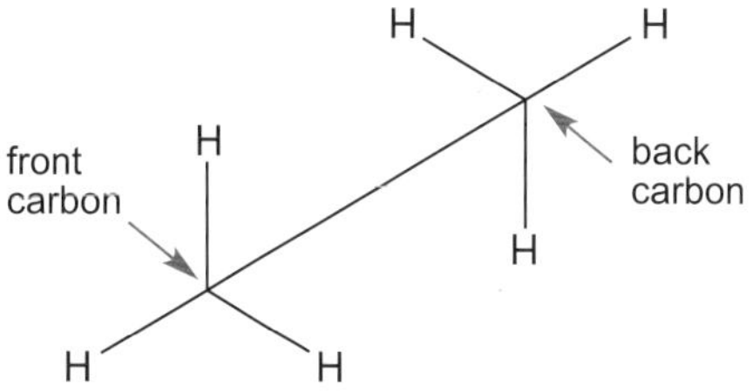

front carbon

back carbon

sawhorse projection

back carbon

front carbon

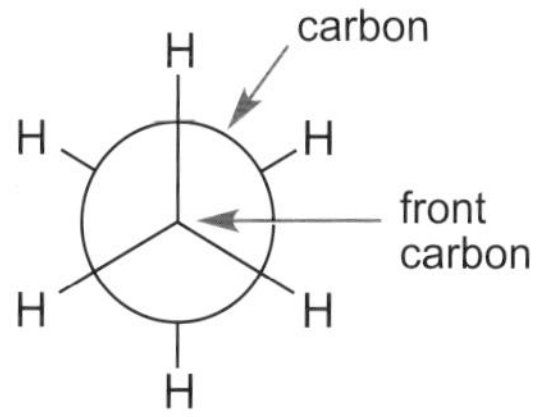

Newman projection

1 kcal/mole

rotate rear carbon 60°

1 kcal/mole

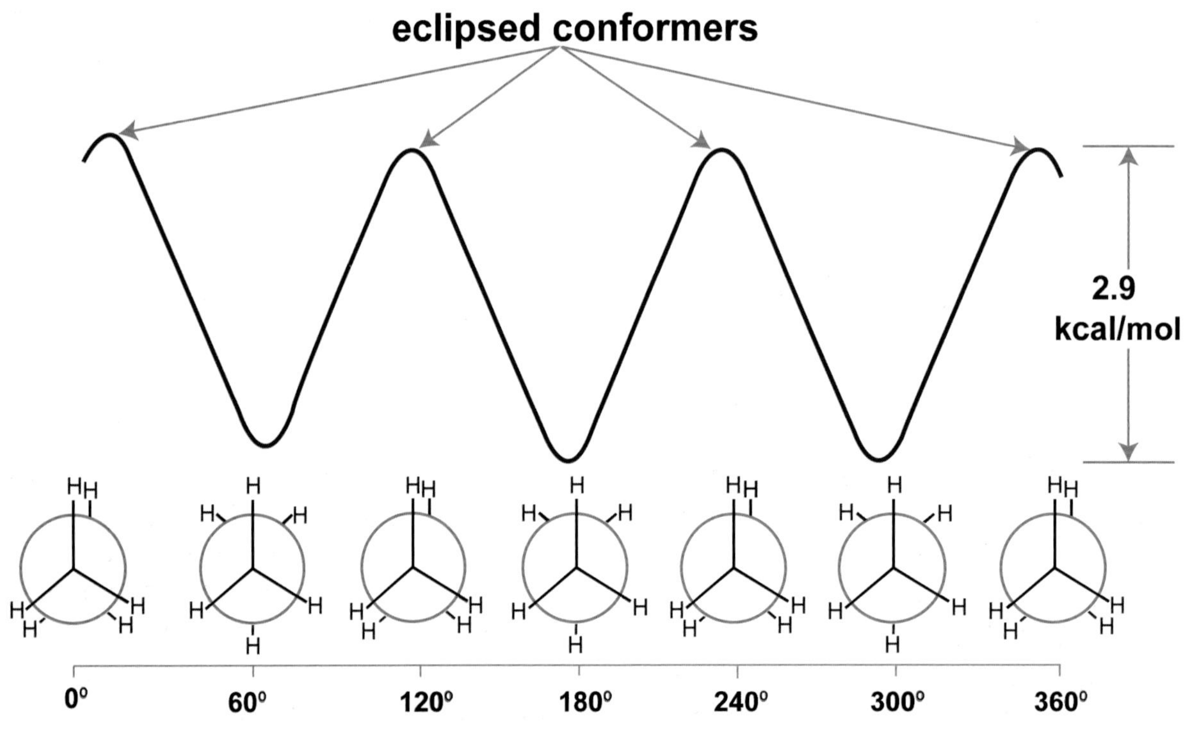

Example 2: Butane

anti conformation

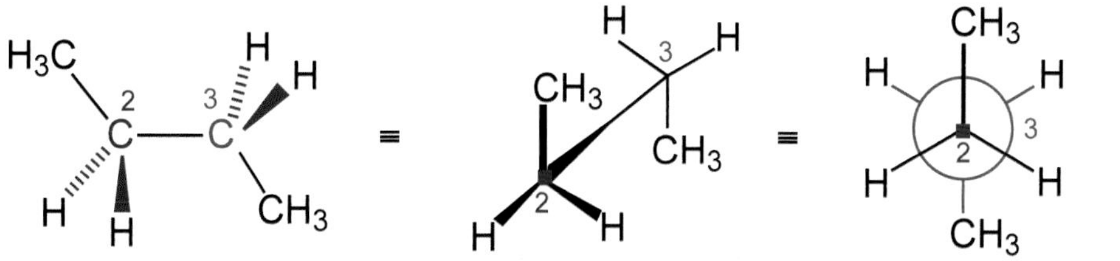

eclipsed conformation

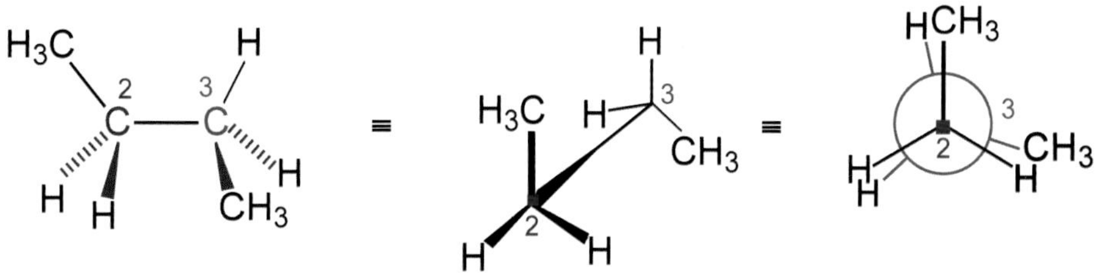

gauche conformation

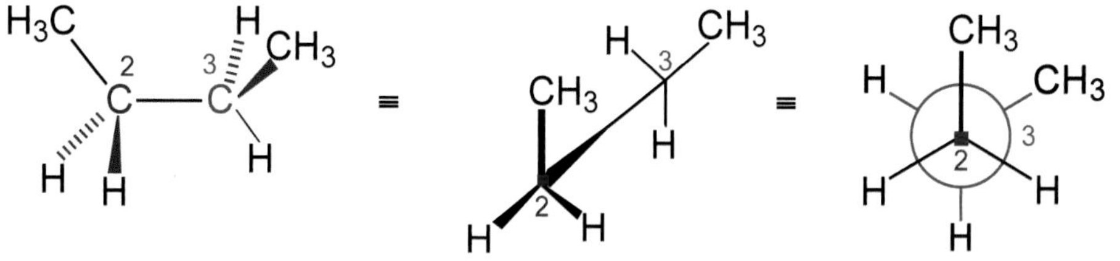

eclipsed conformation

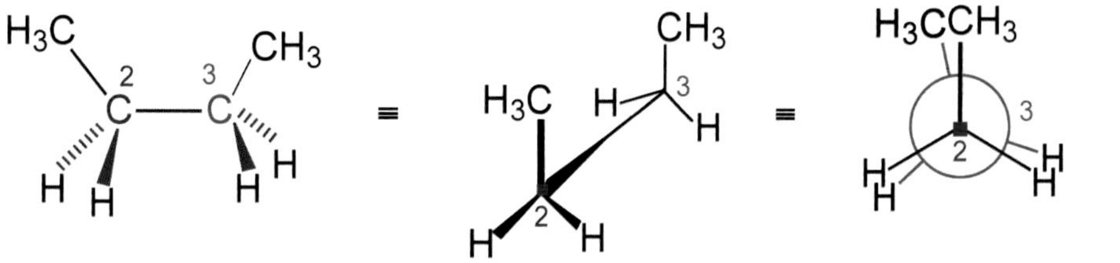

The preceding illustration is a plot of potential energy versus rotation about the C2-C3 bond of butane.

The lowest energy arrangement, the anti conformation, is the one in which two methyl groups (C1 and C4) are as far apart as possible, that is, 180 degrees from each other. When two substituents (i.e. the two methyl groups) are anti and in the same plane, they are *antiperiplanar* to each other.

As rotation around the C2-C3 bond occurs, an eclipsed conformation is reached when there are two methyl-hydrogen interactions and one hydrogen-hydrogen interaction. When the rotation continues, the two methyl groups are 60 degrees apart, thus the gauche conformation. It is still higher in energy than the anti conformation even though it has no eclipsing interactions. The reason, again, is ESR. Because ESR is occurring due to the relative bulkiness (i.e. big size) of the methyl group compared to hydrogens in this molecule, we say that *steric strain* exists between the two close methyl groups.

When two methyl groups completely overlap with each other, the molecule is said to be totally eclipsed and is in its highest energy state (least stable).

At room temperature, these forms easily interconvert: all forms are present to some degree, though the most stable forms dominate.

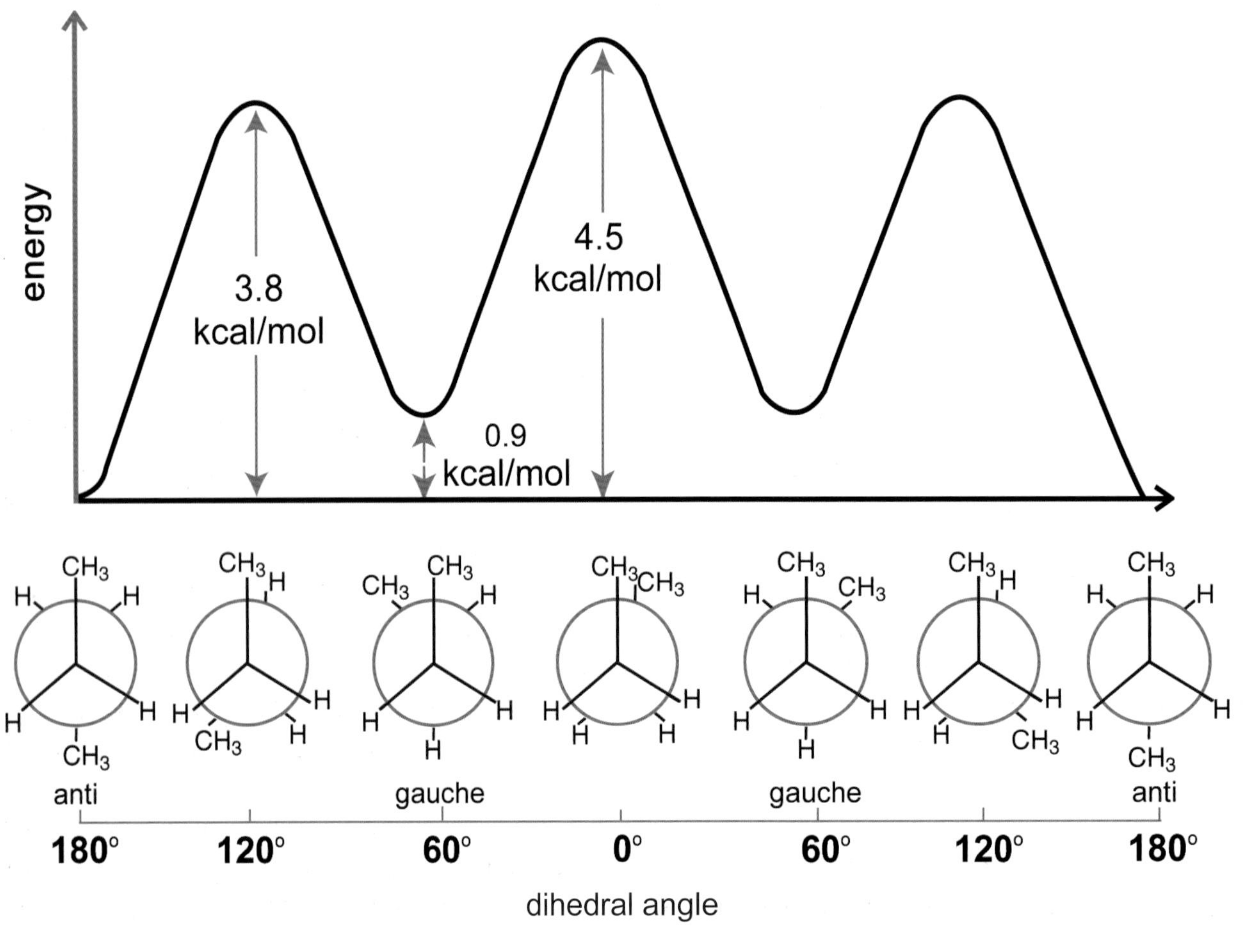

We have seen that conformers rotate about their single bonds. The rotational barrier, or *barrier to rotation*, is the activation energy (CHM 9.5) required to interconvert a subset of the possible conformations called *rotamers*. Butane has three rotamers: two gauche conformers and an anti conformer, where the four carbon centers are coplanar. The three eclipsed conformations with angles between the planes (= *dihedral angles*) of 120°, 0°, and 120° (which is 240° from the first), are not considered to be rotamers, but are instead transition states.

Common Terms

- dihedral angle: torsion (turn/twist) angle
- gauche: skew, synclinal
- **anti**: *trans*, antiperiplanar
- eclipsed: **syn**, *cis*, synperiplanar, torsion angle = 0°

"anti" and "syn" are IUPAC preferred descriptors.

2.5 A Word about IUPAC Nomenclature

IUPAC chemical nomenclature is the set of rules to produce systematic names for chemical compounds. You are responsible for knowing the IUPAC method of naming compounds as there could be 2 questions out of 30 on the DAT which directly rely on nomenclature. IUPAC naming is usually systematic but you will see in upcoming chapters that sometimes the trivial or customary name for a compound is retained as the official IUPAC name.

We have put together this Gold Standard textbook to give you the tools to get an amazing DAT score. However, you will find that sometimes there will be very obscure questions on the DAT, and that can include IUPAC nomenclature. If you will not be satisfied unless you obtain a perfect Organic Chemistry score, then you should review the extensive, detailed rules from the IUPAC website. Fortunately, they have an interactive chart with all the definitions from their fourth major publication, coincidentally named the *Gold Book*, which contains the definitions of a large number of technical terms used in organic chemistry. The extensive summary with interactive map can be found here:

goldbook.iupac.org/Graphs/H02763.3.map.html

We will cover enough nomenclature in our Gold Standard book, and online in our free nomenclature program at dat-prep.com, to get most hard working, insightful students great DAT scores, but if you are aiming for a perfect score, you will also need to review material from the *Gold Book* by IUPAC.

Go online to DAT-prep.com for chapter review Q&A and forum.

ALKANES

Chapter 3

Memorize

* IUPAC nomenclature
* Physical properties
* Bond angles

Understand

* Trends based on length, branching
* Ring strain, ESR
* Complete combustion
* Reactions involving alkenes, alkynes
* Technical categorization of "cyclic alkanes"
* Mechanisms of reactions
* Free radical substitution

Importance

1 to 3 out of the 30 ORG

DAT questions are based on content in this chapter (in our estimation).

* Note that between 30% and 60% of the questions in DAT Organic Chemistry are based on content from 4 chapters: 1, 2, 5 and 6.

Introduction

Alkanes (a.k.a. paraffins) are compounds that consist only of the elements carbon (C) and hydrogen (H) (i.e. hydrocarbons). In addition, C and H are linked together exclusively by single bonds (i.e. they are saturated compounds). Methane is the simplest possible alkane while saturated oils and fats are much larger.

Additional Resources

Free Online Q&A + Forum

Video: Online or DVD

Flashcards

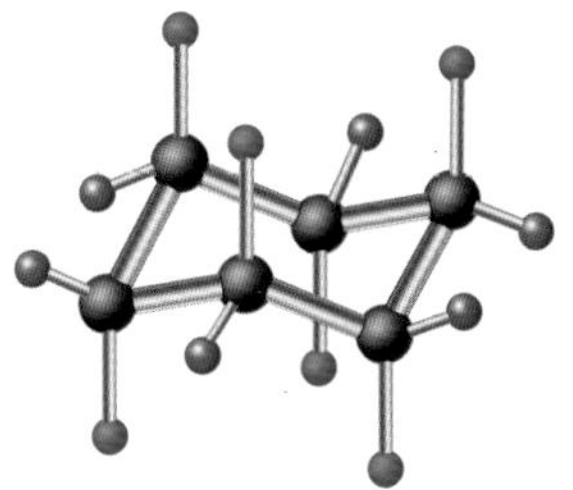

Special Guest

3.1 Description and Nomenclature

Alkanes are hydrocarbon molecules containing only sp^3 hybridized carbon atoms (single bonds). They may be unbranched, branched or cyclic. Their general formula is C_nH_{2n+2} for a straight chain molecule; 2 hydrogen (H) atoms are subtracted for each ring. They contain no functional groups and are fully saturated molecules (= *no double or triple bonds*). As a result, they are chemically unreactive except when exposed to heat or light.

Systematic naming of compounds (= *nomenclature*) has evolved from the International Union of Pure and Applied Chemistry (IUPAC). **The nomenclature of alkanes is the basis of that for many other organic molecules.** The root of the compound is named according to the number of carbons in the longest carbon chain:

C_1 = meth	C_5 = pent	C_8 = oct
C_2 = eth	C_6 = hex	C_9 = non
C_3 = prop	C_7 = hept	C_{10} = dec
C_4 = but		

When naming these as fragments, (alkyl fragments: *the alkane minus one H atom*, symbol: R), the suffix '–yl' is used. If naming the alkane, the suffix '-ane' is used. Some prefixes result from the fact that a carbon with *one* R group attached is a *primary* (normal or n –) carbon, *two* R groups is *secondary* (sec) and with *three* R groups it is a *tertiary* (tert or t –) carbon. Some alkyl groups have special names:

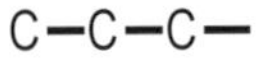

C–C–C– n-propyl (= propyl)   C–C–C–C– n-butyl (= butyl)

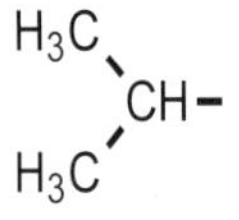

$(H_3C)_2CH–$
isopropyl
(= 2-propyl or propan-2-yl)

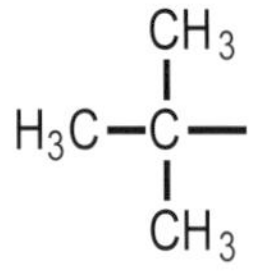

$H_3C–C(CH_3)_2–$
tert-butyl
(= 1,1-dimethylethyl)

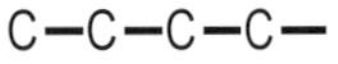

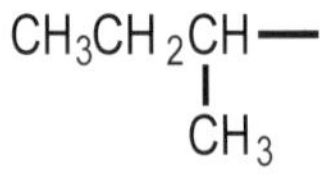

$CH_3CH_2CH(CH_3)–$
sec-butyl
(= 1-methylpropyl)

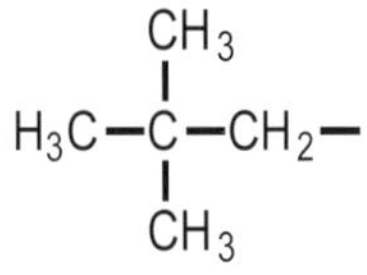

$H_3C–C(CH_3)_2–CH_2–$
neopentyl
(= dimethylpropyl)

Cyclic alkanes are named in the same way (according to the number of carbons), but the prefix 'cyclo' is added. The shorthand for organic compounds is a geometric figure where each corner represents a carbon; hydrogens need not be written, though it should be remembered that the number of hydrogens would exist such that the number of bonds at each carbon is four.

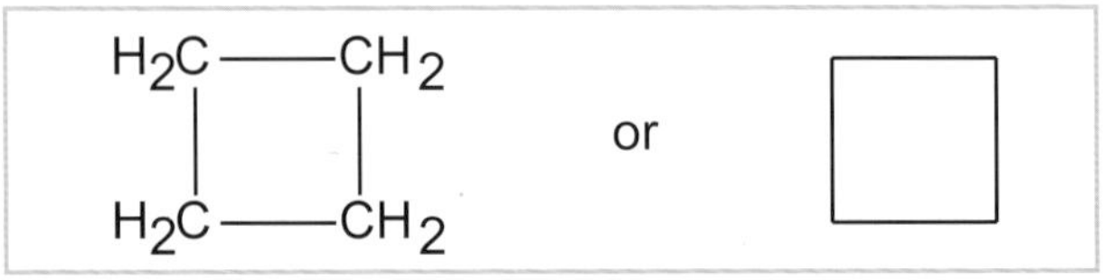

H_2C—CH_2 / H_2C—CH_2 or [square]

cyclobutane

H_2C, H_2C, CH_2, H_2C, CH_2, CH_2 or [hexagon] or [chair]

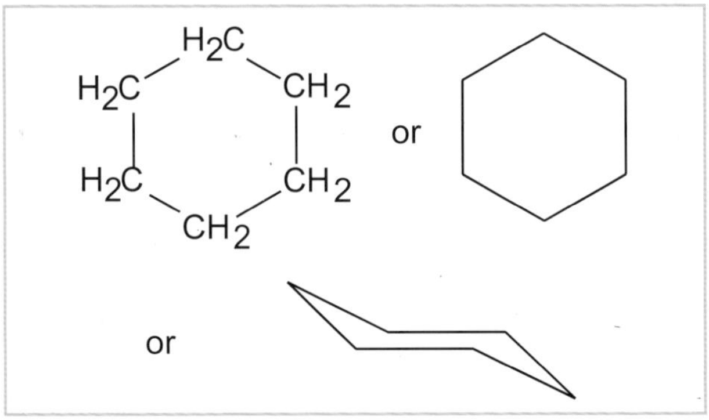

cyclohexane

As mentioned, carbon atoms can be characterized by the number of other carbon atoms to which they are directly bonded. It is very important for you to train your eyes to quickly indentify a primary carbon atom (**1°**), which is bonded to only one other carbon; a secondary carbon atom (**2°**), which is bonded to two other carbons; a tertiary carbon atom (**3°**), which is bonded to three other carbons; and a quaternary carbon atom (**4°**), which is bonded to four other carbons.

HO
4°
1°
3°
2°

The nomenclature for branched-chain alkanes begins by determining the longest straight chain (i.e. *the highest number of carbons attached in a row*). The groups attached to the straight or *main* chain are numbered so as to achieve the lowest set of numbers. Groups are cited in alphabetical order. If a group appears more than once, the prefixes di-(2), tri-(3), tetra-(4) are used. Prefixes such as di-, tri-, tetra- as well as tert-, sec-, n- are not used for alphabetizing purposes. However, cyclo-, iso-, and neo- are considered part of the group name and are used for alphabetizing purposes. If two chains of equal length compete for selection as the main chain, choose the chain with the most substituents.

For example:

CH_3
③ CH_2CHCH_3 ② ①
CH_3CH_2 ⑧ ⑦ — C ⑥ (CH_3; ⑦ CH(H_3C)(CH_3 ⑧)) — C ⑤ (CH_3; CH_3) — C ④ (H) — CH_2CH_3

4,6-Diethyl-2,5,5,6,7-pentamethyloctane (7 substituents) or 3,5-Diethyl-2,3,4,4,7-pentamethyl octane (a bit better for keeners!) NOT 2,5,5,6-Tetramethyl-4-ethyl-6-isopropyl octane (6 substituents)

Naming cycloalkanes:

1. Use the cycloalkane name as the parent name. The only exception is when the alkyl side chain contains a larger number of carbons than the ring. In that case, the ring is considered as a substituent to the parent alkane.

2. Number the substituents on the ring to arrive at the lowest sum. When two or more different alkyl groups are present, they are numbered by an alphabetical order.

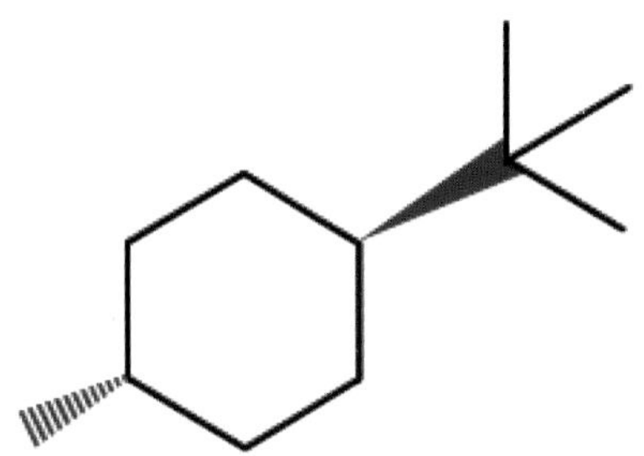

trans-1-tert-butyl-4-methylcyclohexane

3.1.1 Physical Properties of Alkanes

At room temperature and one atmosphere of pressure straight chain alkanes with 1 to 4 carbons are gases (i.e. CH_4 – methane, CH_3CH_3 – ethane, etc.), 5 to 17 carbons are liquids, and more than 17 carbons are solid. Boiling points of straight chain alkanes (= *aliphatic*) show a regular increase with increasing number of carbons. This is because they are nonpolar molecules, and have weak intermolecular forces. Branching of alkanes leads to a dramatic decrease in the boiling point. As a rule, as the number of carbons increase the melting points also increase.

Alkanes are soluble in nonpolar solvents (i.e. benzene, CCl_4 – carbon tetrachloride, etc.), and not in aqueous solvents (= *hydrophobic*). They are insoluble in water because of their low polarity and their inability to hydrogen bond. Alkanes are the least dense of all classes of organic compounds (<< ρ_{water}, 1 g/ml). Thus petroleum, a mixture of hydrocarbons rich in alkanes, floats on water.

3.2 Important Reactions of Alkanes

3.2.1 Combustion

Note that the "heat of combustion" is the change in enthalpy of a combustion reaction. Therefore, the higher the heat of combustion, the higher the energy level of the molecule, the less stable the molecule was prior to combustion.

Combustion may be either complete or incomplete. In complete combustion, the hydrocarbon is converted to carbon dioxide (CO_2) and water (H_2O). If there is insufficient oxygen for complete combustion, the reaction gives other products, such as carbon monoxide (CO) and soot (molecular C). This strongly exothermic reaction may be summarized:

$$C_nH_{2n+2} + \text{excess } O_2 \rightarrow nCO_2 + (n+1)H_2O.$$

3.2.2 Radical Substitution Reactions

Radical substitution reactions with halogens may be summarized:

$$RH + X_2 + \text{uv light}(\,hf\,) \text{ or heat} \rightarrow RX + HX$$

The halogen X_2, may be F_2, Cl_2, or Br_2. I_2 does not react. The mechanism of *halogenation* may be explained and summarized by example:

i. Initiation: This step involves the formation of *free radicals* (highly reactive substances which contain an unpaired electron, which is symbolized by a single dot):

$$Cl{:}Cl + \text{uv light or heat} \rightarrow 2Cl$$

ii. Propagation: In this step, the chlorine free radical begins a series of reactions that form new free radicals:

$$CH_4 + Cl\bullet \rightarrow \bullet CH_3 + HCl$$

$$\bullet CH_3 + Cl_2 \rightarrow CH_3Cl + Cl\bullet$$

iii. Termination: These reactions end the radical propagation steps. Termination reactions destroy the free radicals (coupling).

$$Cl\bullet + \bullet CH_3 \rightarrow CH_3Cl$$

$$\bullet CH_3 + \bullet CH_3 \rightarrow CH_3CH_3$$

$$Cl\bullet + Cl\bullet \rightarrow Cl_2$$

Radical substitution reactions can also occur with halide acids (i.e. HCl, HBr) and peroxides (i.e. HOOH – hydrogen peroxide). Chain propagation (step ii) can destroy many organic compounds fairly quick. This step can be inhibited by using a resonance stabilized free radical to "mop up" (*termination*) other destructive free radicals in the medium. For example, BHT is a resonance stabilized free radical added to packaging of many breakfast cereals in order to inhibit free radical destruction of the cereal (= *spoiling*).

The stability of a free radical depends on the ability of the compound to stabilize the unpaired electron. This is analogous to stabilizing a positively charged carbon (= *carbocation*). Thus, in both cases, a tertiary compound is more stable than secondary which, in turn, is more stable than a primary compound.

Please note that the rate law for free radical substitution reactions was discussed in CHM 9.4.

The relative rate of free radical halogenation: $F_2 > Cl_2 > Br_2 > I_2$. Free radical reactions depend not only on the stability of the intermediate, but also on the number of hydrogens present. The following are examples:

1. When F_2 is treated with UV light and reacted with 2-methylbutane, only one type of product is dominant. Fluorine

radicals are so reactive that it will react mostly with hydrogens type that are most prevalent (hydrogens attached to primary carbons indicated in blue), thus the predominant product will be:

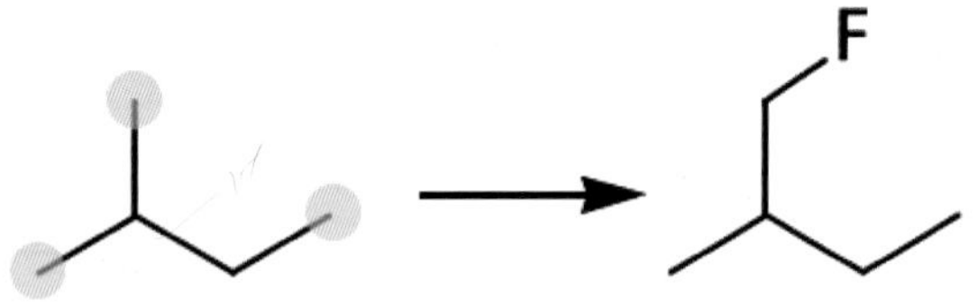

2. When Cl_2 is treated with UV light and reacted with 2-methylbutane, five products are formed. The relative rate of reaction of Br_2 is slower than F_2. Therefore, both abundance of different hydrogens and the relative stability of the primary radical contribute to the types of final products formed.

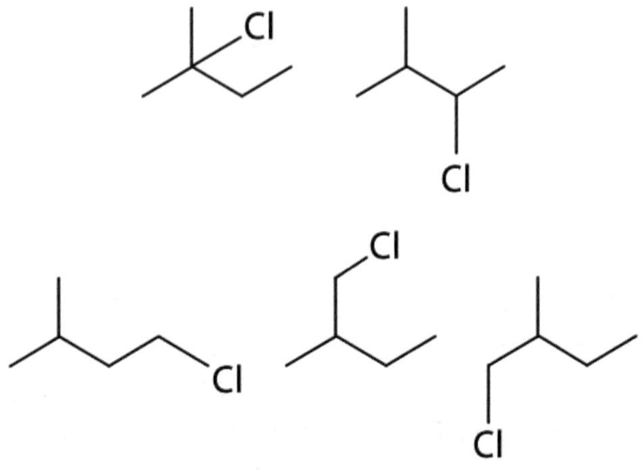

3. When Br_2 is treated with UV light and reacted with 2-methylbutane, only one product is formed because bromine is so selective that it will only react with the most stable primary radical (most substituted carbon atom).

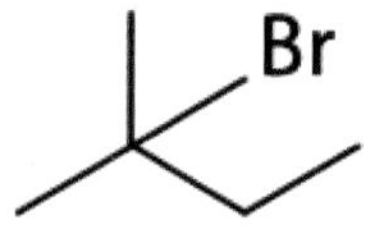

4. I_2 does not react.

The stability of a free radical depends on the ability of the compound to stabilize the unpaired electron. This is analogous to stabilizing a positively charged carbon (= *carbocation*). Thus, in both cases, a tertiary compound is more stable than secondary which, in turn, is more stable than a primary compound.

Also in both cases, the reason for the trend is the same: the charge on the carbon is stabilized by the electron donating effect of the presence of alkyl groups. Alkyl groups are not strongly electron donating, they are normally described as "somewhat" electron donating; however, the combined effect of multiple R groups has an important stabilizing effect that we will see as a critical feature in many reaction types.

$$\bullet CR_3 > \bullet CR_2H > \bullet CRH_2 > \bullet CH_3$$
$$3^o > 2^o > 1^o > \text{methyl}$$

<u>Pyrolysis</u> occurs when a molecule is broken down by heat (*pyro* = fire, *lysis* = separate). C-C bonds are cleaved and smaller chain alkyl radicals often recombine in termination steps creating a variety of alkanes.

3.3 Ring Strain in Cyclic Alkanes

Cyclic alkanes are strained compounds. This **ring strain** results from the bending of the bond angles in greater amounts than normal. This strain causes cyclic compounds of 3 and 4 carbons to be unstable, and thus not often found in nature. The usual angle between bonds in an sp^3 hybridized carbon is 109.5° (= *the normal tetrahedral angle*).

The expected angles in some cyclic compounds can be determined geometrically: 60° in cyclopropane; 90° in cyclobutane and 108° in cyclopentane. Cyclohexane, in the chair conformation, has normal bond angles of 109.5°. The closer the angle is to the normal tetrahedral angle of 109.5°, the more stable the compound. In fact, cyclohexane can be found in a chair or boat conformation or any conformation in between; however, at any given moment, 99% of the cyclohexane molecules would be found in the chair conformation because it is the most stable (lower energy).

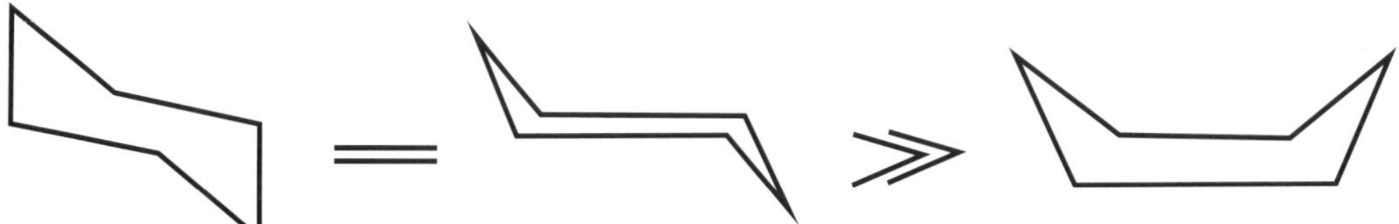

Figure IV.B.3.1: The chair and boat conformations of cyclohexane. Some students like to remember that you sit in a chair because a chair is stable. However, a boat can be tippy and so it's less stable.

It is important to have a clear understanding of electron shell repulsion (ESR). Essentially all atoms and molecules are surrounded by an electron shell (CHM 2.1, ORG 1.2) which is more like a cloud of electrons. Because like charges repel, when there are options, atoms and molecules assume the conformation which minimizes ESR.

For example, when substituents are added to a cyclic compound (i.e. Fig. IV.B.3.2), the most stable position is equatorial (equivalent to the anti conformation, ORG 2.1) which minimizes ESR. This conformation is most pronounced when the substituent is bulky (i.e. isopropyl, t-butyl, phenyl, etc.). In other words, a large substituent takes up more space thus ESR has a more prominent effect.

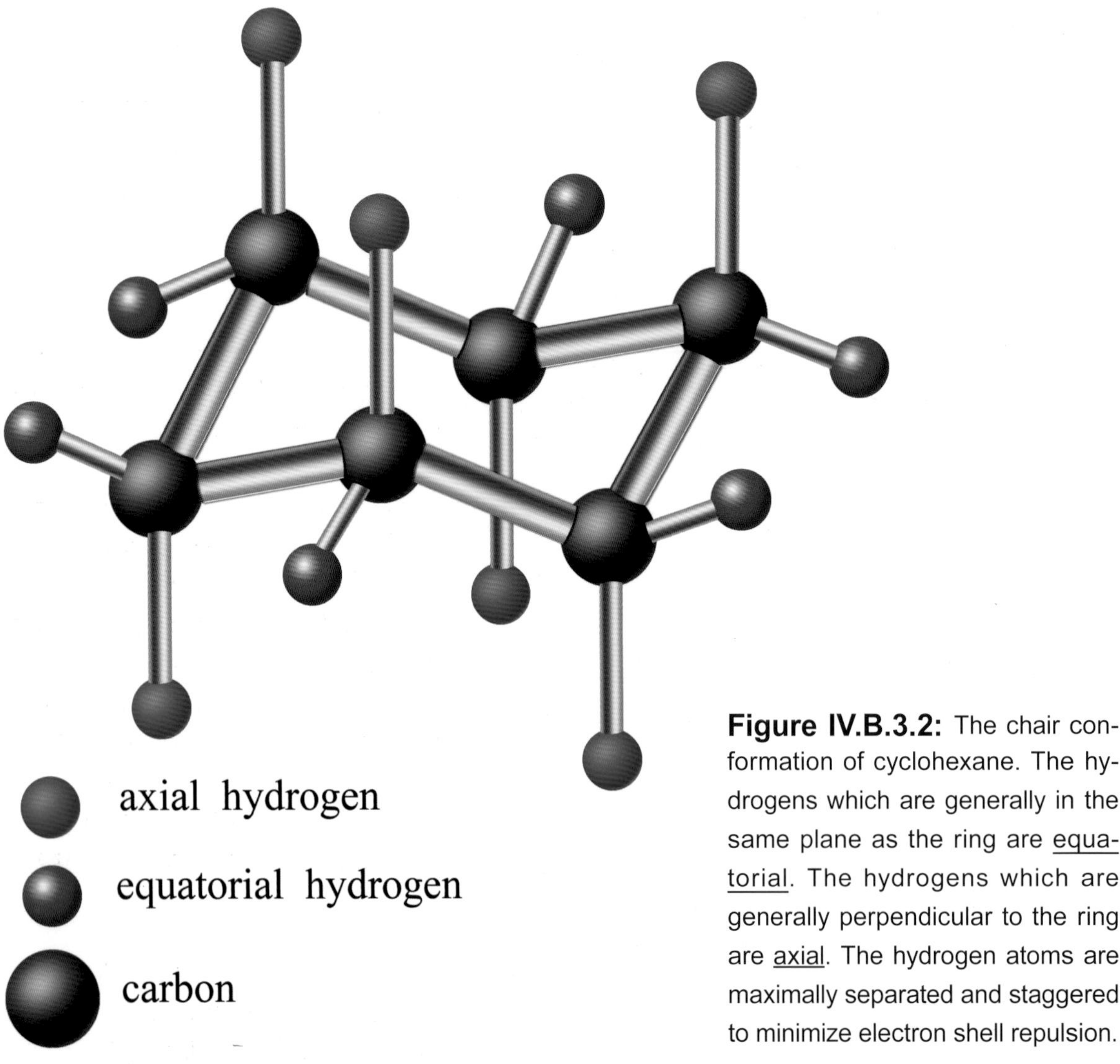

Figure IV.B.3.2: The chair conformation of cyclohexane. The hydrogens which are generally in the same plane as the ring are equatorial. The hydrogens which are generally perpendicular to the ring are axial. The hydrogen atoms are maximally separated and staggered to minimize electron shell repulsion.

3.3.1 A Closer Look at Ring Strain and Conformations of Cycloalkanes

In cycloalkanes, ring strain comes from three factors: (1) angle strain due to bond angle expansion or compression; (2) torsional strain due to the overlapping of adjacent bonds; and (3) steric strain due to the repulsive interactions when atoms approach too close (ESR).

Because this is the source of many test questions, let's review the two types of hydrogen atoms in cyclohexane: those that are perpendicular to the ring are called *axial hydrogens*, and those that are parallel to the plane of the ring are called *equatorial hydrogens*. Each carbon atom has one axial hydrogen atom and one equatorial hydrogen atom. Every ring has two sides, and each side has an alternating axial-equatorial arrangement. The six axial hydrogen bonds are parallel and have an alternating up-down relationship. The six equatorial hydrogen bonds also have an alternating up-down relationship.

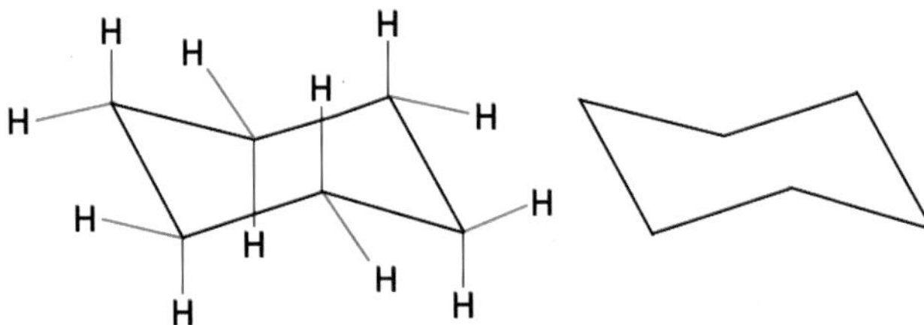

Interconversion of the chair conformations is referred to as *ring flip*, in which each axial and equatorial position becomes interconverted. An axial hydrogen atom in one chair form becomes an equatorial one, and vice versa.

Of course, all conformers between extremes also exist – even if just for a tiny fraction of a second at room temperature. The twist-boat (**C** and **E** in the diagram that follows), the half-chair state (**B**) which is the transition state in the interconversion between the chair (**A**) and twist-boat conformations, and of course, the boat conformer (**D**).

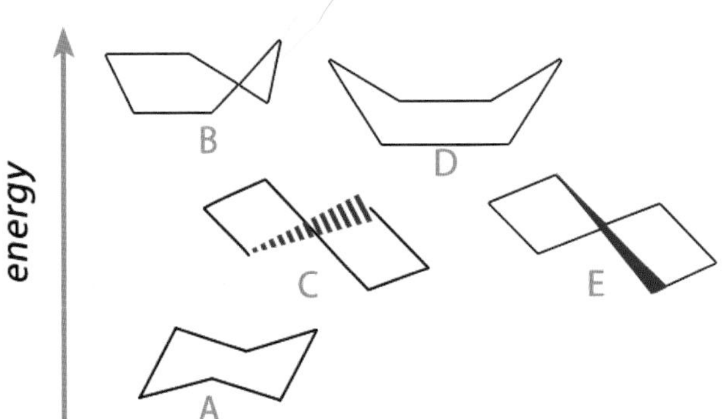

Conformations of mono-substituted cyclohexanes: The two common conformers of a mono-substituted cyclohexane are not equally stable since a substituent is always more stable in an equatorial position than in an axial position. Steric repulsion with other axial substituents (ESR) is present when a substituent is in the axial position, and this is referred to as a *1,3-diaxial interaction*. The axial methyl group on C1 is too close to the axial hydrogens on C3 and C5, resulting in steric strain. Therefore, a bulky substituent can prevent the ring form from adopting certain conformations.

For example, methylcyclohexane has 95% of its conformers with the methyl group at the equatorial position.

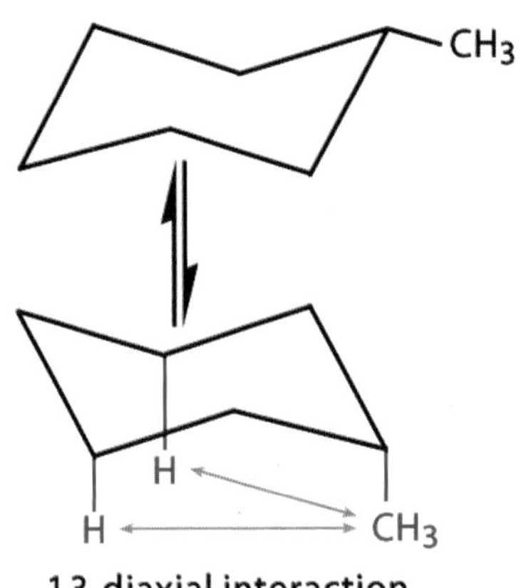

1,3-diaxial interaction

Conformations of di-substituted cyclohexanes: The two common conformers of a di-substituted cyclohexane are more complex since 1,2-dimethylcyclohexane has two isomers: *cis*-1,2-dimethylcyclohexane and *trans*-1,2-dimethylcyclohexane. In the *cis* isomer, both methyl groups are located on the same side of the ring, and the molecule can exist in either of the following two conformations: each has one axial methyl group and one equatorial methyl group. In the *trans* isomer, methyl groups are located on the opposite side of the ring, and the molecule can exist in either of the following two conformations: one conformer has both methyl groups axial and the other conformer has both methyl groups equatorial. However, the conformer on the left side (both axial) is less stable and *trans*-1,2-dimethylcyclohexane will exist almost exclusively in the di-equatorial conformation on the right side.

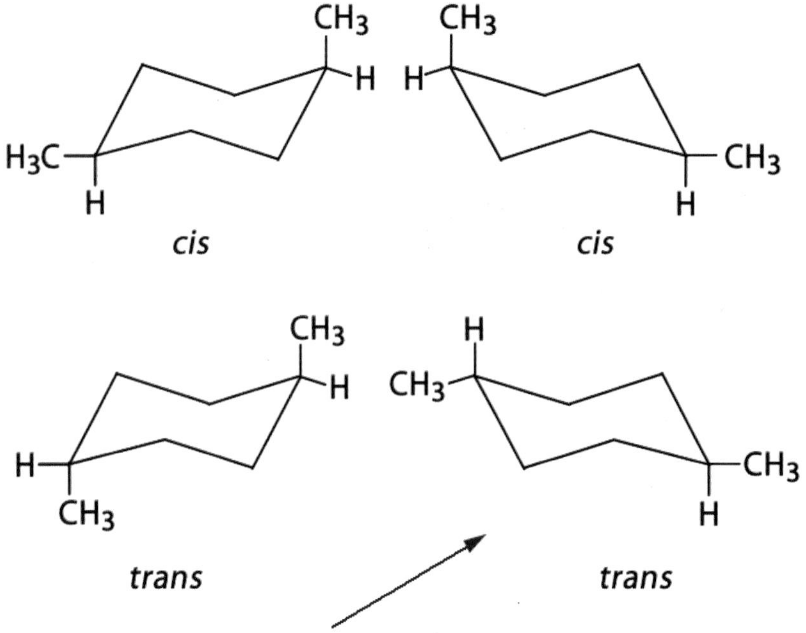

CH_3 CH_3 H H H_3C CH_3 H H

cis *cis*

CH_3 H H CH_3 H CH_3 CH_3 H

trans *trans*

Trans is more stable as it has one conformer with both methyl groups in equatorial positions.

Go online to DAT-prep.com for chapter review Q&A and forum.

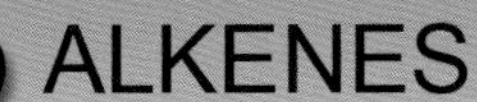

ALKENES

Chapter 4

Memorize	Understand	Importance
* IUPAC nomenclature * Properties and hydrogenation reaction catalysts	* Electrophilic addition, Markovnikoff's rule, oxidation * Concept of nucleophile and electrophile * Markovnikoff and anti-Markovnikoff addition * Mechanisms of reactions	1 to 3 out of the 30 ORG DAT questions are based on content in this chapter (in our estimation). * Note that between 30% and 60% of the questions in DAT Organic Chemistry are based on content from 4 chapters: 1, 2, 5 and 6.

DAT-Prep.com

Introduction

An alkene (a.k.a. olefin) is an unsaturated chemical compound containing at least one carbon-to-carbon double bond.

Additional Resources

Free Online Q&A + Forum

Video: Online or DVD

Flashcards

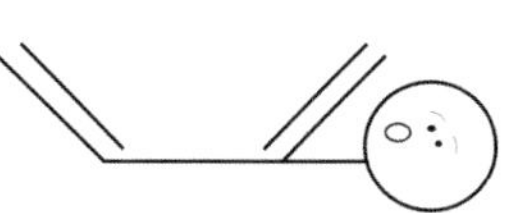

Special Guest

4.1 Description and Nomenclature

Alkenes *(olefins)* are unsaturated hydrocarbon molecules containing carbon-carbon double bonds. Their general formula is C_nH_{2n} for a straight chain molecule; 2 hydrogen (H) atoms are subtracted for each ring. The *functional group* in these molecules is the double bond which determines the chemical properties of alkenes. Double bonds are sp^2 hybridized (*see* ORG 1.2, 1.3). The nomenclature is the same as that for alkanes, except that i) the suffix 'ene' replaces 'ane' and ii) the double bond is (are) numbered in the molecule, trying to get the smallest number for the double bond(s). Always select the longest chain that contains the double bond or the greatest number of double bonds as the parent hydrocarbon. For cycloalkenes, the carbons of the double bond are given the 1– and 2– positions.

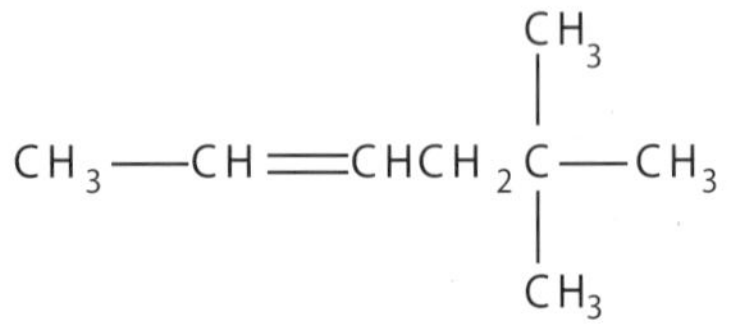

$CH_3—CH=CHCH_2C(CH_3)_2—CH_3$

5,5 - Dimethyl - 2 - hexene

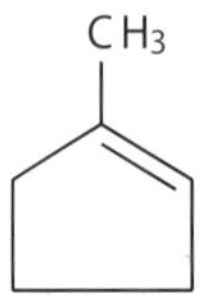

1 - methylcyclopentene

Two frequently encountered groups are sometimes named as if they were substituents.

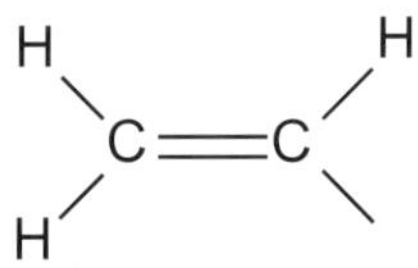

$H_2C=CH—$ or $CH_2=CH—$

the vinyl group

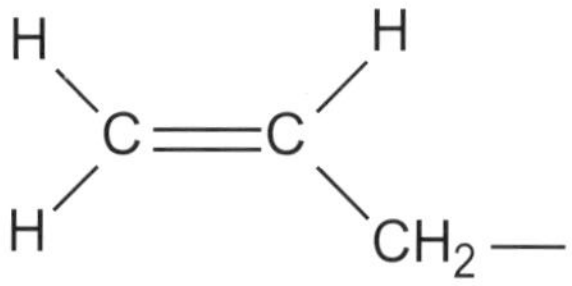

$H_2C=CH—CH_2—$ or $CH_2=CHCH_2—$

the allyl group

Alkenes have similar physical properties to alkanes. *Trans* compounds tend to have higher melting points (due to better symmetry), and lower boiling points (due to less polarity) than its corresponding *cis* isomer. Alkenes, however, due to the nature of the double bond may be polar. The dipole moment is oriented from the electropositive alkyl group toward the electronegative alkene.

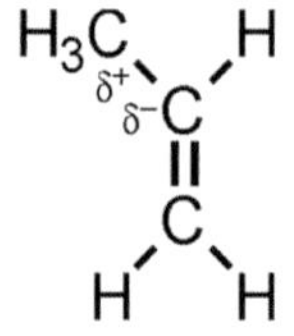

$H_3C(H)C=CH_2$ (δ^+, δ^-)

has a small dipole moment

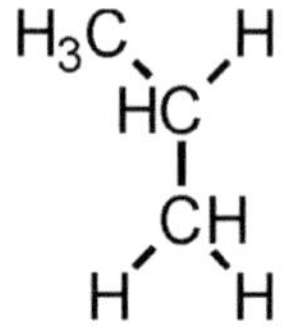

$H_3C(H)HC—CH(H)H$

has no dipole moment

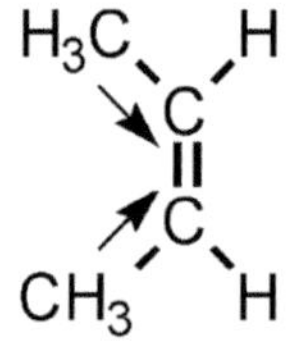

(cis)
small dipole moment

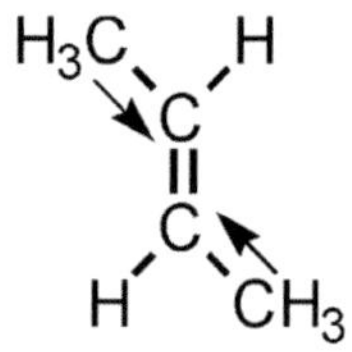

(trans)
no dipole moment

The greater the number of attached alkyl groups (i.e. *the more highly substituted the double bond*), the greater is the alkene's stability. The reason is that alkyl groups are somewhat electron donating, thus they stabilize the double bond.

An alkene with 2 double bonds is a diene, 3 is a triene. A diene with one single bond in between is a conjugated diene. Conjugated dienes are more stable than non-conjugated dienes primarily due to resonance stabilization (see the resonance stabilized conjugated molecule 1,3-butadiene in ORG 1.4). Alkenes, including polyenes (multiple double bonds), can engage in addition reactions (ORG 4.2.1). The notable exceptions include aromatic compounds (conjugated double bonds in a ring; ORG 5.1) which cannot engage in addition reactions which will be discussed in the next chapter.

- Synthesis of Alkenes: The two most common alkene-forming reactions involve elimination reactions of either HX from an alkyl halide or H_2O from alcohol. Dehydrohalogenation occurs by the reaction of an alkyl halide with a strong base. Dehydration occurs by reacting an alcohol with a strong acid.

We will discuss elimination reactions (E1 and E2), which can be used to synthesize alkenes, in the chapter reviewing alcohols (ORG 6.2.4).

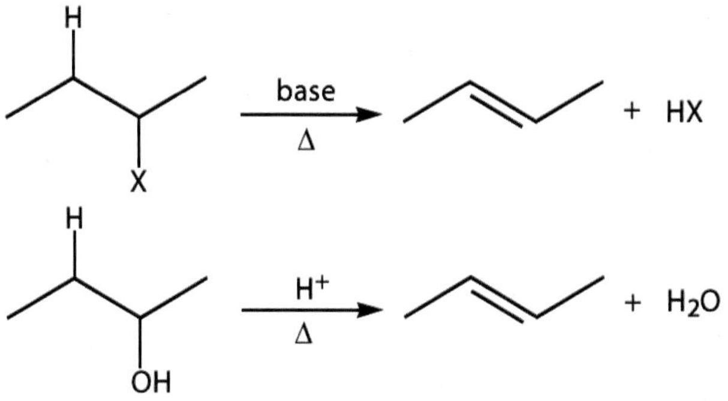

H
X
base
Δ
+ HX

H
OH
H^+
Δ
+ H_2O

Help me!
I'm
DIENE!

4.2 Important Chemical Reactions

4.2.1 Electrophilic Addition

The chemistry of alkenes may be understood in terms of their functional group, the double bond. When electrophiles (*substances which seek electrons*) add to alkenes, carbocations (= *carbonium ions*) are formed. An important electrophile is H^+ (i.e. in HBr, H_2O, etc.). A nucleophile is a molecule with a free pair of electrons, and sometimes a negative charge, that seeks out partially or completely positively charged species (i.e. a carbon nucleus). Some important nucleophiles are OH^- and CN^-.

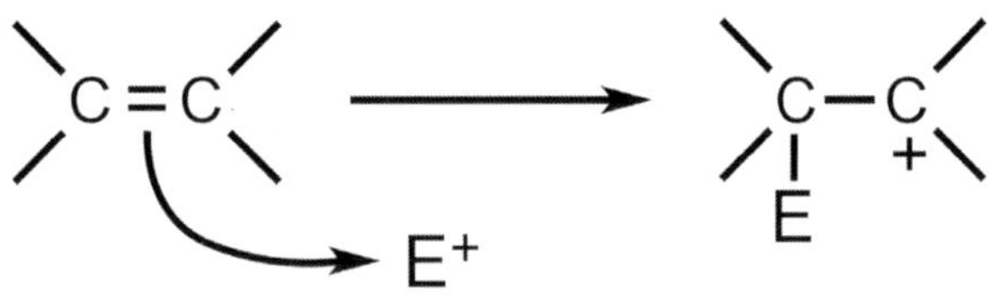

E = electrophile

carbocation (intermediate)

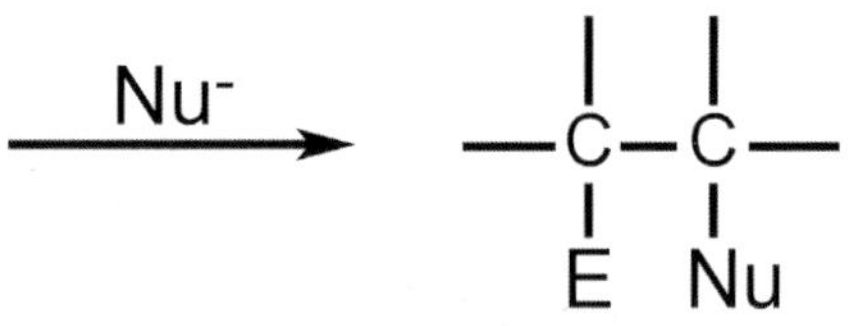

Nu = nucleophile

Note that the carbon-carbon double bond is electron rich (nucleophilic) and can donate a pair of electrons to an electrophile (= "electron loving") during reactions. Electrons from the π bond attack the electrophile. As the π bond is weaker than the σ bond, it can be broken without breaking the σ bond. As a result, the carbon skeleton can remain intact. Electrophilic addition to an unsymmetrically substituted alkene gives the more highly substituted carbocation (i.e. the most stable intermediate). We will soon see that Markovnikoff's rule (or Markovnikov's rule) is a guide to determine the outcome of addition reactions.

Another important property of the double bond is its ability to stabilize carbocations, carbanions or radicals attached to adjacent carbons (*allylic carbons*). Note that all the following are resonance stabilized:

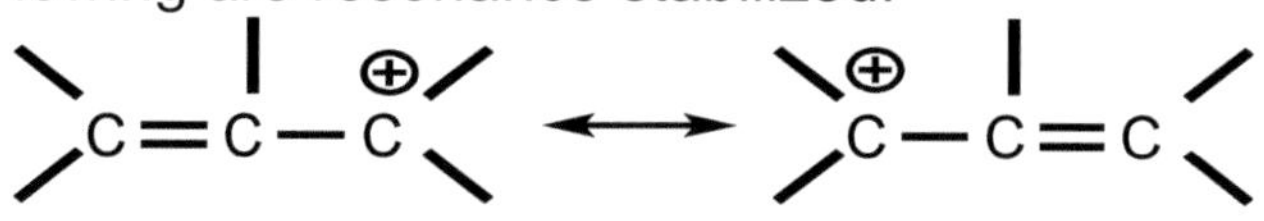

carbocation

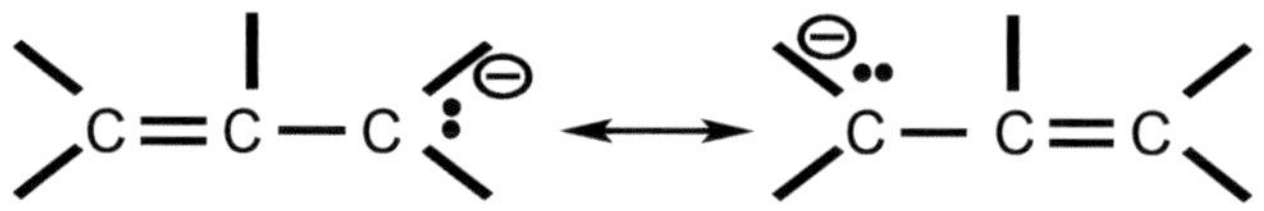

carbanion

carbon radical

The stability of the intermediate carbocation depends on the groups attached to it, which can either stabilize or destabilize it. As well, groups which place a partial or total positive charge adjacent to the carbocation withdraw electrons inductively, by sigma bonds, to destabilize it. More highly substituted carbocations are more stable than less highly substituted ones.

These points are useful in predicting which carbon will become the carbocation, and to which carbon the electrophile and nucleophile will bond. The intermediate carbocation formed must be the most stable. **Markovnikoff's rule** is a result of this, and it states: *the nucleophile will be bonded to the most substituted carbon* (fewest hydrogens attached) *in the product. Equivalently, the electrophile will be bonded to the least sub-*

stituted carbon (most hydrogens attached) *in the product*. An example of this is:

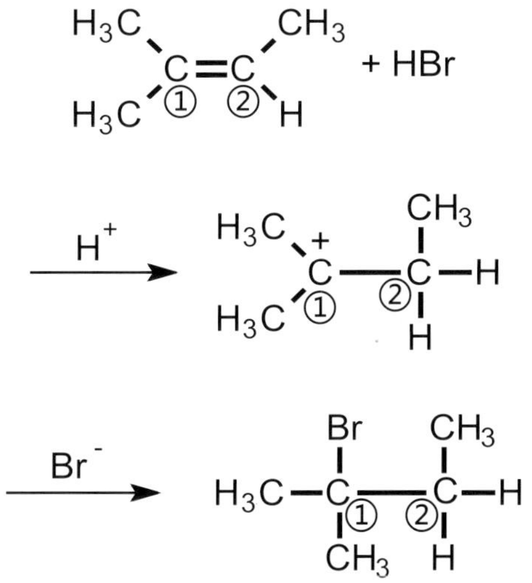

$$(H_3C)_2\overset{①}{C}=\overset{②}{C}H(CH_3) + HBr \xrightarrow{H^+} (H_3C)_2\overset{+}{\underset{①}{C}}-\underset{②}{C}H_2(CH_3) \xrightarrow{Br^-} H_3C-\underset{①}{C}Br(CH_3)-\underset{②}{C}H_2(CH_3)$$

H^+ = electrophile
Br^- = nucleophile
① most substituted carbon
② least substituted carbon
① forms the most stable carbonium ion.

The product, 2-bromo-2-methyl butane, is the more likely or major product (*the Markovnikoff product*). Had the H^+ added to the most substituted carbon (which has a much lower probability of occurrence) the less likely or minor product would be formed (*the anti-Markovnikoff product*). {Memory guide for Markovnikoff's rule: "Hydrogen prefers to add to the carbon in the double bond where most of its friends are" (this works because the least substituted carbon has the most bonds to hydrogen atoms)}

Carbocation intermediate rearrangement: In both *hydride shift* and *alkyl group shift*, H or CH_3 moves to a positively charged carbon, taking its electron pair with it. As a result, a less stable carbocation rearranges to a more stable one (more substituted).

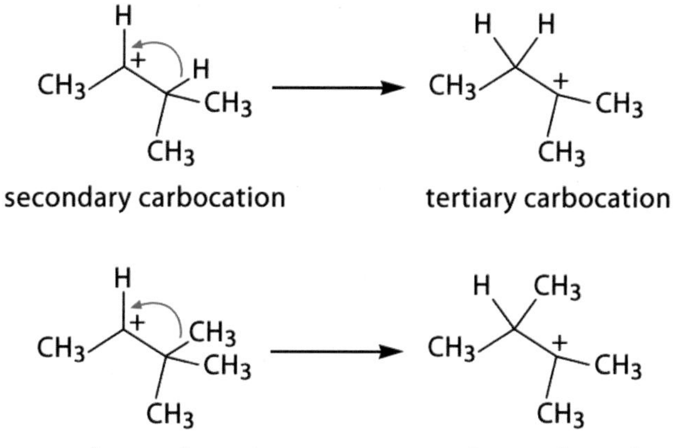

$$CH_3-\overset{+}{C}H-C(H)(CH_3)_2 \longrightarrow CH_3-CH_2-\overset{+}{C}(CH_3)_2$$

secondary carbocation → tertiary carbocation

$$CH_3-\overset{+}{C}H-C(CH_3)_3 \longrightarrow CH_3-CH(CH_3)-\overset{+}{C}(CH_3)_2$$

secondary carbocation → tertiary carbocation

Markovnikoff's rule is true for the ionic conditions presented in the preceding reaction. However, for radical conditions the reverse occurs. Thus *anti-Markovnikoff* products are the major products under free radical conditions.

- Addition of halogens: This is a simple and rapid laboratory diagnostic tool to test for the presence of unsaturation (C=C). Immediate disappearance of the reddish Br_2 color indicates that the sample is an alkene. The general chemical formula of the halogen addition reaction is:

$$C=C + X_2 \rightarrow X-C-C-X$$

The π electron pair of the double bond attacks the bromine, or X_2 molecule, setting up an induced dipole and then displacing the bromide ion. The intermediate forms a cyclic bromonium ion R_2Br , which is then attacked by Br^-, giving the di-bromo addition product.

Since the intermediate is a bromonium ion, the bromide anion can only attack from the opposite side, yielding an anti product.

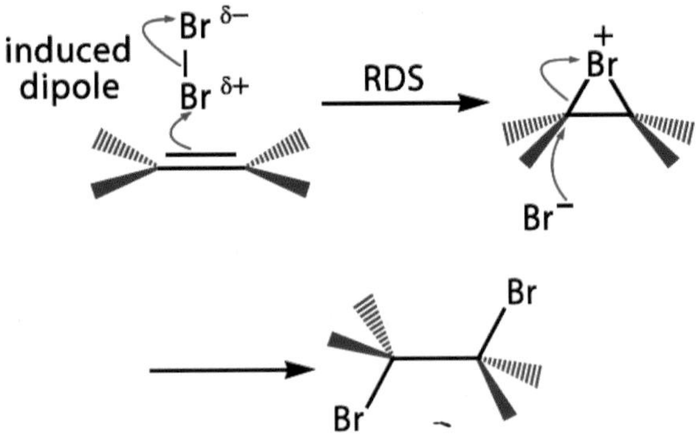

induced dipole $Br^{\delta-}$ / $Br^{\delta+}$ → RDS → Br^+ (bromonium) + Br^- → anti dibromide

RDS = rate determining step (CHM 9.4)

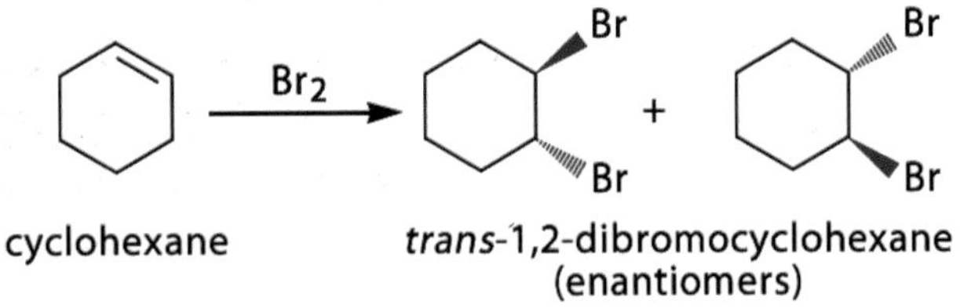

cyclohexane —Br_2→ *trans*-1,2-dibromocyclohexane (enantiomers)

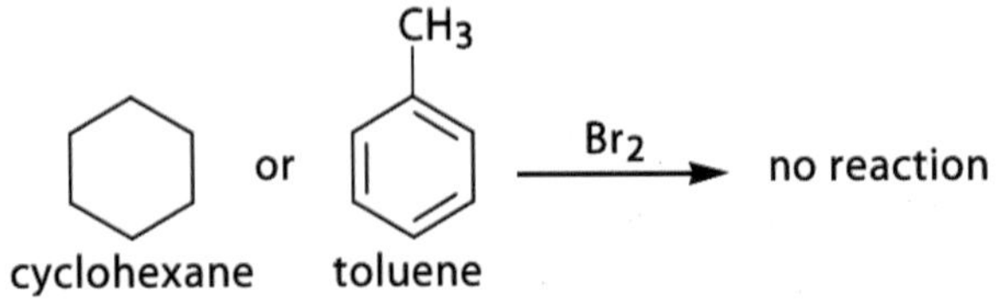

cyclohexane or toluene (CH_3) —Br_2→ no reaction

Halogen addition does not occur in saturated hydrocarbons (i.e. cyclohexane) which lack the electron rich double bond, nor do the reactions occur within an aromatic ring because of the increased stability afforded by conjugation in a ring system due to resonance.

- Halohydrin formation reaction: A halohydrin (or haloalcohol) is a functional group where one carbon atom has a halogen substituent and an adjacent carbon atom has a hydroxyl substituent. This addition, which produces a halohydrin, is done by reacting an alkene with a halogen X_2 in the presence of water. The intermediate forms a cyclic bromonium ion R_2Br . The water molecule competes with the bromide ion as a nucleophile and reacts with the bromonium ion to form the halohydrin. The net effect is the addition of HO-X to the alkene.

In practice, the bromohydrin reaction is carried out using a reagent called NBS. Markovnikoff regiochemistry and anti addition is observed.

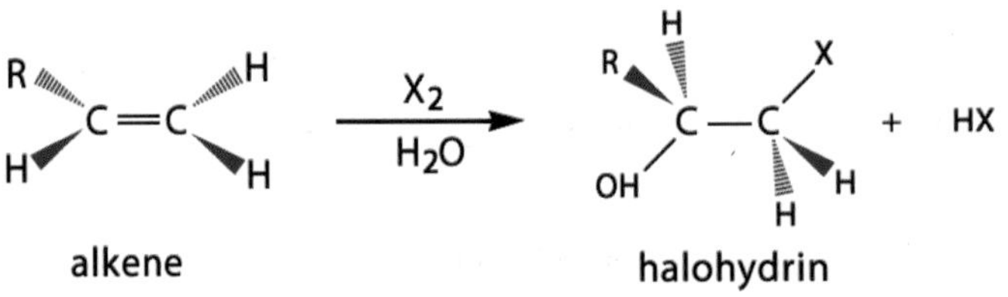

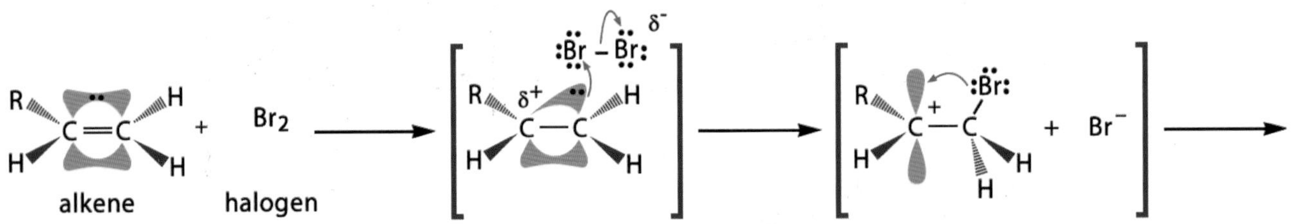

alkene —X_2 / H_2O→ halohydrin + HX

alkene + Br_2 (halogen) → [δ^+ … $:Br-Br:$ δ^-] → [C^+–C–$:Br:$ + Br^-] →

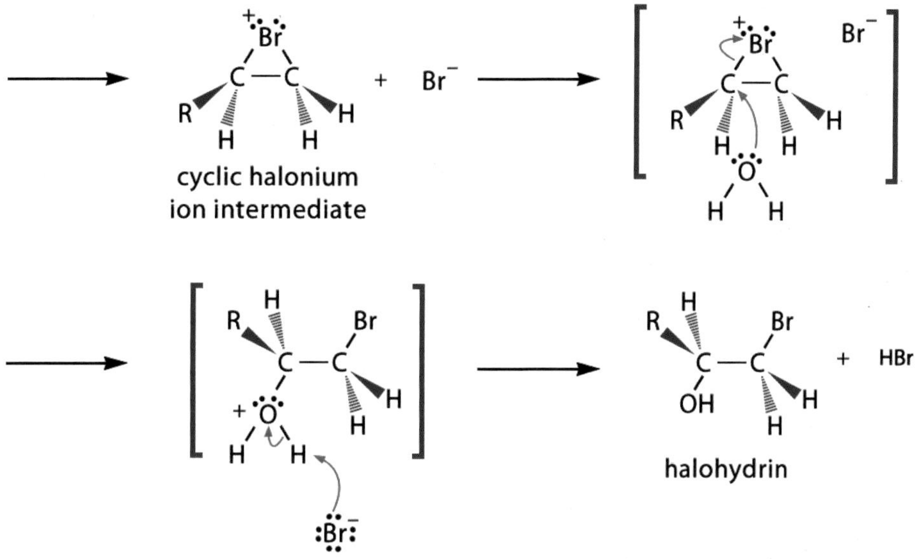

cyclic halonium ion intermediate

halohydrin

• Addition of water by oxymercuration: When an alkene is treated with mercuric acetate $Hg(OAc)_2$, electrophilic addition to the alkene occurs and an alcohol is produced. Instead of forming a bromonium ion as in halohydrin formation, an intermediate mercurinium ion is formed. A nucleophilic attack of the water molecule to the intermediate ion yields the final alcohol product: the hydroxyl group attaches to the more substituted carbon atom. Markovnikoff regiochemistry is observed.

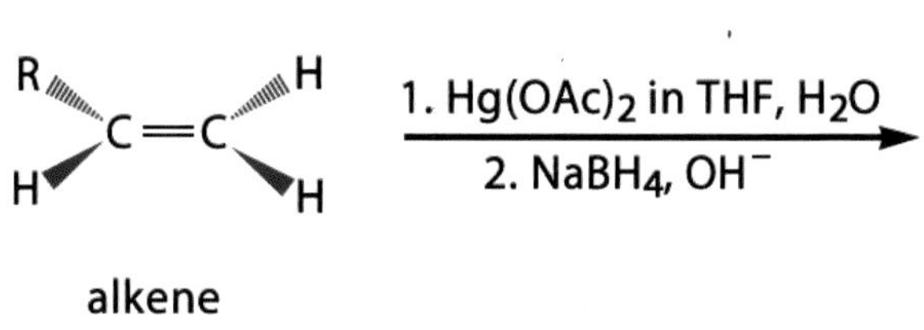

1. $Hg(OAc)_2$ in THF, H_2O
2. $NaBH_4$, OH^-

alkene

alcohol

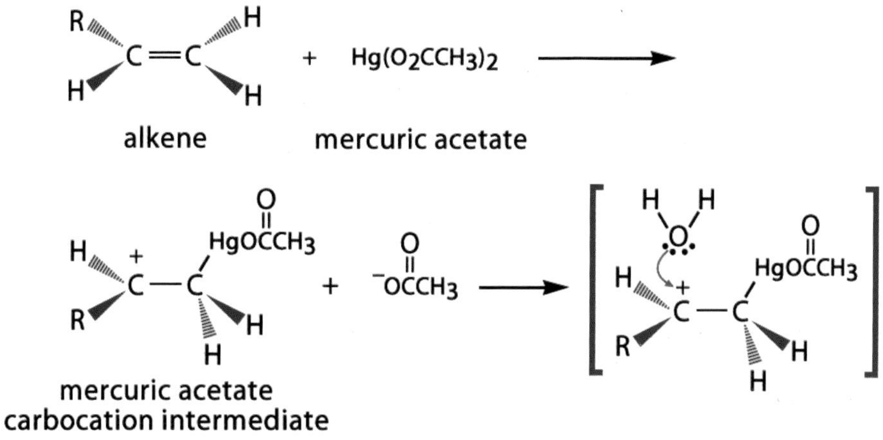

alkene + $Hg(O_2CCH_3)_2$ →

alkene mercuric acetate

mercuric acetate carbocation intermediate

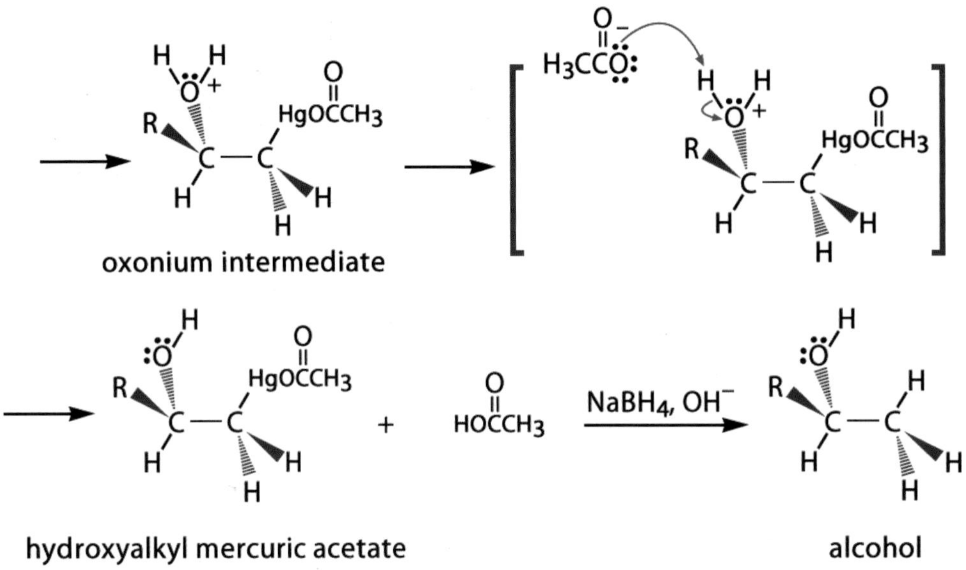

oxonium intermediate

hydroxyalkyl mercuric acetate

NaBH$_4$, OH$^-$

alcohol

• Addition of HX: As we have seen earlier in this section, this reaction occurs via a carbocation intermediate. The halide ion then combines with the carbocation to give an alkyl halide. The proton will add to the less substituted carbon atom, yielding a more substituted (stabilized) carbocation. Markovnikoff regiochemistry is observed. This can be seen in the first two mechanisms shown in this section (ORG 4.2.1).

• Free radical addition of HBr to alkenes: Once a bromine free radical has formed in an initiation step (ORG 3.2.2), it adds to the alkene double bond, yielding an alkyl radical. The regiochemistry of this free radical addition is determined in the first propagation step because, instead of H attacking first in electrophilic addition, the bromine radical adds first to the alkene. Thus anti-Markovnikoff addition is observed.

The stability order of radicals is identical to the stability order of carbocations, tertiary being the most stable and methyl the least.

Notice that the free radical reaction mechanism that follows uses single headed arrows to follow the movement of single electrons, as opposed to the normal arrows that we have seen which follow the movement of electron pairs.

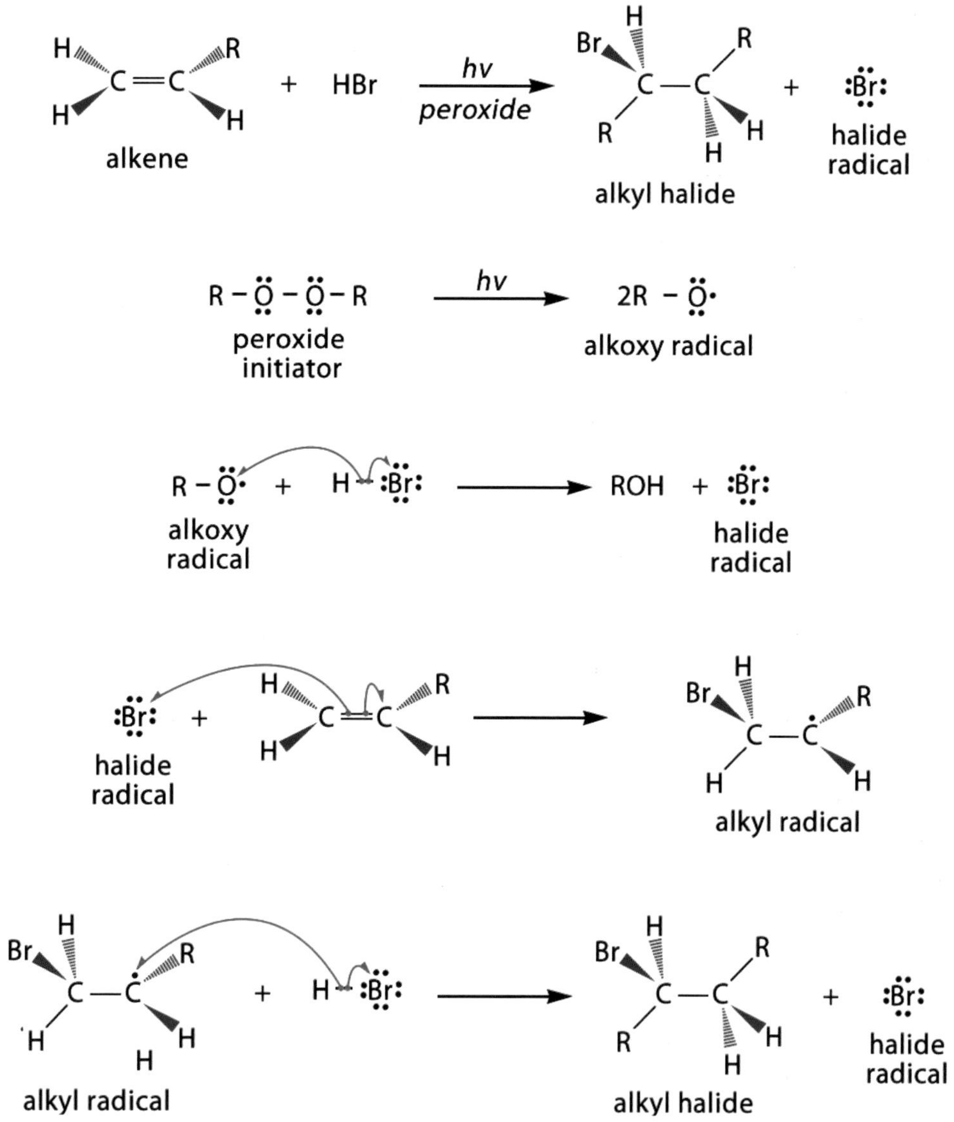

alkene + HBr —(hv, peroxide)→ alkyl halide + halide radical

R–Ö–Ö–R (peroxide initiator) —hv→ 2R–Ö· (alkoxy radical)

R–Ö· (alkoxy radical) + H–:Br: → ROH + :Br: (halide radical)

:Br: (halide radical) + alkene → alkyl radical

alkyl radical + H–:Br: → alkyl halide + :Br: (halide radical)

4.2.2 Oxidation

Alkenes can undergo a variety of reactions in which the carbon-carbon double bond is oxidized. Using potassium permanganate ($KMnO_4$) under mild conditions (*no heat*), or osmium tetroxide (OsO_4), a glycol (= *a dialcohol*) can be produced.

In the following chapters, you will learn how to derive systematic nomenclature (these are names of compounds based on rules as opposed to "common" names often based on tradition). IUPAC (official) nomenclature is usually systematic (i.e. ethane-1,2-diol) but sometimes it is not (i.e. acetic acid). Knowing both the common and the systematic names is the safest way to approach the DAT.

The first reaction that follows is the oxidation of ethene (= ethylene) under mild conditions and the second is the oxidation of 2-butene under abrasive conditions.

$$CH_2 = CH_2 + KMnO_4 \xrightarrow[OH^-]{Cold} \underset{OH}{CH_2} - \underset{OH}{CH_2}$$

Ethylene glycol
(1,2-ethanediol or
ethane-1,2-diol)

Using $KMnO_4$ under more abrasive conditions leads to an oxidative cleavage of the double bond:

$$CH_3CH = CHCH_3 \xrightarrow[heat]{KMnO_4,\ OH^-}$$

$$2CH_3C(=O)O^- \xrightarrow{H^+} 2CH_3C(=O)OH$$

Acetate ion (ethanoate ion) — Acetic acid (ethanoic acid)

Specifically, cold dilute $KMnO_4$ produces 1,2-diols with the syn orientation. Hot, basic $KMnO_4$ leads to oxidative cleavage of the double bonds with the double bond being replaced with a C=O bond and an O atom added to each H atom.

$$CH_3 - CH = CH_2 \xrightarrow{KMnO_4} CH_3 - C(=O)OH + CO_2$$

acetic acid

$$CH_3 - CH = C(CH_3)_2 \xrightarrow{KMnO_4} CH_3 - C(=O)OH + O = C(CH_3)_2$$

acetic acid — acetone

$$CH_2 = CH - CH = CH_2 \xrightarrow{KMnO_4} CO_2 \text{ only}$$

Ozone (O_3) reacts vigorously with alkenes. The reaction (= *ozonolysis*) leads to an oxidative cleavage of the double bond which can produce a ketone and an aldehyde:

$$CH_3C(CH_3) = CHCH_3 \xrightarrow[(2)\ Zn,\ H_2O]{(1)\ O_3}$$

2-Methyl-2-butene

$$CH_3C(CH_3) = O + CH_3CH(=O)$$

Acetone (propanone) — Acetaldehyde (ethanal)

Note that the second step in the reaction uses a reducing agent such as zinc metal. If the starting alkene has a tetra-substituted double bond (i.e. 4 R groups), two ketones will be formed. If it has a tri-substituted double bond, a ketone and an aldehyde will be formed as in the reaction shown. If it has a di-substituted double bond, two aldehydes will be formed.

The hydroboration–oxidation reaction is a two-step organic reaction that converts an alkene into an alcohol by the addition of water across the double bond. The hydrogen and hydroxyl group are added in a syn addition leading to *cis* stereochemistry. Hydroboration–oxidation is an anti-Markovnikoff reaction since the hydroxyl group (not the hydrogen) attaches to the less substituted carbon.

alkene — BH_3 / THF → ^{-}OH / H_2O_2 → alcohol

alkene — BH_3 / THF → [transition state: H---B(H)–H across C=C, δ^- on H, δ^+ on C] →

alkylborane — ^{-}OH / H_2O_2 → alcohol

• Epoxide Formation: Alkenes can be oxidized with peroxycarboxylic acids (i.e. CH_3CO_3H or mCPBA). The product is an oxirane (discussed in ORG 10.1.1, ethers).

$R'''CO_3H$

4.2.3 Hydrogenation

Alkenes react with hydrogen in the presence of a variety of metal catalysts (i.e. Ni – nickel, Pd – palladium, Pt – platinum). The reaction that occurs is an *addition* reaction since one atom of hydrogen adds to each carbon of the double bond (= *hydrogenation*). Both hydrogens add to the double bond from the same metal catalyst surface, thus syn addition is observed. Since there are two phases present in the process of hydrogenation (the hydrogen and the metal catalyst), the process is referred to as a heterogenous catalysis.

A carbon with multiple bonds is not bonded to the maximum number of atoms that potentially that carbon could possess. Thus it is *unsaturated.* Alkanes, which can be formed by hydrogenation, are *saturated* since each carbon is bonded to the maximum number of atoms it could possess (= *four*). Thus hydrogenation is sometimes called the process of saturation.

$$CH_3CH = CH_2 + H_2 \longrightarrow CH_3CH_2 - CH_3$$

Alkenes are much more reactive than other functional groups towards hydrogenation. As a result, other functional groups such as ketones, aldehydes, esters and nitriles are usually unchanged during the alkene hydrogenation process.

4.2.4 The Diels–Alder Reaction

The Diels–Alder reaction is a cycloaddition reaction between a conjugated diene and a substituted alkene (= the dienophile) to form a substituted cyclohexene system.

Diene + Dienophile = Cyclohexene

All Diels-Alder reactions have four common features: (1) the reaction is initiated by heat; (2) the reaction forms new six-membered rings; (3) three π bonds break and two new C-C σ bonds and one new C-C π bond are formed; (4) all bonds break and form in a single step.

The Diels Alder diene must have the two double bonds on the same side of the single bond in one of the structures, which is called the s-*cis* conformation (s-*cis*: *cis* with respect to the single bond). If double bonds are on the opposite sides of the single bond in the Lewis structure, this is called the s-*trans* conformation (s-*trans*: *trans* with respect to the single bond).

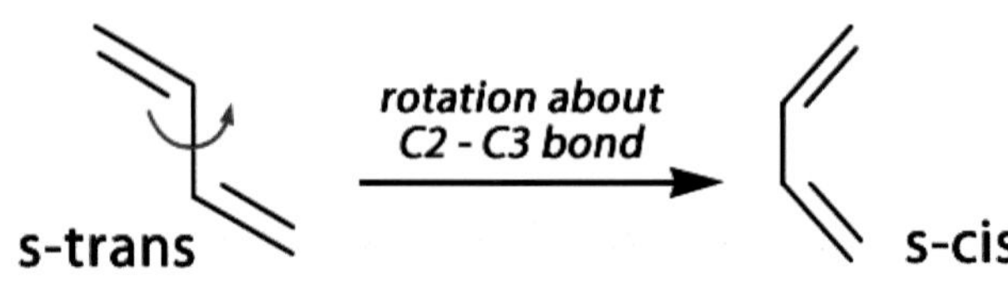

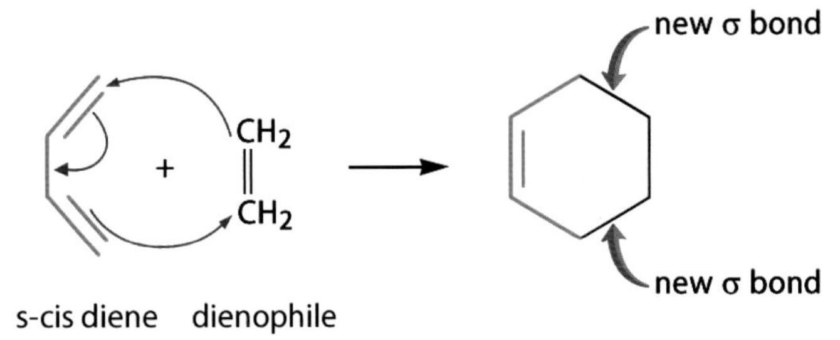

new σ bond

CH_2 CH_2

new σ bond

s-cis diene dienophile

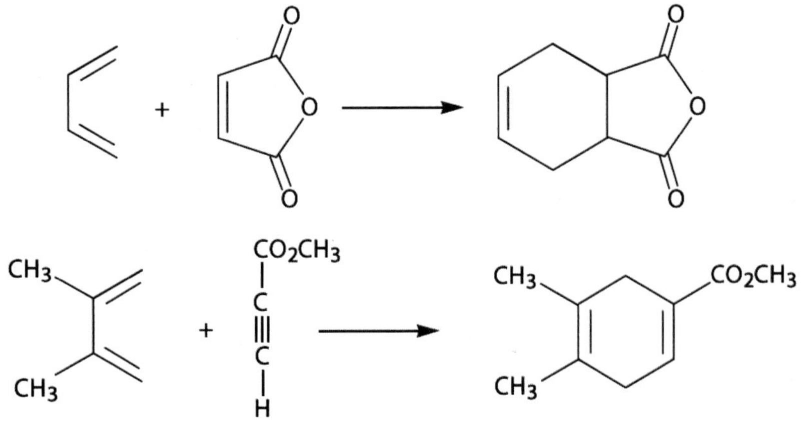

CH_3 CH_3 CO_2CH_3 C C H

CH_3 CH_3 CO_2CH_3

The Diels-Alder reaction is useful because it sometimes creates stereocenters, it always forms a ring, and the reaction is stereospecific (i.e. the reaction mechanism dictates the stereoisomers). For example, a *cis* dienophile generates a ring with *cis* substitution, while a *trans* dienophile generates a ring with *trans* substitution.

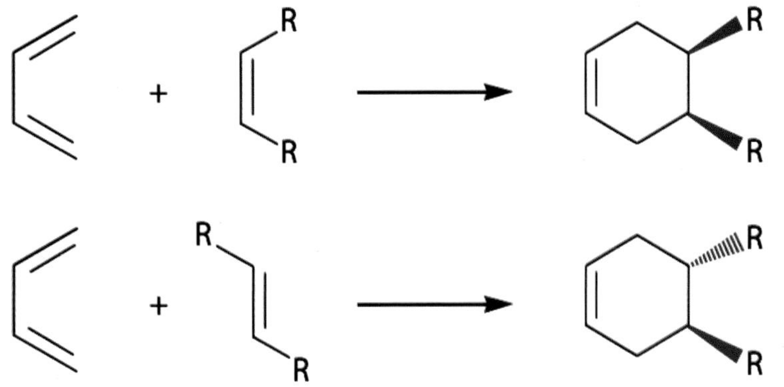

R R R R

R R R R

Diels-Alder reactions are reversible (= "Retro-Diels-Alder").

4.2.5 Resonance Revisited

General Chemistry section 3.2 and Organic Chemistry section 1.4 are important to review before you move on to the next chapter on Aromatics. Many exam questions rely on your understanding of resonance and how it affects stability and reactions. It is helpful to remember that the only difference between different resonance forms is the placement of π or non-bonding electrons. The atoms themselves do not change positions, create new bonds nor are they "resonating" back and forth. The resonance hybrid with its electrons delocalized is more stable than any single resonance form. The greater the numbers of authentic resonance forms possible, the more stable the molecule.

4.3 Alkynes

Alkynes are unsaturated hydrocarbon molecules containing carbon-carbon triple bonds. The nomenclature is the same as that for alkenes, except that the suffix 'yne' replaces 'ene'. Alkynes have a higher boiling point than alkenes or alkanes. Internal alkynes, where the triple bond is in the middle of the compound, boil at higher temperatures than terminal alkynes. Terminal alkynes are relatively acidic.

Basic reactions such as reduction, electrophilic addition, free radical addition and hydroboration proceed in a similar manner to alkenes. Oxidation also follows the same rules and uses the same reactants and catalysts. However, unlike alkenes, alkynes can be partially hydrogenated yielding alkenes with just one equivalent of H_2. The reaction with palladium in Lindlar's catalyst produces the *cis* alkene while sodium or lithium in liquid ammonia will produce the *trans* alkene via a free radical mechanism.

Lindlar, H_2 → H, H (cis alkene)

Lindlar, H_2 → H, H (cis alkene)

$R-C\equiv C-R_1 \xrightarrow{Li/NH_3}$ H, R_1, C = C, R, H

Go online to DAT-prep.com for chapter review Q&A and forum.

AROMATICS

Chapter 5

Memorize

IUPAC nomenclature
Hückel's rule for identifying aromatic compounds

Understand

* Activating and deactivating groups
* Importance of resonance
* Substituent effects on the ring

Importance

2 to 4 out of the 30 ORG

DAT questions are based on content in this chapter (in our estimation).
* Note that between 30% and 60% of the questions in DAT Organic Chemistry are based on content from 4 chapters: 1, 2, 5 and 6.

Introduction

Aromatics are cyclic compounds with unusual stability due to cyclic delocalization and resonance.

Additional Resources

Free Online Q&A + Forum

Video: Online or DVD

Flashcards

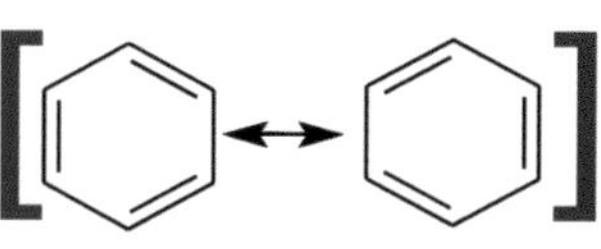

Special Guest

5.1 Description and Nomenclature

Aromatic compounds are cyclic and have their π electrons delocalized over the entire ring and are thus stabilized by π-electron delocalization. Benzene is the simplest of all the aromatic hydrocarbons. The term *aromatic* has historical significance in that many well known fragrant compounds were found to be derivatives of benzene. Although at present, it is known that not all benzene derivatives have fragrance, the term remains in use today to describe benzene derivatives and related compounds.

Benzene is known to have only one type of carbon-carbon bond, with a bond length of ≈ 1.4 Å (angstroms, 10^{-10}m) somewhere between that of a single and double bond. Benzene is a hexagonal, flat symmetrical molecule. All C-C-C bond angles are 120° and all C-C bonds are of equal length - a value between a normal single and double bond length; all six carbon atoms are sp^2 hybridized; and, all carbons have a p orbital perpendicular to the benzene ring, leading to six π electrons delocalized around the ring. The benzene molecule may thus be represented by two different resonance structures, showing it to be the average of the two:

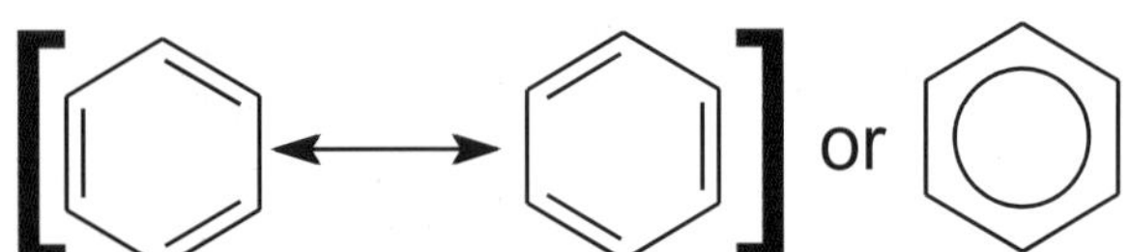

Many monosubstituted benzenes have common names by which they are known. Others are named by substituents attached to the aromatic ring. Some of these are:

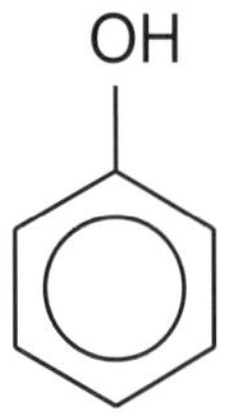

OH — phenol; CH_3 — toluene; NH_2 — aniline

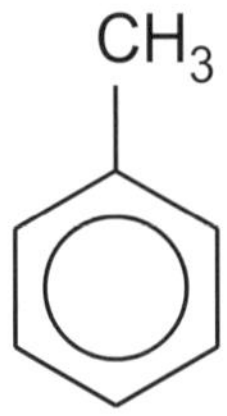

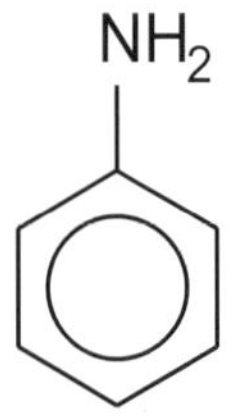

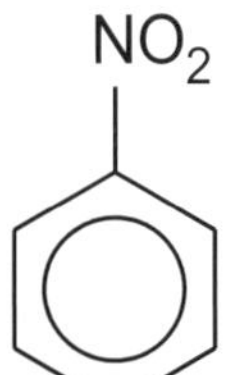

NO_2 — nitrobenzene; CO_2H — benzoic acid

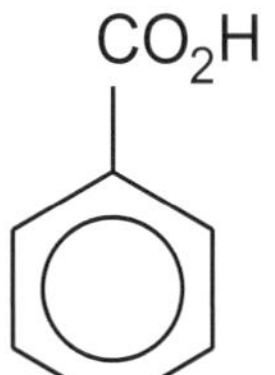

Disubstituted benzenes are named as derivatives of their primary substituents. In this case, either the usual numbering or the ortho-meta-para system may be used. Ortho (*o*) substituents are at the 2nd position from the primary substituent; meta (*m*) substituents are at the 3rd position; para (*p*) substituents are at the 4th position. If there are more than two substituents on the aromatic ring, the numbering system is used. Some examples are:

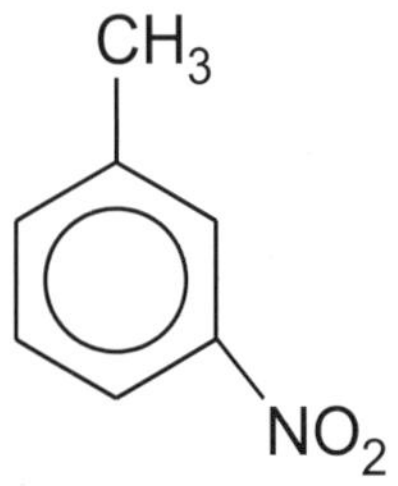

CH_3, NO_2 — m - Nitrotoluene

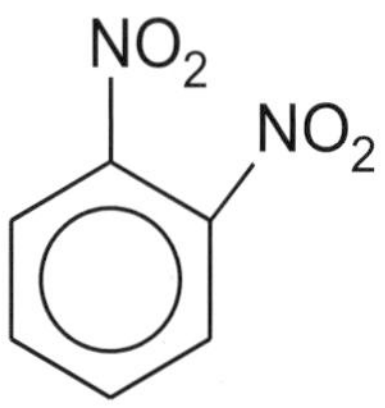

NO_2, NO_2 — o - Dinitrobenzene

NH_2 CH_3

o - Methylaniline
o - Aminotoluene

CO_2H NO_2 OH

3 - nitro - 4 - hydroxybenzoic acid

When benzene is a substituent, it is called a *phenyl or aryl group*. The shorthand for phenyl is Ph. Toluene without a hydrogen on the methyl substituent is called a *benzyl group.*

CH_2

phenyl group benzyl group

Benzene undergoes substitution reactions that retain the cyclic conjugation as opposed to electrophilic addition reactions.

5.1.1 Hückel's Rule

If a compound does not meet all the following criteria, it is likely not aromatic.

1. The molecule is cyclic.
2. The molecule is planar.
3. The molecule is fully conjugated (i.e. p orbitals at every atom in the ring; ORG 1.4).
4. The molecule has 4n + 2 π electrons.

If rules 1., 2. and/or 3. are broken, then the molecule is non-aromatic. If rule 4. is broken then the molecule is antiaromatic.

Notice that the number of π delocalized electrons must be even but NOT a multiple of 4. So 4n + 2 number of π electrons, where n = 0, 1, 2, 3, and so on, is known as Hückel's Rule. Thus the number of pi electrons can be 2, 6, 10, etc. Of course, benzene is aromatic (6 electrons, from 3 double bonds), but cyclobutadiene is not, since the number of π delocalized electrons is 4. Note that a cyclic molecule with conjugated double bonds in a monocyclic (= 1 ring) hydrocarbon is called an annulene. So cyclobutadiene can be called [4] annulene.

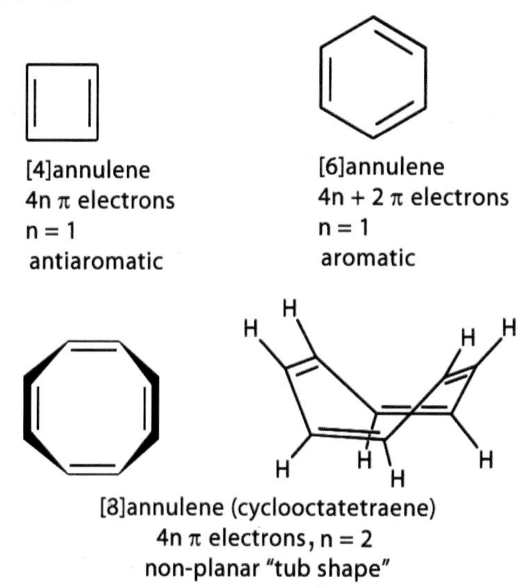

The number of p orbitals and the number of π electrons can be different, which means, whether a molecule is neutral, a cation or an anion, it can be aromatic. Note that aliphatic describes all compounds that are aromatic. A cyclic compound containing only 4n electrons is said to be anti-aromatic.

- Cyclopentadienide anion:

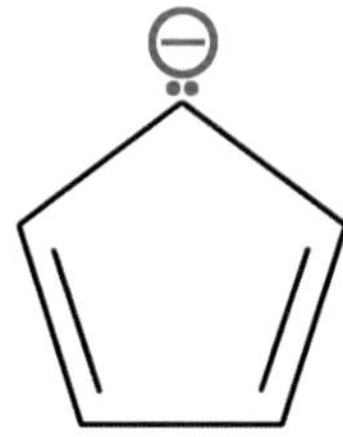

Because of the lone pair, there are 6 π electrons, which meets Hückel's number, so it is aromatic. Thus you can see that if an electron pair is added, or subtracted, a molecule can then become aromatic by fulfilling Hückel's rule. Therefore, if 2 electrons are added to [8]annalene, it will then become a more stable molecule. Specifically, the cyclooctatetraenide dianion ($C_8H_8^{2-}$) is aromatic (thus it has increased stability), and planar, like the cyclopentadienide anion, and both fulfill Hückel's rule.

- Cycloheptatrienyl cation:

CH = CH, HC, CH, CH, CH, CH_2 → CH = CH, HC, CH, CH, CH, CH^+

sp^3 → sp^2 (empty p orbital)

6 π electrons with conjugation through resonance because of the cation, meets Hückel's number, so it is aromatic.

Heterocyclic compounds can be aromatic as well.

- Pyridine:

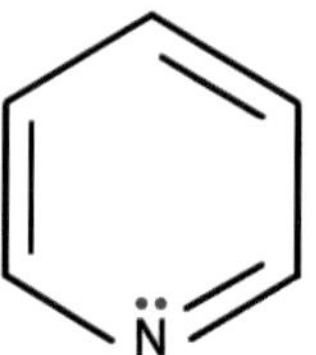

Each sp^2 hybridized carbon atom has a p orbital and contains one π electron. The nitrogen atom is also sp^2 hybridized and has one electron in the p orbital, bringing the total to six π electrons. The nitrogen nonbonding electron pair is in a sp^2 orbital perpendicular to other p orbitals and is not involved with the π system. Thus pyridine is aromatic.

- Pyrrole:

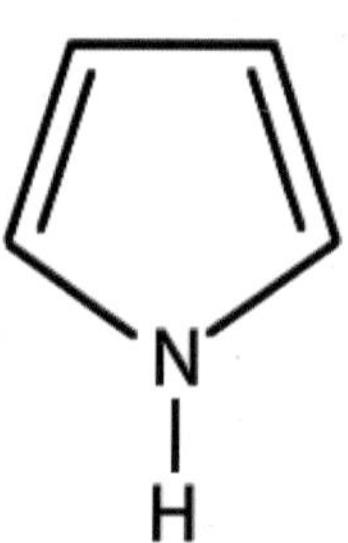

Each sp^2 hybridized carbon atom has a p orbital and contains one π electron. The nitrogen atom is also sp^2 hybridized with its nonbonding electron pair sitting in the p orbital, bringing the total to six π electrons. Thus pyrrole is aromatic.

5.2 Electrophilic Aromatic Substitution

One important reaction of aromatic compounds is known as electrophilic aromatic substitution, which occurs with electrophilic reagents. The reaction is similar to a S_N1 mechanism in that an addition leads to a rearrangement which produces a substitution. However, in this case it is the electrophile (*not a nucleophile*) which substitutes for an atom in the original molecule. The reaction may be summarized:

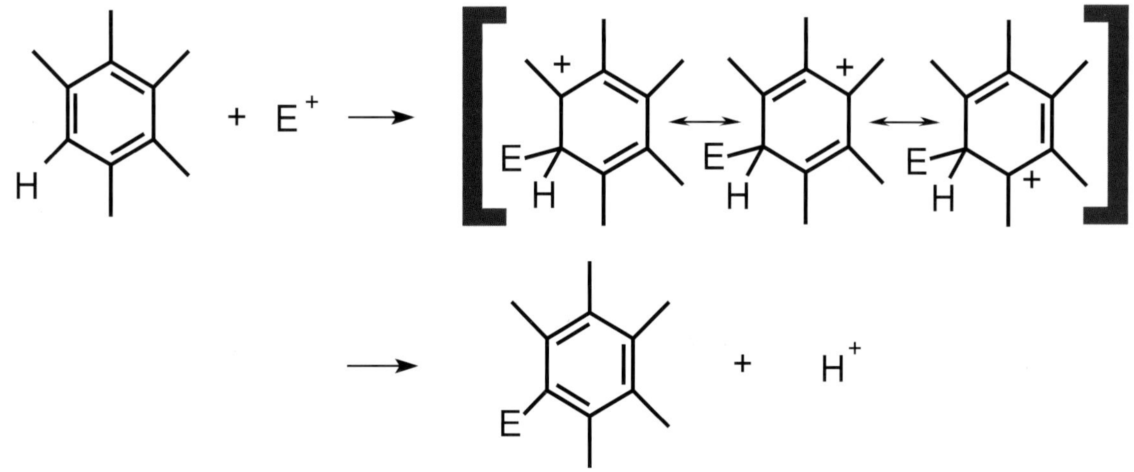

Note that the intermediate positive charge is stabilized by resonance.

It is important to understand that the electrophile used in electrophilic aromatic substitution must always be a powerful electrophile. After all, the resonance stabilized aromatic ring is resistant to many types of routine chemical reactions (i.e. oxidation with $KMnO_4$ – ORG 4.2.2, electrophilic addition with acid - ORG 4.2.1, and hydrogenation - ORG 4.2.3). Remembering that Br, a halide, is already very electronegative (CHM 2.3), Br^+ is an example of a powerful electrophile. In a reaction called bromination, $Br_2/FeBr_3$ is used to generate the Br^+ species which adds to the aromatic ring. Similar reactions are performed to "juice up" other potential substituents (i.e. alkyl, acyl, iodine, etc.) to become powerful electrophiles to add to the aromatic ring.

- Aromatic halogenation: The benzene ring with its 6 π electrons in a conjugated system acts as an electron nucleophile (electron donor) in most chemical reactions. It reacts with bromine, chlorine or iodine to produce mono-substituted products. Fluorine is too reactive and tends to produce multi-substituted products. Therefore, the electrophilic substitution reaction is characteristic of aromaticity and can be used as a diagnostic tool to test the presence of an aromatic ring.

$$C_6H_6 + X_2 \xrightarrow[\text{or } FeX_3]{Fe} C_6H_5X + HX$$

benzene | halogen (X = Cl or Br) | halobenzene | hydrogen halide

• Aromatic nitration: The aromatic ring can be nitrated when reacted with a mixture of nitric and sulfuric acid. The benzene ring reacts with the electrophile in this reaction, the nitronium ion NO_2^+, yielding a carbocation intermediate in a similar way as the aromatic halogenation reaction.

$$C_6H_6 + HNO_3 \xrightarrow[50\ ^\circ C]{H_2SO_4 \text{ catalyst}} C_6H_5NO_2$$

• Aromatic sulfonation: Aromatic rings can react with a mixture of sulfuric acid and sulfur trioxide (H_2SO_4/SO_3) to form sulfonic acid. The electrophile in this reaction is either HSO_3 or SO_3.

$$C_6H_6 \xrightarrow[-H_2O]{H_2SO_4/SO_3} C_6H_5SO_3H$$

• Friedel-Crafts alkylation: This is an electrophilic aromatic substitution in which the benzene ring is alkylated when it reacts with an alkyl halide. The benzene ring attacks the alkyl cation electrophile, yielding an alkyl-substituted benzene product.

There are several limitations to this reaction:

1. The reaction does not proceed on an aromatic ring that has a strong deactivating substituent group.

2. Because the product is attacked even faster by alkyl carbocations than the starting material, poly-alkylation is often observed.

3. Skeletal rearrangement of the alkyl group sometimes occurs. A hydride shift or an alkyl shift may produce a more stable carbocation.

$$R-Cl + FeCl_3 \longrightarrow R^+ + FeCl_4^-$$

$$C_6H_6 + R^+ \longrightarrow [C_6H_6R]^+ \xrightarrow[\text{catalyst regenerated}]{-HCl} C_6H_5R$$

• Friedel-Crafts acylation: An electrophilic aromatic substitution in which the benzene ring is acylated when an acyl group is introduced to the ring. The mechanism is similar to that of Friedel-Crafts alkylation. The electrophile is an acyl cation generated by the reaction between the acyl halide and $AlCl_3$. Because the product is less reactive than the starting material, only mono-substitution is observed.

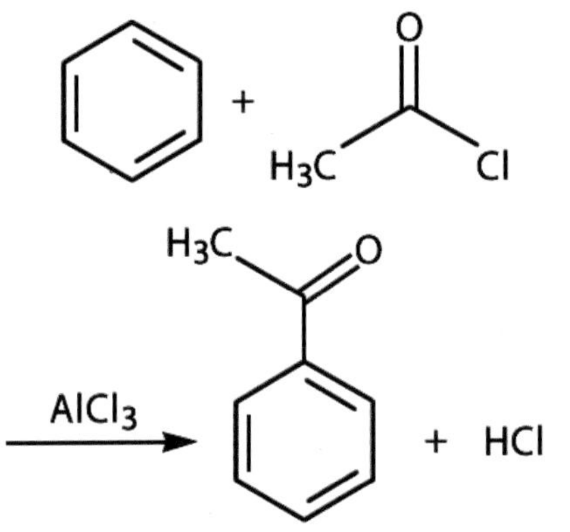

+ H_3C O Cl
H_3C O
$AlCl_3$ + HCl

When groups are attached to the aromatic ring, the intermediate charge delocalization is affected. Thus nature of first substituent on the ring determines the position of the second substituent. Substituents can be classified into three classes: ortho-para (o-p) directing activators, ortho-para directing deactivators, and meta-directing deactivators. As implied, these groups indicate where most of the electrophile will end up in the reaction.

5.2.1 O-P Directors

If a substituted benzene reacts more rapidly than a benzene alone, the substituent group is said to be an activating group. Activating groups can *donate* electrons to the ring. Thus the ring is more attractive to an electrophile. All activating groups are o/p directors. Some examples are $-OH$, $-NH_2$, $-OR$, $-NR_2$, -OCOR and alkyl groups.

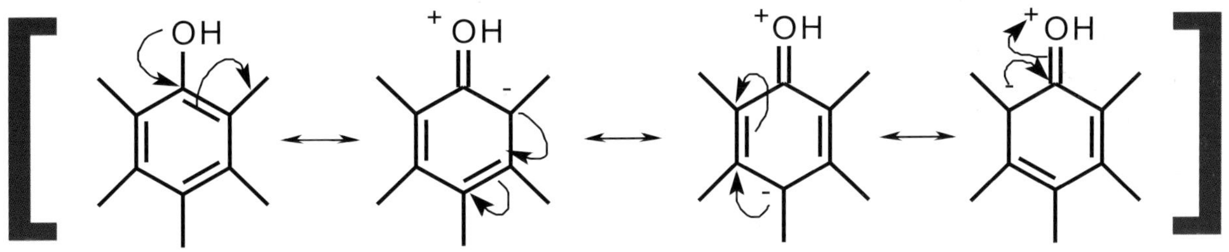

Note that the partial electron density (δ^-) is at the ortho and para positions, so the electrophile favors attack at these positions. Good stabilization results with a substituent at the ortho or para positions:

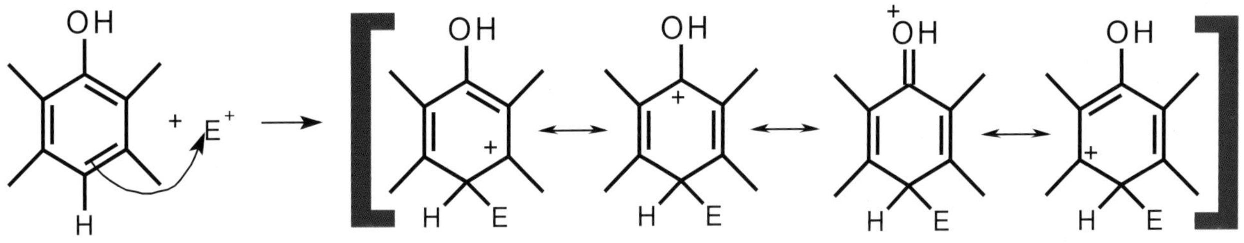

When there is a substituent at the meta position, the –OH can no longer help to delocalize the positive charge, so the o-p positions are favored over the meta:

Note that even though the substituents are o-p directors, probability suggests that there will still be a small percentage of the electrophile that will add at the meta position.

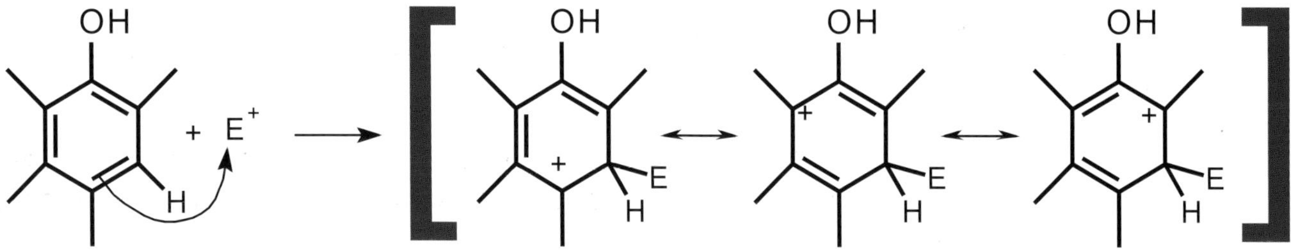

5.2.2 Meta Directors

If a substituted benzene reacts more slowly than the benzene alone, the substituent group is said to be a deactivating group. Deactivating groups can *withdraw* electrons from the ring. Thus the ring is less attractive to an electrophile. All deactivating groups are meta directors, with the exception of the weakly deactivating halides which are o–p directors (-F, -Cl, -Br, -I). Some examples of meta directors are $-NO_2$, $-SO_2$, –CN, $-SO_3H$, -COOH, -COOR, -COR, CHO.

Without any substituents, the partial positive charge density (δ^+) will be at the o–p positions. Thus the electrophile avoids the positive charge and favors attack at the meta position:

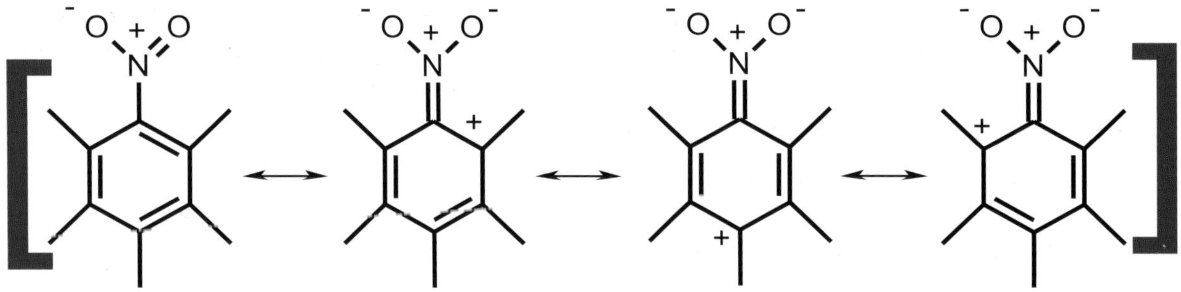

If you are seeking another way to learn, consider logging into your DAT-prep.com account and clicking on Videos to choose the Aromatic Chemistry videos.

With a substituent at the meta position:

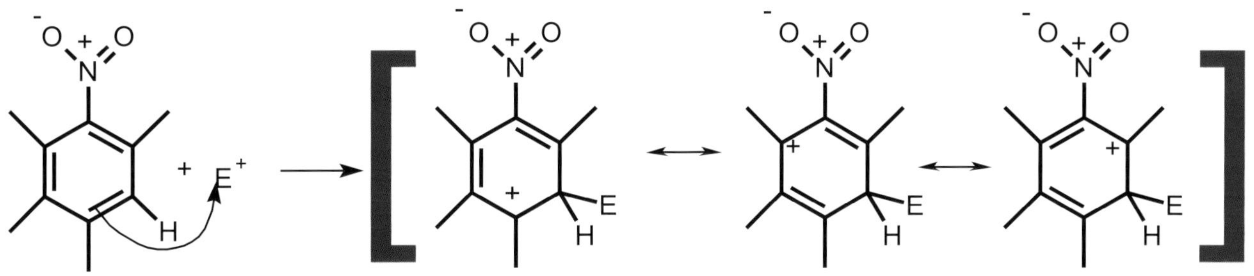

Note that even though the substituents are meta directors, probability suggests that there will still be a smaller percentage of the electrophile that will add at the o–p positions.

5.2.3 Reactions with the Alkylbenzene Side Chain

- Oxidation: Alkyl groups on the benzene ring react rapidly with oxidizing agents and are converted into a carboxyl group. The net result is the conversion of an alkylbenzene into benzoic acid.

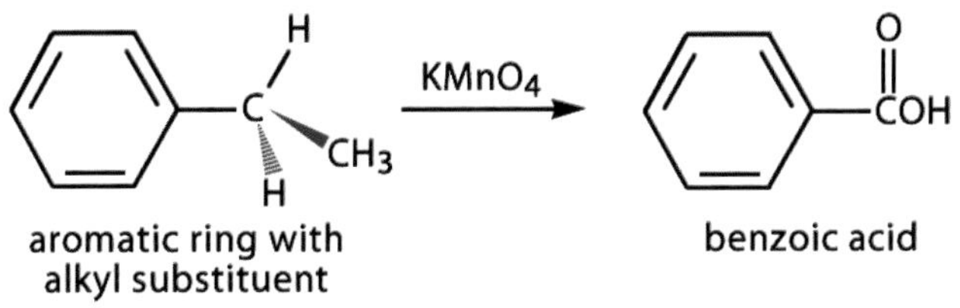

aromatic ring with alkyl substituent —$KMnO_4$→ benzoic acid

- Bromination: NBS (N-bromosuccinimide) reacts with alkylbenzene through a radical chain mechanism (ORG 3.2.2): the benzyl radical generated from NBS in the presence of benzoyl peroxide reacts with Br_2 to yield the final product and bromine radical, which will cycle back into the reaction to act as a radical initiator. The reaction occurs exclusively at the benzyl position because the benzyl radical is highly stabilized through different forms of resonance.

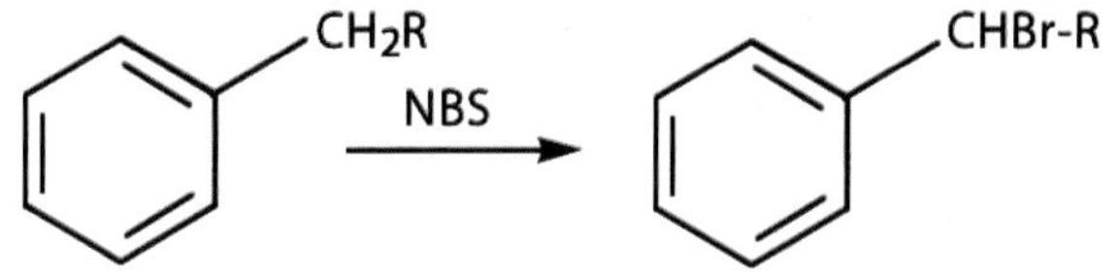

$C_6H_5CH_2R$ —NBS→ $C_6H_5CHBr\text{-}R$

- Reduction: Reductions of aryl alkyl ketones in the presence of H_2 and Pd/C can be used to convert the aryl alkyl ketone generated by the Friedel-Crafts acylation reaction into an alkylbenzene.

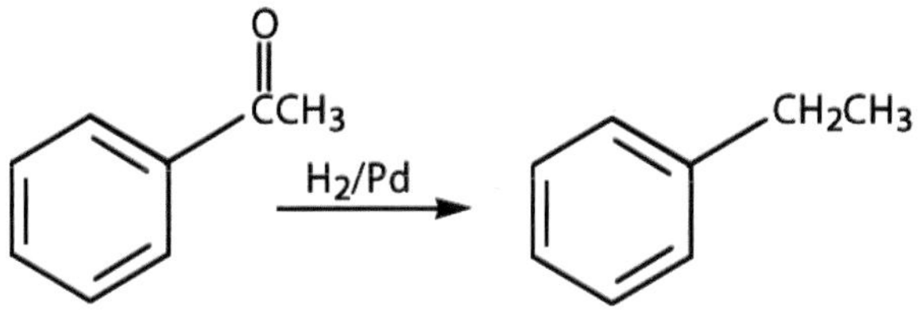

$C_6H_5COCH_3$ —H_2/Pd→ $C_6H_5CH_2CH_3$

Go online to DAT-prep.com for chapter review Q&A and forum.

ALCOHOLS

Chapter 6

Memorize	Understand	Importance
* IUPAC nomenclature * Physical properties * Products of oxidation * Define: steric hindrance	* Trends based on length, branching * Effect of hydrogen bonds * Mechanisms of reactions * Nucleophilic substitution	**4 to 6 out of the 30 ORG** DAT questions are based on content in this chapter (in our estimation). * Note that between 30% and 60% of the questions in DAT Organic Chemistry are based on content from 4 chapters: 1, 2, 5 and 6.

DAT-Prep.com

Introduction

An alcohol is any organic compound in which a hydroxyl group (-OH) is bound to a carbon atom of an alkyl or substituted alkyl group.

Additional Resources

Free Online Q&A + Forum

Video: Online or DVD

Flashcards

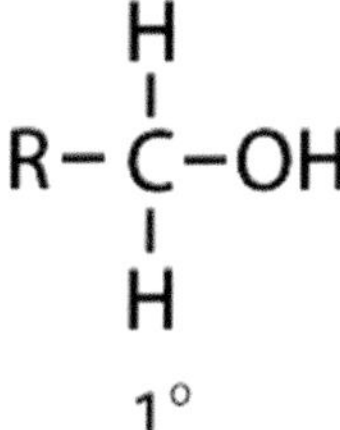

Special Guest

6.1 Description and Nomenclature

The systematic naming of alcohols is accomplished by replacing the –e of the corresponding alkane with –ol.

Alcohols are compounds that have hydroxyl groups bonded to a saturated carbon atom with the general formula ROH. It can be thought of as a substituted water molecule, with one of the water hydrogens replaced with an alkyl group R. Alcohols are classified as primary (1°), secondary (2°) or tertiary (3°):

$R-CH_2-OH$	R_2CH-OH	R_3C-OH
1°	2°	3°

As with alkanes, special names are used for branched groups:

$CH_3-CH(OH)-CH_3$

IUPAC: propan-2-ol
- Isopropanol
- Isopropyl alcohol

$CH_3-C(OH)(CH_3)-CH_3$

IUPAC: 2-methylpropan-2-ol
- 2-methyl-2-propanol
- tert-butanol

The alcohols are always numbered to give the carbon with the attached hydroxy (–OH) group the lowest number (choose the longest carbon chain that contains the hydroxyl group as the parent):

$CH_3CH_2CH_2CH(OH)CH_2CH_3$

3-hexanol NOT 4-hexanol

$CH_3CH_2CH_2CH(CH_3)CH_2CH(OH)CH_2CH(CH_3)CH_3$

2,6-dimethyl-4-nonanol

The shorthand for methanol is MeOH, and the shorthand for ethanol is EtOH. Alcohols are weak acids ($K_a \approx 10^{-18}$), being weaker acids than water. Their conjugate bases are called alkoxides, very little of which will be present in solution:

$$\underset{\text{ethanol}}{C_2H_5OH} + OH^- \rightleftharpoons \underset{\text{ethoxide}}{C_2H_5O^-} + H_2O$$

The acidity of an alcohol decreases with increasing number of attached carbons. Thus CH_3OH is more acidic than CH_3CH_2OH; and CH_3CH_2OH (a primary alcohol) is more acidic than $(CH_3)_2CHOH$ (a secondary alcohol), which is, in turn, more acidic than $(CH_3)_3COH$ (a tertiary alcohol).

Alcohols have higher boiling points and a greater solubility than comparable alkanes, alkenes, aldehydes, ketones and alkyl halides. The higher boiling point and greater solubility is due to the greater polarity and hydrogen bonding of the alcohol. In alcohols, hydrogen bonding is a weak association of the –OH proton of one molecule, with the oxygen of another. To form the hydrogen bond, both a donor, and an acceptor are required:

donor: $CH_3-O-H^{\delta+}$ ---- acceptor: $O^{\delta-}(H)-CH_3$

Sometimes an atom may act as both a donor and acceptor of hydrogen bonds. One example of this is the oxygen atom in an alcohol:

R R R
O O O
H H H
hydrogen bonds

As the length of the carbon chain (= R) of the alcohol molecule increases, the nonpolar chain becomes more meaningful, and the alcohol becomes less water soluble. The hydroxyl group of a primary alcohol is able to form hydrogen bonds with molecules such as water more easily than the hydroxyl group of a tertiary alcohol. The hydroxyl group of a tertiary alcohol is crowded by the surrounding methyl groups and thus its ability to participate in hydrogen bonds is lessened. As well, in solution, primary alcohols are more acidic than secondary alcohols, and secondary alcohols are more acidic than tertiary alcohols. In the gas phase, however, the order of acidity is reversed.

6.1.1 Acidity and Basicity of Alcohols

Alcohols are both weakly acidic and weakly basic. Alcohols can dissociate into a proton and its conjugate base, the alkoxy ion (alkoxide, RO^-), just as water dissociates into a proton and a hydroxide ion. As weak acids, alcohols act as proton donors, thus $ROH + H_2O \rightarrow RO^- + H_3O^+$. As weak bases, alcohols act as proton acceptors, thus $ROH + HX \rightarrow ROH_2^+ + X^-$.

Substituent effects are important in determining alcohol acidity. The more easily the alkoxide ion is accessible to a water molecule, the easier it is stabilized through solvation (CHM 5.3), the more its formation is favored, and the greater the acidity of the alcohol molecule. For example $(CH_3)_3COH$ is less acidic than CH_3OH.

Inductive effects are also important in determining alcohol acidity. Electron-withdrawing groups stabilize an alkoxide anion by spreading out the charge, thus making the alcohol molecule more acidic. Vice versa, electron-donating groups destabilize an alkoxide anion, thus making the alcohol molecule less acidic. For example $(CH_3)_3COH$ is less acidic than $(CF_3)_3OH$.

Since alcohols are weak acids, they do not react with weak bases. However, they do react with strong bases such as NaH, $NaNH_2$, or sodium or potassium metal.

$$CH_3CH_2OH + NaH \rightarrow CH_3CH_2O^-Na^+ + H_2$$

$$CH_3CH_2OH + NaNH_2 \rightarrow CH_3CH_2OH + NH_3$$

$$2CH_3CH_2OH + 2Na \rightarrow 2CH_3CH_2O^-Na^+ + H_2$$

6.1.2 Synthesis of Alcohols

1. **Hydration of alkenes:** Alcohols can be prepared through the hydration of alkenes: (1) Halohydrin (one carbon with a halogen and an adjacent carbon with a hydroxyl substituent) formation yields a Markovnikoff hydration product with anti stereospecificity (i.e. the OH nucleophile adds to the most substituted carbon but *opposite* to the halide); (2) Hydroboration-oxidation yields a syn stereospecific anti-Markovnikoff hydration product (the OH adds to the least substituted carbon); (3) Oxymercuration-reduction yields a Markovnikoff hydration product.

(1) Styrene (CH_2=CH–Ph) $\xrightarrow[H_2O]{X_2 \text{ or NBS}}$ HO–CH(Ph)–CH_2X

(2) Styrene $\xrightarrow[THF]{BH_3}$ H–CH(Ph)–CH_2BH_2 $\xrightarrow[OH^-]{H_2O_2}$ H–CH(Ph)–CH_2OH

(3) Styrene $\xrightarrow[H_2O]{Hg(OAc)_2}$ HO–CH(Ph)–CH_2Hg(OAc) $\xrightarrow{NaBH_4}$ HO–CH(Ph)–CH_2H

2. **Reduction of carbonyl compounds:** An alcohol can be prepared through the reduction of an aldehyde, ketone, carboxylic acid or ester. Aldehydes are converted into primary alcohols and ketones are converted into secondary alcohols in the presence of reducing agents $NaBH_4$ or $LiAlH_4$ (also symbolized as LAH or LithAl). Since $LiAlH_4$ is more powerful and more reactive than $NaBH_4$, it can be used as a reducing agent for the reduction of carboxylic acids and esters to give primary alcohols (see ORG 6.2.2).

$$\underset{\text{ester}}{RC(=O)OR'} \xrightarrow[2.\ H_2O]{1.\ LiAlH_4,\ ether} RCH_2OH + R'OH$$

$$\underset{\text{carboxylic acid}}{RC(=O)OH} \xrightarrow[2.\ H_2O]{1.\ LiAlH_4,\ ether} RCH_2OH$$

3. **Addition reaction with Grignard reagents:** Grignard reagents (RMgX) react with carbonyl compounds to give alcohols. Grignard reagents are created by reacting Mg metal with alkyl (aryl or vinyl) halide.

$$R\text{-}X + Mg \longrightarrow RMgX$$

A number of different alcohol products can be obtained from Grignard reactions with formaldehyde, other aldehydes, ketones or esters. A carboxylic acid does not give an alcohol product because, instead of addition reaction, the carboxylic acid reacts with the Grignard reagent giving a hydrocarbon and magnesium salt of the acid.

- <u>Formaldehyde</u>: Primary alcohol

$$RMgBr + HC(=O)H \xrightarrow[2.\ H_3O^+]{1.\ ether} RCH_2OH$$

- Aldehyde: Secondary alcohol

$$RMgBr + H(R')C{=}O \xrightarrow[2.\ H_3O^+]{1.\ ether} R'(R)C(H)OH$$

- Ketone: Tertiary alcohol

$$RMgBr + R'(R'')C{=}O \xrightarrow[2.\ H_3O^+]{1.\ ether} R'(R'')C(R)OH$$

- Ester: Tertiary alcohol

Two substituents from the Grignard reagent are added to the carbonyl-bearing carbon, giving a tertiary alcohol.

$$2RMgBr + R'C({=}O)OR'' \xrightarrow[2.\ H_3O^+]{1.\ ether} R'(R)C(R)OH + R''OH$$

6.2 Important Reactions of Alcohols

6.2.1 Dehydration

Dehydration (= *loss of water*) reactions of alcohols produce alkenes. The general dehydration reaction is shown in Figure IV.B.6.1.

$$\text{H–C–C–OH}^{\delta^-} \xrightarrow[-H_2O]{+H^+} \text{H–C–C}^+ \xrightarrow{-H^+} \text{C=C}$$

alcohol carbocation alkene

For the preceding reaction to occur, the temperature must be between 300 and 400 degrees Celsius, and the vapors must be passed over a metal oxide catalyst. Alternatively, strong, hot acids, such as H_2SO_4 or H_3PO_4 at 100 to 200 degrees Celsius may be used.

The reactivity depends upon the type of alcohol. A tertiary alcohol is more reactive than a secondary alcohol which is, in turn, more reactive than a primary alcohol. The faster reactions have the most stable carbocation intermediates. The alkene that is formed is the most stable one. A phenyl group will take preference over one or two alkyl groups, otherwise the most substituted double bond is the most stable (= *major product*) and the least substituted is less stable (= *minor product*).

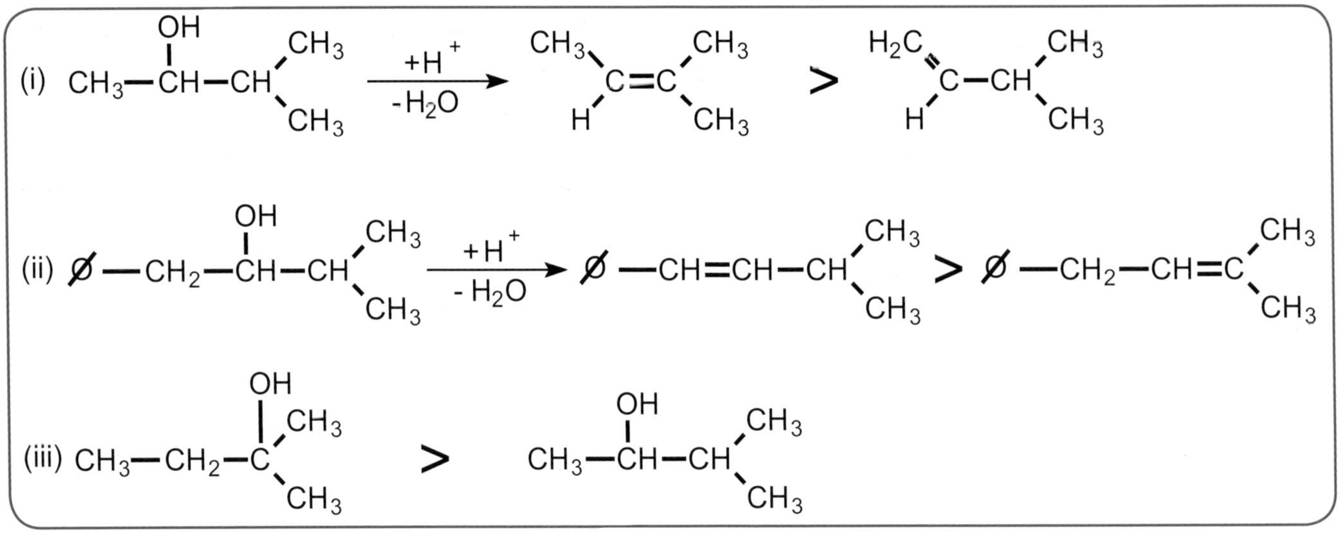

(i) $CH_3-CH(OH)-CH(CH_3)_2 \xrightarrow[-H_2O]{+H^+} (CH_3)(H)C{=}C(CH_3)_2 > H_2C{=}C(H)-CH(CH_3)_2$

(ii) $\phi-CH_2-CH(OH)-CH(CH_3)_2 \xrightarrow[-H_2O]{+H^+} \phi-CH{=}CH-CH(CH_3)_2 > \phi-CH_2-CH{=}C(CH_3)_2$

(iii) $CH_3-CH_2-C(OH)(CH_3)_2 > CH_3-CH(OH)-CH(CH_3)_2$

Figure IV.B.6.2: Dehydration of substituted alcohols. Major and minor products, respectively, are represented in reactions (i) and (ii). An example of a reactant with a greater reaction rate due to more substituents as an intermediate is represented by (iii). ϕ = a phenyl group.

6.2.2 Oxidation-Reduction

In organic chemistry, oxidation (O) is the increasing of oxygen or decreasing of hydrogen content, and reduction (H) is the opposite. Primary alcohols are converted to aldehydes using PCC or $KMnO_4$, under mild conditions (i.e. room temperature, neutral pH). Primary alcohols are converted to carboxylic acids using CrO_3 (the mixture is called a Jones'

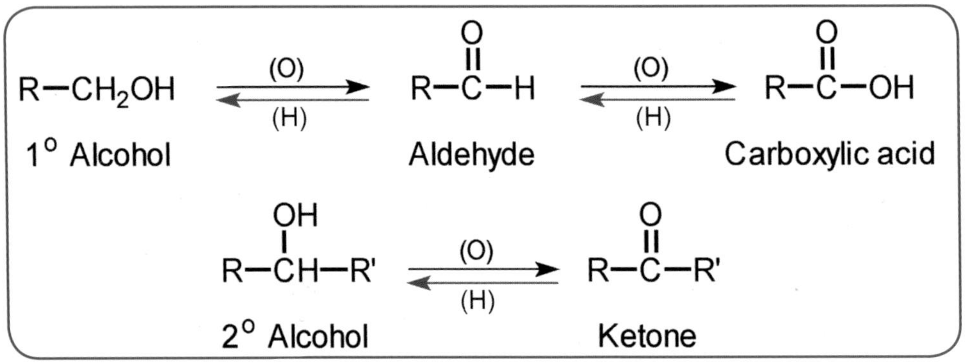

$R-CH_2OH \underset{(H)}{\overset{(O)}{\rightleftharpoons}} R-C(=O)-H \underset{(H)}{\overset{(O)}{\rightleftharpoons}} R-C(=O)-OH$

1° Alcohol — Aldehyde — Carboxylic acid

$R-CH(OH)-R' \underset{(H)}{\overset{(O)}{\rightleftharpoons}} R-C(=O)-R'$

2° Alcohol — Ketone

Figure IV.B.6.3: Oxidation-Reduction. In organic chemistry, traditionally the symbols R and R' denote an attached hydrogen, or a hydrocarbon side chain of any length (which are consistent with the reactions above), but sometimes these symbols refer to any group of atoms.

reagent), $K_2Cr_2O_7$, or $KMnO_4$ under abrasive conditions (i.e. increased temperature, presence of OH-). Secondary alcohols are converted to ketones by any of the preceding oxidizing agents. It is *very* difficult to oxidize a tertiary alcohol. Under acidic conditions, tertiary alcohols are unaffected; they may be oxidized under acidic conditions by dehydration and *then* oxidizing the double bond of the resultant alkene. Classic reducing agents (H) include $LiAlH_4$ (strong), H_2/metals (strong) and $NaBH_4$ (mild).

6.2.3 Substitution

In a substitution reaction one atom or group is *substituted* or replaced by another atom or group. For an alcohol, the –OH group is replaced (*substituted*) by a halide (usually chlorine or bromine). A variety of reagents may be used, such as HCl, HBr or PCl_3. There are two different types of substitution reactions, S_N1 and S_N2.

In the S_N1 (*1st order or monomolecular nucleophilic substitution*) reaction, the transition state involves a carbocation, the formation of which is the rate-determining step. Alcohol substitutions that proceed by this mechanism are those involving benzyl groups, allyl groups, tertiary and secondary alcohols. The mechanism of this reaction is:

(i) $R–L \rightarrow R^+ + L^-$
(ii) $Nu^- + R^+ \rightarrow Nu–R$

The important features of this reaction are:

- The reaction is first order (this means that the rate of the reaction depends only on the concentration of one compound); the rate depends on [R–L], where R represents an alkyl group, and L represents a substituent or ligand.
- There is a racemization of configuration, when a chiral molecule is involved.
- A stable carbonium ion should be formed; thus in terms of reaction rate, benzyl groups = allyl groups > tertiary alcohols > secondary alcohols >> primary alcohols.
- The stability of alkyl groups is as follows: primary alkyl groups < secondary alkyl groups < tertiary alkyl groups.

The mechanism of the S_N2 (*2nd order or bimolecular nucleophilic substitution*) reaction is:

$$Nu^- + R—L \rightarrow [Nu{----}R{----}L]^- \rightarrow Nu—R + L^-$$

There are several important points to know about this reaction:

- The reaction rate is second order overall (the rate depends on the concentration of two compounds); first order with respect to [R-L] and first order with respect to the concentration of the nucleophile [Nu^-].

- Note that the nucleophile adds to the alkyl group by *backside displacement* (i.e. Nu must add to the *opposite* site to the ligand). Thus optically active alcohols react to give an inversion of configuration, forming the opposite enantiomer.

- Large or bulky groups near or at the reacting site may hinder or retard a reaction. This is called *steric hindrance*. Size or steric factors are important since they affect S_N2 reaction rates; in terms of reaction rates, CH_3^- > primary alcohols > secondary alcohols >> tertiary alcohols.

The substitution reactions for methanol (CH_3OH) and other primary alcohols are by the S_N2 reaction mechanism.

6.2.4 Elimination

Elimination reactions occur when an atom or a group of atoms is removed (*eliminated*) from adjacent carbons leaving a multiple bond:

$$-\underset{Y}{\overset{|}{\underset{|}{C}}}-\underset{Z}{\overset{|}{\underset{|}{C}}}- \xrightarrow[\text{(-YZ)}]{\text{elimination}} >C=C<$$

There are two different types of elimination reactions, E1 and E2. In the E1 (Elimination, 1st order) reaction, the rate of reaction depends on the concentration of one compound. E1 often occurs as minor products alongside S_N2 reactions. E1 can occur as major products in alkyl halides or, as in the following example, to an alcohol:

OH, H^+, $\overset{+}{O}H_2$

cyclohexanol

$-H_2O$, H, +, $-H^+$

2° carbocation   cyclohexene

The acid-catalyzed dehydration of alcohols is thus an E1 reaction which yields the more highly substituted alkene as the major product. There is a carbocation intermediate formed during the preceding reaction, thus a tertiary alcohol will react faster and yield an alkene in a more stable way than a secondary or primary alcohol.

Secondary and primary alcohols will only react with acids in very harsh condition (75%-95% H_2SO_4, 100 °C). However, they will react with $POCl_3$ converting the –OH into a good leaving group to yield an alkene. This reaction takes place with an E2 mechanism.

In the E2 (Elimination, 2nd order)

reaction the rate of reaction depends on the concentration of two compounds. E2 reactions require strong bases like KOH or the salt of an alcohol (i.e. *sodium alkoxide*). An alkoxide can be synthesized from an alcohol using either Na(*s*) or NaH (*sodium hydride*) as reducing agents. The hydride ion H^- is a powerful base:

$$R\text{-}OH + NaH \longrightarrow \underset{\text{sodium alkoxide}}{R\text{-}O^-Na^+} + H_2$$

Now the alkoxide can be used as a proton acceptor in an E2 reaction involving an alkyl halide:

$$C_2H_5O^- + H\text{-}CH_2\text{-}CHBr\text{-}CH_3 \text{ (ethoxide + 2-bromopropane)}$$

$$\longrightarrow H_2C{=}CH\text{-}CH_3 \text{ (propene)} + C_2H_5OH \text{ (ehanol)} + Br^-$$

In the preceding reaction, the first step (1) involves the base (ethoxide) removing (*elimination*) a proton, thus carbon has a negative charge (*primary carbanion*, very *unstable*). The electron pair is quickly attracted to the δ^+ neighboring carbon (2) forming a double bond (note that the carbon was δ^+ because it was attached to the electronegative atom Br, *see* ORG 1.5). Simultaneously, Br (*a halide, which are good leaving groups*) is bumped (3) from the carbon as carbon can have only four bonds. {Notice that in organic chemistry the curved arrows always follow the movement of electrons}

The determination of the quality of a leaving group is quite simple: good leaving groups have *strong* conjugate acids. As examples, H_2O is a good leaving group because H_3O^+ is a strong acid, likewise for Br^-/HBr, Cl^-/HCl, HSO_4^-/H_2SO_4, etc.

A decision tree (substitution vs. elimination) is at the back of the book in the section Key Organic Chemistry Reaction Mechanisms.

6.2.5 Conversion of Alcohols to Alkyl Halides

Alcohols can participate in substitution reactions only if the hydroxyl group is converted into a better leaving group by either protonation or the formation of an inorganic ester. Tertiary alcohols can be converted into alkyl halides by a reaction with HCl or HBr. This reaction occurs in an S_N1 mechanism. Primary and secondary alcohols do not react with HCl or HBr readily and are converted into halides by $SOCl_2$ or PBr_3. This reaction occurs in an S_N2 mechanism.

$$RCH_2OH + SOCl_2 \longrightarrow RCH_2Cl + SO_2 + HCl$$

$$RCH_2OH + PBr_3 \longrightarrow RCH_2Br + HOPBr_2$$

Go online to DAT-prep.com for chapter review Q&A and forum.

ALDEHYDES AND KETONES
Chapter 7

Memorize

* IUPAC nomenclature

Understand

* Effect of hydrogen bonds
* Mechanisms of reactions
* Acidity of the alpha H
* Resonance, polarity
* Grignards, organometallic reagents
* Redox reactions

Importance

1 to 3 out of the 30 ORG

DAT questions are based on content in this chapter (in our estimation).
* Note that between 30% and 60% of the questions in DAT Organic Chemistry are based on content from 4 chapters: 1, 2, 5 and 6.

DAT-Prep.com

Introduction

An aldehyde contains a terminal carbonyl group. The functional group is a carbon atom bonded to a hydrogen atom and double-bonded to an oxygen atom (O=CH-) and is called the aldehyde group. A ketone contains a carbonyl group (C=O) bonded to two other carbon atoms: R(CO)R'.

Additional Resources

Free Online Q&A + Forum

Video: Online or DVD

Flashcards

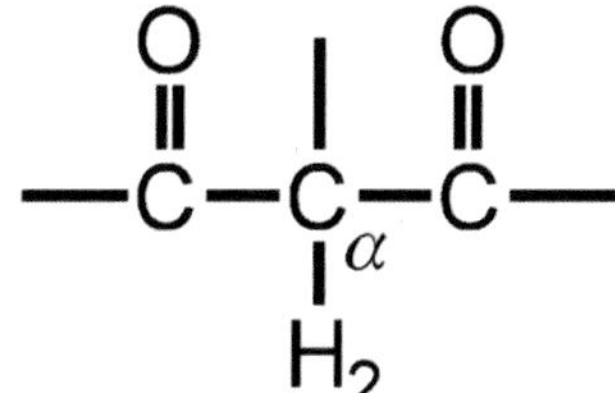

Special Guest

7.1 Description and Nomenclature

Aldehydes and ketones are two types of molecules, both containing the carbonyl group, C=O, which is the basis for their chemistry.

The carbonyl functional group is planar with bond angles of approximately 120°. The carbonyl carbon atom is sp^2 hybridized and forms three σ bonds. The C=O double bond is both stronger and shorter than the C-O single bond.

The general structure of aldehydes and ketones is:

$R-C(=O)-H$ Aldehyde

$R-C(=O)-R'$ Ketone

Aldehydes have at least one hydrogen bonded to the carbonyl carbon, as well as a second hydrogen (= *formaldehyde*) or either an alkyl or an aryl group (= *benzene minus one hydrogen*). Ketones have two alkyl or aryl groups bound to the carbonyl carbon (i.e. the carbon forming the double bond with oxygen).

Systematic naming of these compounds is done by replacing the '–e' of the corresponding alkane with '–al' for aldehydes, and '-one' for ketones. For aldehydes, the longest chain chosen as the parent name must contain -CHO group and the -CHO group must occupy the terminal (C1) position. For ketones, the longest chain chosen as the parent name must contain the ketone group and give the lowest possible number to the carbonyl carbon. Common names are given in brackets:

$CH_3C(=O)-H$ ethanal (acetaldehyde)

$CH_3C(=O)CH_3$ propanone (acetone)

$CH_3C(=O)CH_2CH_2CH_3$ 2-pentanone (methyl propyl ketone)

The important features of the carbonyl group are:

- Resonance: There are two resonance forms of the carbonyl group:

$$R-\overset{\delta^+}{C}(=\overset{\delta^-}{O})-R' \longleftrightarrow R-\overset{+}{C}(-O^-)-R'$$

- Polarity: Reactions about this group may be either nucleophilic, or electrophilic. Since opposite charges attract, nucleophiles (Nu^-) attack the δ^+ carbon, and electrophiles (E^+) attack the δ^- oxygen. In both of these types of reactions, the character of the double bond is altered:

$$R-\overset{\delta^+}{C}(=\overset{\delta^-}{O})-R + E^+ \xrightarrow{\text{Electrophilic}} \left[R-C(=\overset{+}{O}-E)-R \longleftrightarrow R-\overset{+}{C}(-O-E)-R \right]$$

$$Nu^- + R-\overset{\delta^+}{C}(=\overset{\delta^-}{O})-R \xrightarrow{\text{Nucleophilic}} R-C(-O^-)(-Nu)-R$$

- Acidity of the α-hydrogen: The α-hydrogen is the hydrogen attached to the carbon next to the carbonyl group (the α-carbon). The β-carbon is the carbon adjacent to the α-carbon. The α-hydrogen may be removed by a base. The acidity of this hydrogen is increased if it is between 2 carbonyl groups:

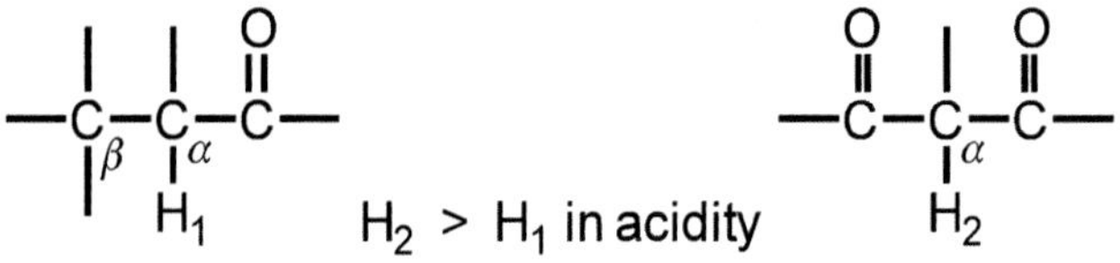

$H_2 > H_1$ in acidity

This acidity is a result of the resonance stabilization of the α-carbanion formed. This stabilization will also permit addition at the β-carbon in α-β unsaturated carbonyls (*those with double or triple bonds*):

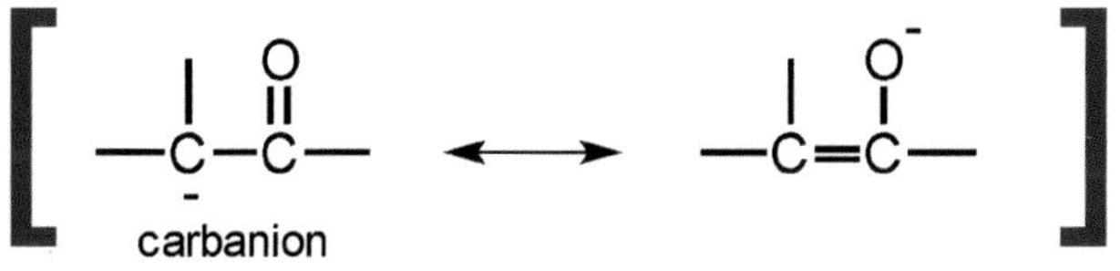

carbanion

resonance stabilization

Nu^-

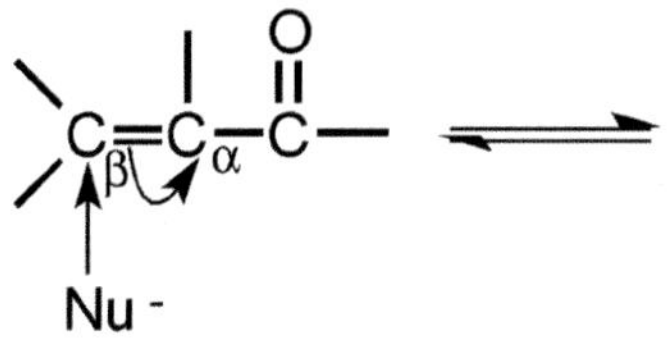

α, β unsaturated carbonyl

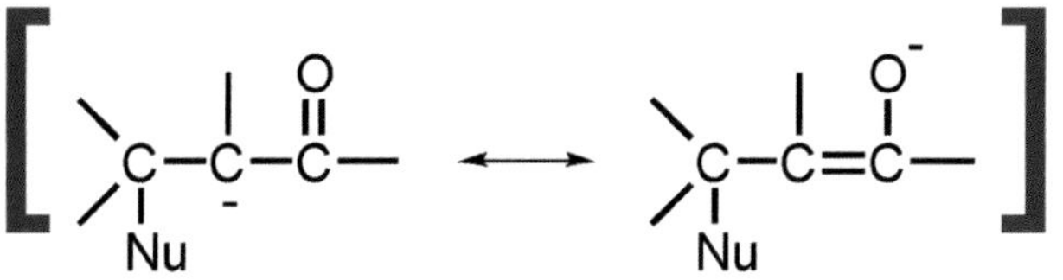

Note that only protons at the α position of carbonyl compounds are acidic. Protons further from the carbonyl carbon (β, gamma - γ, and so on, positions) are not acidic.

- Keto-enol tautomerization: Tautomers are constitutional isomers (ORG 2.1-2.3) that readily interconvert (= *tautomerization*). Because the interconversion is so fast, they are usually considered to be the same chemical compound. The carbonyl exists in equilibrium with the enol form of the molecule (enol = alk***ene*** + alcoh***ol***). The carbonyl exists in equilibrium with the enol form of the molecule. Although the carbonyl is usually the predominant one, if the enol double bond can be conjugated with other double bonds, it becomes stable (conjugated double bonds are those which are separated by a single bond):

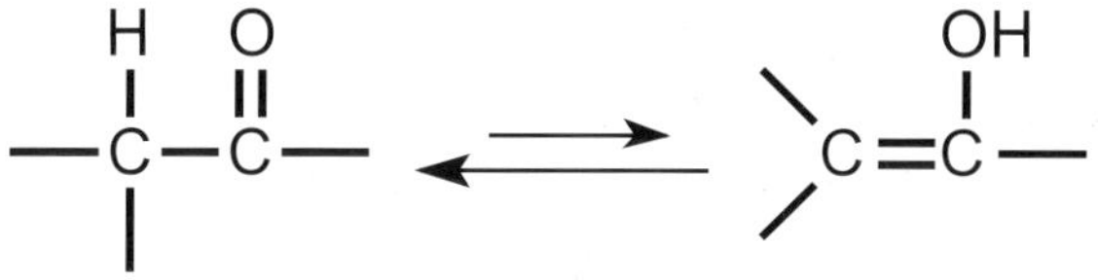

carbonyl enol

- Hydrogen bonds: The O of the carbonyl forms hydrogen bonds with the hydrogens attached to other electronegative atoms, such as O's or N's:

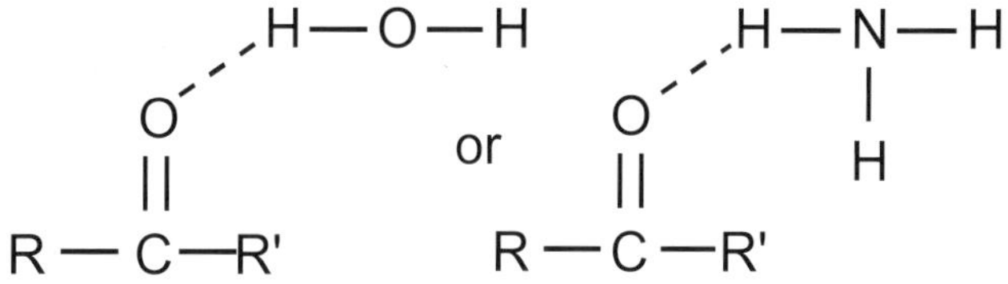

Since there is no hydrogen on the carbonyl oxygen, aldehydes and ketones do not form hydrogen bonds with themselves.

7.2 Important Reactions of Aldehydes & Ketones

7.2.1 Overview

Since the carbonyl group is the functional group of aldehydes and ketones, groups adjacent to the carbonyl group affect the rate of reaction for the molecule. For example, an electron withdrawing ligand adjacent to the carbonyl group will increase the partial positive charge on the carbon making the carbonyl group more attractive to a nucleophile. Conversely, an electron donating ligand would decrease the reactivity of the carbonyl group.

Generally, aldehydes oxidize easier, and undergo nucleophilic additions easier than ketones. This is a consequence of steric hindrance.

Aldehydes will be oxidized to carboxylic acids with the standard oxidizing agents such as $KMnO_4$, CrO_3 (Jones reagent), HNO_3, Ag_2O (Tollens' reagent). Ketones rarely oxidize. When the Tollens' reagent is used, metallic silver Ag is produced if the aldehyde functional group is present in a molecule of unknown structure, thus making it useful as a diagnostic tool. Therefore, the aldehyde will form a silver precipitate while a ketone will not because ketones cannot be oxidized to carboxylic acid.

There are several methods for preparing aldehydes and ketones. We have already seen ozonolysis (ORG 4.2.2) and the classic redox series of reactions (please review ORG 6.2.2). To add to the preceding is a reaction called "hydroformylation" shown for the generation of butyraldehyde by the hydroformylation of propene:

$$H_2 + CO + CH_3CH{=}CH_2 \longrightarrow CH_3CH_2CH_2CHO$$

Primary alcohols can be oxidized to yield aldehydes. The reaction is performed with the mild oxidation reagent PCC.

$$\underset{\text{ethanol}}{CH_3-CH_2-OH} \xrightarrow[CH_2Cl_2]{C_5H_5\overset{+}{N}H[\overset{-}{CrO_3Cl}]\ (PCC)} \underset{\text{ethanal}}{CH_3-\overset{O}{\overset{\|}{C}}H}$$

Secondary alcohols can be oxidized to yield ketones. These reactions are usually performed with PCC, Jones' reagent (CrO_3), and sodium dichromate.

Other reagents include: $K_2Cr_2O_7/H_2SO_4$ or CrO_3/H_2SO_4 or $KMnO_4/OH^-$ or $KMnO_4/H_3O^+$.

Alkenes can be oxidatively cleaved to yield aldehydes when treated with ozone (ORG 4.2.2).

Alkenes can be oxidatively cleaved to

yield ketones when treated with ozone if one of the double bond carbon atoms is di-substituted.

$$CH_3-\underset{\displaystyle CH_3}{\underset{|}{C}}=CH-CH_3 \xrightarrow[2.\ H^+]{1.\ O_3} CH_3-\overset{\displaystyle O}{\overset{\|}{C}}-CH_3 + CH_3-\overset{\displaystyle O}{\overset{\|}{C}}-H$$

Ketones can also be prepared by Friedel-Crafts acylation of a benzene ring with acyl halide in the presence of an $AlCl_3$ catalyst (ORG 5.2).

Hydration of terminal alkynes will yield methyl ketones in the presence of mercuric ion as catalyst and strong acids. The formation of an unstable vinyl alcohol undergoes keto-enol tautomerization (ORG 7.1) to form ketones.

$$R-C\equiv C-R \xrightarrow[HgSO_4]{H_2O + H^{\oplus}} \left[\begin{matrix} R & & \ddot{O}-H \\ & C=C & \\ H & & R \end{matrix} \right]$$

addition — enol tautomer

$$\xrightarrow{\text{tautomerization}} R-\underset{H}{\overset{H}{C}}-\overset{\ddot{O}}{\overset{\|}{C}}-R$$

keto tautomer

There are two classes of reactions that will be investigated: nucleophilic addition reactions at C=O bond, and reactions at adjacent positions.

The most important reaction of aldehydes and ketones is the nucleophilic addition reaction. A nucleophile attacks the electrophilic carbonyl carbon atom and a tetrahedral alkoxide ion intermediate is formed. The intermediate can lead to the protonation of the carbonyl oxygen atom to form an alcohol or expel the carbonyl oxygen atom as H_2O or OH^- to form a carbon-nucleophile double bond.

$$R_2C=O \xrightarrow{Nu^-} \left[R_2C(O^-)Nu \right] \xrightarrow{H^+} R_2C(OH)Nu$$

$$R_2C=O \xrightarrow{NuH_2} \left[R_2C(O^-)\overset{+}{N}uH_2 \right] \longrightarrow R_2C=Nu + H_2O$$

Aldehydes and ketones react with water in the presence of acid or base catalyst to form 1,1-diols, or gem-diols. Water acts as the nucleophile here attacking the carbonyl carbon.

$$CH_3-\overset{\displaystyle O}{\overset{\|}{C}}-H \xrightarrow[H^+]{H_2O} CH_3-\underset{\displaystyle OH}{\underset{|}{\overset{\displaystyle OH}{\overset{|}{C}}}}-H$$

$$CH_3-\overset{\delta^-\ \ddot{O}:}{\overset{\|}{\underset{\delta^+}{C}}}-H + H-\ddot{O}-H \longrightarrow CH_3-\overset{:\ddot{O}:^-}{\overset{|}{\underset{\displaystyle \overset{+}{O}H_2}{\underset{|}{C}}}}-H \longrightarrow CH_3-\underset{\displaystyle OH}{\underset{|}{\overset{\displaystyle OH}{\overset{|}{C}}}}-H$$

Aldehydes and ketones react with HCN to form cyanohydrin. CN^- attacks the carbonyl carbon atom and protonation of O^- foms tetrahedral cyanohydrin product.

$$CH_3-CH_2-\overset{\overset{O}{\|}}{C}H + HCN \rightleftharpoons CH_3CH_2\underset{\underset{CN}{|}}{\overset{\overset{OH}{|}}{C}}-H$$

propanal

$$CH_3-\overset{\overset{O}{\|}}{C}-CH_3 + HCN \rightleftharpoons CH_5\underset{\underset{CN}{|}}{\overset{\overset{OH}{|}}{C}}-CH_3$$

acetone

Reduction of aldehydes and ketones with Grignard reagents yields alcohols. Grignard reagents react with formaldehyde to produce primary alcohols, all other aldehydes to produce secondary alcohols, and ketones to produce tertiary alcohols.

$$\overset{\delta^-}{R}-\overset{\delta^+}{MgX} + R-\overset{\overset{O}{\|}}{C}-H(R) \xrightarrow{H^+} R-\underset{\underset{R}{|}}{\overset{\overset{OH}{|}}{C}}-H(R)$$

$$\overset{\delta^-}{R}-\overset{\delta^+}{Li} + R-\overset{\overset{O}{\|}}{C}-H(R) \xrightarrow{H^+} R-\underset{\underset{R}{|}}{\overset{\overset{OH}{|}}{C}}-H(R)$$

$$R-C\equiv C^-Na^+ + R-\overset{\overset{O}{\|}}{C}-H(R)$$

$$\xrightarrow{H^+} R-C\equiv C-\underset{\underset{H}{|}}{\overset{\overset{OH}{|}}{C}}-H(R)$$

Reducing agents such as $NaBH_4$ and $LiAlH_4$ react with aldehydes and ketones to form alcohols (ORG 6.2.2). The reducing agent functions as if they are hydride ion equivalents and the H:$^-$ attacks the carbonyl carbon atom to form the product.

$LiAlH_4$ or $NaBH_4$

$$+ \; H-\overset{\overset{O}{\|}}{C}-H \longrightarrow H-\underset{\underset{H}{|}}{\overset{\overset{OH}{|}}{C}}-H$$

$$+ \; R'-\overset{\overset{O}{\|}}{C}-H \longrightarrow H-\underset{\underset{R'}{|}}{\overset{\overset{OH}{|}}{C}}-H$$

$$+ \; R'-\overset{\overset{O}{\|}}{C}-R'' \longrightarrow H-\underset{\underset{R'}{|}}{\overset{\overset{OH}{|}}{C}}-R''$$

7.2.2 Acetal (ketal) and Hemiacetal (hemiketal) Formation

Aldehydes and ketones will form hemiacetals and hemiketals, respectively, when dissolved in an excess of a primary alcohol. In addition, if this mixture contains a trace of an acid catalyst, the hemiacetal (hemiketal) will react further to form acetals and ketals.

An acetal is a composite functional group in which two ether functions are joined to a carbon bearing a hydrogen and an alkyl group. A ketal is a composite functional group in which two ether functions are joined to a carbon bearing two alkyl groups.

This reaction may be summarised:

$$R{-}\overset{\overset{\displaystyle O}{\|}}{C}{-}R' \quad + \quad R''OH \quad \underset{-H^+}{\overset{+H^+}{\rightleftharpoons}}$$

aldehyde (R' = H) or ketone (R' = alkyl) — excess alcohol

$$R{-}\underset{OR''}{\overset{OH}{C}}{-}R' \quad \underset{+H_2O}{\overset{+H^+/-H_2O}{\rightleftharpoons}} \quad R{-}\underset{OR''}{\overset{OR''}{C}}{-}R'$$

hemiacetal or hemiketal — acetal or ketal

The <u>first step</u> in the above reaction is that the most charged species (+, the hydrogen) attracts electrons from the δ^- oxygen, leaving a carbocation intermediate. The <u>second step</u> involves the δ^- oxygen from the alcohol *quickly* attracted to the current most charged species (+, carbon). A proton is lost which regenerates the catalyst, and produces the hemiacetal or hemiketal. Now the proton may attract electrons from -OH forming H_2O, a good leaving group. Again the δ- oxygen on the alcohol is attracted to the positive carbocation. And again the alcohol releases its proton, regenerating the catalyst, producing an acetal or ketal.

Aldehydes and ketones can also react with HCN (hydrogen cyanide) to produce stable compounds called cyanohydrins which owe their stability to the newly formed C-C bond.

7.2.3 Imine and Enamine Formation

Imines and enamines are formed when aldehydes and ketones are allowed to react with amines.

When an aldehyde or ketone reacts with a primary amine, an <u>imine</u> (or Schiff base) is formed. A primary amine is a nitrogen compound with the general formula R-NH_2, where R represents an alkyl or aryl group. In an imine the carbonyl group of the aldehyde or ketone is replaced with a C=N-R group.

The reaction may be summarised:

$$-\overset{\delta^+}{C}(=O)- \;+\; R{-}\overset{\delta^-}{N}H_2 \longrightarrow -\underset{\underset{+}{RNH_2}}{\overset{O^-}{C}}- \longrightarrow -\underset{RNH}{\overset{OH}{C}}- \xrightarrow{-H_2O} -\underset{\underset{RN}{\|}}{C}-$$

① ② (electron-movement steps); 1° amine; imine

When an aldehyde or ketone reacts with a secondary amine, an enamine is formed. A secondary amine is a nitrogen with the general formula R_2N-H, where R represents aryl or alkyl groups (these groups need not be identical).

Tertiary amines (of the general form R_3N) do not react with the aldehydes or ketones.

7.2.4 Aldol Condensation

Aldol condensation is a base catalized reaction of aldehydes and ketones that have α-hydrogens. The intermediate, an aldol, is both an ald*ehyde* and a *alcoh*ol. The aldol undergoes a dehydration reaction producing a carbon-carbon bond in the condensation product, an *enal* (= *alk*en*e* + al*dehyde*).

The reaction may be summarised:

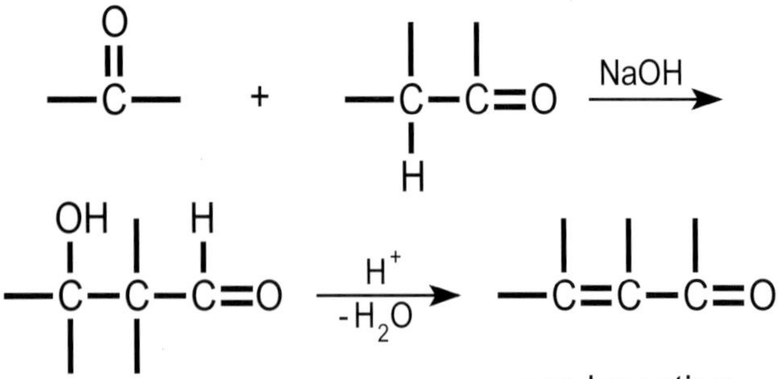

$$-\overset{O}{\overset{\|}{C}}- \; + \; -\underset{H}{C}-C{=}O \xrightarrow{NaOH}$$

$$-\overset{OH}{C}-C-\overset{H}{C}{=}O \xrightarrow[-H_2O]{H^+} -C{=}C-C{=}O$$

Aldol

condensation product

The reaction mechanism:

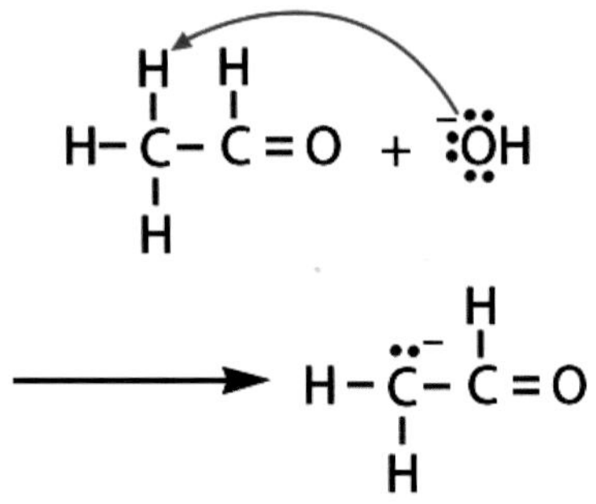

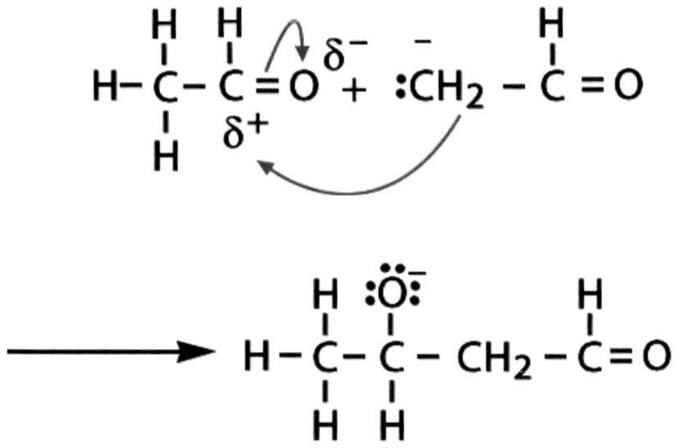

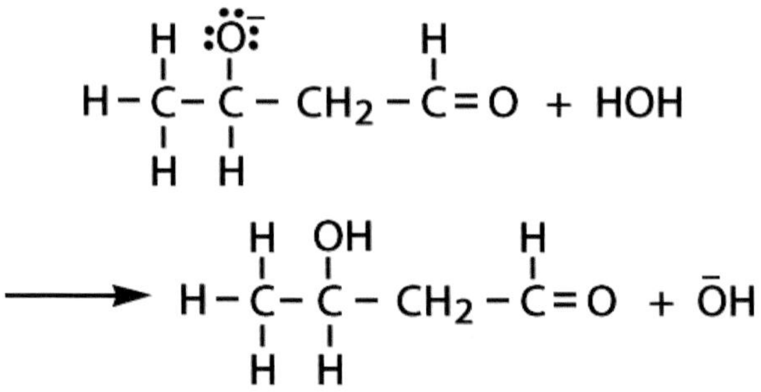

$$H-\underset{H}{\overset{H}{C}}-\overset{H}{C}{=}O + {:}\ddot{O}H^- \longrightarrow H-\underset{H}{\overset{\bullet\bullet -}{C}}-\overset{H}{C}{=}O$$

$$H-\underset{H}{\overset{H}{C}}-\overset{H}{C}{=}O^{\delta-}\,(\delta+) + {:}\overset{-}{C}H_2-\overset{H}{C}{=}O \longrightarrow H-\underset{H}{\overset{H}{C}}-\underset{H}{\overset{:\ddot{O}:^-}{C}}-CH_2-\overset{H}{C}{=}O$$

$$H-\underset{H}{\overset{H}{C}}-\underset{H}{\overset{:\ddot{O}:^-}{C}}-CH_2-\overset{H}{C}{=}O + HOH \longrightarrow H-\underset{H}{\overset{H}{C}}-\underset{H}{\overset{OH}{C}}-CH_2-\overset{H}{C}{=}O + {}^-OH$$

An aldol can now lose H_2O to form a β-unsaturated aldehyde via an E1 mechanism.

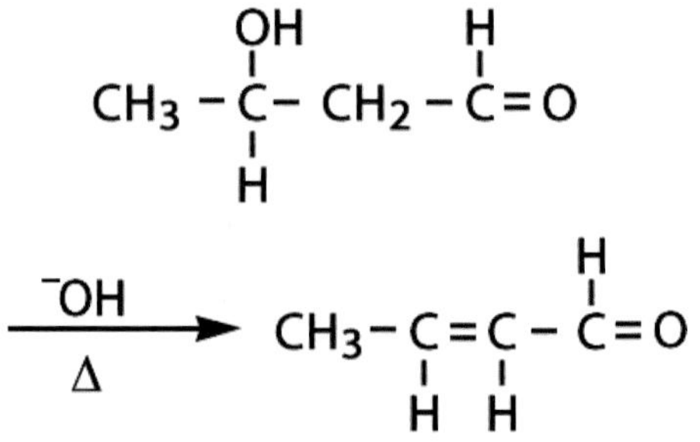

$$CH_3-\underset{H}{\overset{OH}{C}}-CH_2-\overset{H}{C}{=}O \xrightarrow[\Delta]{^-OH} CH_3-\underset{H}{C}{=}\underset{H}{C}-\overset{H}{C}{=}O$$

7.2.5 Conjugate Addition to α-β Unsaturated Carbonyls

α-β unsaturated carbonyls are unusually reactive with nucleophiles. This is best illustrated by example:

—C=C—C=O → H^+ → —C(Nu)—C(H)—C=O

Nu⁻

Examples of relevant nucleophiles includes CN^- from HCN, and R^- which can be generated by a Grignard Reagent (= RMgX) or as an alkyl lithium (= RLi).

For example:

Me, O, ⊖CN → Me, O⊖, CN, H⊕ → Me, O, CN

7.2.6 The Wittig reaction

The Wittig reaction converts aldehydes and ketones into alkenes. A salt is formed, followed by a ylide (**A**) which is a neutral compound, called the Wittig reagent, that eventually attacks the carbonyl carbon of the aldehyde (**B**) or ketone. This forms a four-membered ring intermediate (**E**) which decomposes to form the final product, a Z-alkene (**G**).

$Ph_3\overset{+}{P}$—CH⁻—R_1 (**A**) + H(C=O)R_2 (**B**) ⇌ **C** ⇌ **D** ⇌ **E** → Ph_3PO + **G**

7.2.7 Reduction of Aldehydes and Ketones Revisited

We have already discussed reducing aldehydes and ketones to alcohols (ORG 6.2.2, 7.2.1; $NaBH_4$ and $LiAlH_4$, also symbolized as LAH). However, it is also possible to reduce aldehydes and ketones directly to alkanes using two principle methods:

1. **Clemmensen reduction:** Performed under acidic conditions:

$$R_1C(=O)R_2 \xrightarrow[HCl]{Zn(Hg)} R_1CH_2R_2$$

2. **Wolff-Kishner reduction:** Performed in basic solution and only useful when the product is stable under basic conditions:

$$R_1C(=O)R_2 \xrightarrow{NH_2NH_2} R_1C(=N-NH_2)R_2 \xrightarrow{base} R_1C^{\ominus}(N{=}NH)R_2 \xrightarrow{H_2O}$$

$$R_1CH(N{=}NH)R_2 \xrightarrow[-N_2]{base} R_1CH^{\ominus}R_2 \xrightarrow{H_2O} R_1CH_2R_2$$

Go online to DAT-prep.com for chapter review Q&A and forum.

CARBOXYLIC ACIDS

Chapter 8

Memorize	Understand	Importance
* IUPAC nomenclature	* Hydrogen bonding * Mechanisms of reactions * Relative acid strength * Resonance, inductive effects * Grignards, organometallic reagents * Redox reactions	**1 to 3 out of the 30 ORG** DAT questions are based on content in this chapter (in our estimation). * Note that between 30% and 60% of the questions in DAT Organic Chemistry are based on content from 4 chapters: 1, 2, 5 and 6.

Introduction

Carboxylic acids are organic acids with a carboxyl group, which has the formula -C(=O)OH, usually written -COOH or $-CO_2H$. Carboxylic acids are Brønsted-Lowry acids (proton donors) that are actually, in the grand scheme of chemistry, weak acids. Salts and anions of carboxylic acids are called carboxylates.

Additional Resources

Free Online Q&A + Forum

Video: Online or DVD

Flashcards

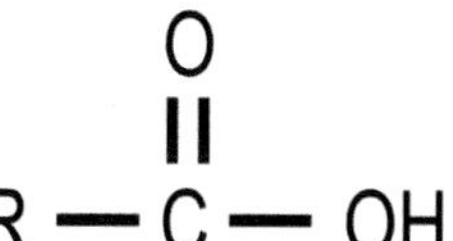

Special Guest

8.1 Description and Nomenclature

Carboxylic acids are molecules containing the *carboxylic group* (carbonyl + hydroxyl), which is the basis of their chemistry. The general structure of a carboxylic acid is:

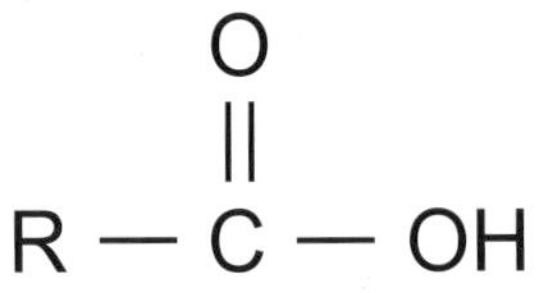

$$R-\overset{\overset{\displaystyle O}{\|}}{C}-OH$$

Systematic naming of these compounds is done by replacing the '–e' of the corresponding alkane with '–oic acid'. The molecule is numbered such that the carbonyl carbon is carbon number one. Many carboxylic acids have common names by which they are usually known (systematic names in italics):

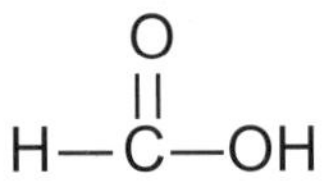

$H-C(=O)-OH$ formic acid, *methanoic acid*

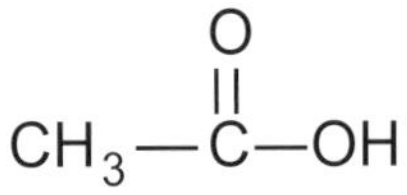

$CH_3-C(=O)-OH$ acetic acid, *ethanoic acid*

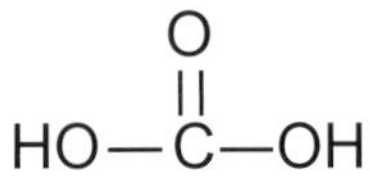

$HO-C(=O)-OH$ carbonic acid, *hydroxymethanoic acid*

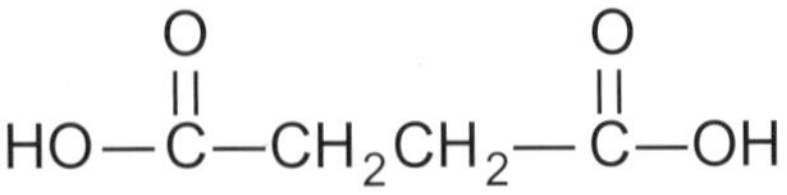

$HO-C(=O)-CH_2CH_2-C(=O)-OH$ succinic acid, *butanedioic acid*

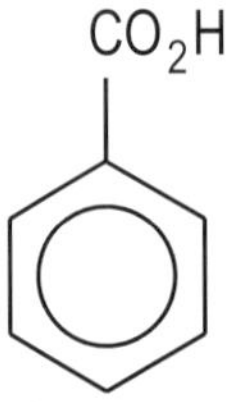

$C_6H_5CO_2H$ benzoic acid, same: *benzoic acid*

Low molecular weight carboxylic acids are liquids with strong odours and high boiling points. The high boiling point is due to the polarity and the hydrogen bonding capability of the molecule. Strong hydrogen bonding has a noticeable effect on boiling points and makes carboxylic acids boil at much higher temperatures than corresponding alcohols. Because of this hydrogen bonding, these molecules are water soluble. Carboxylic acids with more than 6 carbons are only slightly soluble in water, however, their alkali salts are quite soluble due to ionic properties. As well, carboxylic acids are soluble in dilute bases (NaOH or $NaHCO_3$), because of their acid properties. The carboxyl group is the basis of carboxylic acid chemistry, and there are four important features to remember. Looking at a general carboxylic acid:

- The hydrogen (H) is weakly acidic. This is due to its attachment to the oxygen atom, and because the carboxylate anion is resonance stabilized:

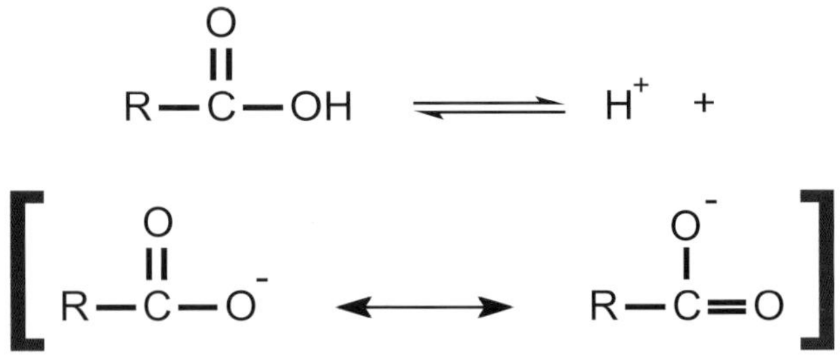

$$R-C(=O)-OH \rightleftharpoons H^+ + \left[R-C(=O)-O^- \longleftrightarrow R-C(-O^-)=O \right]$$

resonance forms

- The carboxyl carbon is very susceptible to nucleophilic attack. This is due to the attached oxygen atom, and the carbonyl oxygen, both atoms being electronegative:

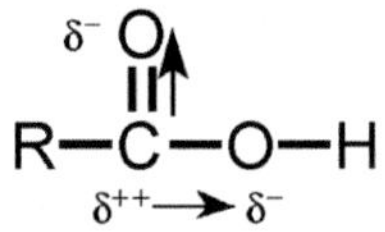

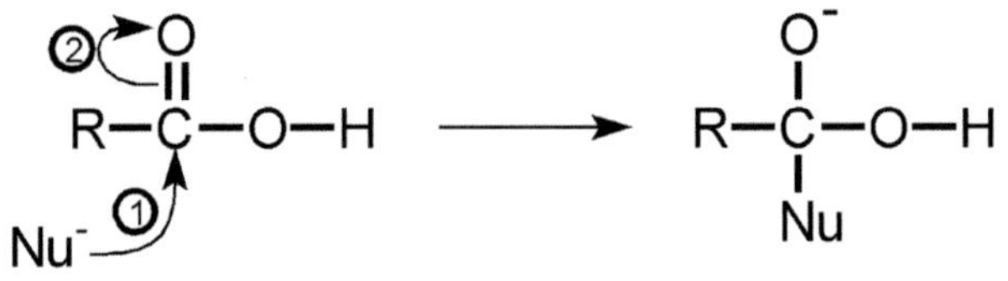

$$R-\overset{\delta^-}{C}(=O)-O-H \quad (\delta^{++} \rightarrow \delta^-)$$

$$Nu^- + R-C(=O)-O-H \longrightarrow R-C(-O^-)(Nu)-O-H$$

- In basic conditions, the hydroxyl group, as is, is a good leaving group. In acidic conditions, the protonated hydroxyl (i.e. water) is an excellent leaving group. This promotes nucleophilic substitution:

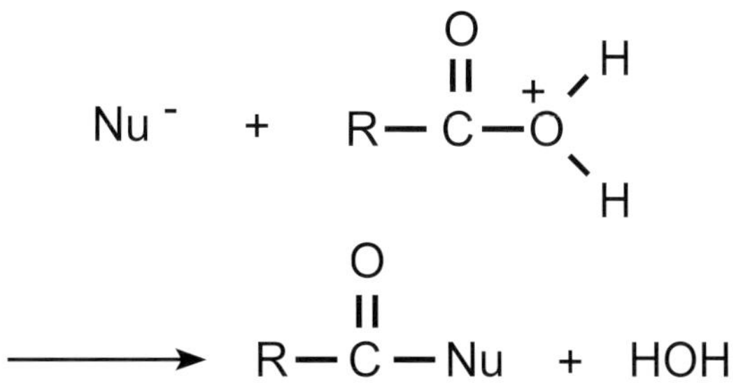

$$Nu^- + R{-}\overset{\overset{\large O}{\|}}{C}{-}\overset{+}{O}H_2 \longrightarrow R{-}\overset{\overset{\large O}{\|}}{C}{-}Nu + HOH$$

- Because of the carbonyl and hydroxyl moieties (i.e. parts), hydrogen bonding is possible both inter- and intramolecularly:

intermolecular (dimerization)

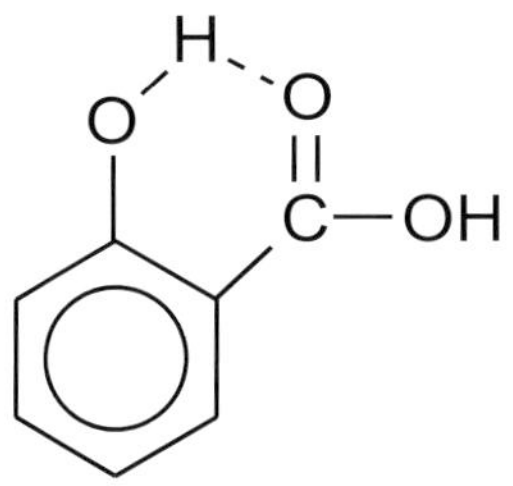

intramolecular

As implied by their name, carboxylic acids are acidic - the most common acid of all organic compounds. In fact, they are colloquially known as organic acids. Organic classes of molecules in order of increasing acid strength are:

alkanes < ammonia < alkynes < alcohols < water < carboxylic acids

In terms of substituents added to benzoic acid, electron-withdrawing groups such as $-Cl$ or $-NO_2$ inductively withdraw electrons and delocalize the negative charge, thereby stabilizing the carboxylate anion and increasing acidity. Electron-donating groups such as $-NH_2$ or $-OCH_3$ donate electrons and concentrate the negative charge, thereby destabilizing the carboxylate anion and decreasing acidity.

The relative acid strength among carboxylic acids depends on the inductive effects of the attached groups, and their proximity to the carboxyl. For example:

$CH_3CH_2{-}C(Cl)_2{-}COOH$ *is a stronger acid than* $CH_3CH_2{-}CH(Cl){-}COOH$.

The reason for this is that chlorine, which is electronegative, withdraws electron density and stabilizes the carboxylate anion. Proximity is important, as:

$CH_3CH_2{-}C(Cl)_2{-}COOH$ *is a stronger acid than* $CH_3{-}C(Cl)_2{-}CH_2COOH$.

Thus the effect of halogen substitution decreases as the substituent moves further away from the carbonyl carbon atom.

8.1.1 Carboxylic Acid Formation

A carboxylic acid can be formed by reacting a Grignard reagent with carbon dioxide, or by reacting an aldehyde with $KMnO_4$ (*see* ORG 6.2.2). Carboxylic acids are also formed by reacting a nitrile (in which nitrogen shares a triple bond with a carbon) with aqueous acid.

Mechanisms to synthesize carboxylic acids:

- Oxidative cleavage of alkenes/alkynes gives carboxylic acids in the presence of oxidizing reagents such as $NaCr_2O_7$ or $KMnO_4$ or ozone.

$KMnO_4$ / H_3O^+

OH

$KMnO_4$ or O_3 → 2

OH

- Oxidation of primary alcohols and aldehydes gives carboxylic acids. Primary alcohols often react with an oxidant such as the Jones' reagent (CrO_3, H_2SO_4). Aldehydes often react with oxidants such as the Jones' reagent or Tollens' reagent $[Ag(NH_3)_2]^+$, also symbolized Ag_2O. Other reagents include: $K_2Cr_2O_7/H_2SO_4$ or CrO_3/H_2SO_4 or $KMnO_4$.

OH $\xrightarrow[OH^-]{KMnO_4}$ OH

H $\xrightarrow{Ag_2O}$ OH

- Hydrolysis of nitriles, RCN, under either strong acid or base conditions can yield carboxylic acids and ammonia (or ammonium salts). Since cyanide anion CN^- is a good nucleophile in S_N2 reactions with primary and secondary alkyl halides, it allows the preparation of carboxylic acids from alkyl halides through cyanide displacement followed by hydrolysis of nitriles. Note that a nitrile hydrolysis reaction increases chain length by one carbon.

$$RCH_2X \xrightarrow{Na^{+-}CN} RCH_2C\equiv N \xrightarrow{H_3O^+} RCH_2COOH + NH_3$$

- Carboxylation of Grignards or other organometallic reagents react with carbon dioxide CO_2 to form carboxylic acids. Alkyl halides react with metal magnesium to form organomagnesium halide, which then reacts with carbon dioxide in a nucleophilic addition mechanism. Protonation of the carboxylate ion forms the final carboxylic acid product. Note that the carboxylation of a Grignard reagent increases chain length by one carbon.

$$RX + Mg \longrightarrow R-Mg-X$$

$$\xrightarrow{CO_2} R-CO_2^{-}\,{}^{+}MgX$$

$$\xrightarrow{H^+} R-C(=O)-OH$$

Grignard reagents are particularly useful in converting tertiary alkyl halides into carboxylic acids, which otherwise is very difficult.

$$(CH_3)_3C-Br \xrightarrow[3)\ H_3O^+]{1)\ Mg,\ ether\quad 2)\ CO_2} (CH_3)_3C-CO_2H$$

8.2 Important Reactions of Carboxylic Acids

Carboxylic acids undergo nucleophilic substitution reactions with many different nucleophiles, under a variety of conditions:

$$Nu^- + R-C(=O)-OH \longrightarrow R-C(=O)-Nu + OH^-$$

If the nucleophile is –OR, the resulting compound is an ester. If it is $-NH_2$, the resulting compound is an amide. If it is Cl from $SOCl_2$, or PCl_5, the resulting compound is an acid chloride.

The typical esterification reaction may be summarized:

$$\underset{\text{alcohol}}{R'O^{*}H} + \underset{\text{acid}}{R-C(=O)-OH} \longrightarrow \underset{\text{ester}}{R-C(=O)-O^{*}R'} + H_2O$$

Notice that an asterix* was added to the oxygen of the alcohol so that you can tell where that oxygen ended up in the product (i.e. the ester). In the lab, instead of an asterix (!), an isotope (CHM 1.3) of oxygen is used as a tracer or label.

The decarboxylation reaction involves the loss of the carboxyl group as CO_2:

$$HO-\overset{O}{\overset{\|}{C}}-\underset{R}{\overset{H}{C}}-\overset{O}{\overset{\|}{C}}-OH \xrightarrow[\text{heat}]{\text{base}} H-\underset{R}{\overset{H}{C}}-\overset{O}{\overset{\|}{C}}-OH + CO_2$$

β – diacid

$$R-\overset{O}{\overset{\|}{C}}-\underset{H}{\overset{H}{C}}-\overset{O}{\overset{\|}{C}}-OH \xrightarrow[\text{heat}]{\text{base}} R-\overset{O}{\overset{\|}{C}}-CH_3 + CO_2$$

β – keto acid

This reaction is not important for most ordinary carboxylic acids. There are certain types of carboxylic acids that decarboxylate easily, mainly:

- Those which have a keto group at the β position, known as β-keto acids.
- Malonic acids and its derivatives (i.e. β-diacids: those with two carboxyl groups, separated by one carbon).
- Carbonic acid and its derivatives.

Carboxylic acids are reduced to alcohols with lithium aluminum hydride, $LiAlH_4$, or H_2/metals (*see* ORG 6.2.2). Sodium borohydride, $NaBH_4$, being a milder reducing agent, only reduces aldehydes and ketones. Carboxylic acids may also be converted to esters or amides first, and then reduced:

$$LiAlH_4 + R-\overset{O}{\overset{\|}{C}}-OH \longrightarrow R-CH_2-OH$$

alcohol

CARBOXYLIC ACID DERIVATIVES
Chapter 9

Memorize

* IUPAC nomenclature

Understand

* Mechanisms of reactions
* Relative reactivity
* Steric, inductive effects

Importance

1 to 3 out of the 30 ORG

DAT questions are based on content in this chapter (in our estimation).
* Note that between 30% and 60% of the questions in DAT Organic Chemistry are based on content from 4 chapters: 1, 2, 5 and 6.

DAT-Prep.com

Introduction

Carboxylic acid derivatives are a series of compounds that can be synthesized using carboxylic acid. For the DAT, this includes acid chlorides, anhydrides, amides and esters.

Additional Resources

Free Online Q&A + Forum

Video: Online or DVD

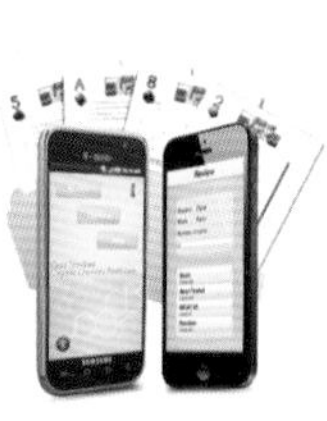

Flashcards

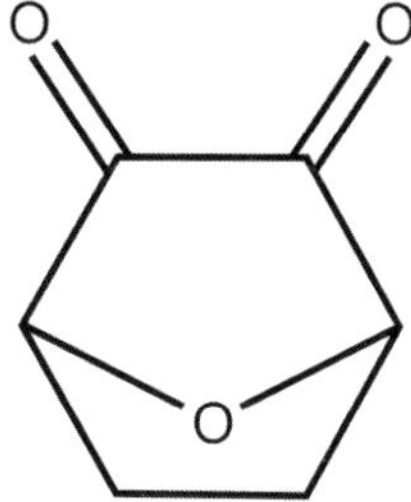

Special Guest

9.1 Acid Halides

The general structure of an acid halide is:

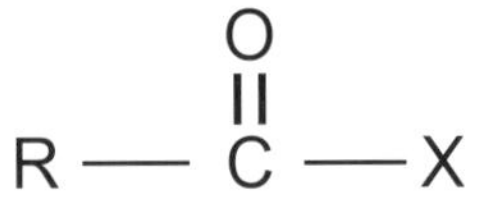

$$R-\overset{\overset{\large O}{\|}}{C}-X \qquad X = \text{Halide}$$

These are named by replacing the 'ic acid' of the parent carboxylic acid with the suffix 'yl halide.' For example:

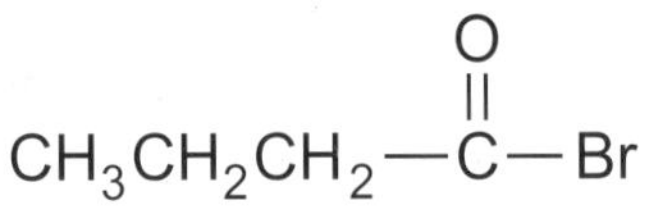

$$CH_3CH_2CH_2-\overset{\overset{\large O}{\|}}{C}-Br \quad \text{Butanoyl bromide}$$

$$CH_3-\overset{\overset{\large O}{\|}}{C}-Cl \quad \text{Acetyl chloride (ethanoyl chloride)}$$

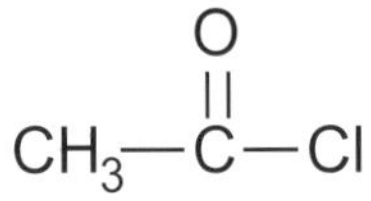

An "acyl" group (IUPAC name: alkanoyl) refers to the functional group RCO-.

Acid chlorides are synthesized by reacting the parent carboxylic acid with PCl_5 or $SOCl_2$. Acid chlorides react with $NaBH_4$ to form alcohols. This can be done in one or two steps. In one step, the acid chloride reacts with $NaBH_4$ to immediately form an alcohol. In two steps, the acid chloride can react first with $H_2/Pd/C$ to form a carboxylic acid; reaction of the carboxylic acid with $NaBH_4$ then produces an alcohol.

Acid halides can engage in nucleophilic reactions similar to carboxylic acids (*see* ORG 8.2); however, acid halides are more reactive (*see* ORG 9.6).

Acyl halides can be converted back to carboxylic acids through simple hydrolysis with H_2O. They can also be converted to esters by a reaction with alcohols. Lastly, acyl halides can be converted to amides ($RCONR_2$) by a reaction with amines.

9.1.1 Acid Anhydrides

The general structure of an acid anhydride is:

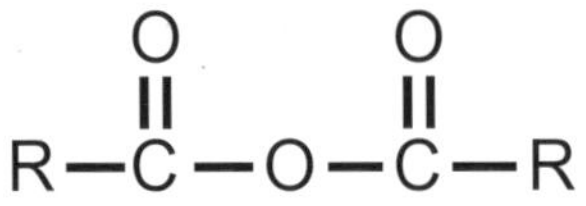

$$R-\overset{\overset{\large O}{\|}}{C}-O-\overset{\overset{\large O}{\|}}{C}-R$$

These are named by replacing the 'acid' of the parent carboxylic acid with the word 'anhydride.' For example:

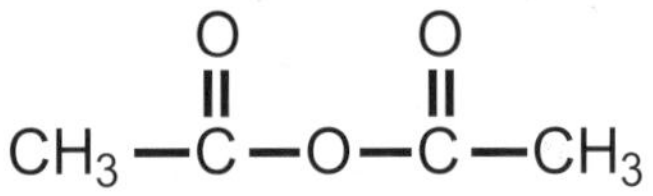

$$CH_3-\overset{\overset{\large O}{\|}}{C}-O-\overset{\overset{\large O}{\|}}{C}-CH_3$$

acetic anhydride
(ethanoic anhydride)

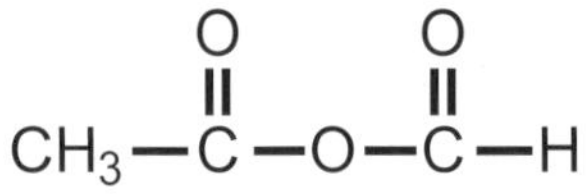

$$CH_3-\overset{\overset{\large O}{\|}}{C}-O-\overset{\overset{\large O}{\|}}{C}-H$$

acetic formic anhydride
(ethanoic methanoic anhydride)

Anhydrides can be synthesized by the reaction of an acyl halide with a carboxylate salt and are a bit less reactive than acyl chlorides.

Both acid chlorides and acid anhydrides have boiling points comparable to esters of similar molecular weight.

9.2 Important Reactions of Carboxylic Acid Derivatives

- Nucleophilic acyl substitution reaction: Carboxylic acid derivatives undergo nucleophilic acyl substitution reactions in which a potential leaving group is substituted by the nucleophile, thereby generating a new carbonyl compound. Relative reactivity of carboxylic acid derivatives toward a nucleophilic acyl substitution reaction is amide < ester < acid anhydride < acid chloride. Note that it is possible to convert a more reactive carboxylic acid derivative to a less reactive one, but not the opposite.

$$Nu^- + R\overset{\delta+}{C}(=\overset{\delta-}{O})LG \longrightarrow RC(=O)Nu + LG^-$$

- Synthesis of acid halides: Acid halides are synthesized from carboxylic acids by the reaction with thionyl chloride ($SOCl_2$), phosphorus trichloride (PCl_3) or phosphorus pentachloride (PCl_5). Reaction with phosphorus tribromide PBr_3 produces an acid bromide.

$$CH_3CH_2CH_2COOH \xrightarrow{SOCl_2} CH_3CH_2CH_2COCl$$

- Reactions of acid halides:

1. **Friedel-Crafts reaction:** A benzene ring attacks a carbocation electrophile -COR which is generated by the reaction with the $AlCl_3$ catalyst, yielding the final product Ar-COR.

$$C_6H_6 + RCCl(=O) \xrightarrow{AlCl_3} C_6H_5CR(=O) + HCl$$

2. **Conversion into acids:** Acid chlorides react with water to yield carboxylic acids. The attack of the nucleophile water followed by elimination of the chloride ion gives the product carboxylic acid and HCl.

$$RC(=O)Cl \xrightarrow{H_2O} RC(=O)OH$$

3. **Conversion into esters:** Acid chlorides react with alcohol to yield esters. The same type of nucleophilic acyl substitution mechanism is observed here. The alkoxide ion attacks the acidchloride while chloride is displaced.

$$RC(=O)Cl \xrightarrow{R'OH} RC(=O)OR'$$

4. **Conversion into amides:** Acid chlorides react with ammonia or amines to yield amides. Both mono- and di-substituted amines react well with acid chlorides, but not tri-substituted amines. Two equivalents of ammonia or amine must be used, one reacting with the acid chloride while the other reacting with HCl to form the ammonium chloride salt.

$$\mathrm{RCOCl} \xrightarrow[\text{base}]{R_2NH} \mathrm{RCONR_2}$$

5. **Conversion into alcohols:** Acid chlorides are reduced by $LiAlH_4$ to yield primary alcohols. The reaction is a substitution reaction of -H for -Cl, which is then further reduced to yield the final product alcohol.

$$\mathrm{RCOCl} \xrightarrow{LiAlH_4} \mathrm{RCOH} \xrightarrow{LiAlH_4} \mathrm{RCH_2OH}$$

Acid chlorides react with Grignard reagents to yield tertiary alcohols. Two equivalents of the Grignard reagent attack the acid chloride yielding the final product, the tertiary alcohol.

$$\mathrm{RCOCl} + 2\,\mathrm{R'MgX} \longrightarrow \mathrm{RR'_2COH}$$

Acid chlorides also react with H_2 in the presence of Lindlar's catalyst ($Pd/BaSO_4$, quinoline) to yield an aldehyde intermediate which can then be further reduced to yield an alcohol.

$$\mathrm{RCOCl} \xrightarrow[Pd/BaSO_4]{H_2} \mathrm{RCOH}$$

6. **Synthesis of acid anhydrides:** Acid anhydrides can be synthesized by a nucleophilic acyl substitution reaction of an acid chloride with a carboxylate anion.

$$\mathrm{CH_3COCl} + \mathrm{CH_3COONa} \longrightarrow \mathrm{CH_3COOCOCH_3} + \mathrm{NaCl}$$

- Reactions of acid anhydrides: The chemistry of acid anhydrides is similar to that of acid chlorides. Since they are more stable, acid anhydrides react more slowly.

1. **Conversion into acids:** Acid anhydrides react with water to yield carboxylic acids. The nucleophile in this reaction is water and the leaving group is a carboxylic acid.

$$\mathrm{RCOOCOR} \xrightarrow{H_2O} \mathrm{RCOOH}$$

2. **Conversion into esters:** Acid anhydrides react with alcohols to form esters and acids as in the following example with ethanoic anhydride.

$$\mathrm{CH_3C(O)OC(O)CH_3} + \mathrm{X{-}O{-}H} \longrightarrow \mathrm{CH_3C(O){-}O{-}X} + \mathrm{CH_3COOH}$$

3. **Conversion into amides:** Ammonia attacks the acid anhydride, yielding an amide and the leaving group carboxylic acid, which is reacted with another molecule of ammonia to give the ammonium salt of the carboxylate anion.

$$\mathrm{RCOOCOR} \xrightarrow[\text{base}]{R_2NH} \mathrm{RCONR_2}$$

4. **Conversion into alcohols:** Acid anhydrides are reduced by $LiAlH_4$ to yield primary alcohols.

$$(RCO)_2O \xrightarrow{[H]} RCH_2OH$$

9.3 Amides

The general structure of an amide is:

$$R-\overset{O}{\overset{\|}{C}}-NR'_2$$

These are named by replacing the '-ic (oic) acid' of the parent anhydride with the suffix '-amide.' If there are alkyl groups attached to the nitrogen, they are named as substituents, and designated by the letter N. For example:

$$CH_3-\overset{O}{\overset{\|}{C}}-N(C_2H_5)_2$$ N,N-diethylacetamide

$$CH_3CH_2-\overset{O}{\overset{\|}{C}}-NH_2$$ propanamide

Unsubstituted and monosubstituted amides form very strong intermolecular hydrogen bonds, and as a result, they have very high boiling and melting points. The boiling points of disubstituted amides are similar to those of aldehydes and ketones. Amides are essentially neutral (no acidity, as compared to carboxylic acids, and no basicity, as compared to amines).

Amides may be prepared by reacting carboxylic acids (or other carboxylic acid derivatives) with ammonia:

$$R-\overset{O}{\overset{\|}{C}}-OH + NH_3 + \text{heat} \xrightarrow{-H_2O} R-\overset{O}{\overset{\|}{C}}-NH_2$$

As well, amides undergo nucleophilic substitution reactions at the carbonyl carbon:

$$R-\overset{O}{\overset{\|}{C}}-NH_2 + NuH \longrightarrow R-\overset{O}{\overset{\|}{C}}-Nu + NH_3$$

Amides can be hydrolyzed to yield the parent carboxylic acid and amine. This reaction may take place under acidic or basic conditions:

$$\underset{\text{amide}}{R-\overset{O}{\overset{\|}{C}}-NHR} + H_2O \xrightarrow{H^+} \underset{\text{acid}}{R-\overset{O}{\overset{\|}{C}}-OH} + \underset{\text{amine}}{RNH_2}$$

$$\underset{\text{amide}}{R-\overset{O}{\overset{\|}{C}}-NHR} + H_2O \xrightarrow{OH^-}$$

$$\underset{\text{carboxylate}}{R-\overset{O}{\overset{\|}{C}}-O^-} + \underset{\text{amine}}{RNH_2} \xrightarrow{H^+} \underset{\text{acid}}{R-\overset{O}{\overset{\|}{C}}-OH}$$

Amides can also form amines by reacting with $LiAlH_4$.

Amides can also be converted to primary amines with the loss of the carbonyl carbon. This is known as a Hofmann rearrangement:

$$RC(=O)NH_2 \xrightarrow[NaOH]{Br_2} [R{-}N{=}C{=}O] \xrightarrow[-CO_2]{H_2O} R{-}NH_2$$

9.3.1 Important Reactions of Amides

Amides are much less reactive than acid chlorides, acid anhydrides or esters.

1. **Conversion into acids:** Amides react with water to yield carboxylic acids in acidic conditions or carboxylate anions in basic conditions.

$$RC(=O)NR'_2 \xrightarrow[heat]{H_2O} RC(=O)OH + R'_2NH$$

2. **Conversion into alcohols:** Amides can be reduced by $LiAlH_4$ to give amines. The net effect of this reaction is to convert an amide carbonyl group into a methylene group ($C{=}O \rightarrow CH_2$).

$$LiAlH_4 + RC(=O)NH_2 \longrightarrow H{-}C(R)(H){-}NH_2$$

9.4 Esters

The general structure of an ester is:

$$R{-}C(=O){-}O{-}R'$$

These are named by first citing the name of the alkyl group, followed by the parent acid, with the 'ic acid' replaced by 'ate.' For example:

$$CH_3{-}C(=O){-}O{-}CH_3$$

methyl acetate
(methyl ethanoate)

The boiling points of esters are lower than those of comparable acids or alcohols, and similar to comparable aldehydes and ketones, because they are polar compounds, without hydrogens to form hydrogen bonds. Esters with longer side chains (R-groups) are more nonpolar than esters with shorter side chains (R-groups). Esters usually have pleasing, fruity odors.

Esters may be synthesized by reacting carboxylic acids or their derivatives with alcohols under either basic or acidic conditions:

$$\underset{\text{alcohol}}{R'O^*H} + \underset{\text{acid}}{R-\overset{\overset{O}{\|}}{C}-OH} \longrightarrow \underset{\text{ester}}{R-\overset{\overset{O}{\|}}{C}-O^*R'} + H_2O$$

As well, esters undergo nucleophilic substitution reactions at the carbonyl carbon:

$$R-\overset{\overset{O}{\|}}{C}-OR' + NuH \longrightarrow R-\overset{\overset{O}{\|}}{C}-Nu + R'OH$$

Esters may also be hydrolyzed, to yield the parent carboxylic acid and alcohol. This reaction may take place under acidic or basic conditions.

$$\underset{\text{ester}}{R-\overset{\overset{O}{\|}}{C}-O^*R'} + H_2O \xrightarrow{H^+} \underset{\text{acid}}{R-\overset{\overset{O}{\|}}{C}-OH} + \underset{\text{alcohol}}{R'O^*H}$$

Esters can be transformed from one ester into another by using alcohols as nucleophiles. This process is known as transesterification:

$$H_2C{=}C(R^1)-C(=O)-OR^2 + R^3R^4N-R^5-OH \xrightarrow[-R^2OH]{\text{catalyst}} H_2C{=}C(R^1)-C(=O)-O-R^5-NR^3R^4$$

Another reaction type involves the formation of ketones using Grignard reagents. The ketone formed is usually only temporary and is further reduced to a tertiary alcohol due to the reactive nature of the newly formed ketone:

$$CH_3-\overset{\overset{O}{\|}}{C}-OC_2H_5 \xrightarrow{CH_3MgI} \left[CH_3-\underset{CH_3}{\overset{OMgI}{C}}-OC_2H_5\right] \xrightarrow{-C_2H_5OMgI} CH_3-\underset{CH_3}{C}{=}O$$

$$CH_3-\underset{CH_3}{C}{=}O \xrightarrow{CH_3MgI} \left[CH_3-\underset{CH_3}{\overset{OMgI}{C}}-CH_3\right] \xrightarrow{HOH} CH_3-\underset{CH_3}{\overset{OH}{C}}-CH_3$$

2-methylpropan-2-ol
(*tert*-butanol)

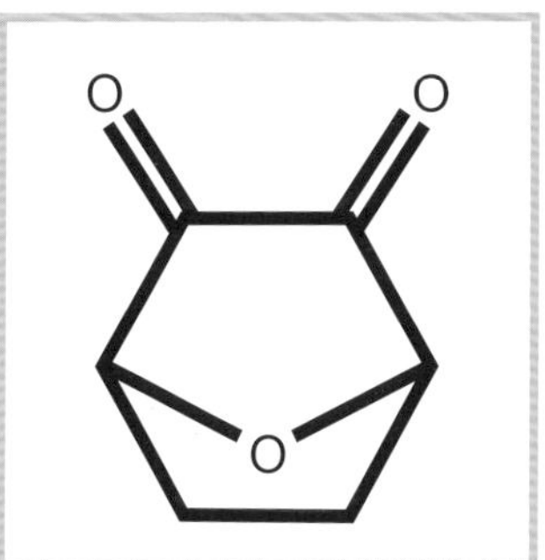

The Ester Bunny

NB: The Ester Bunny is NOT DAT material. In fact for you super-keeners: is the Ester Bunny a real ester? Find out in our Forum!

An important reaction of esters involves the combination of two ester molecules to form an acetoacetic ester (when two moles of ethyl acetate are combined). This is known as the Claisen condensation and is similar to the aldol condensation seen in ORG 7.2.4:

EtO⁻ + H–CH₂–C(=O)OEt ⟶

$CH_3C(=O)OEt$ + ⁻CH₂–C(=O)OEt ⟶

$CH_3C(O^-)(OEt)CH_2C(=O)OEt$ ⟶

$CH_3C(=O)CH_2C(=O)OEt$

- More reactions with esters: Esters have similar chemistry to acid chlorides and acid anhydrides; however, they are less reactive toward nucleophilic substitution reactions.

1. **Conversion into amides:** Esters can react with ammonia or amines to give amides and an alcohol side product.

$$RC(=O)OR' \xrightarrow[\text{base}]{R_2NH} RC(=O)NR_2$$

2. **Conversion into alcohols**: Esters can be easily reduced by $LiAlH_4$ to form primary alcohols. A hydride ion attacks the ester carbonyl carbon to form a tetrahedral intermediate. Loss of the alkoxide ion from the intermediate yields an aldehyde intermediate, which is further reduced by another hydride ion to give a primary alcohol final product.

$$LiAlH_4 + R'C(=O)OR'' \longrightarrow H{-}C(OH)(H){-}R' + R''O{-}H$$

Esters can also be reduced to tertiary alcohols by reacting with a Grignard reagent (or alkyl lithium). Grignard reagents add to the ester carbonyl carbon to form ketone intermediates, which are further attacked by the next equivalent of the Grignard reagent. Thus two equivalents of the Grignard reagent (or alkyl lithium) are used to produce tertiary alcohols.

$$2RLi \text{ or } 2RMgX + R'C(=O)OR'' \longrightarrow R{-}C(OH)(R){-}R'$$

9.4.1 Fats, Glycerides and Saponification

A special class of esters is known as fats (i.e. mono-, di-, and triglycerides). These are biologically important molecules, and they are formed in the following reaction:

$$\underset{\text{fatty acid}}{CH_3(CH_2)_{14}\overset{O}{\overset{\|}{C}}O^*H} + \underset{\text{glycerol}}{\begin{array}{c}CH_2OH\\|\\CH_2OH\\|\\CH_2OH\end{array}} \xrightarrow{-H_2O^*} \underset{\text{monoglyceride}}{\begin{array}{l}CH_2O-\overset{O}{\overset{\|}{C}}-(CH_2)_{14}CH_3\\|\\CH_2OH\\|\\CH_2OH\end{array}} \xrightarrow{-H_2O} \text{II} \xrightarrow{-H_2O} \text{III}$$

Fatty acids (= *long chain carboxylic acids*) are formed through the condensation of C2 units derived from acetate, and may be added to the monoglyceride formed in the above reaction, forming diglycerides, and triglycerides. Fats may be hydrolyzed by a base to the components glycerol and the salt of the fatty acids. The salts of long chain carboxylic acids are called soaps. Thus this process is called *saponification*:

$$\underset{\text{a triglyceride (a fat)}}{\begin{array}{l}CH_2O-\overset{O}{\overset{\|}{C}}-(CH_2)_{14}CH_3\\|\\CH_2O-\overset{O}{\overset{\|}{C}}-(CH_2)_{14}CH_3\\|\\CH_2O-\overset{O}{\overset{\|}{C}}-(CH_2)_{14}CH_3\end{array}} \xrightarrow{3NaOH} \underset{\text{glycerol}}{\begin{array}{c}CH_2OH\\|\\CH_2OH\\|\\CH_2OH\end{array}} + \underset{\text{salt of the fatty acid}}{3\,CH_3(CH_2)_{14}CO_2^-Na^+}$$

9.5 β-Keto Acids

β-keto acids are carboxylic acids with a keto group (i.e. *ketone*) at the β position. Thus it is an acid with a carbonyl group one carbon removed from a carboxylic acid group. Upon heating the carboxyl group can be readily removed as CO_2. This process is called *decarboxylation*. For example:

$$R-\overset{O}{\overset{\|}{C}}-CH_2-\overset{O}{\overset{\|}{C}}-OH \xrightarrow{\text{heat}} R\overset{O}{\overset{\|}{C}}CH_3 + CO_2$$

β – keto acid → ketone

9.6 Relative Reactivity of Carboxylic Acid Derivatives

Any factors that make the carbonyl group more easily attacked by nucleophiles favor the nucleophilic acyl substitution reaction. In terms of nucleophilic substitution, generally, carboxylic acid derivatives are more reactive than comparable non-carboxylic acid derivatives. One important reason for the preceding is that the carbon in carboxylic acids is also attached to the electronegative oxygen atom of the carbonyl group; therefore, carbon is more δ^+, thus being more attractive to a nucleophile. Hence an acid chloride (R-COCl) is more reactive than a comparable alkyl chloride (R-Cl); an ester (R-COOR') is more reactive than a comparable ether (R-OR'); and an amide ($R-CONH_2$) is more reactive than a comparable amine ($R-NH_2$).

Amongst carboxylic acid derivatives, the carbonyl reactivity in order from most to least reactive is:

acid chlorides > anhydrides >> esters
> acids > amides > nitriles

The reasons for this may be attributed to resonance effects and inductive effects. The resonance effect is the ability of the substituent to stabilize the carbocation intermediate by delocalization of electrons. The inductive effect is the substituent group, by virtue of its electronegativity, to pull electrons away increasing the partial positivity of the carbonyl carbon.

Within each carboxylic acid derivative, steric or bulk effects also play an important role. The less the steric hindrance, the more access a nucleophile will have to attack the carbonyl carbon, and vice versa.

9.7 Phosphate Esters

Phosphoric acid derivatives have similar features to those of carboxylic acid derivatives. Phosphoric acid and mono- or di-phosphoric esters are acidic. Under acidic condition, these phosphoric esters can be converted to the parent acid H_3PO_4 and alcohols. To see the structure of phosphate esters, see ORG 12.5.5.

Go online to DAT-prep.com for chapter review Q&A and forum.

ETHERS AND PHENOLS

Chapter 10

Memorize	Understand	Importance
*IUPAC nomenclature	*S_N2 synthesis of ethers *Effect of substituent groups on phenols *Synthesis of oxiranes	**1 to 3 out of the 30 ORG** DAT questions are based on content in this chapter (in our estimation). * Note that between 30% and 60% of the questions in DAT Organic Chemistry are based on content from 4 chapters: 1, 2, 5 and 6.

Introduction

Ethers are composed of an oxygen atom connected to two alkyl or aryl groups of the general formula R–O–R'. A classic example is the solvent and anesthetic diethyl ether, often just called "ether." Phenol is a toxic, white crystalline solid with a sweet tarry odor often referred to as a "hospital smell"! Its chemical formula is C_6H_5OH and its structure is that of a hydroxyl group (-OH) bonded to a phenyl ring thus it is an aromatic compound.

Additional Resources

Free Online Q&A + Forum

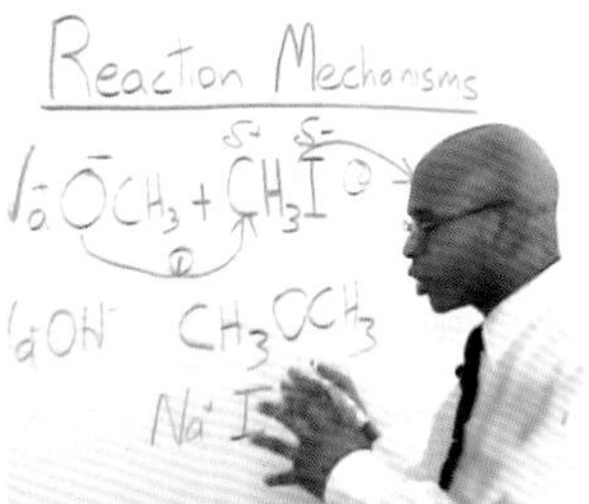

Video: Online or DVD

Flashcards

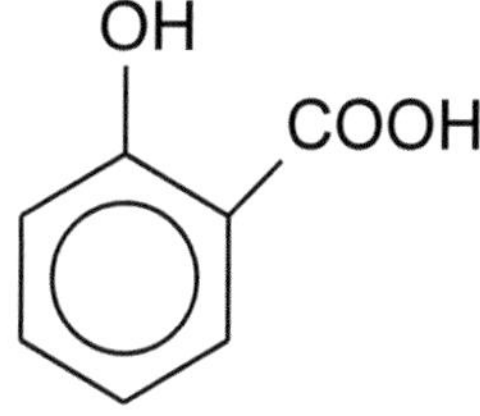

Special Guest

10.1 Description and Nomenclature of Ethers

The general structure of an ether is R-O-R', where the R's may be either aromatic or aliphatic (= *containing only carbon and hydrogen atoms*). In the common system of nomenclature, the two groups on either side of the oxygen are named, followed by the word ether:

$$CH_3 - O - CH_3 \qquad CH_3 - O - \underset{}{CH}(CH_3)CH_3$$

dimethyl ether — methyl isopropyl ether

In the systematic system of nomenclature, the alkoxy (RO-) groups are always named as substituents:

$$CH_3 - O - CH_3 \qquad CH_3 - O - CH(CH_3)CH_3$$

methoxy methane — methoxy isopropane

The boiling points of ethers are comparable to that of other hydrocarbons, which is regarded as relatively low temperatures when compared to alcohols. Ethers are more polar than other hydrocarbons, but are not capable of forming intermolecular hydrogen bonds (those between two ether molecules). Ethers are only slightly soluble in water. However, they can form intermolecular hydrogen bonds between the ether and the water molecules.

Ethers are good solvents, as the ether linkage is inert to many chemical reagents. Ethers are weak Lewis bases and can be protonated to form positively charged conjugate acids. In the presence of a high concentration of a strong acid (especially HI or HBr), the ether linkage will be cleaved, to form an alcohol and an alkyl halide:

$$CH_3 - O - CH_3 + HI \longrightarrow$$
$$CH_3 - OH + CH_3 - I$$

10.1.1 Important Reactions of Ethers

- Williamson ether synthesis: A metal alkoxide can react with a primary alkyl halide to yield an ether in an S_N2 mechanism. The alkoxide, which is prepared by the reaction of an alcohol with a strong base (ORG 6.2.4), acts as a nucleophile and displaces the halide. Since primary halides work best in an S_N2 mechanism, asymmetrical ethers will be synthesized by the reaction between non-hindered halides and more hindered alkoxides. This reaction will not proceed with a hindered alkyl halide substrate:

$$Na^{+}\ {}^{-}OCH_3 + {}^{\delta+}CH_3 - I^{\delta-} \longrightarrow$$
$$CH_3 - O - CH_3 + Na^{+}I^{-}$$

sodium cyclohexanoxide + CH_3I iodomethane (methyl iodide)

→ cyclohexyl methyl ether (methoxycyclohexane) + NaI

In a variant of the Williamson ether synthesis, an alkoxide ion displaces a chloride atom within the same molecule. The precursor compounds are called halohydrins. For example, with 2-chloropropanol, an intramolecular epoxide formation reaction is possible creating the cyclic ether called oxirane (C_2H_4O). Note that oxirane is a three-membered cyclic ether (epoxide).

CH_2OH / Cl—C—H → (KOH, H_2O) → epoxide

Cyclic ethers can also be prepared by reacting an alkene with m-CPBA (meta-chloroperoxybenzoic acid) which can also form an oxirane:

cyclohexene → 1,2-epoxycyclohexane (cyclohexene epoxide)

- Acidic Cleavage: Cleavage reactions of straight chain ethers takes place in the presence of HBr or HI (or even H_2SO_4) and is initiated by protonation of the ether oxygen.

Primary or secondary ethers react by an S_N2 mechanism in which I^- or Br^- attacks the protonated ether at the less hindered site. Tertiary, benzylic and allylic ethers react by an S_N1 or E1 mechanism because these substrates can produce stable intermediate carbocations. Please see the following mechanism:

$$\underset{\text{ether}}{(CH_3)_2CH-O-CH_2CH_3} \xrightarrow[\text{hydrogen halide}]{HI} \underset{\text{alcohol}}{(CH_3)_2CH-OH} + \underset{\text{alkyl halide}}{I-CH_2CH_3}$$

$$\underset{\text{ether}}{(CH_3)_2CH-\ddot{O}-CH_2CH_3} \xrightarrow[\text{hydrogen halide}]{HI} \left[(CH_3)_2CH-\ddot{O}-CH_2CH_3 \quad H^+ \quad :\ddot{I}:^-\right] \longrightarrow$$

$$\underset{\text{dialkyl oxonium ion}}{(CH_3)_2CH-\overset{+}{\ddot{O}}(H)-CH_2CH_3} + \underset{\text{halide ion}}{:\ddot{I}:^-} \longrightarrow \left[(CH_3)_2CH-\overset{+}{\ddot{O}}(H)-CH_2(CH_3) \quad :\ddot{I}:^-\right]$$

$$\longrightarrow \underset{\text{alcohol}}{(CH_3)_2CH-OH} + \underset{\text{alkyl halide}}{I-CH_2CH_3}$$

10.2 Phenols

A phenol is a molecule consisting of a hydroxyl (–OH) group attached to a benzene (aromatic) ring. The following are some phenols and derivatives which are important to biochemistry, medicine and nature:

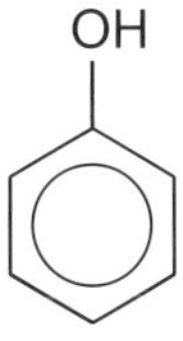

phenol

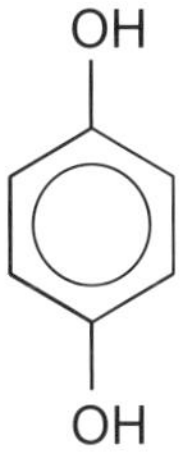

hydroquinone

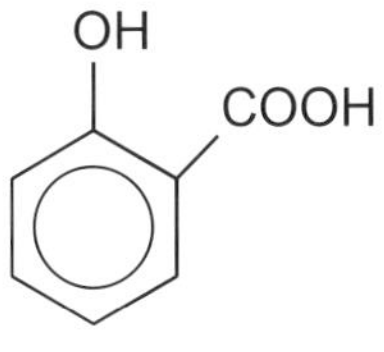

salicylic acid

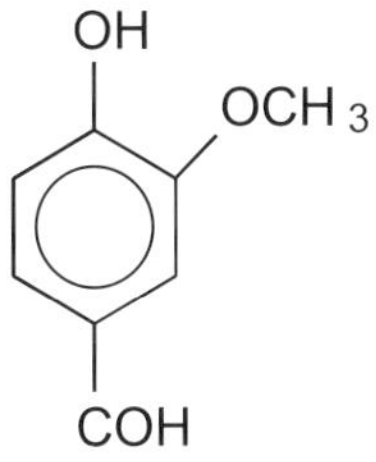

vanillin

Phenols are more acidic than their corresponding alcohols. This is due mainly to the electron withdrawing and resonance stabilization effects of the aromatic ring in the conjugate base anion (the phenoxide ion):

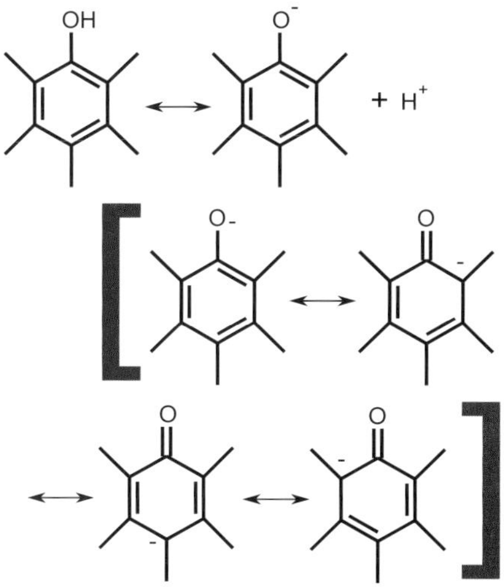

Substituent groups on the ring affect the acidity of phenols by both inductive effects (as with alcohols) and resonance effects. The resonance structures show that electron stabilizing (*withdrawing* or *meta directing*) groups at the ortho or para positions should increase the acidity of the phenol. Examples of these groups include the nitro group (–NO_2), –CN, –CO_2H, and the weakly deactivating o-p directors - the halogens. Destabilizing groups, such as alkyl groups, or other ortho-para directors, will make the compound less acidic. Phenols are ortho-para directors (see ORG Chapter 5).

Phenols can form hydrogen bonds, resulting in fairly high boiling points. Their solubility in water, however, is limited, because of the hydrophobic nature of the aromatic ring. Ortho phenols have lower boiling points than meta and para phenols, as they can form intramolecular hydrogen bonds. However, the para and even the ortho compounds can sometimes form intermolecular hydrogen bonds:

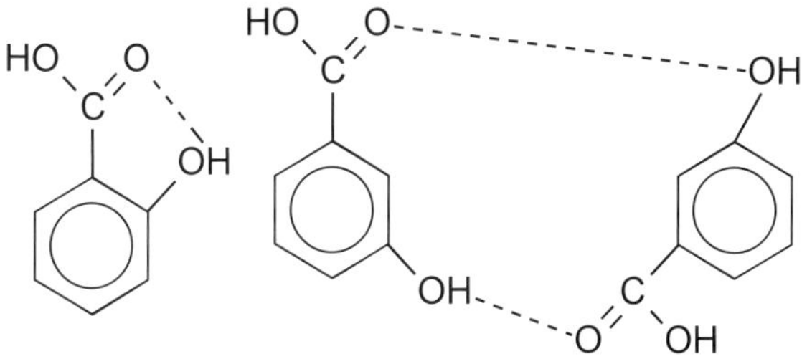

10.2.1 Electrophilic Aromatic Substitution for Phenols

The hydroxyl group is a powerful activating group and an ortho-para director in electrophilic substitutions. Thus phenols can brominate three times in bromine water as follows:

$$\text{C}_6\text{H}_5\text{OH} + 3\,Br_2 \xrightarrow{H_2O} \text{2,4,6-tribromophenol} + 3\,HBr$$

Go online to DAT-prep.com for chapter review Q&A and forum.

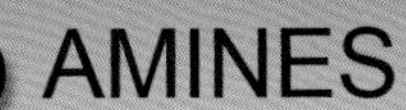

AMINES

Chapter 11

Memorize	Understand	Importance
* IUPAC nomenclature	* Effect of hydrogen bonds * Mechanisms of reactions * Trends in basicity * Resonance, delocalization of electrons * Aromatic amine chemistry	**1 to 3 out of the 30 ORG** DAT questions are based on content in this chapter (in our estimation). * Note that between 30% and 60% of the questions in DAT Organic Chemistry are based on content from 4 chapters: 1, 2, 5 and 6.

DAT-Prep.com

Introduction

Amines are compounds and functional groups that contain a basic nitrogen atom with a lone pair. Amines are derivatives of ammonia (NH_3), where one or more hydrogen atoms are replaced by organic substituents such as alkyl and aryl groups.

Additional Resources

Free Online Q&A + Forum

Video: Online or DVD

Flashcards

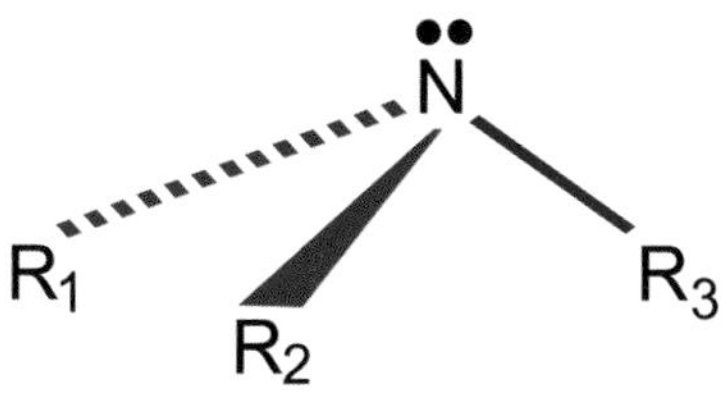

Special Guest

11.1 Description and Nomenclature

Organic compounds with a trivalent nitrogen atom bonded to one or more carbon atoms are called amines. These are organic derivatives of ammonia. They may be classified depending on the number of carbon atoms bonded to the nitrogen:

Primary Amine:	RNH_2
Secondary Amine:	R_2NH
Tertiary Amine:	R_3N
Quaternary Salt:	$R_4N^+ X^-$

In the common system of nomenclature, amines are named by adding the suffix '-amine' to the name of the alkyl group. In a secondary or tertiary amine, where there is more than one alkyl group, the groups are named as N-substituted derivatives of the larger group:

$$CH_3 - \underset{}{\overset{CH_3}{\overset{|}{CH}}} - \overset{CH_3}{\overset{|}{N}} - CH_2 - CH_3$$

N, N-methyl ethyl isopropylamine

In the systematic system of nomenclature, amines are named analagous to alcohols, except the suffix '-amine' is used instead of the suffix '-ol'.

When amines are present with multiple asymmetric substituents, they are named by considering the largest group as the parent name and the other alkyl groups as N-substituents of the parent:

N, N-dimethyl-2-butanamine

The $-NH_2$ group is named as an amino substituent on a parent molecule when amines are present with more than one functional group:

H_2N ... OH (O)

4-aminobutanoic acid

The bonding in amines is similar to the bonding in ammonia. The nitrogen atom is sp^3 hybridized (a common DAT question). Primary, secondary and tertiary amines have a trigonal pyramidal shape (CHM 3.5). The C-N-C bond angle is approximately 108°. Quaternary amines have a tetrahedral shape and a normal tetrahedral bond angle of 109.5°.

With its tetrahedral geometry, amines with three different substituents are considered chiral. Such amines are analogous to chiral alkanes in that the nitrogen atom will possess four different substituents - considering the lone pair of electrons to be the fourth substituent. However, unlike chiral alkanes, chiral amines do not exist in two separate enantiomers. Pyramidal nitrogen inversion between the two enantiomeric forms occurs so rapidly at room temperature that the two forms cannot be isolated.

11.1.1 The Basicity of Amines

Along with the three attached groups, amines have an unbonded electron pair. Most of the chemistry of amines depends on this unbonded electron pair:

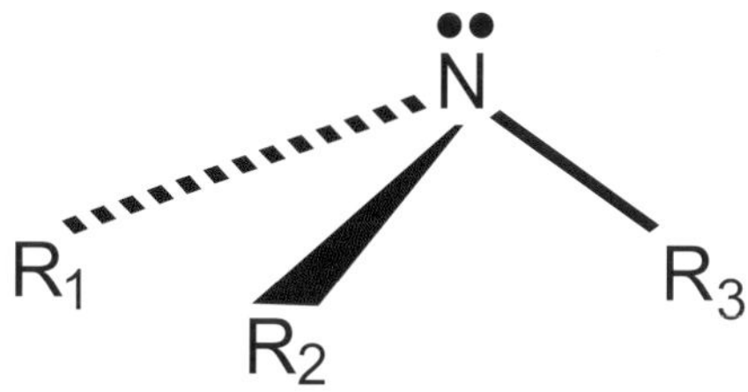

The electron pair is stabilized by the electron donating effects of alkyl groups. Thus the lone pair in tertiary amines is more stable than in secondary amines which, in turn, is more stable than in primary amines. As a result of this electron pair, amines are Lewis bases (see CHM 3.4), and good nucleophiles. In aqueous solution, amines are weak bases, and can accept a proton:

$$R_3N + H_2O \longrightarrow R_3NH^+ + OH^-$$

The ammonium cation in the preceding reaction is stabilized, once again, by the electron donating effects of the alkyl groups. Conversely, should the nitrogen be adjacent to a carbocation, the lone pair can stabilize the carbocation by delocalizing the charge.

The relative basicity of amines is determined by the following:

- If the free amine is stabilized relative to the cation, the amine is less basic.
- If the cation is stabilized relative to the free amine, the amine is more stable, thus the stronger base.

Groups that withdraw electron density (such as halides or aromatics) decrease the availability of the unbonded electron pair. Electron releasing groups (such as alkyl groups) increase the availability of the unbonded electron pair. The base strength then increases in the following series (where Ø represents a phenyl group):

$$NO_2{-}Ø{-}NH_2 < Ø{-}NH_2 < Ø{-}CH_2{-}NH_2 < NH_3 < CH_3{-}NH_2 < (CH_3)_2{-}N{-}H < (CH_3)_3{-}N$$

Note that a substituent attached to an aromatic ring can greatly affect the basicity of the amine. For example, electron withdrawing groups (i.e. $-NO_2$) withdraw electrons from the ring which, in turn, withdraws the lone electron pair (*delocalization*) from nitrogen. Thus the lone pair is less available to bond witha proton; consequently, it is a weaker base. The opposite occurs with an electron donating group, making the amine, relatively, a better base (see ORG Chapter 5).

11.1.2 More Properties of Amines

- The nitrogen atom can hydrogen bond (using its electron pair) to hydrogens attached to other N's or O's. It can also form hydrogen bonds from hydrogens attached to it with electron pairs of N, O, F or Cl:

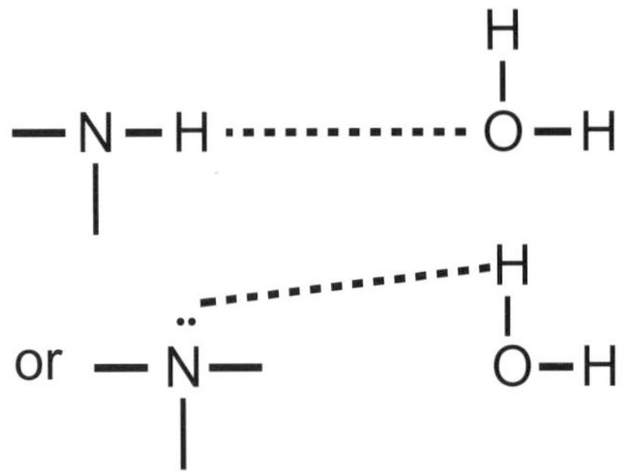

Note that primary or secondary amines can hydrogen bond with each other, but tertiary amines cannot. This leads to boiling points which are higher than would be expected for compounds of similar molecular weight, like alkanes, but lower than similar alcohols or carboxylic acids. The hydrogen bonding also renders low weight amines soluble in water.

- A dipole moment is possible:

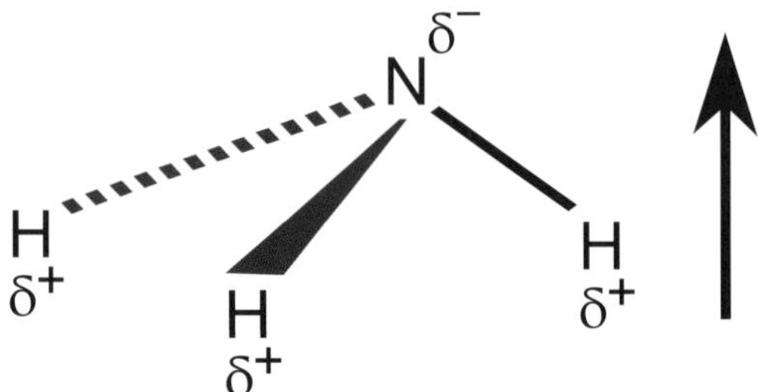

- The nitrogen in amines can contribute its lone pair electrons to activate a benzene ring. Thus amines are ortho-para directors.

- The solubility of quaternary salts decreases with increasing molecular weight. The quaternary structure has steric hindrance and the lone pair electrons on N is not available for H-bonding, thus their solubility is much less than other amines or even alkyl ammonium salts (i.e. $R\text{–}NH_3^+X^-$, $R_2\text{–}NH_2^+X^-$, $R_3\text{–}NH^+X^-$). Quaternary ammonium salts can be synthesized from ammonium hydroxides which are very strong bases.

$$\underset{\text{Quaternary hydroxide}}{(CH_3)_4N^+OH^-} + HCl \longrightarrow \underset{\text{Quaternary salt}}{(CH_3)_4N^+Cl^-} + H_2O$$

11.2 Important Reactions of Amines

- **Amide formation** is an important reaction for protein synthesis. Primary and secondary amines will react with carboxylic acids and their derivatives to form *amides*:

$$R'NH_2 + R-\overset{\overset{\displaystyle O}{\|}}{C}-OH$$

primary or secondary amine; acid

$$\longrightarrow R-\overset{\overset{\displaystyle O}{\|}}{C}-NHR' + H_2O$$

amine

Amides can engage in resonance such that the lone pair electrons on the nitrogen is delocalized. Thus amides are by far less basic than amines.

$$\left[R-\overset{\overset{\displaystyle O}{\|}}{C}-NR_2 \longleftrightarrow R-\overset{\overset{\displaystyle O^-}{|}}{C}=\overset{+}{N}R_2\right]$$

As can be seen, the C–N bond has a partial double bond character. Thus there is restricted rotation about the C–N bond.

- **Alkylation** is another important reaction which involves amines with alkyl halides:

$$RCH_2Cl + \underset{1^\circ, 2^\circ \text{ or } 3^\circ \text{ amine}}{R'NH_2} \longrightarrow RCH_2NHR' + HCl$$

Both amide formation and alkylation make use of the nucleophilic character of the electrons on nitrogen.

Thus ammonia or an alkyl amine reacts with an alkyl halide to yield an amine in an S_N2 mechanism. Ammonia produces a primary amine; a primary amine produces a secondary amine; a secondary amine produces a tertiary amine; and tertiary amine produces a quaternary ammonium salt.

$$H-\overset{\overset{\displaystyle R_1}{|}}{\underset{\underset{\displaystyle R_2}{|}}{N}}: \quad + \quad R_3X$$

primary or secondary amine; halogenoalkane

$$\longrightarrow :\overset{\overset{\displaystyle R_1}{|}}{\underset{\underset{\displaystyle R_2}{|}}{N}}-R_3 \quad + \quad HX$$

alkyl-substituted amine (secondary or tertiary); halogen acid

R1
$R_3—N: + R_4X$
R2
tertiary amine   halogenoalkane

$\longrightarrow R_3—N^+—R_4 + X^-$
(with R_1 above and R_2 below N)
quaternary ammonium cation   halide anion

quaternary ammonium salt

- **Gabriel synthesis:** Primary amines can also be obtained from azide synthesis and Gabriel synthesis in an S_N2 mechanism. The azide ion N_3^-, acting as a nucleophile, displaces the halide ion from the alkyl halide to form RN_3, which is then reduced by $LiAlH_4$ to form the desired primary amine.

$$R\text{-}CH_2\text{-}Cl \xrightarrow[2.\ LiAlH_4]{1.\ NaN_3} R\text{-}CH_2\text{-}NH_2$$

Gabriel amine synthesis occurs via a phthalimide ion displacing the halide from the alkyl halide followed by basic hydrolysis of the N-alkyl phthalimide yielding a primary amine.

$$R\text{-}CH_2\text{-}Cl \xrightarrow{\text{phthalimide } N^- K^+} R\text{-}CH_2\text{-}N(\text{phthalimide}) \xrightarrow{NH_2NH_2} R\text{-}CH_2\text{-}NH_2$$

- **Reductive amination:** Amines can also be synthesized by reductive amination in which an aldehyde or ketone reacts with ammonia, a primary amine or a secondary amine to form a corresponding primary amine, secondary amine or tertiary amine.

$$R_2C{=}O + H\text{-}NH\text{-}R' \xrightarrow{-H_2O} R_2C{=}N\text{-}R' \xrightarrow{+H_2} R_2CH\text{-}NH\text{-}R'$$

- **Reduction of nitriles:** Nitriles can be reduced by $LiAlH_4$ to produce primary amines. This offers a way to convert alkyl halides into primary amines with one more carbon atom.

$$RX \xrightarrow{NaCN} R-C\equiv N$$

$$\xrightarrow[Pt]{H_2(g)} R-CH_2-NH_2$$

- **Reduction of amides:** Amides can also be reduced by $LiAlH_4$ to produce primary amines. Thus carboxylic acids can be converted into primary amines with the same number of carbon atoms.

$$RCOOH \xrightarrow[2.\ NH_3]{1.\ SOCl_2}$$

$$R-C(=O)-NH_2 \xrightarrow[2.\ H^+/\ H_2O]{1.\ LiAlH_4/\ ether}$$

$$R-CH_2-NH_2$$

Go online to DAT-prep.com for chapter review Q&A and forum.

BIOLOGICAL MOLECULES
Chapter 12

Memorize

* Basic structures
* Isoelectric point equation
* Define: amphoteric, zwitterions

Understand

* Effect of H, S, hydrophobic bonds
* Basic mechanisms of reactions
* Effect of pH, isoelectric point
* Protein structure
* Different ways of drawing structures

Importance

0 to 2 out of the 30 ORG

DAT questions are based on content in this chapter (in our estimation).
* Note that between 30% and 60% of the questions in DAT Organic Chemistry are based on content from 4 chapters: 1, 2, 5 and 6.

Introduction

Biological molecules truly involve the chemistry of life. Such molecules include amino acids and proteins, carbohydrates (glucose, disaccharides, polysaccharides), lipids (triglycerides, steroids) and nucleic acids (DNA, RNA).

Additional Resources

Free Online Q&A + Forum

Video: Online or DVD

Flashcards

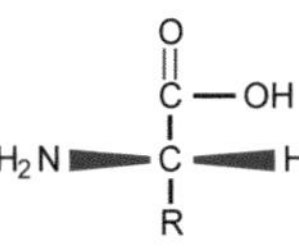

Special Guest

12.1 Amino Acids

Amino acids are molecules that contain a side chain (*R*), a carboxylic acid, and an amino group at the α carbon. Thus the general structure of α-amino acids is:

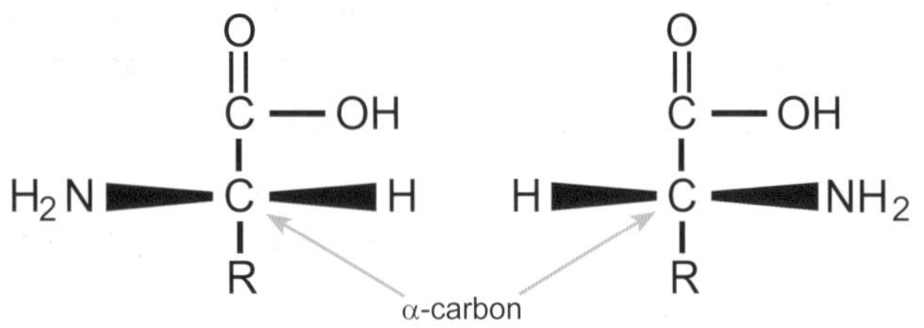

L - amino acid   α-carbon   D - amino acid

Amino acids may be named systematically as substituted carboxylic acids, however, there are 20 important α-amino acids that are known by common names. These are naturally occurring and they form the building blocks of most proteins found in humans. The following are a few examples of α-amino acids:

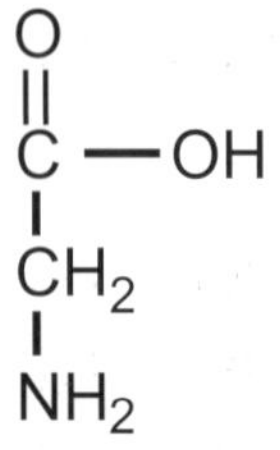

Glycine 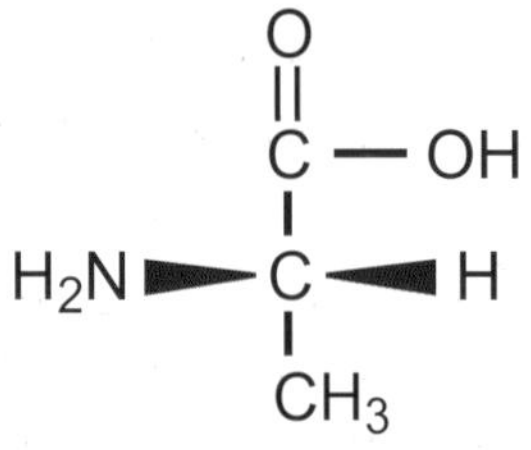   Alanine

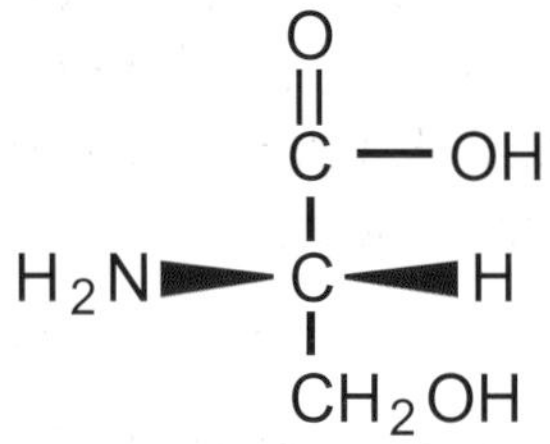

Serine 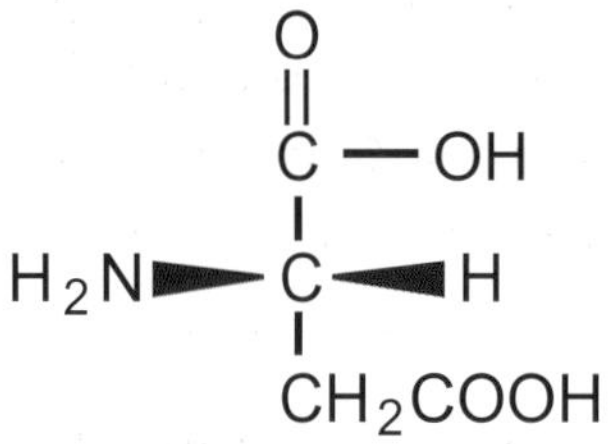   Aspartic acid

Note that the D/L system is commonly used for amino acid and carbohydrate chemistry. The reason is that naturally occurring amino acids have the same relative configuration, the L-configuration, while naturally occurring carbohydrates are nearly all D-configuration. However, the absolute configuration depends on the priority assigned to the side group (*see* ORG 2.3.1 *for rules*).

In the preceding amino acids, the S-configuration prevails (*except glycine which cannot be assigned any configuration since it is not chiral*).

The following mnemonic is helpful for determining the D/L isomeric form of an amino acid: the "CORN" rule. The substituents **CO**OH, **R**, **N**H_2, and H are arranged around the chiral center. Starting with H away from the viewer, if these groups are arranged clockwise around the chiral carbon, then it is the D-form. If counter-clockwise, it is the L-form.

Also note that, except for glycine, the α-carbon of all amino acids are chiral indicating that there must be two different enantiomeric forms.

12.1.1 Hydrophilic vs. Hydrophobic

Different types of amino acids tend to be found in different areas of the proteins that they make up. Amino acids which are ionic and/or polar are hydrophilic, and tend to be found on the exterior of proteins (i.e. *exposed to water*). These include aspartic acid and its amide, glutamic acid and its amide, lysine, arginine and histidine. Certain other polar amino acids are found on either the interior or exterior of proteins. These include serine, threonine, and tyrosine. Hydrophobic amino acids which may be found on the interior of proteins include methionine, leucine, tryptophan, valine and phenylalanine. Hydrophobic molecules tend to cluster in aqueous solutions (= *hydrophobic bonding*). Alanine is a nonpolar amino acid which is unusual because it is less hydrophobic than most nonpolar amino acids. This is because its nonpolar side chain is very short.

Glycine is the smallest amino acid, and the only one that is not optically active. It is often found at the 'corners' of proteins. Alanine is small and, although hydrophobic, is found on the surface of proteins.

12.1.2 Acidic vs. Basic

Amino acids have both an acid and basic components (= *amphoteric*). The amino acids with the R group containing an amino ($-NH_2$) group, are basic. The two basic amino acids are lysine and arginine. Amino acids with an R group containing a carboxyl ($-COOH$) group are acidic. The two acidic amino acids are aspartic acid and glutamic acid. One amino acid, histidine, may act as either an acid or a base, depending upon the pH of the resident solution. This makes histidine a very good physiologic buffer. The rest of the amino acids are considered to be neutral.

The basic $-NH_2$ group in the amino acid is present as an ammonium ion, $-NH_3^+$. The acidic carboxyl $-COOH$ group is present as a carboxylate ion, $-COO^-$. As a result, amino acids are <u>dipolar ions</u>, or *zwitterions*. In an aqueous solution, there is an equilibrium present between the dipolar, the anionic, and the cationic forms of the amino acid:

$$\underset{\text{Acidic}}{H_3\overset{+}{N}-\underset{\underset{CH_3}{|}}{CH}-CO_2H} \underset{H_3O^+}{\rightleftharpoons} \underset{\text{Neutral}}{H_3\overset{+}{N}-\underset{\underset{CH_3}{|}}{CH}-CO_2^-} \underset{H_3O^+}{\rightleftharpoons} \underset{\text{Basic}}{H_2N-\underset{\underset{CH_3}{|}}{CH}-CO_2^-}$$

Therefore the charge on the amino acid will vary with the pH of the solution, and with the isoelectric point. This point is the pH where a given amino acid will be neutral (i.e. have no net charge). For an amino acid with only one amine and one carboxyl group, the isoelectric point can be calculated from the average of the pK_a values of the 2 ionizable groups:

$$\text{isoelectric point} = pI = (pK_{a1} + pK_{a2})/2$$

For an acidic amino acid, the isoelectric point is the average of pK_a values of the carboxyl group and the additional carboxyl group on the side chain. For a basic amino acid, the isoelectric point is the average of pK_a values of the amino group and the additional amino group on the side chain.

Above the isoelectric point (basic conditions), the amino acids will have a net negative charge. Below the isoelectric point (acidic conditions), the amino acids will have a net positive charge.

As this is a common exam question, let's further summarize for the average amino acid: When in a relatively acidic solution, the amino acid is fully protonated and exists as a cation, that is, it has two protons available for dissociation, one from the carboxyl group and one from the amino group. When in a relatively basic solution, the amino acid is fully deprotonated and exists as an anion, that is, it has two proton accepting groups, the carboxyl group and the amino group. At the isoelectric point, the amino acid exists as a neutral, dipolar zwitterion, which means that the carboxyl group is deprotonated while the amino group is protonated.

12.1.3 The 20 Alpha-Amino Acids

1. Nonpolar amino acids: R groups are hydrophobic and thus decrease solubility. These amino acids are usually found within the interior of the protein molecule.

2. Polar amino acids: R groups are hydrophilic and thus increase the solubility. These amino acids are usually found on the protein's surface.

3. Acidic amino acids: R groups contain an additional carboxyl group. These amino acids have a negative charge at physiological pH.

4. Basic amino acids: R groups contain an additional amine group. These amino acids have a positive charge at physiological pH. Note that asparagine and glutamine have amide side chains and are thus not considered basic (see ORG 9.3).

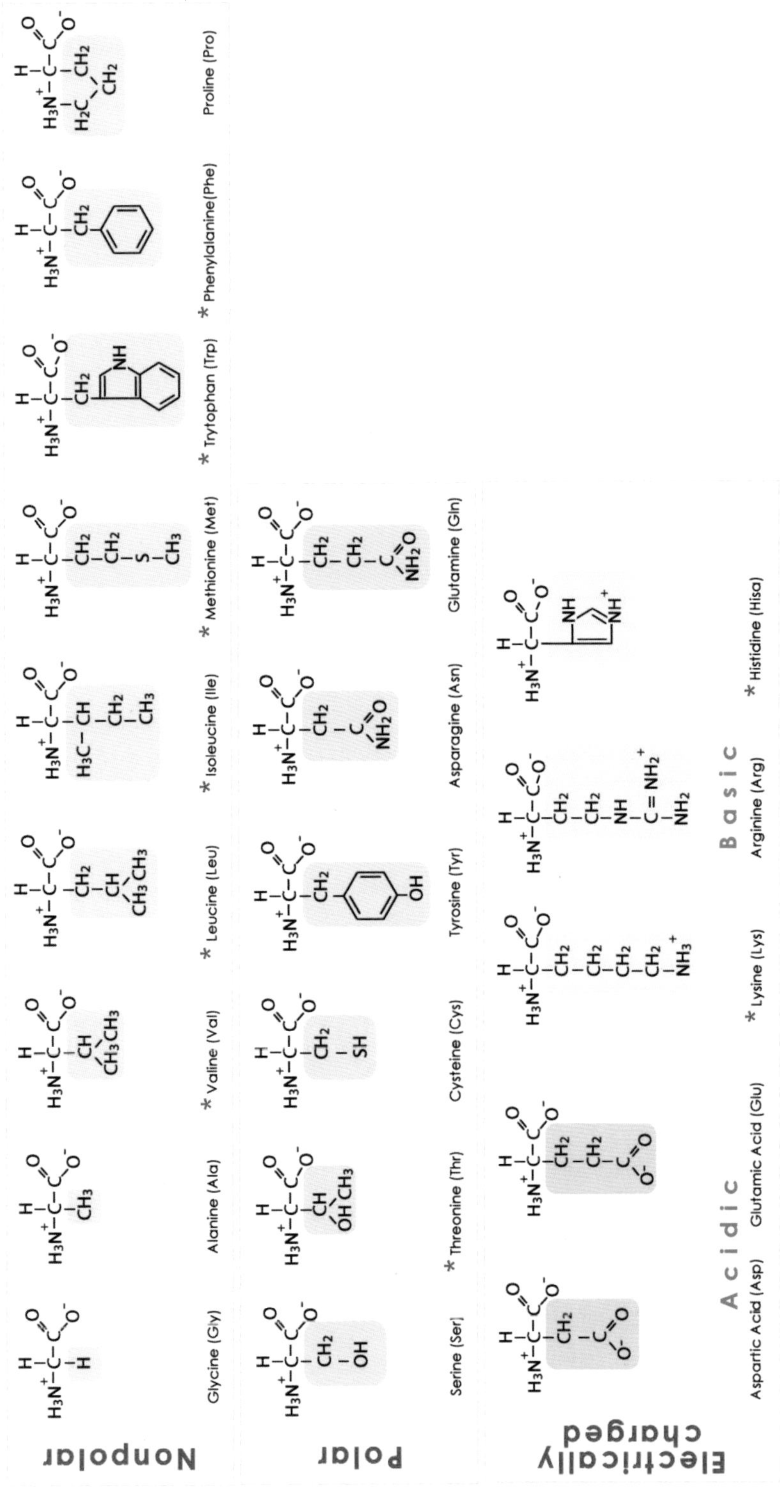

Nonpolar

Glycine (Gly) | Alanine (Ala) | * Valine (Val) | * Leucine (Leu) | * Isoleucine (Ile) | * Methionine (Met) | * Trytophan (Trp) | * Phenylalanine(Phe) | Proline (Pro)

Polar

Serine (Ser) | * Threonine (Thr) | Cysteine (Cys) | Tyrosine (Tyr) | Asparagine (Asn) | Glutamine (Gln)

Electrically charged

Acidic: Aspartic Acid (Asp) | Glutamic Acid (Glu)

Basic: * Lysine (Lys) | Arginine (Arg) | * Histidine (Hisa)

Figure 12.1.3 The 20 Standard Amino Acids. *9 essential amino acids.

12.2 Proteins

12.2.1 General Principles

Proteins are long chain polypeptides which often form higher order structures. Polypeptides are polymers of 40 to 1000 α-amino acids joined together by amide (*peptide*) bonds. These peptide bonds are derived from the amino group of one amino acid, and the acid group of another. When a peptide bond is formed, a molecule of water is released (*condensation = dehydration*). The bond can be broken by adding water (*hydrolysis*).

Since proteins are polymers of amino acids, they also have isoelectric points. Classification as to the acidity or basicity of a protein depends on the numbers of acidic and basic amino acids it contains. If there is an excess of acidic amino acids, the isoelectric point will be at a pH of less than 7. At pH = 7, these proteins will have a net negative charge. Similarly, those with an excess of basic amino acids will have an isoelectric point at a pH of greater than 7. Therefore, at pH = 7, these proteins will have a net positive charge. Proteins can be separated according to their isoelectric point on a polyacrylamide gel (*electrophoresis;* ORG 13.3).

$$\ldots NH-CH(R)-C(=O)-NH-CH(R)-C(=O)-NH-CH(R)-C(=O)\ldots$$

peptide bonds

$$2\ NH_2-CH(R)-CO_2H \underset{\text{hydrolysis}}{\overset{\text{condensation}}{\rightleftharpoons}} NH_2-CH(R)-C(=O)-NH-CH(R)-C(=O)OH + H_2O$$

12.2.2 Protein Structure

Protein structure may be divided into primary, secondary, tertiary and quaternary structures. The primary structure is the sequence of amino acids as determined by the DNA and the location of covalent bonds (*including disulfide bonds*). Secondary, tertiary and quaternary structures all depend on primary structure.

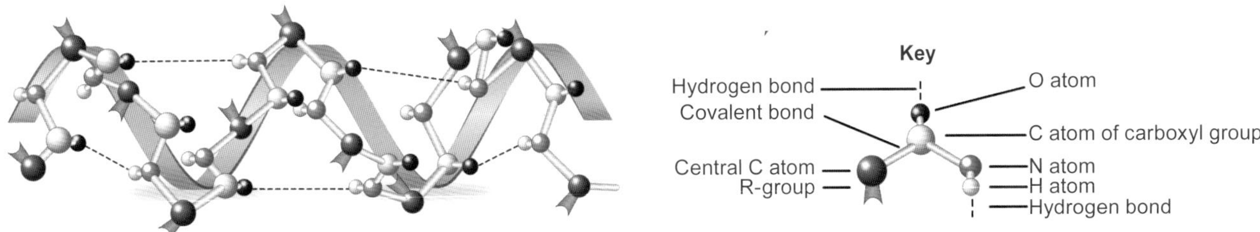

Figure 12.2.2.1: Secondary Structure: α-helix. This is a structure in which the peptide chain is coiled into a helical structure around a central axis. This helix is stabilized by hydrogen bonding between the N-H group and C=O group four residues away. A typical example with this secondary structure is keratin.

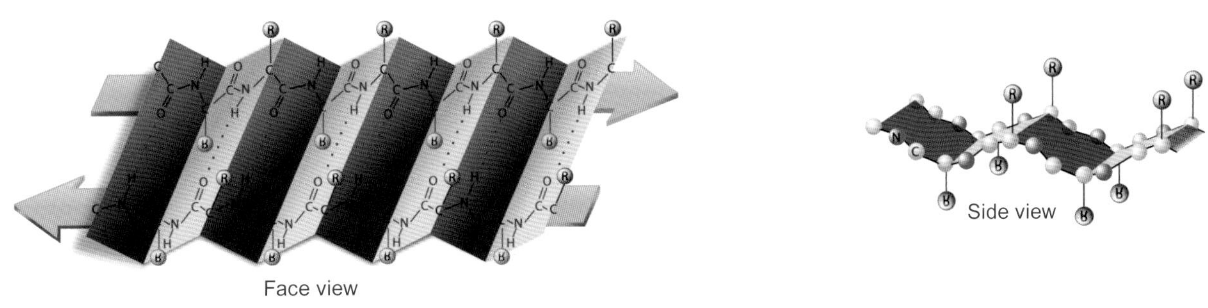

Figure 12.2.2.2: Secondary Structure: Beta pleated sheet. Peptide chains lie alongside each other in a parallel manner. This structure is stabilized by hydrogen bonding between the N-H group on one peptide chain and C=O group on another. A typical example with this secondary structure is produced by some insect larvae: the protein fiber "silk" which is mostly composed of fibroin.

The secondary structure is the orderly inter- or intramolecular *hydrogen bonding* of the protein chain. The resultant structure may be the more stable α-helix (e.g. keratin), or a β-pleated sheet (e.g. silk). Proline is an amino acid which cannot participate in the regular array of H-bonding in an α-helix. Proline disrupts the α-helix, thus it is usually found at the beginning or end of a molecule (i.e. hemoglobin).

The tertiary structure is the further folding of the protein molecule onto itself. This structure is maintained by *noncovalent bonds* like hydrogen bonding, Van der Waals forces, hydrophobic bonding and electrostatic bonding. The resultant structure is a globular protein with a hydrophobic interior and hydrop hilic exterior. Enzymes are classical examples of such a structure. In fact, enzyme activity often depends on tertiary structure.

The covalent bonding of cysteine (*disulfide bonds or bridge*) helps to stabilize the tertiary structure of proteins. Cysteine will form sulfur-sulfur covalent bonds with itself, producing *cystine*.

$$2H_2N-CH(CH_2SH)-CO_2H \xrightarrow{-H_2} HO_2C-CH(NH_2)-CH_2-S-S-CH_2-CH(NH_2)-CO_2H$$

cysteine → cystine

The quaternary structure is when there are two or more protein chains bonded together by noncovalent bonds. For example, hemoglobin consists of four polypeptide subunits (*globin*) held together by hydrophobic bonds forming a globular almost tetrahedryl arrangement.

12.3 Carbohydrates

12.3.1 Description and Nomenclature

Carbohydrates are sugars and their derivatives. Formally they are 'carbon hydrates,' that is, they have the general formula $C_m(H_2O)$ n. Usually they are defined as polyhydroxy aldehydes and ketones, or substances that hydrolyze to yield polyhydroxy aldehydes and ketones. The basic units of carbohydrates are monosaccharides (sugars).

There are two ways to classify sugars. One way is to classify the molecule based on the type of carbonyl group it contains: one with an aldehyde carbonyl group is an *aldose*; one with a ketone carbonyl group is a *ketose*. The second method of classification depends on the number of carbons in the molecule: those with 6 carbons are hexoses, with 5 carbons are pentoses, with 4 carbons are tetroses, and with 3 carbons are trioses. Sugars may exist in either the ring form, as hemiacetals, or in the straight chain form, as polyhydroxy aldehydes. *Pyranoses* are 6 carbon sugars in the ring form; *furanoses* are 5 carbon sugars in the ring form.

In the ring form, there is the possibility of α or β *anomers*. Anomers occur when 2 cyclic forms of the molecule differ in conformation only at the hemiacetal carbon (carbon 1). Generally, pyranoses take the 'chair' conformation, as it is very stable, with all (usually) hydroxyl groups at the equatorial position. *Epimers* are diastereomers that differ in the configuration of only one stereogenic center. For carbohydrates, epimers are 2 monosaccharides which differ in the conformation of one hydroxyl group.

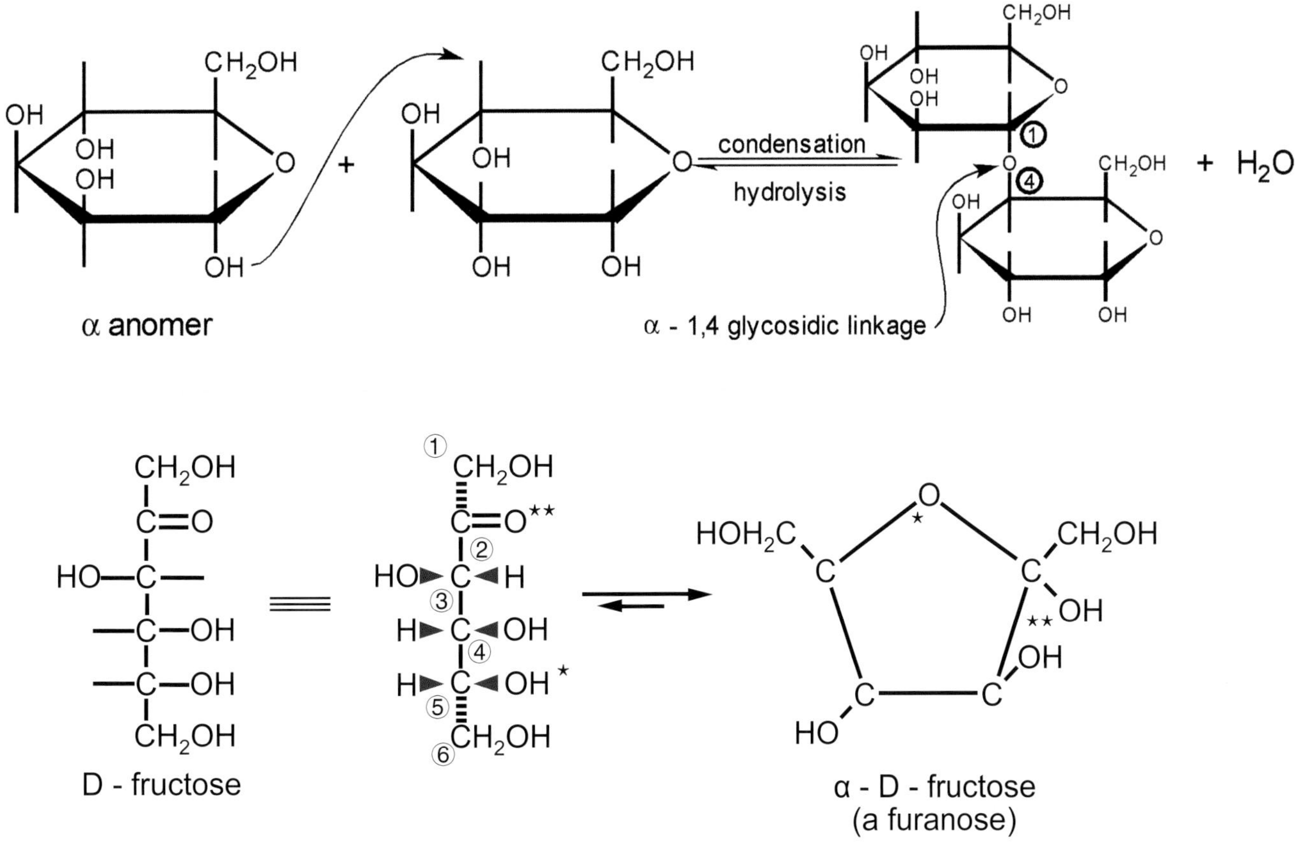

Figure IV.B.12.1 Part I: Names, structures and configurations of common sugars.

To determine the number of possible optical isomers, one need only know the number of asymmetric carbons, normally 4 for hexoses and 3 for pentoses, designated as n. The number of optical isomers is then 2^n, where n is the number of asymmetric carbons (ORG 2.2.2).

Most but not all of the naturally occurring aldoses have the D-configuration. Thus they have the same *relative* configuration as D-glyceraldehyde. The configuration (D or L) is *only* assigned to the highest numbered chiral carbon. The *absolute* configuration can be determined for any chiral carbon. For example, using the rules from Section 2.3.1, it can be determined that the absolute configuration of D-glyceraldehyde is the R-configuration.

The names and structures of some common sugars are shown in Figure IV.B.12.1.

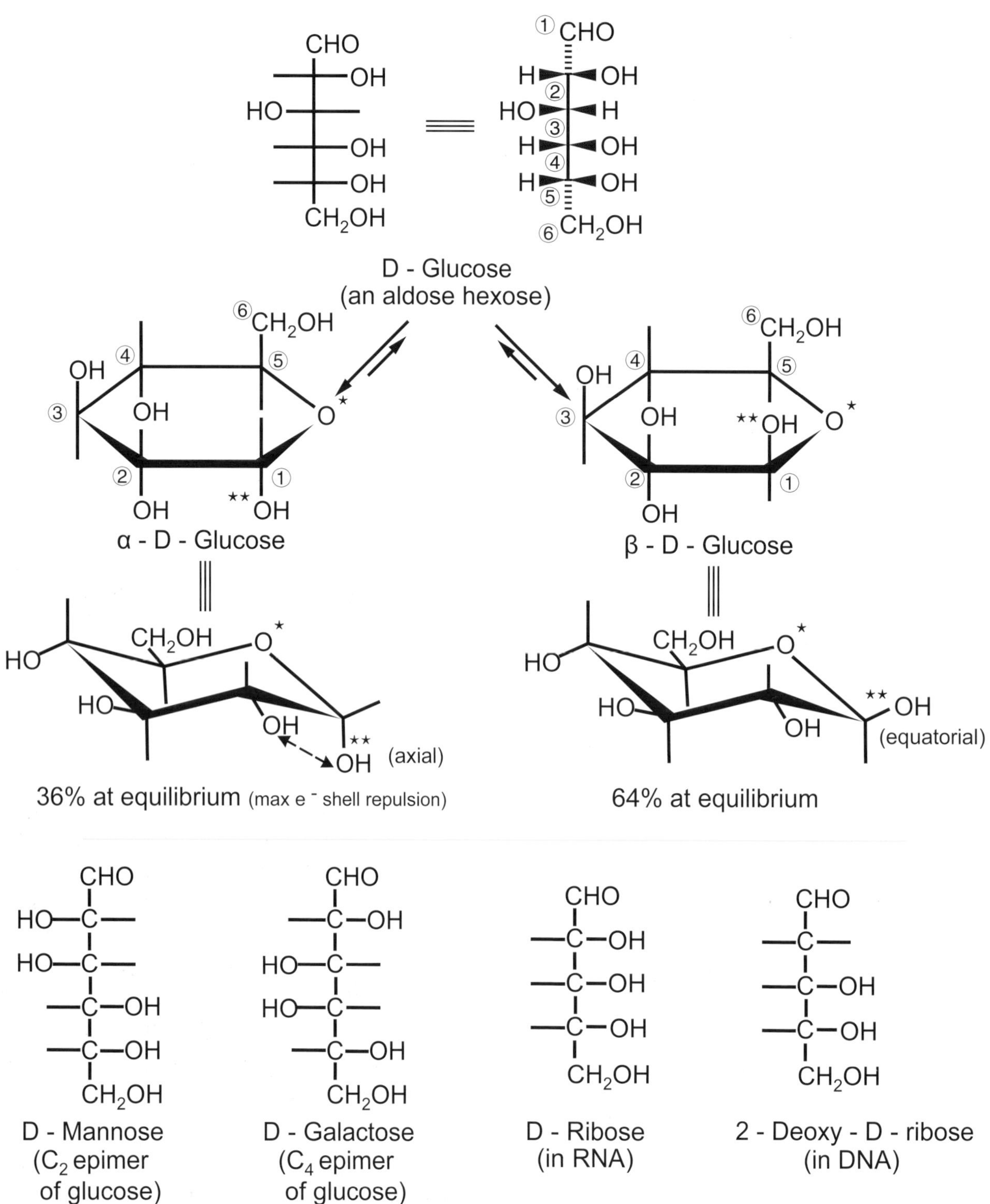

Figure IV.B.12.1 Part II: Names, structures and configurations of common sugars. Though not by convention, H belongs to the end of all empty bonds in the diagrams above.

In the diagram that follows, you will notice a Fischer projection to the far left (*see* ORG 2.3.1). You will also find Fischer projections in the following pages since they are a common way to represent carbohydrates.

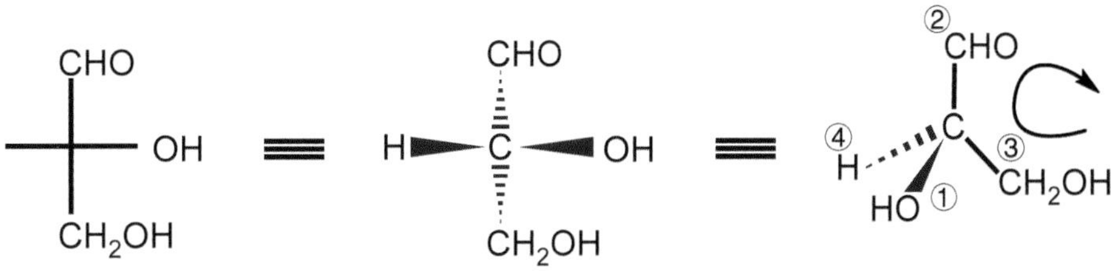

Fischer projection and 3-dimensional representation of D-glyceraldehyde, R-glyceraldehyde (*see* ORG 2.1, 2.2, 2.3 for rules).

12.3.2 Important Reactions of Carbohydrates

Hemiacetal Reaction

Monosaccharides can undergo an intramolecular nucleophilic addition reaction to form cyclic hemiacetals (see ORG 7.2.2). For example, the hydroxyl group on C4 of ribose attacks the aldehyde group on C1 forming a five-membered ring called furanose.

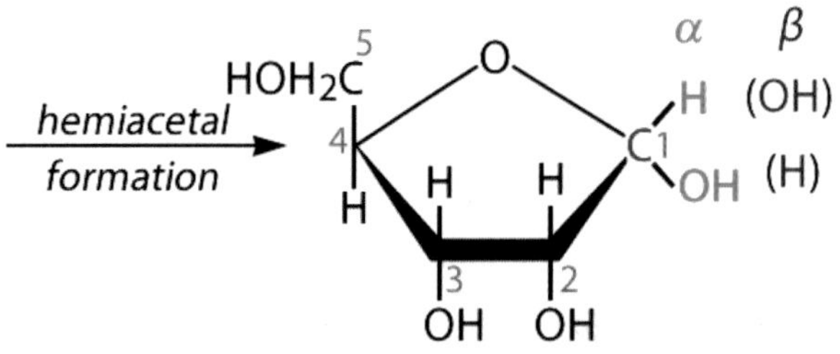

hemiacetal formation

α & β-D-ribofuranose

D-ribose

rotate about C3 - C4 bond

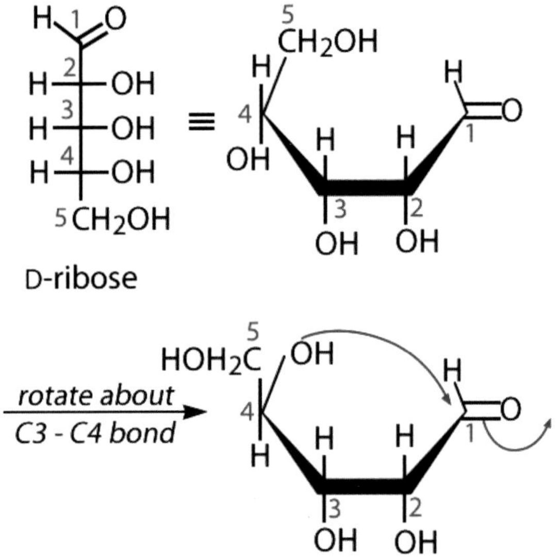

Diastereomers differing in configuration at this newly formed chiral carbon (= C1 where the straight chain monosaccharide converted into a furanose or pyranose) are known as anomers. This newly chiral carbon, which used to be a carbonyl carbon, is known as the anomeric center. When the OH group on C1 is *trans* to CH_2OH, it is called an α anomer. When the OH group on C1 is *cis* to CH_2OH, it is called a β anomer.

Mutarotation is the formation of both anomers into an equilibrium mixture when exposed to water.

Glycosidic Bonds

A disaccharide is a molecule made up of two monosaccharides, joined by a *glycosidic bond* between the hemiacetal carbon of one molecule, and the hydroxyl group of another. The glycosidic bond forms an α-1,4-glycosidic linkage if the reactant is an α anomer. A β-1,4-glycosidic linkage is formed if the reactant is a β anomer. When the bond is formed, one molecule of water is released (condensation). In order to break the bond, water must be added (hydrolysis):

- Sucrose (common sugar) = glucose + fructose
- Lactose (milk sugar) = glucose + galactose
- Maltose (α-1,4 bond) = glucose + glucose
- Cellobiose (β-1,4 bond) = glucose + glucose

Ester Formation

Monosaccharides react with acid chloride or acid anhydride to form esters (see ORG 9.4, 9.4.1). All of the hydroxyl groups can be esterified.

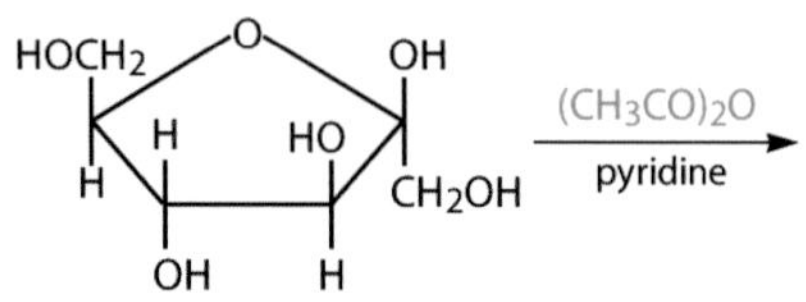

$(CH_3CO)_2O$, pyridine

β-D-fructofuranose

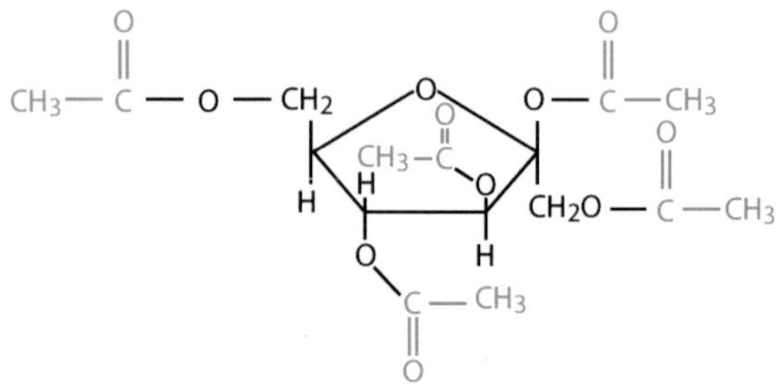

penta-*O-acetyl*-β-D-fructofuranoside

Ether Formation

Monosaccharides react with alkyl halide in the presence of silver oxide to form ethers. All of the hydroxyl groups are converted to -OR groups.

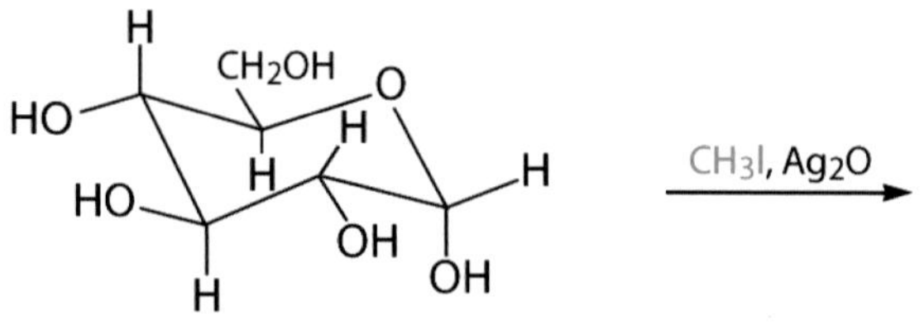

CH_3I, Ag_2O

α-D-glucopyranose

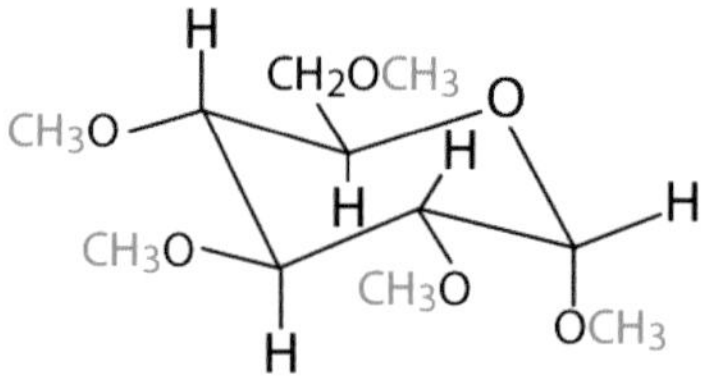

methyl 2, 3, 4, 6-tetra-*O*-methyl-α-D-glucopyranoside

Ether synthesis can also proceed using alcohols (see ORG 10.1):

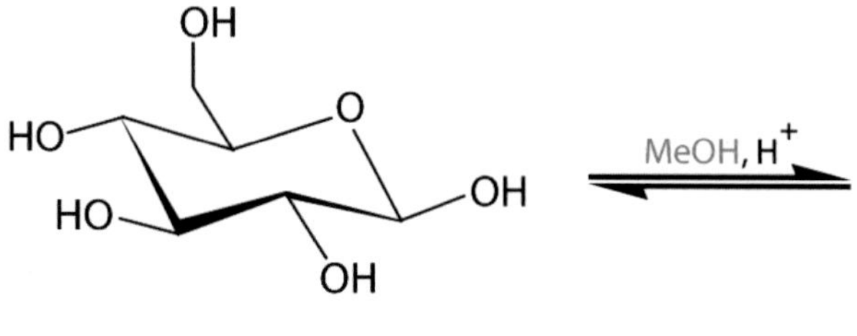

MeOH, H^+

β-D-glucopyranose

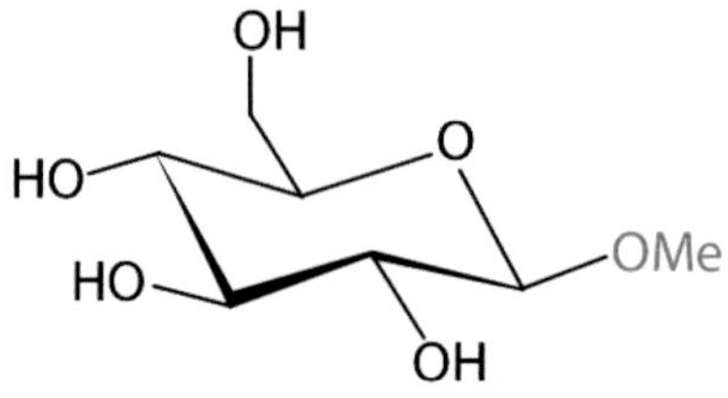

methyl-β-D-glucopyranoside

Reduction Reaction

Open chain monosaccharides are present in equilibrium between the aldehyde/ketone and the hemiacetal form. Therefore, monosaccharides can be reduced by $NaBH_4$ to form polyalcohols (see ORG 6.2.2).

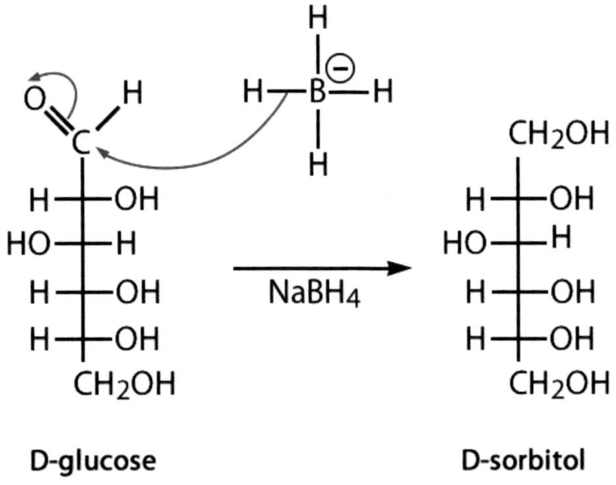

D-glucose **D-sorbitol**

Oxidation Reaction

Again, the hemiacetal ring form is in equilibrium with the open chain aldehyde/ketone form. Aldoses can be oxidized by the Tollens' reagent $[Ag(NH_3)_2]^+$, Fehling's reagent ($Cu_2/Na_2C_4H_4O_6$), and Benedict's reagent ($Cu_2/Na_3C_6H_5O_7$) to yield carboxylic acids. If the Tollens' reagent is used, metallic silver is produced as a shiny mirror. If the Fehling's reagent or Benedict's reagent is used, cuprous oxide is produced as a reddish precipitate.

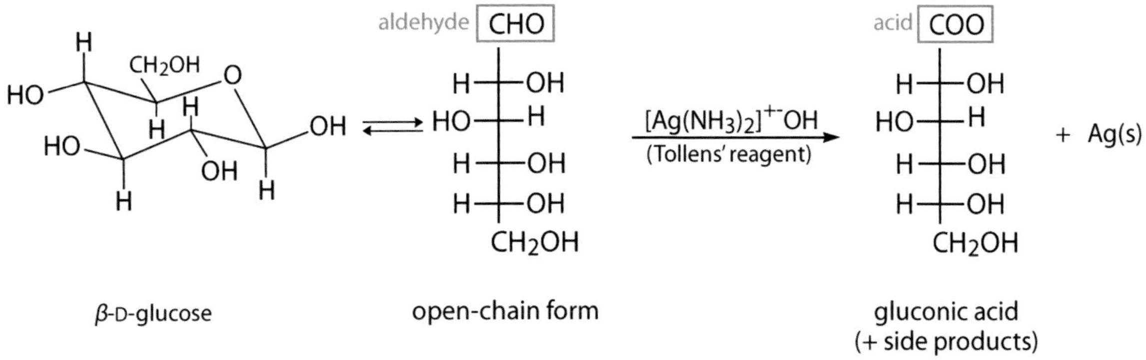

β-D-glucose open-chain form gluconic acid (+ side products)

When aldoses are treated with bromine water, the aldehyde is oxidized to a carboxylic acid group, resulting in a product known as an *aldonic acid*:

D - glucose (an aldose) + Br_2 $\xrightarrow[\text{CaCO}_3,\ \text{pH 5-6}]{H_2O}$ D-Gluconic acid (an aldonic acid) + HBr

Aldoses treated with dilute nitric acid will have both the primary alcohol and aldehyde groups oxidize to carboxylic acid groups, resulting in a product known as an *aldaric acid*:

D-glucose (an aldose) $\xrightarrow[55\text{-}60^{\circ}]{HNO_3}$ D-Glucaric acid (an aldaric acid)

Reducing Sugars/Non-reducing Sugars

All aldoses are reducing sugars because they contain an aldehyde carbonyl group. Some ketoses such as fructose are reducing sugars as well. They can be isomerized through keto-enol tautomerization (ORG 7.1) to an aldose, which can be oxidized normally. Glycosides are non-reducing sugars because the acetal group cannot be hydrolyzed to aldehydes. Thus they do not react with the Tollens' reagent.

12.3.3 Polysaccharides

Polymers of many monosaccharides are called polysaccharides. As in disaccharides, they are joined by glycosidic linkages. They may be straight chains, or branched chains. Some common polysaccharides are:

- Starch (plant energy storage)
- Cellulose (plant structural component)
- Glycocalyx (associated with the plasma membrane)
- Glycogen (animal energy storage in the form of glucose)
- Chitin (structural component found in shells or arthropods)

Carbohydrates are the most abundant organic constituents of plants. They are the source of chemical energy in living organisms, and, in plants, they are used in making the support structures. Cellulose consists of $\beta(1\rightarrow4)$ linked D-glucose. Starch and glycogen are mostly $\alpha(1\rightarrow4)$ glycosidic linkages of D-glucose.

Naturally, "triacyl" refers to the presence of 3 acyl subtituents (RCO-, ORG 9.1). Lipids are a class of organic molecules containing many different types of substances, such as fatty acids, fats, waxes, triacyl glycerols, terpenes and steroids.

Triacyl glycerols are oils and fats of either animal or plant origin. In general, fats are solid at room temperature, and oils are liquid at room temperature. The general structure of a triacyl glycerol is:

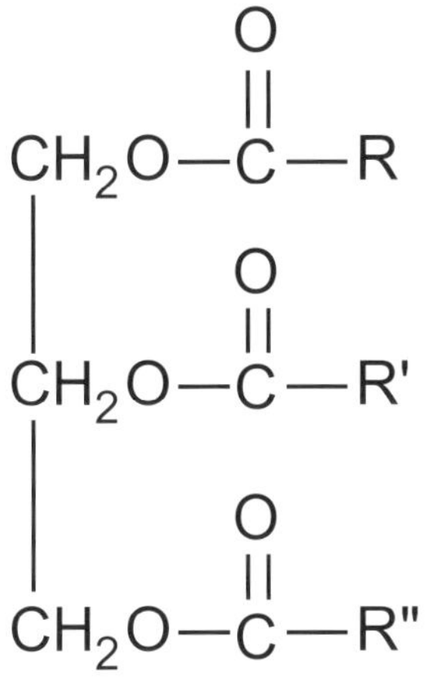

$$\begin{array}{l} CH_2O-\overset{O}{\overset{\|}{C}}-R \\ | \\ CH_2O-\overset{O}{\overset{\|}{C}}-R' \\ | \\ CH_2O-\overset{O}{\overset{\|}{C}}-R'' \end{array}$$

The R groups may be the same or different, and are usually long chain alkyl groups. Upon hydrolysis of a triacyl glycerol, the products are three fatty acids and glycerol (*see* ORG 9.4.1). The fatty acids may be saturated (= no multiple bonds, i.e. *palmitic acid*) or unsaturated (= containing double or triple bonds, i.e. *oleic acid*). Unsaturated fatty acids are usually in the *cis* configuration. Saturated fatty acids have a higher melting point than unsaturated fatty acids. Some common fatty acids are:

$$CH_3(CH_2)_{14}COOH$$

palmitic acid

$$CH_3(CH_2)_{16}COOH$$

stearic acid

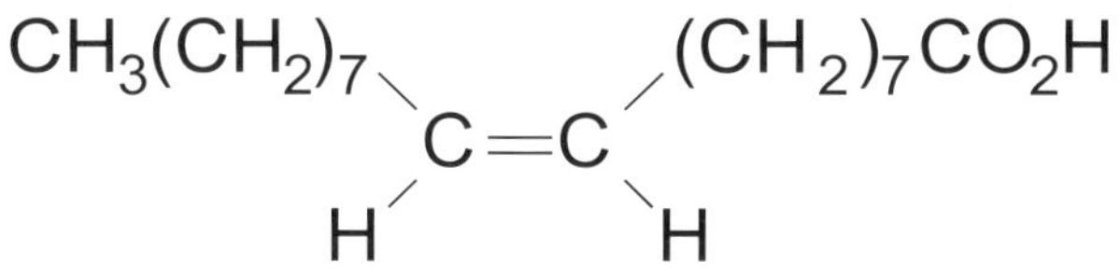

$$\begin{array}{ccc} CH_3(CH_2)_7 & & (CH_2)_7CO_2H \\ & C=C & \\ H & & H \end{array}$$

oleic acid

Soap is a mixture of salts of long chain fatty acids formed by the hydrolysis of fat. This process is called saponification. Soap possesses both a nonpolar hydrocarbon tail and a polar carboxylate head. When soaps are dispersed in aqueous solution, the long nonpolar tails are inside the sphere while the polar heads face outward.

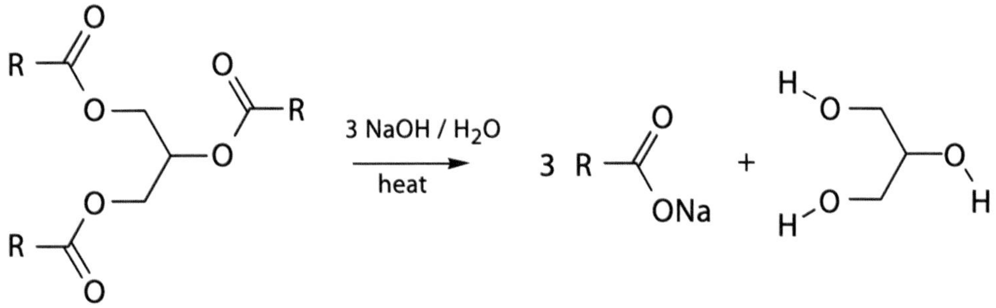

$$\text{triacyl glycerol (R–C(=O)–O– ×3)} \xrightarrow[\text{heat}]{3\ NaOH / H_2O} 3\ R-C(=O)ONa + HOCH_2CH(OH)CH_2OH$$

Soaps are surfactants. They are compounds that lower the surface tension of a liquid because of their amphipathic nature (i.e. they contain both hydrophobic tails and hydrophilic heads).

Of course, the cellular membrane is a lipid bilayer (Biology Chapter 1). The polar heads of the lipids align towards the aqueous environment, while the hydrophobic tails minimize their contact with water and tend to cluster together. Depending on the concentration of the lipid, this interaction may result in micelles (spherical), liposomes (spherical) or lipid bilayers.

Micelles are closed lipid monolayers with a fatty acid core and polar surface. The main function of bile (BIO 9.4.1) is to facilitate the formation of micelles, which promotes the processing or emulsification of dietary fat and fat-soluble vitamins.

Liposomes are composed of a lipid bilayer separating an aqueous internal compartment from the bulk aqueous phase. Liposomes can be used as a vehicle for the administration of nutrients or pharmaceutical drugs.

See BIO 20.4 for illustrations of a lipid bilayer, a liposome and micelles.

12.4.1 Steroids

Steroids are derivatives of the basic ring structure:

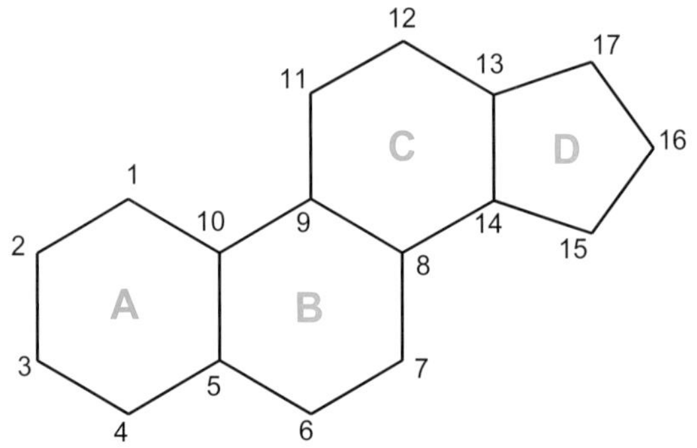

12 13 17 11 C D 16 1 10 9 14 15 2 8 A B 3 5 7 4 6

The IUPAC-recommended ring lettering and carbon numbering are as shown above. Many important substances are steroids, some examples include: cholesterol, D vitamins, bile acids, adrenocortical hormones, and male and female sex hormones.

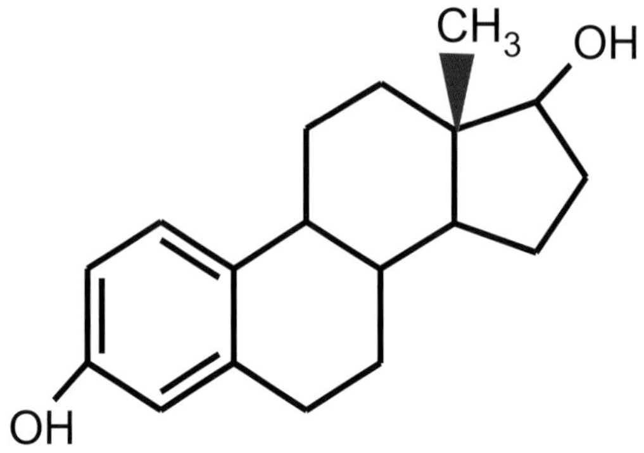

CH_3 OH

OH

Estradiol
(an estrogen)

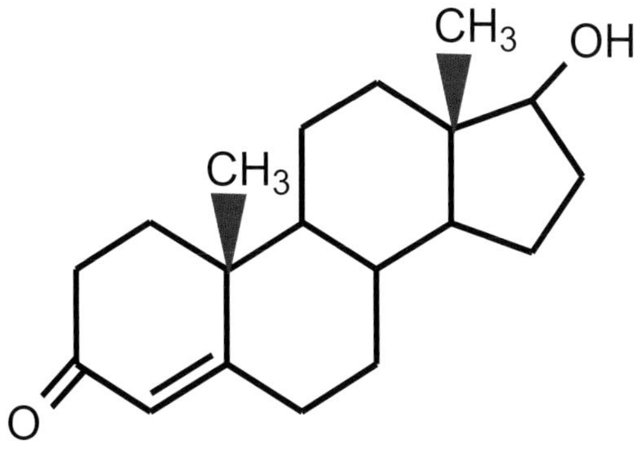

Testosterone
(an androgen)

Since such a significant portion of a steroid contains hydrocarbons, which are hydrophobic, steroids can dissolve through the hydrophobic interior of a cell's plasma membrane. Furthermore, steroid hormones contain polar side groups which allow the hormone to easily dissolve in water. Thus steroid hormones are well designed to be transported through the vascular space, to cross the plasma membranes of cells, and to have an effect either in the cell's cytosol or, as is usually the case, in the nucleus.

12.5 Phosphorous in Biological Molecules

Phosphorous is an essential component of various biological molecules including adenosine triphosphate (ATP), phospholipids in cell membranes, and the nucleic acids which form DNA. Phosphorus can also form phosphoric acid and several phosphate esters:

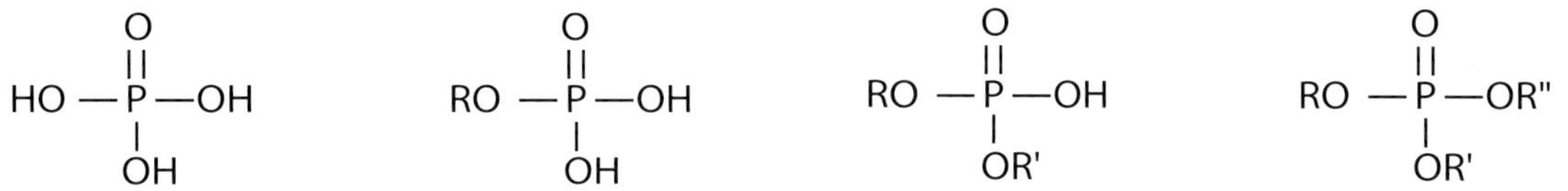

$HO{-}P(=O)(OH){-}OH$

phosphoric acid

$RO{-}P(=O)(OH){-}OH$

$RO{-}P(=O)(OR'){-}OH$

$RO{-}P(=O)(OR'){-}OR''$

phosphate esters

A phospholipid is produced from three ester linkages to glycerol. Phosphoric acid is ester linked to the terminal hydroxyl group and two fatty acids are ester linked to the two remaining hydroxyl groups of glycerol (*see Biology Section 1.1 for a schematic view of a phospholipid*).

In DNA the phosphate groups engage in two ester linkages creating phosphodiester bonds. It is the 5' phosphorylated position of one pentose ring which is linked to the 3' position of the next pentose ring (*see* BIO 1.1.2):

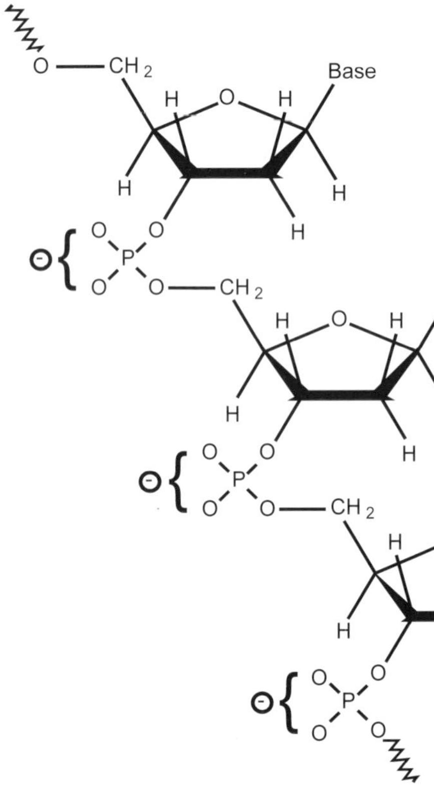

O — CH_2 Base H O H H H H O O P O O — CH_2 Base H O H H H H O O P O O — CH_2 Base H O H H H H O O P O O

In Biology Chapter 4, the production of ATP was discussed.In each case the components ADP and P_i (= *inorganic phosphate*) combined using the energy generated from a coupled reaction to produce ATP. The linkage between the phosphate groups are via *anhydride bonds*:

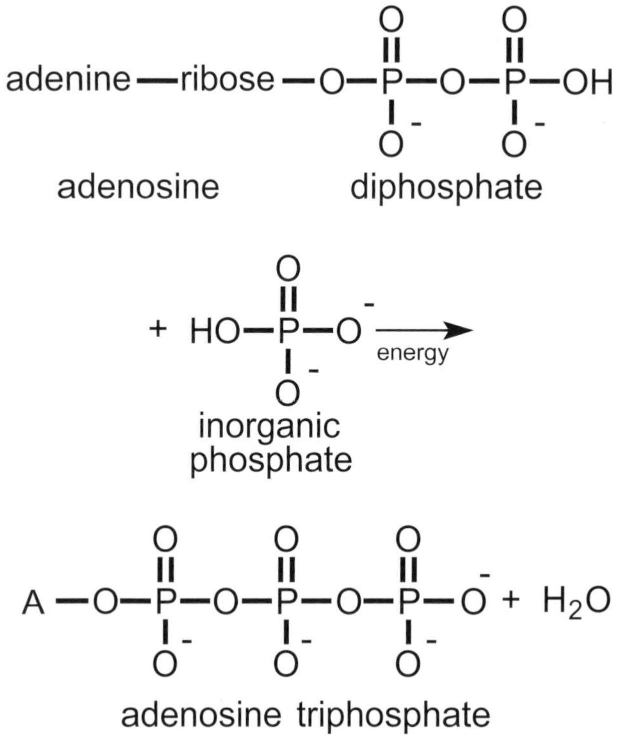

adenine — ribose — O — P(=O)(O⁻) — O — P(=O)(O⁻) — OH

adenosine diphosphate

+ HO — P(=O)(O⁻) — O^- $\xrightarrow{\text{energy}}$

inorganic phosphate

A — O — P(=O)(O⁻) — O — P(=O)(O⁻) — O — P(=O)(O⁻) — O^- + H_2O

adenosine triphosphate

Go online to DAT-prep.com for chapter review Q&A and forum.

SEPARATIONS AND PURIFICATIONS
Chapter 13

Memorize

Definitions of the major techniques
Interactions between organic molecules

Understand

* Different phases in the various techniques
* How to improve separation, purification
* How to avoid overheating (distillation)

Importance

1 to 3 out of the 30 ORG

DAT questions are based on content in this chapter (in our estimation).
* Note that between 30% and 60% of the questions in DAT Organic Chemistry are based on content from 4 chapters: 1, 2, 5 and 6.

Introduction

Separation techniques are used to transform a mixture of substances into two or more distinct products. The separated products may be different in chemical properties or some physical property (i.e. size). Purification in organic chemistry is the physical separation of a chemical substance of interest from foreign or contaminating substances.

Additional Resources

Free Online Q&A + Forum

Video : Online or DVD

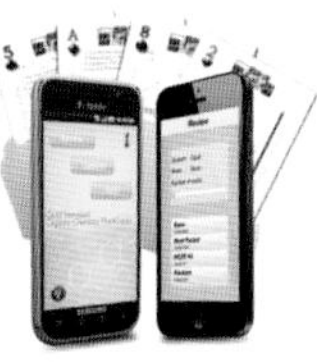

Flashcards

Special Guest

13.1 Separation Techniques

Extraction is the process by which a solute is transferred (*extracted*) from one solvent and placed in another. This procedure is possible if the two solvents used cannot mix (= *immiscible*) and if the solute is more soluble in the solvent used for the extraction.

For example, consider the extraction of solute A which is dissolved in solvent X. We choose solvent Y for the extraction since solute A is highly soluble in it and because solvent Y is immiscible with solvent X. We now add solvent Y to the solution involving solute A and solvent X. The container is agitated. Solute A begins to dissolve in the solvent where it is most soluble, solvent Y. The container is left to stand, thus the two immiscible solvents separate. The phase containing solute A can now be removed.

In practice, solvent Y would be chosen such that it would be sufficiently easy to evaporate (= *volatile*) after the extraction so solute A can be easily recovered. Also, it is more efficient to perform several extractions using a small amount of solvent each time, rather than one extraction using a large amount of solvent.

The main purpose of filtration is to isolate a solid from a liquid. There are two basic types of filtration: gravity filtration and vacuum filtration. In gravity filtration the solution containing the substance of interest is poured through the filter paper with the solvent's own weight responsible for pulling it through. This is often done using a hot solvent to ensure that the product remains dissolved. In vacuum filtration the solvent is forced through the filter with a vacuum on the other side. This is helpful when it is necessary to isolate large quantities of solid.

Sublimation is a process which goes from a heated solid directly into the gas phase without passing through the intermediate liquid phase (CHM 4.3.1). Low pressure reduces the temperature required for sublimation. The substance in question is heated and then condensed on a cool surface (cold finger), leaving the non-volatile impurities behind.

Centrifugation is a separation process that involves the use of centrifugal forces for the sedimentation of mixtures. Particles settle at different rates depending on their size, viscosity, density and shape. Compounds of greater mass and density settle toward the bottom while compounds of lighter mass and density remain on top. This process is most useful in separating polymeric materials such as biological macromolecules.

Distillation is the process by which compounds are separated based on differences in boiling points. Compounds with a lower boiling point are preferably vaporized, condensed on a water cooler, and are separated from compounds with higher boiling points.

1. **Simple distillation** is used to separate liquids whose boiling points differ by at least 25 °C and that boil below 150 °C. The composition of the distillate depends on the composition of the vapors at a given temperature and pressure.

2. **Vacuum distillation** is used to separate liquids whose boiling points differ by at least 25 °C and that boil above 150 °C. The vacuum environment prevents compounds from decomposition because the low pressure reduces the temperature required for distillation.

3. **Fractional distillation** is used to separate liquids whose boiling points are less than 25 °C apart. The repeated vaporization-condensation cycle of compounds will eventually yield vapors that contain a greater and greater proportion of the lower boiling point component.

NOTE: For an illustration of a standard distillation apparatus and to learn more about laboratory techniques and equipment, see General Chemistry Chapter 12.

13.2 Chromatography

Chromatography is the separation of a mixture of compounds by their distribution between two phases: one stationary and one moving. The mobile phase is run through the stationary phase. Different substances distribute themselves according to their relative affinities for the two phases. This causes the separation of the different compounds. Molecules are separated based on differences in polarity and molecular weight.

13.2.1 Gas-Liquid Chromatography

In gas-liquid chromatography, the *stationary phase* is a liquid absorbed to an inert solid. The liquid can be polyethylene glycol, squalene, or others, depending on the polarity of the substances being separated.

The mobile phase is a gas (i.e. He, N_2) which is unreactive both to the stationary phase and to the substances being separated. The sample being analyzed can be injected in the direction of gas flow into one end of a column packed with the stationary phase. As the sample migrates through the column certain molecules will move faster than others. As mentioned the separation of the different types of molecules is dependent on size (*molecular weight*) and charge (*polarity*). Once the molecules reach the end of the column special detectors signal their arrival.

13.2.2 Thin-Layer Chromatography

Thin-layer chromatography (TLC) is a solid-liquid technique, based on adsorptivity and solubility. The *stationary phase* is a type of finely divided polar material, usually silica gel or alumina, which is thinly coated onto a glass plate.

A mixture of compounds is placed on the stationary phase, either a thin layer of silica gel or alumina on glass sheet. Silica gel is a very polar and hydrophobic substance. The mobile phase is usually of low polarity and moves by capillary action. Therefore, if silica gel is used as the stationary phase, nonpolar compounds move quickly while polar compounds have strong interaction with the gel and are stuck tightly to it. In reverse-phase chromatography, the stationary phase is nonpolar and the mobile phase is polar; as a result, polar compounds move quickly while nonpolar compounds stick more tightly to the adsorbant.

There are several types of interactions that may occur between the organic molecules in the sample and the silica gel, in order from weakest to strongest (see CHM 3.4, 4.2):

- Van der Waals force (nonpolar molecules)
- Dipole-dipole interaction (polar molecules)
- Hydrogen bonding (hydroxylic compounds)
- Coordination (Lewis bases)

Molecules with functional groups with the greatest polarity will bind more strongly to the stationary phase and thus will not rise as high on the glass plate.

Organic molecules will also interact with the *mobile phase* (= a solvent), or *eluent* used in the process. The more polar the solvent, the more easily it will dissolve polar molecules. The mobile phase usually contains organic solvents like ethanol, benzene, chloroform, acetone, etc.

As a result of the interactions of the organic molecules with the stationary and moving phases, for any adsorbed compound there is a dynamic distribution equilibrium between these phases. The different molecules will rise to different heights on the plate. Their presence can be detected using special stains (i.e. pH indicators, $KMnO_4$) or uv light (*if the compound can fluoresce*).

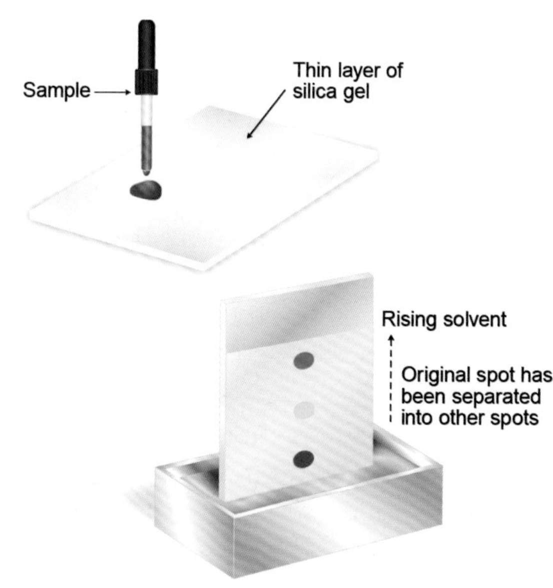

Figure IV.B.13.1: Thin-layer Chromatography.

13.2.3 Column Chromatography

Column chromatography is similar to TLC in principle; however, column chromatography uses silica gel or alumina as an adsorbant in the form of a column rather than TLC which uses paper in a layer-like form. The solvent and compounds move down the column (by gravity) allowing much more separation. The solvent drips out into a waiting flask where fractions containing bands corresponding to the different compounds are collected. After the solvent has evaporated, the compounds can then be isolated. Often the desired compounds are proteins or nucleic acids for which several techniques exist:

1. Ion exchange chromatography – Beads coated with charged substances are placed in the column so that they will attract compounds with an opposing charge.

2. Size exclusion chromatography – The column contains beads with tiny pores which allow small substances to enter, leaving larger molecules to pass through the column faster.

3. Affinity chromatography – Columns are customized to bind a substance of interest (e.g. a receptor or antibody) which allows it to bind very tightly.

13.3 Gel Electrophoresis

Gel electrophoresis is an important method to separate biological macromolecules (i.e. protein and DNA) based on size and charge of molecules. Molecules are made to move through a gel which is placed in an electrophoresis chamber. When an electric current is applied, molecules move at different velocities. These molecules will move towards either the cathode or anode depending on their size and charge (anions move towards anode while cations move towards the cathode. The migration velocity is proportional to the net charge on the molecule and inversely proportional to a coefficient dependent on the size of the molecule. Highly charged, small molecules will move the quickest with size being the most important factor.

There are three main types of electrophoresis:

1. Agarose gel electrophoresis – Used to separate pieces of negatively charged nucleic acids based on their size.

2. SDS-polyacrylamide gel electrophoresis

(SDS-PAGE) – Separates proteins on the basis of mass and not charge. The SDS (sodium dodecyl sulfate) binds to proteins and creates a large negative charge such that the only variable effecting their movement is the frictional coefficient which is solely dependent on mass.

3. Isoelectric focusing – The isoelectric point is the pH at which the net charge of a protein is zero (ORG Chapter 12.1.2). A mixture of proteins can be separated by placing them in an electric field with a pH gradient. The proteins will lose their charge and come to a stop when the pH is equal to their isoelectric point.

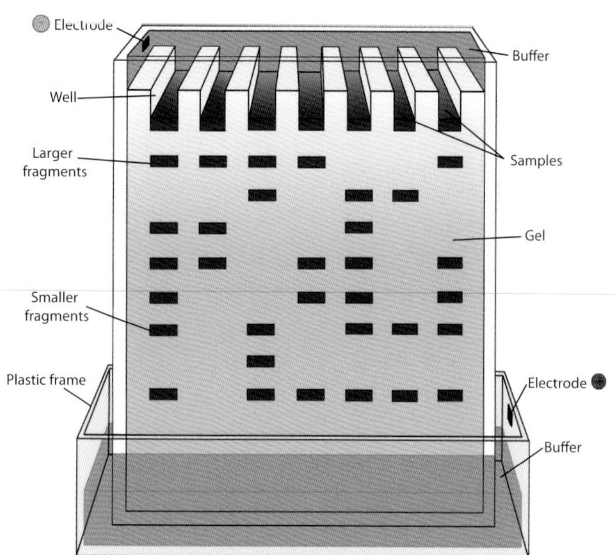

Figure IV.B.13.2: Gel Electrophoresis.

13.4 Recrystallization

Recrystallization is a useful purification technique. A solid organic compound with some impurity is dissolved in a hot solvent, and then the solvent is slowly cooled to allow the pure compound to reform or *recrystallize*, while leaving the impurities behind in the solvent. This is possible because the impurities do not normally fit within the crystal structure of the compound.

In choosing a solvent, solubility data (e.g. K_{sp} at various temperatures, etc.) regarding both the compound to be purified and the impurities should be known. The data should be analyzed such that the solvent would:

- have the capability to dissolve alot of the compound (to be purified) at or near the boiling point of the solvent, while being able to dissolve little of the compound at room temperature. As well, the impurities should be soluble in the cold solvent.
- have a low boiling point, so as to be easily removed from the solid in a drying process.
- not react with the solid.

Go online to DAT-prep.com for chapter review Q&A and forum.

Chapter 14

Memorize

* Key IR absorptions
* NMR rules

Understand

* Basic theory: IR spect., NMR
* Very basic spectrum (graph) analysis
* Deuterium exchange

Importance

1 to 3 out of the 30 ORG

DAT questions are based on content in this chapter (in our estimation).
* Note that between 30% and 60% of the questions in DAT Organic Chemistry are based on content from 4 chapters: 1, 2, 5 and 6.

Introduction

Spectroscopy is the use of the absorption, emission, or scattering of electromagnetic radiation by matter to study the matter or to study physical processes. The matter can be atoms, molecules, atomic or molecular ions, or solids.

Additional Resources

Free Online Q&A + Forum

Video: Online or DVD

Flashcards

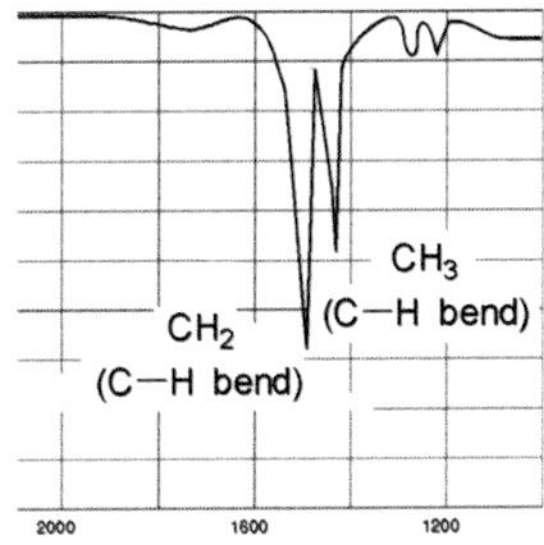

Special Guest

14.1 IR Spectroscopy

In an infrared spectrometer, a beam of infrared (IR) radiation is passed through a sample. The spectrometer will then analyze the amount of radiation transmitted (= % *transmittance*) through the sample as the incident radiation is varied. Ultimately, a plot results as a graph showing the transmittance or absorption (*the inverse of transmittance*) versus the frequency or wavelength of the incident radiation or the wavenumber (= the reciprocal of the wavelength). IR spectroscopy is best used for the identification of functional groups.

The location of an IR absorption band (*or peak*) can be specified in *frequency units* by its wavenumber, measured in cm^{-1}. As the wave number decreases, the wavelength increases, thus the energy decreases (this can be determined using two physics equations which are not required content for the DAT: $v = \lambda f$ and $E = hf$). A schematic representation of the IR spectrum of octane is:

Electromagnetic radiation consists of discrete units of energy called *quanta* or *photons*. All organic compounds are capable of absorbing many types of electromagnetic energy. The absorption of energy leads to an increase in the amplitude of intramolecular rotations and vibrations.

Intramolecular rotations are the rotations of a molecule about its center of gravity. The difference in rotational energy levels is inversely proportional to the moment of inertia of a molecule. Rotational energy is quantized and gives rise to absorption spectra in the microwave region of the electromagnetic spectrum.

Intramolecular vibrations are the bending and stretching motions of bonds within a molecule. The relative spacing between vibrational energy levels increases with the increasing strength of an intramolecular bond. Vibrational energy is quantized and gives rise

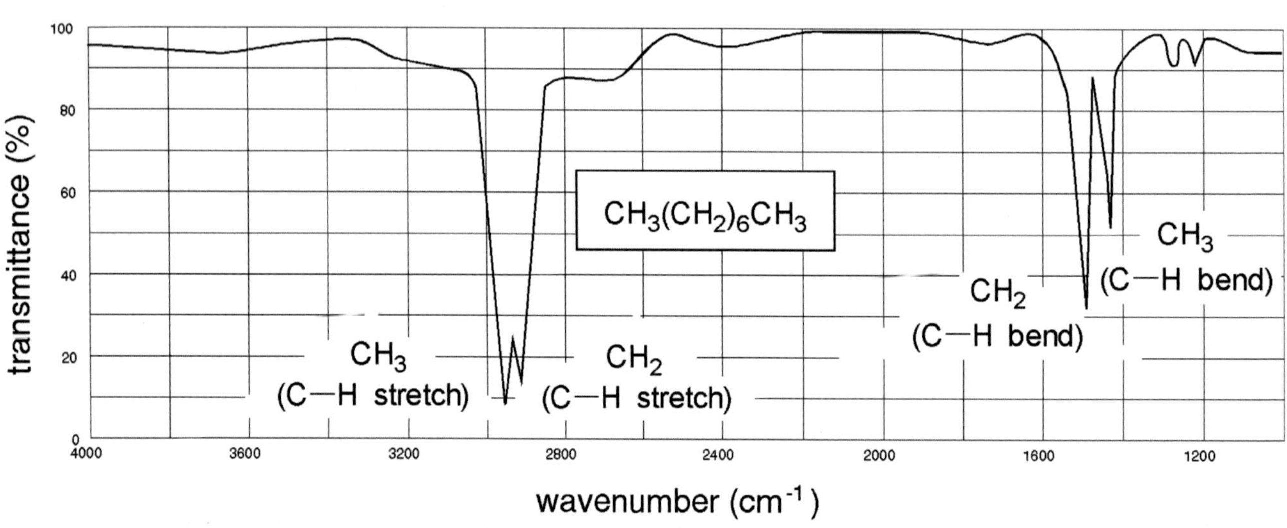

to absorption spectra in the infrared region of the electromagnetic spectrum.

Thus there are two types of bond vibration: stretching and bending. That is, after exposure to the IR radiation the bonds stretch and bend (*or contract*) to a greater degree once energy is absorbed. In general, bending vibrations will occur at lower frequencies (higher wavelengths) than stretching vibrations of the same groups. So, as seen in the sample spectra for octane, each group will have two characteristic peaks, one due to stretching, and one due to bending.

Different functional groups will have transmittances at characteristic wave numbers, which is why IR spectroscopy is useful. Some examples (*approximate values*) of characteristic absorbances are shown in the table.

Group	Frequency Range (cm^{-1})
Alkyl (C–H)	2850 – 2960
Alkene (C=C)	1620 – 1680
Alkyne (C≡C)	2100 – 2260
Alcohol (O–H)	3200 – 3650
Benzene (Ar–H)	3030
Carbonyl (C=O)	1630 – 1780
▶ Aldehyde	1680 – 1750
▶ Ketone	1735 – 1750
▶ Carboxylic Acid	1710 – 1780
▶ Amide	1630 – 1690
Amine (N–H)	3300 – 3500
Nitriles (C≡N)	2220 – 2260

The minimum frequencies that you should memorize for the DAT include the carbonyl and alcohol absorbances.

By looking at the characteristic transmittances of a compound's spectrum, it is possible to identify the functional groups present in the molecule.

Symmetrical molecules or molecules composed of the same atoms do not exhibit a change in dipole moment under IR radiation and thus absorptions do not show up in IR spectra.

14.2 Proton NMR Spectroscopy

Nuclear Magnetic Resonance (NMR) spectroscopy can be used to examine the environments of the hydrogen atoms in a molecule. In fact, using a (*proton*) NMR or

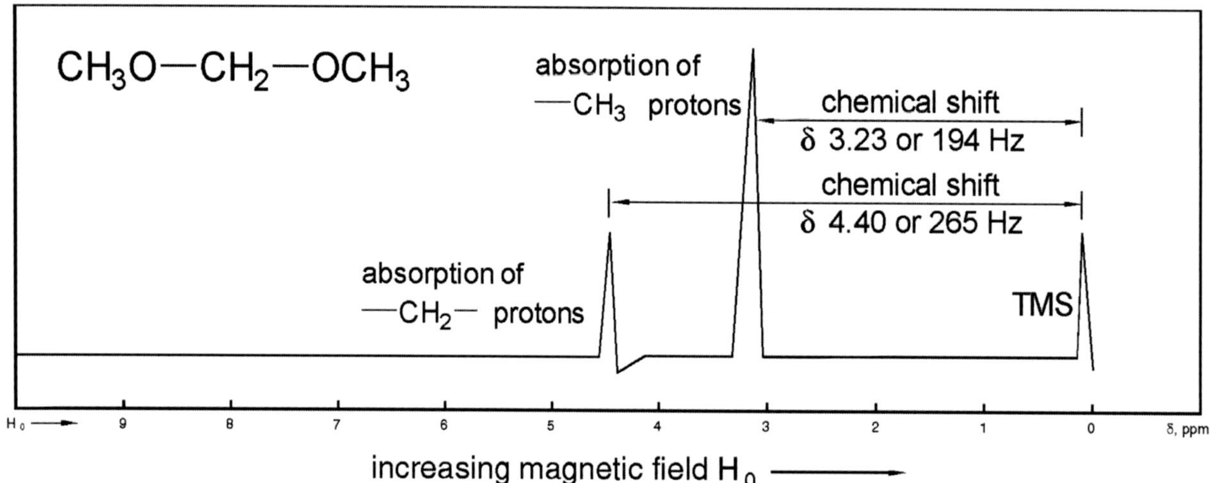

^{1}HNMR, one can determine both the number and types of hydrogens in a molecule. The basis of this stems from the magnetic properties of the hydrogen nucleus (proton). Similar to electrons, the hydrogen proton has a nuclear spin, able to take either of two values. These values are designated as +1/2 and −1/2. As a result of this spin, the nucleus will respond to a magnetic field by being oriented in the direction of the field. NMR spectrometers measure the absorption of energy by the hydrogen nuclei in an organic compound.

A schematic representation of an NMR spectrum, that of dimethoxymethane is shown:

The small peak at the right is that of TMS, tetramethylsilane, shown here:

```
         CH3
          |
CH3 — Si — CH3
          |
         CH3
```

This compound is added to the sample to be used as a reference, or standard. It is volatile, inert and absorbs at a higher field than most other organic chemicals.

The position of a peak relative to the standard is referred to as its *chemical shift*. Since NMR spectroscopy differentiates between types of protons, each type will have a different chemical shift, as shown. Protons in the same environment, like the three hydrogens in $-CH_3$, are called *equivalent protons*.

Dimethoxymethane is a symmetric molecule, thus the protons on either methyl group are equivalent. So, in the example above, the absorption of $-CH_3$ protons occurs at one peak (*a singlet*) 3.23 ppm downfield from TMS. In most organic molecules, the range of absorption will be in the 0–10 ppm (= *parts per million*) range.

The area under each peak is directly related to the number of protons contributing to it, and thus may be used to determine the

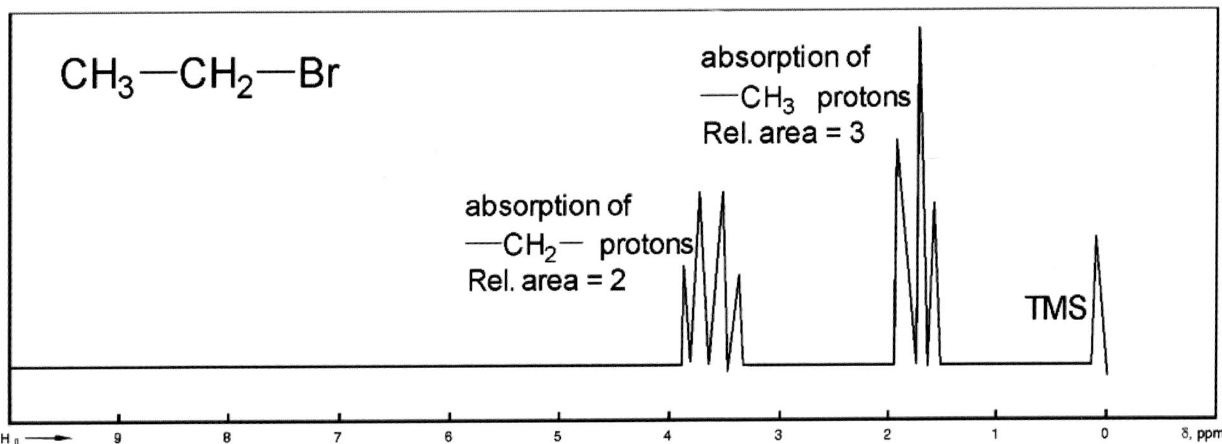

relative number of protons in the molecule. Accurate measurements of the area under the two peaks above yield the ratio 1:3 which represents the relative number of hydrogens (i.e. 1:3 = 2:6).

Let us now examine a schematic representation of the NMR spectrum of ethyl bromide:

It is obvious that something is different. Looking at the molecule, one can see that there are two different types of protons (*either far from Br or near to Br*). However, there are more than two signals in the spectrum. As such, the NMR signal for each group is said to be split. This type of splitting is called spin-spin splitting (= *spin-spin coupling*) and is caused by the presence of neighboring protons (*protons on an adjacent or vicinal carbon*) that are not equivalent to the proton in question. Note that protons that are farther than two carbons apart do not exhibit a coupling effect.

The number of lines in the splitting pattern for a given set of equivalent protons depends on the number of adjacent protons according to the following rule: if there are n equivalent protons in adjacent positions, a proton NMR signal is split into $n + 1$ lines.

Therefore the NMR spectrum for ethyl bromide can be interpreted thus:

- There are two groups of lines (*two split peaks*), therefore there are two different environments for protons.
- The relative areas under each peak is 2:3, which represents the relative number of hydrogens in the molecule.
- There are 4 splits (*quartet*) in the peak which has relatively two hydrogens ($-CH_2$). Thus the number of adjacent hydrogens is $n + 1 = 4$; therefore, there are 3 hydrogens on the carbon adjacent to $-CH_2$.
- There are 3 splits (*triplet*) in the peak which has relatively three hydrogens ($-CH_3$).

Thus the number of adjacent hydrogens is $n + 1 = 3$; therefore, there are 2 hydrogens on the carbon adjacent to $-CH_3$.

The relative areas under each peak may be expressed in three ways: (i) the information may simply be provided to you (*too easy!*); (ii) the integers may be written above the signals (= *integration integers*, i.e. 2,3 in the previous example); or (iii) a step-like *integration curve* above the signals where the relative height of each step equals the relative number of hydrogens.

14.2.1 Deuterium Exchange

Deuterium, the hydrogen isotope ^2H or D, can be used to identify substances with readily exchangeable or acidic hydrogens. Rather than H_2O, D_2O is used to identify the chemical exchange:

$$ROH + DOD \rightleftharpoons ROD + HOD$$

The previous signal due to the acidic $-O\boxed{H}$ would now disappear. However, if excess D_2O is used, a signal as a result of HOD may be observed.

Solvents may also be involved in exchange phenomena. The solvents carbon tetrachloride (CCl_4) and deuteriochloroform ($CDCl_3$) can also engage in exchange-induced decoupling of acidic hydrogens (usu. in alcohols).

14.2.2 ^{13}C NMR

The main difference between proton NMR and ^{13}C NMR is that most carbon 13 signals occur 0–200 δ downfield from the carbon peak of TMS. There is also very little coupling between carbon atoms as only 1.1% of carbon atoms are ^{13}C. There is coupling between carbon atoms and their adjacent protons which are directly attached to them. This coupling of one bond is similar to the three bond coupling exhibited by proton NMR.

Signals will be split into a triplet with an area of 1:2:1 when a carbon atom is attached to two protons. Another unique feature of ^{13}C NMR is a phenomenon called spin decoupling where a spectrum of singlets can be recorded - each corresponding to a singular carbon atom. This allows one to accurately determine the number of different carbons in their respective chemical environments as well as the number of adjacent hydrogens (spin-coupled only).

14.3 Mass Spectrometry

Mass spectrometry (the former expression "mass spectroscopy" is discouraged), unlike other forms of NMR we have seen, destroys the sample during its analysis. The analysis is carried out using a beam of electrons which ionize the sample and a detector to measure the number of particles that are deflected due to the presence of a magnetic field. The reflected particle is usually an unstable species which decomposes rapidly into a cationic fragment and a radical fragment.

Since there are many ways in which the particle can decompose, a typical mass spectrum is often composed of numerous lines, with each one corresponding to a specific mass/charge ratio (m/z, sometimes symbolized as m/e). It is important to note that only cations are deflected by the magnetic field, thus only cations will appear on the spectrum which plots m/z (x-axis) vs. the abundance of the cationic fragments (y-axis). See the figure provided.

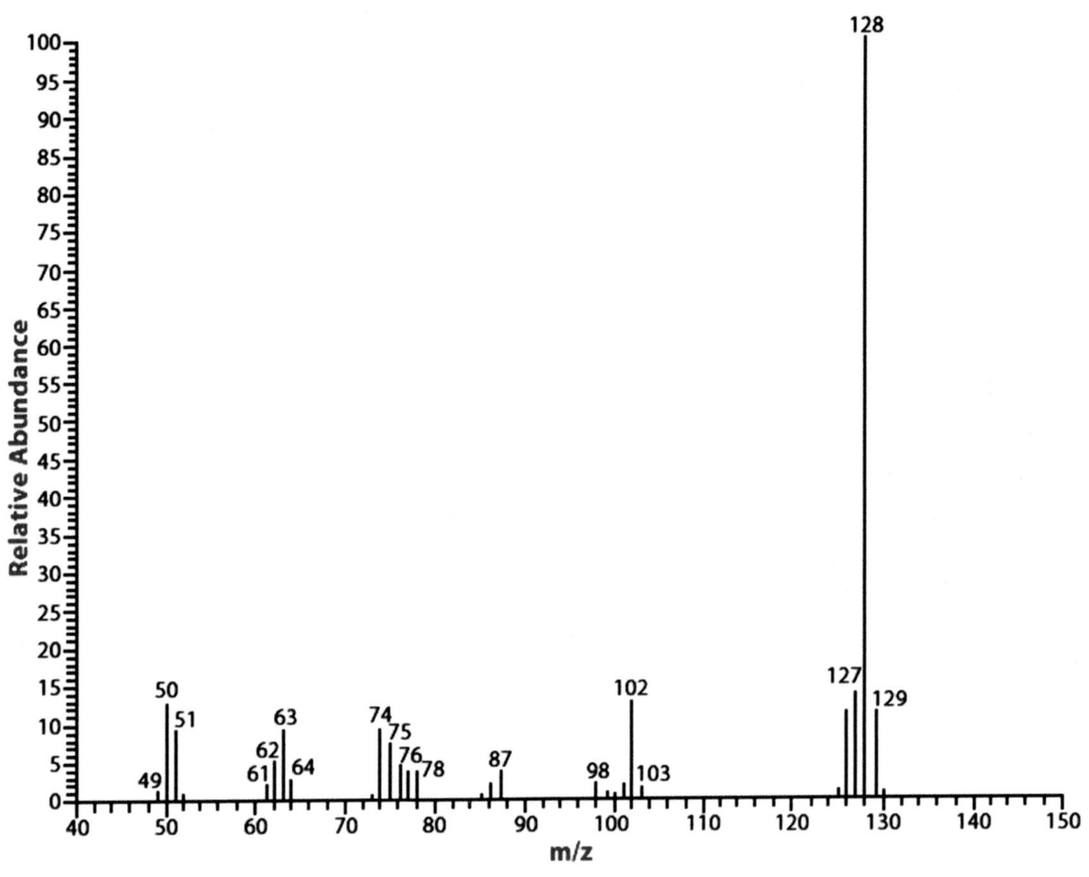

The tallest peak represents the most common ion and is also referred to as the base peak. The molecular weight can be obtained not from the base peak but rather from the peak with the highest m/z ratio, 129 in this case. This is called the parent ion peak and is designated by M^+. By looking at the fragmentation pattern we can ascertain information regarding the compound's structure, something that IR spectroscopy is incapable of achieving.

Go online to DAT-prep.com for chapter review Q&A and forum.

KEY ORGANIC CHEMISTRY REACTION MECHANISMS

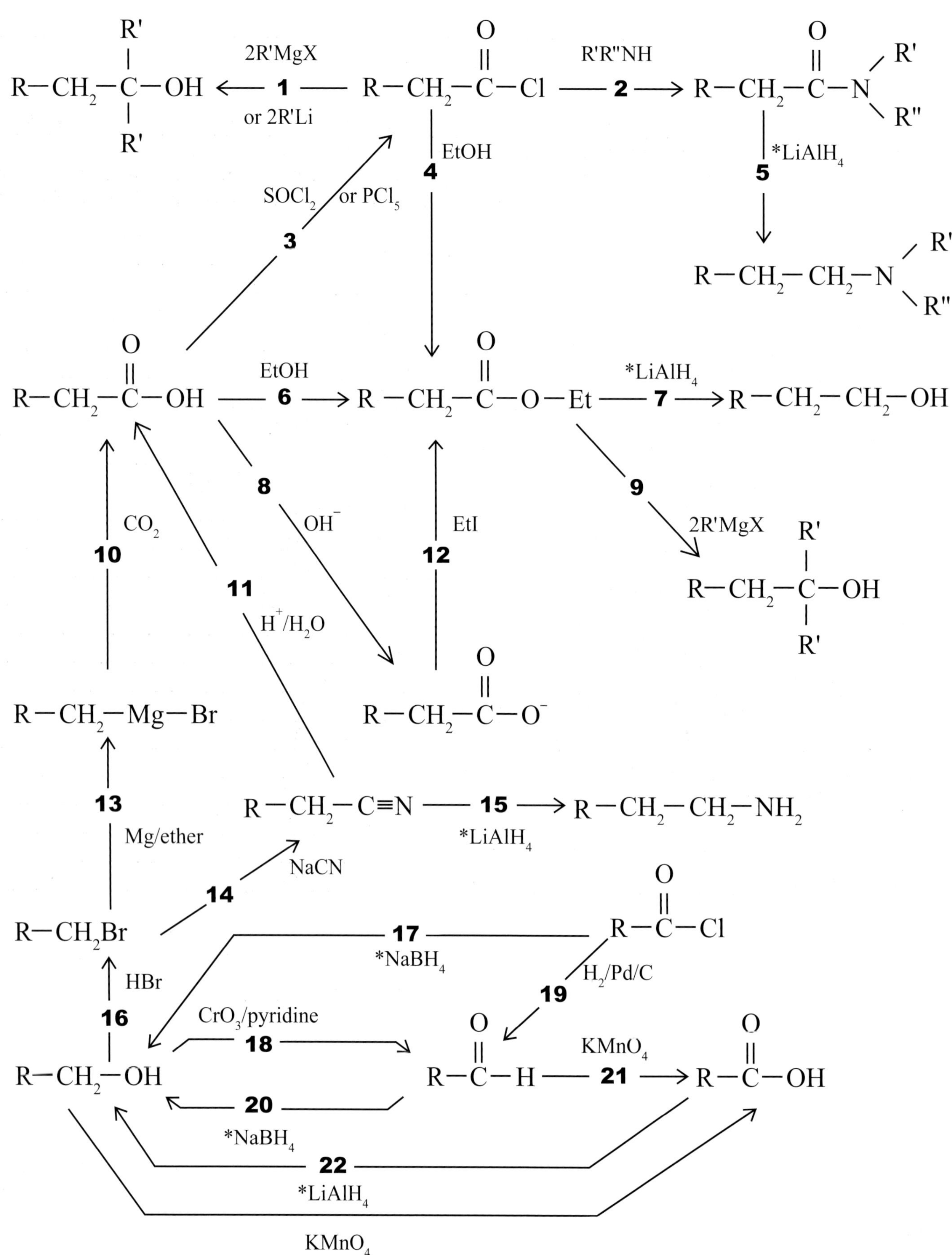
2R'MgX
or 2R'Li
1
R'R''NH
2
EtOH
4
*LiAlH4
5
SOCl2 or PCl5
3
EtOH
6
*LiAlH4
7
8
OH⁻
9
2R'MgX
CO2
10
11
H⁺/H2O
EtI
12
13
Mg/ether
15
*LiAlH4
14
NaCN
17
*NaBH4
19
H2/Pd/C
HBr
16
CrO3/pyridine
18
KMnO4
21
20
*NaBH4
22
*LiAlH4
KMnO4

KEY				
R = alkyl	Et = ethyl	X = halide	R^-MgX^+ = grignard reagent	R^-Li^+ = alkyl lithium
Grignard reagents and alkyl lithiums are special agents since they can create new C—C bonds. *Reduction = addition of hydrogen or subtraction of oxygen. Mild reducing agents add fewer hydrogens/subtract fewer oxygens. Strong reducing agents add more hydrogens/subtract more oxygens. Cross-referencing to The Gold Standard DAT text.				
Most reactions presented can be derived from basic principles (i.e. ORG 1.6, 7.1).				
1) An acid chloride reacts with a grignard reagent to produce a tertiary alcohol. See ORG 9.1				
2) An acid chloride reacts with a primary or secondary amine to produce an amide. See ORG 9.3 & 11.2.				
3) A carboxylic acid reacts with $SOCl_2$ or PCl_5 to produce an acid chloride. See ORG 9.1.				
4) An acid chloride reacts with an alcohol (e.g. ethanol) to produce an ester. See ORG 9.4.				
5) An amide reacts with $LiAlH_4$ to produce an amine. See ORG 8.2, 9.3.				
6) A carboxylic acid reacts with an alcohol (e.g. ethanol) to produce an ester. See ORG 8.2.				
7) An ester reacts with $LiAlH_4$ to produce a primary alcohol. See ORG 8.2, 9.4.				
8) A carboxylic acid reacts with base to produce a carboxylate anion. See CHM 6.3 & ORG 8.1.				
9) An ester reacts with a grignard reagent to produce a tertiary alcohol. See ORG 9.4.				
10) A grignard reagent reacts with carbon dioxide to produce a carboxylic acid. See ORG 8.1.1.				
11) A nitrile reacts with aqueous acid to produce a carboxylic acid. Compare to ORG 10.1.1.				
12) A carboxylate ion reacts with ethyl iodide to produce an ester. Compare to ORG 10.1.1.				
13) An alkyl halide reacts with Mg/ether to produce a grignard reagent. Compare to ORG 10.1.1.				
14) An alkyl halide reacts with NaCN to produce a nitrile. See ORG 6.2.3.				
15) A nitrile reacts with $LiAlH_4$ to produce an amine. See ORG 8.2.				
16) A primary alcohol reacts with HBr to produce an alkyl halide. Compare to ORG 10.1.1.				
17) An acid chloride reacts with $NaBH_4$ to produce a primary alcohol. See ORG 8.2, 9.1.				
18) A primary alcohol reacts with CrO_3/pyridine to produce an aldehyde. See ORG 6.2.2.				
19) A acid chloride reacts with H_2/Pd/C to produce an aldehyde. See ORG 7.1 & 9.1.				
20) An aldehyde reacts with $NaBH_4$ to produce a primary or secondary alcohol. See ORG 7.1, 8.2.				
21) An aldehyde reacts with $KMnO_4$ to produce a carboxylic acid. See ORG 7.2.1.				
22) A carboxylic acid reacts with $LiAlH_4$ to produce a primary alcohol. See ORG 8.2.				

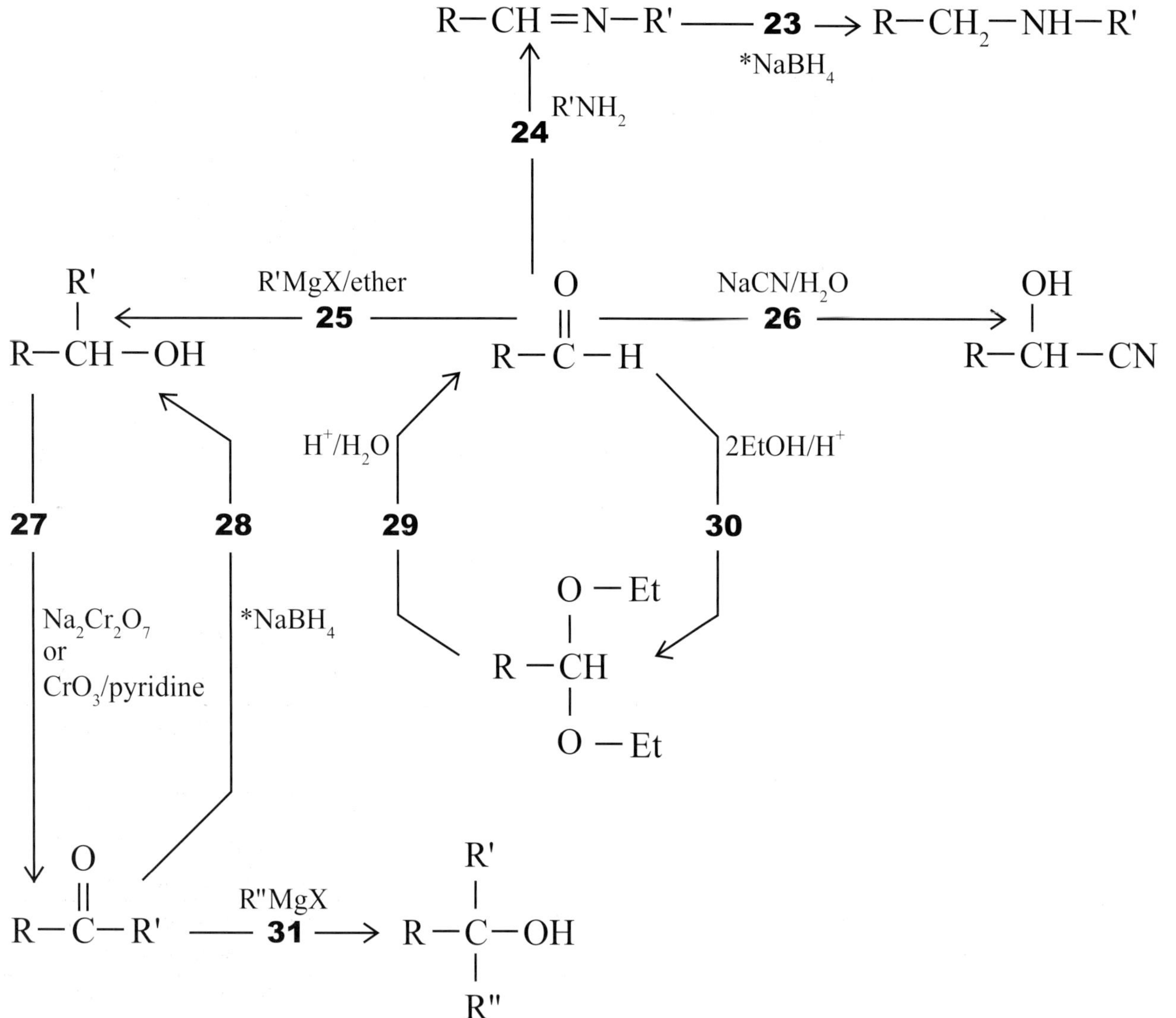

KEY
23) An imine reacts with $NaBH_4$ to produce a secondary amine. See 7.2.3, 8.2.
24) An aldehyde reacts with a primary amine to produce an imine. See ORG 7.2.3.
25) An aldehyde reacts with a grignard reagent and ether to produce a secondary alcohol. See ORG 7.1.
26) An aldehyde reacts with aqueous NaCN. See ORG 7.1.
27) A secondary alcohol reacts with Na_2CrO_7 or CrO_3/pyridine to produce a ketone. See ORG 6.2.2.
28) A ketone reacts with $NaBH_4$ to produce a secondary alcohol. See ORG 7.2.1.
29) An acetal reacts with aqueous acid to produce an aldehyde. See ORG 7.2.2.
30) An aldehyde reacts with an alcohol (e.g. ethanol) and acid to produce an acetal. Note that using with less $EtOH/H^+$, a hemiacetal will form. See ORG 7.2.2.
31) A ketone reacts with a grignard reagent to produce a tertiary alcohol. See ORG 9.1.

List of Common Reagents

Reagent	Comments	Reagent	Comments
$AlCl_3$ aluminum chloride	• Lewis acid • Friedel Crafts	Lindlar catalyst	• heterogeneous catalyst • syn reduction of alkynes to alkenes NOT alkanes
BH_3 borane	• Alkene hydroboration • anti - Markovnikoff	mCPBA meta - chloroperoxybenzoic acid	• epoxidation of alkenes • ketones to esters
CH_2N_2 diazomethane	• Converts carboxylic acids to methyl esters	Mg magnesium metal	• alkyl halide + Mg = Grignard
DCC *N,N'*-dicyclohexyl carbodiimide	• dehydrating agent for peptide couplings	$NaBH_4$ sodium borohydride	• mild reducing agent • aldehydes/ketones to alcohols
DIBAL -H diisobutylaluminum hydride	• reduces esters/nitriles to aldehydes	$NaIO_4$ sodium periodate	• strong ox. agent • cleaves vicinal diols to 2 aldehydes
DMF dimethylformamide	• polar aprotic (= no H^+) solvent • facilitates S_N2	NBS N-bromosuccinimide	• brominations • radical subs. + electrophilic additions
DMSO dimethyl sulfoxide	• polar aprotic solvent • facilitates S_N2	NCS N-chlorosuccinimide	• chlorinations (similar to NBS)
$FeBr_3$ ferric bromide	• Friedel-Crafts • IUPAC: Iron(III)	O_3 ozone	• cleaves double bonds to aldehydes/ketones/acids (depends on workup)
HCN hydrogen cyanide	• makes cyanohydrins • weak acid	$Pb(OAc)_4$ lead tetraacetate	• strong ox. agent, cleaves diols • IUPAC: lead(IV) acetate
$Hg(OAc)_2$ mercuric acetate	• alkene • IUPAC: mercury(II) acetate	PBr_3 phosphorus tribromide	• alcohols to alkyl bromides • carboxylic acids to acyl bromides
K_2CrO_7 potassium dichromate	• mild oxidizing agent • alcohols to aldehydes/ketones	PCC pyridinium chlorochromate	• mild ox. agent • alcohols to aldehydes/ketones
$KMnO_4$ potassium permanganate	• strong oxidizing agent • i.e. hydroxylate alkenes	Pd/C palladium on carbon	• catalyst for hydrogenation i.e. of • unsaturated bonds
LDA lithium diisopropyl amide	• strong base • i.e. carbonyl to enolate	pyrrolidine	• cyclic 2° amine • aldol condensation forming enamines
Li lithium metal	• makes organolithium from alkyl bromide	R_2CuLi organocuprate Gilman reagent	• R replaces X in organic halides • 1,4-addition for unsaturated systems
$LiAlH(OR)_3$	• less reactive $LiAlH_4$ derivative • i.e. esters to aldehydes	$SOCl_2$ thionyl chloride	• chlorinations • i.e. makes acid chlorides
$LiAlH_4$ (LAH, LithAl) lithium aluminum hydride	• strong reducing agent • i.e. esters to alcohols	TsOH toluenesulfonic acid	• p-TsOH (PTSA): strong acid • TSO -, OTs: excellent leaving groups

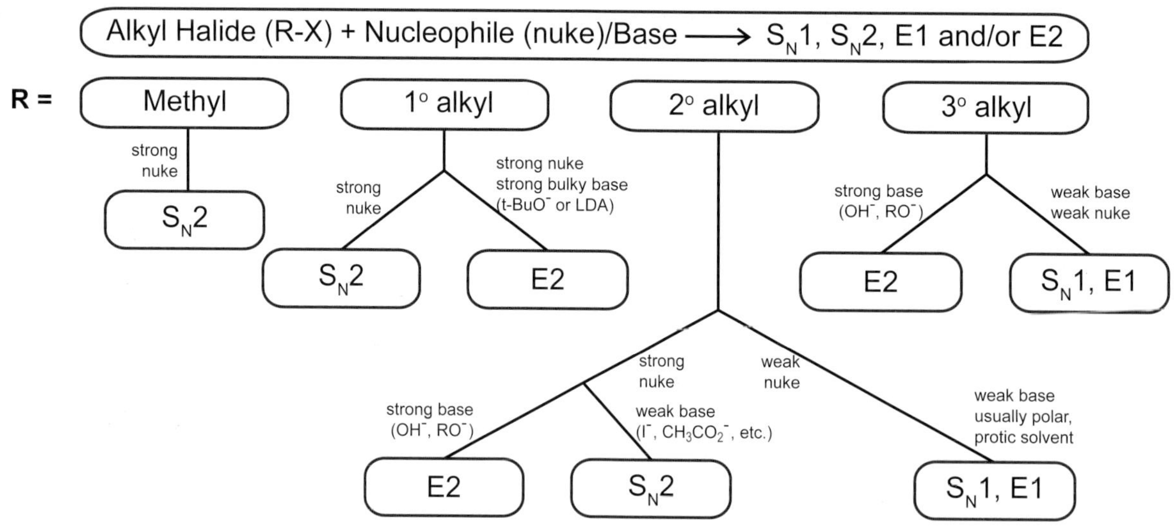

SUBSTITUTION

	S_N1	S_N2
Mechanism	Two steps (carbocation rearrangements possible)	One step (= *concerted*)
Rate law	Rate = k[R–X] (unimolecular, 1st order)	Rate = k[R–X][Nuke] (bimolecular, 2nd order)
Stereochemistry	Loss of stereochemistry (racemization possible)	Stereospecific (inversion due to backside displacement)
Substrate	Cation stability (benzylic > allylic > 3° > 2°) No 1° or methyl R^+ without extra stabilization.	Sterics (methyl > 1° > 2°) No S_N2 with 3°
Nucleophile	Not Important	Strong/Moderate required •strong: RS^-, I^-, R_2N^-, R_2NH, RO^-, CN^- •moderate: RSH, Br^-, RCO_2^-
Leaving group	Very important ($-OSO_2CF_3$ > $-OSO_2F$ >> derivatives of 4-toluenesulfonyl chloride >> –I > –Br > –Cl)	Moderately important (same trend as S_N1)
Solvent	Polar protic (water, most alcohols, formic acid, HF, ammonia)	Polar aprotic (acetonitrile, DMF, HMPA, DMSO - dimethyl sulfoxide)

ELIMINATION

	E1	E2
Mechanism	Two steps (carbocation rearrangements possible)	One step (= *concerted*)
Rate law	Rate = k[R–X] (unimolecular, 1st order)	Rate = k[R–X][Base] (bimolecular, 2nd order)
Stereochemistry	Not stereospecific	Stereospecific (antiperiplanar transition state)
Substrate	Cation stability (benzylic > allylic > 3° > 2°)	Alkene stability (3° > 2° > 1°)
Base	Not important: usually weak (ROH, R_2NH)	Strong base required (RO^-, R_2N^-)
Leaving group	Very important (same trend as S_N1)	Moderately important (same trend as S_N1)
Solvent	Polar protic (water, most alcohols, formic acid, HF, ammonia)	Wide range of solvents
Product ratio	Zaitsev's Rule (or Saytzeff's Rule): The most highly substituted alkene usually predominates. Hofmann Product: Using a sterically hindered base (i.e. t-BuO⁻ or LDA), results in formation of the least substituted alkene (Hofmann product). High temperature favors elimination.	

CHAPTER 1: MOLECULAR STRUCTURE OF ORGANIC COMPOUNDS

1.2 Hybrid Orbitals

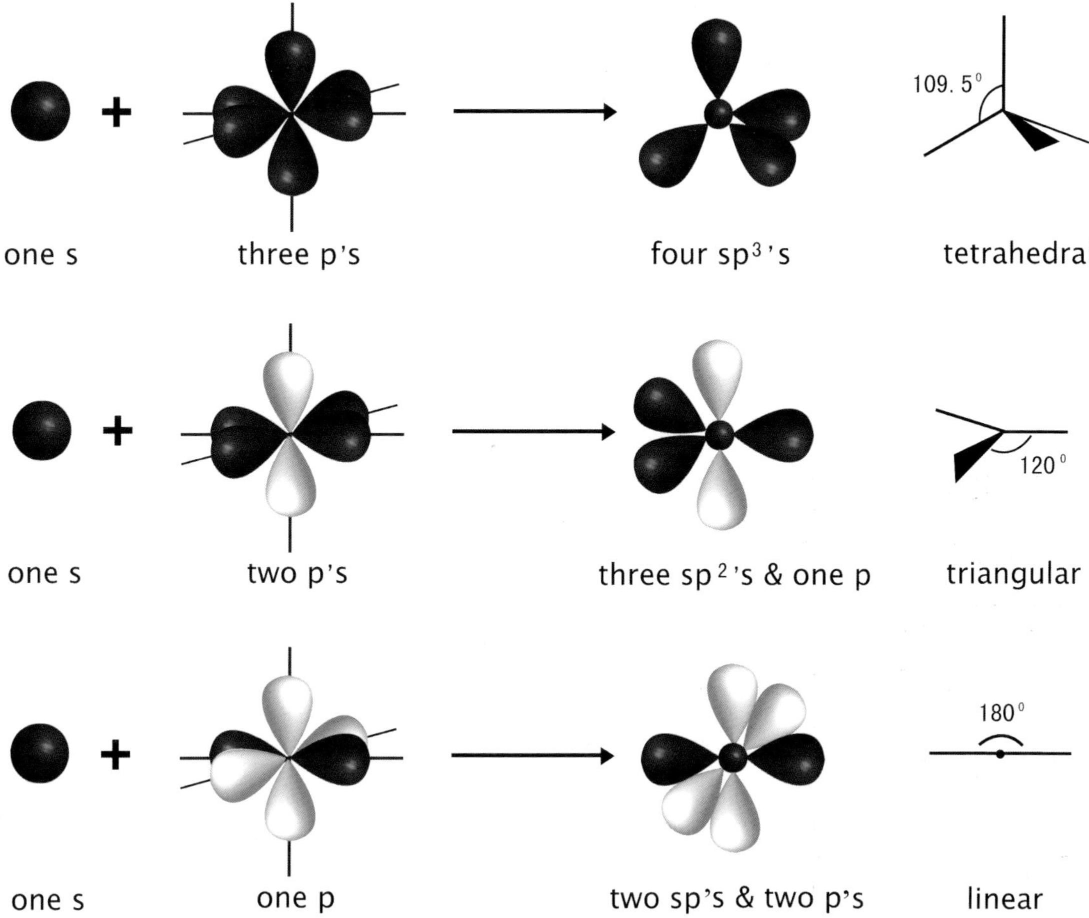

Figure IV.B.1.1: Hybrid orbital geometry

1.6 Ground Rules

"Like charges repel" and "opposites attract" are the basic rules of electrostatics. "Opposites attract" is translated in Organic Chemistry to mean "nucleophile attacks electrophile".

CHAPTER 1: STEREOCHEMISTRY

2.3 Absolute and Relative Configuration

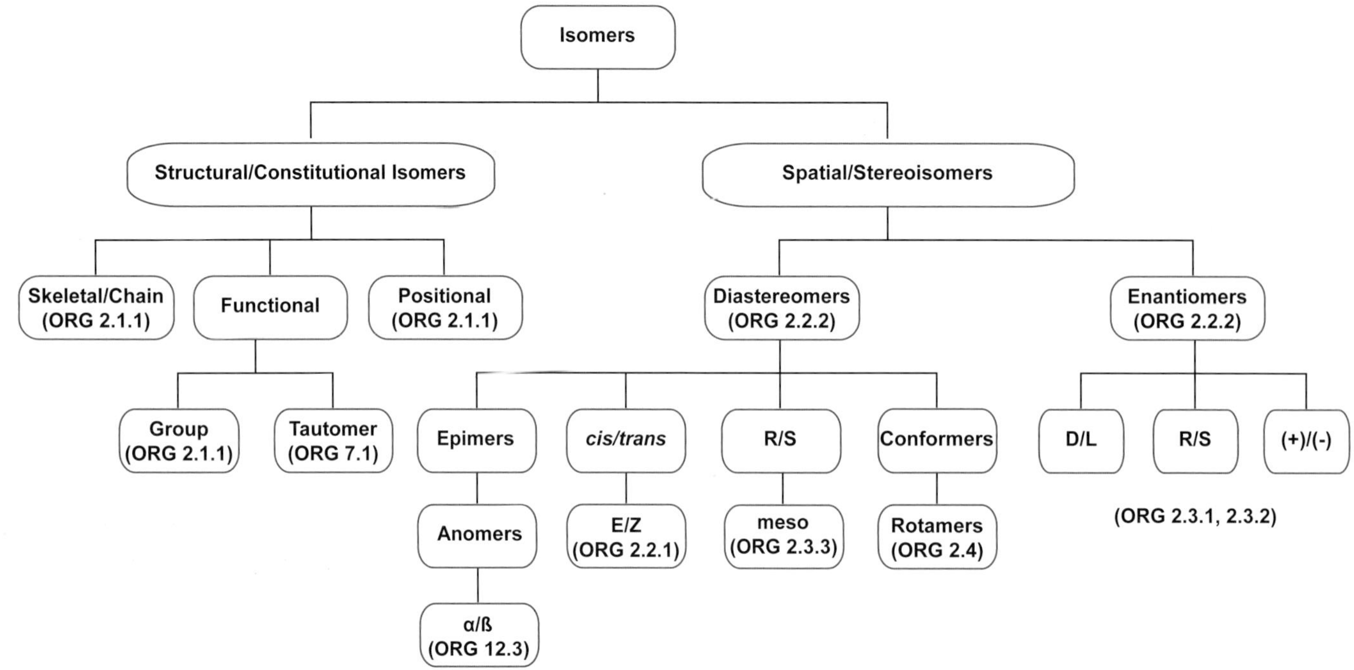

Figure IV.B.2.1.1: Categories of isomers.

2.4 Conformational Isomers

Common Terms

- dihedral angle: torsion (turning/twisting) angle
- gauche: skew, synclinal
- anti: trans, antiperiplanar
- eclipsed: syn, cis, synperiplanar,
  torsion angle = 0°

"anti" and "syn" are IUPAC preferred descriptors.

CHAPTER 3: ALKANES

3.1 Description and Nomenclature

C_1 = meth
C_2 = eth
C_3 = prop
C_4 = but

C_5 = pent
C_6 = hex
C_7 = hept

C_8 = oct
C_9 = non
C_{10} = dec

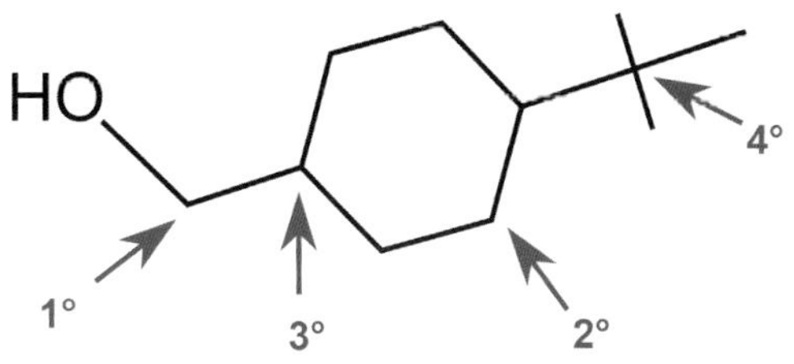

HO
1°
3°
2°
4°

3.3 Ring Strain in Cyclic Alkanes

The expected angles in some cyclic compounds can be determined geometrically: 60° in cyclopropane; 90° in cyclobutane and 108° in cyclopentane. Cyclohexane, in the chair conformation, has normal bond angles of 109.5°. The closer the angle is to the normal tetrahedral angle of 109.5°, the more stable the compound.

CHAPTER 4: ALKENES

4.2.1 Electrophilic Addition

Markovnikoff's rule is a result of this, and it states: *the nucleophile will be bonded to the most substituted carbon* (fewest hydrogens attached) *in the product. Equivalently, the electrophile will be bonded to the least substituted carbon* (most hydrogens attached) *in the product.* Markovnikoff's rule is true for the ionic conditions. Anti-Markovnikoff products are the major products under free radical conditions.

4.2.4 The Diels–Alder Reaction

The Diels–Alder reaction is a cycloaddition reaction between a conjugated diene and a substituted alkene (= the dienophile) to form a substituted cyclohexene system.

Diene + dienophile = cyclohexene

All Diels-Alder reactions have four common features: (1) the reaction is initiated by heat; (2) the reaction forms new six-membered rings; (3) three π bonds break and two new C-C σ bonds and one new C-C π bond are formed; (4) all bonds break and form in a single step.

The Diels Alder diene must have the two double bonds on the same side of the single bond in one of the structures, which is called the s-cis conformation (s-cis: cis with respect to the single bond). If double bonds are on the opposite sides of the single bond in the Lewis structure, this is called the s-trans conformation (s-trans: trans with respect to the single bond).

CH_2 = CH_2
new σ bond
new σ bond
s-cis diene   dienophile

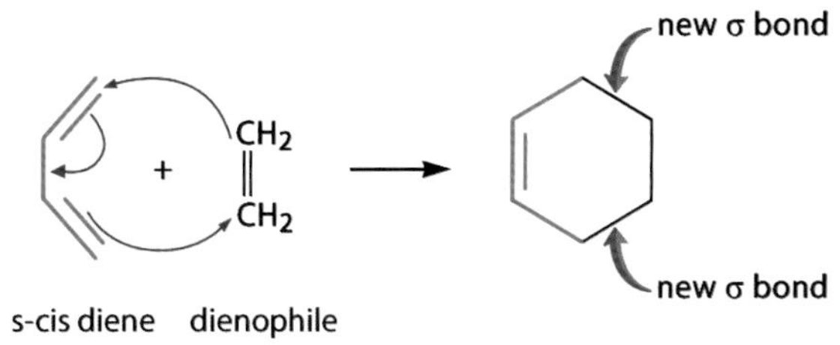

Note that dienes can be divided into 3 classes, depending on the relative location of the double bonds:

1. Cumulated dienes, like allene, have the double bonds sharing a common atom.
2. Conjugated dienes, like 1,3–butadiene, have conjugated double bonds separated by one single bond.
3. Unconjugated dienes (= isolated dienes) have the double bonds separated by two or more single bonds. They are usually less stable than isomeric conjugated dienes.

CHAPTER 5: AROMATICS

5.1.1 Hückel's Rule

If a compound does not meet all the following criteria, it is likely not aromatic.

1. The molecule is cyclic.
2. The molecule is planar.
3. The molecule is fully conjugated (i.e. p orbitals at every atom in the ring; ORG 1.4).
4. The molecule has $4n + 2$ π electrons.

If rules 1., 2. and/or 3. are broken, then the molecule is non-aromatic. If rule 4. is broken then the molecule is antiaromatic.

Notice that the number of π delocalized electrons must be even but NOT a multiple of 4. So $4n + 2$ number of π electrons, where $n = 0, 1, 2, 3$, and so on, is known as Hückel's Rule. Thus the number of pi electrons can be 2, 6, 10, etc.

5.2 Electrophilic Aromatic Substitution

Aromatic halogenation: benzene + X_2 (halogen, X = Cl or Br) —(Fe or FeX_3)→ halobenzene (Ph–X) + HX (hydrogen halide)

Aromatic nitration: benzene + HNO_3 —(H_2SO_4 catalyst, 50 °C)→ nitrobenzene (NO_2)

Aromatic sulfonation: benzene —(H_2SO_4/SO_3, $-H_2O$)→ benzenesulfonic acid (SO_3H)

Friedel-Crafts alkylation: benzene + $H_3C—Cl$ —($AlCl_3$)→ toluene (CH_3) + HCl

Friedel-Crafts acylation: benzene + H_3C–C(=O)–Cl —($AlCl_3$)→ acetophenone (H_3C–C=O) + HCl

EDG	EWG	EWG: Halogens
activates the ring	deactivates the ring	weakly deactivating
O/P Directing	Meta Directing	O/P Directing
i.e. alkyl groups	i.e. nitro ($-NO_2$)	i.e. bromine
acid weakening	acid strengthening	acid strengthening
increase pKa	decrease pKa	decrease pKa

CHAPTER 6: ALCOHOLS

6.1.2 Synthesis of Alcohols

(1) X_2 or NBS, H_2O

(2) BH_3, THF; then H_2O_2, OH^-

(3) $Hg(OAc)_2$, H_2O; then $NaBH_4$

6.2.4 Elimination

$$-\overset{|}{\underset{Y}{C}}-\overset{|}{\underset{Z}{C}}- \xrightarrow[\text{(-YZ)}]{\text{elimination}} \;>C=C<$$

CHAPTER 7: ALDEHYDES AND KETONES

7.2 Important Reactions of Aldehydes & Ketones

$$CH_3-\underset{CH_3}{\underset{|}{C}}=CH-CH_3 \xrightarrow[2.\ H^+]{1.\ O_3} CH_3-\overset{O}{\overset{\|}{C}}-CH_3 + CH_3-\overset{O}{\overset{\|}{C}}-H$$

7.2.6 The Wittig reaction

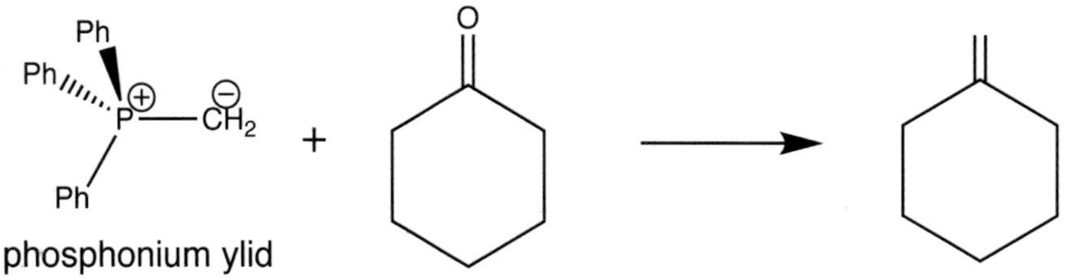

phosphonium ylid

CHAPTER 9: CARBOXYLIC ACID DERIVATES

9.4.1 Fats, Glycerides and Saponification

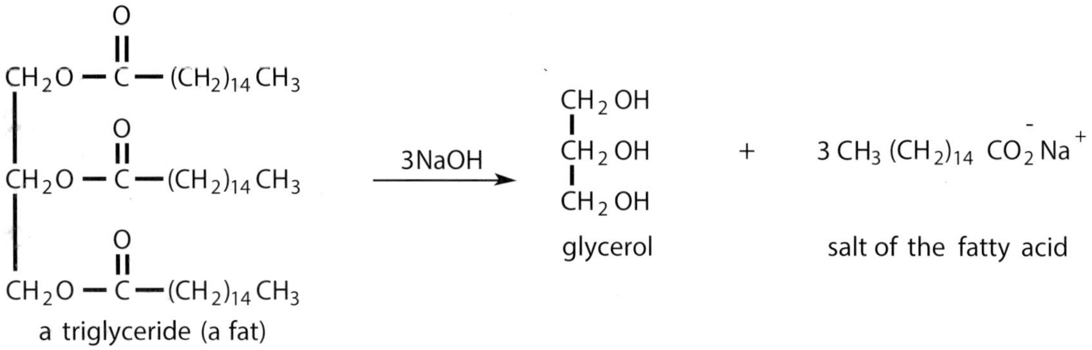

a triglyceride (a fat) $\xrightarrow{3NaOH}$ glycerol + salt of the fatty acid

$$CH_2O-C(=O)-(CH_2)_{14}CH_3,\ CH_2O-C(=O)-(CH_2)_{14}CH_3,\ CH_2O-C(=O)-(CH_2)_{14}CH_3 \xrightarrow{3NaOH} CH_2OH-CH_2OH-CH_2OH + 3\,CH_3(CH_2)_{14}CO_2^-Na^+$$

CHAPTER 12: BIOLOGICAL MOLECULES

12.1 Amino Acids

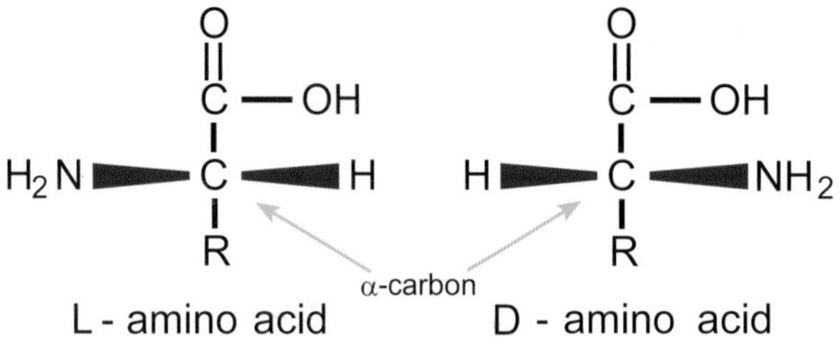

α-carbon

L - amino acid

D - amino acid

12.1.2 Acidic vs. Basic

$$\text{isoelectric point} = pI = (pK_{a1} + pK_{a2})/2$$

CHAPTER 14: SPECTROSCOPY

14.1 IR Spectroscopy

Group	Frequency Range (cm^{-1})
Alcohol (O–H)	3200 – 3650
Carbonyl (C=O)	1630 – 1780

THE GOLD STANDARD

DAT QR & RC

Quantitative Reasoning [Math]
and Reading Comprehension [RC]

Book III of IV

Gold Standard Contributors
• 4-Book GS DAT Set •

Brett Ferdinand BSc MD-CM
Karen Barbia BS Arch
Brigitte Bigras BSc MSc DMD
Ibrahima Diouf BSc MSc PhD
Amir Durmic BSc Eng
Adam Segal BSc MSc
Da Xiao BSc DMD
Naomi Epstein BEng
Lisa Ferdinand BA MA
Jeanne Tan Te
Kristin Finkenzeller BSc MD
Heaven Hodges BSc
Sean Pierre BSc MD
James Simenc BS (Math), BA Eng
Jeffrey Cheng BSc
Timothy Ruger MSc PhD
Petra Vernich BA
Alvin Vicente BS Arch

DMD Candidates

E. Jordan Blanche BS
[Harvard School of Dental Medicine]
Stephan Suksong Yoon BA
[Harvard School of Dental Medicine]

Gold Standard Illustrators
• 4-Book GS DAT Set •

Daphne McCormack
Nanjing Design
· Ren Yi, Huang Bin
· Sun Chan, Li Xin
Fabiana Magnosi
Harvie Gallatiera
Rebbe Jurilla BSc MBA

RuveneCo

The Gold Standard DAT was built for the US DAT.

The Gold Standard DAT is identical to Canadian DAT prep except QR and ORG.
Also, you must practice soap carving for the complete Canadian DAT.

The Gold Standard DAT is identical to OAT prep except PAT, which is replaced by OAT Physics; see our Gold Standard OAT book for Physics review and OAT practice test.

Be sure to register at www.DAT-prep.com by clicking on GS DAT Owners and following the directions for Gold Standard DAT Owners. Please Note: benefits are for 1 year from the date of online registration, for the original book owner only and are not transferable; unauthorized access and use outside the Terms of Use posted on DAT-prep.com may result in account deletion; if you are not the original owner, you can purchase your virtual access card separately at DAT-prep.com.

Visit The Gold Standard's Education Center at www.gold-standard.com.

ISBN 978-1-927338-11-7

Address all inquiries, comments, or suggestions to the publisher. For Terms of Use go to: www.DAT-prep.com

RuveneCo Inc
Gold Standard Multimedia Education
559-334 Cornelia St
Plattsburgh, NY 12901
E-mail: learn@gold-standard.com
Online at www.gold-standard.com

Table of Contents

EXAM SUMMARY

The Dental Admission Test (DAT) consists of 280 multiple-choice questions distributed across quite a diversity of question types in four tests. The DAT is a computer-based test (CBT). This exam requires approximately five hours to complete - including the optional tutorial, break, and post-test survey. The following are the four subtests of the Dental Admission Test:

1. Survey of the Natural Sciences (NS) – 100 questions; 90 min.
    - General Biology (BIO): 40 questions
    - General Chemistry (CHM): 30 questions
    - Organic Chemistry (ORG): 30 questions
2. Perceptual Ability Test (PAT) - 90 questions; 6 subsections; 60 min.
    - Apertures: 15 questions
    - Orthographic or View Recognition: 15 questions
    - Angle Discrimination: 15 questions
    - Paper Folding: 15 questions
    - Cube Counting: 15 questions
    - 3-D Form Development: 15 questions
3. Reading Comprehension (RC) – 50 questions; 3 reading passages; 60 min.
4. Quantitative Reasoning (QR) – 40 questions; 45 min.
    - Mathematics Problems: 30 questions
    - Applied Mathematics/Word Problems: 10 questions

You will get six scores from: (1) BIO (2) CHM (3) ORG (4) PAT (5) QR (6) RC.

You will get two additional scores which are summaries:
(7) Academic Average (AA) = BIO + CHM + ORG + QR + RC
(8) Total Science (TS) = BIO + CHM + ORG

Common Formula for Acceptance:

GPA + DAT score + Interview = Dental School Admissions*

*Note: In general, Dental School Admissions Committees will only examine the DAT score if the GPA is high enough; they will only admit or interview if the GPA + DAT score is high enough. Some programs also use autobiographical materials and/or references in the admissions process. Different dental schools may emphasize different aspects of your DAT score, for example: PAT, BIO, TS, AA. The average score for any section is approximately 17/30; the average AA for admissions is usually 18-20 depending on the dental school; the AA for admissions to Harvard is around 22-23; the 100th percentile is usually 25 meaning that virtually 100% of the approximately 13 000 students who take the DAT every year have an AA less than 25. Only a handful of students score 25/30. Our two student contributors scored 27/30 (AA).

PREFACE

The DAT is challenging, get organized.

dat-prep.com/dat-study-schedule

1. How to study:

1. Study the Gold Standard (GS) books and videos to learn
2. Do GS Chapter review practice questions
3. Consolidate: create and review your personal summaries (= Gold Notes) daily

2. Once you have completed your studies:

1. Full-length practice test
2. Review mistakes, all solutions
3. Consolidate: review all your Gold Notes and create more
4. Repeat until you get beyond the score you need for your targeted dental school

3. Full-length practice tests:

1. ADA practice exams
2. Gold Standard DAT exams
3. TopScore Pro exams
4. Other sources if needed

4. How much time do you need?

On average, 3-6 hours per day for 3-6 months

WARNING: Study more or study more efficiently. You choose. The Gold Standard has condensed the content that you require to excel at the DAT. We have had Ivy League dental students involved in the production of the Gold Standard series so that pre-dent students can feel that they have access to the content required to get a score satisfactory at any dental school in the country. To make the content easier to retain, you can also find aspects of the Gold Standard program in other formats such as:

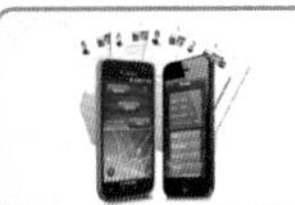

Is there something in the Gold Standard that you did not understand? Don't get frustrated, get online.

dat-prep.com/forum dat-prep.com/QRchanges-2015

Good luck with your studies!

Gold Standard Team

DAT-prep.com

QUANTITATIVE REASONING

FUNDAMENTALS OF THE DAT QUANTITATIVE REASONING

Chapter 1

Memorize	Understand	Not Required
* Basic Rules and Formulas * Conversions and Numerical Relationships * Shortcuts	* Nature of Questions	* Advanced Level Mathematics

Introduction

Beyond the math, the DAT Quantitative Reasoning section stresses proper time management. The more you practice, the more efficient you will become at solving the problems. Knowing what the test covers and building on speed and confidence are thus crucial to your preparation.

Additional Resources

Free Online Forum

1.1 General Introduction

The DAT Quantitative Reasoning Test is a section of speed and mathematical logic. It consists of 40 multiple-choice items and has a time limit of 45 minutes. This means that you have only about one minute to read, analyze, and solve each problem. Nonetheless, the most effective way to prepare for this section is to understand the question types and the concepts that each question assesses. With constant practice, you can then decide which time-saving methods will make you efficient in completing all 40 questions on time.

In general, the DAT QR is meant to gauge your first year college level knowledge of the following math areas:

- Algebra (equations and expressions, inequalities, exponential notation, absolute value, ratios and proportions, and graphical analysis)
- Numerical Calculations (fractions and decimals, percentages, approximations, and scientific notation)
- Conversions (temperature, time, weight, and distance)
- Probability and Statistics
- Geometry
- Trigonometry
- Applied Mathematics (Word) Problems

1.2 Format of the Test

Preparing for the DAT Quantitative Reasoning should also entail familiarizing yourself with the actual set-up of this section: One question is presented at a time and a pop-up on-screen calculator is provided with a click of a button.

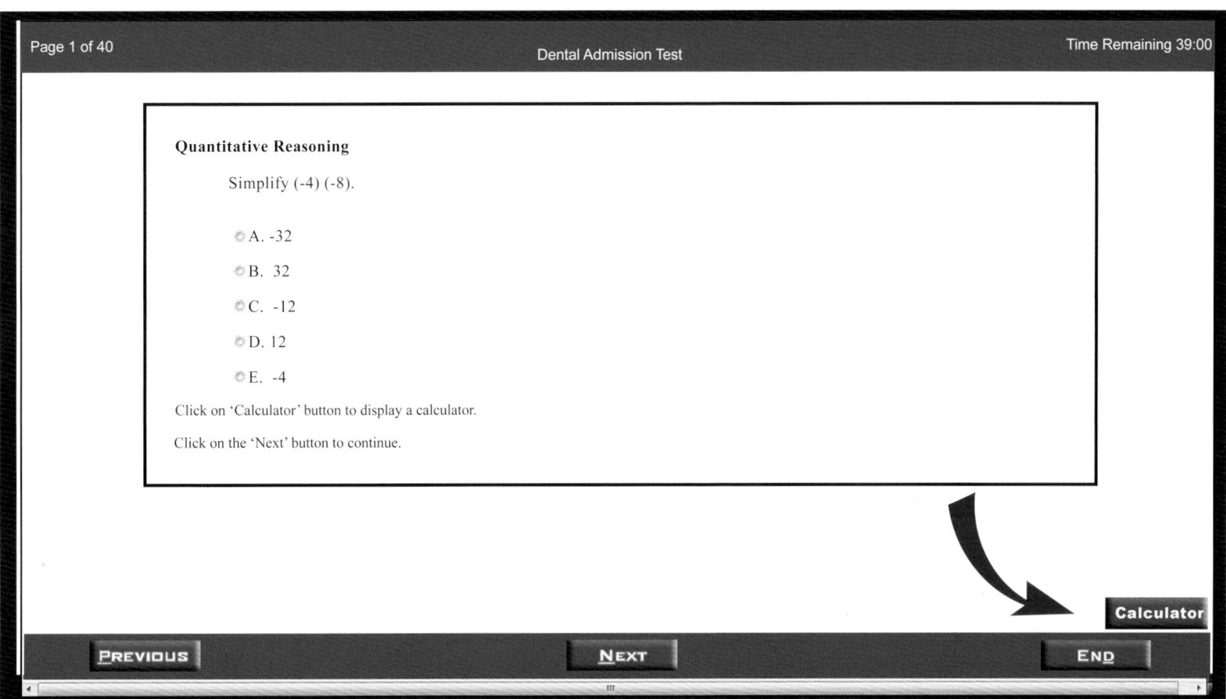

Figure QR.1.1: The Quantitative Reasoning Test Page. The calculator button is provided on every page of the QR section.

The calculator is very basic and the only functions that will be available are addition, subtraction, division, multiplication, the positive/negative (+/-) sign, a period or point sign, the square root key, and 1/x key. These can be operated by using the mouse – not the keyboard. Upon request, you will be given a permanent marker and two laminated sheets on which you can write your calculations manually.

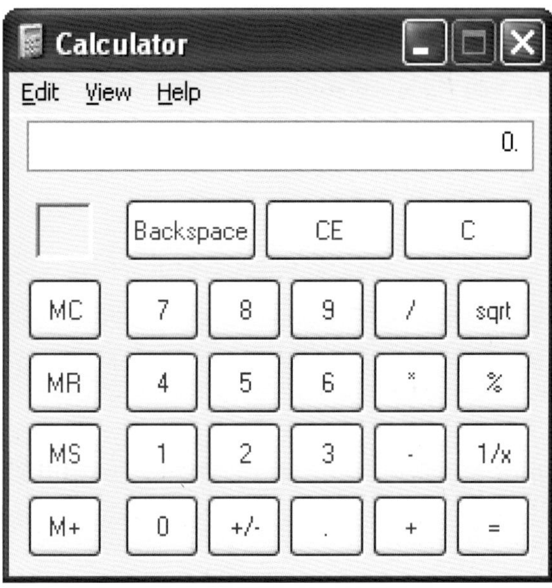

FIGURE QR.1.2: The DAT On-screen Calculator.

1.3 Pending Changes in the DAT QR

Before we delve into the important tips and strategies, you might want to note that the QR section will undergo some changes effective 2015. The following areas will be eliminated:

- Numerical Calculations
- Conversions
- Geometry
- Trigonometry

On the other hand, probability and statistics, as well as data analysis and interpretation, will be retained as critical thinking items but with the following additions:

- Data Sufficiency
- Quantitative Comparison

While the content of this book's edition focuses on the pre-2015 coverage, please take note that the new critical thinking questions will be pretested starting 2013. The results of these trial questions will not be reflected on the candidates' actual QR scores. If you have proof of having purchased this book brand new in 2015, then please email learn@gold-standard.com to access updates online for free.

1.4 How to Do Well in the QR Section

Speed and confidence in solving each problem is central in succeeding in this section. Undoubtedly, the best preparation route is to study the basics and practice with as many questions as you can under timed conditions.

Learn and review the required operations for each of the areas specified by the ADA. Thereafter, make sure that you do all of the chapter review questions plus realistic practice tests, i.e., those which reflect the actual exam.

The ADA offers the *DAT Sample Test Items* as a free download in pdf format and they offer a paid full-length practice test. Taking these tests will give you a clearer idea of the types of questions presented in the real DAT. However, for a simulation of the computer based test (CBT), the Gold Standard program at DAT-prep.com is a good alternative. Top Score Pro is another option. Regardless, you should keep three important things in mind with your QR preparation: Practice makes perfect, specific tips apply to specific topics, and logic does work with math.

1.4.1 Practice Makes Perfect

There are two main goals that you should aim to achieve as you proceed with your practice tests.

1. **Be able to instantly recognize and categorize the area of math involved in a question**

By quickly identifying the type of math problem presented, you can mentally prepare yourself for the different strategies used to solve the question. This gives you a clear direction on how to approach a problem, allowing you to be more time-efficient. When you do your practice tests, you should thus try to adopt the following techniques in order to hone your proficiency in dealing with quantitative items:

- **Ready Formulas**

  If you know your squares, cubes, roots, pi, conversions between units, formulas for the area of a triangle, circle, sphere, cylinder and so forth, you would know which questions you can solve with the least amount of time. By recognizing possible relationships between numbers, you can easily determine the appropriate mathematical formula (and shortcuts!) to use.

  One of the typical questions that show up in the DAT simply asks for the equivalent temperature value of Fahrenheit to Celsius. You can solve this almost instantly if you know the appropriate conversion formula!

- **Guesstimating**

  This strategy is most useful if the values in the answer choices are very spread out yet the question is fairly straightforward. Most questions on the DAT QR will usually have one option that is blatantly wrong. You can then guesstimate (estimate by guesswork) or round off the numbers when doing the calculations. For example, if the question asks you to add 2,301 to 1,203, you could guesstimate and round the given numbers to 2,300 + 1,200 = 3,500. This is much easier to do mentally.

  If you are unsure of your choice, the DAT allows you to mark an answer so you can come back to it later if you have spare minutes left.

- **Working Backwards**

  If you find yourself stuck on a question, you can work backwards from the answer choices by plugging in an option to see if it makes sense. Starting with the middle value would help you decide quickly whether the answer choice is too small or too large.

For questions that frequently slow you down, make sure that you carefully go through the solutions in the answer key. Identify where you fall short. You might just be missing a shortcut. Repeat with more exercises until you are able to master the required manipulations. Remember that the main point of these numerous practices is for you to learn how to pace yourself so that you finish all the questions the first time through with about ten minutes left to spare. This gives you time to go back to questions you skipped earlier.

Moreover, when you practice regularly, you tend to become comfortable with the various strategies. This will also help you identify the areas on which you need further improvement.

2. Become familiar with the tools provided in the actual exam

As already mentioned, the actual DAT provides an on-screen calculator in the QR section. You are not permitted to use anything else except the laminated sheets and marker-pens at the test center.

You should be prepared to deal with possible setbacks. Because the calculator can only be operated by the mouse, this should serve only as a last resort. Using as much mental math as you can is beneficial in order to save time. Likewise, practice writing quickly and neatly as the laminated sheets may be difficult to erase.

1.4.2 Specific Tips Apply to Specific Topics

The next chapters will discuss each of the essential topics listed in the following table. However, this quick "must-know" list can serve as your constant reminder to keep you confidently on track with your QR preparation.

Math Area	Must Know Topics or Skills	Tips
Numbers and Operations	♠ Converting square roots to their exponential forms ♠ Multiplying numbers in scientific notation ♠ Converting units of time (hours to seconds), distance (mi to km, in to cm), temperature (^{0}F to ^{0}C), weight (lbs to kg)	♠ Be comfortable solving without a calculator. ♠ Be on the lookout for common terms that can be cancelled out. ♠ Pay attention to the units given in the problems and the answer choices. ♠ When comparing fractions, convert the denominators to the same value.
Algebra	♠ Solving equations ♠ Solving inequalities and differentiating between "and" or "or"	♠ Understanding the rules in solving algebraic equations is important in solving problems involving angles and triangles.
Geometry	♠ Converting between angles and radians (there are 180 degrees in 1 pi) ♠ 30-60-90 and 45-45-90 triangles ♠ Areas of circle, sphere, triangle, cylinder ♠ Volumes of cylinder, cube, sphere ♠ Identity circle ♠ Sum of interior angles in a polygon: (N-2) x 180 ♠ Graph of a line: y = mx + b (know where the line intercepts the y-axis; know how to find a line that is parallel or perpendicular to any given line) ♠ Circumference, arc length, area of a sector ♠ Distance and midpoint between two points on a coordinate plane	♠ Remember that squares can be bisected to form two 45-45-90 triangles. ♠ Certain polygons such as hexagons are actually made up of smaller triangles. ♠ In dealing with identity circle, remember that any angle over 360 is simply the same as (n-360) where *n* is the angle. ♠ A common question type relating to circumference, arc length, and area of a sector requires solving for the distance covered by a revolution of a wheel.

Trigonometry	♠ Knowing at what points the graph is undefined or 0 ♠ Trigonmetric identities ♠ Remember soh-cah-toa ♠ sin, tan, cos graphs	♠ Problems dealing with distance and angle from a flagpole or some object usually deal with sin/cos/tan. ♠ Similar polygons can be solved through ratios.
Word Problems	♠ Distance = velocity x time ♠ Average velocity = $\frac{\text{total distance}}{\text{total time}}$ (remember you can always re-arrange this equation to find what you need) ♠ Combined work problems: 1/time it takes one person to do the job + 1/time it takes for another person to do the same job = 1/total time it takes to do the job ♠ Simple vs. compound interest	♠ A common question type in this area involves two vehicles moving towards each other or starting at the same point. ♠ Remember that compound interest generates more interest than a simple interest given the same period of time.

1.4.3 Logic Works with Math

Do not feel intimidated when you are confronted with a seemingly unfamiliar problem. Reread the question and understand what is given and what is really asked. Sometimes, the answers are obvious and all you need is to simply use some logical reasoning. With word problems, thinking critically when solving is especially important because the answer is usually not just straight plug-and-chug values.

NOTE

In the succeeding pages, we will review each area specified by the ADA for the Quantitative Reasoning section, as well as techniques, for the respective topics. Each chapter comes with a set of exercises that will help reinforce your knowledge and skills.

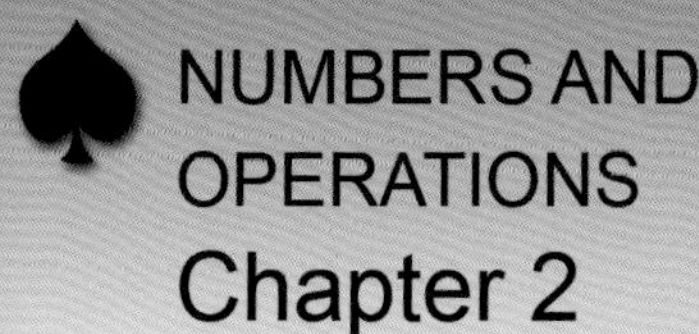

NUMBERS AND OPERATIONS
Chapter 2

Memorize

* Properties of Real Numbers
* Order of Operations
* Rules on Zero
* Important Fraction-Decimal Conversions
* Properties of Exponents

Understand

* Integer, Rational, and Real Numbers
* Basic Operations and Definitions
* Fractions, Mixed Numbers, Decimals and Percentages
* Exponent Manipulations
* Ratios and Proportions

Importance

7 to 9 out of the 40 QR

questions on the DAT are based on content from this chapter (in our estimation).

* This will change in 2015.

Introduction

Study this chapter carefully…

Whether you notice it or not, nearly every problem you will come across in the DAT Quantitative Reasoning section will require you to perform some basic arithmetic. Becoming extremely familiar with the material and key concepts in this chapter will provide the foundation for your overall success.

Time is of the essence on the DAT, so being able to breeze through the basics is crucial, and if you put in the effort now, you will surely thank yourself later.

Let's get started!

Additional Resources

Free Online Forum

2.1 Integers, Rational Numbers, and the Number Line

2.1.1 Integers

Integers are whole numbers without any decimal or fractional portions. They can be any number from negative to positive infinity including zero.

EXAMPLES –2, –1, 0, 1, 2, 3 etc.

2.1.2 Rational Numbers

Rational numbers are numbers that can be written as fractions of integers. "Rational" even contains the word "ratio" in it, so if you like, you can simply remember that these are ratio numbers.

EXAMPLES

$\frac{1}{2}$

$-5 \left(-5 = \frac{-5}{1}\right)$

$1.875 \left(1.875 = \frac{15}{8}\right)$

NOTE

Every integer is also a rational number, but not every rational number is an integer. You can write them as fractions simply by dividing by 1.

A large portion of the problems you will encounter on the Quantitative Reasoning section of the DAT will require you to deal only with rational numbers. Make sure you are extra careful when ratios and fractions are involved because they are notorious for causing mistakes (see section 2.4).

NOTE

If you start with a group of only rational numbers and add, subtract, multiply, and/or divide among them, you will always end up with a rational solution.

Irrational numbers are numbers that cannot be written as fractions of integers. Irrational numbers are normally numbers that have a decimal number that goes on forever with no repeating digits.

EXAMPLES

$\sqrt{2} = 1.4142135623730950...$

$\text{Pi} = \pi = 3.14159265358979...$

2.1.3 Real Numbers and the Number Line

Real numbers are all numbers that can be represented on the number line. These include both rational and irrational numbers.

EXAMPLES

$0, -\frac{1}{3}, \sqrt{2},$ etc.

The **number line** is an infinite straight line on which every point corresponds to a real number. As you move up the line to the right, the numbers get larger, and down the line to the left, the numbers get smaller.

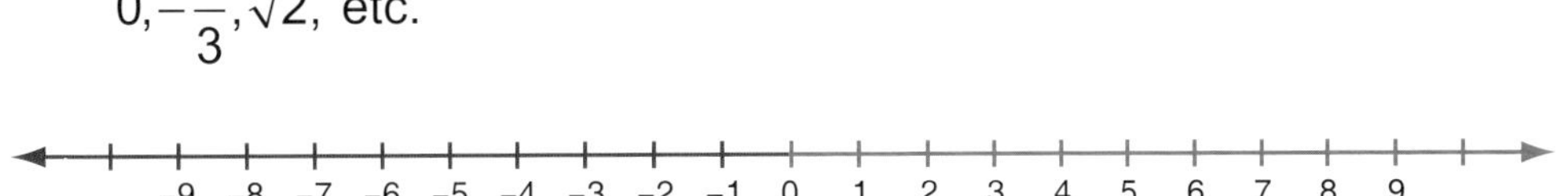

2.2 Basic Arithmetic

2.2.1 Basic Operations

An **operation** is a procedure that is applied to numbers. The fundamental operations of arithmetic are addition, subtraction, multiplication, and division.

A **sum** is the number obtained by adding numbers.

EXAMPLE

The sum of 7 and 2 is 9 since $2 + 7 = 9$.

A **difference** is the number obtained by subtracting numbers.

EXAMPLE

In the equation $7 - 2 = 5$, 5 is the difference of 7 and 2.

A **product** is the number obtained by multiplying numbers.

EXAMPLE

The product of 7 and 2 is 14 since $7 \times 2 = 14$.

A **quotient** is the number obtained by dividing numbers.

EXAMPLE

In the equation $8 \div 2 = 4$, 4 is the quotient of 8 and 2.

Unlike a sum or a product, difference and quotient can result in different numbers depending on the order of the numbers in the expression:

$$10 - 2 = 8 \text{ while } 2 - 10 = -8$$
$$20 \div 5 = 4 \text{ while } 5 \div 20 = 0.25$$

Now, remember that questions on the DAT Quantitative Reasoning test can involve positive and negative numbers. The sum and difference of positive numbers are obtained by simple addition and subtraction, respectively. The same is true when adding negative numbers, except that the sum takes on the negative sign.

EXAMPLES

$(-3) + (-9) = -12$

$(-5) + (-12) + (-44) = -61$

On the other hand, when adding two integers with unlike signs, you need to ignore the signs first, and then subtract the smaller number from the larger number. Then follow the sign of the larger number in the result.

EXAMPLES

$(-6) + 5 = 6 - 5 = -1$

$7 + (-10) = 10 - 7 = -3$

When subtracting two numbers of unlike signs, start by changing the minus sign into its reciprocal, which is the plus sign. Next reverse the sign of the second number. This will make the signs of the two integers the same. Now follow the rules for adding integers with like signs.

EXAMPLES

$(-6) - 5 = (-6) + (-5) = -11$

$7 - (-10) = 7 + 10 = 17$

Multiplication and division of integers are governed by the same rules: If the numbers have like signs, the product or quotient is positive. If the numbers have unlike signs, the answer is negative.

EXAMPLES

$$5 \times 6 = 30$$
$$-5 \times -3 = 15$$
$$81 \div 9 = 9$$
$$-20 \div -4 = 5$$
$$7 \times -4 = -28$$
$$-9 \times 6 = -54$$
$$-15 \div 3 = -5$$
$$16 \div -2 = -8$$

An **expression** is a grouping of numbers and mathematical operations.

EXAMPLE

2 + (3 × 4) × 5 is a mathematical expression.

An **equation** is a mathematical sentence consisting of two expressions joined by an equals sign. When evaluated properly, the two expressions must be equivalent.

EXAMPLE

$2 \times (1+3) = \frac{16}{2}$ is an equation since the expressions on both sides of the equals sign are equivalent to 8.

2.2.2 Properties of the Real Numbers

Whenever you are working within the real numbers (which you always will be on the DAT), these properties hold true. It isn't necessary to memorize the name of each property, but you must be able to apply them all.

Symmetric Property of Equality: The right and left hand sides of an equation are interchangeable, so if $a = b$, then $b = a$.

Transitive Property of Equality: If $a = b$ and $b = c$, then $a = c$. This means that if you have two numbers both equal to one other number, those two numbers are also equal.

Commutative Property of Addition: When adding numbers, switching the position of the numbers will not change the outcome, so $a + b = b + a$.

Associative Property of Addition: When adding more than two numbers, it doesn't matter what order you do the addition in, so $(a + b) + c = a + (b + c)$.

Commutative Property of Multiplication: When multiplying numbers, switching the position of the numbers will not change the outcome, so $a \times b = b \times a$.

Associative Property of Multiplication: When multiplying more than two numbers, it doesn't matter what order you do the multiplication in, so $(a \times b) \times c = a \times (b \times c)$.

Identity Property of Addition: When zero is added or subtracted to any number, the answer is the number itself, so $10b - 0 = 10b$.

Identity Property of Multiplication: When a number is multiplied or divided by 1, the answer is the number itself, so $6a \times 1 = 6a$.

Distributive Property of Multiplication: When multiplying a factor on a group of numbers that are being added or subtracted, the factor may be distributed by multiplying it by each number in the group, so $a(b - c) = ab - ac$.

> Subtraction and division do not follow associative laws.

2.2.3 Order of Operations

Knowing the order of operations is fundamental to evaluating numerical expressions. If you follow it properly, you will always come up with the correct answer! Here it is in list form, to be followed from the top down:

Parentheses
Exponents (including square roots)
Multiplication
Division
Addition
Subtraction

This forms the simple acronym **PEMDAS**, which is a great way to keep the operations straight. Alternatively, some people find it easier to remember the phrase "**P**lease **E**xcuse **M**y **D**ear **A**unt **S**ally."

If you don't like either of these techniques, feel free to come up with your own. It's important to have this down because, as simple as it may seem, being able to carry out the order of operations quickly is crucial to achieving a high score in Quantitative Reasoning.

NOTE

- Multiplication and division have the same rank. It is generally recommended to do them in order from left to right as they appear in the expression, but you can also do them in whatever order that makes most sense to you.
- The same goes for addition and subtraction. Execute them from left to right, or in the order that feels most comfortable.
- When you encounter nested parentheses, evaluate the innermost ones first then work your way outward.

Using PEMDAS, let's evaluate this expression composed only of integers.

$$2^2 + [(3 + 2) \times 2 - 9]$$

First, evaluate the expression contained in the inner set of parentheses.

$$= 2^2 + [(5) \times 2 - 9]$$

You can then choose to strictly follow the PEMDAS order by evaluating the exponent next. Alternately, you can perform the operations within the square brackets, working your way outward, for a more organized procedure as follows:

First, perform the multiplication.

$$= 2^2 + (10 - 9)$$

Then, perform the subtraction.

$$= 2^2 + 1$$

Now evaluate the exponent.

$$= 4 + 1$$

Finally, evaluate the remaining expression.

$$= 5$$

2.3 Rules on Zero

2.3.1 Addition and Subtraction with Zero

Zero is a unique number, and it has special properties when it comes to operations.

Zero is known as the **additive identity** of the real numbers since whenever it is added to (or subtracted from) a number, that number does not change.

Let's examine a simple expression.

$$(3 + 2) - 4$$

We can add or subtract zero anywhere within the expression and the value will not change:

$$(3 - 0 + 2) - 4 + 0$$
$$= (3 + 2) - 4$$

The addition or subtraction of the two zeros has no effect whatsoever on the outcome.

2.3.2 Multiplication and Division with Zero

When adding zero in an expression, it is easy to come up with a practical picture of what the operation represents; you begin with a collection of things and add zero more things to them. When multiplying and dividing with zero, however, such a conceptualization is more difficult. The idea of using zero in this manner is far more abstract.

Fortunately, you don't need to wrestle with trying to picture what multiplication or division with zero looks like. You can simply remember these easy rules:

Multiplying by Zero: The result of multiplying any quantity by zero is *always* equal to zero.

Remember that by the commutative property of multiplication, $a \times b = b \times a$, so if we let $b = 0$, then we have $a \times 0 = 0 \times a$. This means that instead of trying to imagine multiplying a number by zero, you can reverse the thought and consider multiplying zero by a number instead. This second statement is more natural to visualize. You start with nothing, and then no matter how many times you duplicate that nothing, you still end up with nothing.

EXAMPLE

$$3 \times 0 = 0$$
$$123.79 \times 0 = 0$$
$$\left[1.2 + \left(37 - \sqrt{5}\right) \times 2.331\right] \times 0 = 0$$

In the last example, there is no need to go through the order of operations and evaluate the expression inside the parentheses. Because you can see immediately that the entire parenthetical expression is being multiplied by zero, you know that the end result will be zero.

Zero Divided by a Number: The result of dividing zero by any quantity is *always* equal to zero. As with multiplication by zero, if you start with nothing and then take a portion of that nothing, you still end up with nothing.

EXAMPLE

$$0 \div 3 = 0$$
$$0 \div 123.79 = 0$$
$$0 \div \left[1.2 + \left(37 - \sqrt{5}\right) \times 2.331\right] = 0$$

Just like with the multiplication by zero example, you do not need to evaluate the parenthetical expression in order to know that the solution is zero. Especially in the time-constrained setting of the DAT, you should avoid doing such a needless calculation.

Dividing by Zero: Dividing any nonzero quantity by zero results in a solution that is not defined and is therefore undefined.

You should never have to deal with this case on the DAT. If you end up with division by zero in a calculation, you have probably made a mistake. Similarly, you should never end up with zero divided by zero (an undefined quantity). If you do, you should go back and check your work.

2.4 Fractions, Decimals, and Percentages

2.4.1 Fractions

A **fraction** is the quotient of two numbers. It represents parts of a whole and may be seen as a proportion. The number on top is the *numerator*, and the one on the bottom is the *denominator*. Another way of understanding fractions is to consider one as the number of parts present (*numerator*) and the amount of parts it takes to make up a whole (*denominator*). These values can be divided by each other, and this fraction is the quotient.

EXAMPLE

$$\frac{2}{7}$$

In this fraction, 2 is the numerator and 7, the denominator.

Remember, all rational numbers (including integers) can be written as fractions.

2.4.2 Manipulating Fractions

A. Fraction Multiplication

To multiply fractions, simply multiply the numerators together (this will be the new numerator) and then multiply the denominators together (this will be the new denominator).

EXAMPLE

$$\frac{2}{3} \times \frac{4}{5}$$

Multiply the numerators and denominators separately.

$$= \frac{(2 \times 4)}{(3 \times 5)}$$

$$= \frac{8}{15}$$

B. Fraction Division

A **reciprocal** is the number obtained by switching the numerator with the denominator of a fraction. For example, the reciprocal of $\frac{2}{3}$ is $\frac{3}{2}$.

To divide a number by a fraction, multiply that number by the reciprocal of the fraction.

EXAMPLE

$$3 \div \frac{4}{3}$$

Switch the numerator and the denominator in the fraction and multiply. Remember that 3 is really 3 ÷ 1 so the new denominator would be the product of 1 × 4.

$$= \frac{3}{1} \times \frac{3}{4}$$

$$= \frac{9}{4}$$

C. Fraction Addition and Subtraction

With fractions, addition and subtraction are not so easy. You can only add or subtract fractions from each other if they have the same denominator. If they satisfy this condition, then to add or subtract, you do so with the numerators only and leave the denominator unchanged.

EXAMPLE

$$\frac{1}{5} + \frac{3}{5}$$

Both fractions have the same denominator, so add the numerators.

$$= \frac{1 + 3}{5}$$

$$= \frac{4}{5}$$

EXAMPLE

$$\frac{3}{5} - \frac{1}{5}$$

Both fractions have the same denominator, so subtract the numerators.

$$= \frac{3 - 1}{5}$$

$$= \frac{2}{5}$$

What if the denominators of two fractions you are adding or subtracting are not the same? In this case, you must find the Lowest Common Denominator (LCD), the smallest number that is divisible by both of the original denominators.

Ideally, you would like to find the smallest common denominator because smaller numbers in fractions are always easier to work with. But this is not always easy to do, and usually it isn't worth the extra time it will take to do the necessary calculation. The simplest way to find a common denominator is to multiply each fraction by a new fraction in which the numerator and denominator are both the same as the denominator of the other fraction.

EXAMPLE

$$\frac{2}{3} + \frac{2}{7}$$

Don't be confused by the fact that the numerators are the same. We still need to find a common denominator because the denominators are different.

$$= \left(\frac{2}{3} \times \frac{7}{7}\right) + \left(\frac{2}{7} \times \frac{3}{3}\right)$$

$$= \frac{14}{21} + \frac{6}{21}$$

Now that we have the same denominator, we can add the numerators.

$$= \frac{20}{21}$$

This method of finding common denominators utilizes the fact that any number multiplied by 1 is still the same number. The new fractions we introduce are always made of equivalent numerators and denominators, which make the fraction equal to 1, so the values of the original fractions do not change.

D. Comparing Fractions

Another method with which you should be familiar when manipulating fractions is comparing their values (i.e., which of the given fractions is greater than or lesser than the other) when they have different denominators. We will show you three ways to do this.

When you are confronted with only two fractions, finding their common denominator makes the task of evaluating the values easier.

1. Similar to the preceding discussion on adding or subtracting fractions that have different denominators, the fastest way to come up with a common denominator is to multiply both the numerator and denominator of each fraction by the other's denominator.

Let's say you are given the two fractions:

$\frac{4}{5}$ and $\frac{3}{7}$

Multiply the first fraction by 7 over 7 and the second fraction by 5 over 5. (The 7 comes from the fraction $\frac{3}{7}$ while 5 from $\frac{4}{5}$.)

$$\frac{4}{5} \times \frac{7}{7} = \frac{28}{35}$$

$$\frac{3}{7} \times \frac{5}{5} = \frac{15}{35}$$

With both fractions having 35 as the common denominator, you can now clearly see that 28 must be greater than

15. Therefore, $\frac{4}{5}$ is greater than $\frac{3}{7}$.

2. Another way to go about this is through cross-multiplication. Using the same fractions as examples, you first multiply the numerator of the first fraction by the denominator of the second fraction. The product will then serve as the new numerator of the first fraction.

$$\frac{4}{5} \searrow \frac{3}{7} \Rightarrow 4 \times 7 = 28$$

Next, multiply the denominators of the two fractions. The product will now serve as the new denominator of the first fraction.

$$\frac{4}{5} \rightarrow \frac{3}{7} \Rightarrow 5 \times 7 = 35$$

The resulting new fraction would be $\frac{28}{35}$.

Now, let's work on the second fraction. To get its new numerator, this time, multiply the numerator of the second fraction by the denominator of the first fraction. Then multiply the denominators of both fractions.

$$\frac{4}{5} \swarrow \frac{3}{7} \Rightarrow 3 \times 5 = 15$$

$$\frac{4}{5} \leftarrow \frac{3}{7} \Rightarrow 7 \times 5 = 35$$

The second fraction will now become $\frac{15}{35}$. Thus comparing the first and second fractions, we get the same result as we had in the first method.

Because $\frac{28}{35}$ is greater than $\frac{15}{35}$, therefore $\frac{4}{5}$ is greater than $\frac{3}{7}$.

Both procedures follow the same basic principles and prove to be efficient when dealing with two given fractions. But what if you were given three or four fractions?

3. A much simpler way is to convert each fraction to decimals, and then compare the decimals. All you have to do is divide the numerator of the fraction by its own denominator. For big numbers, you can use the calculator provided during the exam. For smaller ones, you could learn to do the calculations in your head or on a board. With a little practice, you can actually train your brain to work fast with arithmetic.

Now let's say a third fraction is introduced to our previous examples: $\frac{4}{5}$, $\frac{3}{7}$, $\frac{9}{13}$. Working on the first fraction, simply divide 4 by 5; on the second fraction, 3 by 7; and on the last, 9 by 13.

$\frac{4}{5} = 4 \div 5 = 0.8$

$\frac{3}{7} = 3 \div 7 = 0.43$

$\frac{9}{13} = 9 \div 13 = 0.69$

Comparing the three fractions in their decimal forms, 0.43 ($\frac{3}{7}$) is the smallest, 0.69 ($\frac{9}{13}$) is the next, and the largest is 0.8 ($\frac{4}{5}$).

E. Reduction and Cancelling

To make calculations easier, you should always avoid working with unnecessarily large numbers. To reduce fractions, you can cancel out any common factors in the numerator and denominator.

EXAMPLE

$$\frac{20}{28}$$

First, factor both the numerator and denominator.

$$= \frac{(4 \times 5)}{(4 \times 7)}$$

Since both have a factor of four, we can cancel.

$$= \frac{5}{7}$$

When multiplying fractions, it is possible to cross-cancel like factors before performing the operation. If there are any common factors between the numerator of the first fraction and the denominator of the second fraction, you can cancel them. Likewise, if there are common factors between the numerator of the second and the denominator of the first, cancel them as well.

EXAMPLE

$$\frac{5}{9} \times \frac{6}{25}$$

First, factor the numerators and denominators.

$$= \frac{5}{(3 \times 3)} \times \frac{(2 \times 3)}{(5 \times 5)}$$

Now, we see that we can cross-cancel 5s and 3s.

$$= \frac{1}{3} \times \frac{2}{5}$$

$$= \frac{2}{15}$$

F. Mixed Numbers

You may encounter numbers on the DAT that have both an integer part and a fraction part. These are called mixed numbers.

EXAMPLE

$$3\frac{1}{2}$$

Mixed numbers should be thought of as addition between the integer and the fraction.

EXAMPLE

$$3\frac{1}{2} = 3 + \frac{1}{2}$$

Now in order to convert a mixed number back to a fraction, all you have to do is consider the integer to be the fraction of itself over 1 and perform fraction addition.

EXAMPLE

$$3\frac{1}{2}$$

$$= \frac{3}{1} + \frac{1}{2}$$

Obtain a common denominator.

$$= \left(\frac{3}{1}\right)\left(\frac{2}{2}\right) + \frac{1}{2}$$

$$= \frac{6}{2} + \frac{1}{2}$$

$$= \frac{7}{2}$$

To add or subtract mixed numbers, you can deal with the integer and fraction portions separately.

EXAMPLE

$$3\frac{1}{2} - 2\frac{1}{2}$$

$$= (3-2) + \left(\frac{1}{2} - \frac{1}{2}\right)$$

$$= 1$$

NOTE

To convert a mixed number to a fraction, keep the denominator of the fraction while multiplying the integer part of the mixed number by the denominator. Then add to the numerator of the mixed number.

EXAMPLE

$$6\frac{2}{5} = (6 \text{ x } 5) + \frac{2}{5} = 30 + \frac{2}{5} = \frac{32}{5}$$

2.4.3 Decimals and Percentages

There are two other ways to represent non-integer numbers that you will encounter on the DAT: As decimals and as percentages.

A. Decimals

Decimal numbers can be recognized by the decimal point (a period) that they contain. Whatever digits are to the left of the decimal point represent a whole number, the integer portion of the number. The digits to the right of the decimal point are the decimal portion.

EXAMPLE

12.34

The integer portion of the number is 12, and .34 is the fractional portion.

The value of the decimal portion of a number operates on a place-value system just like the integer portion. The first digit to the right of the decimal point is the number of tenths (1/10 is one tenth), two digits over is the number of hundredths (1/100 is one hundredth), three digits over is the number of thousandths, then ten-thousandths, etc.

For example, in the decimal 0.56789:

- the 5 is in the tenths position;
- the 6 is in the hundredths position;
- the 7 is in the thousandths position;
- the 8 is in the ten thousandths position;
- the 9 is in the one hundred thousandths position.

Thus, to convert a decimal into a fraction, just drop the decimal point and divide by the power of ten of the last decimal digit. To convert a fraction to a decimal, simply perform the long division of the numerator divided by the denominator.

EXAMPLE

$$0.34 = \frac{34}{100}$$

B. Operations with Decimals

Addition and Subtraction: Adding and subtracting decimals is the same as with integers. The only difference is that you need to take care to line up the decimal point properly. Just like with integers, you should only add or subtract digits in the same place with each other.

EXAMPLE

Add 3.33 to 23.6.

$$\begin{array}{r} 23.60 \\ +\ 03.33 \\ \hline \end{array}$$

Notice how we have carried the decimal point down in the same place. Also, to illustrate the addition more clearly, we have added zeros to hold the empty places. Now perform the addition as if there were no decimal points.

$$\begin{array}{r} 23.60 \\ +\ 03.33 \\ \hline 26.93 \end{array}$$

Multiplication: You can multiply numbers with decimals just as you would with integers, but placing the decimal point in the solution is a little tricky. To decide where the decimal point goes, first count the number of significant digits after the decimal points in each of the numbers being multiplied. Add these numbers together to obtain the total number of decimal digits. Now, count that number of digits in from the right of the solution and place the decimal point in front of the number at which you end.

EXAMPLE

Multiply 3.03 by 1.2.

$$\begin{array}{r} 3.03 \\ \times\ 1.20 \\ \hline \end{array}$$

We have written in a zero as a placeholder at the end of the second number, but be careful not to include it in your decimal count. Only count up to the final nonzero digit in each number (the 0 in the first number counts because it comes before the 3). Thus our decimal digit count is 2 + 1 = 3, and we will place our decimal point in the solution 3 digits in from the right; but first, perform the multiplication while ignoring the decimal.

$$\begin{array}{r} 3.03 \\ \times\ 1.20 \\ \hline 606 \\ +\ 3030 \\ \hline 3636 \end{array}$$

Now, insert the decimal point to obtain the final solution.

$$= 3.636$$

When counting significant digits, remember to consider the following:

1. all zeros between nonzero digits

EXAMPLE

0.45078 → 5 significant figures

2. all zeros in front of a nonzero number

EXAMPLE

0.0056 → 4 significant figures

3. ignore all zeros after a nonzero digit

EXAMPLE

0.2500 → 2 significant figures

NOTE

In DAT Chemistry this last rule is not so simple because in science labs, significant figures (= significant digits = sig figs) represent the accuracy of measurement. This is further discussed in the Appendix to QR A.4 and General Chemistry Chapter 12 in the Gold Standard DAT.

Division: We can use our knowledge of the equivalence of fractions to change a decimal division problem into a more familiar integer division problem. Simply multiply each number by the power of ten corresponding to the smallest significant digit out of the two decimal numbers being divided, and then, perform the division with the integers obtained. {For more information regarding significant digits, see the QR Appendix or General Chemistry Chapter 12.}

This operation is acceptable because it amounts to multiplying a fraction by 1.

EXAMPLE

Divide 4.4 by 1.6

$$\frac{4.4}{1.6}$$

Since the smallest decimal digit in either number is in the tenth place, we multiply the top and bottom by 10.

$$= \frac{4.4}{1.6} \times \frac{10}{10}$$

$$= \frac{44}{16}$$

$$= \frac{11}{4}$$

If you like, you can convert this back to a decimal.

$$= 2.75$$

Rounding Decimals: Rounding decimals to the nearest place value is just like rounding an integer. Look at the digit one place further to the right of the place to which you are rounding. If that digit is 5 or greater, add 1 to the previous digit and drop all the subsequent digits. If it is 4 or less, leave the previous digit alone and simply drop the subsequent digits.

Consider the number 5.3618:

(a) Round to the nearest tenth.

$$= 5.4$$

Since the digit after the tenth place is a 6, we add 1 tenth and drop every digit after the tenth place.

(b) Round to the nearest hundredth.

$$= 5.36$$

Since the digit after the hundredth place is a 1, we do not change any digits. Just drop every digit after the hundredth place.

Fraction-Decimal Conversions to Know: Having these common conversions between fractions and decimals memorized will help you save valuable time on the test.

Fraction	Decimal
1/2	.5
1/3	~ .33
1/4	.25
1/5	.2
1/6	~.167
1/8	.125
1/10	.1

C. Percentages

Percentages are used to describe fractions of other numbers. One percent (written 1%) simply means 1 hundredth. This is easy to remember since "percent" can literally be broken down into "per" and "cent", and we all know that one cent is a hundredth of a dollar.

We can use this conversion to hundredths when evaluating expressions containing percents of numbers, but a percentage has no real meaning until it is used to modify another value. For example, if you see 67% in a problem you should always ask "67% of what?"

EXAMPLE

What is 25% of 40?

$$= .25 \times 40$$
$$= 10$$

To find what percentage a certain part of a value is of the whole value, you can use what is known as the **percentage formula**:

Percent = (Part/Whole) × 100

EXAMPLE

What percentage of 50 is 23?

$$\text{Percentage} = (23/50) \times 100$$
$$= (46/100) \times 100$$
$$= 46\%$$

2.5 Roots and Exponents

2.5.1 Properties of Exponents

To multiply exponential values with the same base, keep the base the same and add the exponents.

EXAMPLE

$$a^2 \times a^3 = a^{2+3} = a^5$$

To divide exponential values with the same base, keep the base the same and subtract the exponent of the denominator from the exponent of the numerator.

EXAMPLE

$$\frac{x^5}{x^3} = x^{5-3} = x^2$$

To multiply exponential values with different bases but the same exponent, keep the exponent the same and multiply the bases.

EXAMPLE

$$2^x \times 3^x = (2 \times 3)^x = 6^x$$

To divide exponential values with different bases but the same exponent, keep the exponent the same and divide the bases.

EXAMPLE

$$\frac{6^x}{2^x} = \left(\frac{6}{2}\right)^x = 3^x$$

To raise an exponential value to another power, keep the base the same and multiply the exponents.

EXAMPLE

$$(x^3)^4 = x^{(3\times4)} = x^{12}$$

Even though all of the preceding examples use only positive integer exponents, these properties hold true for all three of the types described in section 2.5.3.

2.5.2 Scientific Notation

Scientific notation, also called exponential notation, is a convenient method of writing very large (or very small) numbers. Instead of writing too many zeroes on either side of a decimal, you can express a number as a product of a power of ten and a number between 1 and 10. For example, the number 8,765,000,000 can be expressed as 8.765×10^9.

The first number 8.765 is called the coefficient. The second number should always have a base of ten with an exponent equal to the number of zeroes in the original numbers. Moving the decimal point to the left makes a positive exponent while moving to the right makes a negative exponent.

Questions involving scientific notation on the DAT basically boil down to multiplying and dividing the numbers. These problems can pose a challenge in the exam since you cannot input 10^x on the on-screen calculator. The only way to do it is by hand.

In multiplying numbers in scientific notation, the general rule is as follows:

$$(a \times 10^x)(b \times 10^y) = ab \times 10^{x+y}$$

EXAMPLE

To multiply 2.0×10^4 and 10×10^2

(i) Find the product of the coefficients first.

$2.0 \times 10 = 20$

(ii) Add the exponents.

$4 + 2 = 6$

(iii) Construct the result.

20×10^6

(iv) Make sure that the coefficient has only one digit to the left of the decimal point. This will also adjust the number of the exponent depending on the number of places moved.

2.0×10^7

Dividing numbers in scientific notation follows this general rule:

$$\frac{(a \times 10^x)}{(b \times 10^y)} = \frac{a}{b} \times 10^{x-y}$$

Going back to our preceding example, let's divide 2.0 x 10^4 and 10 x 10^2 this time:

(i) Divide the coefficients.

$2.0 \div 10 = 0.2$

(ii) Subtract the exponents.

$4 - 2 = 2$

(iii) Construct the result and adjust the values to their simplest forms.

$0.2 \times 10^2 = 2 \times 10 = 20$

In adding and subtracting numbers written in scientific notation, you need to ensure that all exponents are identical. You would need to adjust the decimal place of one of the numbers so that its exponent becomes equivalent to the other number.

EXAMPLE

Add 34.5×10^{-5} and 6.7×10^{-4}

(i) Choose the number that you want to adjust so that its exponent is equivalent to the other number. Let's pick 34.5 and change it into a number with 10^{-4} as its base-exponent term.

$3.45 \times 10^{-4} + 6.7 \times 10^{-4}$

(ii) Add the coefficients together:

$3.45 + 6.7 = 10.15$

(iii) The exponents are now the same, in this case 10^{-4}, so all you have to do is plug it in:

10.15×10^{-4}

(iv) Adjust the end result so that the coefficient is a number between 1 and 10:

1.015×10^{-3}

The same procedure basically applies to subtraction.

2.5.3 Types of Exponents

Positive Integer Exponents: This is the type of exponent you will encounter most often. Raising a base number *b* to a positive integer exponent *x* is equivalent to making *x* copies of *b* and multiplying them together.

EXAMPLE

$$2^4 = 2 \times 2 \times 2 \times 2 = 16$$

Fractional Exponents: Fractional exponents are also known as roots. Let *x* be the fraction. To raise a base number *b* to the *x* power we make use of the fifth property of exponents in section 2.5.1.

We can write $b^{\frac{n}{d}}$ as $\left(b^{\frac{1}{d}}\right)^n$. The value $b^{\frac{1}{d}}$ is known as the d-th root of *x*. So the base *b* raised to the *x* power is the same as the *d*-th root of *b* raised to the *n* power.

EXAMPLE

$$8^{\frac{2}{3}}$$

$$= \left(8^{\frac{1}{3}}\right)^2$$

The expression inside the parentheses is the cube root of 8. Since $2 \times 2 \times 2 = 8$, the cube root of 8 is 2.

$$= 2^2$$
$$= 4$$

Negative Exponents: The value of a base raised to a negative power is equal to the reciprocal of the base, raised to a positive exponent of the same value. For any exponential value b^{-x}, b^{-x} is equivalent to $\frac{1}{(b^x)}$.

EXAMPLE

$$3^{-2}$$

Take the reciprocal and invert the sign of the exponent.

$$= \frac{1}{(3^2)}$$

$$= \frac{1}{(3 \times 3)}$$

$$= \frac{1}{9}$$

2.5.4 Zero and Exponents

Raising a Number to the Zero: Any number raised to the zero power is equal to 1.

We can see that this follows the rules of exponents (see section 2.5), because $a^0 = a^1 \times a^{-1} = a/a = 1$.

NOTE

The quantity 0^0 (read as zero to the zero power) is 1.

EXAMPLES

$$3^0 = 1$$

$$123.79^0 = 1$$

$$\left[1.2 + \left(37 - \sqrt{5}\right) \times 2.331\right]^0 = 1$$

As with multiplication and division, you should not waste time evaluating the parenthetical expression.

2.6 Ratio and Proportion

2.6.1 What is a Ratio?

A **ratio** is the relation between two numbers. There are multiple ways they can be written, but ratios can always be denoted as fractions.

These are all ways to represent the same ratio:

$$3 \text{ to } 4 = 3:4 = \frac{3}{4}$$

If a ratio is written out in words, the first quantity stated should generally be placed in the numerator of the equivalent fraction and the second quantity in the denominator. Just make sure you keep track of which value corresponds to which category.

2.6.2 Solving Proportions

A **proportion** is a statement of equality between two or more ratios.

Solving for an unknown variable is the most common type of proportion problem. If you have just a ratio on either side of an equation, you can rewrite the equation as the numerator of the first times the denominator of the second equal to the denominator of the first times the numerator of the second. This allows you to find the missing information more easily.

EXAMPLE

Solve for x in the following equation.

$$\frac{2}{3} = \frac{5}{x}$$

Cross multiply to eliminate fractions.

$$\begin{aligned} 2 \times x &= 3 \times 5 \\ 2x &= 15 \\ x &= \frac{15}{2} = 7\frac{1}{2} \end{aligned}$$

This means that the ratio 2 to 3 is equivalent to the ratio 5 to $7\frac{1}{2}$.

Unless it is stated, a proportion does not describe a specific number of things. It can only give you information about quantities in terms of other quantities. But if it is explicitly stated what one of the two quantities is, the other quantity can be determined using the proportion.

A lot of the proportions on the DAT are related to converting units to another type of unit.

EXAMPLE

1ft = 12 inches

How many ft are in 100 inches?

NOTE

We will be doing many examples like this in Chapter 3.

GOLD STANDARD WARM-UP EXERCISES

CHAPTER 2: Numbers and Operations

NOTE

We suggest that you use the default calculator on your PC or Mac computer for all QR Warm-up Exercises. Use only the features described in QR section 1.2. This will help you become accustomed to another element of the DAT QR. It is a good habit to aim to complete practice questions in under 1 minute per question. You will have a bit more time on the real DAT (i.e., 1.1 min./question) but ideally you would leave some time at the end of the exam to review your work.

1. What is the approximate value of $0.125+\sqrt{\frac{1}{9}}$?

A. 0.40
B. 0.46
C. 0.50
D. 0.45
E. 0.30

2. 0.8 is to 0.9 as 80 is to:

A. 9
B. 100
C. 8
D. 10
E. 90

3. If you invest in Bank A, you will receive 19% interest on the amount you invest. If you invest in Bank B, you will receive 21% interest. The maximum amount you can invest in Bank A is $6,430, and the maximum amount you can invest in Bank B is $5,897. How much more interest will you earn if you invest the maximum amount in Bank B than if you invest the maximum amount in Bank A?

A. $16.67
B. $16.30
C. $101.27
D. $111.93
E. $533.00

4. Board C is 3/4 as long as Board B. Board B is 4/5 as long as Board A. What is the sum of the lengths of all three Boards if Board A is 100 m long?

A. 255 m
B. 225 m
C. 240 m
D. 235 m
E. 250 m

5. The proportion of the yellow marbles in a jar of yellow and green jars is 7 out of 9. If there are 999 marbles in the jar, how many of these are yellow?

A. 111
B. 777
C. 2
D. 222
E. 0

6. If 0.25 months is equal to one week, what fraction of a month is equal to one day?

A. 1/7
B. 4/7
C. 7/4
D. 1/30
E. 1/28

7. Which of the following is 6.4% of 1,000?

A. $64^{\frac{3}{4}}$
B. $256^{\frac{3}{4}}$
C. $\left(\frac{64}{100}\right)^2$
D. 0.8^2
E. 6.4 / 100

8. $2+\left[71-8\left(\frac{6}{2}\right)^2\right]$ is what percent of $\sqrt{2500}$?

A. 50%
B. 1%
C. 44%
D. 2%
E. 6%

9. Which is the largest?

A. 0.636
B. 0.136
C. 0.46
D. 0.163
E. 0.3

10. Determine the sum of 9, -5, and 6.

A. 20
B. − 20
C. − 10
D. 10
E. − 6

11. Determine the value of 1.5×10^7 divided by 3.0×10^4.

A. 5.0×10^3
B. 0.5×10^3
C. 5.0×10^{-2}
D. 0.5×10^{-3}
E. 0.5×10^2

GS ANSWER KEY

CHAPTER 2

		Cross-Reference			*Cross-Reference*
1.	B	QR 2.2.3, 2.4.3	7.	B	QR 2.2.3, 2.4.3, 2.5.2
2.	E	QR 2.6.2	8.	D	QR 2.2.3, 2.4.3
3.	A	QR 2.4.3	9.	A	QR 2.4.3
4.	C	QR 2.4.2	10.	D	QR 2.2.1
5.	B	QR 2.6.2	11.	B	QR 2.5.2
6.	E	QR 2.6.1			

* Explanations can be found at the back of the book.

Go online to DAT-prep.com for additional chapter review Q&A and forum.

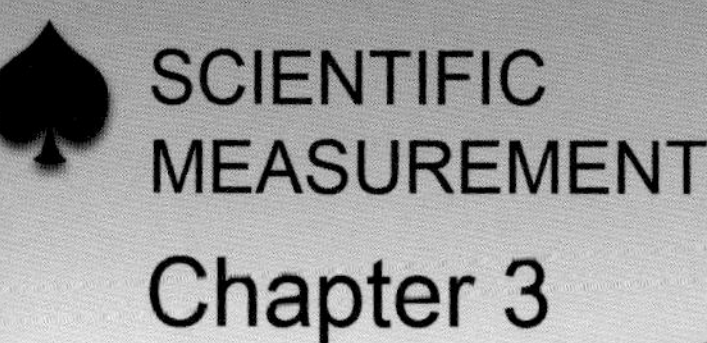

SCIENTIFIC MEASUREMENT

Chapter 3

Memorize

* Conversions between units in the same system (whenever applicable)
* Conversions between certain units in different systems

Understand

* Metric prefixes
* How to convert between units

Importance

2 to 4 out of the 40 QR

questions on the DAT are based on content from this chapter (in our estimation).

* This will change in 2015.

Introduction

While scientific measurement is not a primary focus of the Quantitative Reasoning test, the DAT does use problems involving specific measurements. In order to solve these problems effectively, you must be familiar with British, Metric, and SI units, and some of the relationships between them.

Additional Resources

Free Online Forum

Special Guest

3.1 Systems of Measurement

3.1.1 British Units (Imperial System of Measurement)

You are probably already familiar with several of these units of measurement, but we recommend reviewing them at least once. If you don't know the following information backwards and forwards, you risk losing time on the test.

A. Length: These units are used to describe things like the length of physical objects, the displacement of a physical object, the distance something has traveled or will travel, etc. Area and volume are also measured as the square and cube (respectively) of these units.

Inches	The *inch* is the smallest measurement of length in the British System.
Feet	There are 12 inches in every foot. 1 ft. = 12 in.
Yards	There are 3 feet in every yard. 1 yd. = 3 ft.
Miles	The *mile* is the largest unit of length in the British System. There are 5,280 feet in every mile. 1 mi. = 5,280 ft.

B. Time: These units describe the passage of time.

Seconds	The *second* is the smallest unit of time in the British System.
Minutes	There are 60 seconds in every minute. 1 min. = 60 s.
Hours	There are 60 minutes in every hour. 1 h. = 60 min.
Days	There are 24 hours in every day. 1 day = 24 h.
Years	The *year* is the largest unit of time in the British System. There are 365 days in every year. 1 yr. = 365 days

C. Mass/Weight: Though not technically the same, we can consider mass and weight to be interchangeable for the DAT. The following units describe the amount of matter in an object.

Ounces	The *ounce* is the smallest unit of mass in the British System.

Pounds	There are 16 ounces in every pound. 1 lb. = 16 oz.
Tons	The *ton* is the largest unit of mass in the British System. There are 2,000 pounds in every ton. 1 ton = 2,000 lb.

NOTE

Make sure you memorize the conversions between the different units in each category. You will most likely be required to supply some of this information in order to solve problems on the test.

3.1.2 Metric Units

Measuring with Powers of 10: Unlike the British System, the Metric System has only one unit for each category of measurement. In order to describe quantities that are much larger or much smaller than one of the base units, a prefix is chosen from a variety of options and added to the front of the unit. This changes the value of the unit by some power of 10, which is determined by what the prefix is. The following are the most common of these prefixes:

Milli	One thousandth (10^{-3}) of the base unit
Centi	One hundredth (10^{-2}) of the base unit
Deci	One tenth (10^{-1}) of the base unit
Deca	Ten (10^{1}) times the base unit
Kilo	One thousand (10^{3}) times the base unit

There is a mnemonic that may be used to identify these prefixes:

King	Kilometer	Kilo
Henry	Hectometer	Hecto
Died	Decameter	Deca
Unexpectedly	Unit Base	Unit
Drinking	Decimeter	Deci
Chocolate	Centimeter	Centi
Milk	Milimeter	Milli

As you go down, you divide by 10 and as you go up, you multiply by 10 in order to convert between the units.

EXAMPLE

How many meters is 1 kilometer?

1 km = 1,000 m

From general knowledge, we know that kilo means one thousand. This means there are 1,000 meters in a kilometer. But just in case you get confused, you can also use the clue from the mnemonic. Now we know that **K**ilo is three slots upward from the **U**nit base. Hence we multiply 3 times by 10: 10 x 10 x 10 = 1000.

An even less confusing way to figure out how to do the metric conversions quickly and accurately, is to use a metric conversion line. This is quite handy with any of the common units such as the *meter*, *liter*, and *grams*.

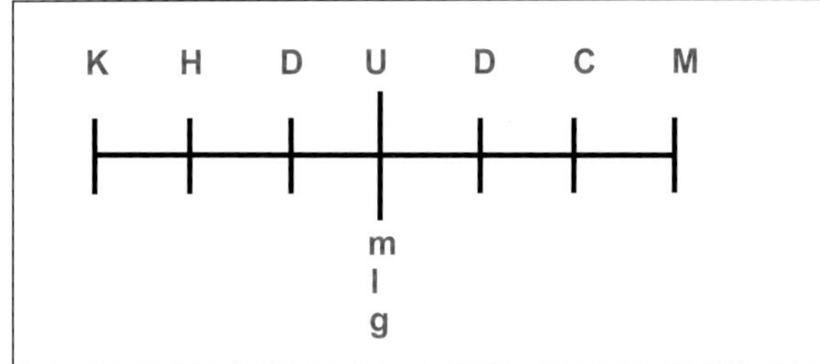

Fig QR 3.1: The Metric Conversion Line. The letters on top of the metric line stands for the "King Henry" mnemonic. On the other hand, the letters below the metric line - **m**, **l**, **g** – stand for the unit bases, **m**eter, **l**iter, or **g**ram, respectively.

To use this device, draw out the metric line as shown in Fig QR 3.1. From the centermost point **U**, the prefixes going to the left represent those that are larger than the base unit (kilo, hecto, deka). These also correspond to the decimal places that you will be moving from the numerical value of the unit to be converted. Those going to the right are for the ones smaller than the unit (deci, centi, milli).

EXAMPLE

How much is 36 liters in milliliters?

Step 1: Place your pen on the given unit, in this case L (liter). Then count the number of places it takes you to reach the unit being asked in the problem (milliliter).

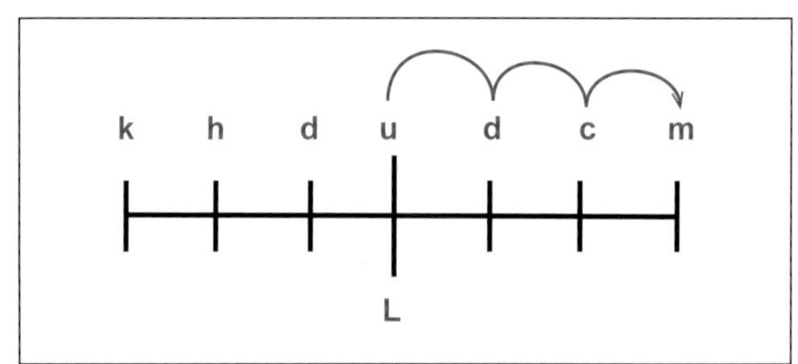

Fig QR 3.2: Converting liter to milliliter using the metric conversion line.

Step 2: Because it took you three places going to the right to move from the liter to the milliliter units, you also need to add three places from the decimal point of the number 36.0.

36 L = 36,000 ml

Now, let's try converting centimeter to kilometer: What is 6.3 cm in km?

1. Place your pen on the **c** (centi) point in the metric line.

2. Moving from **c** to **k** (kilo) takes five places going to the left. This also means moving five places from the decimal point of the number 6.3.
   6.3 cm = .000063 km

Using this method definitely makes doing the metric conversions so much faster than the fraction method!

There are other prefixes that are often used scientifically and may be found in the DAT:

Tera	10^{12}	times the base unit
Giga	10^{9}	times the base unit
Mega	10^{6}	times the base unit
Micro	10^{-6}	of the base unit
Nano	10^{-9}	of the base unit
Pico	10^{-12}	of the base unit

A. Length: As with British length units, these are used to measure anything that has to do with length, displacement, distance, etc. Area and volume are also measured as the square and cube (respectively) of these units.

Meters	The *meter* is the basic unit of length in the Metric System.
Other Common Forms	millimeter, centimeter, kilometer

B. Time: These are units that quantify the passage of time.

Seconds	Just as in the British System, the *second* is the basic unit of time in the Metric System. Minutes, hours, and the other British units are not technically part of the Metric System, but they are often used anyway in problems involving metric units.
Other Common Forms	millisecond

C. Mass: These are units that describe the amount of matter in an object.

Grams	The *gram* is the basic metric unit of mass.
Other Common Forms	milligram, kilogram

3.1.3 SI Units

SI units is the **International System of Units** (abbreviated **SI** from the French *Le Système International d'Unités*) and is a modern form of the metric system. They are used to standardize all the scientific calculations that are done anywhere in the world. The base units are meters, kilograms and seconds. These are the only SI units that may appear on the Quantitative Reasoning test:

Meters	Same as Metric meters
Seconds	Same as Metric and British seconds
Grams	Same as Metric grams (will usually appear as kilograms)

All of these SI units are duplicates from other systems of measurement. There are other distinct units in this system, but it is highly unlikely that they will appear on the QR because they are chemistry and physics units (i.e., moles, kelvin, amperes and candelas).

NOTE

The values of these SI units can be modified by powers of 10 using the same prefixes as in the metric system.

3.2 Conversions

3.2.1 Quick Conversion Formulas

In many instances, having a ready set of memorized formulas saves you time in the test. Here is a quick list of those that you should know for the DAT:

1 inch = 2.54 cm

1 meter = 1.0936 yd

1 mile = 1,760 yards

1 mile = 1.6 km

1 kg = 2.2 lbs

1 kg = 35.27396 oz

1 g = 1000 mg = 0.0353 oz

1 oz = 0.0295735 liter

1 gallon = 128 fl oz

1 hr = 60 min = 3,600 seconds

3 feet = 1 yard = 0.9144 m

12 inch = 1 foot = 0.3048 m

Formula for converting Fahrenheit to Celsius: $\frac{(°F - 32)}{1.8} = °C$

Celsius to Fahrenheit: $°C \times 1.8 + 32 = °F$

3.2.2 Mathematics of Conversions

While it is possible to memorize the conversions between every possible set of units, this would require much more effort than it would be worth. You do need to memorize the basic conversions but there is no point in knowing how many millimeters there are in a mile, for example. Odds are, these obscure conversions won't come up on the test; if they do, the math is simple enough to do without difficulty.

Whether you are converting units between different systems of measurement or simply within a single system, the math involved is the same.

A. The Process: In order to convert a quantity from one type of unit to another type of unit, all you have to do is set up and execute multiplication between ratios. Each conversion that you have memorized from the preceding sections is actually a ratio.

Let's look at the conversion from feet to inches.

"There are 12 inches in 1 foot."

This can be rewritten as a ratio in two ways:

"12 inches to 1 foot" or "1 foot to 12 inches."

$$= \frac{12 \text{ in}}{1 \text{ ft}} \text{ or } \frac{1 \text{ ft}}{12 \text{ in}}$$

When you are performing a conversion, you should treat the units like numbers. This means that when you have a fraction with a certain unit on top and the same unit on bottom, you can cancel out the units leaving just the numbers.

You can multiply a quantity by any of your memorized conversions, and its value will remain the same as long as all of the units, but one, cancel out.

EXAMPLE

How many inches are there in 3 feet?

First, determine which memorized conversion will help. Of course we have a conversion directly between feet and inches, so that is what we'll use.

Next, determine which of the two possible conversion ratios we should use. The goal is to be able to cancel out the original units (in this case, feet), so we want to use whichever ratio has the original units in the denominator (in this case, inches/feet).

$$3 \text{ ft} = 3 \text{ ft} \times \frac{12 \text{ in}}{1 \text{ ft}}$$

Now perform the unit cancellation.

$$= 3 \times \frac{12 \text{ in}}{1}$$

$$= 36 \text{ in}$$

In many instances, you will not have a direct conversion memorized. All you have to do in such a case is multiply by a string of ratios instead of just one.

EXAMPLE

How many inches are there in 5.08 meters?

We cannot convert meters directly into inches, but we can convert meters to centimeters and then centimeters into inches. We can set up both these conversions at the same time and evaluate.

$$5.08\text{ m} = 5.08\text{ m} \times \frac{100\text{ cm}}{1\text{ m}} \times \frac{1\text{ in}}{2.54\text{ cm}}$$

Next, cancel the units.

$$= 5.08 \times \frac{100}{1} \times \frac{1\text{ in}}{2.54}$$

$$= \frac{508\text{ in}}{2.54}$$

$$= 200\text{ in}$$

NOTE

Make sure you check and see that all of your units cancel properly! A lot of unnecessary errors can be avoided simply by paying attention to the units. "Dimensional analysis" is the formal term given to these types of calculations that are solved while keeping an eye on the relations based on units.

GOLD STANDARD WARM-UP EXERCISES

CHAPTER 3: Scientific Measurement

1. How many millimeters are there in 75 meters?
   A. 750 mm
   B. 75 mm
   C. 1000 mm
   D. 75,000 mm
   E. 7,500 mm

2. Which of the following is the shortest distance?
   A. 10 m
   B. 1,000 mm
   C. 10 cm
   D. 0.5 km
   E. 0.1 km

3. A triathlon has three legs. The first leg is a 12 km run. The second leg is a 10 km swim. The third leg is a 15 km bike ride. How long is the total triathlon in meters?
   A. 37,000 m
   B. 3,700 m
   C. 1,000 m
   D. 37 m
   E. 0.037 m

4. If a paperclip has a mass of one gram and a staple has a mass of 0.05 g, how many staples have a mass equivalent to the mass of one paperclip?
   A. 10
   B. 100
   C. 20
   D. 25
   E. 2

5. Which of the following is the number of minutes equivalent to $17\frac{5}{6}$ hours?
   A. 1,080
   B. 1,056
   C. 1,050
   D. 1,020
   E. 1,070

6. The three children in a family weigh 67 lbs., 1 oz., 93 lbs., 2 oz., and 18 lbs., 5 oz. What is the total weight of all three children?
   A. 178.8 lbs.
   B. 178.5 lbs.
   C. 178.08 lbs.
   D. 179.8 lbs.

7. A lawyer charges clients \$20.50 per hour to file paperwork, \$55 per hour for time in court, and \$30 per hour for consultations. How much will it cost for a 90-minute consultation, $\frac{8}{6}$ hours time filing paperwork, and 1 hour in court?
   A. \$110.28
   B. \$100.75
   C. \$88.25
   D. \$127.33
   E. \$95.25

8. If a car moving at a constant speed travels 20 centimeters in 1 second, approximately how many feet will it travel in 25% of a minute?
   A. 10
   B. 15
   C. 12
   D. 9
   E. 39

GS ANSWER KEY

CHAPTER 3

		Cross-Reference			Cross-Reference
1.	D	QR 3.2.2	5.	E	QR 3.2.2
2.	C	QR 3.1.2	6.	B	QR 3.2.2
3.	A	QR 3.2	7.	D	QR 3.1.1, 3.2
4.	C	QR 3.1	8.	A	QR 3.2.2

* Explanations can be found at the back of the book.

Go online to DAT-prep.com for additional chapter review Q&A and forum.

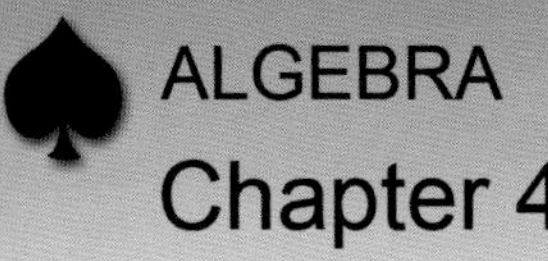

Memorize

* The #1 Rule of Algebra
* Slope-Intercept Form for Linear Equations
* The Quadratic Formula

Understand

* Multiplying Polynomials
* Basic Concepts of Functions
* Manipulating Inequalities
* Basic Equations and Methods of Equation Solving
* Simplifying Equations
* Solving One or More Linear Equations
* Graphing Linear Equations in Cartesian Coordinates
* Factoring and Completing the Square

Importance

7 to 9 out of the 40 QR

questions on the DAT are based on content from this chapter (in our estimation).

* This will change in 2015.

DAT-Prep.com

Introduction 

Becoming comfortable with manipulating and solving algebraic equations is perhaps the single most important skill to have when tackling the Quantitative Reasoning test. This section covers a breadth of important information that will help you deal with any algebraic problem that is thrown at you on the DAT. Almost every problem requires some form of algebra and consequently, you should make it your goal to be confident in all of these concepts.

Additional Resources

Free Online Forum

4.1 Equation Solving and Functions

4.1.1 Algebraic Equations

Before we jump into more complicated algebra, let's review the basics.

A. Terms

Variable: A variable is a symbol - usually in the form of a small letter - that represents a number. It can take on any range of values.

Most problems that are strictly algebraic in nature will provide you with an equation (or equations) containing one or more unknown variables. Based on the information given, the values of the variables will most likely be fixed. Your job is to solve for those values.

Constant: A constant is an expression that contains only numbers and never changes because it has no variables.

Polynomial: A polynomial is an expression (usually part of a function or an equation) that is composed of the sum or difference of some number of terms. Please note that some of the terms can be negative. The **order** of a polynomial is equal to the largest exponent to which a variable is raised in one of the terms.

EXAMPLE $3x^2 + x + 5$

This expression is a polynomial. The variable here is *x*, and the order of the polynomial is 2 because that is the largest exponent to which *x* is raised.

B. Preserving Equality

The #1 Rule of Algebra: Whatever you do to one side of an equation, you *must* do to the other side also!

The equals sign implies equality between two different expressions. When you are given an equation, the equality established must be considered to be always true for that problem (unless you are told otherwise). So if you change one side of the equation and you do not also change the other side in the same way, you fundamentally alter the terms of the equation. The equation will no longer be true.

EXAMPLE

Consider this equation:

$$2x + 3 = 5$$

The following manipulation violates the above rule:

$$(2x + 3) - 3 = 5$$

Here, we have subtracted three from one side but not the other, so the equality no longer holds.

This manipulation, however, does not violate the rule:

$$(2x + 3) - 3 = 5 - 3$$

Here, we have subtracted three from both sides, so the equality still holds true.

NOTE

If two sides of an equation are equal, you can add or subtract the same amount to both sides, and they will still be equal.

EXAMPLE

$a = b$

$a + c = b + c$

$a - c = b - c$

The same rule applies to multiplication and division.

EXAMPLE

$a = b$

$ac = bc$

$a \div c = b \div c$

C. Solving Basic Equations

We can use the rule of algebra described in Part B to help solve algebraic equations for an unknown variable. Keep in mind that addition and subtraction, along with multiplication and division, are inverse operations: They undo each other. First decide the operation that has been applied and then use the inverse operation to undo this (make sure to apply the operation to both sides of the equation). The idea is to isolate the variable on one side of the equation. Then, whatever is left on the other side of the equation is the value of the variable.

EXAMPLE

Solve: $2x + 3 = 5$

$2x + 3 - 3 = 5 - 3$

$2x = 2$

Subtracting 3, however, has not isolated the variable x. Hence, we need to continue undoing by dividing 2 on both sides.

$2x \div 2 = 2 \div 2$

$x = 1$

Here's a little more complicated equation to solve: $2x + 2/3 = 3x - 2$

When you have an equation with the variable on both sides, choose whichever you think will be easier to focus on. In this case, we will isolate x on the right. First, subtract $2x$ from both sides.

$$(2x + 2/3) - 2x = (3x - 2) - 2x$$

$$\Rightarrow 2/3 = x - 2$$

Next, add 2 to both sides to isolate *x*.

$$(2/3) + 2 = (x - 2) + 2$$
$$\Rightarrow 8/3 = x$$

4.1.2 Addition and Subtraction of Polynomials

When adding or subtracting polynomials, the general rules for exponents are applied and like terms are grouped together. You can think of it as similar to collecting the same things together.

EXAMPLE

$$4x^3y + 5z^2 + 5xy^4 + 3z^2$$

$$= 4x^3y + 5xy^4 + (5+3)z^2$$
$$= 4x^3y + 5xy^4 + 8z^2$$

By grouping the similar terms, seeing which terms may be added or subtracted becomes easier.

4.1.3 Multiplying Polynomials

When multiplying two polynomials, you must multiply every term of the first polynomial with every term of the second. The order of this multiplication doesn't matter, but most people find it easiest to keep track by starting with the first term of the first polynomial, multiplying it by every term in the second from left to right, then taking the second term of the first polynomial and doing the same, and so on until all terms have been used. Following this pattern will ensure that every combination of multiplication is done.

EXAMPLE

Evaluate the following expression:

$$(2x + 1)(x^2 - 3x + 2)$$

Begin with the term $2x$ and multiply it by every term of the second polynomial, then do the same with the term 1. To make this clearer, we can even rewrite the expression as follows:

$(2x)(x^2 - 3x + 2) + (1)(x^2 - 3x + 2)$
$= (2x^3 - 6x^2 + 4x) + (x^2 - 3x + 2)$

Combining like terms, we get the following:

$$= 2x^3 - 5x^2 + x + 2$$

4.1.4 Function Basics

Before we can start working with functions, here are some basic definitions, terminology and examples with which you should be familiar.

Function: At its most basic, a function is a mathematical relation that outputs a unique number for every input.

EXAMPLE $f(x) = 2x$

In this case, the function is f; the input variable is x; and the output is $2x$. The notation used here is standard for functions. The denotation of the function (f) comes first, followed by a set of parentheses containing the input variable.

(a) Evaluate f for $x = 2$.

We need to solve for $f(2)$ (pronounced "*f* of two").

$$f(2) = 2 \times 2$$
$$= 4$$

(b) Find $f(-1/2)$.

$$f(-1/2) = 2 \times (-1/2)$$
$$= -1$$

Domain: The domain of a function is the set of possible values that the independent variable or variables (the input) of the function can have.

Range: The range of a function is the set of possible values that the output of the function can have.

EXAMPLE

(a) Find the domain and range of the function f defined by $f(x) = 2x$.

Remember, on the DAT we only need to worry about real numbers. So the largest domain or range we could possibly have is "all real numbers."

To find the domain of the function, look at its output expression (in this case "$2x$") and determine if there are any real number values of the variable (x) for which the expression is not defined. In this case, there are none. For any number x, we can always multiply it by 2 and obtain a new real number value.

Domain = All Real Numbers

To find the range of the function, you also need to look at its output expression. Are there any numbers the output cannot equal? In this case, no; because for any number you can think of, simply inputting half of it will output that number.

Range = All Real Numbers

(b) Find the domain and range of the function f defined by $f(x) = x^2$.

First, find the domain. Is there any number we cannot input into this function? Since x^2 is defined for all real numbers, there are none.

Domain = All Real Numbers

Now, find the range. Are there any numbers we cannot obtain as an output from this function? Since x^2 is always positive for real numbers x, we can never obtain a negative output.

Range = All Non–negative Real Numbers

Remember, this range does include 0. We can also write this as shown in the expression that follows.

$$\text{Range} = [0\ ,\ \infty)$$

The "[" bracket means that 0 is included in the set and the ")" bracket means that ∞ is not included in the set (because infinity is not actually a number). So this notation means the set of all real numbers between 0 and infinity, including 0.

4.2 Inequalities

4.2.1 Inequality Basics

An **inequality** is a statement that describes the relative size of two quantities. This is similar to an equation; except that instead of only saying that two quantities are equal, an inequality can also mean that one quantity is always larger than another.

Inequality Symbols

$>$ is the symbol for "greater than." The quantity on the left of this symbol is always greater than the quantity on the right.

$<$ is the symbol for "less than." The

quantity on the left of the symbol is always less than the quantity on the right.

$\geq$ is the symbol for "greater than or equal to." The quantity on the left of this symbol is always either greater than or equal to the quantity on the right.

$\leq$ is the symbol for "less than or equal to." The quantity on the left of the symbol is always either less than or equal to the quantity on the right.

$|x|$ is the symbol for absolute value. It represents the numerical value of *x* and disregards its sign. Therefore, the absolute value of any real number will always be positive.

EXAMPLE $x > 3$

This inequality states that the variable *x* is greater than 3. So *x* can have any value that is larger than 3, such as 4 or 100.

EXAMPLE $3 \leq x \leq 4$

This is an example of how multiple inequalities can be used in the same statement. It states that *x* is both less than or equal to 4 and greater than or equal to 3. So *x* can have any value between (and including) 3 and 4, such as 3 or 3.5.

4.2.2 Solving Inequalities

A. One-Sided Inequalities

Solving inequalities is almost identical to solving equations. The same rule applies: You always have to do the same thing to both sides. The only difference is that the symbols of inequality are sensitive to inversions of the sign (flipping from positive to negative). Whenever you multiply or divide both sides by a negative number, the inequality symbol changes direction (remember, squaring a negative number falls into this category because you are multiplying by that same negative number). This will never happen with addition and subtraction.

Here is a quick example that might help you understand why the inequality symbol flips for multiplication by a negative number.

EXAMPLE

Say there are two people, person A and person B. Person A has 3 dollars and person B has 2 dollars. In inequality form, we know that $3 > 2$.

Now, instead of having money, let's say for some reason person A now *owes* 3 dollars and person B *owes* 2 dollars. As you can see, we have simply multiplied both quantities by -1. Now, which person has more money and which has less? Obviously -3 dollars is less than -2 dollars; so as an inequality, this reads as $-3 < -2$.

So, simply multiplying by a negative number has caused the direction of the inequality symbol to switch.

With this principle in mind, we can now solve inequalities. Just like with equations, all we have to do is isolate the variable on one side.

EXAMPLE

Solve the following inequality for x:

$2 - 3x \leq .5x - 1.$

First, choose the side on which you want to isolate the variable. We'll use the left side.

$$(2 - 3x) - 2 \leq (.5x - 1) - 2$$
$$\Rightarrow (-3x) - .5x \leq (.5x - 3) - .5x$$
$$\Rightarrow (-7/2)x \leq -3$$
$$\Rightarrow (-2/7)(-7/2)x \geq -3 \times (-2/7)$$
$$\Rightarrow x \geq 6/7$$

B. Absolute Inequalities

In solving absolute inequalities, the inequality symbol used ($<$, $\leq$, $>$, $\geq$) is a significant consideration in writing the solution set. The following rules should apply:

- If the symbol is $>$ (or $\geq$), meaning that the absolute value is greater than the number on the other side of the inequality, the connecting word is "or."

If $a > 0$, then the solutions to $|x| > a$ are $x > a$ or $x < -a$.

EXAMPLE

Solve for the following inequality:

$|x + 2| > 7.$

In this case, the absolute value $|x + 2|$ is greater than 7. Hence,

$\Rightarrow x + 2 > 7$ or $x + 2 < -7$
$\Rightarrow x > 5$ or $x < -9$

You can think of "great-or" as a way of memorizing this rule.

- If the symbol is $<$ (or $\leq$), meaning that the absolute value is less than the number on the other side of the inequality, the connecting word is "and."

If $a < 0$, then the solutions to $|x| < a$ are $x < a$ and $x > -a$. This can also be written as $-a < x < a$.

Similarly, in the inequality $|x + 2| < 7$, the side containing the absolute value is less than 7 and should thus indicate the connective "and" in the solution.

EXAMPLE

Solve: $|x + 2| < 7.$

$\Rightarrow x + 2 < 7$ and $x + 2 > -7$

$\Rightarrow x < 5$ and $x > -9$

$\Rightarrow -9 < x < 5$

This time, you can think of "less th-and" to remember this rule.

C. Two-Sided Inequalities

Though it is odd to see equations with more than one equals sign, two-sided inequalities are common. You can solve them by splitting them up into two one-sided inequalities and solving these individually.

EXAMPLE

Solve the following inequality for x:

$$12 > 3x > 6.$$

Breaking this inequality into two, we obtain $12 > 3x$ and $3x > 6$. We must solve these:

(i) $(12)/3 > (3x)/3$
$\Rightarrow 4 > x$

(ii) $(3x)/3 > (6)/3$
$\Rightarrow x > 2$

These two inequalities can be recombined to form the new two-sided inequality $4 > x > 2$.

4.3 Simplifying Equations

In order to make solving algebraic equations easy and quick, you should simplify terms whenever possible. The following are the most common and important ways of doing so.

4.3.1 Combining Terms

This is the most basic thing you can do to simplify an equation. If there are multiple terms being added or subtracted in your equation that contain the same variables, you can combine them.

EXAMPLE

Simplify the equation: $3x + 4xy - 2 = xy + 1$

Notice that there are two terms we can combine that contain xy and two terms we can combine that are just constants.

$(3x + 4xy - 2) - xy = (xy + 1) - xy$
$\Rightarrow 3x + 3xy - 2 = 1$

$(3x + 3xy - 2) + 2 = 1 + 2$
$\Rightarrow 3x + 3xy = 3$

$\Rightarrow \left(\frac{3x + 3xy}{3}\right) = \frac{3}{3}$
$\Rightarrow x + xy = 1$

Always make sure to look for like terms to combine when you are solving an algebra problem.

4.3.2 Variables in Denominators

When you are trying to manipulate an equation, having variables in the denominators of fractions can make things difficult. In order to get rid of such denominators entirely, simply multiply the entire equation by the quantity in the denominator. This will probably cause other terms to become more complicated, but you will no longer have the problem of a variable denominator.

EXAMPLE

Simplify the expression: $\frac{3}{2x} + 5x = 4$.

The problem denominator is 2*x*, so we multiply both sides by 2*x*.

$$(\frac{3}{2x} + 5x)2x = (4)2x$$

$$\Rightarrow 3 + 10x^2 = 8x$$

When there are different denominators containing variables, cross multiply the denominator to cancel out.

EXAMPLE

$$\frac{5}{(x+3)} = \frac{2}{x} - \frac{1}{3x}$$

Multiply 3x on both sides:

$$\frac{5}{(x+3)}(3x) = \frac{2}{x} - \frac{1}{3x}(3x)$$

$$\frac{15x}{(x+3)} = 6 - 1$$

Multiply (x+3) on both sides:

$$\frac{15x}{(x+3)}(x+3) = 5(x+3)$$

$$15x = 5x + 15$$

$$15x - 5x = 5x + 15 - 5x$$

$$10x = 15$$

$$x = \frac{15}{10} = \frac{3}{2}$$

4.3.3 Factoring

If every term of a polynomial is divisible by the same quantity, that quantity can be factored out. This means that we can express the polynomial as the product of that quantity times a new, smaller polynomial.

EXAMPLE

Factor the following expression:

$$2x^3 - 4x^2 + 4x$$

Every term in this polynomial is divisible by $2x$, so we can factor it out of each term. The simplified expression, then, is

$$2x(x^2 - 2x + 2).$$

To verify that you have properly factored an expression, multiply out your solution. If you get back to where you started, you've done it correctly.

4.4 Linear Equations

4.4.1 Linearity

Linear equation is an equation that describes relationships between variables in which every term is a scalar or a scalar multiple of a variable. In a linear equation, there can neither be variables raised to exponents nor variables multiplied together.

(a) $3x + 2y = z + 5$

This equation is linear.

(b) $3x^2 - 2xy = 1$

This equation is not linear. The terms $3x^2$ and $2xy$ cannot appear in a linear equation.

The reason such equations are called "linear" is that they can be represented on a Cartesian graph as a straight line (see section 4.5).

4.4.2 Solving Linear Equations with Multiple Variables

In the previous sections we have only considered equations, inequalities, and functions with single variables. In many cases though, Quantitative Reasoning problems will require you to deal with a second variable.

NOTE

Everything in this section applies to inequalities as well as equations. Just remember to be wary of multiplication and division by negative numbers!

A. Isolating a Variable

When you have a single equation with two variables, you will not be able to solve for specific values. What you can do is solve for one variable in terms of the other. To do this, pick a variable to isolate on one side of the equation and move all other terms to the other side.

EXAMPLE

Solve the following for y: $4y - 3x = 2y + x - 6$.

Let's isolate y on the left side:

$$(4y - 3x) + 3x - 2y = (2y + x - 6) + 3x - 2y$$

$$\frac{(2y)}{2} = \frac{(4x - 6)}{2}$$

$$y = 2x - 3$$

Now we know the value of y, but only in relation to the value of x. If we are now given some value for x, we can simply plug it in to our solution and obtain y. For example, if $x = 1$ then $y = 2 - 3 = -1$.

B. Solving Systems of Equations

How do you know if you will be able to solve for specific values in an equation or not? The general rule is that if you have the same number of unique equations as variables (or more equations), you will be able find a specific value for every variable. So for the example in Part A, since we have two variables and only one equation, in order to solve for the variables, we would need one more unique equation.

In order for an equation to be unique, it must not be algebraically derived from another equation.

EXAMPLE

$$300 = 30x - 10y$$
$$30 = 3x - y$$

From the above example, the two equations describe the same line and therefore are not unique since they are scalar multiples of each other.

There are two strategies you should know for solving a system of equations:

I. **Substitution.** This strategy can be used every time, although, it will not always be the fastest way to come up with a solution. You begin with one equation and isolate a variable as in Part A. Next, wherever the isolated variable appears in the second equation, replace it with the expression this variable is equal to. This effectively eliminates that variable from the second equation.

If you only have two equations, all you need are two steps. Once you have followed the procedure above, you can solve for the second variable in the second equation and substitute that value back into the first equation to find the value of the first variable. If you have more than two variables and equations, you will need to continue this process of isolation and substitution until you reach the last equation.

EXAMPLE

Solve the following system of equations for *x* and *y*.

$$4y - 3x = 2y + x - 6$$
$$3x + y \; = 12$$

We have already isolated *y* in the first equation, so the first step is done. The new system is as follows:

$$y = 2x - 3$$
$$3x + y = 12$$

Next, we substitute $2x - 3$ for y in the second equation.

$$3x + (2x - 3) = 12$$
$$\Rightarrow 5x - 3 = 12$$
$$\Rightarrow 5x = 15$$
$$\Rightarrow x = 3$$

Now, we have a value for *x*, but we still need a value for *y*. Substitute 3 for *x* in the *y*-isolated equation.

$$y = 2(3) - 3$$
$$y = 3$$

So our solution to this system of equations is $x = 3$, $y = 3$.

II. **Equation Addition or Subtraction.** You will not always be able to apply this strategy, but in some cases, it will save you from having to do all of the time-consuming substitutions of Strategy I. The basic idea of equation addition or subtraction is exactly what you would expect: Addition or subtraction of equations directly to each other.

Say you have two equations, A and B. Because both sides of any equation are by definition equal, you can add, say, the left side of equation A to the left side of equation B and the right side of equation A to the right side of equation B without changing anything. In performing this addition, you are doing the same thing to both sides of equation B.

The purpose of performing such an

addition is to try and get a variable to cancel out completely. If you can accomplish this, you can solve for the other variable easily (assuming you only have two variables, of course). Before adding the equations together, you can manipulate either of them however you like (as long as you maintain equality) in order to set up the cancellation of a variable.

If the only way to cancel out a variable is by subtracting the equation, this may be done as well.

EXAMPLE

Use equation addition or subtraction to solve the following for x and y.

$$2x - 2y = 1$$
$$4x + 5y = 11$$

If we multiply the first equation by two, we will have 4x present in each equation. Then if we subtract, the 4x in each equation will cancel.

$$\begin{array}{r} 4x - 4y = 2 \\ -\ (4x + 5y = 11) \\ \hline 0x - 9y = -9 \\ \Rightarrow y = 1 \end{array}$$

Now, we can substitute this value of y into whichever equation looks simpler to solve for x (either one will work though).

$$2x - 2(1) = 1$$
$$\Rightarrow 2x = 3$$
$$\Rightarrow x = \frac{3}{2}$$

So our solution to this system of equations is $y = 1,\ x = \frac{3}{2}$.

4.5 Graphing Linear Functions

4.5.1 Linear Equations and Functions

Every linear equation can be rewritten as a linear function. To do so, simply isolate one of the variables as in Section 4.4.2A. This variable is now a function of the variables on the other side of the equation.

EXAMPLE

Rewrite the equation $3y - 2x = 6$ as a function of x.

$$3y - 2x = 6$$
$$\Rightarrow 3y = 2x + 6$$
$$\Rightarrow y = \frac{2}{3}x + 2$$

Now that we have isolated y, it is actually a function of x. For every input of x, we get a unique output of y. If you like, you can rewrite y as $f(x)$.

$$f(x) = \frac{2}{3}x + 2$$

4.5.2 Cartesian Coordinates in 2D

The Cartesian coordinate system is the most commonly used system for graphing. A Cartesian graph in two dimensions has two axes: The *x*-axis is the horizontal one, and the *y*-axis is the vertical one. The independent variable is always along the *x*-axis and the dependent variable is along the *y*-axis. The independent variable is controlled and the output depends on the independent variable. The further right you go on the *x*-axis, the larger the numbers get; and on the *y*-axis, the numbers get larger the further up you go. A point on the graph is specified as an ordered pair of an *x* value and a *y* value like this: (x, y). This point exists *x* units from the origin (the point (0, 0) where the axes cross) along the *x*-axis, and *y* units from the origin along the *y*-axis.

EXAMPLE

Find the point $(3, -1)$ on the Cartesian graph shown.

To plot this point, simply count three units to the right along the *x*-axis and one unit down along the *y*-axis.

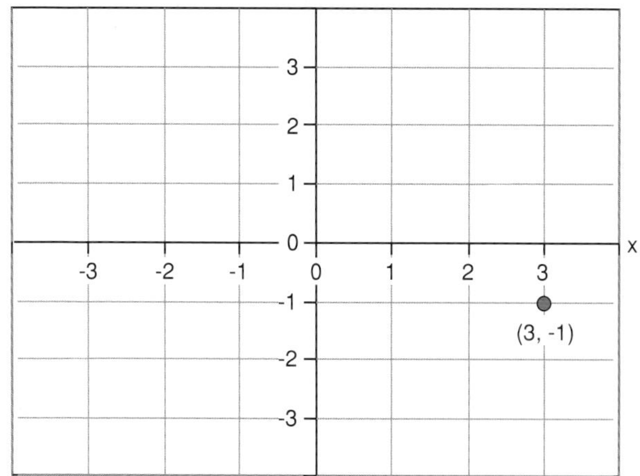

4.5.3 Graphing Linear Equations

In order to graph a straight line in Cartesian coordinates, all you need to know is two points. Every set of two points has only one unique line that passes through both of them.

To find two points from a linear equation, simply choose two values to plug in for one of the variables. It is best to pick values that will make your calculations easier, such as 0 and 1. Plugging in each of these values, we can solve for *y* and obtain two points.

EXAMPLE

Graph the line defined by $2x + y = 3$.

First, let's plug in $x = 0$ and $x = 1$ to find two points on the line.

$$2(0) + y = 3$$
$$\Rightarrow y = 3$$
$$2(1) + y = 3$$
$$\Rightarrow y = 1$$

Now, we have two points: (0, 3) and (1, 1). To graph the line, all we have to do is plot these points on a graph and draw a straight line between them.

4.5.4 Slope-Intercept Form

There are two pieces of information that are very useful in the graphing of a linear equation: The slope of the line and its *y*-intercept.

Slope refers to the steepness of a line. It is the ratio (Slope = rise/run) of the number of units along the y-axis to the number of units along the x-axis between two points.

EXAMPLE

$$y = 5x + 3 \text{ and } y = 5x + 10$$

These two equations would be parallel to each other since both slopes (m)=5.

$$y = 3x + 6 \text{ and } y = -\frac{1}{3x} + 3$$

These two equations are perpendicular. The line of the first equation has a positive slope and the perpendicular line has a decreasing slope and therefore allows both equations to have opposite signs.

The ***y*-intercept** of a line is the *y*-coordinate of the point at which the line crosses the *y*-axis. The value of *x* where the line intersects, is always zero and its coordinates will be (0, *y*).

One of the standard forms of a linear equation is the slope-intercept form, from which the slope and the *y*-intercept of the line are immediately obvious. This form resembles $y = mx + b$. Here m and b are constants such that m is the slope of the line and b is the *y*-intercept.

EXAMPLE

Rewrite the following equation in slope-intercept form: $2y + 5x = 8$.

$$\Rightarrow 2y = -5x + 8$$
$$\Rightarrow y = -\frac{5}{2}x + 4$$

This is now in slope-intercept form. In this case, the slope m is $-\frac{5}{2}$ and the *y*-intercept is 4.

Slope-intercept form is also useful for constructing the equation of a line from other information. If you are given the slope and the intercept, obviously you can simply plug them in to $y = mx + b$ to get the equation. It is also very simple to obtain the slope and intercept if you know two points on the line, (x_1, y_1) and (x_2, y_2). The slope can be obtained directly from this information:

Slope = rise/run = $(y_2 - y_1)/(x_2 - x_1)$

Once the slope m is obtained, you only need to solve for b. To do so, plug in one of the points as well as m into the slope-intercept equation. You can then solve for b.

EXAMPLE

Find the equation for the line passing through (1, 1) and (2, 3).

First, determine the slope.

$$m = \frac{(3-1)}{(2-1)} = 2$$

Now plug m and a point into the slope-intercept equation to find b.

$$y = mx + b$$
$$\Rightarrow 1 = 2(1) + b$$
$$\Rightarrow -1 = b$$

Plugging in all of this information, we now have a complete equation.

$$y = 2x - 1$$

4.6 Quadratic Equations

A **quadratic equation** is an equation that can be written in the form $ax^2 + bx + c = 0$ where a, b, and c are constants. This is a second-degree polynomial set equal to zero, and it will always have two solutions, although they are not always unique.Being asked to solve a quadratic equation is a standard type of algebra problem, so you should be very familiar with the techniques listed in the following subsections.

4.6.1 Factoring and Completing the Square

A. Factoring

Factoring is the simplest and easiest way to solve a quadratic equation, but you will not always be able to use this method. Only special quadratics can be solved this way. Still, you should always try and use this method first.

The goal is to factor the quadratic into

two first-degree polynomials so you have $(ax + b)(cx + d) = 0$. Once you have obtained this form, you know that either $(ax + b) = 0$ or $(cx + d) = 0$, so the two solutions are $x = -\frac{b}{a}$ and $x = -\frac{d}{c}$.

There is no single quick way to factor a quadratic this way. Instead, you should do many sample exercises to develop the ability to think logically and come up with the solution. As a guide, think about what values must be multiplied to obtain the constants a, b, and c of your quadratic.

More specifically, for $ax^2 + bx + c$, if the value of a is 1, your two polynomials will be $(x + m)$ and $(x + n)$ where $b = m + n$ and $c = m \times n$. Therefore, try to think about what numbers multiply together to give c and add together to give b.

EXAMPLE

Solve the quadratic equation:

$$x^2 + 3x + 2 = 0$$

To factor, we need two numbers that add to 3 and multiply to 2. We know that these numbers must both be positive since a positive and a negative number would yield a negative number when multiplied, and two negative numbers would yield a negative number when added.

Also, the two numbers must be less than 3 because otherwise their sum would have to be larger than 3. After some thought, it is clear that the numbers we are looking for are 1 and 2 since $1 + 2 = 3$ and $1 \times 2 = 2$.

$$\Rightarrow (x + 1)(x + 2) = 0$$

$$\Rightarrow (x + 1) = 0 \text{ and } (x + 2) = 0$$

$$\Rightarrow x = -1 \text{ and } x = -2$$

B. Completing the Square

This method can be a little tricky. The basic idea is to manipulate the quadratic so that you can write the portion with the variables as the square of a first-order polynomial. Then you can take the square root and find the solutions. To accomplish this for a generic quadratic $ax^2 + bx + c = 0$, follow these steps:

Step 1 Move c to the other side of the equation.

$$ax^2 + bx = -c$$

Step 2 Divide through by the leading coefficient a.

$$x^2 + \left(\frac{b}{a}\right)x = -\frac{c}{a}$$

Step 3 Take half of $\left(\frac{b}{a}\right)$, i.e., the coefficient of x. Square it, and add it to both sides of the equation.

$$x^2 + \left(\frac{b}{a}\right)x + \left(\frac{b}{2a}\right)^2 = -\frac{c}{a} + \left(\frac{b}{2a}\right)^2$$

This allows you to write the polynomial as a square, namely $\left(x + \frac{b}{2a}\right)^2$.

$$\left(x + \frac{b}{2a}\right)^2 = -\frac{c}{a} + \left(\frac{b}{2a}\right)^2$$

Step 4 Take the square root of both sides and solve for x.

$$x+\frac{b}{2a}=\pm\sqrt{\left[-\frac{c}{a}+\left(\frac{b}{2a}\right)^2\right]}$$

$$x=-\frac{b}{2a}\pm\sqrt{\left[-\frac{c}{a}+\left(\frac{b}{2a}\right)^2\right]}$$

Following the variables in this general version can be difficult, so let's look at an example.

EXAMPLE

Solve the following quadratic by completing the square:

$$2x^2+4x-8=0$$

Step 1 $2x^2+4x=8$

Step 2 $x^2+2x=4$

Step 3 $x^2+2x+1=4+1=5$

$\Rightarrow\sqrt{(x+1)^2}=\sqrt{5}$

Step 4 $x + 1 = \pm\sqrt{5}$

$\Rightarrow x = -1\pm\sqrt{5}$

4.6.2 The Quadratic Formula

If you do not want to or cannot use one of the methods in Part 4.6.1 to solve your quadratic equation, you can simply plug numbers into the quadratic formula to come up with a solution (CHM 6.6.1).

For a generic quadratic equation $ax^2 + bx + c = 0$, these are the solutions:

$$x=\frac{-b\pm\sqrt{b^2-4ac}}{2a}$$

Sometimes, doing the arithmetic necessary to compute this formula can take a lot of time, so factoring and completing the square are usually better options if you feel comfortable with them. They will save you time on the test.

When there is no first degree term $ax^2 + c = 0$, we can solve the equation by isolating x^2. Such that,

$$x^2=-\frac{c}{a}.$$

Therefore, $x=\pm\sqrt{-\frac{c}{a}}$.

GOLD STANDARD WARM-UP EXERCISES

CHAPTER 4: Algebra

1. If $\frac{x}{2} - 1 < x$, then which must be true?

A. $2 > x$

B. $-\frac{1}{2} < x$

C. $-2 < x$

D. $-2 > x$

E. $2 < x$

2. If $f(x) = \frac{12}{4x^3 - 6x + 5}$, then $f(2)$ equals:

A. 12/17

B. 12/49

C. 12/9

D. 12/15

E. 12/25

3. $13xy^2z$ is to $39y$ as $9xyz^6$ is to:

A. $3z^5$

B. $27z$

C. $9y$

D. $27z^5$

E. $9z^6$

4. At what point do the lines $y = 2x - 1$ and $6x - 5y = -3$ intersect?

A. (2, 3)

B. (0.5, 0)

C. (−1,−3)

D. (−0.5, −2)

E. (1/4,-3/4)

5. Loubha has a total of \$.85. If she has two less dimes than nickels, how many dimes and nickels does she have?

A. 5 nickels, 7 dimes

B. 6 nickels, 4 dimes

C. 1 nickel, 8 dimes

D. 4 nickels, 2 dimes

E. 7 nickels, 5 dimes

6. If $2.5 \times 10^3(3 \times 10^x) = 0.075$, then x equals:

A. −3

B. −5

C. 0

D. −4

E. 2

7. If $y = 3x^2 - 5x - 7$, then which of the following represents x?

A. $\dfrac{-5 \pm \sqrt{3y+46}}{3}$

B. $\dfrac{5 \pm \sqrt{12y+109}}{6}$

C. $\dfrac{-5 \pm \sqrt{12y+109}}{6}$

D. $\dfrac{5 \pm \sqrt{12y+109}}{36}$

E. $\dfrac{5 \pm \sqrt{3y+46}}{3}$

8. A plank of wood is leaning against the left side of a house with vertical walls. Both are on level ground. If the plank touches the ground 7 feet away from the base of the house, and touches the house at a point 5 feet above the ground, at what slope is the plank lying?

A. –5/7
B. 7/5
C. –7/5
D. 5/7
E. 2

9. If $n + n = k + k + k$ and $n + k = 5$, then $n = ?$

A. 9
B. 6
C. 5
D. 3
E. 2

GS ANSWER KEY

Chapter 4

	Cross-Reference		*Cross-Reference*
1. C	QR 4.2.2A	6. B	QR 4.3.1
2. E	QR 4.1.4	7. B	QR 4.6.2
3. D	QR 4.3.2, 4.3.3	8. D	QR 4.5.4
4. A	QR 4.4.2A, 4.4.2B	9. D	QR 4.3.1, 4.4.2A, 4.4.2B
5. E	QR 4.4.2B		

* Explanations can be found at the back of the book.

Go online to DAT-prep.com for additional chapter review Q&A and forum.

GOLD NOTES

GEOMETRY
Chapter 5

Memorize	Understand	Importance
The Pythagorean Theorem **Perimeter, Area, and Volume Formulas** **Properties of Triangles**	* **Points in Cartesian Coordinates** * **Parallel and Perpendicular Lines** * **Similar Polygons** * **Types of Triangles and Angles** * **Problems with Figures and Solids**	**3 to 5 out of the 40 QR** **questions on the DAT are based on content from this chapter (in our estimation).** * **This will change in 2015.**

DAT-Prep.com

Introduction

Geometry is a very visual branch of mathematics dealing with lines and shapes and relations in space, so drawing and labeling pictures can be extremely helpful when you are confronted with geometric problems. But don't forget about algebra! More often than not, these problems are simply algebraic equations in disguise.

Additional Resources

Free Online Forum

5.1 Points, Lines and Angles

5.1.1 Points and Distance

Knowing your way around the Cartesian coordinate systems begins with understanding the relationships between simple points. As discussed in section 4.5, points on a graph are represented as an ordered pair of an x and y coordinate, (x, y).

A. Addition and Subtraction of Points

To add or subtract two points, simply add or subtract the two x values to obtain the new x value and add or subtract the two y values to obtain the new y value.

EXAMPLE

Add the points (2, 3) and (1, –5).

$$(2, 3) + (1, -5)$$
$$= (2 + 1, 3 - 5)$$
$$= (3, -2)$$

Graphically, addition of points is easy to visualize. All you are doing when you add two points is treating the first point as the new origin. You then plot the second point in terms of this new origin to find the sum of the two points.

You can add more than two points in the same way. Just add all of the x values together, and then add all of the y values together.

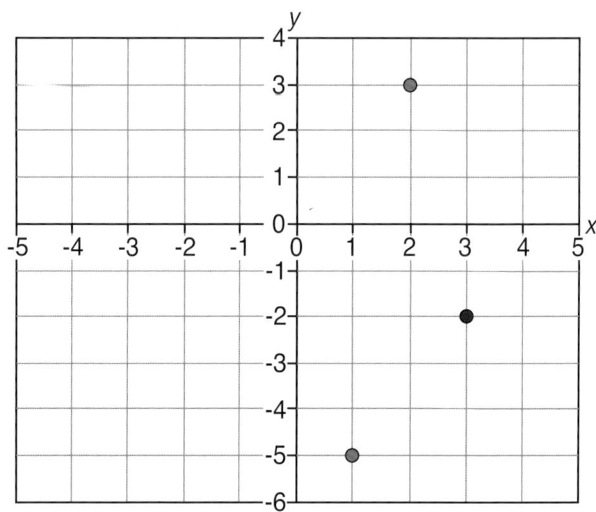

B. Distance between Points

Finding the distance between two points requires the use of the Pythagorean Theorem. This theorem is probably the most important tool you have for solving geometric problems.

Pythagorean Theorem: $x^2 + y^2 = z^2$

This theorem describes the relationship between the lengths of the sides of a right triangle. The lengths x and y correspond to the two legs of the triangle adjacent to the right angle, and the length z corresponds to the hypotenuse of the triangle. For a further discussion of the Pythagorean Theorem and right triangles, see section 5.2.2.

In order to find the distance between two points (x_1, y_1) and (x_2, y_2), consider there to be a line segment connecting them. This line segment (with length z equivalent to the distance between the points) can be thought of as the hypotenuse of a right triangle. The other two sides extend from the points: One is parallel to the x-axis; the other, to the y-axis (with lengths x and y, respectively).

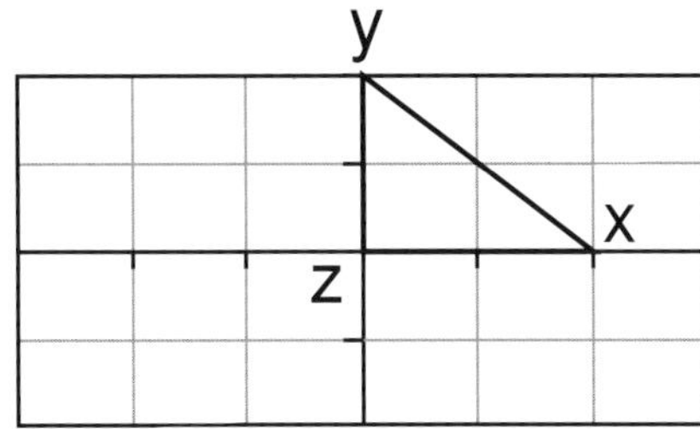

To find the distance between the two points, simply apply the Pythagorean Theorem.

$$x = (x_2 - x_1)$$
$$y = (y_2 - y_1)$$
$$z = \sqrt{(x^2 + y^2)}$$

Plugging in the point coordinates will yield z, the distance between the two points.

EXAMPLE

Find the distance between the points (5, 0) and (2, –4).

$$x = (2 - 5) = -3$$
$$y = (-4 - 0) = -4$$
$$z = \sqrt{(-3^2 + -4^2)}$$
$$= \sqrt{(9 + 16)} = \sqrt{25} = 5$$

So the distance between the points is $z = 5$.

5.1.2 Line Segments

A. Segmentation Problems

These problems are a kind of geometry-algebra hybrid. You are given a line segment that has been subdivided into smaller segments, and some information is provided. You are then asked to deduce some of the missing information.

In a segmentation problem, some of the information you are given may be geometric, and some may be algebraic. There is not, however, a clear algebraic equation to solve. You will need to logically determine the steps needed to reach a solution.

EXAMPLE

The line segment QT of length $4x + 6$ is shown in the figure that follows. Point

S is the midpoint of QT and segment RS has length $x - 1$. What is the length of line segment QR?

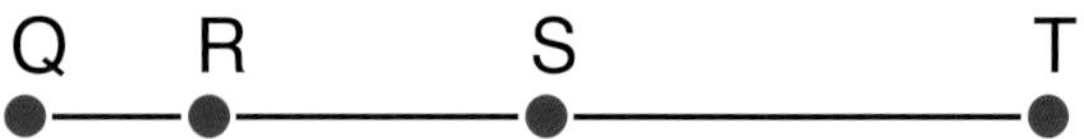

First, determine what information you know. The length of QT and RS are given. Also, since we have a midpoint for QT, the length of QS and ST are simply half of the length of QT.

Now, determine an algebraic relationship regarding the length of QR, which is what we are looking for. We can see that the length of QR is simply QS with the RS segment removed.

$$QR = QS - RS$$

Plugging in our information, we get the following:

$$QR = \frac{(4x+6)}{2} - (x-1)$$
$$= 2x + 3 - x + 1$$
$$= x + 4$$

Before you start working out a solution, it can be extremely helpful to list the information you are given. This will help you understand and organize the problem, both in your own mind and on the page.

B. Segments in the Plane

In segmentation problems, you only have to deal with one dimension. However, line segments can also turn up in problems dealing with a two dimensional Cartesian graph.

To determine the length of a line segment in a plane, simply find the distance between its endpoints using the Pythagorean Theorem (see section 5.1.1).

Any line segment in a plane corresponds to a single linear equation. This can be determined as in chapter 4 from any two points on the line segment. Knowing this linear equation can help you find other points on the line segment.

5.1.3 Angles

An **angle** is formed by the intersection of two lines.

In problems that are not trigonometric, angles are almost always measured in degrees. A full circle makes 360°.

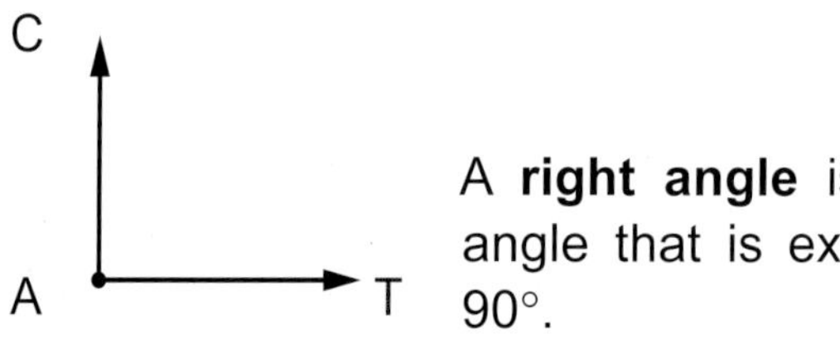

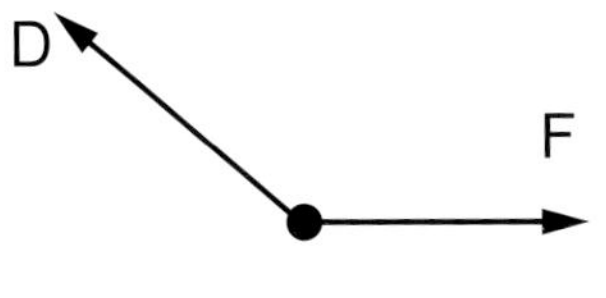

An **obtuse angle** is an angle that is greater than 90°.

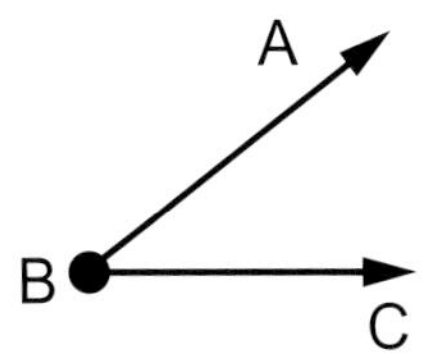

An **acute angle** is an angle that is less than 90°.

A **straight angle** is an angle that is exactly 180°.

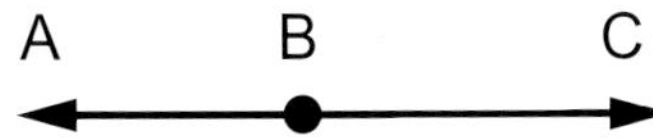

A **vertical angle** is the angle opposite of each other that is formed by two intersecting lines. The two angles across from each other are equal in measure. The following example shows that angles 1 and 3 are vertical angles and equal to each other. Same are angles 2 and 4. At the same time, adjacent vertical angles 1 and 4 or 2 and 3 are also supplementary angles and will form 180°.

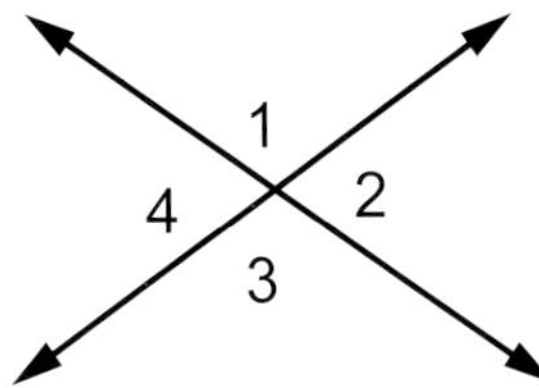

Complementary angles are two angles that add up to 90°. The example that follows shows that angles A and B add up to 90°.

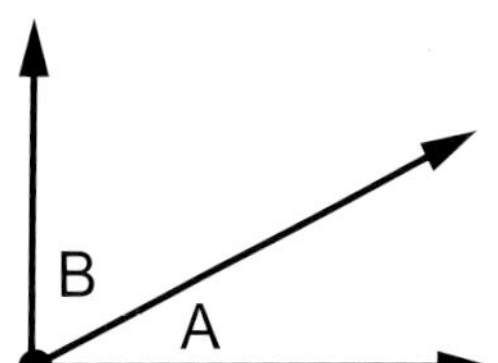

Supplementary angles are two angles that add up to 180°. This example shows that angles A and B add up to 180°.

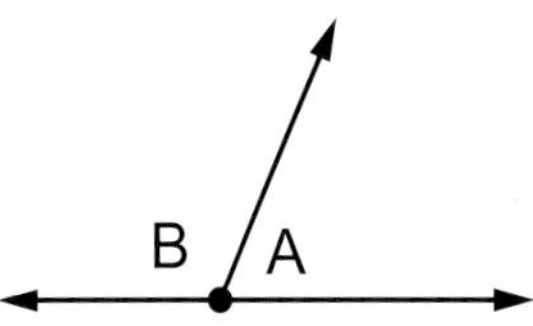

A. Angles and Lines in the Plane

If two lines are **parallel**, they have the same slope. Such lines will never intersect, and so they will never form angles with one another.

If two lines are **perpendicular**, their intersection forms only 90° angles. If the slope of a given line is a/b, then the slope of any perpendicular line is $-b/a$.

EXAMPLE

Consider the line defined by $y = 2x + 3$.

(a) Give the equation for a parallel line:

$$y = 2x + 2.$$

Any line that still has a slope of 2 will suffice. So, in slope-intercept form, any line of the form $y = 2x + a$ will be a parallel line.

(b) Give the equation for the perpendicular line that intersects the given line at the y-axis.

In this case, there is only one solution since the line can only intersect the y-axis once. The solution will be a line with the same y-intercept (which is 3) and the negative reciprocal slope (which is –½).

$$y = -\frac{1}{2}x + 3$$

The standard kind of angle-line problem deals with a setup of two parallel lines that are cut by a transversal, like the one in the following.

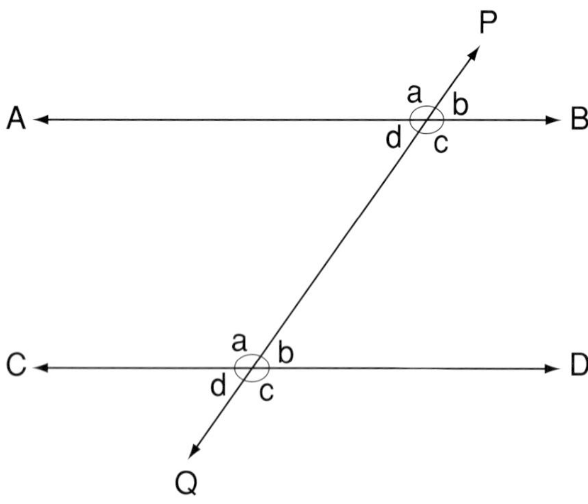

The trick with these problems is to realize that there are only ever two values for the angles.

First, think of the two areas of intersection as exact duplicates of each other. The upper left angles are equivalent, as are the upper right, the lower left, and the lower right. Using just this information, you automatically know the value of the twin of any angle that is given to you.

Also, angles that are opposite each other are equivalent. So the lower left angle is the same as the upper right and vice versa.

The other fact you can use to determine unknown angles is that the angle along a straight line is 180°. When you are given an angle a, you can find supplement b by subtracting 180° – a.

EXAMPLE

In the figure that follows, if angle a is 35°, what is the value of angle b?

Angle b is the twin of the supplement of a, so b is equal to 180° – a.

$$b = 180^\circ - 35^\circ = 145^\circ$$

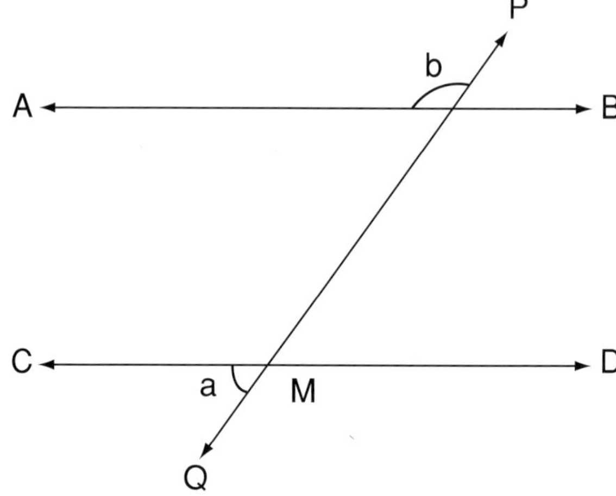

B. Properties of Parallel Line Angles

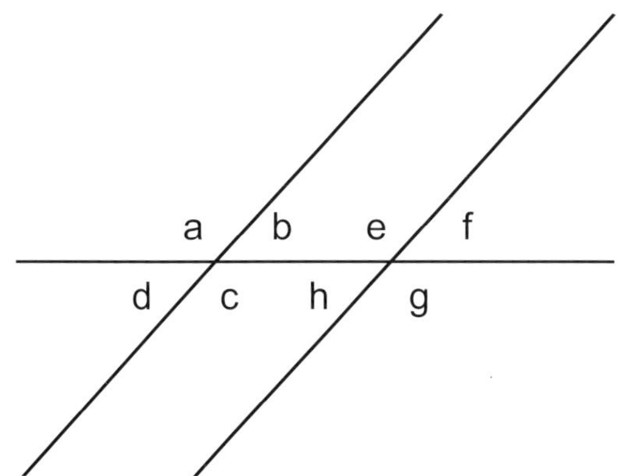

When two parallel lines are cut by a transversal line:

1. both pairs of acute angles as well as obtuse angles are equal: $a = e, b = f, d = h, c = g$.
2. alternate interior angles are equal in measure as well: $c = e, b = h$.

C. Interior Angles of a Polygon

Sometimes you may be dealing with a shape that you are not familiar with and do not know the total of all interior angles. If the polygon has *x* sides, the sum, S, is the total of all interior angles for that polygon. For a polygon with *x* sides, the sum may be calculated by the following formula:

$$S = (x - 2)\,(180^\circ)$$

EXAMPLE

A triangle has 3 sides, therefore,

$S = (3 - 2) \times 180^\circ$
$S = 180^\circ$

A rectangle has 4 sides,

$S = (4 - 2) \times 180^\circ$
$S = 360^\circ$.

Given the total angles for a polygon, you can determine each interior angle of a polygon by dividing the sum of the polygon by the number of sides.

EXAMPLE

A rectangle has a sum of 360°. Given that $x = 4$, $360^\circ \div 4 = 90^\circ$. Therefore, each angle in a rectangle is 90°.

NOTE

The assumption here is that all angles of a given polygon have the same measure, which may not always be the case on the DAT. In order to apply this, be certain that the polygon has equal angles.

5.2 2D Figures

Make sure you know how to find the area, perimeter, side lengths, and angles of all the figures in this section. There are all kinds of ways to combine different shapes into the same problem; but if you can deal with them all individually, you'll be able to break down any problem thrown your way!

5.2.1 Rectangles and Squares

A **rectangle** is a figure with four straight sides and four right angles. In rectangles, opposite sides always have the same length, as do the two diagonals that can be drawn from corner to corner.

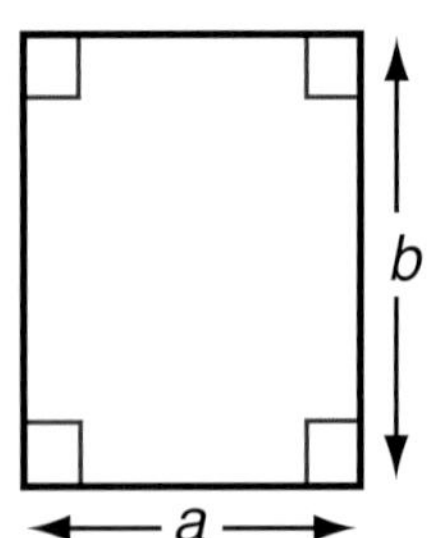

Perimeter: The perimeter of a rectangle is equal to the sum of its sides.

$$\text{Perimeter} = a + b + a + b = 2a + 2b$$

Area: The area of a rectangle is equal to the product of its length and width.

$$\text{Area} = \text{Length} \times \text{Width} = a \times b$$

A **square** is a rectangle with all four sides of the same length, so $a = b$.

The perimeter of a square is

$$P = a + a + a + a = 4a.$$

The area of a square is

$$A = a \times a = a^2.$$

5.2.2 Types of Triangles

While there are a wide variety of types of triangles, every one shares these properties:

(i) The sum of the interior angles of a triangle is always equal to 180°. In the following figure, *a*, *b*, and *c* are interior angles.

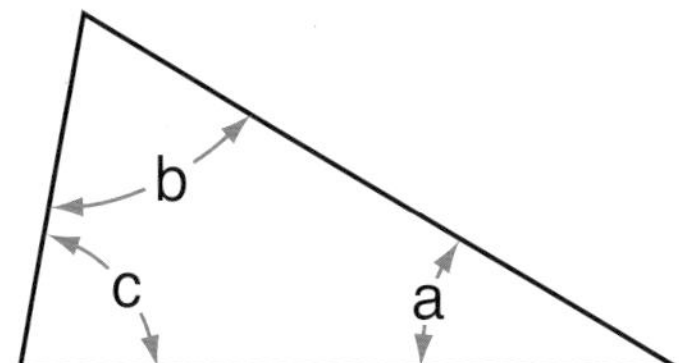

(ii) The sum of the exterior angles of a triangle is always equal to 360°. The following figure shows *d, e,* and *f* to be exterior angles.

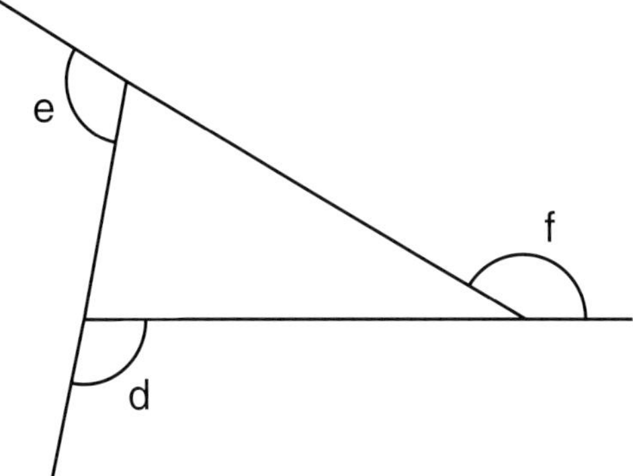

(iii) The value of an exterior angle is equal to the sum of the opposite two interior angles.

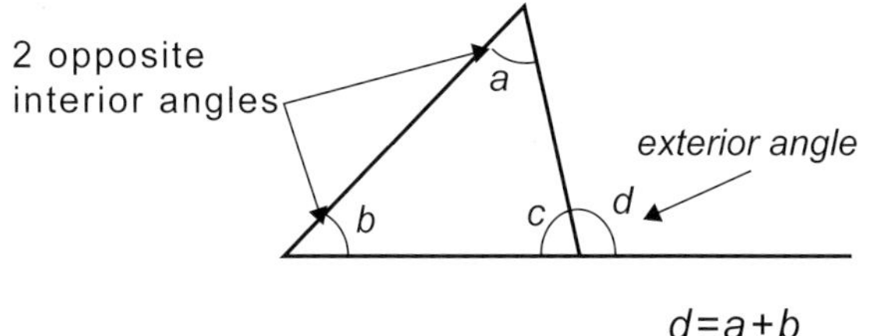

EXAMPLE

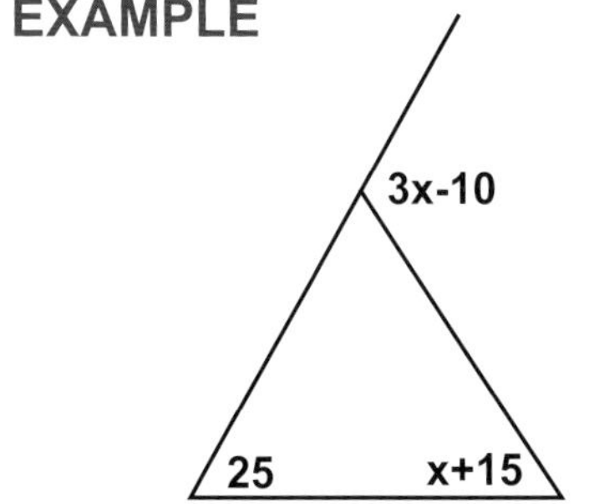

$$3x - 10 = 25 + x + 15$$
$$2x = 10 + 25 + 15$$
$$2x = 50$$
$$x = 25$$

(iv) The perimeter of a triangle is equal to the sum of its sides.

(v) The area of a triangle is always half the product of the base and the height.

$$\text{Area} = \frac{1}{2}\,\text{Base} \times \text{Height}$$

You can pick any side of the triangle to function as the base, and the height will be the line perpendicular to that side that runs between it and the opposite vertex.

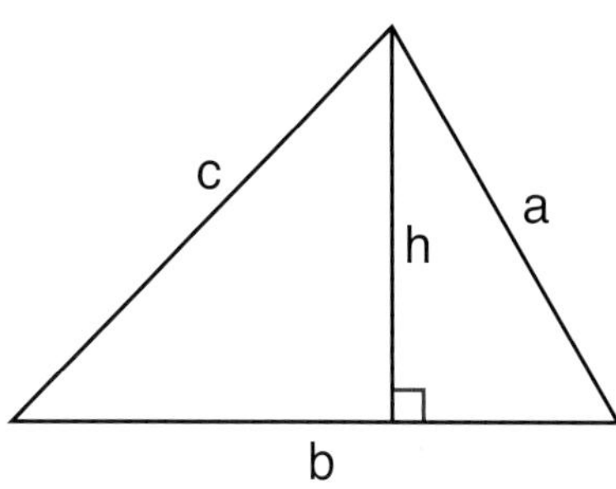

(vi) The sum of any two sides of a triangle is always greater than or equal to the third side. So if *a*, *b*, and *c* are the three sides of a triangle,

$$a + b \geq c.$$

If the sum of two sides is equal to the length of the third side, the triangle is a line segment. This property is known as the **triangle inequality**.

(vii) The difference of any two sides of a triangle is always smaller than the third side. So if a, b and c are three sides of a triangle, $a - b < c$.

What are the possible values for x?

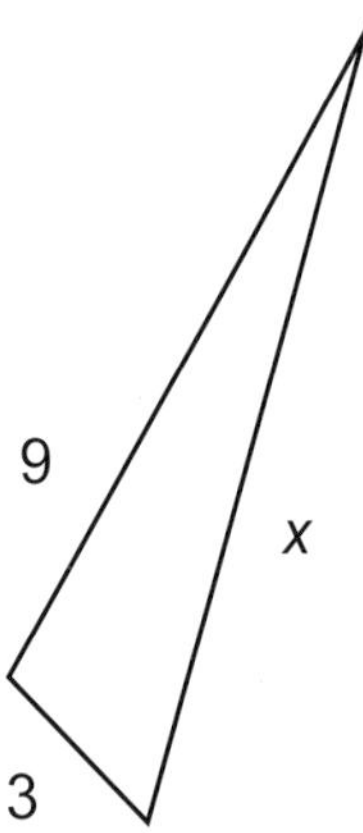

Therefore, $x < (9 + 3)$ and $x > (9 - 3)$, $6 < x < 12$.

A. Right Triangles

A **right triangle** is a triangle that contains a right angle. The other two angles in a right triangle add up to 90°.

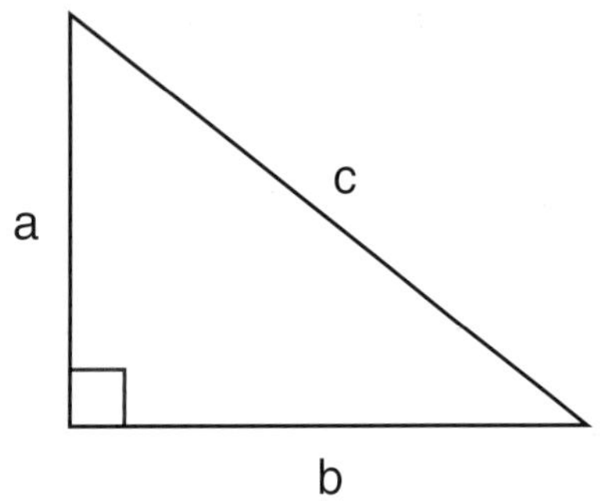

The two short legs of a right triangle (the legs that come together to form the right angle) and the hypotenuse (the side opposite the right angle) are related by the Pythagorean Theorem:

$$a^2 + b^2 = c^2$$

To find a missing side of the triangle, plug the values you have into the Pythagorean Theorem and solve algebraically.

The two legs of a right triangle are its base and height. So to find the area, compute as thus shown.

$$\text{Area} = \frac{1}{2}(a \times b)$$

Special Cases: There are a few cases of right triangles you should know. First, the ratios of side lengths 3:4:5 and 5:12:13 are often used. Identifying that a triangle corresponds to one of these cases can save you precious time since you will not have to solve the Pythagorean Theorem.

There are also two special ratios of interior angles for right triangles: 30°–60°–90° and 45°–45°–90°. The sides of a 30°–60°–90° triangle have the ratio $1:\sqrt{3}:2$ and the sides of a 45°–45°–90° triangle have the ratio $1:1:\sqrt{2}$.

NOTE

Pythagorean Theorem

Knowing any two sides of a right triangle lets you find the third side by using the Pythagorean formula: $a^2 + b^2 = c^2$.

3-4-5 triangle: if a right triangle has two legs with a ratio of 3:4, or a leg to a hypotenuse ratio of either 3:5 or 4:5, then it is a 3-4-5 triangle.

5-12-13 triangle: if a right triangle has two legs with a ratio of 5:12, or a leg to a hypotenuse ratio of either 5:13 or 12:13, then it is a 5-12-13 triangle.

45°-45°-90° triangle: if a right triangle has two angles that are both 45°, then the ratio of the three legs is $1:1:\sqrt{(2)}$.

30°-60°-90° triangle: if a right triangle has two angles of 30° and 60°, then the ratio of the three legs is $1:\sqrt{(3)}:2$.

B. Isosceles Triangles

An **isosceles triangle** is a triangle that has two equal sides. The angles that sit opposite the equal sides are also equal.

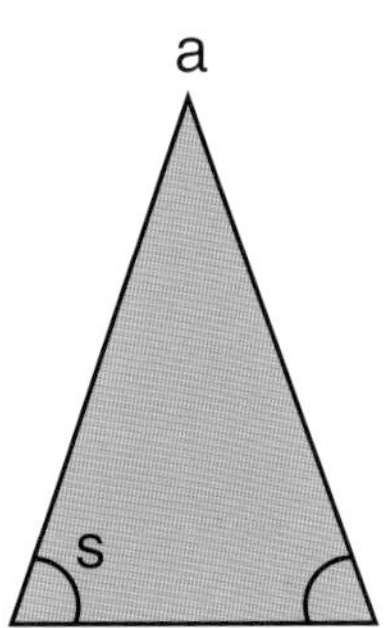

For an isosceles triangle, use the odd side as the base and draw the height line to the odd vertex. This line will bisect the side, so it is simple to determine the height using the Pythagorean Theorem on one of the new right triangles formed.

C. Equilateral Triangles

An **equilateral triangle** is a triangle with all three sides equal. All three interior angles are also equal, so they are all 60°.

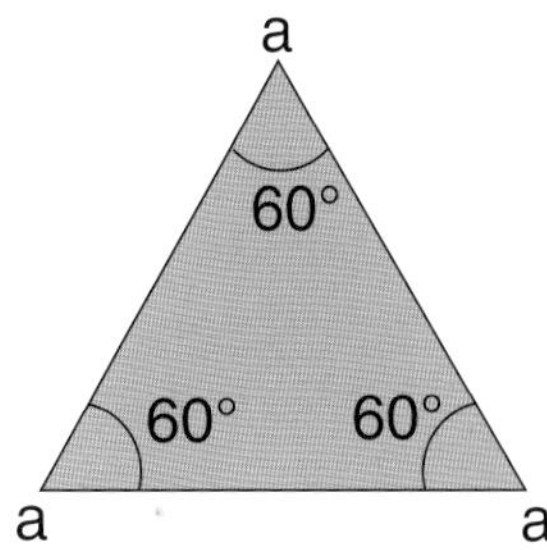

Drawing a height line from any vertex will divide the triangle into two 30°–60°–90° triangles, so you can easily solve for the area.

D. Scalene Triangles

A **scalene triangle** is any triangle that has no equal sides and no equal angles. To find the value for the height of this kind of triangle requires the use of trigonometric functions (see Chapter 6).

E. Similar Triangles

Two triangles are **similar** if they have the same values for interior angles. This means that ratios of corresponding sides will be equal. Similar triangles are triangles with the same shape that are scaled to different sizes.

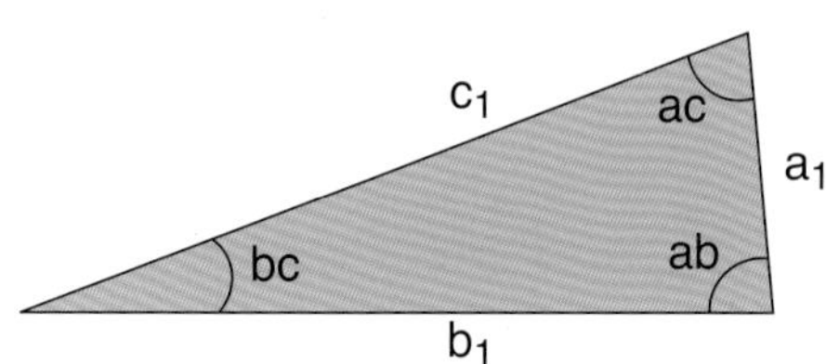

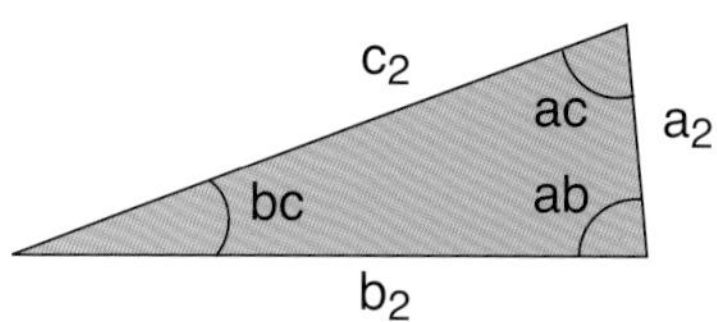

To solve for values in a triangle from information given about a similar triangle, you will need to use ratios. The ratios of corresponding sides are always equal, for example $\frac{a_1}{a_2} = \frac{b_1}{b_2}$. Also, the ratio of two sides in the same triangle is equal to the corresponding ratio in the similar triangle, for example $\frac{a_1}{b_1} = \frac{a_2}{b_2}$.

5.2.3 Circles

A **circle** is a figure in which every point is the same distance from the center. This distance from the center to the edge is known as the **radius** (*r*). The length of any straight line drawn from a point on the circle, through the center, and out to another point on the circle is known as the **diameter** (*d*). The diameter is twice the radius.

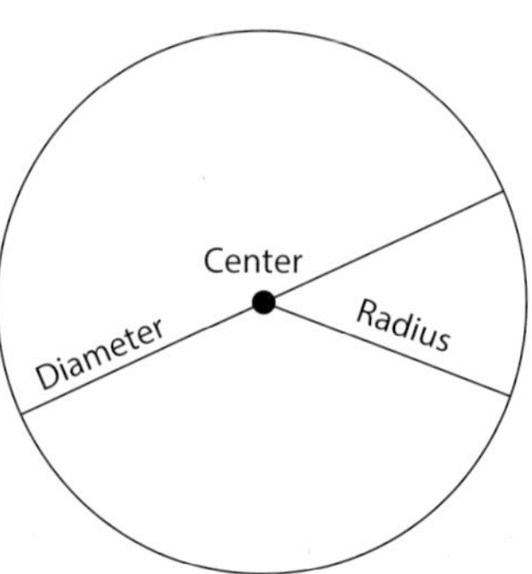

$$d = 2 \times r \quad \text{or} \quad r = \frac{1}{2}d$$

There are no angles in a circle.

Circumference: The circumference of a circle is the total distance around a circle. It is equal to pi times the diameter.

$$\text{Circumference} = \pi \times d = 2\pi \times r$$

Area: The area of a circle is equal to pi times the square of the radius.

$$\text{Area} = \pi \times r^2 = \frac{1}{4}\pi \times d^2$$

Length: Length of an arc is defined as a piece of circumference formed by an angle of *n* degrees measured as the arc's central angle in a circle of radius *r*.

$$L = \frac{n^\circ}{360^\circ} \times 2\pi r$$

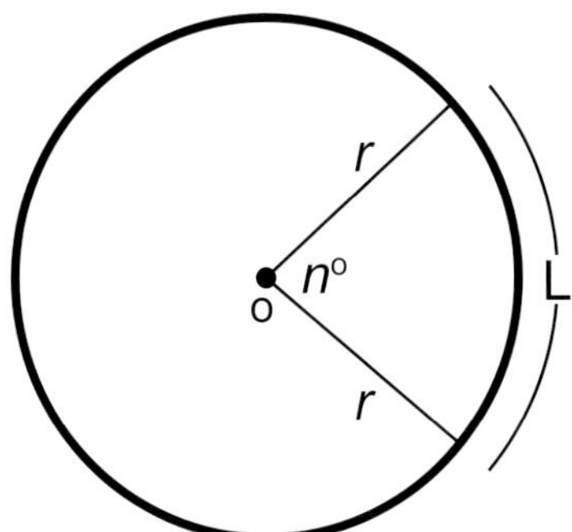

Area of a sector: The area of a sector is a portion of the circle formed by an angle of *n* degree measured as the sector's central angle in a circle of radius *r*.

$$\text{Area (sector)} = \frac{1}{2}r^2\theta \text{ (in radians)}$$

$$\text{Area (sector)} = \frac{n^\circ}{360^\circ} \times \pi r^2 \text{ (in degrees)}$$

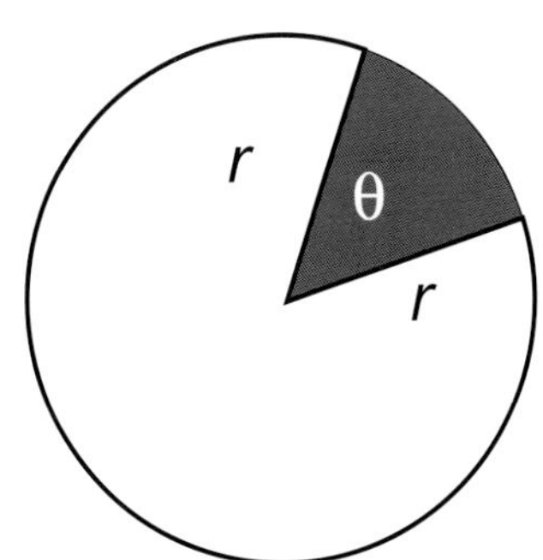

5.2.4 Trapezoids and Parallelograms

A. Trapezoids

A **trapezoid** is a four-sided figure with one pair of parallel sides and one pair of non-parallel sides.

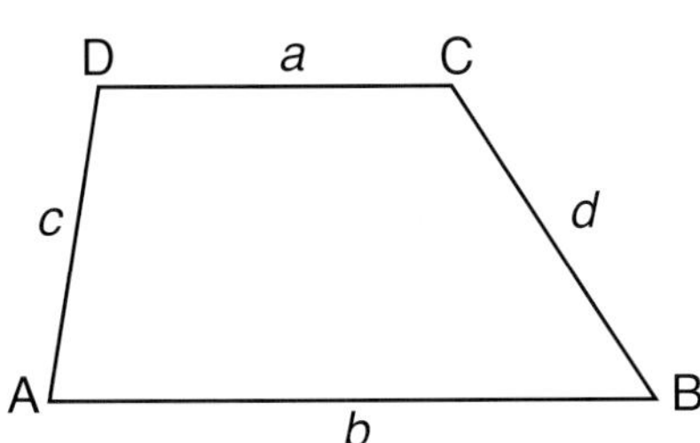

Usually the easiest way to solve trapezoid problems is to drop vertical lines down from the vertices on the smaller of the two parallel lines. This splits the figure into two right triangles on the ends and a rectangle in the middle. Then, to find information about the trapezoid, you can solve for the information (side length, area, angles, etc.) of these other shapes.

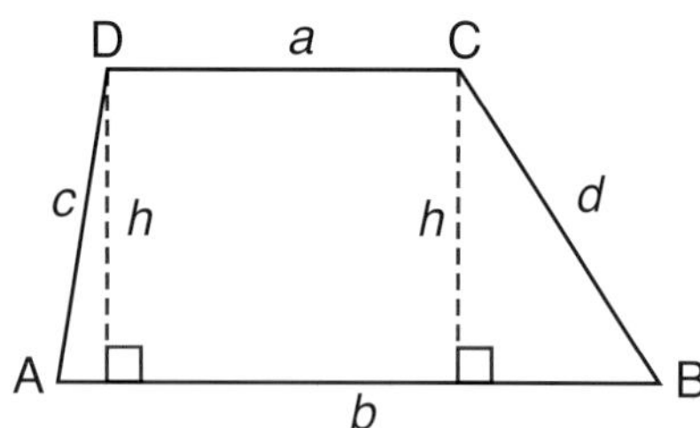

1. The area of a trapezoid is calculated as

$$\frac{a+b}{2}h$$

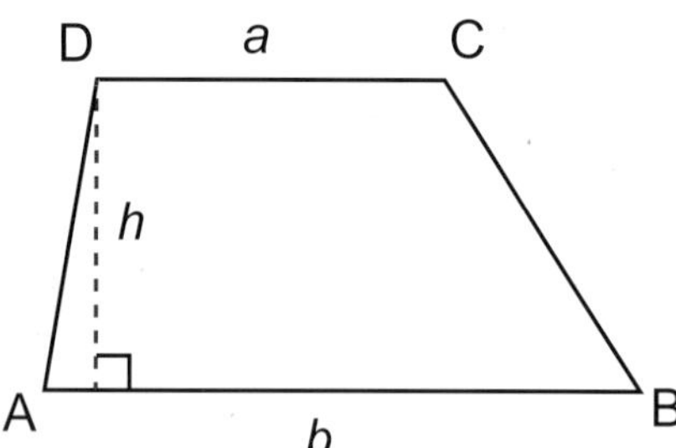

2. The upper and lower base angles are supplementary angles (i.e., they add up to 180°).

Angle A + Angle D = 180°
Angle B + Angle C = 180°

Sometimes it can be useful to draw a line from vertex to vertex and construct a triangle that way, but this usually only makes sense if the resulting triangle is special (i.e. isosceles).

Isosceles Trapezoids: Just like isosceles triangles, **isosceles trapezoids** are trapezoids with two equal sides. The sides that are equal are the parallel sides that form angles with the base of the trapezoid. Similarly, if the left and right sides are of the same lengths, these angles are the same as well.

In this isosceles trapezoid, ABCE means that Angle A = Angle D, Angle B = Angle C, and Diagonal AC = Diagonal BD.

The perimeter $= a + b + 2c$

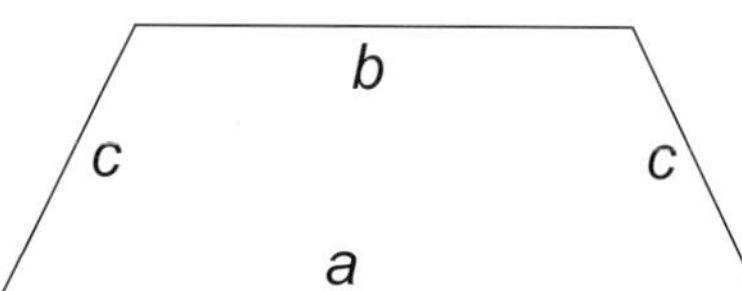

B. Parallelograms

A **parallelogram** is a quadrilateral that has two sets of parallel sides. A square, for example, is a special kind of parallelogram, as is a rhombus (which has four sides of equal length but, unlike a square, has two different pairs of angle values).

Area: The area of a parallelogram is simply the base times the height.

$$\text{Area} = (\text{Base}) \times (\text{Height})$$

The height of a parallelogram can be found by dropping a vertical from a vertex to the opposite side and evaluating the resulting right triangle.

The sum of all the angles in a parallelogram is 360°. Opposite angles are equivalent, and adjacent angles add up to 180°.

5.3 3D Solids

In three dimensions, it doesn't always make sense to talk about perimeters. Shapes with defined edges (such as boxes and pyramids) still have them, but rounded shapes (such as spheres) do not. Instead, we are generally concerned with the values of surface area and volume.

5.3.1 Boxes

Boxes are the three-dimensional extension of rectangles. Every angle in a box is 90°, and every box has six rectangular faces, twelve edges, and eight vertices. Opposite (and parallel) faces are always of the same length, height, and width, as are opposite (and parallel) edges.

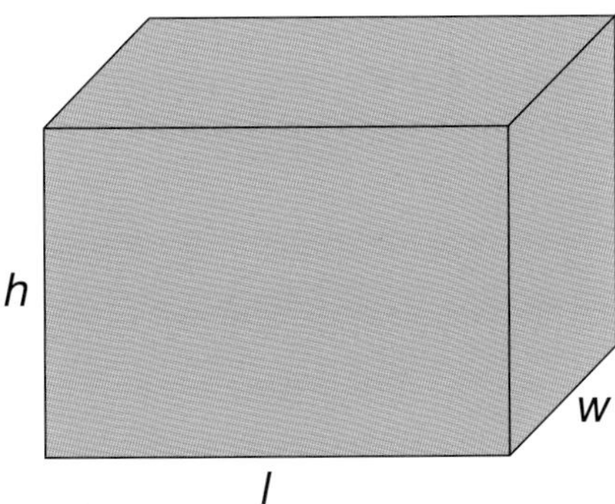

Perimeter: The perimeter of a box is the sum of its edges. There are, however, only three different lengths and four edges corresponding to each one. So to find the perimeter, we can simply take the sum of four times each the width, length, and height.

$$\text{Perimeter} = 4l + 4w + 4h = 4(l + w + h)$$

Surface Area: The surface area of a box is the sum of the area of each of its faces. Since there is one duplicate of each unique face, we only need to find three products, double them, and add them together.

$$\begin{aligned}\text{Surface Area} &= 2lw + 2wh + 2lh \\ &= 2(lw + wh + lh)\end{aligned}$$

Volume: Calculating the volume of a box can be visualized as taking the surface of any of its rectangular faces and dragging it through space, like you were blowing a box-shaped bubble. So you start with the product of a width times a height, and then you multiply that by a length.

$$\text{Volume} = l \times w \times h$$

5.3.2 Spheres

The definition of a sphere is basically identical to that of a circle, except that it is applied in three dimensions rather than two: It is a collection of points in three dimensions that are all of the same distance from a particular center point. Again, we call this distance the radius, and twice the radius is the diameter. A sphere has no vertices or edges, so it has no circumference.

Surface Area: Surface Area $= 4\pi \times r^2$

Volume: Volume $= (4/3)\pi \times r^3$

5.3.3 Cylinders

Spheres may be the 3D equivalent of circles, but if you start with a circle and extend it into the third dimension, you obtain the tube shape known as a cylinder. Cylinders have two parallel circular faces, and their edges are connected by a smooth, edgeless surface.

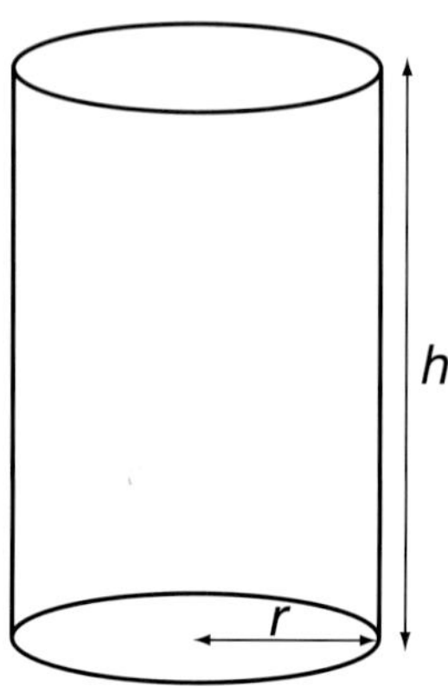

Surface Area: The surface area of a cylinder is composed of three parts: The two circular faces and the connecting portion. To find the total area of a cylinder, add the areas of these two parts. We already know how to calculate area for circles; and for the connecting surface, all we need to do is extend the circumference of one of the circles into three dimensions. So, multiply the circumference by the height of the cylinder.

Surface Area $= 2(\pi \times r^2) + (2\pi \times r) \times h$

Volume: The volume of a cylinder is equal to the area of one of its bases (circle) multiplied by the height.

Volume $= (\pi \times r^2) \times h$

5.3.4 Cones

A cone is like a cylinder, except that instead of having a circle on either end; it has a circle on one and a single point on the other. The height of the cone is the distance from the center of the circle to the single vertex, and the slant length is the distance from the edge of the circle to the vertex.

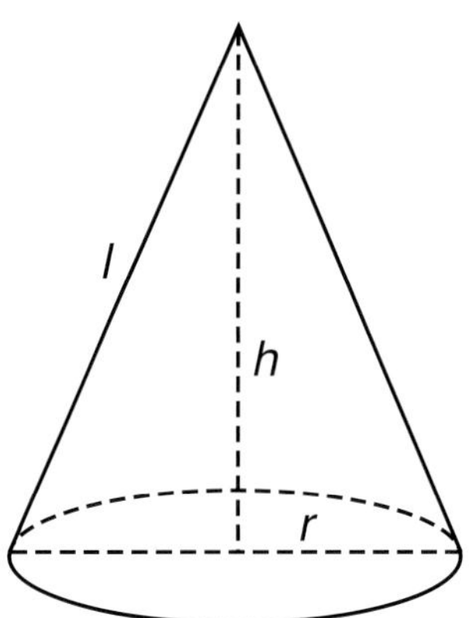

Surface Area: To find the surface area of a cone, we use the same strategy as we did with a cylinder. We find the surface area of the circle and add it to the surface area of the smooth lateral portion. The area of the circle can be found from the radius as usual, and the area of the lateral portion is ½ the circumference of the circle times the slant length.

$$\text{Surface Area} = (\pi \times r^2) + \frac{1}{2}c \times l$$
$$= (\pi \times r^2) + \frac{1}{2}(2\pi \times r) \times l$$

Volume: To find the volume of a cone, we need the radius of the circle and the cone's height.

$$\text{Volume} = (1/3)\pi \times r^2 \times h$$

5.3.5 Other Solids

There are all kinds of different solids that can be constructed out of basic 2D figures and the solids we've already discussed. If you are able to deal with all of these individually though, you will be able to break down and tackle any wacky solid that might be thrown at you.

5.3.6 Vertices

You have now heard the word "vertex" used in different instances with similar meanings. Just for clarification, we may define the vertex as: (1) the point at which the sides of an angle intersect; (2) the points on a triangle or pyramid opposite to and farthest away from its base; and finally, (3) a point on a polyhedron (a solid bounded by faces/polygons) common to three or more sides.

GOLD STANDARD WARM-UP EXERCISES

CHAPTER 5: Geometry

1. The area of a circle is 144π. What is its circumference?

A. 6π
B. 24π
C. 72π
D. 12π
E. 36π

2. How many cubes with edges of length 6 inches will fit inside a cubical box with an edge of length 1 yard?

A. 216
B. 36
C. 18
D. 108
E. 72

3. The points (2,–3) and (2,5) are the endpoints of a diameter of a circle. What is the radius of the circle?

A. 64
B. 4π
C. 16
D. 8
E. 4

4. A cylinder of radius 1 foot and height 1 foot is full of water. The water is poured into a cyclinder of radius 1 foot and height 6 inches until it is full. How many cubic feet of the water will be left over?

A. 0.6π
B. 0.4π
C. 0.64π
D. 0.5π
E. 0.75π

5. A and B are similar 45°-45°-90° triangles. If B has an area of 12 square feet, and A has three times the area of B, what is the length of A's hypotenuse?

A. $\sqrt{72}$ feet
B. 36 feet
C. 72 feet
D. 12 feet
E. 6 feet

6. Leslie drives from Highway 1 to the parallel Highway 2 using the road that crosses them, as in the given figure below. Leslie misses the turn onto Highway 1 at point Q and drives 2 km further, to point P. Driving in a straight line from point P to get back to Highway 1, how much further will Leslie travel?

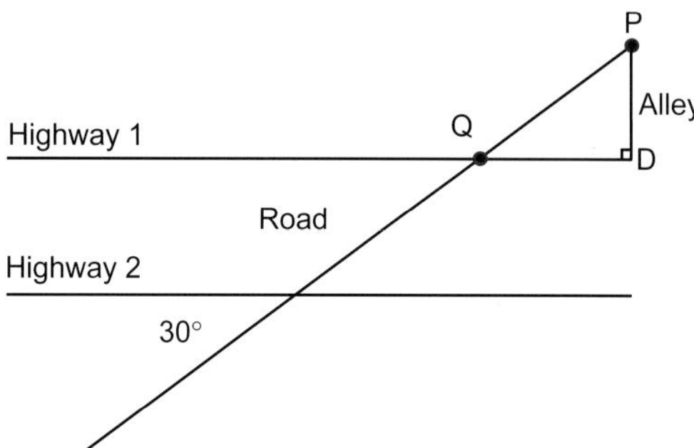

A. 1/2 km
B. $\sqrt{3}$ km
C. 1 km
D. 2 km
E. $2\sqrt{3}$ km

7. A circle is inscribed in a square with a diagonal of length 5. What is the area of the circle?

A. $\frac{25}{8}\pi$
B. $\frac{25}{2}\pi$
C. $\frac{25}{16}\pi$
D. $\frac{25}{4}\pi$
E. 50π

8. A circle is drawn inside a larger circle so that they have the same center. If the smaller circle has 25% the area of the larger circle, which of the following is the ratio of the radius of the small circle to that of the larger circle?

A. $\frac{1}{8}$
B. $\frac{3}{4}$
C. $\frac{1}{4}$
D. $\frac{1}{25}$
E. $\frac{1}{2}$

9. A circle passes through the point (0,0) and the point (10,0). Which of the following could NOT be a third point on the Circle?

A (1, –3)
B (2, 4)
C (7, 4)
D (5, 0)
E (2, –4)

10. A rectangular picture 4½ feet wide and 3½ feet long is enclosed by a border 3 inches wide. What is the total area, in square feet, of the picture and border?

A. 12
B. 15
C. 15¾
D. $17\frac{13}{16}$
E. 20

11. Mary wants to wallpaper a room. It has one bay window that measures 3 feet by 4 feet, and a door that measures 3 feet by 7 feet. The room is 12 feet by 12 feet, and is 10 feet tall. If only the walls are to be covered, and rolls of wallpaper are 100 square feet, what is the minimum number of rolls that she will need?
   A. 4 rolls
   B. 5 rolls
   C. 6 rolls
   D. 7 rolls
   E. 8 rolls

12. In order to protect her new car, Stacey needs to build a new garage. The concrete floor needs to be 64.125 square feet and is 9.5 feet long. How wide does it need to be?
   A. 7.25 feet
   B. 8.25 feet
   C. 6.75 feet
   D. 6.25 feet
   E. 7.50 feet

GS ANSWER KEY

CHAPTER 5

		Cross-Reference			*Cross-Reference*
1.	B	QR 5.2, 5.2.3	7.	A	QR 5.2, 5.2.1, 5.2.3
2.	A	QR 5.3, 5.3.1	8.	E	QR 5.2, 5.2.3
3.	E	QR 5.2, 5.2.3	9.	D	QR 5.1, 5.1.1, 5.2.3
4.	D	QR 5.3, 5.3.3	10.	E	QR 5.2, 5.2.1
5.	D	QR 5.2, 5.2.2	11.	B	QR 5.3, 5.3.1
6.	C	QR 5.1, 5.1.3	12.	C	QR 5.3, 5.3.1

* Explanations can be found at the back of the book.

Go online to DAT-prep.com for additional chapter review Q&A and forum.

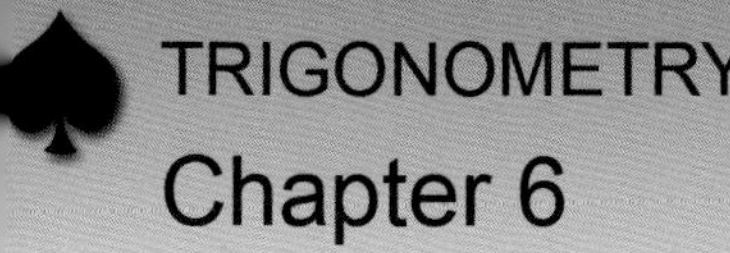

TRIGONOMETRY

Chapter 6

Memorize	Understand	Importance
Formulas for Sine, Cosine, and Tangent Important Values of Sine and Cosine Important Identities Polar Coordinate Conversions	* Graphing Sine, Cosine, and Tangent * Secant, Cosecant, and Cotangent * The Unit Circle * Degrees vs. Radians * Inverse Trigonometric Functions * Graphing in Polar Coordinates * Distance and Midpoint Formulas	**3 to 5 out of the 40 QR** questions on the DAT are based on content from this chapter (in our estimation). * This will change in 2015.

Introduction

Trigonometry is the most conceptually advanced branch of mathematics with which you will need to be familiar for the Quantitative Reasoning test. But don't let that scare you. Basically, everything in this section boils down to right triangles, and after Chapter 6, you'd be a triangle pro!

Additional Resources

Free Online Forum

6.1 Basic Trigonometric Functions

The trigonometric functions describe the relationship between the angles and sides of right triangles. The angle in question is generally denoted by θ, the Greek letter theta, but you will never see the right angle used as θ.

We call the leg connecting to the vertex of θ the *adjacent side* ("b" in the diagram), and the leg that does not touch the *opposite side* ("a" in the diagram). The edge across from the right angle is called the *hypotenuse*.

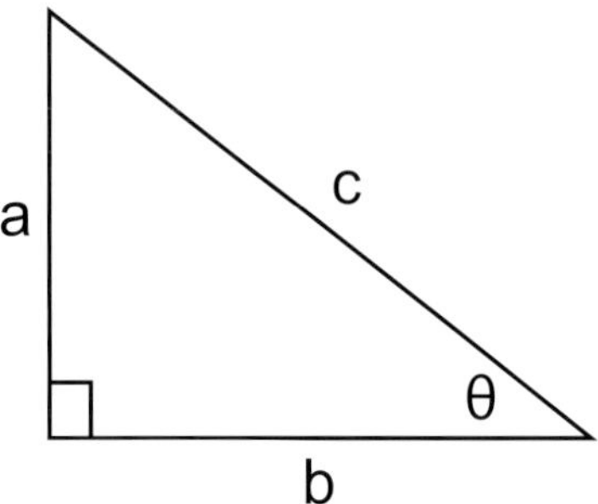

6.1.1 Sine

A lot of people like to use the mnemonic device "SOH-CAH-TOA" to remember how to evaluate the three basic trigonometric functions: Sine, cosine, and tangent. The first three letters, "SOH," refer to the first letter of each word in the following equation.

$$\text{Sine} = \frac{\text{Opposite}}{\text{Hypotenuse}}$$

Sine of an angle θ is written sin(θ). So to calculate this value, simply divide the length of the opposite side by the length of the hypotenuse.

EXAMPLE

What is sin(θ) in the following triangle?

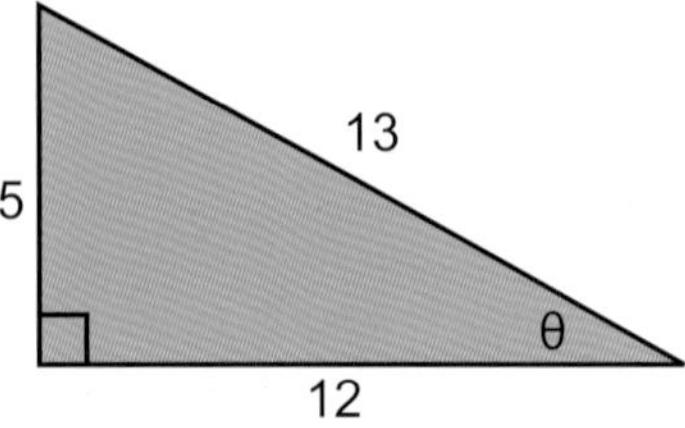

The opposite side has length 5, and the hypotenuse has length 13, so

$$\sin(\theta) = \frac{5}{13}$$

6.1.2 Cosine

The second set of three letters in SOH-CAH-TOA refers to the equation for the cosine of an angle.

$$\text{Cosine} = \frac{\text{Adjacent}}{\text{Hypotenuse}}$$

The abbreviation for the cosine of an angle is $\cos(\theta)$.

EXAMPLE

In the 5–12–13 triangle in Section 6.1.1, what is $\cos(\theta)$?

Dividing the adjacent side by the hypotenuse, we obtain the following solution:

$$\cos(\theta) = \frac{12}{13}$$

6.1.3 Tangent

The final three letters in SOH-CAH-TOA refer to the equation for finding the tangent of an angle.

$$\text{Tangent} = \frac{\text{Opposite}}{\text{Adjacent}}$$

You can also find the tangent of an angle if you know the value for sine and cosine. Notice that the hypotenuse cancels out if you divide sine and cosine.

$$\text{Tangent} = \frac{\text{Sine}}{\text{Cosine}}$$

You can also manipulate this equation to express sine or cosine in terms of the tangent.

EXAMPLE

In the 5–12–13 triangle in Section 6.1.1, what is $\tan(\theta)$?

Dividing the opposite side by the adjacent side, we obtain:

$$\tan(\theta) = \frac{5}{12}$$

6.1.4 Secant, Cosecant, and Cotangent

These three functions are far less commonly used than sine, cosine, and tangent, but you should still be familiar with them. They are not very hard to remember because they are just the reciprocals of the main three functions.

$$\text{Cosecant} = \frac{1}{\text{Sine}} = \frac{\text{Hypotenuse}}{\text{Opposite}}$$

$$\text{Secant} = \frac{1}{\text{Cosine}} = \frac{\text{Hypotenuse}}{\text{Adjacent}}$$

$$\text{Cotangent} = \frac{1}{\text{Tangent}} = \frac{\text{Adjacent}}{\text{Opposite}}$$

The abbreviations for these functions are sec, csc, and cot, respectively.

6.2 The Unit Circle

6.2.1 Trig Functions on a Circle

As you can see from the equations in Section 6.1, the trigonometric functions are ratios of side lengths. This means that every angle has a value for each of the functions that *does not* depend on the scale of the triangle.

In Section 6.1 we looked at examples with a 5–12–13 triangle. Our solutions were as follows:

$$\sin(\theta) = \frac{5}{13}$$

$$\cos(\theta) = \frac{12}{13}$$

$$\tan(\theta) = \frac{5}{12}$$

Let's compare these results with the trigonometric functions for the similar triangle 10, 24, 26, which clearly has longer sides but the same angle θ:

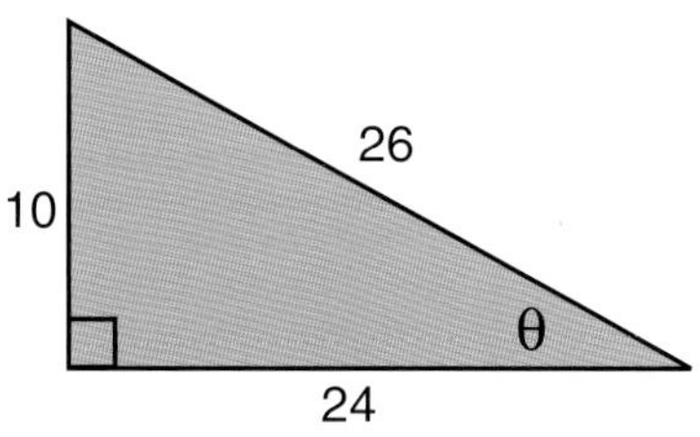

$$\sin(\theta) = \frac{10}{26} = \frac{5}{13}$$

$$\cos(\theta) = \frac{24}{26} = \frac{12}{13}$$

$$\tan(\theta) = \frac{10}{24} = \frac{5}{12}$$

As you can see, the trigonometric values for the angle remain the same.

Also, the absolute value of sine and cosine is never greater than 1 for any angle. This makes perfect sense because the hypotenuse of a triangle is always its longest side, and for sine and cosine, the hypotenuse is in the denominator.

If we plot the graph of sine and cosine for θ from 0° to 360° in Cartesian Coordinates with $x = \cos(\theta)$ and $y = \sin(\theta)$, we obtain a circle of radius 1. This is known as the **unit circle**, as shown in the succeeding picture. The angle formed at the vertex of the x-axis is equal to θ.

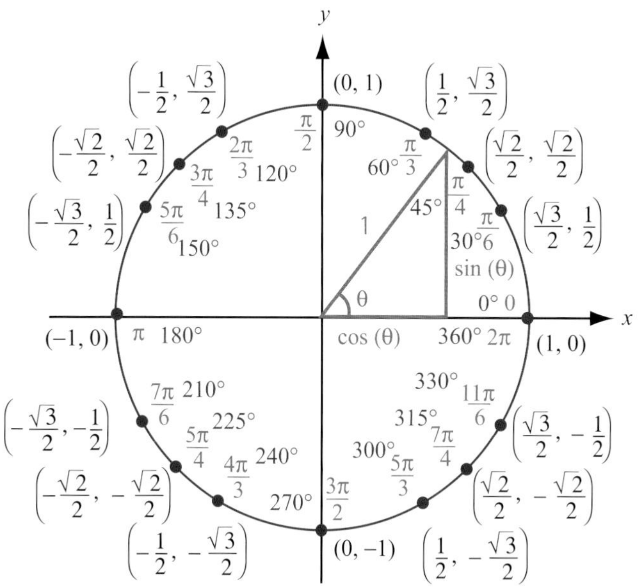

When simply dealing with right triangle figures, we never use negative numbers because negative length does not make sense. With the unit circle, though, legs of the triangle can be in negative space on the Cartesian plane. This can result in negative values for sine and cosine.

6.2.2 Degrees and Radians

Up until this point, we have measured angles using degrees. When dealing with trigonometric functions, however, it is often more convenient to use the unit-less measurement of **radians**. There are 2π radians in 360°, so one trip around the unit circle is an increase in θ by 2π radians.

$$2\pi \text{ radians} = 360°$$

This translates to 1 radian = $\frac{360}{2\pi}$, but you will usually be working with radians in multiples of π, so it is not necessary to memorize this.

Here is a list of important angles (in degrees and radians) and their sine and cosine values to memorize from the unit circle:

Degrees	Radians	Sine	Cosine
0°	0	0	1
30°	$\frac{\pi}{6}$	$\frac{1}{2}$	$\frac{(\sqrt{3})}{2}$
45°	$\frac{\pi}{4}$	$\frac{1}{\sqrt{2}}$	$\frac{1}{\sqrt{2}}$
60°	$\frac{\pi}{3}$	$\frac{(\sqrt{3})}{2}$	$\frac{1}{2}$
90°	$\frac{\pi}{2}$	1	0

Note that $\frac{1}{\sqrt{2}}$ is the same as $\frac{\sqrt{2}}{2}$.

These major angles repeat for each quadrant of the unit circle, but the signs of the sine and cosine values change. Moving counterclockwise around the circle and beginning with the upper right, the quadrants are labeled I, II, III, and IV.

Quadrant	Sine	Cosine
I	+	+
II	+	–
III	–	–
IV	–	+

NOTE

How many degrees are there in $\frac{3(\pi)}{4}$ radians?

Because 2π radians = 360°, this makes 1(π) radian = 180°.

Solution:

$$1\pi \text{ radian} = 180°$$

$$\frac{3\pi}{4} = \frac{3\pi}{4} \times \frac{180°}{\pi} = 135°$$

How many radians are there in 270°?

Solution:

$$1\pi \text{ radian} = 180°$$

$$270° \times \frac{\pi}{180°} = \frac{3\pi}{2}$$

6.2.3 Graphing Trig Functions

Looking at the unit circle, it is very apparent that the trigonometric functions are **periodic**. This means that they continue to repeat the same cycle infinitely. After you go once around the circle, a full 360°, you end up right back at the beginning and begin to cycle through again.

A. Sine

As you can see from the table in 6.2.2, the sine function increases for the first 90°. For the next 90° it decreases while staying positive, then it continues to decrease into the negatives, and finally for the last 90°, it increases from −1 back to 0. From this information, we can picture the general shape of the graph, and we know that the period of the function is a full 360° or 2π radians.

The graph itself looks like this:

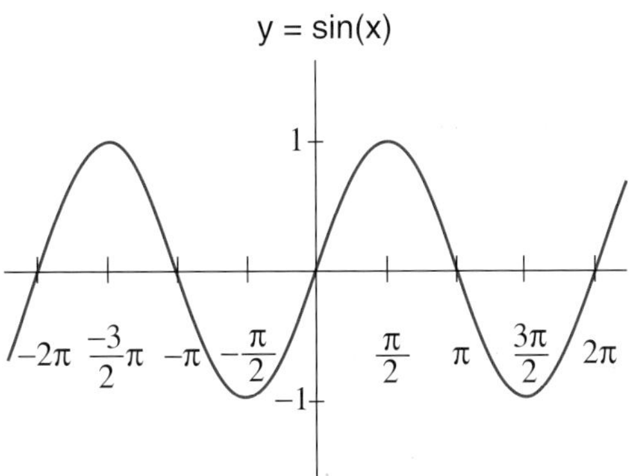

As you can see in the graph, the sine function reaches a maximum at $\frac{\pi}{2} + 2\pi \times n$, has an x-intercept at $\pi \times n$, and a minimum at $\frac{3\pi}{2} + 2\pi \times n$ where n is any integer.

B. Cosine

The cosine function is identical to the sine function, except that it is shifted along the x-axis by half a period. So rather than starting at 0 and increasing, it starts at one and decreases. The period is still 2π radians.

The graph looks like this:

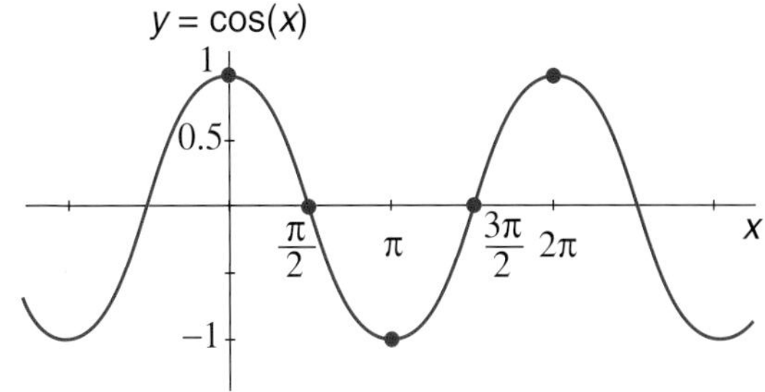

Just like with the sine function, you can see where the maxima, minima, and intercepts of the cosine function are from the graph. It reaches a maximum at $2\pi \times n$, an x-intercept at $\frac{\pi}{2} + \pi \times n$, and a minimum at $2\pi \times n + \pi \times n$ where n is any integer.

C. Tangent

The graph of the tangent function differs from sine and cosine graphs in a few important ways. First of all, the tangent function repeats itself every π radian instead of every 2π. So it is π-periodic rather than 2π-periodic. Also, it has vertical **asymptotes**, vertical lines that the function approaches but never crosses, at $(n)\left(\frac{\pi}{2}\right)$ for every odd integer n. The value of the tangent goes infinity as it approaches an asymptote from left to right; and negative infinity as it approaches from right to left.

Remember, the tangent function is the ratio of the sine function to the cosine function, so the asymptotes occur when the cosine of an angle is equal to zero, where $\cos(x) = 0$, because division by zero is undefined. 0/0 is never possible for the tangent function, so it is irrelevant.

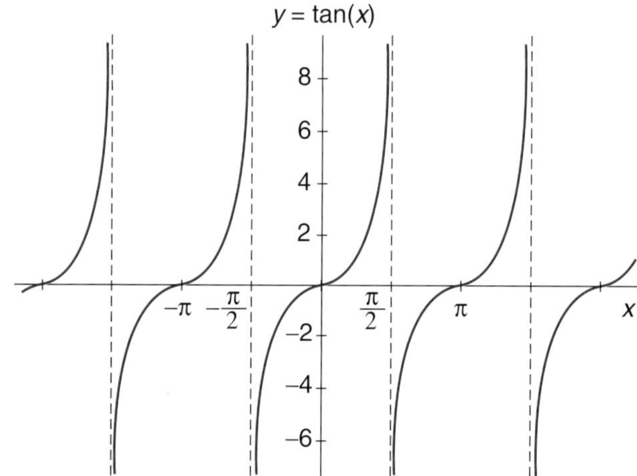

6.3 Trigonometric Problems

6.3.1 Inverse Trig Functions

We have discussed the formulas for finding the value of trigonometric functions for different angles, but how can you find the value of an angle if all you know is the value of one of the functions? This is where the inverse trigonometric functions come into play.

The **inverse** of a trigonometric function takes an input value x and outputs an angle. The value of the inverse trigonometric function of x is equal to the angle. To represent an inverse function, we write -1 in superscript like we would an exponent. But remember, this is not actually an exponent.

Inverse sine is represented as $\sin^{-1}$ and it is defined as such:

$$\sin(\sin^{-1}(x)) = x$$

So, $\sin(\theta) = x$ and $\sin^{-1}(x) = \theta$.

Now that we have inverse functions in our toolbox, we can begin to solve algebraic problems that contain trigonometric functions.

Solve the following equation for x.

$$\pi - \tan 2x = \left(\frac{4}{3}\right)\pi$$

$$\Rightarrow -\tan 2x = \left(\frac{1}{3}\right)\pi$$

$$\Rightarrow \tan 2x = \frac{-\pi}{3}$$

$$\Rightarrow 2x = \tan^{-1}\left(\frac{-\pi}{3}\right)$$

We did not list values for tangent in the tables in Section 6.2.2, but we can use the sine and cosine values to find them. Remember that tan = sin/cos. We can use the values for $\frac{\pi}{3}$ in quadrant IV:

$$\Rightarrow 2x = \frac{-\left(\frac{\sqrt{3}}{2}\right)}{\frac{1}{2}}$$

$$\Rightarrow 2x = -\sqrt{3}$$

$$\Rightarrow x = -\frac{\sqrt{3}}{2}$$

6.3.2 Trigonometric Identities

There are a few other identities that can be extremely useful in the manipulation of equations involving trigonometric functions. If you encounter such an equation and it seems like it would be difficult to solve using only inverses, you should try to apply these identities. You may have to do some algebraic work, though, before you can apply them.

(i) $\sin^2\theta + \cos^2\theta = 1$

This identity follows directly from the Pythagorean Theorem. Since the sine and cosine compose the legs of a right triangle and the hypotenuse has length 1, this identity always holds.

(ii) $\tan^2\theta + 1 = \sec^2\theta$

(iii) $\cot^2\theta + 1 = \csc^2\theta$

(iv) $\sin(2\theta) = 2\sin\theta\cos\theta$

(v) $\cos(2\theta) = 1 - 2\sin^2\theta$

(vi) $\tan(2\theta) = \dfrac{2\tan\theta}{1-\tan^2\theta}$

EXAMPLE

Simplify the following equation:

$$\sin^2(x) + \sin^2(x) \times \cos^2(x) = \sec^2(x)$$

Since the only functions on the left side at this point are sines and cosines, let's factor out a $\sin^2(x)$ and then try to use identity (i).

$$\sin^2(x)[\sin^2(x) + \cos^2(x)] = \sec^2(x)$$
$$\sin^2(x) \times 1 = \sec^2(x)$$

Now let's replace $\sec^2(x)$ using identity (ii).

$$\sin^2(x) = \tan^2(x) + 1$$

We can even simplify this further using the equation for tangent (= sin/cos) and then multiply each side by $\cos^2(x)$.

$$\sin^2(x) = \frac{\sin^2(x)}{\cos^2(x)} + 1$$

$$\sin^2(x)\cos^2(x) = \left(\frac{\sin^2(x)}{\cos^2(x)} + 1\right)\cos^2(x)$$

$$\sin^2(x)\cos^2(x) = \cos^2(x) + \sin^2(x)$$

By using identity (i) again, we have

$$\sin^2(x)\cos^2(x) = 1$$

6.3.3 The Pythagorean Theorem

The Pythagorean Theorem is fundamental to trigonometry.

If a problem requires you to set up an equation involving trigonometric functions, whether it is from an arbitrary right triangle or the unit circle, you will most likely need to use the Pythagorean Theorem. Remember, it is the primary relationship we have in relating the lengths of sides in a right triangle, so now we can relate side length to trigonometric functions.

6.4 Polar Coordinates

So far, we have only discussed graphs using Cartesian coordinates. As we have seen, the Cartesian system makes it easy to work with straight lines, but this does not hold true for all types of curves.

There is another important two-dimensional system that uses what are known as **polar coordinates**. Instead of plotting a point using the two legs of a right triangle (the x and y coordinates in the Cartesian system), polar coordinates use the hypotenuse of the triangle (r) and the angle from the x-axis (θ). Instead of two distance components, polar coordinates use one radial distance component (the distance from the origin) and an angle component. A point is written as the ordered pair (r, θ).

Conversions: Sometimes, it is necessary to convert points between polar and Cartesian coordinates. Here are the identities to use:

(i) $r^2 = x^2 + y^2$

(ii) $x = r \times \cos(\theta)$

(iii) $y = r \times \sin(\theta)$

EXAMPLE

Convert the Cartesian point (3,4) to polar coordinates.

Before we can find θ we need to find the value for r using (i).

$$r^2 = 3^2 + 4^2$$
$$\Rightarrow r^2 = 25$$
$$\Rightarrow r = 5$$

Now we can find θ using either (ii) or (iii).

$$3 = 5 \times \cos(\theta)$$
$$\Rightarrow 3/5 = \cos(\theta)$$
$$\Rightarrow \theta = \cos^{-1}(3/5)$$
$$\Rightarrow \theta \approx 53^\circ$$

Combining this information, we see that the Cartesian point (3,4) is the point (5, 53°) in polar coordinates.

EXAMPLE

Convert $x^2 + y^2 = 4$ to polar coordinates and graph.

This conversion happens to be extremely simple. All we need to do is apply (i) directly.

$$\Rightarrow r^2 = 4$$
$$\Rightarrow r = 2$$

Notice that in this equation, r does not depend on θ. It contains simply all points that are 2 units away from the origin.

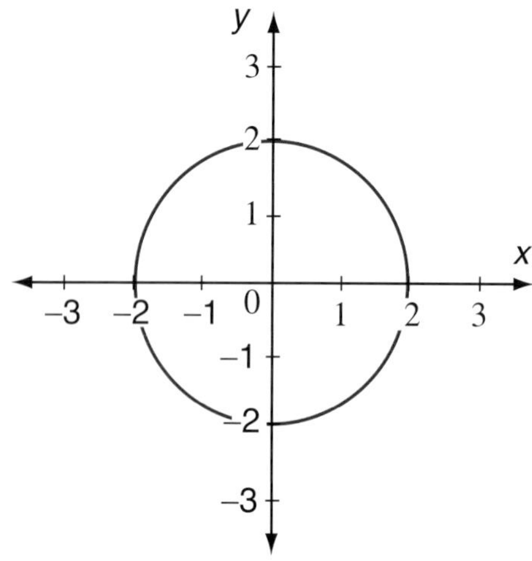

In polar coordinates, a circle of radius x centered at the origin results when $r = x$ for any constant x.

6.5 Additional Helpful Formulas

Sum or Difference of Two Angles

For angles α and β, the following sum and difference identities may be applied:

1. $\sin(\alpha + \beta) = \sin\alpha\cos\beta + \cos\alpha\sin\beta$

2. $\sin(\alpha - \beta) = \sin\alpha\cos\beta - \cos\alpha\sin\beta$

3. $\cos(\alpha + \beta) = \cos\alpha\cos\beta - \sin\alpha\sin\beta$

4. $\cos(\alpha - \beta) = \cos\alpha\cos\beta + \sin\alpha\sin\beta$

5. $\tan(\alpha+\beta) = \dfrac{\tan\alpha + \tan\beta}{1 - \tan\alpha\tan\beta}$

6. $\tan(\alpha-\beta) = \dfrac{\tan\alpha - \tan\beta}{1 + \tan\alpha\tan\beta}$

Cofunction Identities

$$\sin\left(\frac{\pi}{2}-\theta\right)=\cos\theta \qquad \cos\left(\frac{\pi}{2}-\theta\right)=\sin\theta$$

$$\tan\left(\frac{\pi}{2}-\theta\right)=\cot\theta \qquad \cot\left(\frac{\pi}{2}-\theta\right)=\tan\theta$$

$$\sec\left(\frac{\pi}{2}-\theta\right)=\csc\theta \qquad \csc\left(\frac{\pi}{2}-\theta\right)=\sec\theta$$

Odd-Even Identities

For angle θ at which the functions are defined:

1. $\sin(-\theta) = -\sin(\theta)$
2. $\cos(-\theta) = \cos(\theta)$
3. $\tan(-\theta) = -\tan(\theta)$
4. $\cot(-\theta) = -\cot(\theta)$
5. $\sec(-\theta) = \sec(\theta)$
6. $\csc(-\theta) = -\csc(\theta)$

GOLD STANDARD WARM-UP EXERCISES

CHAPTER 6: Trigonometry

1. In a right triangle ABC with right angle at C, hypotenuse AB = 7 cm and side AC = 2 cm, approximately what is the measure of the angle at A?

   A. 17°
   B. 1°
   C. 0.5°
   D. 73°
   E. 16°

2. What percentage of the unit circle is represented by the angle $8\pi/5$?

   A. 1.6%
   B. 80%
   C. 0.25%
   D. 160%
   E. 502%

3. Which of the following is the value of $-\cos(\pi/2)$?

   A. 0
   B. −1
   C. 1
   D. $1/\sqrt{2}$
   E. $\sqrt{2}$

4. The tangent of one of the acute angles in a right triangle is 3/2. If the leg opposite this angle has a length of 12, what is the length of the hypotenuse?

   A. 8
   B. $6\sqrt{13}$
   C. $4\sqrt{13}$
   D. 18
   E. $3\sqrt{13}$

5. $\cos(x) - \sin(x) = 0$, $x = ?$

   A. 45°
   B. 30°
   C. 180°
   D. 60°
   E. 270°

6. If the secant of an angle is 5/4, what is the tangent of the angle?

   A. 9/16
   B. 1/2
   C. 4/5
   D. 3/4
   E. $\sqrt{41}/25$

7. The value of $\cos(\pi/6)$ equals the value of:

   A. $\sin(\pi/2)$

   B. $\sin(\pi/4)$

   C. $\sin(\pi)$

   D. $\sin(\pi/6)$

   E. $\sin(\pi/3)$

8. The sine of an angle is negative, and the tangent of the same angle is positive. In which quadrant does the angle lie?

   A. First

   B. Second

   C. Third

   D. Fourth

   E. Any

GS ANSWER KEY

CHAPTER 6

		Cross-Reference			*Cross-Reference*
1.	D	QR 6.3, 6.3.1	5.	A	QR 6.3, 6.3.2
2.	B	QR 6.2, 6.2.1	6.	D	QR 6.3, 6.3.2
3.	A	QR 6.5	7.	E	QR 6.2, 6.2.3
4.	C	QR 6.1, 6.1.3, 6.3, 6.3.3	8.	C	QR 6.2, 6.2.1

* Explanations can be found at the back of the book.

Go online to DAT-prep.com for additional chapter review Q&A and forum.

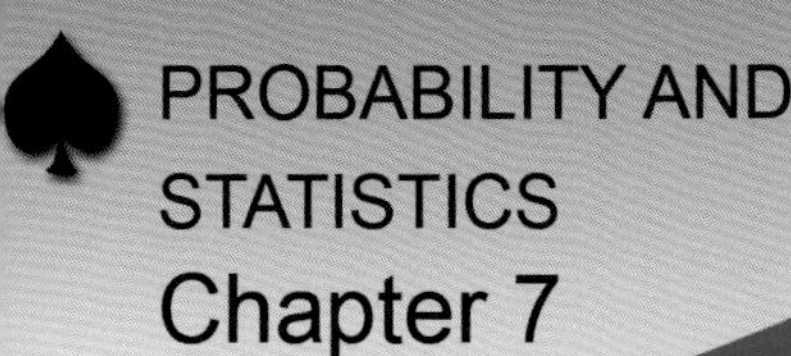

PROBABILITY AND STATISTICS
Chapter 7

Memorize

* Formula for Average
* Formula for Probability

Understand

* Determining Probabilities
* Combining Probabilities of Multiple Events
* Mode, Median, Variance, Standard Deviation and its Corresponding Graph
* Correlation Coefficient
* Permutations and Combinations

Importance

3 to 5 out of the 40 QR

questions on the DAT are based on content from this chapter (in our estimation).

* This will change in 2015.

DAT-Prep.com

Introduction

Probability and statistics are relatively minor subjects on the Quantitative Reasoning test, but they can be tricky. Please do note that effective 2015, more of these items will be given on the DAT.

This section will help you keep things straight such as when to multiply and when to add probabilities – simple questions that can often be the most confusing.

Additional Resources

Free Online Forum

7.1 Probability

7.1.1 What is Probability?

Probability is a measure of the likelihood that something will happen.

In mathematics, probability is represented as a ratio of two numbers. The second number - the denominator - corresponds to the total number of possible outcomes the situation can have. The first number - the numerator - corresponds to the number of ways the particular outcome in question can occur.

$$\text{Probability} = \frac{(\text{number of ways the outcome can occur})}{(\text{number of possible outcomes})}$$

Let's look at a simple example.

Let's consider the flipping of a coin. Of course, we know that there are only two possible outcomes of a coin flip, heads or tails. So the total number of outcomes is 2, which will be our denominator.

Say we want to find the probability that a flipped coin will be heads. There is only one way this outcome can come about, so the numerator will be 1. Therefore, the probability of flipping heads is 1 in 2:

$$\text{Probability of Heads} = \frac{1}{2}$$

It is important to note that the quantity in the numerator of a probability ratio is a subset of the quantity in the denominator. The number of ways an outcome can occur is always less than or equal to the total number of outcomes. This means that a probability will never be more than 1, since 1 would mean the outcome is the *only* possibility. Also, the sum of the probabilities of all possible outcomes will always be 1.

Let's look at a slightly more complicated example.

Say you have a typical six-sided die with the sides labeled 1 through 6. If you roll the die once, what is the probability that the number will not be divisible by 3?

Let's begin by finding the total number of outcomes. Be careful here. The only outcomes we wish to determine the probability of are rolls of numbers divisible by 3, but the total number of possible outcomes is not affected by this restriction. There are still 6 in total, one for each number it is possible to roll.

Now we want to know how many ways out of these 6 we can roll a number that is not divisible by 3. Well, the only two numbers that are divisible by 3 that are possibilities are 3 and 6. So 1, 2, 4, and 5 are not. This means that there are 4 ways for the outcome to occur.

$$\text{Probability} = \frac{4}{6}$$

Reducing fractions is usually fine when working with probability; just know that if you do, the numerator and denominator will not necessarily correspond to the number of possibilities anymore.

$$\text{Probability} = \frac{2}{3}$$

The simplest way to complicate a probability problem is to allow for multiple correct outcomes. To find the total probability, simply add the individual probabilities for each correct outcome. For the above example, the total probability is actually the sum of the probabilities of rolling 1, 2, 4, and 5.

7.1.2 Combining Probabilities

What if you are asked to find the probability that multiple events will occur?

The solution to such a problem will still be a ratio in which the numbers represent the same quantities as before. The new difficulty is figuring out how many different outcome possibilities there are. Luckily, there is an easy way to calculate this. All you have to do is find the probability of each individual event and then multiply them together.

Why does this work? Think about it this way: For each possible outcome of the first event, there is still every possible outcome for the second. So the total number of possibilities will be the number of outcomes in the first times the number of outcomes in the second.

EXAMPLE

Let's go back to the flipping coin! If you flip it twice, what is the probability that the first flip will turn up heads and the second tails?

When dealing with multiple events, always focus on one event at a time before combining. So start with the first flip. We know that the probability it will be heads is ½. Now for the second flip, the probability it will be tails is also ½.

Now to find the probability that both of the events will occur, we multiply the individual probabilities:

$$\text{Probability} = \frac{1}{2} \times \frac{1}{2}$$
$$= \frac{1}{4}$$

Probability questions will not always be as clear-cut as this. Let's look at another coin flip example.

EXAMPLE

If you flip a coin twice, what is the probability that it will come up heads exactly one time?

This question seems almost identical to the previous example, but be careful! The difference is that the phrasing of this question does not specify particular outcomes for the individual events.

Let's solve this in two ways:

(i) Let's combine both events into one. To find the total number of possible outcomes, multiply the totals of each event, so there are $2 \times 2 = 4$ possibilities. Now count the number of ways we can flip heads once. Well, we could have heads on the first flip and tails on the second, so that is 1, or we could have tails then heads, so that is 2. Therefore, the probability of flipping heads exactly once is 2 to 4.

$$\text{Probability} = \frac{2}{4}$$

(ii) Now let's treat the events separately. Ask yourself: What are the odds that an outcome of the first event will be compatible with flipping heads once? The answer is $\frac{2}{2}$ since we can still achieve the overall desired outcome with the second flip no matter what the first flip is.

Now what are the odds that an outcome of the second event will be compatible with flipping heads once? Since you already have a first flip determined, there is only one outcome for the second flip that will give the desired result. If the first flip was heads we need a tails flip, and if the first flip was tails we need a heads flip. So the odds for the second flip are ½ .

$$\text{Probability} = \frac{2}{2} \times \frac{1}{2}$$
$$= \frac{2}{4}$$

There are all kinds of confusing ways probability problems can be written. You have to be extra careful to break them down and determine exactly what is being asked because the test writers love to try and trick you. Double and triple-check that you have the setup right for probability problems because it is so easy to accidentally overlook something.

NOTE

When you want to know the probability of event A or B, the probabilities must be added. If you want to know the probability of events A and B, the probabilities must be multiplied.

7.2 Statistics

7.2.1 Averages

When given a collection of numbers, the **average** is the sum of the numbers divided by the total number of numbers.

$$\text{Average} = \frac{(\text{sum of numbers})}{(\text{number of numbers})}$$

EXAMPLE

What is the average of the set {4, 7, 6, 7}?

Add up the numbers and, since there are 4 of them, divide by 4.

$$\text{Average} = \frac{(4+7+6+7)}{4} = \frac{24}{4} = 6$$

The average may or may not actually appear in the set of numbers, but it is a common way to think of the typical value for the set.

7.2.2 Mode, Median, Mean

Here are a few other statistics terms you should know:

The **mode** of a set of values is the number that appears the most times. Mode can be bimodal or multimodal. Simply stated, bimodal means that two numbers are repeated the most while multimodal indicates two or more numbers are repeated the most.

The **median** of a set of values is the number that appears exactly in the center of the distribution. This means there are an equal number of values greater than and less than the median.

Arithmetic mean is just another name for the average of a set of numbers. The terms are interchangeable.

EXAMPLE

Find the mode, median, and mean of the following set: {3, 5, 11, 3, 8}.

Let's begin with the mode. All we need

to do is see which value or values repeat the most times. In this case, the only one that repeats is 3.

Mode = 3

To find the median we always need to first arrange the set in numerical order.

{3, 3, 5, 8, 11}

Now the median is whichever number lies in the exact center.

Median = 5

Since the mean is the same as the average, we add the values and divide by 5.

$$\text{Mean} = \frac{(3+3+5+8+11)}{5} = \frac{30}{5} = 6$$

NOTE

If a set has an even number of values, there will be no value exactly in the center. In this case, the median is the average of the two values that straddle the center.

Example

Given: 3, 4, 5, 6, 6, 8, 9, 10, 10, 12

The median is the average of the two middle data: $\frac{(6+8)}{2} = 7$

7.3 More Tools for Probability and Statistics

7.3.1 The Correlation Coefficient

The correlation coefficient r indicates whether two sets of data are associated or *correlated*. The value of r ranges from -1.0 to 1.0. The larger the absolute value of r, the stronger the association. Given two sets of data X and Y, a positive value for r indicates that as X increases, Y increases. A negative value for r indicates that as X increases, Y decreases.

Imagine that the weight (X) and height (Y) of everyone in the entire country was determined. There would be a strong positive correlation between a person's weight and their height. In general, as weight increases, height increases (*in a population*). However, the correlation would not be perfect (i.e. $r < 1.0$). After all, there would be some people who are very tall but very thin, and others who would be very short but overweight. We might find that $r = 0.7$. This would suggest there is a strong positive association between weight and height, but it is not a perfect association.

If two sets of data are correlated, does that mean that one *causes* the other? Not necessarily; simply because weight and height are correlated does not mean that if you gained weight you will necessarily gain height! Thus association does not imply causality.

Note that a correlation greater than 0.8 is generally described as strong, whereas a correlation that is less than 0.5 is generally described as weak. However, the interpretation and use of these values can vary based upon the "type" of data being examined. For example, a study based on chemical or biological data may require a stronger correlation than a study using social science data.

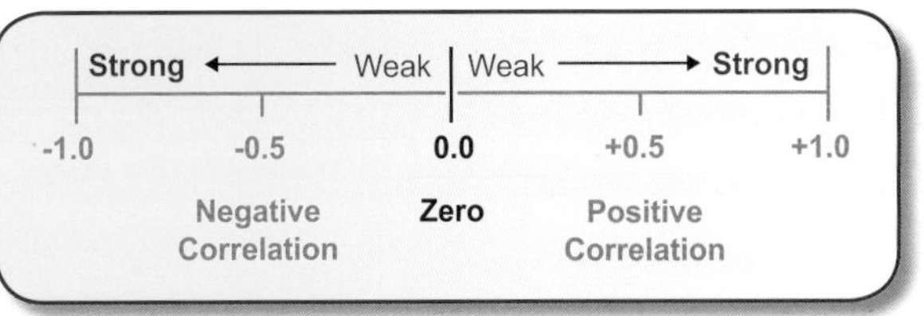

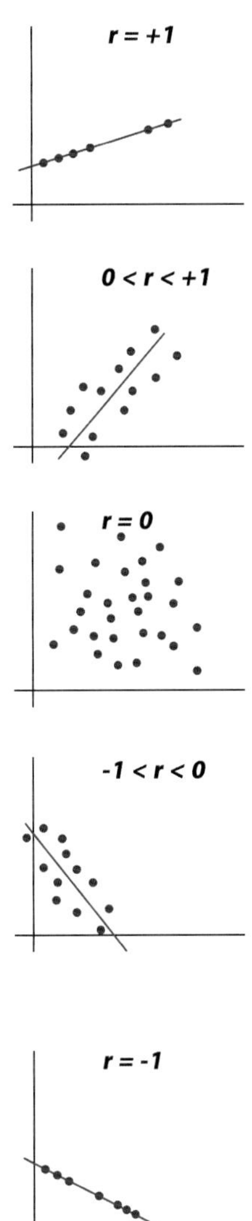

Varying values of the correlation coefficient (r) based on data plotted for two variables (= scatter diagrams). In red is the line of "best fit" (= *regression line;* Appendix A.1.3).

7.3.2 The Standard Deviation

When given a set of data, it is often useful to know the average value, *the mean*, and the *range* of values. As previously discussed, the mean is simply the sum of the data values divided by the number of data values. The range is the numerical difference between the largest value and the smallest value.

Another useful measurement is the *standard deviation*. The standard deviation indicates the dispersion of values around the mean. Given a bell-shaped distribution of data (i.e., the height and weight of a population, the GPA of undergraduate students, etc.), each standard deviation (SD) includes a given percentage of data. For example, the mean +/– 1 SD includes approximately 68% of the data values, the mean +/– 2 SD includes 95% of the data values, and the mean +/– 3 SD includes 99.7% of the data values.

For example, imagine that you read that the mean GPA required for admission to Belcurve University's Dental School is 3.5 with a standard deviation of 0.2 (SD = 0.2). Thus approximately 68% of the students admitted have a GPA of 3.5 +/– 0.2, which means between 3.3 and 3.7. We can also conclude that approximately 95% of the students admitted have a GPA of 3.5 +/– 2(0.2), which means between 3.1 and 3.9. Therefore the standard deviation becomes a useful measure of the dispersion of values around the mean 3.5.

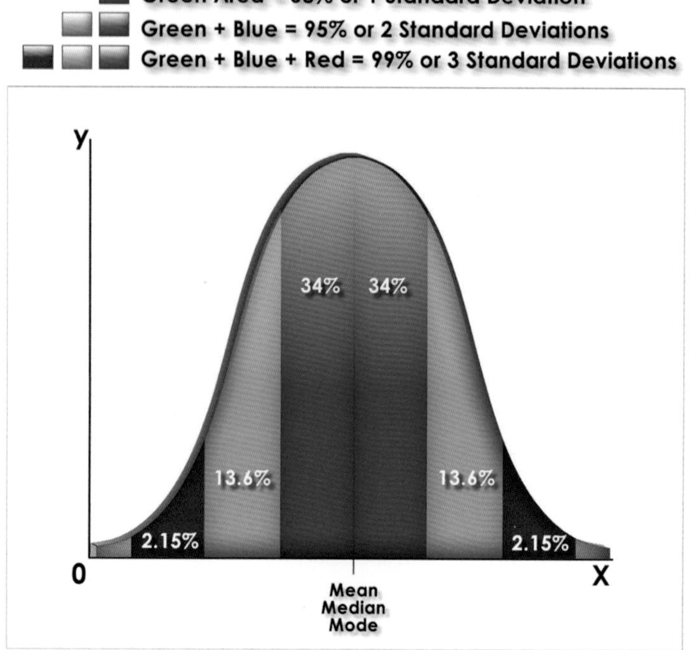

Figure 7.1: The Normal Curve (also referred to as: the Normal Distribution Curve).

7.3.3 Variance

Variance is another measure of how far a set of numbers is spread out or, in other words, how far numbers are from the mean. Thus variance is calculated as the average of the squared differences from the mean.

There are three steps to calculate the variance:

1. Determine the mean (the simple average of all the numbers)
2. For each number: subtract the mean and square the result (the squared difference)
3. Determine the average of those squared differences

The variance is also defined as the square of the standard deviation. Thus unlike standard deviation, the variance has units that are the square of the units of the variable itself. For example, a variable measured in meters will have a variance measured in meters squared. Note: for those of you aiming for a perfect QR score, the equations for standard deviation and variance can be found at the end of this chapter.

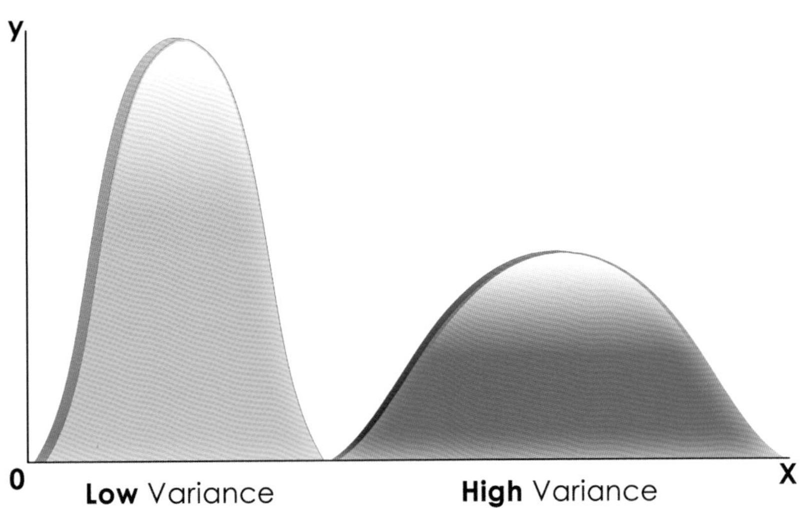

Figure 7.2: Variance.

7.3.4 Equations for Standard Deviation and Variance

Standard deviation and variance problems are common for DAT QR; however, because of time constraints, it is not likely that you would need to calculate the standard deviation or variance using the formulas in this section. However, if you are aiming for a perfect score then it is prudent to have all the tools at your disposal.

First, let's revisit the mean or average of a data set.

In statistics, a sample is a subset of a population. Typically, the population is very large, making an analysis of all the values in the population impractical or impossible. The sample is a subset of manageable size. Samples are collected and statistics are calculated so one can make inferences or extrapolations from the sample to the population.

For any data set, the mean can be calculated:

Sample Mean	Population Mean
$\bar{X} = \frac{\sum x}{n}$	$\mu = \frac{\sum x}{N}$

$\sum$ = the sum of

$\sum x$ = the sum of all data values

n = the number of data items in the sample

N = the number of data items in the population

The standard deviation (SD) - a measure of the dispersion of a set of data from its mean - is calculated using the following formula:

Sample SD	Population SD
$s = \sqrt{\frac{\sum (x - \bar{X})^2}{n-1}}$	$\sigma = \sqrt{\frac{\sum (x - \mu)^2}{N}}$

x = each value in the sample or population

n - 1 = "degrees of freedom" and is used to compensate for the fact that the more accurate population mean (μ) is usually unknown.

HYPOTHETICAL EXAMPLE

The number of times students completed the DAT before obtaining a QR score of 25 or higher: 3, 2, 4, 1, 4, 4. Find the standard deviation and variance of the data set.

Step 1: Calculate the mean and deviation of this small data set. Note that because n = 6, this is very likely a subset of all students who scored 25 or higher in QR, we regard this as a sample size and we use the equations accordingly.

x	$\bar{X}$	$(x-\bar{X})$	$(x-\bar{X})^2$
3	3	0	0
2	3	-1	1
4	3	1	1
1	3	-2	4
4	3	1	1
4	3	1	1

Step 2: Using the deviation, calculate the standard deviation by squaring both sides of the relevant equation:

$$s^2 = \frac{(0+1+1+4+1+1)}{(6-1)} = \frac{8}{5}$$

$$= 1.6$$

Since $s^2 = 1.6$, the standard deviation of the sample $s = 1.265$. And the variance of the sample $(= s^2) = 1.6$.

The Coefficient of Variation

A standard deviation of 1.265 with a mean of 3, as we calculated, is much different than a standard deviation of 1.265 with a mean of 20. By calculating how the standard deviation relates to the mean (= coefficient of variation = CV), we can have a standard way of determining the relevance of the standard deviation and what it suggests about the sample. The closer the CV is to 0, the greater the uniformity of the data. The closer the CV is to 1, the greater the variability of the data.

$$CV = \frac{s}{\bar{X}}$$

Using our example of a standard deviation of 1.265 and a mean of 3, you will see that the coefficient of variation is rather large, indicating that the data has a great deal of variability with respect to the mean and there is no general consensus among the sample.

$$CV = \frac{s}{\bar{X}} = \frac{(1.265)}{(3)} = 0.42$$

Using the example of a standard deviation of 1.265 and a mean of 20, we see that the coefficient of variation is rather small, indicating that the data has a greater deal of uniformity with respect to the mean and there is a general consensus among the sample.

$$CV = \frac{s}{\bar{X}} = \frac{(1.265)}{(20)} = 0.06$$

7.3.5 Simple Probability Revisited

Let's apply a formula to simple probability. If a phenomenon or experiment has n equally likely outcomes, s of which are called successes, then the probability P of success is given by $P = \frac{s}{n}$.

EXAMPLE

- if "heads" in a coin toss is considered a success, then

  $P(\text{success}) = \frac{1}{2}$;

- if a card is drawn from a deck and diamonds are considered successes, then

  $P(\text{success}) = \frac{13}{52}$. It follows that $P(\text{success}) = 1 - P(\text{failure})$.

7.3.6 Permutations

Suppose n is a positive integer. The symbol $n!$, read *n-factorial*, is defined as follows:

$$n! = (n)(n-1)(n-2)\ldots(3)(2)(1)$$

By definition $0! = 1$.

A permutation of a set is an *ordered* arrangement of the elements in that set. The number of permutations of n objects is $n!$. For example, using 5 different amino acids, the number of possible permutations creating different outcomes (*oligopeptides*) is: $5! = (5)(4)(3)(2)(1) = 120$.

Suppose you have 7 books and place 3 on a shelf. The first slot can be filled by any of 7 choices, the second slot can be filled by one less or 6 choices, and again there is one less choice for the third slot leaving 5 books from which to choose. The total number of ways to fill the 3 slots on the shelf is thus $(7)(6)(5) = 210$.

The general rule is that the number of permutations of n things taken r at a time is n_r, where $n_r = n!/(n-r)!$. In the preceding example, $n = 7$ and $r = 3$ thus,

$$\begin{aligned} n_r &= 7!/(7-3)! \\ &= (7)(6)(5)(4)(3)(2)(1)/(4)(3)(2)(1) \\ &= (7)(6)(5)(4!)/(4!) \\ &= (7)(6)(5) = 210 \end{aligned}$$

NOTE

Permutations may be simplified if it is found in both the numerator and the denominator.

In the given example, 4! could be canceled out, leaving you with $(7)(6)(5) = 210$. This will save you time on the DAT and you will not have to waste too much effort expanding a permutation.

For the DAT, it is very important to pay

attention to the wording of the problem and identify what is known about the problem. In this example, we know that there are 7 books and as each is placed on the shelf, there is 1 less book to choose from. Since the outcome of the first depends on the outcome of the second, these events are considered dependent. This is called sampling without replacement.

In the case where the object is being put back into your sample after each event, the amount of possible outcomes does not change from one event to another. If the outcome of the first event does not affect the outcome of the second, the two events are independent of each other. This is called sampling with replacement.

7.3.7 Combinations

Permutations are important when the *order* of selection matters (e.g., *simply by changing the order of the amino acids, the activity of the oligopeptide or the* <u>*outcome*</u> *changes*). Combinations are important when the order of selection does not matter (e.g., *as long as there is a red book, a green book, and a blue book on the shelf, the order does not matter*).

Since the order does not matter, there are fewer combinations than permutations. In fact, the combination C_r is given by:

$$C_r = \frac{n_r}{r!} = \frac{n!}{\left[r!(n-r)!\right]}$$

For example, once again consider a total of 7 books where there are only 3 slots on the shelf. This time you are told that the order the books appear on the shelf is not relevant. The number of different combinations is therefore

$$C_r = \frac{n_r}{r!} = \frac{n!}{\left[r!(n-r)!\right]} = \frac{7!}{\left[3!(7-3)!\right]}$$

$$= \frac{210}{3!} = \frac{210}{6} = 35$$

7.3.8 Probability Tree

The probability tree may be used as another means to solve probability of independent and dependent events. It is a very useful visual that will show all possible events. Each branch represents a possible outcome and its probability. Depending on what the question is asking for, the probabilities of each event may be added or multiplied to determine the combined probability of events.

Suppose that you were observing the probability of choosing 2 balls from a basket that contained 8 red and 4 white balls. What is the probability of picking 2 red balls without replacement?

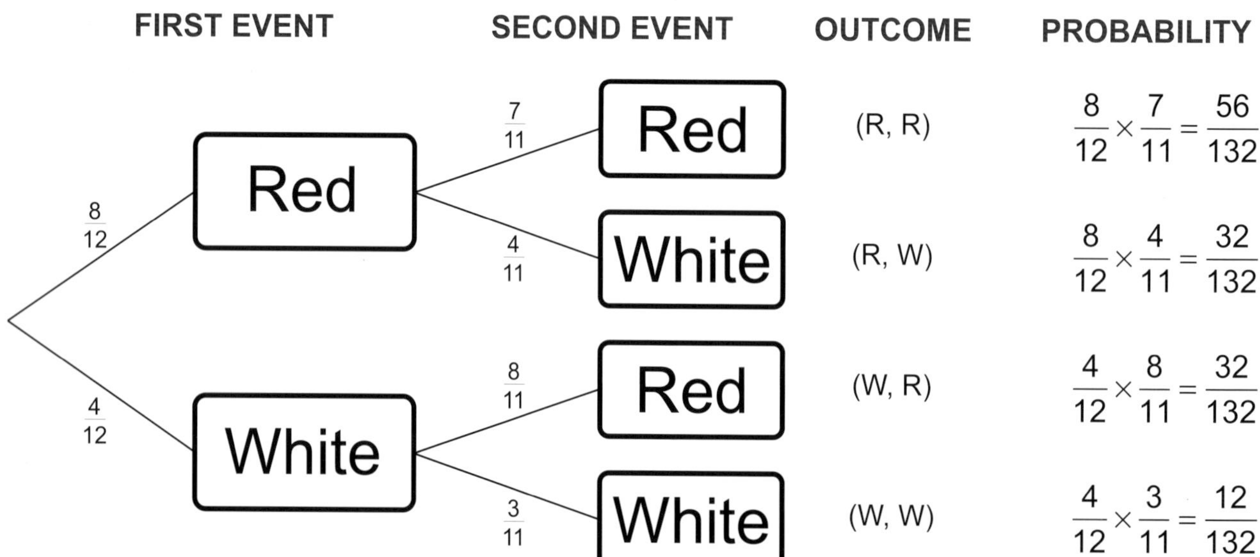

Thus the probability of picking 2 red balls without replacement (R, R) is: $\frac{8}{12} \times \frac{7}{11} = \frac{56}{132} = \frac{14}{33}$

If the question had asked the probability of having at least 1 white ball without replacement, the answer would be $\frac{8}{12} \times \frac{4}{11} + \frac{4}{12} \times \frac{8}{11} + \frac{4}{12} \times \frac{3}{11} = \frac{76}{132} = \frac{19}{33}$. Notice that this answer represents all outcomes NOT given by (R, R) and so it is numerically 1 - P(R, R).

GOLD STANDARD WARM-UP EXERCISES

CHAPTER 7: Probability and Statistics

1. A jar contains 4 red marbles and 6 blue marbles. What is the probability that a marble chosen at random will be red?

   A. 4/6
   B. 4/10
   C. 2/6
   D. 6/10
   E. 2/4

2. In how many different ways can six different objects be arranged in a line?

   A. 120
   B. 30
   C. 720
   D. 36
   E. 6

3. A box contains 6 yellow balls and 4 green balls. Two balls are chosen at random without replacement. What is the probability that the first ball is yellow and the second ball is green?

   A. 5/12
   B. 1/10
   C. 6/25
   D. 1
   E. 4/15

4. An English teacher wants to prepare a class reading list that includes 1 philosophy book, 1 work of historical fiction, and 1 biography. She has 3 philosophy books, 2 works of historical fiction, and 4 biographies to choose from. How many different combinations of books can she put together for her list?

   A. 32
   B. 288
   C. 28
   D. 9
   E. 24

5. An unemployment office's survey shows that the distribution of the local residents' annual income is a bell curve. 2,516 residents are within one standard deviation of the local average annual income. How many residents were in the survey's sample?

   A. 3,700
   B. 2,648
   C. 2,524
   D. 2,523
   E. 7,862

6. The average time it takes 3 students to complete a test is 35 minutes. If 1 student takes 41 minutes to complete the test and another takes 37 minutes, how many minutes does the third student take to complete the test?

   A. 4
   B. 38
   C. 27
   D. 39
   E. 43

7. A small library receives a shipment of gray books, blue books, black books, and brown books. If the librarian decides to shelve all the books of one color on Monday, all of the books of another color on Tuesday, and the rest of the books on Wednesday, in how many different ways can the book shelving be completed?

   A. 3
   B. 4
   C. 8
   D. 12
   E. 24

8. A list of four integers has the following properties: the range is equal to 14, the median is equal to 7, and the mean is equal to 8. One of the numbers is 9. What are the other three numbers?

   A. 1, 7, 15
   B. 2, 5, 16
   C. −11, 3, 7
   D. 0, 0, 23
   E. −12, 2, 7

9. When you roll a die, what is the probability to first get a 3 and then a 1 or a 2?

   A. 1/6
   B. 1/8
   C. 1/32
   D. 1/16
   E. 1/18

GS ANSWER KEY

Chapter 7

		Cross-Reference			Cross-Reference
1.	B	QR 7.1.1	6.	C	QR 7.2, 7.2.1
2.	C	QR 7.3.4	7.	D	QR 7.3.5
3.	E	QR 7.1, 7.1.2	8.	B	QR 7.2
4.	E	QR 7.3, 7.3.5	9.	E	QR 7.1, 7.1.2
5.	A	QR 7.3.2			

* Explanations can be found at the back of the book.

Go online to DAT-prep.com for additional chapter review Q&A and forum.

APPENDIX

CHAPTER 7: Probability and Statistics

Advanced DAT-30 Passage: ANOVA, Scheffe Test and Chi-Square

NOTE

This section is not for all students. This content is "low yield" meaning that it takes a lot of energy to review it properly but the questions pop up on the DAT rarely. If you have the time and the will to aim for a perfect score, this additional statistics review is followed by questions so that the material can be learned in an interactive way. As per usual, explanations are at the back of the book. You should decide if you wish to read these sections based on the requirements of the dental program(s) you wish to attend. If you are preparing for the 2015 DAT or beyond, we suggest that you review this section and go online to dat-prep.com for further suggested reading.

Student's *t*-test and ANOVA

The *t*-test (= Student's t-test) and analysis of variance (= ANOVA) are statistical procedures that assume normal distributions (= *parametric*) and make use of the mean and variance to determine the significance of the differences of the means of two or more groups of values.

The *t*-test uses the mean, the variance and a "Table of Critical Values" for the "*t*" distribution. The *t*-test is used to determine the significance of the difference between the means of two groups based on a standard that no more than 5% of the difference is due to chance or sampling error, and that the same difference would occur 95% of the time should the test be repeated. Rarely, a more rigorous standard of 1% (= .01 level) is used and, as a result, the same difference would occur 99% of the time should the test be repeated.

EXAMPLE

The experiment or treatment group ($\bar{X}$ = 73.30, SD = 3.91) scored significantly higher than the control group ($\bar{X}$ = 67.30, SD = 4.32), $t(75) = 4.90$, $p < .05$. Note that the number in parenthesis (75) after the *t* value is the number of cases adjusted for the values that are free to vary = "degrees of freedom" = $n - 1$. The *p* value (= probability value or alpha level) expresses statistical significance.

In the preceding example, *p* is most important and indicates at what level a statistically significant difference exists (i.e .05 level; this will be discussed further).

There are one sample and two sample *t*-tests:

1. a one sample *t*-test is a hypothesis test for answering questions about the mean where the data are a random sample of independent observations from an underlying normal distribution where the variance is unknown;

2. a two sample *t*-test is a hypothesis test for answering questions about the mean where the data are collected from two random samples of independent observations, each from an underlying normal distribution where the variances of the 2 populations are assumed to be equal.

Analysis of variance (ANOVA) is a parametric statistical measure used for determining whether differences exist among two or more groups. ANOVA uses the mean, the variance and a "Table of Critical Values for the *F* Distribution". Statistical significance is usually based on the .05 level.

ANOVA can be used for several different types of analyses:

- One-way ANOVA - assumes there are two variables with one variable a dependent, interval or ratio variable (numerical data that show quantity and direction), and one variable, an independent, nominal variable or factor such as an ethnicity code or sex code.

- *N*-way ANOVA - assumes there are more than two variables with one variable a dependent, interval or ratio variable and two or more, independent, nominal variables or factors such as ethnicity code or sex code.

- Multiple Regression - assumes there are more than two variables with one variable a dependent, interval or ratio variable and two or more, independent, interval or ratio variables such as test scores, income, GPA, etc.

- Analysis of Covariance - assumes there are more than two variables with one variable a dependent, interval or variable and two or more variables are a combination of independent, nominal, interval or ratio variables.

Scheffe Test

The Scheffe test is used with ANOVA to determine which variable among several independent variables is statistically the most different.

Effect Size

For both *t*-test and one-way ANOVA procedures, a secondary statistical procedure called effect size is sometimes used to determine the level of significance. This could be used in an experimental study comparing the means of two groups, a control group and an experimental group. Effect size is calculated by taking the difference in the means of the two groups and dividing it by the standard deviation of the control group. In education experiments, an effect size of +.20 (20% of the standard deviation) would be considered a minimum for significance; an effect size above +.50 is considered very strong.

Chi-Square

t-test and analysis of variance are parametric statistical procedures that assume that the distributions are normal or nearly normal and is used when variables are continuous such as test scores and GPAs. Chi-square is a nonparametric statistical procedure used to determine the significance of the difference between groups when data are nominal and placed in categories such as gender or ethnicity. This procedure compares what is observed against what was expected.

Categories of Chi-Square (χ^2):

1. Chi-Squared Goodness of Fit Test is a test for comparing a theoretical distribution, such as a Normal distribution, with the observed data from a sample.

2. Chi-Squared Test of Association allows the comparison of two attributes in a sample of data to determine if there is any relationship between them. If the value of the test statistic for the chi-squared test of association is too large, then there is a poor agreement between the observed and expected frequencies and the null hypothesis of independence or no association is rejected.

3. Chi-Squared Test of Homogeneity is used to determine if a single categorical variable has the same distribution in 2 (or more) distinct populations from 2 (or more) samples.

Null Hypothesis, Alternative Hypothesis

Consider the following two types of statistical hypotheses:

- **Null hypothesis** (= H_0) is usually the hypothesis that sample observations result purely from chance. {Remember: "If *p* is low, H_0 has to go!"}

- **Alternative hypothesis** (= H_1 or H_a) is the hypothesis that sample observations are influenced by some non-random cause.

For example, suppose we wanted to determine whether a coin was fair and balanced. A null hypothesis might be that half the flips would result in heads and half, in tails. The alternative hypothesis might be that the number of heads and tails would be very different. Symbolically, these hypotheses would be expressed as

H_0: probability = 0.5
H_a: probability < 0.5 or > 0.5

Suppose we flipped the coin 100 times, resulting in 85 heads and 15 tails. Given this result, we would be inclined to reject the null hypothesis. That is, we would conclude that the coin was probably not fair and balanced.

Z Scores and p values

The *z* score (= standard score = *z* value) is a test of statistical significance that helps you decide whether or not to reject the null hypothesis. The *p*-value is the probability that you have falsely rejected the null hypothesis. *Z* scores are measures of standard deviation. For example, a *Z* score of +3.0 is interpreted as "+3.0 standard deviations away from the mean". *P* values are probabilities. Both statistics are associated with the standard normal distribution.

Very high or a very low (negative) *z* scores (i.e. very small p values) are found in the tails of the normal distribution. The p value associated with a 95% confidence level is 0.05 and the associated *z* values are approximately -2 and +2 (see the normal curve in section 7.3.2).

One and Two-sided Tests

A one-sided test (= one-tailed test of significance) is a statistical hypothesis test in which the values for which we can reject the null hypothesis H_0 are located entirely in one tail of the probability distribution. In other words, the critical region for a one-sided test is the set of values less than the critical value of the test, or the set of values greater than the critical value of the test.

A two-sided test (= two-tailed test of significance) is a statistical hypothesis test in which the values for which we can reject the null hypothesis, H_0 are located in both tails of the probability distribution. In other words, the critical region for a two-sided test is the set of values less than a first critical value of the test and the set of values greater than a second critical value of the test.

Errors

Two types of errors can result from a decision rule:

- **Type I error**. A Type I error occurs when the researcher rejects a null hypothesis when it is true. The probability of committing a Type I error is called the significance level or alpha (= α). The confidence level is 1 − α.

- **Type II error**. A Type II error occurs when the researcher accepts a null hypothesis that is false. The probability of committing a Type II error is called beta (= β). The probability of not committing a Type II error is called the "power of the test" = 1 - β.

10. What is the meaning of $p < .05$?

A. The probability of obtaining the data if the null hypothesis were true is less than 5%.

B. There is a 5% chance of making a type I error.

C. There is a less than a 1 in 20 probability of the result occurring by chance alone if the null hypothesis were true.

D. All of the above.

11. The ANOVA test is based on which assumption(s)?

I. The samples are randomly selected

II. The populations are statistically significant

III. The populations are normally distributed

A. III only
B. II and III only
C. I, II, and III only
D. I, and III only

12. The chi-square goodness of fit test can be used to test for:

A. credibility.
B. probability.
C. differentiability.
D. normality.

13. The null hypothesis is:

A. the assumption that a significant result is very unlikely.
B. the analysis of the pattern between the variables being tested.
C. the assumption there is no relationship or difference between the variables being tested.
D. the assumption that there is a relationship or difference between the variables being tested.

14. Which of the following is consistent with the null hypothesis and the alternative hypothesis?

A. It is possible for neither hypothesis to be true
B. Exactly one hypothesis must be true
C. Both hypotheses must be true
D. It is possible for both hypotheses to be true

15. In a two-tailed test of significance:

A. results in either of two directions can lead to the rejection of the null hypothesis.
B. no results lead to the rejection of the null hypothesis.
C. results in only one direction can lead to the rejection of the null hypothesis.
D. a standard deviation leads to the rejection of the null hypothesis.

16. If the Gold Standard was trying to prove that their materials are more effective at getting high DAT scores compared to older methods of preparation, they would conduct a:

A. one-tailed test.
B. two-tailed test.
C. Chi-Squared Test of Homogeneity.
D. Chi-Squared Test of Association.

17. The alternative hypothesis can be:

A. one-sided.

B. two- sided.

C. one or two- sided.

D. neither one nor two- sided.

18. A type II error occurs when:

A. the test is biased.

B. the sample mean differs from the population mean.

C. the null hypothesis is incorrectly accepted when it is false.

D. the null hypothesis is incorrectly rejected when it is true.

19. The value set for α is known as:

A. the significance level.

B. the rejection level.

C. the confidence level.

D. the acceptance level.

20. When someone asks "how significant" the sample evidence is, they are referring to the:

A. causality.

B. value of β.

C. sample value.

D. p-value.

ANSWER KEY

ADVANCED TOPICS - CHAPTER 7

		Cross-Reference			*Cross-Reference*
10.	D	QR Appendix	16.	A	QR Appendix
11.	A	QR Appendix	17.	C	QR Appendix
12.	D	QR Appendix	18.	C	QR Appendix
13.	C	QR Appendix	19.	A	QR Appendix
14.	B	QR Appendix	20.	D	QR Appendix
15.	A	QR Appendix			

P = paragraph; *S* = sentence; *E* = equation; *T* = table; *F* = figure

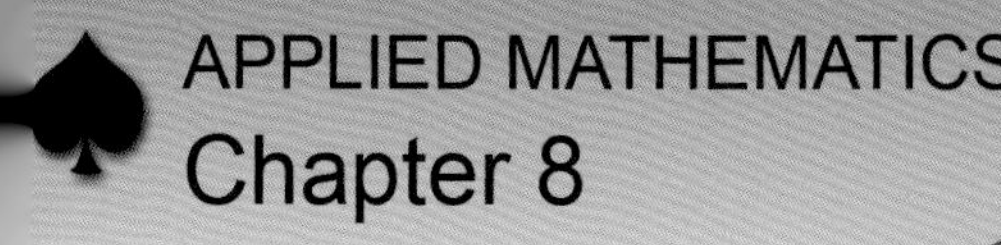

Memorize

Law of Reflection
Property of Elliptical Mirrors
Equations for Velocity and Interest

Understand

* Ellipses
* Rates of Change
* Velocity Problems, Interest Problems, Work Problems, Age Problems
* Strategies for Word Problems

Importance

8 to 12 out of the 40 QR

questions on the DAT are based on content from this chapter (in our estimation).

* This will change in 2015.

Introduction

Ten of the forty Quantitative Reasoning questions on the DAT are applied mathematics or word problems. There is a huge range of types of word problems that you might encounter on the test. This chapter covers those that require extra explanation, as well as convenient strategies for dealing with any type that gets thrown your way.

Additional Resources

Free Online Forum

8.1 Optics

Optics is the branch of physics that deals with light. Problems of this variety show up on the Quantitative Reasoning test because reflection of light is all about angles.

8.1.1 Reflection

Reflection occurs when light hits a surface and bounces off. An uneven surface reflects light diffusely, scattering it, but an even surface like a mirror reflects light in a very precise way. This is why you can see your image in a mirror but not in, say, a wall.

Law of Reflection: This law says that the angle of incidence is always equal to the angle of reflection.

If you draw a line perpendicular to the mirror at the point where the light hits (= the "normal" line), the **angle of incidence** (θ_i) is the angle formed by that line and the incoming light ray. Similarly, the **angle of reflection** (θ_r) is the angle formed by the perpendicular and the reflected light ray.

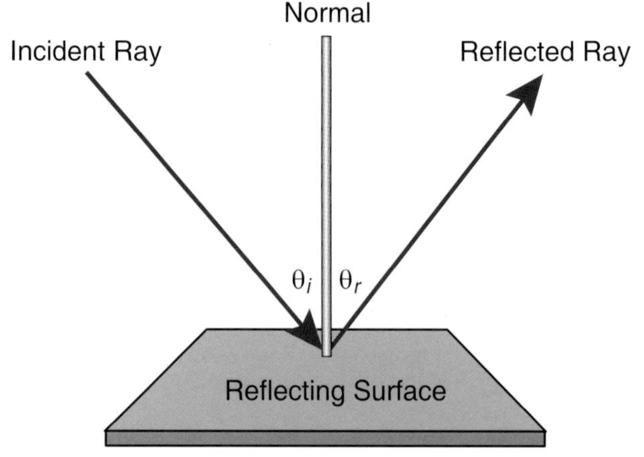

Using the law of reflection, you can easily turn any plane mirror problem into a geometry and/or trigonometry problem involving lines and angles.

8.1.2 Elliptical Mirrors

The law of reflection still applies to curved mirror surfaces. The only problem is knowing how to draw the perpendicular line at the point of incidence. Dealing with unusually curved mirrors is usually too complicated for the Quantitative Reasoning test, but you may still encounter questions about an elliptical mirror.

An **ellipse** is an oval-shaped figure. It has two points in its interior that are equally spaced on either side of the center (called the **foci**) such that, for any point on the perimeter of the ellipse, the sum of the distances to the foci is always the same. The line passing through both foci from one end of the perimeter to the other is known as the **major axis**. The line perpendicular to the major axis passing through the midpoint is the **minor axis**. A circle is a special ellipse for which both foci are the same point.

Property: If a light ray passes through a focus of an elliptical mirror, it will always reflect off the inside of the mirror and pass through the other focus.

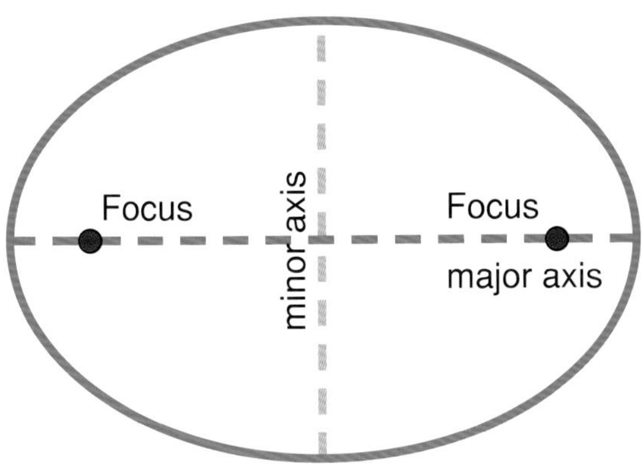

NOTE

The length of the major axis is the same as the distance a light ray will travel between one focus and the other if it is reflected once on the way.

8.2 Word Problems

8.2.1 Rates of Change

A rate of change is an amount by which one variable changes in relationship to another variable. Usually, a rate of change specifies how some value changes as time progresses. All rates of change can be written as fractions, so rate of change problems almost always boil down to algebra problems involving fraction manipulation.

EXAMPLE

A glass can hold 10 oz of liquid. Water is being poured in at a rate of 3 oz every 2 seconds. How long will it take for the glass to reach $^2/_3$ full?

The rate in this problem translates to the fraction 3 oz/2 sec. We want to find the time "t" it will take for $^2/_3$ of 10 oz to be poured in, so we set up an algebraic equation:

$$\frac{3\text{ oz}}{2\text{ sec}} \times t = \frac{2}{3} \times 10\text{ oz}$$

$$\Rightarrow t = \frac{2\text{ sec}}{3\text{ oz}} \times \frac{20\text{ oz}}{3}$$

$$\Rightarrow t = \frac{40}{9}\text{ sec}$$

8.2.2 Distance, Time and Velocity

A specific type of rate of change with which you should be familiar is **velocity**. Velocity is the distance an object travels in a specific direction per unit of time. Do not get this confused with **speed,** which is a value that is independent of the direction of travel.

$$\text{Velocity} = \frac{\text{Distance}}{\text{Time}}$$

You can use this equation to solve for any one of the three values if you know the other two.

EXAMPLE

A jogger runs the first 100 meters of a 5 km race in 24 seconds. If the jogger maintains the same pace until the end of the race, how long will it take him to run the entire race?

We are given a distance and a time, so we can easily find the velocity of the jogger.

$$V = \frac{100\text{ m}}{24\text{ sec}}$$

The distance in question is in kilometers, so we need to convert this velocity.

$$V = \frac{.1\text{ km}}{24\text{ sec}}$$

Now we need to apply our velocity formula once more. We have a velocity and a distance, but we ultimately want to find the time.

$$\frac{.1\text{ km}}{24\text{ sec}} = \frac{5\text{ km}}{t}$$
$$\Rightarrow 5\text{ km} \times 24\text{ sec} = .1\text{ km} \times t$$
$$\Rightarrow \frac{(5 \times 24\text{ sec})}{.1} = t$$
$$\Rightarrow t = 1200\text{ sec} = 20\text{ min}$$

Velocity problems can also involve a geometric component if a specific direction (or directions) of travel is included, so be on the lookout! {Vectors are discussed in the QR Appendix (A.6)}

8.2.3 Simple and Compound Interests

Questions dealing with simple and compound interests are very straightforward on the DAT. These questions are essentially plug-and-chug problems. Make sure you differentiate between simple and compound interests.

Simple interest is calculated based on just the initial amount of money invested. Thus the formula for simple interest can be expressed as:

I = PRT

where I is the interest earned from the investment, P is the principal or the amount of money invested, R is the rate of interest (usually in the form of percentage) charged on the principal, and T is the time.

EXAMPLE

Johnny borrowed $15,000 from the bank at 5% simple interest per year. How much does Johnny owe the bank in one year?

I = PRT

= ($15,000)(0.05)(1)

= $750 owed

Compound interest is computed based on the amount of money invested and all interests accumulated during the past periods. Interests may be compounded monthly, semiannually, or annually. The simplest way to approach these questions is to treat each period as a simple interest problem.

EXAMPLE

Joe borrowed $12,000 from the bank at 10% interest compounded annually. How much does he owe the bank in 3 years?

After the first year:

$I = PRT$

$= (\$12,000)(0.1)(1)$

= \$1,200 in interest for the first year.

After the second year:

$I = PRT$

$= (\$12,000 + \$1,200)(0.1)(1)$

= \$1,320 in interest for the second year.

After the third year:

$I = PRT$

$= (\$12,000 + \$1,200 + \$1,320)(0.1)(1)$

= \$1,452 in interest for the third year.

Total interest:

\$1,200 + \$1,320 + \$1,452 = \$3,972 total interest owed after three years.

NOTE

Be comfortable with rearranging the Interest equation. The DAT can ask you to solve for any one of the interest rate, time, or principal.

8.2.4 Work Problems

Work problems are almost guaranteed to show up on the DAT. Fortunately, they are rather simple and can be solved with the following equation:

$$\frac{1}{(t1)} + \frac{1}{(t2)} = \frac{1}{(T)}$$

where *t1* = time it takes for A to finish the task, *t2* = time it takes for B to finish the task, and T = total time.

EXAMPLE

Jack takes 5 hours to paint a house while Joan takes 10 hours to do the same task. How long would it take to paint one house if Jack and Joan worked together?

$$\left(\frac{1}{5\ hours}\right) + \left(\frac{1}{10\ hours}\right) = \left(\frac{1}{total\ time}\right)$$

$$\left(\frac{2}{10\ hours}\right) + \left(\frac{1}{10\ hours}\right) = \left(\frac{1}{total\ time}\right)$$

$$\left(\frac{3}{10\ hours}\right) = \left(\frac{1}{total\ time}\right)$$

Cross multiply:

3(total time) = 10 hours

total time = 10/3 or 3 ⅓ hours if Jack and Joan work together.

8.2.5 Age Problems

Age problems are simply algebraic expressions disguised as word problems. There are two methods in approaching these problems.

Problem: Kim is 20 years older than Joe. In 5 years, Kim will be 5 years older than twice Joe's age. How old is Kim today?

Method 1:

Let K = Kim's age and J = Joe's age

We can set up the first statement as:

K = J + 20

The second statement can be set up as:

(K + 5) – 5 = 2(J + 5)

Let's rearrange the first equation to K - 20 = J since we are solving for Kim's age. Then substitute the first equation into the second equation. We get,

(K + 5) – 5 = 2(K – 20 + 5)
K = 2(K – 15)
K = 2K – 30
K = 30

Kim is 30 years old while Joe is 10 years old.

Method 2:

Plug and chug the answers provided. Sometimes the quickest way to solving these types of problems are through trial and error.

8.3 Word Problem Strategies

8.3.1 What You Need and What You Know

Identify the Problem Type: The first thing you should do when you encounter a word problem is ask, "What type of problem is it?" If you can identify it as a rate, geometry, probability, or some other kind of problem, you will have an immediate idea of what might need to be done.

What You Need: Next, go through the problem and pick out exactly what information the problem is asking you to find. Are you looking for the distance traveled, the probability of heads, the measure of an angle? Whatever it may be, write it down on the laminated note board provided during the test.

What You Know: After you have identified what you are looking for, you should go back and look at what information you are given. The problem will always provide enough information to solve the problem (sometimes even more than enough), but it can often be a little confusing to keep all of it in your mind at once. It may not even be presented in an easy to understand form; for example, ratios and rates are much clearer if you rewrite them as concise fractions. It can be extremely helpful to quickly list out what you know on the note board.

8.3.2 Draw a Picture

If a word problem has any kind of geometric component, it can be difficult to keep it straight in your mind. Drawing a simple picture of the situation will solve this problem, but beyond that, a picture can even help you to see connections you would not have otherwise noticed.

Some problems do not lend themselves to pictorial representations. In such cases, you should not spend time worrying about drawing one. If it seems difficult to draw or if you can't even figure out what to draw, then a picture probably would not be helpful.

8.3.3 Set Up the Math

This is the part where you have to bring your math knowledge and skills to the table. You have your lists of what you need and know, you have your picture, and now you have to find a way to solve the problem.

It is up to you to make the connections, but before you start tossing numbers around you should take a moment to set up the math. This means you should write out the equations and relationships you will need before you start evaluating. This way, you can easily keep track of the work you are doing in case you make a mistake, and all you need to do in the end to find the solution is plug in values and crank out some basic algebra and arithmetic.

GOLD STANDARD WARM-UP EXERCISES

CHAPTER 8: Applied Mathematics

1. If it takes thirty minutes to walk 1.5 miles, how many miles will be covered in 3 hours?

   A. 12
   B. 4.5
   C. 9
   D. 7.5
   E. 2.25

2. A ray of light passes through one focus of an elliptical mirror with a major axis of length 8. At the point of reflection, it is 6 units away from the other focus. At this point, how far is the ray of light from the first focus?

   A. 2
   B. 4
   C. 6
   D. 8
   E. 10

3. A ray of light passes through the foci of an elliptical mirror at $(\sqrt{5}, 0)$. It is reflected at the endpoint of the minor axis, the point (0, 2). What is the length of the major axis?

   A. $2\sqrt{5}$
   B. 3
   C. 4
   D. 6
   E. $\sqrt{29}$

4. A small pipe allows water to flow at 5 gallons per minute. A larger pipe allows water to flow at 15 gallons per minute. If both pipes are used, how many minutes will it take to fill a 180 gallon tank with water?

   A. 18
   B. 9
   C. 24
   D. 12
   E. 30

5. A beam of light originates at the outer edge of a circular mirror of radius 5 and passes through the center. How far does it travel before being reflected?

   A. 10
   B. 1
   C. 5
   D. 2.5
   E. 15

6. A truck travels 150 miles in 3 hours during the morning, and 180 miles in 3 hours during the afternoon. What is its average speed for the day?

   A. 37 mph
   B. 36 mph
   C. 65 mph
   D. 110 mph
   E. 55 mph

7. The beam from a lighthouse sweeps out $\frac{\pi}{4}$ radians every 5 seconds. 500 meters away from the shore, a ship is directly approaching at a rate of 100 meters per minute. If this speed is maintained, how many complete revolutions will the beam make before the ship reaches the shore?

A. 5

B. 60

C. 7.5

D. 75

E. 300

8. The bottom of a square basement window with a diagonal length of 1 meter is level with the ground, as shown in the following figure. A ray of light originates at its lower left-hand corner and travels diagonally up to the upper right-hand corner, where it is reflected downwards. How many meters from the corner of the window (point D) is the ray when it reaches the ground again, at point E?

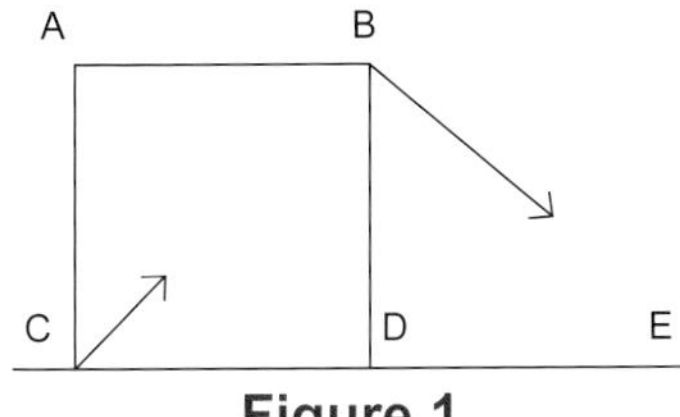

Figure 1

A. $2/\sqrt{2}$

B. 1/2

C. 1

D. $1/\sqrt{2}$

E. 2

9. The average age of a wife, her husband and daughter three years ago was 27 years and that of her husband and daughter five years ago was 20 years. What is the wife's present age?

A. 36

B. 40

C. 37

D. 42

E. 38

10. Hiking up a mountain took 5 hours, but down only 1½ hours. If the distance each way was 3.3 miles, what is the difference between the two hiking rates in km/s?

A. 5.63×10^{-4} km/s

B. 6.84×10^{-4} km/s

C. 9.03×10^{-4} km/s

D. 6.16×10^{-4} km/s

E. 6.43×10^{-4} km/s

GS ANSWER KEY

Chapter 8

		Cross-Reference			Cross-Reference
1.	C	QR 8.2.2	6.	E	QR 8.2.2
2.	A	QR 8.1, 8.1.2	7.	C	QR 8.2, 8.2.2
3.	D	QR 8.1.2	8.	D	QR 8.1, 8.1.1
4.	B	QR 8.2, 8.2.1	9.	B	QR 8.2.1
5.	A	QR 8.1, 8.1.1	10.	B	QR 8.2, 8.2.2

* Explanations can be found at the back of the book.

Go online to DAT-prep.com for additional chapter review Q&A and forum.

Appendix A

DAT MATH REVIEW

In the preceding science review and QR sections, several mathematical concepts were presented (i.e. trigonometry, rules of logarithms, the quadratic equation, statistics, etc.). The purpose of this section is to review the DAT mathematical concepts *not* presented elsewhere, though there may be some overlap for emphasis.

A.1 Basic Graphs

A.1.1 The Graph of a Linear Equation

Equations of the type $y = ax + b$ are known as *linear equations* since the graph of y (= *the ordinate*) versus x (= *the abscissa*) is a straight line. The value of y where the line intersects the y axis is called the *intercept* b. The constant a is the *slope* of the line. Given any two points (x_1, y_1) and (x_2, y_2) on the line, we have:

$$y_1 = ax_1 + b$$

and

$$y_2 = ax_2 + b.$$

Subtracting the upper equation from the lower one and dividing through by $x_2 - x_1$ gives the value of the slope,

$$a = (y_2 - y_1)/(x_2 - x_1).$$

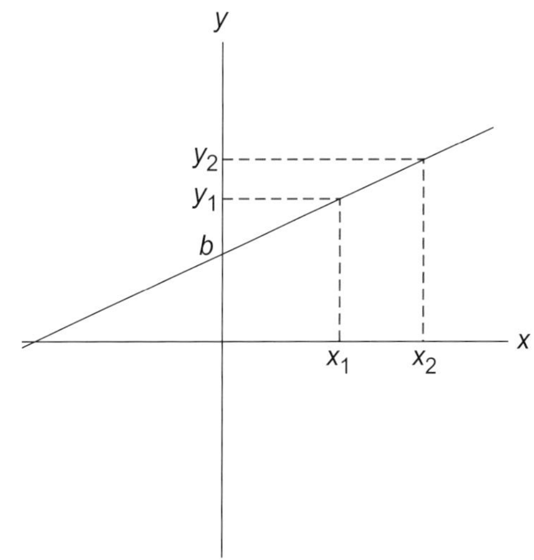

A.1.2 Reciprocal Curve

For any real number x, there exists a unique real number called the multiplicative inverse or *reciprocal* of x denoted $1/x$ or x^{-1} such that $x\,(1/x) = 1$. The graph of the reciprocal $1/x$ for any x is:

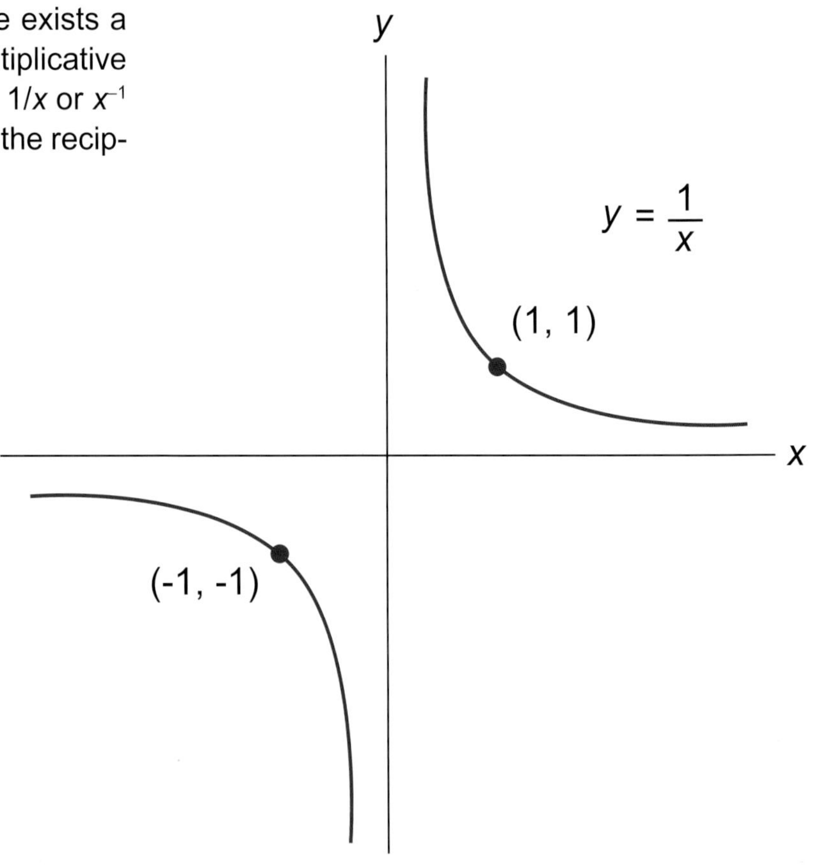

A.1.3 Miscellaneous Graphs

There are classical curves which are represented or approximated in the science text as follows: Sigmoidal curve (CHM 6.9.1, BIO 7.5.1), sinusoidal curve (QR 6.2.3), and hyperbolic curves (CHM 9.7 Fig III.A.9.3, BIO 1.1.2).

If you were to plot a set of experimental data, often one can draw a line (A.1.1) or curve (A.1.2/3, A.2.2) which can "best fit" the data. The preceding defines a *regression* line or curve. The main purpose of the regression graph is to predict what would likely occur outside of the experimental data.

A.2 Exponents and Logarithms

A.2.1 Rules of Exponents

$a^0 = 1$	$a^1 = a$
$a^n\, a^m = a^{n+m}$	$a^n/a^m = a^{n-m}$
$(a^n)^m = a^{nm}$	$a^{\frac{1}{n}} = \sqrt[n]{a}$

A.2.2 Exponential and Logarithmic Curves

The exponential and logarithmic functions are *inverse functions*. That is, their graphs can be reflected about the $y = x$ line.

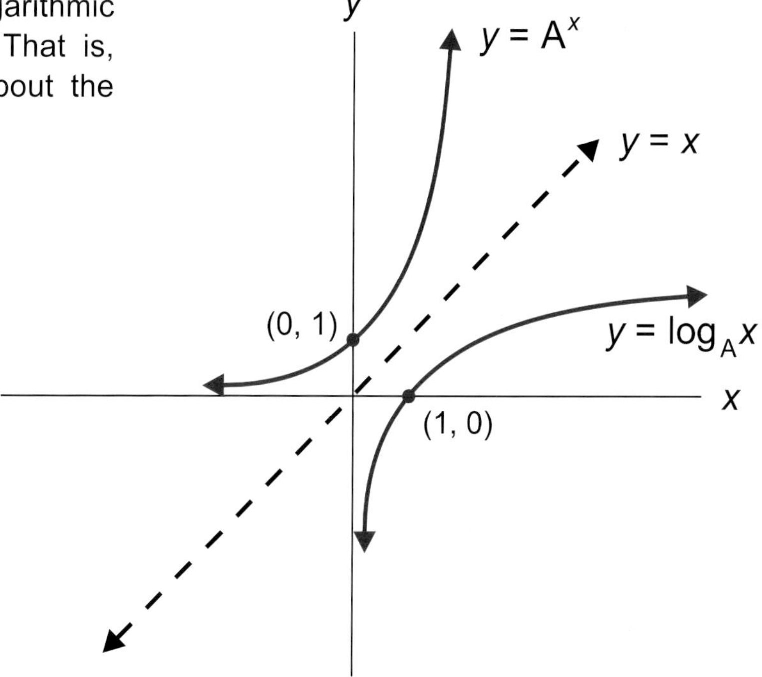

Figure A.1: Exponential and Logarithmic Graphs. $A > 0$, $A \neq 1$.

A.2.3 Log Rules and Logarithmic Scales

The rules of logarithms were discussed in context of Acids and Bases in General Chemistry (CHM 6.5.1). These rules also apply to the "natural logarithm" which is the logarithm to the base *e*, where "*e*" is an irrational constant approximately equal to 2.7182818. The natural logarithm is usually written as ln *x* or loge *x* . The natural logarithm is used in the Nernst equation (BIO 5 Appendix). In general, the power of logarithms is to reduce wide-ranging numbers to quantities with a far smaller range.

For example, the graphs commonly seen in this text, including the preceding one, are drawn to a unit or *arithmetic scale.* In other words, each unit on the *x* and *y* axes represents exactly *one* unit. This scale can be adjusted to accommodate rapidly changing curves. For example, in a unit scale the numbers 1 (= 10^0), 10 (= 10^1), 100 (= 10^2), and 1000 (= 10^3), are all far apart with varying intervals. Using a logarithmic scale, the sparse values suddenly become separated by one unit: Log $10^0 = 0$, log $10^1 = 1$, log $10^2 = 2$, log $10^3 = 3$, and so on.

In practice, logarithmic scales are often used to convert a rapidly changing curve (e.g. an exponential curve) to a straight line. It is called a *semi-log* scale when either the abscissa *or* the ordinate is logarithmic. It is called a *log-log* scale when both the abscissa *and* the ordinate are logarithmic.

A.3 Simplifying Algebraic Expressions

Algebraic expressions can be factored or simplified using standard formulae:

$$a(b + c) = ab + ac$$
$$(a + b)(a - b) = a^2 - b^2$$
$$(a + b)(a + b) = (a + b)^2 = a^2 + 2ab + b^2$$
$$(a - b)(a - b) = (a - b)^2 = a^2 - 2ab + b^2$$
$$(a + b)(c + d) = ac + ad + bc + bd$$

A.4 Significant Digits, Experimental Error

If we divide 2 by 3 on a calculator, the answer on the display would be 0.6666666667. The leftmost digit is the *most significant digit* and the rightmost digit is the *least significant digit*. The number of digits which are really significant depends on the accuracy with which the values 2 and 3 are known.

For example, suppose we wish to find the sum of two numbers a and b with experimental errors (or *uncertainties*) Δa and Δb, respectively. The uncertainty of the sum c can be determined as follows:

$$c \pm \Delta c = (a \pm \Delta a) + (b \pm \Delta b)$$

$$= a + b \pm (\Delta a + \Delta b)$$

thus

$$\Delta c = \Delta a + \Delta b.$$

The sign of the uncertainties are not correlated, so the same rule applies to subtraction. Therefore, *the uncertainty of either the sum or difference is the sum of the uncertainties.*

Now we will apply the preceding to significant digits. A measurement or calculation of 3.7 has an implicit uncertainty. Any number between 3.65000... and 3.74999... rounds off to 3.7, thus 3.7 really means 3.7 ± 0.05. Similarly, 68.21 really means 68.21 ± 0.005. Adding the two values and their uncertainties we get: (3.7 ± 0.05) + (68.21 ± 0.005) = 71.91 ± 0.055. The error is large enough to affect the first digit to the right of the decimal point; therefore, the last digit to the right is not significant. The answer is thus 71.9.

The rule for significant digits states that *the sum or difference of two numbers carries the same number of significant digits to the right of the decimal as the number with the least significant digits to the right of the decimal.* For example, 105.64 – 3.092 = 102.55.

Multiplication and division is somewhat different. Through algebraic manipulation, the uncertainty or experimental error can be determined:

$$c \pm \Delta c = (a \pm \Delta a)(b \pm \Delta b)$$

After some manipulation we get

$$\Delta c/c = \Delta a/a + \Delta b/b.$$

The preceding result also holds true for division. Thus for (10 ± 0.5)/(20 ± 1), the fractional error in the quotient is:

$$\Delta c/c = \Delta a/a + \Delta b/b = 0.5/10 + 1/20$$
$$= 0.1 \text{ (10\% error)}$$

Thus the quotient including its absolute error is $c \pm \Delta c = 0.5(1 \pm 0.1) = 0.5 \pm 0.05$.

The rule for significant digits can be derived from the preceding and it states that *the product or quotient of two numbers has the same number of significant digits as the number with the least number of significant digits.*

A.5 Properties of Negative and Positive Integers

Positive + Positive = Positive

$$5 + 4 = 9$$

Negative + Negative = Negative

$$(-6) + (-2) = -8$$

Positive + Negative = Sign of the highest number and then subtract

$$(-5) + 4 = -1$$
$$(-8) + 10 = 2$$

Negative − Positive = Negative

$$(-7) - 10 = -17$$

Positive − Negative = Positive + Positive = Positive

$$6 - (-4) = 6 + 4 = 10$$

Negative − Negative = Negative + Positive = Sign of the highest number and then subtract

$$(-8) - (-7) = (-8) + 7 = -1$$

Negative × Negative = Positive

$$(-2) \times (-5) = 10$$

Positive/Positive = Positive

$$8/2 = 4$$

Negative × Positive = Negative

$$(-9) \times 3 = -27$$

Positive/Negative = Negative

$$64/(-8) = -8$$

A.6 Scalars and Vectors

NOTE

Translational motion is the movement of an object (or particle) through space without turning (rotation). Displacement, velocity and acceleration are key vectors - specified by magnitude and direction - often used to describe translational motion. Being able to manipulate and resolve vectors is helpful for some DAT problems. For example, vectors are useful to determine if a molecule has a dipole based on bond polarity (i.e. CHM, ORG). They also help resolve a boat's velocity while it is moving across a river with a downstream current (QR). Because of its rarity on the DAT, we consider acceleration to be an Advanced DAT-30 Topic.

Scalars, such as speed, have magnitude only and are specified by a number with a unit (55 miles/hour). Scalars obey the rules of ordinary algebra. Vectors, like velocity, have both magnitude and direction (100 km/hour, west). Vectors are represented by arrows where:

(i) the length of the arrow indicates the magnitude of the vector, and;

(ii) the arrowhead indicates the direction of the vector. Vectors obey the special rules of vector algebra. Thus vectors can be moved in space but their orientation must be kept the same.

Addition of Vectors: Two vectors *a* and *b* can be added geometrically by drawing them to a common scale and placing them head to tail. The vector connecting the tail of a to the head of *b* is the sum or resultant vector *r*.

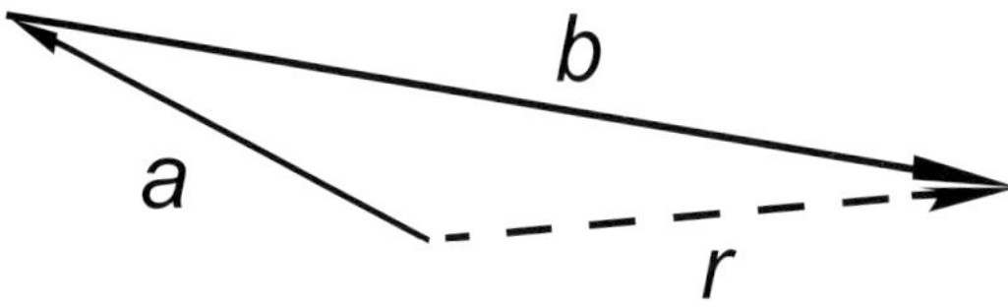

Figure III.B.1.1: The vector sum $a + b = r$.

Subtraction of Vectors: To subtract the vector *b* from *a*, reverse the direction of *b* then add to *a*.

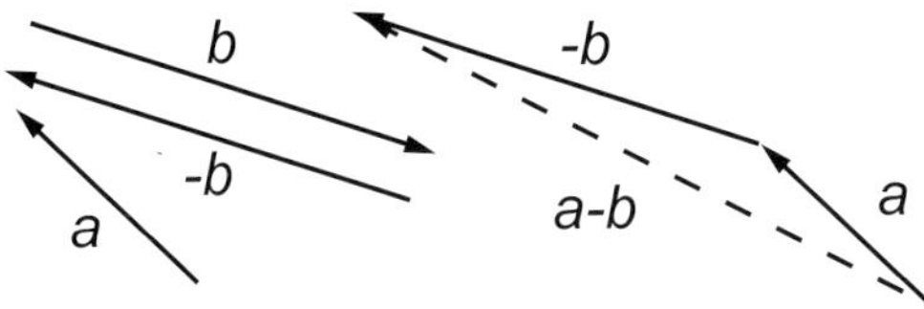

Figure III.B.1.2: The vector difference $a - b = a + (-b)$.

Resolution of Vectors: Perpendicular projections of a vector can be made on a coordinate axis. Thus the vector *a* can be resolved into its *x*–component (a_x) and its *y*–component (a_y).

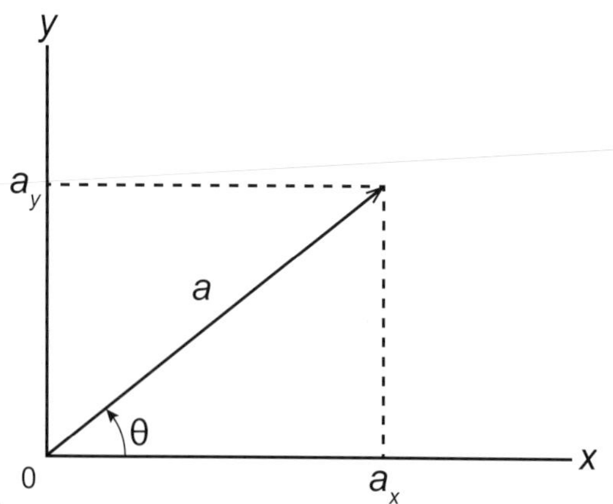

Figure III.B.1.3: The resolution of a vector into its scalar components in a coordinate system.

Analytically, the resolution of vector a is as follows:

$$a_x = a \cos\theta \text{ and } a_y = a \sin\theta$$

Conversely, given the components, we can reconstruct vector *a*:

$$a = \sqrt{a_x^{\,2} + a_y^{\,2}} \text{ and } \tan\theta = a_y / a_x$$

A.7 Common Values of Trigonometric Functions

There are special angles which produce standard values of the trigonometric functions. These values should be memorized.Several of the values are derived from the following triangles:

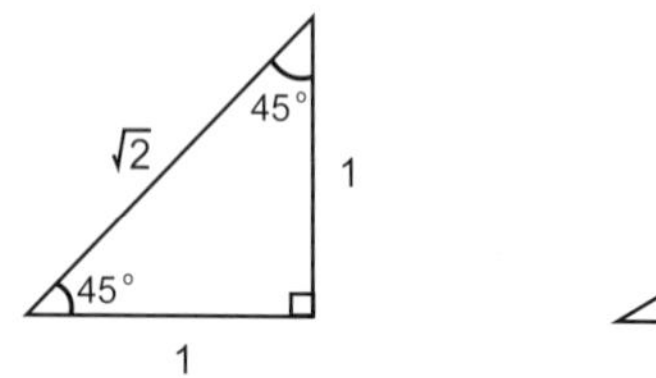

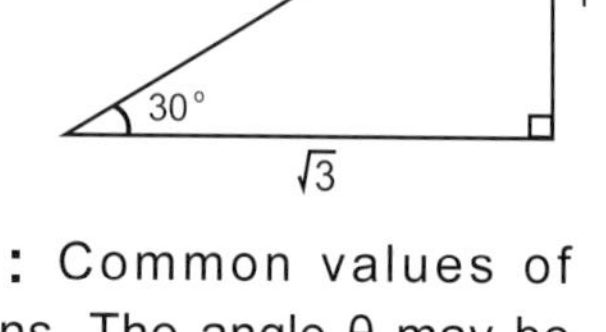

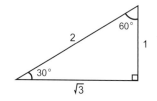

Table III.B.1.1: Common values of trigonometric functions. The angle θ may be given in radians (*R*) where $2\pi^R = 360° = 1$ revolution. Recall $\sqrt{3} \approx 1.7$, $\sqrt{2} \approx 1.4$.

Note that 1° = 60 arcminutes, 1 arcminute = 60 arcseconds

θ	sin θ	cos θ	tan θ
0°	0	1	0
30°	1/2	$\sqrt{3}/2$	$1\sqrt{3}$
45°	$1\sqrt{2}$	$1\sqrt{2}$	1
60°	$\sqrt{3}/2$	1/2	$\sqrt{3}$
90°	1	0	∞
180°	0	-1	0

Each trigonometric function (i.e. sine) contains an inverse function (i.e. $\sin^{-1}$), where if $\sin\theta = x$, $\theta = \sin^{-1}x$. Thus $\cos 60° = 1/2$, and $60° = \cos^{-1}(1/2)$. Some texts denote the inverse function with "arc" as a prefix. Thus arcsec (2) = $\sec^{-1}(2)$.

A.8 Distance and Displacement

Distance is the amount of separation between two points in space. It has a magnitude but no direction. It is a scalar quantity and is always positive.

Displacement of an object between two points is the difference between the final position and the initial position of the object in a given referential system. Thus, a displacement has an origin, a direction and a magnitude. It is a vector.

The sign of the coordinates of the vector displacement depends on the system under study and the chosen referential system. The sign will be positive (+) if the system is moving towards the positive axis of the referential system and negative (–) if not.

The units of distance and displacement are expressed in length units such as feet (ft), meters (m), miles and kilometers (km).

A.9 Speed and Velocity

Speed is the rate of change of distance with respect to time. It is a scalar quantity, it has a magnitude but no direction, like distance, and it is always positive.

Velocity is the rate of change of displacement with respect to time. It is a vector, and like the displacement, it has a direction and a magnitude. Its value depends on the position of the object. The sign of the coordinates of the vector velocity is the same as that of the displacement.

The **instantaneous velocity** of a system at a given time is the slope of the graph of the displacement of that system vs. time at that time. The magnitude of the velocity decreases if the vector velocity and the vector acceleration have opposite directions.

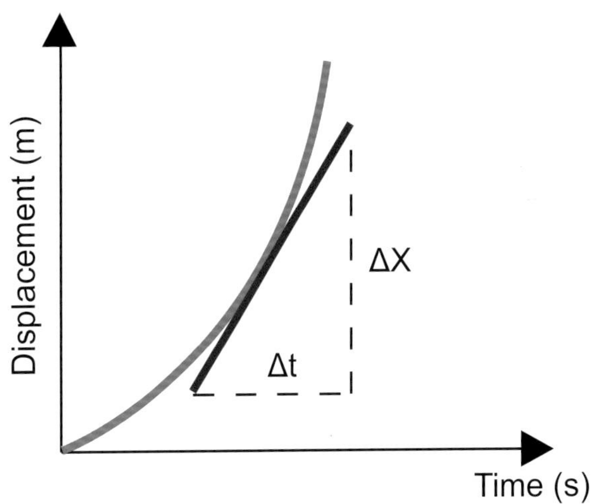

Figure III.B.1.4: Displacement vs. time.

The units of speed and velocity are expressed in length divided by time such as feet/sec., meters/sec. (m/s) and miles/hour.

Dimensional Analysis: remember from High School math that a slope is "rise over run" meaning it is the change in the y-axis divided by the change in the x-axis (see Appendix A.1.1). This means when we pay attention to the units, we get, for example, m/s which is velocity.

A.10 Acceleration: Advanced DAT-30 Content from A.10 to A.12

Acceleration (*a*) is the rate of change of the velocity (*v*) with respect to time (*t*):

$$a = v/t$$

Like the velocity, it is a vector and it has a direction and a magnitude.

The sign of the vector acceleration depends on the net force applied to the system and the chosen referential system. The units of acceleration are expressed as velocity divided by time such as meters/sec^2. The term for negative acceleration is **deceleration**.

A.10.1 Average and Instantaneous Acceleration

The average acceleration *av* between two instants *t* and $t' = t + \Delta t$, measures the result of the increase in the speed divided by the time difference,

$$a_v = \frac{v' - v}{\Delta t}$$

The instantaneous acceleration can be determined either by calculating the **slope** (*see* Appendix A.1.1) of a velocity vs. time graph at any time, or by taking the limit when Δt approaches zero of the preceding expression.

$$av = \lim_{\Delta t \to 0} \frac{v' - v}{\Delta t}$$

Math involving "limits" does not exist on the DAT. So let's discuss what this definition is describing in informal terms. The limit is the value of the change in velocity over the change in time as the time approaches 0. It's like saying that the change in velocity is happening in an instant. This allows us to talk about the acceleration in that incredibly fast moment: the instantaneous acceleration which can be determined graphically.

Consider the following events illustrated in the graph (Fig. III.B.1.4): your car starts at rest (0 velocity and time = 0); you steadily accelerate out of the parking lot (the change in velocity increases over time = acceleration); you are driving down the street at constant velocity (change in velocity = 0 and thus acceleration is 0 divided by the change in time which means: a = 0); you see a cat dart across the street safely which made you slow down temporarily (change in velocity is negative thus negative acceleration which, by definition, is deceleration); you now enter the on-ramp for the highway so your velocity is now increasing at a faster and faster rate (increasing acceleration). You can examine the instantaneous acceleration at any one point (or instant) during the period that your acceleration is increasing.

To determine the displacement (*not* distance), take the area under the graph or curve. To calculate area: a rectangle is base (*b*) times height (*h*); a triangle is ½*b* × *h*; and for a curve, they can use graph paper and expect you would count the boxes under the curve to estimate the area.

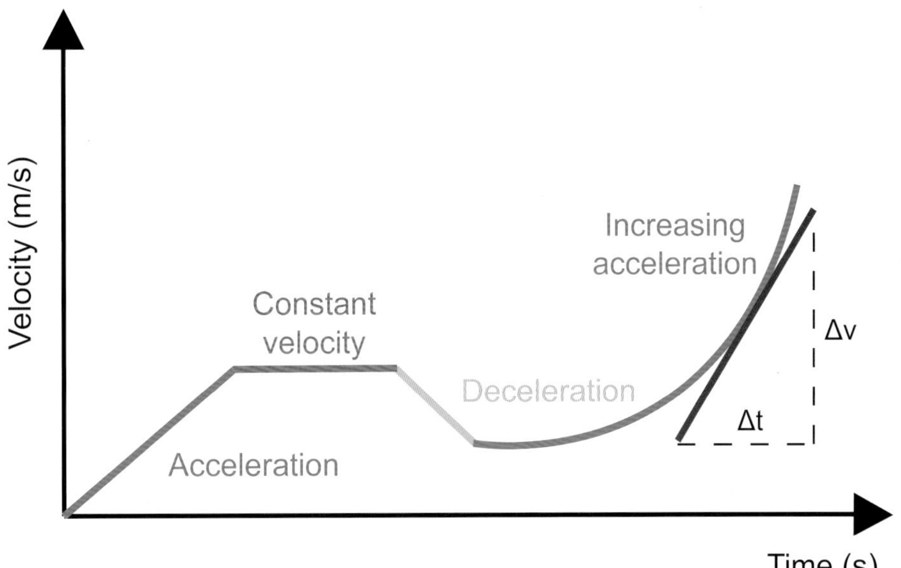

Figure III.B.1.4: Velocity vs. time. Note that at constant velocity, the slope and thus the acceleration are both equal to zero.

A.11 Uniformly Accelerated Motion

The magnitude and direction of the acceleration of a system are solely determined by the exterior forces acting upon the system. If the magnitude of these forces is constant, the magnitude of the acceleration will be constant and the resulting motion is a **uniformly accelerated motion**. The initial displacement, the velocity and the acceleration at any given time contribute to the overall displacement of the system:

$x = x_0$ – displacement due to the initial displacement x_0.

$x = v_0 t$ – displacement due to the initial velocity v_0 at time t.

$x = ½at^2$ – displacement due the acceleration at time t.

The total displacement of the uniformly-accelerated motion is given by the following formula:

$$x = x_0 + v_0 t + ½at^2$$

The translational motion is the motion of the center of gravity of a system through space, illustrated by the above equation.

A.12 Equations of Kinematics

Kinematics is the study of objects in motion with respect to space and time. There are three related equations. The first is above, the others are:

$$v = v_0 + at \text{ and } v^2 = v_0^2 + 2ax$$

where v is the final velocity.

Chapter Review Solutions - QR

Question 1 B

See: QR 2.2.3, 2.4.3

According to the rules of order of operations, we work with the square root first: $0.125 + \sqrt{\frac{1}{9}} = 0.125 + \frac{1}{3}$. Since the answers are in decimal form, this problem is easiest to solve if all values are in decimal form. From the list of fraction-to-decimal conversions, $\frac{1}{3} \approx 0.33$, and so, $0.125 + \frac{1}{3} \approx 0.125 + 0.33 = 0.455$. All of the answers have only two decimal places, so we must round this answer off to the hundredths decimal place. The digit in the thousandths decimal place is a 5, and so the digit in the hundredths decimal place increases by 1 to become 6. 0.455 therefore rounds off to 0.46.

Quick Solution:

$$0.125 + \sqrt{\frac{1}{9}} = 0.125 + \frac{1}{3} \approx 0.125 + 0.333$$

$$= 0.458 \approx 0.46.$$

Question 2 E

See: QR 2.6.2

This is a proportion problem, so there will be two equivalent ratios. We construct the first ratio as $\frac{0.8}{0.9}$ and the second as $\frac{80}{x}$. If we set them equal, we get $\frac{0.8}{0.9} = \frac{80}{90}$, and cross-multiplication gives us $0.8x = (0.9)(80)$, or $0.8x = 72$. Therefore, $x = \frac{72}{0.8} = 90$.

Quick Solution: 80 differs from 0.8 by a factor of 100. This means that the answer must be related to 0.9 by the same factor: $x = 100(0{:}9) = 90$

Question 3 A

See: QR 2.4.3

The interest earned by investing $5,897 in Bank B is 21% of $5,897, or (0.21)($5, 897) = $1238.37. The interest earned by investing $6,430 in Bank A is 19% of $6,430, or (0.19)($6,430) = $1221.70. Subtracting the smaller from the larger, we get $1238.37 − $1221.70 = $16.67.

Question 4 C

See: QR 2.4.2

We must work backwards to find the lengths of boards B and C. Board B is 4/5 as long as Board A, which is $\frac{4}{5}(100m) = 80m$. Board C is 3/4 as long as this, which is $\frac{3}{4}(80m) = 60m$. To find the sum of these lengths, we add the three values: $100m + 80m + 60m = 240m$.

Question 5 B

See: QR 2.6.2

This is a proportion problem in which the following are given: The proportion of the yellow marbles in the jar of yellow and green marbles is 7 out of 9. This makes the ratio of the number of yellow marbles to green marbles 7:2. The total number of marbles is 999. Therefore, the number of yellow marbles = (7/9) × 999 = 777 marbles.

Question 6 E

See: QR 2.6.1

This is a ratio problem involving different units. The given ratio is 0.25 months per week. We need to re-write this as a fraction: 0.25 months per week $= \frac{25}{100}$ months/week $= \frac{1}{4}$ months/week. This ratio tells us that there are four weeks in one month. We can express the number of months corresponding to one day using an intermediate relationship. There are 7 days in one week, which we can express with the ratio $\frac{1}{7}$ weeks/day. To express the number of months per day, we must multiply the first ratio by the second: $(\frac{1}{4}$ months/week$)(\frac{1}{7}$ weeks/day$) = \frac{1}{28}$ months/day. Notice that the weeks units cancel so that the only units left are months and days. If we had used a ratio expressing the number of days per week (the reciprocal of weeks per day), $\frac{7}{1}$ days/week, this cancellation would not occur and the final answer would not have the correct units of months per day.

Quick Solution: To convert a ratio that expresses a relationship between months and weeks to one that expresses a relationship between months and days, multiply it by a ratio that expresses a relationship between weeks and days:

$$(\frac{1}{4}\ \text{months/week})(\frac{1}{7}\ \text{weeks/day}) = \frac{1}{28}\ \text{months/day}.$$

Question 7 B

See: QR 2.2.3, 2.4.3, 2.5.2

The first step in this problem is to find the value of 6.4% of 1,000. We convert the percentage to a decimal (0.064) and multiply by 1,000:0.064(1,000) = 64. Next, we find which of the answer choices is equal to this value. Choice A is obviously incorrect because 64 taken to any power besides 1 does not equal 64. The order of operations tells us that we must perform the calculation inside the parentheses first in choice C, which is a decimal (0.64). Squaring this value does not give us 64. It is easy to see that choice D will also be a decimal. Choice E begins with a small number (6.4) and divides it by a much larger number, so we know that the answer will be even smaller, and therefore not equal to 64. The correct choice is B. To check this, note that $256^{3/4} = (256^{1/4})^3 = (4)^3$ (because $4 \times 4 \times 4 \times 4 = 256$) and $(4)^3 = 64$.

Question 8 D

See: QR 2.2.3, 2.4.3

First, simplify the expressions according to the rules of the order of operations:

$$2 + \left[71 - 8\left(\frac{6}{2}\right)^2\right] = 2 + (70 - 8(3)^2)$$
$$= 2 + (71 - 8(9))$$
$$= 2 + (71 - 72)$$
$$= 2 + (-1) = 1$$

and $\sqrt{2500} = 50$. So, we need to find the percentage of 50 that is constituted by 1. Using the formula

Percent = Part/Whole × 100

$$\frac{1}{50} \times 100 = 0.02 \times 100 = 2,$$

we see that the answer is 2%.

Question 9 A

See: QR 2.4.3

The tenths decimal place is the largest occupied in each number. Comparing the digits in this decimal place, it is clear that the .6 in .636 is the largest.

Question 10 D

See: QR 2.2.1

Following the rule of adding like and unlike signs:

$= 9 + -5 + 6$
$= 4 + 6$
$= 10$

Question 11 B

See: QR 2.5.2

Dividing the coefficients 1.5 and 3.0 gives an answer of 0.5. Then the correct exponent value is determined by subtracting the exponents involved, which are 7 and 4. The final answer in scientific notation is 0.5×10^3.

Question 1 D

See: QR 3.2.2

Construct a ratio comparing millimeters to meters using the definition of the prefix "milli." Remember that we want to convert from meters to millimeters, so the denominator of the fraction we use for this ratio must contain the units of meters: $\frac{1000\,\text{mm}}{1\,\text{m}}$. Now multiply this ratio and the given value: $75\,\text{m}\left(\frac{1000\,\text{mm}}{1\,\text{m}}\right) = 75{,}000\,\text{mm}$.

Question 2 C

See: QR 3.1.2

Start with any of the choices and compare it to the rest:

0.1km = 100m > 10 m

0.5 km > 0.1 km > 10 m

10 cm < 10 m

1000mm = 1m > 10 cm

Question 3 A

See: QR 3.2

The total length of the triathlon is 12 km + 10 km + 15 km = 37 km. Express the ratio of kilometers to meters as a fraction, with kilometers in the denominator to cancel the units of 37 km: $\frac{1000\text{ m}}{1\text{ km}}$.

Now multiply: $37\text{ km}\left(\frac{1000\text{ m}}{1\text{ km}}\right) = 37{,}000\text{ m}$.

Question 4 C

See: QR 3.1

Construct an equation that expresses an unknown number of staples, times the weight of each, equals the weight of one paperclip:

$$0.05x = 1$$

$$x = \frac{1}{0.05} = 20$$

Question 5 E

See: QR 3.2.2

Convert the mixed number to an improper fraction:

$$17\frac{5}{6} = \frac{107}{6}$$

Convert using the fact that 60 minutes equals 1 hour:

$$\left(\frac{107}{6}\text{hours}\right)\left(\frac{60\,\text{minute}}{1\,\text{hour}}\right) = 1070\,\text{minutes}$$

Question 6 B

See: QR 3.2.2

Add like units:

$$67\text{ lbs.} + 93\text{ lbs.} + 18\text{ lbs.} = 178\text{ lbs.}$$

$$1\text{ oz.} + 2\text{oz.} + 5\text{oz.} = 8\text{oz.}$$

Convert to pounds the part of the total weight that is in ounces and add to the rest of the weight:

$$(8\,\text{oz.})\left(\frac{1\text{ lbs.}}{16\text{ 0z.}}\right) = 0.5\text{ lbs.}$$

$$178\text{ lbs.} + 0.5\text{ lbs.} = 178.5\text{ lbs.}$$

Question 7 D

See: QR 3.1.1, 3.2

Given that the charges are:

$20.50 per hour to file paper,
$55 per hour for time in court,
$30 per hour for consultations,

a 90-minute consultation = $30 + $15 = $45.

8 /6 hours = 80 minutes time filing paper work = $20.50 + $6.83 = $27.33

Since 20 minutes = $6.83

1 hour in court = $55

Total charges = $45 + $27.33 + $55 = $127.33

Question 8 A

See: QR 3.2.2

Multiply by all ratios necessary to convert centimeters to feet (via inches) and seconds to minutes, and divide by 4 to calculate the speed for only 25% of a minute:

$$(20\text{ cm/sec.})\left(\frac{1}{2.54}\text{ in./cm}\right)$$

$$\left(\frac{1}{12}\text{ ft./in.}\right)(60\text{ sec./min.})\left(\frac{1}{4}\right) \approx 10\text{ ft./min.}$$

Question 1 C

See: QR 4.2.2A

Combine like terms:

$$\frac{x}{2} - 1 - \frac{x}{2} < x - \frac{x}{2}$$

$$-1 < \frac{x}{2}$$

$$-1(2) < \left(\frac{x}{2}\right)(2)$$

$$-2 < x$$

Question 2 E

See: QR 4.1.4

Substitute 2 for x in the function:

$$f(2) = \frac{12}{4(2)^3 - 6(2) + 5}$$

$$= \frac{12}{4(8) - 12 + 5}$$

$$= \frac{12}{32 - 12 + 5} = \frac{12}{25}$$

Question 3 D

See: QR 4.3.2, 4.3.3

Create a ratio with the first two values and simplify:

$$\frac{13xy^2z}{39y} = \frac{xyz}{3}$$

The unknown ratio must also be equal to this value. Let k represent the variable and cross-multiply:

$$\frac{9xyz^6}{k} = \frac{xyz}{3}$$
$$3(9xyz^6) = (xyz)k$$
$$\frac{27xyz^6}{xyz} = k$$
$$27z^5 = k$$

Question 4 A

See: QR 4.4.2A, 4.4.2B

Substitute the first equation into the second, replacing y:

$$6x - 5y = -3$$
$$6x - 5(2x - 1) = -3$$
$$6x - 10x + 5 = -3$$
$$-4x + 5 = -3$$
$$-4x = -8$$
$$x = 2$$

Substitute this value back into either equation to find y:

$$y = 2x - 1$$
$$y = 2(2) - 1$$
$$y = 3$$

Question 5 E

See: QR 4.4.2B

We will need to write equations that correspond to the sentences. Let d represent the number of dimes, and n represent the number of nickels. Since there are two less dimes than nickels,

$$d = n - 2.$$

The amount of money a group of coins is worth is equal to the value of the coins times the number of coins. The total value of Loubha's nickels is $\$0.05n$ and the total value of her dimes is $\$0.10d$. These add up to all of the money she has:

$$\$0.05n + \$0.10d = \$0.85.$$

Substitute the first equation into the second for n:

$$\$0.05n + \$0.10(n - 2) = \$0.85$$
$$\$0.05n + \$0.10n - \$0.20 = \$0.85$$
$$\$0.15n = \$0.85 + \$0.20$$
$$\$0.15n = \$1.05$$

$$n = \$1.05 / \$0.15$$
$$n = 7$$

There are 7 nickels. We can plug this into either of the two original equations, but the first is easiest to use:

$$d = n - 2$$
$$d = 7 - 2$$
$$d = 5$$

NOTE: In this particular problem, the fastest way is to just try the different answers until one fits the requirements. We have shown the work in case it was a different question type then you would still know the approach.

Question 6 B

See: QR 4.3.1

Simplify the expression:

$$(2.5 \times 10^3)(3 \times 10^x) = 0.075$$
$$(2.5 \times 3)(10^3 \times 10^x) = 0.075$$
$$(7.5)(10^{3+x}) = 0.075$$

Divide both sides of the equation 7.5, or simply note that 0.075 is one–hundredth $(\frac{1}{100}) = 10^{-2}$ of 7.5:

$$10^{3+x} = 10^{-2}$$
$$3 + x = -2$$
$$x = -5$$

Question 7 B

See: QR 4.6.2

y is a quadratic equation, so we can use the quadratic formula to solve for x, but, first, the equation must be in standard form:

$$3x^2 - 5x - 7 - y = 0$$

The term $-y$ does not have any powers of x, so it becomes part of the constant term: $a = 3, b = -5, c = -7 - y$. Applying the quadratic formula,

$$\frac{-(-5) \pm \sqrt{(-5)^2 - 4(3)(-7-y)}}{2(3)}$$

$$= \frac{5 \pm \sqrt{25 + 84 + 12y}}{6}$$

$$= \frac{5 \pm \sqrt{109 + 12y}}{6}$$

Question 8 D

See: QR 4.5.4

If we think of the plank as a straight line in a coordinate system, we can use the points at which its ends are located to find its slope. The origin can be anywhere we choose, and the base of the house's left wall is a good choice. This point of the house must be located at (0, 0), and so the base of the plank, 7 feet to the left, is located at (–7, 0). The point at which the plank touches the left wall is 5 feet above the origin, at (0, 5). The slope of the plank is therefore

$$m = \frac{0 - 5}{-7 - 0} = \frac{-5}{-7} = \frac{5}{7}$$

Question 9 D

See: QR 4.3.1, 4.4.2A, 4.4.2B

It is given that $2n = 3k$, which implies that $\frac{2}{3}n = k$. $n + k = 5$ can therefore be rewritten:

$$n + \frac{2}{3}n = 5$$

$$\frac{5}{3}n = 5$$

$$n = 3$$

Question 1 B

See: QR 5.2, 5.2.3

Using the given information to write an equation, we have:

$$\pi r^2 = 144\pi$$

We need the value of the radius to find the circumference, so we solve for r:

$$r^2 = \frac{144\pi}{\pi}$$

$$r = \sqrt{144}$$

$$r = 12$$

The formula for the circumference of a circle gives us:

$$2\pi r = 2\pi(12) = 24\pi$$

Question 2 A

See: QR 5.3, 5.3.1

We need to divide the volume of the box by the volume of one of the smaller cubes. One edge of the large box is 1 yard, or 36 inches, so its volume is $(36\text{ in})^3 = 46656$ in. The volume of the cube is $(6\text{ in})^3 = 216\text{ in}^3$

$$\frac{46656\,\text{in}^3}{216\,\text{in}^3} = 216$$

Question 3 E

See: QR 5.2, 5.2.3

The length of the radius is half of the length of the diameter, which is $d = \sqrt{(2-2)^2 + (-3-5)^2} = \sqrt{0 + 64} = 8$

units long. The radius is therefore equal to 4.

Question 4 D

See: QR 5.3, 5.3.3

The difference in volume of the cylinders will give us the difference in the amount of water they can hold. The larger cylinder has volume $\pi(1)^2(1)^2 = \pi\text{ ft}^3$ and the smaller cylinder has volume $\pi(1)^2(0.5) = 0.5\pi\text{ ft}^3$. The difference is $\pi\text{ ft}^3 - 0.5\pi\text{ ft}^3 = 0.5\pi\text{ ft}^3$.

Question 5 D

See: QR 5.2, 5.2.2

Triangle A has an area of $\frac{bh}{2} = 3(12\text{ ft}^2) = 36\text{ft}^2$, which means that its base times its height is equal to 72 square feet. The base and height of all 45°–45°–90° triangles are the same, so

$(b \times h)/2 = (b \times b)/2 = 36$. Solving for b gives us $b = \sqrt{72}$. Using the Pythagorean Theorem, we can solve for the hypotenuse. h2 = $(\sqrt{72})2 + (\sqrt{72})2 = 144$, therefore $h = \sqrt{144} = 12$.

Question 6 C

See: QR 5.1, 5.1.3

The angle PQD has a measure equal to that of the given angle, 30 degrees, because the highways are parallel and the road forms a transversal across them. The hypotenuse of the right triangle PQD is 2 km long, and the alley, which forms the leg of the triangle that is opposite angle PQD, has a length of

$$(2\text{ km})\sin(30°) = 1\text{ km}$$

Question 7 A

See: QR 5.2, 5.2.1, 5.2.3

The relationship between the length of a side *s* and the length of the diagonal d of a square is

$$d = s\sqrt{2}$$

The length of a side of the given square is therefore

$$s = \frac{d}{\sqrt{2}} = \frac{5}{\sqrt{2}}$$

This is always the length of the diagonal of the inscribed circle, which has a radius of length $\frac{5}{\sqrt{2}} \div 2 = \frac{5}{2\sqrt{2}}$. The area of the circle is therefore

$$\pi\left(\frac{5}{2\sqrt{2}}\right)^2 = \frac{25\pi}{8}$$

Question 8 E

See: QR 5.2, 5.2.3

Represent the areas of the large and small circle by πr_L^2 and πr_S^2, respectively. 25% is equivalent to $\frac{1}{4}$, so

$$\pi r_S^2 = \frac{1}{4}(\pi r_L^2)$$

$$r_S^2 = \frac{1}{4}r_L^2$$

$$\sqrt{r_S^2} = \sqrt{\frac{1}{4}r_L^2}$$

$$r_S = \frac{1}{2}r_L$$

and the ratio of the radii is $\frac{r_S}{r_L} = \frac{\frac{1}{2}r_L}{r_L} = \frac{1}{2}$.

Question 9 D

See: QR 5.1, 5.1.1, 5.2.3

(0, 0), (10, 0), and any given point except (5, 0) can be connected by an arc, which can form part of a circle. (0, 0), (10, 0), and (5, 0) can only be connected by a line, which can never form part of a circle.

Question 10 E

See: QR 5.2, 5.2.1

The 3-inch border at each end of both dimensions adds 6 in., or 0.5 ft. to both the length and the width of the picture. The total area of both picture and border is therefore: (5)(4) = 20 sq. ft.

Question 11 B

See: QR 5.3, 5.3.1

The four walls have a total area of 4(10)(12) = 480 sq. ft. The total area of the door and bay window are (3)(7) + (3)(4) = 21 + 12 = 33 sq. ft. The total surface area that needs to be covered with wallpaper is therefore 480 – 33 = 447 sq. ft. The number of wallpaper rolls needed is $\frac{447}{100} = 4.47$, which rounds up to 5.

Question 12 C

See: QR 5.3, 5.3.1

The surface area of the floor is given by its length times its width, so its width is given by the surface area divided by the length:

$$\frac{64.125}{9.5} = 6.75\text{ feet}$$

Question 1 D

See: QR 6.3, 6.3.1

The lengths of the hypotenuse and the side adjacent to angle A are given, so we can use the inverse cosine of the ratio of these sides to fnd the angle:

$$\cos^{-1}\left(\frac{2}{7}\right) \approx 73°$$

Question 2 B

See: QR 6.2, 6.2.1

A circle covers a total of 2π radians, and

$$\frac{\frac{8\pi}{5}}{2\pi} = \frac{4}{5}$$

which is equivalent to 80%.

Question 3 A

See: QR 6.5

$$-\cos\left(\frac{\pi}{2}\right) = \cos\left(\frac{\pi}{2}\right) = 0$$

Question 4 C

See: QR 6.1, 6.1.3, 6.3, 6.3.3

In a right triangle, the tangent of an angle represents the ratio of sides $\frac{opposite}{adjacent}$, so the given values form the proportion $\frac{3}{2} = \frac{12}{x}$, where x is the side adjacent the angle in Question. Cross-multiplication gives us 3x = 24, or x = 8, and we can fnd the length of the hypotenuse using the Pythagorean Theorem:

$$12^2 + 8^2 = c^2$$
$$144 + 64 = c^2$$
$$\sqrt{208} = c$$
$$\sqrt{4 \times 4 \times 13} = c$$
$$4\sqrt{13} = c$$

Question 5 A

See: QR 6.3, 6.3.2

Simplifying the expression, we get: Cos (x) = sin(x). The only angle for which the sine and cosine are equal is 45º. This can be inferred from the fact that the legs of a 45°–45°–90° triangle are of equal lengths.

Question 6 D

See: QR 6.3, 6.3.2

Using the identity $\tan^2(x) + 1 = \sec^2(x)$,

$$\tan^2(x) + 1 = \left(\frac{5}{4}\right)^2$$
$$\tan^2(x) = \frac{25}{16} - \frac{16}{16}$$
$$\tan(x) = \sqrt{\frac{9}{16}}$$
$$\tan(x) = \frac{3}{4}$$

Question 7 E

See: QR 6.2, 6.2.3

The cosine of an angle is equal to the sine of its complement. $\frac{\pi}{6}$, or $\left(\frac{\pi}{6}\right)\left(\frac{180°}{\pi}\right) = 30°$, is the complement of $\frac{\pi}{3} = 60°$.

Question 8 C

See: QR 6.2, 6.2.1

On the unit circle, the sine of an angle is equivalent to the *y*-coordinate of the terminal side of the angle, so the angle must lie in one of the quadrants in which *y* is negative: The third or fourth. The tangent of an angle is represented by the quotient of the *y*-coordinate and *x*-coordinate of the angle's terminal side, so it is positive in quadrants in which *x* and *y* have the same sign: The third and first. Therefore, the angle must be located where the two possible regions overlap: The third quadrant.

Question 1 B

See: QR 7.1.1

There are four red marbles, and a total of 4 red + 6 blue = 10 marbles, so the probability is $\frac{4}{10}$.

Question 2 C

See: QR 7.3.4

Each ordering of the objects is different, so it is necessary to calculate of the number of permutations in which all 6 objects are used. $6! = 720$

Question 3 E

See: QR 7.1, 7.1.2

With a total of 10 balls and 6 yellow balls, the probability that the first ball is yellow is $\frac{6}{10} = \frac{3}{5}$. After the first ball is chosen, there are 9 left, of which 4 are green. The probability of choosing a green ball at this point is therefore $\frac{4}{9}$. The total probability is

$$\left(\frac{3}{5}\right)\left(\frac{4}{9}\right) = \frac{4}{15}$$

Question 4 E

See: QR 7.3, 7.3.5

Multiply all possible choices: $3 \times 2 \times 4 = 24$

Question 5 A

See: QR 7.3.2

The 2516 residents represent 68% of the total number of residents x:

$$2516 = 0.68x$$

$$3700 = x$$

Question 6 C

See: QR 7.2, 7.2.1

If the third student takes x minutes to complete the test:

$$\frac{41 + 37 + x}{3} = 35$$

$$78 + x = 105$$

$$x = 27$$

Question 7 D

See: QR 7.3.5

There are 4 different book colors, so there are 4 different choices for books to shelve on Monday. There are only 3 choices on Tuesday. On Wednesday, the rest of the books will be shelved, so there is only 1 choice. This gives a total of $4 \times 3 \times 1 = 12$ different ways to shelve the books.

Question 8 B

See: QR 7.2

Label the numbers a, b, c, d from smallest to largest. The range is the difference between the largest and smallest:

$$d - a = 14$$

The median is the average of the two middle numbers:

$$\frac{b + c}{2} = 7$$

and so

$$b + c = 14$$

The mean is the average of all of the numbers:

$$\frac{a + b + c + d}{4} = 8$$

Simplifying this equation and substituting 14 for $b + c$:

$$a + b + c + d = 32$$

$$a + 14 + d = 32$$

$$a + d = 18$$

Adding this equation and the equation that represents the range:

$$(a + d) + (d - a) = 18 + 14$$

$$2d = 32$$

$$d = 16$$

Therefore:

$$16 - a = 14$$

$$a = 2$$

Now, we have 3 of the numbers and can use the simplified equation for the mean to find the fourth, which we can call x:

$$2 + 9 + 16 + x = 32$$

$$x = 5$$

Question 9 E

See: QR 7.1, 7.1.2

A die has a total of 6 possible sides. There is only one side that displays a 3, so the probability of rolling a 3 is $\frac{1}{6}$. Similarly, the probability of rolling any other number is also $\frac{1}{6}$. The probability of rolling a 1 or a 2 is the sum of their individual probabilities: $\frac{1}{6} + \frac{1}{6} = \frac{1}{3}$. Because this probability is independent of the probability of first rolling a 3, we multiply the results to get the total probability: $\left(\frac{1}{6}\right)\left(\frac{1}{3}\right) = \frac{1}{18}$.

Question 10 D

See: QR Chap 7 Appendix

The p value (= **p**robability value or alpha level) expresses statistical significance. The probability of committing a Type I error is called the significance level or alpha (= α). All answer choices are accurately describing $p<.05$.

Question 11 A

See: QR Chap 7 Appendix

The t-test (= Student's t-test) and analysis of variance (= ANOVA) are statistical procedures that assume normal distributions (= *parametric*) and make use of the mean and variance to determine the significance of the differences of the means of two or more groups of values. Whether there is evidence that the samples or data were random or that differences in the populations are significant would be the result of a statistical analysis but not an assumption.

Question 12 D

See: QR Chap 7 Appendix

Chi-Squared Goodness of Fit Test is a test for comparing a theoretical distribution, such as a Normal distribution, with the observed data from a sample.

Question 13 C

See: QR Chap 7 Appendix

Null hypothesis (= H_0) is usually the hypothesis that sample observations result purely from chance. In other words, the null hypothesis says that there is no significant difference between specified populations, any observed difference being due to sampling or experimental error. This is most consistent with answer choice C which states that it is "the assumption that there is no relationship or difference between the variables being tested".

Question 14 B

See: QR Chap 7 Appendix

Either the null hypothesis is true or the alternative hypothesis is true but never both.

Question 15 A

See: QR Chap 7 Appendix

A two-sided test (= two-tailed test of significance) is a statistical hypothesis test in which the values for which we can reject the null hypothesis, H_0 are located in both tails of the probability distribution.

Question 16 A

See: QR Chap 7 Appendix

Test scores follow a normal curve or normal distributions (= *parametric*). Chi-square is a nonparametric statistical procedure. The question is looking at one parameter: are Gold Standard students scoring higher than other students: one-tailed test.

Question 17 C

See: QR Chap 7 Appendix

Again, let's return to flipping a coin.

H_0: probability = 0.5

H_a: probability < 0.5 or > 0.5

Thus the alternative hypothesis could be that heads occur more often, or that heads occur less often as would be predicted by the null hypothesis would suggest that the event is not random.

Question 18 C

See: QR Chap 7 Appendix

A Type II error occurs when the researcher accepts a null hypothesis that is false. Traditionally, a Type I error is considered to be more serious.

Question 19 A

See: QR Chap 7 Appendix

A Type I error occurs when the researcher rejects a null hypothesis when it is true. The probability of committing a Type I error is called the significance level or alpha (= α). The confidence level is $1 - \alpha$.

Question 20 D

See: QR Chap 7 Appendix

The p value (= **p**robability value or alpha level) expresses statistical significance. The probability of committing a Type II error is called beta (= β).

Question 1 C

See: QR 8.2.2

The walking speed is $\frac{1.5\text{mi}}{0.5\text{hr.}} = 3\text{mi./hr.}$, and in 3 hours, (3 hr.) (3 mi./hr.) = 9 mi. will be covered.

Question 2 A

See: QR 8.1, 8.1.2

Since the ray passes through one focus, it must pass through the other after being reflected. The length of any such path is always equal to the length of the major axis, so if the distance between the point of reflection and the second focus is 6, the distance between the point of reflection and the first focus must be 8 − 6 = 2.

Question 3 D

See: QR 8.1.2

The distance from the given focus to the point of reflection is

$$\sqrt{(\sqrt{5} - 0)^2 + (0 - 2)^2}$$
$$= \sqrt{(\sqrt{5})^2 + (2)^2}$$
$$= \sqrt{5 + 4}$$
$$= \sqrt{9} = 3$$

The second focus must be located at $(-\sqrt{5}, 0)$. By symmetry, this focus is also 3 units from the point of reflection. The sum of these lengths is the total distance traveled by the ray of light, and is equal to the length of the major axis.

Question 4 B

See: QR 8.2, 8.2.1

Combined, the two pipes fill the tank at a rate of 5 + 15 = 20 gal./min.. The time t needed to fill the tank is:

$$t = \frac{180\text{ gal.}}{20\text{ gal./min.}} = 9\text{ min.}$$

Question 5 A

See: QR 8.1, 8.1.1

The beam of light will be reflected on the opposite side of the mirror, and because it passes through the center, its path is a diagonal of the circle, which has length $2r = 2(5) = 10$.

Question 6 E

See: QR 8.2.2

The truck's speed during the morning is

$$\frac{150\text{ mi}}{3\text{ hrs}} = 50\text{ mph}$$

and its speed during the afternoon is

$$\frac{180\text{ mi}}{3\text{ hrs}} = 60\text{ mph}$$

The average speed is

$$\frac{50\text{ mph} + 60\text{ mph}}{2} = 55\text{ mph}$$

Question 7 C

See: QR 8.2, 8.2.2

The ship will reach the shore in

$$\frac{500\text{ km}}{100\text{ km / min}} = 5\text{ min}$$

This is a total of

$$(5\text{ min.})(60\text{ sec./min.}) = 300\text{ sec},$$

which makes up

$$\frac{300\text{ sec}}{5\text{ sec}} = 60$$

intervals of 5 seconds each. In this time, the lighthouse beam sweeps out

$$60\left(\frac{\pi}{4}\right) = 15\pi\text{ radians},$$

which is equivalent to

$$\frac{15\pi}{2\pi} = 7.5\text{ revolutions.}$$

Question 8 D

See: QR 8.1, 8.1.1

As the diagonal of a square intercepts the corners of the square at a 45° angle, a ray travelling diagonally across a square must intercept the corner at the same angle. The Law of Reflection tells us that the ray is reflected at 45° as well, so BDC and BED are congruent 45°–45°–90° triangles. The distance DE, which represents the ray's distance from point D, must be equal to CD. The length of the diagonal of a square is the length of the side times the square root 2, so CD and DE must have length $\frac{1}{\sqrt{2}}$.

Question 9 B

See: QR 8.2.1

Let w, h, d represent the current ages of the wife, husband, and daughter, respectively. Three years ago, they were $w - 3, h - 3, d - 3$ years old. The average of these is:

$$\frac{(w - 3) + (h - 3) + (d - 3)}{3} = 27$$

Five years ago, the husband and daughter were $h - 5, d - 5$ years old, and the average of these ages is:

$$\frac{(h - 5) + (d - 5)}{2} = 20$$

Simplify these fractions to get:

$$w + h + d = 90,$$
$$h + d = 50$$

Now, subtract the second equation from the first:

$$w + h + d - (h + d) = 90 - (50)$$
$$w = 40$$

Question 10 B

See: QR 8.2, 8.2.2

Use the formula $\text{rate} = \frac{\text{distance}}{\text{time}}$, where the distance is 3.3 miles. The downhill rate minus the uphill rate is:

$$\begin{aligned} r2 - r1 &= \frac{3.3}{1.5} - \frac{3.3}{5} \\ &= \frac{10(3.3)}{15} - \frac{3(3.3)}{15} \\ &= \frac{7(3.3)}{15} \\ &= 1.54 \text{ miles per hour} \end{aligned}$$

Given that 1 mile = 1.6 km:

$$\frac{1.54\text{mi}}{1\text{hr}} \times \frac{1.6\text{km}}{1\text{mi}} \times \frac{1\,\text{hr}}{3600\,\text{s}}$$
$$= \frac{2.464\text{ km}}{3600\,\text{s}}$$
$$= 6.84 \times 10^{-4}\text{ km/s}$$

DAT-Prep.com

READING COMPREHENSION

THE STRUCTURE OF THE READING COMPREHENSION SECTION

Chapter 1

Understand

* Key concepts in academic reading, question types, study reading strategies

DAT-Prep.com

Introduction

The DAT Reading Comprehension entails two main tasks: (1) locating key information in academic texts and (2) identifying concepts in order to make reasonable inferences about the subject under discussion. These require certain skills that some candidates may already have while others may still need to develop.

In any case, your first step in confronting this section is to familiarize yourself with the features and structure of the test. This will help you determine the approach that you need to adopt in your RC preparation.

Let's start reading!

Additional Resources

Free Online Forum

1.1 Overview

The third section of the DAT is the **Reading Comprehension Test**. This section primarily assesses your ability to locate key details and infer fundamental concepts in scholarly texts. Recall and analysis of written information are skills that are requisite to the problem-solving demands in the basic sciences. Thus the stimulus passages given in the Reading Comprehension section replicate the kind of scientific reading required in dental college.

Prior knowledge of science topics and concepts is NOT REQUIRED to competently answer the test questions, and the best preparation really is, well...reading. However, it is regular study reading from a variety of academic references throughout your high-school and undergraduate studies that makes for a strong foundation in this section. Nevertheless, you should not neglect to prepare for this test as it accounts for one of the five standard scores that make up the Academic Average score in the DAT.

In a report published by the ADA in May 2011, 39 of the 58 surveyed U.S. dental schools indicated that they consider the Reading Comprehension as the third most important DAT score of an applicant, following the Academic Average and Total Science scores, in their admissions criteria.[1] Half of the 10 Canadian dental schools likewise include this score in the DAT, next to Perceptual Ability and Academic Average, as a significant factor in their selection process.

By acquainting yourself with the nature and scope of this section, you will be able to anticipate vulnerable areas. As long as you are quick to address your weaknesses, increasing your chances of doing well in this section is very much possible.

---

[1] ADA Survey Center, *2009-10 Survey of Dental Education Tuition, Admission, and Attrition Volume 2* (Chicago, Illinois: American Dental Association, 2011), http://www.ada.org/sections/professionalResources/pdfs/survey_ed_vol2.pdf.

1.2 Format and Content of the Test

The Reading Comprehension Test is composed of 50 multiple-choice questions and has a time limit of 60 minutes. It consists of three reading passages of approximately 1,500 words in length.

This section comes right after the optional 15-minute break subsequent to the Perceptual Ability Test. A passage is then presented on the computer screen in full-page view. {Please note that the Canadian

DAT remains a paper test and is 50 minutes long. The Reading Comprehension Test is only included in the English DAT in Canada.}

The subsequent screens will show one question at a time, with the reading passage in a parallel window right under it. Every time the page moves to the next question, the reading passage reloads and goes back to its beginning sentence or paragraph.

On average, there are 16 to 17 questions per passage, although this can occasionally range from 15 to 20. Each question requires an answer choice from four to five options.

The Reading Passage

A passage is placed in a smaller window with a vertical scroll bar that allows the test-taker to move the text up and down. Paragraphs are also numbered. The "NEXT" button at the bottom-center of the window leads to the questions in the succeeding pages.

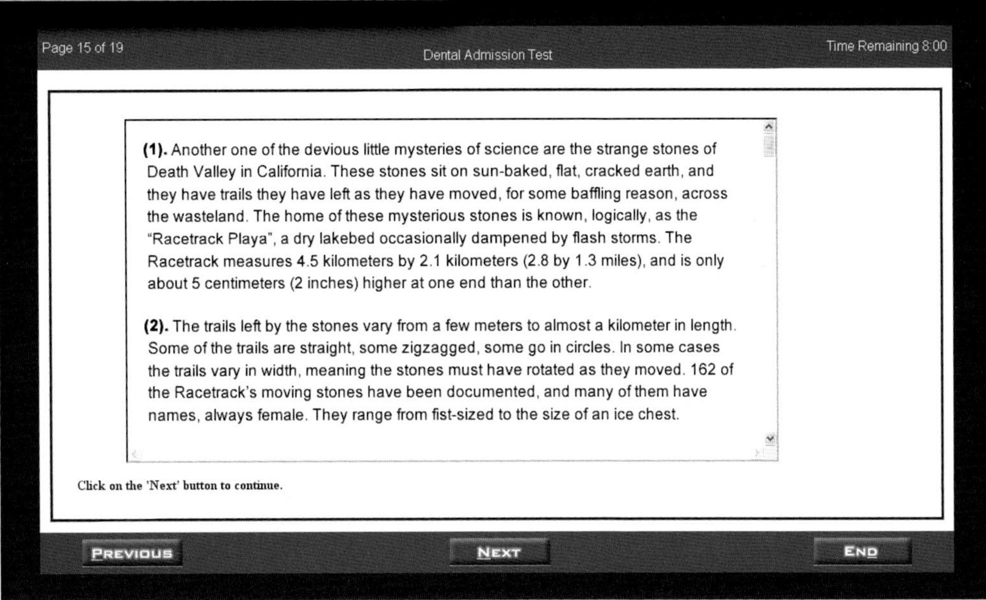

Page 15 of 19
Dental Admission Test
Time Remaining 8:00
(1). Another one of the devious little mysteries of science are the strange stones of Death Valley in California. These stones sit on sun-baked, flat, cracked earth, and they have trails they have left as they have moved, for some baffling reason, across the wasteland. The home of these mysterious stones is known, logically, as the "Racetrack Playa", a dry lakebed occasionally dampened by flash storms. The Racetrack measures 4.5 kilometers by 2.1 kilometers (2.8 by 1.3 miles), and is only about 5 centimeters (2 inches) higher at one end than the other.
(2). The trails left by the stones vary from a few meters to almost a kilometer in length. Some of the trails are straight, some zigzagged, some go in circles. In some cases the trails vary in width, meaning the stones must have rotated as they moved. 162 of the Racetrack's moving stones have been documented, and many of them have names, always female. They range from fist-sized to the size of an ice chest.
Click on the 'Next' button to continue.
PREVIOUS
NEXT
END

Figure RC.1.1: Screenshot of a Reading Passage.

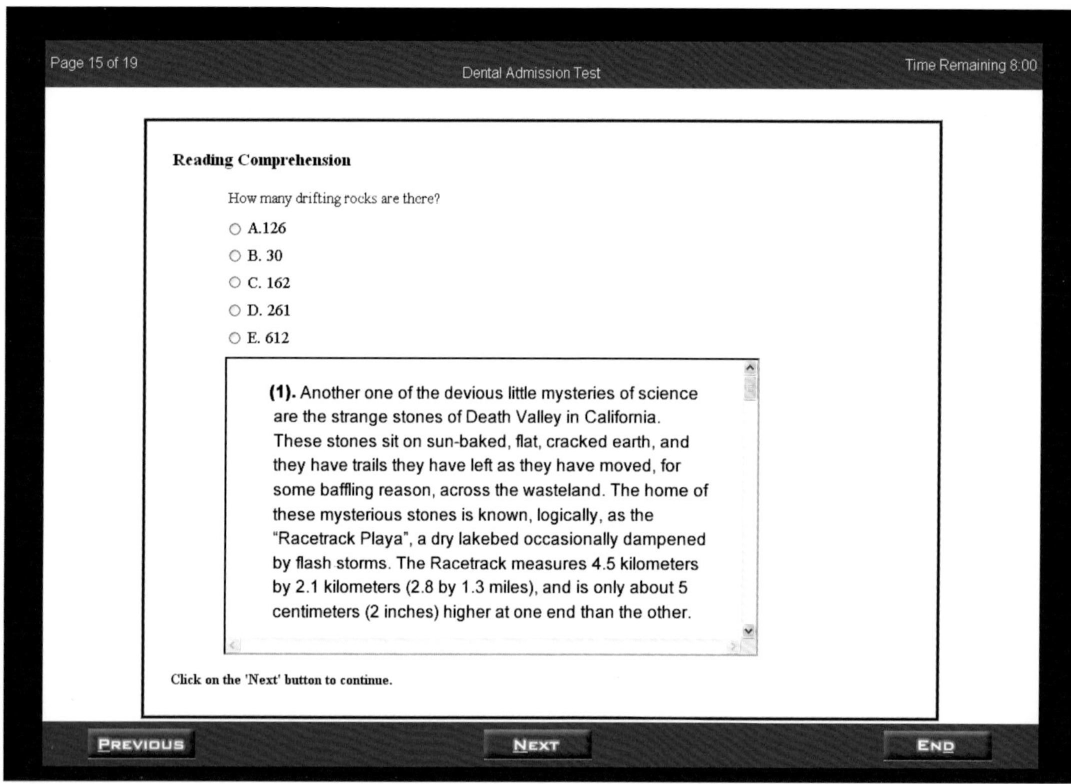

Figure RC.1.2: Screen Window View of the Questions. Take note that for each question, the entire reading passage is still provided in a smaller screen with the scroll bar.

Unlike the Biology, Chemistry and Quantitative Reasoning sections, the ADA has not published any recommended text to review for the Reading Comprehension Test. However, the DAT User's Manual describes the subject matter as "developed from aspects of dental, basic, or clinical science not covered in an undergraduate college curriculum."[2]

In addition, students who have taken the past exams reported coming across the following topics:

---

[2] Dental Admission Testing Program, *Report 3 2011: User's Manual 2009* (Chicago, Illinois: American Dental Association Department of Testing Services, 2011), http://www.ada.org/sections/educationAndCareers/pdfs/dat_users_manual.pdf.

Science Topics

- Aging
- Antibiotics
- Bone fractures
- Brain functions, glutamate receptors
- Contraception
- Einstein-related topic
- Enzymes, telomerases
- Fungi
- Gene therapy, genetic cancer, epithelial-mesenchymal transition
- Helico bacteria (H.Pylori)
- Herbal medicine
- Hurricanes
- Physics involving calculations
- Subatomic particles
- Tooth development
- Transcription/Translation, recent studies on mRNA, voltage-gated ion channels, messenger

Non-science topics

- Ethics
- Floating Bridges
- Piano
- The Stock Market

Please note that you do neither have to know nor study these topics in order to do well on the exam. Rather, these merely serve as examples to give you a glimpse of the subject matters typically found on the test.

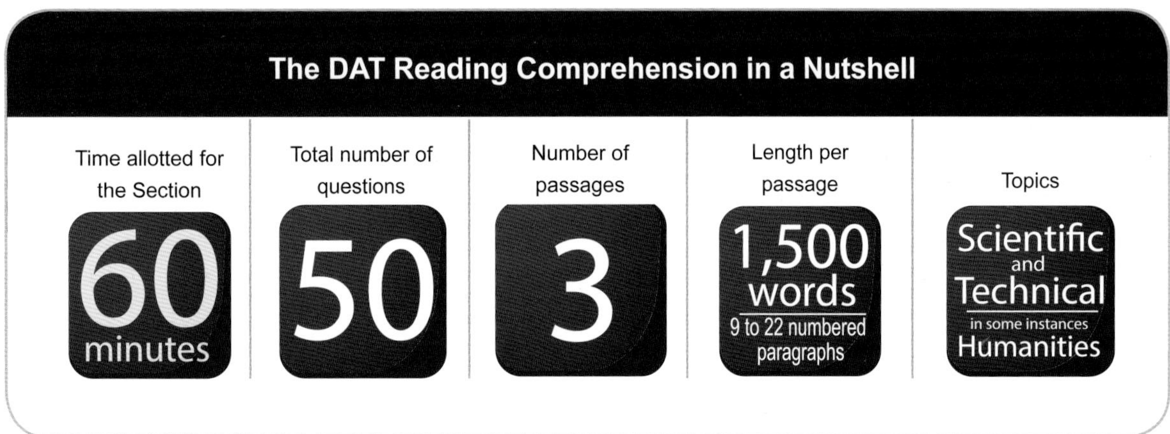

The DAT Reading Comprehension in a Nutshell
Time allotted for the Section
60 minutes
Total number of questions
50
Number of passages
3
Length per passage
1,500 words
9 to 22 numbered paragraphs
Topics
Scientific and Technical
in some instances
Humanities

Chapter 2

Understand

* **Reading comprehension techniques: predicting, skimming, paraphrasing, visualizing, contextual clues**

Introduction

Questions in the DAT Reading Comprehension test mostly require careful attention to specific terms, methods and or core ideas in a passage. On some occasions, you may need to slow down and evaluate certain details with an analytical perspective.

Reading techniques such as predicting, skimming, and paraphrasing should form the backbone of your preparation. The earlier you utilize these skills, The earlier you utilize these skills, the earlier you will be able to identify which strategies are the most effective for you.

Additional Resources

Free Online Forum

2.1 Factors Affecting Preparation and Performance in the Test

In the preceding chapter, we have discussed the format and content of the DAT Reading Comprehension test.

Knowing what to expect in this section is quite important because the difficulty of a test is oftentimes subjective to the test-taker. For instance, some passages may appear lengthy because paragraphs in the RC section are numbered, making short but several paragraphs look longer. Being confronted with a seemingly lengthy passage may set an anxious examinee to panic, consequentially affecting focus and confidence in overcoming the whole test.

However, if you very well know beforehand that a reading passage will only have 1500 words at the maximum, and assuming that you have adequately practiced your reading speed for this section, you can calmly proceed with the exam.

Likewise, the difficulty of a specific passage depends on a candidate's background. Someone who is not used to reading dense articles whether in the sciences or humanities often find the RC section a real challenge. Moreover, humanities in the DAT RC context specifically refer to philosophical texts that deal with moral values or socio-political principles. Readings based on culture or the arts are also common. A student with a strong science background may find these readings difficult because of limited exposure to such topics.

Applicants who have English as their second language doubly struggle in the RC section because the language used in these passages is largely technical.

Building your skills effectively for this section indeed depends on a number of factors. However, familiarity with science topics, exposure to technical and scholarly reading, timing and the ability to focus are all key components to success. While no specific presumed knowledge is required to answer any of the questions, you still need to remain focused on cultivating these core skills, which will be tested in the actual exam.

2.2 Developing Comprehension Skills

2.2.1 One Year or More before the DAT

Strengthening your reading comprehension skills is beneficial to your overall preparation for the DAT: you are more likely to overcome better the cognitive rigor of the different test sections. By exposing yourself to various topics, your stored knowledge will also expand. This will be particularly important when you start interviewing for dental school and present yourself as a well-rounded individual.

Therefore, read! Be known as a "voracious reader"! Read materials that interest you, as well as those that DO NOT necessarily excite you. After all, dental school involves a lot of reading and absorbing enormous amounts of information.

Contrary to approaching creative and opinion pieces, some extent of background knowledge makes reading scientific articles a less agonizing experience. You tend to understand technical concepts better and quicker if you have been introduced to the topic before. At least once every week, for 1 – 3 hours, you should read among the following (either from a university library or online):

- **Scientific Articles**

Suggested Resources:

✓ **Dental Journals**
The Journal of the American Dental Association (http://jada.ada.org/)
The Journal of Contemporary Dental Practice (http://www.thejcdp.com/)
Journal of Dental Research (http://jdr.sagepub.com/)
The Directory of Open Access Journals (http://www.doaj.org/) This free-access site lists the links to online dental journals.

✓ **Dental Research and News Sources**
Pubmed has several articles that have free Full Text content: http://www.ncbi.nlm.nih.gov/pubmed/
ADA Science News (http://ada.org/272.aspx)
ADA Publications and Resources (http://ada.org/293.aspx)

✓ **Science Magazines**
The Scientific American (http://www.scientificamerican.com/sciammag/)
Discover Magazine (http://discovermagazine.com/)

Active reading tends to improve comprehension and speed. With scientific articles, the following techniques usually prove to be helpful:

1. **Predicting**
   This is equivalent to preliminary skimming. Upon seeing the title of what you are about to read, you can usually guess the article's content, especially if you are familiar with the subject matter from prior knowledge. Likewise, awareness of textual types (e.g., expository*, argumentative) could help predict to which the succeeding discussions may lead.

2. **Skimming**
   This is a technique for spotting clues within the text itself. You run your eyes quickly through the content for an overview of what to expect in the material, occasionally slowing down on seemingly salient parts. As you skim over the words and the paragraphs, you should continually ask yourself…

   - Is this article about a description of some characteristic?
   - Is the article about an origin, a discovery or a scientific process or method?
   - Does the author organize his or her ideas through definitions and examples, classification, or cause and effect?

   By using this technique, you can figure out certain parts that are not essential and detect parts where you need to dedicate some attention for a better understanding of the details. Lastly, skimming will confirm your earlier prediction, which was initially based on the article's title.

3. **Paraphrasing**
   In order to test your general understanding of reading material, restate the main idea of each relevant paragraph. By the end of the article, you will have a clearer outline of the author's central point. Taking the whole by its smaller parts is less overwhelming than having to swallow everything in a single glance.

4. **Visualizing**
   Quite frequently, the procedures and the apparatus described in scientific papers are very specific. For descriptions of the parts of an instrument, doing a sketch proves to be of great benefit. Similarly, you can create a skeletal outline of the steps in an experiment, a research investigation, or a process.

---

*Expository texts can range from textbooks to scientific journals, encyclopedia, and biographies. These articles are meant to inform, describe, explain or define concepts, theories and methods.

- **Humanities Articles**

For exposure to a variety of the humanities topics and themes, include Arts and Culture articles in your weekly plate of exploratory reading:

✓ **Humanities and Culture Magazines or Journals**
The New Yorker - Culture section
(http://www.newyorker.com/arts/)
Digital Humanities
(http://www.digitalhumanities.org/dhq/)
The Culture Magazine
(http://www.culturemachine.net/)

Paraphrasing is a reading technique that is highly applicable to selections from the humanities and any texts that demand inference. However, you should go beyond just getting the main idea. The following are also vital questions that you need to actively ask yourself when reading non-scientific articles:

- What are the primary supporting facts and/or evidences that support the author's thesis?
- For which type of audience would the article appeal?
- What is the author's tone?
- What is the author's attitude or opinion toward the subject?
- What is the author's purpose for writing the article?

2.3 One Year or Less before the DAT

Read section 2.2.1 one more time! Even at this point in your preparation, being a voracious reader - with all that it entails - should be your goal. Besides reading, you need to practice.

The best strategy is to take the ADA's *DAT Sample Test Items*, which can be downloaded for free from the ADA website. Although this is not a full-length test, you should still do this section within the prescribed time limit (approximately 1.2 minutes per question). Your main objective is to gauge your current skills against the requirements of the real test. You should be able to determine this by reviewing your mistakes.

If you performed well and understood the source of your errors then you will only require ADA and the Gold Standard (GS) DATs in order to complete your preparation. If, on the other hand, you struggled in the test or struggled to understand your mistakes then you may need additional work on strategies, practice or a formal course for or without credit. An optional RC program can be found at DAT-prep.com.

Basic Preparation Tools	Practice Exams (Full-length)
• ADA *DAT Sample Items* • GS book and online	• DAT Practice Test (ADA) • GS QR/RC + PAT/GS-1 books and online • Top Score Pro

2.3 Advice for ESL Students

The same preparation applies for candidates with English as a second language (ESL). Depending on your English skills, you may or may not benefit from an English reading or writing summer course. Of course, you would have the option of deciding whether or not you would want to take such a course for credit.

However, vocabulary may be a chief obstacle, so getting used to academic and rhetorical language is imperative. The dictionary will have to be a constant help buddy in the beginning; but as you progress in your speed and vocabulary, you need to wean yourself from the dictionary and start counting on context clues.

2.4 Contextual Reading

Contextual reading compels you to make a logical guess about the meaning of an unknown word based on the other words and phrases found within the immediate sentences in the paragraph. Writers themselves use this technique to make lucid points. Several cues easily offer probable definitions to uncommon terms:

1) Examples
Cue words: includes, consists of, such as

Equine *animals, such as horses and zebras, have long been used not only to aid in man's work but also to assist in therapy.*

Using the example clue (use of "such as"), the word equine means:
A. mammal.
B. reptile.
C. horse group.
D. dog.

2) Synonyms
Cue words: is similar to, just as, also means

*Calling my cousin an "eccentric weirdo" is **tautologous**! It is similar to telling a ghost that he is dead twice.*

The cue word "is similar to" indicates that tautologous means:
A. repetitive.
B. alien.
C. scary.
D. ridiculous.

3) Antonyms and Contrasts
Cue words: unlike, contrary to/in contrast, on the other hand, as opposed to

*Contrary to the playwright's **euphemisms** about the King's corrupt leadership, the merchant was quite direct in criticizing the latter's injustices.*

Based on the contrasting descriptions used in the sentence, the word euphemism refers to:

A. corruption.
B. indirect speech.
C. criticism.
D. politics.

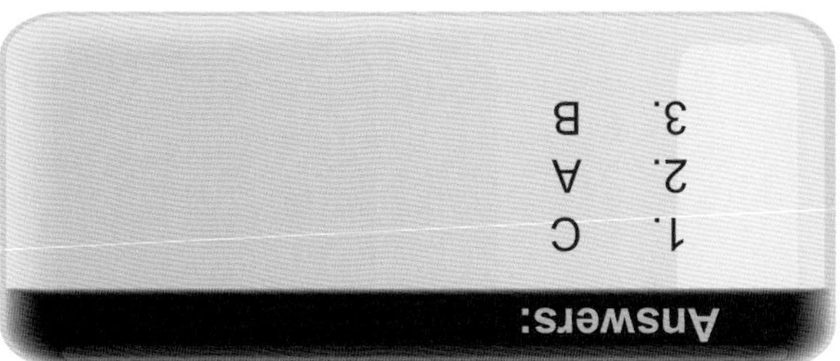

4) Sense of the sentence
Oftentimes, you only need to observe how the words or phrases relate within the sentence in order to fairly conclude what the difficult word means. Take careful note of the descriptions in the paragraph. Use your logic in determining the most probable meaning of a newly-encountered term.

*March 21, 1894 marks a rare series of **syzygies** in the history of astronomical events. A few hours before Mercury transits the sun as seen from Venus, a partial lunar eclipse is witnessed from Earth. From Saturn, both Mercury and Venus could be seen simultaneously transiting the* *sun. Such planetary spectacles can also be observed by the naked human eye during full moons and new moons as the sun, our planet Earth, and the moon periodically aligns.*

Based on the context of the discussion in the paragraph, the closest meaning of syzygies could be:

A. planetary collisions.
B. lunar eclipses.
C. planetary alignments.
D. historical changes.

5) Root Words, Prefixes, and Suffixes

Certain root words and word parts carry specific meanings. Being acquainted with these, combined with the other clues discussed earlier, helps you figure out the most probable meaning of an unfamiliar word.

Answer: C

Descriptions in the paragraph mention "lunar eclipse," "Mercury transits the sun" and "the sun, our planet earth, and the moon periodically aligns." These should serve as primary clues in determining a general definition of syzygies.

(D) Historical changes is obviously the least likely option. (A) Planetary collisions may sound related; however, nothing in the paragraph indicates a collision of the planets. This should now narrow down your choice between (B) lunar eclipses and (C) planetary alignments. Now common knowledge tells us that a lunar eclipse occurs when three celestial bodies such as the sun, the moon and the Earth align. On the other hand, a full moon or a new moon does not necessarily result to a lunar eclipse. This makes C the more logical answer!

Common Root Words of Scientific Terms

The following is a list of root words, prefixes, and suffixes, which you would generally find in scientific literature. A prefix is a group of letters added to the beginning of a word; a suffix is added to the end of a word.

Prefixes

A
aden- gland
adip- fat
aero- air
agri- field; soil
alb- white
alg-/algia- pain
alto- high
ambi- both
ameb- change; alternation
amni- fetal membrane
amphi-; ampho- both
amyl- starch
ana- up; back; again
andro- man; masculine
anemo- wind
angi- blood vessel; duct
ante- before; ahead of time
anter- front
antho- flower
anthropo- man; human
aqu- water
archaeo- primitive; ancient
arteri- artery
arthr- joint; articulation
aster-; astr- ; astro- star
ather- fatty deposit
atmo- vapor
audi- hear
aur- ear
auto- self

B
bacter-/bactr- bacterium; stick; club
baro- weight
bath- depth; height
bene- well; good
bi- (Latin) two; twice
bi-/bio- (Greek) life; living
brachi- arm
brachy- short
brady- slow
branchi- fin
bronch- windpipe

C
calor- heat
capill- hair
capit- head
carcin- cancer
cardi-/cardio- heart
carn- meat; flesh
carp- fruit
carpal- wrist
cata- breakdown; downward
caud- tail

Prefixes

cente- pierce
centi- hundredth
centr- center
cephal- head
cerat- horn
cerebr- brain
cervic- neck
chel- claw
chem- dealing with chemicals
chir- hand
chlor- green
chondr- cartilage
chrom-/chromo- color
chron- time
circa-; circum- around; about
cirru- hairlike curls
co- with; together
cocc- seed; berry
coel- hollow
coll- glue
coni- cone
contra- against
corp- body
cort-/cortic- outer layer
cosmo- world; order; form
cotyl- cup
counter- against
crani- skull
cresc-/cret- begin to grow
crypt- hidden; covered
cumul- heaped
cuti- skin
cyt- cell; hollow container

D
dactyl- finger
deca- ten
deci- tenth
deliquesc- become fluid
demi- half
dendr- tree
dent- tooth
derm- skin
di-/dipl- (Latin) two; double
di-/dia- (Greek) through; across; apart
dia- (Latin) day
digit- finger; toe
din- terrible
dis- apart; out
dorm- sleep
dors- back
du-/duo- two
dynam- power
dys- bad; abnormal; difficult

E
ec- out of; away from
echin- spiny; prickly
eco- house
ecto- outside of
en-/endo-/ent- in; into; within
encephal- brain
enter- intestine; gut
entom- insects
epi- upon; above; over
erythro- red
eso- inward; within; inner

Prefixes

F
ferro- iron
fibr- fiber; thread
fiss- split
flor- flower
flu-; fluct-; flux flow
foli- leaf
fract- break

G
gastr- stomach
geo- land; earth
gloss- tongue
gluc-/glyc- sweet; sugar
glut- buttock
gnath- jaw
gymno- naked; bare
gyn- female
gyr- ring; circle; spiral

H
halo- salt
hapl- simple
hecto- hundred
hem- blood
hemi- half
hepar/hepat- liver
herb- grass; plants
hetero- different; other
hex- six
hibern- winter
hidr- sweat
hipp- horse
hist- tissue
holo- entire; whole
homo- (Latin) man; human
homo- (Greek) same; alike
hort- garden
hydr- water
hygr- moist; wet
hyper- above; beyond; over
hyph- weaving; web
hypno- sleep
hypo- below; under; less
hyster- womb; uterus

I
ichthy- fish
infra- below; beneath
inter- between
intra- within; inside
iso- equal; same

K
kel- tumor; swelling
kerat- horn
kilo- thousand
kine- move

L
lachry- tear
lact- milk
lat- side
leio- smooth
leuc-/leuk- white; bright; light
lign- wood
lin- line

Prefixes

lingu- tongue
lip- fat
lith-; -lite stone; petrifying
loc- place
lumin- light

M
macr- large
malac- soft
malle- hammer
mamm- breast
marg- border; edge
mast- breast
med- middle
meg- million; great
mela-/melan- black; dark
mes- middle; half; intermediate
met-/meta- between; along; after
micro- small; millionth
milli- thousandth
mis- wrong; incorrect
mito- thread
mole- mass
mono- one; single
mort- death
morph- shape; form
multi- many
mut- change
my- muscle
myc- fungus
mycel- threadlike
myria- many
moll- soft

N
nas- nose
necr- corpse; dead
nemat- thread
neo- new; recent
nephro- kidney
neur- nerve
noct-/nox- night
non- not
not- back
nuc- center

O
ob- against
ocul- eye
oct- eight
odont- tooth
olf- smell
oligo- few; little
omni- all
onc- mass; tumor
opthalm- eye
opt- eye
orb- circle; round; ring
ornith- bird
orth- straight; correct; right
oscu- mouth
oste- bone
oto- ear
ov-/ovi- egg
oxy- sharp; acid; oxygen

P
pachy - thick

Prefixes

paleo- old; ancient
palm- broad; flat
pan- all
par-/para- beside; near; equal
path- disease; suffering
pent- five
per- through
peri- around
permea- pass; go
phag- eat
pheno- show
phon- sound
photo- light
phren- mind; diaphragm
phyc- seaweed; algae
phyl- related group
physi- nature; natural qualities
phyt- plant
pino- drink
pinni- feather
plan- roaming; wandering
plasm- formed into
platy- flat
pleur- lung; rib; side
pneumo- lungs; air
poly- many; several
por- opening
port- carry
post- after; behind
pom- fruit
pre- before; ahead of time
prim- first
pro- forward; favoring; before
proto- first; primary
pseudo- false; deceptive
psych- mind
pter- having wings or fins
pulmo- lung
puls- drive; push
pyr- heat; fire

Q
quadr- four
quin- five

R
radi- ray
ren- kidney
ret- net; made like a net
rhe- flow
rhin- nose
rhiz- root
rhodo- rose
roto- wheel
rubr- red

S
sacchar- sugar
sapr- rotten
sarc- flesh
saur- lizard
schis-/schiz- split; divide
sci- know
scler- hard
semi- half; partly
sept- partition; seven
sex- six
sol- sun

Prefixes

solv- loosen; free
som-/somat- body
somn- sleep
son- sound
spec-/spic- look at
spir- breathe
stat- standing; staying
stell- stars
sten- narrow
stern- chest; breast
stom- mouth
strat- layer
stereo- solid; 3-dimensional
strict- drawn tight
styl- pillar
sub- under; below
super-/sur- over; above; on top
sym-/syn- together

T
tachy- quick; swift
tarso- ankle
tax- arrange; put in order
tele- far off; distant
telo- end
terr- earth; land
tetr- four
thall- young shoot
toxico- poison
top- place
trache- windpipe
trans- across
tri- three
trich- hair
turb- whirl

U
ultra- beyond
uni- one
ur- urine

V
vas- vessel
vect- carry
ven-/vent- come
ventr- belly; underside
vig- strong
vit-/viv- life
volv- roll; wander

X
xanth- yellow
xero- dry
xyl- wood

Z
zo- animal
zyg- joined together
zym- yeast

Suffixes

A
-ap/-aph -touch
-ary/-arium -place for something
-ase -forms names of enzymes

B
-blast -sprout; germ; bud

C
-cell -chamber; small room
-chrome -color
-chym -juice
-cid/-cis -cut; kill; fall
-cul/-cule -small; diminutive
-cyst -sac; pouch; bladder
-cyte -cell; hollow container

D
-duct -lead

E
-elle -small
-emia -blood
-en -made of
-eous -nature of; like
-err -wander; go astray

F
-fer -bear; carry; produce
-fid -divided into
-flect/-flex -bend

G
-gam -marriage
-gene -origin; birth
-gest -carry; produce; bear
-glen -eyeball
-glob -ball; round
-gon -angle; corner

H
-hal/-hale -breathe; breath
-helminth -worm

I
-iac -person afflicted with disease
-iasis -disease; abnormal condition
-ism -a state or condition
-ist -person who deals with...
-itis -inflammation; disease
-ium -refers to a part of the body

K
-kary -cell nucleus

L
-less -without
-log -word; speech
-logist -one who studies...
-logy -study of...
-lys/-lyt/-lyst -decompose; split; dissolve

M
-mer -part
-meter/-metry measurement
-mot -move

Suffixes

N
-ner -moist; liquid
-node -knot
-nom/-nomy -ordered knowledge; law

O
-oid -form; appearance
-oma -abnormal condition; tumor
-orium/-ory -place for something
-osis -abnormal condition

P
-pathy -disease; suffering
-ped -foot
-ped -child
-phil -loving; fond of
-phone -sound
-phore; pher -bear; carry
-phyll -leaf
-phyte -plant
-plast -form
-pod -foot

R
-rrhage -burst forth
-rrhea -flow

S
-scop -look; device for seeing
-septic -infection; putrefaction
-sis -condition; state
-sperm -seed
-spher -ball; round
-spire -breathe
-spor -seed
-stasis -placed
-stome -mouth

T
-the/-thes -put
-thel -cover a surface
-therm -heat
-tom -cut; slice
-trop -turn; change
-troph -nourishment; one who feeds

U
-ul/-ule -diminutive; small
-ura -tail
-verge -turn; slant
-vor -devour; eat

Z
-zoa -animal

DAT READING COMPREHENSION STRATEGIES
Chapter 3

Understand

* **DAT-specific exam strategies and approaches**
* **Types of questions**

DAT-Prep.com

Introduction

Speed reading is a critical skill in the Reading Comprehension test. The DAT RC specifically calls for mental endurance and efficiency. For one, this section comes after the Perceptual Ability Test – which can already be mentally exhausting! For another, questions on the DAT RC require you to QUICKLY spot key details, delineate facts from opinion, and as the term "comprehension" implies, understand the central point of the written piece.

In this chapter, we will show you clear and specific strategies and build your skills with dozens of exercises. This will be followed by three separate mini-RC tests and then a full-length practice RC test. Let's begin . . .

Additional Resources

Free Online Forum

3.1 How to Approach the Reading Comprehension Section

Three passages to read – each with approximately 1500 words – and a total of 50 questions to answer in 60 minutes! How do you complete this test on time and ace it?

Indeed, time management poses a major challenge to many test-takers. The DAT RC, however, is not merely about speed reading. This section will also require mental endurance after a demanding one-hour Perceptual Ability Test. Likewise, efficiency in locating relevant information and understanding key ideas are integral factors that will help you overcome the demands of this section.

Nevertheless, students have aced the section using different strategies. There is no "one size fits all" strategy to obtain a great score. The key is to be able to start early with your preparation so you can identify which strategy specifically works for you. A systematic approach with clear strategies – some sort of a game plan – is vital in achieving an excellent RC score.

Ideally, you should make a concerted effort to try the various strategies that we present to you during separate timed practice tests. Then you can compare the various scores which you have obtained. This will help you narrow down the specific strategies that apply to your own experience. From that point onward, you should remain consistent.

Ample Preparation Time + Clear Strategies + Simulated Practice Tests

3.1.1 Methods in Reading Passages during the Exam

Generally, you would need to read carefully but swiftly. You will have about 20 minutes per passage. Every 30 minutes, you should check the timer on the computer to be sure that you have completed approximately 25 questions. Of course you can judge time in any way you want (20, 25, 30-minute intervals, etc.). But decide on a system during practice and commit to that system on test day.

Be sure to reach a speed where you have at least 10 minutes to spare. If you have time at the end, you can return to properly evaluate the questions you skipped or marked. Of course, if you find that you are getting behind the set pace, then you consistently guess the answers to time-consuming questions in order to catch up.

In the meantime, you should try to apply each of the strategies that we will discuss in this section in order to determine which gives you your optimal performance. Different DAT students have boosted their RC scores with completely different techniques. With constant practice, you will be able to determine which of the following is best for you.

1. **Questions First, Passage Once**

   Some candidates like to get a glimpse of the questions prior to reading the text. Others read the questions but not the answer choices yet. Then they read the passage and answer questions as they read the information. The point of doing this is to survey the kind of reading technique that will work best in attacking the passage and which other strategy to employ.

   You may find it more efficient to work in this manner. Try one of the practice exams using this strategy and if you find it easier to answer the questions correctly, you should use the same method on the actual DAT.

2. **Passage First, Questions Next**

   Some examinees prefer to carefully read through the passage once while noting the key details. Remember that the DAT is a computerized exam, and you will be provided with laminated note boards at your test center upon request. You can take brief notes of the major ideas and concepts in each paragraph along with their keywords. You can use boxes and or circles to categorize the important details and then, make meaningful connections between the main concepts and their supporting information by using arrows. This is also called "mapping."

   This strategy allows you to mark significant information in specific paragraphs so that they are easier to locate when answering relevant questions later. At the same time, you can see where the discussion is going as you construct each part of the "map." Ideally, you should be able to make a reasonable conclusion of the author's central thesis once you complete the "map."

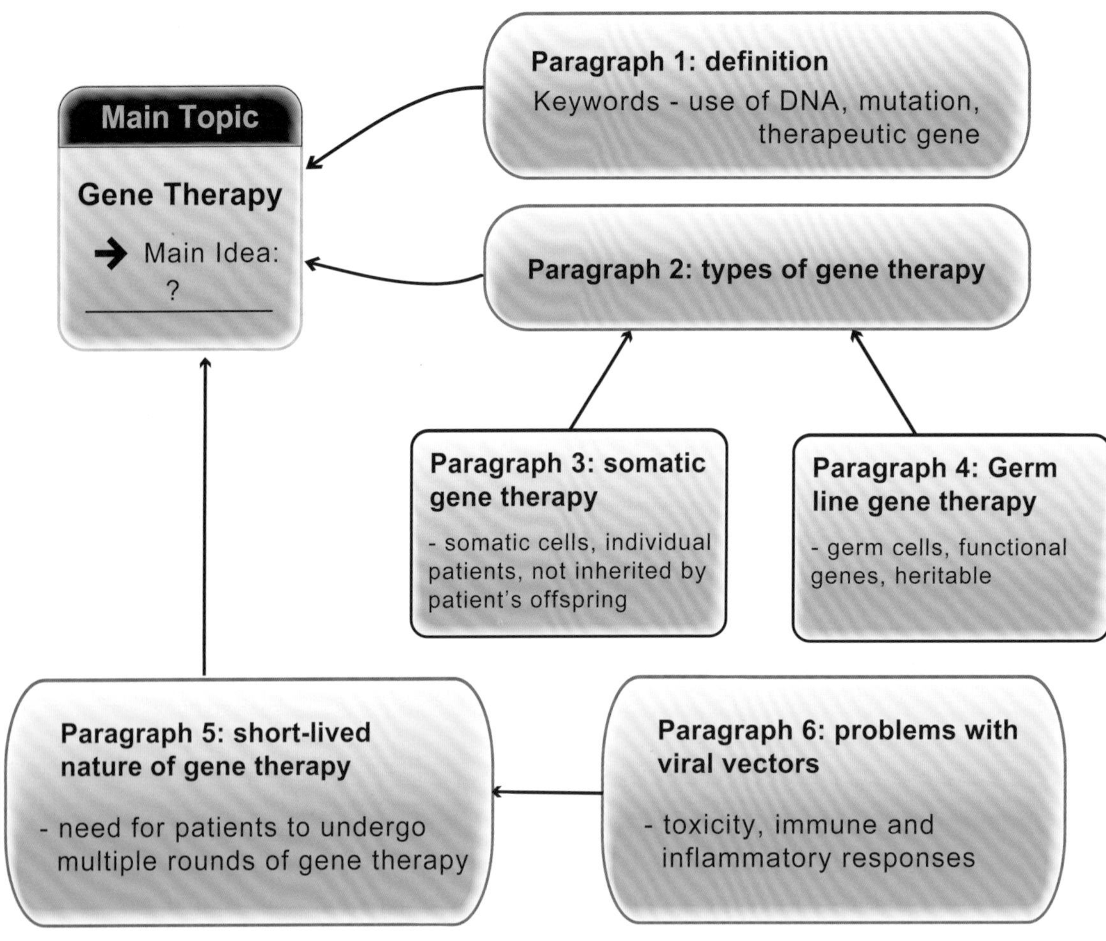

Figure RC 3.1: Mapping a Passage. Start with the main box using the passage's title as the main topic. You can then use circles and boxes to help you categorize the main concepts and their supporting details respectively. By the time that you complete "mapping" Paragraph 6, you can safely infer that the passage's main idea is roughly about the disadvantages of gene therapy.

3. **Questions and Passage at the Same Time**

   This approach may not always work with questions that greatly require identifying the central idea of a passage. However, for questions that merely ask you to locate data such as dates, names, terminologies or definitions, this exam reading method is time-saving.

   You read each question as you proceed with the test, and then skim through the different paragraphs to find the correct answer.

4. **Read the Opening and Closing Paragraphs**

   In many cases, you would need to combine one or two of the preceding approaches in dealing with the passages. Going over the first and last paragraphs of a passage gives you a "bracket" to work within.

   Once you get an initial feel of the passage, you can decide on the appropriate strategy that will speed up your performance during the exam.

We have also established that reading diverse material in the period leading up to the exam will be useful since the stimulus material will be from a variety of sources. Create a mindset that, in the exam, you are prepared for “edutainment": After completing a passage, look forward to what you can learn and discover in the next one. Having properly prepared and then begin the exam with the right attitude will give you an edge.

In any case, the most logical means to find out which strategy or which combination of strategies would augment your test-taking skills is to do simulated practice. The more you practice, the more you are inclined to be comfortable with a particular strategy or modify a technique to suit your own strengths or weaknesses.

3.1.2 Basic Question and Answer Techniques

Understanding the “science” of answering multiple choice questions is another vital skill in dealing with not only the Reading Comprehension section, but also with the DAT exam as a whole. The following are general techniques used in answering such questions.

1. Process of Elimination (PoE): eliminate any answers that are obviously

wrong. In many cases, there may be two very similar answer choices that appear to be correct. You would need to pay close attention to the subtle differences in order to determine the actual answer. Dismissing the obvious ones first from your choices would certainly save you a lot of precious time. If you have second thoughts about your remaining choices, the exam's program allows you to mark an answer so you can go back to it later - if you have enough time left - and decide on your final choice.

2. Never lose sight of the question: by the time students read answer choices C and D, some have forgotten the question and are simply looking for "true" sounding statements. Therefore, they tend to choose an option, which presents a statement that may be true but does not answer the question, and is therefore incorrect. For example,

   Answer Choice D: Most people are of average height. → This is a true statement.

   However, the question was: What is the weight of most people?

   Therefore, the true statement becomes the incorrect answer!

   Continually check the question and check or cross out right or wrong answers.

3. Paying attention to details: a common decoy in most timed multiple-choice exams, and especially in the DAT RC, is to offer options that are in close proximity – either within the same sentence or paragraph – where the correct answer is found. At other times, either the phrasing of the statements in the answer choices or the language used in the passage itself is complicated. Hence you need to stay focused on the facts and thoroughly understand both the information and the question presented.

EXAMPLE

Question: What is the most effective treatment for OLP?

A. Corrective dentistry
B. Regular dental consultations
C. Systemic corticosteroids
D. Non-randomized clinical trials

Text: Although systemic corticosteroids are probably the most effective treatment modality for patients with diffuse erosive OLP (oral lichen planus) or multi-site disease, the literature on their use is limited to non-randomized clinical trials. Thus oral hygiene and corrective dentistry play a major role in the management of OLP and consultation with a dentist or oral medicine specialist is helpful.

Answer: Getting the facts straight in this test item can be tricky. The question is simply asking for the most effective treatment, regardless of its actual use or availability of helpful alternatives. Thus the correct answer is C.

4. Verbatim Statements: Literal and direct quotes from the stimulus material characterize several of the correct answer choices in the real DAT. This is because topics in the reading passages mostly deal with scientific and literal matters.

The next question-and-answer techniques, which we will discuss, are rarely required in the DAT RC. However, these are common "tricks" in multiple choice questions, which are worth getting yourself familiar with – just in case they do come up in the exam.

5. Beware of the extreme: words such as always, never, perfect, totally, and completely are often (but not always) clues that the answer choice is incorrect.

6. Mean Statements: mean or politically incorrect statements are unlikely to be included in a correct answer choice. For example, if you see any of the following statements in an answer choice, you can pretty much guarantee that it is not the correct answer:

   Parents should abuse their children.
   Poor people are lazy.
   Religion is socially destructive.
   Torture is usually necessary.

3.2 DAT-specific RC Exam Strategies

While the preceding methods and techniques are effective in tackling the RC section, there are strategies that specifically address the types of questions presented in the DAT.

1. **Scan and Locate (SaL)**

   You will most probably make the most use of this strategy. When you scan, you simply locate specific details that ask the basic "who, what, when, where, and how." Basically, you will be looking for proper nouns and numerical figures. It is similar to browsing the telephone directory to look up an address or contact number.

If you have been practicing the reading techniques recommended in Chapter 2, this strategy might become almost second nature to you. This is probably the easiest skill to develop, yet a very important one. Efficiently locating a specific detail trains you to differentiate material information from immaterial ones; those that add something new from those that simply restate an idea.

Scanning will work even without a preview of the questions. You simply proceed with each question – one at a time – and rapidly find the data being asked by scrolling down and up the passage, then move on to the next. Note the scanned details – either mentally or by writing them down – and remember that these are key to the passage's overall discussion. For example, the answer to a question "Which of the following experiments resulted in the widespread cure of such disease?" must be pertinent to the passage. You can then use this as one of your bases to understand the main idea better or to determine the author's purpose.

2. **Skim for Ideas (SI)**

The main difference between scanning and skimming is that you search for words or numerical values in the former while sentences and ideas in the latter. Skimming is mostly useful when the information that you are looking for is not explicitly stated in the passage. Therefore, you randomly seek for supporting data, more keywords, examples or explanations. Whenever you find one, slow down and read for the precise information you need.

3. **Outline and Annotate (OA)**

Outlining is more or less the same as the reading technique "paraphrasing" discussed in Chapter 2. You can use this strategy as a conjunction either after you have shortly gone over the questions or as you go along assessing the passage first. The advantage, on the other hand, of doing an initial glimpse of the different questions is that you get to have a heads-up as to whether the passage will simply require scanning information or demand an in-depth understanding of concepts. In most instances, this strategy tends to work best with inference questions.

Essentially, you jot down key terms and ideas of each numbered paragraph. Please note, however, that the Canadian

DAT does not allow the use of any paper other than the answer sheet provided. For the American DAT, as mentioned earlier, you can ask for a note board, which is provided in the test center. Doing so helps you to read actively and then later, to find keywords or points without having to search aimlessly. Your notes can also include any one or more of the following that you deem relevant:

- brief remarks of each paragraph's main idea
- definition of key terms
- hypothetical examples or interpretations of important concepts
- your observations of the author's tone, writing style, attitude toward the subject, or devices used to illustrate a point
- your own questions or doubts about ambiguous points in the paragraph

Some candidates also find it helpful to do the following: just before you read from each passage, think of someone young that you know - for example, a younger brother, sister, cousin, etc. Imagine that once you finish reading the stimulus material, you will have to explain it to them in words that they understand. The idea is to encourage active reading, attention and focus.

An alternative scenario, if it does not stress you out too much, would be to imagine that you will need to give a speech in class regarding the passage right after you read it once. Keep that imagery during your evaluation of the material, so you have a heightened sense of awareness of what you are reading.

Gold Standard DAT RC Key Methods and Strategies

- Scan and Locate (SaL)
- Skim for Ideas (SI)
- Outline and Annotate (OA)
- Process of Elimination (PoE)
- Attention to Details
- Never lose sight of the question

3.3 Types of Questions

Questions in the DAT Reading Comprehension section can be loosely classified into two main categories: detail-oriented and concept-oriented.

1. Detail-oriented

Questions of this type chiefly test your accurate identification of facts or key concepts found in the passage.

A. Recall Questions

You will need to search the passage for terms, synonyms, proper names, dates, statistical numbers, locations, characteristics, descriptions, definitions, etc.

B. Exception or Negative Questions

These are fundamentally the same as the Recall Questions; but this time, the false statement serves as the correct answer.

2. Concept-oriented

These require you to understand, conclude, or judge what could be reasonably inferred from the author's views or from the evidence demonstrated in the passage.

A. Math-related Questions

This question type occasionally comes out in the RC section and calls for simple math logic, interpretation, or a quick calculation of numerical data mentioned in the passage.

B. True or False Statements

These come in two forms:

- Two Statements

Normally, a test question presents two statements, which are derived from the passage. You need to evaluate them as either both true or false, or either one of them is true or false.

- Statement and Reason

You will be presented with a cause and effect statement that requires you to judge whether the reason supports the statement or not, or both are unrelated.

C. Evaluation Questions

Some questions ask you to consider the validity, accuracy, or value of the author's ideas and/or the facts presented in the text. These heavily demand inference skills.

D. **Application Questions**

These questions challenge your higher cognitive skills through generalization of the concepts presented in the passage. Use the given information to solve new problems described in the questions.

Now let's dissect and understand each question type in the following sections.

3.3.1 Recall Questions

Literal types of questions commonly appear similar to any one of the following examples:

- Term: What is the most common form of cancer?
- Statistical Number: Which of the following shows the number of times that the city was hit by an earthquake?
- Location: At which of the following countries was surgery first recognized as a legitimate medical practice?
- Synonyms: A meteor is also known as...
- Characteristics: Which of the following clinical methods characterizes the treatment used by the doctor?
- Description: The law of conservation is stated in the passage as...
- Definition: As used in the passage, which of the following best defines "dentistry"?

Since these are primarily detail questions, most of them can be easily answered using "scan and locate" (SaL), as well as "skim for ideas" (SI) strategies.

Now let's do some exercises to ensure that you can successfully deal with these question types. Please take a piece of paper to cover the answers while you are responding to the questions. Notice that just as in the real exam, questions do not necessarily follow the chronological order of information discussed in the passage.

Read the following excerpts and promptly locate the details asked in the questions that follow.

PASSAGE 1

(1). As early as February 21, 1775, the Provincial Congress of Massachusetts appointed a committee to determine what medical supplies would be necessary should colonial troops be required to take the field. Three days later, the Congress voted to "make an inquiry where fifteen doctor's chests can be got, and on what terms"; and on March 7, it directed the committee of supplies "to make a draft in favor of Dr. Joseph Warren and Dr. Benjamin Church, for five hundred pounds, lawful money, to enable them to purchase such articles for the provincial chests of medicine as cannot be got on credit."

(2). A unique ledger of the Greenleaf apothecary shop of Boston reveals that this pharmacy on April 4, 1775, supplied at least 5 of the 15 chests of medicines. The account, in the amount of just over £247, is listed in the name of the Province of the Massachusetts Bay, and shows that £51 was paid in cash by Dr. Joseph Warren. The remaining £196 was not paid until August 10, after Warren had been killed in the Battle of Bunker Hill.

(3). The 15 medicine chests, including presumably the five supplied by Greenleaf, were distributed on April 18—three at Sudbury and two each at Concord, Groton, Mendon, Stow, Worcester, and Lancaster. No record has been found to indicate whether or not the British discovered the medical chests at Concord, but, inasmuch as the patriots were warned of the British movement, it is very likely that the chests were among the supplies that were carried off and hidden. The British destroyed as much of the remainder as they could locate.

1. What is the name of the pharmacy from which the committee purchased the medicine chests?

Answer: ____________________

2. In whose account were the medical supplies listed?

Answer: ____________________

3. What amount would approximately represent the price of one medicine chest?

Answer: ____________________

4. Three of the medicine chests were distributed at which location?

Answer: ____________________

5. The Provincial Congress of Massachusetts decided to canvass for 15 doctor's chests on which date?

Answer: ____________________

PASSAGE 2

(1). The term bioinformatics was coined by Paulien Hogeweg and Ben Hesper in 1978 for the study of informatic processes in biotic systems. Its primary use since at least the late 1980s has been in genomics and genetics, particularly in those areas of genomics involving large-scale DNA sequencing. Over the past few decades rapid developments in genomic and other molecular research technologies and developments in information technologies have combined to produce a tremendous amount of information related to molecular biology.

(2). It is the name given to these mathematical and computing approaches used to glean understanding of biological processes that bioinformatics has become known as the application of computer science and information technology to the field of biology. Bioinformatics now entails the creation and advancement of databases, algorithms, computational and statistical techniques and theory to solve formal and practical problems arising from the management and analysis of biological data.

6. Bioinformatics can be defined as what?

Answer: ______________________

Answers:

1. Greenleaf
   Strategy: SaL; P2 S1*
   (P stands for Paragraph, S stands for Sentence; the corresponding numbers point to the paragraph number and the sentence within that paragraph)
2. The Province of the Massachusetts Bay
   Strategy: SaL; P2 S2
3. £51
   Strategy: SaL and SI; P2 S2
4. Sudbury
   Strategy: SaL and SI; P3 S1
5. February 24, 1775
   Strategy: SaL and SI; P1 S2.
   The Provincial Congress of Massachusetts voted to "make an inquiry where fifteen doctor's chests can be got, and on what terms" three days after it appointed a committee for the medical supplies on February 21, 1775. February 21 plus 3 days makes February 24.

7. Who coined the term "bioinformatics"?

   Answer: ____________________

8. What would characterize the main functions of bioinformatics?

   Answer: ____________________

9. In what year did bioinformatics become useful to genomics and genetics?

   Answer: ____________________

10. In which particular area of genomics is bioinformatics useful?

    Answer: ____________________

Answers:

6. Bioinformatics is the application of computer science and information technology to the field of biology.
   Strategy: SaL; P2 S1
7. Paulien Hogeweg and Ben Hesper
   Strategy: SaL; P1 S1
8. Use of mathematical and computing approaches to understand biological processes
   Strategy: SI; P2 S1
9. 1980s
   Strategy: SI; P1 S2
10. large-scale DNA sequencing
    Strategy: SaL; P1 S2

3.3.2 Exception or Negative Questions

The following are some of the most common examples of this question type:

Each of the following characteristics generally pertains to modern art EXCEPT one. Which one is the EXCEPTION?

Which of the following symptoms was NOT mentioned in the passage?

Which of the following statements is false?

In these questions, using the "process of elimination" technique would be ideal in choosing the best answer out of multiple choices. There will be a number of instances when a statement would sound valid in a real world situation but is not discussed in the passage. At other times, an option would be correct but points to another closely-related concept. Therefore, you should "never lose sight of the question" as well.

PASSAGE 3

(1). Resistance to antibiotics is one of the critical complications in the treatment of infectious diseases. Enterococcal resistance to gentamicin, which is the effective antibiotic in this case, highlights the importance and the priority of the matter. Enterococci are among the most common microorganisms responsible for nosocomial infections in the hospital intensive care units and also the causative infectious agent in urinary and bile tract systems, resulting in bacteremia in infants and acute endocarditis in adults, in addition to dental and gingival infections. Therefore, isolation and identification of different enterococcal species and determination of their resistance pattern and their prevalence as well as obtaining their genetic patterns are of utmost importance. Examples of these methods include antibiogram by disk diffusion agar for determination of gentamicin resistance, evaluation of the genetic pattern utilizing DNA isolation, and observation of formed bands using electrophoresis on agarose gel 0.8% by ultraviolet. A general and comprehensive method for obtaining an ideal outcome by these methods can also be tested.

(2). Enterococci are gram-positive cocci, usually detected in feces. These bacteria grow in blood agar or BHI containing 5% blood, and are often non-hemolytic but sometimes α- or β-hemolytic. They do not produce any gases and are PYR, LAP, and bile escolin positive. They grow in 6.5% NaCl medium and can bear the 10-45°C temperature range. The Moller Hinton medium is utilized for testing enterococcal resistance against gentamicin. In previous studies, the bacteria from diluted culture in 0.5 McFarland solution was cultured in Moller Hinton medium and the 100 μg gentamicin was placed on it and after 24 hours the resistance degree was reported by measuring the hallow around the disk. For determination of enterococcal resistance genetic pattern, the molecular and DNA derivation was used afterwards.

(3). For plasmid derivation in alkaline lysis method, plasmids are turned to deluxe rapidly. Generally, when the antibiotic concentration required for bacterial death or its growth inhibition is higher, the microorganism shows resistance to it. Plasmids are naturally circular chromosomes without any small proteins, and are seen in bacteria as well as the bacterial genome. Their genome is composed of double-stranded DNA and their replication is dependent on the host cells but independent of the bacterial genome. Most of them are replicated in bacterial reproduction cycles. Plasmids bear many genes that the bacterium usually needs their productions and for this, their high quantities are justifiable.

1. The following are methods used for testing enterococcal resistance against gentamicin EXCEPT one. Which is the EXCEPTION?

A. Antibiogram by Disk Diffusion Agar Test
B. The Moller Hinton medium
C. Fecal Analysis
D. Plasmid derivation in Alkaline Lysis method

2. Enterococci cause the following infections EXCEPT:

A. nosocomial infection.
B. bacteremia.
C. acute endocarditis.
D. urinary tract infection.
E. gingivitis.

3. Which is NOT a characteristic of enterococci?

A. Detected in feces
B. Do not produce any gases
C. Gram-positive cocci
D. Naturally circular chromosomes

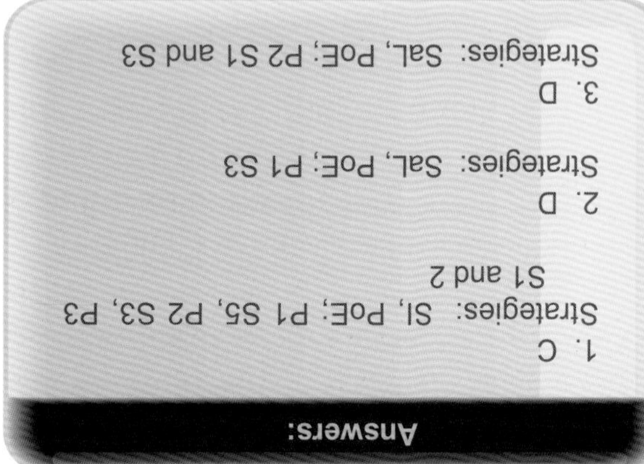

PASSAGE 4

(1). According to Linda Hutcheon, one of the main features that distinguishes postmodernism from modernism is the fact the it "takes the form of self-conscious, self-contradictory, self-undermining statement." One way of creating this double or contradictory stance on any statement is the use of parody: citing a convention only to make fun of it. As Hutcheon explains, "Parody—often called ironic quotation, pastiche, appropriation, or intertextuality—is usually considered central to postmodernism, both by its detractors and its defenders." Unlike Fredric Jameson, who considers such postmodern parody as a symptom of the age, one way in which we have lost our connection to the past and to effective political critique, Hutcheon argues that "through a double process of installing and ironizing, parody signals how present representations come from past ones and what ideological consequences derive from both continuity and difference."

4. Each of the following is another name for parody EXCEPT one. Which is the EXCEPTION?

A. Black Comedy
B. Ironic Quotation
C. Pastiche
D. Appropriation
E. Intertextuality

5. Which of the following is NOT a form of a postmodern statement?

A. Self-replicating
B. Self-conscious
C. Self-contradictory
D. Self-undermining

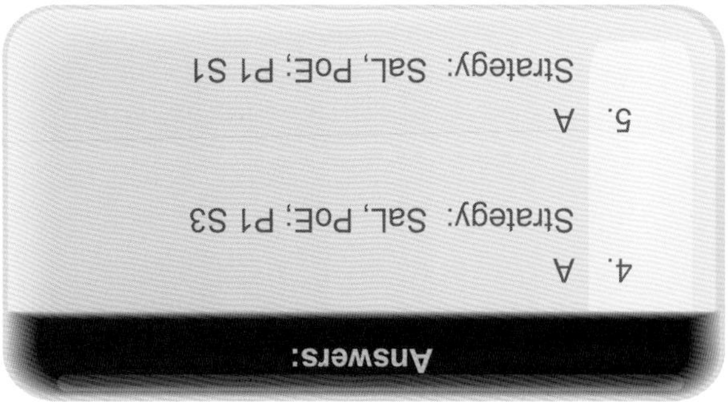

3.3.3 Math-related questions

These questions assess your comprehension of subtle mathematical relationships within a descriptive text. The following short exercises will give you an overview of how to deal with this question type.

PASSAGE 5

(1). All ordinary matter is made up of combinations of chemical elements, each with its own atomic number, indicating the number of protons in the atomic nucleus. Additionally, elements may exist in different isotopes, with each isotope of an element differing in the number of neutrons in the nucleus. A particular isotope of a particular element is called a nuclide. Some nuclides are inherently unstable. That is, at some point in time, an atom of such a nuclide will spontaneously transform into a different nuclide. This transformation may be accomplished in a number of different ways, including radioactive decay, either by emission of particles [usually electrons (beta decay), positrons or alpha particles] or by spontaneous fission, and electron capture.

(2). While the moment in time at which a particular nucleus decays is unpredictable, a collection of atoms of a radioactive nuclide decays exponentially at a rate described by a parameter known as the half-life, usually given in units of years when discussing dating techniques. After one half-life has elapsed, one half of the atoms of the nuclide in question will have decayed into a "daughter" nuclide or decay product. In many cases, the daughter nuclide itself is radioactive, resulting in a decay chain, eventually ending with the formation of a stable (nonradioactive) daughter nuclide; each step in such a chain is characterized by a distinct half-life. In these cases, usually the half-life of interest in radiometric dating is the longest one in the chain, which is the rate-limiting factor in the ultimate transformation of the radioactive nuclide into its stable daughter. Isotopic systems that have been exploited for radiometric dating have half-lives ranging from only about 10 years (e.g., tritium) to over 100 billion years.

(3). In general, the half-life of a nuclide depends solely on its nuclear properties; it is not affected by external factors such as temperature, pressure, chemical environment, or presence of a magnetic or electric field. (For some nuclides which decay by the process of electron capture, such as beryllium-7, strontium-85, and zirconium-89, the decay rate may be slightly affected by local electron density, therefore these isotopes may not be as suitable for radiometric dating.) But in general, the half-life of any nuclide is essentially a constant. Therefore, in any material containing a radioactive nuclide, the proportion of the original nuclide to its decay product(s) changes in a predictable way as the original nuclide decays over time. This predictability allows the relative abundances of related nuclides to be used as a clock to measure the time from the incorporation of the original nuclide(s) into a material to the present.

1. Based on information in the passage, how much would be left of a 5-gram radioactive nuclide parent that decays to a daughter nuclide after 3 half-lives?

Answer: ____________________

Answers:

1. 0.625 gram
Strategies: OA, quick calculation; P2
The passage indicates that one-half of the atoms of a parent nuclide will decay to a daughter nuclide. Thus if a parent nuclide starts out as having a value of 5 grams, it will be left with 2.5 grams after the passage of 1 half-life; 1.25 grams after the passage of two half-lives; and 0.625 after 3 half lives.

PASSAGE 6

(1). Piano music is divided by bar lines into small sections called measures. It also has numbers near the beginning of the music. These numbers are called the time signature. The time signature is related to the rhythm of the music. Each time signature contains 2 numbers: the top number tells you the number of beats or counts in each measure. The number at the bottom tells you which type of note gets the beat. A 4 at the bottom means that the QUARTER NOTE gets one beat. The 4/4 time signature is a very common time signature.

(2). The WHOLE NOTE is a white note with no stem. It receives 4 counts, or 4 beats (1-2-3-4). The HALF NOTE is a white note with a stem. It receives 2 counts (1-2). That means in the same time that you play one whole note, you could play two half notes. The QUARTER NOTE is a black note with a stem. It receives one count, or one beat. You can play 2 quarter notes in the time it takes to play a half note, or you could play 4 quarter notes in the time it takes to play a whole note.

(3). Now for the DOTTED NOTE. A dot can be slapped onto any note: whole notes, half notes, quarter notes, eighth notes, etc. Putting a dot behind a note changes the duration of the note by increasing it by half of its original value. For example: A whole note is worth 4 counts; A dotted whole note would increase the duration of the note by half of its original value (+2), so a dotted whole note would be worth 6 counts. A dotted half note would be worth 3 counts. A dotted quarter note would be worth 1 and a half counts.

2. In a 2/4 time signature, how many half notes can fit in a measure?

Answer: ______________________

3. Two quarter notes and one half note is equivalent to what note?

Answer: ______________________

4. Two dotted quarter notes would be worth how many counts?

Answer: ______________________

5. If an eighth note is worth half a count, how many eighth notes would it take a whole note?

Answer: ______________________

The "piano passage" on the actual DAT is regarded as the hardest passage, and candidates generally cringe upon encountering it. This is important to practice with - just in case.

Answers:

2. 1
   Strategy: SI; P1 and P2
   In the 2/4 time signature, the '2' tells us that there are 2 beats in every measure, and the '4' tells us that the quarter note gets one beat. Since a half note is worth 2 counts, this means that only 1 half note can fit a measure with 2/4 time signature.

3. Whole Note
   Strategies: SaL, quick calculation; P2
   One quarter note is equivalent to 1 beat, so two quarter notes equal 2 beats. One half note gets 2 beats. This means that combining two quarter notes and one half note yield 4 beats, which is equivalent to a whole note.

4. 3 quarter notes or 1 half note and 1 quarter note
   Strategies: SaL, quick calculation; P3, last sentence
   A dotted quarter note is worth 1 and a half counts. 1 and a half counts multiplied by 2 is 3 counts, which is either 3 quarter notes (1 beat each) or 1 half note (2 beats) and 1 quarter note (1 beat).

5. 8
   Strategies: SaL, quick calculation; P2
   Since a whole note is equivalent to 4 counts, this would be equivalent to 8 half counts or 8 eighth notes.

3.3.4 True or False Statements

These frequently require scanning (SaL), skimming (SI), and close attention to the surrounding details. Study the following short passages and validate the corresponding statements as any one of the following:

A. *Both statements are true.*
B. *Both statements are false.*
C. *The first statement is true. The second statement is false.*
D. *The first statement is false. The second statement is true.*

PASSAGE 7

(1). Thermodynamics is a 'phenomenal' science, in the sense that the variables of the science range over macroscopic parameters such as temperature and volume. Whether the microphysics underlying these variables are motive atoms in the void or an imponderable fluid is largely irrelevant to this science. The developers of the theory both prided themselves on this fact and at the same time worried about it. Clausius, for instance, was one of the first to speculate that heat consisted solely of the motion of particles (without an ether), for it made the equivalence of heat with mechanical work less surprising. However, as was common, he kept his "ontological" beliefs separate from his statement of the principles of thermodynamics because he didn't wish to (in his words) "taint" the latter with the speculative character of the former.

1. Macroscopic parameters refer to the philosophy underlying thermodynamics. Microphysics refers to empirical variables, such as temperature and volume.

Answer: ____________________

Answer:

1. B

Strategies: Sl, SaL; P1 S1 and S2

Let's have a quick refresher with the RC strategies that we used here: Sl stands for Skimming for Ideas. SaL stands for Scan and Locate. P refers to Paragraph and S to Sentence, which means that P1 S1 and S2 directs you to review Paragraph 1 Sentences 1 and 2 of the passage to find the correct answer.

PASSAGE 8

(1). Industrial noise is usually considered mainly from the point of view of environmental health and safety, rather than nuisance, as sustained exposure can cause permanent hearing damage. Traditionally, workplace noise has been a hazard linked to heavy industries such as ship-building and associated only with noise induced hearing loss (NIHL). Modern thinking in occupational safety and health identifies noise as hazardous to worker safety and health in many places of employment and by a variety of means.

(2). Noise can not only cause hearing impairment (at long-term exposures of over 85 decibels (dB), known as an exposure action value, but it also acts as a causal factor for stress and raises systolic blood pressure. Additionally, it can be a causal factor in work accidents, both by masking hazards and warning signals, and by impeding concentration. Noise also acts synergistically with other hazards to increase the risk of harm to workers. In particular, noise and dangerous substances (e.g. some solvents) that have some tendencies towards ototoxicity may give rise to rapid ear damage.

2. Occupational noise is associated only with noise induced hearing loss and heavy industries such as ship-building. Aside from hearing impairment, noise can also cause stress and elevation of systolic blood pressure.

Answer: ____________

Answer:

2. D
Strategies: SI, attention to details; P1 S2 and P2 S1

PASSAGE 9

(1). A violin consists of a body or corpus, a neck, a bridge, a soundpost, four strings, and various fittings. The fittings are the tuning pegs, tailpiece and tailgut, endpin, possibly one or more fine tuners on the tailpiece, and perhaps a chinrest, either attached directly over the tailpiece or to the left of it.

(2). The body of the violin is made of two arched plates fastened to a "garland" of ribs with animal hide glue. The rib garland includes a top block, four corner blocks (sometimes omitted in cheap mass-produced instruments,) a bottom block, and narrow strips called linings, which help solidify the curves of the ribs, and provide extra gluing surface for the plates. The ribs are what is commonly seen as the "sides" of the box. From the top or back, the body shows an "hourglass" shape formed by an upper bout and a lower bout. Two concave C-bouts between each side's corners form the waist of this figure, providing clearance for the bow.

3. Four corner blocks in the rib garland may not be found in mass-produced violins.

A chinrest is normally provided in the violin.

Answer: ______________________

Answer:

3. C
Strategies: SaI, attention to details; P1 S2 and P2 S2

PASSAGE 10

(1). The study of bacteria practically began with the use of the microscope. It was toward the close of the seventeenth century that the Dutch microscopist, Leeuwenhoek, working with his simple lenses, first saw the organisms which we now know under this name, with sufficient clearness to describe them. Beyond mentioning their existence, however, his observations told little or nothing. Nor can much more be said of the studies which followed during the next one hundred and fifty years. During this long period many a microscope was turned to the observation of these minute organisms, but the majority of observers were contented with simply seeing them, marveling at their minuteness, and uttering many exclamations of astonishment at the wonders of Nature.

(2). A few men of more strictly scientific natures paid some attention to these little organisms. Among them we should perhaps mention Von Gleichen, Muller, Spallanzani, and Needham. Each of these, as well as others, made some contributions to our knowledge of microscopical life, and among other organisms studied those which we now call bacteria. Speculations were even made at these early dates of the possible causal connection of these organisms with diseases, and for a little the medical profession was interested in the suggestion. It was impossible then, however, to obtain any evidence for the truth of this speculation, and it was abandoned as unfounded, and even forgotten completely, until revived again about the middle of the 19th century. During this century of wonder a sufficiency of exactness was, however, introduced into the study of microscopic organisms to call for the use of names, and we find Muller using the names of Monas, Proteus, Vibrio, Bacillus, and Spirillum, names which still continue in use, although commonly with a different significance from that given them by Muller. Muller did indeed make a study sufficient to recognize the several distinct types, and attempted to classify these bodies. They were not regarded as of much importance, but simply as the most minute organisms known. It was Louis Pasteur who brought bacteria to the front, and it was by his labors that these organisms were rescued from the obscurity of scientific publications and made objects of general and crowning interest.

4. Louis Pasteur was the first to recognize the existence of microscopic organisms. Muller was the first to classify the different kinds of bacteria.

Answer: ____________________

5. Speculations were made of the possible causal connection of microscopic organisms with diseases during the mid-18th century.
Despite little interest in the significant role of microscopic organisms to diseases, some organisms were specifically named by the mid-19th century.

Answer: ____________________

Answers:

4. B
Strategies: SI, attention to details; P1 S2 and P2 S2
Leeuwenhoek was the first to recognize the existence of microscopic organisms in general while Pasteur was the one who did important work specifically about the bacteria. Muller, on the other hand, classified and named the different microscopic organisms - not bacteria.

5. A
Strategies: SI; P2 S4 and S6

With questions that present a statement and a reason, careful attention to the specified details is necessary. A common decoy used is mixing up two different pieces of information from the passage, making the combination of the statement and its reason appear to be correct.

In the succeeding excerpts, let's test your acute observation of the written details. Assess the respective questions as any one of the following:

A. *Both the statement and reason are correct and related.*
B. *Both the statement and the reason are correct but NOT related.*
C. *The statement is correct but the reason is NOT.*
D. *The statement is NOT correct, but the reason is correct.*
E. *NEITHER the statement NOR the reason is correct.*

PASSAGE 11

(1). One of the boldest and most determined of all the early explorers was Ferdinand Magellan, a young Portuguese nobleman. He felt sure that somewhere on that long coast which so many explorers had reached he would find a strait through which he would be able to pass, and which would lead into the Indian Ocean; and so Magellan formed the idea of circumnavigating the globe.

(2). He applied to the King of Portugal for aid; but as the Portuguese king was not willing to help him, he went to Spain, where his plan found favor.

(3). The Spanish king gave him a fleet of five vessels, and on September 20, 1519, he set sail for the Canary Islands. Continuing the voyage toward Sierra Leone, the vessels were becalmed, and for a period of three weeks they advanced only nine miles. Then a terrific storm arose, and the sailors, who had grumbled and found fault with everything during the entire voyage, broke into open mutiny. This mutiny Magellan quickly quelled by causing the principal offender to be arrested and put in irons.

(4). The voyage was then continued, and land was at last sighted on the Brazilian coast, near Pernambuco.

(5). The fleet then proceeded down the coast as far as Patagonia, where the weather grew so very cold that it was decided to seek winter quarters and postpone the remainder of the journey until spring. This was done, Magellan finding a sheltered spot at Port St. Julian, where plenty of fish could be obtained and where the natives were friendly.

(6). These native Patagonians Magellan described as being very tall, like giants, with long, flowing hair, and dressed scantily in skins.

(7). Great hardships had been endured by the crew. Food and water had been scarce, the storms had been severe, and suffering from cold was intense. The sailors did not believe there was any strait, and they begged Magellan to sail for home. It was useless to try to influence this determined man. Danger made him only the more firm. Magellan told them that he would not return until he had found the opening for which he was looking.

(8). Then the mutiny broke out anew. But Magellan by his prompt and decisive action put it down in twenty-four hours. One offender was killed, and two others were put in irons and left to their fate on the shore when the ships sailed away.

(9). As soon as the weather grew warmer the ships started again southward. After nearly two months of sailing, most of the time through violent storms, a narrow channel was found, in which the water was salt. This the sailors knew must be the entrance to a strait.

6. Ferdinand Magellan sought the aid of the King of Portugal because the Spanish King did not support his plan of circumnavigating the globe.

Answer: ______________________

7. Mutiny broke out again because the sailors found fault with everything during the entire voyage.

Answer: ______________________

8. Magellan formed the idea of circumnavigating the globe because he felt sure that he would find a strait through which he would be able to pass, and which would lead into the Pacific Ocean.

Answer: ______________________

Answers:

6. E
Strategies: Sal, attention to details; P2
The statement and the reason are reversed.

7. B
Strategies: Sl, attention to details; P3 S3, P7 and P8 S1
Details about the first mutiny was mixed up with the second mutiny.

8. C
Strategies: Sal, attention to details; P1 S2
The erroneous detail in the statement's reason is "Pacific Ocean," which should be "Indian Ocean."

PASSAGE 12

(1). Niels Henrik David Bohr was a Danish physicist who made fundamental contributions to understanding atomic structure and quantum mechanics, for which he received the Nobel Prize in Physics in 1922. Bohr mentored and collaborated with many of the top physicists of the century at his institute in Copenhagen. He was part of a team of physicists working on the Manhattan Project. Bohr married Margrethe Nørlund in 1912, and one of their sons, Aage Bohr, grew up to be an important physicist who in 1975 also received the Nobel Prize. Bohr has been described as one of the most influential scientists of the 20th century.

(2). Bohr's legacy to physics and its interpretation is a controversial one. He contributed decisively to the development of atomic and nuclear physics in many ways (especially to quantum theory from 1913 to 1925), and he is widely recognized as possessing remarkable insight into the nature of physical problems. Yet his theoretical approach and interpretive outlook sometimes have been questioned as vague, unclear, or inconsistent. Scholarship from 1970 to 2007 emphasized both the radical successes and some of the interpretive challenges of Bohr's work.

9. Bohr's legacy to physics and its interpretation is controversial because his theoretical approach and interpretive outlook have been questioned as vague, unclear, or inconsistent.

Answer: __________________

10. Niels Henrik David Bohr received the Nobel Prize in Physics in 1975 for his fundamental contributions to understanding atomic structure and quantum mechanics.

Answer: __________________

Answers:

9. A
Strategy: SaL; P2 S1 and S3

10. D
Strategies: SaL, attention to details: P1 S1 and S4
The erroneous detail in the statement is the year 1975, which should 1922.

3.3.5 Evaluation Questions

Evaluation Questions mainly ask you to identify key concepts and/or facts either directly taken from the text or inferred from it. This type of question can be further subcategorized into tone, implication, and main idea questions.

- **Tone Questions**

  These entail judging the attitude or opinion of the author towards the subject.

  What is the overall tone of the passage?
  With which statement would the author of the passage agree?

- **Implication Questions**

  Based on clues and evidences in the passage, you may be asked to draw conclusions about ideas such as what would follow if the author is correct in his/her argument or what a particular discovery might lead to.

  A court jester is most likely to equate which of the following modern-day jobs?
  Which of the following is the best description of a "rocket" locomotive?
  From statements in the passage, it can be inferred that the author probably is a(n)...
  Which of the following sentences could best be added to the specific paragraph x?

- **Main Idea Questions**

  These test your comprehension of the theme of the article. Questions may ask you for the main idea, central idea, purpose, a possible title for the passage, and so on. You may be asked to determine which statement best expresses the author's arguments or conclusions.

  What is the main idea of the passage?
  What would be the best title for this passage?
  Which of the following sentences best fits the passage?
  Which of the following sentences is the best conclusion for the closing paragraph?
  With which statement would the author of the passage agree? (This question may border between Tone and Main Idea Questions.)

An ideal strategy for these questions would be to outline and annotate (OA). Likewise, watch out for extreme words and mean statements among the answer options.

Constant practice should help develop these strategies for the slow reader. Again, remember that the most important part of any practice is to set aside enough time to single out your mistakes, try to understand why you keep getting the wrong answers, and if you have to, modify your strategies in order to optimize your results in the actual test.

In order to get a clear gauge of your possible challenges with these question types, consider the following short passages, answer the different guide questions, and study the explanations provided.

PASSAGE 13

(1). Freud wrote several important essays on literature, which he used to explore the psyche of authors and characters, to explain narrative mysteries, and to develop new concepts in psychoanalysis (for instance, *Delusion and Dream in Jensen's Gradiva* and his influential readings of the Oedipus myth and Shakespeare's ***Hamlet*** in ***The Interpretation of Dreams***). The criticism has been made, however, that in his and his early followers' studies "what calls for elucidation are not the artistic and literary works themselves, but rather the psychopathology and biography of the artist, writer or fictional characters." Thus many psychoanalysts among Freud's earliest adherents did not resist the temptation to psychoanalyze poets and painters sometimes to Freud's chagrin. Later analysts would conclude that "clearly one cannot psychoanalyze a writer from his text; one can only appropriate him."

1. What would be the best title for this passage?

A. Freudian Analysis of Literary Works
B. The Interdisciplinary Work of Freud on Classical Literature
C. Criticisms on the Psychoanalysis of Literature
D. Pitfalls of Psychoanalysis in Art and Literature

2. With which statement would the author of the passage agree?

A. Freud's work has been influential both in psychology and literature.
B. One cannot always conclude about a writer's psyche based on his literary work alone.
C. Many psychoanalysts were wrong in their findings about art and literature.
D. Psychology and Literature can never go hand in hand.

PASSAGE 14

(1). In 1831 we have Faraday at the climax of his intellectual strength, forty years of age, stored with knowledge and full of original power. Through reading, lecturing, and experimenting, he had become thoroughly familiar with electrical science: he saw where light was needed and expansion possible. The phenomena of ordinary electric induction belonged, as it were, to the alphabet of his knowledge: he knew that under ordinary circumstances the presence of an electrified body was sufficient to excite, by induction, an unelectrified body. He knew that the wire which carried an electric current was an electrified body, and still that all attempts had failed to make it excite in other wires a state similar to its own.

(2). What was the reason of this failure? Faraday never could work from the experiments of others, however clearly described. He knew well that from every experiment issues a kind of radiation, luminous, in different degrees to different minds, and he hardly trusted himself to reason upon an experiment that he had not seen. In the autumn of 1831, he began to repeat the experiments with electric currents, which, up to that time, had produced no positive result. And here, for the sake of younger inquirers, if not for the sake of us all, it is worthwhile to dwell for a moment on a power which Faraday possessed in an extraordinary degree. He

Answers:

1. C

Strategy: OA

A title generally embodies the content, i.e., the overall idea of a specific work. Hence this question calls for understanding of the excerpt's main idea. In this paragraph, the author introduces Freud's work in analyzing various literary works then moves on to discuss various criticisms in using psychoanalysis when appraising literature and art. The keywords are "criticisms" and "psychoanalysis."

2. B

Strategies: OA (paraphrasing); extreme statements

This question requires distinguishing the author's opinion on the subject from the passage's general topic. One effective way is to watch out for structure words. A few examples are "thus," "nevertheless," "needless to say," "moreover," "however," "therefore," "on the other hand," etc. Sentences that start with these cues usually signal the author's opinion. In this example, the structure word "thus" is found in the third sentence of the paragraph: "Thus 'many psychoanalysts among Freud's earliest adherents did not resist the temptation to psychoanalyze poets and painters sometimes to Freud's chagrin.'" The author reinforces his/her view of the psychoanalysts' failure to provide faithful assessment of aesthetic works by immediately citing an example of other analysts' criticism: "Later analysts would conclude that 'clearly one cannot psychoanalyze a writer from his text; one can only appropriate him.'"

united vast strength with perfect flexibility. His momentum was that of a river, which combines weight and directness with the ability to yield to the flexures of its bed. The intentness of his vision in any direction did not apparently diminish his power of perception in other directions; and when he attacked a subject, expecting results, he had the faculty of keeping his mind alert, so that results different from those which he expected should not escape him through pre-occupation.

3. Which of the following sentences is the best conclusion for the closing paragraph?

   A. Faraday finally sought the advice of other scientists working on a similar experiment.
   B. Unfortunately, Faraday had to abandon his work.
   C. Luckily, Faraday found the missing element that would make his experiment successful.
   D. And so, Faraday persevered in conducting his experiments with electric currents.

4. Which of the following sentences best fits the passage?

   A. Faraday was a genius in electrical science.
   B. Faraday's failure was directly related to his refusal to collaborate with other scientists.
   C. Faraday was a man of great intellectual insights and determination.
   D. Faraday was a stubborn scientist.

Answers:

3. D
Strategy: OA or SI
The overall tone of the passage is that of optimism and admiration for Faraday's perseverance and intellectual independence. A and B are exact opposites of the statements in P2 S2 to S3 and P2 S7 respectively. C does not have enough clue or clear evidence as basis. D matches the characteristics described by the author about Faraday.

4. C
Strategy: OA or SI
This is a main idea question, which means that the best choice should be the statement that most represents the central point of the passage. Paragraph 1 discusses the extent of Faraday's knowledge especially about electrical science. Paragraph 2 illustrates Faraday's persistence despite failures in his experiments. Therefore, the most encompassing idea about the passage is that of Option C. A and B, although true, are only mentioned in specific parts of Paragraph 1 and Paragraph 2 respectively. D misinterprets the author's characterization of Faraday.

PASSAGE 15

(1). This project was inspired by a number of visits I made to various science and engineering museums in order to investigate the design of small electronic consumer devices. The research trips were unsuccessful, but only in the sense that my original expectations had not been met. I found that the objects on display in most cases looked exactly like the final product that would then be presented to the market. I had expected to see unfinished hotchpotches of machines, exposed working components and a cacophony of tangled cables. I was also hoping for a look beyond, or behind, the scenes of the design process and into a space manufacturers might ordinarily keep from public view. Instead, the objects that I came across were merely empty shells, made only to demonstrate the aesthetic of the product's design.

5. What is the overall tone of the passage?

- **A.** Disgust
- **B.** Disappointment
- **C.** Businesslike
- **D.** Curious

6. From statements in the passage, it can be inferred that the author probably is a(n):

- **A.** art critic.
- **B.** tourist.
- **C.** auctioneer.
- **D.** engineer.

Answers:

5. B
Strategy: SI; P1 S2 and S6

6. A
Strategy: SI; P1 S1 and last sentence
In both sentences, the author referred to "design" and "aesthetic of the product's design." A tourist would not be too critical; an auctioneer would have mentioned something about a bid; and, an engineer would not keep considering the "aesthetics of a product's design."

3.3.6 Application Questions

These are questions involving concepts that were introduced in the passage and how they would apply to general or real world situations. Usually, a situation or function is given, and you will be made to identify which particular theory, process, or instrument would best fit the description or offer a solution. You should use the information presented in the passage to solve new problems described in the questions; reevaluate the passage based on new facts associated with the questions.

Possible effective strategies could include "scan and locate" (SaL), "skim for ideas" (SI), "outline and annotate" (OA) or sketch the described apparatus or process in order to concretize the concepts.

PASSAGE 16

(1). There still exists among ourselves an activity, which on the technical plane gives us quite a good understanding of what a science we prefer to call 'prior' rather than 'primitive,' could have been on the plane of speculation. This is what is commonly called 'bricolage' in French. In its old sense the verb 'bricoler' applied to ball games and billiards, to hunting, shooting and riding. It was however always used with reference to some extraneous movement: a ball rebounding, a dog straying or a horse swerving from its direct course to avoid an obstacle. And in our own time the 'bricoleur' is still someone who works with his hands and uses devious means compared to those of a craftsman.

(2). The 'bricoleur' is adept at performing a large number of diverse tasks; but, unlike the engineer, he does not subordinate each of them to the availability of raw materials and tools conceived and procured for the purpose of the project. His universe of instruments is closed and the rules of his game are always to make do with 'whatever is at hand', that is to say with a set of tools and materials which is always finite and is also heterogeneous because what it contains bears no relation to the current project, or indeed to any particular project, but is the contingent result of all the occasions there have been to renew or enrich the stock or to maintain it with the remains of previous constructions or destructions.

(3). The set of the bricoleur's means cannot therefore be defined in terms of a project (which would presuppose besides, that, as in the case of the engineer, there were, at least in theory, as many sets of tools and materials or 'instrumental sets', as there are different kinds of projects). It is to be defined only by its potential use or, putting this another way and in the language of the 'bricoleur' himself, because the elements are collected or retained on the principle that 'they may always come in handy'. Such elements are specialized up to a point, sufficiently for the 'bricoleur' not to need the equipment and knowledge of all trades and professions, but not enough for each of them to have only one definite and determinate use. They each represent a set of actual and possible relations; they are 'operators' but they can be used for any operations of the same type.

1. Which of the following constructions below would NOT be an example of "bricolage"?

- **A.** Scrapbooking
- **B.** Surrealistic Poetry
- **C.** Junk Art
- **D.** A Land Survey
- **E.** Decorative Food Servings

2. Which activity would NOT be an illustration of "bricolage"?

- **A.** Stage sets made up of scrap metal for a theatrical performance
- **B.** A birdhouse constructed from toothpicks and various wood scraps
- **C.** A well-designed deck with pre-cut lumber
- **D.** A quilt sewn together with various leftover fabrics
- **E.** A maze constructed from the various hedges and shrubs in the garden

3. The Digital Era and Computer Apps have given bricolage a refreshing outlook due to advanced manipulation of popular media. Which entries BEST represent a type of digital "bricolage"?

- **A.** Using digital audio loops (cut and paste) for recording mixes and remixes
- **B.** GPS used in other contexts such as cruise ships, restaurants, etc.
- **C.** Photoshopped pictures, which distort the original to something humorous
- **D.** Constructing a website

Answers:

1. D
   Strategy: SI; P1 last sentence, P2 S1, P3 S1
   Scrapbooking, surrealistic poetry, junk art, and decorative food servings all entail "working with hands" and using "devious means." On the other hand, land surveying would require using instruments, calculations and some engineering background.

2. C
   Strategy: SaL or OA; P1 and P2
   Descriptions in the passage suggest that bricolage would involve making do with "whatever is at hand." Only a well-designed deck with lumber cut to a specific shape or size would not fit this description.

3. A
   Strategy: SaL; P2 last sentence
   "His universe of instruments is closed and the rules of his game are always to make do with 'whatever is at hand', that is to say with a set of tools and materials which is always finite and is also heterogeneous because what it contains bears no relation to the current project, or indeed to any particular project, but is the contingent result of all the occasions there have been to renew or enrich the stock or to maintain it with the remains of previous constructions or destructions."

3.4 Reading Comprehension (RC) Mini Tests with Answer Key, Explanations and Strategies

Now that we have outlined the structure of the DAT Reading Comprehension section, the types of questions, and most importantly, the approach and strategies that will help you excel, you can proceed to test yourself with our GS RC mini tests.

As described earlier, the DAT RC is comprised of three passages. A mini test presents only one passage at a time. The objective is to get you started in applying the techniques discussed in sections 3.1 to 3.3, and allow you to assess your current level of competence. We strongly suggest that you ALWAYS time yourself for every practice test. Otherwise, you would be eliminating one of the major components of your preparation making it more difficult to get a top DAT RC score.

At the end of each mini test, you should work through the answers and explanations. The answer key specifies the **Question Type** and the **Strategies** that are appropriate for the question. Keep notes of your wrong answers and then go back to the specific section(s) in this chapter, reviewing and analyzing how you can still improve on your next attempts. Only when you feel ready, you can try to get an initial run of the whole RC exam by taking the full-length GS RC Practice Test at the end of the Reading Comprehension chapters. As you progress with your review, you should also consider full-length practice tests (i.e. NS, PAT, RC and QR in one sitting) including those from the ADA, Gold Standard and TopScore.

Before you proceed, let's reiterate some important abbreviations and references in our answer keys:

OA	Outline and Annotate	Discussed in Section 3.3
SaL	Scan and Locate	Discussed in Section 3.3
SI	Skim for Ideas	Discussed in Section 3.3
PoE	Process of Elimination	Discussed in Section 3.2
Attention to details		Discussed in Section 3.2
Never lose sight of the question		Discussed in Section 3.2
P	Paragraph	P1 would mean Paragraph 1 and so forth
S	Sentence	S1 would mean Sentence 1 and so forth

*A note on "Recall Questions": Most recall questions do not need detailed explanations and only require you to re-read a specific paragraph and sentence. Hence only the paragraph and sentence numbers are provided in the answer key explanations of some of these questions.

From this point, advance to the next pages ONLY when you are ready. Please give each attempt your best shot. Good luck!

RC Mini Test 1

The following is a sample mini test which is comparable to the level of difficulty required for the Reading Comprehension Test of the DAT. Please note that this sample would roughly be 1/3 of the actual Reading Comprehension Test portion of the DAT.

You have 20 minutes to complete this portion of the DAT Mini Test; the actual test is 60 minutes. Please time yourself accordingly.

BEGIN ONLY WHEN YOUR TIMER IS READY.

Passage 1

NASA Science Balloons

(1). Balloons may seem like an old-fashioned technology to most of the public, but they are very much alive and well. Weather balloons have been commonplace for decades, and the military still makes considerable use of them. The public is very familiar with hot-air sport ballooning, as well as with the exciting record-breaking flights across continents and oceans, using very high-tech balloon technologies. While the "great age" of manned balloon flights into the stratosphere is history, balloons continue to be important tools for scientific research. Unmanned stratospheric balloons are used for astronomy and climate studies, and balloons are also potentially an important tool for exploring other planets.

(2). The US National Science Foundation set up a scientific balloon program in 1961, originally based in Boulder, Colorado. In 1963, the balloon program was moved to Palestine, Texas, halfway between Dallas and Houston, since at the time the area was largely unpopulated and balloon payloads falling out of the sky were unlikely to land on a house. The US National Aeronautics & Space Administration (NASA) picked up the balloon program in 1982. The Palestine operation is now designated the "Columbia Scientific Balloon Facility (CSBF)" – the name having been changed from the "National Scientific Balloon Facility" in 2005 in honor of the crew of the space shuttle Columbia, which burned up on reentry in 2003.

(3). The CSBF is directed by the Physical

Sciences Laboratory of New Mexico State University at Las Cruces. However, population growth near Palestine has forced the CSBF to perform more launches at remote sites. Launches are regularly performed at Fort Sumner, New Mexico; Lynn Lake, Manitoba, Canada; McMurdo Station, Antarctica; Fairbanks, Alaska; and Alice Springs, Australia. Special launches have also been performed from a number of other locales. The CSBF has performed over 2,000 balloon flights since its inception. At its peak, in the 1970s, the CSBF was performing up to 80 missions a year, but the organization's launch rate is now much lower, a few dozen missions a year. Partly this is because the feasible missions have mostly been done, but it is also due to funding limitations. However, the CSBF is not in danger of extinction, since researchers know that it is much easier, quicker, and cheaper to use a balloon than a spacecraft to fly a payload into near-space conditions. The fact that balloon payloads, unlike satellite payloads, are usually recovered intact for re-use is another plus.

(4). The modern "zero-pressure balloon" vehicle used by the CSBF is generally similar to the SKYHOOK balloons originally invented by Otto Winzen. It is made from special polyethylene film, typically 0.8 mil thick, fabricated from longitudinal panels sealed with tapes. A scientific balloon typically has a volume of 1.08 million cubic meters (38 million cubic feet) and can carry 1,700 kilograms (3,750 pounds) of suspended load to 39 kilometers (128,000 feet). At this altitude, the scientific payload is above 99.7% of the atmosphere's mass. The "flight train" consists of the balloon and a scientific instrument package hitched to the balloon through a parachute pack. A NASA zero-pressure science balloon is inflated through the traditional roller system, with enough lifting gas provided for 10% lift over the load and balloon mass, and the gas expanding as the balloon rises.

(5). Data from the payload and balloon are telemetered directly to ground stations or through satellite links. Occasionally they are also recorded on board via film, magnetic tape, or solid-state digital storage media. Radio commands are used for instrument and balloon control. Balloon position is obtained by direct visual tracking, airplane tracking, or use of Global Position System (GPS) navigation receivers. The flight ends when the parachute and payload are separated via radio command, usually from a tracking aircraft. During separation, the balloon is destroyed by tearing open a set of rip panels, permitting the payload to parachute to the ground. With recent improvements in design, materials, and quality control, the large zero-pressure balloon has become an extremely reliable vehicle, with very high mission success rates. One drawback, however, is its limited mission endurance. While long-standing studies on cosmic rays, atmospheric circulation, and weather continue, much recent effort has been devoted to the atmospheric chemistry, and to astronomy at wavelengths – such as the infrared, ultraviolet, and X-ray bands – that are blocked by the atmosphere.

(6). An alternative approach, the "constant volume" or "superpressure" balloon, features a relatively unyielding plastic envelope filled at relatively high pressure, ensuring retention of a constant volume. A superpressure balloon does not need ballast, or at least not as much as a zero-pressure balloon, and can float at high altitudes for many months. The CSBF is now working on a superpressure "Ultra-Long Duration Balloon (ULDB)" that can stay at altitude for several months, orbiting the Earth several times. Raven Industries conducted a flight of a prototype ULDB in October 1999, but the balloon ruptured when it reached altitude. A second prototype, a tenth the size of a full-scale ULDB, was launched in June 2000 and was a success, remaining aloft for 27 hours. The full-scale ULDB design features an envelope with an inflated diameter of 59 meters (193 feet) and a height of 35 meters (115 feet). It is intended to remain aloft with 900 kilograms (a ton) of payload at altitudes of 35 kilometers (115,000 feet) for up to 100 days. The first full-scale ULDB test flight took place in late February 2001 from an Alice Springs, Australia launch site, but sprung a leak and was destroyed a few hours after launch. Subsequent launches took place roughly once a year, with mixed results. NASA still plans to begin operational ULDB launches in 2010.

(7). The superpressure balloon concept is not entirely new, going back at least to the US Air Force's "Global Horizontal Sounding Technique (GHOST)" balloon program, with eighty-eight GHOST balloons about 3 meters (10 feet) in diameter released over a period of ten years beginning in 1966. They all carried a small payload, the primary goal of the mission being to simply track the balloons to map high-altitude winds. In 1966, A GHOST balloon was the first balloon to circle the Earth, taking ten days to make the journey. Some of the GHOST balloons were said to have remained aloft for a year. Later in the program, they relayed their data through satellites. This project provided new results on the seasonal variations of global air currents.

(8). Balloons have proven very useful for scientific research on Earth; there are those who believe they are potentially very useful for exploring other planets as well. Robot "rovers" have been sent to the Moon and Mars since the 1960s, but such machines tend to be expensive and have limited range, and due to the long communications time-lag over interplanetary distances, they have to be smart enough to navigate without running into obstacles or falling off cliffs. If a planet has an atmosphere, however, a balloon would have many advantages over a rover. A robot balloon, or "aerobot", would be much cheaper and lighter than a rover, with the light weight reducing booster launch costs. An aerobot could cover a great deal of ground, and its view from a height would give them the ability to examine wide swathes of terrain with far more detail than would be obtained by an orbiting satellite. For exploratory missions, the aerobot's relative lack of directional control would not be a big concern, since there would be generally no need to direct it to a specific location. While the French were working on planetary aerobots, NASA's Jet Propulsion Laboratory (JPL) had become interested in the idea as well, with a JPL team performing several balloon flights in the Earth's atmosphere during the 1990s to validate technology. The JPL team envisioned a simple "Mars weather balloon" to validate the technology operationally; to be followed by a large superpressure balloon flight; and finally a solar-powered Mars blimp. NASA hasn't committed to an aerobot mission yet, but the agency has collaborated with the Centre National d'Études Spatiales (CNES) on the development of a series of low-cost "Scout" missions to Mars, and a Mars aerobot is on the list of options. A company named Global Aerospace Corporation performed an investigation of a Mars aerobot for NASA, with the aerobot envisioned as carrying both a science gondola and a set of small drop probes that could be released to provide detailed inspection of a number of sites.

- Adapted from "NASA Science Balloons" (http://www.vectorsite.net/avbloon_5.html#m1) Thanks to Greg Goebel.

1. Of the regular balloon launch sites, which of the following is NOT listed in the article?

A. Fort Sumner
B. Lynn Lake
C. Columbia
D. Alice Springs
E. Fairbanks

2. The US National Science Foundation set up a scientific balloon program in 1961. NASA set up a similar program in 1963.

A. Both statements are true.
B. Both statements are false.
C. The first sentence is true. The second sentence is false.
D. The first sentence is false. The second sentence is true.
E. The passage does not contain enough information to make a judgment.

3. Of the balloons discussed in the passage, which is NOT mentioned? Which is the EXCEPTION?

A. Zero-pressure balloons
B. Hot air balloons
C. Superpressure balloons
D. Weather balloons
E. Anisotropic balloons

4. Which balloon provided new results on the seasonal variations of global air currents?

A. Ultra-Long Duration balloon
B. GHOST balloons
C. Anisotropic balloons
D. Zero-pressure balloons
E. Aerobot balloons

5. Which of the following is NOT true about the modern zero-pressure balloons used by CSBF?

- **A.** It can remain aloft for 27 hours.
- **B.** It has a typical volume of 1.08 million cubic meters.
- **C.** It is typically 0.8 mil thick, made of special polyethylene film.
- **D.** It can typically carry 3750 pounds of suspended load.
- **E.** None of the above

6. Which of the following acronyms is NOT correct?

- **A.** JPL - Jet Propulsion Laboratory
- **B.** GHOST - Global Horizontal Sounding Technique
- **C.** ULDB - Ultra-Long Duration Balloon
- **D.** CSBF - Columbia Super Balloon Facility
- **E.** NASA - National Aeronautics & Space Administration

7. In the 1970s, CSBF was performing up to:

- **A.** 80 missions a year.
- **B.** 88 missions a year.
- **C.** 70 missions a year.
- **D.** 800 missions a year.
- **E.** 90 missions a year.

8. The space shuttle Columbia burned up on reentry in which of the following years?

- **A.** 2005
- **B.** 1982
- **C.** 1962
- **D.** 2003
- **E.** 2000

9. Based on statements in the passage, it can be inferred that a "payload" is:

- **A.** a tracking device.
- **B.** a communication device.
- **C.** a data collection device.
- **D.** the total weight of all of the balloons.
- **E.** total balloon contents.

10. Which of the following is NOT true concerning the latest ULDBs? Which is the EXCEPTION?

- **A.** It has an inflated diameter of 193 feet.
- **B.** It has an inflated height of 115 feet.
- **C.** It can carry up to a ton of payload.
- **D.** It can carry a ton of payload for 100 days.
- **E.** It can carry a ton of payload at altitudes over 200,000 feet.

11. Which of the following was the first balloon to circle the Earth?

- **A.** ULDB
- **B.** Aerobot
- **C.** GHOST
- **D.** SKYHOOK
- **E.** Solar-powered blimp

12. The primary goal of a GHOST balloon was:

- **A.** to interlink with satellites.
- **B.** to map high-altitude winds.
- **C.** to understand atmospheric chemistry.
- **D.** to study cosmic rays.
- **E.** to provide geographical surveillance.

13. Balloon payloads are usually recovered intact.
Satellite payloads, on the other hand, are much cheaper to use.

- **A.** Both statements are true.
- **B.** Both statements are false.
- **C.** The first statement is true, the second statement is false.
- **D.** The first statement is false, the second statement is true.

14. The first full-scale ULDB test flight took place in late February 2001 from which of the following locations?

- **A.** Fort Sumner
- **B.** Lynn Lakes
- **C.** Fairbanks
- **D.** Alice Springs
- **E.** Palestine

15. From the following list of popular narratives, which would be the most relevant to the article?

- **A.** Moby Dick
- **B.** Hamlet
- **C.** Ulysses
- **D.** 20,000 Leagues Under the Sea
- **E.** Around the World in 80 days

16. Which of the following would NOT be an advantage of a Mars Aerobot over a Mars Rover? Which is the EXCEPTION?

- **A.** Cost
- **B.** Range
- **C.** Predictability of direction
- **D.** Weight
- **E.** Details of view

17. The improved large zero-pressure balloon has very low mission success rates. Yet, this version has very high mission endurance.

A. Both statements are true.
B. Both statements are false.
C. The first statement is true, while the second statement is false.
D. The first statement is false, while the second statement is true.

If time remains, you may review your work. If your allotted time (20 minutes) is complete, please proceed to the Answer Key.

RC Mini Test 1 Answer Key

1. C
2. C
3. E
4. B
5. A
6. D
7. A
8. D
9. C
10. E
11. C
12. B
13. C
14. D
15. E
16. C
17. B

RC Mini Test 1 Explanations and Strategies

1. Question Type: *Exception/Negative Question*
   Strategies: *SaL, PoE; P3 S3, P2 last sentence*

   (A) Fort Sumner, (B) Lynn Lake, (D) Alice Springs and (E) Fairbanks are all mentioned in Paragraph 3. On the other hand, Columbia was the name of the space shuttle that burned up in 2003 as indicated in the last sentence of Paragraph 2.

2. Question Type: *True False Statement (Two Statements)*
   Strategies: *SaL, attention to details; P2 S1 to S3*

   The third sentence of Paragraph 2 states that NASA picked up the balloon program in 1982, not 1963.

3. Question Type: *Exception/Negative Question*
   Strategies: *SaL, PoE*

   Paragraph 4 discusses (A) zero-pressure balloons and Paragraph 6 (C) superpressure balloons. (D) Weather balloons is mentioned in P1 S2 and (B) hot air balloons in P1 S3. Only (E) anisotropic balloons are not mentioned anywhere in the passage.

4. Question Type: *Recall*
   Strategy: *SaL; P7 last sentence*

5. Question Type: *Exception/Negative Question*
   Strategies: *SaL, PoE, attention to details*

   The modern zero-pressure balloons are discussed in Paragraph 4, specifically Statement B in S3, Statement C in S2, and Statement

D in S3. On the other hand, Statement A is mixed up with the information in P6 S5, which supposedly pertains to the ULDB superpressure balloon – not the zero-pressure balloons used by CSBF.

6. Question Type: *Exception/Negative Question*
Strategies: *SaL, PoE, attention to details*

JPL is mentioned in P8 S7, GHOST in P7 S1, ULDB in P6 S3, and NASA in P2 S3. CSBF is indeed mentioned in P2 S4 but as Columbia Scientific Balloon Facility – not Columbia Super Balloon Facility.

7. Question Type: *Recall*
Strategy: *SaL; P3 S6*

8. Question Type: *Recall*
Strategy: *SaL; P2 last sentence*

9. Question Type: *Evaluation Question*
Strategies: *SI, attention to details; P5 S1 to S5*

Several contextual cue words in the first 5 sentences of Paragraph 5 hint that a payload functions as a data collection device: "Data from the payload and balloon are telemetered," "recorded on board via film, magnetic tape, or solid-state digital storage media," "direct visual tracking, airplane tracking, or use of Global Position System (GPS) navigation receivers."

10. Question Type: *Exception/Negative Question*
Strategies: *SaL, PoE; P6*

Each answer choice is mentioned in the following specific sentences in Paragraph 6: A and B inS6; C and D in S7. Only the data in E cannot be found in the paragraph or anywhere in the passage.

11. Question Type: *Recall*
Strategies: *SaL; P7 S3*

12. Question Type: *Recall*
Strategy: *SaL; P7 S2*

13. Question Type: *True False Statement (Two Statements)*
Strategies: *SaL, PoE, attention to details; P3 S8 and last sentence*

The first statement is true as indicated in P3 last sentence. However, the second statement is false: balloon payloads - NOT satellite payloads - are cheaper.

14. Question Type: *Recall*
Strategy: *SaL; P6 S7*

15. Question Type: *Evaluation Question (Main Idea)*
Strategies: *SI, prior knowledge*

This question can be easily answered with simple inference and familiarity with the titles presented in the different choices. Understanding that the passage is about air balloons or balloon flights, the narrative that has this same theme should match as the correct answer.

16. Question Type: *Exception/Negative Question*
Strategies: *SI, PoE, attention to details; P8 S4 to S6*

Answering this question may require more attention to details because the answer choices are paraphrased from lines in the passage. (A) Cost would equate "aerobot would be much cheaper"; (B) Range would be "could cover a great deal of ground"; (C) Predictability of direction would be "lack of directional control," which is not considered as an aerobot's advantage over a rover – therefore, the correct answer; (D) weight is "lighter than a rover"; and (E) Details of view is "the ability to examine wide swathes of terrain with far more detail."

17. Question Type: *True False Statement (Two statements)*
Strategies: *SaL, attention to details; P5 S7 and S8*

The information in the two statements are reversed.

Would you like to discuss any of the answers or strategies in this section? Go to www.dat-prep.com/forum to share and learn.

RC Mini Test 2

The following is a sample mini test which is comparable to the level of difficulty required for the Reading Comprehension Test of the DAT. Please note that this sample would roughly be 1/3 of the actual Reading Comprehension Test portion of the DAT.

You have 20 minutes to complete this portion of the DAT Mini Test; the actual test is 60 minutes. Please time yourself accordingly.

BEGIN ONLY WHEN YOUR TIMER IS READY.

Passage 2

Symbiosis

(1). Symbiosis (from Ancient Greek sýn "with" and bíōsis "living") is a close and often long-term interaction between different biological species. In 1877, Bennett used the word symbiosis (which previously had been used for people living together in community) to describe the mutualistic relationship in lichens. In 1879, the German mycologist Heinrich Anton de Bary defined it as "the living together of unlike organisms." The definition of symbiosis is controversial among scientists. Some believe symbiosis should only refer to persistent mutualisms, while others believe it should apply to all types of persistent biological interactions (i.e., mutualistic, commensalistic, or parasitic).

(2). Some symbiotic relationships are obligate, meaning that both symbionts entirely depend on each other for survival. For example, many lichens consist of fungal and photosynthetic symbionts that cannot live on their own. Others are facultative, meaning that they can but do not have to live with the other organism. Symbiotic relationships include those associations in which one organism lives on another (ectosymbiosis, such as mistletoe), or where one partner lives inside the other (endosymbiosis, such as lactobacilli and other bacteria in humans or zooxanthelles in corals).

(3). Endosymbiosis is any symbiotic relationship in which one symbiont lives within the tissues of the other, either in the intracellular or extracellular space. Examples are rhizobia, nitrogen-fixing bacteria that live in root nodules on legume roots; actinomycete nitrogen-fixing bacteria called Frankia, which live in alder tree root nodules; single-celled algae inside reef-building corals; and bacterial endosymbionts that provide essential nutrients to about 10%–15% of insects. Ectosymbiosis, also referred to as exosymbiosis, is any symbiotic relationship in which the symbiont lives on the body surface of the host, including the inner surface of the digestive tract or the ducts of exocrine glands. Examples of this include ectoparasites such as lice, commensal ectosymbionts such as the barnacles that attach themselves to the jaw of baleen whales, and mutualist ectosymbionts such as cleaner fish.

(4). Mutualism is any relationship between individuals of different species where both individuals derive a benefit. Generally, only lifelong interactions involving close physical and biochemical contact can properly be considered symbiotic. Mutualistic relationships may be either obligate for both species, obligate for one but facultative for the other, or facultative for both. Many biologists restrict the definition of symbiosis to close mutualist relationships. A large percentage of herbivores have mutualistic gut fauna that help them digest plant matter, which is more difficult to digest than animal prey. Coral reefs are the result of mutualisms between coral organisms and various types of algae that live inside them. Most land plants and land ecosystems rely on mutualisms between the plants, which fix carbon from the air, and mycorrhizal fungi, which help in extracting minerals from the ground.

(5). An example of mutual symbiosis is the relationship between the ocellaris clownfish that dwell among the tentacles of Ritteri sea anemones. The territorial fish protects the anemone from anemone-eating fish, and in turn the stinging tentacles of the anemone protect the clownfish from its predators. A special mucus on the clownfish protects it from the stinging tentacles. Another example is the goby fish, which sometimes lives together with a shrimp. The shrimp digs and cleans up a burrow in the sand in which both the shrimp and the goby fish live. The shrimp is almost blind, leaving it vulnerable to predators when above ground. In case of danger the goby fish touches the shrimp with its tail to warn it. When that happens, both the shrimp and goby fish quickly retract into the burrow.

(6). One of the most spectacular examples of obligate mutualism is between the siboglinid tube worms and symbiotic bacteria that live at hydrothermal vents and cold seeps. The worm has no digestive tract and is wholly reliant on its internal symbionts for nutrition. The bacteria oxidize either hydrogen sulfide or methane, which the host supplies to them. These worms were discovered in the late 1980s at the hydrothermal vents near the Galapagos Islands and have since been found at deep-sea hydrothermal vents and cold seeps in all of the world's oceans. There are also many types of tropical and sub-tropical ants that have evolved very complex relationships with certain tree species.

(7). Commensalism describes a relationship between two living organisms where one benefits and the other is not significantly harmed or helped. It is derived from the English word commensal, used for human social interaction. The word derives from the medieval Latin word, formed from "com" and "mensa," meaning "sharing a table." Commensal relationships may involve one organism using another for transportation (phoresy) or for housing (inquilinism), or it may also involve one organism using something that another created after its death (metabiosis). Examples of metabiosis are maggots, which feast and develop on corpses, and hermit crabs using gastropod shells to protect their bodies.

(8). A parasitic relationship is one in which one member of the association benefits while the other is harmed. Parasitic symbioses take many forms, from endoparasites that live within the host's body to ectoparasites that live on its surface. In addition, parasites may be necrotrophic, which is to say they kill their host, or biotrophic, meaning they rely on their host's surviving. Biotrophic parasitism is an extremely successful mode of life. Depending on the definition used, as many as half of all animals have at least one parasitic phase in their life cycles, and it is also frequent in plants and fungi. Moreover, almost all free-living animals are host to one or more parasite taxa. An example of a biotrophic relationship would be a tick feeding on the blood of its host.

(9). Amensalism is the type of symbiotic relationship that exists where one species is inhibited or completely obliterated and one is unaffected. This type of symbiosis is relatively uncommon in rudimentary reference texts, but is omnipresent in the natural world. An example is a sapling growing under the shadow of a mature tree. The mature tree can begin to rob the sapling of necessary sunlight and, if the mature tree is very large, it can take up rainwater and deplete soil nutrients. Throughout the process the mature tree is unaffected. Indeed, if the sapling dies, the mature tree gains nutrients from the decaying sapling. Note that these nutrients become available because of the sapling's decomposition, rather than from the living sapling, which would be a case of parasitism.

(10). While historically, symbiosis has received less attention than other interactions such as predation or competition, it is increasingly recognized as an important selective force behind evolution, with many species having a long history of interdependent co-evolution. In fact, the evolution of all eukaryotes (plants, animals, fungi, and protists) is believed under the endosymbiotic theory to have resulted from a symbiosis between various sorts of bacteria. Up to 80% of vascular plants worldwide form symbiotic relationships with fungi, for example, in arbuscular mycorrhiza.

(11). The biologist Lynn Margulis, famous for her work on endosymbiosis, contends that symbiosis is a major driving force behind evolution. She considers Darwin's notion of evolution, driven by competition, to be incomplete and claims that evolution is strongly based on co-operation, interaction, and mutual dependence among organisms. According to Margulis and Dorion Sagan, "Life did not take over the globe by combat, but by networking."

(12). Symbiosis played a major role in the co-evolution of flowering plants and the animals that pollinate them. Many plants that are pollinated by insects, bats, or birds have highly specialized flowers modified to promote pollination by a specific pollinator that is also correspondingly adapted. The first flowering plants in the fossil record had relatively simple flowers. Adaptive speciation quickly gave rise to many diverse groups of plants, and, at the same time, corresponding speciation occurred in certain insect groups. Some groups of plants developed nectar and large sticky pollen, while insects evolved more specialized morphologies to access and collect these rich food sources. In some taxa of plants and insects the relationship has become dependent, where the plant species can only be pollinated by one species of insect.

1. Understory vegetation grows beneath the breeding colonies of herons. As the heron's population becomes dense, the trees on which they build their nests eventually die down due to the bird's heavy toxic excrements. The herons may suffer from the loss of their nesting trees, but they do not necessarily get hurt or benefit from the damaged vegetation. This type of symbiotic relationship is described to be:

A. commensalism.
B. parasitism.
C. amensalism.
D. ectosymbiosis.

2. In the example of mutual symbiosis between the shrimp and the goby fish, what is the primary benefit of their relationship?

A. Protection
B. Shelter
C. Nutrition
D. Transportation
E. Propagation

3. Each of the following are considered mutually beneficial symbionts EXCEPT one. Which one is the EXCEPTION?

   A. Rhizobia
   B. Bacterial endosymbionts
   C. Lice
   D. Frankia
   E. Lactobacilli

4. Which of the following best describes symbiosis?

   A. The ability of unlike organisms to live together
   B. Close relationship between two different species
   C. Lifelong close physical and biochemical contact of different species
   D. Persistent biological interactions in a community of diverse species
   E. Long-term mutually beneficial relationships of different biological species

5. Termites can chew and ingest wood, but they rely on their intestinal flagellates trichonympha to break down their food for them and chemically digest cellulose into sugars. The termite, in turn, provides food, shelter and constant internal environment to the trichonympha. Both cannot survive in the absence of the other. This type of relationship is an example of:

   A. inquilinism.
   B. necrotrophic parasitism.
   C. biotrophic parasitism.
   D. obligate mutualism.
   E. facultative mutualism.

6. Most orchids are plants that depend on their hosts for physical support and not nutrition. To which of the following symbiotic interaction would orchids belong?

   A. Ectoparasitism
   B. Biotrophic parasitism
   C. Facultative mutualism
   D. Metabiosis
   E. Inquilinism

7. Historically, symbiosis has received less attention than predation and competition. Yet, it is believed as an important selective force behind the evolution of eukaryotes.

   A. Both statements are true.
   B. Both statements are false.
   C. The first sentence is true while the second sentence is false.
   D. The first sentence is false while the second sentence is true.

8. Ectosymbiosis is the same as:

   A. ectoparasitism.
   B. endosymbiosis.
   C. mistletoe.
   D. exosymbiosis.
   E. phoresy.

9. Bennett first used the word "symbiosis" to describe the mutualistic relationship of:

   A. lichens.
   B. coral reefs.
   C. unlike organisms.
   D. lactobacilli

10. A parasite is said to be biotrophic when:

   A. it survives on a dead host.
   B. it relies on the host's survival.
   C. it lives within the host's body.
   D. it feeds on the host's blood.

11. The biologist Lynn Margulis contradicts Darwin's notion of evolution because the latter assumes co-operation, interaction, and mutual dependence among organisms.

   A. Both the statement and reason are correct and related.
   B. Both the statement and the reason are correct but NOT related.
   C. The statement is correct, but the reason is NOT.
   D. The statement is NOT correct, but the reason is correct.
   E. NEITHER the statement NOR the reason is correct.

12. Adaptive speciation caused the flowering plants and their pollinators to undergo the following developments EXCEPT one. Which one is the EXCEPTION?

- **A.** Specialized morphology of pollinators
- **B.** Diversity of the plant species
- **C.** Pollination by insects, bats, or birds
- **D.** Obligate relationship of some plants and insects

13. Eukaryotes include the following EXCEPT:

- **A.** plants.
- **B.** animals.
- **C.** fungi.
- **D.** bacteria.
- **E.** protists.

14. An obligate symbiotic relationship is described to be that:

- **A.** both symbionts cannot live on their own.
- **B.** both symbionts can but do not have to live with the other organism.
- **C.** one of the two symbionts can live on its own.
- **D.** one of the symbionts lives on the other.
- **E.** both symbionts are protective of the other.

15. The definition of symbiosis is controversial among scientists because some believe that symbiosis should refer to all types of persistent biological interactions.

- **A.** Both the statement and reason are correct and related.
- **B.** Both the statement and the reason are correct but NOT related.
- **C.** The statement is correct, but the reason is NOT.
- **D.** The statement is NOT correct, but the reason is correct.
- **E.** NEITHER the statement NOR the reason is correct.

16. Who is the first scientist to provide a definition for symbiosis?

- **A.** Lynn Margulis
- **B.** Bennett
- **C.** Charles Darwin
- **D.** Heinrich Anton de Bary
- **E.** Dorion Sagan

17. Parasitic symbioses involve only relationships in which one member of the association lives within the host's body.

Half of all animals have at least one parasitic phase in their life cycles.

A. Both statements are true.
B. Both statements are false.
C. The first sentence is true while the second sentence is false.
D. The first sentence is false while the second sentence is true.

18. Any symbiotic relationship in which one symbiont lives within the tissues of the other, either in the intracellular or extracellular space is known as:

A. phoresy.
B. inquilinism.
C. metabiosis.
D. endosymbiosis.
E. endoparasitism

If time remains, you may review your work. If your allotted time (20 minutes) is complete, please proceed to the Answer Key.

RC Mini Test 2 Answer Key

1. C	7. A	13. D
2. A	8. D	14. A
3. C	9. A	15. A
4. C	10. B	16. D
5. D	11. C	17. D
6. E	12. C	18. D

RC Mini Test 2 Explanations and Strategies

1. Question Type: *Application Question*
   Strategies: *SI, OA; P9*

   The first sentence in Paragraph 9 defines "amensalism" as the type of symbiotic relationship where one species is inhibited or completely destroyed while the other one is unaffected. The example given in this question closely matches the situation of the sapling and the mature tree, cited in Paragraph 9. Although the herons' existence eventually caused damage to the understory vegetation, the herons in return neither benefited nor got harmed from the lost vegetation. Therefore, the correct answer is C.

   (A) Commensalism is roughly the opposite of this, i.e., one species benefits and the other is not significantly harmed or helped. This is also unlike (B) parasitism, where one member in the relationship benefits from either the existence or annihilation of another. On the other hand, (D) ectosymbiosis refers to a symbiotic relationship in which the symbiont feeds on the body surface of the host. This cannot be the correct answer because the herons do not live or feed on the vegetation.

2. Question Type: *Evaluation Question*
   Strategy: *SaL; P5 last 2 sentences*

   Cue words in the statements such as the shrimp being "vulnerable to predators" and the goby fish touches the shrimp with its tail "to warn" strongly suggest that their relationship is based on protection. The context of the paragraph likewise alludes to symbiotic relationships that work around protection.

3. Question Type: *Evaluation Question*
   Strategies: *OA, prior knowledge; P3 S2 and last sentence*

   Contextual clues in Paragraph 3 suggest that rhizobia, Frankia, bacterial endosymbionts provide nutrients (benefits) to their hosts while lactobacilli are generally known as "good" (in the biological context, "mutually beneficial") bacteria. Lice, on the other hand, are parasites and considered as pests – therefore, NOT "good."

4. Question Type: *Evaluation Question (Implication)*
   Strategies: *SaL or OA, PoE, attention to details; P1 S1*

   What makes this question tricky is that the passage offers several definitions of the term "symbiosis." However, A is a definition merely given by Heinrich Anton de Bary as indicated in P1 S3; D is only one of the opinions about symbiosis by some scientists, according to P1 last sentence; and E is loosely a definition from Bennett in P1 S2. This narrows down the choice between B and C. One easy way to determine the best option is to quickly and smartly locate the most conclusive statement that describes "symbiosis." This can be found in P4 S2, "Generally, only lifelong interactions involving close physical and biochemical contact can properly be considered symbiotic." This closely points to C. B, on the other hand, offers a very general definition.

   Another strategy would be to infer how symbiosis mainly works in the various relationships described in the different paragraphs and then choose the most inclusive definition among the answer choices: C.

5. Question Type: *Application*
   Strategies: *OA/paraphrasing; P6*

   The example in this question is similar to the case of the siboglinid tube worms and symbiotic bacteria discussed in Paragraph 6. The relationship illustrated refers to obligate mutualism: both symbionts entirely depend on each other for survival (P2 S1).

   The other answers are wrong based on each of their definitions:
   (A) Inquilinism pertains to a relationship between two living organisms where one benefits through housing without causing harm or profiting the other either.
   (B) Necrotrophic parasitism is a kind of parasitism that eventually kills the host.
   (C) Biotrophic parasitism only benefits the parasite for as long as the host is alive.
   (E) Facultative mutualism means that both members of the relationship can but do not have to live with the other.

6. Question Type: *Application Question*
   Strategy: *SI or OA; P2, P7, P8*

   Inquilinism is a form of commensalism described as a relationship between two living organisms where one benefits through physical shelter (housing) while the other is not significantly harmed or helped. This type of symbiotic interaction fits the description of an orchid to its host. (A) Ectoparasitism is a close choice. However, ectoparasites live on the surface of their host primarily for nourishment and in the process, cause harm. The other options are off-tangent.

7. Question Type: *True False Statement (Two Statements)*
   Strategies: *SaL, attention to details; P10*

   The first statement is almost verbatim of the first half of P10 S1: "While historically, symbiosis has received less attention than other interactions such as predation or competition. . ." The second statement is a paraphrase of the second half of P10 S2 and S3.

8. Question Type: *Recall*
   Strategy: *SaL; P3 S3*

9. Question Type: *Recall*
   Strategy: *SaL; P1 S2*

10. Question Type: *Recall*
    Strategy: *SaL; P8 S3*

11. Question Type: *True False Statements (Statement and Reason)*
    Strategies: *SI, attention to details; P11 S2*

    The information provided in the reason is reversed.

12. Question Type: *Exception/Negative Question*
    Strategies: *SI, PoE, never lose sight of the question; P12*

    Options A, B, and D are simple paraphrase of the information found in P12 S4 and S5. Pollination by insects, bats, or birds, on the other hand, is not an offshoot of adaptive speciation but rather, a "standard" activity or function of pollinators. The question is specifically asking for the developments, which arose from adaptive speciation, in the flowering plants and their pollinators – not what each already does. Therefore, the answer is C.

13. Question Type: *Exception/Negative Question*
    Strategies: *SaL, PoE; P10 S2*

    In P10 S2, the eukaryotes are specifically identified in a parenthesis to include plants, animals, fungi, and protists. Nowhere in the passage indicates bacteria as a eukaryote.

14. Question Type: *Recall*
    Strategy: *SaL; P2 S1*

15. Question Type: *True False Statement (Statement and Reason)*
    Strategy: *SaL; P1 last 2 sentences*

16. Question Type: *Recall*
    Strategies: *SaL, PoE; P1 S3*

    Bennett was the first to use the term "symbiosis," not define it. Dorion Sagan and Lynn Margulis are the ones who said that "life did not take over the globe by combat, but by networking." Charles Darwin was only mentioned in the passage in relation to Margulis' contention about the theory of evolution.

17. Question Type: *True False Statements (Two Statements)*
    Strategies: *SaL, PoE, attention to details; P8 S2 and S5*

The first statement presents an incomplete definition of parasitic symbioses, which should include endoparasitism (living within a host's body), ectoparasitism (living on the surface of a host), necrotrophic parasitism (killing the host) and biotrophic parasitism (relying on the host's survival).

18. Question Type: *Recall*
    Strategy: *SaL, P3 S1*

Would you like to discuss any of the answers or strategies in this section? Go to www.dat-prep.com/forum to share and learn.

RC Mini Test 3

The following is a sample mini test which is comparable to the level of difficulty required for the Reading Comprehension Test of the DAT. Please note that this sample would roughly be 1/3 of the actual Reading Comprehension Test portion of the DAT.

You have 20 minutes to complete this portion of the DAT Mini Test; the actual test is 60 minutes. Please time yourself accordingly.

BEGIN ONLY WHEN YOUR TIMER IS READY.

Passage 3

Empirical Science

(1). A scientist, whether theorist or experimenter, puts forward statements, or systems of statements, and tests them step by step. In the field of the empirical sciences, more particularly, he constructs hypotheses, or systems of theories, and tests them against experience by observation and experiment. I suggest that it is the task of the logic of scientific discovery, or the logic of knowledge, to give a logical analysis of this procedure; that is, to analyze the method of the empirical sciences.

(2). But what are these "methods of the empirical sciences"? And what do we call "empirical science"?

(3). According to a widely accepted view — to be opposed in this book — the empirical sciences can be characterized by the fact that they use "inductive methods," as they are called. According to this view, the logic of scientific discovery would be identical with inductive logic, i.e. with the logical analysis of these inductive methods.

(4). It is usual to call an inference "inductive" if it passes from singular statements (sometimes also called "particular" statements), such as accounts of the results of observations or experiments, to universal statements, such as hypotheses or theories.

(5). Now it is far from obvious, from a logical point of view, that we are justified in inferring universal statements from singular ones, no matter how numerous; for any conclusion drawn in this way may always turn out to be false: no matter how many instances of white swans we may have observed, this does not justify the conclusion that all swans are white.

(6). The question whether inductive inferences are justified, or under what conditions, is known as the problem of induction. The problem of induction may also be formulated as the question of the validity or the truth of universal statements which are based on experience, such as the hypotheses and theoretical systems of the empirical sciences. For many people believe that the truth of these universal statements is "known by experience"; yet it is clear that an account of an experience — of an observation or the result of an experiment — can in the first place be only a singular statement and not a universal one. Accordingly, people who say of a universal statement that we know its truth from experience usually mean that the truth of this universal statement can somehow be reduced to the truth of singular ones, and that these singular ones are known by experience to be true; which amounts to saying that the universal statement is based on inductive inference. Thus to ask whether there are natural laws known to be true appears to be only another way of asking whether inductive inferences are logically justified.

(7). Yet if we want to find a way of justifying inductive inferences, we must first of all try to establish a principle of induction. A principle of induction would be a statement with the help of which we could put inductive inferences into a logically acceptable form. In the eyes of the upholders of inductive logic, a principle of induction is of supreme importance for scientific method: ". . . this principle," says Reichenbach, "determines the truth of scientific theories. To eliminate it from science would mean nothing less than to deprive science of the power to decide the truth or falsity of its theories. Without it, clearly, science would no longer have the right to distinguish its theories from the fanciful and arbitrary creations of the poet's mind."

(8). Now this principle of induction cannot be a purely logical truth like a tautology or an analytic statement. Indeed, if there were such a thing as a purely logical principle of induction, there would be no problem of induction; for in this case, all inductive inferences would have to be regarded as purely logical or tautological transformations, just like inferences in deductive logic. Thus the principle of induction must be a synthetic statement; that is, a statement whose negation is not self-contradictory but logically possible. So the question arises why such a principle should be accepted at all, and how we can justify its acceptance on rational grounds.

(9). Some who believe in inductive logic are anxious to point out, with Reichenbach, that "the principle of induction is unreservedly accepted by the whole of science and that no man can seriously doubt this principle in everyday life either." Yet even supposing this were the case — for after all, "the whole of science" might err — I should still contend that a principle of induction is superfluous, and that it must lead to logical inconsistencies.

(10). That inconsistencies may easily arise in connection with the principle of induction should have been clear from the work of Hume, also, that they can be avoided, if at all, only with difficulty. For the principle of induction must be a universal statement in its turn. Thus if we try to regard its truth as known from experience, then the very same problems which occasioned its introduction will arise all over again. To justify it, we should have to employ inductive inferences; and to justify these we should have to assume an inductive principle of a higher order; and so on. Thus the attempt to base the principle of induction on experience breaks down, since it must lead to an infinite regress.

(11). Kant tried to force his way out of this difficulty by taking the principle of induction (which he formulated as the "principle of universal causation") to be "a priori valid." But I do not think that his ingenious attempt to provide an a priori justification for synthetic statements was successful.

(12). My own view is that the various difficulties of inductive logic here sketched are insurmountable. So also, I fear, are those inherent in the doctrine, so widely current today, that inductive inference, although not "strictly valid," can attain some degree of "reliability" or of "probability." According to this doctrine, inductive inferences are "probable inferences." "We have described," says Reichenbach, "the principle of induction as the means whereby science decides upon truth. To be more exact, we should say that it serves to decide upon probability. For it is not given to science to reach either truth or falsity . . . but scientific statements can only attain continuous degrees of probability whose unattainable upper and lower limits are truth and falsity." At this stage I can disregard the fact that the believers in inductive logic entertain an idea of probability that I shall later reject as highly unsuitable for their own purposes. I can do so because the difficulties mentioned are not even touched by an appeal to probability. For if a certain degree of probability is to be assigned to statements based on inductive inference, then this will have to be justified by invoking a new principle of induction, appropriately modified. And this new principle in its turn will have to be justified, and so on. Nothing is gained, moreover, if the principle of induction, in its turn, is taken not as "true" but only as "probable." In short, like every other form of inductive logic, the logic of probable inference, or "probability logic," leads either to an infinite regress, or to the doctrine of apriorism.

(13). The theory to be developed in the following pages stands directly opposed to all attempts to operate with the ideas of inductive logic. It might be described as the theory of the deductive method of testing, or as the view that a hypothesis can only be empirically tested — and only after it has been advanced.

(14). Before I can elaborate this view (which might be called "deductivism," in contrast to "inductivism") I must first make clear the distinction between the psychology of knowledge which deals with empirical facts, and the logic of knowledge which is concerned only with logical relations. For the belief in inductive logic is largely due to a confusion of psychological problems with epistemological ones. It may be worth noticing, by the way, that this confusion spells trouble not only for the logic of knowledge but for its psychology as well.

- from Karl Popper's ***Logic of Scientific Discovery***

1. The problem of induction is best represented by which of the following equations?

   A. X = Z always
   B. X = Z many times, so X must be the same as Z
   C. X never equals Z, so X is unique and apart from Z
   D. X is sometimes Z, but only in certain situations
   E. X is derived from Z on the basis of logic

2. Of the following, which is tested by a scientist against experience with observation and experiment?

   A. Inductive logic
   B. Deductive logic
   C. Empirical sciences
   D. Hypotheses and theories
   E. None of the above

3. The idea of an "infinite regress" results from the idea that a theory is:

   A. after experience.
   B. before experience.
   C. deductively sound.
   D. inductively inferred.
   E. a priori.

4. With which of the following statements would the author of the passage agree?

   A. Deductive logic should be preferred over inductive logic.
   B. The methods of empirical science are marked by circular reasoning.
   C. Inductive logic is questionable and suspect.
   D. Tautological statements support observation and hypotheses.
   E. Scientists need to justify inductive inferences.

5. Based on usage in this passage, which of the following best defines “empirical”?

    A. Arbitrary
    B. Inferable
    C. Falsifiable
    D. Observable
    E. More than one of the above

6. Which of the following analogies best represents the idea of infinite regress?

    A. A bridge connected to another bridge
    B. A circle within another circle
    C. A snake eating its own tail (uberous)
    D. A mirror turned towards another mirror
    E. A vessel with many interconnected chambers

7. Inductive logic, by its nature, supposedly passes from the “singular event” to:

    A. the hypothetical derived.
    B. the a priori established.
    C. the universally true.
    D. the testable observation.
    E. the experimental deduced.

8. The author’s tone and type of audience are which of the following terms?

    A. Critical - Scientific Community
    B. Arcane - General Populace
    C. Careful - Students
    D. Witty - Academic
    E. Profound - Logicians

9. The principle of induction serves to decide upon probability in science because it is given to science to reach either truth or falsity.

    A. Both the statement and reason are correct and related.
    B. Both the statement and the reason are correct but NOT related.
    C. The statement is correct but the reason is NOT.
    D. The statement is NOT correct, but the reason is correct.
    E. NEITHER the statement NOR the reason is correct.

10. Reichenbach organizes a principle of induction around:

- **A.** the establishment of logical inferences.
- **B.** social consensus of the scientific community.
- **C.** logically derived a priori formulations.
- **D.** other inductive tautologies.
- **E.** None of the above

11. Of the following, which according to the passage are the functions of the principle of induction?

1. Characterizes empirical science as tautological
2. Justifies inductive inferences as a logical form
3. Determines the truth of scientific theories
4. Distinguishes science from creative art

- **A.** All of the above
- **B.** 2, 3 and 4 only
- **C.** 2 and 3 only
- **D.** 3 only
- **E.** 4 only

12. The problem of induction is basically:

- **A.** how to refine this logical process.
- **B.** how to avoid this process in favor of deduction.
- **C.** whether its applications are logically faulty.
- **D.** whether inductive inferences are justified or under what conditions.
- **E.** how there is an inherent contradiction in inductive inferences.

13. In the last paragraph, the statement to "make clear the distinction between the psychology of knowledge which deals with empirical facts, and the logic of knowledge which is concerned only with logical relations" can be inferred to be the author's juxtaposition between:

- **A.** what is observable and what is testable.
- **B.** what is hypothetical and what is logically sound.
- **C.** what is testable and what is inductive.
- **D.** what is observable and what is logically sound.
- **E.** what is inductive and what is universally true.

14. What is the task of the logic of scientific discovery?

- **A.** To analyze the method of empirical sciences
- **B.** To put forward statements and test them step by step
- **C.** To test scientific theories against experience by observation and experiment
- **D.** To employ inductive logic
- **E.** All of the above

15. Which of the following is the best description of a synthetic statement?

- **A.** A statement based on experience
- **B.** A universal statement based on inductive inference
- **C.** The power to decide the truth or falsity of a theory
- **D.** A statement whose negation is not self-contradictory but logically possible
- **E.** A purely logical or tautological transformation

If time remains, you may review your work. If your allotted time (20 minutes) is complete, please proceed to the Answer Key.

RC Mini Test 3 Answer Key

1. B	6. D	11. B
2. D	7. C	12. D
3. D	8. A	13. D
4. C	9. C	14. A
5. D	10. B	15. D

RC Mini Test 3 Explanations and Strategies

1. Question Type: *Evaluation Question (Main Idea)*
   Strategy: *OA*

   The whole passage is about how inductive logic compiles on examples in order to move from the singular examples to the universal. A is incorrect because that would posit the problem of induction as an exact correspondence between entities or phenomena. C is also incorrect because this equation suggests an inequality, subtraction or difference of phenomena or entities. This is closer to deduction, not induction. D is incorrect because it gives X a contextually determined essence. E is a made up phrase, simply made to distract the test taker.

2. Question Type: *Recall*
   Strategy: *SaL; P1 S2*

3. Question Type: *Evaluation Question (Implication)*
   Strategy: *SaL or OA, P10 last 2 sentences, P12 last sentence*

   The idea of infinite regress can be inferred based on the author's discussion in Paragraph 10: a theory supported through induction must be inductively inferred as well, resulting to an endless chain of induction. After Experience or A Posteriori, as well as Before Experience or A Priori, are related but not as specific to the idea of infinite regress. C is quite the contrary, and can be ruled out.

4. Question Type: *Evaluation Question (Tone and Main Idea)*
   Strategies: *OA, attention to details in P3*

   Early in the passage, the author expresses his opposition to the inductive method: "According to a widely accepted view — to be opposed in this book — the empirical sciences can be characterized by the fact that they use 'inductive methods'." This statement would readily give a clear hint of the author's tone – that of contradiction, which is closest to viewing inductive logic as "questionable and suspect."

   Another strategy is to paraphrase the main idea of each significant paragraph in order to have a clear outline of the author's overall point.

   (1). I suggest that it is the task of the logic of scientific discovery, or the logic of knowledge, to give a logical analysis of this procedure; that is, to analyze the method of the empirical sciences.

   (3). The author explicitly contradicts the inductive method.

   (4). Induction starts with the specific "particular" or "singular" to the general or "universal."

   (5). This method is not justified because "any conclusion drawn in this way may always turn out to be false."

   (6). The problem of the inductive method is that the truth of the universal statements is questionable and cannot be justified because they are based on a particular observation or a singular result of an experiment. In other words, a universal statement cannot be justified by a singular experience or event.

   (7). In order to justify the inductive method, a principle of induction must first be established. (A principle of induction would be a statement with the help of which we could put inductive inferences into a logically acceptable form.)

   (8). Ideally, a principle of induction must present a synthetic statement - a statement whose negation is not self-contradictory but logically possible.

   (9). The author believes that a principle of induction is superfluous (unnecessary), and that it must lead to logical inconsistencies. On the other hand, Reichenbach asserts that "the principle of induction is unreservedly accepted by the whole of science and that no man can seriously doubt this principle in everyday life either."

   (10). The principle of induction is prone to infinite regress.

   (11). Kant fails to provide an a priori justification for synthetic statements.

   (12). Inductive logic is problematic in several ways: inductive inference, although not "strictly valid," can attain some degree of "reliability" or of "probability"; "probability logic," leads either to an infinite regress, or to the doctrine of apriorism.

(13). The author introduces the idea of deductivism.

(14). The author distinguishes his idea of "the psychology of knowledge which deals with empirical facts (from) the logic of knowledge which is concerned only with logical relations.

The preceding brief notes clearly indicate that the author's concern in this excerpt is questioning the validity of inductive logic. Therefore, the most reasonable answer to this question would be C.

The author does mention his preference to deductivism over inductivism. However, this is not elaborated in the passage. A, then, would not be an accurate answer. (B) Circular reasoning in empirical science is not asserted in the passage either.

Although tautology in relation to logic is mentioned, the idea that (D) tautological statements support observation and hypotheses is off-tangent in the context of the passage. Lastly, the author does not seek that (E) "scientists need to justify inductive inferences." Rather, he dismisses the use of such method as resulting to infinite regress.

5. Question Type: *Evaluation Question (Implication)*
   Strategies: *OA, PoE; P1, P3, P4, P6*

   (A) Arbitrary is the term used by the author to describe poetic creations. This can be readily eliminated then. On the other hand, inferring from paragraphs that refer to "empirical" or "empirical science" often suggests the following key ideas: "experience by observation and experiment" (P1 S2); "the empirical sciences can be characterized by the fact that they use 'inductive methods'" (P3 S1), correlating to the notion in Paragraph 4 that induction entails "observations or experiments." These lead to D (observable) as the best choice.

   Although (B) inference is repeatedly mentioned in the passage, this is used in reference to the inductive method per se, not empirical science. (C) Falsifiable is an element of theory, which limits scope, i.e., the theory does not include everything, thus this is prescriptive evaluation and reservations of a given theory, not a definition in itself. E can thus be eliminated as well.

6. Question Type: *Application Question*
   Strategies: *OA/paraphrasing, PoE; P10 and P12*

   Since "infinite regress" is the idea that inductive logic which is inferred is based on an inference, and that inference is based on another inference and so on, the best analogy would be (D) of a mirror turned towards a mirror reproducing its own representation. The notion of (C) a snake eating its own tail, comes close to representing the tautological reasoning sometimes used to support inductive modes of logic: Premise = CLAIM = Premise. However, the idea of something eating up its own self suggests an end, therefore not "infinite."

   The analogy of (A) a bridge connected to another bridge is also close but is only limited to one extension – not one after another. (B)

A circle within a circle suggests related but separate inferences – not a continuation. This is the same with the idea in E. These make all the other options incorrect.

7. Question Type: *Evaluation Question (Implication); Recall*
Strategies: *Paraphrasing, SaL; P4*

This question is merely a paraphrase of the general idea found in Paragraph 4, which states induction starts with the specific – "particular" or "singular" – to the general or "universal."

8. Question Type: *Evaluation Question (Tone)*
Strategy: *SI*

The author makes clear from the beginning that he is opposed to the idea of inductive logic. He then devotes a majority of his succeeding discussions in pointing out the problems of induction. He is therefore, critical. In addition, constant references to empirical science and experiments make this passage generally suited for the scientific community, which can include students or the academic audience and logicians as well.

However, (D) witty does not characterize the tone of the author. (C) Careful and (E) profound may be reasonable descriptions of the quality of the author's writing, but they are not as encompassing and specific.

(B) Arcane connotes ambiguous or difficult to understand, which is illogical to have something written in this language to be meant for the general populace. Thus B is wrong.

9. Question Type: *True False Statements (Statement and Reason)*
Strategy: *SaL; P12 S4 to S6*

10. Question Type: *Recall*
Strategies: *SaL, attention to details; P9 S1*

As the passage states in a quote from Reichenbach, " the principle of induction is unreservedly accepted by the whole of science and that no man can seriously doubt this principle in everyday life." This amounts to a social consensus of the inductive method. Answer A is nonsense. E (None of the Above) can be ruled out. D may be true, in the idea of infinite regress, but the question states "the principle of induction." C is more or less philoso-babble constructed in the answers to distract the test taker.

11. Question Type: *Recall; Evaluation (Implication)*
Strategies: *SI, paraphrasing; P7 and P8 S1*

This question pertains to the discussion of establishing a principle of induction found in Paragraph 7. According to the author, "a principle of induction would be a statement with the help of which we could put inductive inferences into a logically acceptable form" (Statement 2). For Reichenbach, this principle "determines the truth of scientific theories" (Statement 3) and "distinguish(es) (scientific) theories from the fanciful and arbitrary creations of the poet's mind" (Statement 4).

P8 S1 would eliminate Statement 1: "Now this principle of induction cannot be a purely logical truth like a tautology or an analytic statement." Therefore, the best answer is B.

12. Question Type: *Recall*
    Strategy: *SaL; P6 S1*

13. Question Type: *Evaluation (Implication)*
    Strategies: *OA/paraphrasing, inference*

    This question requires clearly understanding what "empirical" mainly connotes in the passage. As already determined and explained in Question No. 5, empirical or empirical facts would indicate something "observable." Additionally, the author makes a significant remark in Paragraph 8 that for a method, such as that of induction, to work, a synthetic statement must result: one that is logically valid or possible. Hence, the correct answer is D: the author juxtaposes "what is observable (empirical facts) and what is logically sound (logical relations)."

    A is incorrect because logical relations is not indicated in the passage as "testable." B is also wrong because hypothetical does not directly characterize an "empirical fact." Hypothesis is only part of this process. C is primarily incorrect because of the term "induction" being correlated to logic. The author explicitly opposes this view. E sounds correct; however, it must be noted that the author has not established the concept of logic to be "universally true." Therefore, E is an erroneous statement.

14. Question Type: *Recall*
    Strategy: *SaL; P1 last sentence*

    The two key phrases here are "empirical facts" and "logical relations" - meaning "observations" and "logic as a system of itself." Therefore, an analysis of the method of empirical sciences – as explicitly stated in the last sentence of Paragraph 1 – is the best answer. B and C are corollaries or peripheral statements that simply relate to the passage in general while D goes against the main idea of the author.

15. Question Type: *Recall*
    Strategy: *SaL; P8 S3*

Would you like to discuss any of the answers or strategies in this section? Go to www.dat-prep.com/forum to share and learn.

Gold Standard DAT RC Practice Test

Reading Comprehension Test

Time Limit: 60 Minutes

Passage 1

Scientific Analysis and Reasoning

(1). Unlike some other classical figures (Auguste Comte and Émile Durkheim, for example) Max Weber did not attempt, consciously, to create any specific set of rules governing social sciences in general, or sociology in particular. Compared to Durkheim and Marx, Weber was more focused on individuals and culture and this is clear in his methodology. Whereas Durkheim focused on the society, Weber concentrated on the individuals and their actions; and whereas Marx argued for the primacy of the material world over the world of ideas, Weber valued ideas as motivating actions of individuals, at least in the big picture.

(2). Weber was concerned with the question of objectivity and subjectivity. Weber distinguished social action from social behavior, noting that social action must be understood through how individuals subjectively relate to one another. Study of social action through interpretive means must be based upon understanding the subjective meaning and purpose that the individual attaches to their actions. Social actions may have easily identifiable and objective means, but much more subjective ends and the understanding of those ends by a scientist is subject to yet another layer of subjective understanding (that of the scientist). Weber noted that the importance of subjectivity in social sciences makes creation of full-proof, universal laws much more difficult than in natural sciences and that the amount of objective knowledge that social sciences may achieve is precariously limited. Overall, Weber supported the goal of objective science, but he noted that it is an unreachable goal – although one definitely worth striving for.

> *There is no absolutely "objective" scientific analysis of culture . . . All knowledge of cultural reality . . . is always knowledge from particular points of view . . . An "objective" analysis of cultural events, which proceeds according to the thesis that the ideal of science is the reduction of empirical reality to "laws," is meaningless. . . [because]. . . the knowledge of social laws is not knowledge of social reality but is rather one of the various aids used by our minds for attaining this end.*
>
> - Max Weber, "Objectivity" in ***Social Science,*** 1897

(3). The principle of "methodological individualism," which holds that social scientists should seek to understand collectivities (such as nations, cultures, governments, churches, corporations, etc.) solely as the result and the context of the actions of individual persons, can be traced to Weber, particularly to the first chapter of ***Economy and Society***, in which he argues that only individuals "can be treated as agents in a course of subjectively understandable action." In other words, Weber argued that social phenomena can be understood scientifically only to the extent that they are captured by models of the behavior of purposeful individuals, models which Weber called "ideal types," from which actual historical events will necessarily deviate due to accidental and irrational factors. The analytical constructs of an ideal type never exist in reality, but provide objective benchmarks against which real-life constructs can be measured.

> *We know of no scientifically ascertainable ideals. To be sure, that makes our efforts more arduous than in the past, since we are expected to create our ideals from within our breast in the very age of subjectivist culture.*
>
> \- Max Weber, 1909

(4). Weber's methodology was developed in the context of a wider debate about methodology of social sciences, the *Methodenstreit* (debate over methods). Weber's position was close to historicism, as he understood social actions as being heavily tied to particular historical contexts and its analysis required the understanding of subjective motivations of individuals (social actors). Thus Weber's methodology emphasizes the use of comparative historical analysis. Therefore, Weber was more interested in explaining how a certain outcome was the result of various historical processes rather than predicting an outcome of those processes in the future.

(5). Such views by Max Weber find their parallel in the field of twentieth-century scientific thoughts. Jacob Bronowski, writer of the book and the 1973 BBC television documentary series, ***The Ascent of Man***, was a mathematician, biologist, historian of science, theatre author, poet and inventor. In the 1950s, he wrote an essay entitled *The Nature of Scientific Reasoning*, which similarly discusses subjectivity, this time among scientific theories, as the following excerpt would show:

(6). "No scientific theory is a collection of facts. It will not even do to call a theory true or false in the simple sense in which every fact is either so or not so. The Epicureans held that matter is made of atoms 2000 years ago and we are now tempted to say that their theory was true. But if we do so we confuse their notion of matter with our own. John Dalton in 1808 first saw the structure of matter as we do today, and what he took from the ancients was not their theory but something richer - their image: the atom. Much of what was in Dalton's mind was as vague as the Greek notion, and quite as mistaken. But he suddenly gave life to the new facts of chemistry and the ancient theory together, by fusing them to give what neither had: a coherent picture of how matter is linked and built up from different kinds of atoms. The act of fusion is the creative act.

(7). All science is the search for unity in hidden likenesses. The search may be on a grand scale, as in the modern theories which try to link the fields of gravitation and electromagnetism. But we do not need to be browbeaten by the scale of science. There are discoveries to be made by snatching a small likeness from the air too, if it is bold enough. In 1935, the Japanese physicist Hideki Yukawa wrote a paper which can still give heart to a young scientist. He took as his starting point the known fact that waves of light can sometimes behave as if they were separate pellets. From this he reasoned that the forces which hold the nucleus of an atom together might sometimes also be observed as if they were solid pellets. A schoolboy can see how thin Yukawa's analogy is, and his teacher would be severe with it. Yet Yukawa, without a blush, calculated the mass of the pellet he expected to see, and waited. He was right; his meson was found, and a range of other mesons, neither the existence nor the nature of which had been suspected before. The likeness had borne fruit.

(8). The scientist looks for order in the appearances of nature by exploring such likenesses. For order does not display itself of itself, if it can be said to be there at all, it is not there for the mere looking. There is no way of pointing a finger or camera at it; order must be discovered and, in a deep sense, it must be created. What we see, as we see it, is mere disorder.

(9). This point has been put trenchantly in a fable by Karl Popper. Suppose that someone wishes to give his whole life to science. Suppose that he therefore sat down, pencil in hand, and for the next twenty, thirty, forty years recorded in notebook after notebook everything that he could observe. He may be supposed to leave out nothing: today's humidity, the racing results, the level of cosmic radiation and the stock market prices and the look of Mars, all would be there. He would have compiled the most careful record of nature that has ever been made; and, dying in the calm certainty of a life well-spent, he would of course leave his notebooks to the Royal Society. Would the Royal Society thank him for the treasure of a lifetime of observation? It would not. The Royal Society would treat his notebooks exactly as the English bishops have treated Joanna Southcott's box. It would refuse to open them at all, because it would know without looking that the notebooks contain only a jumble of disorderly and meaningless items."

- Part of this passage is adapted from J. Bronowski, *The Nature of Scientific Reasoning*

1. In the excerpt from Jacob Bronowski's essay, the author starts with "No scientific theory is a collection of facts." Which of the following reasons can NOT be inferred to be applicable to this statement?

   A. Theories are sometimes developed from other earlier theories.
   B. Facts from one era of history may differ from facts of later histories.
   C. Scientific theory can be a creative act through fusion of theories.
   D. Facts are immutable throughout time, while theories are not.

2. Weber's concept of methodological individualism is BEST exemplified by how one:

   A. conceives collective institutions as the product of individual actions.
   B. focuses on how social action can be understood through subjective interpretation.
   C. interprets "ideal types" on the basis of debate over methods.
   D. stands in stark contrast to social realities interpreted by Marx and Durkheim.
   E. represents as an agent in subjective social actions.

3. Jacob Bronowski is identified as all of the following EXCEPT a(n):

   A. mathematician.
   B. biologist.
   C. author.
   D. poet.
   E. philosopher.

4. The fable by Karl Popper can be inferred to express the idea that in scientific study:

   A. order must be discovered and created.
   B. a clear focus is needed to sort out the mess of variables.
   C. indiscriminate research findings will not be applauded by the scientific community.
   D. what we see, as we see it, is mere disorder.
   E. the Royal Society, in reality, regard scientific theories to be meaningless.

5. "Methodenstreit" means:

   A. methodology of social sciences.
   B. methodological individualism.
   C. debate over methods.
   D. scientific analysis and reasoning.
   E. social action.

6. According to Bronowski, science is characterized by a number of ideas. Which of the following is NOT an idea advanced in his essay?

- **A.** Science looks for order in the appearance of Nature.
- **B.** Science looks for unity in hidden likenesses.
- **C.** Science proceeds to build theory through testing and observation.
- **D.** Science is selective in its searches for order and likeness.

7. All knowledge of cultural reality is always knowledge from certain points of view.

Social phenomena can be understood scientifically only to the extent that they are captured by "ideal types."

- **A.** Both statements are true.
- **B.** Both statements are false.
- **C.** The first statement is true.
  The second statement is false.
- **D.** The first statement is false.
  The second statement is true.

8. Hideki Yukawa discovered:

- **A.** that light waves could behave like pellets.
- **B.** the meson.
- **C.** that the nucleus of an atom was not held together similar to pellets.
- **D.** the link between gravitation and electromagnetism.
- **E.** that scientific theory is creative.

9. The notion of an objective scientific analysis of culture is unattainable because it will always be marked by subjective perspectives.

- **A.** Both the statement and reason are correct and related.
- **B.** Both the statement and the reason are correct but NOT related.
- **C.** The statement is correct but the reason is NOT.
- **D.** The statement is NOT correct, but the reason is correct.
- **E.** NEITHER the statement NOR the reason is correct.

10. Weber's opinion toward objectivity in the social sciences is that:

- **A.** it is practically non-existent.
- **B.** it is nothing more than an ideal.
- **C.** it is masked by our very own subjectivity.
- **D.** objective knowledge is limited.
- **E.** it is more focused on individuals and culture.

11. Weber's "ideal types" are:

- **A.** striving for objectivity through subjective means.
- **B.** ideal methodologies for understanding social action.
- **C.** socially-constructed realities based on subjective interpretation.
- **D.** models of social behavior.
- **E.** deviations due to accidental and irrational factors.

12. It can be inferred from the passage that "Methodenstreit" was:

- **A.** a concern of how to properly define social action.
- **B.** an argument of how to proceed theoretically in the study of social sciences.
- **C.** a theoretical quagmire of evaluating objectivity.
- **D.** a postulation of proof concerning subjectivity.

13. Which of the following concepts DOES NOT point out a difference of Weber from other classical figures in the social sciences?

- **A.** Weber focused on individuals and their social actions.
- **B.** Weber valued the ideas that drive individual actions.
- **C.** Weber created standards albeit subjective for understanding society.
- **D.** Weber was concerned with the question of objectivity and subjectivity.
- **E.** Weber noted that social action must be understood through how individuals subjectively relate to one another.

14. Which of the following sociological studies would be reasonably expected to interest Weber?

- **A.** A report on repercussions of President Bush's "War on Terrorism" policy
- **B.** A subjective study of social behavior among victims of domestic violence
- **C.** An analysis of Napoleon Bonaparte's motivation for waging the Napoleonic Wars
- **D.** A research report on culture presenting the different findings and impressions of the researchers

15. According to Bronowski, the order of Nature must be:

- **A.** discovered.
- **B.** understood.
- **C.** fused.
- **D.** deduced.
- **E.** debated.

16. Weber wrote the first chapter of ***Economy and Society*** in:

- **A.** 1808.
- **B.** 1897.
- **C.** 1909.
- **D.** 1935.
- **E.** 1973.

17. The view that matter has primacy over ideas was promoted by:

- **A.** Dalton.
- **B.** the Epicureans.
- **C.** Comte.
- **D.** Marx.
- **E.** Durkheim.

Passage 2

Drifting Rocks

(1). Another one of the devious little mysteries of science are the strange stones of Death Valley in California. These stones sit on sun-baked, flat, cracked earth, but for some baffling reason, they have moved across the wasteland. They have, in fact, left trails of their movement.

(2). The home of these mysterious stones is known, logically, as the "Racetrack Playa", a dry lakebed occasionally dampened by flash storms. The Racetrack measures 4.5 kilometers by 2.1 kilometers (2.8 by 1.3 miles), and is only about 5 centimeters (2 inches) higher at one end than the other.

(3). The trails left by the stones vary from a few meters to almost a kilometer in length. Some of the trails are straight; some are zigzagged; some go in circles. In some cases, the trails vary in width, meaning the stones must have rotated as they moved. One hundred sixty two of the Racetrack's moving stones have been documented, and many of them have names, always female. They range from fist-sized to the size of an ice chest.

(4). In 1948, two US Geological Survey geologists suggested that the little desert whirlwinds known as "dust devils" might be responsible for moving the stones around. Then George Stanley, a geologist of Fresno State College in California, suggested the stones might have become frozen in ice sheets during the winter and slid around with the sheets on an underlying slick of water.

(5). Between 1968 and 1975, two geologists, Robert Sharp of the California Institute of Technology and Dwight Carey of the University of California at Los Angeles, made careful measurements of the positions of 30 rocks in an attempt to answer the mystery of the drifting rocks once and for all. They tried to pound stakes around some of the rocks, on the principle that if the motion were caused by floating ice, the stakes would hold the ice in place. The mystery only seemed to deepen. In one case, a rock drifted out of the stakes while another remained where it was, and in other cases rocks moved near other rocks that remained stationary.

(6). Sharp and Carey never really managed to link the movement of a rock to any event and finally gave up. By this time, research has become somewhat restricted by the fact that the Racetrack is now a protected Wilderness area. The US National Park Service was trying to protect the Racetrack, which was suffering from increasing numbers of intruders who were not always considerate of the special nature of the place. Sometimes park rangers find citizens dancing naked on the dried mud, apparently obtaining inspiration from the place's cosmic energies. Drug runners also occasionally use it as a landing strip, though ranger vigilance has largely eliminated this practice. Rangers had to dig a trench to keep four-wheel drive vehicles out and kept the place tidied up.

(7). Meanwhile, researchers continue to puzzle over the drifting rocks. One early suggestion was that the rocks were driven by gravity, sliding down a gradual slope over a long period of time. But this theory was discounted when it was revealed that the northern end of the playa is actually several centimeters higher than the southern end and that most of the rocks were in fact traveling uphill.

(8). Nonetheless, John B. Reid, Jr. of Hampshire College in Amherst, Massachusetts, is a partisan of the ice floe theory while Paula Messina, assistant professor of geology at San Jose State University in California, thinks they move in the wind over a slick of mud when the Racetrack is wet. Reid does not buy the wind theory, basing his objections on studies performed by him and his students in the late 1980s and early 1990s, when they measured the force required to move some of the Racetrack's bigger rocks and determined that wind speeds of hundreds of kilometers per hour would be required to budge them – though it has been pointed out that Reid's measurements, taken in dry conditions, may not have accurately reflected what would happen when the Racetrack was wet.

(9). Though no one has yet been able to conclusively identify just what makes the rocks move, for the past ten years, Dr. Paula Messina has made it her quest to understand what has bewildered geologists for decades. "It's interesting that no one has seen them move, so I am kind of sleuthing to see what's really going on here," says Dr. Messina.

(10). Many scientists had dedicated much of their careers to the racing rocks, but the remoteness of the area kept their research limited in scope. No one had been able to map the complete set of trails before the advent of a quick, portable method known as global positioning. Dr. Messina was the first to have the luxury of this high technology at her fingertips.

(11). In 1996, armed with a hand-held GPS unit, she digitally mapped the location of each of the 162 rocks scattered over the playa. "I'm very fortunate that this technology was available at about the same time the Racetrack captured my interest," she says. "It took only ten days to map the entire network – a total of about 60 miles." Since then, she has continued to chart the movements of each rock within a centimeter of accuracy. Walking the length of a trail, she collects the longitude and latitude points of each, which snap into a line. She then takes her data back to the lab where she is able to analyze changes in the rocks' positions since her last visit.

(12). She has found that two components are essential to their movement: wind and water. The fierce winter storms that sweep down from the surrounding mountains carry plenty of both. The playa surface is made up of very fine clay sediments that become extremely slick when wet. "When you have pliable, wet, frictionless sediments and intense winds blowing through," offers Dr. Messina, "I think you have the elements to make the rocks move."

(13). At an elevation of 3,700 feet, strong winds can rake the playa at 70 miles per hour. But Dr. Messina is quick to point out that sometimes even smaller gusts can set the rocks in motion. The explanation for this lies in her theory, which links wind and water with yet another element: bacteria.

(14). After periods of rain, bacteria lying dormant on the playa begin to "come to." As they grow, long, hairlike filaments develop and cause a slippery film to form on the surface. "Very rough surfaces would require great forces to move the lightest-weight rocks," she says. "But if the surface is exceptionally smooth, as would be expected from a biogeologic film, even the heaviest rocks could be propelled by a small shove of the wind. I think of the Racetrack as being coated by Teflon, under those special conditions."

(15). In science, hypotheses are often based on logic. But over the years, Dr. Messina has discovered that on the Racetrack, logic itself must often be tossed to the wind. "Some of the rocks have done some very unusual things," she says. In her initial analysis, she hypothesized that given their weight, larger rocks would travel shorter distances and smaller, lighter rocks would sail on further, producing longer trails. It also seemed reasonable that the heavier, angular rocks would leave straighter trails and rounder rocks would move more erratically.

(16). What she discovered surprised her. "I was crunching numbers and found that there was absolutely no correlation between the size and shape of the rocks and their trails. There was no smoking gun, so this was one of the big mysteries to me." What appears as a very flat, uniform terrain is in fact a mosaic of microclimates. In the southeastern part of the playa, wind is channeled through a low pass in the mountains, forming a natural wind tunnel. This is where the longest, straightest trails are concentrated. In the central part of the playa, two natural wind tunnels converge from different directions, creating turbulence. It is in this area that the rock trails are the most convoluted. "What I think is happening," proposes Dr. Messina, "is that the surrounding topography is actually what is guiding the rocks and telling them where to go."

(17). Some people have suggested attaching radio transmitters to the rocks or erecting cameras to catch them "in the act" in order to put an end to the speculation. But as Death Valley National Park is 95 percent designated wilderness, all research in the park must be noninvasive. It is forbidden to erect any permanent structures or instrumentation. Further, no one is permitted on the playa when it is wet because each footprint would leave an indelible scar.

(18). As for Dr. Messina, she is content in the sleuthing. "People frequently ask me if I want to see the rocks in action and I can honestly answer that I do not," she says. "Science is all about the quest for knowledge, and not necessarily knowing all the answers. Part of the lure of this place is its mystery. It's fine with me if it remains that way."

- Adapted from "Drifting Rocks" (http://www.vectorsite.net/tamyst.html) Thanks to Greg Goebel.

18. The Racetrack Playa has an elevation of:

- **A.** 5 centimeters.
- **B.** 60 miles.
- **C.** 10000 meters.
- **D.** 3,700 feet.
- **E.** 31,00 feet.

19. John B. Reid, Jr. believed in the same theory that George Stanley suggested in the late 1940s.

Robert Sharp and Dwight Carey disproved that the movement of the rocks was caused by floating ice.

- **A.** Both statements are true.
- **B.** Both statements are false.
- **C.** The first sentence is true while the second sentence is false.
- **D.** The first sentence is false while the second sentence is true.

20. In Messina's final hypothesis, she attributed the explanation behind the drifting rocks to be caused by:

- **A.** bacteria-based slippery clay.
- **B.** wind tunnels.
- **C.** the terrain's topography.
- **D.** ice floe.
- **E.** mysterious forces.

21. The approximate sizes of the rocks have been described to range:

A. from a few centimeters to 200 centimeters.
B. from fist-sized to the size of an ice chest.
C. from 100 centimeters up to a meter in size.
D. from 200 centimeters up to 500 centimeters.
E. The passage does not contain any description of size besides varied.

22. Suppose that Reid and his students were able to conduct their measurements in wet conditions with successful results. This would undermine another assertion made in the passage that:

A. floating ice causes the movements of the rocks.
B. the "dust devils" are causing the rocks to move.
C. the stones, frozen in ice sheets during the winter, slide around with the sheets on an underlying slick of water.
D. the wind is responsible for moving the stones over a slick of mud whenever the Racetrack is wet.

23. Winter storm winds come into the playa of up to:

A. 80 mph gusts.
B. 70 mph gusts.
C. 90 mph gusts.
D. 60 mph gusts.
E. This information is not within the passage.

24. Dr. Messina's GPS unit has an x and y co-ordinate accuracy of:

A. one centimeter.
B. ten centimeters.
C. five centimeters.
D. twenty centimeters.
E. This information is not contained in the passage.

25. How many drifting rocks are there in total?

A. 126
B. 30
C. 162
D. 261
E. 612

26. The theory that the rocks were sliding down a gradual slope over a long period of time was proven to be true when it was revealed that wind speeds of hundreds of kilometers per hour would be required to budge them.

A. Both the statement and reason are correct and related.
B. Both the statement and the reason are correct but NOT related.
C. The statement is correct but the reason is NOT.
D. The statement is NOT correct, but the reason is correct.
E. NEITHER the statement NOR the reason is correct.

27. Many of the moving stones in the Racetrack Playa have names which are:

A. mythological.
B. scientific.
C. Native American.
D. female.
E. male.

28. Which of the following is the BEST reason that makes Dr. Messina's theory relatively strong?

A. Limited variables
B. Multiple causes
C. Use of GPS
D. Singular effects
E. More accurate measurements

29. Reid's main contention with Messina concerning the drifting rocks concerns:

A. ice.
B. mud.
C. direction.
D. wind speed.
E. trails.

30. Attaching radio transmitters to the rocks is not permitted on the Racetrack because rain or snow would negate any data collected from radios.

A. Both the statement and reason are correct and related.
B. Both the statement and the reason are correct but NOT related.
C. The statement is correct but the reason is NOT.
D. The statement is NOT correct, but the reason is correct.
E. NEITHER the statement NOR the reason is correct.

31. Which of the following statements concerning Sharp and Carey is NOT true? Which is the EXCEPTION?

- **A.** They made careful measurements of 30 rocks on the Playa.
- **B.** They used stakes to try to hold the rocks in place.
- **C.** Both had insignificant and contradictory results.
- **D.** Both are part of the US Geological Survey.
- **E.** Both gave up in their research.

32. What Messina found from her GPS analysis was that:

- **A.** wind tunnels of variable strength move the rocks around the slippery mud in a random pattern.
- **B.** a combination of mud, slipperiness, wind, wet clay and bacteria account for the random distributions.
- **C.** there was absolutely no correlation between the size and shape of the rocks and their trails.
- **D.** the icefloe and dust devil theories could be ruled out based on trail positioning.
- **E.** all prior theories lack the necessary GPS and computer analysis, therefore theoretically dubious.

33. Each of the following describes the rock trails EXCEPT one. Which one is the EXCEPTION?

- **A.** Straight
- **B.** Back and forth
- **C.** Circling
- **D.** Zigzagged
- **E.** Varying in width

Passage 3

Forensic Dentistry

(1). Bite marks are an important and sometimes controversial aspect of forensic odontology. Forensic odontology is the study of dental applications in legal proceedings. The subject covers a wide variety of topics including individual identification, mass identification, and bite mark analysis. The study of odontology in a legal case can be a piece of incriminating evidence or an aspect of wide controversy. There have been many cases throughout history, which have made use of bite marks as evidence.

(2). Bite marks are usually seen in cases involving sexual assault, murder, and child abuse and can be a major factor in leading to a conviction. Biting is often a sign of the perpetrator seeking to degrade the victim while also achieving complete domination. Bite marks can be found anywhere on a body, particularly on soft, fleshy tissue such as the stomach or buttocks. In addition, bite marks can be found on objects present at the scene of a crime. Bite marks are commonly found on a suspect when a victim attempts to defend him or herself.

(3). Even though using bite mark evidence began around 1870, the first published account involving a conviction based on bite marks as evidence was in the case of Doyle v. State, which occurred in Texas in 1954. The bite mark in this case was on a piece of cheese found at the crime scene of a burglary. The defendant was later asked to bite another piece of cheese for comparison. A firearms examiner and a dentist evaluated the bite marks independently and both concluded that the marks were made by the same set of teeth. The conviction in this case set the stage for bite marks found on objects and skin to be used as evidence in future cases.

(4). Another landmark case was People v. Marx, which occurred in California in 1975. A woman was murdered by strangulation after being sexually assaulted. She was bitten several times on her nose. Walter Marx was identified as a suspect and dental impressions were made of his teeth. Impressions and photographs were also taken of the woman's injured nose. These samples along with other models and casts were evaluated using a variety of techniques, including two-dimensional and three-dimensional comparisons, and acetate overlays. Three experts testified that the bite marks on the woman's nose were indeed made by Marx, and he was convicted of voluntary manslaughter.

(5). Although there are many cases in which bite mark evidence has been critical to the conviction or exoneration of criminal defendants, there is continuing dispute over its interpretation and analysis.

(6). Factors that may affect the accuracy of bite mark identification include time-dependent changes of the bite mark on living bodies, effects of where the bite mark was found, damage on soft tissue, and similarities in dentition among individuals. Other factors include poor photography, impressions, or measurement of dentition characteristics.

(7). For bites on human skin, a potential bite injury must be recognized early, as the clarity and shape of the mark may change in a relatively short time in both living and dead victims. Bite marks most often appear as elliptical or round areas of contusion or abrasion, occasionally with associated indentations.

(8). Once the mark is initially evaluated, it should be examined by a forensic odontologist to determine if the dimensions and configuration are within human ranges. Since a large proportion of individuals (80-90%) secrete the ABO blood groups in their saliva, swabbing the area and a control area elsewhere on the body should be completed before the body is washed. Although there have been descriptions of using fingerprint dusting methods, photography is the primary means of recording and preserving the bite mark and is critically important in documenting the evidence. When there are indentations in the skin, or to preserve the three-dimensional nature of the bitten area, impressions should be taken to fabricate stone models. This is done by fabricating custom impression trays and taking an impression of the mark and surrounding skin with standard dental impression material. These impressions are then poured in dental stone to produce models. After the initial analysis is complete, there may be a need to preserve the actual skin bearing the mark. A ring of custom tray material can be made to fit like a hoop, closely approximating the skin, which can then be attached to the skin with cyanoacrylate adhesive and stabilized with sutures. When the pathologist completes the autopsy, the bite mark can be excised with the supporting framework in place.

(9). Studies have also been performed in an attempt to find the simplest, most efficient, and most reliable way of analyzing bite marks. Most bite mark analysis studies use porcine skin (pigskin), because it is comparable to the skin of a human, and it is considered unethical to bite a human for study in the United States. Limitations to the bite mark studies include differences in properties of pigskin compared to human skin and the technique of using simulated pressures to create bite marks. Although similar histologically, pigskin and human skin behave in dynamically different ways due to differences in elasticity. Furthermore, postmortem bites on nonhuman skin, such as those used in the experiments of Martin-de-las-Heras et al., display different patterns to those seen in antemortem bite injuries. In recognition of the limitations of their study, Kouble and Craig suggest using a G-clamp on an articulator in future studies to standardize the amount of pressure used to produce experimental bite marks instead of applying manual pressure to models on pigskin. Future research and technological developments may help reduce the occurrence of such limitations.

(10). Kouble and Craig compared direct methods and indirect methods of bite mark analysis. In the past, the direct method compared a model of the suspect's teeth to a life-size photograph of the actual bite mark. In these experiments, direct comparisons were made between dental models and either photographs or "fingerprint powder lift-models." The "fingerprint powder lift" technique involves dusting the bitten skin with black fingerprint powder and using fingerprint tape to transfer the bite marks onto a sheet of acetate. Indirect methods involve the use of transparent overlays to record a suspect's biting edges. Transparent overlays are made by free-hand tracing the occlusal surfaces of a dental model onto an acetate sheet. When comparing the "fingerprint powder lift" technique against the photographs, the use of photographs resulted in higher scores determined by a modified version of the ABFO scoring guidelines. The use of transparent overlays is considered subjective and irreproducible because the tracing can be easily manipulated. On the other hand, photocopier-generated overlays where no tracing is used is considered to be the best method in matching the correct bite mark to the correct set of models without the use of computer imaging.

(11). While the photocopier-generated technique is sensitive, reliable, and inexpensive, new methods involving digital overlays have proven to be more accurate. Two recent technological developments include the 2D polyline method and the painting method. Both methods use Adobe Photoshop. Use of the 2D polyline method entails drawing straight lines between two fixed points in the arch and between incisal edges to indicate the tooth width. Use of the painting method entails coating the incisal edges of a dental model with red glossy paint and then photographing the model. Adobe Photoshop is then used to make measurements on the image. A total of 13 variables were used in analysis. Identification for both methods were based on canine-to-canine distance (1 variable), incisor width (4 variables), and rotational angles of the incisors (8 variables). The 2D polyline method relies heavily on accurate measurements, while the painting method depends on precise overlaying of the images. Although both methods were reliable, the 2D polyline method gave efficient and more objective results.

(12). Nevertheless, bite mark analysis is not without its critics. Recently, the scientific foundation of forensic odontology, and especially bite mark comparison, has been called into question. A 1999 study, frequently referenced in news stories but difficult to actually locate, by a member of the American Board of Forensic Odontology found a 63 percent rate of false identifications. However, the study was based on an informal workshop during an ABFO meeting, which many members did not consider a valid scientific setting.

(13). An investigative series by the Chicago Tribune entitled "Forensics under the Microscope" examined many forensic science disciplines to see if they truly deserve the air of infallibility that has come to surround them. The investigators concluded that bite mark comparison is always subjective and no standards for comparison have been accepted across the field. The journalists discovered that no rigorous experimentation has been conducted to determine error rates for bite mark comparison, a key part of the scientific method. Critics of bite mark comparison cite the case of Ray Krone, an Arizona man convicted of murder on bite mark evidence left on a woman's breast. DNA evidence later implicated another man and Krone was released from prison. Similarly, Roy Brown was convicted of murder due in part to bite mark evidence, and freed after DNA testing of the saliva left in the bite wounds matched someone else.

- Portions of this passage are adapted from "Experimental Studies of Forensic Odontology to Aid in the Identification Process" by Susmita Saxena, Preeti Sharma, and Nitin Gupta. *Journal of Forensic Dental Sciences*, 2010 Jul-Dec; 2(2): 69–76.

34. Recent investigation into bite mark analysis shows that this procedure suffers from:

- **A.** a shortage of methods to actually quantify the identification of a person's teeth.
- **B.** a lack of rigorous experimentation to determine error rates.
- **C.** failure to follow the scientific method at a paradigmatic level.
- **D.** a lack of willing research associates, concerned with such analysis.
- **E.** a shortage of replication studies, to help confirm analysis results.

35. A 1999 study claims a bite mark false identification rate of:

- **A.** 36%.
- **B.** 33%.
- **C.** 63%.
- **D.** 66%.
- **E.** The passage does not indicate this information.

36. Which of the following is NOT a factor that may affect the accuracy of bite mark identification? Which is the EXCEPTION?

- **A.** Time-dependent changes of the bite mark on living bodies
- **B.** Effects of where the bite mark was found
- **C.** Damage on soft tissue
- **D.** Jaw alignment ratios in proportion to dental symmetry
- **E.** Poor photography, impressions, or measurement of dentition characteristics

37. Which of the following sentences would be the best conclusion for the closing paragraph?

- **A.** When reporting on bite mark evidence, dentists should be transparent about the inherent obstacles to accurate analysis.
- **B.** Despite issues on the accu-racy of bite mark analysis procedures, several legal precedents allow for the admissibility of such evidence.
- **C.** Indeed, an opinion is worth nothing unless the evidence is clearly describable and accurate when presented in court.
- **D.** After all, bite mark analysis has almost non-existent valid rules, regulations, or processes for accreditation to standardize the evidence they provide in court.
- **E.** Despite dentistry being a scientific field, forensic odontology remains a subjective science prone to errors.

38. Of the 2D polyline method of identification, which of the following set of variables used in analysis is correct?

- **A.** Canine-to-canine distance (2 variables), incisor width (3 variables), and rotational angles of the incisors (8 variables)
- **B.** Canine-to-canine distance (1 variable), incisor width (4 variables), and rotational angles of the incisors (8 variables)
- **C.** Canine-to-canine distance (1 variable), incisor width (8 variables), and rotational angles of the incisors (4 variables)
- **D.** Canine-to-canine distance (4 variables), incisor width (1 variable), and rotational angles of the incisors (8 variables)
- **E.** Canine-to-canine distance (8 variables), incisor width (1 variable), and rotational angles of the incisors (4 variables)

39. A direct method of identification would be the "fingerprint powder lift" technique.

An indirect method of identification would be the use of transparent overlays.

- **A.** Both statements are true.
- **B.** Both statements are false.
- **C.** The first statement is true. The second statement is false.
- **D.** The first statement is false. The second statement is true.

40. Which of the following methods do Kouble and Craig suggest to address the problems posed with the use of pigskin in bite mark analysis?

- **A.** Experimenting with other animal forms such as cows or horses to determine error rates
- **B.** Using a G-clamp manipulator to increase the standard intensity of pressure used
- **C.** Using a comparison of both direct and indirect methods in relation to pressure used
- **D.** Using a G-clamp on an articulator to standardize the amount of pressure used
- **E.** Keeping the pigskin at the same temperature as the victim kept in the forensic lab

41. Forensic odontology was first publicly recognized in:

- **A.** 1780.
- **B.** 1954.
- **C.** 1975.
- **D.** 1945.
- **E.** 1870.

42. Which legal proceedings context concerning bite mark identification is NOT mentioned in the passage? Which is the EXCEPTION?

- **A.** Manslaughter
- **B.** Kidnapping
- **C.** Child Abuse
- **D.** Sexual Abuse
- **E.** Burglary

43. Suppose an investigator is skeptical over the bite mark evidence presented against a murder suspect. How would a forensic odontoligst BEST convince the investigator that the procedure performed is reliable?

- **A.** Bite marks found on the victim's body were deep, indicating that the act was deliberate and premeditated.
- **B.** A second set of dental impressions was obtained from the suspect himself.
- **C.** The autopsy was performed 24 hours after the crime was committed.
- **D.** The marked area was swabbed for traces of saliva and submitted for DNA testing.
- **E.** Photocopier-generated overlays were employed to match the murderer's correct bite mark.

44. Which of the following persons was convicted of burglary based on bite mark evidence left on a piece of cheese?

A. Marx
B. Krone
C. Doyle
D. Brown
E. Martin-de-las-Heras

45. The use of transparent overlays is considered subjective and irreproducible because there are differences between pigskin and human skin.

A. Both the statement and reason are correct and related.
B. Both the statement and the reason are correct but NOT related.
C. The statement is correct but the reason is NOT.
D. The statement is NOT correct, but the reason is correct.
E. NEITHER the statement NOR the reason is correct.

46. What is The BEST method for bite mark analysis to date?

A. Transparent overlays
B. Photography
C. Fingerprint dusting
D. 2D polyline method
E. Painting method

47. The 2D polyline method employs Adobe Photoshop in bite mark analysis identification.

The painting method uses AUTOCAD in bite mark analysis identification.

A. The first statement is true, while the second statement is false.
B. The first statement is false, while the second statement is true.
C. Both statements are true.
D. Both statements are false.
E. There is not enough information within the passage to make a judgment.

48. ABFO stands for:

A. American Board of Forensic Odontologists.
B. American Board of Forensic Odontology.
C. Associated Board for Forensic Odontology.
D. Associated Board of Forensic Odontologists.
E. American Board for Forensic Odontology.

49. Which of the following bite mark analysis techniques were NOT used in the case of the People vs. Marx? Which is the EXCEPTION?

- **A.** Acetate overlays
- **B.** Two dimensional comparisons
- **C.** The "fingerprint lift method"
- **D.** Three dimensional comparisons
- **E.** Other models and casts

50. The experiments of Martin-de-las-Heras et al., found that:

- **A.** the use of G-Clamp on an articulator standardized the amount of pressure in bite mark analysis.
- **B.** postmortem bites on nonhuman skin displayed the same patterns as antemortem bites.
- **C.** transparent overlays and tracing could easily be sketched in error.
- **D.** postmortem bites on nonhuman skin displayed different patterns from antemortem bites.
- **E.** the 2D polyline method without tracing is the most efficient method to date.

Practice Test 1 Answer Key

1. D	18. D	35. C
2. A	19. C	36. D
3. E	20. C	37. B
4. A	21. B	38. B
5. C	22. B	39. A
6. C	23. B	40. D
7. A	24. A	41. B
8. B	25. C	42. B
9. A	26. E	43. D
10. B	27. D	44. C
11. D	28. B	45. B
12. B	29. D	46. D
13. C	30. C	47. A
14. C	31. D	48. B
15. A	32. C	49. C
16. C	33. B	50. D
17. D	34. B	

Practice Test 1 Explanations and Strategies

1. Answer: D
   Question Type: *Exception/Negative Question; Evaluation Question (Main Idea)*
   Strategies: *SI, PoE; P6*

   This question requires a careful inference of the basic premises of an author's view. By using the process of elimination, the correct statements can be inferred and are mentioned in Paragraph 6. D, being the exception, is the correct answer, which is supported by the phrase "which every fact is either so or not so" in Sentence 2 of Paragraph 6.

2. Answer: A
   Question Type: *Evaluation Question (Implication)*
   Strategies: *SI, paraphrasing, never lose sight of the question; P3 S1*

This is another inference question that requires you to carefully understand the essence of a theoretical concept. All options are mentioned in the passage at one point or another. Thus you need to remain focused on what the question is truly asking, which can be found in the first sentence of Paragraph 3: "The principle of 'methodological individualism,' which holds that social scientists should seek to understand collectivities (such as nations, cultures, governments, churches, corporations, etc.) solely as the result and the context of the actions of individual persons. . ."

3. Answer: E
   Question Type: *Exception/Negative Question*
   Strategy: *SaL; P5 S2*

4. Answer: A
   Question Type: *Evaluation Question (Main Idea)*
   Strategies: *SI, inference; P8*

   Although D is close and a direct quote in the passage, it is the preceding quote in that penultimate paragraph which provides the best answer (A) stating, "The scientist looks for order in the appearances of nature by exploring such likenesses. For order does not display itself of itself, if it can be said to be there at all, it is not there for the mere looking. There is no way of pointing a finger or camera at it; order must be discovered and, in a deep sense, it must be created". We cannot just infer D and leave it at that, but infer that the answer to this disorder is through discovery and creation of order, from the jumble of appearance. The fable is supposed to illustrate this preceding idea.

   The other answers are also partially correct but lack the overall explanatory power of A.

5. Answer: C
   Question Type: *Recall*
   Strategy: *SaL; P4 S1*

6. Answer: C
   Question Type: *Exception/Negative Question*
   Strategies: *SaL, inference; P7, P8*

   A, B and D are ideas advanced by Bronowski as can be found in the following, respectively: P8 S1, P7 S1, and P8 S2. He never mentions theory-building through testing and observation, even though one could infer that this method underlies "science."

7. Answer: A
   Question Type: *True or False Statements*
   Strategy: *SaL; P2 S2 of quoted paragraph; P3 S2*

8. Answer: B
   Question Type: *Evaluation (Implication)*
   Strategies: *SI, inference, prior knowledge; P7 S10*

   The answer to this question can be tricky unless you are familiar with the subject from prior knowledge. This is because Yukawa's discovery is presented in the passage in narrative form rather than as a straightforward description. Hence you need to be careful in reading the paragraph where this is discussed (P7) in order to infer the correct answer.

"Yukawa, without a blush, calculated the mass of the pellet he expected to see, and waited. He was right; his meson was found, and a range of other mesons, neither the existence nor the nature of which had been suspected before." The other statements are corollaries, hypotheses, or distractions.

9. Answer: A
Question Type: *True or False Statements (Statement and Reason)*
Strategy: *SI; P2 quoted paragraph*

The answer is supported by Weber's own quote:

"There is no absolutely 'objective' scientific analysis of culture... All knowledge of cultural reality... is always knowledge from particular points of view."

Here, "particular points of view" expresses "perspective."

10. Answer: B
Question Type: *Evaluation Question (Main idea)*
Strategies: *SI, inference; P2 last sentence and quoted paragraph*

This question requires a keen understanding of the gist of Weber's view on objectivity in the social sciences. This can be best inferred in Paragraph 2 as follows:

"Overall, Weber supported the goal of objective science, but he noted that it is an unreachable goal – although one definitely worth striving for. . . An 'objective' analysis of cultural events, which proceeds according to the thesis that the ideal of science is the reduction of empirical reality to 'laws,' is meaningless. . . [because]. . . the knowledge of social laws is not knowledge of social reality but is rather one of the various aids used by our minds for attaining this end."

11. Answer: D
Question Type: *Recall*
Strategy: *SI; P3 S2*

"In other words, Weber argued that social phenomena can be understood scientifically only to the extent that they are captured by models of the behavior of purposeful individuals, models which Weber called 'ideal types.'"

12. Answer: B
Question Type: *Evaluation Question (Main Idea)*
Strategies: *SI, inference; P4 S1*

This question requires you to deduce the meaning of the term in question in its paraphrased form. A, C, and D are partially correct, but only to the extent that they can be included in B, meaning any debate about methodology used in a given discipline or science, is one that sets up standards for the proper theoretical approach – or how to proceed theoretically, in adopting a methodology for the study.

13. Answer: C
Question type: *Recall*
Strategy: *SI; P1 and P2*

C is the opposite of the idea expressed in Sentence 1 of Paragraph 1. The rest are either verbatim or can be inferred from Paragraphs 1 and 2.

14. Answer: C
Question Type: *Application Question*
Strategies: *SI, inference; P4 S3*

The answer to this question cannot be found in an exact statement in the passage. However, you are required to use the information provided in the passage as basis for evaluating the given options.

Paragraph 4 of the passage makes clear that Weber is more concerned in studying the motivating factors of individual actions, rather than in determining the effect of such actions: "Weber's methodology emphasizes the use of comparative historical analysis. Therefore, Weber was more interested in explaining how a certain outcome was the result of various historical processes rather than predicting an outcome of those processes in the future."
Option C obviously complements Weber's methodology.

15. Answer: A
Question Type: *Recall*
Strategy: *SaL; P8 S3*

16. Answer: C
Question Type: *Recall*
Strategy: *SaL; P3 S1 and quoted paragraph*

17. Answer: D
Question Type: *Recall*
Strategy: *SaL; P1 last sentence*

18. Answer: D
Question Type: *Recall*
Strategy: *SaL; P13 S1*

19. Answer: C
Question Type: *True or False Statements (Two Statements)*
Strategies: *SI, attention to details; P4 S2*

The statements given in this question are paraphrased from different parts of the passage. This requires locating the relevant paragraphs and then inferring the main ideas.

The first statement is derived from information contained in Paragraph 4 Sentence 2 and Paragraph 8 Sentence 1. Essentially, both George Stanley in the late 1940s and John B. Reid, Jr. in the 80s and 90s attributed the movement of the rocks to the floating ice sheets.

The second statement is derived from the last two sentences of Paragraph 5 and Sentence 1 of Paragraph 6. Although Sharp and Carey were not able to prove anything, nothing was also conclusive in the measurements they conducted.

20. Answer: C
    Question Type: *Recall*
    Strategy: *SaL; P16 S1*

21. Answer: B
    Question Type: *Recall*
    Strategy: *SaL; P3 last sentence*

22. Answer: B
    Question Type: *Application Question*
    Strategies: *OA, inference; P8 S2, P13 S1*

    This question requires that you infer the implications behind the theories brought forward in the passage.

    In Paragraph 8, although Reid was able to discount the factor of the wind in the rocks' movements, results of his study were only based on dry conditions. This still leaves the possibility of the wind being a factor in the drifting rocks phenomenon during the wet weather.

    On the other hand, had Reid's findings been proven consistent on wet conditions, this might even give more credit to the floating ice theory as the wind would be eliminated as a contributing factor in the rocks' movements in ANY condition. This eliminates option A.

    B cannot be the best answer because "dust devils" only occur on dry conditions. Results derived from dry conditions are already enough to discount the "dust devils" as the driving force behind the drifting rocks.

    C is also wrong. The statement in this option has nothing to do with the contention about the wind as a factor in the rocks' movements.

    This leaves D as the most possible answer. According to Reid's study, "wind speeds of hundreds of kilometers per hour would be required to budge (the rocks)." In Paragraph 13, strong winds are measured to yield a force of only 70 miles per hour.

23. Answer: B
    Question Type: *Recall*
    Strategy: *SaL; P13 S1*

24. Answer: A
    Question Type: *Recall*
    Strategy: *SI; P11 S4*

25. Answer: C
    Question Type:*Recall*
    Strategy: *SaL; P3 S3*

26. Answer: E
    Question Type: *True or False Statements (Statement and Reason)*
    Strategies: *SaL, inference; P7 S2 and S3, P8 S2*

    The information given in this question is almost verbatim of certain parts in the passage. What is tricky here is that the first statement is obviously wrong. Paragraph 7 indeed explains that the theory of the rocks sliding down a gradual slope due to gravity was discounted when it was discovered that the rocks were in fact traveling uphill. On the other hand, the second statement is true as indicated in

Paragraph 8. However, Reid's conclusion about the wind speeds has more to do with the wind and the "dust devil" theories and does not have a direct link to the rock's sliding movement. Hence, this bit of information is still an incorrect reason in relation to the gravity theory. This makes (E) neither the statement NOR the reason correct.

27. Answer: D
    Question Type: *Recall*
    Strategy: *SaL; P3 S3*

28. Answer: B
    Question Type: *Evaluation Question (Implication)*
    Strategies: *OA, inference; P6 S1, P8, P10 to P16*

    It must be noted that the other researchers who conducted measurements in the Playa either failed to prove anything or focused on only one possible cause of the rocks' movements.

    Sharp and Carey never really managed to link the movement of a rock to any event and finally gave up.

    John Reid was able to disprove the wind theory but ironically did not come up with a proof to support the ice floe theory.

    On the other hand, Messina conducted several observations for a span of ten years to trace the cause behind the "drifting rocks" mystery. Rightfully so for a subject as complex and variable as the rocks in the Playa, Dr. Messina came up with a number of plausible explanations as denoted in Paragraphs 12, 13, and 16.

29. Answer: D
    Question Type: *Recall*
    Strategy: *SaL; P8 S1*

30. Answer: C
    Question Type: *True or False Statement (Statement and Reason)*
    Strategy: *SaL; P17*

31. Answer: D
    Question Type: *Exception/Negative Question*
    Strategy: *SaL; P4 S1, P5, P6 S1*

    Option A is supported by Sentence 1 of Paragraph 5, Option B by Sentence 2, and Option C by the last two sentences. Option E is also supported by Sentence 1 of Paragraph 6. On the other hand, the two geologists from US Geological Survey were never named in Sentence 1 of Paragraph 4 while Sharp and Carey were clearly identified with California Institute of Technology and University of California at Los Angeles, respectively.

32. Answer: C
    Question Type: *Recall*
    Strategy: *SaL; P16 S1*

33. Answer: B
    Question Type: *Recall*
    Strategy: *SaL; P3 S2 S3*

34. Answer: B
    Question Type: *Recall*
    Strategies: *SI, attention to details; P13 S3*

35. Answer: C
Question Type: *Recall*
Strategy: *SaL; P12 S3*

36. Answer: D
Question Type: *Exception/Negative Question*
Strategy: *SaL; P6*

"Jaw alignment ratios in proportion to dental symmetry" does not constitute "similarities in dentition among individuals."

37. Answer: B
Question Type: *Evaluation Question (Main Idea)*
Strategy: *OA; P1, P3, P4, P10, P11, P12*

This question requires your overall understanding of the passage's main message. By looking at significant clues in the different paragraphs, you will realize that the main purpose of the author is to illustrate that despite the various contentions on the methods used in bite mark analysis, they all boil down to the fact that the evidence they bring about is after all, admissible in court.

This is clearly conveyed from the beginning of the passage (P1 last two sentences): "The study of odontology in a legal case can be a piece of incriminating evidence or an aspect of wide controversy. There have been many cases throughout history, which have made use of bite marks as evidence." The last sentence of Paragraph 3 further supports this view stating, "The conviction in this case set the stage for bite marks found on objects and skin to be used as evidence in future cases."

While the statement in A sounds ideal, no specific part in the passage indicates the author advocating this view.

C is obviously off on a tangent.

Option D is countered by Paragraph 10 Sentence 7 in defense of standardization of the bite marks analysis procedure: "the use of photographs resulted in higher scores determined by a modified version of the ABFO scoring gui-delines."

Option E can likewise be contended by the fact that the passage presented scientific methods used in bite mark evidence and oppositions were made mostly by journalists (non-scientific). The 1999 study cited in Sentence 3 of Paragraph 12 also casts doubt to the real persona (and hence credibility) of the member of the American Board of Forensic Odontology who was "frequently referenced in news stories but difficult to actually locate."

38. Answer: B
Question Type: *Recall*
Strategy: *SaL; P11 S7*

39. Answer: A
Question Type: *Recall*
Strategy: *SaL; P10 S3, S5*

40. Answer: D
Question Type: *Recall*
Strategies: *SaL, attention to details; P9 S6*

41. Answer: B
    Question Type: *Recall*
    Strategies: *SaL, never lose sight of the question; P3 S1*

    This question can be tricky, and you have to be careful in identifying that what is being asked is the date when forensic odontology (dental applications in legal proceedings) was first publicly recognized. This could have only been possible with the publication of the case of Doyle v. State in 1954.

42. Answer: B
    Question Type: *Recall*
    Strategies: *SaL, attention to details; P2 S1, P3 S2, P4 last sentence*

43. Answer: D
    Question Type: *Application Question*
    Strategies: *SI or OA, attention to details; P8 S2, P13*

    This question can be easily answered if you have been paying close attention to the information presented in the last paragraph of the passage. It should be noted that the significant evidence that reversed the court's sentences to Krone and Brown was DNA testing. Swabbing of the saliva specimen, which is essential in DNA testing, in bite mark analysis procedure is further supported by Sentence 2 of Paragraph 8.

    Option A is quite subjective and therefore, not convincing. Option B is a plausible method to confirm a dental match of a suspect; so is E. However, a DNA match still qualifies as stronger evidence. C describes one of the factors affecting the accuracy of bite mark analysis. The best answer is D.

44. Answer: C
    Question Type: *Recall*
    Strategy: *SaL; P3*

45. Answer: B
    Question Type: *True or False Statements (Statement and Reason)*
    Strategies: *SI, inference; P9 S4, P10 S8*

    A quick review of Paragraphs 9 and 10 would prove that both the statement and reason in this question convey correct information. However, the reason for the use of transparent overlays being subjective and irreproducible is because the tracing can be easily manipulated. Thus, the reason given in the question is not related.

46. Answer: D
    Question Type: *Recall*
    Strategies: *SaL, PoE, attention to details; P11 last sentence*

    Reviewing the last sentence of Paragraph 11 would help eliminate option E. Sentence 8 of Paragraph 10 likewise negates option A as the correct answer. Sentence 3 Paragraph 8 indicates (C) Fingerprint dusting as merely one of the methods and (B) photography as the primary means - not the best method - of recording and preserving bite marks. This leaves D as the best answer.

47. Answer: A
Question Type: *True or False Statements (Two Statements)*
Strategy: *SaL; P11 S3*

48. Answer: B
Question Type: *Recall*
Strategies: *SaL, attention to details; P12 S3*

49. Answer: C
Question Type: *Recall*
Strategies: *SaL, attention to details; P4*

50. Answer: D
Question Type: *Recall*
Strategies: *SI, inference; P9 S5*

Would you like to discuss any of the answers or strategies in this test? Go to www.dat-prep.com/forum to share and learn.

THE GOLD STANDARD

DAT PAT & GS-1

Perceptual Ability Test [PAT]
and GS Full-length Practice Test [GS-1]

Book IV of IV

Gold Standard Contributors
• 4-Book GS DAT Set •

Brett Ferdinand BSc MD-CM
Karen Babia BS Arch
Brigitte Bigras BSc MSc DMD
Ibrahima Diouf BSc MSc PhD
Amir Durmić BSc Eng
Adam Segal BSc MSc
Da Xiao BSc DMD
Naomi Epstein BEng
Lisa Ferdinand BA MA
Jeanne Tan Te
Kristin Finkenzeller BSc MD
Heaven Hodges BSc
Sean Pierre BSc MD
James Simenc BS (Math), BA Eng
Jeffrey Chen BSc
Timothy Ruger MSc PhD
Petra Vernich BA
Alvin Vicente BS Arch

DMD Candidates

E. Jordan Blanche BS
[Harvard School of Dental Medicine]
Stephan Suksong Yoon BA
[Harvard School of Dental Medicine]

Gold Standard Illustrators
• 4-Book GS DAT Set •

Daphne McCormack
Nanjing Design
· Ren Yi, Huang Bin
· Sun Chan, Li Xin
Fabiana Magnosi
Harvie Gallatiera
Rebbe Julie Jurilla BSc MBA
Jonathan Jurilla MEd-ESL

RuveneCo

The Gold Standard DAT was built for the US DAT.

The Gold Standard DAT is identical to Canadian DAT prep except QR and ORG. Also, you must practice soap carving for the complete Canadian DAT.

The Gold Standard DAT is identical to OAT prep except PAT, which is replaced by OAT Physics; see our Gold Standard OAT book for Physics review and OAT practice test.

Be sure to register at www.DAT-prep.com by clicking on GS DAT Owners and following the directions for Gold Standard DAT Owners. Please Note: benefits are for 1 year from the date of online registration, for the original book owner only and are not transferable; unauthorized access and use outside the Terms of Use posted on DAT-prep.com may result in account deletion; if you are not the original owner, you can purchase your virtual access card separately at DAT-prep.com.

Visit The Gold Standard's Education Center at www.gold-standard.com.

ISBN 978-1-927338-12-4

Address all inquiries, comments, or suggestions to the publisher. For Terms of Use go to: www.DAT-prep.com

RuveneCo Inc
Gold Standard Multimedia Education
559-334 Cornelia St
Plattsburgh, NY 12901
E-mail: learn@gold-standard.com
Online at www.gold-standard.com

Table of Contents

EXAM SUMMARY

The Dental Admission Test (DAT) consists of 280 multiple-choice questions distributed across quite a diversity of question types in four tests. The DAT is a computer-based test (CBT). This exam requires approximately five hours to complete - including the optional tutorial, break, and post-test survey. The following are the four subtests of the Dental Admission Test:

1. Survey of the Natural Sciences (NS) – 100 questions; 90 min.
    - General Biology (BIO): 40 questions
    - General Chemistry (CHM): 30 questions
    - Organic Chemistry (ORG): 30 questions
2. Perceptual Ability Test (PAT) - 90 questions; 6 subsections; 60 min.
    - Apertures: 15 questions
    - Orthographic or View Recognition: 15 questions
    - Angle Discrimination: 15 questions
    - Paper Folding: 15 questions
    - Cube Counting: 15 questions
    - 3-D Form Development: 15 questions
3. Reading Comprehension (RC) – 50 questions; 3 reading passages; 60 min.
4. Quantitative Reasoning (QR) – 40 questions; 45 min.
    - Mathematics Problems: 30 questions
    - Applied Mathematics/Word Problems: 10 questions

You will get six scores from: (1) BIO (2) CHM (3) ORG (4) PAT (5) QR (6) RC.

You will get two additional scores which are summaries:
(7) Academic Average (AA) = BIO + CHM + ORG + QR + RC
(8) Total Science (TS) = BIO + CHM + ORG

Common Formula for Acceptance:

GPA + DAT score + Interview = Dental School Admissions*

*Note: In general, Dental School Admissions Committees will only examine the DAT score if the GPA is high enough; they will only admit or interview if the GPA + DAT score is high enough. Some programs also use autobiographical materials and/or references in the admissions process. Different dental schools may emphasize different aspects of your DAT score, for example: PAT, BIO, TS, AA. The average score for any section is approximately 17/30; the average AA for admissions is usually 18-20 depending on the dental school; the AA for admissions to Harvard is around 22-23; the 100th percentile is usually 25 meaning that virtually 100% of the approximately 13 000 students who take the DAT every year have an AA less than 25. Only a handful of students score 25/30. Our two student contributors scored 27/30 (AA).

PREFACE

The DAT is challenging, get organized.

dat-prep.com/dat-study-schedule

1. How to study:

1. Study the Gold Standard (GS) books and videos to learn
2. Do GS Chapter review practice questions
3. Consolidate: create and review your personal summaries (= Gold Notes) daily

2. Once you have completed your studies:

1. Full-length practice test
2. Review mistakes, all solutions
3. Consolidate: review all your Gold Notes and create more
4. Repeat until you get beyond the score you need for your targeted dental school

3. Full-length practice tests:

1. ADA practice exams
2. Gold Standard DAT exams
3. TopScore Pro exams
4. Other sources if needed

4. How much time do you need?

On average, 3-6 hours per day for 3-6 months

WARNING: Study more or study more efficiently. You choose. The Gold Standard has condensed the content that you require to excel at the DAT. We have had Ivy League dental students involved in the production of the Gold Standard series so that pre-dent students can feel that they have access to the content required to get a score satisfactory at any dental school in the country. To make the content easier to retain, you can also find aspects of the Gold Standard program in other formats such as:

Is there something in the Gold Standard that you did not understand? Don't get frustrated, get online.

dat-prep.com/forum dat-prep.com/QRchanges-2015

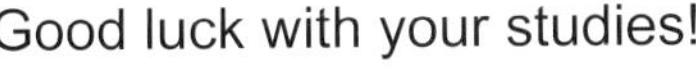
Good luck with your studies!

Gold Standard Team

DAT-Prep.com

DENTAL SCHOOL ADMISSIONS

PART I

MPROVING
EMIC STAN

IMPROVING ACADEMIC STANDING

1.1 Lectures

Before you set foot in a classroom you should consider the value of being there. Even if you were taking a course like 'Basket Weaving 101', one way to help you do well in the course is to consider the value of the course to **you**. The course should have an *intrinsic* value (i.e. 'I enjoy weaving baskets'). The course will also have an *extrinsic* value (i.e. 'If I do not get good grades, I will not be accepted...'). Motivation, a positive attitude, and an interest in learning give you an edge before the class even begins.

Unless there is a student 'note-taking club' for your courses, your attendance record and the quality of your notes should both be as excellent as possible. Be sure to choose a seat in the classroom that ensures you will be able to hear the professor adequately and see whatever she may write. Whenever possible, do not sit close to friends!

Instead of chattering before the lecture begins, spend the idle moments quickly reviewing the previous lecture in that subject so you would have an idea of what to expect. Try to take good notes and pay close attention. The preceding may sound like a difficult combination (especially with professors who speak and write quickly); however, with practice you can learn to do it well.

And finally, do not let the quality of teaching affect your interest in the subject nor your grades! Do not waste your time during or before lectures complaining about how the professor speaks too quickly, does not explain concepts adequately, etc. When the time comes, you can mention such issues on the appropriate evaluation forms! In the meantime, consider this: despite the good or poor quality of teaching, there is always a certain number of students who **still** perform well. You must strive to count yourself among those students.

1.2 Taking Notes

Unless your professor says otherwise, if you take excellent notes and learn them inside out, you will *ace* his course. Your notes should always be up-to-date, complete, and separate from other subjects.

To be safe, you should try to type or write everything! You can fill in any gaps by comparing your notes with those of your friends. You can create your own shorthand symbols or use standard ones. The following represents some useful symbols:

|·|	*between*
=	*the same as*
≠	*not the same as*
∴	*therefore*
Δ	*difference, change in*
cf.	*compare*
c̄ or w	*with*
c̄out or w/o	*without*
esp.	*especially*
∵	*because*
i.e.	*that is*
e.g.	*for example*

Many students rewrite their notes at home. Should you decide to rewrite your notes, your time will be used efficiently if you are paying close attention to the information you are rewriting. In fact, a more useful technique is the following: during class, write your notes only on the right side of your binder. Later, rewrite the information from class in a complete but condensed form on the left side of the binder (*this condensed form should include mnemonics, which we will discuss later*).

Some students find it valuable to use different colored pens. Juggling pens in class may distract you from the content of the lecture. Different colored pens would be more useful in the context of rewriting one's notes.

Of course, typing can be more efficient but time should still be set aside to actively condense and organize notes after class. If the professor has supplied handouts, ideally you would condense those notes as well to include only the most important information or content that you find challenging to remember.

1.3 The Principles of Studying Efficiently

If you study efficiently, you will have enough time for extracurricular activities, movies, etc. The bottom line is that your time must be used efficiently and effectively.

During the average school day, time can be found during breaks, between classes, and after school to quickly review notes in a library or any other quiet place you can find on campus. Simply by using the available time in your school day, you can keep up to date with recent information.

You should design an individual study schedule to meet your particular needs. However, as a rule, a certain amount of time every evening should be set aside for more in-depth studying. Weekends can be allotted for special projects and reviewing notes from the beginning.

On the surface, the idea of regularly reviewing notes from the beginning may sound like an insurmountable task that would take forever! The reality is just the opposite. After all, if you continually study the information, by the time midterms approach you would have seen the first lecture so many times that it would take only moments to review it. On the other hand, had you not been reviewing regularly, it would be like reading that lecture for the first time!

You should study wherever you feel most comfortable and effective (i.e., library, at home, etc.). Should you prefer studying at home, be sure to create an environment, which is conducive to the task at hand.

Studying should be an active process to memorize, synthesize, and understand a given set of material. Memorization and comprehension are best achieved by the **elaboration** of course material, **attention, repetition,** and practicing **retrieval** of the information. All these principles are carried out in the following techniques.

1.4 Studying from Notes and Texts

Successful studying from either class notes or textbooks can be accomplished in three simple steps:

- **Preview the material:** Read all the relevant headings, titles, and sub-titles to give you a general idea of what you are about to learn. You should never embark on a trip without knowing where you are going!

- **Read while questioning:** Passive studying is when you sit in front of a book and just read. This can lead to boredom, lack of concentration, or even worse - difficulty remembering what you just read! Active studying involves reading while actively questioning yourself. For example, how does this fit in with the 'big picture'? How does this relate to what we learned last week? What cues about these words or lists will make it easy for me to memorize them? What type of question would my professor ask me? If I was asked a question on this material, how would I answer?

- **Recite and consider:** Put the notes or text away while you attempt to recall the main facts. Once you are able to recite the important information, consider how it relates to the entire subject.

N.B. If you ever sit down to study and you are not quite sure with which subject to begin, always start with either the most difficult subject or the subject you like least (usually they are one and the same!).

1.5 Study Aids

The most effective study aids include practice exams, mnemonics and audio MP3s.

Practice exams (*exams from previous semesters*) are often available from the library, upper level students, online or directly from the professor. They can be used like maps, which guide you through your semester. They give you a good indication as to what information you should emphasize when you study; what question types and exam format you can expect; and what your level of progress is.

Practice exams should be set aside to do in the weeks and days before 'the real thing.' You should time yourself and do the exam in an environment free from distractions. This provides an ideal way to uncover unexpected weak points.

Mnemonics are an effective way of memorizing lists of information. Usually a word, phrase, or sentence is constructed to symbolize a greater amount of information (i.e. LEO is A GERC = Lose Electrons is Oxidation is Anode, Gain Electrons is Reduction at Cathode). An effective study aid to active studying is the creation of your own mnemonics.

Audio MP3s can be used as effective tools to repeat information and to use your time efficiently. Information from the left side of your notes (*see 1.2 Taking Notes*) or your summarized typed notes including mnemonics, can be dictated and recorded. Often, an entire semester of work can be summarized in one 90-minute recording.

Now you can listen to the recording on an MP3 player or an iPod while waiting in line at the bank, or in a bus or with a car stereo on the way to school, work, etc. You can also listen to recorded information when you go to sleep and listen to another one first thing in the morning. You are probably familiar with the situation of having heard a song early in the morning and then having difficulty, for the rest of the day, getting it out of your mind! Well, imagine if the first thing you heard in the morning was: "Hair is a modified keratinized structure produced by the cylindrical down growth of epithelium..."! Thus MP3s become an effective study aid since they are an extra source of repetition.

Some students like to **record lectures**. Though it may be helpful to fill in missing notes, it is not an efficient way to repeat information.

Some students like to use **study cards** (flashcards) on which they may write either a summary of information they must memorize or relevant questions to consider. Then the cards are used throughout the day to quickly flash information to promote thought on a course material. Smartphone apps, like the ones designed by Gold Standard, can make flashcards more interactive.

1.5.1 Falling Behind

Imagine yourself as a marathon runner who has run 25.5 km of a 26 km race. The finishing line is now in view. However, you have fallen behind some of the other runners. The most difficult aspect of the race is still ahead.

In such a scenario, some interesting questions can be asked: Is now the time to drop out of the race because 0.5 km suddenly seems like a long distance? Is now the time to reevaluate whether or not you should have competed? Or is now the time to remain faithful to your goals and to give 100%?

Imagine one morning in mid-semester, you wake up realizing you have fallen behind in your studies. What do you do? Where do you start? Is it too late?

You should see the situation as one of life's challenges. Now is the worst time for doubts, rather, it is the time for action. A clear line of action should be formulated such that it could be followed.

For example, you might begin by gathering all pertinent study materials like a complete set of study notes, relevant text(s), sample exams, etc. As a rule, to get back into the thick of things, notes and sample exams take precedence. Studying at this point should take a three pronged approach: i) a regular, consistent review of the information from your notes from the beginning of the section for which you are responsible (i.e., *starting with the first class*); ii) a regular, consistent review of course material as you are learning it from the lectures (*this is the most efficient way to study*); iii) regular testing using questions given in class or those contained in sample exams. Using such questions will clarify the extent of your progress.

It is also of value, as time allows, to engage in extracurricular activities, which, you find helpful in reducing stress (e.g., sports, piano, creative writing).

THE DENTAL SCHOOL INTERVIEW

2.1 Introduction

The application process to most dental schools includes interviews. Only a select number of students from the applicant pool will be given an offer to be interviewed. The dental school interview is, as a rule, something that you achieve. In other words, after your school grades, DAT scores and/or references, and autobiographical materials have been reviewed, you are offered the ultimate opportunity to put your best foot forward: a personal interview.

Depending on the dental school, you may be interviewed by one, two or several interviewers (i.e., panel or committee interview). You may be the only interviewee or there may be others (i.e., a group interview). There may be one or more interviews lasting from 20 minutes to two hours. Some dental schools are introducing the multiple mini-interview (MMI) which includes many short assessments in a timed circuit. Despite the variations among the technical aspects of the interview, in terms of substance, most dental schools have similar objectives. These objectives can be arbitrarily categorized into three general assessments: (i) your personality traits, (ii) social skills, and (iii) knowledge of dentistry as a profession.

Personality traits such as maturity, integrity, compassion, originality, curiosity, self-directed learning, intellectual capacity, confidence (not arrogance!), and motivation are all components of the ideal applicant. These traits will be exposed by the process of the interview, your mannerisms, and the substance of what you choose to discuss when given an ambiguous question. For instance, bringing up specific examples of academic achievement related to school and related to self-directed learning would score well in the categories of intellectual capacity and curiosity, respectively. Nevertheless, highlighting significant insights about support to and interaction with patients in say, a recent involvement in community service might set you apart from equally qualified candidates as more emotionally matured and compassionate.

Motivation is a personality trait, which may make the difference between a high and a low or moderate score in an interview. A student must clearly demonstrate that he or she has the energy and eagerness to survive (typically) four long years of dental school and beyond! If you are naturally shy or soft-spoken, you will have to give special attention to this category. In other instances, a student must display the desire to learn and the zest to think critically in a problem-based learning framework.

Social skills such as leadership, ease of communication, ability to relate to others and work effectively in groups, volunteer work, cultural and social interests, all constitute skills that are often viewed as critical for future dentists. It is not sufficient to say in an interview: "I have good social skills"! You must display such skills via your interaction with the interviewer(s) and by discussing specific examples of situations that clearly portray your social skills.

Knowledge of dental medicine includes at least a general understanding of what the field of dentistry involves, the curriculum you are applying to, and knowledge of common dental issues like the dental amalgam controversy, consumer safety issues, oral cancer, latest technologies used in dental procedures, special needs services, the health care system, and ethical decision-making issues involving patient autonomy, confidentiality, and practice values. It is striking to see the number of students who apply to dental school each year whose knowledge of dentistry is limited to headlines and popular TV shows! It is not logical for someone to dedicate their lives to a profession they know little about.

Doing volunteer work in a hospital or a community clinic is a good start. Alternatively, job shadowing at a private dental office or a relative who is an orthodontist can help expose you to the daily goings-on of a dental career. The key is to get a good grasp of the profession in diverse settings – from the public health care delivery system to private practice to dental specialties. Here are some more suggestions: (i) keep up-to-date with the details of dentistry-related controversies in the news. You should also be able to develop and support opinions of your own; (ii) skim through a dental journal at least once; (iii) read dental articles in a popular science magazine (i.e., Scientific American, Discover, Popular Science, etc.); (iv) keep abreast of changes in dental school curricula in general and specific to the programs to which you have applied. You can access such information online or at most university libraries and by writing individual dental schools for information on their programs; (v) get involved in a laboratory research project.

2.2 Preparing for the Interview

If you devote an adequate amount of time for interview preparation, the actual interview will be less tense for you and you will be able to control most of the content of the interview.

Reading from the various sources mentioned in the preceding sections would be helpful. Also, read over your curriculum vitae and/or any autobiographical materials you may have prepared. Note highlights in your life or specific examples that reflect the aforementioned personality traits, social skills or your knowledge of dental medicine. Zero in on qualities or stories that are important, memorable, interesting, amusing, informative or "all of the above"! Once in the interview room, you will be given the opportunity to elaborate on the qualities you believe are important about yourself. Be ready to respond to an interviewer should they ask you: “What do you want to know about us?” In many cases, students tend to concentrate on preparing their most brilliant answers to various interview questions that they tend to overlook another means for the admission committee to gauge an applicant’s sincere interest in the course and the university itself – by letting the applicant himself or herself ask and/or clarify essential information about the school and how the program could ultimately help advance a successful career in dentistry.

Once you have received the invitation, do not lose time to get to know the dental college with which you will be having the interview. Go online or call and inquire about the structure of the interview (e.g., one-on-one, group, MMI, etc.). Ask them if they can tell you who will interview you. Many schools have no qualms volunteering such information. Now you can determine the person's expertise by either asking or looking through staff members of the different faculties or dental specialties at that university or college. A periodontist, an academician, and a general practitioner all have different areas of expertise and will likely orient their interviews differently. Thus you may want to read from a source, which will give you a general understanding of their specialty.

Choose appropriate clothes for the interview. Every year some students dress for a dental school interview as if they were going out to dance! Dentistry is still considered a conservative profession; you should dress and groom yourself likewise. First impressions are very important. Your objective is to make it as easy as possible for your interviewer(s) to imagine you as a dentist.

Do practice interviews with people you respect but who can also maintain their objectivity. Let them read this entire chapter on dental school interviews. They must understand that you are to be evaluated *only* on the basis of the interview. On that basis alone, they should be able to imagine you as an ideal candidate for a future dentist.

2.3 Strategies for Answering Questions

Always remember that the interviewer controls the *direction* of the interview by his questions; you control the *content* of the interview through your answers. In other words, once given the opportunity, you should speak about the topics that are important to you; conversely, you should avoid volunteering information that renders you uncomfortable. You can enhance the atmosphere in which the answers are delivered by being polite, sincere, tactful, well-organized, outwardly oriented and maintaining eye contact. Motivation, intellectual interest, and a positive attitude must all be evident.

As a rule, there are no right or wrong answers. However, the way in which you justify your opinions, the topics you choose to discuss, your mannerisms and your composure all play important roles. It is normal to be nervous. It would be to your advantage to channel your nervous energy into a positive quality, like enthusiasm.

Do not spew forth answers! Take your time - it is not a contest to see how fast you can answer. Answering with haste can lead to disastrous consequences as what happened to this student in an actual interview:

Q: *Have you ever doubted your interest in dentistry as a career?*

A: *No! Well . . . ah . . . I guess so. Ah . . . I guess everyone doubts something at some point or the other . . .*

Retractions like that are a bad signal, but it illustrates an important point: there are usually no right or wrong answers in an interview; however, there are right or wrong ways of answering. Through this example we can conclude the following: listen carefully to the question, try to relax, and think before you answer!

Do not sit on the fence! If you avoid giving your opinions on controversial topics, it will be interpreted as indecision, which is a negative trait for a prospective dentist. You have a right to your opinions. However, you must be prepared to defend your point of view in an objective, rational, and informative fashion. It is also important to show that, despite your opinion, you understand both sides of the argument. If you have an extreme or unconventional perspective and if you believe your perspective will not interfere with your practice of dentistry, you must let your interviewer know that.

Imagine a student who is uncomfortable with the idea of cosmetic dentistry as a legitimate medical practice. If asked about her opinion on cosmetic dentistry, she should clearly state her opinion objectively, show she understands the opposing viewpoints, and then use data to reinforce her position. If she feels that her opinion would not interfere with her objectivity when practicing dentistry, she might volunteer: "If I were in a position where my perspective might interfere with an objective management of a patient, I would refer that patient to another dentist."

Carefully note the reactions of the interviewer in response to your answers. Whether the interviewer is sitting on the edge of her seat wide-eyed or slumping in her chair while yawning, you should take such cues to help you determine when to continue, change the subject, or when to stop talking. Also, note the more subtle cues. For example, gauge which topic makes the interviewer frown, give eye contact, take notes, etc.

Lighten up the interview with a well-timed story. A conservative joke, a good analogy, or anecdote may help you relax and make the interviewer sustain his interest. If it is done correctly, it can turn a routine interview into a memorable and friendly interaction.

It should be noted that because the system is not standardized, a small number of interviewers may ask overly personal questions (i.e., about relationships, religion, etc.) or even questions that carry sexist tones (e.g., *What would you do if you got pregnant while attending dental school?*). Some questions may be frankly illegal. If you do not want to answer a question, simply maintain your composure, express your position diplomatically, and address the interviewer's real concern (i.e., *Does this person have the potential to be a good dentist?*). For example, you might say in a non-confrontational tone of voice: "I would rather not answer such a question. However, I can assure you that whatever my answer may have been, it would in no way affect either my prospective studies in dentistry or any prerequisite objectivity I should have to be a good dentist."

2.4 Sample Questions

There are an infinite number of questions and many different categories of questions. Different dental schools will emphasize different categories of questions. Arbitrarily, ten categories of questions can be defined: ambiguous, medically related, academic, social, stress-type, problem situations, personality-oriented, based on autobiographical material, miscellaneous, and ending questions. We will examine each category in terms of sample questions and general comments.

Ambiguous Questions:

* * *Tell me about yourself.*

How do you want me to remember you?

What are your goals?

There are hundreds if not thousands of applicants, why should we choose you?

Convince me that you would make a good dentist.

Why do you want to study dentistry?

COMMENTS: These questions present nightmares for the unprepared student who walks into the interview room and is immediately asked: "Tell me about yourself." Where do you start? If you are prepared as previously discussed, you will be able to take control of the interview by highlighting your qualities or objectives in an informative and interesting manner.

Dentistry/Health Care Questions:

What are the pros and cons to our health care system?

If you had the power, what changes would you make to our health care system?

How are dentists responsible for educating the general public about oral health?

Do dentists make too much money?

Is it ethical for medical practitioners to strike?

What is the difference between the Hippocratic Oath and the Dentist's Pledge?

How important is dentistry in relation to the health profession in general?

Do you know of any controversial bill concerning dental health care that was recently passed in Congress?

COMMENTS: The health care system, esthetic dentistry, confidentiality, patient autonomy, health insurance, and other ethical issues are very popular topics in this era of technological advances, skyrocketing health care costs, and ethical uncertainty. A well-informed opinion can set you apart from most of the other interviewees.

Questions Related to Academics:

Why did you choose your present course of studies?

What is your favorite subject in your present course of studies? Why?

Would you consider a career in your present course of studies?

Can you convince me that you can cope with the workload in dental school?

How do you study/prepare for exams?

Do you engage in self-directed learning?

What is Problem-Based Learning or PBL?

How do you feel about the online delivery format in dental education?

COMMENTS: Dental schools like to see applicants who are well-disciplined, committed to dentistry as a career, and who exhibit self-directed learning (i.e., such a level of desire for knowledge that the student may seek to study information independent of any organized infrastructure). Beware of any glitches in your academic record. You may be asked to give reasons for any grades they may deem substandard. On the other hand, you should volunteer any information regarding academic achievement (i.e., prizes, awards, scholarships, particularly high grades in one subject or the other). At some point, you may also be asked to discuss aspects that you mentioned in your personal statement.

Questions Related to Social Skills or Interests:

Give evidence that you relate well with others.

Give an example of a leadership role you have assumed.

Have you done any volunteer work?

Have you engaged in any sports?

What are the prospects for a lasting peace in Afghanistan? Libya? The Sudan? The Middle-East?

COMMENTS: Questions concerning social skills should be simple for the prepared student. If you are asked a question that you cannot answer, say so. If you pretend to know something about a topic in which you are completely uninformed, you will make a bad situation worse.

Stress-Type Questions:

How do you handle stress?

What was the most stressful event in your life? How did you handle it?

The night before your final exam, your father has a heart-attack and is admitted to a hospital, what do you do?

COMMENTS: The ideal dentist has positive coping methods to deal with the inevitable stressors of a dental practice. Stress-type questions are a legitimate means of determining if you possess the raw material necessary to cope with dental school and dentistry as a career. Some decide to introduce stress into the interview and see how you handle it. For example, they may decide to ask you a confrontational question or try to back you into a corner (e.g., You do not know anything about dentistry, do you?). Alternatively, the interviewer might use silence to introduce stress into the interview. If you have completely and confidently answered a question and silence falls in the room, do not retract previous statements, mutter, or fidget. Simply wait for the next question. If the silence becomes unbearable, you may consider asking an intelligent question (e.g., a specific question regarding their curriculum).

Questions on Problem Situations:

You are about to administer anesthesia to a sixteen-year-old patient. She suddenly expresses apprehension about the procedure and confesses that she is pregnant. She begs you to keep the information in utmost confidentiality. Would you still inform the girl's parents?

How would you deal with a group member who does not submit his assigned tasks for a small group project?

You have a very nervous patient who is about to undergo a dental treatment. What would you do to ease the anxiety?

Your patient is at the top of his career. How do you tell him that he has oral cancer?

COMMENTS: As for the other questions, listen carefully and take your time to consider the best possible response. Keep in mind that the ideal dentist is not only knowledgeable, but is also compassionate, empathetic, and is objective enough to understand both sides of a dilemma. Be sure such qualities are clearly demonstrated.

Personality-Oriented Questions:

If you could change one thing about yourself, what would it be?

How would your friends describe you?

What do you do with your spare time?

What is the most important event that has occurred to you in the last five years?

If you had three magical wishes, what would they be?

What are your best attributes?

COMMENTS: Of course, most questions will assess your personality to one degree or the other. However, these questions are quite direct in their approach. Forewarned is forearmed!

Questions Based on Autobiographical Materials:

COMMENTS: Any autobiographical material you may have provided to the dental school is fair game for questioning. You may be asked to discuss or elaborate on any point the interviewer may feel is interesting or questionable.

Miscellaneous Questions:

Should the federal government reinstate the death penalty? Explain.

What do you expect to be doing 10 years from now?

How would you attract dentists to rural areas?

Why do you want to attend our dental school?

What other dental schools have you applied to?

Have you been to other interviews?

COMMENTS: You will do fine in this grab-bag category as long as you stick to the strategies previously iterated.

Ending Questions:

What would you do if you were not accepted to a dental school?

How do you think you did in this interview?

Do you have any questions?

COMMENTS: The only thing more important than a good first impression is a good finish in order to leave a positive lasting impression. They are looking for students who are so committed to dentistry that they will not only re-apply to dental school if not accepted, but they would also strive to improve on those aspects of their application that prevented them from being accepted in the first attempt. All these questions should be answered with a quiet confidence. If you are given an opportunity to ask questions, though you should not flaunt your knowledge, you should establish that you are well-informed. For example: "I have read that you have changed your curriculum to a more patient-oriented and self-directed learning approach. I was wondering how the dental students are getting along with these new changes." Be sure, however, not to ask a question unless you are genuinely interested in the answer.

2.4.1 Interview Feedback: Questions, Answers and Feedback

Specific interview questions can be found online for free at studentdoctor.net and futuredoctor.net. Dr. Ferdinand reproduced and captured the intense experience of a medical school interview on video which, of course, is very similar to the content, process and interaction of a dental school interview. "The Gold Standard Medical School Interview: Questions, Tips and Answers + MMI" DVD was filmed live in HD on campus in front of a group of students. A volunteer is interviewed in front of the class and the entire interview is conducted as if it were the real thing. After the interview, an analysis of each question and the mindset behind it is discussed in an open forum format. If you are not sure that you have the interviewing skills to be accepted to dental school, then it is a must-see video.

$\mathcal{A} + \mathcal{B} = ?$

DAT-Prep.com

UNDERSTANDING THE DAT

PART II

THE STRUCTURE OF THE DAT

1.1 Introduction

The Dental Admission Test (DAT) is required by all dental schools in the United States and its territories, for applicants seeking entry into the D.M.D. program (Doctor of Dental Medicine), or its equivalent the D.D.S. (Doctor of Dental Surgery). The test is standardized by the American Dental Association (ADA) through its Department of Testing Services and is available throughout the year by testing appointments in Prometric Test Centers around the US, Guam, Puerto Rico, the US Virgin Islands, and Canada.

In most instances, the weight given to DAT scores in the admissions process varies from school to school. However, results in the different sections of the test tend to be used in a way similar to your university GPA (i.e. your academic standing). Some schools consider the Academic Average and Total Science scores as significant criteria in their selection of candidates. Others combine the PAT with the Academic Average and Total Science scores, and a few others give as much emphasis to the Reading Comprehension score. Consult programs directly about their evaluation guidelines.

1.1.1 When to Take the DAT

Taking the DAT requires registering with the ADA and meeting their eligibility requirements. Usually, applicants have successfully completed at least one year of undergraduate studies, including the prerequisite courses in biology, general chemistry, and organic chemistry at the time of application. Note that the majority of the applicants complete two or more years of college before taking the DAT.

Upon approval of your application, the Department of Testing Services (DTS) will notify you, through email or letter, of the procedure in securing a testing appointment with the Prometric Contact Center. As a registered examinee, you will have the next twelve months from your application and payment to confirm a testing date.

Prospective students commonly arrange for their DAT roughly a year before their intended matriculation into dental school. However, varying circumstances may call for careful planning when choosing the appropriate time for you to take this exam. The following are common factors to consider:

1. The Admissions Cycle

Most dental schools begin reviewing applications around June, the majority of successful candidates start receiving acceptance letters as early as the 1st of December. Getting over the DAT hurdle well ahead of the submission deadlines will put you in a more favorable position in several ways: you will have ample time to procure any supplemental materials that the schools might request; you will have a less stressful time preparing for your interview; and, you would have a better chance of belonging to the initial bulk of the entering classes.

Many schools observe a rolling admissions process - they continue to accept applications until all vacant spots are filled. Applicants with remarkable credentials who wait until the last minute may miss admission into their schools of preference if the number of early applicants who satisfactorily meet the entry requirements quickly closes the enrollment seats.

2. Course Requirements

Dental colleges usually impose certain curricular prerequisites as part of their entry requirements. Some applicants opt to take their DAT a year before completing any required coursework. They can then focus on improving their GPAs in the remaining semesters. Others take the opposite route. You should weigh which schedule would work best for you. In any case, be sure to check the individual schools regarding their rules and criteria for DAT scores – some might consider scores received three years before the date of your application, while others may only look at scores from two years ago.

3. Contingent Results

If you are not satisfied with your DAT score, the ADA permits you to retake the exam 90 days later. As a precaution, you should provide some allowance for such an event.

1.1.2 Retaking the DAT

To reiterate, an applicant who is unsatisfied with his or her DAT scores must wait 90 days before retesting. If approved, students are permitted to retake the DAT once per twelve-month period. Results of the four most recent DATs taken, as well as the total number of attempts, are reported on the official score reports. Admissions committees may consider either the best, or the most recent marks. There is currently no limit as to the number of times to take the DAT.

For the most up-to-date guidelines on registration, scheduling and pertinent information about the DAT, consider consulting your undergraduate advisor and accessing the following:

US:
www.ada.org/dat.aspx
Canada:
www.cda-adc.ca/en/dental_profession/dat/index.asp
Prometric Centers:
www.prometric.com/ADA

1.2 The Format of The DAT

Part of doing well in a standardized test includes being familiar with the format of the actual exam, what it covers, and what skills and level of knowledge are being assessed. Accurate information of this sort helps identify your study needs and as a result, allows you to judge which prep materials and courses would help to address your weak areas.

The Dental Admission Test measures your general academic aptitude, understanding of scientific information, and visual discrimination. Memory, comprehension, and problem solving are essential cognitive skills needed for this exam.

The DAT is a timed computer-based test divided into four sections. All questions are in multiple choice format with four or five options per question. You are to work on only one section at a time. A timer is visible on the upper right hand corner of the computer screen. If you are unsure of your answer on a specific item, you may click the "Mark" button. You can then review your marked and/or incomplete responses if you have enough time left. Otherwise, a message that says "The time limit for this test has expired" will appear and you will have to move on to the next segment of the test.

REMEMBER

Once you exit a test section, you cannot go back to it.

The test center administrator provides two laminated note boards and two low-odor, fine-tip permanent markers. The laminated sheets are 8.5" x 11" in size with one side in the form of graph paper and the other side just a blank page. Should you require additional pieces, you only need to raise your hand so that the test center administrator will replace them with new ones. No scratch paper is permitted within the testing area during the exam.

The following table shows the sequence of the different DAT test sections:

Optional Tutorial	
Time	15 minutes
Survey of Natural Sciences	
Time	90 minutes
Number of Questions	100
Perceptual Ability Test	
Time	60 minutes
Number of Questions	90
Optional Break	
Time	15 minutes
Reading Comprehension Test	
Time	60 minutes
Number of Questions	50
Quantitative Reasoning Test	
Time	45 minutes
Number of Questions	40
Optional Post-Test Survey	
Time	15 minutes

The Natural Sciences on the DAT collectively include biology, general and organic chemistry at introductory university levels. The subject material is apportioned as follows:

Biology	40 items
General Chemistry	30 items
Organic Chemistry	30 items

Some pages contain an Exhibit button that allows you to open a new window showing the periodic table.

The Perceptual Ability Test or PAT comes after the Survey of Natural Sciences. It is comprised of the following six areas:

Apertures	15 figures; 5 answer choices each
View Recognition	15 problem sets; 4 answer choices each
Angle Discrimination	15 patterns; 4 answer choices each
Paper Folding	15 problem sets; 5 answer choices each
Cube counting	15 questions; 5 answer choices each
3D Form Development	15 problem sets; 4 answer choices each

Keep in mind that using pencils, fingers, and note boards as measuring devices are prohibited during this section.

You can choose whether or not to take the 15-minute break. If you choose to take it, the timer will continue to monitor the minutes remaining on the upper right hand corner of the computer screen. Once 15 minutes has elapsed, the test will resume automatically. If you decide to continue without any break, you can click the "End" button and you will be immediately directed to the Reading Comprehension (RC) section.

The RC Test presents three passages of about 1,500 words each. An average of 16 to 17 questions accompanies every reading text. The computer screen displays on the same page the individual question on the upper half of the page and the corresponding reading passage in a scrollable box on the lower half of the page.

The Quantitative Reasoning Test (QRT) is the last exam section of the DAT. It covers Number Operations, Algebra, Geometry, Trigonometry, Probability and Statistics, and Applied Mathematics problems. In this particular section only, a basic four-function calculator appears on the computer screen.

Overall, you will have a total of 4 hours and 15 minutes without the three optional portions of the test or 5 hours if you go through each segment. The Canadian DAT has a slightly different format, which we will present in the next section.

1.2.1 The Canadian DAT

The Dental Aptitude Test in Canada is a paper and pencil exam that assesses general academic knowledge, comprehension of scientific information, two and three dimensional visual perception, and manual dexterity. It can be taken either in English or in French, depending on which is required by the school where you are applying. Of the ten accredited Canadian dental schools, only the Université de Montréal and the Université Laval in Quebec offer the dental program in French at present. On the other hand, the University of Toronto and the University of Western Ontario accept scores from the American DAT while McGill University no longer includes the DAT scores in their admissions criteria.

Unlike the American DAT, which can be scheduled almost any time of the year in more than 70 Prometric locations, the Canadian DAT is administered only twice a year. The test is normally conducted on a Saturday in November and in February at test centers in the ten Canadian dental schools and thirteen additional sites across Canada. The Canadian Dental Association (CDA) also gives consideration to candidates who cannot take the exam on a Saturday schedule for religious reasons.

Commonly, candidates who plan to matriculate into dental school within one year write the November exam. Most retakers and those applying a year farther, attempt the February DAT. Some schools recognize DAT results obtained five years prior to the application while others, two or three years.

1.2.2 Content and Sequence of the Canadian DAT

Both the English and the French DAT have identical test sections: Survey of Natural Sciences, Perceptual Ability Test, and Manual Dexterity Test. However, only the English DAT contains the Reading Comprehension Test. Additionally, the Manual Dexterity Test is an optional portion of the DAT. At this time, the University of British Columbia, the University of Toronto, the University of Dalhousie, and the University of Western Ontario do not require the Manual Dexterity Test Score. Applicants are, therefore, advised to base their options of the exams according to the qualifications set by the dental program(s) to which they seek acceptance.

The typical order of the test sections in the English Canadian DAT is as follows:

1. Manual Dexterity Test

In this section, you will be given a cylindrical bar of soap of about 15 cm long and a pattern, which specifies the shape of the two

The Canadian DAT Testing Schedule	
Manual Dexterity Test (MDT)	
Time	30 minutes
Carving Pattern	1
Section Break*	
Survey of Natural Sciences	
Time	60 minutes
Questions	70
Stretch Break*	
Perceptual Ability Test	
Time	60 minutes
Questions	90
Section Break*	
Reading Comprehension Test	
Time	50 minutes
Questions	50

* The duration of each section break depends on the invigilators, although these typically last between 5 to 15 minutes. No formal lunch break is provided.

ends and the middle portions of the soap – for example, square, triangle, or fluted. You will have five minutes to study the figure during which you will not be allowed to do anything to the soap. Once the 30-minute carving time starts, YOU CAN NO LONGER REPLACE YOUR SOAP, so be careful not to chip any edges when cutting it; or worse, break the soap itself. You are permitted to use surgical gloves, but you must supply your own. You can also request for a pencil to mark your soap.

Four areas serve as the basis in scoring the carved pattern:

1. **Pattern reproduction** – completeness and accuracy of measurements
2. **Planes** – flatness and smoothness
3. **Angles** – sharpness and accuracy of lines, corners, and angles
4. **Sectional relationship** – symmetry and orientation

2. Survey of Natural Sciences

The Natural Sciences section covers only Biology and General Chemistry and none of the Organic Chemistry component found in the American DAT. The breakdown of the test items is as follows:

Biology	40 items
General Chemistry	30 items

3. Perceptual Ability Test

The Perceptual Ability Test consists of angle discrimination, form development, cube counting, orthographic projections and apertures.

4. Reading Comprehension Test (English DAT only)

Similar to the RC Test in the American DAT, this section presents three reading passages of 1,500 words in length and an average of 16 to 17 questions each. However, the time limit is 10 minutes shorter with a total of 50 minutes for all 50 RC questions in the Canadian DAT.

Because this is a paper test, you can mark, highlight, and/or write notes on the test booklet. All answers, however, must be written on the answer sheet.

General Comparison of the American and Canadian DAT		
	American DAT	**Canadian DAT**
Name of the Test	• Dental Admission Test	• Dental Aptitude Test
Testing Method	• Computer	• Paper
Total Test Time	4 hours and 15 minutes and 3 15-minute optional breaks	Approximately 4 hours; breaks in between sections
Total Number of Questions	280 questions	210 questions + MDT for the English DAT; 160 questions + MDT for the French DAT
Survey of Natural Sciences	100 questions; 90 minutes 1) Biology (40) 2) General Chemistry (30) 3) Organic Chemistry (30)	70 questions; 60 minutes 1) Biology (40) 2) General Chemistry (30)
Perceptual Ability Test	90 questions; 60 minutes 1) apertures 2) view recognition 3) angle discrimination 4) paper folding 5) cube counting 6) 3D form development	90 questions; 60 minutes 1) apertures 2) angle discrimination 3) cubes 4) form development 5) orthographic projections
Reading Comprehension	50 questions; 60 minutes • 3 reading passages	50 questions; 50 minutes (English DAT) • 3 reading passages
Quantitative Reasoning	40 Questions; 45 minutes	NONE
Manual Dexterity (Soap Carving)	NONE	30 minutes (optional)*
Administering Body	American Dental Association	Canadian Dental Association
Test Frequency	Almost any time throughout the year	Every November and February
Official Practice Materials	• 1 full-length Practice Test (available in print and web based format) • 1 Sample Test (available as free download in PDF format from the ADA website)	• DAT Preparation Kit (includes materials for the MDT and DAT Preparation Manual with sample tests); consider practicing with at least 20 CDA soaps
*Consult with the dental school where you are applying before choosing to disregard this section.		

REMEMBER

Prohibited Items in the Examination Room:
books, slide rulers, paper, calculators and rulers or other measuring and calculating devices.

1.3 English as a Second Language (ESL)

Many ESL students will need to pay extra attention to the Reading Comprehension Test of the DAT. Although specific advice for all students will be presented in the sections that follow, extra tips are discussed for ESL students in Section 3.2.3 of the Reading Comprehension part of this book series.

Having said that, DAT scores are subjected to a statistical analysis to check that each question is fair, valid and reliable. Test questions in development are scrutinized in order to minimize gender, ethnic or religious bias, and to affirm that the test is culturally fair.

Depending on your English skills, you may or may not benefit from an English reading summer course. Certainly, you have the option of deciding whether or not you would want to take such a course for credit.

1.4 How the DAT is Scored

The DAT reports eight standard scores. The first six scores are from the individual tests themselves, i.e. biology, general chemistry, organic chemistry, perceptual ability, reading comprehension, and quantitative reasoning. The multiple choice questions are first scored right or wrong resulting in a raw score. Note that wrong answers are worth the same as unanswered questions so ALWAYS ANSWER ALL THE QUESTIONS even if you are not sure of certain answers. The raw score is then converted to a scaled score ranging from 1 (lowest) to 30 (highest). A test section that is skipped will be scored 1. This is neither a percentage nor a percentile. The test is not based on a curve. Essentially, DAT performance is measured using an ability-referenced system. Based on standard scores, an individual examinee's abilities (i.e. knowledge and problem solving skills) are directly compared to that of the other DAT examinees'. It is not possible to accurately replicate this scoring system at home.

The remaining two scores are Total Science and Academic Average. The Total Science score is the standard score for the 100 questions in the Survey of Natural Sciences as a whole – NOT THE AVERAGE OF THE STANDARD SCORES of the Science subtests. This is derived from the sum of your raw scores each in biology, general chemistry, and organic chemistry. The total score is then converted to a standard score for Total Science. In contrast, a score in the Academic Average is the rounded average of the standard scores from the reading comprehension (RC), quantitative reasoning (QR), biology (BIO), general chemistry (CHM), and organic chemistry (ORG) tests. Here is an example of an Academic Average calculation:

QR – 19
RC – 21
BIO – 22
CHM – 21
ORG – 20

TOTAL: 103 ÷ 5 = 20.6; rounded up to the nearest whole, the Academic Average for these scores would be 21.

Standards for interviews or admissions may vary for the individual scores, Total Science and the Academic Average. For example, one particular dental school may establish a cutoff (minimum) of 17 for all sections. In other cases, admissions committees assess candidates against a mean of DAT scores in a particular batch of applicants; therefore, the range can vary from year to year. Contact individual programs for specific score requirements.

The DAT may include a small number of questions, called pretest questions, which will not be scored. These questions are trial questions which may be used in the future. If you see a question that you think is off the wall, unanswerable or inappropriate for your level of knowledge, it could well be one of these questions, so never panic! And of course, answer every question because guessing may provide a 25% chance of being correct while not answering provides a 0% chance of being correct!

1.4.1 Average, Good, and High DAT Scores

Because the DAT employs an ability-referenced measurement, there are no established cutoff scores, or Pass and Fail marks. Rather, the standard score indicates your test performance relative to all the students who did the same test on the same day. This means that the national average of 17 on the scored sections is not always a guarantee for acceptance in a dental program. In most instances, what is considered "average" depends on the entering batch of a particular academic year. This could range from as low as 16 to as high as 22 in the Academic Average and 14 to 22 in the Perceptual Ability Test. Likewise, a "good" score may be good enough for admittance to one dental school but below the cutoff of another. The best way to find out is to consult the websites of the dental institutions to which you intend to apply.

Your main aim is to achieve the scores that will put you on a competitive footing among all the other applicants. Statistics of enrollees entering dental school in 2011 report a majority with scores around 19 to 20 in the Academic Average, PAT, and Total Science. Section scores of 21 and above are generally perceived to be highly competitive.

***Source:** Predoctoral Dental Applicants and Enrollees Graphs published online by ADEA (American Dental Education Association).

1.4.2 When are the Scores Released?

Right after completing the DAT, an unofficial score report is immediately generated at the Prometric Test Center. This report will then be audited for accuracy and verified by the Department of Testing Services. Official scores are forwarded within three to four weeks to the dental schools, which are indicated in the DAT application of the examinee. The ADA also sends the scores to the appropriate standardized application service such as the Associated American Dental Schools Application Service (AADSAS) or the Texas Medical and Dental Schools Application Service (TMDSAS) in case the specified dental schools participate in any one of these services. Scores are then posted to the examinee's dental school application and then forwarded to the respective faculties within one week. In such a case, you can confirm the proper submission of your official DAT scores by logging into your ADEA AADSAS application.

Requests of additional copies and/or recipients mean additional fees and transmittal time. For more details about this process, please check the ADA website.

1.4.3 DAT Scores in Canada

Similar to the American DAT, scores from the Canadian DAT are reported as standard scores ranging from 1 to 30. The test is based on the number of correct answers and does not penalize wrong answers. However, a blank answer sheet will be reported as zero. Therefore, DO NOT LEAVE ANY QUESTION UNANSWERED, even if you only have to guess.

A standard score of 15 is considered the national average. However, since there are only a few dental schools operating in Canada, admissions tend to be quite competitive. Any score above 20 would be ideal.

Total Science is the weighted average from the Biology and Chemistry scores; Academic Average is the arithmetic mean of the scores in Biology, Chemistry and Reading Comprehension. The Manual Dexterity or Carving Test uses a criterion-referenced measurement, i.e., scores are scaled on a complete or perfect mastery of a defined set of skills at one end and the complete absence of those skills at the other end. In order to be graded for this section, the carving must be two-thirds complete and correct. Otherwise, an incomplete or incorrect pattern will be penalized. The perfect score for this section is 30.

About six to eight weeks from the testing date, CDA mails the official DAT transcripts to the examinee (student transcript) and up to five schools that are specified in the DAT registration form. The student copy contains a detailed explanation of the test scores. Requests for additional copies after registration entail additional fees. Check the CDA website for detailed information.

THE RECIPE FOR DAT SUCCESS

2.1 The Important Ingredients

- Time, Motivation
- Read from varied sources/Check SDN and premed101 websites for advice (read essential sources; familiarize with the actual test content and the skills demanded)
- A review of the basic DAT sciences

DAT-Specific Information

- The Gold Standard DAT Books
- optional: The Gold Standard Natural Sciences DVDs, smartphone apps/ flashcards, MP3s or online programs (DAT-prep.com)
- optional: speed reading/comprehension course if necessary

DAT-Specific Problems

- Gold Standard (GS) chapter review problems in the book and online
- Gold Standard DAT tests (full lengths GS-1 and GS-2; GS free mini)
- Official DAT Practice Test (Web-based or Print format) and Sample Test Items (free download in PDF format from the ADA website)
- TopScore Pro: 3 full length practice DATs

2.2 The Proper Mix

1) Study regularly and start early. Creating a study schedule is often effective. Adhering to it is even more productive. Even the best study plans will unlikely yield the scores that you want if you do not follow your own preparation regimen. A lot of material needs to be covered and you will need sufficient time to review. Starting early will highlight your weak areas and give you ample time

to remedy them. This will also reduce your stress level in the weeks leading up to the exam and may make your studying easier. Make sure that you get a good grasp of what each section of the test is designed to assess.

Depending on your English skills and the quality of your science background, a good rule of thumb is: 3-6 hours/day of study for 3-6 months.

2) Keep focused and enjoy the material you are learning. Forget all past negative learning experiences, so you can open your mind to the information with a positive attitude. Given an open mind and some time to consider what you are learning, you will find most of the information tremendously interesting. Motivation can be derived from a sincere interest in learning and by keeping in mind your long-term goals.

3) Preparation for the Sciences: The Gold Standard (GS) DAT books are the most comprehensive review guides for the DAT ever to be sold in bookstores. Thus the most directed and efficient study plan is to begin by reviewing and understanding the science sections in the GS. While doing your science survey, you should take notes specifically on topics that are marked Memorize or Understand on the first page of each chapter. Your notes - we call them Gold Notes (!!) - should be very concise (no longer than one page per chapter). Every week, you should study from your Gold Notes at least once.

As you are incorporating the information from the science review, do the practice problems in the books and/or those included in the free chapter review questions online at DAT-prep.com. This is the best way to more clearly define the depth of your understanding and to get you accustomed to the questions you can expect on the DAT.

4) Preparation for the PAT: This section in the DAT requires a keen eye for details. Developing this skill starts with acquiring visualization techniques and applying them in several practice problem sets until you get used to seeing the different angles and dimensions of various figures. Go through the GS PAT chapters and familiarize yourself with the six subsections of the test. As you go along with your review, you will be able to adapt our techniques and strategies to identify the correct options.The more practice, the more you are likely to sharpen your perceptual acuity.

5) Preparation for Reading Comprehension: Begin by reading the advice and techniques given in GS RC. Time yourself and practice, practice, practice with various resources for this section as needed (in the book, online at DAT-prep.com, TopScore, and of course, the ADA materials). You should be sure to understand each and every mistake you make so as to ensure there will be improvement.

6) Preparation for Quantitative Reasoning: Similar to your preparation for the section on the Sciences, take note of the scope and demands of the test, which are listed on the first page of GS QR. Your aim is to determine your deficiencies and work on the foundations that will help address these.

7) Do practice exams. Ideally, you would finish your science review in The Gold Standard text and/or the science review DVDs at least a couple of months prior to the exam date. Then each week you can do a practice exam under simulated test conditions and thoroughly review each exam after completion. Scores in practice exams should improve over time. Success depends on what you do between the first and the last exam. You can start with ADA's DAT Sample Test Items then continue with the GS and TopScore practice exams and then complete the DAT Practice Test from ADA. You should do practice exams as you would the actual test: in one sitting within the expected time limits. Doing practice exams serves two important purposes in your preparation. First, it will increase your confidence and allow you to see what is expected of you. It will make you realize the constraints imposed by time limits in completing the entire test. Second, it will allow you to identify the areas in which you may be lacking.

Some students can answer all DAT questions quite well if they only had more time. Thus you must time yourself during practice and monitor your time during the test. On average, you will have a little less than a minute per question for Natural Sciences, a little over 30 seconds per question for the PAT, 20 minutes per passage and its accompanying questions for the RC, and 1.1 minutes per question for QR. In other words, every 30 minutes, you should check to be sure that you have completed an approximate number of questions for that section; for example, 34 questions or more in the first 30 minutes for Science, 70 or more in the next, and so on. If not, then you always guess on "time consuming questions" in order to catch up and, if you have time at the end, you return to properly evaluate the questions you skipped. Set aside at least the equivalent of a full day to review the explanations for EVERY test question. Do NOT dismiss any wrong answer as a "stupid mistake." You made that error for a reason, so you must work that out in your mind to reduce the risk that it occurs again. You can reduce your risk by test-proofing answers (i.e. spending 5-10 seconds being critical of your response) and by considering the following questions:

1. Why did you get the question wrong (or correct)?
2. What question-type or passage-type gives you repeated difficulty?
3. What is your mindset when looking

at a particular visual figure?

4. Did you monitor your time during the test?
5. Are most of your errors at the beginning or the end of the test?
6. Did you eliminate answer choices when you could?
7. For the Reading Comprehension Test, did you effectively scan for the detail questions? Did you comprehend the fundamental concepts presented in each passage?
8. Was your main problem a lack of content review or a lack of practice?
9. In which specific science or QR content areas do you need improvement?
10. Have you designed a study schedule to address your weaknesses?

8) Remember that the DAT will primarily measure your basic knowledge and understanding of concepts. Evidently, a lot of material in the GS books must simply be memorized; for example, some very basic science equations, rules of logarithms, trigonometric functions, the phases in mitosis and meiosis, naming organic compounds and many, many basic science facts. Nonetheless, for the most part, your objective should be to try to understand, rather than memorize, the biology, chemistry, and math material you review. This may appear vague now, but as you immerse yourself in the review chapters and practice material, you will more clearly understand what is expected of you.

9) Relax once in a while! While the DAT requires a lot of preparation, you should not forsake all your other activities. Try to keep exercising, maintain a social life and do things you enjoy. If you balance work with things that relax you, you will study more effectively overall.

2.3 It's DAT Time!

1) On the night before the exam, try to get a good night sleep. The DAT can be physically draining and it is in your best interest to be well rested when you do the exam.

2) Avoid last minute cramming. On the morning of the exam, do not begin studying ad hoc. You will not learn anything effectively, and noticing something you do not know or will not remember might reduce your confidence and lower your score unnecessarily. Just get up, eat a good breakfast, consult your Gold Notes (the top level information that you personally compiled) and go do the exam.

3) Eat breakfast! You need the food energy to get through the exam.

4) If you are taking an afternoon schedule, eat a light lunch. Avoid greasy food that will make you drowsy. You do not want to feel sleepy while taking the test. A chocolate bar or other sweet highly caloric food could, however, be very useful during the break when you may be tired for the last section. The 'sugar low' will hit you only after you have completed the exam when you do not have to be awake!

5) Make sure you answer all the questions! You do not get penalized for incorrect answers, so always choose something even if you have to guess. If you run out of time, pick a letter and use it to answer all the remaining questions. The ADA performs statistical analyses on every test so no one letter will give you an unfair advantage. Just choose your "lucky" letter and move on!

6) Pace yourself. Do not get bogged down trying to answer a difficult question. If the question is very difficult, mark it, guess, move on to the next question and return later if you have enough time remaining.

7) Remember that some of the questions may be thrown out as inappropriate, used solely to calibrate the test or trial questions. If you find that you cannot answer some of the questions, do not despair. It is possible they could be questions used for these purposes.

8) Do not let others psyche you out! Some people might be leaving an earlier exam saying, 'It went great. What a joke!' Ignore them. Often these types may just be trying to boost their own confidence or to make themselves look good in front of their friends. Just focus on what you have to do and tune out the other examinees.

9) Relax during the short break. You need the time to recuperate and rest.

10) Before reading the RC passage, some students find it more efficient to quickly read the questions first. In this way, as soon as you read something in the passage which brings to mind a question you have read, you can answer immediately. Otherwise, if you read the text first and then the questions, you may end up wasting time searching through the text for answers.

11) Read the text and questions carefully! Often students leave out a word or two while reading, which can completely change the sense of the problem. Pay special attention to words in italics, CAPS, bolded, or underlined. You will certainly find the word "EXCEPT" in CAPS in a question on the real DAT!

12) You must be both diligent and careful with the way you choose the correct answer because you will not be given extra time to make corrections when time expires.

13) Consider your choice of clothing on test day. Be ready for too much heat or an overzealous air conditioning unit.

14) Some problems involve algebraic manipulation of equations and/or numerical calculations. Be sure that you know what all the variables in the equation stand for and that you are using the equation in the appropriate circumstance. In chemistry and QR, the use of dimensional analysis will help you keep track of units and solve some problems where you might have forgotten the relevant equations.

15) The final step in problem solving is to ask yourself: is my answer reasonable? This is where your intuition serves as a guide. But to be frank, 'intuition' in the context of the DAT is really learned through the experience of a comprehensive review and completing many practice problems and tests.

We, at The Gold Standard, will do our best - on paper and online - to guide you through the content and strategies you can use to be successful. Let's continue . . .

DAT-prep.com

PAT

PERCEPTUAL ABILITY

THE RELEVANCE OF THE PERCEPTUAL ABILITY TEST

Chapter 1

Memorize	Understand	Not Required
The Paper Folding Quadrant The Gold Standard Cube Formula	* The Purpose of the Test * Three-dimensional Objects * Three-dimensional (3D) and Two-dimensional (2D) Views * Rules on Apertures	* Formal training or academic course

Introduction

This section is a test of your visual acumen rather than formal knowledge. Nevertheless, understanding the concepts involved in the six subtests of the PAT is paramount to your successful performance in this test.

Additional Resources

Free Online Forum

1.1 The Importance of the PAT Score

The Perceptual Ability Test (PAT) is the only section in the DAT that does not require academic knowledge or training. It is designed to be used as a predictor of an applicant's performance in the preclinical operative skills and restorative dentistry practical laboratory classes. The ability to perceive small differences is also important in selecting candidates for dental schools that require eye-to-hand fine motor coordination in their curriculum.

Just as perceptual aptitude is not typically correlated with general grade point average (GPA) in dental school, the PAT score is likewise NOT included in the computation of the DAT academic average score. The importance of your performance in this test varies from school to school wherein the minimum requirement can be as low as 16 to as high as 20. Needless to say, the best way to determine the extent of your preparation for the PAT is to consult directly with the institution to which you are applying.

1.2 How to Prepare for the Perceptual Ability Test

Preparing for the PAT is somewhat different from the rest of the DAT sections as it is more about perceptual *ability* rather than knowledge. Your ability to visualize patterns and mentally manipulate 2D and 3D objects will be measured in at least four of the subtests. Central to your approach is a clear understanding of the concepts governing each subsection, and primary in your general preparation for the PAT is getting acquainted with the content and structure of the test.

1.2.1 The Format and Content of the PAT

As already mentioned, six divisions comprise this exam, namely the apertures, view recognition, angle discrimination, paper folding, cube counting, and 3D form development. In total, you will be given 60 minutes to complete 90 questions – which are further divided to15 questions per subsection. This means that you will have 40 seconds to answer each question.

However, keep in mind that not all six parts require equal amounts of time. You might find some sections to be more challenging and thus more time-consuming than the others. Since the PAT is administered as a single segment – meaning, there are no section breaks – you can skip the questions that you think will require relatively more time for you to complete. You can then come back to these questions once you have worked your way through the whole section. Remember that an "easy" question counts just as equally as a "hard" question. Also, knowing that you have completed at least all of the "easy" questions will give you more peace of mind as you spend the rest of the allotted time working on the harder questions.

The Six PAT Subsections	
Apertures	You will be presented with a 3-D object and you must determine through which of the five openings this object can pass.
View Recognition	Two projections of an object will be presented in each question. You are to determine the third.
Angle Discrimination	Each question will show four angles labeled 1 - 4. You are required to rank them from the smallest to the largest.
Paper Folding	A series of folds – usually two to three times – on a piece of paper will be illustrated in each question. One or more holes will then be punched at specific locations of the paper. Your task is to mentally unfold the paper and determine the resulting pattern of holes.
Cube Counting	For every two to four questions, you will be shown a stack of cubes. You will be asked to imagine that the stack as a whole is painted on all sides except for the bottom. You will then determine how many cubes have a particular number of sides painted.
Pattern Folding	A flat, unfolded pattern is presented in a question. You will have to choose the correct 3D figure that it represents once folded.

1.2.2 Practice, Practice, Practice

As with most undertakings that call for skills development, repetition is the key to success. Many candidates, at least in the beginning, will often find themselves running out of time in the PAT section. But with constant practice, you can train your brain to visualize these patterns and objects. Complete the first to second practice tests at a comfortable pace and record the precise time it took you to finish an entire subsection. This will give you a clear idea of your current level in terms of skills and speed. From there, you can create a more realistic study schedule for the PAT, and even the DAT as a whole.

For every practice set, go through each question and understand not only why an option is correct, but also why the other answer choices are wrong. Oftentimes in the actual test, you will arrive at the correct answer by eliminating the wrong ones first. Eventually, you will be able to perceive these problems much quicker and more efficiently.

It is also imperative that you do not stress out on this section. The PAT requires the most visualization out of all the sections on the DAT. If you are anxious and tired, you will not be able to solve the problems efficiently.

Finally, take note that you are not allowed to bring any item into the testing room: NO calculators, rulers, and pencils. You will be provided with a dry erase board and a marker, but you are not permitted to use your fingers or the note boards as measuring devices during this section.

1.2.3 Living the PAT

If the PAT is supposed to test your real life visual skills, then let real life improve your PAT performance. Whether you are indoors or outdoors right now, look around. There are angles everywhere. There are objects behind other objects: notice that even though you can't see all of the objects behind, you can make logical inferences about their shapes.

Look at a cup. Notice the linear vertical lines that make out its outline. Notice how the top – which you know is really circular – seems more and more elliptical as you lower the angle of your view.

Can you pick out any acute or obtuse angles within your field of view? Which ones are clearly smaller than others? What allows you to know this to be true?

Paper folding (hole punching) and pattern folding do not appear as naturally as some of the other sections. If you are struggling with either of these two sections, you should try to actually do the folding in "real life" at least a few times. It would be especially meaningful if you tried it for an actual problem where you were having difficulty imagining the correct answer. Going through the process might help you to visualize the answer in a new way.

Looking at complex 3D objects from different angles is a normal part of life. Thinking about the edges, outlines, shapes, etc. as you are looking at objects does not come naturally. Try it in your free time, or when you are waiting in line somewhere, just as a temporary exercise to prepare for the PAT.

The more that you do PAT problems, the more you can see PAT in your surroundings. This sharpens your "instinct" for this section of the DAT.

In the succeeding pages, we will review each of the subsections specified by the ADA for the Perceptual Ability Test, as well as techniques for the respective topics. Each chapter comes with a set of exercises that will help reinforce your understanding and skills. Additional PAT chapter review questions and explanations are also available online at DAT-prep.com.

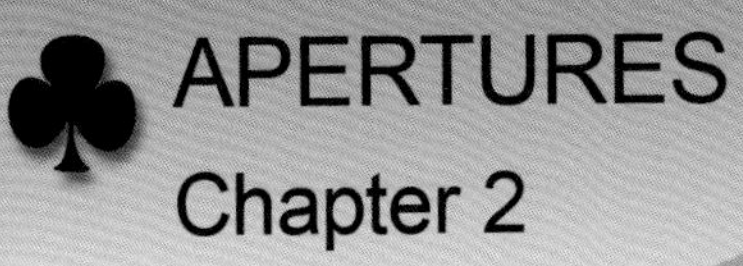

APERTURES

Chapter 2

Understand

* The Six Standard Views
* Mirror Outlines of 3D Objects
* Aperture Rules

DAT-Prep.com

Introduction

An aperture generally refers to an opening or a hole. This explains why Apertures in the PAT is also known as the Keyhole or the Key and Hole section. In this section, an aperture is the shape of an opening to a pathway, through which a three-dimensional object fits exactly and therefore, passes through without leaving any gaps.

In other words, an aperture of a three-dimensional object does not only have the same shape but also corresponds to the exact scale of the object. This basically tests your visual keenness to measure and differentiate irregularly shaped objects, as well as perceive their subtle details.

Additional Resources

Free Online Forum

2.1 About the Aperture Test

The first subsection of the Perceptual Ability Test is called "Apertures" or "Aperture Passing." Its more popular name among DAT candidates is "Keyhole." Each question in this test presents a three-dimensional object as the main reference (the "key"), followed by a choice of five outlines, representing possible passages ("holes") into which the object can go through in a single continuous motion.

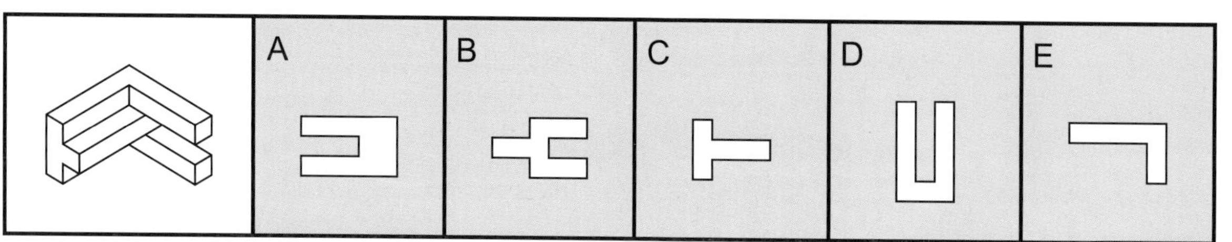

Figure PAT 2.1: Sample ***Aperture*** question that appears on the DAT. The correct answer is **A.**

The purpose of this subsection is to test a candidate's ability to visualize the two-dimensional view of a given object from three directions: the top, front, and right. This entails mentally rotating, turning, and flipping an object; the main objective of which is to identify the aperture that would match one of these three visualized 2D outlines of the object and perform the insertion with perfect ease.

2.2 Understanding Three-dimensional Objects and Views

One essential point that you need to understand is that a three-dimensional object has a total of six standard views namely the top, the bottom, the front, the rear or back, and the right and left sides as illustrated in Figures PAT 2.2 and 2.2-A.

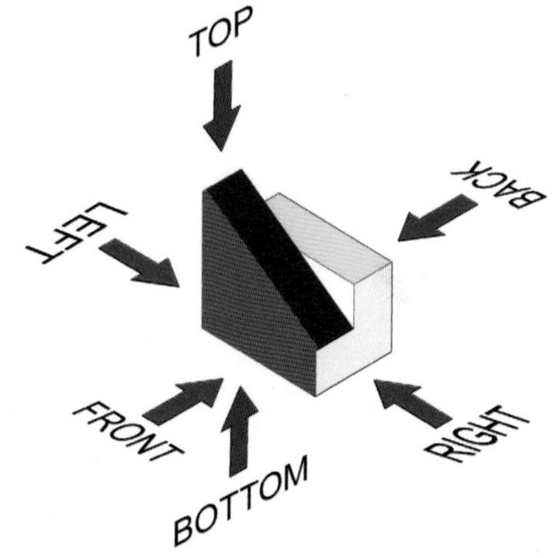

Figure PAT 2.2: The six sides (TOP, BOTTOM, FRONT, BACK, RIGHT, LEFT) in three-dimensional view.

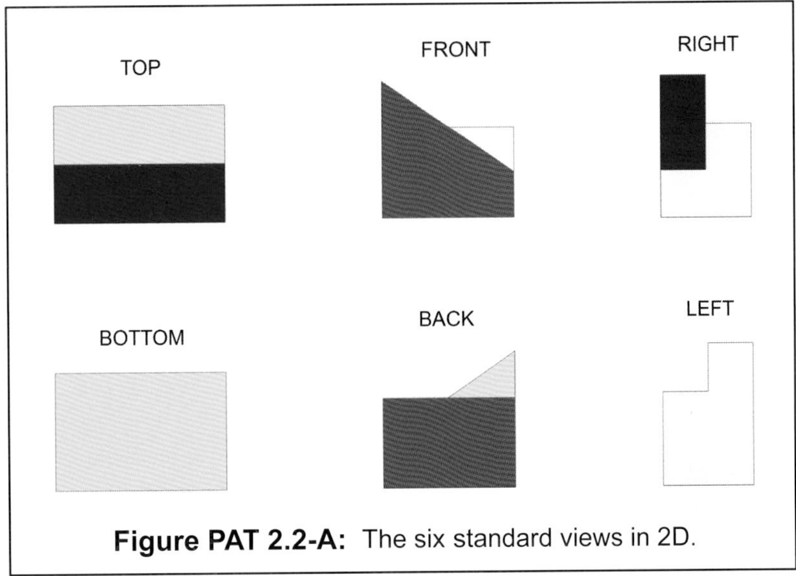

Figure PAT 2.2-A: The six standard views in 2D.

Slopes are some of the commonly confusing shapes to gauge from a two-dimensional perspective. They usually appear as rectangles or squares from certain points of view. See section 2.2.3 for a detailed discussion of understanding irregular shapes in 2D.

In this specific PAT subsection, however, each view is assumed to mirror the outline of its opposite side (top-bottom, front-back and right side-left side). If you focus on the outlines of the six standard views, the total height and width of the top and bottom are essentially the same.

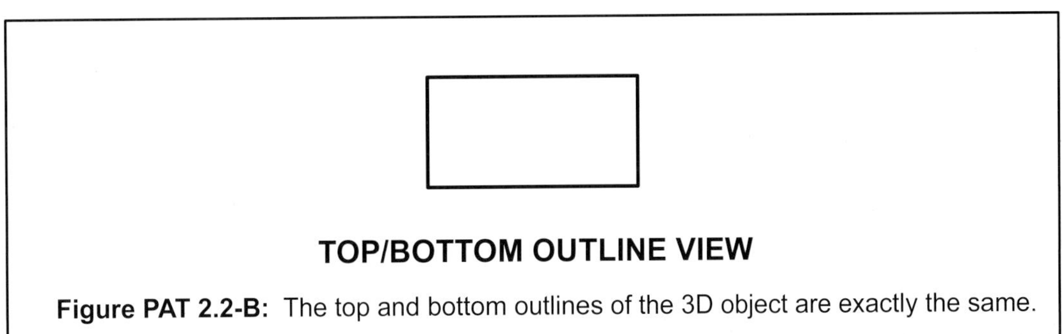

Figure PAT 2.2-B: The top and bottom outlines of the 3D object are exactly the same.

The back view is just the flip side of the front view, as is the case with the right and left views. Their only differences would be the angle from where one side is viewed.

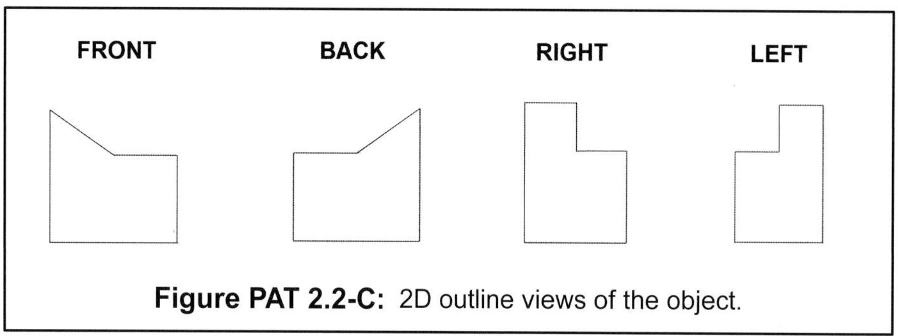

Figure PAT 2.2-C: 2D outline views of the object.

Hence, visualizing accurately the three basic outlines (top, front, and right) of a given 3D model is the most important skill that you should develop for the PAT Aperture test.

From this point onwards, we will refer to only three essential views: the top/bottom, the front/back, and the right/left views. Now let's try exploring a more complicated looking object.

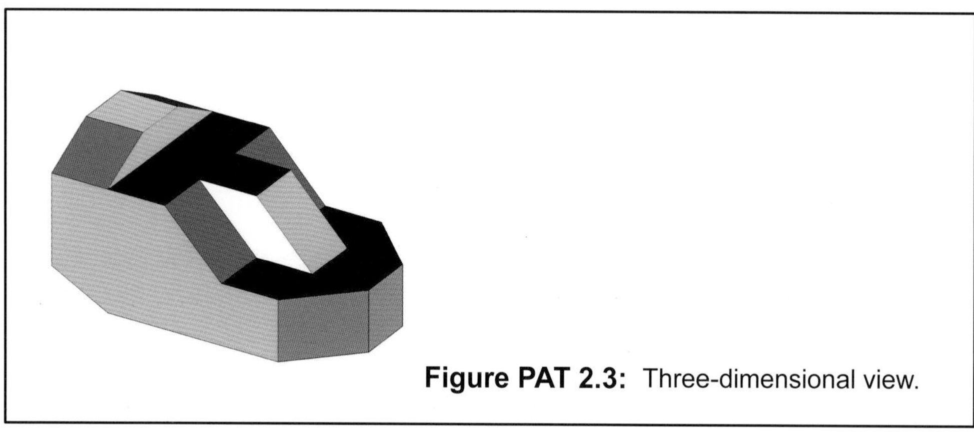

Figure PAT 2.3: Three-dimensional view.

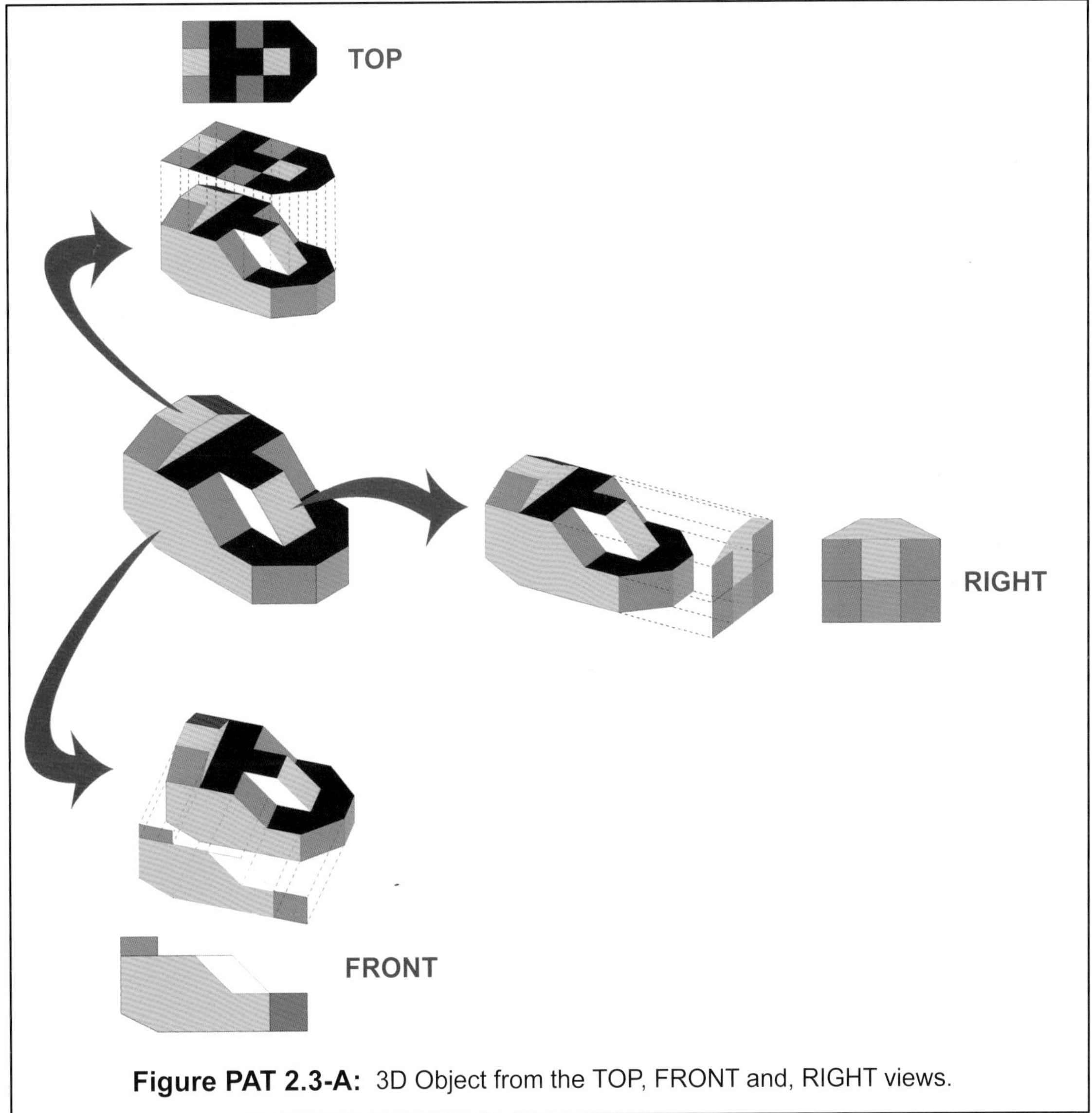

Figure PAT 2.3-A: 3D Object from the TOP, FRONT and, RIGHT views.

This time, try to either draw or imagine the outlines of the top, front, and right views. These outlines represent the shapes of the openings into which the object can pass through. Just remember that any of these apertures could be presented in the test in an upside down or flipped position. Nevertheless, the basic outline of a certain view never changes.

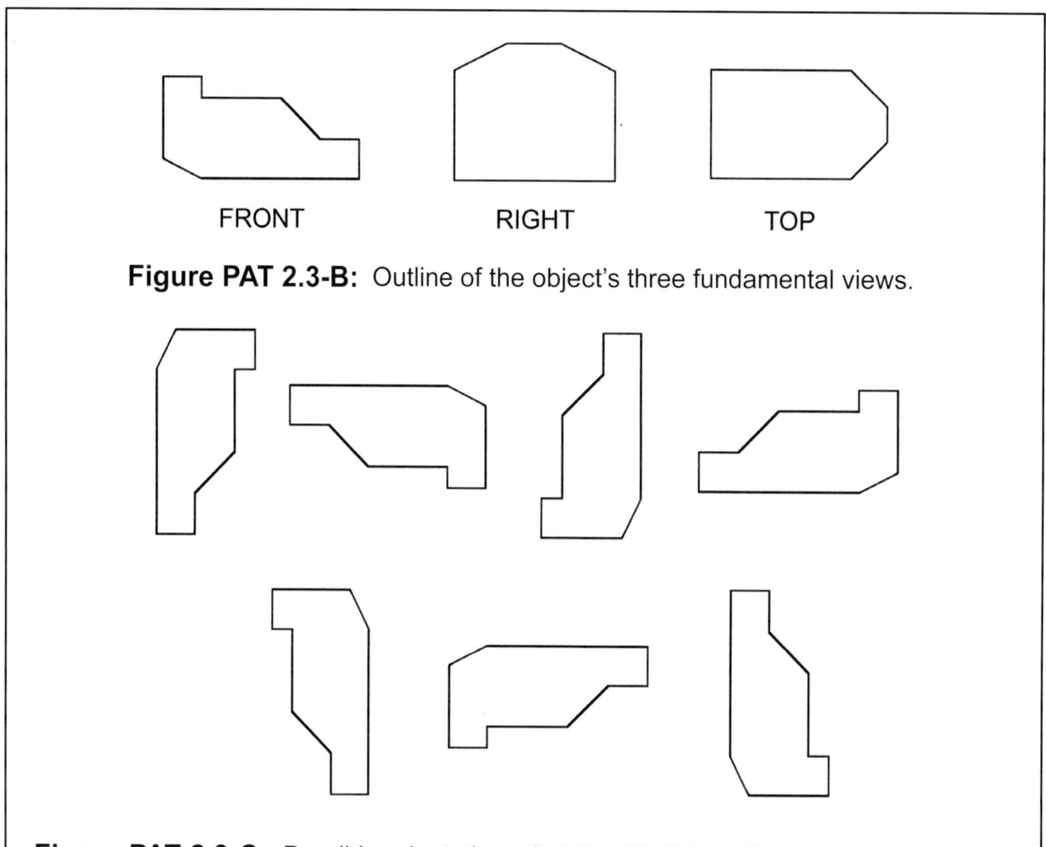

Figure PAT 2.3-B: Outline of the object's three fundamental views.

Figure PAT 2.3-C: Possible orientations that the FRONT outline could be presented in the test. Take some time to review each option above so that it begins to become part of the way you think when reviewing answer choices during the exam.

This time, let's try assessing a 3D object without any color and see if you can now comfortably determine its top, front and right outlines.

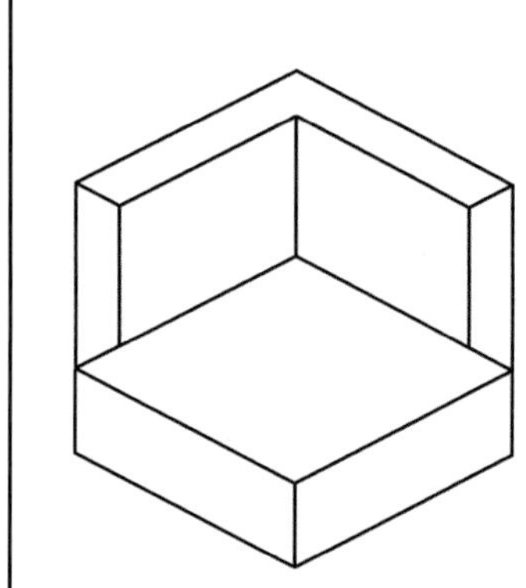

Figure PAT 2.4: 3D object in black and white as it could appear in a real exam question. Can you visualize the top, front, and right outline views of this object?

N.B. Your imagination is a muscle. All of our exercises have been carefully chosen to help you flex that muscle. So please take your time, focus and give a full effort with each exercise before reviewing the answers. This is your path to improvement.

A critical aspect in evaluating Figure PAT 2.4 is understanding how the L-shaped component is attached behind the box. Your first clue is the way its edges are drawn relative to the edges of the box.

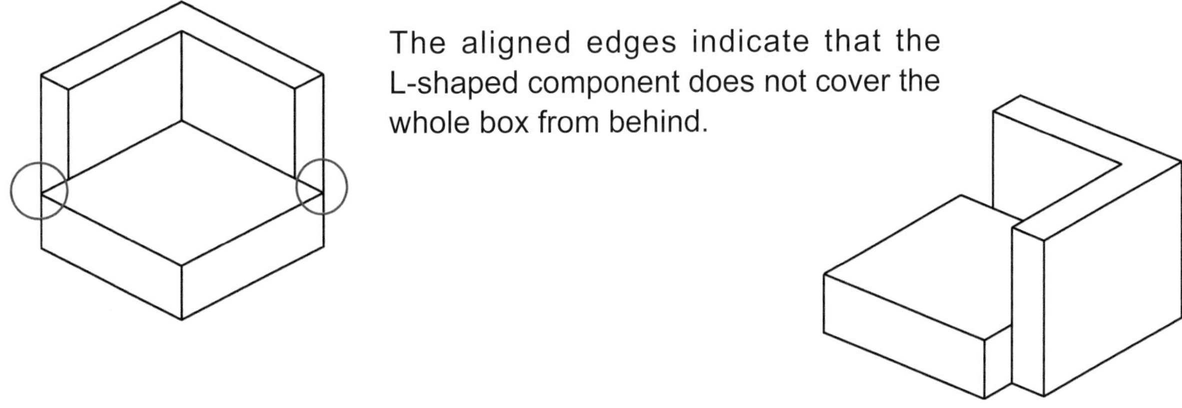

The aligned edges indicate that the L-shaped component does not cover the whole box from behind.

Alternate Scenario

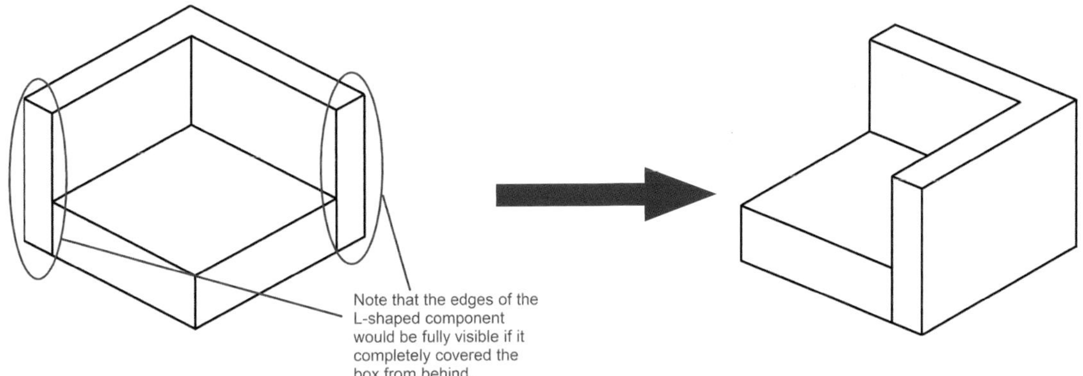

Note that the edges of the L-shaped component would be fully visible if it completely covered the box from behind.

Now let's start examining the front view of Figure PAT 2.4 and determine the shape of its outline. In order to aid us in distinguishing each view, let's assign colors to the parts corresponding to a specific side.

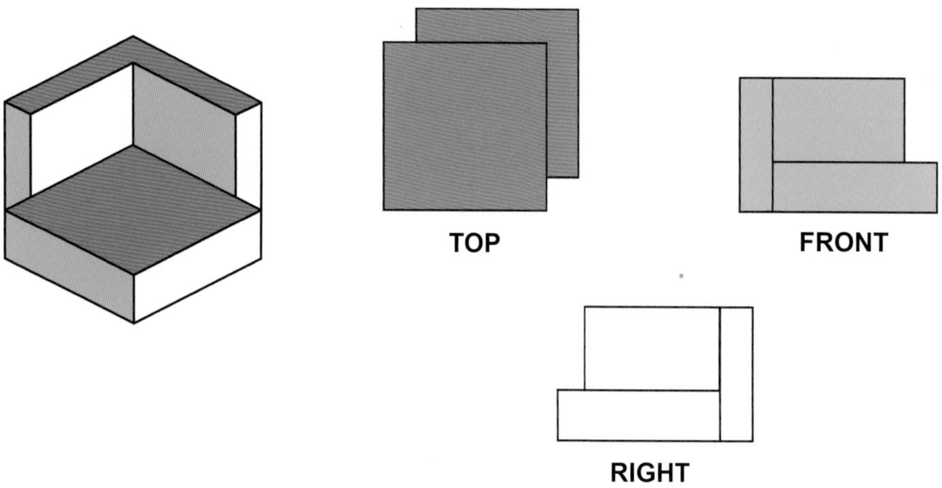

Based on these three basic views, the object's outlines would look like the following:

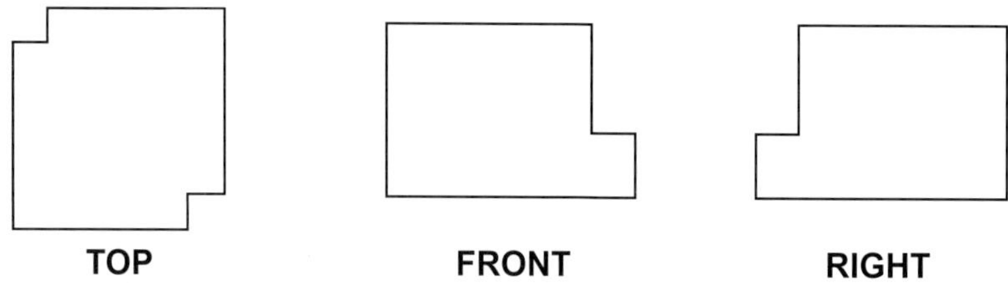

While several strategies may be applied with the Apertures section, **FOCUSING ON THE OUTLINES** of the object itself and on its three basic views is the most fundamental approach in determining the correct aperture for a 3D object.

Now let's do some short exercises to make sure that you have understood and can now focus on the three basic outlines of 3D objects. Draw the TOP, FRONT, and RIGHT outline views of each given object in the appropriate spaces provided. If, at this point, you find that drawing their opposite views – that is, the bottom, back and left, respectively – help you visualize the outlines better, you are free to do so.

1.

TOP/BOTTOM

FRONT/BACK

RIGHT/LEFT

2.

TOP/BOTTOM

FRONT/BACK

RIGHT/LEFT

3.

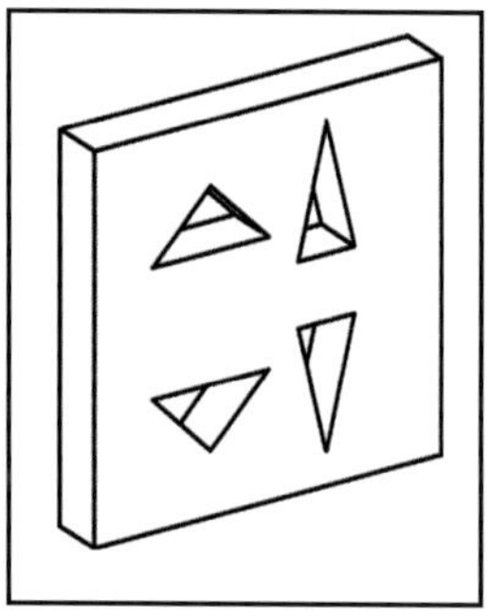

TOP/BOTTOM

FRONT/BACK

RIGHT/LEFT

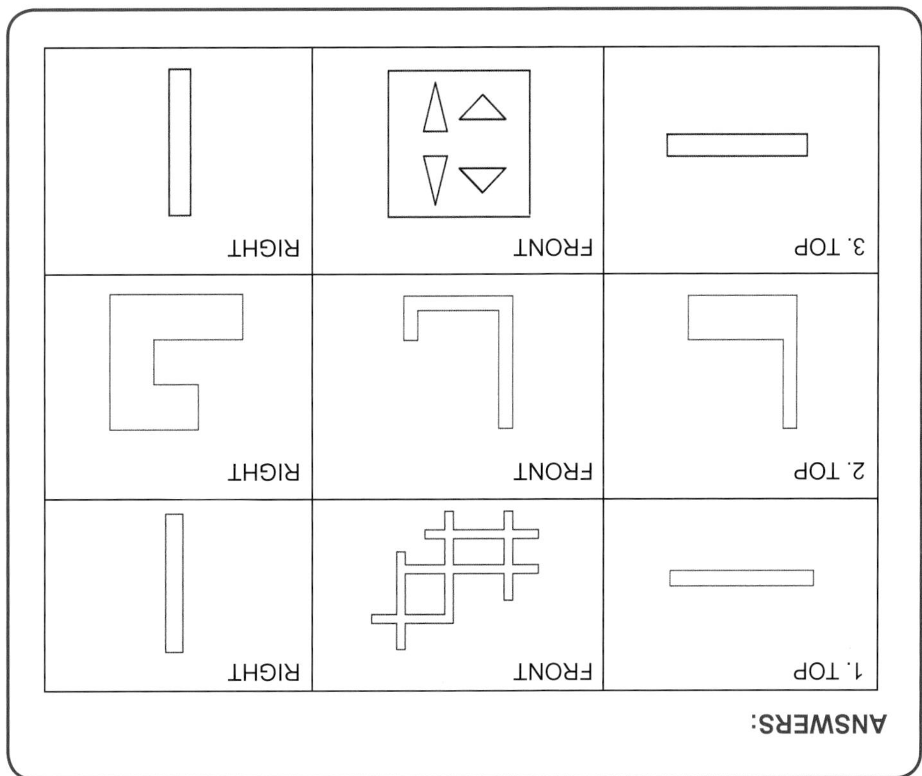

Now that we have narrowed down the important views and outlines to consider (TOP, FRONT, and RIGHT) when determining the correct apertures of a given object, let's start evaluating specific 3D objects in detail using these three fundamental views. Familiarizing yourself with the different views of various objects, especially the confusing ones, will make visualizing on the PAT not only so much easier but also so much faster.

2.2.1 Cylinders

Cylinders have three significant parts: two flat ends (also called *bases*) and one curved surface. The important thing to remember about cylinders is that their flat ends, which can be circular or elliptical in shape, will always show a rounded outline from a 180-degree view (see Figure PAT 2.6) while the curved surface, straight edges (see Figure PAT 2.7).

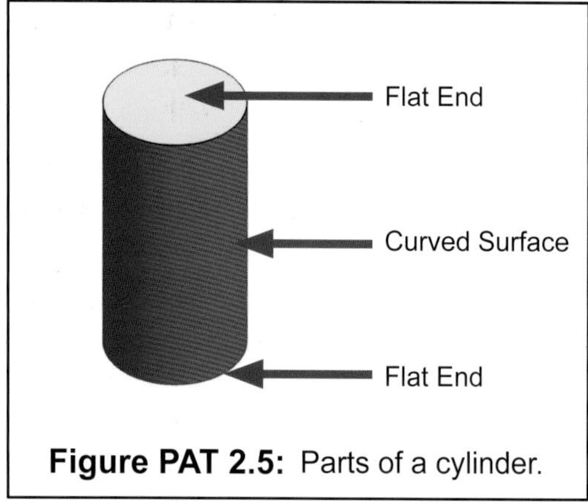

Figure PAT 2.5: Parts of a cylinder.

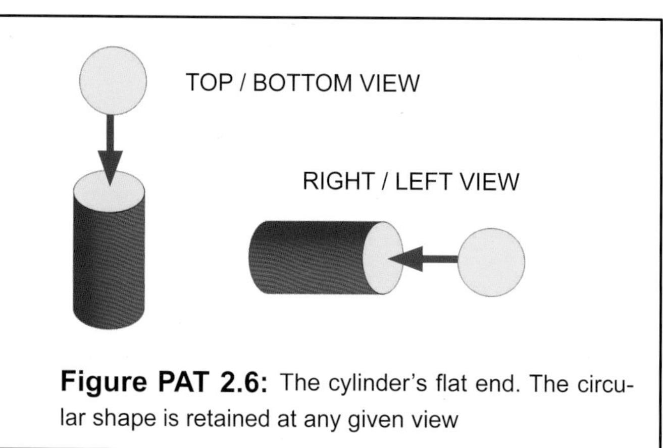

Figure PAT 2.6: The cylinder's flat end. The circular shape is retained at any given view

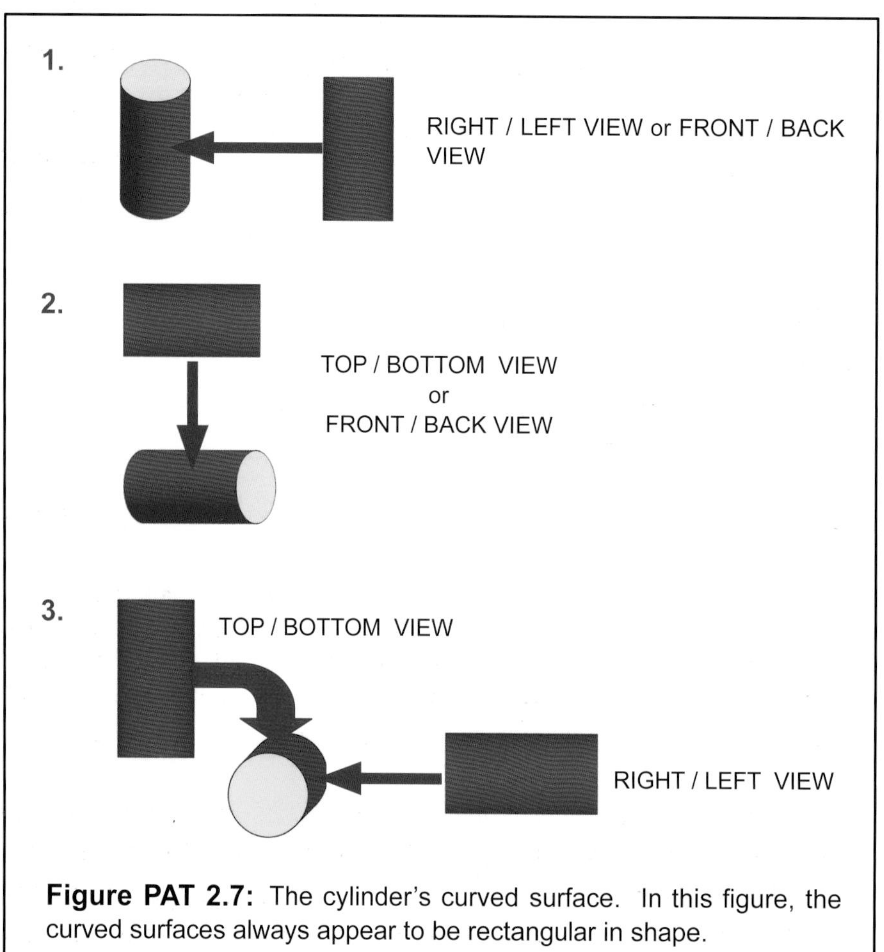

Figure PAT 2.7: The cylinder's curved surface. In this figure, the curved surfaces always appear to be rectangular in shape.

Looking at Figure PAT 2.7, you would observe that the shape of a curved surface stays proportionally the same in two views when in upright position (the front/back and right/left views) and in horizontal position (the top/bottom and front/back views). Even from an oblique view of the cylinder, only the orientation changes – vertical from the top/bottom view and horizontal from the right/left view – but the rectangle shape basically stays the same.

Inversely, the base always stays rounded in shape and from only one view, which could be the top/bottom, the right/left view, or the front/back view depending on how the cylinder is positioned.

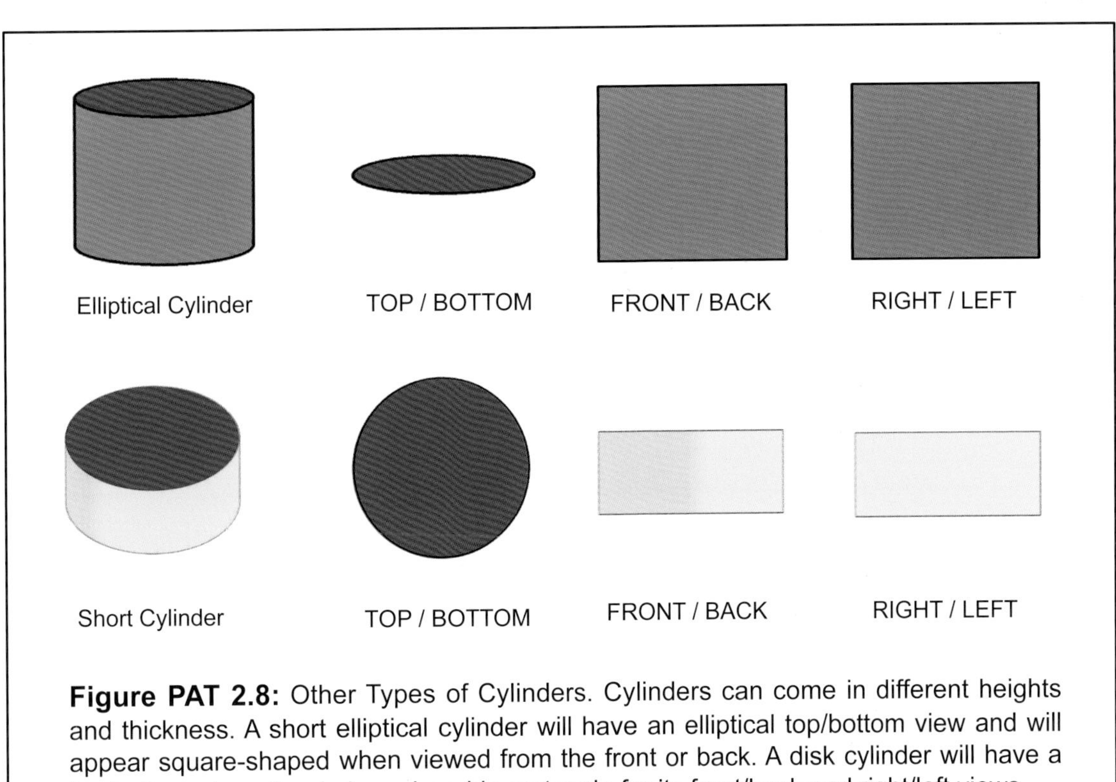

Figure PAT 2.8: Other Types of Cylinders. Cylinders can come in different heights and thickness. A short elliptical cylinder will have an elliptical top/bottom view and will appear square-shaped when viewed from the front or back. A disk cylinder will have a top/bottom view of a circle and a wide rectangle for its front/back and right/left views.

The cylinder shape will be presented in the actual test in a variety of sizes and orientations. They can also be shown as the main surface of an object or as one of the components. The best way to deal with this shape is to first, determine the correct contours of its bases and curved surface in the three fundamental views. Next, you need to gauge their respective dimensions. Finally, critical to these visualizations is your ability to stay focused on the outlines of the different views.

Let's take a look at two Aperture questions featuring this three-dimensional shape. Again, remember that you can effectively determine the correct answers if you stay focused on the outlines of the object's three basic views.

Choose the correct aperture to each object:

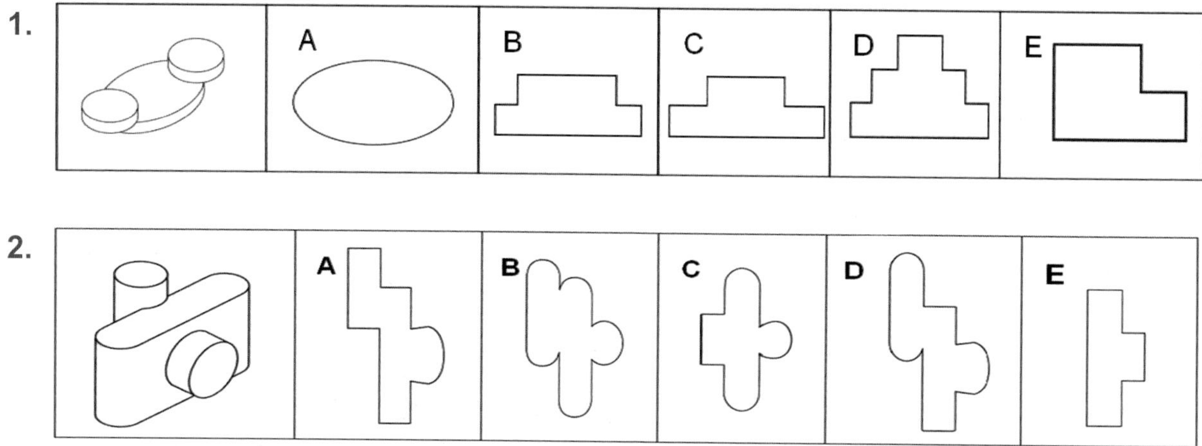

ANSWERS:

1. B. The 3D object in this question is composed of three cylinders: two small circular parts and one elliptical main surface. This should be easy to answer if you can easily recall that the curved surfaces of cylinders always show straight edges.

In this question, all three cylinders have the same orientation – that is, the top/bottom views show the bases of the two small parts as rounded and the bigger component as elliptical while the curved surfaces show up as short rectangles for the smaller circles and a wide rectangle for the elliptical one from the front/back and right/left views.

This means that A is the only aperture that shows the top/bottom view. At first glance, A is obviously incorrect. Because the two circular cylinders are attached passed the edges of the elliptical cylinder, the circular shapes should be visible on the top/bottom outline. A shows only the elliptical shape, therefore, wrong. This narrows down the choices to B, C, D, and E.

Since the remaining options all show straight edges, you can start visualizing the front/back and the right/left views and outlines.

Please cover the solution while you are considering your answer.

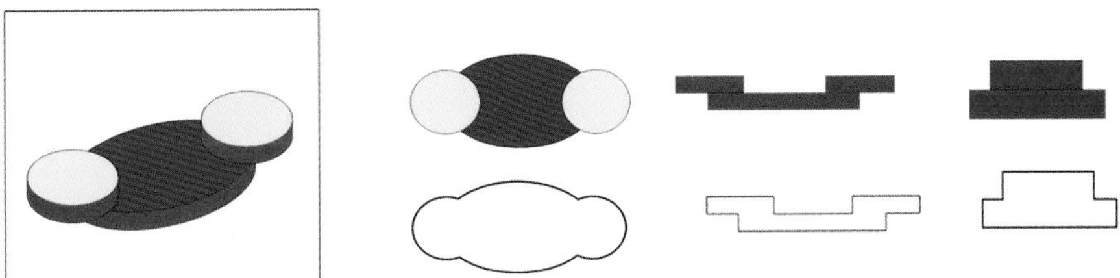

Figure PAT 2.9: Three Fundamental Views of Object 1.

* For clarification purposes, we have included the Top/Bottom view in the illustration.

From Figure PAT 2.9, we gather that all the shapes from the front/back and right/left views are rectangular. You can now eliminate D because it shows a square outline on top of the figure. E is also off the mark.

B and C show the object's outline from the right/left view. B outlines a wider rectangle on top than the one below it. This is correct because from both the right and left views, the elliptical cylinder will now have a narrower dimension than its front or back surface. C is wrong because it shows the opposite case. Your ability to spot these proportions in an object's outline as a whole will be tested quite often on the PAT Apertures questions.

---

2. C. The 3D object in this question is also comprised of three cylinders – this time, of different sizes, shapes, and orientations. These can be confusing to the untrained eye. However, distinguishing such differences as reflected on their various views and outlines is a skill that is frequently tested on the PAT; hence, you should practice working and visualizing similar types of questions as much as you can to help you overcome this challenge.

Looking at the given figure, the attachment on the left is a long cylinder in the upright position. The main surface is a narrow elliptical – also in the upright position, and the protrusion on the left is a short, circular cylinder in the horizontal position. This means that the top/bottom view will show the shapes of a circle, an oblong, and a rectangle, respectively. (Remember that the circular protrusion is horizontally positioned from the main elliptical object. Hence it would show its curved surface – rectangular – from the top or bottom view.) This eliminates A and B.

On the other hand, the front view will show three different sizes of rectangles. The right view is tricky: it will indeed show the circular protrusion on the center of the elliptical cylinder. However, because it is a solid protrusion and not a hole, this will be negligible from the outline view (see Figure PAT 2.10). The main surface (the elliptical object) will now appear as a rectangle while the long cylinder attachment will only have a small square as its visible part on top of the rectangle. This will now prove E as an incorrect choice.

Between C and D, you only need to evaluate the correct placement of the circle, the oblong, and the rectangle from the top view. Based on the outline view on Figure PAT 2.10, C is the best answer.

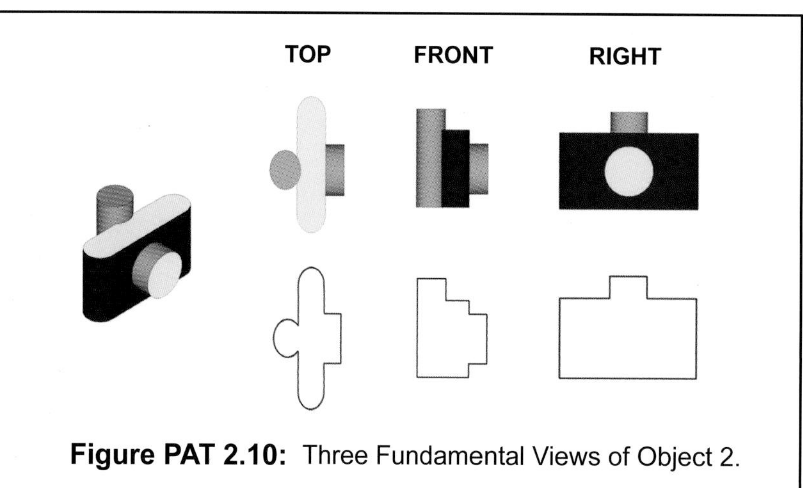

Figure PAT 2.10: Three Fundamental Views of Object 2.

2.2.2 Spheres

This shape seldom appears on the actual DAT, but it would be worth knowing that because a sphere is globular in shape, it thus appears as a circle at any angle.

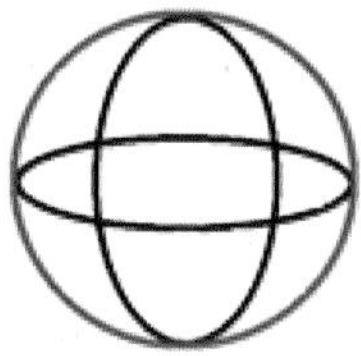

Figure PAT 2.11: 3D and outline views of the sphere. Take note that the shape remains circular from any of the three fundamental views.

2.2.3 Slopes

Familiarizing yourself with the different types of slopes and curves is one of the most important aspects of your preparation for this PAT subsection. These shapes frequently appear as protrusions, angled cuts, and/or attachments in an object. They are quite confusing when presented in combination with other shapes. They are also mostly found on the difficult questions of the PAT Apertures in order to gauge your visual scrutiny of details.

The following are some of the most common types, which you might encounter on the actual test. Again, the outlines of the top, front, and right views should be your main focus.

1. Convex Slopes

With slopes that curve outward, you have to be keen on how the curved and straight edges appear in the two-dimensional view of specific sides.

In Figure PAT 2.12, note how the arc on the slope's upper edge appears straight while the lower edge curved from the top view. The right view shows the reverse.

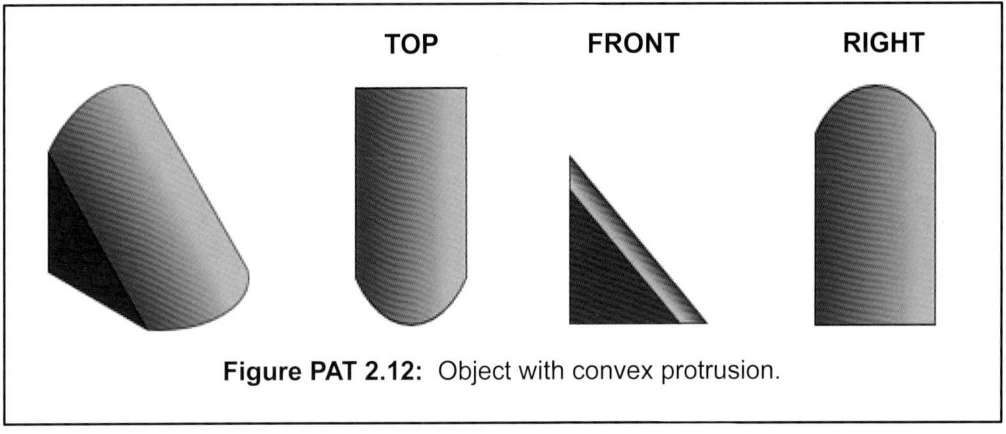

Figure PAT 2.12: Object with convex protrusion.

The front view is another area that requires close attention. The triangular base (i.e. flat surface) of the object will definitely appear; but you must also remember that the curvature of the convex slope protrudes outward. Hence this bulge will be visible from the front or back view. The question is, what shape will it manifest?

Now a convex protrusion is very much like the curved surface of a cylinder. As illustrated in section 2.2.1, curved surfaces always appear with flat edges in the two-dimensional views. Therefore, this will show as a linear layer on top of the triangle's hypotenuse, making the front-back outline a larger triangle than the actual size of the base.

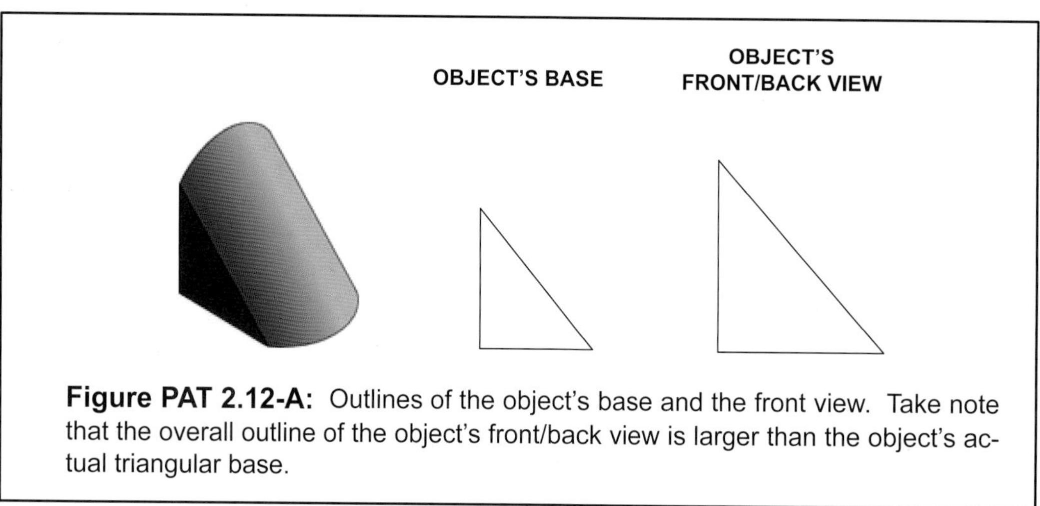

Figure PAT 2.12-A: Outlines of the object's base and the front view. Take note that the overall outline of the object's front/back view is larger than the object's actual triangular base.

Of course, convex slopes can come in various forms. In Figure PAT 2.13, the top and right views yield square outlines because the upper and lower edges of the slope are both straight. Being able to spot these details and differences are vital in choosing an object's correct aperture in the exam.

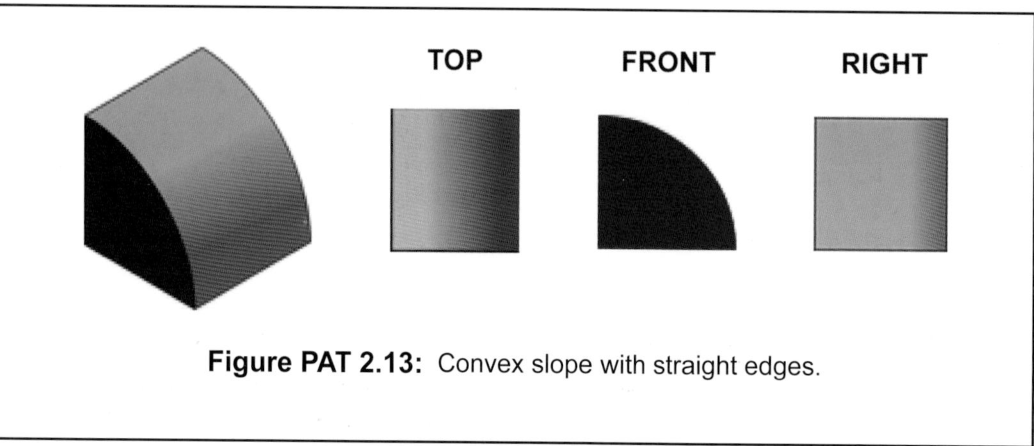

Figure PAT 2.13: Convex slope with straight edges.

2. Concave Slopes

Contrary to convex slopes, objects with concave components have depressions (i.e. "if it goes in like a cave, it's concave"). They DO NOT show bulges in any view. Instead, the concave surface may be completely invisible to at least one view. Hence, they are mostly irrelevant in visualizing the outline views of an object. The most fundamental approach, in this case, is to be attentive to the basic contour of the object's edges.

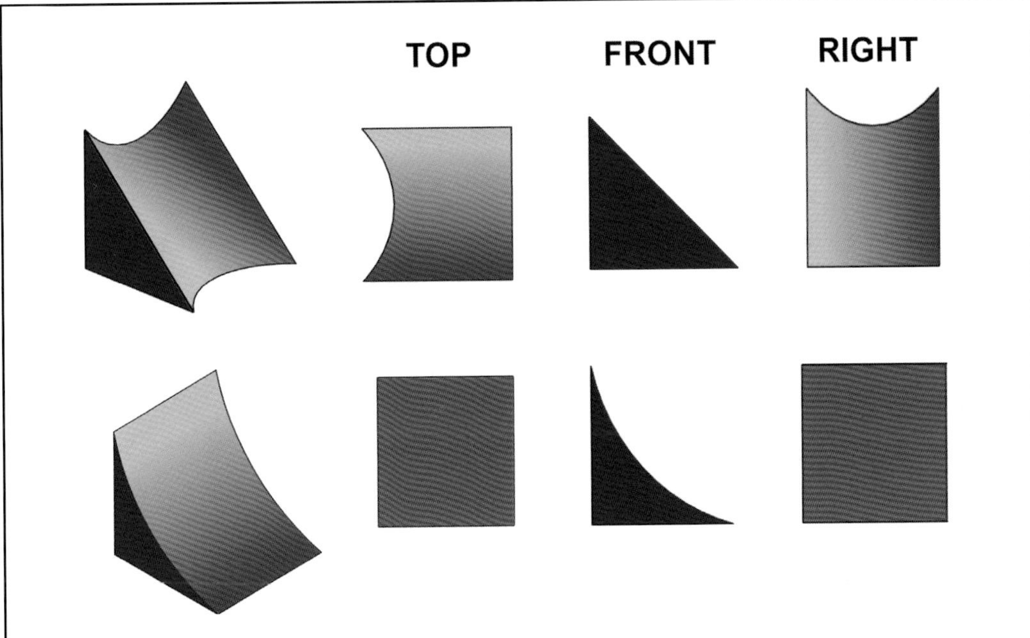

Figure PAT 2.14: Top, Front, and Right Views of Objects with Concave Parts. Take note how the curvatures appear in the different views.

3. Linear Slopes

With objects that have linear edges on their slopes, the DAT often uses these in the PAT Apertures questions to test your eye on proportions. This is primarily because the height or the length of an object can vary, depending on the degree of the inclination. The steeper the slope, the more area of the slanting surface becomes visible on a 180 degree view. The lower the inclination, the lesser area shows up, making the object look shorter in a particular two-dimensional view.

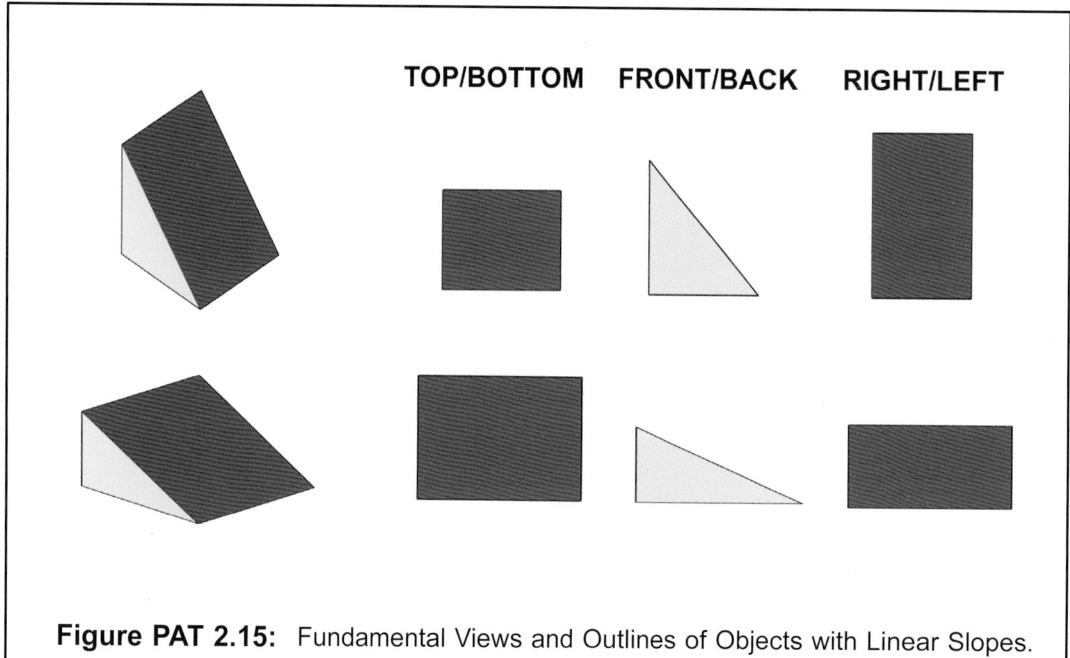

Figure PAT 2.15: Fundamental Views and Outlines of Objects with Linear Slopes. A steeper tilt shows a taller right/left view while a lower inclination forms a shorter one.

You must realize by now that the actual length of the slanting surface cannot be a reliable basis in judging an object's height in the 2D views. Similar to the second model in Figure PAT 2.15, an object with a mild slope can appear shorter from the right view even if the slanting surface may be longer.

One "trick" that will keep you from getting confused is to concentrate on the outline of the mirroring views. As explained in section 2.2, in this particular PAT subsection, each view will always have the same dimensions as its opposite side. In Figure PAT 2.16 for example, you can get the exact picture of the right view by estimating the height and width of the left outline. You can do the same procedure in determining the top view.

Now you have another strategy that you can utilize for the Apertures test (!): if you find a shape or an object to be confusing, you can move your sight to the opposite views and see if you could figure out the correct outline that you are looking for.

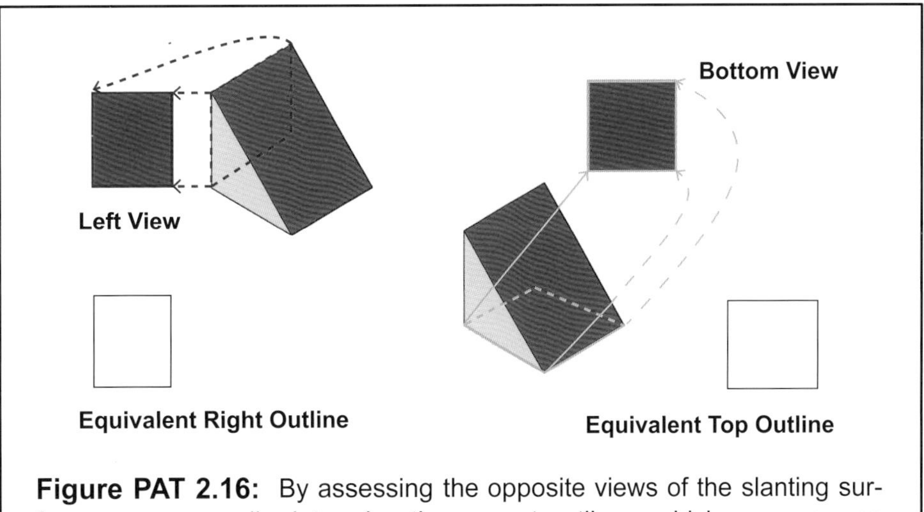

Figure PAT 2.16: By assessing the opposite views of the slanting surface, you can easily determine the correct outlines, which can serve as possible apertures for the object.

The pyramid and the star are another set of 3D objects that are confusing because of the sloping parts. Just keep in mind that a pyramid will always have the triangle shape on all its sides (front-back and top-bottom views). However, the top view in a classic "square" pyramid will be a square – just like its base, which is the bottom view.

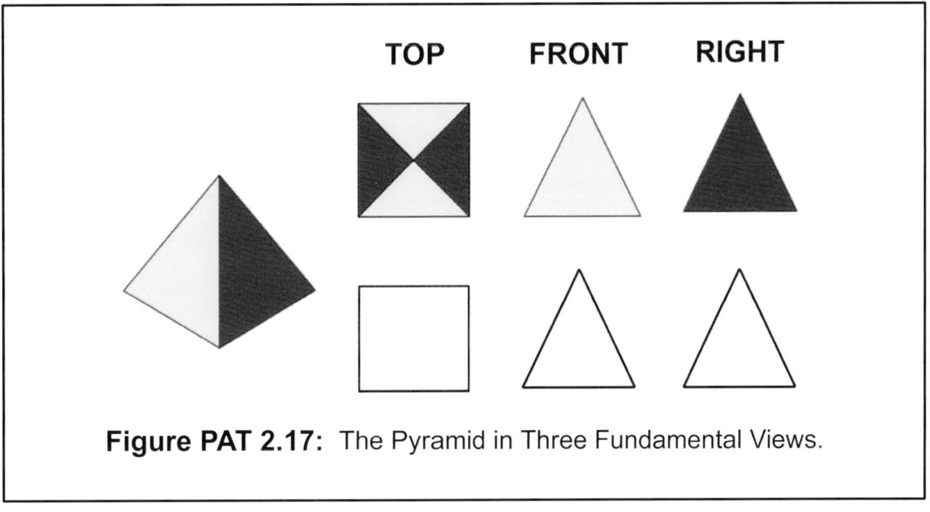

Figure PAT 2.17: The Pyramid in Three Fundamental Views.

Please note that there are other *rare* bases for pyramids which could be triangular, rectangular or which could have more than 4 corners.

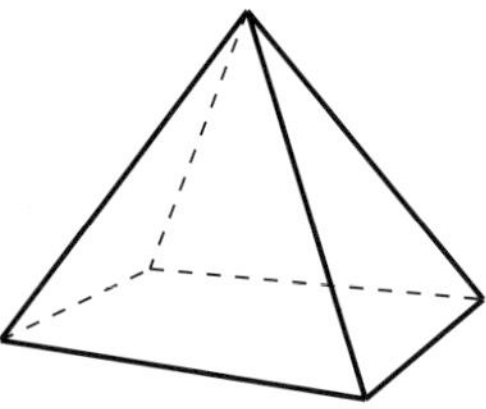

rectangular-based pyramid

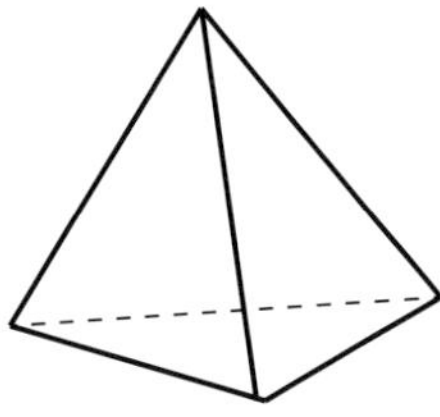

triangular-based pyramid

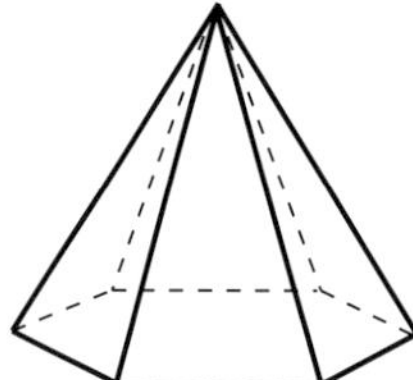

hexagonal-based pyramid

With star-shaped objects, the top-bottom view takes the form of the star. The two other views (front and right) have straight edges, with the height and width depending on the object's depth.

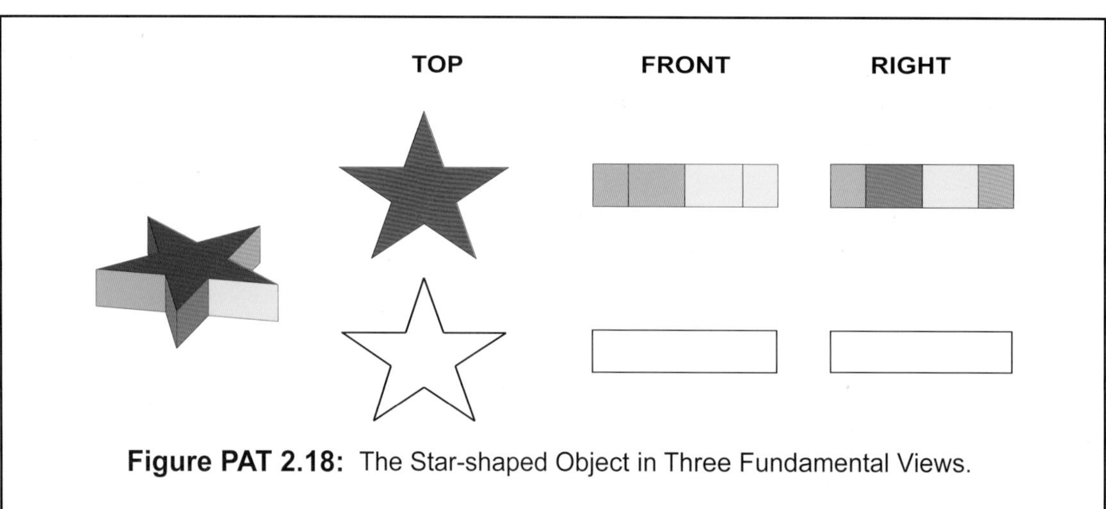

Figure PAT 2.18: The Star-shaped Object in Three Fundamental Views.

4. Angled Cuts

Angled cuts work practically the same as the linear slopes. The "cut" shows up only on one of the fundamental views – usually the front view – of the object. Again, the trick is to consider the opposite outlines of the three fundamental views in order to determine the precise dimensions of the correct aperture.

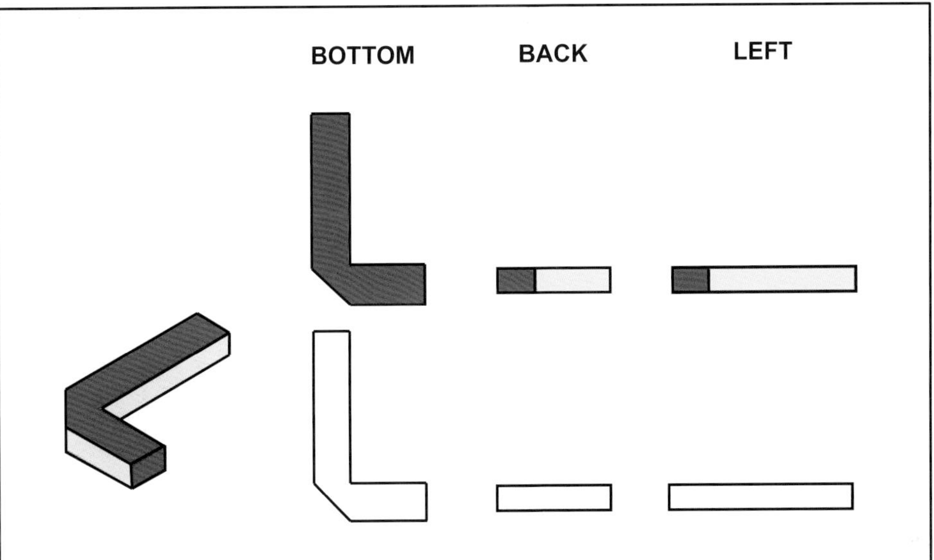

Figure 2.19: Object with an angled cut on its base. Take note that the slope does not show on the two views (front/back and right/left).

Now let's test the extent of your understanding and visual skills in assessing 3D objects in the Apertures test so far. The following are three typical questions that you will encounter in the PAT section. You can time yourself on every question in order to get a clear idea of your current level.

You have 40 seconds to complete each question in the PAT section, so you can give yourself 2 minutes to choose your answers for the 3 questions below. The three fundamental views and their outlines are provided in the answer key which follows on the next page.

If at the end of this short exercise, you still find the different objects to be confusing, please access the Lessons section of dat-prep.com for further explanations and exercises.

1.

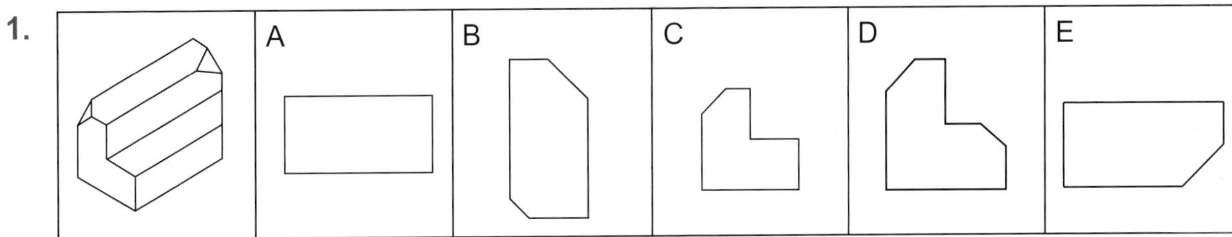

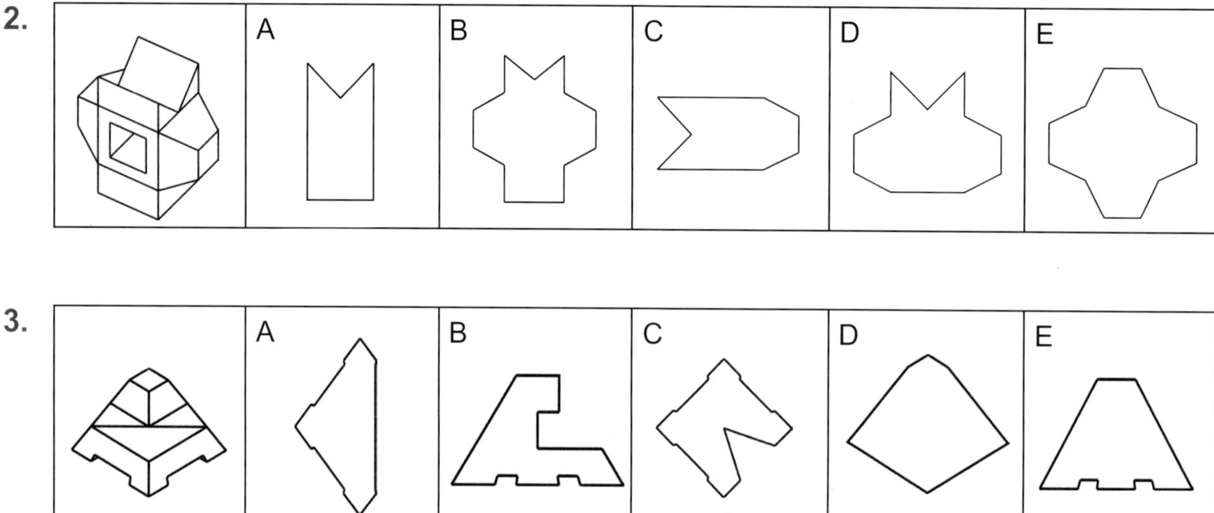
2.
A
B
C
D
E
3.
A
B
C
D
E

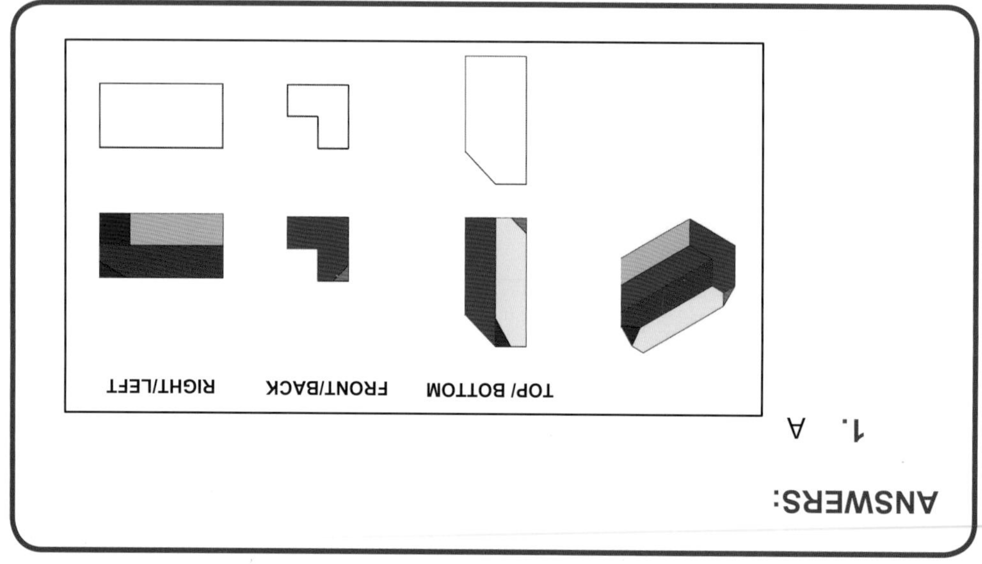
ANSWERS:
1. A
TOP/ BOTTOM
FRONT/BACK
RIGHT/LEFT

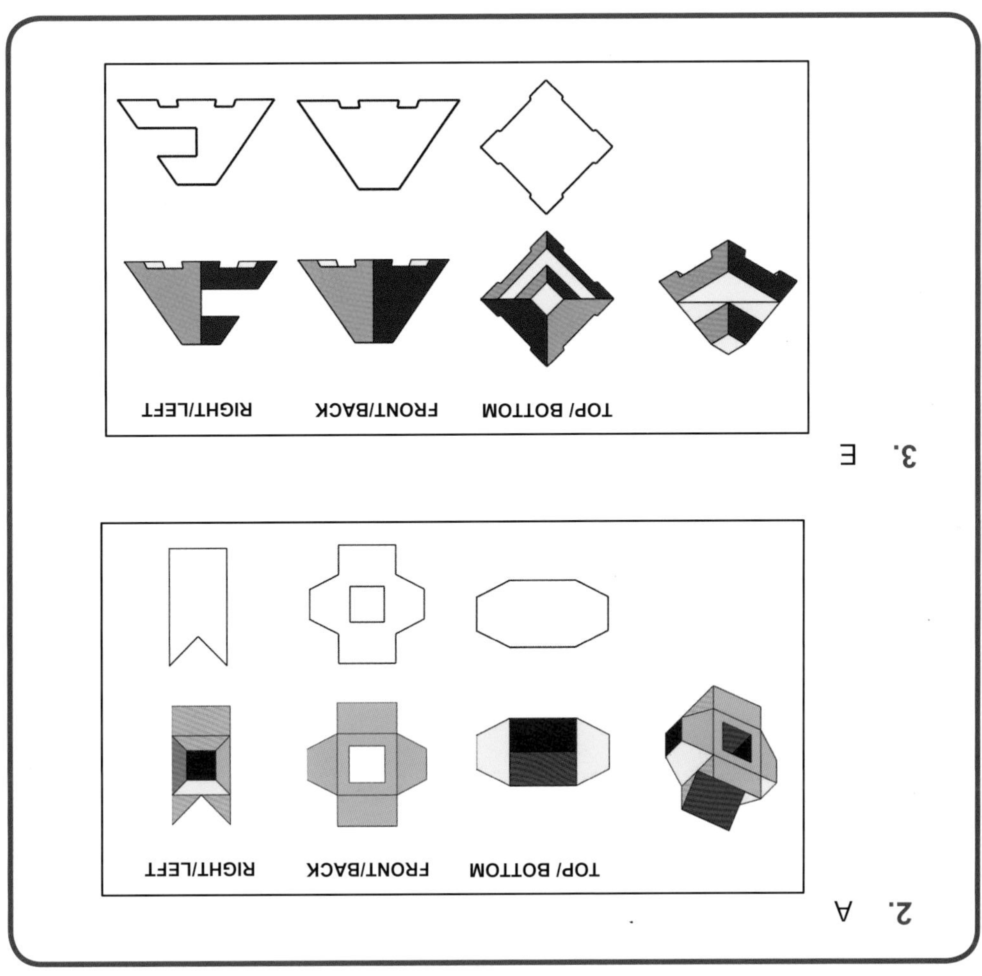
2. A
TOP/ BOTTOM
FRONT/BACK
RIGHT/LEFT
3. E
TOP/ BOTTOM
FRONT/BACK
RIGHT/LEFT

2.2.4 Perspectives and Distances

The three-dimensional objects given in the Apertures questions can be presented in a variety of perspectives. Neither technical knowledge nor in-depth understanding of the different types of perspectives is necessary. Nevertheless, you do need to grasp the basic concept that the size of an object becomes smaller as it moves away from view.

This is mostly true with certain parts of an object such as the protrusions, the slopes, and the holes. Some components may be partially covered such as the rectangle just below the square towering the object in Figure PAT 2.20. In other cases, the whole object itself can display a different contour or size than its actual appearance. In Figure PAT 2.21 for example, the cube, presented in what is called a "three-point perspective", can give an illusion that it could fit a hexagonal-shaped aperture.

Certainly, differences in perspective points can be confusing, and the best way to deal with this is to expose yourself to as much visual stimuli as you can lay your eyes on. You must be thorough but quick, and sharp but careful. Practice with DAT PAT-style questions as often and as regularly as you can.

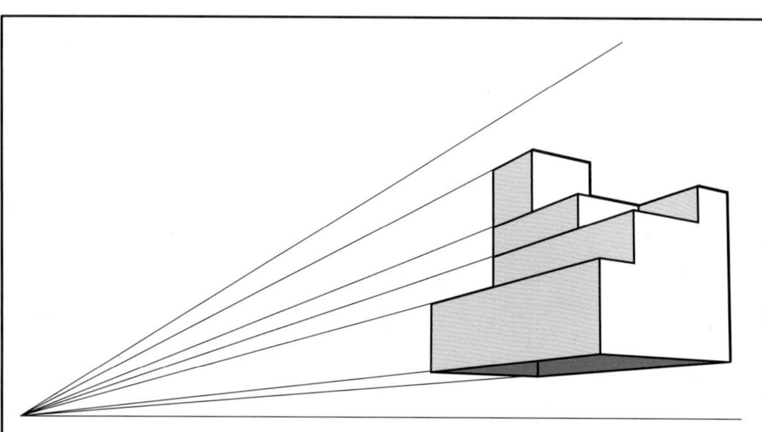

Figure PAT 2.20: Object in One-Point Perspective.

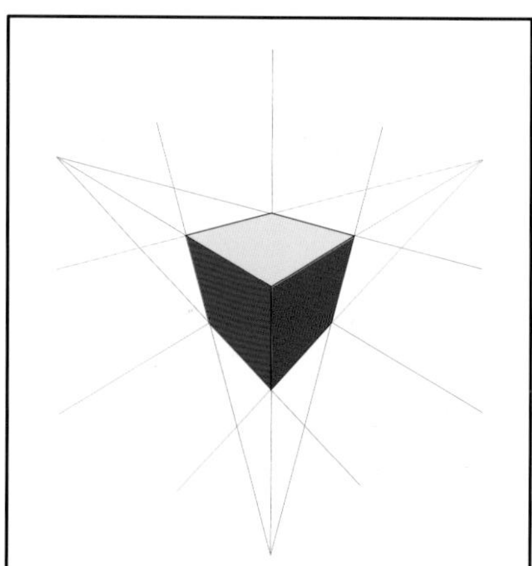

Figure PAT 2.21: Cube in Three-Point Perspective.

The next critical aspect of your preparation for the PAT Apertures is getting acquainted with its specific rules, which we will discuss in detail in the next section.

2.3 Understanding the Rules for PAT Apertures

Among the six subsections of the Perceptual Ability Test, only the Apertures have specific rules that dictate the manner by which you select the answer to each question. It is thus very important that you fully understand them and incorporate these into your strategies.

Rule 1. **Before performing the insertion into an aperture, the irregularly shaped object may be rotated in any direction. The object may be entered through the aperture on a side not shown in the question.**

This rule requires your knowledge and understanding of the six standard views and the three essential outlines as discussed in section 2.2. Moreover, while the rule does say that the object can be rotated in "any" direction, this is rather confusing because the solid object can only be inserted through the aperture in one of the three directions namely the top (or bottom), the front (or back) and the right (or left) sides. This is highly related to rule no. 2.

Rule 2. **Once the object is introduced to the opening, it should pass completely through the hole without further rotating the object in any direction.**

The most important thing to remember with this rule is that the correct aperture is always the exact shape of the object's outline. Rule number 3 explains this further.

Rule 3. **Both the three-dimensional object and its corresponding aperture are drawn to the same scale. It may be possible for one of the answer choices to have the correct shape yet be too small or too big for the object. However, the differences are large enough to be seen by the naked eye.**

Pay attention to proportions! The actual DAT stresses proportions more than anything else for this subsection. As soon as you set your eyes on the 3D object given in the question, start visualizing the outline of its three fundamental views. Make sure that one of these views corresponds to one of the "keyholes" presented. Do not forget that protruding elements are also part of the outline.

Most test center administrators are quite strict about enforcing the rules. Some students have managed to use their marker or a finger as rough "rulers" to assess proportions. Of course, we cannot recommend such a technique.

Rule 4. **No irregularities are hidden in any portion of the object. In case the figure has indentations, the hidden portion would be symmetric with the visible part.**

In section 2.2, we have discussed that each view is assumed to mirror the outline of its opposite side. While a hole or a protrusion on one side of the view would usually be reflected on its reverse part, there are cases, such as with the concave slopes and the angled cuts in section 2.2.3 for example, when the irregular portion may prove irrelevant in considering the outline of the object. Figure PAT 2.22 makes a very simple illustration of this rule.

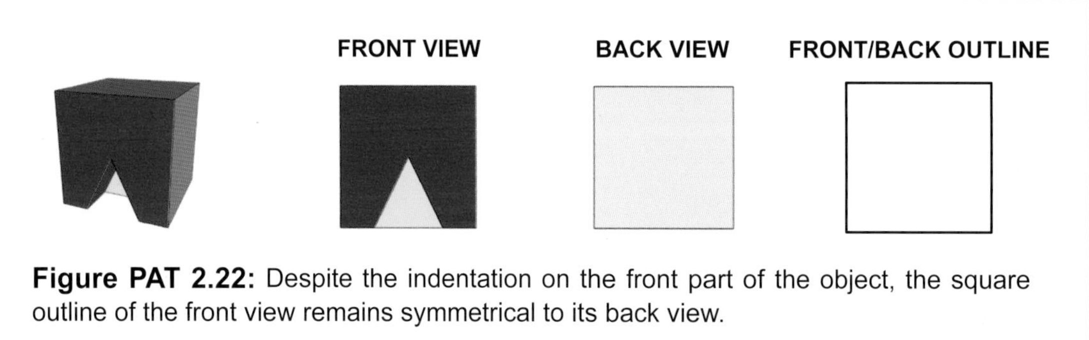

Figure PAT 2.22: Despite the indentation on the front part of the object, the square outline of the front view remains symmetrical to its back view.

Rule 5. **For each question, only one aperture matches the exact shape and size of one of the two-dimensional views of the object.**

This rule may be quite obvious, but several questions on the DAT have two almost identical answer choices. Your ability to spot the tiny details such as the exact shape of one of the edges and the direction of the slants is a critical skill that must be developed.

2.3.1 Applying the Rules

Now that we have analyzed each rule in this PAT subsection, let us try applying them with the following example:

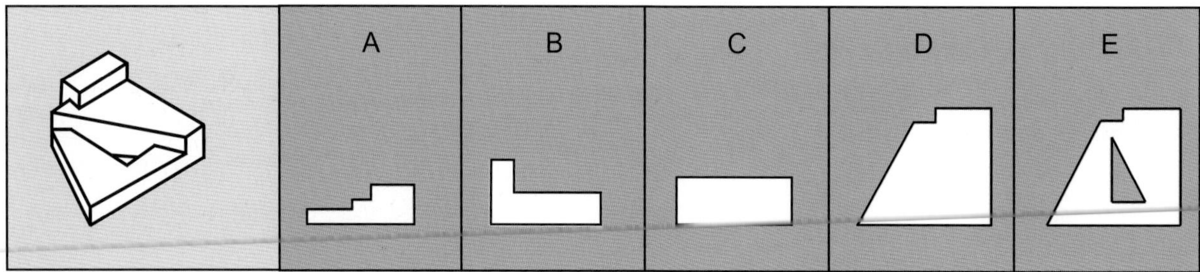

Step 1. Find the outlines of the object from the three fundamental views.

There are three sides of the object that are visible: the TOP, FRONT and SIDE VIEWS as shown in Figure 1. Remember that you need not worry about the hidden sides since according to Rule 4, no irregularities are hidden in the object. If ever the figure would have symmetric indentations, the hidden portion would be symmetric with the visible part (See figure 2).

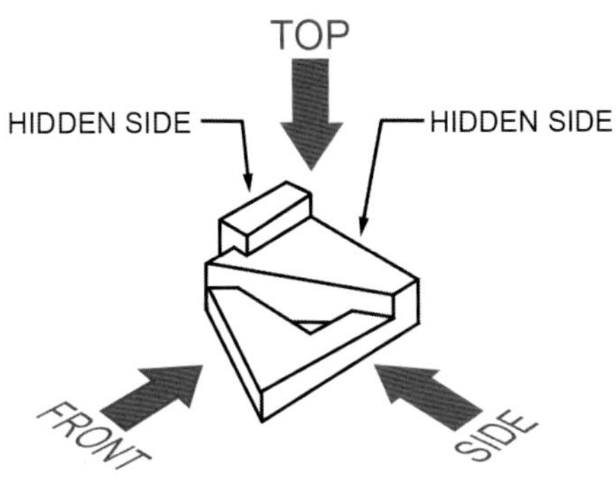

Figure 1

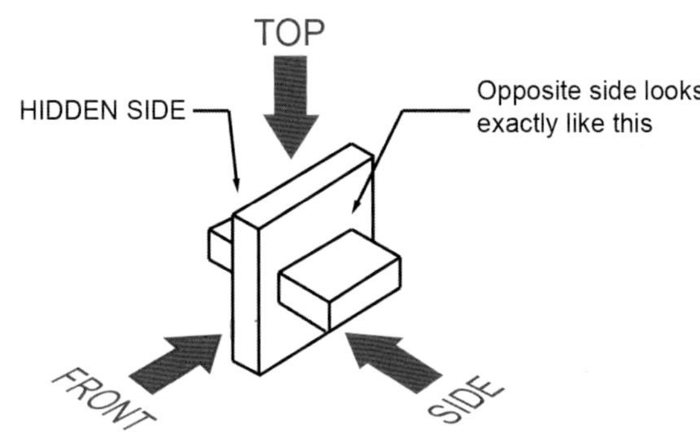

Figure 2. Symmetrical Object

Imagine how the object looks like when viewed from the three different points. This is to distinguish the outlines of the object. Do not get confused by the other parts of the object. Focus on the outlines.

Figure 3 shows the object from Figure 1 when viewed from each point.

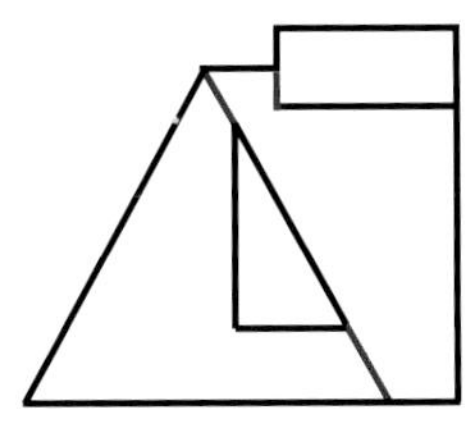

Fig. 3a. Top View

Fig. 3b. Front View

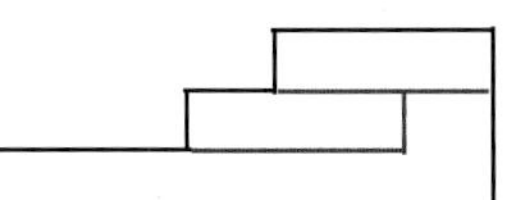

Fig. 3c. Side View

Figure 3

Figure 4 shows the outlines only of the object when viewed from each point.

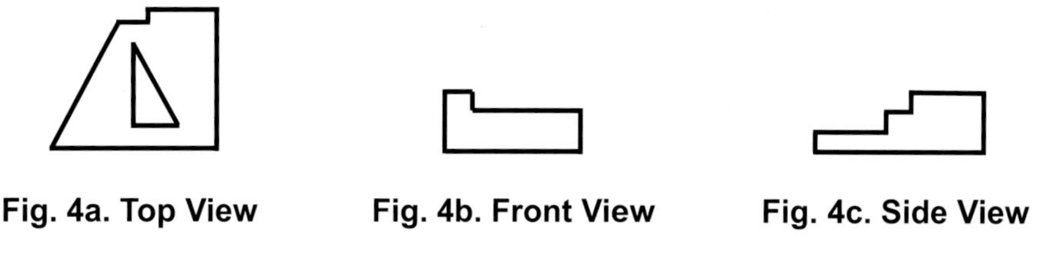

Fig. 4a. Top View **Fig. 4b. Front View** **Fig. 4c. Side View**

Figure 4

Step 2. Find the correct aperture from the given options.

Let us start by trying the outline of the side view. Only one choice from the **side** view's outline may fit – this is aperture A.

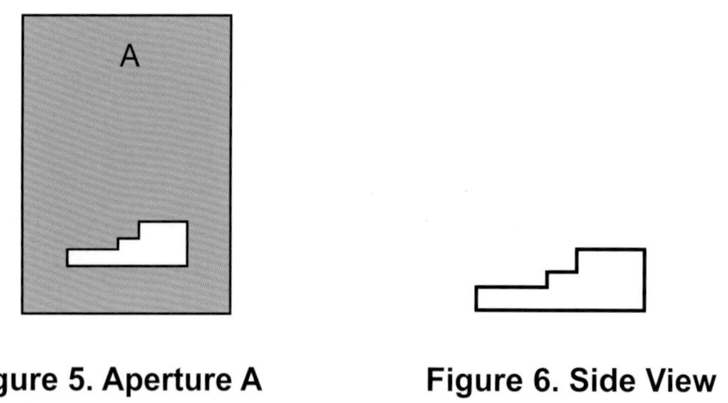

Figure 5. Aperture A **Figure 6. Side View**

Aperture A (Figure 5) looks exactly like the side view outline (Figure 6) but obviously smaller, so this is not the correct answer according to Rule 3.

Next let us try the **front** view outline. Only one choice fits – this is aperture B.

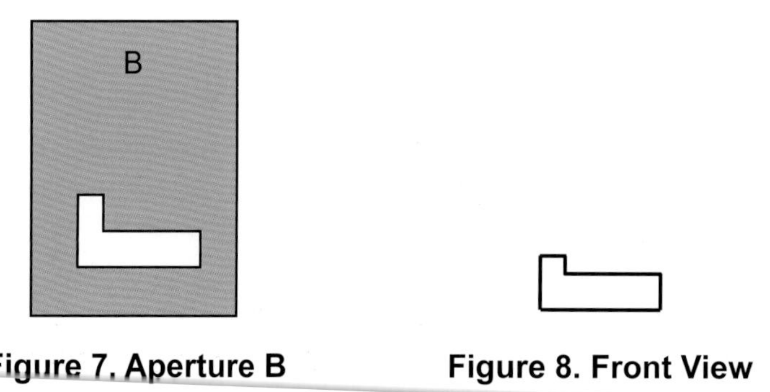

Figure 7. Aperture B **Figure 8. Front View**

Aperture B (Figure 7) looks close to the front view outline (Figure 8) but there is obviously a slight difference in the upper left part, so this is still not the correct answer.

Let us try the last option, which is the **top** view outline. Two possible choices seem to match the top view outline. These are apertures D and E.

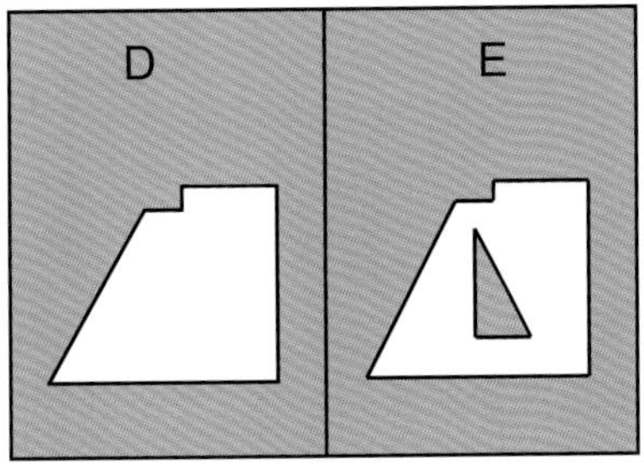

Figure 9. Aperture D and E

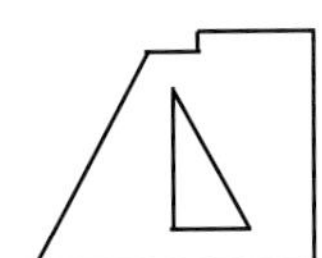

Figure 10. Top View

The top view outline shows a hole in the center but regardless of whether a hole is there or not, the object will fit to both apertures D and E. You might argue that in this question, two answers are possible. This is not possible because Rule 5 clearly states that only one aperture is correct for each object. In a case like this, the aperture that can accommodate all the features of the object should be the answer. Therefore, the best answer is E.

Remember that the object can pass through aperture E if the bottom is inserted first. If aperture E is oriented in a reversed direction as illustrated in Figure 11, the object will still pass through the aperture if the top is inserted first.

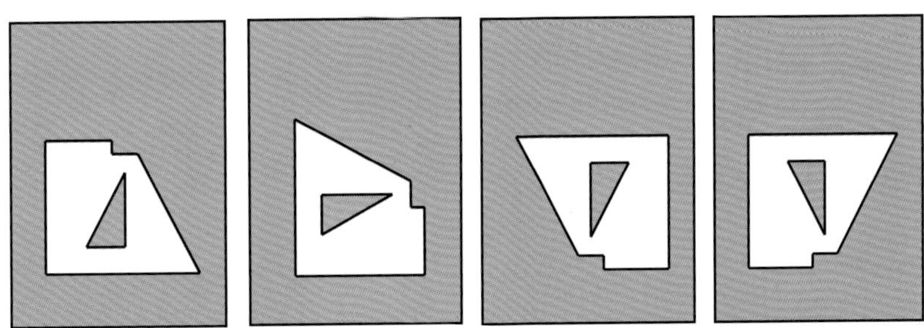

Figure 11. Aperture E is still the correct answer if it looks like these.

Both of these two options of aperture E may also be rotated in any direction. Remember therefore, that some or all of the choices in the actual test may be rotated.

REMINDER: Everything should be done as quickly as possible with approximately 40 seconds to answer each question.

Now let's try with a few more exercises to help you apply the different strategies and rules, which we have discussed in this chapter.

2.4 Mini Exercises

1. This object is made up of basic shapes and requires you to pay attention to proportions.

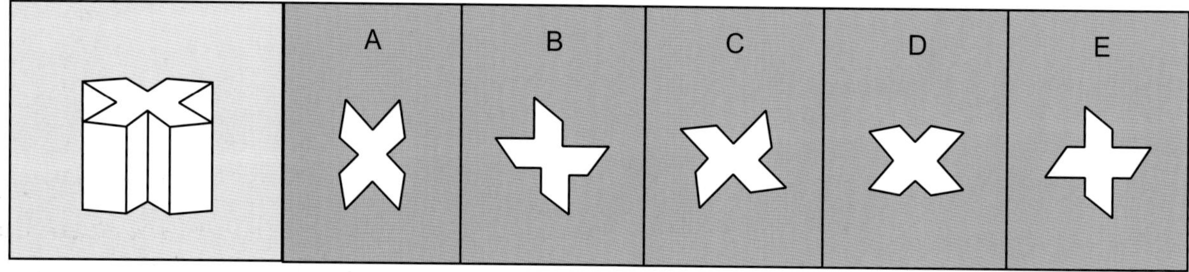

2. This object has attachments or components with basic shapes but requires you to consider the rotated or mirrored view.

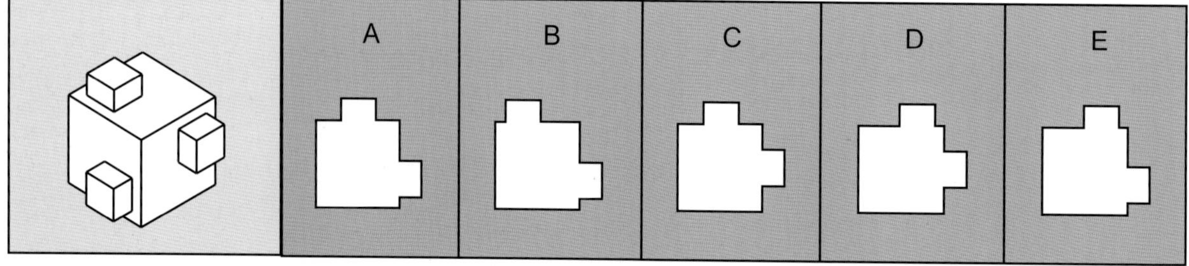

3. The shape of the object looks complex, and the options require you to pay attention to the proportions, as well as consider the rotated or mirrored views.

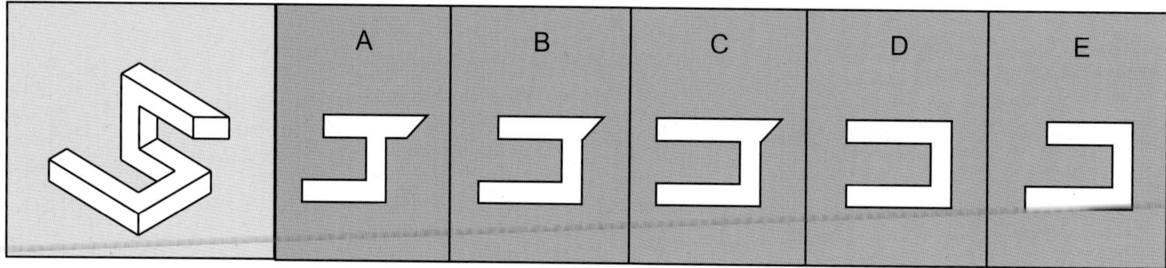

4.

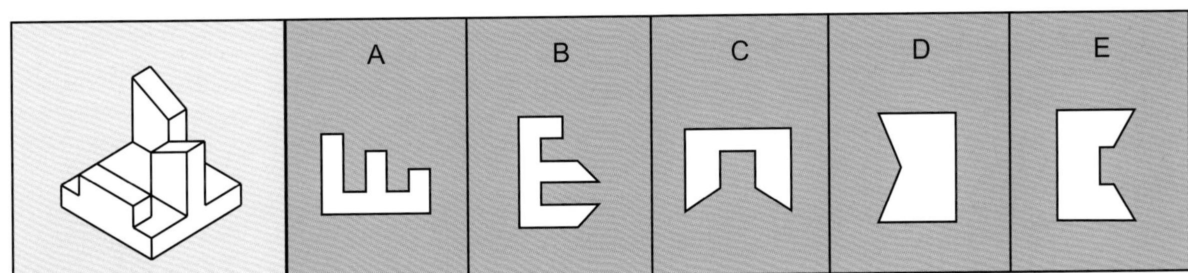

2.4.1 Answer Key and Explanations

1. Answer: A

The aperture in this question resembles the letter X. You need to concentrate on this basic shape, which is the largest surface of the 3D figure. Only A and D most resemble the letter X. The only difference between the two is that option D is smaller in size and its inner edges are smaller compared to the figure. Instantly, you know that A is the right answer.

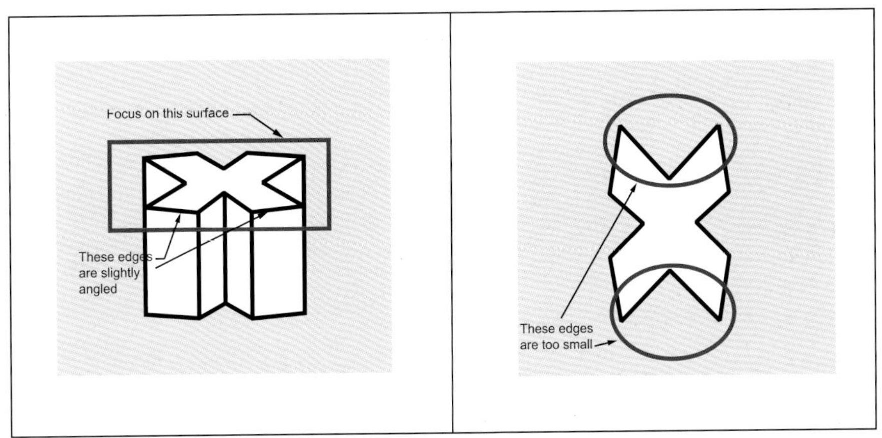

2. Answer: E

All of the options are viewed from a single direction: the left view (mirror image of the right side view). The main differences between the given apertures are the distances of the attached small cubes, so you only need to focus on these. Notice that the cubes are not centered but are placed near the edges of the big cube.

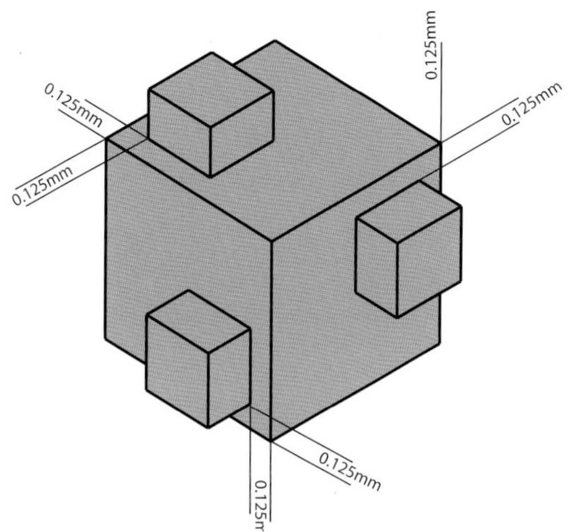
0.125mm
0.125mm
0.125mm
0.125mm
0.125mm
0.125m

By comparing each option to the 3D figure, you will easily identify that A is wrong because the small cube on top is positioned at the center. Options C and D are also incorrect because the cubes on the side are both located at the center. The upper cube of B is way too far from the edge adjacent to the face where the side cube is located; thus, incorrect. This leaves option E as the right answer.

3. Answer: B

All of the choices in this question are viewed from one direction: the top view. You can simply proceed to comparing each option to the 3D figure. Option A has shorter components therefore, wrong. B follows the outline of the object's top view: the upper arm is shorter than the lower arm; the pointed edge is shown. B is the correct answer.

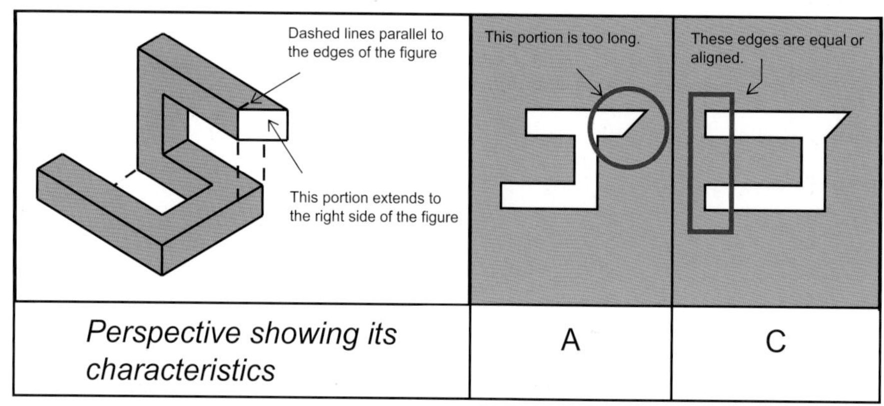
Dashed lines parallel to the edges of the figure
This portion extends to the right side of the figure
This portion is too long.
These edges are equal or aligned.
Perspective showing its characteristics
A
C

Options C and D are both incorrect because all portions of the aperture are aligned or equal in length. E does not have the angled extension and therefore, incorrect.

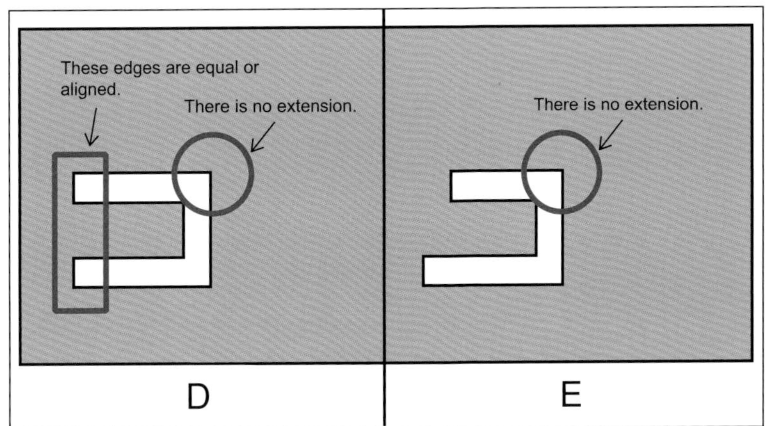

4. Answer: E

This is a complicated looking figure so you need to study it carefully. Take note of the height of the components, which are like towers; the distance of these towers from one another; and the thickness of the square base.

The best strategy here is the process of elimination. Option A is viewed from the left side. However, it shows the wrong aperture because the two taller towers should be equal in height. B is also incorrect because the sloping edges should be

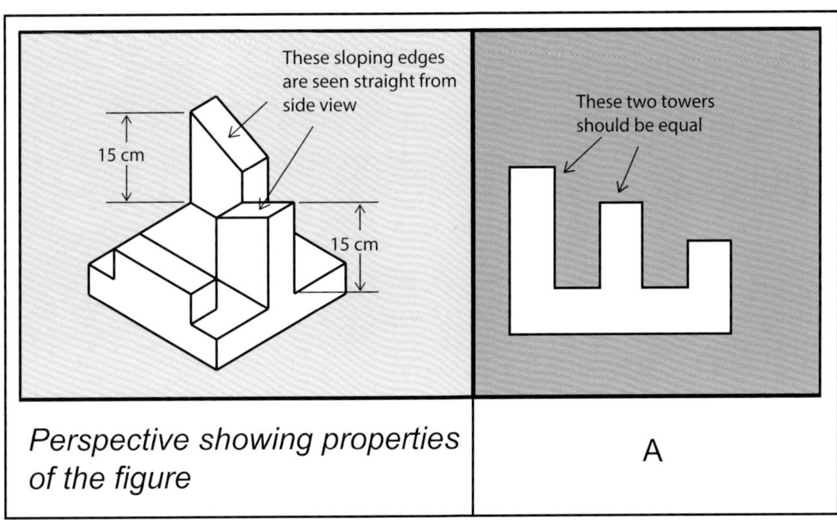

Perspective showing properties of the figure

seen as straight from the right side view. Option C might have the correct taller towers from the front view, but the small tower/protrusion is not considered. Thus it is wrong. The sloping edges in option D are too wide, which makes this a wrong answer as well. The only option left is E (taken from the front view and rotated 90 degrees clockwise) and thus the correct answer.

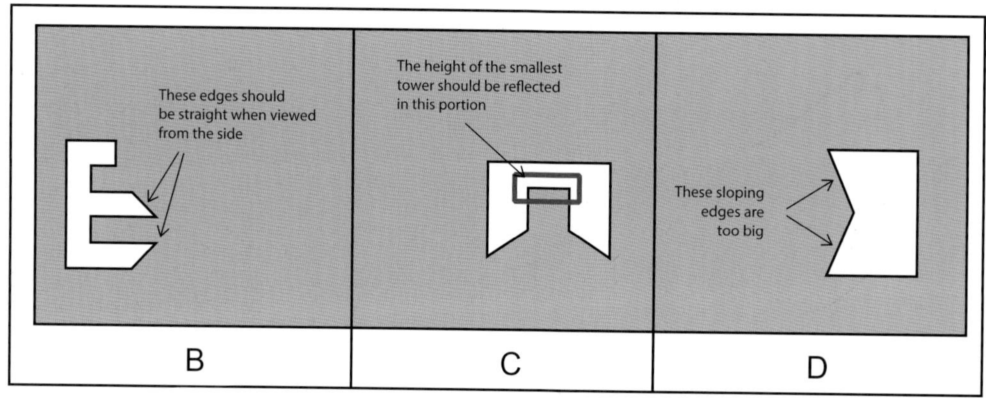
These edges should be straight when viewed from the side
The height of the smallest tower should be reflected in this portion
These sloping edges are too big
B
C
D

GOLD STANDARD WARM-UP EXERCISES

CHAPTER 2: Apertures

The following questions represent one of the six subsections in the Perceptual Ability Test of the DAT. While this serves as a review of the discussions in this chapter, the level of difficulty of each question closely parallels the actual test.

You have 10 minutes to complete this portion of the DAT Mini Test; the actual test is 60 minutes.

Please time yourself accordingly.

BEGIN ONLY WHEN YOUR TIMER IS READY

1.

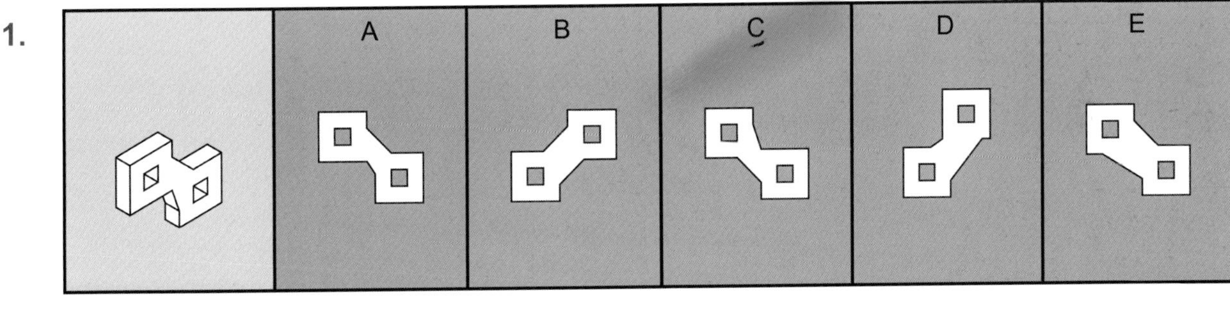

2.

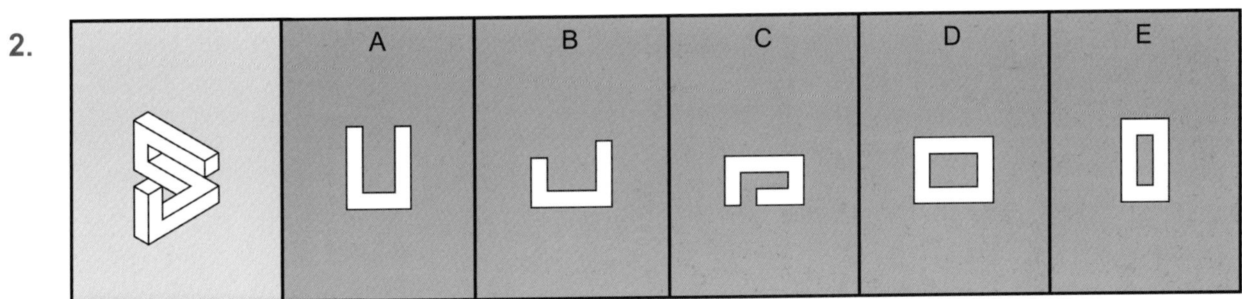

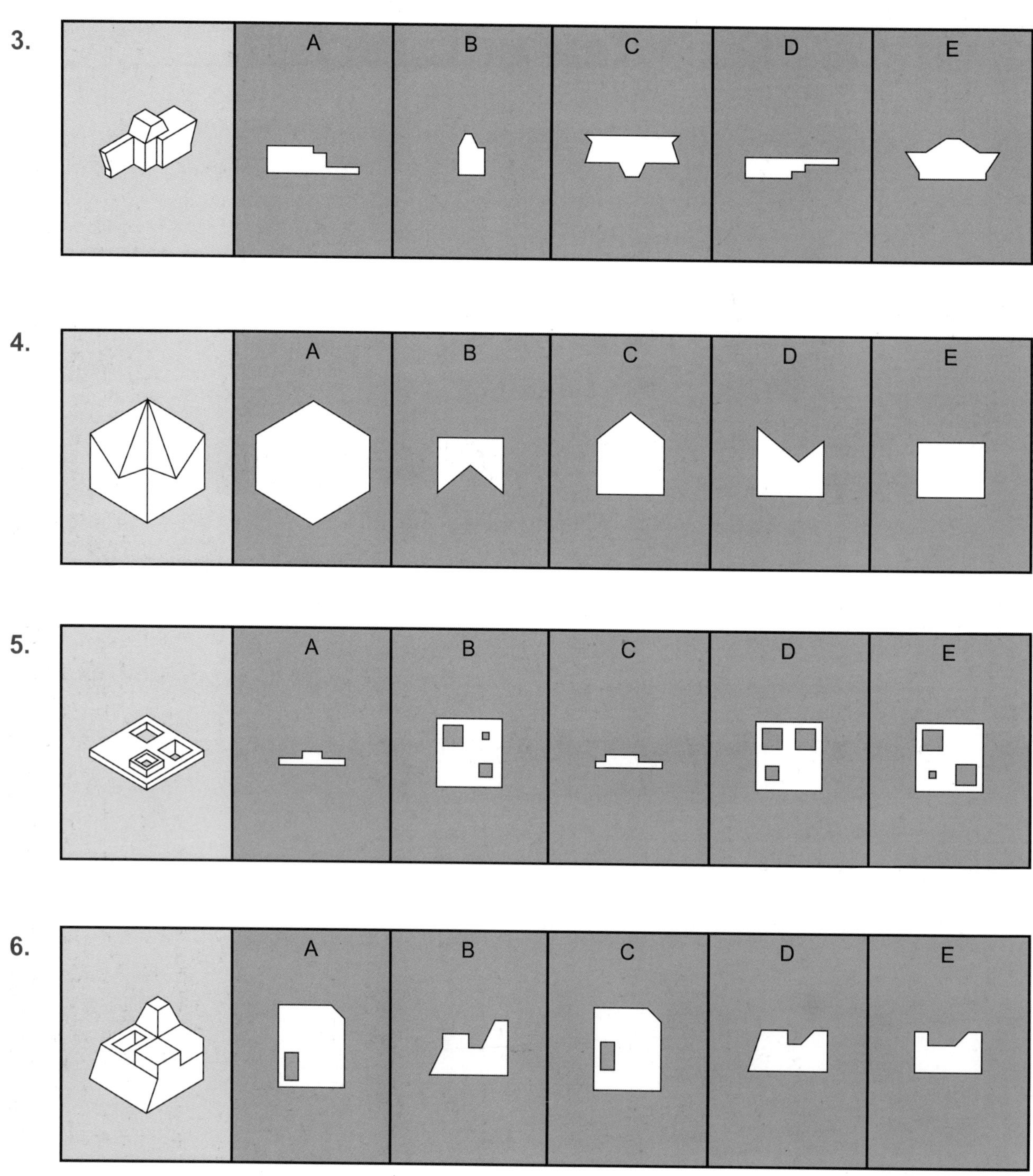
3.
A
B
C
D
E
4.
A
B
C
D
E
5.
A
B
C
D
E
6.
A
B
C
D
E

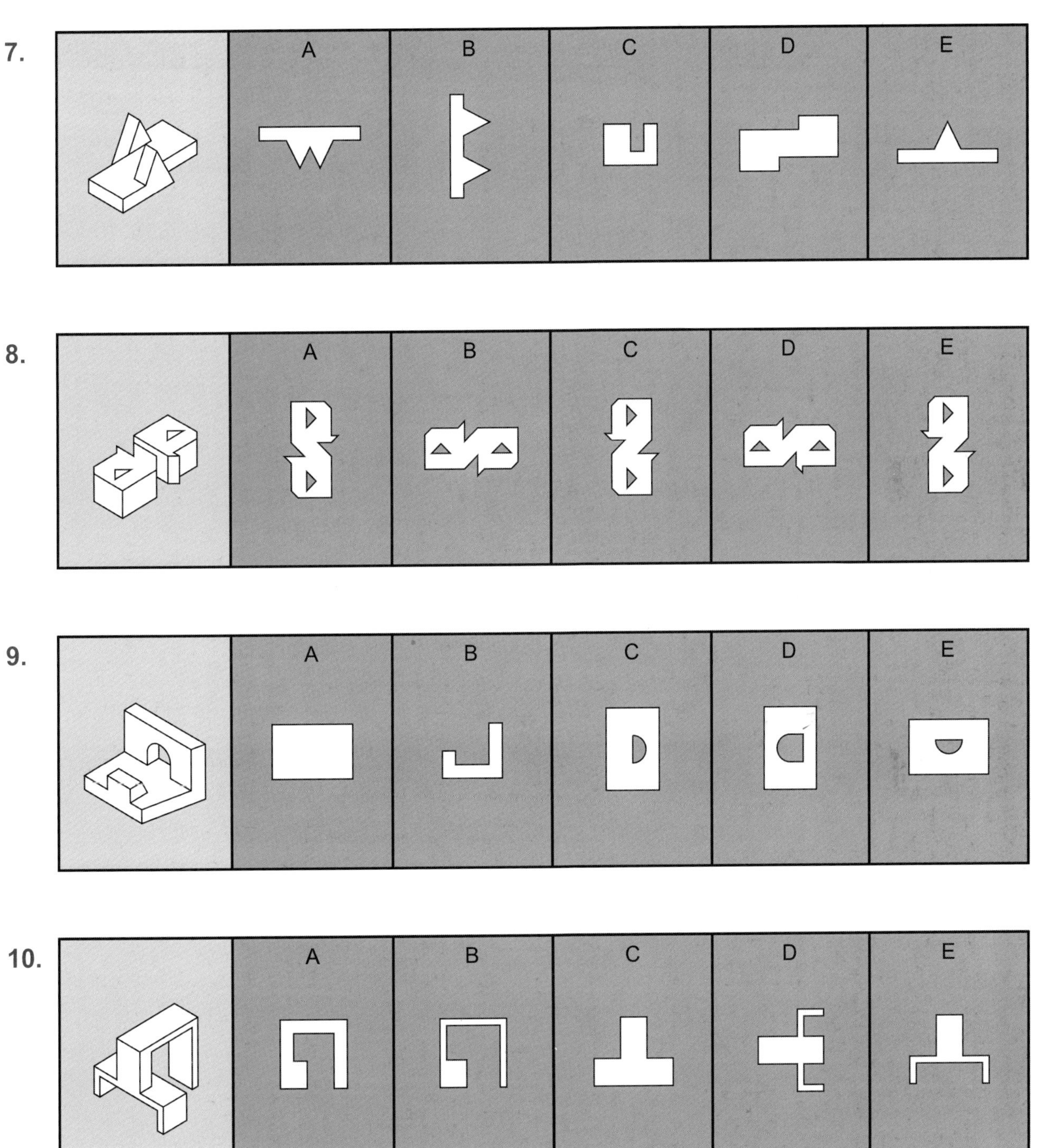
7.
A
B
C
D
E
8.
A
B
C
D
E
9.
A
B
C
D
E
10.
A
B
C
D
E

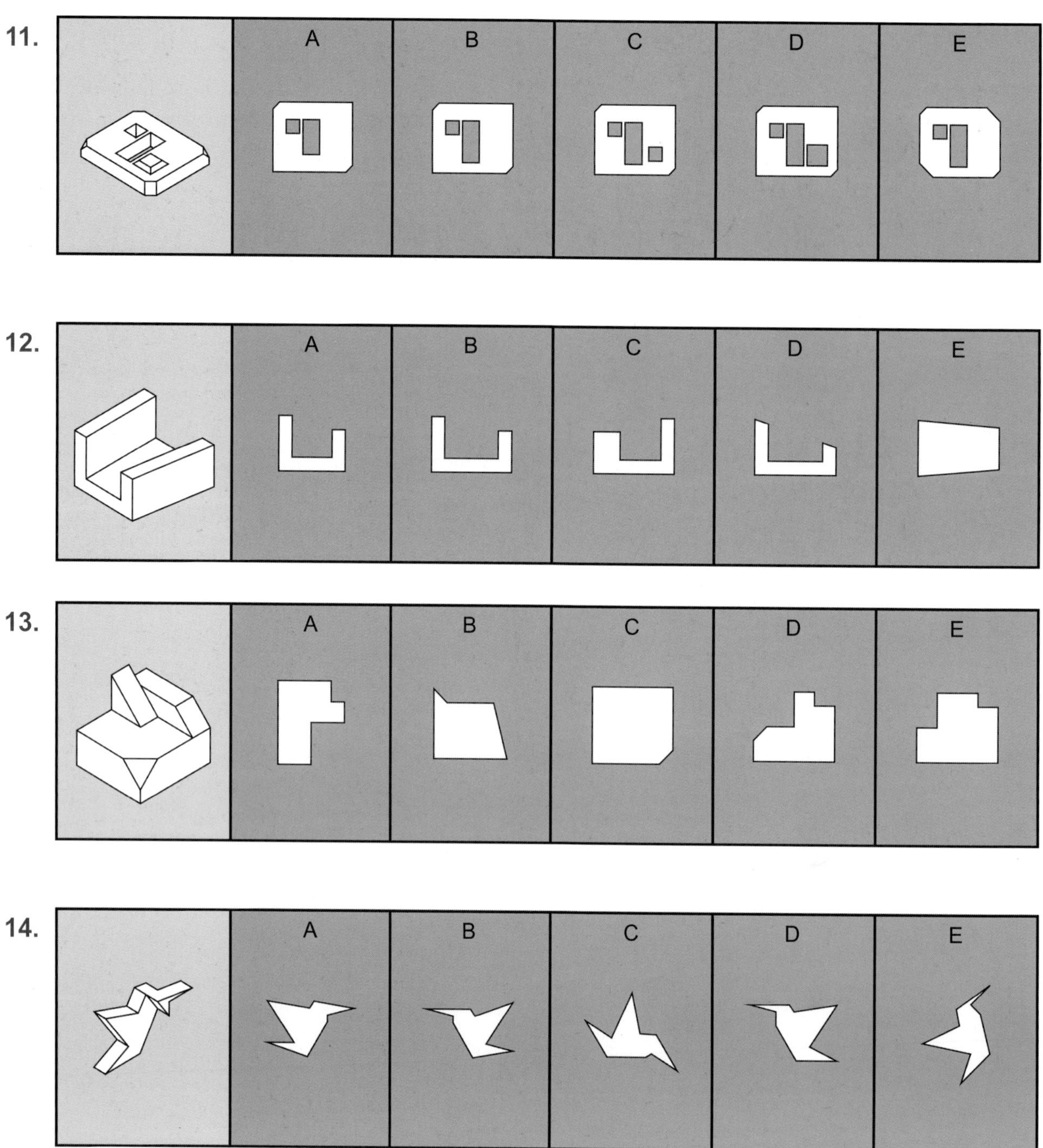
11.
A
B
C
D
E
12.
A
B
C
D
E
13.
A
B
C
D
E
14.
A
B
C
D
E

15.

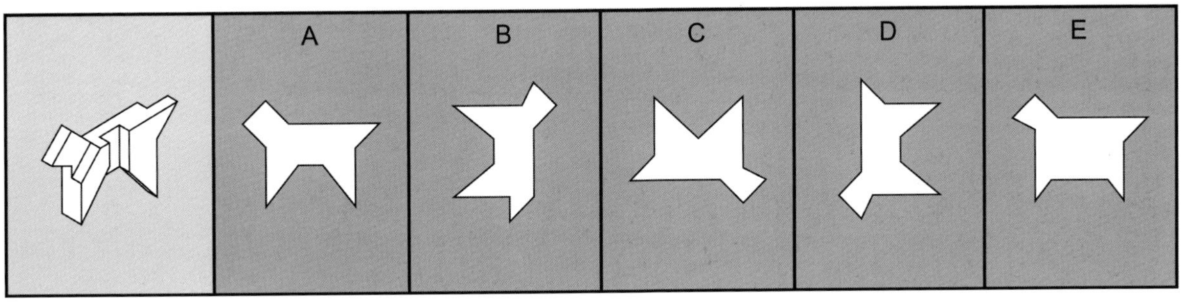

	A	B	C	D	E

If time remains, you may review your work. If your allotted time is complete, please proceed to the Answer Key.

GS ANSWER KEY

CHAPTER 2

1.	A	9.	C
2.	E	10.	D
3.	A	11.	B
4.	E	12.	C
5.	B	13.	A
6.	C	14.	E
7.	A	15.	D
8.	E		

* Explanations can be found in the Lessons section at www.dat-prep.com.

Go online to DAT-prep.com for additional chapter review Q&A and forum.

Go online to DAT-prep.com for additional chapter review Q&A and forum.

ORTHOGRAPHIC PROJECTION

Chapter 3

Understand

* Orthographic Projection
* The Projection Grid
* Hidden Lines

Introduction

An orthographic projection is a representation of a three-dimensional object in flat or two-dimensional perspectives: usually the top, front and right side (end) views. The top view would often indicate the width and depth of the object; the front view, its height and width; and the end view, its depth and height. This second section of the PAT is essentially a view recognition test - the views are orthographic projections. For practical reasons, students commonly refer to this section as the TFE (Top/Front/End) Section.

In the drawing, solid lines represent the edges hence the object's skeletal shape. Dotted lines signify a hidden edge, also known as a hidden line, denoting that either a folded or an extended part of the object exists but becomes invisible from a two-dimensional view. Therefore, this section demands your scrutiny to compare, contrast, and to logically match the adjacent solid and dotted lines.

Additional Resources

Free Online Forum

3.1 About the View Recognition Test

Most DAT candidates refer to the View Recognition test as the Top/Front/End (TFE) section. In this PAT subsection, three-dimensional objects are represented in their detailed two-dimensional forms through the three standard views, namely the top view, front view, and end view (this time, the "right view" is identified as the "end view").

This test assesses your ability to translate the two-dimensional views of a 3D object and mentally reconstruct the object in its entirety. Each question will show two out of the three possible projections of the 3D object. Your task is to determine the missing view.

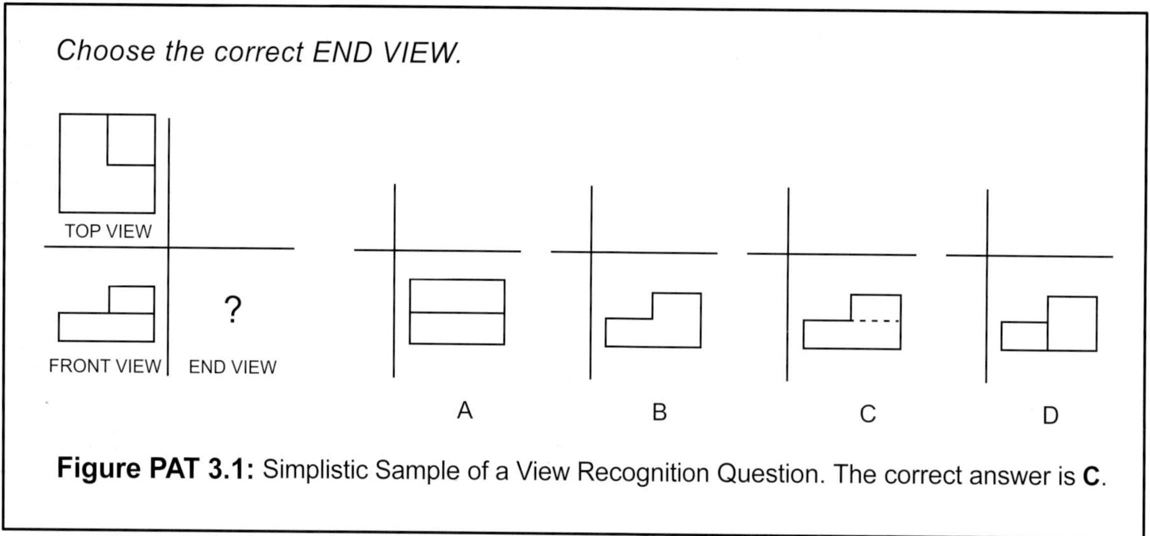

Figure PAT 3.1: Simplistic Sample of a View Recognition Question. The correct answer is **C**.

Visualizations in the View Recognition test are very much similar to the Apertures section. Both require your acute perception of the three fundamental views. The main difference is that with View Recognition, you must now consider the details – not just the outlines – of the objects including the holes and the edges of surfaces, which may not be directly visible in a particular view because they are behind another surface. These hidden details are indicated by dotted lines. Solid lines, on the other hand, signify edges that can be directly seen from that specific view.

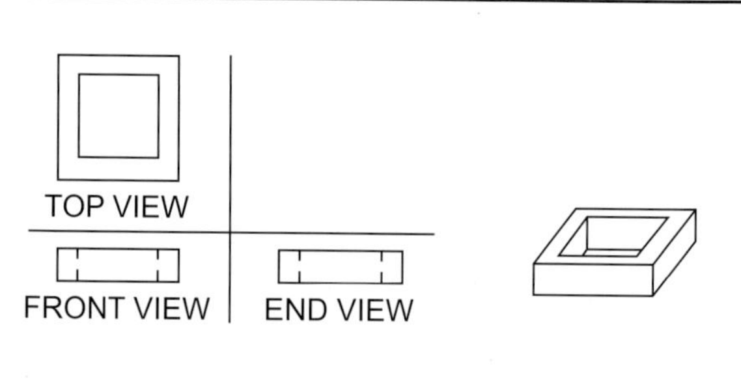

Figure PAT 3.2: Top, Front, and End Views of an Object with Hidden Edges. The dotted lines on the front and end views represent the intersections of the surfaces of the square cavity behind the outer surfaces of the object.

3.2 Understanding Orthographic Projection

A common approach to this test involves matching the lines in each of the given views to the lines or edges of the correct figure among the answer choices. Adopting this method entails a clear understanding of how the three different views in the drawing relate to the actual 3D object that they symbolize. Let us start by getting a good grasp of what View Recognition is really all about.

Technically, view recognition is known as *orthographic projection*. Orthographic projection is a means of drawing an object as viewed in at least three different directions in order to help a person visualize what the individual parts look like. The most common views presented in orthographic drawings are the top, front, and end (right side) views. A better way to comprehend the principles of orthographic projection is to imagine an object being placed in a glass cube with its surface reflected (i.e. projected) onto the crystal faces of the cube.

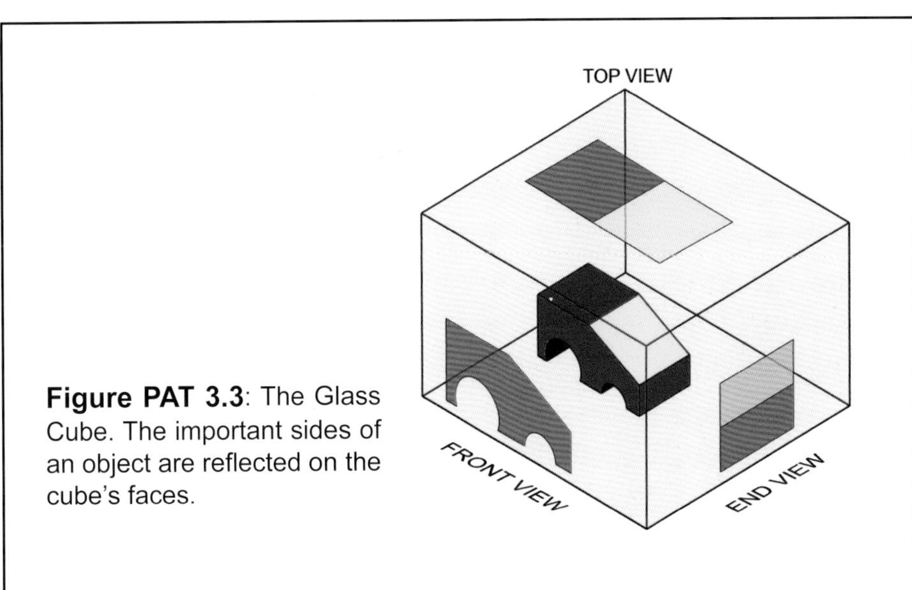

Figure PAT 3.3: The Glass Cube. The important sides of an object are reflected on the cube's faces.

Imagine unfolding the cube so that the three views of the object can now be seen on the same plane.

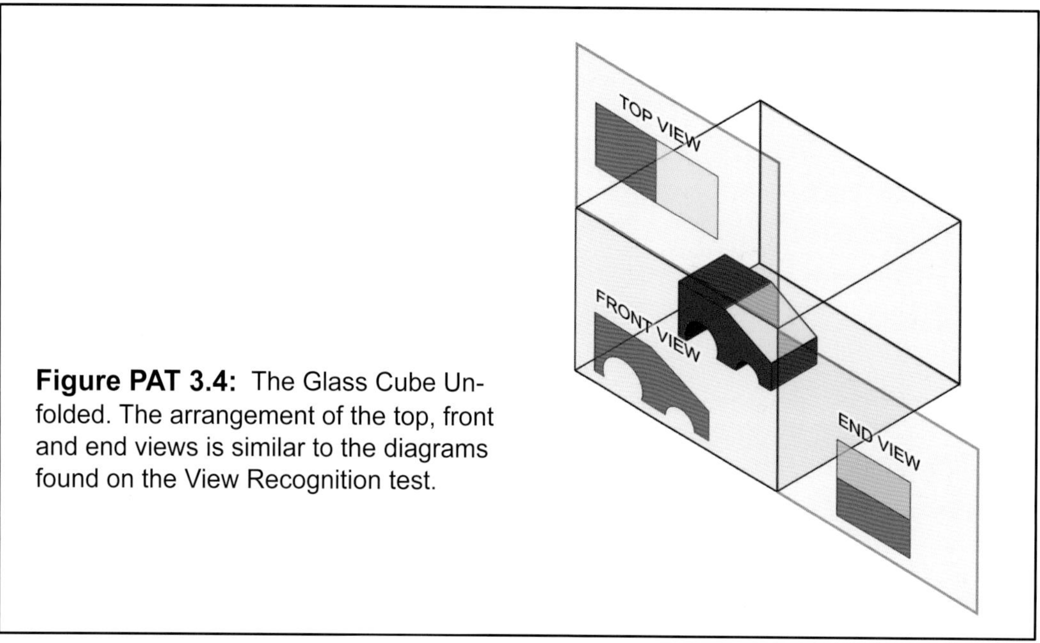

Figure PAT 3.4: The Glass Cube Unfolded. The arrangement of the top, front and end views is similar to the diagrams found on the View Recognition test.

Now that the glass cube is unfolded, the three views should be able to exhibit the following characteristics:

1. The **front view** shows the **width** and **height** dimensions of the object.
2. The **top view** shows the **width** and **depth** dimensions of the object.
3. The **end view** shows the **height** and **depth** dimensions of the object.
4. **Each view** is relatively **aligned to the other views**: the top view parallels vertically with the front view and share the same width dimension, in the same manner that the front view aligns horizontally with the end view and share the same height dimension.

Paying attention to the proportions of the figures from the given views and the answer choices is indeed a logical approach to this test. Oftentimes, options will only vary in the sizes or lengths of an edge or a line. You should thus reinforce this technique with a systematic procedure in interpreting the orthographic representations. We will discuss some of these in the succeeding sections.

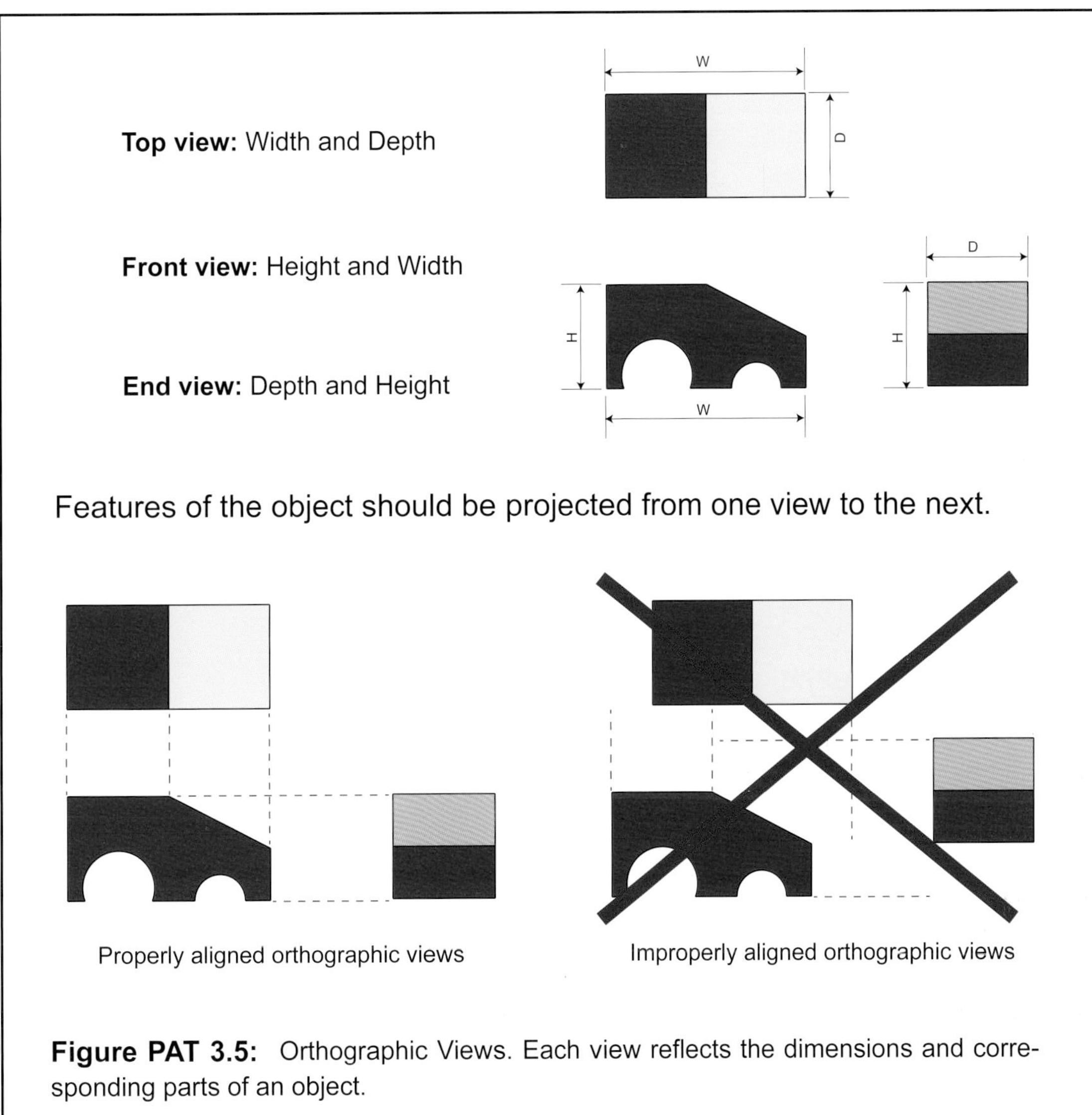

Top view: Width and Depth
Front view: Height and Width
End view: Depth and Height
W
D
H
Features of the object should be projected from one view to the next.
Properly aligned orthographic views
Improperly aligned orthographic views

Figure PAT 3.5: Orthographic Views. Each view reflects the dimensions and corresponding parts of an object.

3.3 How to Find the Missing Views

Identifying one of the orthographic (two-dimensional) views presented in the test necessitates recognizing the shape of the actual three-dimensional object. This skill takes time and regular, structured practice to develop. Nonetheless, one effective method that you can adopt is constructing a projection grid of the two given views in order to determine the form of the third view.

3.3.1 The Projection Grid

This method requires that you draw construction lines that will function as your guide in establishing the features of the missing view. All lines from the intersections and corners of the two views must be extended on the missing spot of the quadrant.

1. To find the FRONT VIEW

Extend all vertical lines from the top view and all horizontal lines from the end view, including those from the dotted lines, and allow them to cross each other on the front view. Spot the intersections and mark them.

1. All solid and dotted lines and intersections projected downwards should be aligned with any tips, edges and intersections of the object on the front view.
2. All horizontal solid and dotted lines as well as intersections projected from the end view, which may intersect with the vertical lines from the top, can be the significant corners and intersections of the front view.
3. Angled lines viewed from the top may also be a hint for an inclination on the front view.
4. Hidden edges or lines covered by any solid line may no longer be viewed as dotted lines but as a solid line from the front view.

TOP VIEW

?

FRONT VIEW

END VIEW

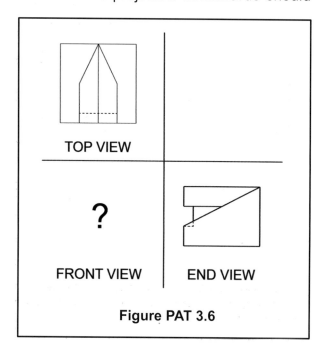

Figure PAT 3.6

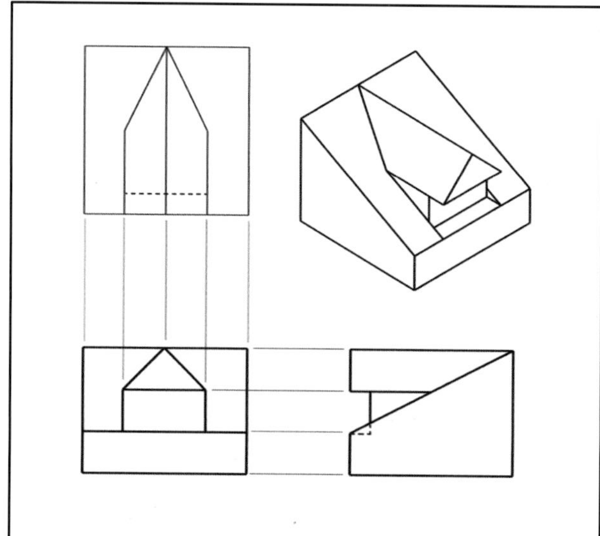

Figure PAT 3.6-A: Sketch the top and side views and make projections as shown.

Keep in mind that the front view, among the three 2D views, shows the most characteristics of an object. Usually, this view contains the least amount of hidden lines.

2. To find the TOP VIEW

In doing the projections for the top view, it is necessary that you mark the main intersections by locating the lines from the front to the end view. For example, mark only the intersection created by the center and outermost lines from the front with that of the end view.

1. Rotate the end view 90 degrees counterclockwise.
2. Vertical lines – both solid and dotted lines – from the front view should be projected upwards. Intersection points should also be extended as vertical lines in the projection.
3. All solid and dotted lines, as well as intersections from the end view should be projected horizontally to the left.
4. The intersections created from these lines should serve as your guide in determining the corners and edges of the top view.
5. Most lines from the inner portion of the end view figure become hidden on the top view. Lines coming from the right area of the end view become the upper portion of the top view.

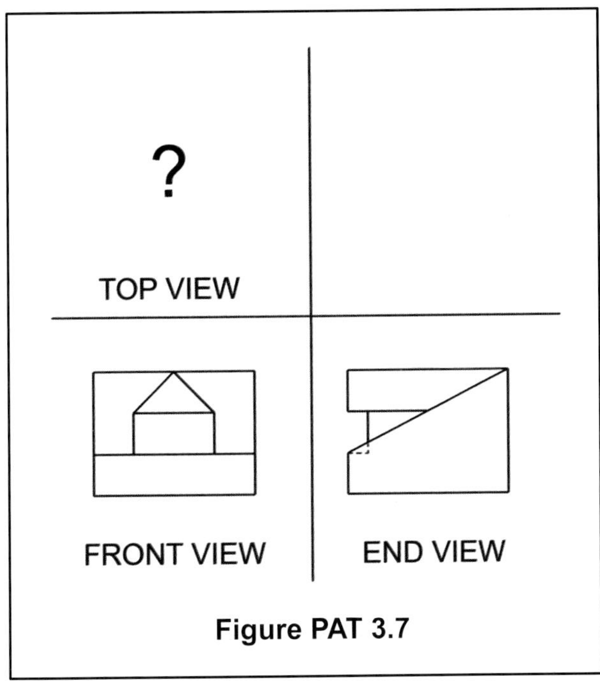

Figure PAT 3.7

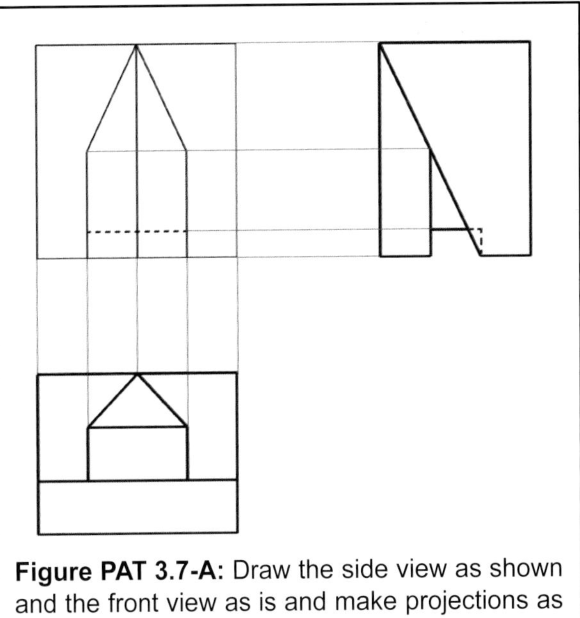

Figure PAT 3.7-A: Draw the side view as shown and the front view as is and make projections as shown.

3. To find the END VIEW

1. Rotate the top view 90 degrees clockwise.
2. The upper part of the top view will now become the right part of the end view.
3. The intersections of the vertical lines from the rotated top view and the horizontal lines from the front view are crucial.

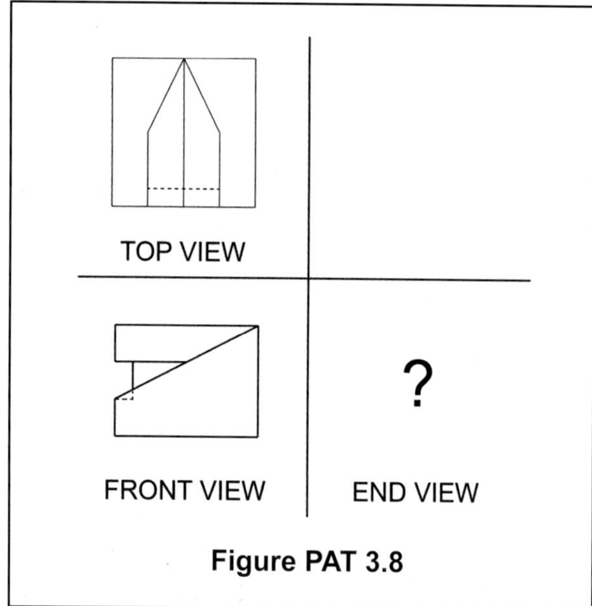

Figure PAT 3.8

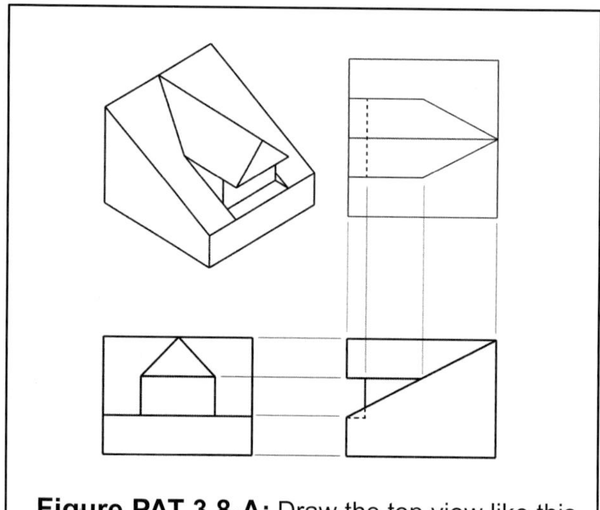
Figure PAT 3.8-A: Draw the top view like this and the front view as is and make projections as shown.

Please note that this method may take time in the beginning. The key is to practice consistently so that you will eventually become comfortable with the various steps and concepts of creating projections. In the meantime, let's try applying this approach to the sample question from Figure 3.1.

Choose the correct END VIEW.

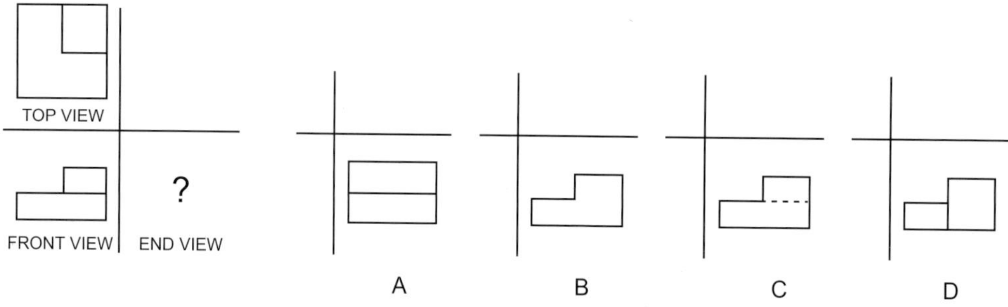

From the given views, the top figure shows that within the square is a smaller square located on the upper right. On the front view, the smaller rectangle, also located at the upper right, is about half the size of the bigger rectangle.

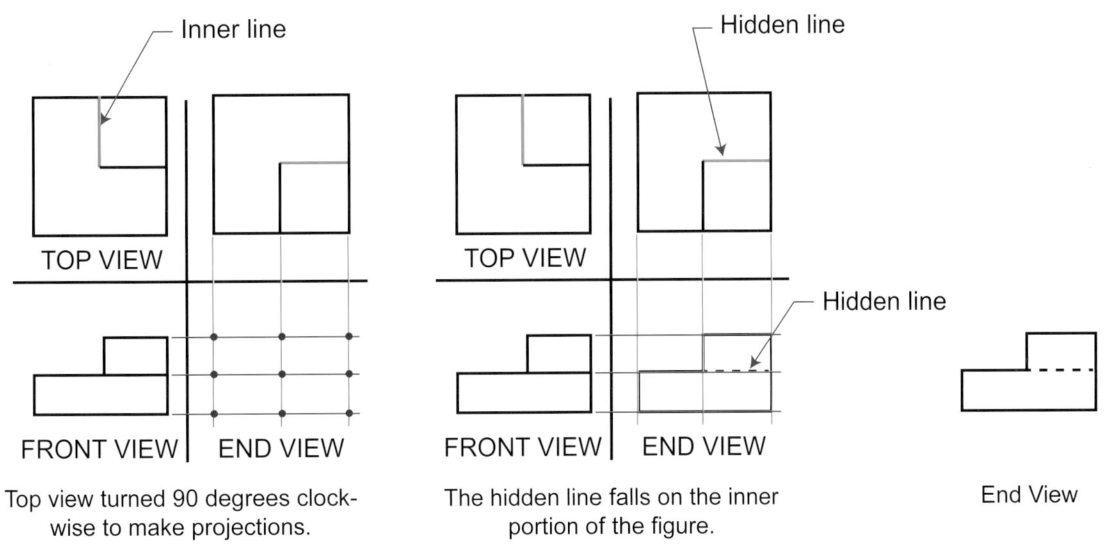

Top view turned 90 degrees clockwise to make projections.

The hidden line falls on the inner portion of the figure.

End View

Given the top and front views, you can start making projections to get the end view. First, turn the top view 90 degrees clockwise. Use construction lines for projections (blue lines are from the top view and red lines are from the front). Take note that all vertical lines on the top view and all horizontal lines on the front view should be projected. The intersections of these lines would be the significant points or corners of the end view.

Carefully eliminate irrelevant intersections by verifying from the front and top views. You should also consider any inner vertical or horizontal lines on the top and front views – these should be hidden from the end view. In this case, it is the green-colored line.

3.3.2 The Hidden Lines

Sometimes, an object will have a component or a feature located at the back, so this becomes invisible from the front view. To indicate the presence of this feature, dotted lines are used in its place.

Hidden lines are one of the most confusing details to visualize in the test. One way to deal with them is to remember that they represent one of three things:

1. the edge view of a hidden surface (see Figure PAT 3.1)
2. an intersection of two surfaces that is behind another surface (see Figure PAT 3.2)
3. the outer edge of a curved surface that is hidden (see Figure PAT 3.6).

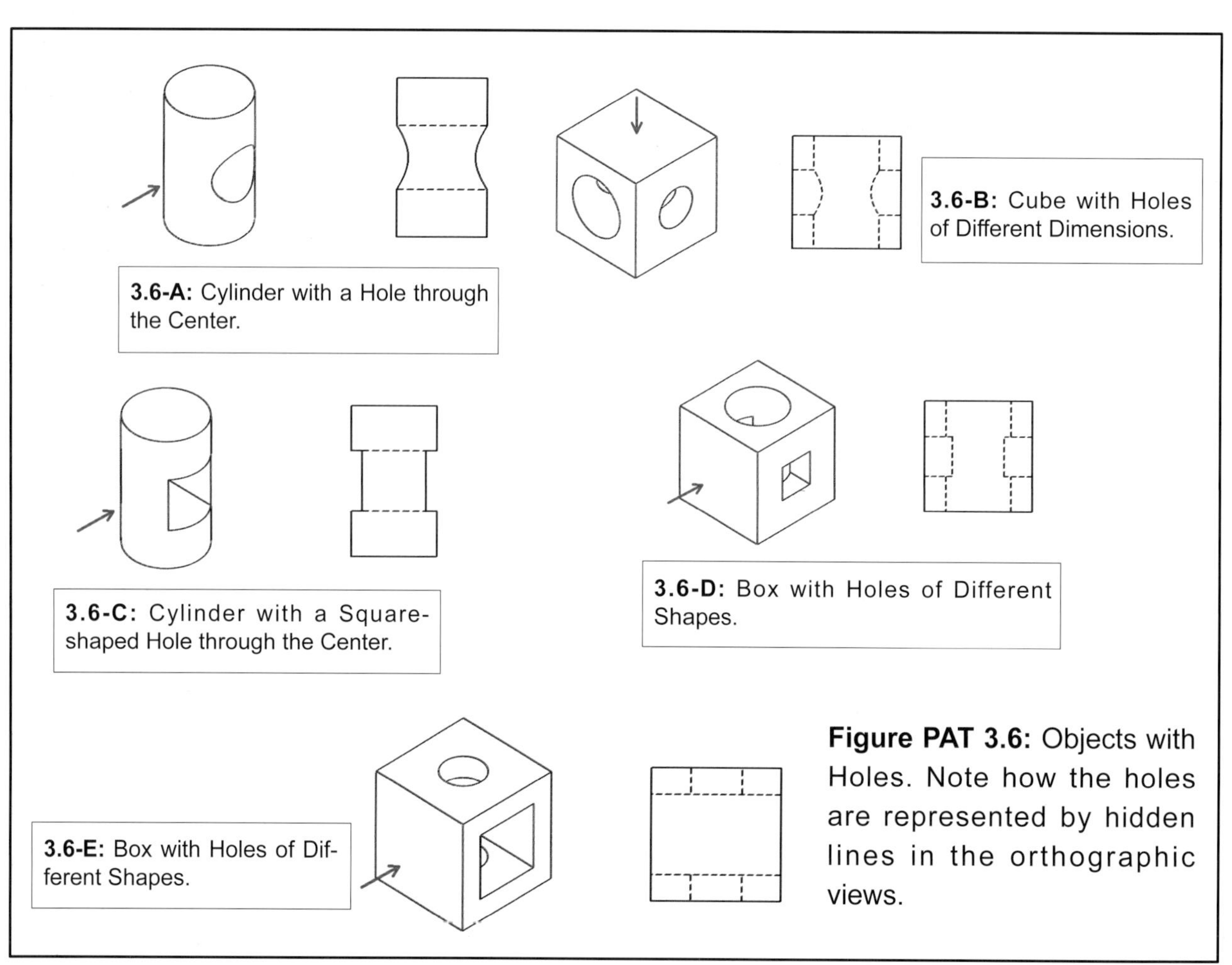

3.6-A: Cylinder with a Hole through the Center.
3.6-B: Cube with Holes of Different Dimensions.
3.6-C: Cylinder with a Square-shaped Hole through the Center.
3.6-D: Box with Holes of Different Shapes.
3.6-E: Box with Holes of Different Shapes.

Figure PAT 3.6: Objects with Holes. Note how the holes are represented by hidden lines in the orthographic views.

3.3.3 Visualizing Three-Dimensional Objects in Two-Dimensional Views

You can also think of the View Recognition test as the opposite of the Apertures test. The former requires you to visualize the three-dimensional form of the given 2D views while the latter compels you to do the opposite.

Both PAT subsections, on the other hand, share the same concepts and principles governing the 3D objects and their corresponding 2D views. Judging the distances of the object's components and the shapes of sloping surfaces are critical sections to review for both tests: their shapes and the placement of their edges tend to vary on certain views.

For example, a circle viewed from the top should have straight edges both from the front and the end views, but retains its rounded shape from the top view. Likewise, a protrusion situated at the back portion of the object will appear on top of the object's surface in the 2D front view (see the FRONT VIEW of the object in Figure PAT 3.1). If you find these details confusing, you should go back and review sections 2.2 to 2.2.3 of Chapter 2.

During the early stage of your preparation for the PAT, take time and try to visualize the views of the 3D object as they are projected into the top, front, and end views. It also helps to mentally map out the top-front-end views of everyday objects whenever possible to get your eyes and mind used to visualizing 3D objects in their 2D views and vice versa.

3.4 Mini Exercises

1. Choose the correct END VIEW

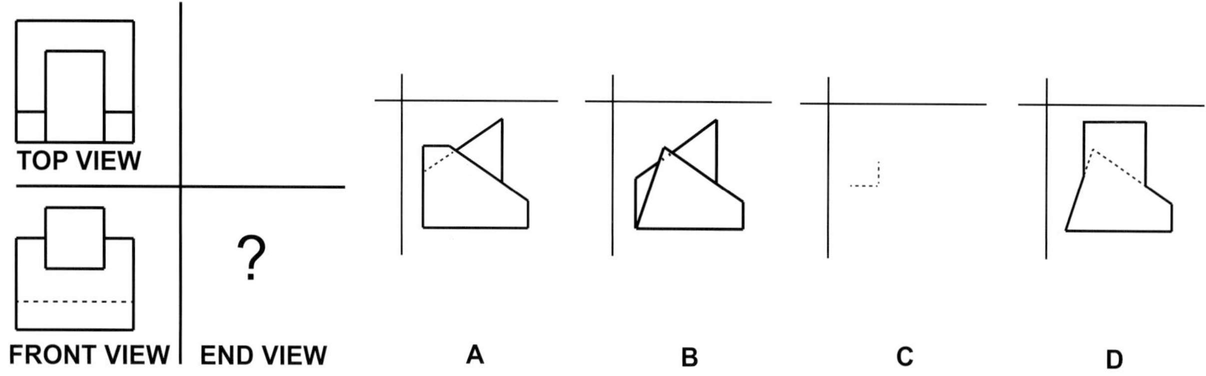

2. Choose the correct FRONT VIEW

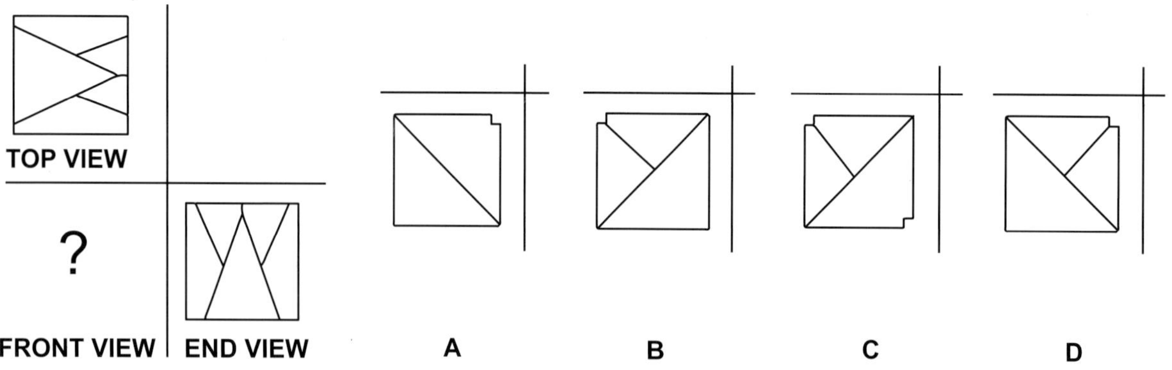

3. Choose the correct FRONT VIEW

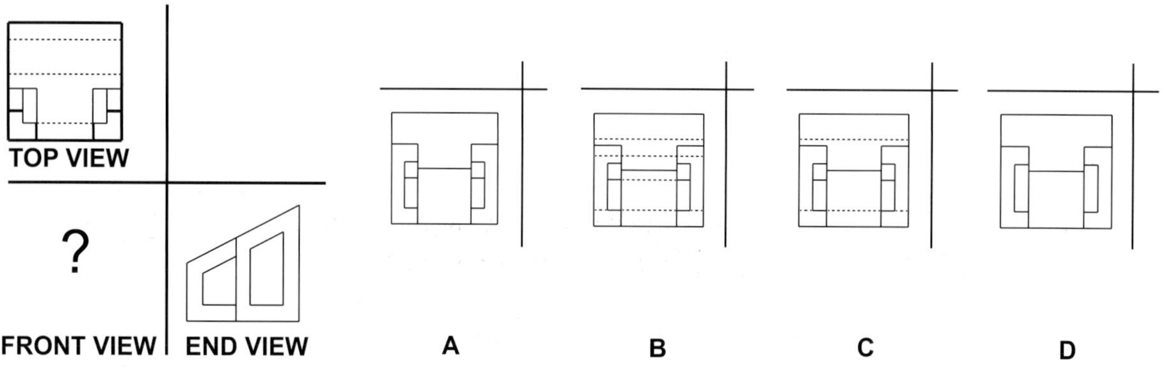

4. Choose the correct FRONT VIEW

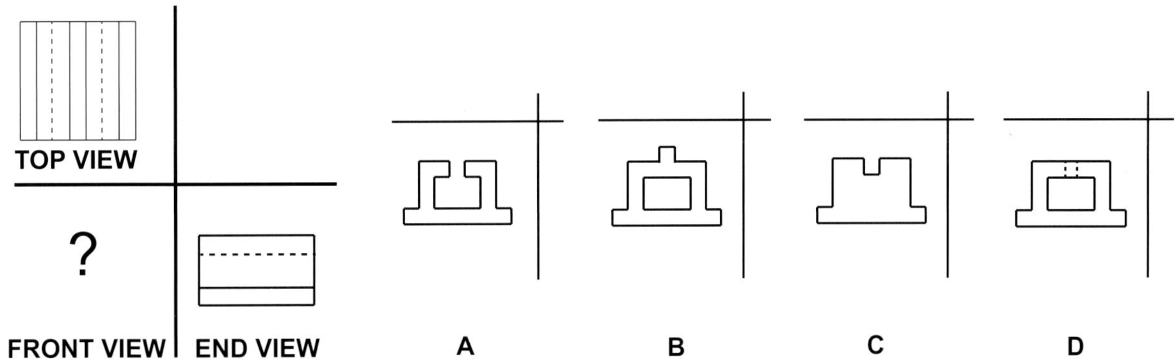

5. Choose the correct TOP VIEW

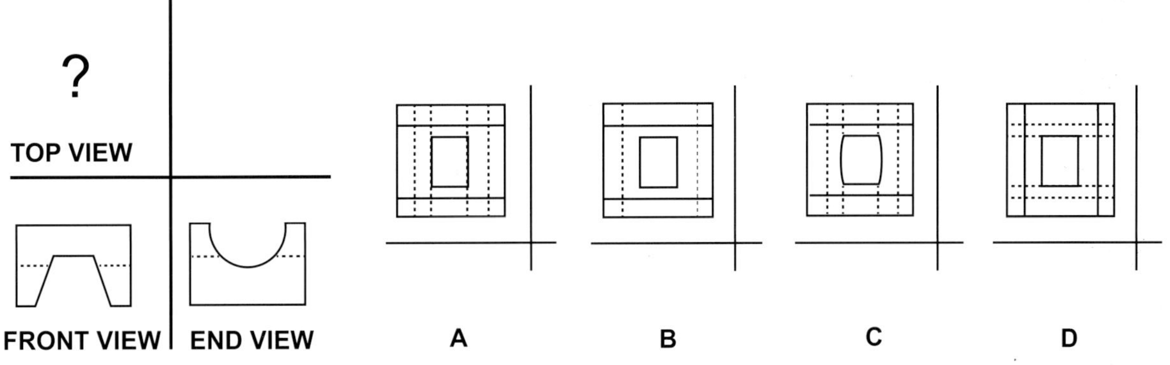

ANSWERS: 1.A 2.D 3.B 4.A 5.A

Explanations for the mini exercises can be accessed by clicking Lessons in the top Menu when you are logged into www.dat-prep.com.

GOLD STANDARD WARM-UP EXERCISES

CHAPTER 3: Orthographic Projection

The following questions represent one of the six subsections in the Perceptual Ability Test of the DAT. While this serves as a review of the discussions in this chapter, the level of difficulty of each question closely parallels the actual test.

You have 10 minutes to complete this portion of the DAT Mini Test; the actual test is 60 minutes.

Please time yourself accordingly.

BEGIN ONLY WHEN YOUR TIMER IS READY

1. Choose the correct TOP VIEW.

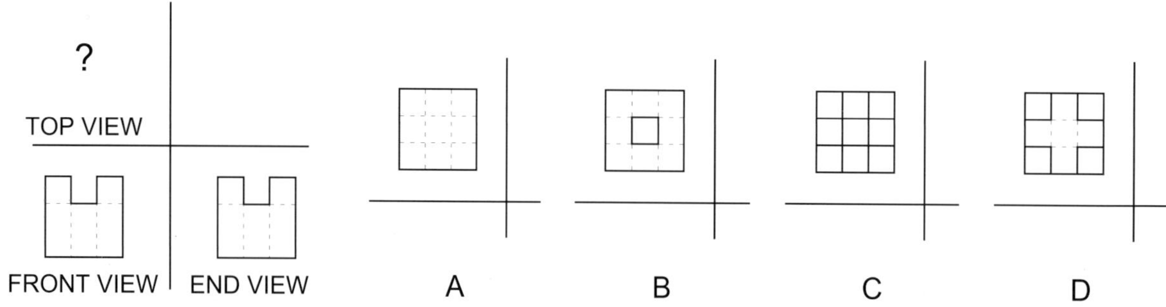

2. Choose the correct END VIEW.

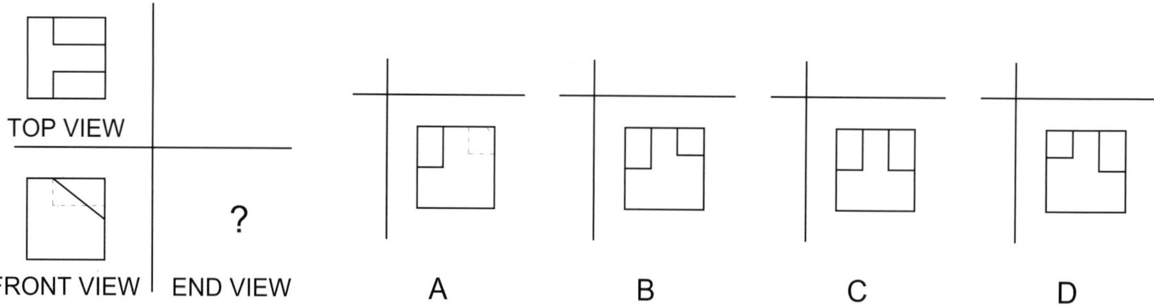

3. Choose the correct FRONT VIEW.

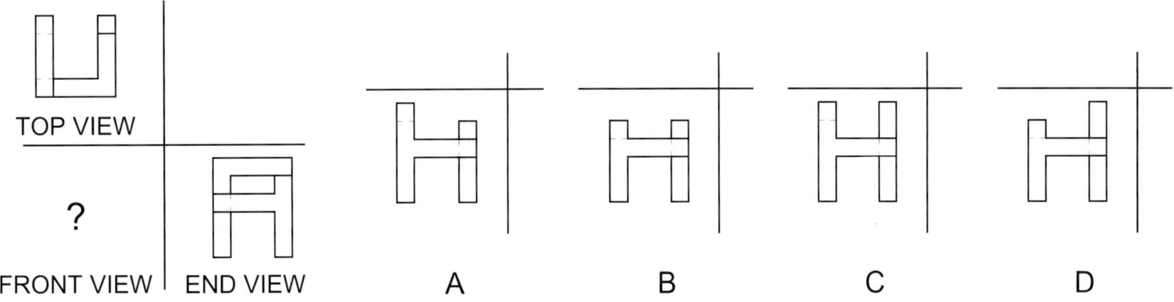

4. Choose the correct END VIEW.

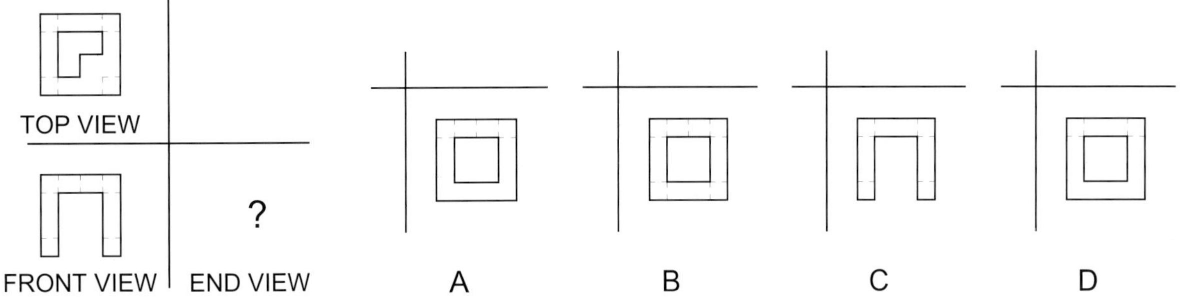

5. Choose the correct FRONT VIEW.

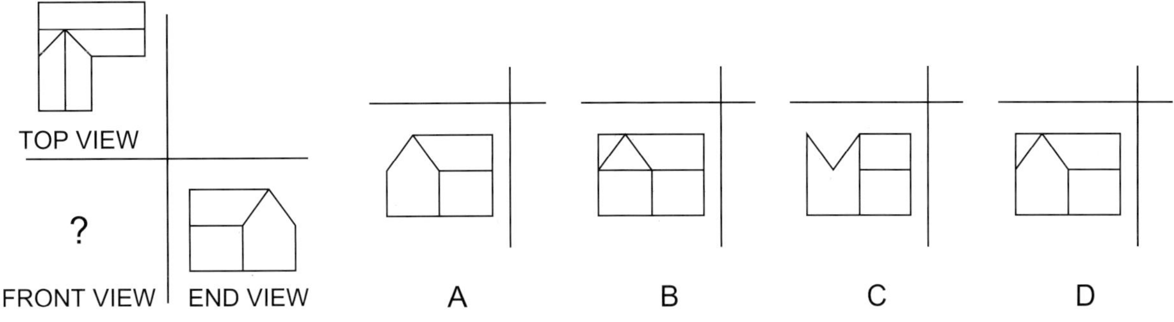

6. Choose the correct END VIEW.

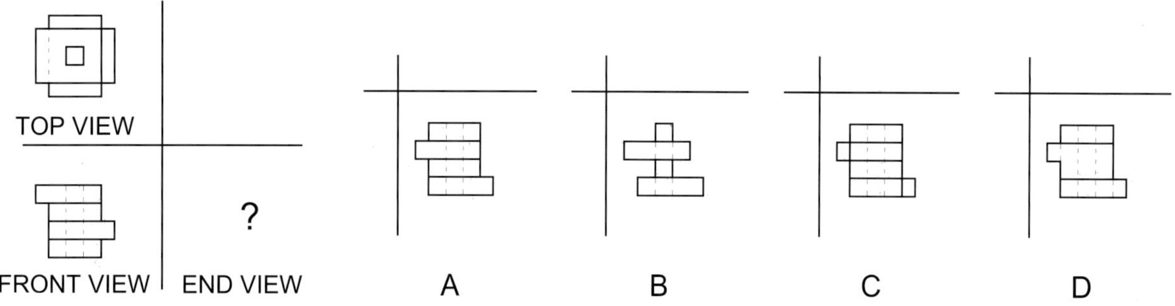

7. Choose the correct TOP VIEW.

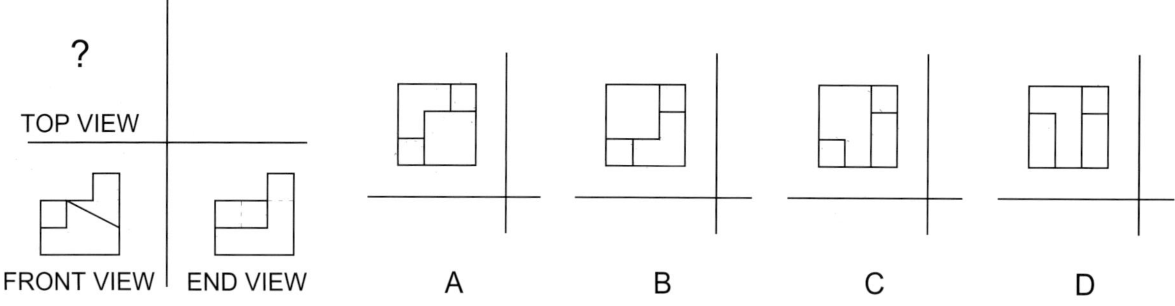

8. Choose the correct END VIEW.

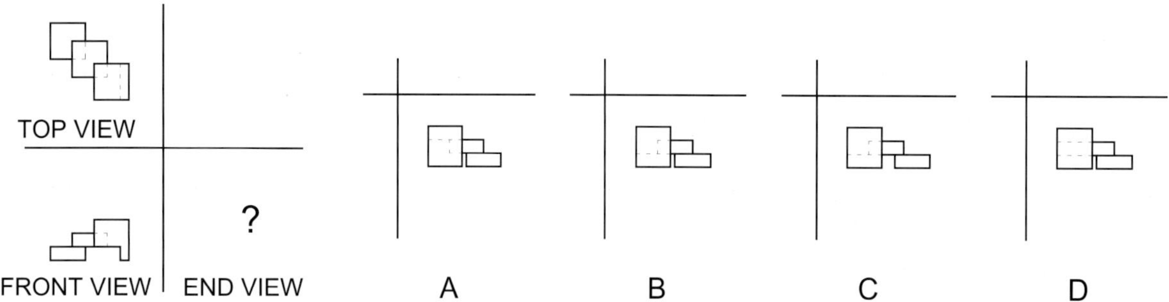

9. Choose the correct END VIEW.

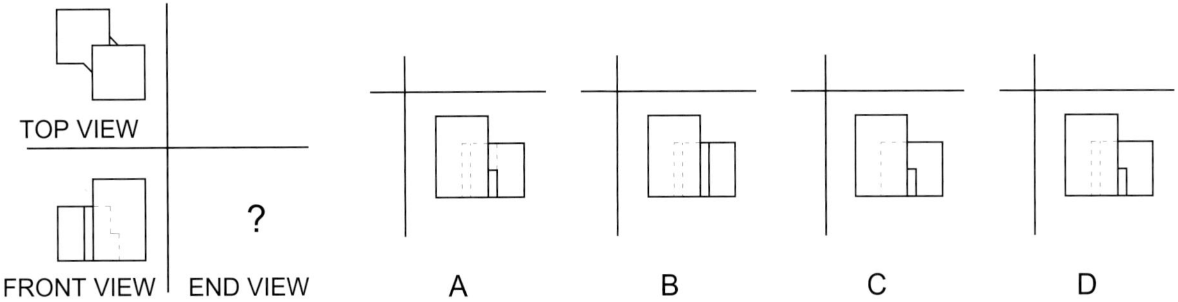

10. Choose the correct FRONT VIEW.

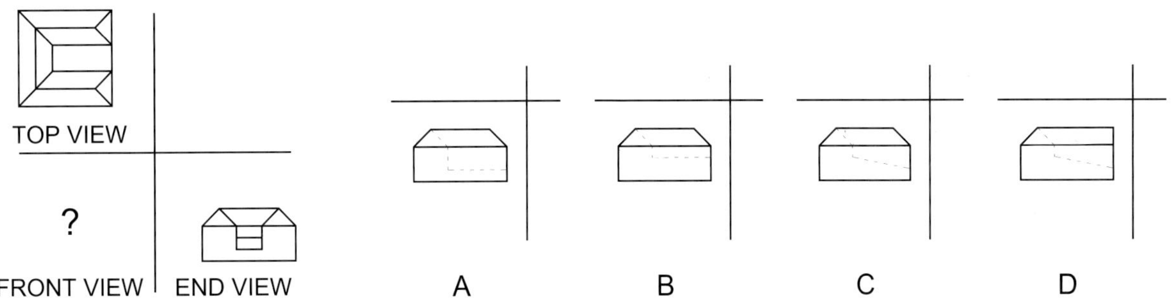

11. Choose the correct TOP VIEW.

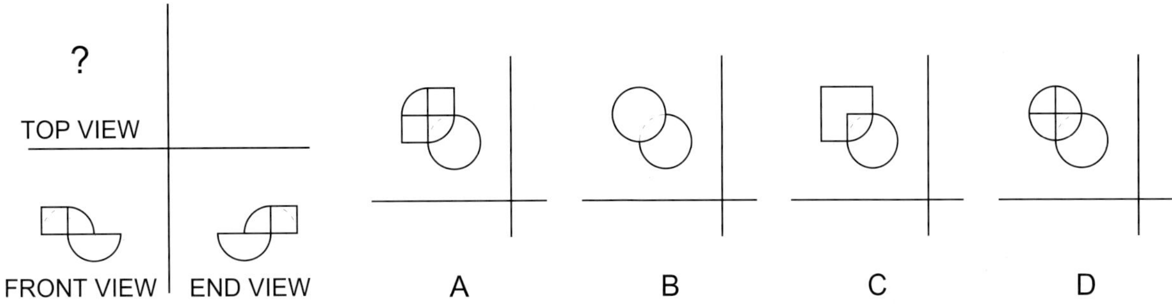

12. Choose the correct TOP VIEW.

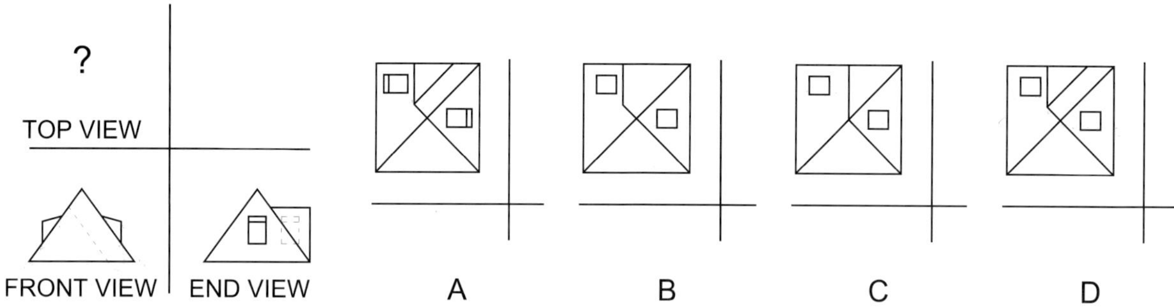

13. Choose the correct END VIEW.

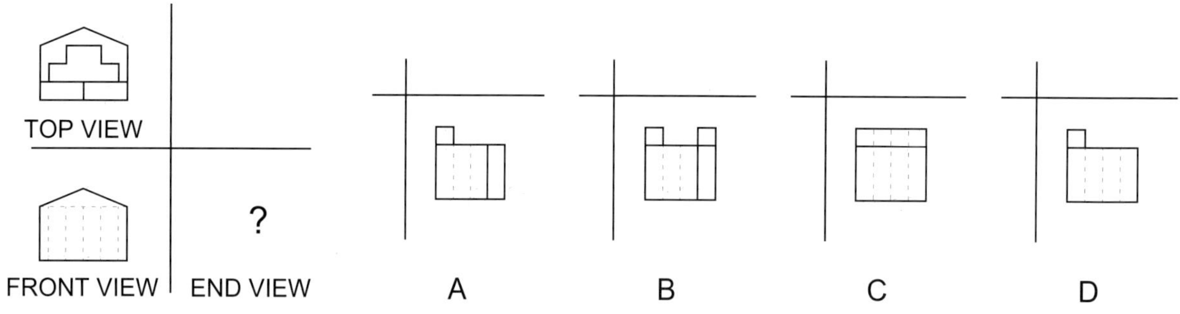

14. Choose the correct END VIEW.

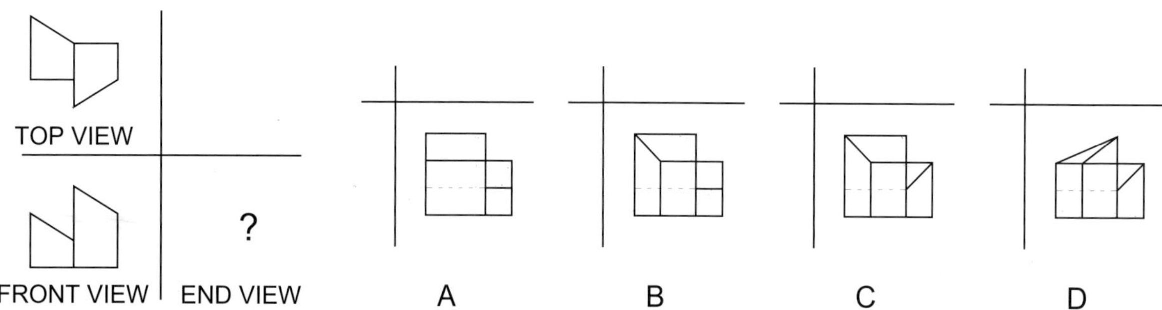

15. Choose the correct TOP VIEW.

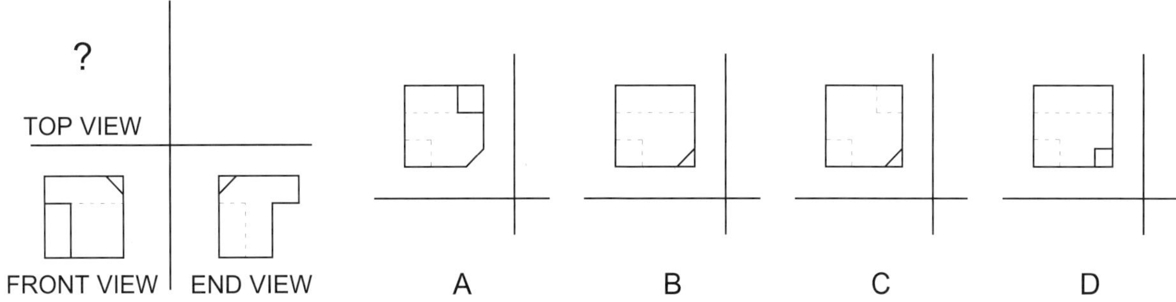

If time remains, you may review your work. If your allotted time is complete, please proceed to the Answer Key.

GS ANSWER KEY

Chapter 3

1.	C	9.	D
2.	B	10.	C
3.	A	11.	A
4.	A	12.	D
5.	D	13.	A
6.	A	14.	C
7.	A	15.	B
8.	B		

* Explanations can be found in the Lessons section at www.dat-prep.com.

Go online to DAT-prep.com for additional chapter review Q&A and forum.

Go online to DAT-prep.com for additional chapter review Q&A and forum.

ANGLE DISCRIMINATION

Chapter 4

Understand

* Key Strategies for Acute and Obtuse Angles

DAT-Prep.com

Introduction 

An angle is the space between two lines that intersect at a common endpoint, called *the vertex*. Angles become smaller when the lines are brought closer to each other and become larger when moved farther away. The Angle Discrimination Section tests your ability to rank the angles of the figures from the smallest to the largest. This section is more commonly referred to as Angle Ranking.

Additional Resources

Free Online Forum

4.1 About the Angle Discrimination Test

Angle Discrimination is the third subsection in the DAT PAT test that examines your visual reasoning and spatial abilities. This test consists of 15 multiple choice questions, which ask examinees to identify the relative sizes of four interior angles from the smallest to the largest. This is the reason why most candidates refer to this PAT subsection as "angle ranking."

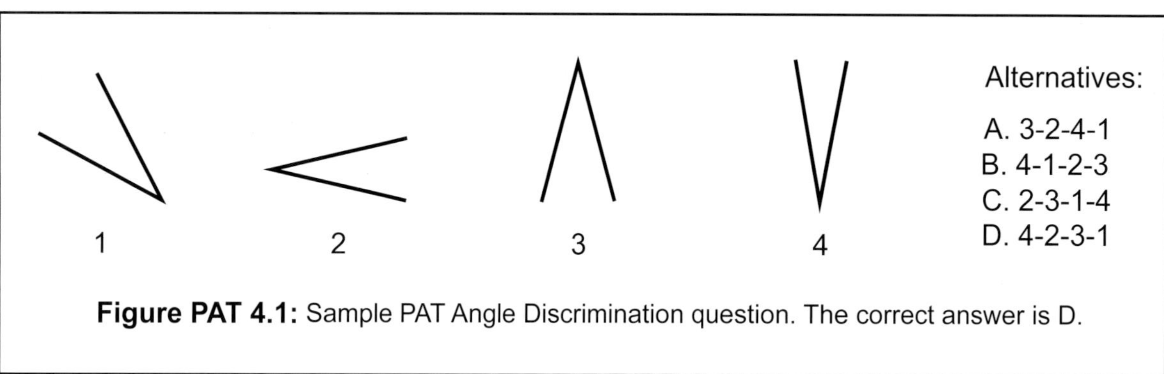

Figure PAT 4.1: Sample PAT Angle Discrimination question. The correct answer is D.

4.2 How to Prepare for this PAT Section

For the purpose of clarity, let us first briefly describe the different parts of an angle.

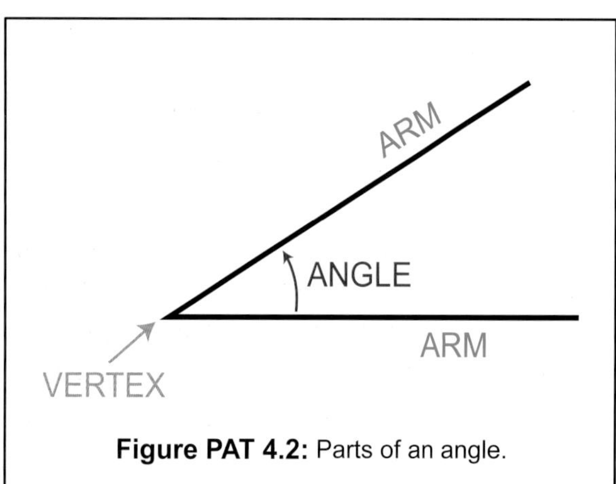

Figure PAT 4.2: Parts of an angle.

The two straight lines of an angle are called the *arms*. The point where these two arms intersect is called the *vertex*. The space between the vertex and the two arms is considered as the *angle*. The angle shown in the diagram represents the interior angle which is the smaller of the two possible angles between 2 arms. Thus the interior angle must always be less than 180°, which would be a straight line. This DAT PAT section is only concerned with interior angles.

There are several kinds of angles, but the most important ones with which you should be familiar in this test are the acute

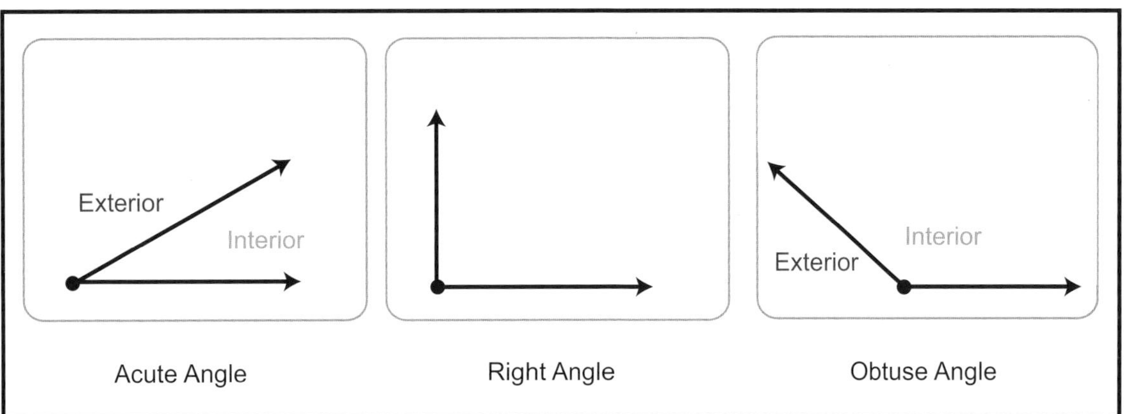

(smaller than 90°) and obtuse (greater than 90° but less than 180°) angles. The key here is to frequently practice looking at the slight differences involving these two types of angles: the "darker" the vertex of an acute angle, the smaller its angle; the nearer an angle to becoming a straight line, the bigger its angle.

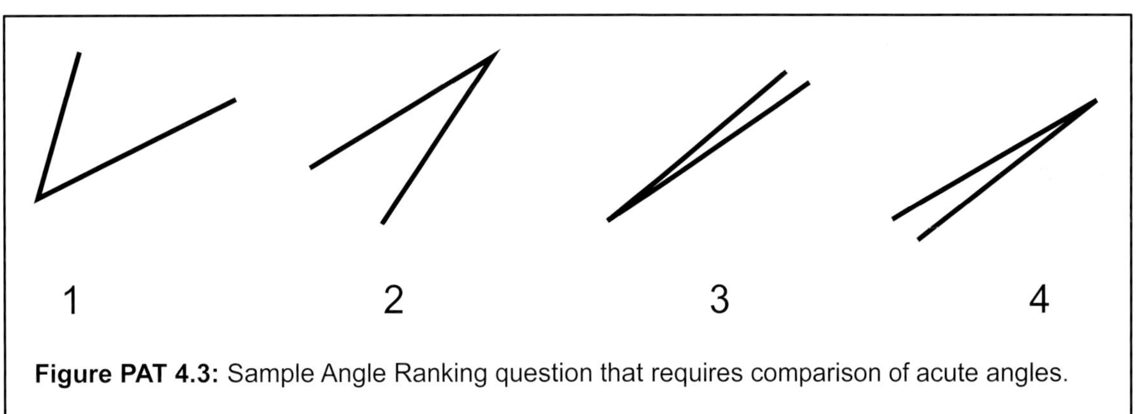

Figure PAT 4.3: Sample Angle Ranking question that requires comparison of acute angles.

In Figure PAT 4.3, angles 3 and 4 are obviously the closest possible choices for the smallest angle. If you examine their vertices, you would notice that angle 3 has a darker vertex than angle 4, making the former the smallest among the four angles.

On the other hand, for questions involving obtuse angles, you would want to look for the figure that nearly resembles a straight line to determine the largest angle. The smallest angle would have its two arms closest to each other.

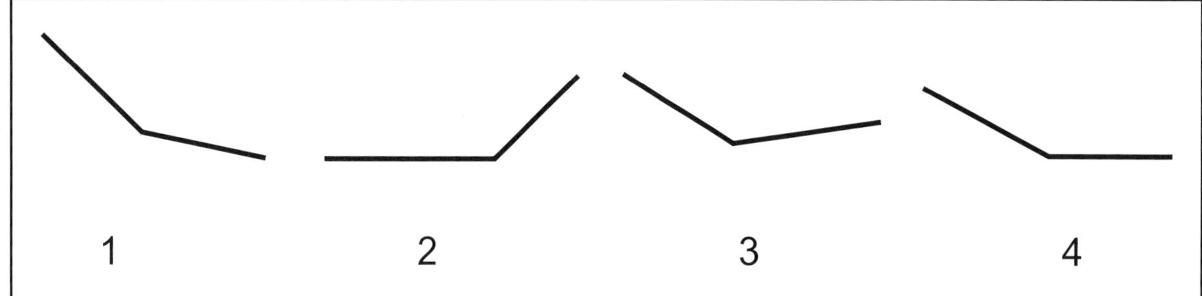

Figure PAT 4.4: Sample Angle Ranking question that requires comparison of obtuse angles. The largest angle is 1.

Of course, if this is your first encounter with angle ranking questions, you might find the initial attempts to be quite difficult – just like any other new endeavor. But like most of the DAT sections, consistent practice (in the book and online at DAT-prep.com) is paramount to your success in this test.

The point of frequently doing these exercises is for you to try as many techniques as you can so that you would finally settle on the one strategy that will not only make you visually keen with angles, but also help you increase your speed in answering the questions. In other words, you need to train your eyes to QUICKLY SPOT the minute differences between at least two closely similar angles.

Now let's discuss specific strategies that you can adopt for this PAT subsection.

4.3 Strategies

1. Process of Elimination

Remember that your main task in this test is to rank the angles from the smallest to the largest for all 15 Angle Discrimination questions. Thus identifying these two extremes should be your first strategy. Often, at least one of the two, either the smallest or the largest, would be easy to identify. This will make eliminating some of the options easier. For example, if the smallest angle is represented in one or two of the answer choices, you can instantly discard the remaining choices. Then check if the largest angle is represented in the answer choices you have considered. You can occasionally determine the correct answer at this point.

Quite often, you will find yourself down to two angles that are difficult to compare. Generally, you need to focus on the intersections (the inner portion) of the angles, not on their lines. Likewise, try not to stare at the angles for too long. Doing this will only make all the angles look like they are all of the same size.

In other cases, you may need to use different techniques depending on how the angles are presented in a question.

2. Extend a horizontal line

When comparing obtuse angles, one method that you can temporarily do, in the beginning, is to place your hand or a piece of paper on one of the arms of the angle. Please note though that touching the computer screen during the actual test is prohibited; hence, you should eventually move from this "physical" method to purely visualizations. In any case, the objective is to create a base – a horizontal point of reference – so that you can compare, this time, from the outer angles.

Taking Figure PAT 4.5 as an example, the two obtuse angles might be difficult to compare because they are positioned in different directions. In this instance, (mentally) extending a line on one of the arms tends to make the outer angles clearer and easier to gauge. Angle 1 shows a farther distance from the horizontal line, which indicates that it has a smaller angle than Angle 2.

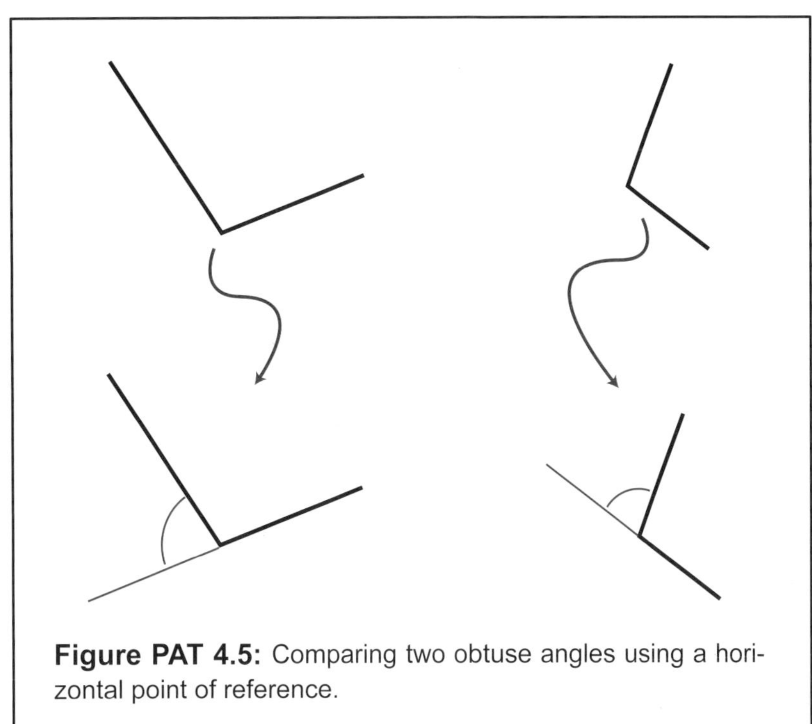

Figure PAT 4.5: Comparing two obtuse angles using a horizontal point of reference.

3. Create an isosceles triangle

Another option is to mentally adjust the image provided to create an isosceles triangle which has two arms that are equal in length. Then, compare the base of these triangles; the longer the base, the bigger the angle. In some questions, it is not necessary to extend any arms because all of the arms of all of the given angles are already the same length. In such cases, creating the base is even simpler.

There are also a number of popular strategies that have either been originated or popularized by former DAT candidates. The following methods are the most well-known up to the date of this publication.

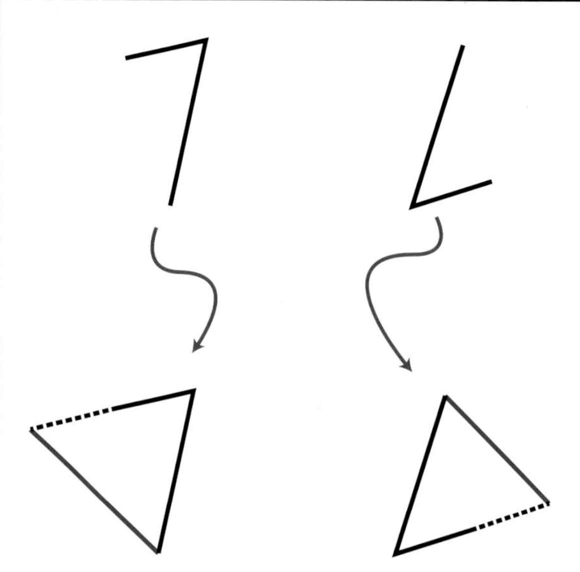

Figure PAT 4.6: Mentally converting similar angles into isosceles triangles can accentuate the differences by focusing on their bases. The smaller base points to the smaller angle which, in this case, is on the right. This technique is reliable if the arms of the triangles are of equal lengths.

4.3.1 Other Useful Techniques

1. The "Hill" Technique

This technique was designed by Justin Orlandini Temple, popularly referred to as Orlo on the Student Doctor Network DAT forum (www.studentdoctor.net). It has earned a great number of commendations from candidates who have improved their Angle Ranking scores after using the said technique.

To use this method, you have to visualize one side of the angle as the ground and the other side as a hill. Then imagine you are riding a bicycle you want to safely ride down that hill. For acute angles, you should be looking from the outside of the angle: the safest hill to ride down, which is not as steep, will be the smallest angle. The steepest hill to ride down will be the largest angle.

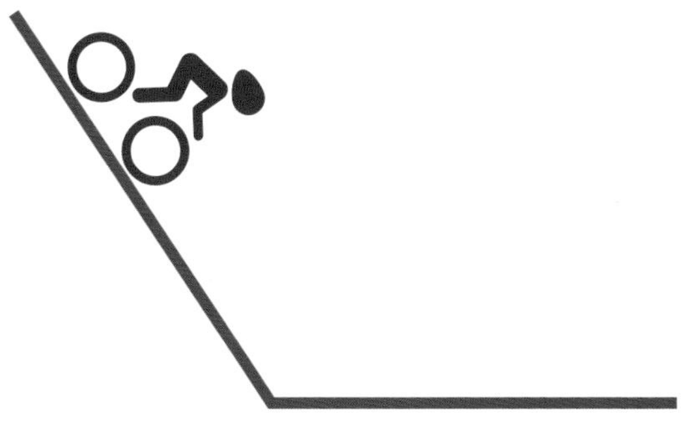

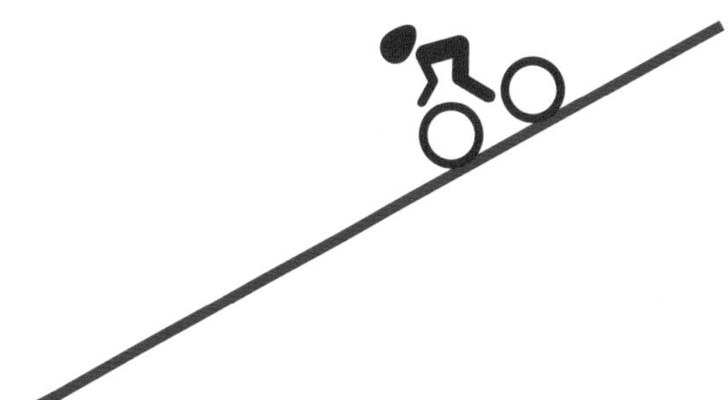

For obtuse angles, you should be looking from the inside of the angle: the safest hill (closest to 180 degrees) to ride down will be the largest angle. The steepest hill to ride down will be the smallest angle.

Let it roll: If you do not like the imagery of riding a bike downhill during an exam (!!), you can imagine a ball rolling down the hill. If it rolls slowest when the angle is acute, then it is smallest, and vice-versa for an obtuse angle.

2. The Laptop Technique

This technique was also designed by Justin Orlandini Temple. It involves visualizing each angle as an open laptop. Select the longer arm as the base of the laptop and the shorter arm as the screen. Imagine that the base of the laptop is flat on the table in front of you. The laptop (angle) that is easiest to close is the smallest angle.

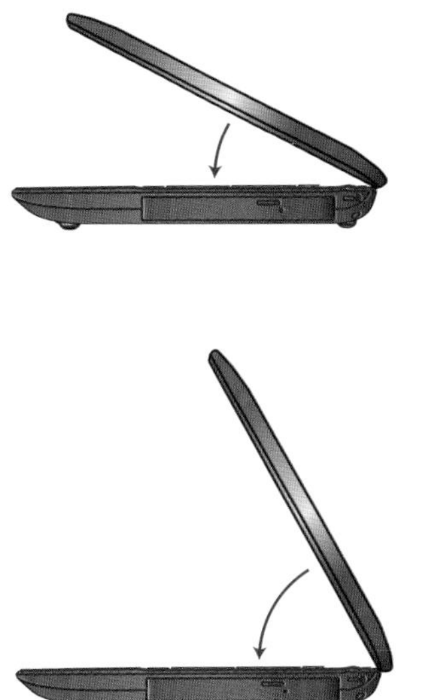

3. The Rapid Eye Technique

Most candidates recommend this technique when estimating closely related angles. You need to focus on the interior portion of the angle then quickly move your eyes back and forth from one to the other of the two closest angles.

4. Get Back and Glance

This technique combines 2 observations that some candidates have had: (1) when they back away from the computer screen, they can get a better impression of the problem; and (2) they only need a few seconds to decide which is the biggest and which is the smallest angle – even when choosing between 2 very similar angles. This method relies more on instinct than logical decision making. The truth is, some students are able to use this skill with little practice and get great scores; whereas, other students need practice and relaxation techniques to tap into this "reflex".

5. Caution

Both the given angles and the options on the PAT can be misleading and can cause faulty reasoning. Beware of different forms of perceptual interferences such as oblique positioning and different lengths of arms of the given angles. These can affect your visual sensibility.

It is essential to understand that the length of an angle's arm is independent of its angular measurement. Once again, constant practice and exposure to various angle ranking problems can greatly enhance your ability to move from one angle to another with sharp eyes. You can take 20-25 minutes every day practicing DAT-style problems. Again, the point is to try to use different techniques and determine which is easier and faster for you to use.

Ideally, you would genuinely attempt each of the strategies during practice. After some experience, you will find a combination of strategies that works best for you.

4.4 Mini Exercises and Explanations

At this point, you would want to apply some of the techniques for yourself on some DAT-style Angle Ranking questions. Before you do so, let us first discuss one sample question before taking on the mini exercises.

Rank the following angles from the smallest to the largest:

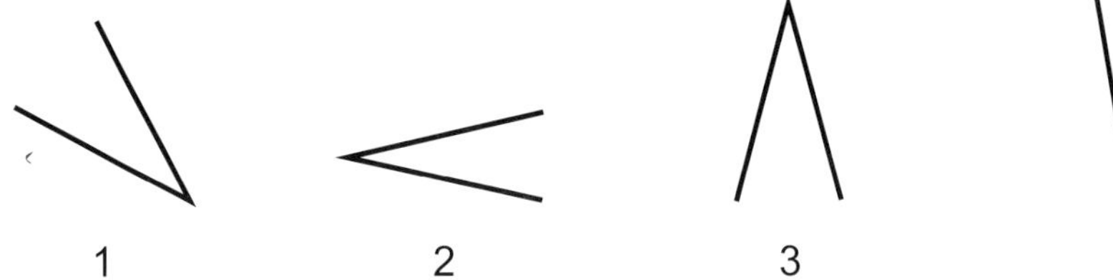

Alternatives:

A. 3-2-4-1
B. 4-1-2-3
C. 2-3-1-4
D. 4-2-3-1

The correct answer is **D**.

As discussed earlier, it is usually best to pick the largest angle first and then the smaller one or the reverse. This is because the smallest and largest angles get noticed quickly.

We can see that the largest angle is 1 and the smallest is 4. Now look for the choices that start with 4 and end with 1. Any other options that do not start or end with these can never be the right answer. In our given example, A and C should be excluded from the alternatives.

The next task is to find what the second and third angles are. Some questions on the PAT show obvious differences between angles 2 and 3. Most, however, are "too close to call." Angles are generally perceived as the hardest section because the angles are so close and difficult to distinguish. This section can be highly instinctual and there is just no magic bullet. Hence do not spend too much time glaring at the angles for an extra 15-30 seconds as this will be even more visually confusing. Since you are dealing with acute angles here, look for the darker vertex – which is 2. The correct answer is thus D.

Though the process of elimination can be very helpful at times, of course there will be challenging questions where the answer choices are designed to confuse you. This is why having experience with different strategies will allow you to pull a specific tool out of the toolbox when you need it most.

4.4.1 Mini Exercises

This section requires you to evaluate the four INTERIOR angles and rank each item from SMALL to LARGE in terms of degrees. From the alternatives, select the one with the correct order.

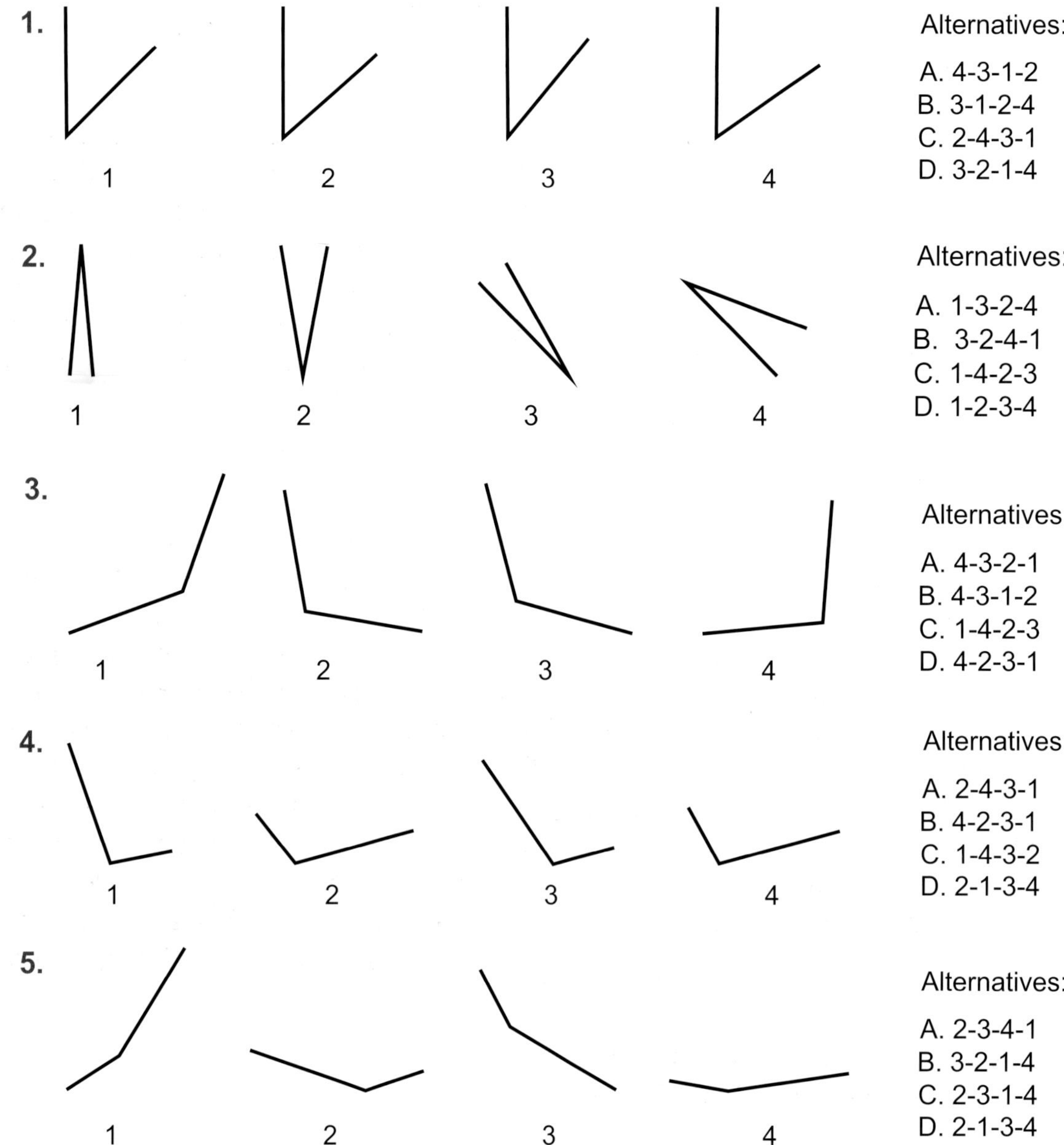

4.4 Mini Exercises and Explanations

1. Answer: B

By focusing on the intersection of the two lines, you will know which angle is smaller than the other. In this item, number 3 seems to be the smallest. So you can readily eliminate options A and C. Next you need to compare angles 1 and 2. Angle 1 is clearly smaller, so the sequence should be 3-1-2-4. The correct answer is B.

2. Answer: C

If all angles on the question were acute such as in this case, you can look for the darkest angle to determine the smallest among the figures. This means that the two lines are so close to one another, making the angle look darker.

In this question, the first angle is the smallest. You can now get rid of choice B. Among the remaining angles, 4 is the biggest so you can discard option C now. If you are still having a hard time determining the smaller angle, compare the openings (you can only do this if the lines of both angles are equal in length). Number 3 is smaller than 2, yielding the sequence 1-3-2-4. Thus the correct answer is A.

3. Answer: D

Angles 2 and 3 are similar in direction; so are 1 and 4. Between 2 and 3, 2 is smaller whereas 4 is smaller than 1. With this information, option C is eradicated from the choices. Next to number 4 should be 2. From here, you can instantly decide that D is the right answer.

4. Answer: C

Similar to question 3, compare first the similarly positioned angles. Between 2 and 4, 4 is smaller, and then 1 is smaller than 3. Now compare 1 and 4 since they are the smaller angles. The angle in number 1 is smaller than 4. Next, angle 4 is smaller than angle 3. Therefore, the sequence should be 1-4-3-2, which is C.

5. Answer: C

With angles that are all obtuse, finding the largest angle first would be the easiest to do. You should be looking for the angle which is closest to a straight line. In this item, angle 4 is the biggest. You can then narrow down your choices to B, C and D, which have 4 as the biggest angle. Now compare 2 and 3 since all of the remaining choices start with these two. Notice that number 2 is more bent than 3. Finally, between 1 and 3, angle 3 is smaller. Hence, the correct sequence is 2-3-1-4, which is choice C.

GOLD STANDARD WARM-UP EXERCISES

CHAPTER 4: Angle Discrimination

The following questions represent one of the six subsections in the Perceptual Ability Test of the DAT. While this serves as a review of the discussions in this chapter, the level of difficulty of each question closely parallels the actual test.

You have 10 minutes to complete this portion of the DAT Mini Test; the actual test is 60 minutes.

Please time yourself accordingly.

BEGIN ONLY WHEN YOUR TIMER IS READY

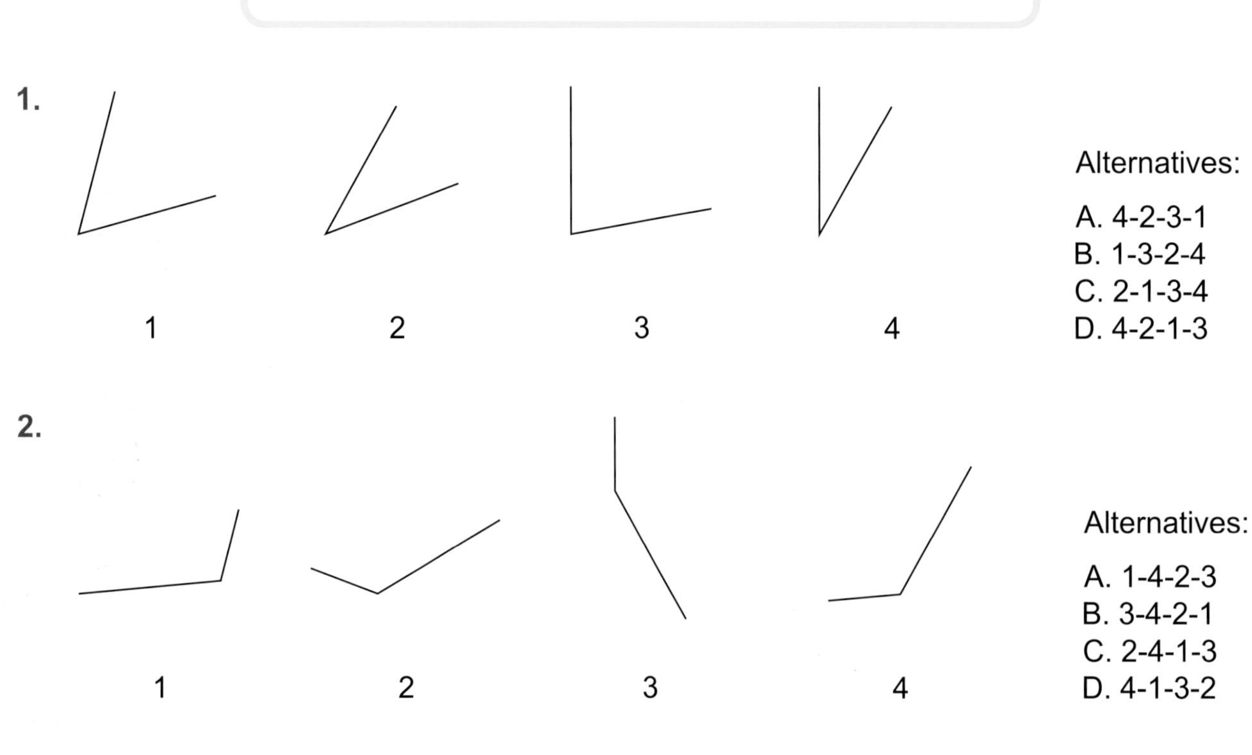

3.

  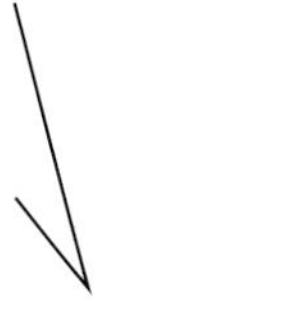

1 2 3 4

Alternatives:

A. 3-1-4-2
B. 2-1-4-3
C. 1-4-3-2
D. 4-2-3-1

4.

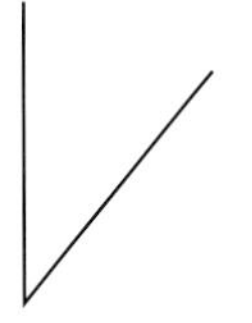  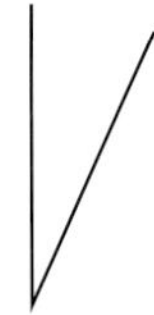 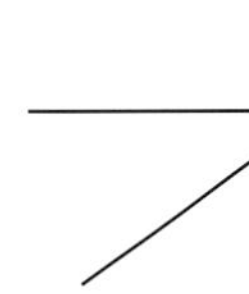 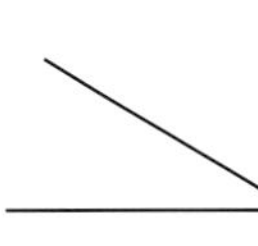

1 2 3 4

Alternatives:

A. 3-2-1-4
B. 2-3-2-4
C. 2-4-3-1
D. 3-1-4-2

5.

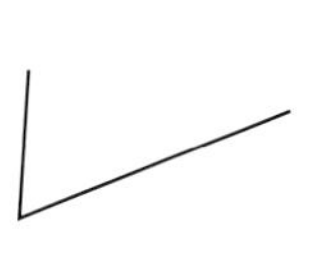 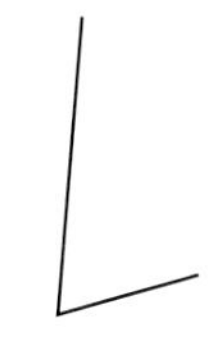 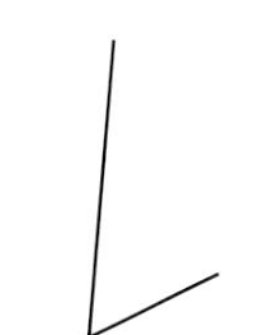 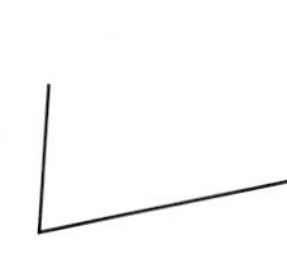

1 2 3 4

Alternatives:

A. 4-3-1-2
B. 1-2-3-4
C. 2-1-4-3
D. 3-1-2-4

6.

 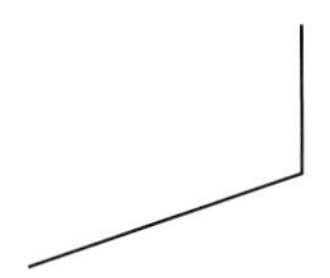 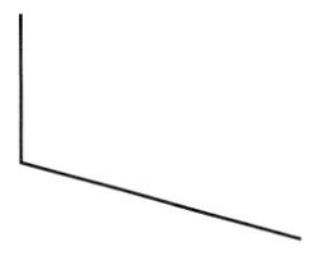 

1 2 3 4

Alternatives:

A. 3-4-2-1
B. 2-4-1-3
C. 1-4-3-2
D. 4-3-2-1

7.

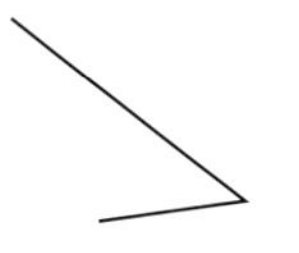 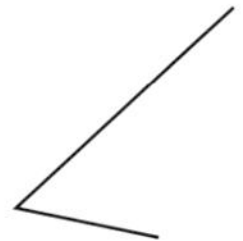 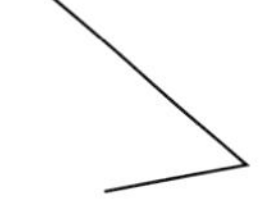 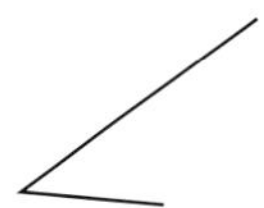

1 2 3 4

Alternatives:

A. 3-1-4-2
B. 4-1-3-2
C. 3-2-1-4
D. 1-4-3-2

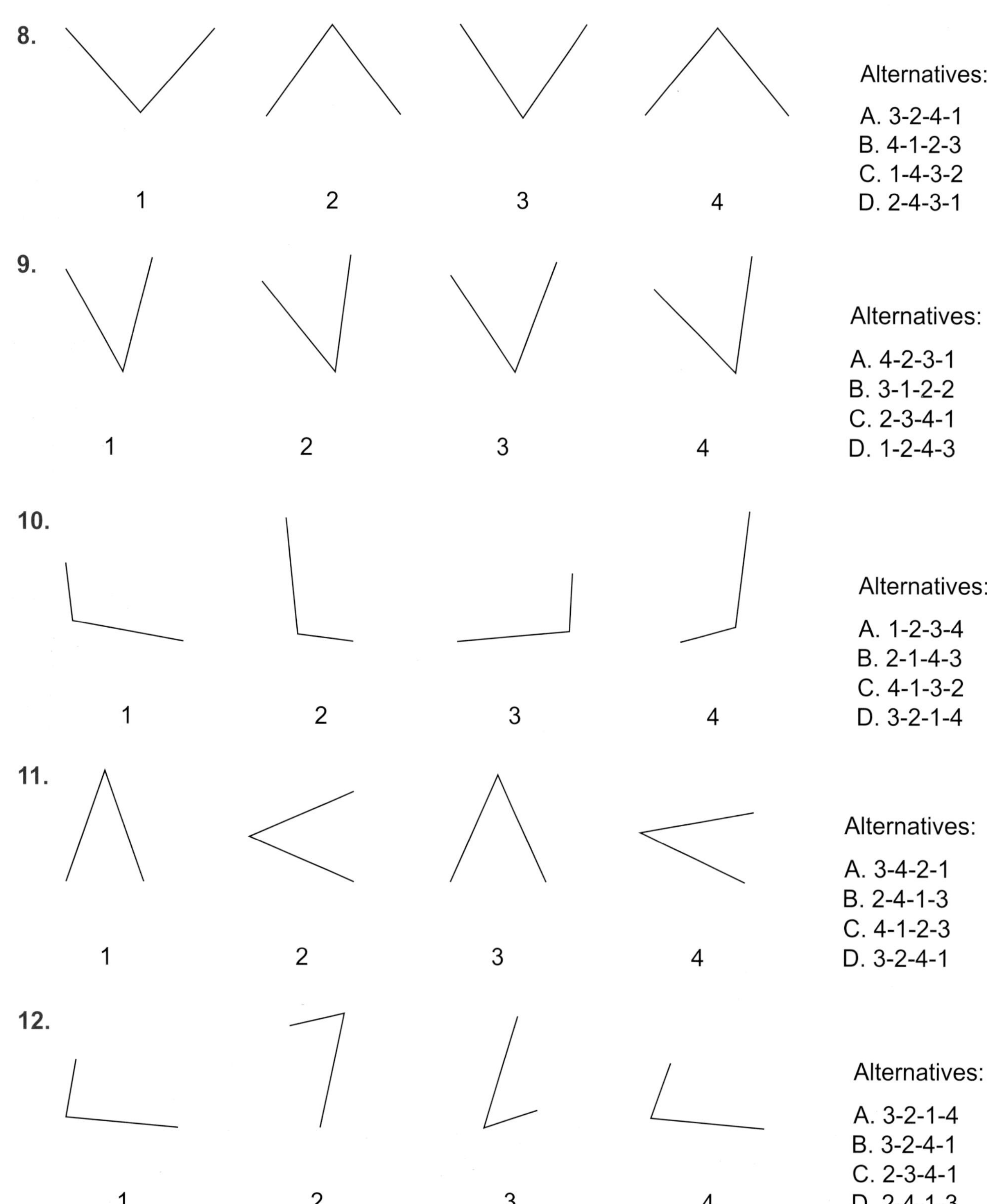
8.
1
2
3
4
Alternatives:
A. 3-2-4-1
B. 4-1-2-3
C. 1-4-3-2
D. 2-4-3-1
9.
1
2
3
4
Alternatives:
A. 4-2-3-1
B. 3-1-2-2
C. 2-3-4-1
D. 1-2-4-3
10.
1
2
3
4
Alternatives:
A. 1-2-3-4
B. 2-1-4-3
C. 4-1-3-2
D. 3-2-1-4
11.
1
2
3
4
Alternatives:
A. 3-4-2-1
B. 2-4-1-3
C. 4-1-2-3
D. 3-2-4-1
12.
1
2
3
4
Alternatives:
A. 3-2-1-4
B. 3-2-4-1
C. 2-3-4-1
D. 2-4-1-3

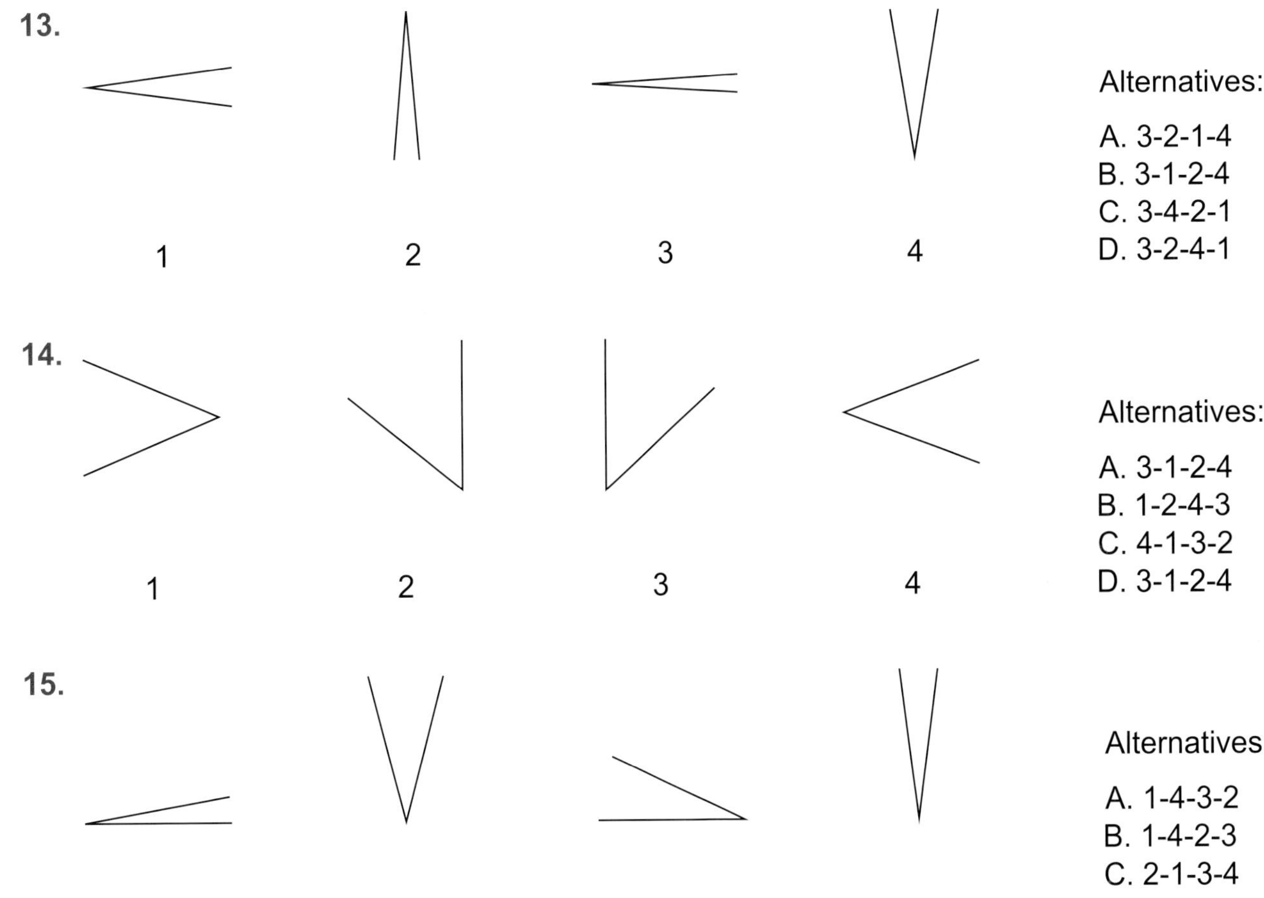

If time remains, you may review your work. If your allotted time is complete, please proceed to the Answer Key.

GS ANSWER KEY

CHAPTER 4

1.	D	9.	D
2.	A	10.	D
3.	B	11.	C
4.	C	12.	B
5.	D	13.	A
6.	C	14.	C
7.	B	15.	A
8.	A		

* Explanations can be found in the Lessons section at www.dat-prep.com.

Go online to DAT-prep.com for additional chapter review Q&A and forum.

Go online to DAT-prep.com for additional chapter review Q&A and forum.

PAPER FOLDING

Chapter 5

Memorize

* The Hole Sequences in the Paper Folding Quadrants

Understand

* Folding Patterns
* Linear and Diagonal Folds
* Half Hole-punch

Introduction

A folded paper that is punched with a hole in it will create a pattern of more than one hole when unfolded. The Paper Folding Section, also known as the Hole Punching Section, entails considering a square sheet of paper on a flat surface; observing how it is folded and by how many times; looking at the spot where a hole is punched; and then, visualizing the resulting pattern of the holes once the paper is fully spread. This section essentially examines your ability to foresee where the holes end up in the paper.

Additional Resources

Free Online Forum

5.1 About the Paper Folding Test

The Paper Folding test is commonly referred to as the "hole punching" section. It primarily measures your ability to mentally manipulate three-dimensional diagrams.

Similar to the other PAT subsections, this test includes 15 multiple-choice questions. Each item presents a pattern of a square piece of paper being folded and eventually hole-punched in specific places. You will need to mentally unfold the paper in order to determine the answer choice with the correct placement of holes.

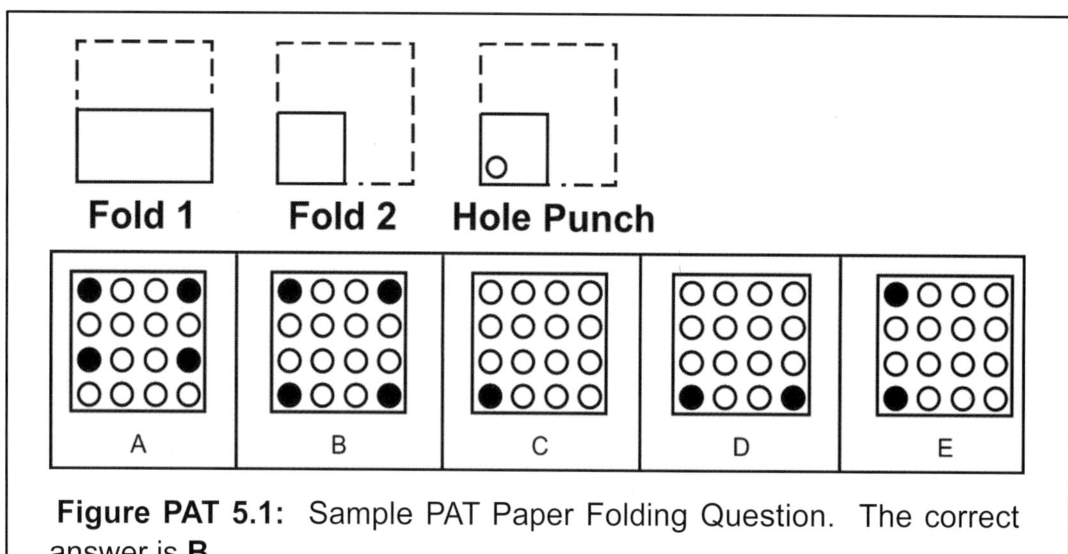

Figure PAT 5.1: Sample PAT Paper Folding Question. The correct answer is **B**.

Basic in your review for this PAT subsection is to understand how a paper is folded. In each question, the sequence of the folding pattern is shown similar to Figure PAT 5.2.

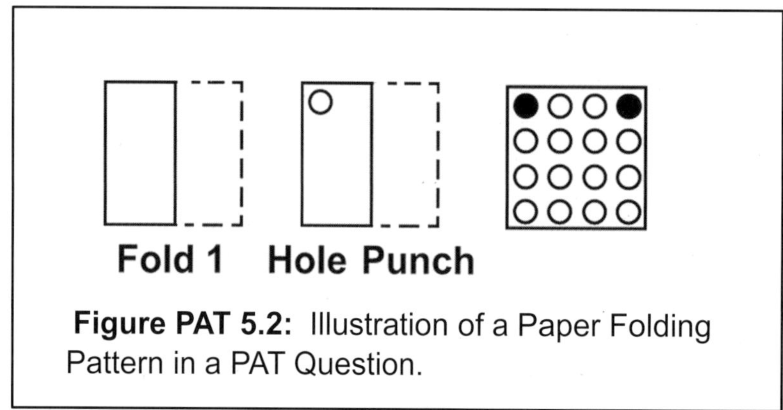

Figure PAT 5.2: Illustration of a Paper Folding Pattern in a PAT Question.

The solid outline on each square represents the position of the folded paper while the broken lines indicate the portion of the paper before it was folded. It is important to note that the paper is neither turned nor twisted after each fold. Now let's look at this procedure from an isometric view.

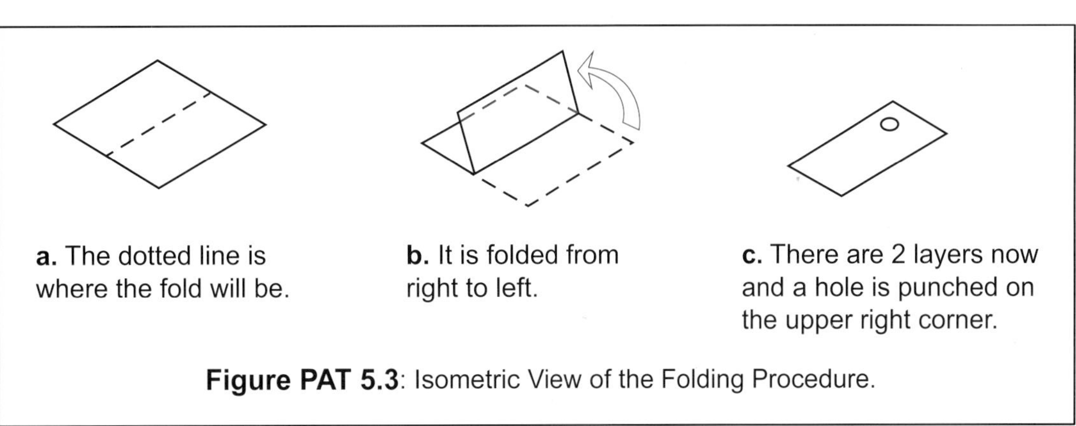

a. The dotted line is where the fold will be.
b. It is folded from right to left.
c. There are 2 layers now and a hole is punched on the upper right corner.

Figure PAT 5.3: Isometric View of the Folding Procedure.

Each question will then require you to identify the resulting pattern of the punched hole or holes from among five options. The most common method in answering these questions is to work the folding procedure backwards, starting with the paper with a hole already punched through it. From there, you would unfold the figure in the reverse sequence. For each step, mentally locate the portion of the paper where the hole or holes should now take their places.

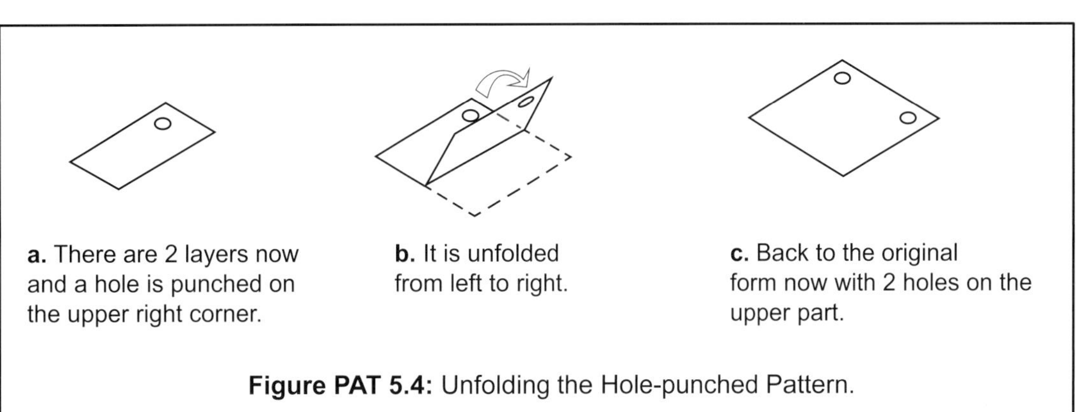

a. There are 2 layers now and a hole is punched on the upper right corner.
b. It is unfolded from left to right.
c. Back to the original form now with 2 holes on the upper part.

Figure PAT 5.4: Unfolding the Hole-punched Pattern.

Besides knowing the paper folding procedure in this test, understanding the patterns involved in the various questions is also important.

5.2 Understanding the Paper Folding Pattern

The Paper Folding test is essentially about patterns and symmetry. The fundamental premise is that in every piece of square paper given in the questions, there are potentially 16 holes that can be punched. These holes are evenly distributed by four in four smaller squares or quadrants (see Figure PAT 5.5). From this arrangement, we can assign a sequence number for each hole that describes its specific location within the quadrants.

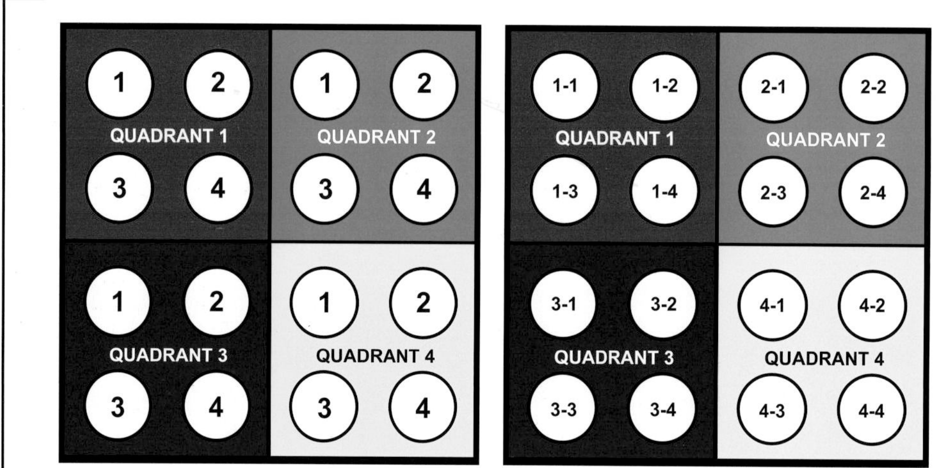

Figure PAT 5.5: Gold Standard Paper Folding Quadrants and the Sequence of Holes.

The first numeral in our sequence number represents the quadrant where the hole belongs. The second numeral is the location of the hole within the quadrant. Hence they are organized as follows:

Quadrant 1	Quadrant 2	Quadrant 3	Quadrant 4
1-1: Hole Number 1 of Quadrant 1	2-1: Hole Number 1 of Quadrant 2	3-1: Hole Number 1 of Quadrant 3	4-1: Hole Number 1 of Quadrant 4
1-2: Hole Number 2 of Quadrant 1	2-2: Hole Number 2 of Quadrant 2	3-2: Hole Number 2 of Quadrant 3	4-2: Hole Number 2 of Quadrant 4
1-3: Hole Number 3 of Quadrant 1	2-3: Hole Number 3 of Quadrant 2	3-3: Hole Number 3 of Quadrant 3	4-3: Hole Number 3 of Quadrant 4
1-4: Hole Number 4 of Quadrant 1	2-4: Hole Number 4 of Quadrant 2	3-4: Hole Number 4 of Quadrant 3	4-4: Hole Number 4 of Quadrant 4

Formalizing the order of the holes like this eventually makes visualizing the different paper folding patterns easier and more precise. Now that we have established a basic sequence of the holes, we can now focus on the folding action itself.

5.2.1 Folding Patterns

While a piece of paper can be folded in numerous possible ways, these can actually be classified in just two general folding systems: the linear and the diagonal.

1. The Linear Fold

A linear manner of folding can be horizontal or vertical. In any of these procedures, the sequence of holes in each quadrant remains intact. This means that any of the 16 hole-sequences can appear in the resulting hole-punching pattern.

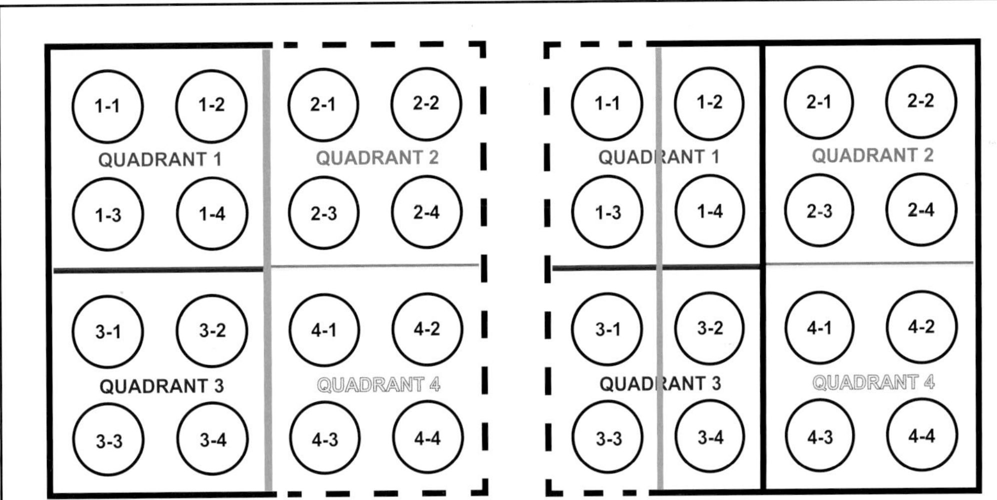

Figure PAT 5.6-A: Examples of Vertical Linear Folds. The tangerine line indicates where the vertical fold is made on the paper.

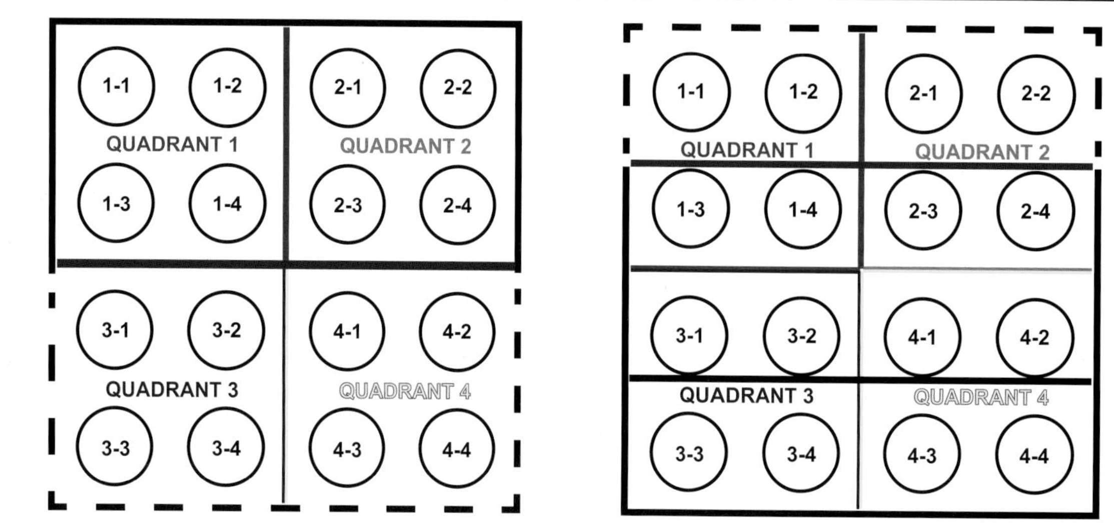

Figure PAT 5.6-B: Two Examples of Horizontal Linear Folds. The purple line indicates the part of the paper where the horizontal fold is made.

2. The Diagonal Fold

In contrast to the linear fold, a diagonal fold causes some hole sequences to be eliminated from certain possible hole-punching patterns UNLESS the punch is made on the fold itself (see discussion in section 5.2.2). A diagonal fold leaning towards the upper right edge of the paper makes the hole sequences 2-2, 2-3, 3-2, and 3-3 irrelevant (see Figure 5.7-A). The one leaning towards the upper left edge of the paper discounts hole sequences 1-1,1-4, 4-1, and 4-4 (see Figure 5.7-B).

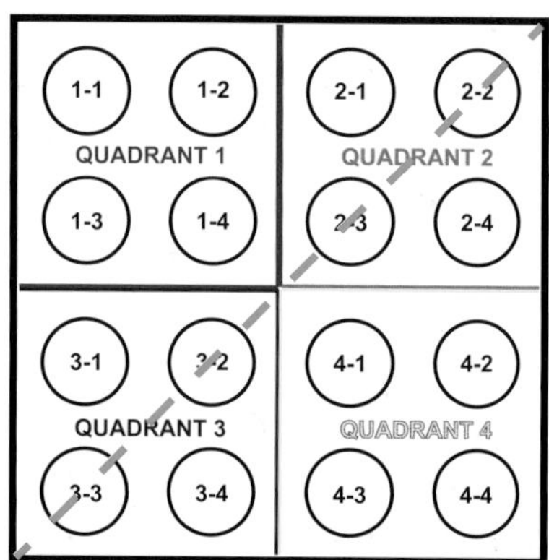

Figure PAT 5.7-A: Diagonal Fold Leaning to the Right.

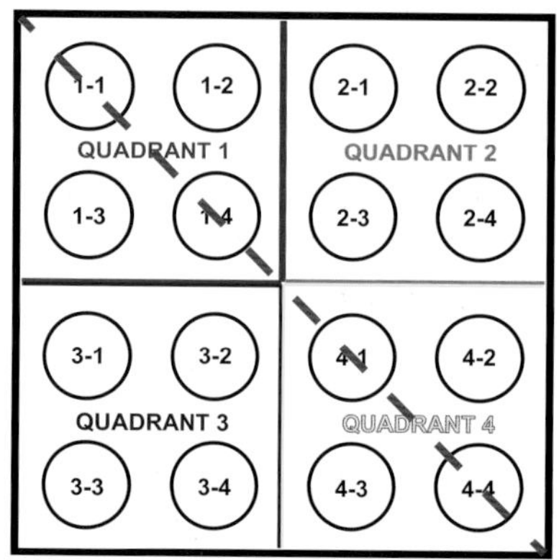

Figure PAT 5.7-B: Diagonal Fold Leaning to the Left.

5.2.2 The Symmetrical Pattern of Hole Punches

Another approach to this section is to think of each fold as a line of symmetry – that is, a hole punched on one side of the fold will be reflected on the other side of the line upon unfolding. In many cases, however, this system may not be as simple as it sounds.

Not all holes are punched on a "full" layer (see Figure PAT 5.2). Some holes are punched on the fold itself, such as demonstrated in Figure PAT 5.8, making the hole look sliced in half. Nevertheless, the line of symmetry will still apply in this kind of punch: a "half-punch" will generate its symmetrical half and yield one whole punched hole (not two) in the process.

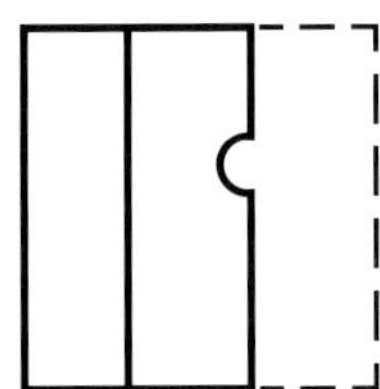

There are 2 layers and 1 hole punched.

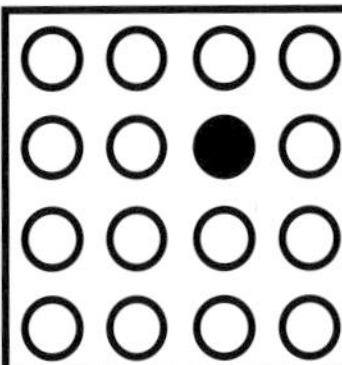

Total number of holes is still 1.

1 hole punched through 2 layers of paper but on the fold.

Figure PAT 5.8: The Half Hole-Punch. A hole is made on the fold itself.

Moreover, whenever a hole is punched along the fold itself, it immediately highlights the exact location of that hole from the quadrants. For example, in Figure PAT 5.8, the hole-punch is made on Hole 2-3; hence the answer is a hole on that very spot itself. Taking note of this as you try to visualize the resulting pattern of the paper folds will highly aid in distinguishing the correct answer choice in case you find yourself stuck on two closely similar options during the actual test.

Several questions on the DAT PAT also combine the linear and diagonal folds. Keeping track of the overlapping layers of paper in each fold is thus very important. Some holes are punched through several layers while others are punched through a single layer. Practicing with an actual piece of paper in the beginning would help. Eventually though, you will need to adopt a strategy that will wean you off the physical manipulations. We will discuss this strategy in the next section.

5.2.3 The Importance of Counting the Layers

Being able to quickly determine the number of holes produced by the punches helps you narrow down the answer choices in a time-efficient manner. To give you a clearer idea, let's take the following sample problem as a concrete reference.

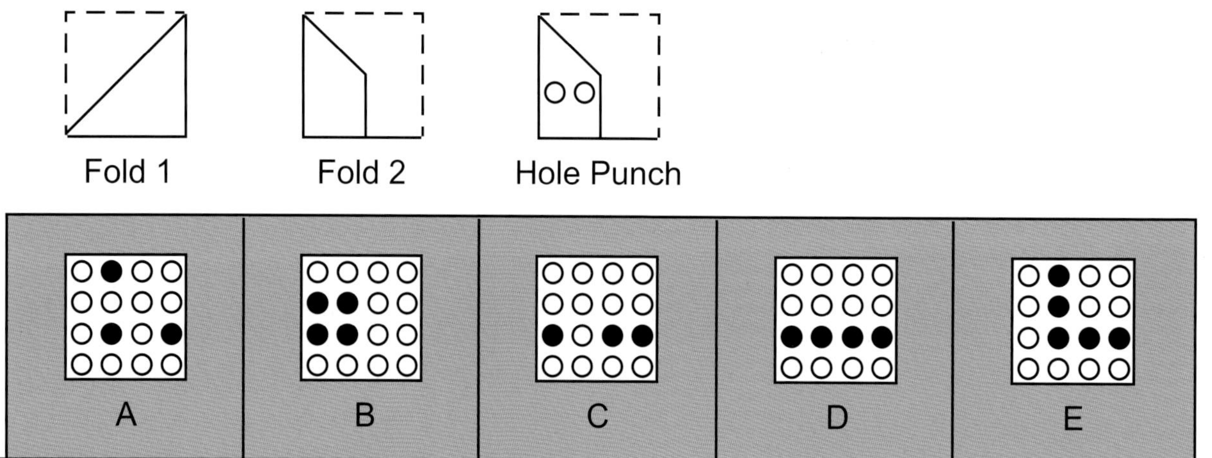

The first thing that you should do to answer this question is to count the number of layers from the first fold (Fold 1) to the last (Fold 2). To accurately track the folding sequence, it may help to draw a dotted line, representing the previous layer that is now hidden from view.

Fold 1 makes 2 layers.

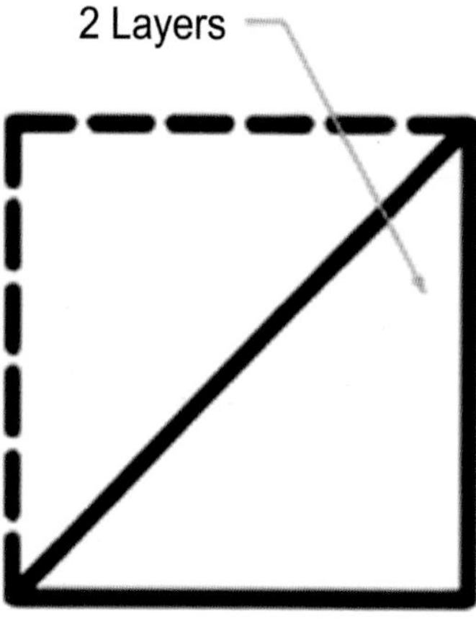

Now because Fold 1 makes a second fold, you might think that Fold 2 will simply yield another 2 layers. BE CAREFUL – this is not as simple as you might think. Take note that after the paper was folded to the left on Fold 2, Quadrant 1 of the paper remains 2 layers while the upper left half of Quadrant 3 is 2 layers and the lower right half, 4 layers.

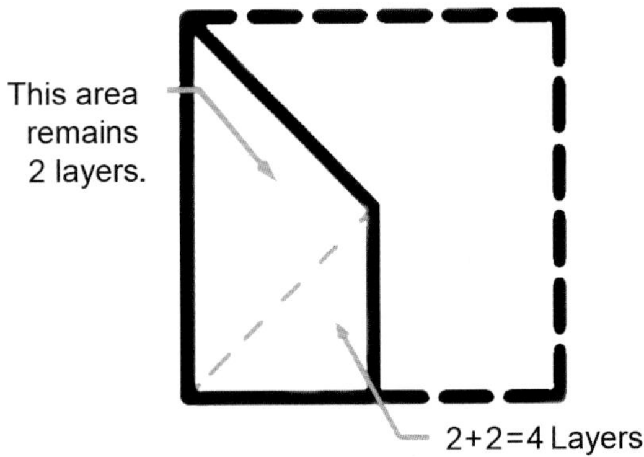
This area
remains
2 layers.
2+2=4 Layers

Next, observe that one of the holes is punched on the fold itself.

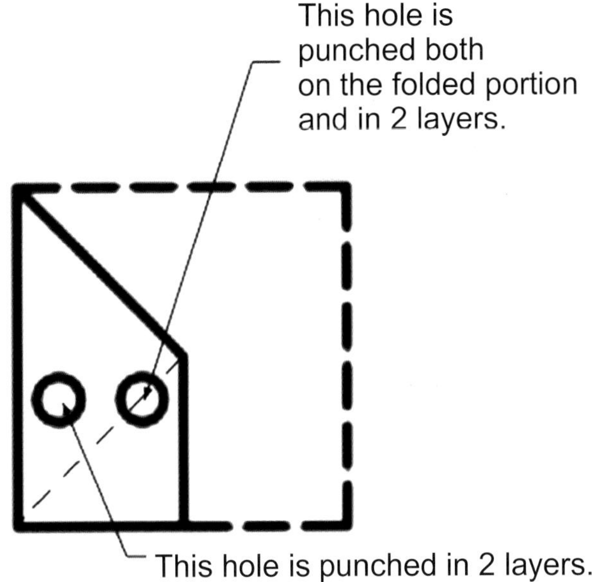
This hole is
punched both
on the folded portion
and in 2 layers.
This hole is punched in 2 layers.

The first hole, in the 3-1 location, is punched on a two-layer area. This means that this hole will be symmetrically reflected on the opposite side of the paper, specifically Hole 4-2. You can also think of this in mathematical terms: multiply the number of holes by the number of layers to get the total number of punched holes produced in a fold. You can now be certain that there should be at least 2 punched holes in the resulting pattern.

The second hole, on the other hand, requires some careful analysis. The hole is punched on the 3-2 location and it also falls on two areas:

1. the 2 layers from Fold 2: 2 layers multiplied by 1 hole makes 2 holes
2. the fold itself from Fold 1, which is now hidden: as discussed in section 5.2.2, a punch made on the hole itself makes only 1 hole

In total, the resulting pattern should have 5 holes. The only option with 5 holes is E, making it the best answer.

Alternatively, you can figure out the resulting hole-punched pattern using the 4-quadrant diagram. The following figures show how the hole-punches on the 3-1 and 3-2 spots create the 5-hole, L-shaped pattern from our sample problem.

Fold 1: Diagram Showing Possible Patterns of Symmetrical Hole-sequences Produced by the Diagonal Fold.

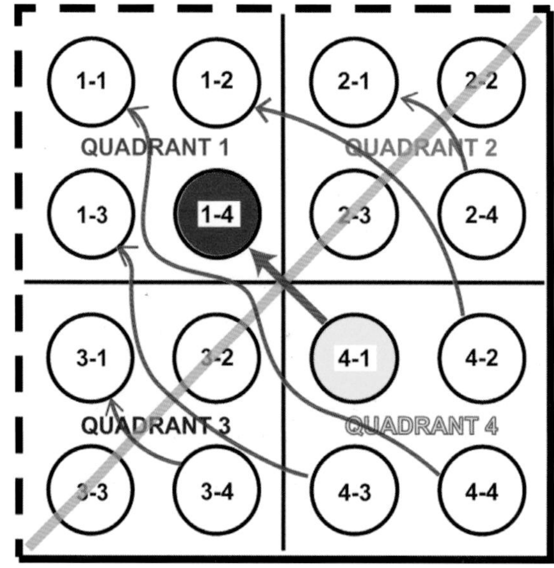

From the figure Fold 1, you will note that the following hole-sequences are expected to possibly create symmetrical patterns:

- 2-4 and 2-1
- 4-2 and 1-2
- 4-1 and 1-4
- 4-4 and 1-1
- 4-3 and 1-3
- 3-4 and 3-1

This time, figure Fold 2 shows the possible symmetrical hole-punched patterns generated by the vertical fold to the left. Take note that a three-point combination is created on 3 patterns:

- 4-1, 3-2, and 1-4
- 4-3, 3-4, and 1-3
- 4-4, 3-3, and 1-1

This is due to the overlapping layers of the diagonal fold on the first instance and the vertical fold on the second. On the other hand, take note that the following patterns from the diagonal fold on Fold 1 are also possible to show up on Fold 2:

- 2-4 and 2-1
- 4-2 and 1-2

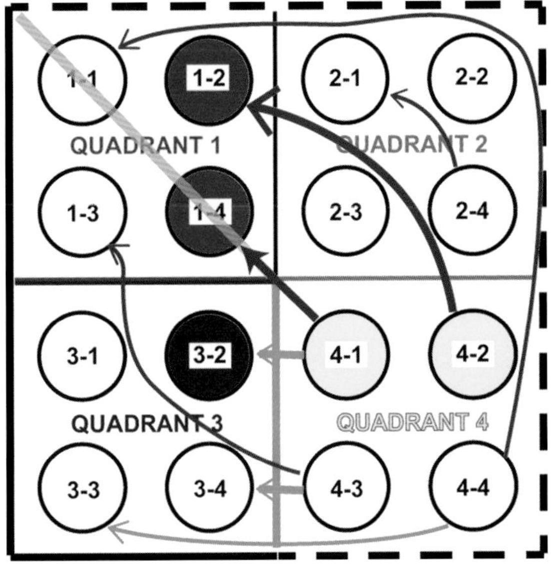

Fold 2: Diagram Showing Possible Patterns of Symmetrical Hole-sequences Produced by the Vertical Fold.

Now you can be certain that hole-sequences 3-2, 4-1, and 1-4 are part of the resulting pattern. On the other hand, take note that Hole 3-1 has already overlapped with Hole 3-4 during the diagonal fold. The vertical fold of the paper going to the left did not move this overlapping spot. Instead, the original 3-1 spot is now replaced by the overlapping holes of 4-2 and 1-2. This results to a final pattern that includes hole-sequences 1-2, 1-4, 3-2, 4-1, and 4-2.

To summarize, these are some of the strategies that you can use with the hole-punching PAT subsection:

1. Counting the layers brought about by the folds:
    - Count the number of layers on every fold
    - Separately count the number of layers for each hole-punch
    - Draw dashed lines to indicate hidden lines and edges

> To determine the number of holes created by a punch, multiply the number of holes by the number of layers where it is punched.

2. If the hole-punch is on the fold itself, immediately note the hole's location from the four quadrants.

3. Note the direction of the fold because this suggests the trend of the holes. Make sure you are familiar with the positions of the holes from the quadrants.

> Remember that the hole-punches follow a symmetrical pattern. Make sure to pay attention to the retained layer of the punched holes as well as the mirror locations of the hole-sequences.

Now that we have discussed the essential concepts and strategies involved in the PAT Paper Folding test, it is time for you to start applying them. Do as many exercises as possible. Your goal in the beginning is not to ace each and every question but to understand what makes your answers incorrect. In the process, you would hopefully find the approach that works best for you.

5.4 Mini Exercises

Choose the correct pattern that results from the following folding sequences:

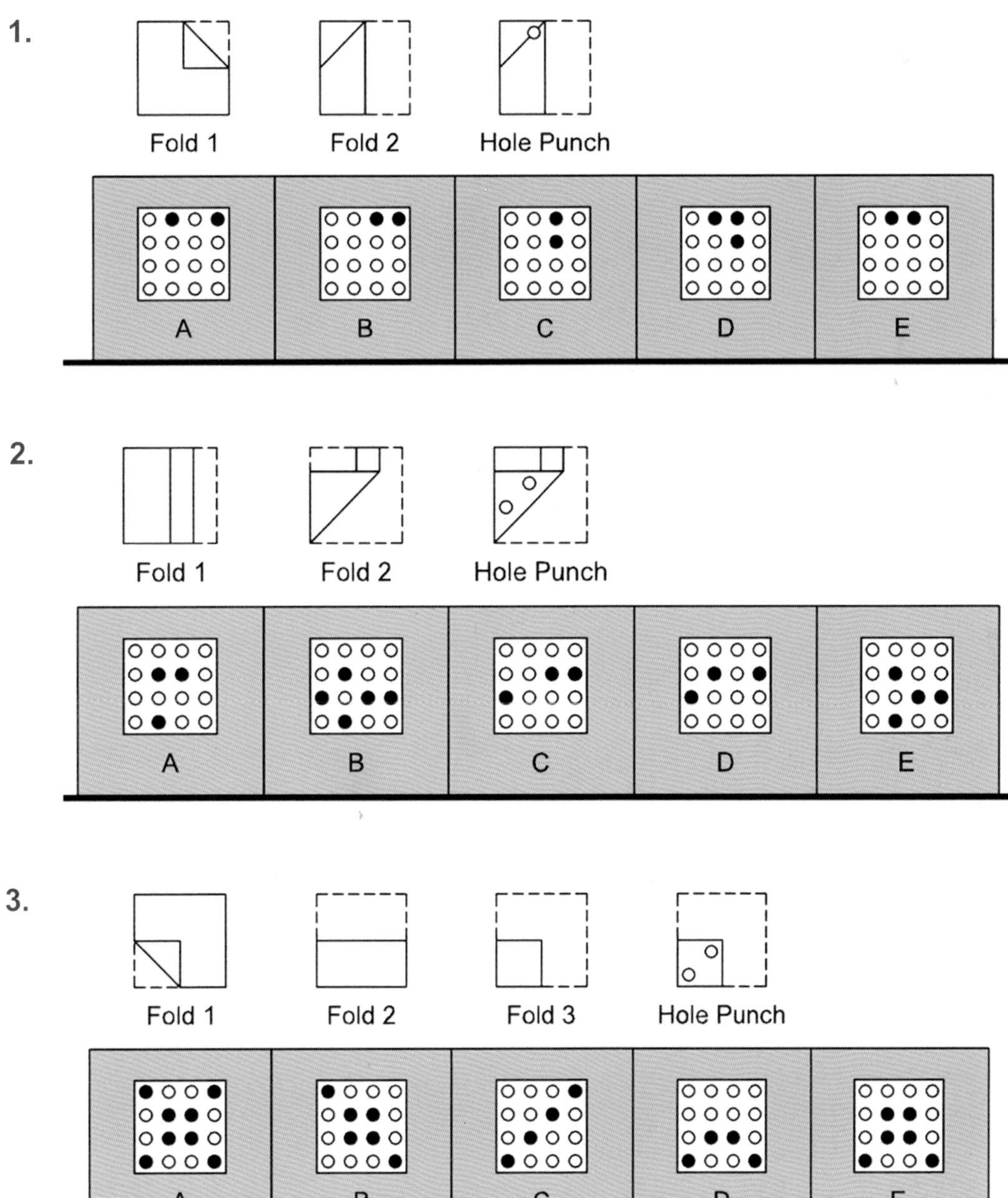

4.

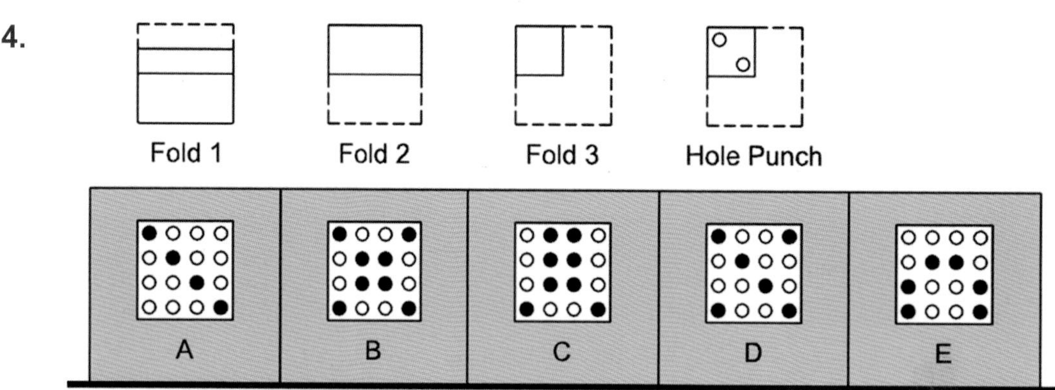

5.4.1 Answer Key and Explanations

1. Answer: B

Closely follow the folding of the paper, especially the number of layers on each fold. Fold 1 creates 2 layers. At this point, take note also that the diagonal fold is made along the lines of holes 2-1 and 2-4.

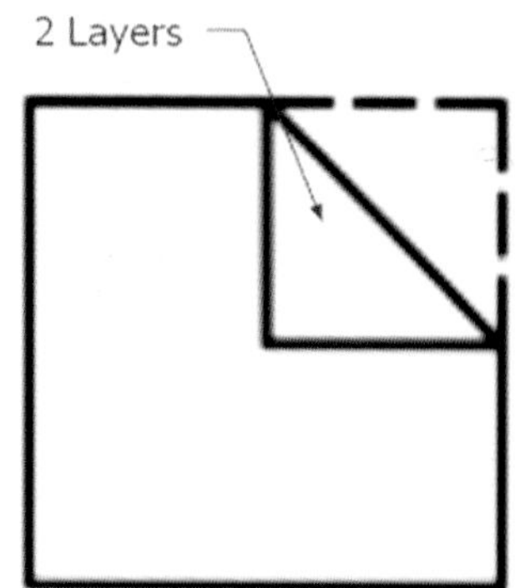

Fold 2 generates 3 areas, each with a differing number of layers. The upper left half of Quadrant 1 is 1 layer, its lower right half is 3 layers, and the whole area of Quadrant 3 is 2 layers. The hole-punch was made on the upper right spot of Quadrant 1 (the 1-2 location), so we will not worry about Quadrant 3 from here on.

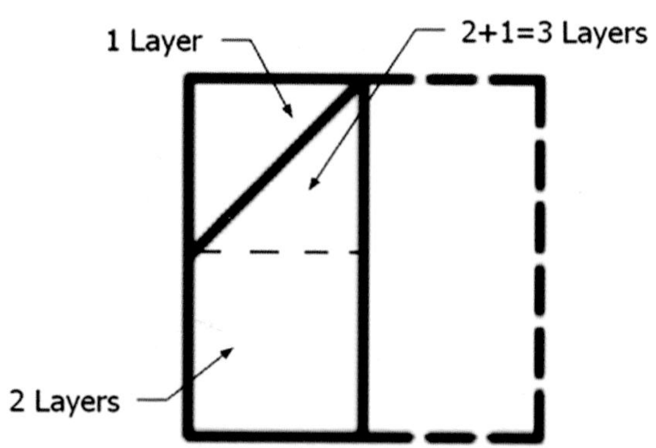

Two folds are made but only one hole is punched on the entire paper, and it is on a folded area. Remember that when a hole is punched on a folded portion, it will create just 1 hole.

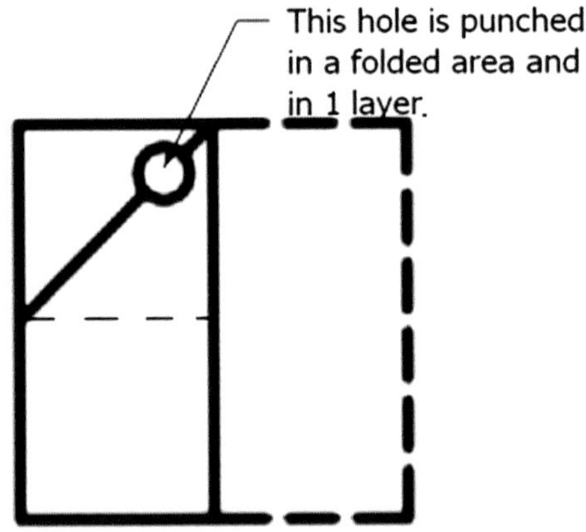
This hole is punched
in a folded area and
in 1 layer.

3 layers (on half of the 1-2 location) multiplied by a half-hole is 1.5; add, 1 layer (on the other half of the 1-2 location) multiplied a half hole is .5. There should be a total of 2 punched holes. You can easily delete option D.

Next, take note that we earlier identified the Fold 1 to have been made on the line that includes holes 2-1 and 2-4. This time, notice that the hole was punched on the 2-1 spot (only in reverse since the paper was folded going to the left on Fold 2). If you unfold the paper, the hole on the folded part is located at the upper left of Quadrant 2, which is hole 2-1. This spot is symmetrical to the hole 1-2 of Quadrant 1. Therefore, the correct answer is B.

2. Answer: B

In this question, sketching the hidden edges of the folds would greatly help in determining the number of layers. Plot the 4 quadrants with their corresponding hole-sequences if you have to.

Carefully observe the number of layers where each hole is punched. The hole-punch on the 1-4 spot has 3 layers while the bottom hole (on the 3-1 spot) is punched in 2 layers. Using the layer-counting strategy, the following formula would prove that the total number of holes in the resulting pattern should be 5:

3 layers × 1 hole = 3
2 layers × 1 hole = 2
3 + 2 = 5 holes

Only option B has 5 holes, so it is the correct answer.

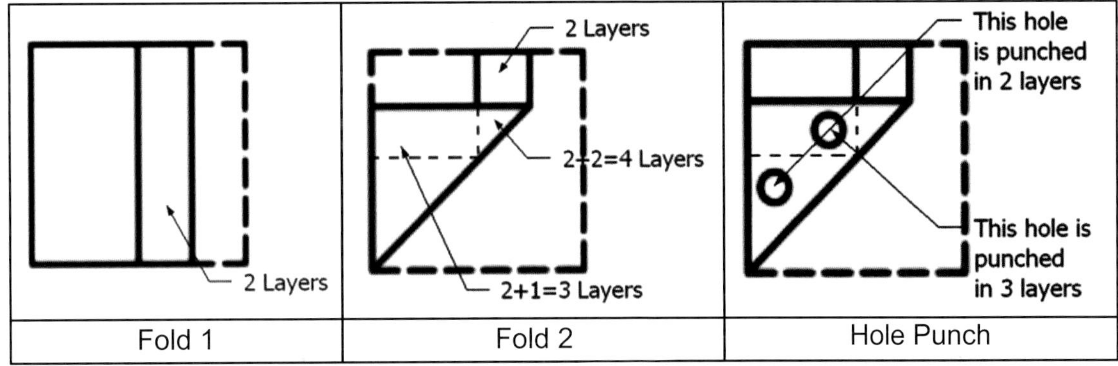
2 Layers
2 Layers
2+2=4 Layers
2+1=3 Layers
This hole is punched in 2 layers
This hole is punched in 3 layers
Fold 1
Fold 2
Hole Punch

3. Answer: A

Your knowledge of the hole-sequences in the quadrants will be highly useful in this question. Drawing dashed lines will also aid you in knowing the precise number of layers where the holes are punched.

Take note that the paper is folded three times. First look at the upper hole (on the 3-2 spot) and trace back the number of layers on this hole-punch from Fold 1 (2 layers) to Fold 2 (1 layer added) to Fold 3 (2 layers added). Hole-punch on the 3-2 spot is therefore 5-layered.

Now trace back the layers on the lower hole (on the 3-3 spot) from Fold 1 (none) to Fold 2 (1 layer) to Fold 3 (2 layers added). This hole-punch has 3 layers. You should then be looking for a folding pattern with 8 holes. Easily, you would know that the correct answer is A.

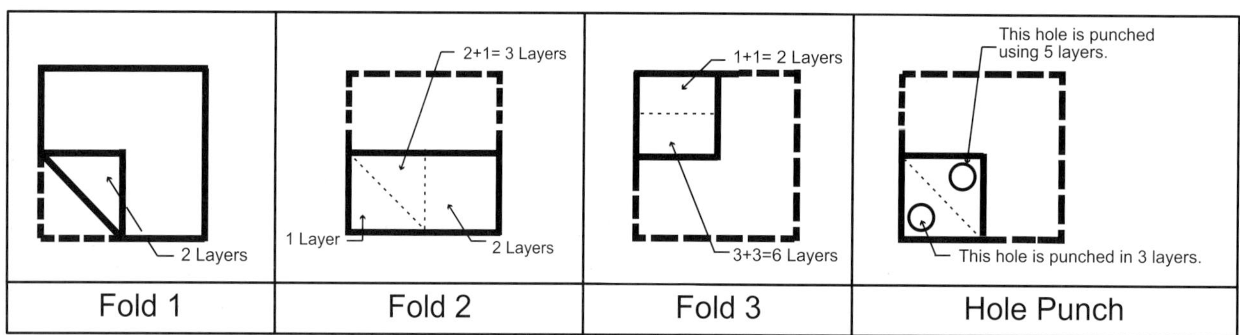

4. Answer: C

In answering this question, it is important to remember the direction of the folding. This way, you would not get confused in counting the number of layers in each area.

Similar to question 3, the paper is folded three times. First, determine the number of layers on the upper hole (on the 1-1 spot): Fold 1 (none), Fold 2 (1 layer), Fold 3 (1 layer added). This hole-punch has 2 layers.

The lower hole (on the 1-4 spot) has 2 layers on Fold 1, 1 layer added on Fold 2, and 3 layers added on Fold 3. Thus the lower hole-punch has 6 layers. The pattern that we will be looking for should have a total of 8 holes. This narrows down your answer choices to B and C.

Now let's go back to the upper hole-punch and evaluate the symmetrical patterns of the holes. (It would be good to draw a diagram of the 4 quadrants here.)

Take note that because the paper is already folded on Fold 1, Holes 1-1 and 1-2, 2-1 and 2-2 are instantly eliminated from the pattern of the upper hole-punch ONLY. You will note later that Holes 1-2 and 2-1 will still show up for the lower hole-punch.

In the meantime, you can only start on Fold 2: the hole-sequence that lands on this spot is 3-3. On Fold 3, Hole 4-4 joins the layer.

Next, let's evaluate the lower hole-punch. On Fold 1, the symmetrical Holes 1-2 and 1-4 make up the 2 layers. On Fold 2, Hole 3-2 goes with the third layer. On Fold 3, 3 symmetrical holes - Holes 2-1, 2-3, and 4-1- should be included.

The correct pattern should include Holes 1-2, 1-4, 2-1, 2-3, 3-2, 3-3, 4-1 and 4-4. The right answer is C.

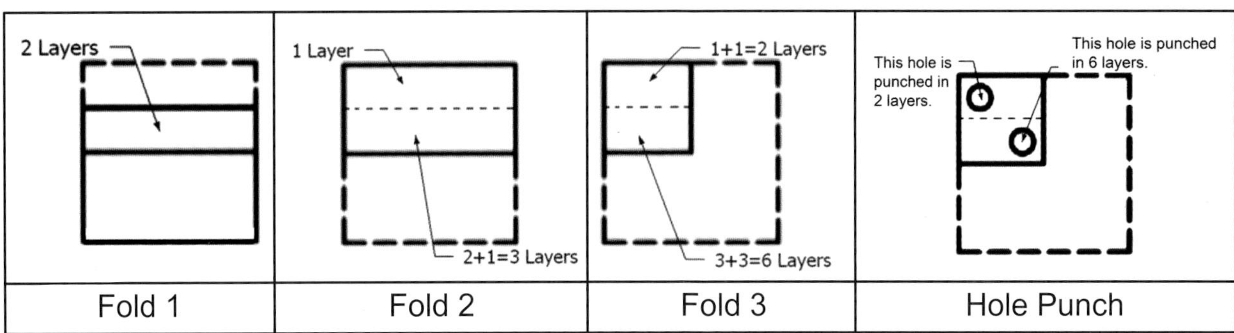

GOLD STANDARD WARM-UP EXERCISES

CHAPTER 5: Paper Folding

The following questions represent one of the six subsections in the Perceptual Ability Test of the DAT. While this serves as a review of the discussions in this chapter, the level of difficulty of each question closely parallels the actual test.

You have 10 minutes to complete this portion of the DAT Mini Test; the actual test is 60 minutes.

Please time yourself accordingly.

BEGIN ONLY WHEN YOUR TIMER IS READY

1.

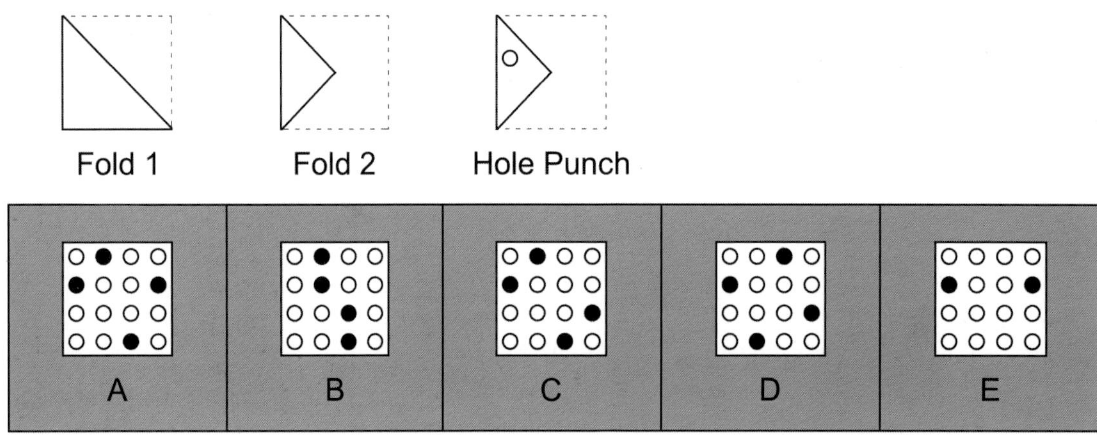

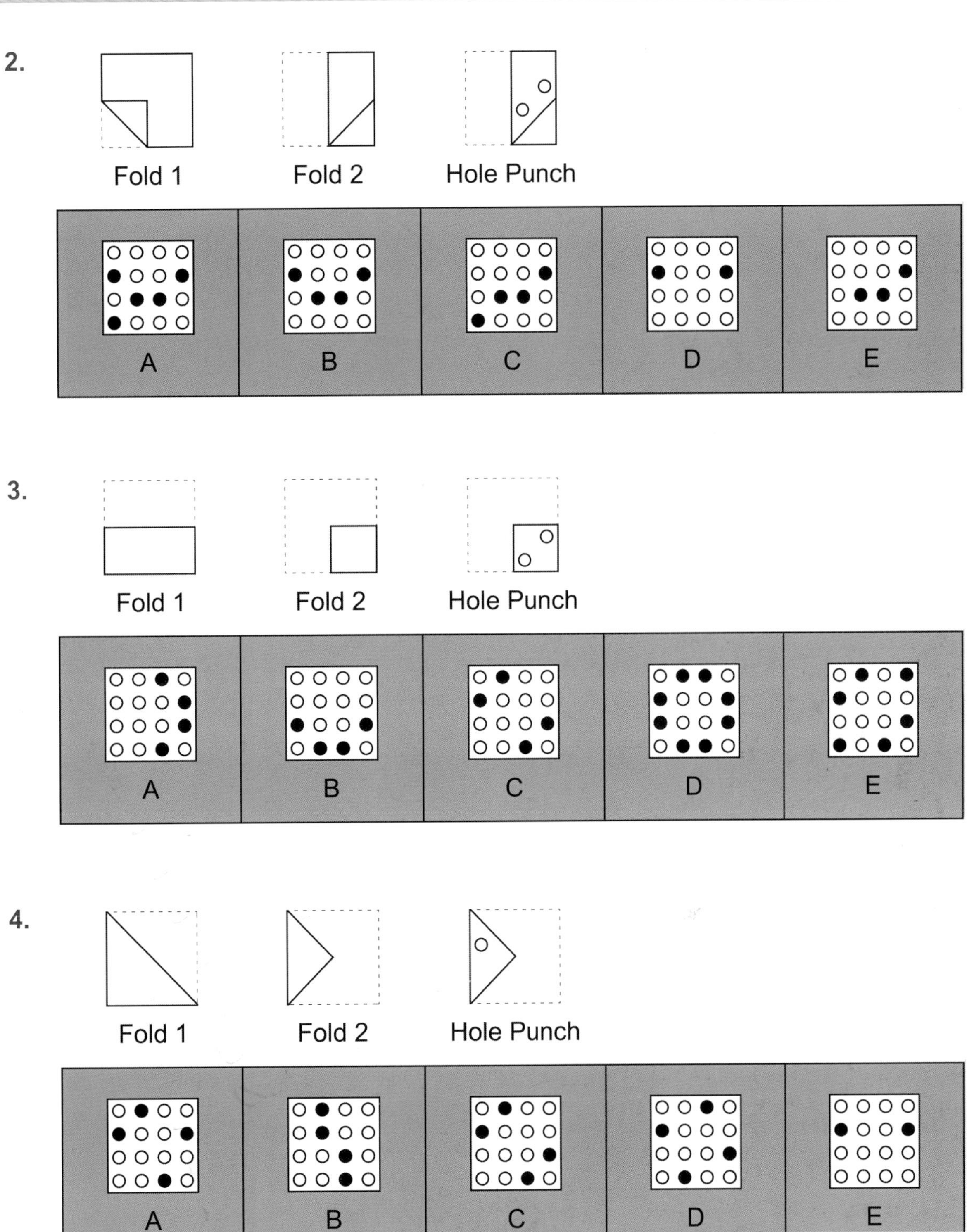
2.
Fold 1
Fold 2
Hole Punch
A
B
C
D
E
3.
Fold 1
Fold 2
Hole Punch
A
B
C
D
E
4.
Fold 1
Fold 2
Hole Punch
A
B
C
D
E

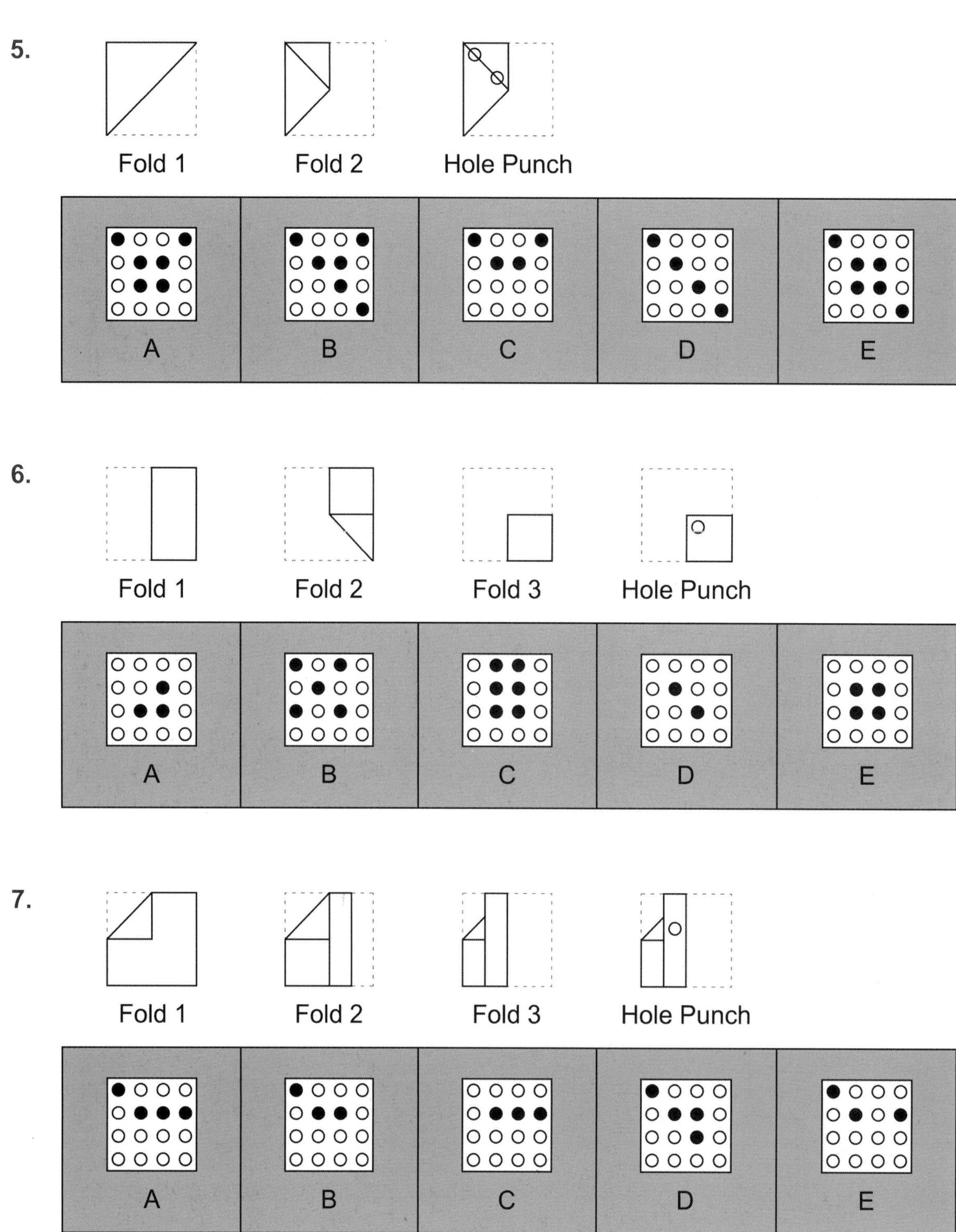
5.
Fold 1
Fold 2
Hole Punch
A
B
C
D
E
6.
Fold 1
Fold 2
Fold 3
Hole Punch
A
B
C
D
E
7.
Fold 1
Fold 2
Fold 3
Hole Punch
A
B
C
D
E

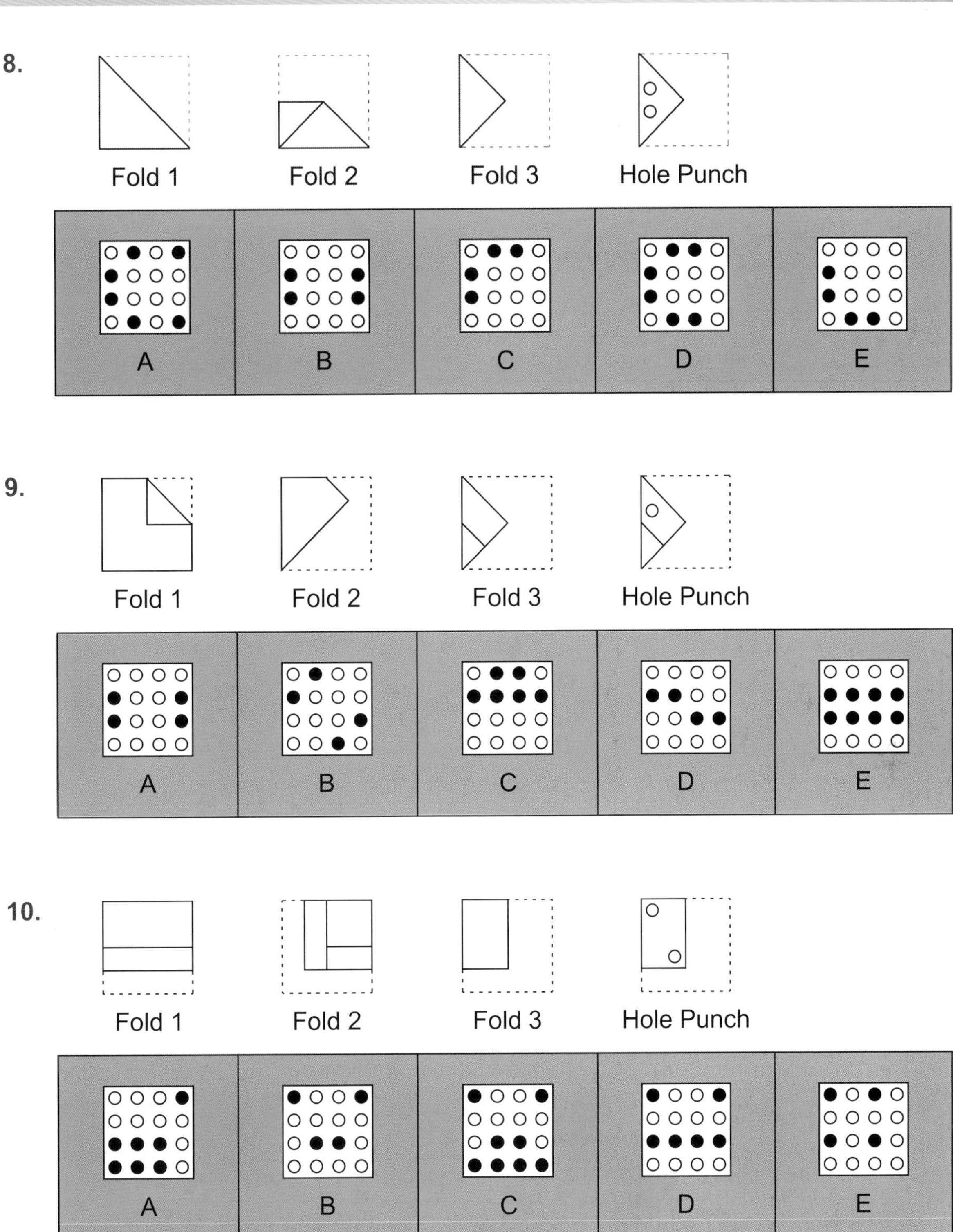
8.
Fold 1
Fold 2
Fold 3
Hole Punch
A
B
C
D
E
9.
Fold 1
Fold 2
Fold 3
Hole Punch
A
B
C
D
E
10.
Fold 1
Fold 2
Fold 3
Hole Punch
A
B
C
D
E

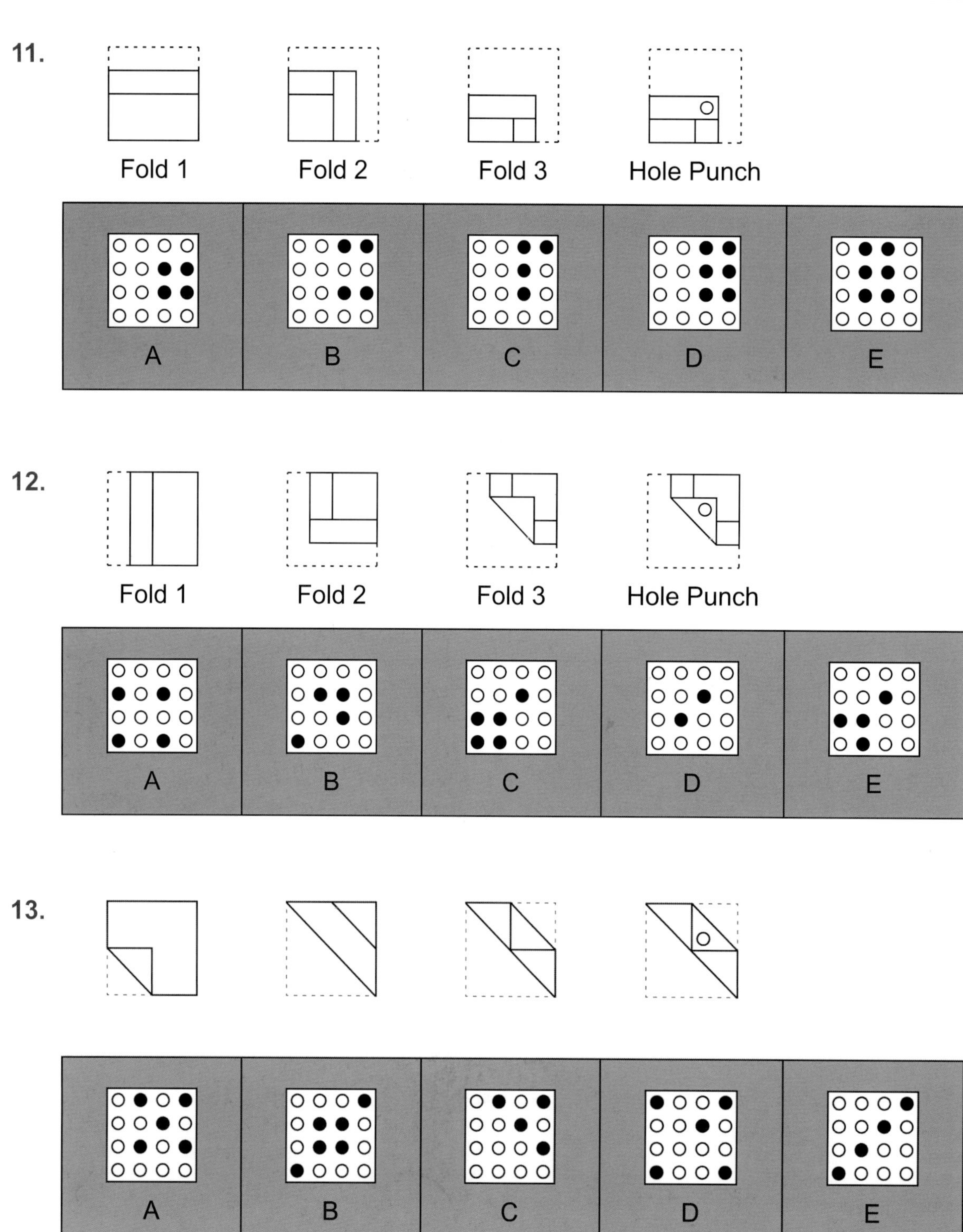
11.
Fold 1
Fold 2
Fold 3
Hole Punch
A
B
C
D
E
12.
Fold 1
Fold 2
Fold 3
Hole Punch
A
B
C
D
E
13.
A
B
C
D
E

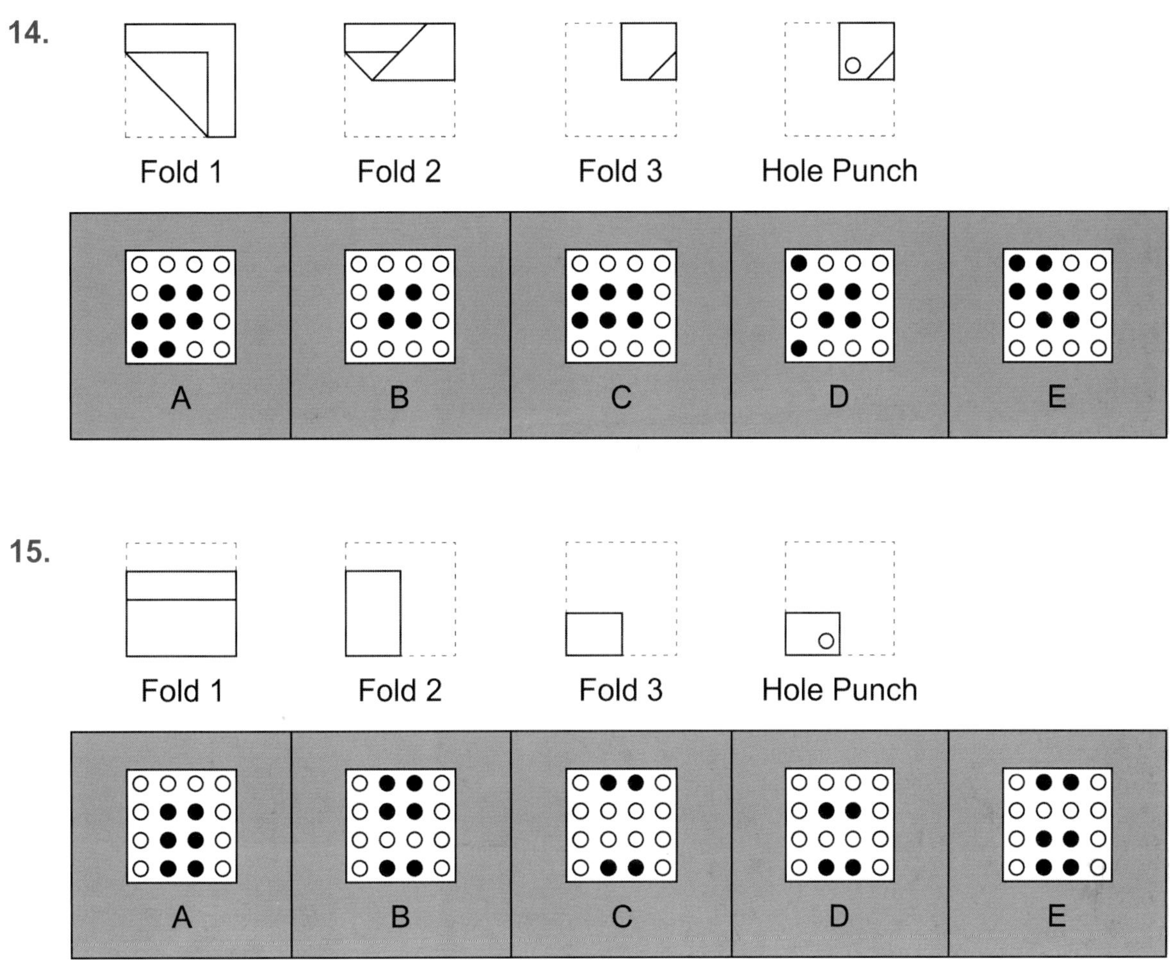

If time remains, you may review your work. If your allotted time is complete, please proceed to the Answer Key.

GS ANSWER KEY

CHAPTER 5

1.	D	9.	D
2.	A	10.	D
3.	B	11.	C
4.	C	12.	B
5.	D	13.	A
6.	C	14.	C
7.	B	15.	A
8.	A		

* Explanations can be found in the Lessons section at www.dat-prep.com.

Go online to DAT-prep.com for additional chapter review Q&A and forum.

Go online to DAT-prep.com for additional chapter review Q&A and forum.

CUBE COUNTING
Chapter 6

Memorize

* The Gold Standard Cube Counting Formula

Understand

* Three Assumptions of the Cube Formations
* Examples of Cubes with 1 to 5 Exposed Sides

Introduction

A cube is a three-dimensional object with six square faces. Cube counting involves assessing three-dimensional cubes of the same size, stacked in a certain formation, and thereafter, painted on all sides except the base, which rests on a surface.

When cubes are piled over the other or one behind another, some may become invisible behind or under the others. Nonetheless, you should include the painted surfaces of these hidden cubes when counting. This section obviously challenges your thorough attention to details.

Additional Resources

Free Online Forum

6.1 About Cube Counting

The fifth subsection of the PAT consists of 15 multiple-choice questions that involve cube-counting. Formations of stacked cubes are presented, followed by two to four questions that ask you to identify the total count of cubes, which have a particular number of sides painted.

In Figure 1, how many cubes have two of their exposed sides painted?

A. 1 cube
B. 2 cubes
C. 3 cubes
D. 4 cubes
E. 5 cubes

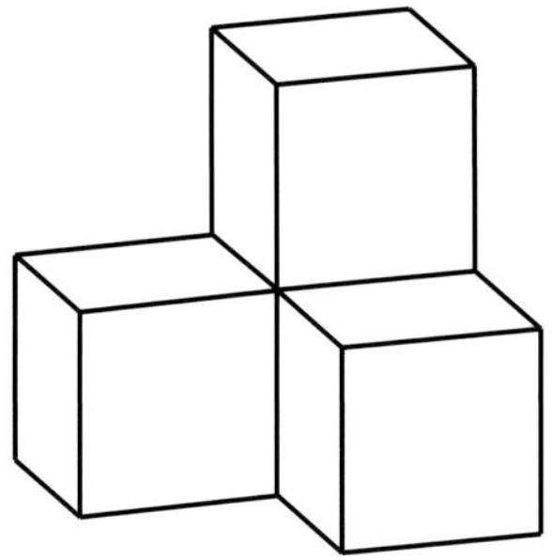

Figure PAT 6.1: Simplistic Sample Figure and Cube Counting Question in the PAT. The correct answer is **A**.

You are to imagine that each figure in the test is constructed by bonding identical cubes together. Thereafter, the cubes are painted on all of their exposed surfaces, excluding the bases. The number of painted sides per cube can range from zero to five.

6.2 Understanding the Cube Formations

Most candidates find this PAT subsection to be relatively easy because the questions merely involve simple counting and a keen eye for details. Nevertheless, you have to keep in mind that some cubes may be "invisible" – that is, they are piled either behind or under other cubes. Essentially, there are three assumptions of cube formations:

1. A cube that serves as a base supporting another cube on top of it may be hidden from view if there are four other cubes attached to it. This type of cube is usually found "inside" the stacks. At other times, it is located at the back of the pile.
2. The stack of cubes is assumed to be continuous where there are no gaps in between.
3. There are no floating cubes.

6.3 Cube Counting Strategies

It is important to note that for every model given in this test, the corresponding set of questions follows a chronological sequence that starts by asking for the smallest number to the most number of cubes with their X number of sides exposed. Continuing from our sample question in Figure PAT 6.1, these are the complete set of questions pertaining to the figure:

1. In Figure 1, how many cubes have two of their exposed sides painted?

   A. 1 cube
   B. 2 cubes
   C. 3 cubes
   D. 4 cubes
   E. 5 cubes

2. In Figure 1, how many cubes have four of their exposed sides painted?

   A. 1 cube
   B. 2 cubes
   C. 3 cubes
   D. 4 cubes
   E. 5 cubes

3. In Figure 1, how many cubes have five of their exposed sides painted?

   A. 1 cube
   B. 2 cubes
   C. 3 cubes
   D. 4 cubes
   E. 5 cubes

This means that when evaluating the cube formations, beginning with the inner portion and the bottom of the figure would be quite logical since these are the areas where you would find most of the cubes with only 1 exposed side painted.

Visualize the hidden cubes and determine how many other cubes connect to it. Focus on the number of cubes attached rather than the cube itself. Using the dry erase board provided in the test center, sketch the figure and mark the cubes with the number of exposed sides, which you have already identified. You can also designate numbers on cubes from the bottom front to the upper rear cubes, depending on your preference to avoid confusion.

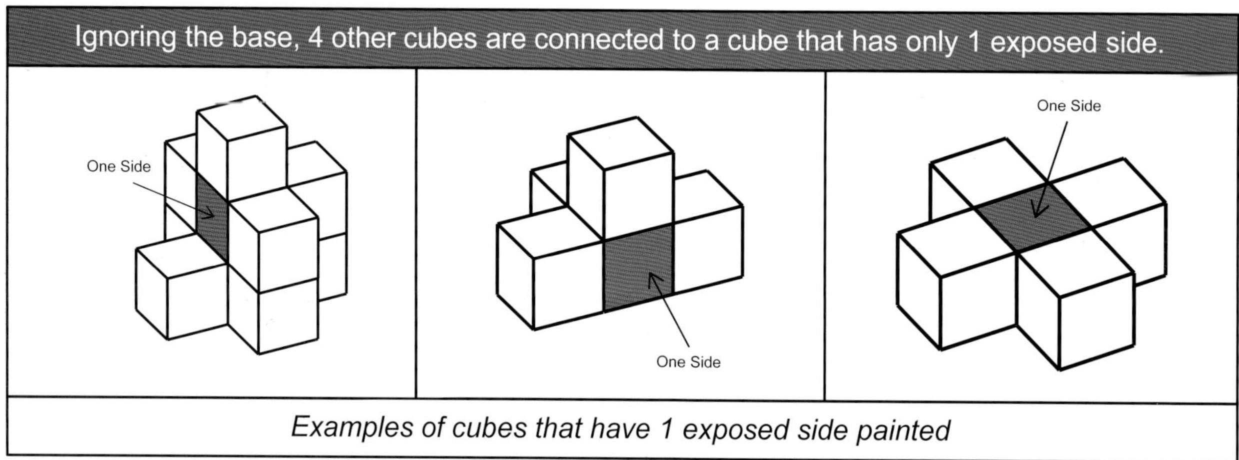
Ignoring the base, 4 other cubes are connected to a cube that has only 1 exposed side.
One Side
One Side
One Side

Examples of cubes that have 1 exposed side painted

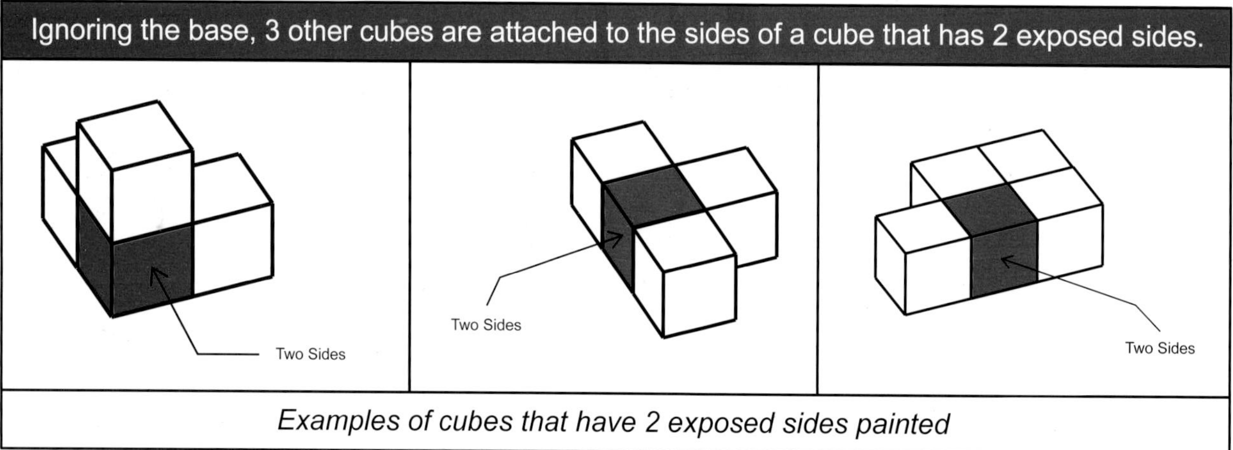
Ignoring the base, 3 other cubes are attached to the sides of a cube that has 2 exposed sides.
Two Sides
Two Sides
Two Sides

Examples of cubes that have 2 exposed sides painted

Ignoring the base, 2 other cubes are connected to the sides of a cube that has 3 exposed sides.

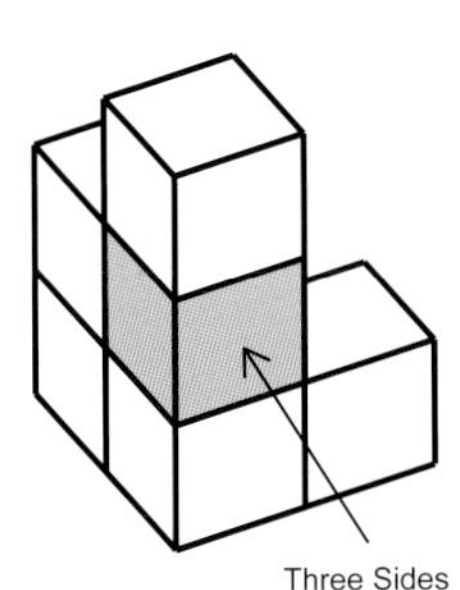

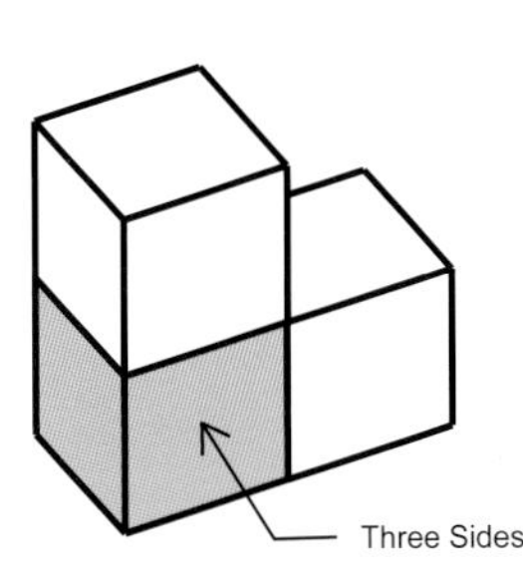

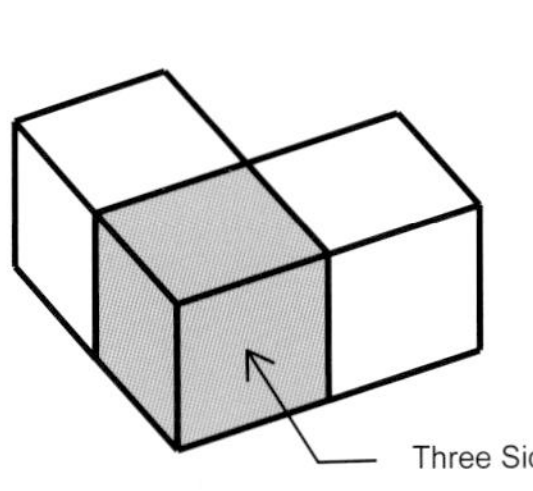

Examples of cubes that have 3 exposed sides painted

Ignoring the base, only 1 cube is attached to a cube that has 4 exposed sides.

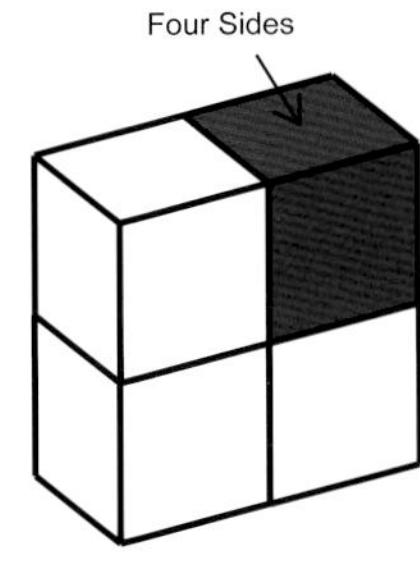

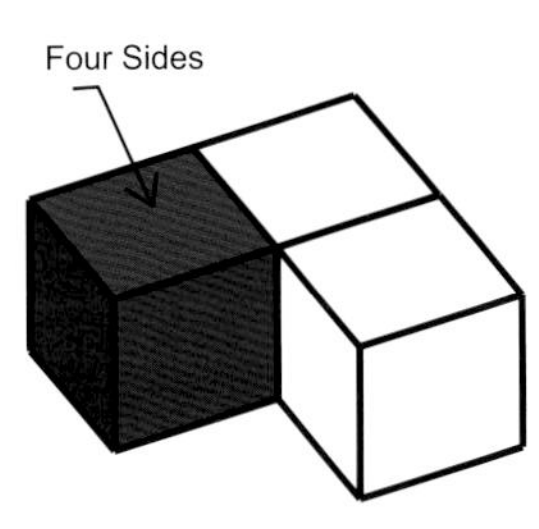

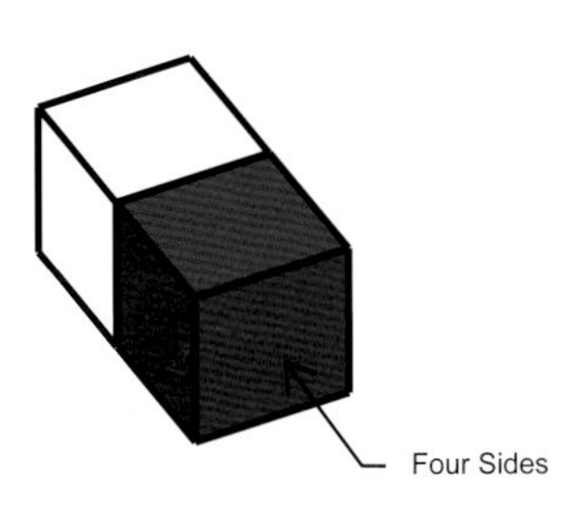

Examples of cubes that have 4 exposed sides painted

A cube that has 5 of its exposed sides painted should be found on top without any cube connected to it except the one acting as its base.

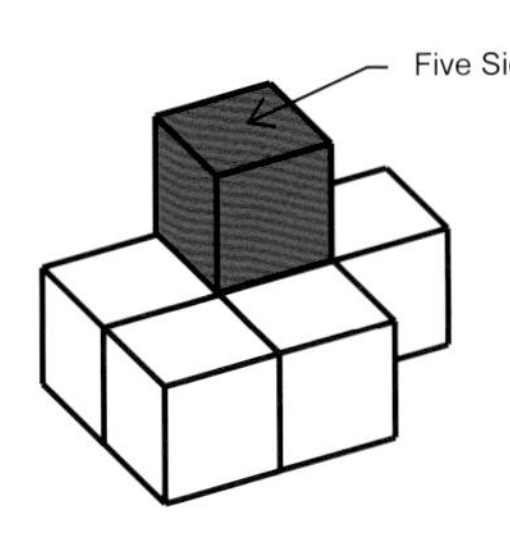

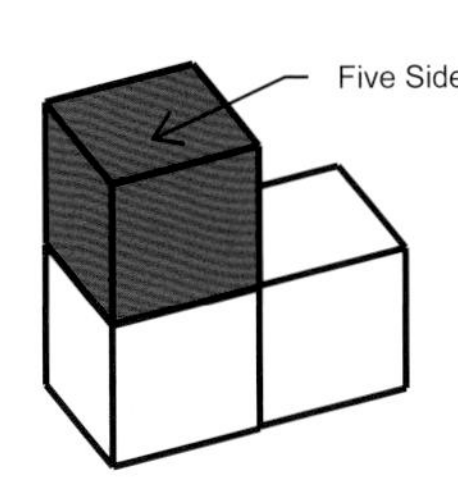

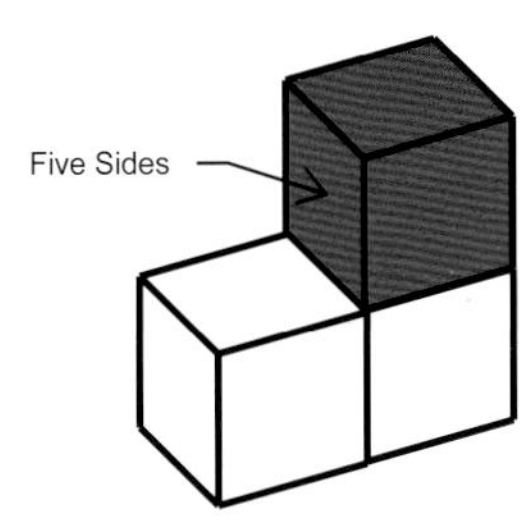

Examples of cubes that have 5 exposed sides painted

6.3.1 The Gold Standard Cube Counting Formula

Using a simple mathematical principle, you can simply scan each cube and calculate the sides that can be painted. We know that a cube can only have six sides. But because the bottom of these cubes rests on a parallel plane (remember the third assumption: no floating cubes), you should always consider just five sides when you calculate the number of sides exposed.

Now determine the number of other cubes surrounding a cube. Subtract these from 5 (representing the five sides of the cube that can be possibly exposed or attached to). The difference is the number of sides painted.

6 sides of a regular cube – 1 side (its base) = 5 exposed sides to consider
Number of cubes attached = n

$5 - n$ = number of exposed sides painted

6.4 Mini Exercises

PROBLEM A

1. In Figure A, how many cubes have two of their exposed sides painted?

A. 1 cube
B. 2 cubes
C. 3 cubes
D. 4 cubes
E. 5 cubes

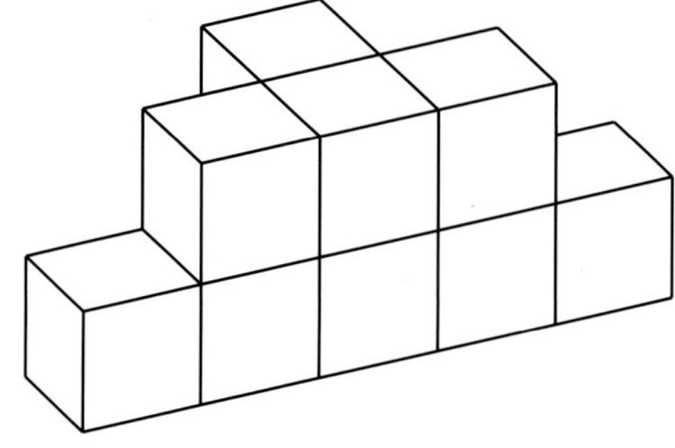

Figure A

2. In Figure A, how many cubes have four of their exposed sides painted?

A. 1 cube
B. 2 cubes
C. 3 cubes
D. 4 cubes
E. 5 cubes

PROBLEM B

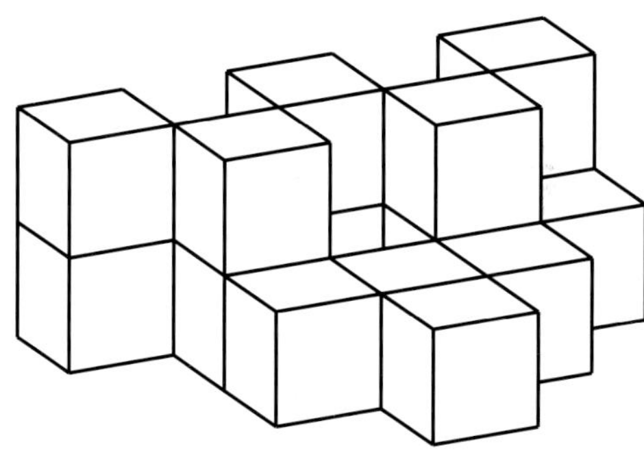

Figure B

3. In Figure B, how many cubes have two of their exposed sides painted?

A. 1 cube
B. 2 cubes
C. 3 cubes
D. 4 cubes
E. 5 cubes

4. In Figure B, how many cubes have three of their exposed sides painted?

A. 1 cube
B. 2 cubes
C. 3 cubes
D. 4 cubes
E. 5 cubes

5. In Figure B, how many cubes have four of their exposed sides painted?

A. 1 cube
B. 2 cubes
C. 3 cubes
D. 4 cubes
E. 5 cubes

6.4.1 Answer Key and Explanations

1. Answer: C

In this question, keep in mind that when looking for cubes that have 2 of their exposed sides painted, you should identify those cubes that have 3 other cubes attached to it. These are mostly located at the inner portion of the figure. The 3 cubes are colored red in the diagram for easy viewing. The correct answer is C.

2. Answer: E

For cubes that have more exposed sides painted, lesser number of cubes are attached to it. This question asks for cubes having 4 of their exposed sides painted hence search for cubes located at the outer portion or the edges of the figure. There are 5 cubes that have 4 of their exposed sides painted. Therefore, the correct answer is E.

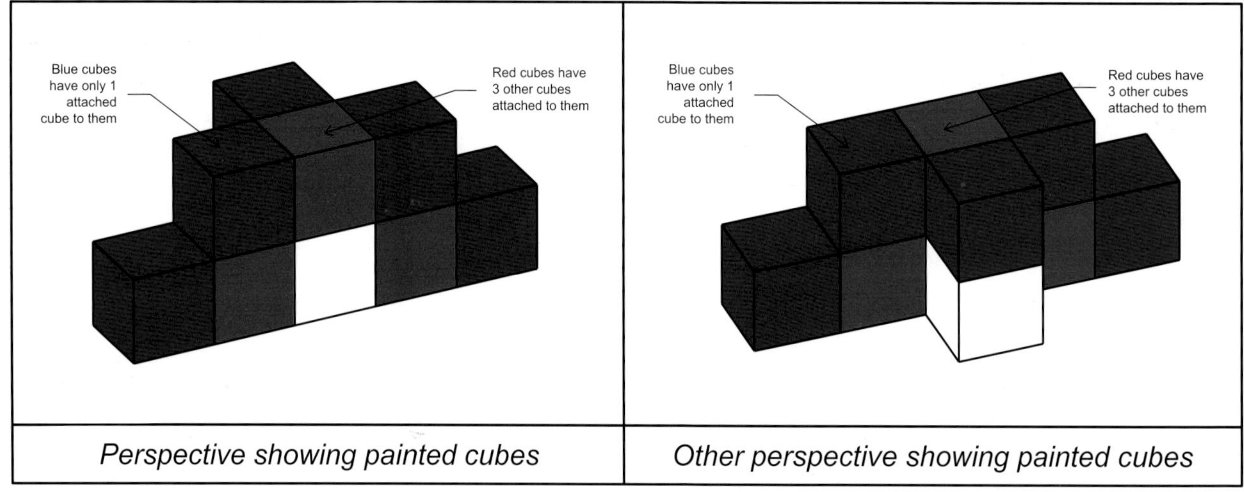

Perspective showing painted cubes	*Other perspective showing painted cubes*

3. Answer: B

This question requires that you look for the number of cubes that have 2 of their exposed sides painted. These cubes are frequently positioned at the bottom or in between cubes. There are only 2 red cubes in the figure, which means that the correct answer is B.

4. Answer: E

If the question asks for the number of cubes with 3 of their sides exposed, look for cubes having 2 cubes attached. In this case, all green cubes are located at the bottom of the figure. There are a total of 5 green cubes that have 3 exposed sides painted. Thus, the correct answer is E.

5. Answer: C

This question asks for the total number of cubes that have 4 of their exposed sides painted. Bear in mind that only 1 cube should be attached to this cube excluding the base. They are typically situated at the edge or at the corner of the figure. Hence, the correct answer is C because there are only 3 cubes having 4 of their sides exposed.

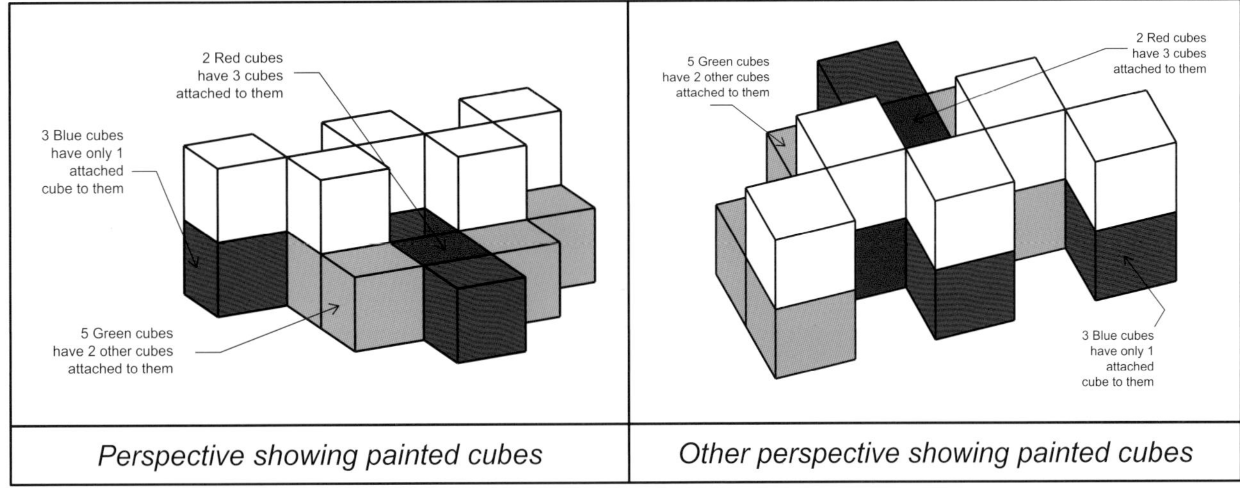

Perspective showing painted cubes | *Other perspective showing painted cubes*

GOLD STANDARD WARM-UP EXERCISES

Chapter 6: Cube Counting

The following questions represent one of the six subsections in the Perceptual Ability Test of the DAT. While this serves as a review of the discussions in this chapter, the level of difficulty of each question closely parallels the actual test.

You have 10 minutes to complete this portion of the DAT Mini Test; the actual test is 60 minutes.

Please time yourself accordingly.

BEGIN ONLY WHEN YOUR TIMER IS READY

Problem A

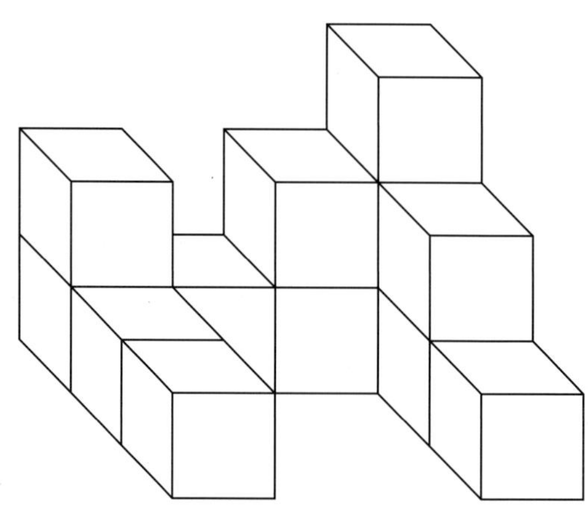
Figure A

1. In Figure A, how many cubes have two of their exposed sides painted?

   A. 1 cube
   B. 2 cubes
   C. 3 cubes
   D. 4 cubes
   E. 5 cubes

2. In Figure A, how many cubes have three of their exposed sides painted?

   A. 1 cube
   B. 2 cubes
   C. 3 cubes
   D. 4 cubes
   E. 5 cubes

3. In Figure A, how many cubes have four of their exposed sides painted?

   A. 1 cube
   B. 2 cubes
   C. 3 cubes
   D. 4 cubes
   E. 5 cubes

Problem B

4. In Figure B, how many cubes have three of their exposed sides painted?

   A. 1 cube
   B. 2 cubes
   C. 3 cubes
   D. 4 cubes
   E. 5 cubes

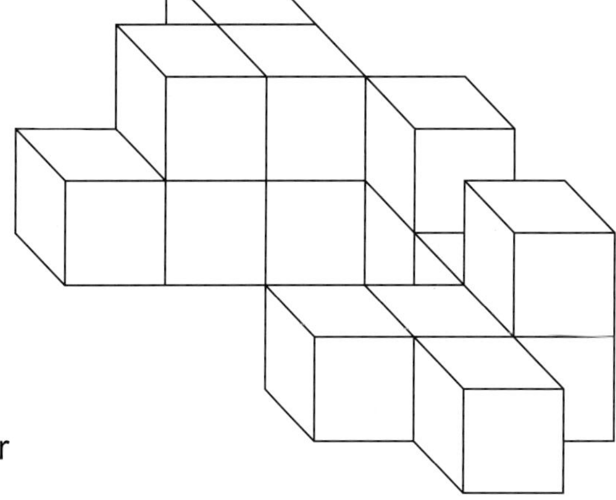

Figure B

5. In Figure B, how many cubes have four of their exposed sides painted?

   A. 1 cube
   B. 2 cubes
   C. 3 cubes
   D. 4 cubes
   E. 5 cubes

Problem C

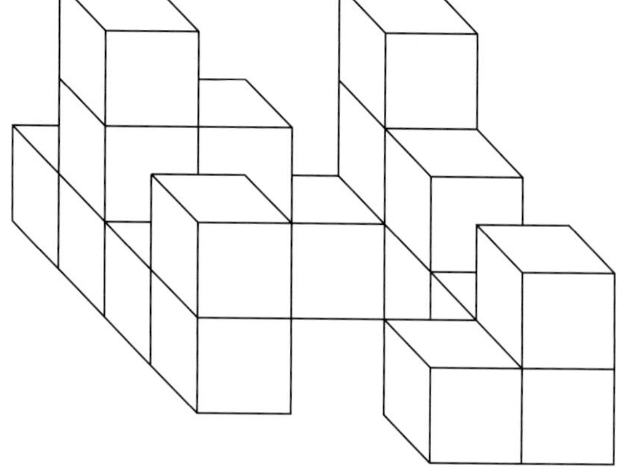

Figure C

6. In Figure C, how many cubes have two of their exposed sides painted?

   A. 1 cube
   B. 2 cubes
   C. 3 cubes
   D. 4 cubes
   E. 5 cubes

7. In Figure C, how many cubes have four of their exposed sides painted?

   A. 1 cube
   B. 2 cubes
   C. 3 cubes
   D. 4 cubes
   E. 5 cubes

8. In Figure C, how many cubes have five of their exposed sides painted?

   A. 1 cube
   B. 2 cubes
   C. 3 cubes
   D. 4 cubes
   E. 5 cubes

Problem D

9. In Figure D, how many cubes have two of their exposed sides painted?

   A. 1 cube
   B. 2 cubes
   C. 3 cubes
   D. 4 cubes
   E. 5 cubes

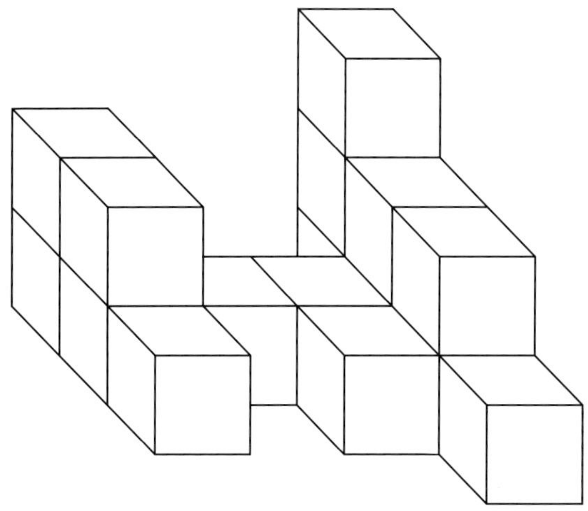

Figure D

10. In Figure D, how many cubes have four of their exposed sides painted?

   A. 1 cube
   B. 2 cubes
   C. 3 cubes
   D. 4 cubes
   E. 5 cubes

Problem E

11. In Figure E, how many cubes have one of their exposed sides painted?

   A. 1 cube
   B. 2 cubes
   C. 3 cubes
   D. 4 cubes
   E. 5 cubes

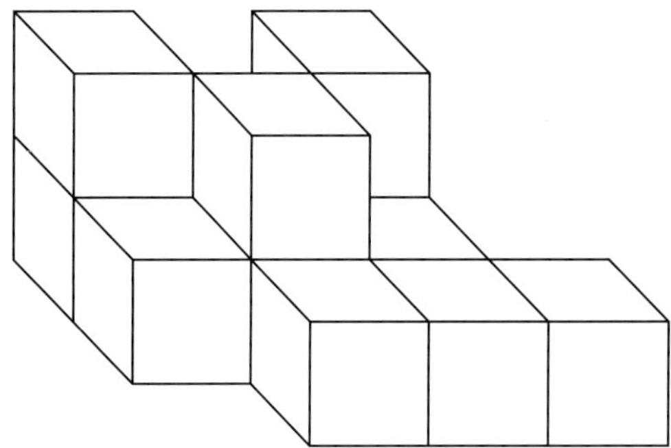

Figure E

12. In Figure E, how many cubes have three
of their exposed sides painted?

A. 1 cube
B. 2 cubes
C. 3 cubes
D. 4 cubes
E. 5 cubes

13. In Figure E, how many cubes have five of their exposed sides painted?

A. 1 cube
B. 2 cubes
C. 3 cubes
D. 4 cubes
E. 5 cubes

Problem F

14. In Figure F, how many cubes have two of their exposed sides painted?

A. 1 cube
B. 2 cubes
C. 3 cubes
D. 4 cubes
E. 5 cubes

15. In Figure F, how many cubes have four of their exposed sides painted?

A. 1 cube
B. 2 cubes
C. 3 cubes
D. 4 cubes
E. 5 cubes

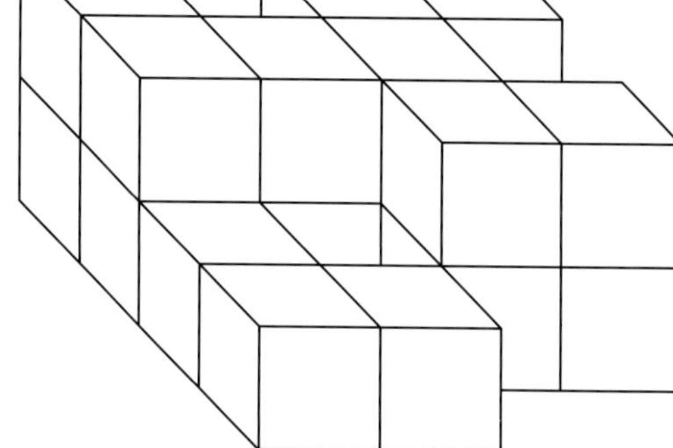

Figure F

If time remains, you may review your work. If your allotted time is complete, please proceed to the Answer Key.

GS ANSWER KEY

Chapter 6

1.	E	9.	A
2.	B	10.	E
3.	D	11.	A
4.	D	12.	D
5.	E	13.	C
6.	D	14.	D
7.	D	15.	D
8.	D		

* Explanations can be found in the Lessons section at www.dat-prep.com.

Go online to DAT-prep.com for additional chapter review Q&A and forum.

Go online to DAT-prep.com for additional chapter review Q&A and forum.

3D FORM DEVELOPMENT

Chapter 7

Understand

* **The Folding Pattern**
* **Significant Parts of the Unfolded Figure**

Introduction

Form Development requires mentally constructing the unfolded pattern of a three-dimensional object into its formed shape. Different flat patterns represent various figures, which can include a shaded dice, a diamond, and any irregular shape.

Just as the other preceding sections in the PAT, the 3D Form Development section tests your ability to spot fine differences but this time, actively perceiving an object spatially and in multiple probable forms.

Additional Resources

Free Online Forum

7.1 About 3D Form Development

The last subsection of the PAT is the 3D Form Development test – also known as Pattern Folding. Each question presents a flat pattern figure. You are to imagine folding it into a three-dimensional figure, which can turn out to be a dice, a cube, or an irregularly-shaped object.

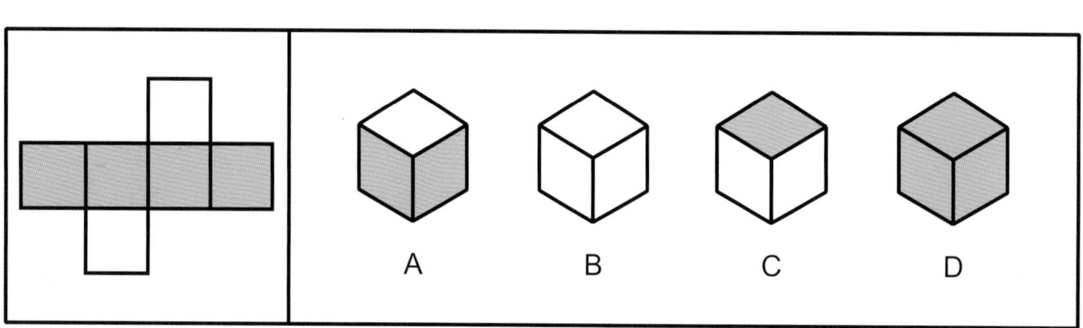

Figure PAT 7.1: Sample Pattern Folding Question on the PAT. One of the figures in the four options (A, B, C, or D) can be formed from the flat pattern shown on the left. The correct answer is **A.**

This test aims to measure your spatial skills: the ability to mentally manipulate 3D figures. Take note that the orientation of the 3D figures may vary in each question, so you need to be visually sharp on such details.

7.2 How to Prepare for this Subsection

Most candidates find this part of the PAT to be quite difficult. Some patterns can be very complex, and solving them can take so much time. Generally, you should get familiar with common geometric figures like the circle, triangle, square and rectangle. Try to explore the differences in their shapes and how each one looks like from various directions. Distinguishing trapezoids from parallelograms and other irregular shapes in 3D views also makes a good foundation in building your skills in 3D form development.

Identifying the significant parts of an unfolded pattern and understanding how a figure is folded are likewise paramount to your preparation for this test. Usually, the base is the largest portion of the figure. It is located at the center of the unfolded object but falls on the bottom once folded. Keep in mind that the direction of the fold should be inward. The base can also have the most number of components attached to it.

7.2.1 Numbering the Parts

Sometimes, sketching helps you visualize the object better. You may also designate numbers to represent the surfaces of the unfolded figure. This way, you can mark and remember which side is connected to another.

Let us try applying a numbering system on the following sample question.

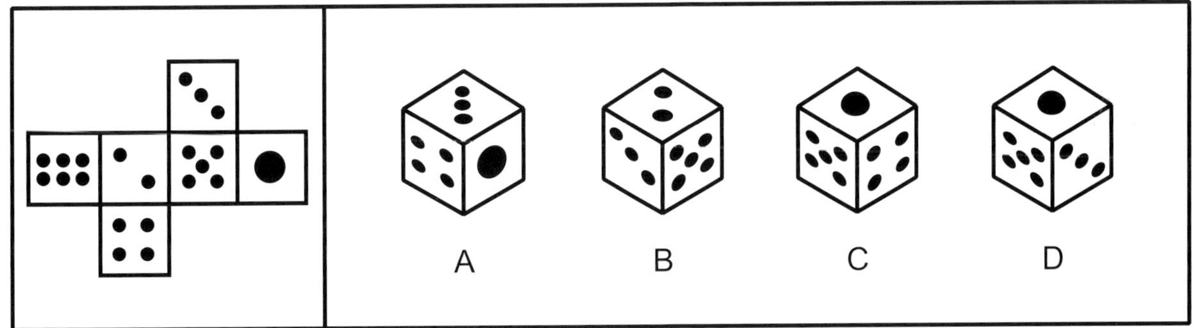

Start by looking for two surfaces that are not placed beside each other. These are parts that are located at least one side apart from each other. Looking at the flat pattern, these are 1 and 2 (the numbering used here corresponds to the number of circles found in a component), 3 and 4, and 5 and 6. If you see any of these sides beside each other in any of the answer choices, you can eliminate those options. Looking at the given options in the question, A should be discounted from the alternatives. So now we are left with only three options.

The next step is to find the correct answer by mentally folding the flat pattern. First, you can assign a reference side or a base. The reference side is where all the components should converge and it should end up at the bottom since the fold should be done inward.

Let's start evaluating option B. We are looking at a cube with a top having 2 circles. Looking at the image on the left, the bottom should be surface 1 (remember that the opposite side of 2 is 1). Let us fold it one part at a time using the isometric view.

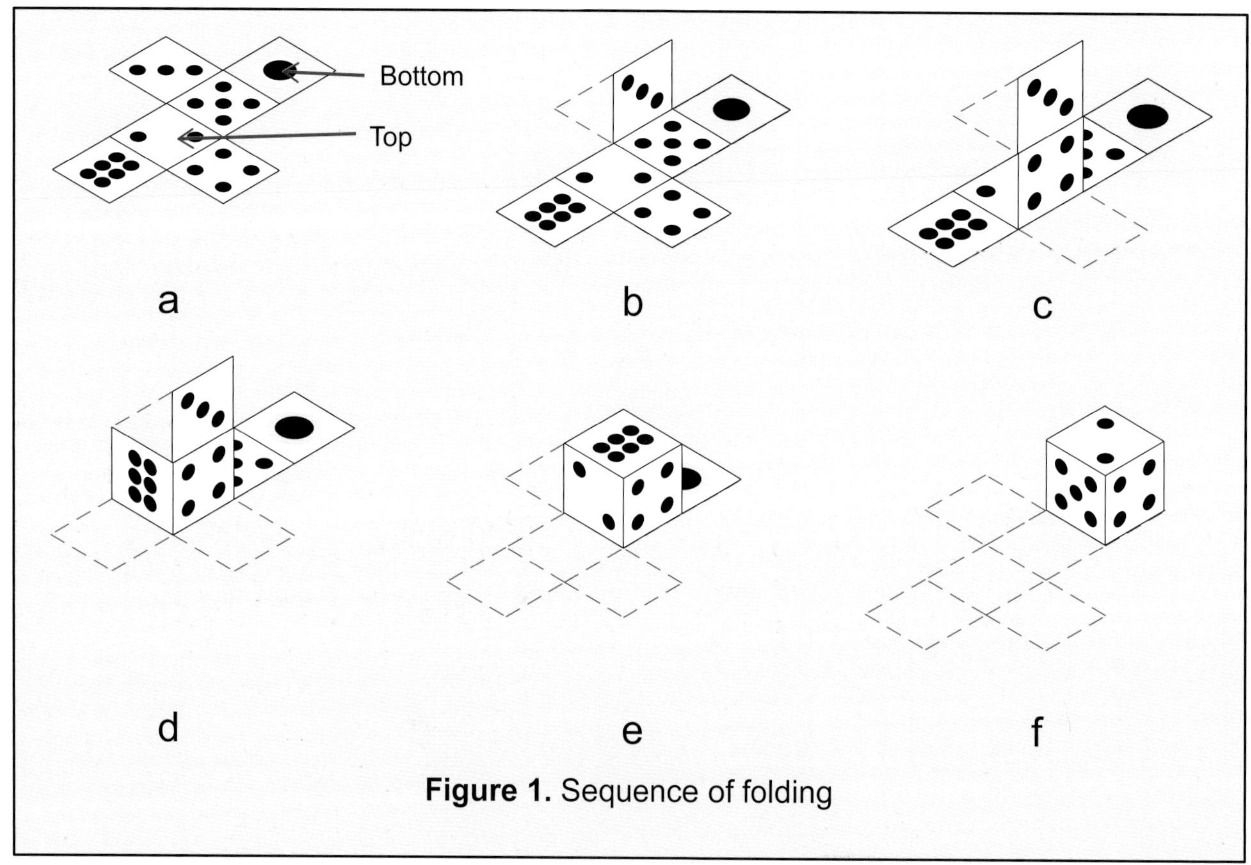

Figure 1. Sequence of folding

Figure 1f shows how the 3D object looks like after being fully folded. None of the options matches it. This does not automatically mean however that choice B is incorrect because we have not seen the other side yet. It is therefore important to know how the object appears from all sides.

If we rotate choice B to see the other side, it will look like Figure 2. B is, indeed, not the correct answer.

We are now down to two choices (C and D). This time, you can try finding the correct answer either mentally or by making sketches. Figure 3 shows the possible views of the object with surface 1 on top.

Looking at C and D, the only one that matches Figure 3d is D. The correct answer therefore is D.

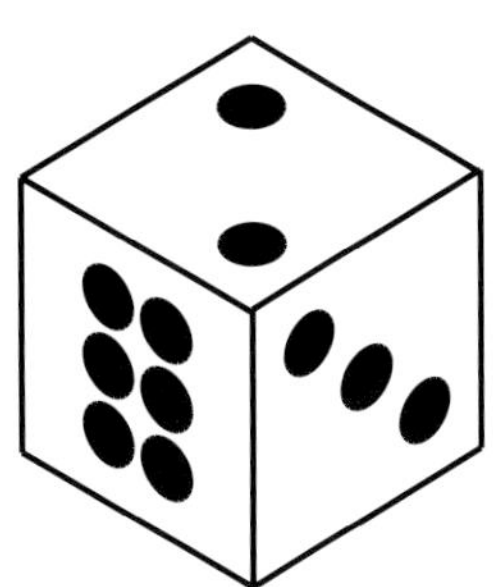

Figure 2

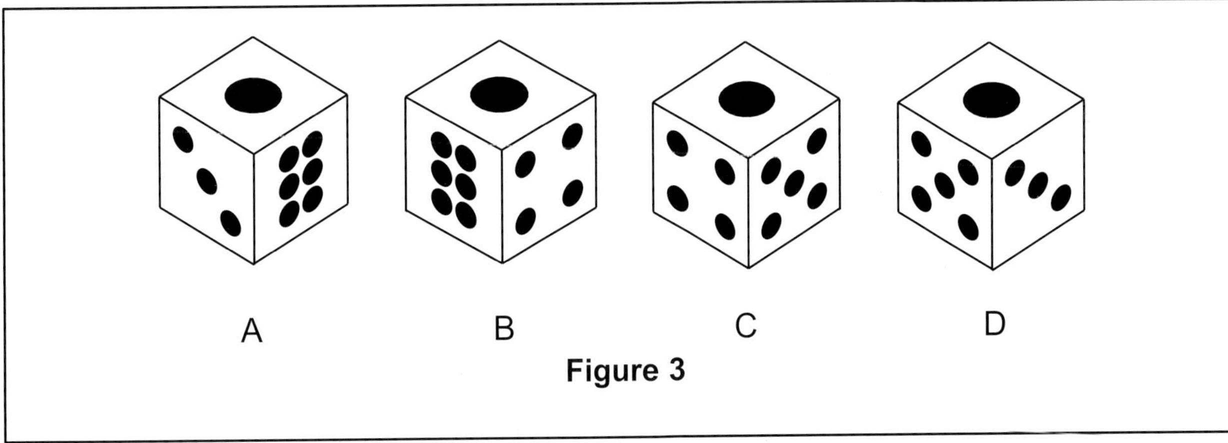

Figure 3

Now let's take a more complex-looking pattern.

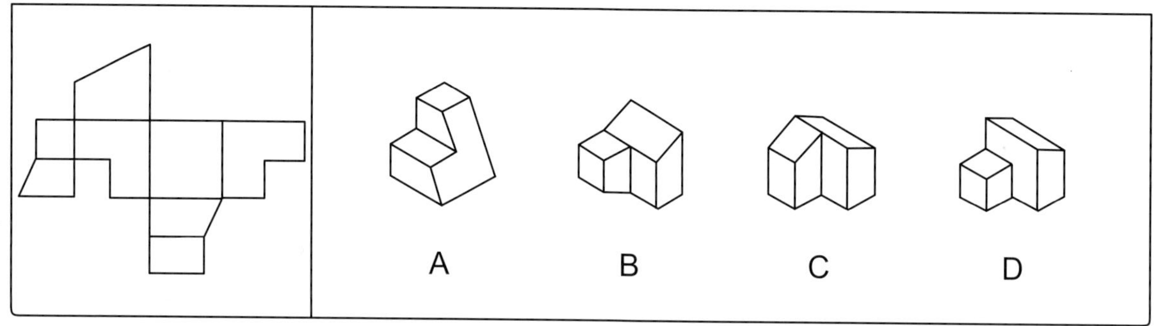

First, number each part of the flat pattern. Then choose a base for the object: it should be the largest part of the pattern and should have the most number of components attached to it. In this case, it is surface 5.

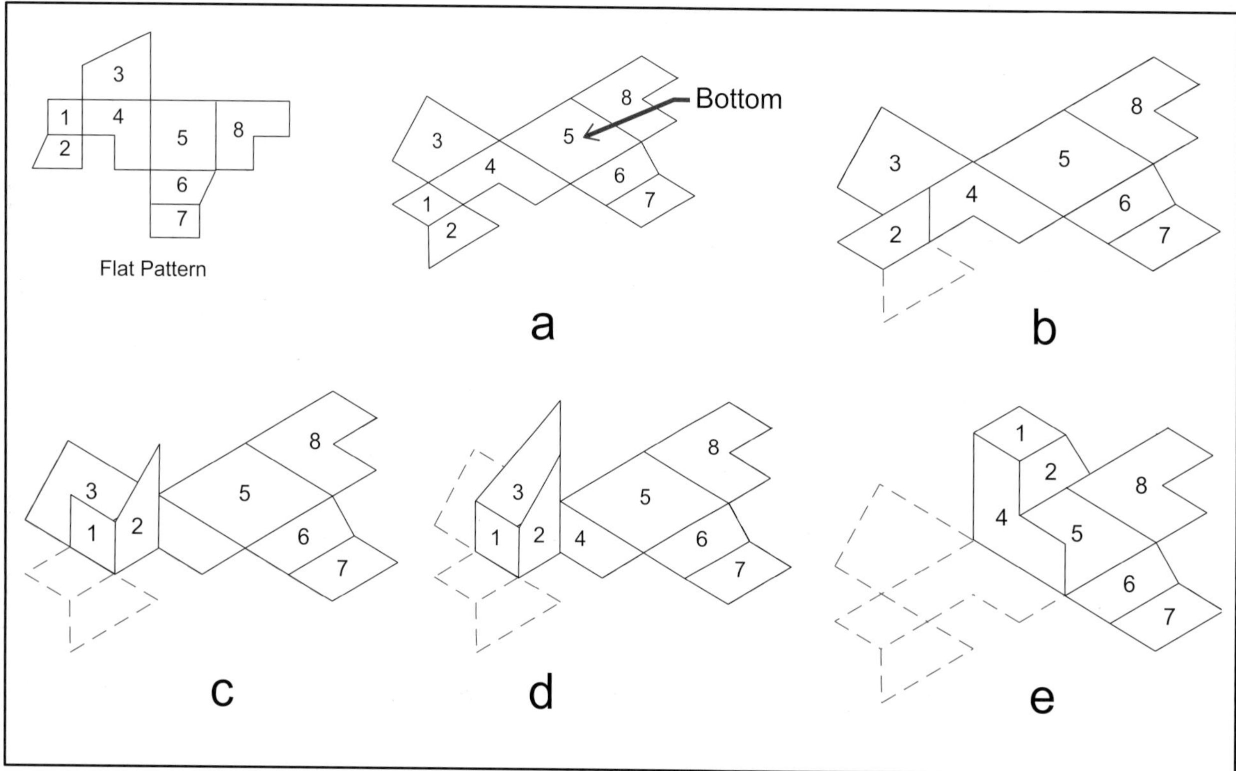

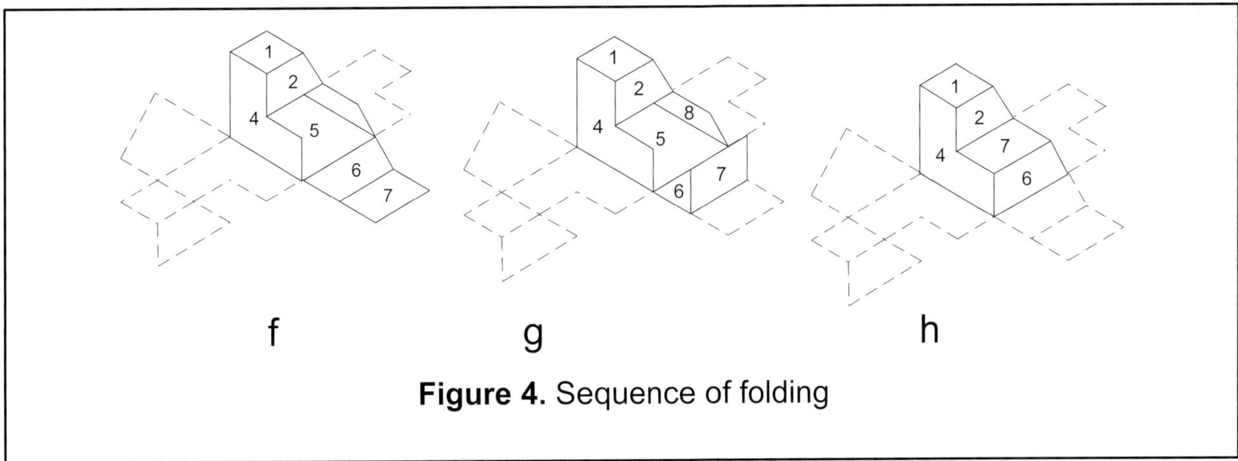

Figure 4. Sequence of folding

Figure 4h reflects how the 3D object looks like after the folds are completed. However, we cannot see a match among the options. We should then explore how the object would look like from all directions.

If we are going to rotate our folded object 90 degrees clockwise, it will look like Figure 5b.

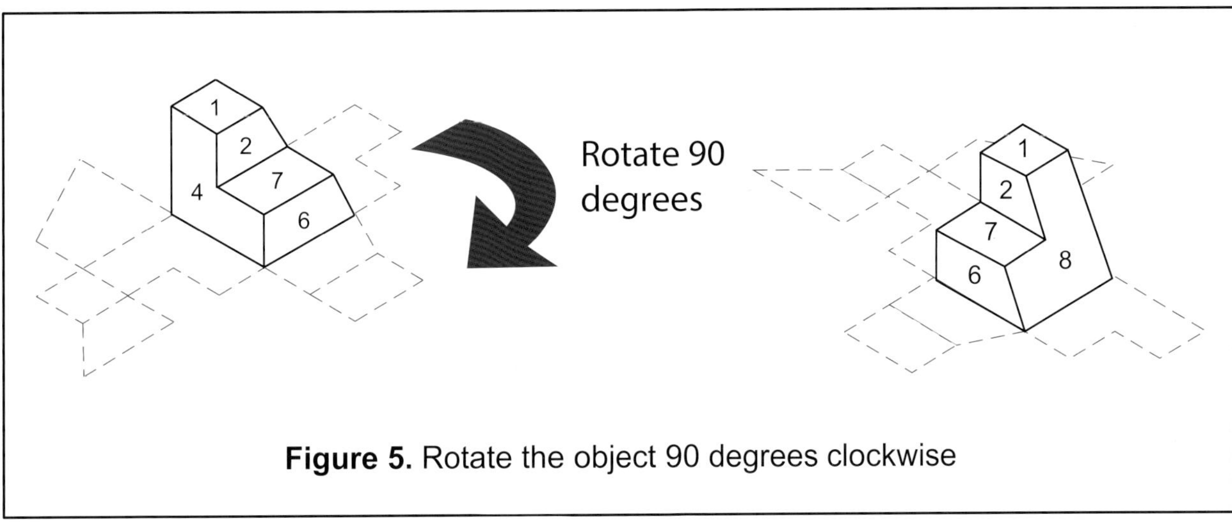

Figure 5. Rotate the object 90 degrees clockwise

Figure 5b is identical to choice A. Therefore, the correct answer is A.

There are also patterns that have at least two identical parts. With such patterns, you should keep in mind that identical parts are most often located opposite each other once the pattern is folded. In Figure 6a, we can see that the parts numbered 2 and 6 are identical. After several folds, it will look like Figure 6f.

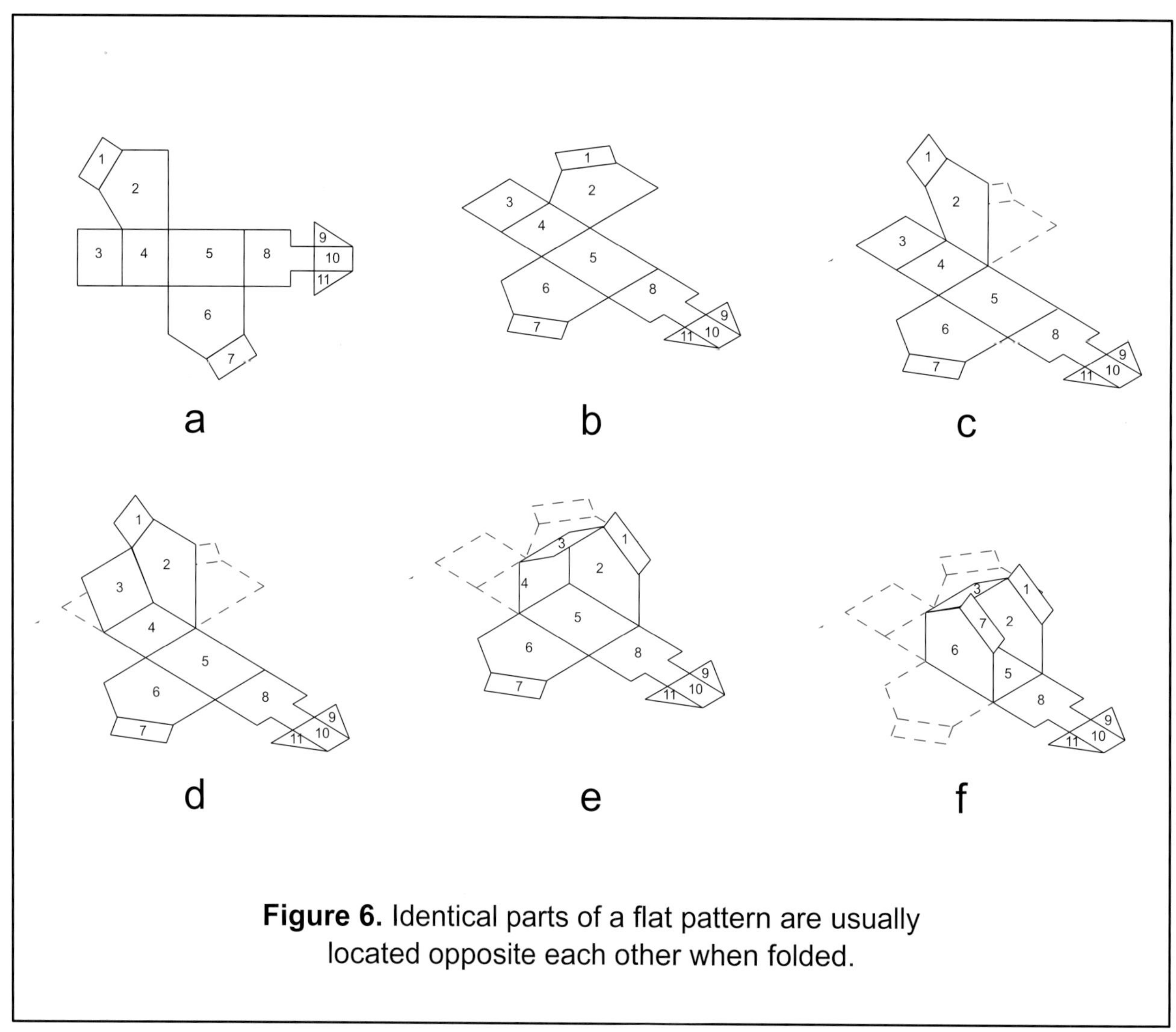

Figure 6. Identical parts of a flat pattern are usually located opposite each other when folded.

After a few more folding, the finished product and correct answer can be any of the images in Figure 7.

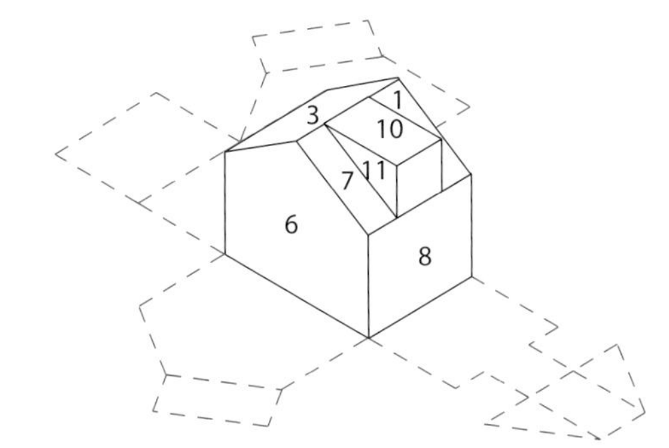

a. Correct answer

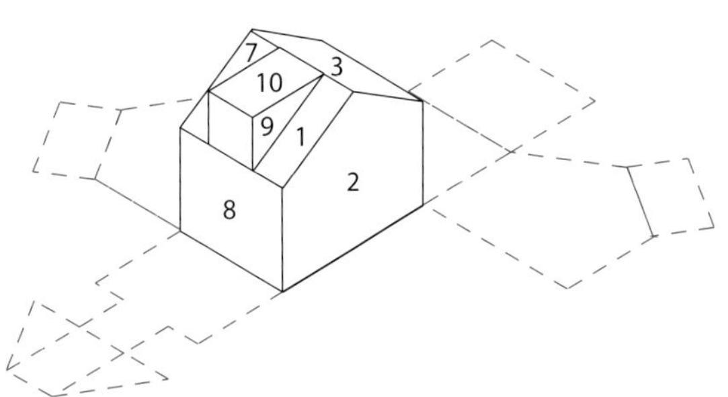

b. Correct answer when rotated 90 degrees clockwise

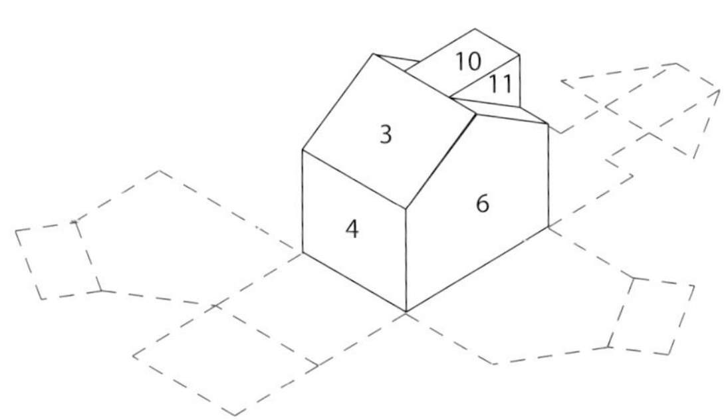

c. Correct answer when rotated 90 degrees counterclockwise

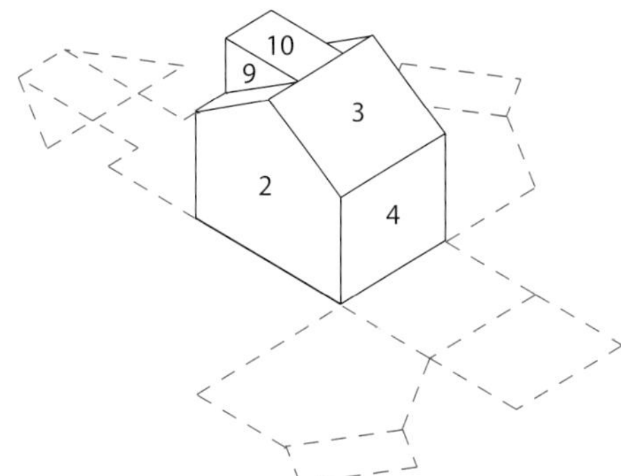

d. Correct answer when rotated 180 degrees

Figure 7

7.2.2 Various Pattern Folding Strategies

Several techniques have been popularized in tackling the 3D Pattern Folding test. You do not need to master all of them but it would be worth trying them out. You can modify some of them or even discover your own techniques in the process. What is most important is for you to find a method that makes you more efficient in answering the questions.

Nevertheless, here are some known strategies for this PAT subsection:

1. Side-counting Technique

This technique is commonly used for irregular shapes. First, count all the sides of each irregular shape from the flat figure. Then count the number of sides of the 3D shape from the answer choices. You can then use the process of elimination by discounting, one at a time, the choices that do not match the number of sides from the given flat figure.

2. Comparing Substructures in the Most Pronounced Shape

This technique involves mainly looking for the largest irregular shape in the given flat figure. Examine the largest irregular shape by its width and length. Then check if the selected irregular shape from the flat figure is represented in the answer choices. Compare the obvious differences and proceed with the elimination technique if needed.

3. Top-Front-End Technique

Practicing with as many questions as you can using this technique is important because this can be tricky. You can start by looking at two projections: top and front, front and end, or top and end. The most common – and the easiest – projection to look at is the front view, and then you can determine its top and end view. The Top-Front-End technique is suitable for dice, shaded cubes, and shaded irregular shapes. When you first see the given figure, be quick to find where your eyes should focus. Look for the widest and highest dimensions to be able to determine essential characteristics to be used as points of reference. Eliminating the wrong answers will then become easy for you.

For dice figures, you can also use the number of points on each side as the point of reference to identify the correct answer. For shaded figures, you can use the shaded region as a point of reference to determine the correct 3D form from the answer choices.

The following section contains five "mini" exercises on which you can try applying the approaches and techniques, which we have discussed so far. Even as early as now, timing yourself during these short exercises would prove beneficial. Note the time it took you to answer one question. This will give you a clearer view of your current level of performance in the test.

7.4 Mini Exercises

1.

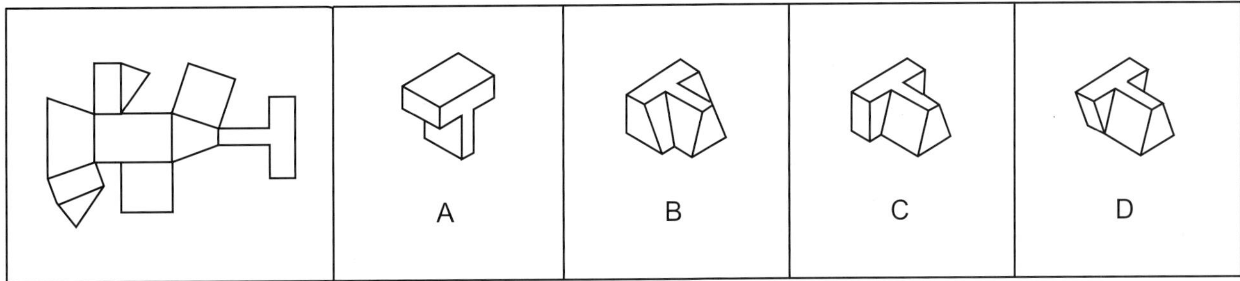

2.

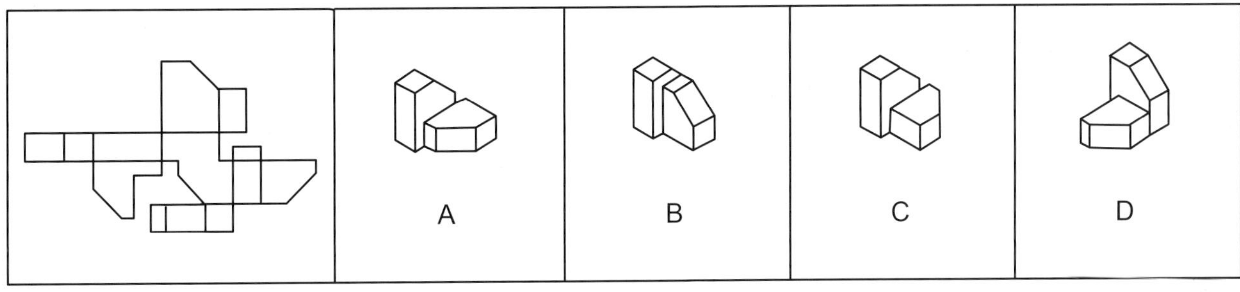

3.

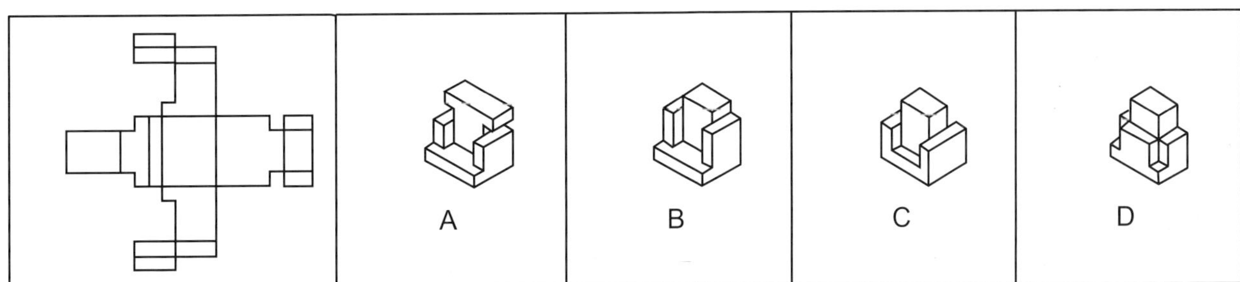

4.

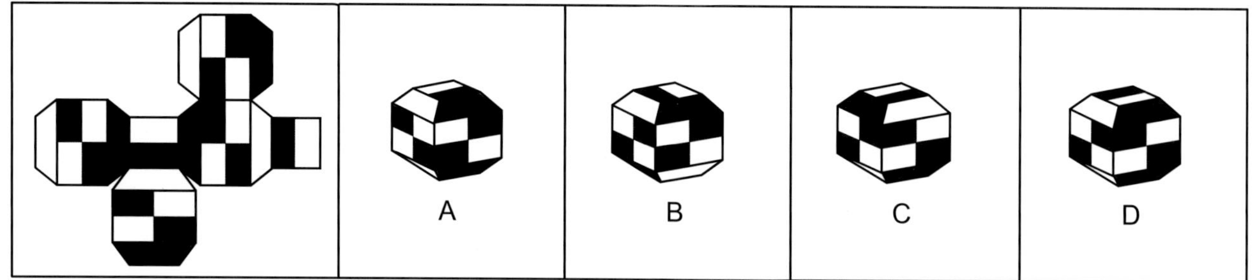

5.

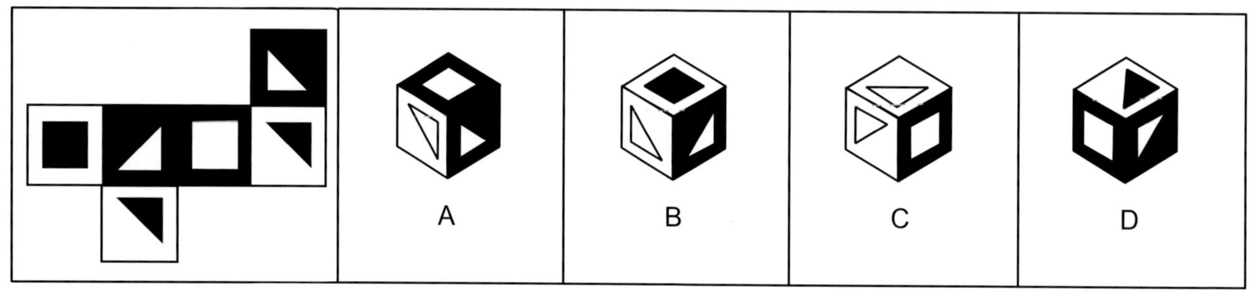

7.4.1 Answer Key and Explanations

1. Answer: D

The figure in this question has a total of 10 components or surfaces. Different types of shapes are also spotted within the figure. There are big and small rectangles, triangles, two kinds of trapezoids and a T-shaped component. Given these characteristics, you can check which option is correct. A depicts 2 T-shaped components hence incorrect. B, on the other hand, has 3 kinds of trapezoids instead of just 2. C has 2 kinds of trapezoids, but the triangular components are not seen. Thus the correct answer is D.

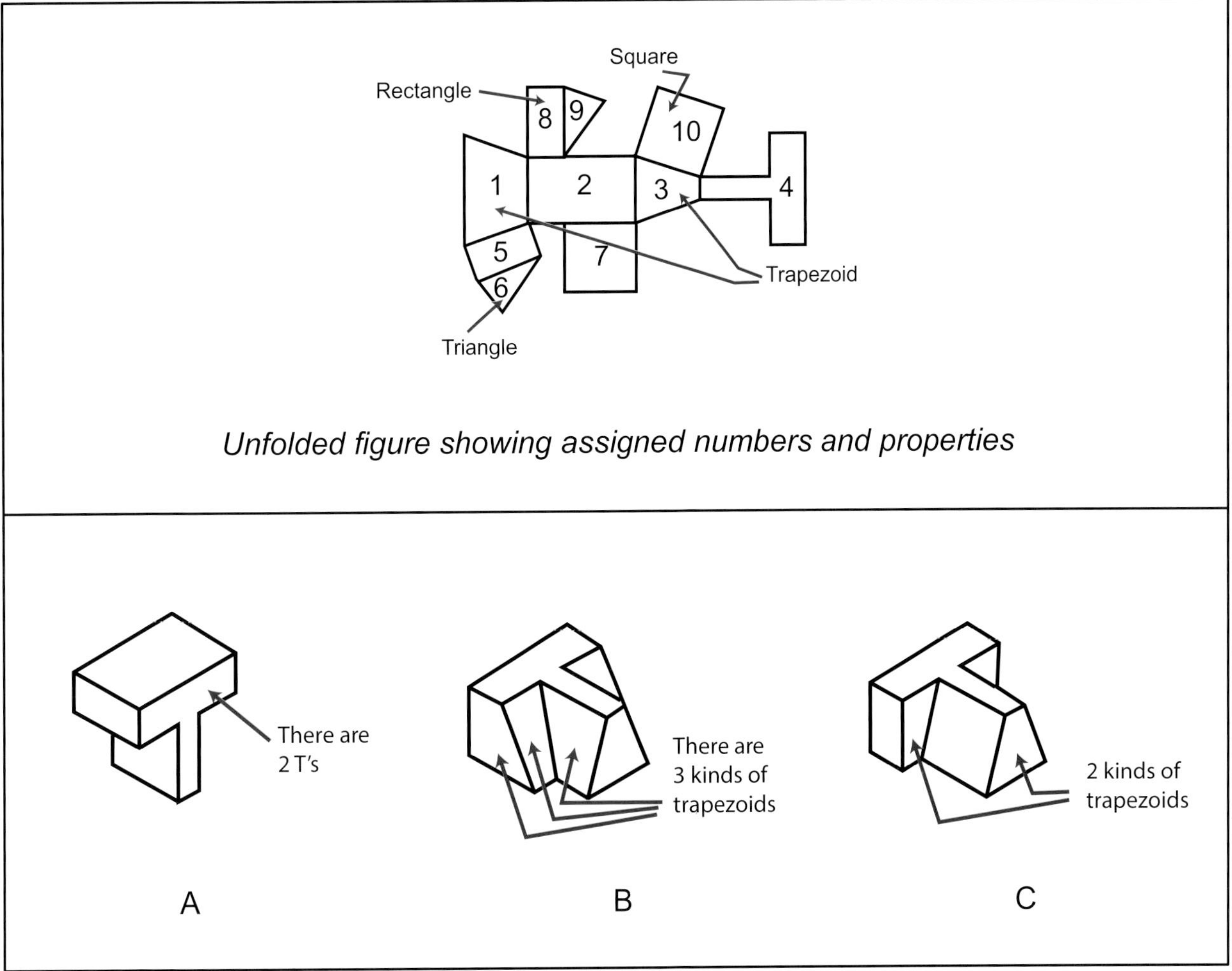

Unfolded figure showing assigned numbers and properties

2. Answer: A

The unfolded figure here has unique components such as surfaces 4 and 5. Surface 5 can be used as the base of the 3D figure. With these properties, you can already compare it with the given choices. The correct answer is A.

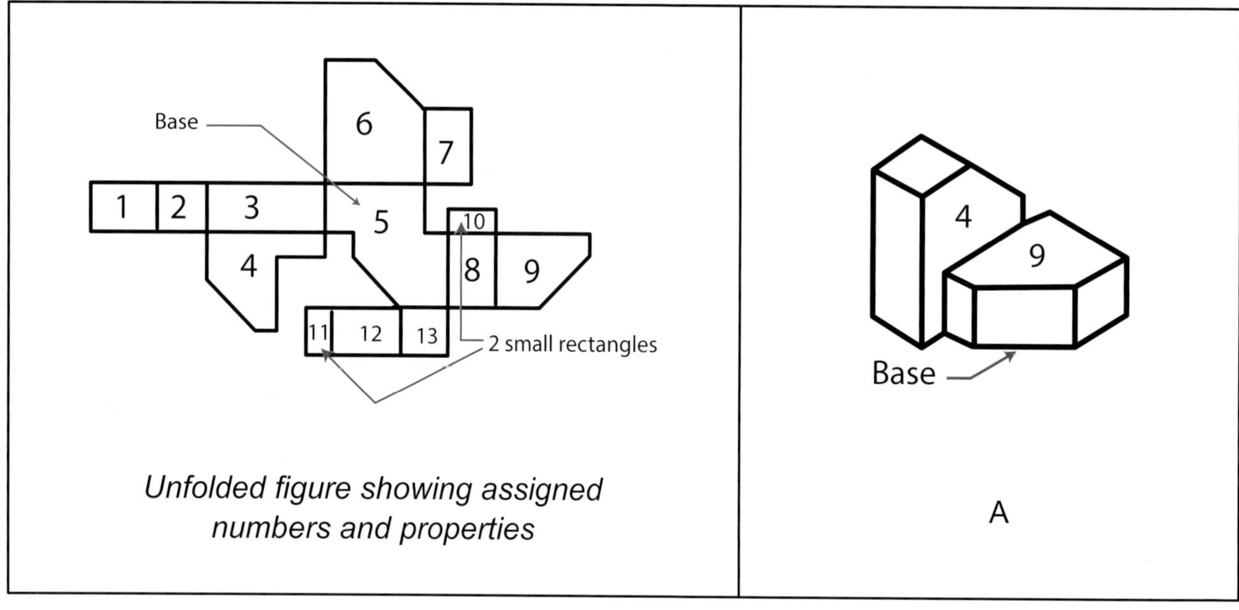

Unfolded figure showing assigned numbers and properties

A

3. Answer: B

The figure in this question shows differing shapes like L, T and various sizes of rectangles. You can directly compare each option based on these observations. A is obviously wrong because it has a different T-shaped side. B is the correct answer because the L and T-shaped surfaces are evident. Both C and D are wrong because C does not have the L or T-shaped component while D has more than 16 components.

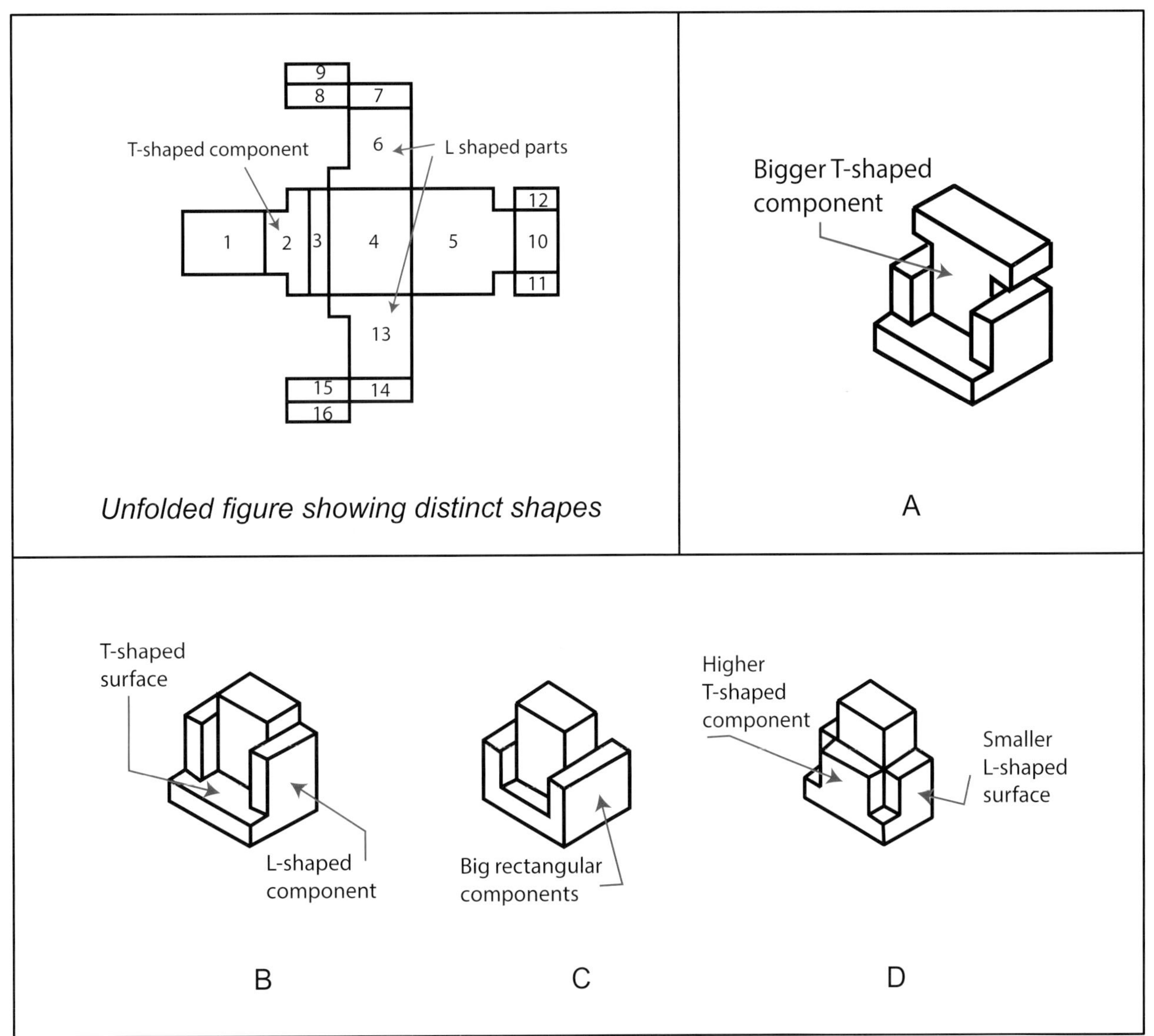

Unfolded figure showing distinct shapes

4. Answer: C

Remember that shaded figures are usually folded downwards. You also need to take note of the adjacent or connecting planes of the figure. Take note of the shaded rectangles that should be connected when folded as well as the orientation of these shadings. A and D have the rectangular shading aligned with the shaded trapezoid, and this is wrong. B also has a different shading arrangement compared to the unfolded figure. Thus the correct answer is C.

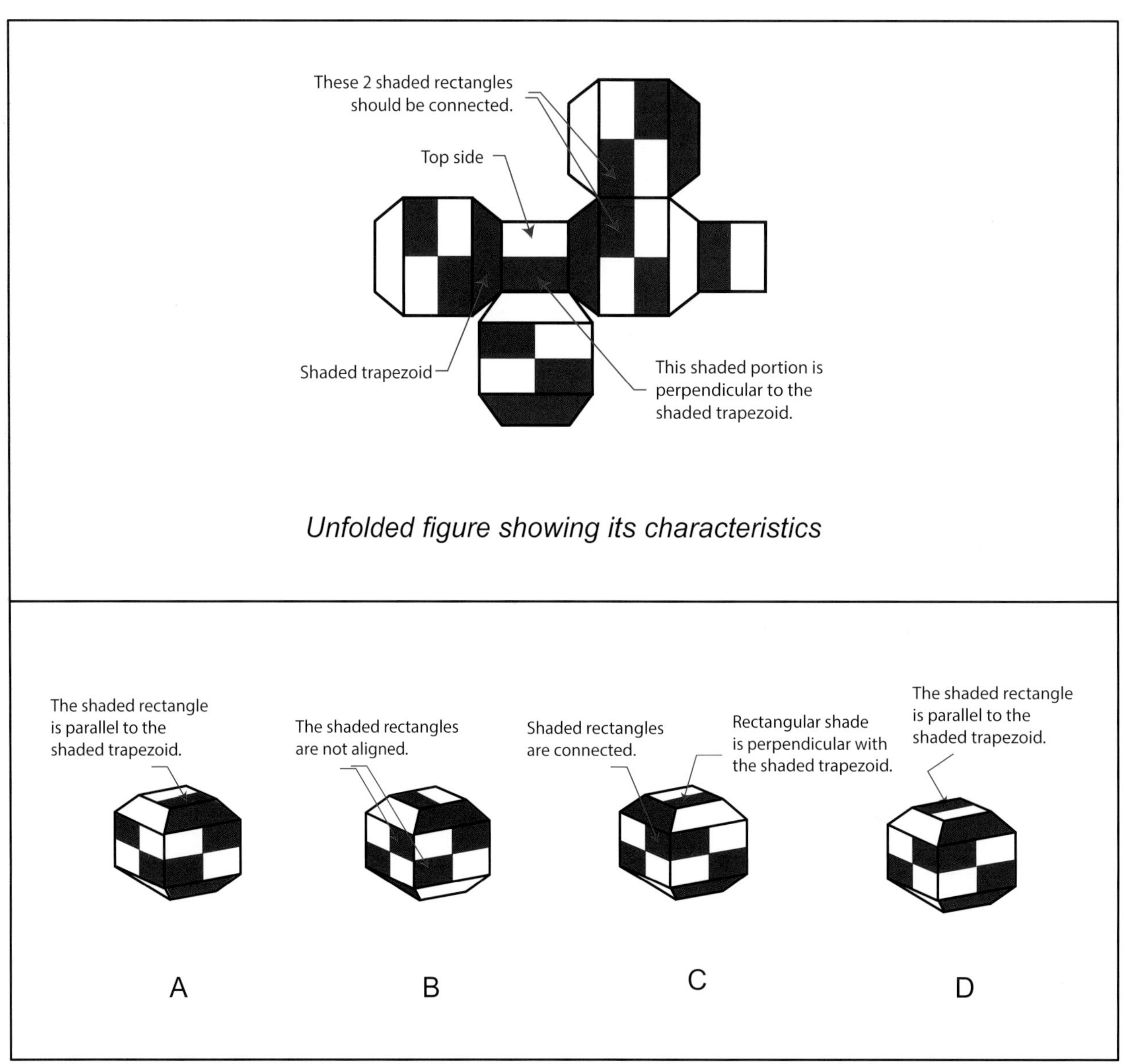
These 2 shaded rectangles should be connected.
Top side
Shaded trapezoid
This shaded portion is perpendicular to the shaded trapezoid.
Unfolded figure showing its characteristics
The shaded rectangle is parallel to the shaded trapezoid.
The shaded rectangles are not aligned.
Shaded rectangles are connected.
Rectangular shade is perpendicular with the shaded trapezoid.
The shaded rectangle is parallel to the shaded trapezoid.
A
B
C
D

5. Answer: D

This number may look difficult at first glance, but this is actually quite easy. What matters here is the position of the shaded sides since this is basically just a cube. You would observe that each of options A, B and C has a white side with a white triangle. These are totally wrong and therefore, the correct answer is D.

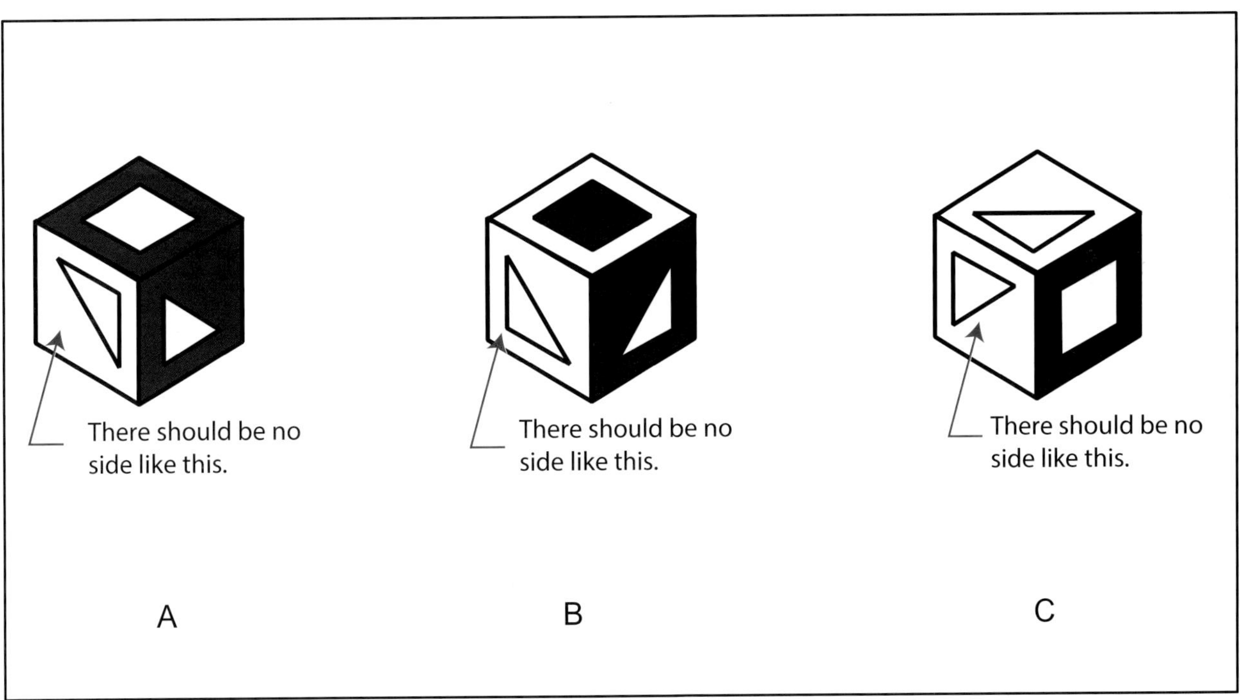
There should be no side like this.
There should be no side like this.
There should be no side like this.
A
B
C

GOLD STANDARD WARM-UP EXERCISES

Chapter 7: 3D Form Development

The following questions represent one of the six subsections in the Perceptual Ability Test of the DAT. While this serves as a review of the discussions in this chapter, the level of difficulty of each question closely parallels the actual test.

You have 10 minutes to complete this portion of the DAT Mini Test; the actual test is 60 minutes.

Please time yourself accordingly.

BEGIN ONLY WHEN YOUR TIMER IS READY

1.

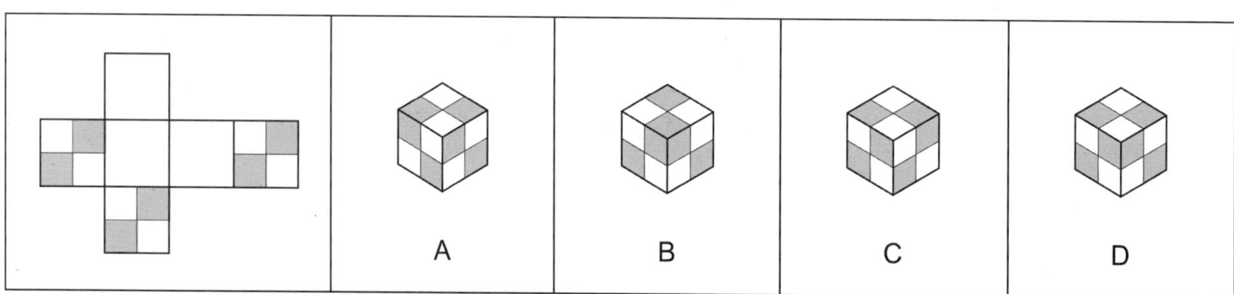

2.

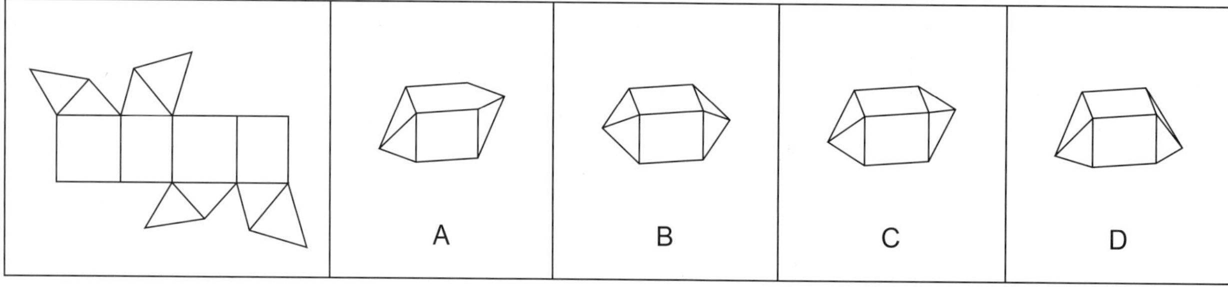

3.

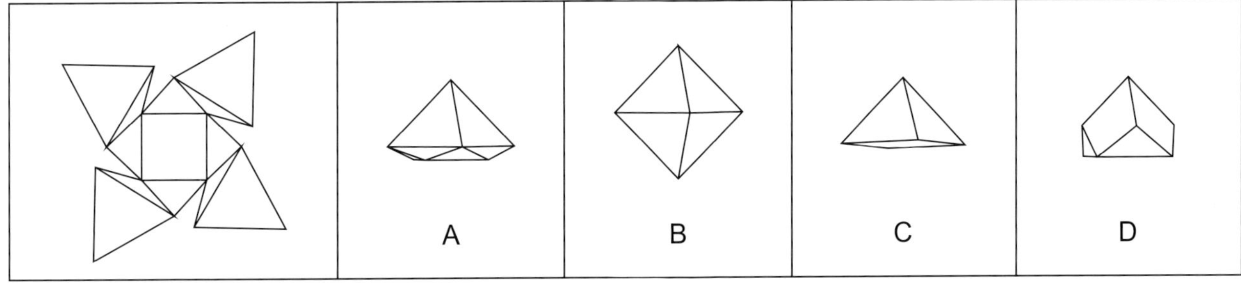

4.

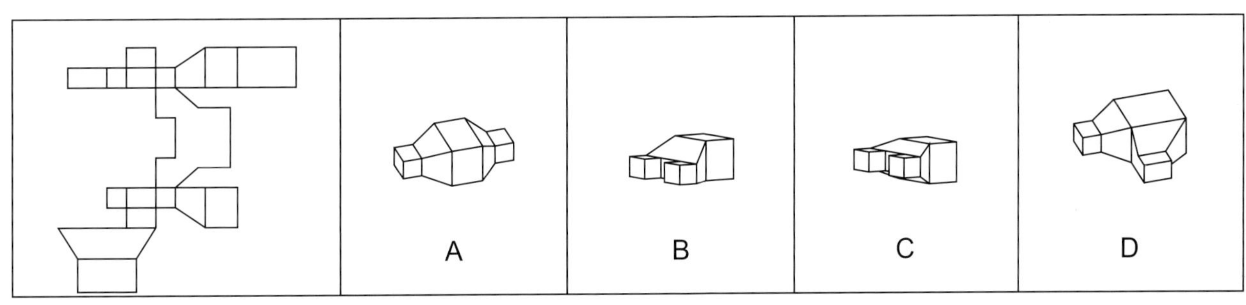

5.

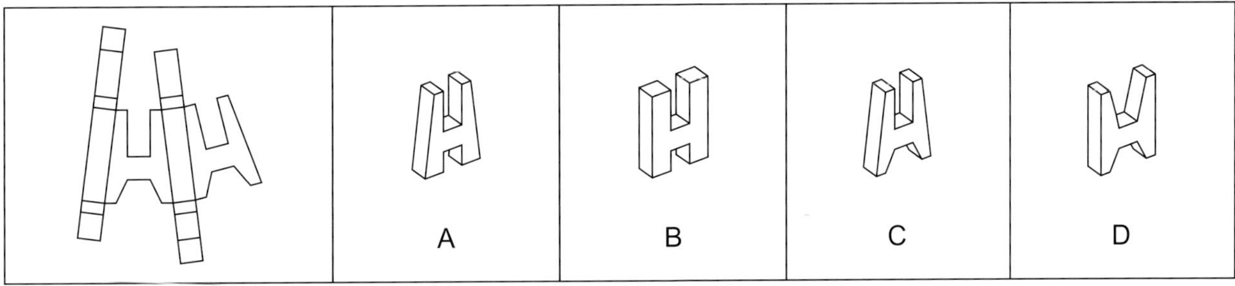

6.

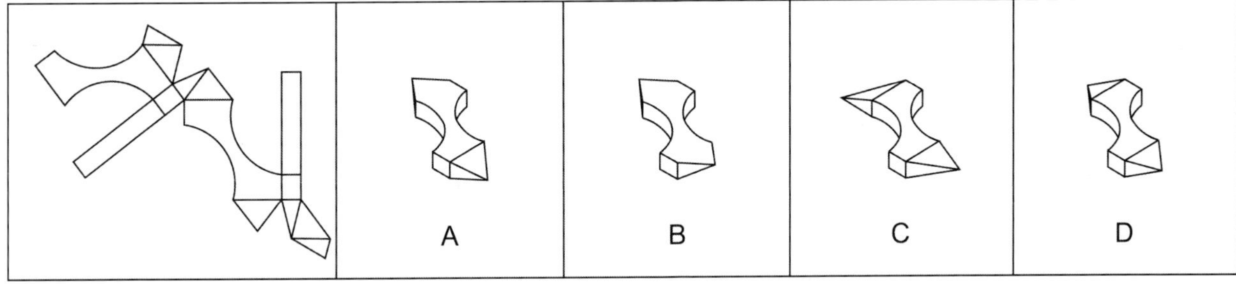

7.

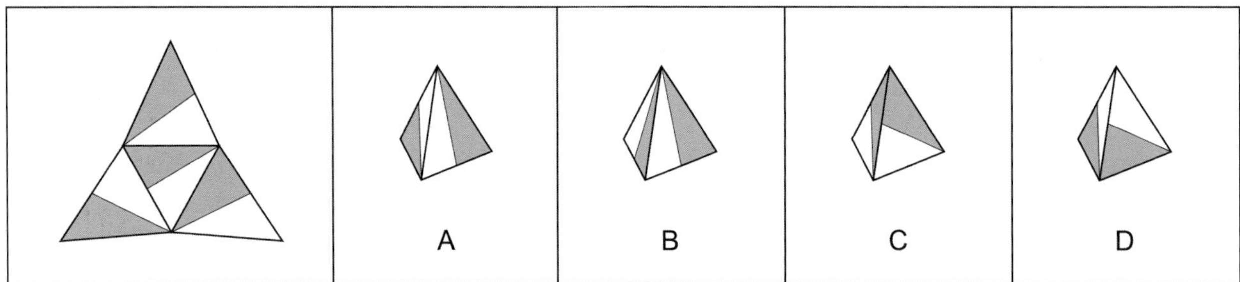

8.

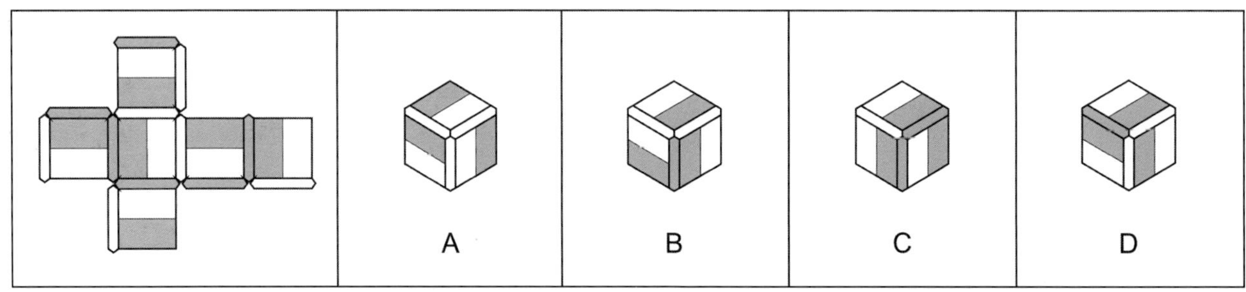

9.

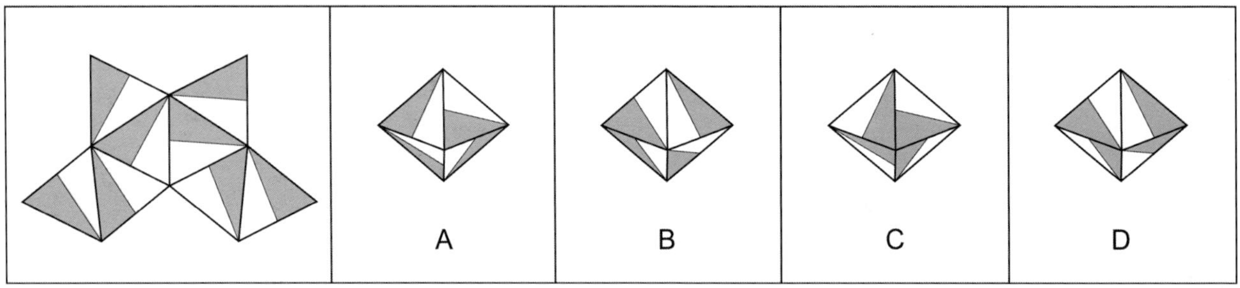

10.

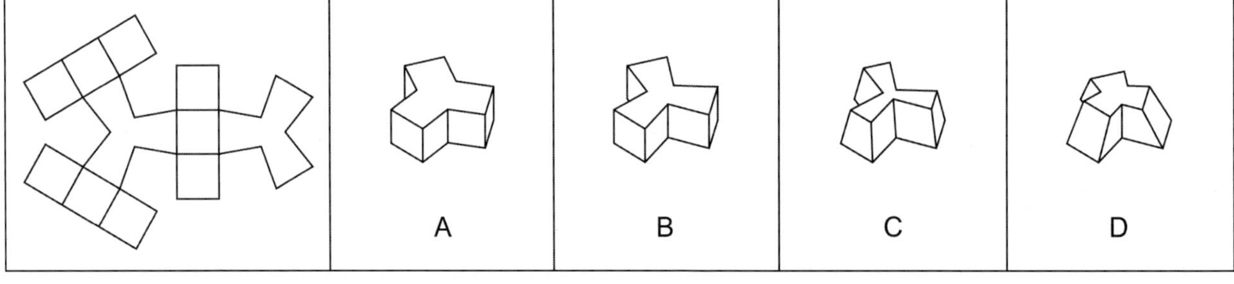

11 .

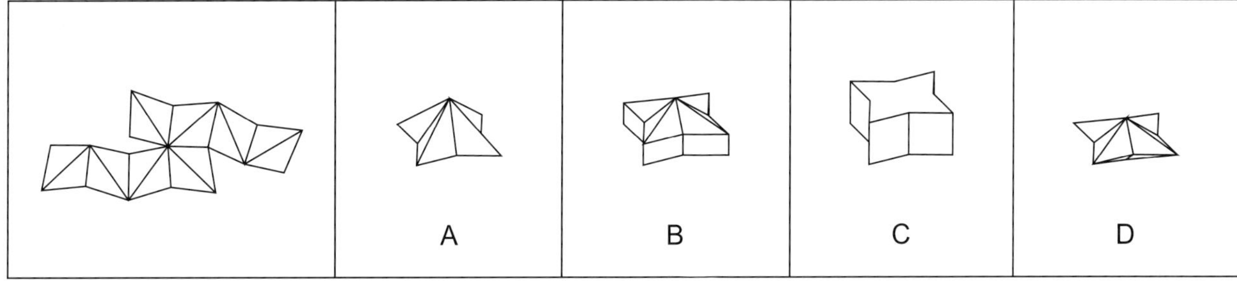

12.

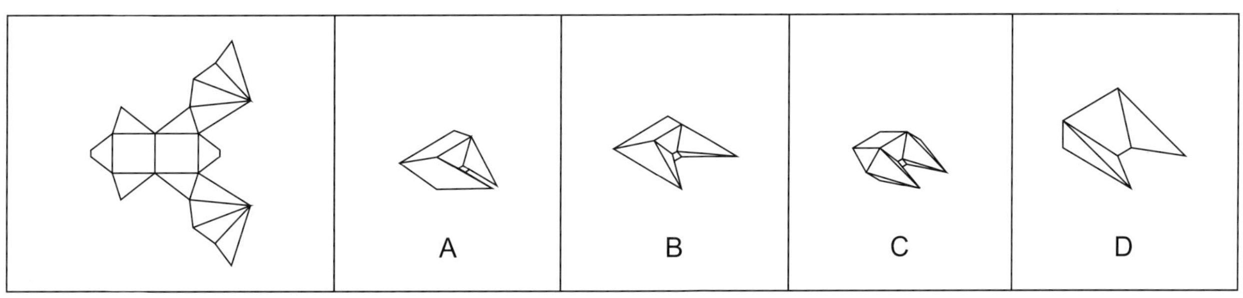

13.

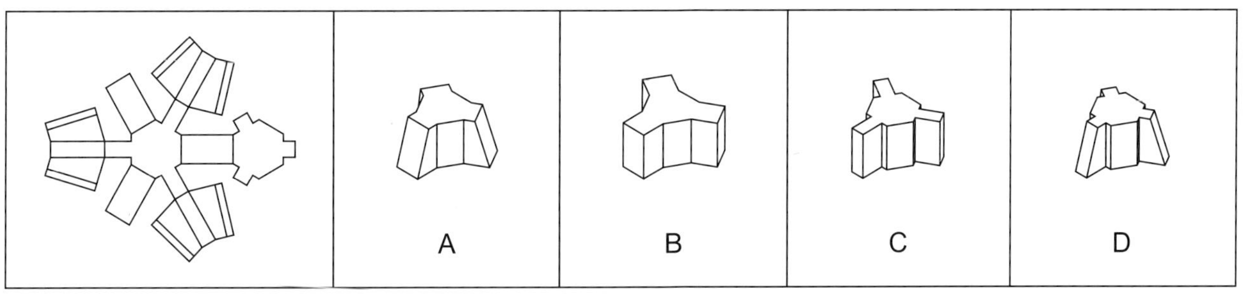

14.

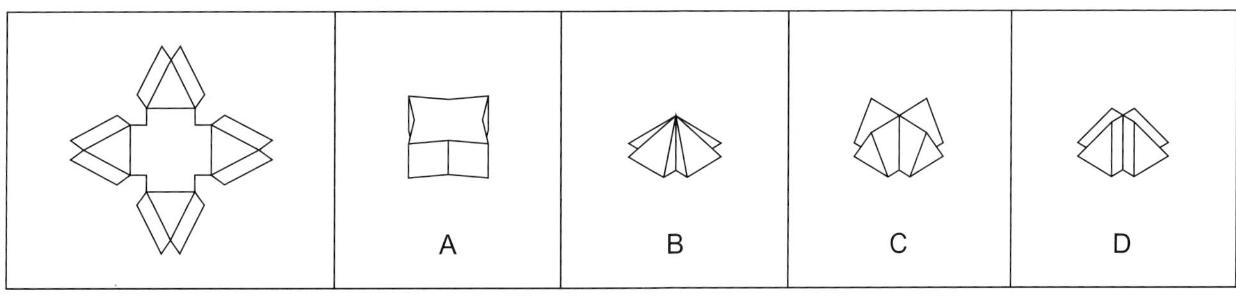

15.

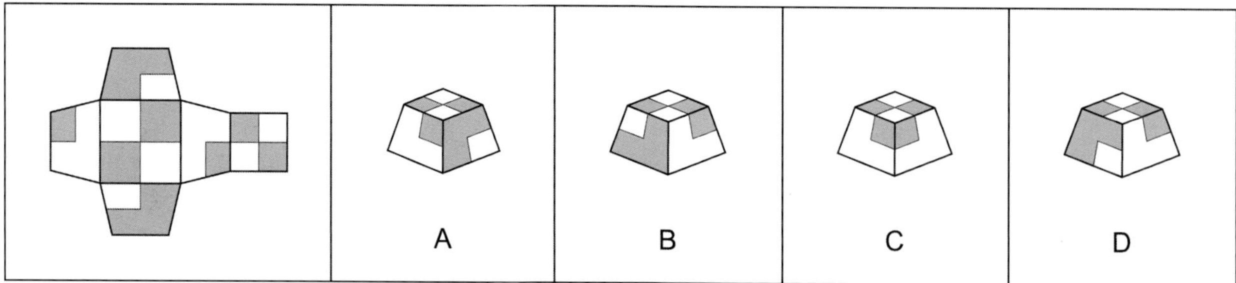

If time remains, you may review your work. If your allotted time is complete, please proceed to the Answer Key.

GS ANSWER KEY

CHAPTER 7

1.	D	9.	C
2.	C	10.	B
3.	A	11.	D
4.	B	12.	C
5.	C	13.	D
6.	D	14.	D
7.	B	15.	A
8.	A		

* Explanations can be found in the Lessons section at www.dat-prep.com.

Go online to DAT-prep.com for additional chapter review Q&A and forum.

Go online to DAT-prep.com for additional chapter review Q&A and forum.

Gold Standard DAT PRACTICE TEST 2013-2014

GS-1

Survey of the Natural Sciences   Time limit: 90 minutes

This GS-1 exam has 100 multiple choice questions.
Biology: 1-40; General Chemistry: 41-70; and Organic Chemistry: 71-100

Please do not begin until your timer is ready.

1. Which of the following represents a genetic mutation in which bases are added or deleted in numbers other than multiples of three?

A. Inversion
B. Duplication
C. Frame shift
D. Translocation
E. Point mutation

2. All of the following are functions of the human spleen EXCEPT one. Which one is the EXCEPTION?

A. Produces platelets.
B. Filters damaged red blood cells.
C. Filters bacteria.
D. Stores erythrocytes.
E. Stores antigen presenting cells.

3. Which of the following statements is true concerning inspiration?

A. The internal pressure is positive with respect to the atmosphere.
B. The diaphragm and accessory muscles relax.
C. It is a passive process.
D. The thoracic cage moves inward, while the diaphragm moves downward.
E. The phrenic nerve is stimulated.

4. PKU disease is a recessive autosomal genetic condition. DNA isolated from parents reacted with normal specific and abnormal specific probes in the following manner:

	normal specific	abnormal specific
mother	reaction	reaction
father	no reaction	reaction

A male offspring of the couple represented in the table above could potentially be which of the following?
I. PKU disease positive
II. PKU disease negative, PKU gene carrier
III. PKU disease negative, PKU gene non-carrier

A. I only
B. I and II only
C. I and III only
D. II and III only
E. I, II and III

5. A conjoint and open vascular bundle will be observed in the transverse section of which of the following?

A. Monocot twig
B. Monocot root
C. Monocot stem
D. Dicot root
E. Dicot stem

6. Match and choose the correct option:

I. Cuticle	i. guard cells
II. Bulliform cells	ii. single layer
III. Stomata	iii. waxy layer
IV. Epidermis	iv. empty colorless cell

A. I-i, II-iv, III-iii, IV-ii
B. I-i, II-ii, III-iii, IV-iv
C. I-iii, II-iv, III-i, IV-ii
D. I-iii, II-ii, III-i, IV-iv
E. I-iii, II-ii, III-iv, IV-i

7. The mechanism by which blastomeres differentiate into germ cells is referred to as:

A. induction.
B. determination.
C. specialization.
D. differentiation.
E. neurulation.

8. Prokaryotic organisms make up the:

A. Protists.
B. Protists and Eubacteria.
C. Archaebacteria and Protists.
D. Archaebacteria, Eubacteria, and Protists.
E. Eubacteria and Archaebacteria.

9. Calcitonin lowers calcium levels in blood by inhibiting the action of:

A. osteoclasts.
B. osteoblasts.
C. osteocytes.
D. osteons.
E. osteomeres.

10. All of the following are characteristics of most enzymes EXCEPT one. Which one is the EXCEPTION?

A. They affect the equilibrium of reaction.
B. They affect the rate of reaction.
C. They are specific to particular substrates.
D. They lower the energy of activation of a chemical reaction.
E. They are composed of simple or complex proteins.

11. Implantation of the developing embryo into the uterine lining occurs during:

A. fertilization.
B. cleavage.
C. blastulation.
D. gastrulation.
E. neurulation.

12. The antarctic tundra:

A. is characterized by deciduous needleleaf trees.
B. is characterized by evergreen needleleaf trees.
C. is divided by the tree line.
D. contains numerous species of reptiles.
E. is unforested because it is both cold and dry.

13. In which of the following blood vessels would pO_2 be the highest?

A. Hepatic portal system
B. Left pulmonary artery
C. Renal vein
D. Inferior vena cava
E. Pulmonary vein

14. Filtration of plasma occurs in the Bowman's capsule of the nephron. What is the driving force for this initial filtration step in the kidney?

A. An ionic gradient formed by a countercurrent multiplier system
B. Blood pressure
C. A chemiosmotic gradient across the semipermeable tubular membrane
D. Contraction of smooth muscles surrounding the Bowman's capsule
E. Vacuoles in the podocytes

15. Consider the following table.

Table 1: Experimental data presenting the rates of protein degradation (Rxn rate) with varying concentration of trypsin and the enzyme inhibitor inhibitin.

Trial#	[trypsin] mmol/L	Rxn rate mmol(Ls)$^{-1}$	[inhibitin] mmol/L
1	5.6×10^{-4}	5.40	0
2	7.4×10^{-3}	5.45	3.6×10^{-6}
3	5.6×10^{-4}	1.98	7.2×10^{-6}
4	7.4×10^{-3}	2.02	1.1×10^{-5}
5	8.3×10^{-5}	0.04	1.4×10^{-5}

On statistical analysis, researchers confirmed that there was no significant difference between the rate of reaction determined for Trial # 1 and Trial # 2. The most likely explanation is:

A. the concentration of inhibitin was 0.
B. the concentration of inhibitin was significantly elevated.
C. the concentration of trypsin was significantly elevated.
D. the concentration of trypsin was significantly decreased.
E. the concentration of trypsin was 0.

16. Which of the following statements could be used to correctly describe the overall polymerase chain reaction (PCR)?

A. It is an anabolic reaction that breaks down new DNA strands.
B. It is an anabolic reaction that synthesizes new DNA strands.
C. It is a catabolic reaction that breaks down new DNA strands.
D. It is a catabolic reaction that synthesizes new DNA strands.
E. It is neither anabolic nor catabolic.

17. The medication AZT is an analog of thymidine which has an $-N_3$ group in the place of an –OH at the 3' position of the sugar. Thus AZT will act to disrupt which process of the retrovirus HIV?

A. Transcription
B. Reverse transcription
C. Translation
D. Endocytosis
E . Exocytosis

18. The genetic basis of human blood types includes recessive (Z^O) and codominant alleles (Z^A and Z^B). Determine which of the following genotypes produce blood that agglutinates when combined with type O serum.

I. Z^AZ^A
II. Z^AZ^B
III. Z^AZ^O

A. I only
B. III only
C. I and II only
D. I and III only
E . I, II and III

19. Which of the following structures of the ear is responsible for maintaining a sense of equilibrium?

A. The organ of Corti
B. The vestibulo-cochlear apparatus
C. The semicircular canals
D. The Eustachian tube
E . The ossicles

20. Plasmodesmata:

A. are considered to be the desmosomes of plant cells.
B. connect to intermediate fibers of the cytoskeleton.
C. encircle cells like a belt.
D. connect actin fibers of one cell to the extracellular matrix of another.
E. connect the cytoplasm of one plant cell to that of another.

21. Exocytosis is directly associated with all of the following EXCEPT one. Which one is the EXCEPTION?

A. Porosomes
B. Chloride and calcium channels
C. Clathrin-coated vesicles
D. “Kiss-and-run” fusion
E. SNARE proteins

22. Which of the following observations would support the hypothesis that the movement of dopamine into a cell is mediated by a transporter protein in the plasma membrane?

A. A hypotonic cell bathed in dopamine leads to increased dopamine uptake by the cell.
B. A cell bathed in an isotonic dopamine solution has no net uptake of dopamine.
C. The rate of dopamine influx increases proportionally with the extracellular dopamine concentration.
D. The rate of dopamine influx reaches a plateau, despite increasing extracellular concentration.
E. Cyclic AMP concentration remains steady.

23. The early earth was a harsh environment. The present day organisms that could possibly have survived that type of environment are:

A. eubacteria.
B. protobionts.
C. blue-green algae.
D. archeabacteria.
E. eukaryotic organisms.

24. A time versus population-size graph with exponential growth may be graphed with what shaped curve?

A. S
B. k
C. C
D. J
E. N

25. Consider the diagram below.

Prot = proteins which are the only ions which cannot cross the membrane *m*. Thus the membrane is semipermeable.

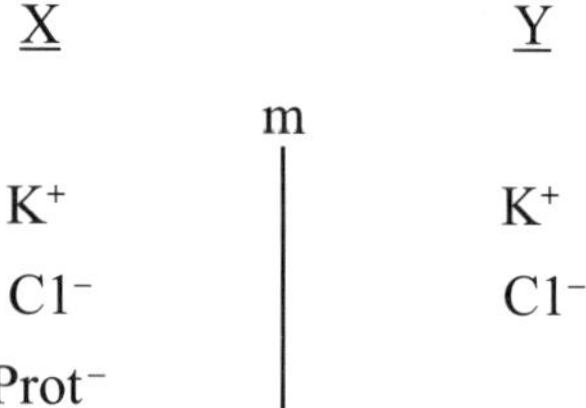

Assuming that the total concentrations of anions and cations on both sides of the membrane are initially equal, how would Cl^- ions be expected to act?

A. They would not move at all because no electro chemical gradient exists.
B. They would diffuse across the membrane from Y to X along its chemical gradient.
C. They would diffuse across the membrane from X to Y along the electrochemical gradient.
D. They would diffuse across the membrane from Y to X along its electrical gradient.
E. Cl^- ions from both sides of the membrane would diffuse across the membrane, but would stop net movement once the electrochemical gradient no longer existed.

26. After sexual maturation, the primordial germ cells in the testes are initially called:

A. spermatids and are haploid.
B. primary spermatocytes and are diploid.
C. primary spermatocytes and are haploid.
D. spermatogonia and are diploid.
E. spermatogonia and are haploid.

27. In which order of priority are the human body's nutrient stores utilized for energy production during fasting and subsequent starvation?

A. Glycogen, protein, fat
B. Fat, glycogen, protein
C. Glycogen, fat, protein
D. Fat, protein, glycogen
E. Protein, fat, glycogen

28. Which of the following hormones, found in the human menstrual cycle, are produced in the ovary?

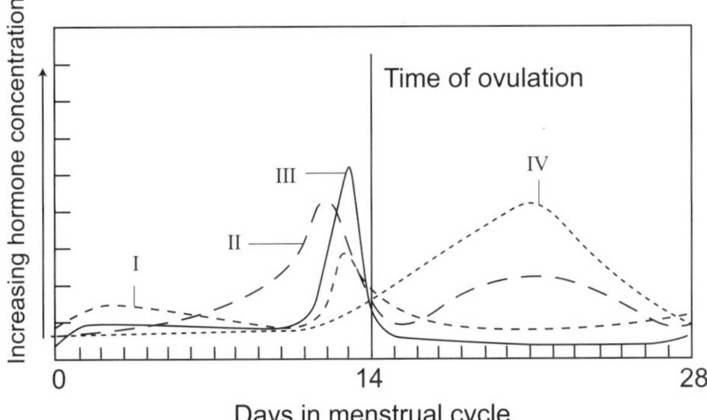

A. I and II
B. II and III
C. III and IV
D. I and III
E. II and IV

29. The K_m is the substrate concentration at which an enzyme-catalyzed reaction occurs at half its maximal velocity, $V_{max}/2$. What effect would a competitive reversible inhibitor be expected to have on V_{max} and K_m?

A. V_{max} would stay the same, but K_m would decrease.
B. V_{max} would stay the same, but K_m would increase.
C. K_m would stay the same, but V_{max} would decrease.
D. Both V_{max} and K_m would decrease.
E. Both V_{max} and K_m would increase.

30. Down's syndrome, in which 2N = 47, is one of the most common forms of chromosomal abnormalities. This results from the failure of one pair of homologous chromosomes to separate during meiosis. During which of the meiotic phases would this likely occur?

A. Metaphase I
B. Metaphase II
C. Anaphase I
D. Anaphase II
E. Telophase

31. What sequence of bases would tRNA have, in order to recognize the mRNA codon CAG?

A. GTC
B. UAG
C. CAG
D. GCU
E. GUC

32. The difference between the bacterium Lactobacillus and the eukaryote Trichomonas is that Lactobacillus has no:

A. ribosomes.
B. cell wall.
C. plasma membrane.
D. lysosomes.
E. RNA.

33. Bile, a chemical which emulsifies fat, is produced by the:

A. liver.
B. gallbladder.
C. common bile duct.
D. pancreas.
E. duodenum.

34. During the dark phase of photosynthesis, the molecule that is oxidized and the molecule that is reduced, respectively, are:

A. NADP and water.
B. water and CO_2.
C. water and NADP.
D. $NADPH_2$ and CO_2.
E. CO_2 and water.

35. Which of the following are LEAST appropriately matched?

A. Reduction - gain of electrons
B. Anabolic reactions - expend energy
C. Exergonic reaction-catabolism
D. Endergonic reaction - anabolism
E. Activation energy - entropy

36. At what level(s) of protein structure could you expect to find hydrogen bonds?

A. Primary
B. Secondary
C. Tertiary
D. Only A and B
E. Only B and C

37. In cardiovascular physiology, ejection fraction (EF) represents which of the following?

A. Blood pressure / heart rate
B. Stroke volume × heart rate
C. Stroke volume / heart rate
D. Stroke volume × end diastolic volume
E. Stroke volume / end diastolic volume

38. Assuming that parasites and their hosts coevolve in an "arms race," we might deduce that the parasite is "ahead" if local populations are more capable of attacking the host population with which they are associated than other populations. Whereas the host may be "ahead" if local populations are more resistant to the local parasite than to other populations of the parasite. The preceding suggests that one result of interspecific interactions might be:

A. genetic drift within sympatric populations.
B. genetic drift within allopatric populations.
C. genetic mutations within sympatric populations.
D. genetic mutations within allopatric populations.
E. genetic mutations within migrating populations.

39. Each of the following statements are true regarding evidence consistent with the endosymbiotic theory EXCEPT one. Which one is the EXCEPTION?

A. Mitochondria and chloroplasts reproduce independently of their eukaryotic host cell.
B. Mitochondria and chloroplasts possess their unique DNA which is circular like prokaryotic DNA.
C. The thylakoid membranes of chloroplasts resemble the photosynthetic membranes of cyanobacteria.
D. The ribosomes of mitochondria and chloroplasts resemble those of prokaryotes in both size and sequence.
E. Animal cells do not have chloroplasts and plant cells do not have mitochondria.

40. The wrist bones are also referred to as which of the following?

A. Carpals
B. Metacarpals
C. Phalanges
D. Tarsals
E. Metatarsals

41. Using the information in the table, calculate the enthalpy change for the following process:

$$C_{graphite} \rightarrow C_{diamond}$$

Table 1

	Graphite	Diamond
Enthalpy of combustion to yield oxide (ΔH_c) kJ mol^{-1}	-393.3	-395.1

A. 1.8 kJ mol^{-1}.
B. −1.8 kJ mol^{-1}.
C. 1.0 kJ mol^{-1}.
D. −1.0 kJ mol^{-1}.
E. 0 kJ mol^{-1}.

42. H_2SO_3 acts as a Lewis acid probably because sulfurous acid:

A. is a proton donor.
B. donates a pair of electrons from another species.
C. reacts with NaOH which is a strong base.
D. possesses oxygen atoms.
E. accepts a pair of electrons from another species.

43. What is the percent by mass of oxygen in sulfurous acid (H_2SO_3)?

A. 31.9%
B. 19.7%
C. 39.0%
D. 58.5%
E. 68.8%

44. 20 mL of 0.05 M Mg^{2+} in solution is desired. It is attempted to achieve this by adding 5 mL of 0.005 M $MgCl_2$ and 15 mL of $Mg_3(PO_4)_2$. What is the concentration of $Mg_3(PO_4)_2$?

A. $\dfrac{(0.015)}{[(.05)(.02)-(.005)(.005)]}$

B. $(0.015)[(0.05)(.02) - (.005)(.005)]$

C. $\left[\dfrac{(.05)(.02)-(.005)(.005)}{(0.015)}\right]$

D. $\dfrac{(0.045)}{[(.05)(.02)-(.005)(.005)]}$

E. $\dfrac{[(.05)(.02)-(.005)(.005)]}{(0.045)}$

45. What would be the pH of a 1.0 M solution of an unknown salt hydroxide given that the metal is monovalent and the K_b of the salt is 1.0×10^{-6}?

A. 11
B. 8.0
C. 7.5
D. 13.0
E. 14.0

46. A sample of white phosphorus (P_4) was reacted with excess Cl_2 gas to yield 68.75 grams of phosphorus trichloride. How many discrete P_4 molecules were there in the sample?

A. $\left[\dfrac{\left(\frac{69}{138}\right)}{4}\right](6.0\times10^{23})$

B. $\dfrac{\left[\dfrac{\left(\frac{69}{138}\right)}{4}\right]}{(6.0\times10^{23})}$

C. $\left[\dfrac{\left(\frac{69}{138}\right)}{8}\right](6.0\times10^{23})$

D. $\dfrac{(6.0\times10^{23})}{\left[\dfrac{\left(\frac{69}{138}\right)}{4}\right]}$

E. $\dfrac{(6.0\times10^{23})}{\left[\dfrac{\left(\frac{69}{138}\right)}{8}\right]}$

47. Which of the following is the strongest reducing agent?

Electrochemical reaction	E° value (V)
$MnO_2 + 4H^+ + 2e^- \rightleftharpoons Mn^{2+} + 2H_2O$	+1.23
$Fe^{3+} + e^- \rightleftharpoons Fe^{2+}$	+0.771
$Cr^{3+} + e^- \rightleftharpoons Cr^{2+}$	–0.410

reduces oxidizes

A. Cr^{3+}
B. Cr^{2+}
C. Mn^{2+}
D. MnO_2
E. Fe^{3+}

48. As the atomic number increases as one moves across the periodic table, the numerical value for electron affinity generally:

A. remains neutral though the electron affinity increases.
B. becomes more positive because of the decreasing effective nuclear charge.
C. becomes more negative because of the increasing effective nuclear charge.
D. becomes more positive because of the increasing atomic radius.
E. becomes more negative because of the increasing atomic radius.

49. HCl has a higher boiling point than either H_2 or Cl_2. The likely reason is that HCl:

A. exhibits weak dipole-dipole interactions, unlike H_2 and Cl_2.
B. has a greater molecular mass than either H_2 or Cl_2.
C. is less polar than either H_2 or Cl_2.
D. is a smaller molecule than H_2 and Cl_2.
E. is a strong acid.

50. Which of the following molecules can be involved in hydrogen bond formation but cannot form hydrogen bonds with molecules of its own kind?

A. C_2H_5OH
B. HCOOH
C. CH_3OCH_3
D. HF
E. H_3O^+

51. Reaction I was carried out in the dark and stopped before equilibrium was reached. The partial pressure of Cl_2 was found to be 35 atm and the mole fraction of HCl found to be 0.40. If the total pressure of the system is 100 atm, what is the partial pressure of H_2?

Reaction I

$H_2 + Cl_2 \rightleftharpoons 2HCl$

A. 10 atm
B. 25 atm
C. 65 atm
D. 75 atm
E. 85 atm

52. A fossil was discovered in the forests of Africa and when examined, it was found that it had a carbon-14 activity of 10.8 disintegrations per minute per gram (dpm g^{-1}). If the average activity of carbon-14 in a living organism is 43.0 dpm g^{-1}, approximately how many half-lives have passed since the death of the organism?

A. 8
B. 6
C. 4
D. 3
E. 2

53. Uranium ^{238}U is radioactive. One of the intermediates in its decay is obtained via 3 alpha emissions, 2 beta emissions and 3 gamma emissions. What is the identity of this intermediate?

A. $^{238}_{84}Po$
B. $^{232}_{88}Ra$
C. $^{226}_{84}Po$
D. $^{226}_{88}Ra$
E. $^{238}_{86}Po$

54. Given the following information:

$2Fe \rightleftharpoons 2Fe^{2+} + 4e^-$ $E^\circ = +0.440$ V

$O_2 + 2H_2O + 4e^- \rightleftharpoons 4OH^-$ $E^\circ = +0.401$ V

Determine the E° for the overall reaction:

$2Fe(s) + O_2(g) + 2H_2O(l) \rightarrow 2Fe^{2+}(aq) + 4OH^-(aq)$

A. +0.382 V
B. +0.841 V
C. −0.058 V
D. −1.702 V
E. −0.673 V

55. Given that the K_{sp} of FeX_2 is 5.0×10^{-16} where "X" is an unknown anion, what is its solubility in moles per liter?

A. 1.0×10^{-2}
B. 2.1×10^{-3}
C. 3.4×10^{-3}
D. 5.0×10^{-6}
E. 6.1×10^{-3}

56. Which of the following is a plausible structure for white phosphorus (P_4)?

A. 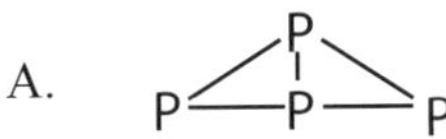

B. 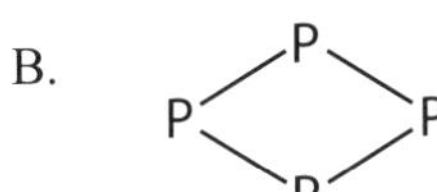

C. 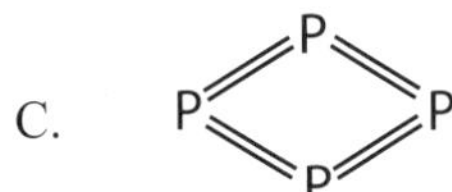

D. 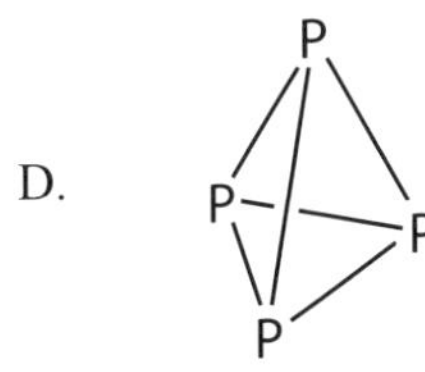

E. 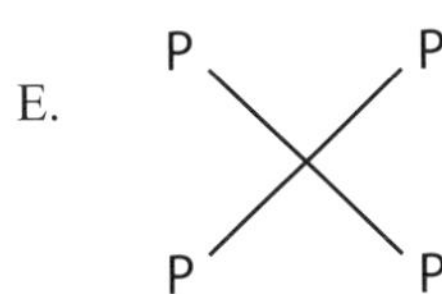

57. All of the following can be used to describe metals EXCEPT one. Which one is the EXCEPTION?

A. Excellent conductors of heat
B. Form positive ions by losing electrons
C. Ductile and malleable
D. Low ionization energy
E. Good conductors of electricity, but less well than metalloids

58. When s-block carbonates decompose, a gas is obtained which is heavier than air and does not support a lighted splint. What gas is it?

A. O_2
B. CO
C. CO_2
D. CO_3
E. C

59. Li_2O is often considered to be covalent in nature because of the unusually high electronegativity of lithium. Which of the following would be a plausible Lewis dot structure for the compound?

A. Li—Li—Ö
B. Li—Ö—Li
C. Li=O=Li
D. ·Li—Ö—Li·
E. ·Li—O—Li·

60. In the following electrolytic cell, which solution(s) could be used such that the electrode at A is the anode?

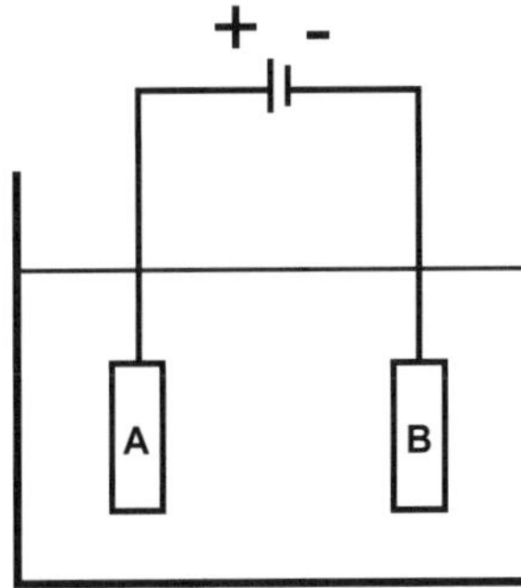

A. Molten NaCl
B. $CuSO_4$
C. $FeBr_2$
D. All of the above
E. None of the above

61. Given that the K_a of the indicator methyl-orange (HMe) is 4.0×10^{-4}, a solution of pH = 2 containing methyl-orange would be what color?

HMe	⇌	H^+	+	Me^-
Red		Colorless		Yellow

A. Orange
B. Yellow
C. Colorless
D. Pink
E. Red

62. Consider the following reaction:

$FeCl_2(aq) + H_2S(g) \rightarrow FeS(s) + 2HCl(aq)$

When sulfur is precipitated, what type of reaction has occurred?

A. Oxidation-reduction
B. Neutralization
C. Disproportionation
D. Displacement
E. Double replacement

63. Which of the following electron configurations of atoms in neutral form corresponds to that of a Group II metal?

A. $1s^2, 2s^3$
B. $1s^2$
C. $1s^2, 2s^2, 2p^6, 3s^2$
D. $1s^2, 2s^2, 2p^2$
E. $1s^2, 2s^2, 2p^6, 3s^2, 3p^6, 3d^4, 4s^2$

64. What is the K_{a2} expression for hydrogen sulfide (H_2S) as an acid?

A. $[H^+][S^{2-}]$

B. $\dfrac{[H^+][S^{2-}]}{[HS^-]}$

C. $[H^+]^2[S^{2-}]$

D. $\dfrac{[H^+]^2[S^{2-}]^2}{[HS^-]}$

E. $\dfrac{[2H^+]^2[2S^{2-}]}{[HS^-]}$

65. At a given temperature T in kelvin, the relationship between the three thermodynamic quantities including the change in Gibbs free energy (ΔG), the change in enthalpy (ΔH) and the change in entropy (ΔS), can be expressed as follows:

$\Delta G = \Delta H - T\Delta S$

The sublimation of carbon dioxide occurs quickly at room temperature. What might be predicted for the three thermodynamic quantities for the reverse reaction?

A. Only ΔS would be positive.
B. Only ΔS would be negative.
C. Only ΔH would be negative.
D. Only ΔG would be positive.
E. All 3 would be negative.

66. Water has a specific heat of 4.18 J/g•°C while glass (Pyrex) has a specific heat of 0.78 J/g•°C. If 40.0 J of heat is added to 1.00 g of each of these, which will experience the larger temperature increase?

A. They both will experience the same change in temperature because only the mass of a substance relates to the increase in temperature.
B. Neither would necessarily experience a temperature increase.
C. It would depend on the source of the heat added.
D. Water
E. Glass

67. 50 grams of glucose ($C_6H_{12}O_6$) and 50 grams of sucrose ($C_{12}H_{22}O_{11}$) were each added to beakers of water (beaker 1 and beaker 2, respectively). Which of the following would be true?

A. Boiling point elevation for beaker 1 would be greater than the boiling point elevation for beaker 2.
B. Boiling point elevation for beaker 1 would be less than the boiling point elevation for beaker 2.
C. The same degree of boiling point elevation will occur in both beakers.
D. No boiling point elevation would be observed in either of the beakers.
E. Boiling point depression would occur in both beakers but to different degrees.

68. Which of the following would cause a gas to more closely resemble an ideal gas?

A. Decreased pressure
B. Decreased temperature
C. Decreased volume
D. Increased pressure
E. Increased volume

69. The data in Table 1 were collected for Reaction I:

Reaction I

2X + Y → Z

Table I

Exp.	[X] in M	[Y] in M	Initial rate of reaction
1	0.050	0.100	2×10^{-4}
2	0.050	0.200	8×10^{-4}
3	0.200	0.100	8×10^{-4}

What is the rate law expression for Reaction I?

A. Rate = $k[X]^2[Y]$
B. Rate = $k[X]^2[Y]^2$
C. Rate = $k[X][Y]^2$
D. Rate = $k[X][Y]$
E. Rate = $k[2X][Y]$

70. What piece of laboratory equipment is best for accurately measuring the volume of a liquid?

A. Graduated cylinder
B. Erlenmeyer flask
C. Beaker
D. Evaporating dish
E. More than one of the above

71. Morphine is illustrated below.

HO
O
H
N—CH_3
HO

How many chiral carbons are there in morphine?

A. 5
B. 6
C. 7
D. 8
E. More than 8

72. Using 2 equivalents of the first and 1 equivalent of the second, respectively, which of the following pairs of compounds can be used to form the following tertiary alcohol?

OH

A. Propyl lithium and methyl butanoate
B. Butyl magnesium bromide and propyl butanoate
C. Butyl lithium and pentyl pentanoate
D. Pentyl magnesium chloride and propyl propanoate
E. Propyl magnesium bromide and hexyl pentanoate

73. Rank the following compounds from most to least basic:

I. $CH_3CH_2^-$
II. $CH_3CH_2O^-$
III. $CH_3CH_2NH_2$

A. I > II > III
B. II > III > I
C. III > II > I
D. II > I > III
E. I > III > II

74. Four compounds – allyl alcohol, benzoic acid, 2-butanone and butyraldehyde - were identified and stored in separate bottles. By accident, the labels were lost from the sample bottles. The following information was obtained via infrared spectroscopy and was used to identify and relabel the sample bottles.

Infrared absorption peaks (cm^{-1})

Bottle I	Bottle II	Bottle III	Bottle IV
1700 (sharp)	1710	1730 (sharp)	3333 (broad)
–	3500 – 3333 (broad)	2730	1030 (small)

Which of the following most accurately represents the contents of bottles I, II, III, and IV, respectively?

A. Butyraldehyde, 2-butanone, benzoic acid, allyl alcohol
B. Benzoic acid, butyraldehyde, allyl alcohol, 2-butanone
C. 2-Butanone, butyraldehyde, allyl alcohol, benzoic acid
D. 2-Butanone, benzoic acid, butyraldehyde, allyl alcohol
E. Benzoic acid, allyl alcohol, butyraldehyde, 2-butanone

75. What is the structure of formic acid?

A. H — C (=O — O — H)

B. H — O (=C = O — H)

C. O = C = O (with H above and H below C)

D. H — C (=O)(— O — H)

E. C (=O)(— O — H, — H)

76. Phenols are soluble in a strongly basic sodium hydroxide solution, and insoluble in dilute sodium bicarbonate. Phenol has a pKa = 10.0. The introduction of an ortho bromine atom into the phenol would have the effect of:

A. lowering the pKa and thus decreasing the acidity of the phenol.
B. lowering the pKa and thus increasing the acidity of the phenol.
C. increasing the pKa and thus decreasing the acidity of the phenol.
D. increasing the pKa and thus increasing the acidity of the phenol.
E. no effect on the pKa nor the acidity of the phenol.

77. What is the product of the following acid catalyzed reaction?

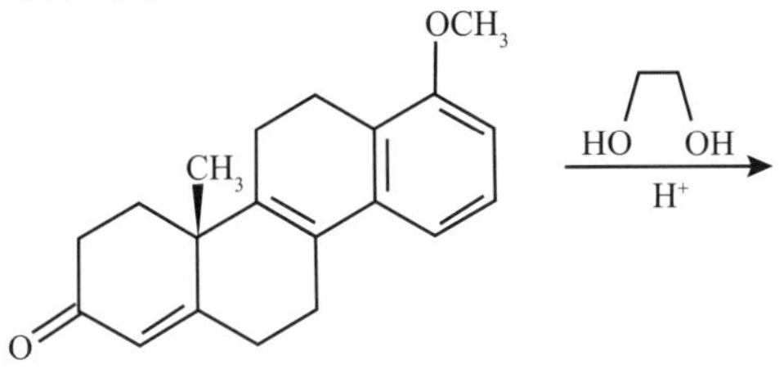

OCH_3 ; CH_3 ; O ; HO OH ; H^+

A. 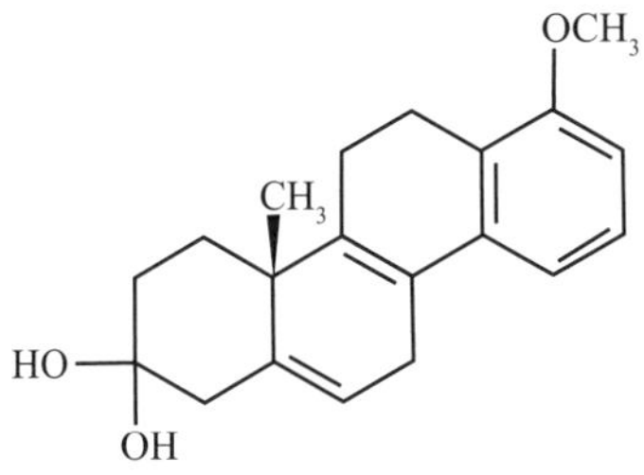 OCH_3 ; CH_3 ; HO ; OH

B. 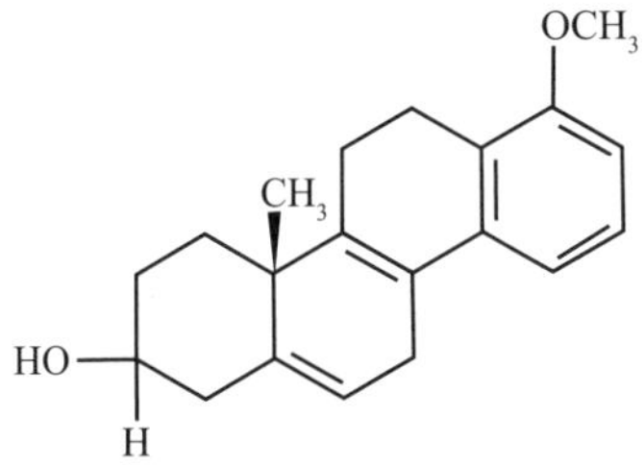 OCH_3 ; CH_3 ; HO ; H

C. 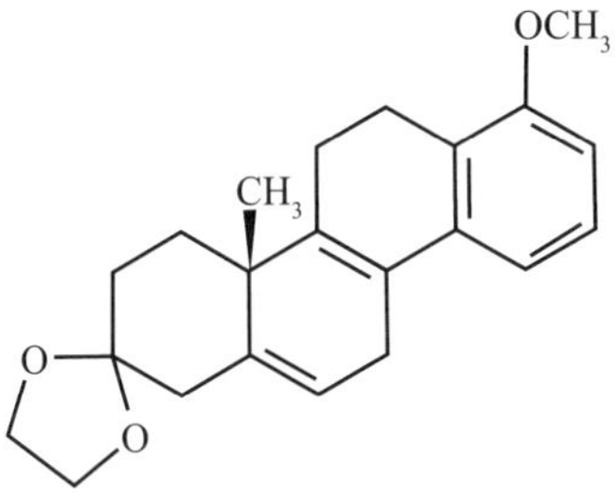 OCH_3 ; CH_3 ; O ; O

D. 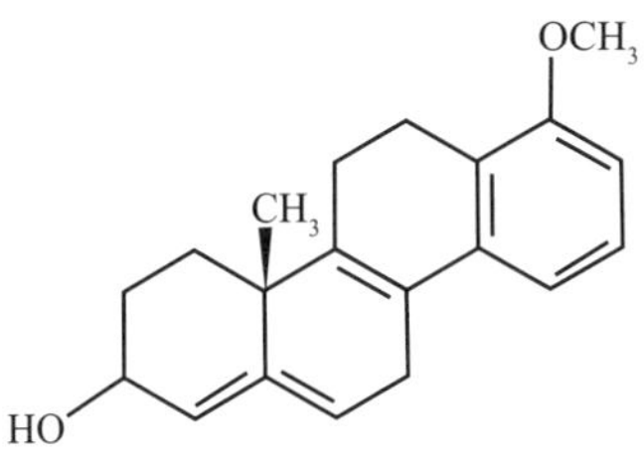 OCH_3 ; CH_3 ; HO

78. The efficiency of the distillation process in producing a pure product is improved by repeating the process, increasing the length of the column and avoiding overheating. All of the following can prevent overheating EXCEPT one. Which one is the EXCEPTION?

A. Boiling chips
B. Boiling slowly
C. Adding a vacuum
D. Adding a nucleophile
E. Decreasing the vapor pressure

79. Cyclic ethers, or epoxides, are important chemical compounds that are composed of a 3–membered ring containing an oxygen atom and 2 carbon atoms. What are the bond angles in the epoxide ring?

A. 109.5°
B. 60°
C. 108°
D. 110°
E. 120°

80. Which hydrogen(s) labeled below – directly bonded to a carbon – is (are) most acidic?

$NH_2CH_2CH_2CH_2COOH$
1 2 3 4

A. 1
B. 2
C. 3
D. 4
E. 1, 2 and 3 are equally acidic.

81. Which of the following would explain the non-separation of cortisol from cortisone by gas-liquid chromatography (GLC)?

A. The solid material in the column of the GLC, through which substances pass in their mobile phase, absorbs cortisol and cortisone equally well.
B. Cortisol and cortisone have relatively high boiling points.
C. Cortisol and cortisone have very similar melting points.
D. Cortisol moves through the column of the GLC, through which substances pass in their mobile phase, at a much quicker rate than cortisone.
E. Cortisone moves through the column of the GLC at a much quicker rate than cortisol.

82. Which of the following represents the amino acid methionine at its isoelectric point?

A. $CH_3-S-CH_2-CH_2-C(H)(NH_3^+)-COO^-$

B. $CH_3-S-CH_2-CH_2-C(H)(NH_3^+)-COOH$

C. $CH_4^+-S-CH_2-CH_2-C^-(NH_2)-COOH$

D. $CH_4^+-S-CH_2-CH_2-C^-(NH_3^+)-COO^-$

83. Consider the following schematic of a ^1H NMR:

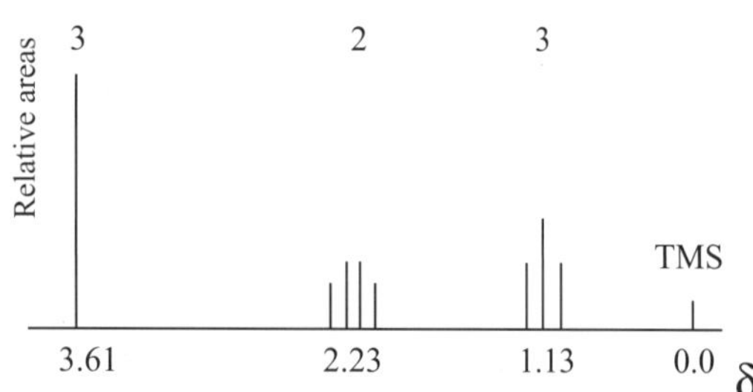

Which of the following compounds is most consistent with the ^1H NMR above?

A. C_4H_6O
B. $CH_3COCH_2OCH(CH_3)_2$
C. $CH_3CH_2COOCH_3$
D. $CH_3CH_2OCH_2CH_2CH_3$
E. $CH_3COCH_2OCH_3$

84. Choose the correct structure for:

$CH_3CH_2CH(CH_3)CH(CH(CH_3)_2)CH_2CH = C(CH_3)_2$

A.

B.

C.

D.

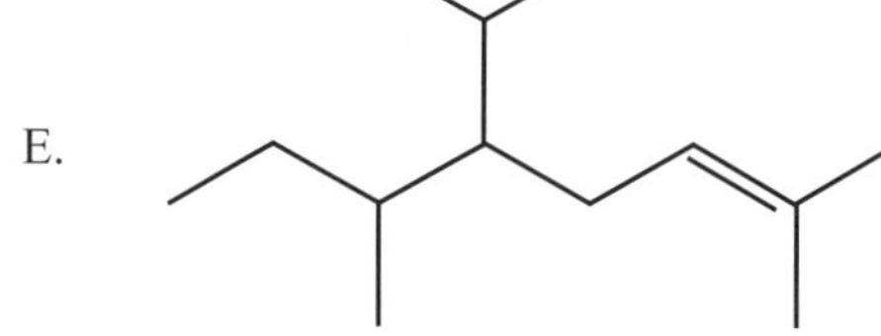

E.

85. The solvent used to do an extraction should do all of the following EXCEPT one. Which one is the EXCEPTION?

A. It must be sparingly soluble in the liquid from which the solute is to be extracted.
B. It must readily dissolve the substance to be extracted.
C. It must react chemically with the solute to form a product.
D. It must be easily separated from the solute after extraction.
E. None of the above.

86. How many possible structural isomers are there for C_4H_8?

A. 2
B. 4
C. 5
D. 6
E. 16

87. Which of the following statements is consistent with the acid-catalyzed dehydration of tertiary alcohols?

A. Formation of the carbocation is a slow step.
B. Protonation of the OH functional group is rapid and reversible.
C. Deprotonation of the carbocation is a fast step.
D. Cleavage of the C–O bond occurs in the rate determining step.
E. All of the above

88. Consider the following reaction:

The preceding reaction can be classified most closely as which of the following?

A. Enamine formation
B. Decarboxylation reaction
C. Enzymatic cleavage
D. Sp-sp hybridization
E. Imine formation

89. How many of the following compounds contain at least 1 chiral carbon and how many exhibit optical activity, respectively?

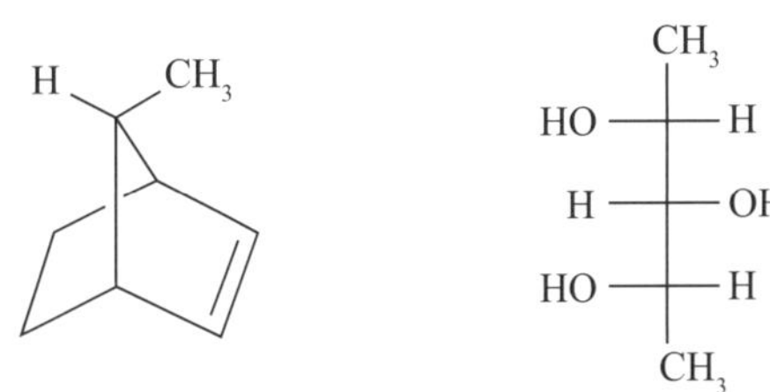

A. 4 compounds possess at least 1 chiral carbon; 1 compound is optically active.
B. 4 compounds possess at least 1 chiral carbon; 2 compounds are optically active.
C. 2 compounds possess at least 1 chiral carbon; 1 compound is optically active.
D. 2 compounds possess at least 1 chiral carbon; 2 compounds are optically active.
E. 3 compounds possess at least 1 chiral carbon; 3 compounds are optically active.

90. Consider the following reaction:

$(CH_3)_2C = CH_2 + HCl \rightarrow$ Product

Which of the following compounds best exemplifies the major organic product of the above reaction?

A. $(CH_3)_2CHCH_2Cl$
B. $(CH_3)_2CClCH_3$
C. $CH_2{=}CCl{-}CH_2CH_3$
D. $CH_3{-}CCl_2{-}CH_2CH_3$
E. $(ClCH_2)_2CHCH_3$

91. Acid catalysts such as *p*–toluensulfonic acid are often used to dehydrate alcohols. The role of the acid catalyst is to:

A. increase ΔG° and increase the activation energy for the dehydration reaction.
B. increase ΔG° and lower the activation energy for the dehydration reaction.
C. maintain ΔG° at the same value and lower the activation energy for the dehydration reaction.
D. lower ΔG° and increase the activation energy for the dehydration reaction.
E. lower ΔG° and lower the activation energy for the dehydration reaction.

92. Which of the following is the most accurate representation of the reaction coordinate diagram for the solvolysis of t–butyl bromide?

Note that [ ]* represents the intermediate.

A.

B.

C.

D.

93. The free energy changes for the equilibria *cis* ⇌ *trans* of 1,2–, 1,3–, and 1,4– dimethylcyclohexane are shown below.

The most stable diastereomer in each case would be:

A. IA, IIB, IIIA
B. IB, IIB, IIIB
C. IA, IIA, IIIA
D. IA, IIB, IIIB
E. IB, IIA, IIIB

94. What is the hybridization of C1 in coniine?

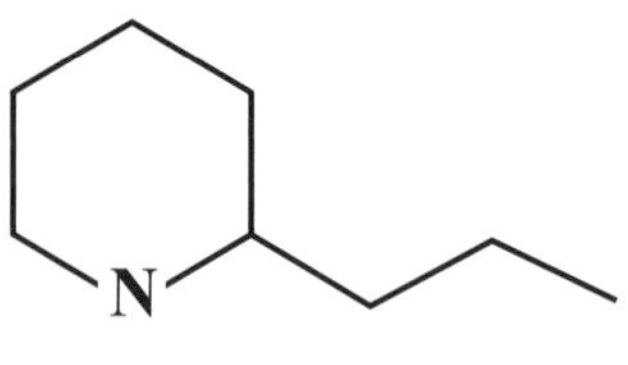

Coniine

A. sp
B. sp^2
C. sp^3
D. sd^4
E. None of the above

95. Which of the following would be the least reactive diene in a Diels-Alder reaction?

A. 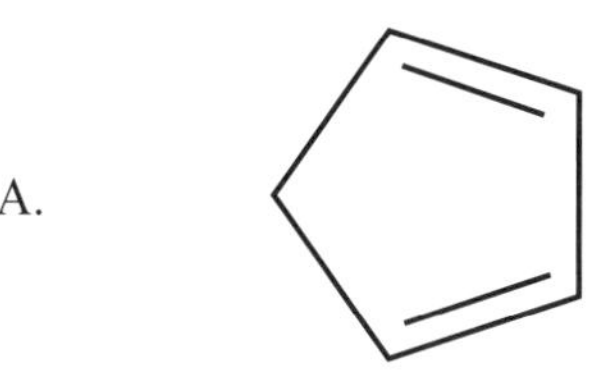

B. 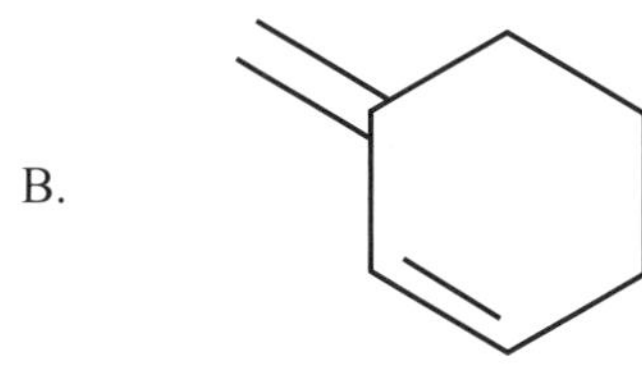

C. 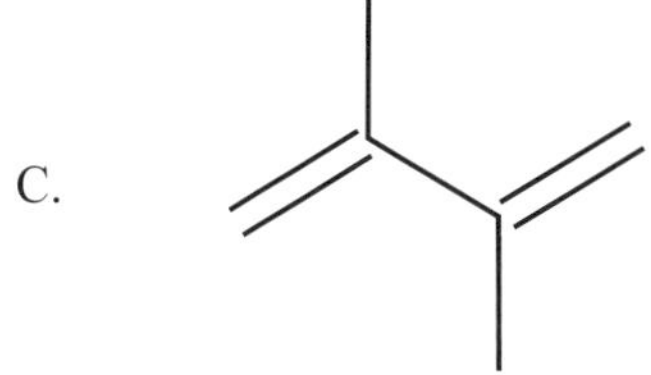

D. 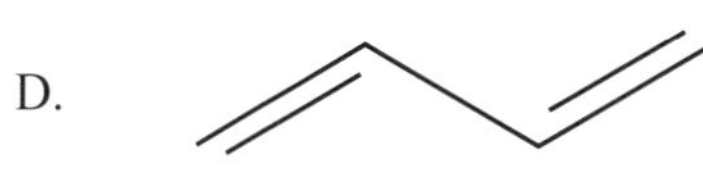

E. 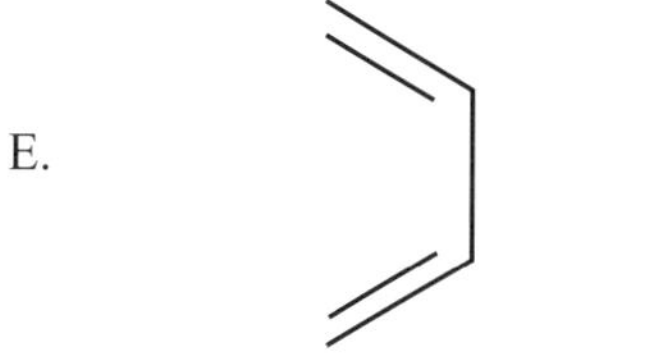

96. A student used a distillation apparatus to separate ethyl acetate from 1–butanol because of the difference in boiling points of these 2 compounds. This difference is most likely attributed to which of the following factors?

A. Hydrogen bonding
B. Bond hybridization
C. Temperature scanning
D. Increments of 5 degrees
E. Resonance stabilization

97. All of the following are true regarding allene (C_3H_4) EXCEPT one. Which one is the EXCEPTION?

A. The C–H bond angles are 120°.
B. The hybridization of the carbon atoms are sp and sp^2.
C. The bond angle formed by the three carbons is 180°.
D. The central carbon of allene forms two sigma bonds and two pi bonds.
E. Allene is a conjugated diene.

98. Which of the following is aromatic?

A. 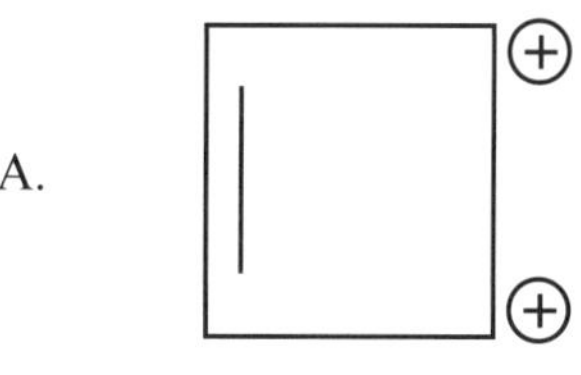

B. 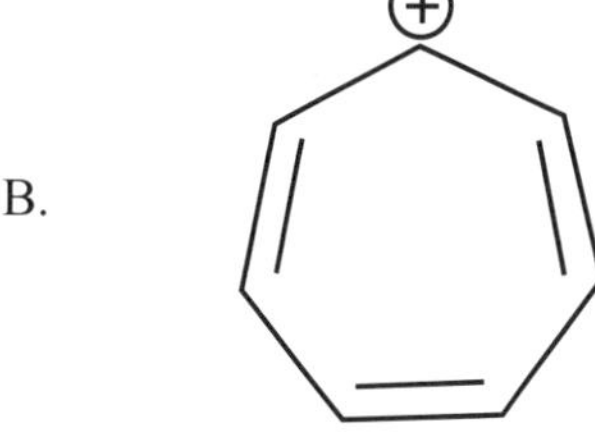

C. 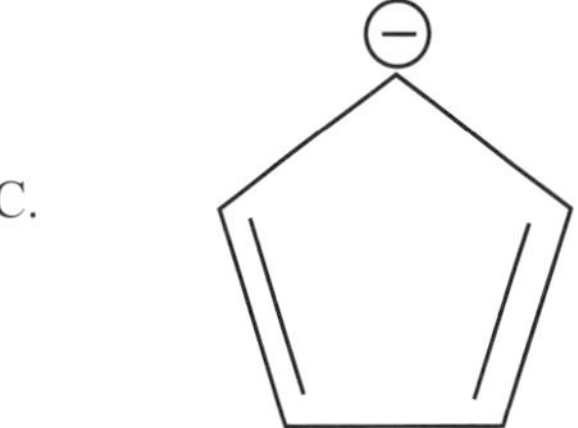

D. 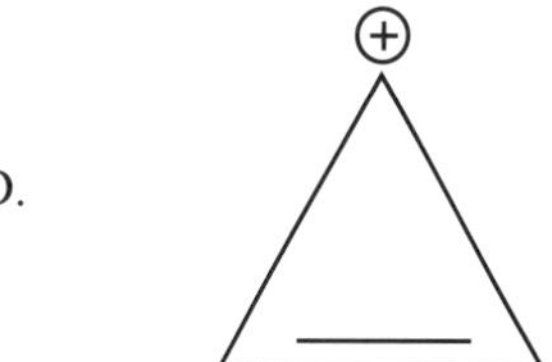

E. All of the above

99. Which of the following represents the product from the reaction shown below?

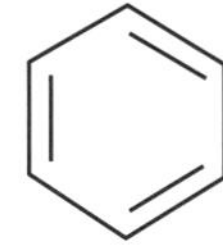

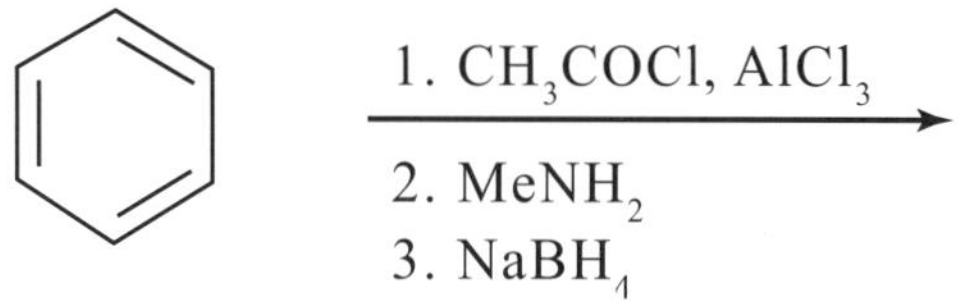

1. CH_3COCl, $AlCl_3$
2. $MeNH_2$
3. $NaBH_4$

A. 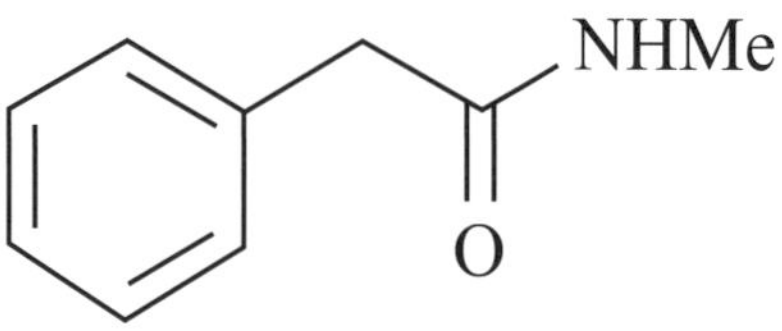 NHMe, O

B. 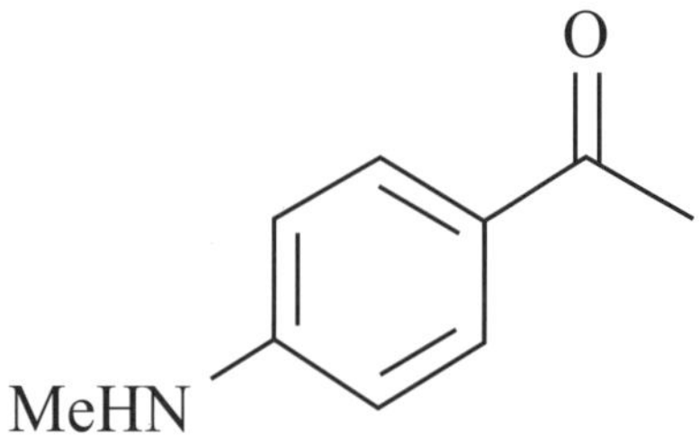 O, MeHN

C. 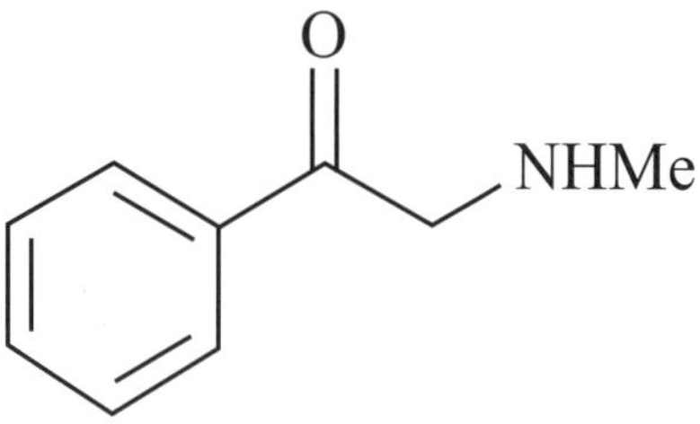 O, NHMe

D. 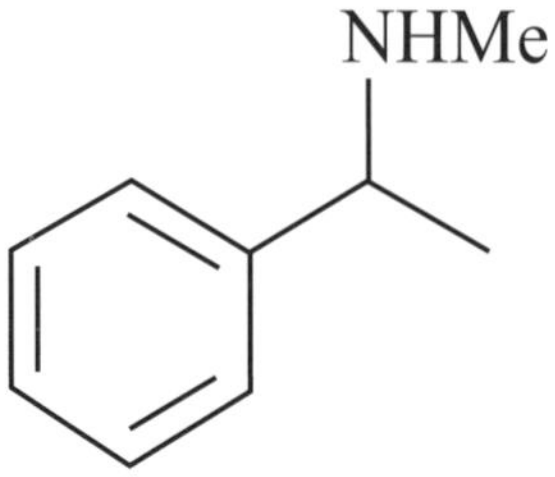 NHMe

E. 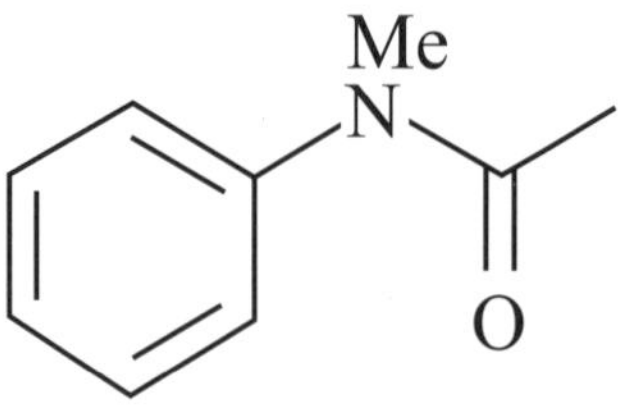 Me, N, O

100. Each of the following structures is a resonance form of the molecule shown below EXCEPT one. Which one is the EXCEPTION?

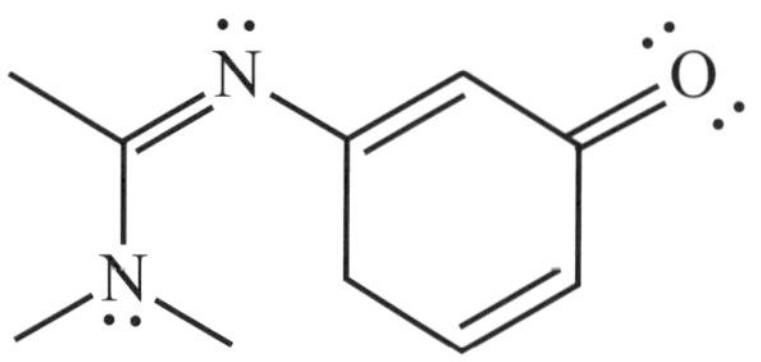

A.

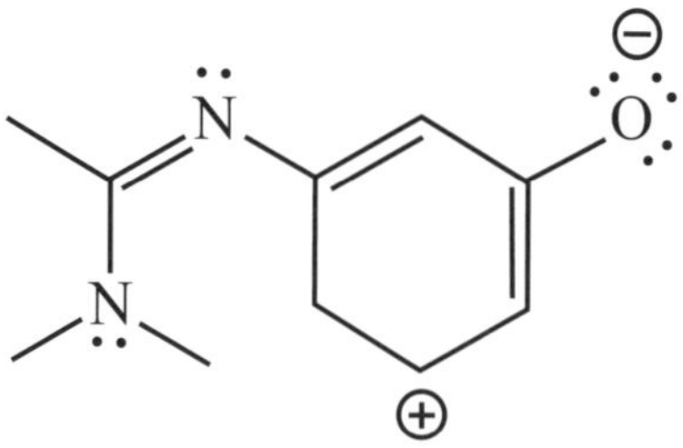

B.

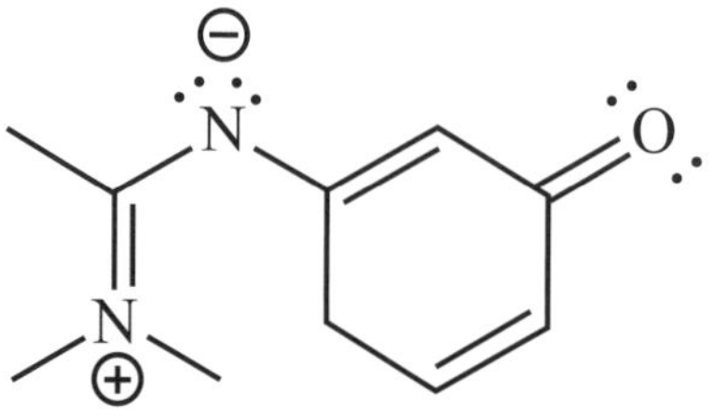

C.

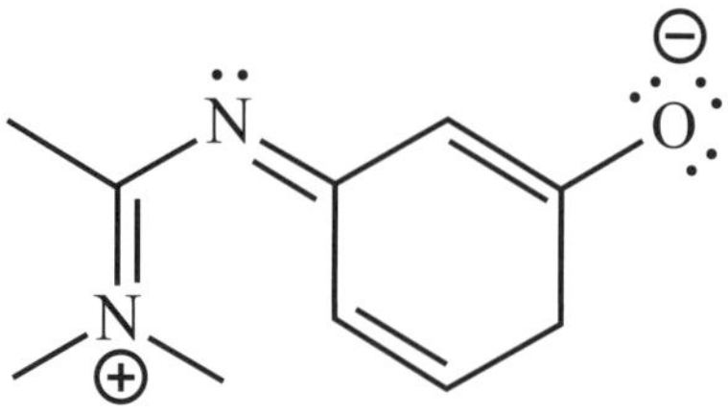

D.

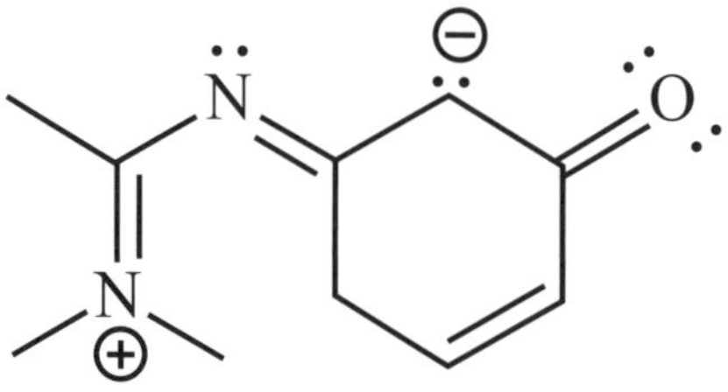

E.

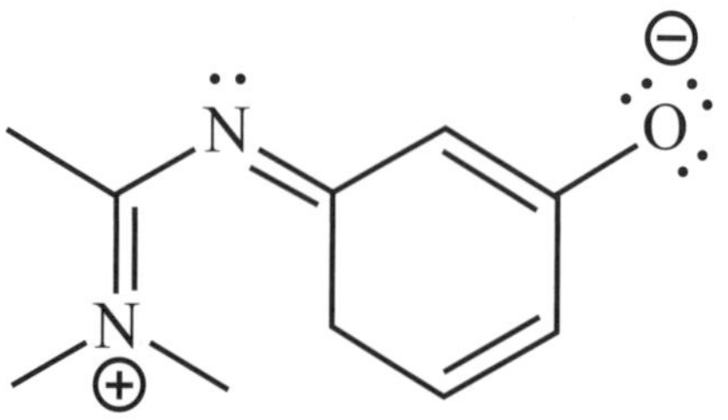

END OF THIS TEST SECTION.

Perceptual Ability Test

Time limit: 60 minutes

Part 1

For questions 1 through 15:

This visualization test is composed of items modeled in the sample question below. A three-dimensional object is presented on the left, followed by five choices of apertures or openings.

The task is the same in each question. First, you have to mentally rotate the given object to see how it looks from different directions. Next, select the aperture from the five options that would allow the object to pass smoothly if the correct side were inserted first. Lastly, mark the letter of your choice on the answer sheet.

Rules:

1. The given object may be entered through the aperture from a direction that is different from the one shown in the question.
2. Once the object is introduced to the opening, it must pass completely through the hole without rotating the object in any direction.
3. Both the three-dimensional object and the corresponding apertures are drawn to the same scale. It may be possible for an aperture to have the correct shape yet be too small or too big for the object. However, the differences are large enough to be seen by the naked eye.
4. No irregularities are hidden in any portion of the object. In case the figure has symmetric indentations, the hidden portion would be symmetric with the visible part.
5. For each question, only one aperture matches the exact shape and size of one of the two-dimensional views of the object.

Example: (The answer to this example should not be marked on the answer sheet.)

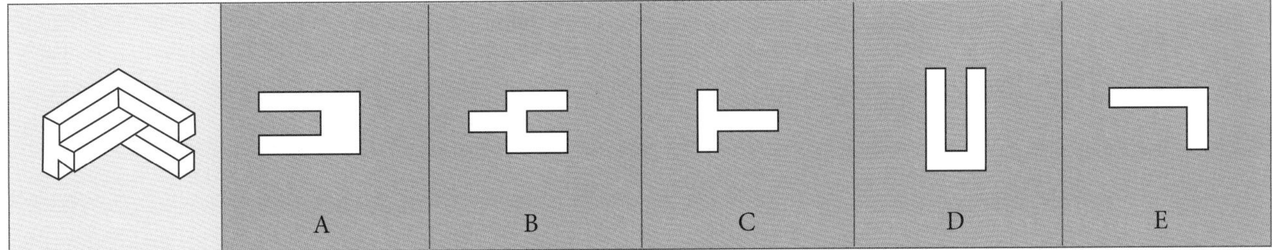

The correct answer is A.

For the object to pass all the way through the aperture, it has to be rotated first at 180 degrees from right to left and then, the side on the right is inserted first.

Please proceed to the questions.

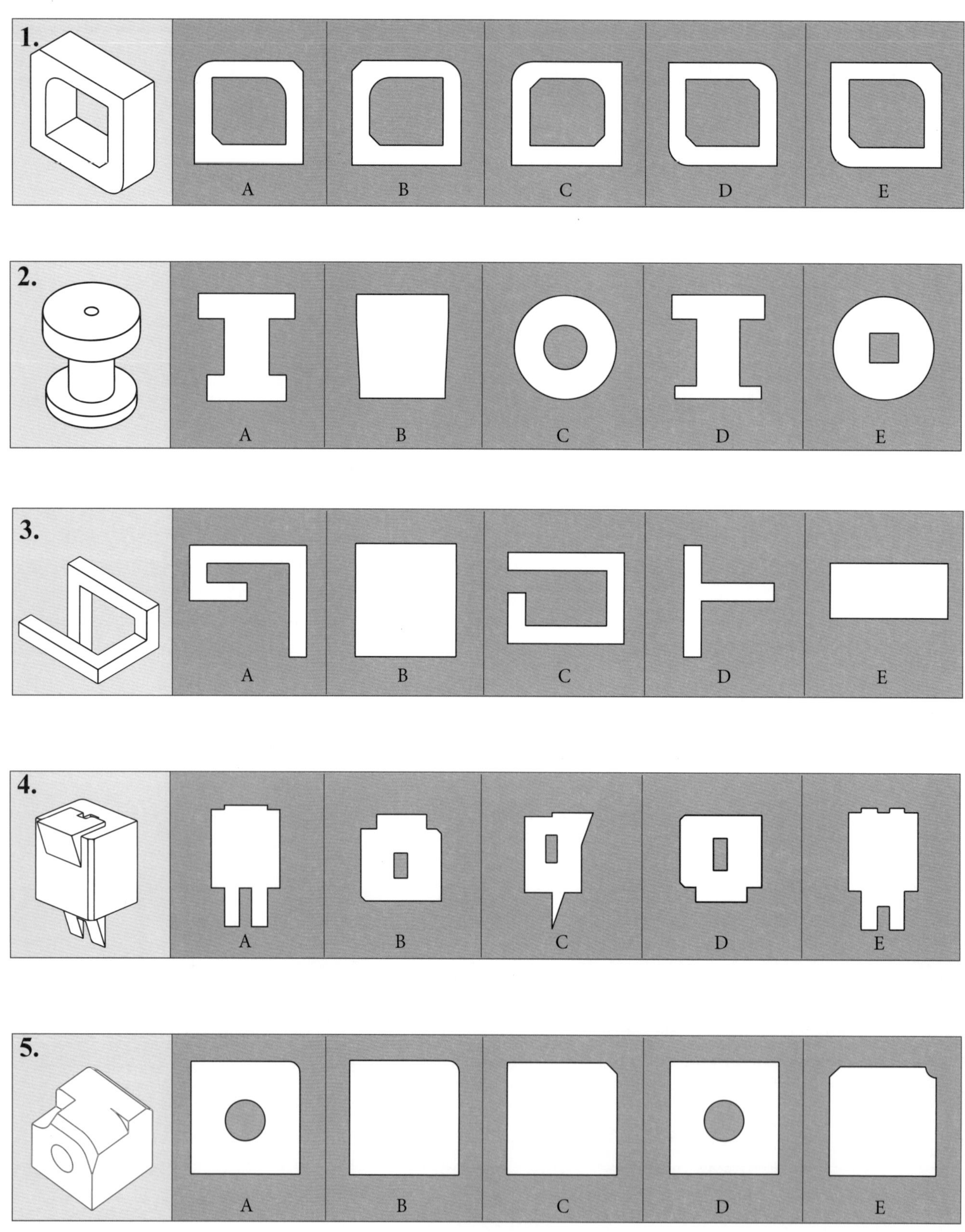
1.
A
B
C
D
E
2.
A
B
C
D
E
3.
A
B
C
D
E
4.
A
B
C
D
E
5.
A
B
C
D
E

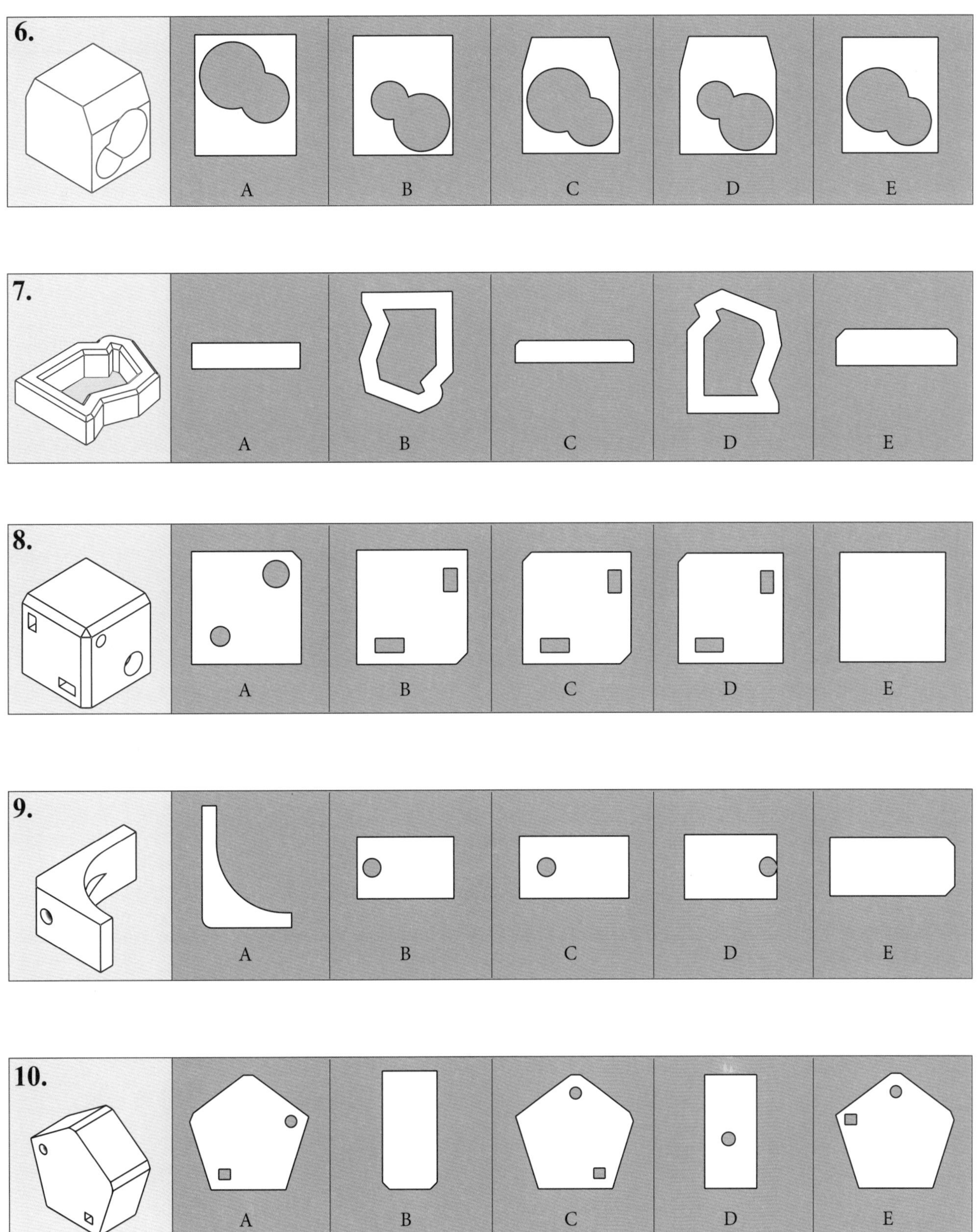
6.
A
B
C
D
E
7.
A
B
C
D
E
8.
A
B
C
D
E
9.
A
B
C
D
E
10.
A
B
C
D
E

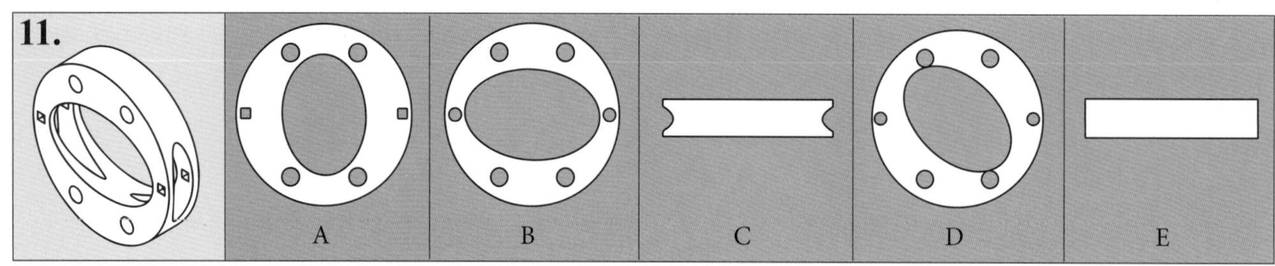

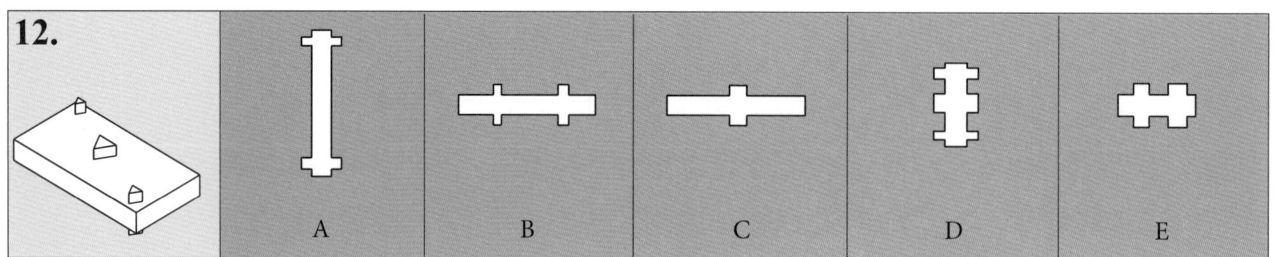

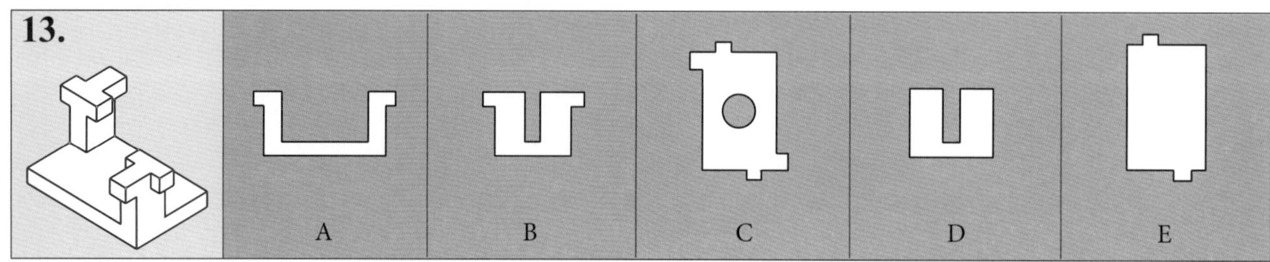

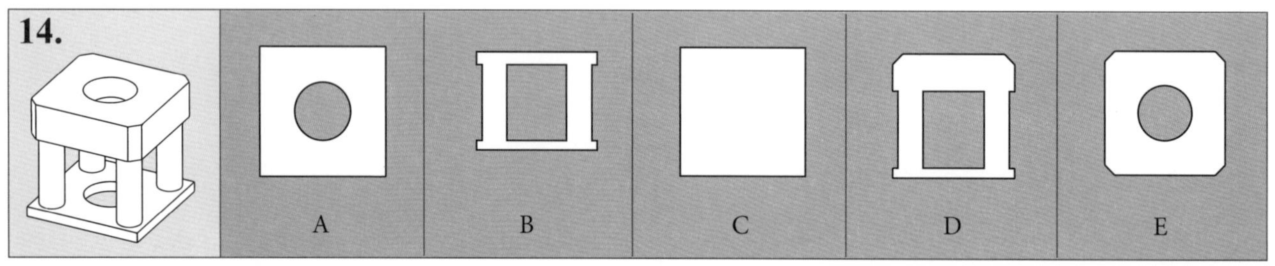

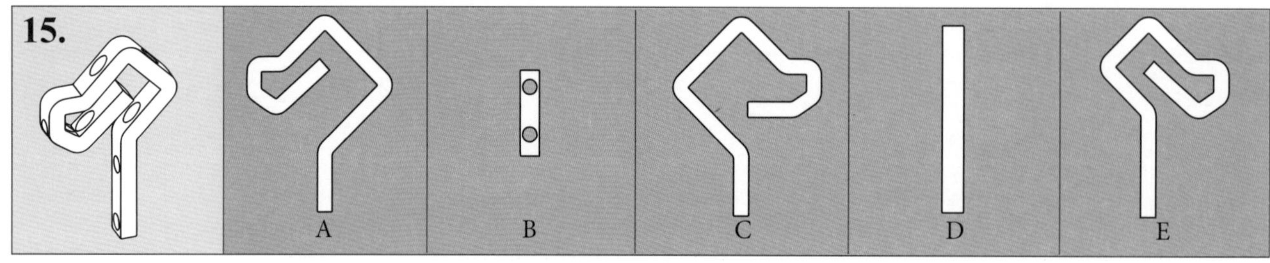

DO NOT STOP - READ DIRECTIONS FOR PART 2 AND CONTINUE

Part 2

For questions 16 through 30:

The following figure shows the top, front, and end views of a basic solid object. These are flat perspectives where only points along the parallel lines of the object's surface are shown. The projection looking DOWN on the object (TOP VIEW) is in the upper left-hand corner of the illustration. The projection looking at the object from the FRONT (FRONT VIEW) is in the lower left-hand corner. The projection looking at the object from the RIGHT side (END VIEW) is in the lower right-hand corner. The positions of these views are ALWAYS the same in each question and are also labeled accordingly.

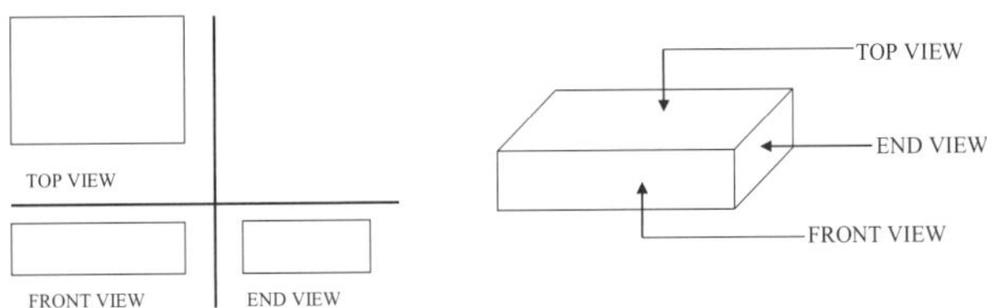

If the object had a hole in it, the views would look like as such:

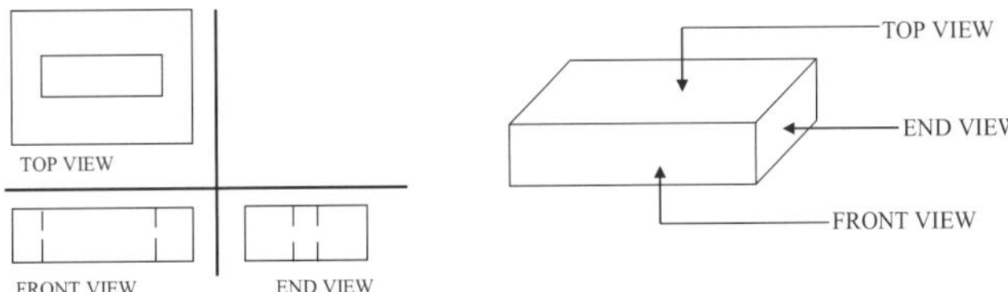

Points that are not visible on the surface of the object in a particular view are represented by DOTTED lines.

In the succeeding questions, two views are presented, followed by four options to complete the set. Pick the correct choice that corresponds to the missing view and mark it on the answer sheet.

Example: Choose the correct END VIEW. (The answer to this example should not be marked on the answer sheet.)

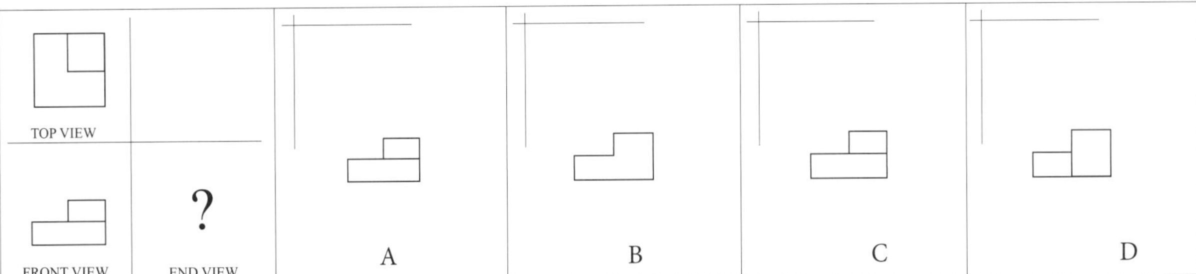

The correct answer is C.

The front view shows a smaller block on the base and no hole (because no dotted lines are shown). The top view shows that the block is a square and located on the upper left corner of the base. These characteristics correspond to the outline shown in option C if viewed from the right side of the object.

Please note that the problems given in the succeeding items do not always require you to choose the end view. The top view or front view may also be asked.

Please proceed to the questions.

16. Choose the correct TOP VIEW.

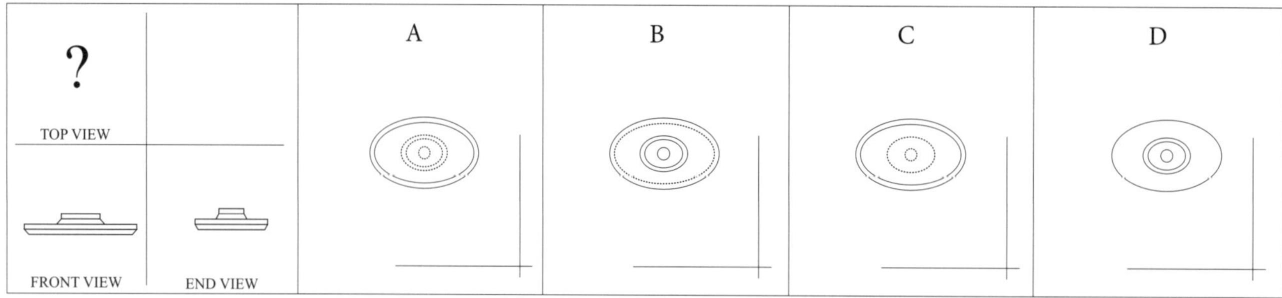

17. Choose the correct TOP VIEW.

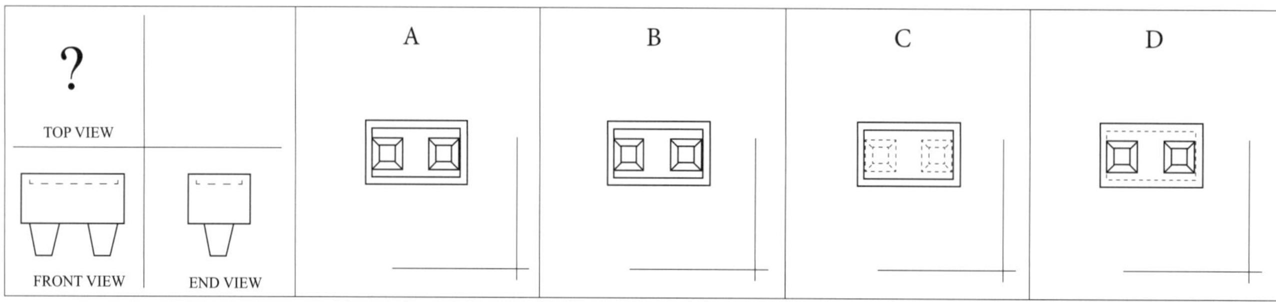

18. Choose the correct END VIEW.

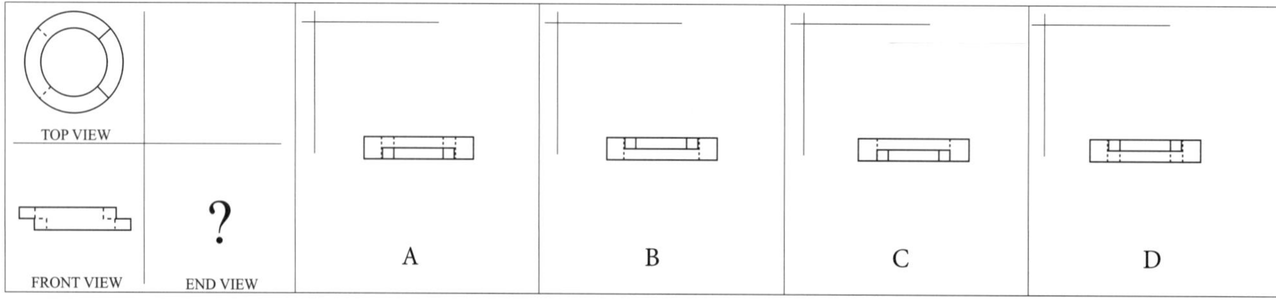

19. Choose the correct END VIEW.

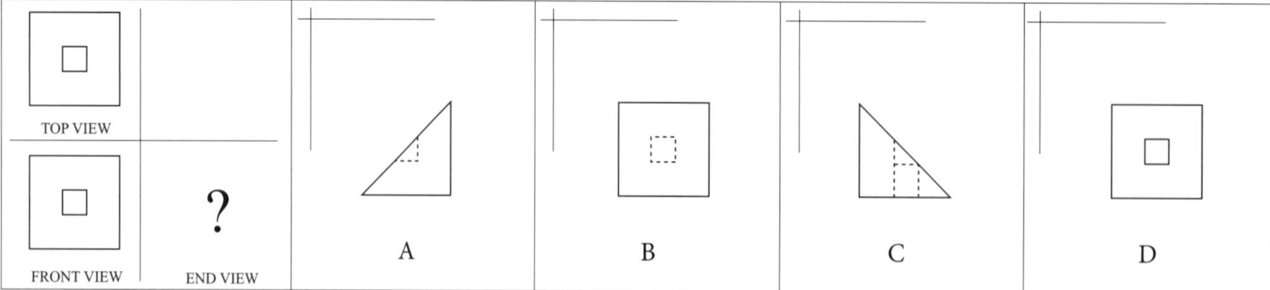

20. Choose the correct FRONT VIEW.

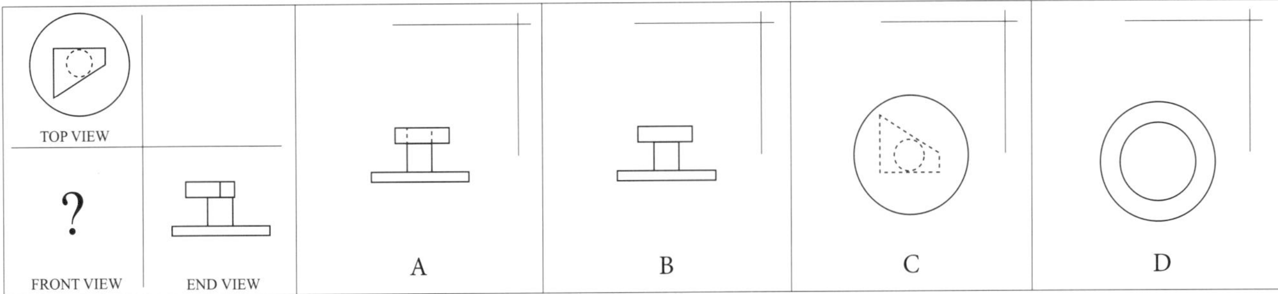

21. Choose the correct TOP VIEW.

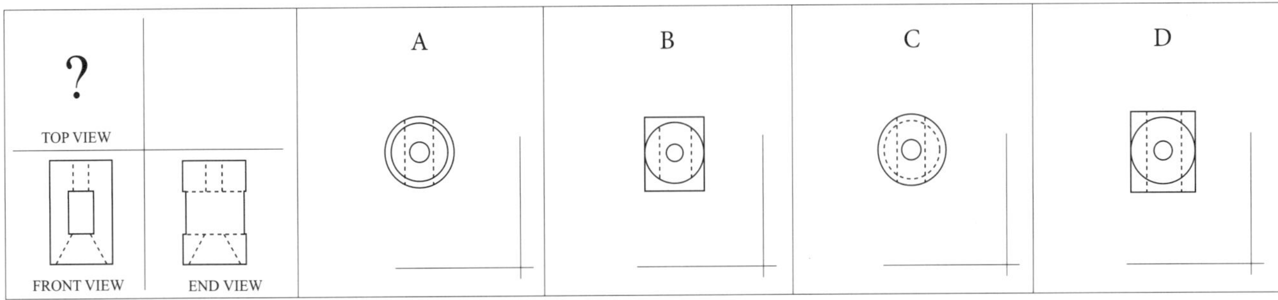

22. Choose the correct FRONT VIEW.

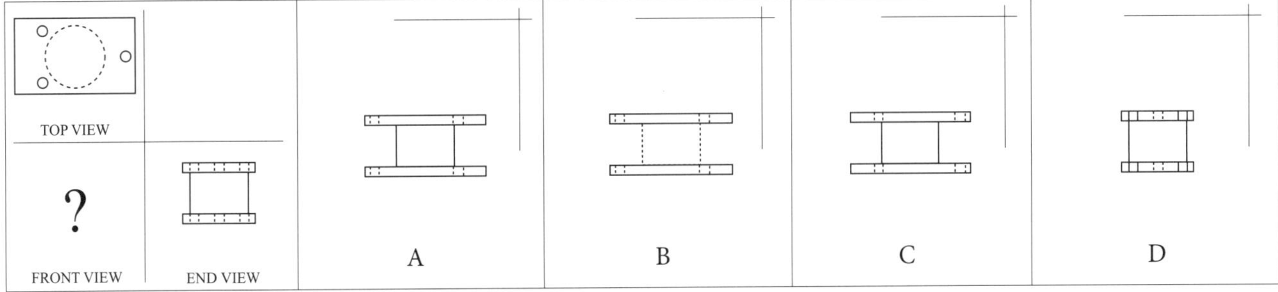

23. Choose the correct TOP VIEW.

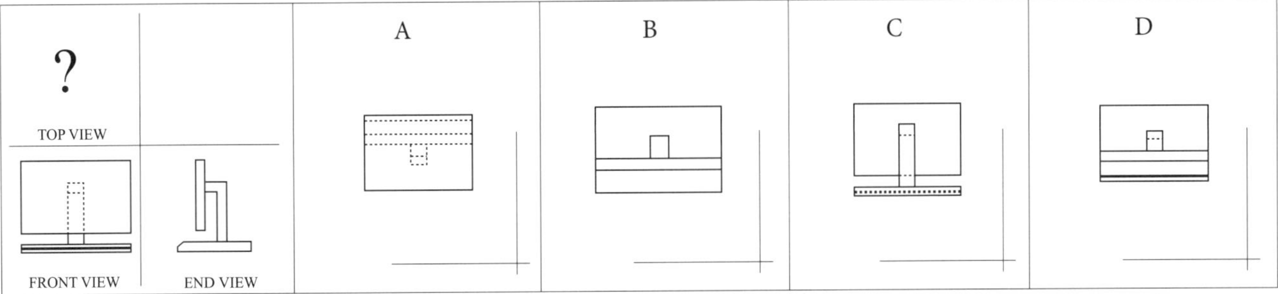

24. Choose the correct END VIEW.

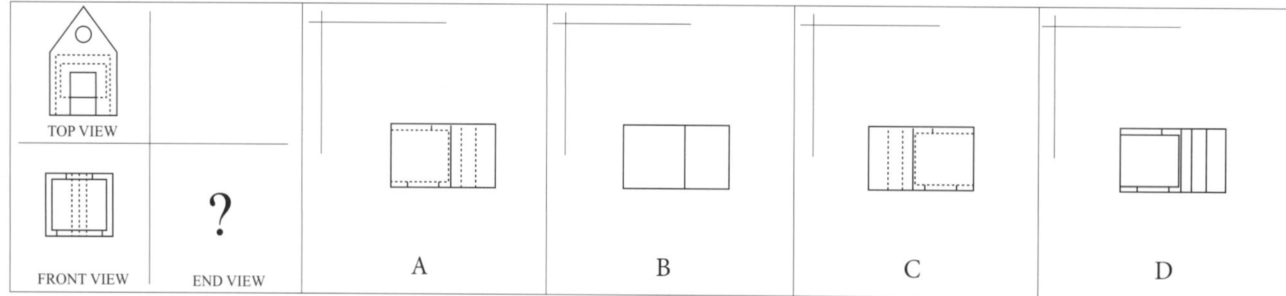

25. Choose the correct FRONT VIEW.

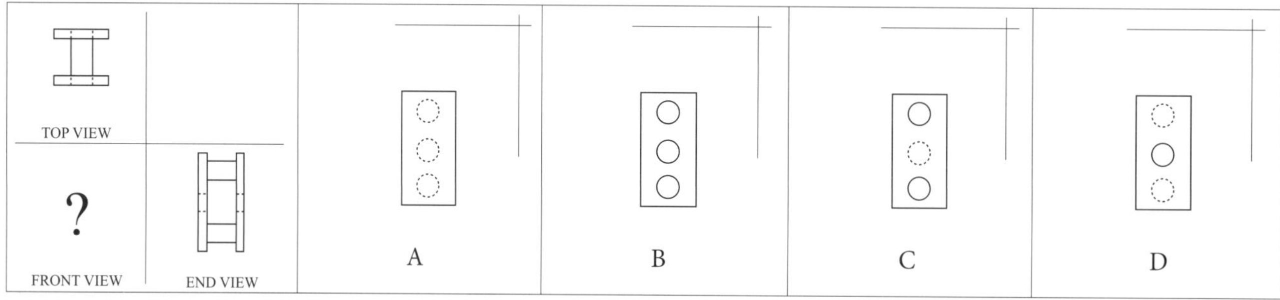

26. Choose the correct END VIEW.

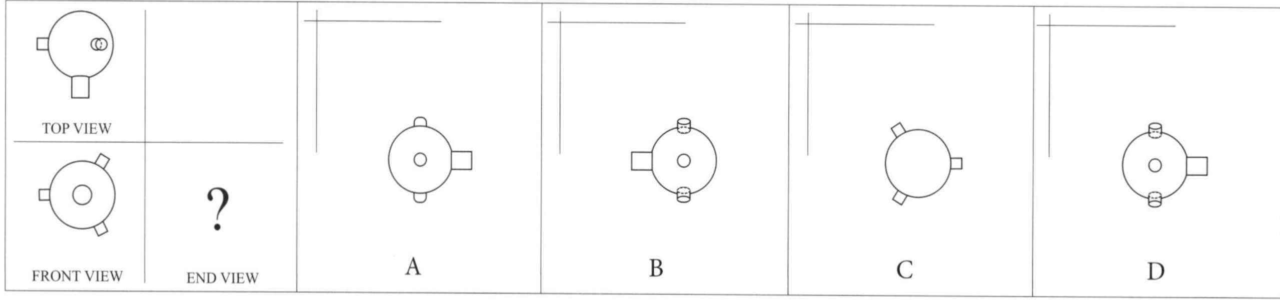

27. Choose the correct TOP VIEW.

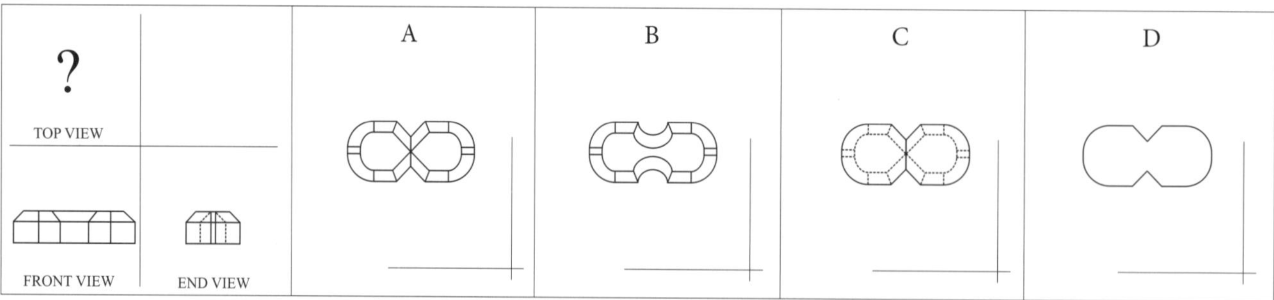

28. Choose the correct FRONT VIEW.

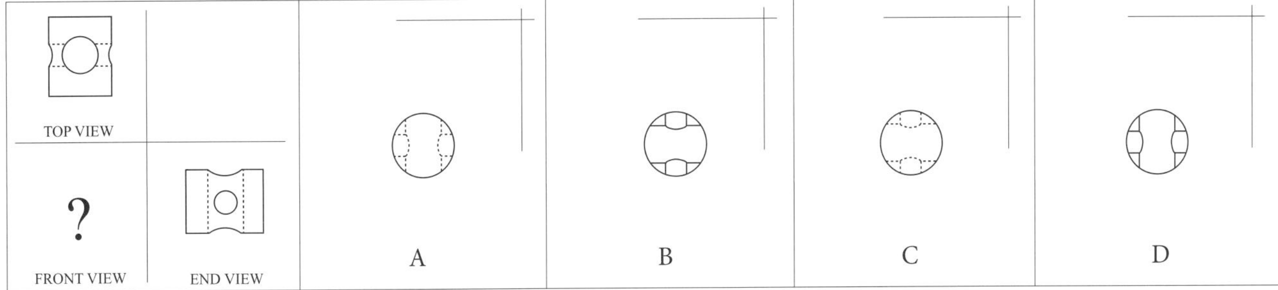

29. Choose the correct TOP VIEW.

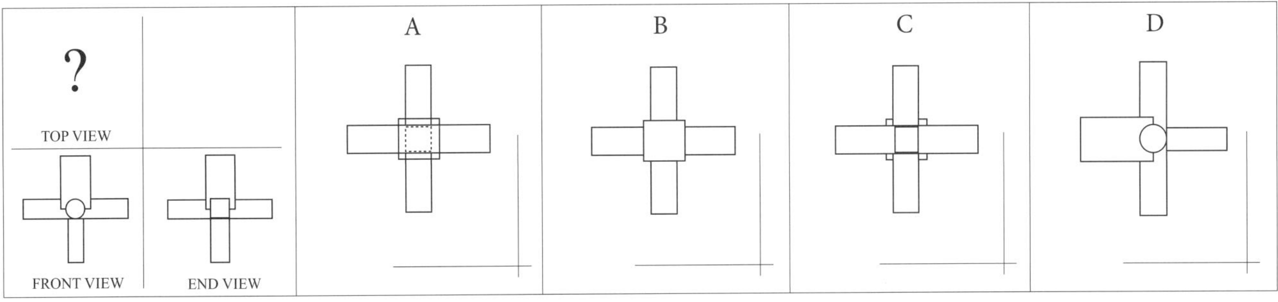

30. Choose the correct TOP VIEW.

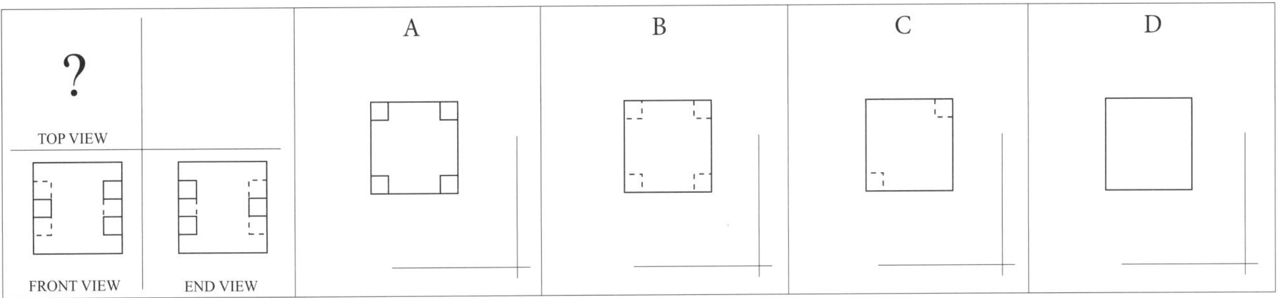

DO NOT STOP - READ DIRECTIONS FOR PART 3 AND CONTINUE

Part 3

For questions 31 through 45:

This section requires you to evaluate the four INTERIOR angles and rank each item from SMALL to LARGE in terms of degrees. From the alternatives, select the one with the correct order. Indicate your choice on the answer sheet.

Example:

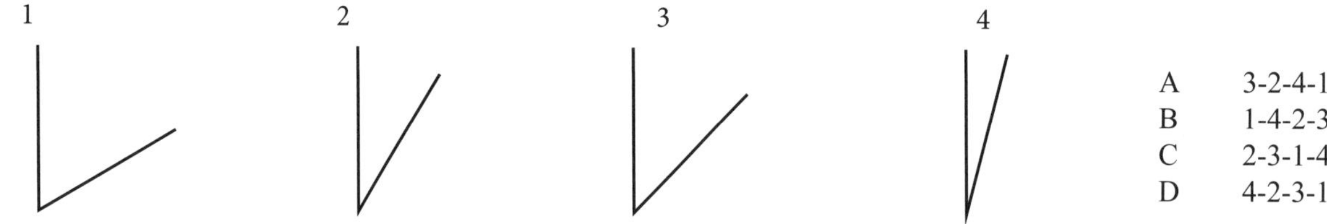

The correct answer is D.

The correct order of the angles from small to large is 4-2-3-1.

Please proceed to the questions.

31. 1 2 3 4

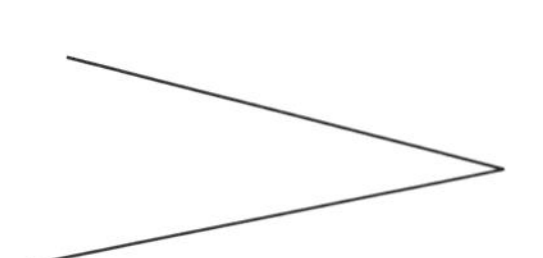
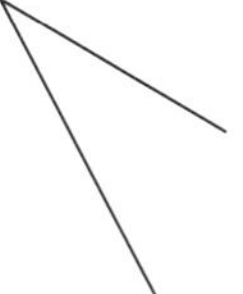
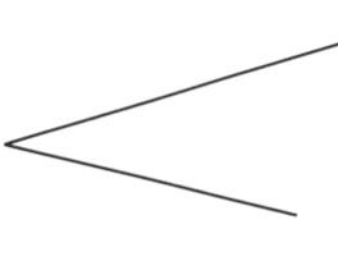

A 3-1-4-2
B 2-3-1-4
C 2-1-3-4
D 1-3-4-2

32. 1 2 3 4

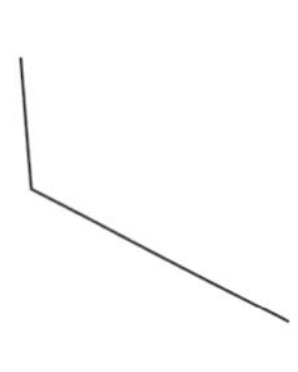
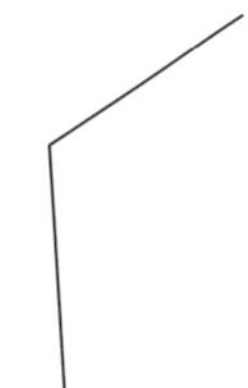

A 1-2-4-3
B 2-1-4-3
C 4-3-2-1
D 3-4-1-2

33. 1 2 3 4

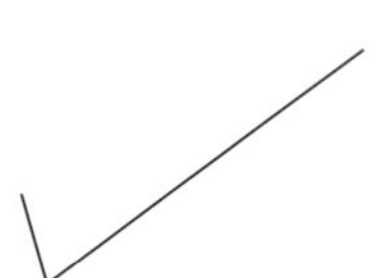
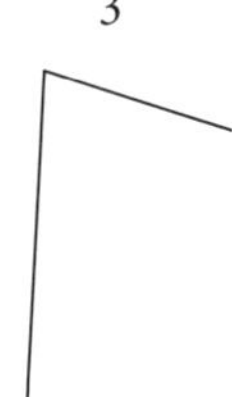

A 2-1-3-4
B 1-2-4-3
C 3-2-1-4
D 4-3-1-2

34. 1 2 3 4

A 2-1-3-4
B 1-2-3-4
C 4-3-1-2
D 4-3-2-1

35. 1 2 3 4

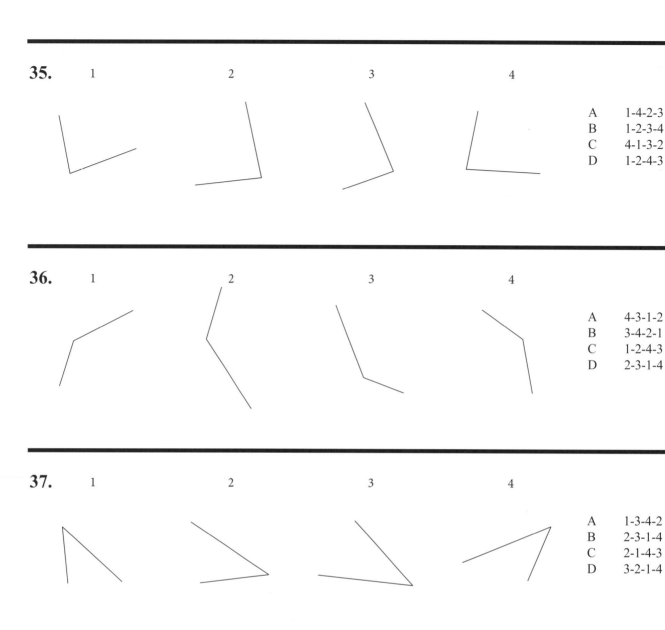

A 1-4-2-3
B 1-2-3-4
C 4-1-3-2
D 1-2-4-3

36. 1 2 3 4

A 4-3-1-2
B 3-4-2-1
C 1-2-4-3
D 2-3-1-4

37. 1 2 3 4

A 1-3-4-2
B 2-3-1-4
C 2-1-4-3
D 3-2-1-4

38. 1 2 3 4

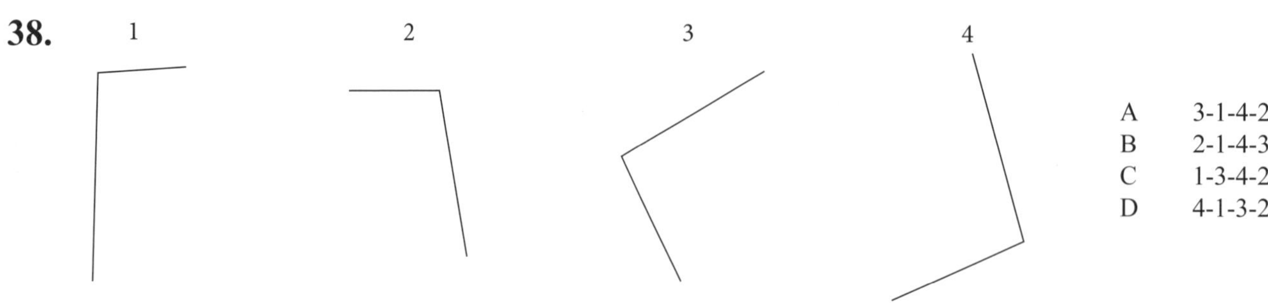

A 3-1-4-2
B 2-1-4-3
C 1-3-4-2
D 4-1-3-2

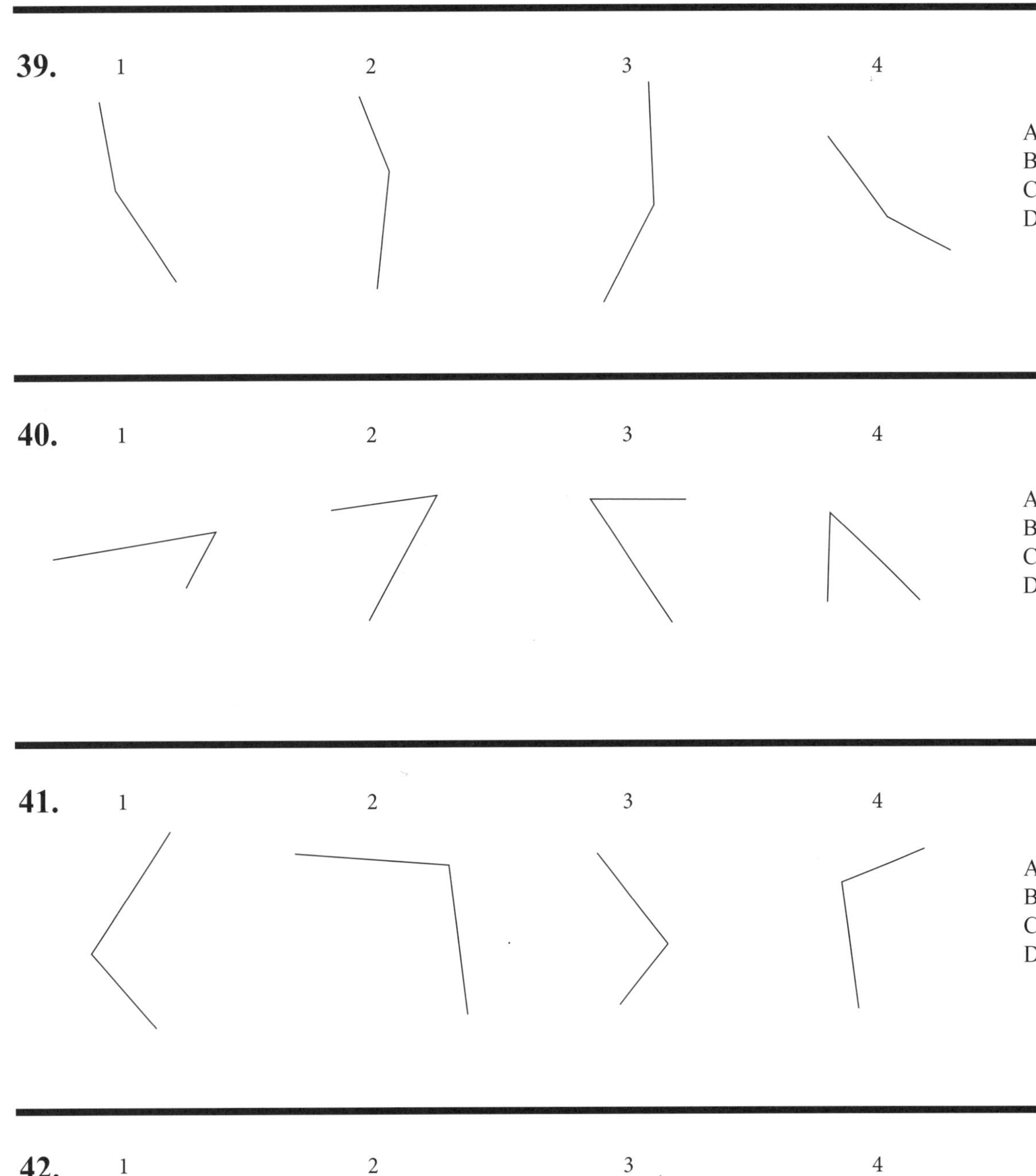

42. 1 2 3 4

A 2-1-3-4
B 2-1-4-3
C 1-2-3-4
D 3-1-2-4

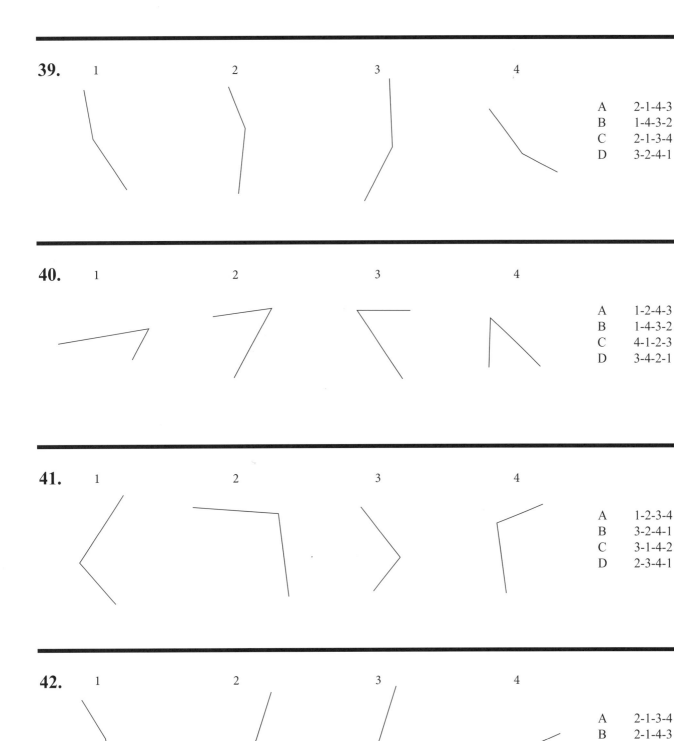

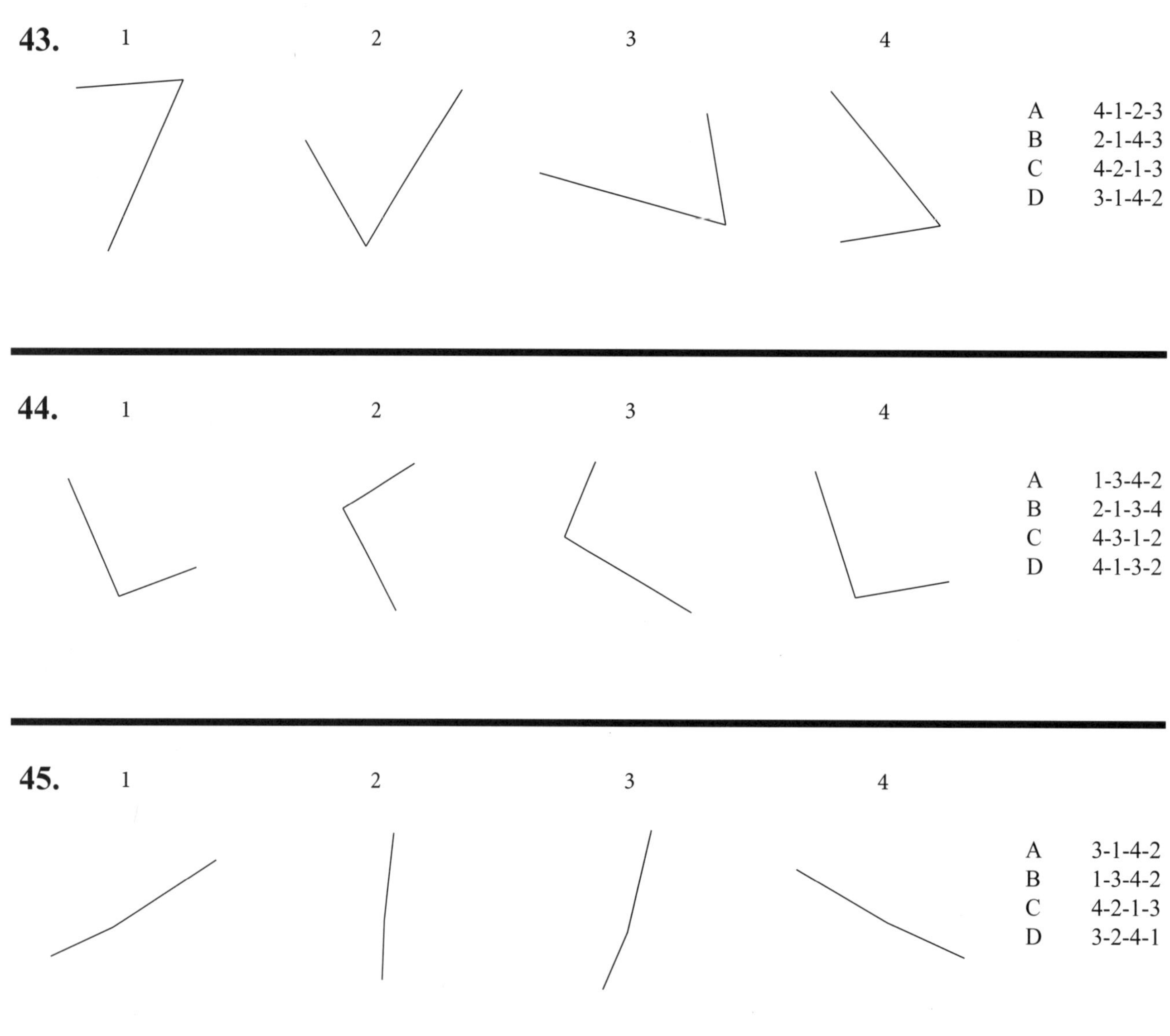

DO NOT STOP - READ DIRECTIONS FOR PART 4 AND CONTINUE

Part 4

For questions 46 through 60:

Each question in this section presents the following scenario:

A square-shaped paper is folded one or more times. The broken lines in the next figures represent the main outline of the paper; the solid lines signify the position of the paper as it is being folded. Take note that the paper is never turned or twisted. This means that the folded paper always stays within the boundaries of the original square.

Each question shows the paper folded multiple times. After the last fold, the paper is punched with a hole. Your task is to visualize unfolding the paper and identifying the position of the holes on the unfolded square. Only one pattern is correct for each question.

Example 1:(The answer to this example should not be marked on the answer sheet.)

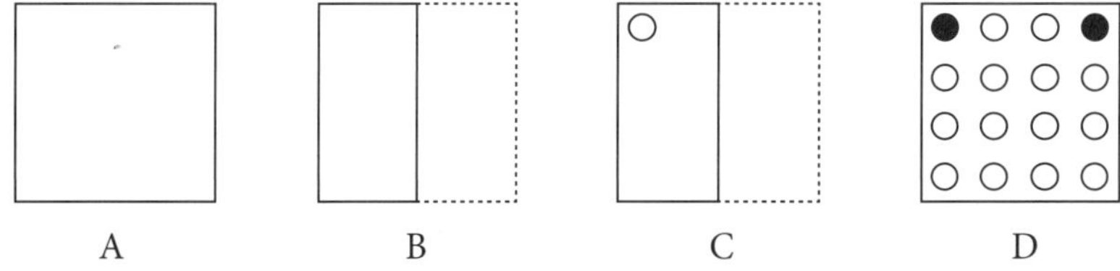

In Example 1, Figure A shows the unfolded paper. Figure B shows the paper now folded in half. Figure C shows where the hole is punched on the folded paper. Figure D shows the resulting pattern of the holes, indicated by the darkened circles, on the original square.

Example 2 shows how a question appears on the test.

Example 2:

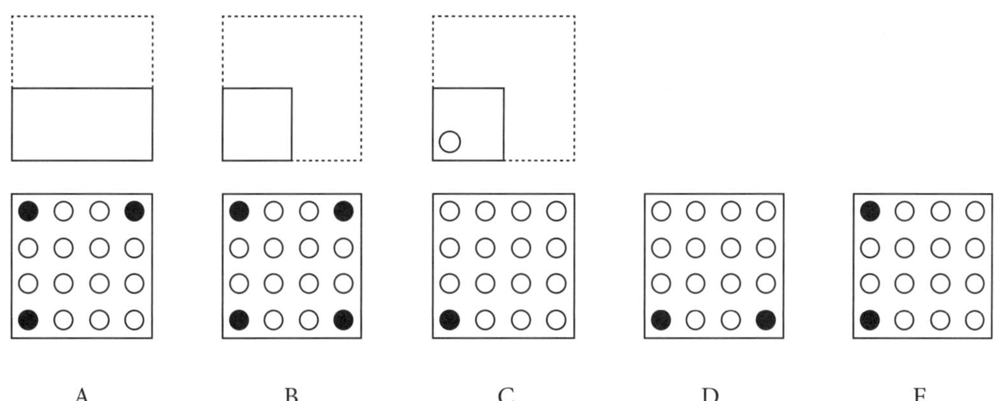

A B C D E

The correct answer is B.

The paper was four layers when punched, resulting to the holes placed in each of the four corners.

Please proceed to the questions.

46.

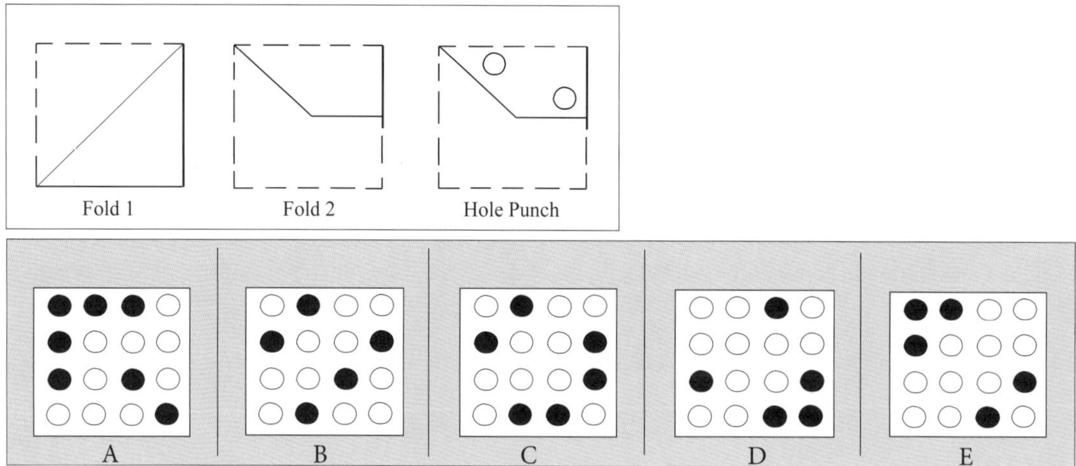

Fold 1
Fold 2
Hole Punch
A
B
C
D
E

47.

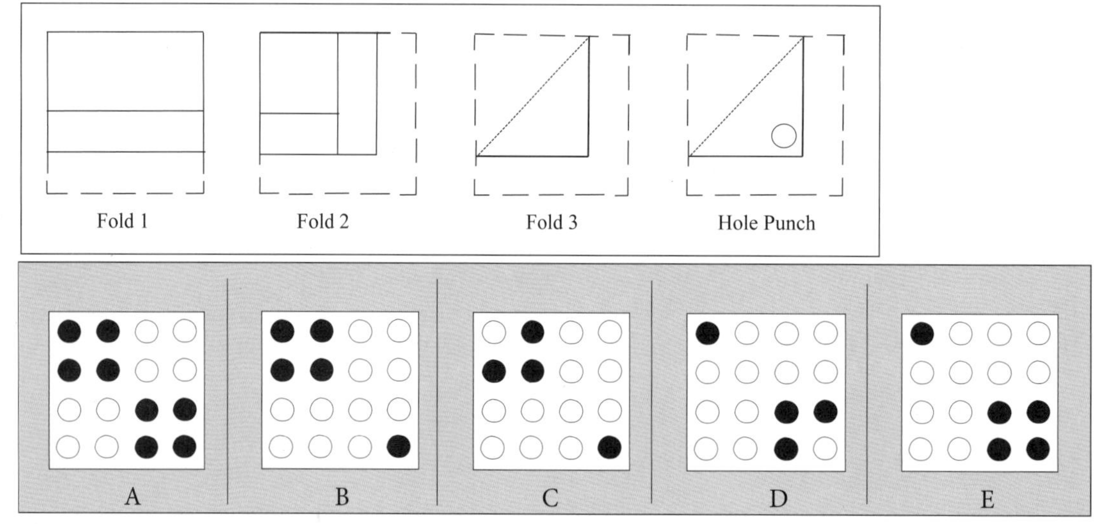

Fold 1
Fold 2
Fold 3
Hole Punch
A
B
C
D
E

48.

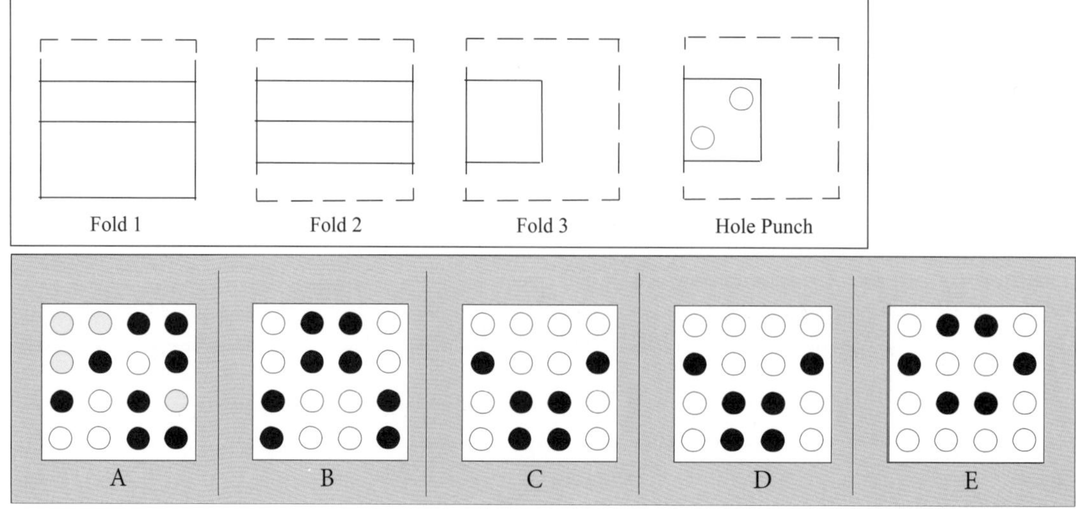

Fold 1
Fold 2
Fold 3
Hole Punch
A
B
C
D
E

49.

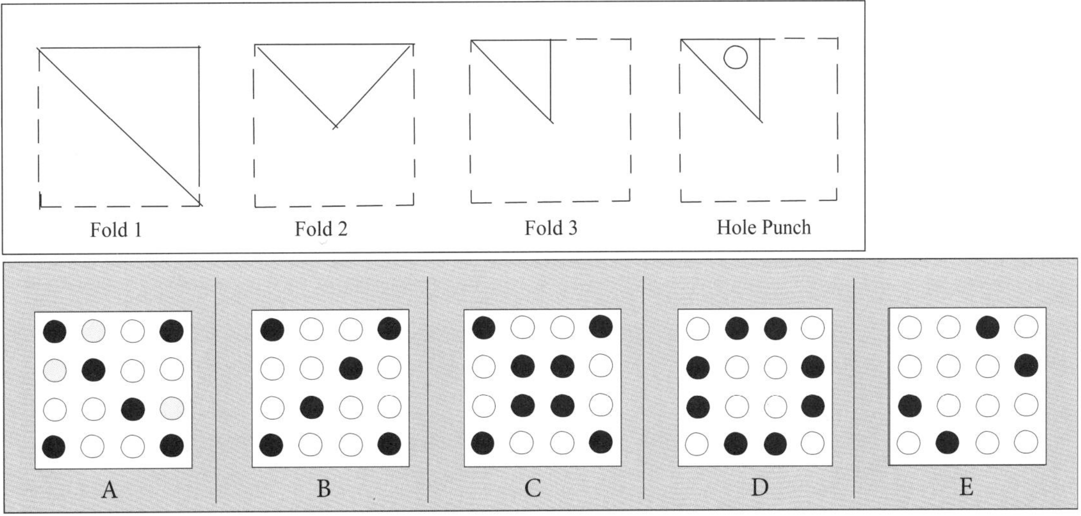
Fold 1
Fold 2
Fold 3
Hole Punch
A
B
C
D
E

50.

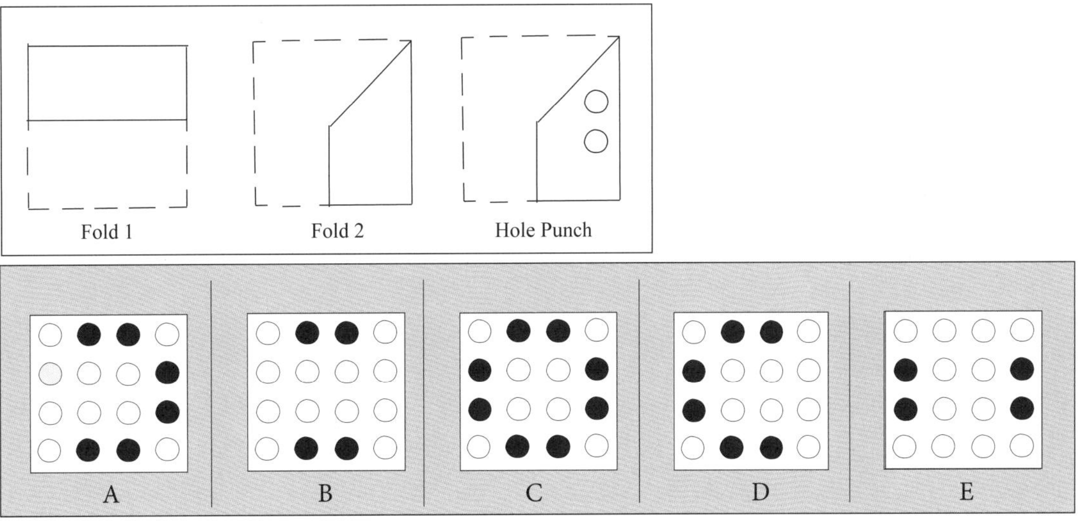
Fold 1
Fold 2
Hole Punch
A
B
C
D
E

51.

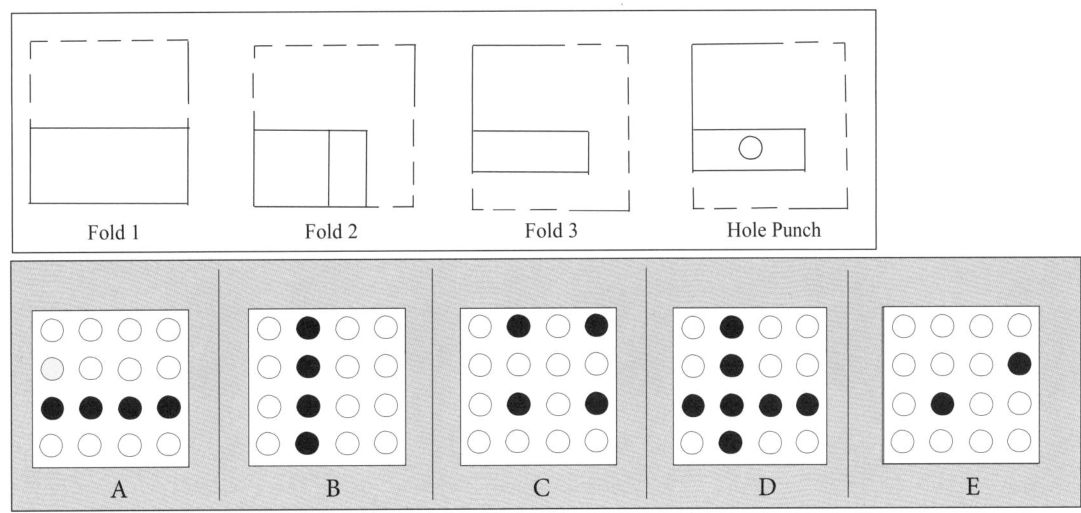
Fold 1
Fold 2
Fold 3
Hole Punch
A
B
C
D
E

52.

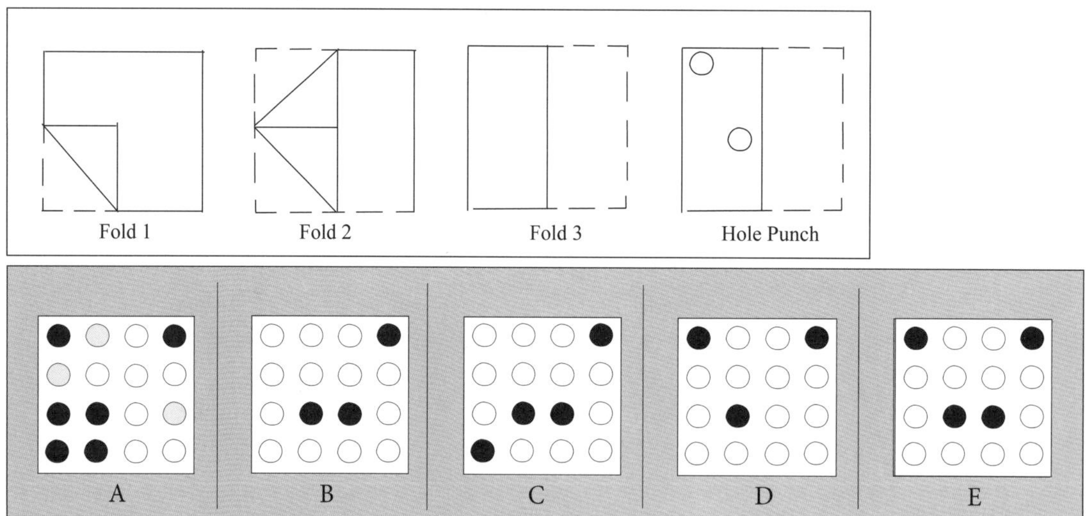
Fold 1
Fold 2
Fold 3
Hole Punch
A
B
C
D
E

53.

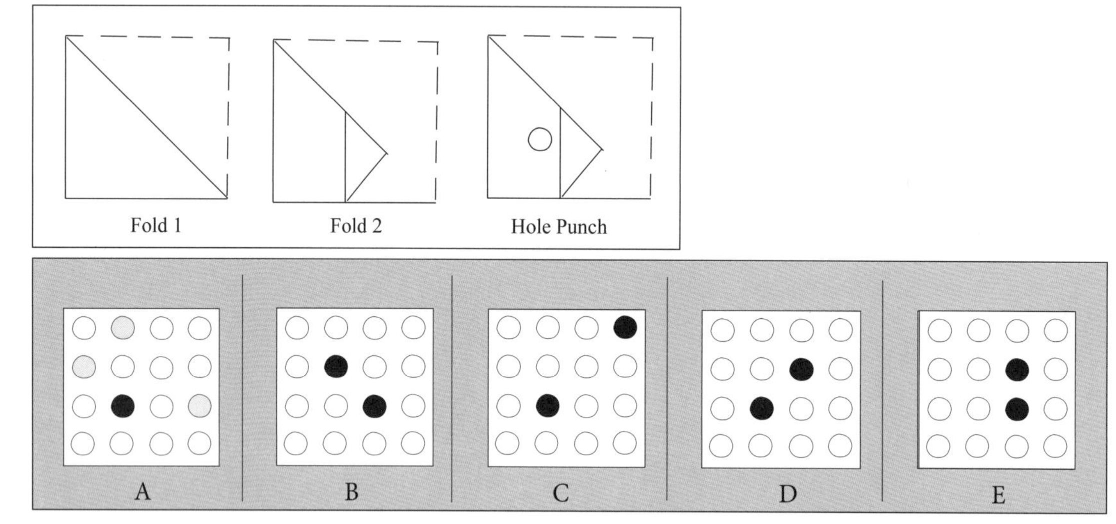
Fold 1
Fold 2
Hole Punch
A
B
C
D
E

54.

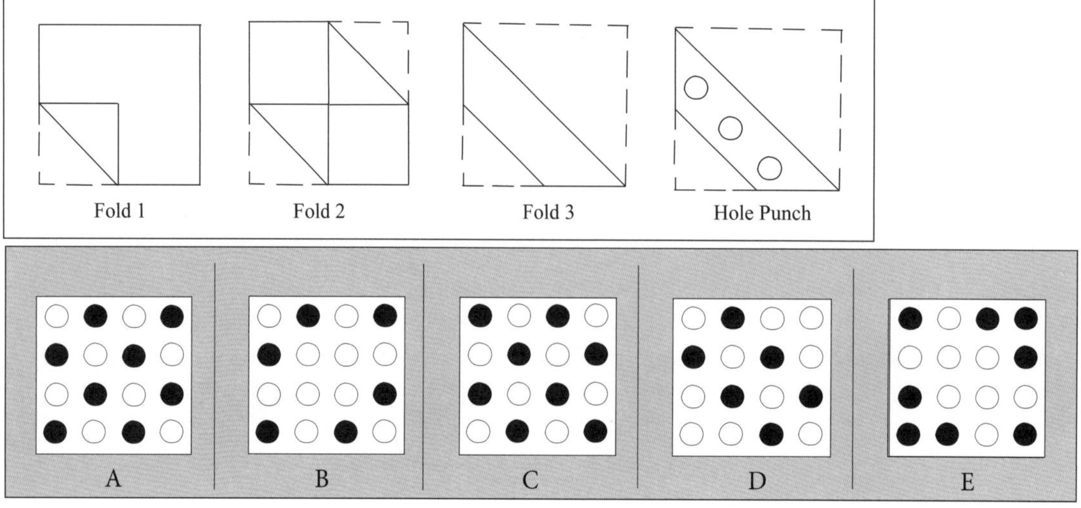
Fold 1
Fold 2
Fold 3
Hole Punch
A
B
C
D
E

55.

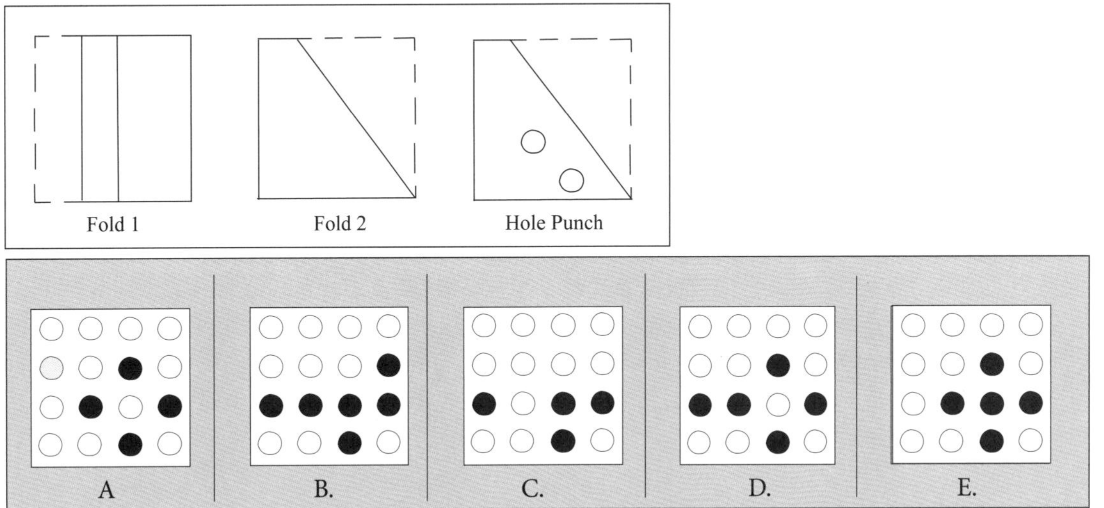

Fold 1
Fold 2
Hole Punch
A
B.
C.
D.
E.

56.

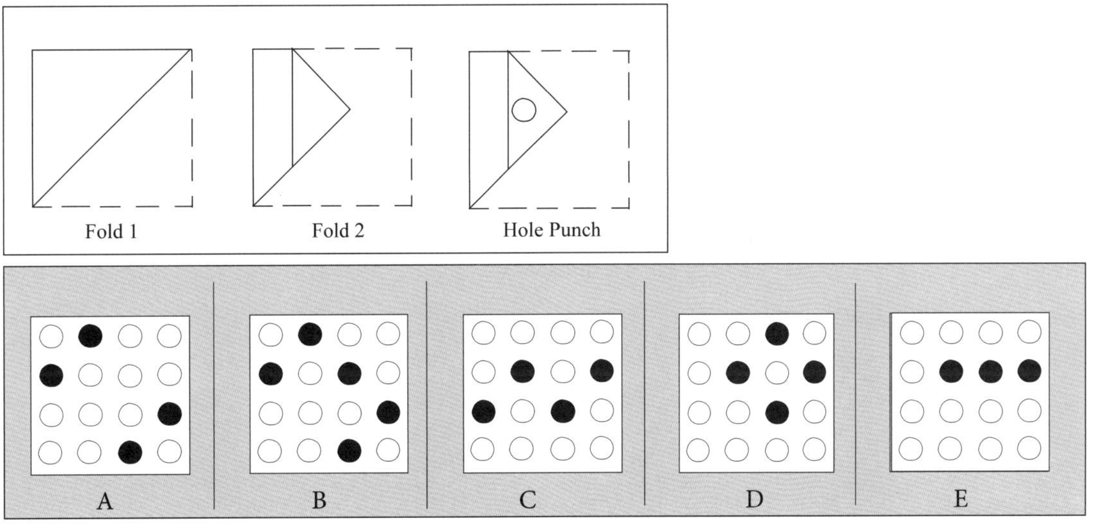

Fold 1
Fold 2
Hole Punch
A
B
C
D
E

57.

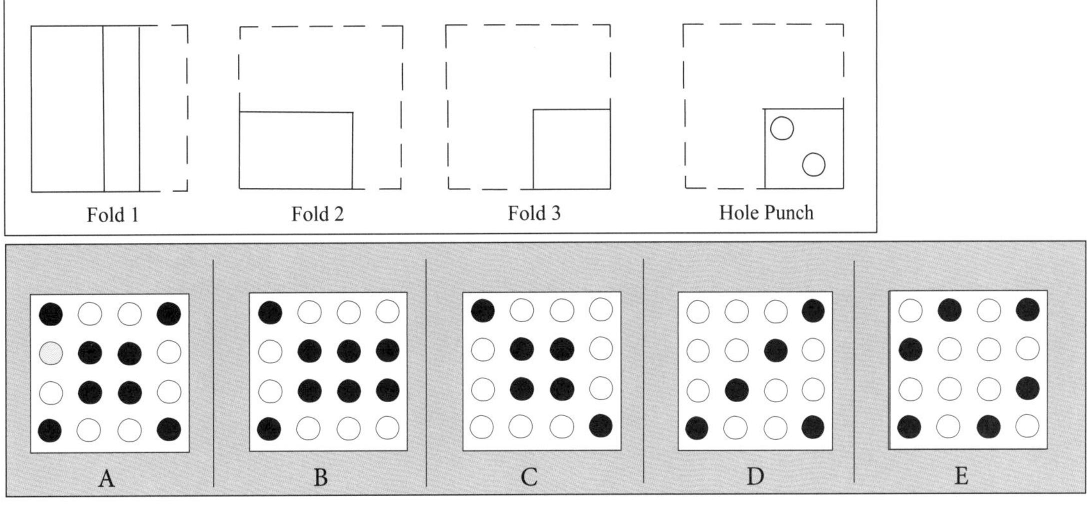

Fold 1
Fold 2
Fold 3
Hole Punch
A
B
C
D
E

58.

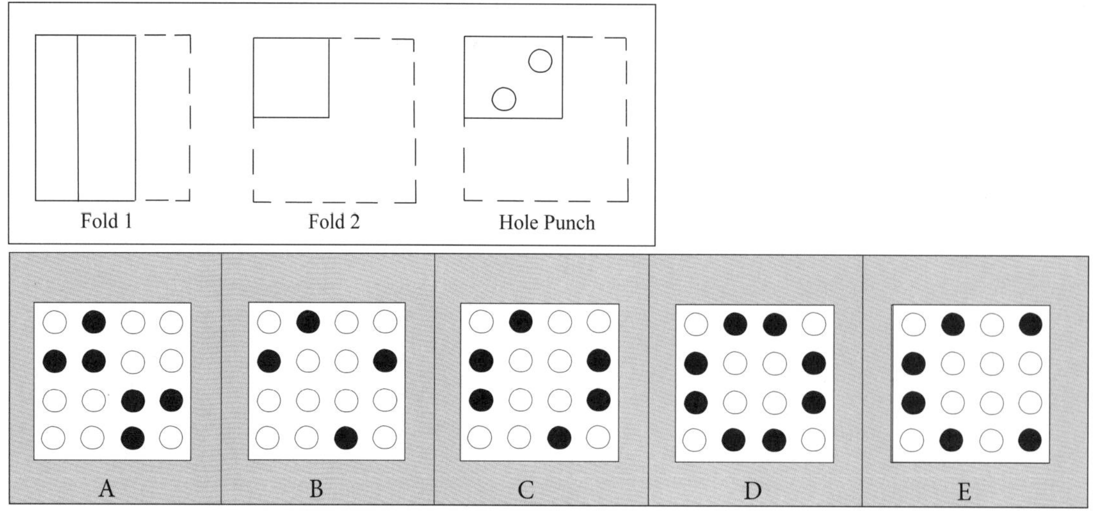

59.

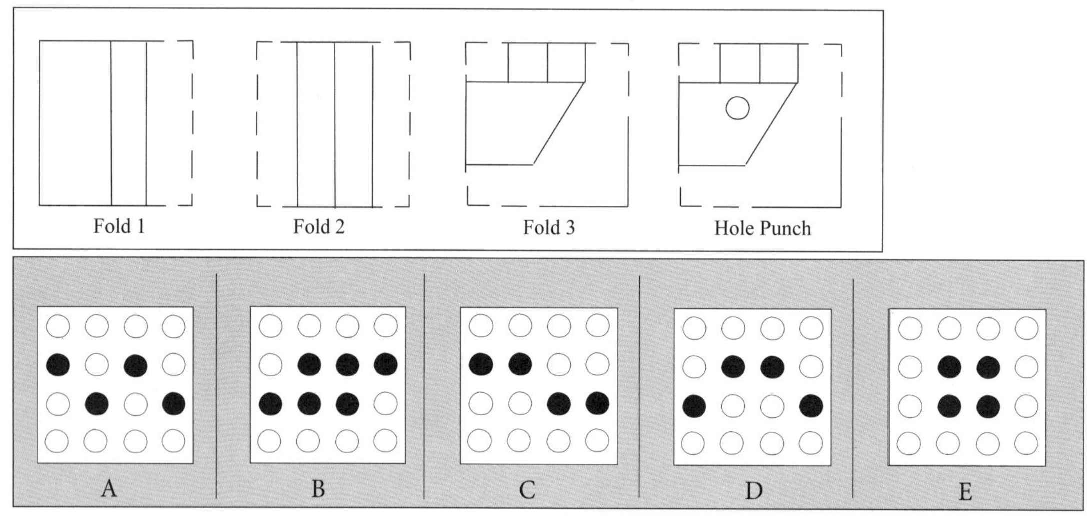

60.

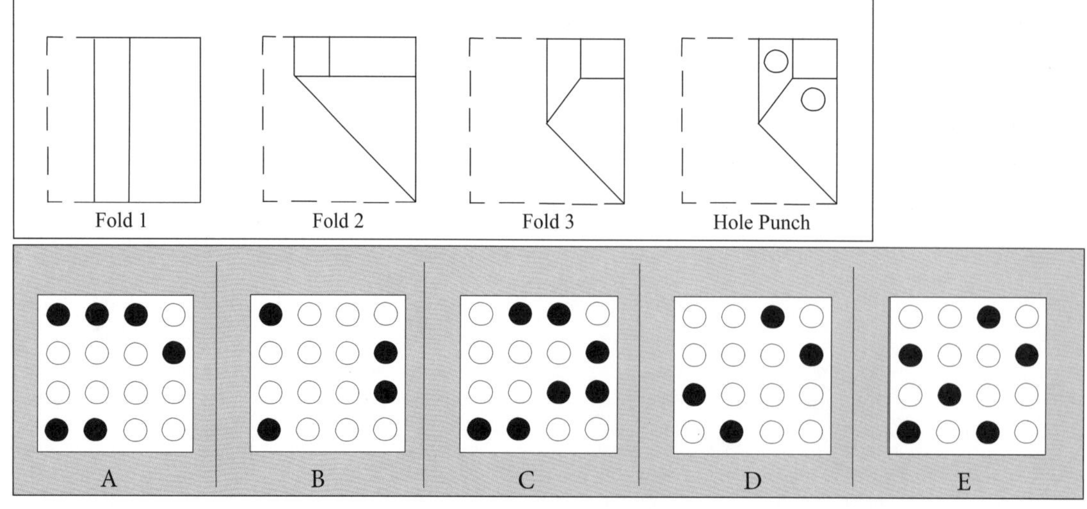

DO NOT STOP - READ DIRECTIONS FOR PART 5 AND CONTINUE

Part 5

For questions 61 through 75:

Each figure is constructed by stacking cubes on top of each other. Once they are stacked, all of the exposed surfaces, excluding the bottom surfaces, are painted. The number of painted sides per cube can range from zero to five. Do not forget that there are cubes "hidden" behind the other cubes.

For the questions in this section, you are required to evaluate each figure and conclude how many cubes have:

only **one** of their sides painted.
only **two** of their sides painted.
only **three** of their sides painted.
all **five** of their sides painted.

Remember: No problem will have zero (0) as the correct answer.

Example: (The answer to this example should not be marked on the answer sheet.)

In figure 1, how many cubes have two of their exposed sides painted?

A. 1 cube
B. 2 cubes
C. 3 cubes
D. 4 cubes
E. 5 cubes

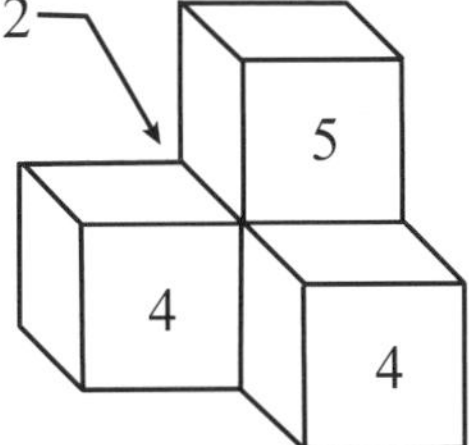

The correct answer is A.

There are four cubes in Figure 1. Three are visible, and one is hidden supporting the top cube. Two sides of the invisible cube are painted; five sides of the top cube are painted; and for each of the remaining two cubes, four of their sides are painted .

Note: The numbers in the cubes indicating the number of exposed sides shown in the sample (Figure 1) are not shown in the actual questions. However, it is important to remember that after the cubes are stacked together, each one is PAINTED ON ALL VISIBLE SIDES EXCEPT THE BOTTOM.

Please proceed to the questions.

PROBLEM A

61. In Figure A, how many cubes have two of their exposed sides painted?

A. 1 cube
B. 2 cubes
C. 3 cubes
D. 4 cubes
E. 6 cubes

62. In Figure A, how many cubes have three of their exposed sides painted?

A. 1 cube
B. 3 cubes
C. 4 cubes
D. 5 cubes
E. 6 cubes

63. In Figure A, how many cubes have four of their exposed sides painted?

A. 1 cube
B. 2 cubes
C. 3 cubes
D. 5 cubes
E. 6 cubes

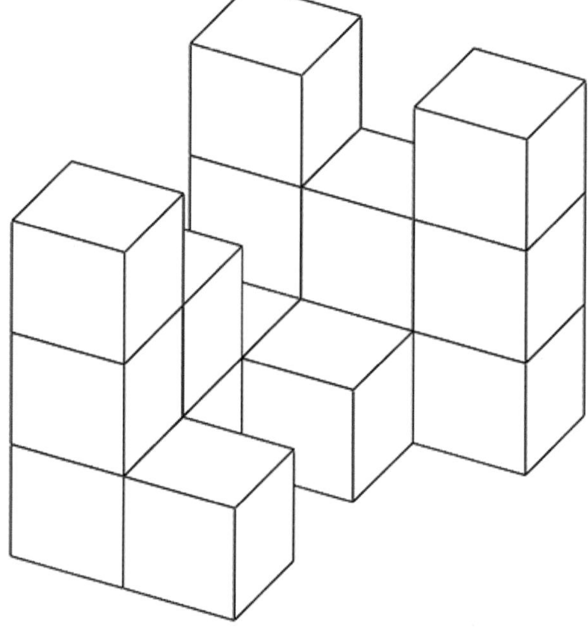

FIGURE A

PROBLEM B

64. In Figure B, how many cubes have one of their exposed sides painted?

A. 1 cube
B. 2 cubes
C. 3 cubes
D. 4 cubes
E. 5 cubes

65. In Figure B, how many cubes have three of their exposed sides painted?

A. 2 cubes
B. 3 cubes
C. 4 cubes
D. 6 cubes
E. 7 cubes

66. In Figure B, how many cubes have four of their exposed sides painted?

A. 2 cubes
B. 3 cubes
C. 4 cubes
D. 6 cubes
E. 7 cubes

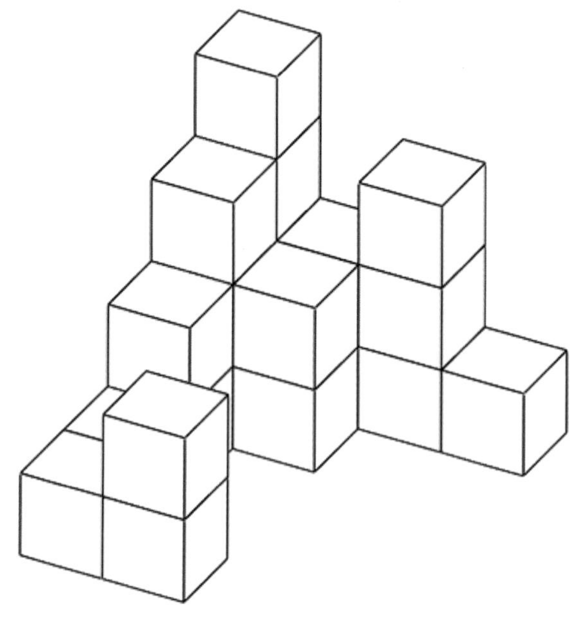

FIGURE B

PROBLEM C

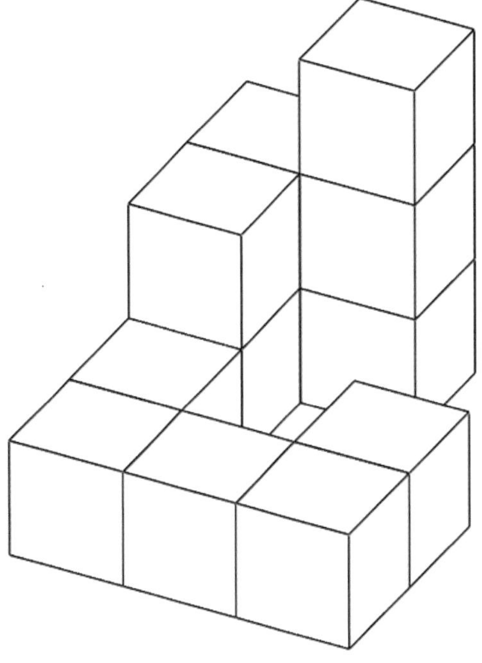

FIGURE C

67. In Figure C, how many cubes have two of their exposed sides painted?

A. 2 cubes
B. 3 cubes
C. 4 cubes
D. 5 cubes
E. 6 cubes

68. In Figure C, how many cubes have three of their exposed sides painted?

A. 1 cube
B. 2 cubes
C. 4 cubes
D. 6 cubes
E. 7 cubes

PROBLEM D

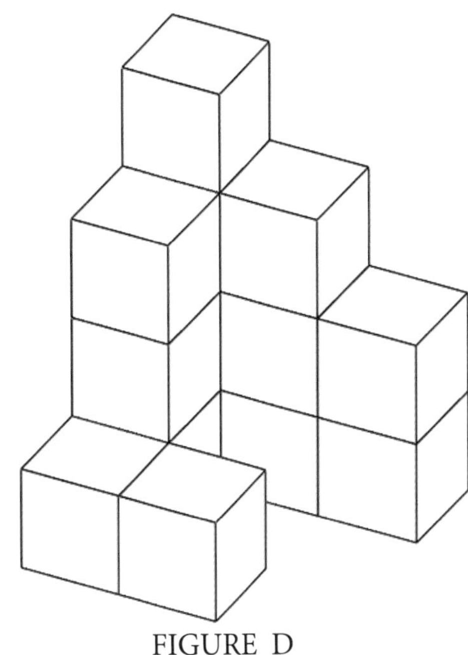

FIGURE D

69. In Figure D, how many cubes have two of their exposed sides painted?

A. 2 cubes
B. 3 cubes
C. 4 cubes
D. 6 cubes
E. 7 cubes

70. In Figure D, how many cubes have three of their exposed sides painted?

A. 2 cubes
B. 3 cubes
C. 5 cubes
D. 6 cubes
E. 7 cubes

PROBLEM E

71. In Figure E, how many cubes have two of their exposed sides painted?

A. 1 cube
B. 2 cubes
C. 3 cubes
D. 5 cubes
E. 6 cubes

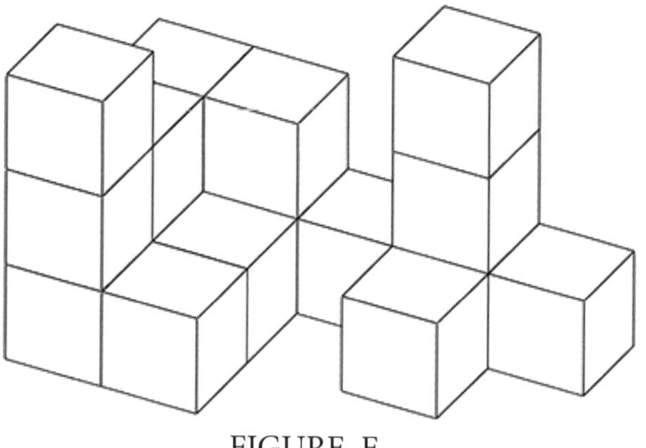

FIGURE E

72. In Figure E, how many cubes have three of their exposed sides painted?

A. 1 cube
B. 2 cubes
C. 3 cubes
D. 4 cubes
E. 5 cubes

73. In Figure E, how many cubes have four of their exposed sides painted?

A. 1 cube
B. 2 cubes
C. 4 cubes
D. 5 cubes
E. 6 cubes

PROBLEM F

74. In Figure F, how many cubes have two of their exposed sides painted?

A. 1 cube
B. 2 cubes
C. 3 cubes
D. 5 cubes
E. 6 cubes

75. In Figure F, how many cubes have three of their exposed sides painted?

A. 1 cube
B. 3 cubes
C. 4 cubes
D. 6 cubes
E. 7 cubes

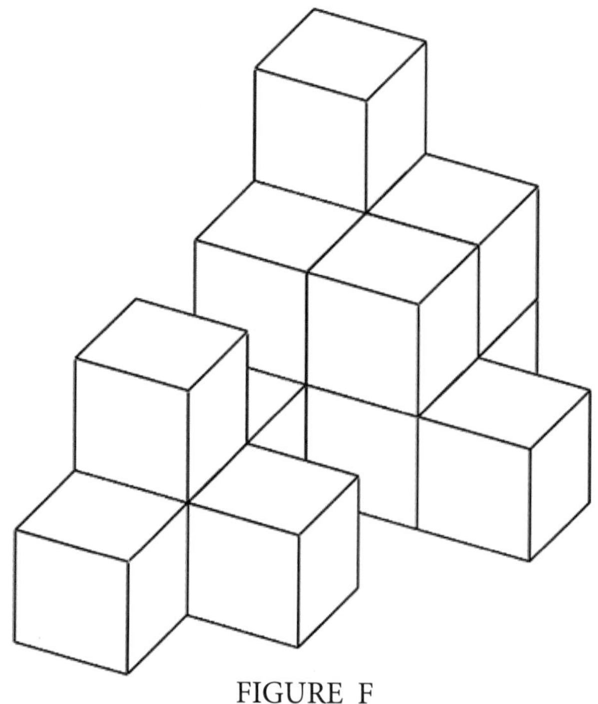

FIGURE F

DO NOT STOP - READ DIRECTIONS FOR PART 6 AND CONTINUE

Part 6

For questions 76 through 90:

Each question in this section will present a flat pattern, which will then be folded into a three-dimensional model. Four options of the resulting actual figure are given. Only one model is correct in every set.

Some figures will have shaded portions similar to the pattern shown in the example below. The shaded areas are not necessarily the "sides" of a figure. They can be the top or the bottom of the figure as well.

Example: (Do not mark the answers to this example on your answer sheet.)

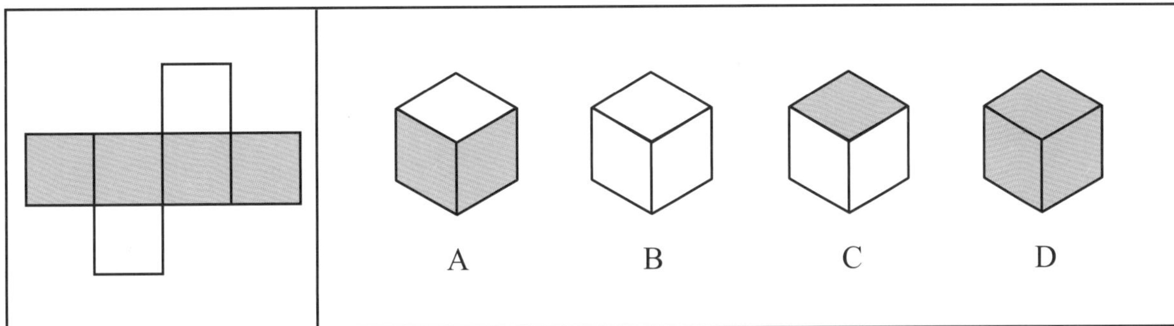

The correct answer is A.

From the given figures A, B, C, or D, the shaded parts obviously form as the sides of the box. The resulting model will then have all four sides shaded while the top and bottom will be white. This makes A the best answer.

Please proceed to the questions.

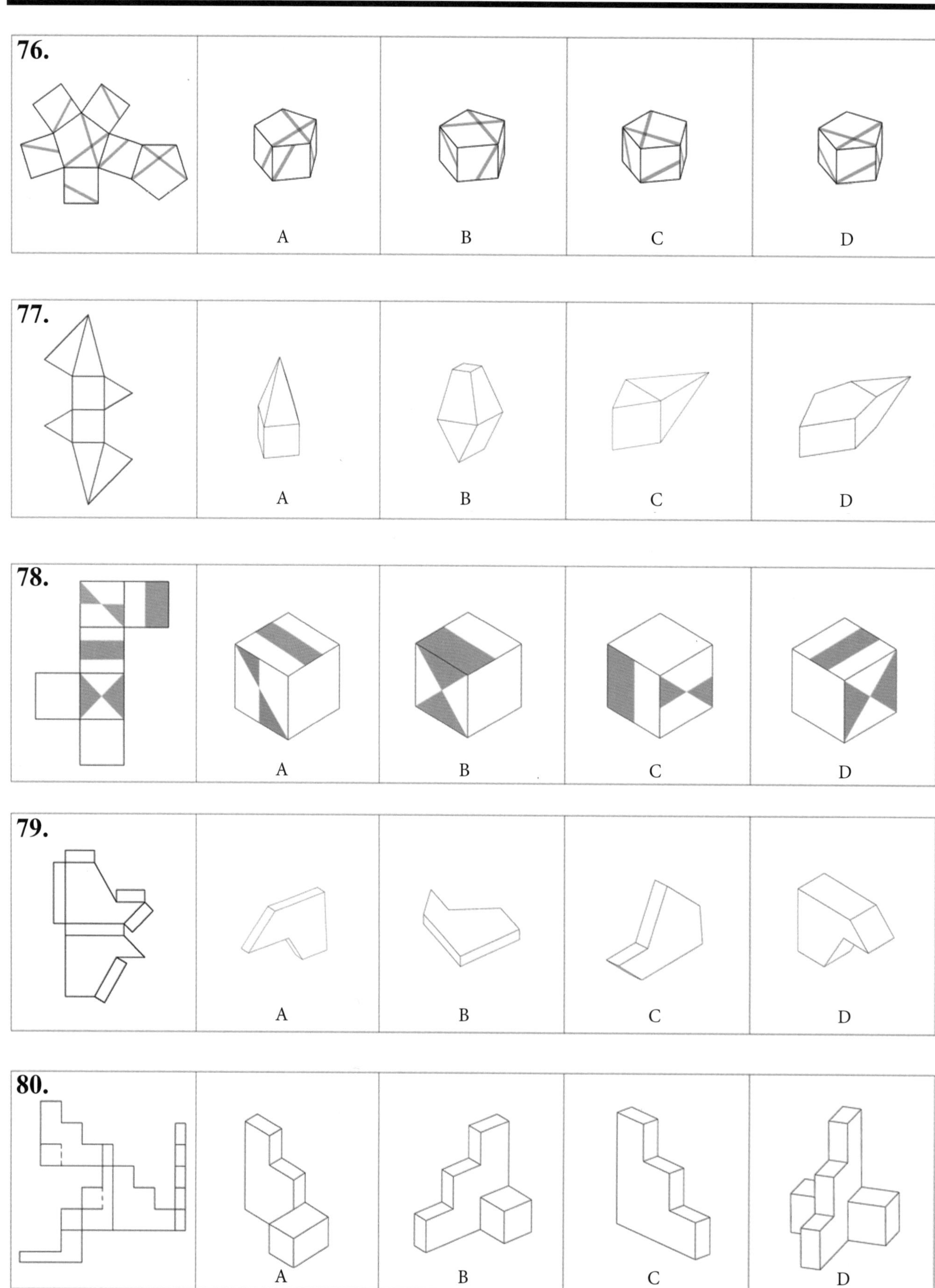
76.
A
B
C
D
77.
A
B
C
D
78.
A
B
C
D
79.
A
B
C
D
80.
A
B
C
D

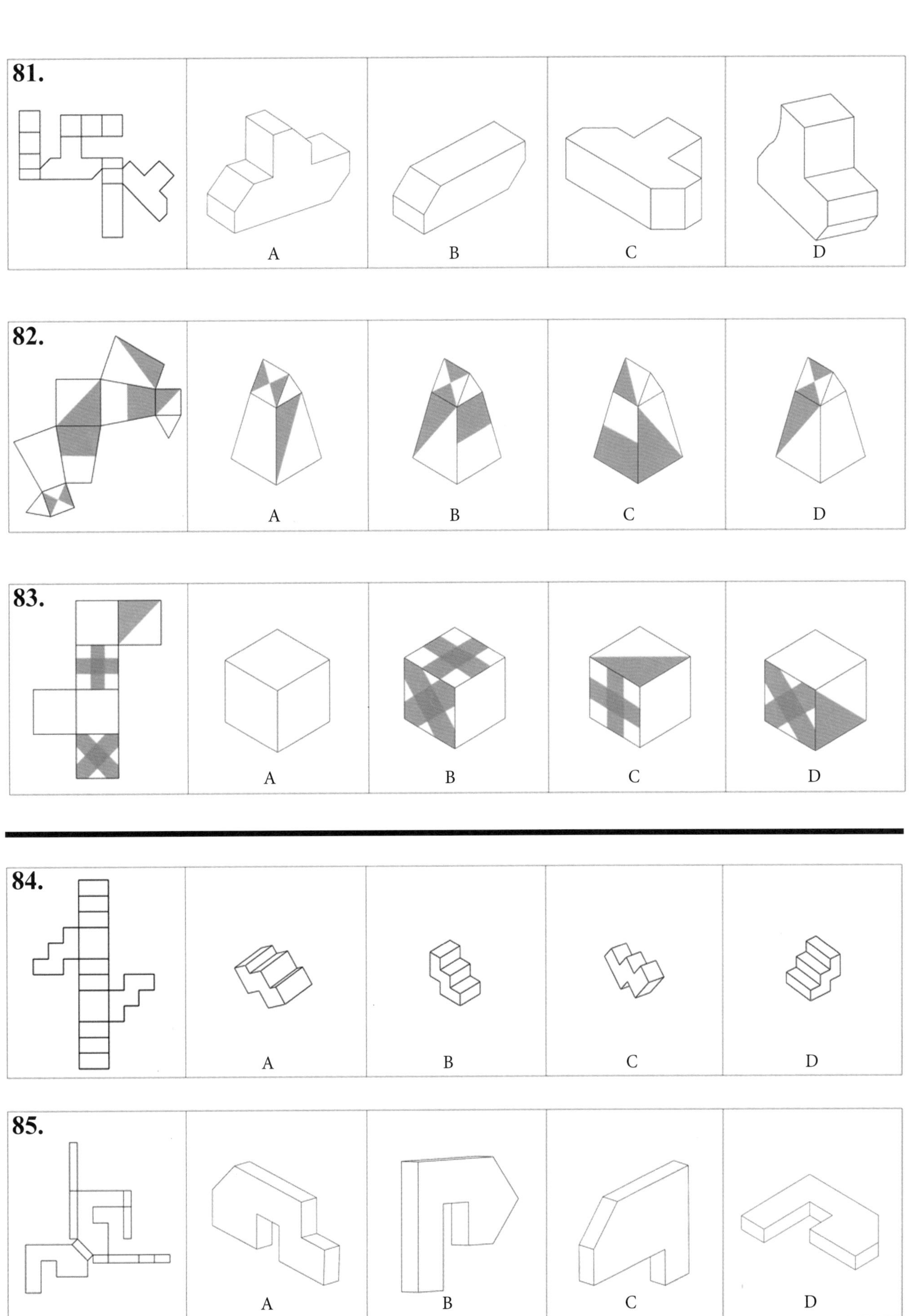
81.
A
B
C
D
82.
A
B
C
D
83.
A
B
C
D
84.
A
B
C
D
85.
A
B
C
D

86.

A B C D

87.

A B C D

88.

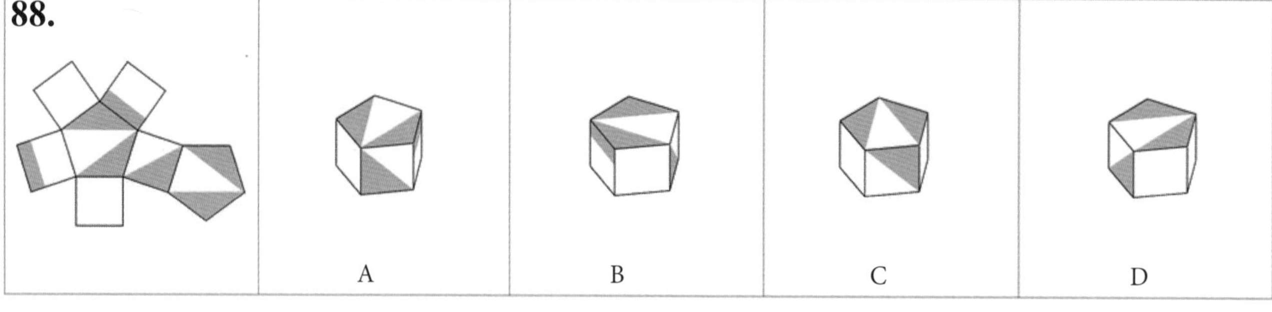

89.

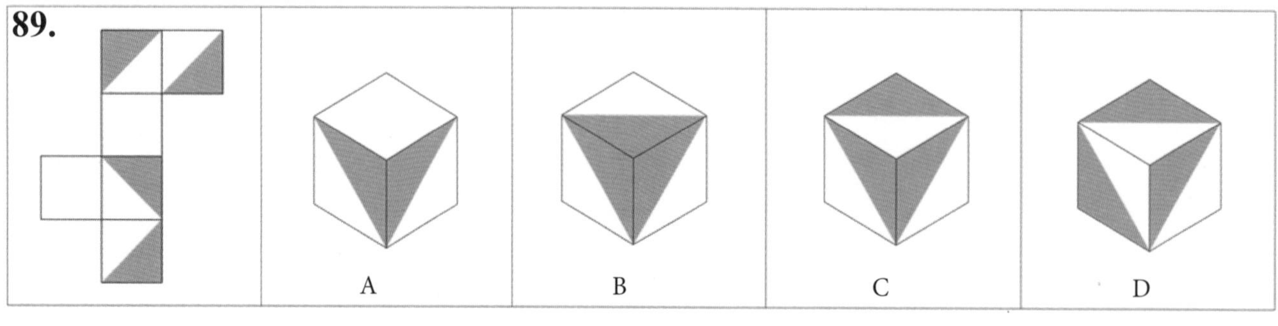

90.

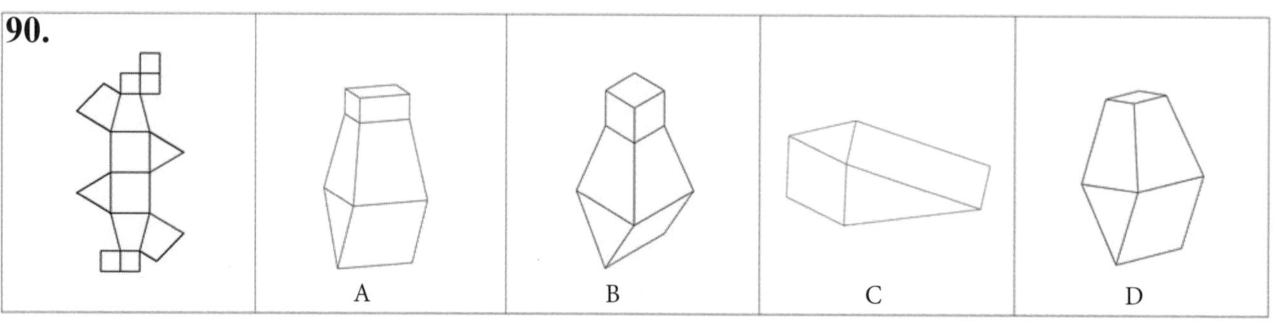

END OF THIS TEST SECTION.

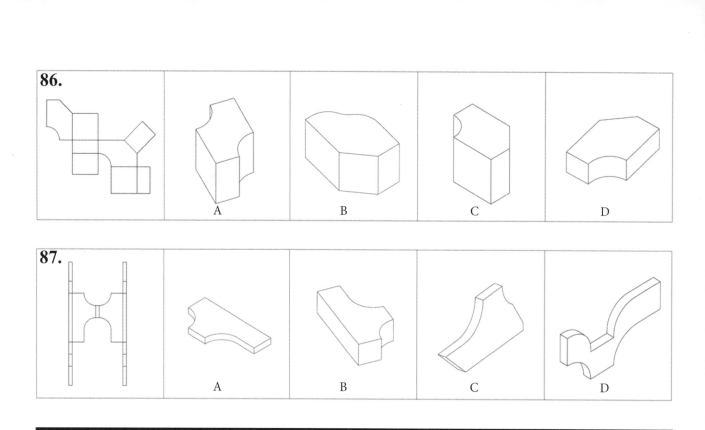

Passage 1

Cosmic Rays

(1) The earliest telescopes were optical telescopes, allowing astronomers to view the Universe in visible light. In the 20th century, astronomers extended the range of telescopes to cover the entire electromagnetic spectrum, from radio and infrared regions, into the ultraviolet, X ray, and gamma ray bands. However, electromagnetic radiation isn't the only sort of particle that falls from the sky: ionized atomic nuclei hit the Earth's atmosphere continuously, with such "cosmic rays" providing hints on energetic processes in the Universe. Since the middle of the 20th century, astronomers have been setting up instrument systems to help determine the origin of cosmic rays.

(2) After the discovery of radioactivity at the beginning of the 20th century, scientists then discovered that there seemed to be a pervasive background radiation that was present almost everywhere. The radiation was believed to be coming from the Earth itself. In 1910, a Jesuit pries named Theodor Wulf (1868 – 1946) went up the Eiffel Tower in Paris to measure radiation levels with an "electroscope." This was a simple device consisting of a sealed gas-filled globe with a metal rod inserted in the top, connected to two thin gold leaves inside the globe. A static electric charge could be used to form the two leaves to spread apart; any radiation passing through the globe would ionize the gas, causing the charge on the leaves to discharge so that they would gradually fall back together.

(3) If the radiation was actually coming from the Earth, it would be weaker at the top of the tower – but the radiation levels were surprisingly high. Wulf suggested that this mysterious radiation might be coming from the upper atmosphere or space. He suggested that balloon flights might be conducted to confirm this notion.

(4) In 1911 – 1912 an Austrian physicist named Victor Hess (1883 – 1964) made a series of ten balloon flights with an electroscope to investigate. Hess did discover that radiation increased with altitude. There was widespread skepticism over his findings, but a German researcher named Werner Kollhoerster made five Time flights of his own and provided confirmation. Kollhoerster's last flight was on 28 June 1914; that was the day Serbian extremists assassinated the heir to the throne of the Austro-Hungarian Empire, setting off World War I, which put pure scientific research on the back burner until the end of the war in 1918.

(5) After the conflict in 1922, the American experimental physicist Robert Millikan (1868 – 1953) conducted studies of his own on the matter, launching automated balloons from Texas and performing studies from the top of tall Pike's Peak in Colorado. He reported no rise in the level of radiation; his findings were correct, but it turned out that the level of cosmic radiation in those regions was unusually low. Hess and Kollhoerster hotly contested Millikan's findings; although Millikan was not noted for being flexible in his judgments, he was very thorough, and so he conducted further studies in the mountains of California in 1925. He was forced to concede that the radiation did exist, naming it "cosmic rays."

(6) That would prove to be his only really positive contribution to the debate. Millikan insisted that cosmic rays were high-energy gamma rays, but in 1929 Kollhoerster and his colleague Walter Boethe built a "coincidence counter," using two proportional counter tubes that would go off when a single particle passed through both. After recording the passage of cosmic-ray particles through the two tubes, they placed a slab of gold between them, assuming it would block the cosmic rays. It would have if they had been photons; but it didn't, meaning they were charged particles with mass.

(7) Millikan insisted that their experiment was in error. Kollhoerster and Boethe suggested that if cosmic rays were charged particles, not photons, then they would be deflected by the Earth's magnetic field, with the cosmic-ray flux strongest at the poles and weakest at the equator. Studies by various researchers, including Millikan, were afflicted by equipment and other problems and gave ambiguous results, but in 1932 one of Millikan's ex-students, Arthur Holly Compton (1892 – 1962), announced the results of a careful series of observations to show that cosmic rays did vary with latitude as would be expected if they were charged particles. Millikan bitterly attacked Compton's results and then, confronted with new evidence that confirmed Compton's conclusions, abruptly reversed himself, claiming that he and Compton were (and had been) in complete agreement.

(8) The entire subject of cosmic rays ended up being an embarrassment to Millikan. Although he could be hidebound, he was still one of the finest experimental physicists of his generation. He was simply off his game when it came to cosmic ray studies, and he would hardly mention them in his memoirs. There was a widespread belief for a time that he had discovered cosmic rays, but Hess's work was well documented, and Hess received the Nobel Prize for physics in 1936 for the discovery.

(9) A consensus emerged that cosmic rays were generally charged atomic nuclei moving at a high velocity through space that strike the Earth's atmosphere, generating a "cascade" of a million to a billion secondary particles known as an "air shower," with the particles scattered over an ellipse hundreds of meters wide when it hits ground. The particles in the air showers proved to be a gold mine for particle physicists, since the cascades contained short-lived particles not easily found in the laboratory. In the postwar period, up to the early 1950s, cosmic rays were investigated with balloons that carried stacks of photographic emulsions to high altitude to record the traces of these particles.

(10) Cosmic rays hit the Earth at a rate of about one thousand a second per square meter, and their energies don't seem to have any upper bound, though their numbers do unsurprisingly fall off as the energy level increases. About 90% are hydrogen nuclei (protons), 9% are helium nuclei (alpha particles), and the remaining 1% are (mostly) various heavier nuclei. Since they are charged particles, their paths through space are scrambled by galactic magnetic fields, making it difficult to determine the location of their origin.

(11) There are two classes of cosmic rays, those with energies below 10^{16} electron-volts (eV) and those above that level up to 10^{20} eV or more. Astronomers believe the two classes arise from separate processes. The low energy cosmic rays are common, while the more interesting high energy cosmic rays are rare, with the entire Earth intercepting one about once every second. The low energy cosmic rays are not seen as particularly mysterious: the great Italian – American physicist Enrico Fermi suggested that ordinary charged particles could be accelerated to such energies over long periods of time by magnetic fields in our Galaxy. They are also produced by the solar wind from the Sun. Low energy cosmic rays are also not seen as particularly interesting and for the most part, users of modern cosmic ray observatories regard them as "background noise" that has to be screened out.

(12) In contrast, nobody has any clear idea of where the superpowerful cosmic rays come from. They are so powerful that they have been said to have energies comparable to a brick thrown through a plate glass window; pretty impressive performance for a submicroscopic particle. They are generally referred to as "ultra-high energy cosmic rays (UHECRs)". Galactic magnetic fields aren't strong enough to push them around, and since they hit the Earth from all directions instead of along the plane of the Milky Way in our sky, they appear to be produced by extragalactic sources, possibly by supernovas or other "cosmic catastrophes" – though some physicists have suggested they may arise from exotic processes, such as the decay of "magnetic monopoles."

(13) As earlier mentioned, about 1% of cosmic rays are "mostly" relatively heavy nuclei. However, that 1% includes a thin flux of very high-energy gamma rays, in the 10^{12} eV range, that cause air showers very similar to those created by cosmic rays, with about one gamma-ray event for every 100,000 cosmic ray events. Millikan's assertion that cosmic rays were gamma rays wasn't completely wrong – but it was very close to completely wrong. These gamma rays aren't diverted by galactic magnetic fields and so can be traced back to a source by mapping the geometry of the air shower.

(14) There are four ways to observe cosmic rays: by observing the track of faint blue "Cerenkov radiation" left by the air shower particles using something similar to a reflecting telescope; by picking up the "footprint" of the air shower using an array of particle detectors, including proportional counter tubes, scintillation detectors, and wire chambers (Somewhat confusingly, some particle detectors also observe Cerenkov light, though with the light created by passage of particles through a sealed tank of water instead of the atmosphere.); by sensing the faint fluorescence (more properly "luminescence", but the term "fluorescence" has stuck) of atmospheric nitrogen gas in the wake of the air shower; and, by picking up the radio energy generated by the air shower. This is not a popular approach, but the LOFAR low-frequency radio telescope mentioned previously has been used for this purpose.

(15) It is of course possible to build "hybrid" detector systems that use more than one of these methods. Particle detector and radio detector systems work round the clock; air Cerenkov and fluorescence detectors can only really work on clear, moonless nights.

1. Cosmic rays are considered to be:

A. footprints of the air shower.
B. random gamma rays.
C. ionized atomic nuclei.
D. short-lived particles.
E. magnetic monopoles.

2. Which of the following devices was first designed to measure radiation?

A. Balloon flights
B. Optical telescope
C. Electroscope
D. Wire chamber
E. Coincidence counter

3. Which of the following scientists is credited with beginning research on cosmic rays?

A. Victor Hess
B. Werner Kollhoerster
C. Walter Boethe
D. Arthur Holly Compton
E. Theodor Wulf

4. Which of the following represents the number of times that balloon flights were conducted manually?

A. 4
B. 7
C. 16
D. 15

5. Who of the following was awarded the Noble Prize for the discovery of cosmic rays?

A. Theodor Wulf
B. Robert Millikan
C. Arthur Holly Compton
D. Werner Kollhoerster
E. Victor Hess

6. Cosmic rays hit the Earth at which of the following rates?

A. One million a second per square meter
B. One thousand a second per square meter
C. One hundred a second per square meter
D. Varies with magnetic field
E. One billion a second per square meter

7. Which of the following statements are true about the composition of cosmic rays?

A. About 90% are hydrogen nuclei (alpha particles), 9% are helium nuclei (protons), and the remaining 1% are (mostly) various heavier nuclei.
B. About 90% are hydrogen nuclei (protons), 9% are helium nuclei (alpha particles), and the remaining 1% are (mostly) various heavier nuclei.
C. About 90% are hydrogen nuclei (protons), 9% are helium nuclei (alpha particles), and the remaining 1% are (mostly) various lighter nuclei.
D. About 90% are helium nuclei (protons), 9% are hydrogen nuclei (alpha particles), and the remaining 1% are (mostly) various heavier nuclei.
E. About 9% are hydrogen nuclei (protons), 90% are helium nuclei (alpha particles), and the remaining 1% are (mostly) various heavier nuclei.

8. How do users of modern cosmic ray observatories regard low energy cosmic rays?

A. Similar to a laminar flow
B. Background noise
C. Constituent of alpha particle dispersion
D. Proton particle dispersions

9. From where do ultra-high energy cosmic rays most possibly originate?

A. Cosmic dispersion and flow
B. Supernovas, cosmic catastrophes, or decay of magnetic poles
C. Scattering cascades that hit the ground
D. Solar wind from the sun
E. Intergalactic star and sun events

10. Of the 1% of relatively heavy nuclei found in cosmic rays, a thin flux is comprised of which of the following?

A. Alpha particles
B. Magnetic monopoles
C. Protons
D. Neurons
E. Gamma rays

11. Between approximately what years were cosmic rays investigated using balloons that carry photographic emulsions and record traces of particles in air showers?

A. 1918 – 1950
B. 1922 – 1950
C. 1910 – 1914
D. 1910 – 1915
E. 1922 – 1925

12. What does the LOFAR telescope measure?

A. Gamma rays
B. Alpha particles
C. Supernovas
D. Radio energy generated by the air shower
E. Protons

13. Which of the following declarations by Millikan was very close to being completely wrong?

A. Supernovas are one cause of cosmic rays.
B. Alpha particles account for all of cosmic rays.
C. Cosmic Rays are gamma rays.
D. There is a divided mix between protons and alpha particles within the nuclei.
E. Air showers are caused by magnetic mono poles.

14. Which of the following best typifies the two classes of cosmic rays?

A. Those with energies below 10^{13} electron-volts (eV) and those above that level up to 10^{20} eV or more
B. Those with energies below 10^{16} electron-volts (eV) and those above that level up to 10^{22} eV or more
C. Those with energies below 10^{16} electron-volts (eV) and those above that level up to 10^{20} eV or more
D. Those with energies below 10^{16} electron-volts (eV) and those above that level up to 10^{20} eV or more
E. Those with energies below 10^{14} electron-volts (eV) and those above that level up to 10^{20} eV or more

15. Particle detectors are able to pick up Cerenkov radiation and "footprints" of the air shower.

The LOFAR low-frequency radio telescope is used to detect the fluorescence of atmospheric nitrogen gas from air shower.

A. Both statements are true.
B. Both statements are false.
C. The first sentence is true while the second sentence is false.
D. The first sentence is false while the second sentence is true.

Passage 2

Artificial Neural Networks

(1) Artificial Neural Networks are a tool for computation that is based on the neuron's interconnection in the human brain's nervous system as well as that of other organisms. It is also called neural nets, artificial neural nets, or simply ANN.

(2) An artificial neural net is a non-linear type of processing system which is made to perform various kinds of tasks, especially those that do not have an exact algorithm. ANN strives to simulate the firing of synapses. Hence, artificial neural nets can be designed to solve problems based on sample data and teaching methods fed to it, which it uses as a basis for computation and output. With regards to the received training, various tasks can be operated by means of utilizing artificial neural networks that are constructed identically. Just as long as there are proper training modes, a sort of logical generalization is possible in the use and function of artificial neural networks. Generalization is the capability to recognize patterns and similarities among various inputs. Noise-corrupted patterns can also be recognized by generalization. Naturally, the equivalence of an Artificial Neural Network is BNN, which means Biological Neural Networks.

(3) One important factor of neural networks is the neural nets. Commonly, the term "neural net" pertains solely to artificial systems like artificial neural networks. However, the biological variants of neural net cannot be taken for granted because these exist apart from the artificial variant of neural net. Neural nets are not linear mathematically speaking. They cannot be described as a straight arrow, nor a simple cause-effect, stimulus-response type of relationship or model. They can be thought of as layered spatially with a linear type of effect or result of processing. Each layer has something to do with the layer it follows or is imbricated with. There is a representation of combinations of multiplicity. This makes the net a complex system.

(4) Of course, the most complex system is the biological neural system. A common neural system of a human body or that of another organism has billions of cells that interconnect with every neuron. This aspect cannot be achieved by even the latest artificial system; this multitude of complexity is why it is not likely to produce an exact reproduction of biological systems behavior.

(5) The neuron is the basic foundation from which the network systems are constructed for both Biological Neural Networks and Artificial Neural Networks. Every neuron is a system that handles signals out of inputs since it is a MIMO system (multiple-input, multiple-output). After receiving the signal, a resultant signal is produced, and then the signal is transmitted to all of the outputs. The neurons that can be found in an artificial neural network are formed into layers. The first layer is known as the input layer, which functions with interaction with the environment in order to handle input. On the other hand, the final layer is called the output layer, which handles the output in order to tender the data that has been processed. Those layers that do not have any kind of interaction with the input or the output (or the environment in general) are known as hidden layers as these lie in the layers between the output layer and the input layer. These hidden layers make the system complex due to their multiplicity and non-linear relationship, though combined in unique packets or interactions with each other.

(6) Neurons are commonly known as PE or Processing Elements as these can have different forms. The term Processing Elements is used in order to treat it differently from the biological equivalents. There is a certain network pattern into which the Processing Elements are linked. When it comes to artificial systems, PE are only electrical unlike the biological neurons that are chemical. PE may be analog, digital, or hybrid. Analog elements move in time, so to speak, while digital elements move in space, while hybrid elements simulate both temporal and spatial movements. But then again, in order to duplicate the synapse effect, there are multiplicative weights assigned to the connections. Calibration of these weights is necessary to tender the right system output. We can think of weights as the amount of information fed through multiple inputs.

(7) Two equations that define the key concept of Processing Elements represent the McCulloch-Pitts model of a neuron. The simple input and output relationship known as the McCulloch-Pitts neuron, the linear system and the step activation function are characterized by the Perceptron. However, there were some people who did not feel the early success of this work as well as the research for artificial neural networks in general. Among them were Seymore Papert and Marvin Minsky. They had a book entitled Perceptrons, published in 1969 and this was utilized for the discrediting of the artificial neural networks research. One point that Papert and Minsky highlighted was that Perceptron did not classify the non-linear patterns that can be separated from the input space.

(8) There are two main alternative uses of artificial neural nets: algorithmic solution and expert system. Algorithmic solution is raised when there is enough information regarding the data as well as the underlying theory. Unknown solutions can be directly calculated through analyzing the data as well as the data's theoretical relationship. For ease of calculation, ordinary von Neumann computer applications can be utilized. Expert system, on the other hand, is utilized when there is not enough theoretical background and data needed for the creation of any form of reliable problem model. This can be considered a stochastic model. It represents random distributions or patterns, which may bring generalizations or results that can be further tested or refined with guided assumptions or theories.

(9) Moreover, the use of artificial neural networks can be maximized in instances where there is abundant data but little amount of underlying theory, guidance or direction, if you will. When it comes to neural networks, a priori assumptions for the problem space, as well as information regarding the statistical distribution, are not required. Assumptions characterized by patterns are not needed by the neural networks. They can produce results without a distributive framework. Even so, the use of a priori information can still aid on speeding the training when used as statistical distribution of the input space.

(10) Overtraining usually becomes an issue when there are too many training examples and the system is overwhelmed to the extent of not using the useful generalizations. Overtraining can also transpire when there are so many neurons within the network, and the computation capacity exceeds its limit. Despite what sounds like high tech artificial intelligence gibberish or slang, artificial neural networks are used in many contexts. Artificial Neural Networks have been used in sales forecasting, industrial process control, customer research, and data validation, risk management and target marketing. They have also been used in medicine in diagnostics and as you might have guessed, in software games as AI. Though seemingly artificial, there are a number of scientists who believe that artificial neural networks may someday be "conscious," –resembling some of the popular media stereotypes, which we have all seen in helpful robots, cars, and "friendly" space ship computers.

(11) A historical view of ANN and BNN can be summarized as follows:

Late 1800's. There were attempts of scientific study pertaining to how the brain of human beings works. These were usually philosophical works of logic and rationalism.

1890. The first work regarding the activity pattern of the human brain was published by William James.

1943. A neuron model was developed by Warren McCulloch and Walter Pitts. This model, which is broken into a summation over weighted inputs and sum output function, is still utilized these days in the field of artificial neural networking.

1949. The Organization of Behavior was published by Donald Hebb. This work shows an outline of a law for the learning of synaptic neurons. As a commemoration of his work, this law was later renamed as Hebbian Learning.

1951. The first Artificial Neural Network was made by Marvin Minsky while he was at Princeton.

1958. It was one year after the death of John von Neumann when The Computer and the Brain was published. His work showcased propositions about several radical changes in the means, which researchers use to model the brain.

1958. Frank Rosenblatt created the Mark I Perceptron computer at Cornell University. It was an attempt to utilize the techniques of neural network for recognition of characters.

1960. Frank Rosenblatt created the book entitled Principles of Neurodynamics. This contained his ideas and researches about brain modeling.

1974. Paul John Webros discovered the backpropagation algorithm.

1986. The backpropagation algorithm was rediscovered by David Rumelhart, Geoffrey Hinton, and R. J. Williams through their book Learning Internal Representation by Error Propagation. As a gradient descent algorithm, backpropagation is utilized for the purpose of curve-fitting and finding weights that minimize errors in artificial neural networks.

1987. Slated for artificial neural networks researches, the Institute of Electrical and Electronics Engineers (IEEE) began its annual international ANN conference. The INNS or the International Neural Network Society was created.

1988. The INNS Neural Networking journal began its publication.

16. Which of the following CANNOT be performed by ANN?

A. Analyze data
B. Solve problem
C. Recognize patterns among assorted inputs
D. Replicate exact biological systems behavior
E. Calculate unknown solutions

17. Stochastic generalizations from ANN are produced from random patterns.
ANN do not require a priori information.

A. Both statements are true.
B. Both statements are false.
C. The first sentence is true while the second sentence is false.
D. The first sentence is false while the second sentence is true.

18. ANN strives to simulate:

A. systems of complexity.
B. transmission of input-output information.
C. data collation.
D. computer logic.
E. algorithms.

19. The Neural Net is:

A. linear.
B. causal.
C. effects-oriented.
D. layered.
E. cause-oriented.

20. What produces complexity within the neural net?

A. Imbrications of variance
B. Hidden layers
C. Multitudinal velocities
D. Multiple inputs
E. Complex interactions

21. MIMO stands for:

A. Multitude Inertia, Mass Organization
B. Main Inertia, Mass Organization
C. Multiple Inputs, Multiple Outputs
D. Main Inputs, Main Outputs
E. Mass Internalization, Multiple Inertia

22. ANN utilizes algorithms. ANN strives to emulate BNN.

A. Both statements are true.
B. Both statements are false.
C. The first sentence is true while the second sentence is false.
D. The first sentence is false while the second sentence is true.

23. The following network patterns in artificial systems are linked with neurons. Which one is the exeption?

A. Electrical
B. Temporal
C. Digital
D. Analog
E. Hybrid

24. Hybrid PE tend to move:

A. in time.
B. in conjunction with layers.
C. in space.
D. in time and space.
E. in a linear fashion.

25. Overtraining is the result of:

A. exceeding the maximum computation capacity.
B. too much data but not enough underlying theory.
C. too many useful generalizations.
D. expert systems using a priori assumptions.
E. algorithmic complexity.

26. ANN utilizing "Expert Systems" represent models that are:

A. guided by theory.
B. lacking in statistical data.
C. trained by a priori assumptions.
D. overtrained.
E. random and stochastic.

27. Which factor characterizes both the Artificial and the Biological Neural Networks?

A. The linear system
B. Multiplicative weights
C. The neuron as basic foundation
D. Processing Elements
E. The step activation function

28. Which of the following best describes the use of backpropagation?

A. Finding errors in a learning application
B. Minimizing error functions in neural nets
C. Limiting training to a priori assumptions
D. Introducing feedback loops
E. Propagating errors to increase learning

29. Which of the following is NOT true concerning the history of ANN?

A. Minsky created the first ANN.
B. Papert and Minsky created the Perceptron.
C. The law for the learning of synaptic neurons was renamed after Donald Hebb.
D. McCullogh and Pitts created the neuron model.
E. The book Learning Internal Representation by Error renewed interest in backpropagation algorithm.

30. The weighted functions in PE can be thought of as:

A. resultant outputs from data.
B. the quantity of data into multiple inputs.
C. hidden layers of complexity.
D. theory or a priori assumptions.
E. calibrated generalizations.

31. Based on usage in this passage, which of the following refers to "a priori"?

A. Inherent mental structures
B. Assumed theories
C. Guided training
D. Expert systems
E. Overtrained generalizations

32. The best results from ANN are produced with the use of:

A. much theory, little data.
B. much data, little theory.
C. much data and theory.
D. non-linear patterns.

33. Analog Processing Elements can be thought to work in:

A. expert systems.
B. space.
C. layers.
D. time.
E. generalized patterns.

34. The difference between algorithmic and expert systems basically concerns:

A. the amount of data.
B. the amount of training.
C. the amount of theory.
D. the amount of generalization.
E. the amount of neurons.

35. ANN can generalize the following EXCEPT:

A. noise.
B. similarities among assorted inputs.
C. linear computations.
D. random patterns.
E. complex distributions.

Passage 3

Music and Mathematics

(1) Many music theorists use mathematics to understand music. Indeed, musical sounds seem to display an inherent order of number properties. Although the ancient Chinese, Egyptians and Mesopotamians are known to have studied the mathematical principles of sound, the Pythagoreans of ancient Greece are the first researchers known to have investigated the expression of musical scales in terms of numerical ratios, particularly the ratios of small integers.

(2) The Greek octave had only five notes, coinciding with the principle of perfect fifths. Pythagoras discovered that differences in the ratio of the length between two strings create variations in pitch. The ratio 2:3 creates the musical fifth, 3:4 the fourth, and so on. Moreover, the ancient Greeks learned that a note with a given frequency could only be combined and played harmoniously with other notes whose frequencies were integer multiples of the first. These would eventually signify the ratio of the wavelength or frequency of a given note to another and thus, the creation of chords.

(3) In addition, Pythagoras pointed out that each note is a fraction of a string. Thus, if a musician had a string that played an A, then the next note is 4/5 the length (or 5/4 the frequency) which is approximately a C. The rest of the octave has the fractions 3/4 (approximately D), 2/3 (approximately E), and 3/5 (approximately F), before reaching 1/2 which is the octave A. With a guitar, the octave is the 12th Fret, and in terms of distance, mathematically it should be half the distance between the bridge at the lower end of the guitar and the nut where the strings cross over at the top of the guitar. Shortening the length between the two produces a higher pitch or tone – envision the strings in a piano, which range from the lower tones-longer strings to the higher tones-shorter strings.

(4) In the Western system of musical notation, the frequency ratio 1:2 is generally identified as the octave. Two different notes in this relation are often considered as fundamentally the same and only vary in pitch but not in character. Octaves of a note occur at 2n times the frequency of that note (where n is an integer), such as 2, 4, 8, 16, etc. and the reciprocal of that series. For example, 50 Hz and 400 Hz are one and two octaves away from 100 Hz because they are ½ (or 2 -1) and 4 (or 22) times the frequency, respectively. Hence, notes an octave apart are given the same note name – the name of a note an octave above A is also A. This is called octave equivalency, the assumption that pitches one or more octaves apart are musically equivalent in many ways, leading to the convention "that scales are uniquely defined by specifying the intervals within an octave."

(5) The application of mathematical concepts to music did not merely involve notes and harmony. The attempt to structure and communicate new ways of composing and hearing music has led some composers to incorporate the golden ratio and Fibonacci numbers into their work.

(6) In mathematics and the arts, two quantities are in the golden ratio if the ratio of the sum of the quantities to the larger quantity is equal to the ratio of the larger quantity to the smaller one. The Fibonacci numbers are the numbers in the following integer sequence: 0,1,1,2,3,5,8,13,21,34, 55,89,144. By definition, the first two Fibonacci numbers are 0 and 1, and each subsequent number is the sum of the previous two. The most important feature in the sequence of Fibonacci ratios – the ratio of a Fibonacci number with its bigger adjacent – is that it converges to a constant limit known as the golden ratio of 0.61803398...

(7) The golden section is employed by musicians to generate rhythmic changes or to develop a melody line. James Tenney reconceived his piece For Ann (rising), which consists of up to twelve computer-generated upwardly glissandoing tones , having each tone start with the golden ratio (in between an equal tempered minor and major sixth) below the previous tone, so that the combination tones produced by all consecutive tones are a lower or higher pitch already, or soon to be, produced.

(8) In Béla Bartok's Music for Strings, Percussion and Celesta, the xylophone progression occurs at the intervals 1:2:3:5:8:5:3:2:1 – a sort of bell curve of a golden ratio. French composer Erik Satie used the golden ratio in several of his pieces, including Sonneries de la Rose+Croix. The golden ratio is also apparent in the organization of the sections in the music of Debussy's Reflets dans l'eau (Reflections in Water), from Images (1st series, 1905), in which "the sequence of keys is marked out by the intervals 34, 21, 13 and 8, and the main climax sits at the phi position."

(9) Also, many works of Chopin, mainly Etudes (studies) and Nocturnes are formally based on the golden ratio. This results in the biggest climax of both musical expression and technical difficulty after about 2/3 of the piece. The mathematician Michael Schneider analyzed the waveform of the Amen break and found that the peaks are spaced at intervals in the golden ratio.

(10) An emerging and modern connection between music and mathematics is being made from the relationship of fractals and the generation of melodic form. Fractals are visual representations of certain mathematical functions, which show increasing detail upon magnification. A very important phenomenon of fractals is that they manifest self-similarity at all scales. Benoit Mandelbrot, one of the fathers of fractal geometry (and the man who coined the term fractal), loosely defines fractals as "shapes that are equally complex in their details as in their overall form. That is, if a piece of a fractal is suitably magnified to become of the same size as the whole, it should look like the whole, either exactly, or perhaps only slightly deformed." Today, we see fractal imagery all over the net in graphic design. Its self-replicating form is also found in nature: imagine broccoli, or even the circulatory system as fractal. Composers are also taking this idea to music.

(11) One would expect that the construction of such complex shapes would require complex rules, but in reality, the algorithms (equations) that generate fractals are typically extraordinarily simple. Their visual results, however, show great richness. The seeming paradox is easily demystified: these algorithms involve "loops."

(12) The key to the richness of detail that fractals exhibit is something that mathematicians call iteration. Most equations that we learned in school are linear – that is, the input is proportional to the output. For example, the equation x2 - 1 = 0 is a linear equation. The equations that generate fractals, however, are nonlinear. Nonlinear equations involve iteration, which means that the solution of the equation is repeatedly fed back into itself. It is an arresting thought that something produced from a purely mathematical procedure can be so aesthetically pleasing.

(13) Algorithms (or, at the very least, formal sets of rules) have been used to compose music for centuries; the procedures used to plot voice-leading in Western counterpoint, for example, can often be reduced to algorithmic determinacy. The term is usually reserved, however, for the use of formal procedures to make music without human intervention, either through the introduction of chance procedures or the use of computers.

(14) Many algorithms that have no immediate musical relevance are used by composers as creative inspiration for their music. Algorithms such as fractals, L-systems, statistical models, and even arbitrary data (e.g. census figures, GIS coordinates, or magnetic field measurements) are fair game for musical interpretation. The success or failure of these procedures as sources of "good" music largely depends on the mapping system employed by the composer to translate the non-musical information into a musical data stream.

(15) There is no universal method to sort different compositional algorithms into categories. One way to do this is to look at the way an algorithm takes part in the compositional process. The results of the process can then be divided into music composed by computer and music composed with the aid of computer. Music may be considered composed by computer when the algorithm is able to make choices of its own during the creation process.

(16). Another way to sort compositional algorithms is to examine the results of their compositional processes. Algorithms can either provide notational information (sheet music) for other instruments or provide an independent way of sound synthesis (playing the composition by itself). There are also algorithms creating both notational data and sound synthesis.

(17). Algorithmic techniques have also been employed in a number of systems intended for direct musical performance, with many using algorithmic techniques to generate infinitely variable improvisations on a predetermined theme. An early example was the 1982 computer game Ballblazer of Lucasfilm Games, where the computer improvised on a basic jazz theme composed by the game's musical director Peter Langston; later in the life of that company, now rechristened LucasArts, an algorithmic iM-USE engine was developed for their flagship game, Dark Forces. Similar generative music systems have caught the attention of noted composers. Brian Eno has produced a number of works for the Koan generative music system, which produces ambient variations for web-pages, mobile devices, and for standalone performance.

36. In a musical scale, 13 notes separate each octave of 8 notes. The 5th note and 3rd note comprise the basic foundation of the chords. These are based on the whole tone, which is two steps from the 1st note of the scale. The pattern represents:

A. The Greek octave.
B. The Fibonacci sequence.
C. Fractals.
D. An algorithmic technique.
E. The golden section.

37. Which of the following phenomena in Nature would NOT resemble the self-replicating form of a fractal?

A. Snow flakes
B. Lightning
C. Circulatory system
D. Wind
E. Broccoli

38. In terms of tone, the middle point on a string in a guitar is known as:

A. a half-tone.
B. the middle 5th.
C. C Major.
D. an octave.

39. Which of the following statements is the best interpretation of the principle of the golden ratio?

A. Each two measures add up to make the next one sequentially proportionate to the lower measure.
B. The length of a whole relates to its large part in the same way that the large part relates to the small part.
C. The proportion of the smaller parts is exponentially derivative to the larger parts.
D. The whole is an expanding sequence of the smaller parts.

40. The key to the richness of details exhibited by fractals are what mathematicians call:

A. non-linear equations.
B. iteration.
C. loops.
D. regeneration.
E. magnified details.

41. The paradox of fractals is stated to be that:

A. its algorithms involve loops.
B. the richness of fractals is self-replicating.
C. the construction of complex shapes requires extraordinarily simple equations.
D. something produced from a purely mathematical procedure can be so aesthetically pleasing.
E. their visual results show great richness.

42. In Béla Bartók's Music for Strings, Percussion and Celesta, the xylophone progression demonstrates:

A. the Fibonacci numbers inverted.
B. a bell curve of a golden ratio.
C. he harmonic ratios of the Pythagoreans.
D. the golden ratio starting at phi and going downwards.
E. a combination of the golden ratio and the Fibonacci numbers.

43. The ancient Greeks measured notes and harmony using frequency ratios. Modern musicians use the golden section to generate rhythmic changes or to develop a melody line.

A. Both statements are true.
B. Both statements are false.
C. The first statement is true, the second statement is false.
D. The first statement is false, the second statement is true.

44. Based on statements in the passage, if one note has a frequency of 400 Hz, the note an octave below it, would be which of the following frequencies?

A. 200 Hz
B. 400 Hz
C. 600 Hz
D. 800 Hz
E. All of the above

45. What makes fractals an important phenomenon in musicology?

A. Their algorithms are very simple.
B. They can produce pleasant music from a purely mathematical procedure.
C. Composers use them as creative inspiration for their music.
D. They manifest self-similarity at all scales.

46. What is the main idea of the passage?

A. Math can be found in all music.
B. Music can be defined using mathematical techniques.
C. Either the golden ratio or the Fibonacci numbers occur in all music.
D. There is an intricate yet measurable relationship between music and math.
E. The form and content of music and mathematics are essentially the same.

47. Algorithms in music usually refer to:

A. formal procedures to make music without human intervention.
B. formal sets of rules that produce fractals.
C. equations.
D. the mapping system of a composer.
E. notational data and sound synthesis.

48. The name of a note an octave above A is also A because a note with a given frequency could only be combined with another note whose frequency is an integer multiple of the first.

A. Both the statement and reason are correct and related.
B. Both the statement and the reason are correct but NOT related.
C. The statement is correct but the reason is NOT.
D. The statement is NOT correct, but the reason is correct.
E. NEITHER the statement NOR the reason is correct.

49. Which of the following would be the best conclusion for the closing paragraph?

A. Indeed, such developments serve to prove that mathematics is as much an art as it is a science.
B. Still, whatever connects music with mathematics, both of them remain two different disciplines.
C. Over the years, mathematics and music do not form such strong opposites as they are commonly considered to do; after all, certain connections and similarities between them explain why some musicians like mathematics and why mathematicians generally love music.
D. Although a less popular notion, mathematical applications have indeed greatly contributed to the world's reservoir of beautiful musical creations.

50. The Pythagoreans investigated musical scales in terms of:

A. mathematical iterations.
B. ratios of small integers.
C. harmonic proportions.
D. rough trigonometry.
E. basic fractions.

1. Stephen is 4ft tall, and he is growing ½ in. every two months. John is 3ft 10in and is growing 1in. every three months. If these rates remain constant, how tall will Stephen and John be when they are the same height?

A. 4ft 6in
B. 4ft 10in
C. 5ft
D. 5ft 6in
E. 6ft

2. Which of the following are possible values of x if $x^2 - 7x + 5 = -7$?

A. -3
B. 3
C. 4
D. A and C
E. B and C

3. What is the mean value of the set {7 , 7 , 8 , 10 , 13}?

A. 7
B. 8
C. 9
D. 10
E. 11

4. If an equilateral triangle has a base of length 3, what is the measure of the angle between the base and the left side?

A. 60°
B. 45°
C. 30°
D. 90°
E. Insufficient information to draw a conclusion

5. If a six-sided die is rolled three times, what is the probability that every roll will turn up an even number?

A. 3/2
B. 1/2
C. 1/6
D. 1/8
E. 1/16

6. If f is a function that satisfies $f(x) = 2f(x)$ for all real numbers x, which of the following must be true of $f(1)$?

A. $f(1) = 2$
B. $f(1) = 1$
C. $f(1) = 0$
D. Either $f(1) = 1$ or $f(1) = 0$
E. Insufficient information to draw a conclusion

7. A certain blueberry bush can produce a maximum of 400 berries in a season. If one year it produces only 30% of its maximum yield and the next year it produces 85%, how many berries does it produce over the two-year period?

A. 200
B. 340
C. 400
D. 460
E. 600

8. If 2 km is equal to 1.2 miles, then 3.5 miles is approximately equal to how many km?

A. 2.7
B. 4.75
C. 5.4
D. 5.8
E. 12

9. Which of the following is the value of $\cot\left(\frac{7\pi}{6}\right)$?

A. -1
B. -1/2
C. $\sqrt{2}$
D. $\sqrt{3}$
E. $\frac{(\sqrt{3})}{2}$

10. Consider the point p with coordinates (5 , 1) in the Cartesian plane. What is sin θ where θ is the angle between the x-axis and the line from the origin to p?

A. 1/50
B. $\frac{1}{\sqrt{26}}$
C. 1/5
D. 1/2
E. $\frac{\sqrt{3}}{2}$

11. If a cup of sand has a mass of 360 g, about how many cups are in 20 kg of sand?

A. .06
B. 18
C. 55.6
D. 100
E. 720

12. Which of the following is the best approximation for $\frac{\left[\left(7.2\times10^{3}\right)\left(4.61\times10^{8}\right)\right]}{\left(2.23\times10^{7}\right)}$?

A. 1.5×10^{-4}
B. 1.5×10^{-2}
C. 1.5×10^{3}
D. 1.5×10^{4}
E. 1.5×10^{5}

13. What is the length of a diagonal of a rectangle with sides length 3 and 5?

A. 4
B. $\sqrt{15}$
C. $\sqrt{34}$
D. 8
E. 15

14. Three days, 14 hours, and 26 minutes is equal to how many minutes?

A. 3266
B. 4026
C. 4826
D. 5126
E. 5186

15. Which of the following is the length of each side of a square inscribed in a circle with a radius of 3?

A. 3
B. $3\sqrt{2}$
C. 5.2
D. 6
E. 9

16. 3x is to 6y as 5xy is to:

A. 10x
B. 10y
C. 10x/y
D. $10x^2$
E. $10y^2$

17. Which of the following is the value of x if $(3x + 2)^2 - x = 6$?

A. 1/5
B. 2/5
C. 1
D. 2/3
E. 2/7

18. Which of the following is the length of the side labeled S in the right triangle below?

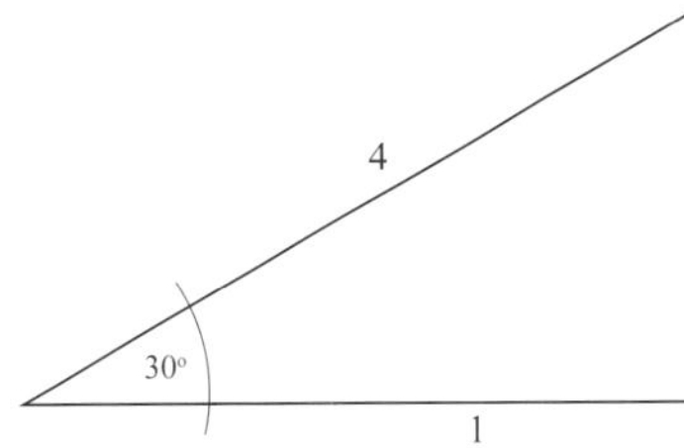

A. 1/2
B. $\frac{\sqrt{3}}{2}$
C. $\sqrt{2}$
D. 2
E. $2\sqrt{3}$

19. Which of the following is equal to sin x if csc x = $\frac{2}{\sqrt{3}}$ and if $\frac{3\pi}{2} < x < 2\pi$?

A. $-\frac{\sqrt{3}}{2}$

B. -1/2

C. 1/2

D. $\frac{\sqrt{3}}{2}$

E. $\frac{1}{\sqrt{2}}$

20. If $(2/x) + 3 > 5 - (1/x)$, then which must be true?

A. $(1/x) > (2/3)$
B. $(1/x) < (2/3)$
C. $(3/2) > x$
D. $(3/2) < x$
E. A and C

21. A cylinder has a height of 10 cm and a base diameter of 6 cm. Which of the following is the best approximation of the total surface area, in cm^2?

A. 245
B. 220
C. 180
D. 120
E. 60

22. A car is travelling at 65 mph. What fraction of an hour will it take for the car to travel 25 miles?

A. 1/4
B. 5/13
C. 1/2
D. 2/3
E. 23/30

23. While shopping for clothing John purchases three pairs of pants at \$39.99 each, four shirts at \$15.75 each, and a dozen socks at \$3.00 a pair. Which of the following best approximates John's total purchase?

A. \$60
B. \$200
C. \$220
D. \$240
E. \$300

24. Which of the following is 75% of 7/2?

A. 11/6
B. 21/8
C. 5/2
D. 3
E. 13/4

25. If the planet Earth has a mass of 5.97×10^{24} kg, and the planet Jupiter has a mass of 1.90×10^{27} kg, approximately how many times more massive is Jupiter than Earth?

A. 3.2×10^{-3}
B. 3.2×10^{1}
C. 3.2×10^{2}
D. 3.2×10^{3}
E. 3.2×10^{51}

26. How many pounds does 4.5 kg equal if 1 kg is equal to 2.2 pounds?

A. 2
B. 4.5
C. 7.2
D. 9
E. 9.9

27. Which of the following represents the distance between the points (-2 , 1) and (10 , 6) in the Cartesian plane?

A. $2\sqrt{3}$
B. $2\sqrt{11}$
C. 13
D. 17
E. $12\sqrt{5}$

28. Taylor has a container with 12 blue marbles and 8 yellow marbles. If she draws two marbles in a row without replacement, what is the probability that both marbles are yellow?

A. 14/95
B. 14/57
C. 4/19
D. 5/19
E. 1/3

29. Which of the following equations describe a line passing through points (-1 , 3) , (1 , 0) and (5 , -6) in the Cartesian plane?

A. $y = -(3/2)x + 1$
B. $y = (3/2)x + 3/2$
C. $3y + 3x = 5$
D. $y + 2x = 2/3$
E. $2y + 3x = 3$

30. Which of the following is equivalent to the fraction $\dfrac{\left[2-\left(\dfrac{6}{5}\right)\right]}{\left[1+\left(\dfrac{2}{5}\right)\right]}$?

A. 1
B. 1/2
C. 4/7
D. 11/5
E. 2

31. In a college classroom of 143 students the ratio of women to men was 4 to 7. How many of the students were male?

A. 13
B. 36
C. 52
D. 81
E. 91

32. Which of the following is smallest?

A. $\dfrac{1}{\sqrt{3}}$
B. 11/23
C. 2/3
D. 3/5
E. 7/13

33. Which of the following is equal to x if $\left(\dfrac{.06}{2.7}\right)\left(\dfrac{81}{x}\right) = 5.4$?

A. 1/3
B. 1
C. 2
D. 9/5
E. 20/3

34. A tree that is 4 meters tall will grow in height by a maximum of 40% for every subsequent year. Which of the following represents the best approximation of the maximum increase in height the tree can have over the next 3 years?

A. 1.6
B. 4.8
C. 6.4
D. 7.0
E. 11.0

35. Which of the following is the value of x if $x \neq -2$, $x \neq 3$, and $\dfrac{2}{\left[3(x+2)\right]} + \dfrac{3}{(x-3)} = \dfrac{(5x-1)}{(x^2-x-6)}$?

A. 3/4
B. 15/4
C. 15
D. -2
E. -6

36. To the nearest multiple of 10, which of the following best approximates 17.4×9.7?

A. 100
B. 160
C. 170
D. 180
E. 200

37. On a trip to and from the grocery store Sid travelled at an average speed of 28 mph. If it took him 18 minutes to get to the store and 12 minutes to get back home, what was his average speed on the way home?

A. 20 mph
B. 24 mph
C. 28 mph
D. 30 mph
E. 35 mph

38. A jar contains 3 green balls and 6 red balls. If 3 balls are drawn without replacement, what is the probability that the first 2 will be green and the third will be red?

A. 1/11
B. 1/12
C. 1/13
D. 1/14
E. 1/15

39. If 2 cups of water, 1 cup of 90% apple juice and 3 cups of 60% apple juice are mixed, what is the percentage of apple juice in the mixture?

A. 45%
B. 50%
C. 60%
D. 75%
E. 90%

40. On a math quiz, 1/3 of the 36 students in the class scored a 10, 1/12 scored a 9, ¼ scored an 8, and the rest scored a 7. What was the median quiz score?

A. 10
B. 9.5
C. 9
D. 8
E. 7

Answer Keys & Solutions

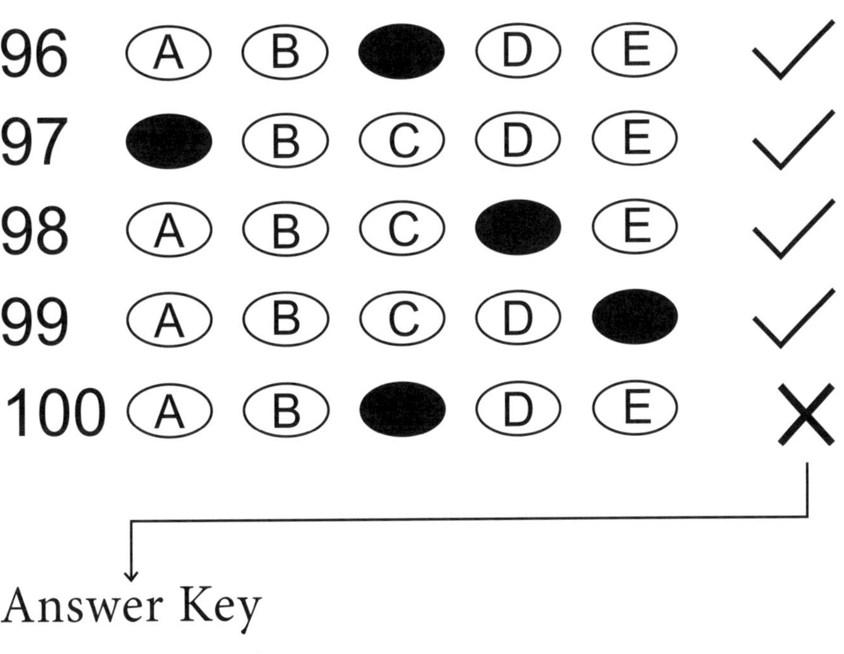

Answer Document
96 A B D E
97 B C D E
98 A B C E
99 A B C D
100 A B D E

Answer Key

100 A P1, L6-8; KW: proton; C. ↔ not

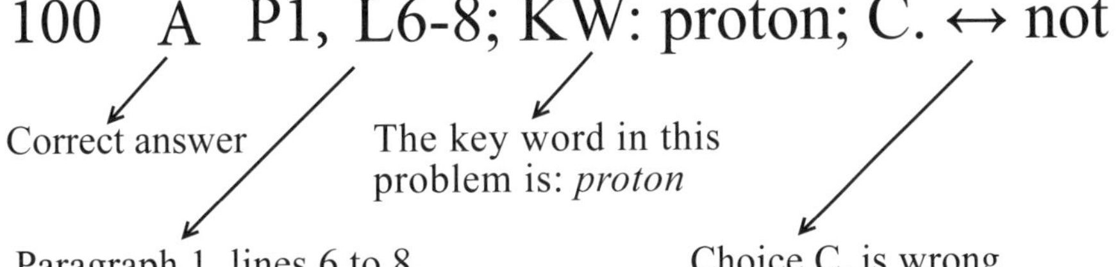

Correct answer
The key word in this problem is: *proton*
Paragraph 1, lines 6 to 8, is where the answer can be found
Choice C. is wrong because of the word "*not*"

GS-1: Natural Sciences Test

#	Answer	*Cross-reference*
1.	C	BIO 15.5
2.	A	BIO 7.5, 8.3
3.	E	BIO 12.4
4.	B	BIO 15.1, 15.3
5.	E	BIO 17.1, 17.2 , 17.2.3
6.	C	BIO 17.1, 17.2
7.	B	BIO 14.5.1
8.	E	BIO 2.2, BIO 16.6.4
9.	A	BIO 6.3.3, 5.4.4
10.	A	BIO 4.1, CHM 9.7; CHM 9.7
11.	C	BIO 14.5
12.	E	BIO 19.7
13.	E	BIO 7.2, 7.3, 7.5.1
14.	B	BIO 7.5.2, 10.3
15.	C	BIO 4.3, 2.5, 2.5.1
16.	B	BIO 4.1, 15.7, Chapter 15 Appendix
17.	B	BIO 1.2.2, BIO 3, BIO 20.5
18.	E	BIO 15.2
19.	C	BIO 6.2.3
20.	E	BIO 1.4.1, 17.6.4
21.	C	BIO 1.1.3
22.	D	BIO 1.1.1, 4.1
23.	D	BIO 2.2, BIO 16.6.4
24.	D	BIO 19.2
25.	E	BIO 1.1, 5.1.1, 5.1.3
26.	D	BIO 14.2
27.	C	BIO 4.4
28.	E	BIO 14.3
29.	B	BIO 4.2
30.	C	BIO 14.2
31.	E	BIO 1.2.2, 3.0
32.	D	BIO 2.2
33.	A	BIO 9.4.1
34.	D	BIO 17.6.3, 17.6.6
35.	E	BIO 4.1, 4.7; CHM 8.2, 10.1, 10.2
36.	E	BIO 20.2.2
37.	E	BIO 7 Appendix
38.	B	BIO 16.3, 19.2-19.4 and Appendix
39.	E	BIO 16.4.2, 17
40.	A	BIO 11.3, 11.3.3
41.	A	CHM 8.3, 1.4
42.	E	CHM 3.4, 6.1
43.	D	CHM 1.4
44.	E	CHM 5.3.1
45.	A	CHM 6.6, 6.5
46.	A	CHM 1.3, 1.5
47.	B	CHM 10.1
48.	C	CHM 2.3
49.	A	CHM 4.2, 4.3.2
50.	C	CHM 4.2, ORG 10.1
51.	B	CHM 4.1.7
52.	E	CHM 11.4
53.	D	CHM 11
54.	B	CHM 10.1, 10.2
55.	D	CHM 5.3.2
56.	D	CHM 3.5
57.	E	CHM 2.4, 2.4.1
58.	C	CHM 1.1-1.5
59.	B	CHM 2.3
60.	D	CHM 10.4
61.	E	CHM 6.9
62.	E	CHM 1.5.1, 5.2, 6.2, 6.9.1
63.	C	CHM 2.1, 2.2, 2.3
64.	B	CHM 6.1
65.	D	E; CHM 8.10
66.	E	CHM 8.7
67.	A	CHM 5.1.1, 5.1.2
68.	A	CHM 4.1.2, 4.1.8
69.	C	CHM 9.3
70.	A	CHM 12.3.1
71.	A	ORG 2.1, 2.2, 2.3
72.	E	ORG 1.6, 7.1, 8.1, 9.4
73.	A	CHM 6.3, ORG 1.6, 4.2.1, 6.2.4, 11.1.1
74.	D	ORG 4.2, 7.1, 8.1, 14.1
75.	D	ORG 1.1, 8.1
76.	B	CHM 6.3, ORG 5.2.2, 10.2
77.	C	ORG 7.2.2
78.	D	ORG 13.3, CHM 12
79.	B	CHM 3.5, ORG 3.3, 10.1
80.	C	ORG 7.1
81.	A	ORG 13.2.1
82.	A	ORG 12.1.2
83.	C	ORG 14.2
84.	E	ORG 3.1, 4.1
85.	C	ORG 13
86.	C	ORG 2.1, 2.2, 2.3
87.	E	ORG 6.2.4
88.	E	ORG 7.2.3
89.	A	ORG 2.3.1, 2.3.2, 2.3.3
90.	B	ORG 4.2.1
91.	C	CHM 9.5, 9.7, 9.8, 9.10, ORG 6.2.1
92.	C	CHM 8.2, 8.10, 9.5
93.	E	ORG 3.3, 12.3.2 F
94.	C	CHM 3.5; ORG 1.2, 1.3
95.	B	ORG 4.2.4
96.	A	ORG 4.2.2, 6.1, 9.4, 13.1; CHM 12
97.	E	CHM 3.5; ORG 1.2, 1.3, 4.1, 4.2
98.	E	ORG 5.1.1
99.	D	ORG 1.6, 5.2, 5.2.1, 5.2.2, 6.2.2, 7.2.3
100.	C	CHM 3.5; ORG 1.2, 1.3

To estimate your standard score, sign in to dat-prep.com then click Tests in the top Menu. Cross-references above refer to subsections from chapters in the Gold Standard Book Set.

GS-1: Perceptual Ability Test

1.	E	24.	A	47.	E	70.	B
2.	D	25.	D	48.	B	71.	C
3.	D	26.	B	49.	D	72.	E
4.	B	27.	B	50.	A	73.	C
5.	A	28.	A	51.	B	74.	C
6.	E	29.	A	52.	C	75.	C
7.	B	30.	B	53.	E	76.	B
8.	D	31.	D	54.	A	77.	C
9.	C	32.	C	55.	D	78.	D
10.	A	33.	B	56.	D	79.	B
11.	C	34.	C	57.	B	80.	B
12.	D	35.	A	58.	E	81.	C
13.	B	36.	D	59.	C	82.	A
14.	A	37.	B	60.	A	83.	D
15.	E	38.	A	61.	D	84.	B
16.	B	39.	D	62.	E	85.	D
17.	C	40.	C	63.	B	86.	C
18.	D	41.	B	64.	C	87.	A
19.	A	42.	C	65.	D	88.	C
20.	B	43.	A	66.	B	89.	A
21.	C	44.	B	67.	A	90.	A
22.	C	45.	A	68.	E		
23.	D	46.	C	69.	D		

GS-1: Reading Comprehension Test

1.	C	18.	B	35.	C
2.	C	19.	D	36.	B
3.	E	20.	B	37.	D
4.	D	21.	C	38.	D
5.	E	22.	A	39.	B
6.	B	23.	B	40.	B
7.	B	24.	D	41.	C
8.	B	25.	A	42.	B
9.	B	26.	E	43.	A
10.	E	27.	C	44.	A
11.	B	28.	B	45.	D
12.	D	29.	B	46.	D
13.	C	30.	B	47.	A
14.	D	31.	B	48.	C
15.	C	32.	B	49.	D
16.	D	33.	D	50.	B
17.	A	34.	C		

GS-1: Quantitative Reasoning Test

		Cross-reference
1.	A	QR 3.2, 3.2.1, 8.2, 8.2.1
2.	E	QR 4.6, 4.6.1
3.	C	QR 7.2, 7.2.2
4.	A	QR 5.2, 5.2.2
5.	D	QR 7.1
6.	C	QR 4.1, 4.1.4
7.	D	QR 2.4.3, 8.3
8.	D	QR 2.6
9.	D	QR 6.1, 6.1.4, 6.2, 6.2.1
10.	B	QR 5.1, 5.1.1, 5.2, 5.2.2, 6.1, 6.1.1
11.	C	QR 2.6, 3.2, 3.2.1
12.	E	QR 2.5, 2.5.2
13.	C	QR 5.2, 5.2.2, 6.3, 6.3.3
14.	E	QR 3.1, 3.1.1
15.	B	QR 5.2, 5.2.3, 6.3, 6.3.3
16.	E	QR 2.4, 2.4.2
17.	B	QR 4.1, 4.1.1, 4.3, 4.3.1
18.	E	QR 6.1, 6.1.2
19.	B	QR 6.1, 6.1.4, 6.2, 6.2.1
20.	E	QR 4.2, 4.2.2
21.	A	QR 5.3, 5.3.3
22.	B	QR 2.6
23.	B	QR 2.2, 2.2.3
24.	B	QR 2.4, 4.2
25.	C	QR 2.5, 2.5.2
26.	E	QR 2.6
27.	C	QR 4.5, 4.5.2, 5.1, 5.1.1
28.	A	QR 7.1, 7.1.2
29.	E	QR 4.5, 4.5.4
30.	C	QR 2.4, 2.4.2
31.	E	QR 2.6
32.	B	QR 2.4, 2.4.1
33.	A	QR 2.4, 2.41, 2.4.2
34.	D	QR 8.2, 8.2.3
35.	B	QR 4.3, 4.3.1, 4.3.3
36.	C	QR 2.2, 2.2.1
37.	E	QR 3.1, 3.1.1, 8.2, 8.2.2
38.	D	QR 7.1, 7.1.2
39.	A	QR 2.4.3, 8.3, 8.3.3
40.	D	QR 7.2, 7.2.2

To estimate your standard score, sign in to dat-prep.com then click Tests in the top Menu. Cross-references above refer to subsections from chapters in the Gold Standard Book Set.

GS-1
SOLUTIONS

Question 1 C

See: BIO 15.5

Mutations are rare, inheritable, random changes in the genetic material (DNA) of a cell. Mutations are much more likely to be either neutral (esp. silent mutations) or negative (i.e. cancer) than positive for an organism's survival. Nonetheless, such a change in the genome increases genetic variability. Only mutations of gametes, and not somatic cells, are passed on to offspring. The following are some forms of mutations:

- Point mutation is a change affecting a single base pair in a gene
- Deletion is the removal of a sequence of DNA, the regions on either side being joined together
- Inversion is the reversal of a segment of DNA
- Translocation is when one chromosome breaks and attaches to another
- Duplication is when a sequence of DNA is repeated.
- Frame shift mutations occur when bases are added or deleted in numbers other than multiples of three. Such deletions or additions cause the rest of the sequence to be shifted such that each triplet reading frame is altered.

Question 2 A

See: BIO 7.5, 8.3

The spleen contains white pulp and red pulp. While the white pulp contains leukocytes (including antigen presenting cells) which filter red blood cells as well as foreign particles, the red pulp stores erythrocytes. It does not, however, produce platelets which are formed from fragments of large bone marrow cells or megakaryocytes.

Question 3 E

See: BIO 12.4

Inspiration is active and requires the contraction of the diaphragm by the phrenic nerve. The diaphragm will thus move downward, while the thoracic cage is pushed outwards increasing the volume of the chest cavity. This will thus cause a negative internal pressure which will allow air to enter the lungs. Hence, only answer choice **E.** is correct.

Question 4 B

See: BIO 15.1, 15.3

The reaction indicates that the allele for the normal and abnormal gene exists in the mother (Aa) and 2 abnormal alleles exist in the father (aa). As such, a Punnett square can be produced for this couple.

A = chromosome with normal gene

a = chromosome with abnormal gene

	a	**a**
A	Aa	Aa
a	aa	aa

Hence, 50% of boys will manifest the disease: boys (actually either sex since this is not sex-linked) could be either Aa or aa.

Question 5 E

See: BIO 17.1, 17.2 , 17.2.3

The vascular bundle is scattered in monocots. In dicot stems, it is common that the xylem and phloem tissues are present on the same radius and just opposed to each other in conjoint vascular bundles (ring patterned). Depending on the number and position of phloem group, conjoint vascular bundles can be of two types: collateral type and bi-collateral type.

Collateral vascular bundles are very common and seen in stems of dicotyledons (with some exceptions). Cambium may be present or absent in between xylem and phloem patches making the vascular bundle open or closed, respectively.

Bi-collateral vascular bundles contain two (= bi) patches of phloem on either sides of the xylem on the same radius. The outer phloem or external phloem remains towards the periphery of the central cylinder and the inner or internal phloem remains towards the center.

Question 6 C

See: BIO 17.1, 17.2

The cuticle is a continuous layer of waxy substances covering the outer surfaces of the epidermis of plants, it contains cutin and protects against water loss (or gain) and other damage. The term is also used for the hard outer covering or case of certain organisms such as arthropods and turtles.

The epidermis is a single-layered group of cells that covers plants' leaves, flowers, roots and stems.

Stomata, the plural of stoma, refers to the minute pores in the epidermis of the leaf or stem of a plant that allows movement of gases in and out of the intercellular spaces.

Even if you had never heard of bulliform cells, you should have gotten the answer correct by knowing the preceding plant structures.

Bulliform cells are large, bubble-shaped, empty-looking, colorless epidermal cells that occur in groups on the upper surface of the leaves of many grasses. During drought, the loss of moisture through vacuoles leads the leaves of many grass species to close as the two edges of the grass blade fold up toward each other. Once adequate water is available, these bulliform cells enlarge and the leaves open again.

Question 7 B

See: BIO 14.5.1

First off, it is important to know that a blastomere represents the first week of cell replication. The point at which a blastomere is committed to becoming a germ cell is different from the point at which the germ cell actually starts to function as a germ cell (i.e. producing cell-specific proteins). Determination is the point at which a cell is committed to becoming a particular type of cell, although it may not display any specific characteristics that would yet identify it as a specific type of cell. After determination, a cell will differentiate into a particular type of cell, and the fully differentiated cell is called *specialized*. Determination is the crucial point at which the fate of the blastomere is decided.

Question 8 E

See: BIO 2.2, BIO 16.6.4

Protists are a diverse group of eukaryotic microorganisms thus they have nuclei. The protists do not have much in common besides a relatively simple organization - either they are unicellular, or they are multicellular without specialized tissues. This simple cellular organization distinguishes the protists from other eukaryotes, such as fungi, plants and animals.

Question 9 A

See: BIO 6.3.3, 5.4.4

Osteoclasts are responsible for the release of calcium to the blood.

Question 10 A

See: BIO 6.3.3, 5.4.4; CHM 9.7

The equilibrium of a catalyzed reaction remains constant (constant amount of reactants and products); the rate at which equilibrium occurs increases.

Question 11 C

See: BIO 14.5

Implantation of the developing embryo into the uterine lining occurs during blastulation whereby the embryo has developed into a blastocyst.

Question 12 E

See: BIO 19.7

The tree line is the ecological boundary between forest and tundra and thus does not divide the tundra. Tundra can be further subdivided into alpine, arctic or Antarctic (frozen). Tundra is known for permafrost and short growing seasons but "frozen" or "antarctic" tundra is incapable of supporting vegetation because it is too cold and dry. Most of Antarctica (the continent) is covered by ice fields.

Question 13 E

See: BIO 7.2, 7.3, 7.5.1

Oxygen from lungs → pulmonary vein → heart → aorta → arteries to body tissues → body tissues (capillaries) → veins from body tissues (includes renal) → vena cava → heart → pulmonary arteries → lungs. Note that a portal system or portal vein shuttles blood from one capillary bed to another.

Question 14 B

See: BIO 7.5.2, 10.3

Blood (or hydrostatic) pressure is proportional to the filtration rate.

Question 15 C

See: BIO 4.3, 2.5, 2.5.1

There are two main differences between Trials 1 and 2 in Table 1: (1) the [inhibitin] is increased by a relatively small amount (approx. 10^{-6} mmol/L); (2) the [trypsin] is increased by a relatively large amount (by a factor of 10). Answer choices **B**. and **D**. cannot account for the constant rate observed for the two reactions since a significant increase in inhibitor, or decrease in enzyme should cause a decrease in the reaction rate. However, a significant increase in [trypsin] (difference #2) with a concomitant minor increase in [inhibitin] could allow the enzyme to overcome the effects of the inhibitor, resulting in a constant rate of reaction.

Question 16 B

See: BIO 4.1, 15.7, Chapter 15 Appendix

This question requires knowledge of the definition of anabolism and catabolism. A catabolic reaction involves the breakdown of macromolecules, whereas an anabolic reaction involves the synthesis of macromolecules from individual building blocks (BIO 4.1). PCR entails the synthesis (amplification) of a new DNA strand using a DNA template and free nucleotides, therefore, it is an anabolic reaction that synthesizes new DNA strands.

Background: The polymerase chain reaction (PCR) is a powerful biological tool that allows the rapid amplification of any fragment of DNA without purification. In PCR, RNA primers are made to flank the specific DNA sequence to be amplified. These RNA primers are then extended to the end of the DNA molecule with the use of a heat-resistant DNA polymerase. The newly synthesized DNA strand is then used as the template to undergo another round of replication.

Question 17 B

See: BIO 1.2.2, BIO 3, BIO 20.5

The question states that AZT is an analog of thymidine and differs from thymidine in that it lacks the 3'–OH group. This OH group is crucial in the synthesis of DNA strands because it is required to form the 5'–3' phosphodiester linkage which holds the DNA backbone together (BIO 1.2.2). Consequently, since there is a 3'–N_3

rather than a 3'–OH, once this nucleotide analog is incorporated into the DNA, synthesis of the DNA strand will be blocked as no subsequent nucleotide will be able to form a bond with the 3' carbon atom. Moreover, the retroviral RNA must be converted to DNA in a process known as reverse transcription. In this case, the RNA strand will serve as a template to generate a single strand of DNA. Hence, it is reverse transcription of the viral RNA that will be disrupted by AZT. Recall that conventional transcription uses uridine instead of thymidine, and so AZT would not affect the conversion of DNA to RNA (BIO 3).

Question 18 E

See: BIO 1.2.2, BIO 3

An antibody-antigen interaction involving serum and red blood cells leads to clumping or agglutination. Type O blood is the "universal donor" because the red blood cells have no antigens. However, type O serum contains anti-A and anti-B antigens. I, II and III contain red blood cells with either some A or B or both antigens, thus resulting in antibody-antigen interaction with type O serum.

Question 19 C

See: BIO 6.2.3

The semicircular canals, which are found in the inner ear, are responsible for maintaining a sense of equilibrium.

Question 20 E

See: BIO 1.4.1, 17.6.4

In multicellular plants, the structural functions of cell junctions are provided for by cell walls. The analogues of communicating cell junctions in plants are called plasmodesmata (BIO 17.6.4). 1. Communicating junctions, like gap junctions in animal cells, are narrow tunnels which allow the free passage of small molecules and ions. One gap junction channel is composed of two connexons (or hemichannels) which connect across the intercellular space (BIO 1.4.1).

Question 21 C

See: BIO 1.1.3

Receptor-mediated endocytosis is mediated by clathrin-coated vesicles (CCVs). Exocytotic vesicles are usually not clathrin coated, most of them have no coat at all.

In exocytosis, the transient vesicle fusion with the cell membrane forms a structure shaped like a pore (= *porosome*). Porosomes contain many different types of protein including chloride and calcium channels, actin, and SNARE proteins that mediate the docking and fusion of vesicles with the cell membrane. The primary role of SNARE proteins is to mediate vesicle fusion through full fusion exocytosis or open and close (= "kiss-and-run fusion") exocytosis.

Question 22 D

See: BIO 1.1.1, 4.1

Answer choices **A** and **C** are consistent with simple diffusion. Answer choice **C** is equivocal. Answer choice **D** suggests the presence of a transporter (carrier mediated transport) because there must be a limited number of carriers, if the concentration of dopamine gets too high, the carriers would be saturated thus the rate of crossing the membrane would level off (plateau).

Question 23 D

See: BIO 2.2, BIO 16.6.4

The Archaea (AKA archeabacteria) are a domain of single-celled microorganisms. These microbes have no cell nucleus or any other membrane-bound organelles. Initially, archaea were termed "extremophiles" because of their ability to live in harsh or extreme environments, but they have since been found to also live in a broad range of habitats.

Protobionts are systems that are considered to have possibly been the precursors to prokaryotic cells.

Question 24 D

See: BIO 19.2

J-shaped curves are a classic representation of exponential growth. The J-shaped curve is characteristic of populations that are introduced into a new or unfilled environment, or alternatively, whose numbers have been drastically reduced by a catastrophic event and are rebounding.

Question 25 E

See: BIO 1.1, 5.1.1, 5.1.3

The question essentially provides the following information: (i) the concentration of potassium (the only cation) on both sides of the membrane is equal; (ii) the concentration of the anions on side X (Cl^- and $Prot^-$) must be equal to side Y (Cl^- alone). Therefore:

$$Cl^-_x + Prot^-_x = Cl^-_y$$

Thus:

$$Cl^-_x < Cl^-_y$$

Since $[Cl^-]_y > [Cl^-]_x$, there exists a chemical gradient for diffusion (BIO 1.1.1) from Y to X (i.e. answer choice **A.** is incorrect). The electrical gradient depends on the membrane potential (BIO 5.1.3). The electrical and chemical gradients balance at an equilibrium which is dynamic (answer choice **E.**; other answer choices do not take into account the dynamic equilibrium).

Note: The Gibbs–Donnan effect (also known as the Donnan effect or Gibbs–Donnan equilibrium) is the name for the behavior of charged particles near a semi-permeable membrane to sometimes fail to distribute evenly across the two sides of the membrane.

Question 26 D

See: BIO 14.2

Spermatogonia (diploid) are male germ cells which can produce primary spermatocytes.

Each primary spermatocyte duplicates its DNA and eventually undergoes meiosis I to produce two haploid secondary spermatocytes. Each of the two secondary spermatocytes further undergo meiosis II to produce two spermatids (haploid). Thus 1 primary spermatocyte produces 4 spermatids. The spermatids then undergo spermiogenesis to produce spermatozoa.

Question 27 C

See: BIO 4.4

Glucose (from glycogen) is the first and most common source to produce ATP. Amino acids, which requires the breakdown of protein in muscle which would be fed into the Krebs cycle, would only be used when all else fails.

Question 28 E

See: BIO 14.3

You must be familiar with the graph of the menstrual cycle in order to know which curve is referring to which hormone. There are four hormones involved: luteinizing hormone (LH), follicle stimulating hormone (FSH), estrogen and progesterone. If the menstrual cycle is understood well, you should immediately know that both estrogen and progesterone are secreted by the corpus luteum which came from the ovary. Alternatively, if the pituitary hormones are known, it is easy to eliminate LH and FSH because they are secreted by the anterior pituitary. Notice the LH surge before ovulation (III) which remains low in the 2nd part of the menstrual cycle.

Question 29 B

See: BIO 4.2

In this case, the inhibitor (I) binds the active site of the enzyme (E) reversibly and thus, it can be displaced by the substrate (S). Therefore, if [S] is gradually increased for a given [I], the inhibitor will be displaced from the active site of the enzyme and the effect of the inhibitor will be overcome as the enzyme reaches its normal maximal velocity (V_{max}). On the other hand, the K_m of the enzyme, which represents the [S] at half V_{max} should increase. In our example, the same V_{max} for the enzyme will be reached if enough S is added, however, this increase in [S] needed to overcome the effect of the inhibitor will raise the K_m accordingly. You should be aware that the larger the K_m, the less efficient the enzyme because a higher [S] is required to reach a given velocity of the reaction.

Question 30 C

See: BIO 14.2

Down's syndrome, or trisomy 21, is caused by the presence of triplicate copies of chromosome 21 in the afflicted individual. Since a normal genotype consists of two chromosome 21s, the overall number of chromosomes in a Down's syndrome patient is increased by one (46 + 1 = 47N). In both meiosis and mitosis, the separation of chromosomes (in meiosis I) or sister chromatids (in mitosis and meiosis II) occurs during anaphase, thereby eliminating answer choices **A.** and **B.** Recall that meiosis is divided into two steps. During the reduction division, the homologous chromosomes pair at the equatorial plate and separate to form two daughter cells consisting of a haploid (N) number of chromosomes. During the second meiotic division, the chromosomes line up at the center of the cell (just as they would in mitosis) and the sister chromatids separate to form two daughter cells of a haploid number of chromosomes. Since the homologous chromosomes pair up only in meiosis 1, we expect that the failure of chromosomes 21 to separate will occur, with a greater likelihood, in Anaphase I.

Question 31 E

See: BIO 1.2.2, 3.0

You must know that A pairs with T and C pairs with G. However, the question is asking about RNA, not DNA. In RNA, T is replaced by U. Therefore, the complementary sequence of CAG is GUC.

Question 32 D

See: BIO 2.2

The question is asking for a feature that *eukaryotes* have that *prokaryotes* (i.e. bacteria) do not have. A cell wall is listed, however, a cell wall is a feature that the *prokaryote* has that some eukaryotes have (i.e. plants and fungi).

One of the major differences between *prokaryotes* and *eukaryotes* is that *prokaryotes* contain no membrane bound organelles. Therefore, a *eukaryote* would have lysosomes, while a *prokaryote* would not.

Question 33 A

See: BIO 9.4.1

This is very simple question. You should know that the liver produces bile and the gallbladder stores it.

Question 34 D

See: BIO 17.6.3, 17.6.6

During dark phase (= dark stage/reaction = light independent stage/reaction), the reduced $NADPH_2$ transfers its hydrogens to CO_2 which is reduced to carbohydrate. The dark stage takes place in the stroma of the chloroplast. Unlike the light stage, the dark stage is controlled by enzymes and therefore affected by temperature. The enzyme is ribulose bisphosphate carboxylase oxygenase (RUBISCO).

Question 35 E

See: BIO 4.1, 4.7; CHM 8.2, 10.1, 10.2

Endergonic is defined as "absorbing energy in the form of work." In metabolism, an endergonic process is anabolic (energy is stored) which is usually coupled with ATP. Reduction is defined as a gain in electrons (GERC: Gain Electrons Reduction Cathode). Anabolic reactions refers to the set of metabolic pathways that construct molecules from smaller units using energy. Activation energy can be defined as the minimum energy required to start a chemical reaction. It's relationship to entropy is nowhere as clear as the other answer choices.

Question 36 E

See: BIO 20.2.2

The primary structure refers to the amino acid linear sequence of the protein held together by covalent peptide bonds. Keep in mind that the primary structure is the order of the amino acids in the protein. For this reason, even post-translational modifications such as disulfide formation, phosphorylations and glycosylations are considered a part of the primary structure (these are all types of covalent bonding).

The dipeptide cystine is composed of two cysteine amino acids joined by a disulfide bond (= bridge) and can help to stabilize the tertiary structure and to some degree, the quaternary structure of proteins (and rarely involved in secondary structure). H-bonding, which is non-covalent, is prominent in secondary and tertiary protein structures.

Question 37 E

See: BIO 7 Appendix

Even if you had forgotten the equation, because EF is a fraction (often given as a %), it has no units, so the numerator and denominator must have the same unit.

EF = stroke volume / end diastolic volume

Cardiac output = stroke volume × heart rate

Question 38 B

See: BIO 16.3, 19.2-19.4 and Appendix

The question discusses evolution within two different species. Within a species, the passage distinguishes between "local" populations and "other" populations which suggests that the populations live apart (= *allopatric*; BIO 16.3). Since the local population evolves differently (i.e. "*more capable of attacking the host . .* ."), genetic drift may be implicated. Recall that genetic mutations are usually either negative or neutral with regard to the organism's survival (BIO 15.5). Note: interspecific means 'between different species' whereas intraspecific means 'within the same species'.

Question 39 E

See: BIO 16.4.2, 17

Answer choice **E** is both irrelevant and untrue since plant cells have both chloroplasts and mitochondria.

Question 40 A

See: BIO 11.3, 11.3.3

Some common relations in brackets: carpals (wrist), metacarpals (palm), phalanges (fingers), tarsals (ankle), metatarsals (foot), phalanges (toes).

Question 41 A

See: CHM 8.3, 1.4

From Table I we are not given ΔH formation; rather, we are provided with a different parameter which the table describes as the enthalpy of combustion ΔHc of carbon. The end product of combustion (the oxide) of carbon is carbon dioxide. Now we can use Hess's Law knowing that the ΔHc for $C_{graphite} = -393.3$ kJ mol^{-1} and for $C_{diamond} = -395.1$ kJ mol^{-1}. We can summarize the process as follows:

$C_{graphite} \rightarrow CO_2$ ΔHc = −393.3 kJ mol^{-1}

$CO_2 \rightarrow C_{diamond}$ ΔHc = 395.1 kJ mol^{-1}

$C_{graphite} \rightarrow C_{diamond}$ ΔHc = 1.8 kJ mol^{-1}

{Notice the change in direction of the equation for $C_{diamond}$ was necessary in order to cancel the CO_2; thus the sign for ΔHc was changed from negative to positive}

Question 42 E

See: CHM 3.4, 6.1

By definition, a Lewis acid is a chemical species which accepts an electron pair (CHM 3.4). Answer choice **A.** is the Bronsted-Lowry definition of an acid (CHM 6.1).

Question 43 D

See: CHM 1.4

The relative atomic mass of O is ≈ 16; that of H is 1.0; and that of S is ≈ 32. Thus the relative molecular mass of H_2SO_3 is (2 × 1.0) + 32 + (16 × 3) = 82. The mass of the molecular oxygen (16 × 3 = 48) is more than half of 82. There is only one answer choice (**D.**) which is greater than 0.5! Alternatively, you can do it the old fashioned way: 48/82 + calculate!

Question 44 E

See: CHM 5.3.1

On the Surface:

x = molarity of $Mg_3(PO_4)_2 \rightarrow$ Solve for x

$(.005M\ Mg^{2+})(.005\ L) + (3x)(.015\ L) = (.05M\ Mg^{2+})(.02\ L)$

Note the 3 in front of x because there are 3 potential Mg^{2+} generated from each $Mg_3(PO_4)_2$ in aqueous solution. Solve for x:

$(3x)(.015\ L) = (.05M\ Mg^{2+})(.02\ L) - (.005M\ Mg^{2+})(.005\ L)$

$x = [(.05)(.02) - (.005)(.005)] / (0.045)$

Thus x = 0.022 M.

Going Deeper: a detailed calculation follows . . .

Let's begin with the total number of moles of Mg^{2+} present in the final solution: 0.05 moles/L × 0.02 L = 0.001 moles of Mg^{2+}. Next, let's look at the number of moles of Mg^{2+} obtained from $MgCl_2$: 0.005 moles/L × 0.005 L = 0.000025 moles of Mg^{2+}. Now we know the number of moles of Mg^{2+} we need supplied from $Mg_3(PO_4)_2$: (0.001 – 0.000025) moles = 0.000975 moles. Thus from the 15 mL of $Mg_3(PO_4)_2$ we need 0.000975 moles of Mg^{2+}. But each mole of $Mg_3(PO_4)_2$ contains 3 moles of Mg^{2+} Therefore, the concentration of $Mg_3(PO_4)_2$ = [(0.000975 moles)/(0.015 L)] × 1/3 = 0.022 mol L^{-1} = 2.2×10^{-2} M.

Sometimes on the real DAT, they will not calculate the answer; they will just confirm that you know how to set up the solution such as the answer choices in this question.

Question 45 A

See: CHM 6.6, 6.5

Using $K_b = ([X^+][OH^-]) / [XOH]$; X is most probably a Group I metal since it is monovalent (= univalent = a valence of one).

Assuming that $[X^+] = [OH^-]$ approximately

$K_b = [OH^-]^2 / [XOH]$, where XOH approximates 1.0 M at equilibrium, thus:

$1.0 \times 10^{-6} = [OH^-]^2 / 1$

$[OH^-]^2 = 1.0 \times 10^{-6}$

$[OH^-] = 1.0 \times 10^{-3}$ mol dm^{-3}

$pOH = -\log[OH^-] = -\log(1.0 \times 10^{-3}) = -(-3) = 3$

Using pH + pOH = 14, we get:

pH = 14 – pOH = 14 – 3 = 11

Question 46 A

See: CHM 1.3, 1.5

Using Number of moles = (Mass)/(Relative molecular mass)

For PCl_3: Number of moles = (68.75 g)/[(31.0 + 35.5 × 3) g mol^{-1}] = 68.75/137.5 = 1/2

Equation: $P_4\ (s) + 6Cl_2 \rightarrow 4PCl_3$

Thus, Number of moles of P_4 = 1/4 × Number of moles PCl_3 = 1/4 × 1/2 mole = 1/8 mole

Using 1 mole of particles = 6.0×10^{23} particles (Avogadro's # = 6.023×10^{23} particles/mole)

1/8 mole P_4 = 1/8 × 6.0 × 10^{23} = 3/4 × 10^{23} = 0.75 × 10^{23} P_4 molecules

Question 47 B

See: CHM 10.1

The reduced species of the electrochemical equilibrium with the most negative E° value is the strongest reducing agent (CHM 10.1). Memory aside (!), it is of value to note that a reducing agent reduces the other substance, thus a reducing agent is oxidized. Note that only answer choices **B.** and **C.** are oxidized (= *lose electrons*). When you write the two relevant equations as oxidations, instead of reductions like the table provided, you will note that only answer choice **B.** has a positive E° value indicating the spontaneous nature of the reaction. The table provided demonstrates half-reactions written as reduction potentials. In order to write the oxidation, simply reverse the reaction and change the sign of E°:

Oxidation: $Cr^{2+} \rightarrow Cr^{3+} + e^-$ E° = 0.410

Question 48 C

See: CHM 2.3

As one moves across the periodic table, the atomic radius decreases as a result of the increasing effective nuclear charge (*without an increase in the number of atomic orbitals*). In other words, the nucleus becomes more and more positive from left to right on the periodic table resulting in the drawing of negatively charged orbital electrons nearer and nearer to the nucleus. As a result, atoms will accept electrons more readily as we go across the periodic table and the electron affinity (EA) becomes more negative (*less positive*). For example, halogens have very negative EA values because of their strong tendencies to form anions. Alkaline earths have positive EA values.

Question 49 A

See: CHM 4.2, 4.3.2

Any dipole-dipole interaction (ie, due to the separation of charges or difference in electronegativities between H and Cl) present requires energy to be broken before the HCl can enter the gaseous phase, thereby making HCl more difficult to boil (*i.e. the boiling point is elevated*). Neither Cl_2 nor H_2 have a separation in charge. Note that for the molecule HF, the boiling point is even greater due to H-bonding which is an even stronger intermolecular force than simple dipole-dipole interactions.

Question 50 C

See: CHM 4.2, ORG 10.1

Ethers possess a highly electronegative atom (*oxygen*), but no hydrogen atom is directly bonded to an oxygen or any other electronegative atom. As a result, another molecule with an electropositive hydrogen (i.e. water) can form hydrogen bonds with the oxygen atom of an ether, but the ether's hydrogen atoms will not be involved in hydrogen bonding.

Question 51 B

See: CHM 4.1.7

Keep in mind that: Partial pressure = Mole fraction × Total pressure

Since the total pressure is 100 atm, the mole fraction of 0.40 for HCl represents 40 atm; we are given 35 atm for Cl_2, thus 100 – (40 + 35) = 25 atm.

Question 52 E

See: CHM 11.4

Using Fraction of activity remaining = (Final activity)/(Initial activity)

Fraction of activity remaining = (10.8 dpm g^{-1})/(43.0 dpm g^{-1}) = 1/4, approximately

Using Fraction of activity remaining = $(1/2)^{\text{number of half-lives}}$

$1/4 = (1/2)^x$, thus x = 2

Question 53 D

See: CHM 11

Recall that an alpha particle is a helium nucleus (^4_2He) and a beta particle is an electron ($^0_{-1}e^-$).

Equation I: $^{238}_{92}U \rightarrow ^x_yZ + 3\,^4_2He + 2\,^0_{-1}e^- + 3$ (gamma rays)

Since the sum of the atomic numbers and mass numbers on either side of the equation must be equal:

$238 = x + (3 \times 4) + (2 \times 0) + (3 \times 0)$

$x = 226$

$92 = y + (3 \times 2) + (2 \times -1) + (3 \times 0)$

$y = 88$

Thus, from the answer choices, Z = Ra; note that gamma rays are a form of electromagnetic radiation (CHM 11) and thus have no charge and no mass.

Question 54 B

See: CHM 10.1, 10.2

Written as standard reduction potentials, we get:

$O_2 + 2H_2O + 4e^- \leftrightarrow 4OH^-$ $E^o = +0.401$ V Cathode (gain of electrons)

$2Fe^{2+} + 4e^- \leftrightarrow 2Fe$ $E^o = -0.440$ V Anode (loss of electrons)

$E^o_{reaction} = E^o_{reduction} - E^o_{oxidation}$

$E^o_{reaction} = +0.401 - (-0.440) = +0.841$ V

Question 55 D

See: CHM 5.3.2

Equation: $FeX_2 \leftrightarrow Fe^{2+} + 2X^-$

Solubility s can be calculated using the above equation and $K_{sp} = [Fe^{2+}][X^-]^2$:

$K_{sp} = (s)(2s)^2 = 4s^3$

Thus $s^3 = (K_{sp}/4) = (5.0 \times 10^{-16})/4 = (1.25 \times 10^{-16})$

$= 0.125 \times 10^{-15} = 1/8 \times 10^{-15}$

s = [cube root (1/8)] × [cube root (10^{-15})] = $1/2 \times 10^{-5}$

= 5.0×10^{-6} mol L^{-1}

The calculation can be done in under a minute without a calculator.

Question 56 D

See: CHM 3.5

P: 3 bonds

Phosphorus is in Group V. It can therefore either have a valency of 3 or 5 (*you can memorize this or determine it through VSEPR modeling*). Answer choice **D.**, which has three bonds to each phosphorous, is the only answer which fulfils this requirement.

Question 57 E

See: CHM 2.4, 2.4.1

Metals have high melting points and densities. They are excellent conductors of heat and electricity due to their valence electrons being able to move freely. This fact also accounts for the major characteristic properties of metals: large atomic radius, low ionization energy, high electron affinities and low electronegativity. Groups IA and IIA are the most reactive of all metal species. Of course, metals tend to be shiny and solid (with the exception of mercury, Hg, a liquid at STP). They are also ductile (they can be drawn into thin wires) and malleable (they can be easily hammered into very thin sheets). Metals form positive ions by losing electrons.

Metalloids (or semimetals) conduct better than nonmetals but not as well as metals.

Question 58 C

See: CHM 1.1-1.5

Let us use the process of elimination. Answer choice **A.** is false because it would support a lighted splint (*translation: fire burns in the presence of oxygen!*). Answer choice **B.** (molecular weight or MW = 28 g/mol) is somewhat lighter that air which is mostly nitrogen (78%, MW = 28 g/mol) with oxygen (21%, MW = 32 g/mol). Answer choice **D.** is really an anion (*carbonate*) not a gas (P2) and answer choice **E.** is a solid. Thus we are left with carbon dioxide (MW = 44 g/mol) which is heavier than air and does not support a lighted splint.

Question 59 B

See: CHM 2.3

Lithium only has one valent electron (Group I, PT; CHM 2.3). Therefore, one would expect only one covalent bond per lithium atom with no extra valent electrons on the lithium (that is, no lone pairs nor single electrons).

Question 60 D

See: CHM 10.4

A is the positively charged electrode i.e. anode in the diagram so the electrolyte used is irrelevant.

Question 61 E

See: CHM 6.9

Since the pH is less than the pK_a of the indicator, the undissociated form predominates.

$pH = 2; pK_a = -\log K_a = -\log(4 \times 10^{-4}) = 4 - \log(4) > 2$

{for the math see CHM 6.5.1, and the end of CHM 6.6.1}

Since the pH of the solution is less than the pK_a of the indicator, reduced pH means increased $[H^+]$, looking at Reaction I and remembering Le Chatelier's Principle, if the stress is on the right side of the equilibrium (i.e. increased $[H^+]$), the reaction shifts to the left which gives the red color (i.e. increased [HMe]).

Going Deeper: Note that from the math described, we know that the pK_a of methyl orange must be between 3 and 4 which suggests that if the pH of the solution is 2, it must be red, if it a pH of 5 (for example), it must be yellow. However, if the pH is between 3 and 4, the color would be a combination of yellow and red which would mean orange. Normally, indicators switch between their 2 colors (i.e. red and yellow in this example) over a pH range of about 2.

Question 62 E

See: CHM 1.5.1, 5.2, 6.2, 6.9.1

Answer choice **A.** can be eliminated since the oxidation numbers of the atoms in the reactants and products remain constant (CHM 1.6). A neutralization (answer choice **B.**) would involve an acid/base reaction, however, only acid is present in the equation. The precipitation of sulfur involves the replacement of the chlorine atoms with sulfur (CHM 1.5.1; cf. CHM 5.2, 6.2, 6.9.1) to form FeS(s), and, the replacement of sulfur atoms with chlorine to form HCl (= double replacement; CHM 1.5.1, also called *metathesis*).

Question 63 C

See: CHM 2.1, 2.2, 2.3

The roman numerals of the Group A atoms (which include the metals; see CHM 2.3F) indicate the number of electrons in the outer shell of the atom. In this case, both answer choices **B.** and **C.** have 2 valence electrons; however, answer choice **B.** represents the structure of He, a nonmetal. Answer choice **E.** has a d orbital. Keep in mind that in general, a transition metal is one which forms one or more stable ions which have incompletely filled d orbitals. Thus answer choice **E.** is Cr (not a Group II metal) but the more stable state would have the d orbital half filled thus $3d^5$, $4s^1$.

Question 64 B

See: CHM 6.1

K_{a2} is the expression describing the further dissociation of the conjugate base from the K_{a1} expression; in other words, the dissociation of the second proton. For the reaction:

$HS^- \rightarrow H^+ + S^{2-}$

K_{a2} = [products] / [reactants] = $[H^+][S^{2-}] / [HS^-]$.

Question 65 D

See: E; CHM 8.10

$\Delta G = \Delta H - T\Delta S$

"The sublimation of carbon dioxide occurs quickly at room temperature" means that it is spontaneous and so ΔG must be negative (by definition). Sublimation means:

Solid CO_2 + heat $\rightarrow$ vapor

Entropy (randomness) is clearly increasing (thus positive ΔS) because we are moving from a structured, ordered solid to randomly moving gas particles. Heat is required so it is endothermic meaning ΔH is positive. The question is asking about the reverse reaction so all 3 signs are reversed: ΔG is now positive; ΔH is now negative; ΔS is now negative.

Going deeper: Notice that a negative ΔS multiplied by a $-T$ (see the Gibbs free energy equation) creates a positive term which overshadows the effect of the negative ΔH and thus ΔG is still positive. Also, please keep in mind that sometimes the real DAT will provide the Gibbs free energy equation but sometimes they won't.

Question 66 E

See: CHM 8.7

The easiest way to objectively answer the question is to round the figures which can be done because the values of the specific heats are so far apart thus: 4 J/g•°C for water and 1 J/g•°C for glass. Using dimensional analysis (paying attention to the units):

Water: (40 J)/(4 J/g•°C) = 10 °C for 1 gram.

Glass: (40 J)/(1 J/g•°C) = 40 °C for 1 gram.

Question 67 A

See: CHM 5.1.1, 5.1.2

This question tests your understanding of *colligative properties.* From the equation

$T_b = K_B m$, where K_B is constant, or the molality is the factor to be considered. Recall that m = (Number of moles solute)/(1000 g solvent) and number of moles = (Mass of substance present)/(Relative molecular mass). Since glucose has a smaller relative molecular mass than sucrose, there will be a greater number of moles of glucose present when equal masses of the two substances are used. Therefore, the molality of glucose is greater and hence the boiling point elevation is greater.

Question 68 A

See: CHM 4.1.2, 4.1.8

A gas most closely approaches ideality at very low pressures (*thus making the relative volume that the gas particles occupy and the attractive forces between them negligible*) and at high temperatures (*so that the energy loss in inelastic collisions is negligible*). {*Plow and Thigh !*}

Question 69 C

See: CHM 9.3

By looking at Table 1, we can see that when the concentration of X is quadrupled (factor of 4^1) while [Y] is unchanged (Exp. 1 and 3), the rate is increased by a factor of $4 = 4^1$. Thus the order of the reaction with respect to X is 1. When the concentration of Y is doubled (factor of 2^1) while [X] remains the same (Exp. 1 and 2), the rate of reaction is quadrupled (factor of $4 = 2^2$). Thus, the order of reaction with respect to Y is 2. The rate equation is Rate = [X] $[Y]^2$. {*Notice that the stoichiometric coefficients are not relevant*}

Question 70 A

See: CHM 12.3.1

A buret would be better but a graduated cylinder is by far the best on the list.

Question 71 A

See: ORG 2.1, 2.2, 2.3

A chiral carbon or stereogenic carbon center (or stereocenter) must be bonded to 4 different substituents. For this reason, ignore all carbons with double bonds (notice double bonds in the rings labeled A and C) and ignore all carbons bonded to hydrogen twice (some in rings B and E). We are left with 5 centers of chirality which are all in rings B and C (C5, C6, C9, C13 and C14; note that 13 is not labeled in the diagram but it is clearly in ring B between 12 and 14).

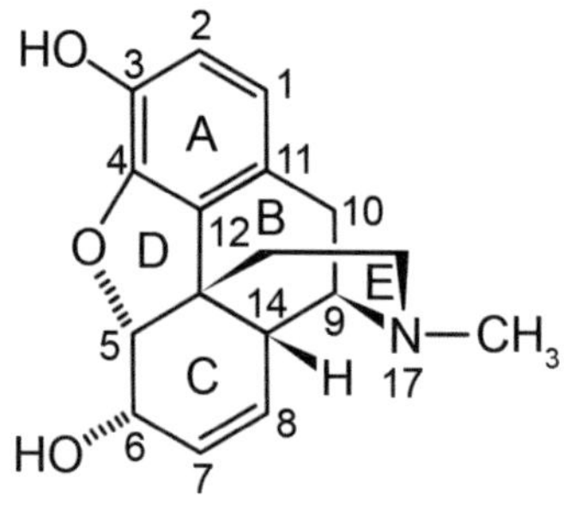

Question 72 E

See: D; ORG 1.6, 7.1, 8.1, 9.4

Keep in mind that alkyl lithiums and Grignard reagents (i.e. RMgBr) general partially negative carbons which will be attracted to partially positive carbons thus creating carbon-carbon bonds.

First identify the compound as 4-propyl-4-octanol and consider quickly sketching it in a way that resembles the tertiary alcohol in the mechanism provided so that you can more easily compare the various R groups. Doing so reveals 2 propyl groups attached to the central carbon meaning that there is either a propyl lithium or propyl MgBr (Grignard) being used. The 4-propyl-4-octanol also has a butyl group (R') which must originate from the ester thus it must be pentanoate. The nature of R" is irrelevant since it is part of the leaving group and thus is not found in the product.

The General Reaction Mechanism:

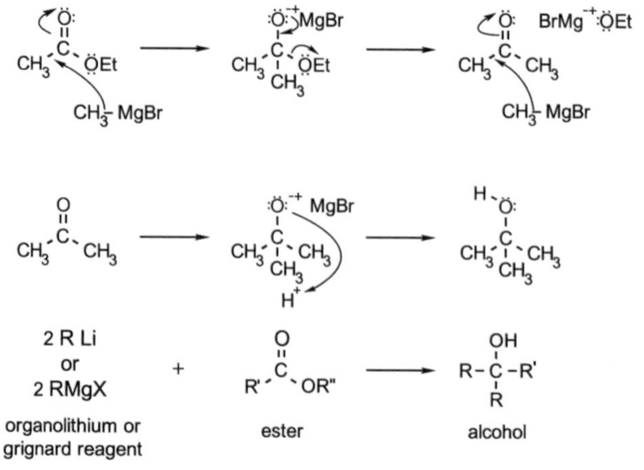

In case you were tripped up by nomenclature, here is hexyl pentanoate:

Question 73 A

See: CHM 6.3, ORG 1.6, 4.2.1, 6.2.4, 11.1.1

A base can be defined as a proton (H^+) acceptor. The strongest base would more likely carry a negative charge (opposites attract) and would create the most stable product. Alkanes are very stable and it is extremely difficult to remove a proton. Furthermore, primary anions (I) are extremely unstable thus it strongly wants a proton. This is followed by an ethoxide group (II) and then a compound that does not even have a negative charge (III; it has an electronegative N which would not be as attractive for a proton as a negatively charged O or C).

Question 74 D

See: ORG 4.2, 7.1, 8.1, 14.1

This question tests your memory of a couple of the IR absorption peaks. The absolute minimum to memorize are the bands for an alcohol (OH, 3200 – 3650) and that for the carbonyl group (C = O, 1630 – 1780) because these are the two most encountered functional groups in DAT organic chemistry.

Bottle II has a peak at 1710 (carbonyl) 3333 - 3500 (hydroxyl) = carboxylic acid (i.e. benzoic acid). Bottle IV has a peak at 3333 so it must be the alcohol. Without doing anything else, there is only one possible answer, **D**.

{*For fun, draw the structures of the four compounds*; allyl, ORG 4.2, add -OH to make it an alcohol; benzoic acid - ORG 8.1; the four carbon ketone 2-butanone (= *methyl ethyl ketone*) and the four carbon aldehyde butyraldehyde (= *butanal*) - ORG 7.1}

Question 75 D

See: ORG 1.1, 8.1

Formic acid (HCOOH) is a carboxylic acid whose structure is shown by answer choice **D**. Note that answer choices **A**., **B**. and **E**. can be quickly discounted because carbon needs to form 4 bonds to be neutral (ORG 1.1). Similarly, oxygen needs 2 bonds to be neutral, eliminating answer choice **B**.

Question 76 B

See: CHM 6.3, ORG 5.2.2, 10.2

When a compound becomes more acidic, Ka increases (CHM 6.3) thus pKa decreases because pKa = – log Ka. That's all!

The following information is for the curious minded (!) but was certainly not needed in order to answer the question: (i) substituents affect the acidity of phenols (ORG 10.2); (ii) halides (i.e. Br) are weakly deactivating groups but they are O-P Directors (ORG 5.2.2); (iii) activating groups (O-P Directors except halides) decrease the acidity of the phenol (ORG 10.2); (iv) in summary, where EDG = electron donating group and EWG = electron withdrawing group, we get:

EDG	EWG	EWG: Halogens
activates the ring	deactivates the ring	weakly deactivating
O/P Directing	Meta Directing	O/P Directing
i.e. alkyl groups	i.e. nitro ($-NO_2$)	i.e. bromine
acid weakening	acid strengthening	acid strengthening
increase pKa	decrease pKa	decrease pKa

The Reasoning: Electron withdrawing groups can stabilize the negative charge on oxygen which encourages oxygen to lose a proton (i.e. become more acidic). One more time for fun! When a compound becomes more acidic, Ka increases (CHM 6.3) thus pKa decreases because pKa = – log Ka. That's all!

Question 77 C

See: ORG 7.2.2

This question provides us with only one answer which could possibly have the correct geometry! Nonetheless, let's work through the mechanism.

The story goes something like this: The catalyst (H^+), being the most charged substance is implicated first. Thus the electrons from the electronegative oxygen (O in the carbonyl, C = O) are attracted to the proton (H^+) and bonds. To remain neutral oxygen loses its pi bond with carbon, leaving only a single bond and secondary carbocation. The δ – charge on the oxygen from the *diol* (= a compound with 2 alcohol – OH – groups) attacks the positively charged carbocation. The extra hydrogen on the oxygen which now attaches to carbon is kicked out as a proton (regenerating our catalyst). Now we have our "*hemi-ketal*": the ketone has been converted into a hydroxyl group and the diol (*minus one hydrogen*).

Next, the proton strikes again! It can be attracted to the hydroxyl group which falls off as water (*a great leaving group*), thus we have a secondary carbocation, again. Now we have a partial negative charge (the oxygen of the free arm of the diol) and a positive charge (the carbocation) in close proximity in the same molecule! In a very fast *intra*molecular reaction, the nucleophile meets the carbon nucleus and regenerates the proton catalyst. The product is answer choice **C**., a ketal.

Question 78 D

See: ORG 13.3, CHM 12

Overheating may destroy the pure compounds or increase the percent impurities. Some of the methods which are classically used to prevent overheating include boiling slowly, the use of boiling chips (= ebulliator, which makes bubbles) and the use of a vacuum which decreases the vapor pressure and thus the boiling point. A nucleophile could only create unwanted products and thus prevent the isolation of a pure product from the original mixture.

Going Deeper: Boiling chips, or boiling stones, are small chunks of inert material. A few are added to a liquid before it is heated and they tend to promote steady, even boiling. In theory, a liquid should boil when it is heated at its boiling point. The temperature should remain constant because the excess heat is dissipated in overcoming the heat of vaporization required to move liquid molecules into the gas phase. In practice, spontaneous formation of gas bubbles within the liquid can be slow which could lead to super-heating and ultimately, large violent bubbles. Boiling chips produce small gas bubbles where the liquid molecules can evaporate and initiate boiling at a steady even rate.

Question 79 B

See: CHM 3.5, ORG 3.3, 10.1

Since epoxides are by definition 3-membered rings, they will have the same geometry as cyclopropane. Hence, their bond angles should be 60° (ORG 3.3).

Question 80 C

See: ORG 7.1

The α carbon is the carbon adjacent to the carbon of the carbonyl group of the molecule and it has increased acidity because of the resonance stabilization of the anion.

Note that the carboxylic acid hydrogen is the most acidic hydrogen of this molecule but that hydrogen is not directly bonded to a carbon.

Question 81 A

See: ORG 13.2.1

If the material in the GLC absorbs each compound equally well, then they cannot be separated by this method.

Note that GLC is similar to fractional distillation - both processes separate the components of a mixture primarily based on boiling point (or vapor pressure) differences. Fractional distillation is usually used to separate components of a mixture on a large scale, whereas GLC can be used on a much smaller scale. Neither is directly dependent on the melting point.

Question 82 A

See: ORG 12.1.2

This is a common type of DAT question. You should be familiar with the concept of isoelectric point from the organic chemistry review.

The isoelectric point is defined as the pH at which an amino acid is immobile in an electric field due to the neutrality of the molecule (note that the negative charge on the carboxyl group cancels out the positive charge on the amino group). If we are in a medium which is more acidic (= lower pH) than the isoelectric point, the carboxyl group will become protonated to give a molecule with an overall positive charge. At a pH greater than the isoelectric point, the amino group will lose its proton and give a negatively charged methionine.

Note that the acidic component ($-COOH$) of the amino acid acted like an acid by donating a proton (and becoming $-COO^-$). The basic component of the amino acid ($-NH_2$) acted like a base and received a proton ($-NH_3^+$). But overall, being the isoelectric point, the molecule is neutral.

Question 83 C

See: ORG 14.2

Observe that the ^{1}H NMR spectrum has 3 groups of lines or peaks; thus there are 3 groups of chemically equivalent protons. Additionally, since the relative areas of the peaks is 3:2:3, the number of protons in the groups is in the ratio 3:2:3.

Next, there is spin-spin splitting in two of the peaks. One peak is a triplet, indicating the presence of 2 adjacent non-equivalent protons. The other peak is a quadruplet, indicating the presence of 3 adjacent non-equivalent protons. Since the 3rd peak is not split, the protons that caused it must not be adjacent to any non-equivalent protons. The only choice consistent with these requirements is $CH_3CH_2COOCH_3$.

Question 84 E

See: ORG 3.1, 4.1

$CH_3CH_2CH(CH_3)CH(CH(CH_3)_2)CH_2CH{=}C(CH_3)_2$

- Eliminate **D** by noticing at the right end of the molecule there is a double bond followed by a **C** with 2 methyl groups attached. The location of the double bond also helps to orient the direction of the molecule and avoid potential traps.
- In the middle of the molecule, there are 2 methyl groups attached to a CH which is in turn attached to a CH so this eliminates answer **C**: $CH(CH(CH_3)_2)$
- And finally, to the far left, **A** and **B** start as though the molecule has 2 methyl groups attached to a CH which is incorrect since the molecule begins with 1 methyl: CH_3CH_2
- Of course, you can come to the solution any way you are comfortable but this is one systematic way to avoid traps.

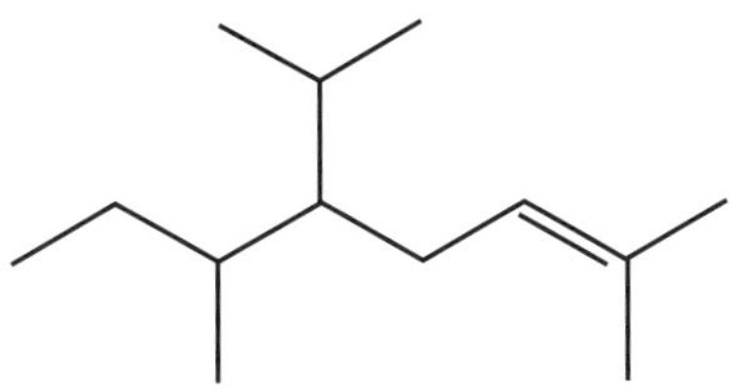

Question 85 C

See: ORG 13

All of the answer choices are useful to help an extraction to occur except answer choice **C**. Ideally, a solvent dissolves the solute (for example, when you add salt in water) but you do not expect nor would the objective be to create a molecule between the water and the solute because that would change the nature of the solute (i.e. salt or caffeine, etc).

Aside: it is important to note that it is more efficient to perform several small extractions using a small amount of solvent each time rather than one extraction using a large amount of solvent.

Question 86 C

See: ORG 2.1, 2.2, 2.3

Two of the structures below are (Z)–2–butene and (E)–2–butene which are stereoisomers of each other, not structural isomers. They have the same molecular formula, same connectivity, but different spatial arrangement. These would constitute stereoisomers thus there would be only 5 structural isomers in all. See isomers below:

1. (E) and (Z) 2–butene;
2. 1–butene;
3. 2–methyl–propene;
4. cyclobutane; and,
5. methyl–cyclopropane (not illustrated)

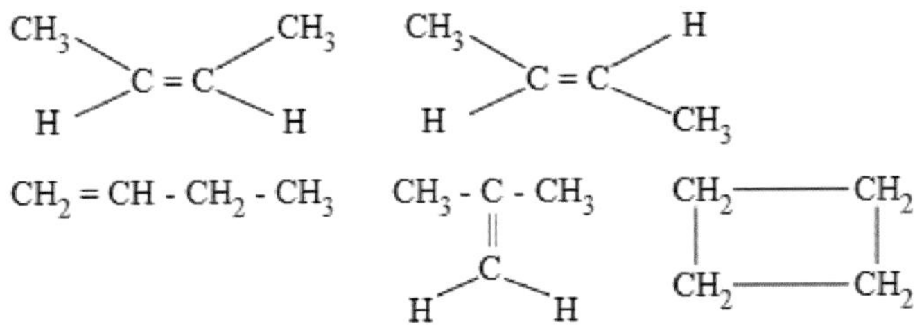

$CH_3(H)C=C(H)CH_3$ (cis) $CH_3(H)C=C(H)CH_3$ (trans)

$CH_2=CH-CH_2-CH_3$ $CH_3-C(=CH_2)-CH_3$ $CH_2-CH_2-CH_2-CH_2$ (ring)

Question 87 E

See: ORG 6.2.4

This is Elimination 1st order, E1, meaning that: (a) 2 atoms will be eliminated from the original molecule (turning a single bond into a double bond); and (b) the "1" means that the rate determining step depends on the concentration of 1 molecule. The rate determining step (RDS) is the slowest step in a reaction mechanism.

1. FAST: the proton is attracted to the partial negative charge on oxygen in –OH forming a great leaving group (water). Answer **B**.
2. SLOWEST: the oxygen in the water substituent pulls electrons away from the central carbon to get rid of its formal positive charge and now neutral water leaves the tertiary carbocation. Answers **A** and **D**.
3. FAST: electrons in a neighboring C–H bond are attracted to the carbocation forming a C = C bond and kicking out the proton which is regenerated (= catalyst).

Question 88 E

See: ORG 7.2.3

This is a typical imine formation, which involves the nucleophilic attack of the amino hydrogen on the central carbonyl carbon of the reactant on the left, followed by a dehydration. Since H_2O is being removed, this reaction is considered a dehydration, not a decarboxylation (= loss of CO_2). In addition, answer choice **C**. is incorrect because cleavage would consist of the reverse reaction (i.e. the formation of two molecules from one, through the breaking of bonds). The N and C in the imine are sp^2 hybridized, eliminating answer choice **D**. An enamine is formed when a secondary amine is used but the reaction in this problem uses a primary amine.

Question 89 A

See: ORG 2.3.1, 2.3.2, 2.3.3

A stereogenic or chiral carbon is a carbon atom which is asymmetric which means that it is attached to four different atoms or groups. Having a chiral carbon is usually a prerequisite for a molecule to have chirality, though the presence of a chiral carbon does not necessarily make a molecule chiral (i.e. a meso compound). A meso compound has an internal plane of symmetry which bisects the molecule and thus it displays no optical activity.

The 1st and 4th molecules happen to be named pentane-2,3,4-triol or 2,3,4-pentanetriol. Notice the position of the chiral carbons (asterix *) as well as the absence of an internal plane of symmetry. Notice that if the molecule was folded along the dotted line, the top part would not match the bottom part: no symmetry within the molecule.

Going Deeper: the following information would not affect your answer but it will help to train your eyes. Keep in mind that a Fisher projection is a 2D way to represent 3D molecules in which all horizontal lines are actually pointing towards the viewer. Notice the perspective of the viewer we placed above the 3D image of the molecule. Notice that the first OH group is to the left of the viewer which you can see in the Fisher projection also. It is also easy to see why the 3rd OH group is to the right of the viewer. But notice the 2nd OH group (on carbon–3) in the 3D representation of the molecule is pointing away from the viewer. But in order to do a Fisher projection, the horizontal groups must point towards the viewer. The only way to do this is to rotate the bond 180 degrees so that they point towards the viewer but, of course, the 2nd OH now ends up on the right side.

The second molecule happens to be named 1,3–difluorocyclohexane. Notice the position of the chiral carbons (asterix *) as well as the internal plane of symmetry (meso compound). Notice that each chiral carbon is attached to: (1) **H**; (2) **F**; (3) a carbon attached to a carbon attached to **F**; (4) a carbon attached to a carbon that is not attached to **F**.

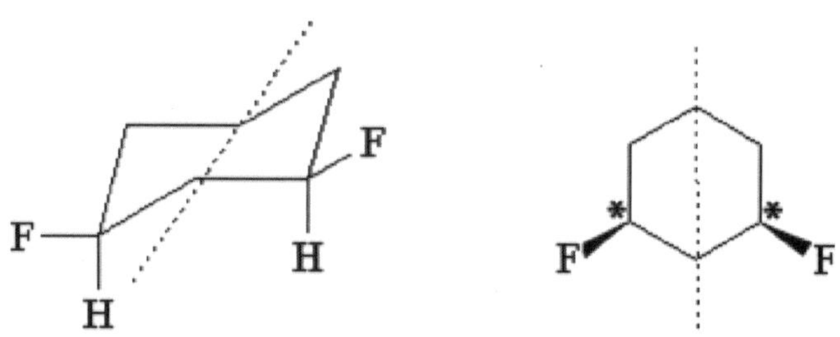

The 3rd molecule has 2 chiral carbons * but has an internal plane of symmetry (meso). Notice that the ring has a double bond on the right side but none on the left: this fact is important to understand how the 2 carbons became chiral.

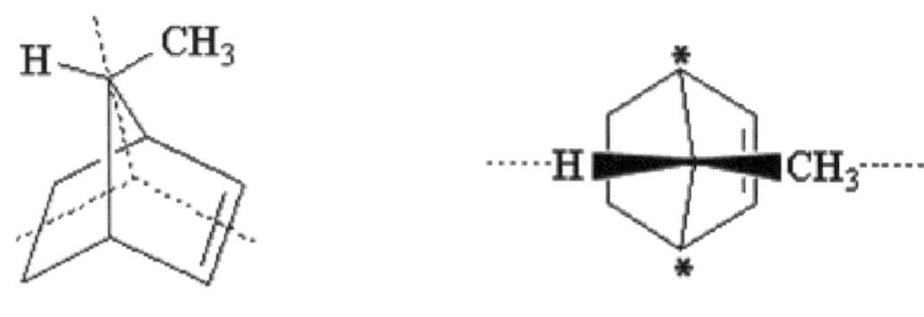

The fourth molecule (pentane-2,3,4-triol) shows an internal plane of symmetry with chiral carbons noted *.

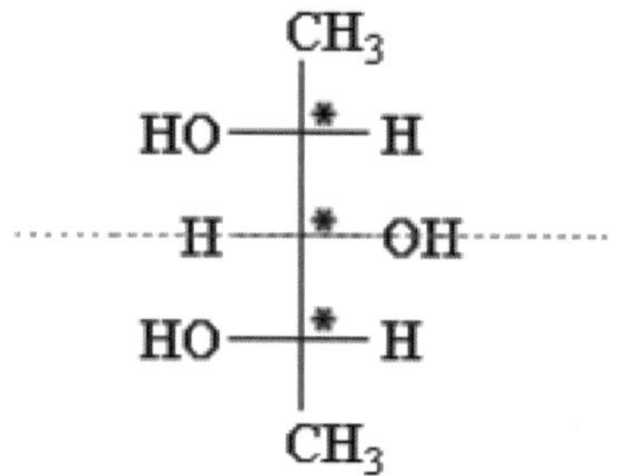

Question 90 B

See: ORG 4.2.1

This question asks us to remember 'Mark's rule': alkene + acid → under ionic conditions (i.e. no: uv, hf, increased energy/heat), hydrogen adds preferentially to where its buddies are (= *the greatest number of other H's at the double bond* = a simplification of Markovnikoff's rule. Thus answer choice **B.** is the major product and **A.** is the minor product.

Question 91 C

See: CHM 9.5, 9.7, 9.8, 9.10, ORG 6.2.1

This question tests your understanding of a catalyst: they speed up the rate of a reaction (kinetics), they decrease the activation energy, they do not affect K_{eq}, they are not used up in a reaction, and finally, they do not affect thermodynamics, ΔG^o (CHM 9.5, 9.7, 9.8, 8.10). If you're interested in dehydration of alcohols (!) see ORG 6.2.1.

Question 92 C

See: CHM 8.2, 8.10, 9.5

When a compound reacts with the solvent, the process is referred to as a *solvolysis* reaction.

Because of the stability of tertiary compounds, one compound is in rate-determining step: t–butyl bromide in solution can simply dissociate into Br^- and the stable t–butyl .

Now a nucleophile would be happy to *quickly* mate with the positive carbocation (*nucleophilic substitution, first*** order* = S_N1). If the nucleophile is hydroxide, or water, then the product would be the tertiary alcohol tert–butanol $(CH_3)_3C$-OH {*note –OH substituted –Br*}. If the nucleophile is ethoxide, or ethanol, then the product would be the ether $(CH_3)_3C$-OCH_2CH_3. {*The preceding product can be named t–butyl ethyl ether, or, ethoxy t–butane*; see ORG 10.1}

The solvolysis reaction occurs spontaneously, which means $\Delta G < 0$, which also means that the great likelihood is that $\Delta H < 0$. The latter is called an *exothermic* reaction. Since energy is released, the reactants must have a higher energy and the products must have a lower energy. The only possible answers are **A.** and **C.** However, the intermediate in **A.** has a low energy which indicates stability implying that any further reaction is not likely to be spontaneous (from the mechanism just described we know this to be false, untrue and unpleasant to hear!). Answer choice **C.** suggests a higher energy intermediate which would be happy to engage in a further reaction to create a low energy, very stable final product.

Question 93 E

See: ORG 3.3, 12.3.2 F

This question tests two concepts.

1. Just like atoms or molecules, groups attached to a ring have electrons in their outermost shells. Like charges

repel. Thus *electron shell repulsion* means substituents want to be maximally apart.

2. There are two positions for substituents of a ring: *axial* and *equatorial*. Equatorial substituents are maximally apart.

Question 94 C

See: CHM 3.5; ORG 1.2, 1.3
C1 is the first carbon in cyclic coniine which is the carbon in the ring attached to the propyl substituent (or ligand). It has 4 bonds: 1 to propyl, one to N, one to the carbon in the ring 'above' and one bond to H which is not shown in the structure but assumed to be there in this neutral molecule. Thus 4 bonds to carbon (1s + 3p) must be $4sp^3$ hybridized bonds.

For your interest: notice that C1 is the only chiral carbon in coniine.

Question 95 B

See: ORG 4.2.4
The Diels–Alder reaction is a cycloaddition reaction between a conjugated diene and a substituted alkene (= the dienophile) to form a substituted cyclohexene system.

Diene + dienophile = cyclohexene

All Diels-Alder reactions have four common features: (1) the reaction is initiated by heat; (2) the reaction forms new six-membered rings; (3) three π bonds break and two new C–C σ bonds and one new C–C π bond are formed; (4) all bonds break and form in a single step.

The Diels Alder diene must have the two double bonds on the same side of the single bond in one of the structures, which is called the s-cis conformation (s–cis: cis with respect to the single bond). If double bonds are on the opposite sides of the single bond in the Lewis structure, this is called the s-trans conformation (s-trans: trans with respect to the single bond).

Answer choices **C** and **D** can gain the correct s–cis conformation by rotation about a C–C bond. Here is an example:

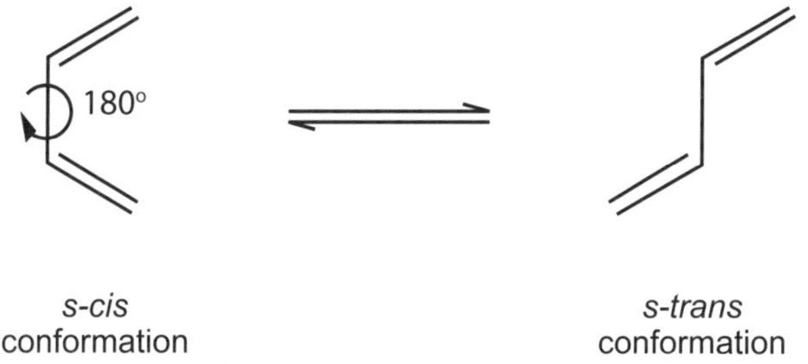

{Side Note: in the preceding equilibrium, 98% would be in the more stable s-trans conformation of 1,3–butadiene (answer choice **D**) in order to minimize electron shell repulsion. Nonetheless, both conformations are possible.}

Notice that the diene in answer choice **B** can never gain the correct conformation because the C–C bond between the alkenes is constrained within the ring. In fact, answer choice **B** is unreactive in a Diels-Alder reaction because 3 methylenecycloxenene is 100% s-trans:

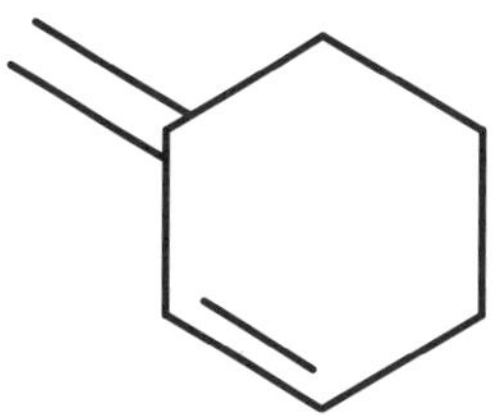

On the other hand, notice that answer choice A, cyclopentadiene, is constrained by the ring and is thus 100% s–cis (i.e. both double bonds are 'permanently' on the same side of the single bond between them):

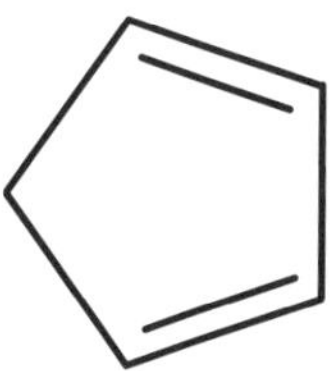

Question 96 A

See: ORG 4.2.2, 6.1, 9.4, 13.1; CHM 12
Distillation is the process by which compounds are separated based on differences in boiling points. Alcohols (1–butanol) have a partially negatively charged oxygen and a partially positively charged hydrogen which can engage in hydrogen bonding which increases the boiling point. Esters (ethyl acetate) have a partially negative oxygen but no partially positive hydrogen so no hydrogen bonding with itself. For this same reason, esters are more volatile than carboxylic acids of similar molecular weight.

Question 97 E

See: CHM 3.5; ORG 1.2, 1.3, 4.1, 4.2
Consider the structure of allene and review the answer choices.

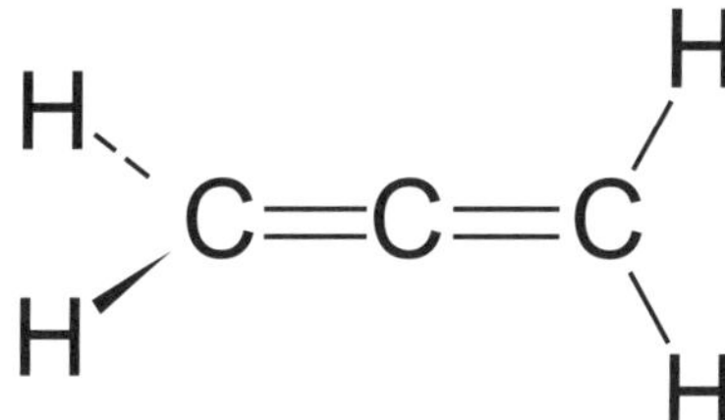

Notice that the 2 carbons at the end of the molecule are in the center of a triangle: trigonal planar 120° sp^2 hybridization with neighboring atoms (ORG 1.2,1.3; CHM 3.5). Notice that the C in the center of allene is in the middle of a line: linear 180° sp hybridization.

Note that dienes can be divided into 3 classes, depending on the relative location of the double bonds:

1. Cumulated dienes, like allene, have the double bonds sharing a common atom.
2. Conjugated dienes, like 1,3–butadiene, have conjugated double bonds separated by one single bond.
3. Unconjugated dienes (= isolated dienes) have the double bonds separated by two or more single bonds. They are usually less stable than isomeric conjugated dienes.

Question 98 E

See: ORG 5.1.1
If a compound does not meet all the following criteria, it is likely not aromatic.

1. The molecule is cyclic.
2. The molecule is planar.
3. The molecule is fully conjugated (p orbitals at every atom in the ring).
4. The molecule has 4n + 2 π electrons.

Notice that the number of π delocalized electrons must be even but NOT a multiple of 4. So 4n + 2 number of π electrons, where n = 0, 1, 2, 3, and so on, is known as Hückel's Rule.

Thus the number of pi electrons can be 2, 6, 10, etc.

Of course, benzene is aromatic (6 electrons, from 3 double bonds), but cyclobutadiene is not, since the number of π delocalized electrons is 4. However, the cyclobutadienide (2–) ion is aromatic (6 electrons).

A, **B**, **C** and **D** are all cyclic and planar. **A**, **B** and **D** have positive charges that will attract the negative pi electrons from neighboring carbons creating resonance forms delocalizing the pi electrons over all carbons in the ring. Answer choice **C** has an extra pair of p orbital electrons and thus, again, all carbons would be involved in the delocalization of pi electrons. In terms of the total number of electrons for each molecule, **A** has 2 π electrons (i.e. 1 double bond), **B** has 6 π electrons, **C** also has 6 π electrons (2 double bonds and 1 lone pair) and **D** has 2 π electrons (i.e. 1 double bond).

Question 99 D

See: ORG 1.6, 5.2, 5.2.1, 5.2.2, 6.2.2, 7.2.3
Note that Me = methyl = CH_3.

Step 1: Friedel Crafts acylation using aluminium chloride produces acetophenone (other names: phenyl methyl ketone, phenylethanone). It is the simplest aromatic ketone.

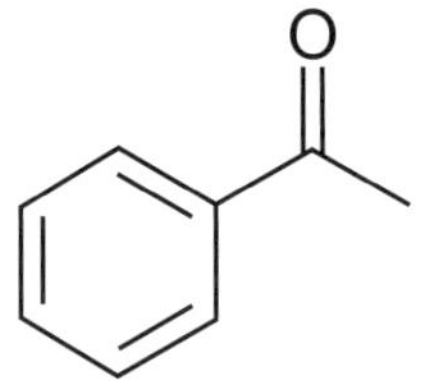

Step 2. When an aldehyde or a ketone reacts with a primary amine, an imine (Schiff base) is formed. Thus the primary amine $MeNH_2$ condenses with acetophenone to form an N-methylimine [Ph(Me)C=NMe] and water as the inorganic by-product.

Step 3. Sodium borohydride, a mild reducing agent compared to lithium aluminium borohydride, reduces the imine turning the double bond into a single bond to give the secondary amine.

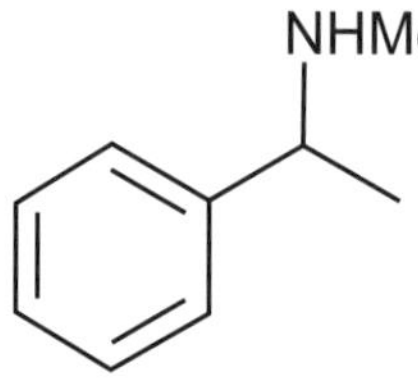

NHMe

Question 100 C

See: CHM 3.5; ORG 1.2, 1.3
First, let's number the carbons in the ring. Oxygen is attached to C1 and so N is attached to C3. So in the original molecule, we see that there are double bonds in the ring between C2 = C3 and C5 = C6. All of the answer choices follow the rules of drawing resonance structures except answer choice **C**. Let's carefully follow the electrons for answer choice **C** and thus we can understand what went wrong.

Our starting material:

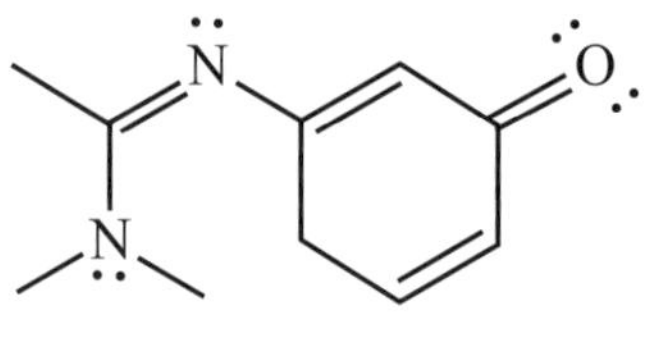

Keep in mind that oxygen is the most electronegative atom in the molecule and thus 'wishes' to withdraw electrons to itself.

1. The nitrogen is positively charged because it contributed its lone pair of electrons to carbon.
2. Carbon's double bond with the 2nd nitrogen breaks and thus nitrogen has a negative charge and an extra lone pair (note: this describes answer choice **B**.).

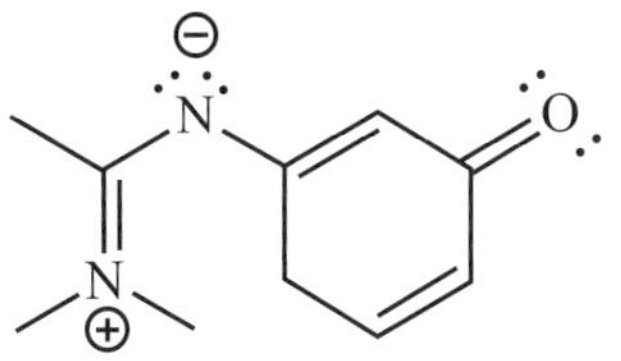

3. Nitrogen's lone pair bonds with C3 which breaks C3 = C2 so now C2 has a lone pair and a formal negative charge (C2 is secondary carbanion and this describes answer choice **D**).

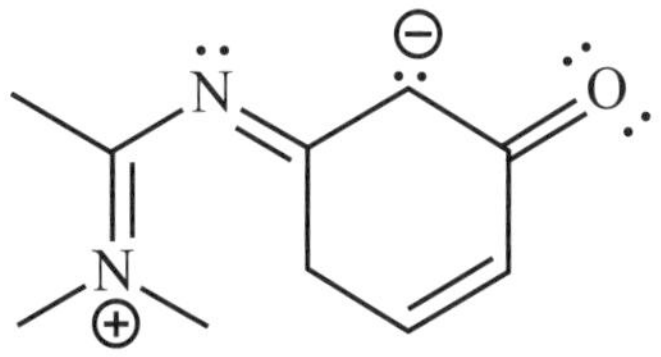

4. Remember that oxygen wants the electrons more than any other atom in this molecule. C2's lone pair bonds with C1 as C = O breaks so now oxygen has the lone pair and the formal negative charge (this describes answer choice **E**).

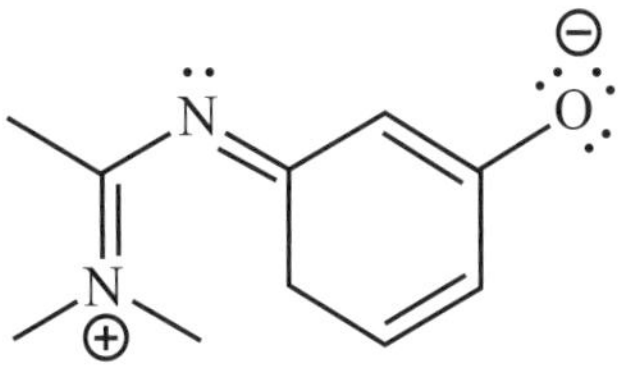

5) We just worked out why answer choice **E** is correct. Well, the only difference between **E** and **C** is that **E** correctly has the double bond C5 = C6 like the starting material but answer choice C incorrectly places the double bond at C4 = C5. That would only be possible if C6 had a + charge and C4 had a – charge.

6) And finally, answer choice **A** is like the starting material except, instead of oxygen pulling electrons from nitrogen along 'the top' (!!) of the molecule, oxygen pulls electrons from the C5 = C6 double bond creating a C6 = C1 double bond, a lone pair on oxygen and a secondary carbocation at C5 (because it lost its bond).

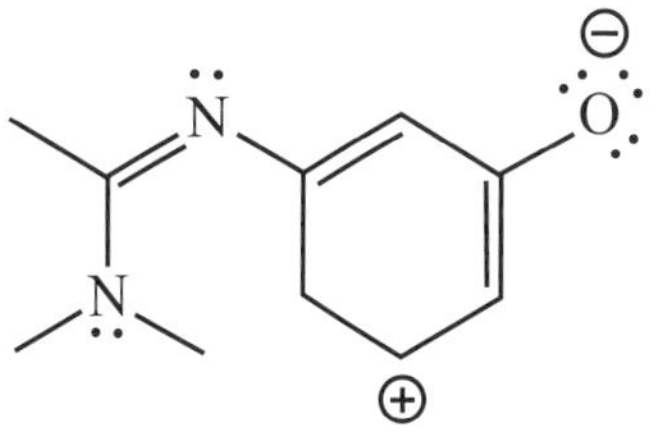

PART 1

Question 1 E

First: *Scan the choices*. The choices seem to be viewed on either front or rear so you focus directly in these sides. You may also rotate the object at different angles. You will instantly identify the correct answer **E**, which is the rear side.

Second: *Check the largest surface area and its details*. Notice that the bottom right, outer curved edge and inner diagonal of the front side becomes the bottom left of the rear side. This eliminates **A**, **B** and **C** choices. Furthermore, the upper left outer diagonal and inner curved edge of the front side becomes the upper right of the rear side.

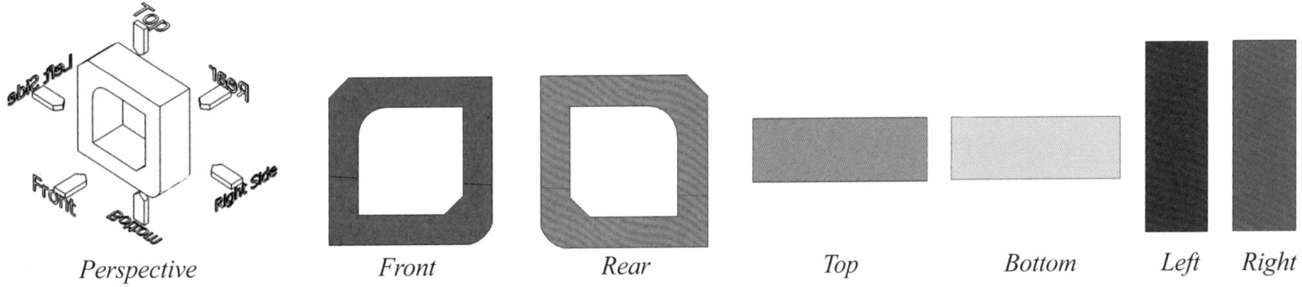

Perspective *Front* *Rear* *Top* *Bottom* *Left* *Right*

Question 2 D

First: *Focus on the outline of the object.* The outline means the silhouette of the object. You can immediately get rid of **C** and **E** since the center hole of the 3D object is obviously a small circle.

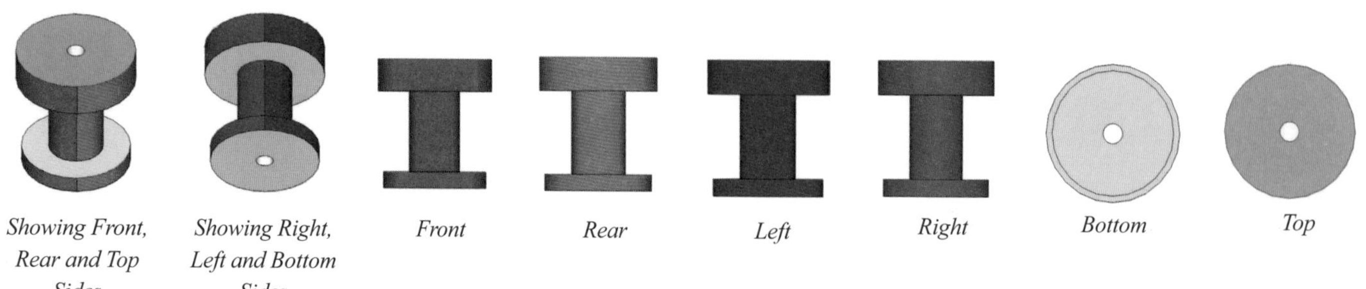

Showing Front, Rear and Top Sides *Showing Right, Left and Bottom Sides* *Front* *Rear* *Left* *Right* *Bottom* *Top*

Second: *Check details.* Observe that the thickness of the bottom cylinder is approximately half of the upper cylinder. The diameter of the hole at the center is about one-eighth of the upper cylinder. You can now readily eliminate choices **A** and **B**, leaving **D** as the answer.

Question 3 D

First: *Consider the standard views.* Examine the 3D object carefully and recognize that it has straight edges. Visualize how the object would look from different standard views. The following illustrations will show that the object's front view is just a mirror image of the rear view. The same with right-left views and bottom-top views.

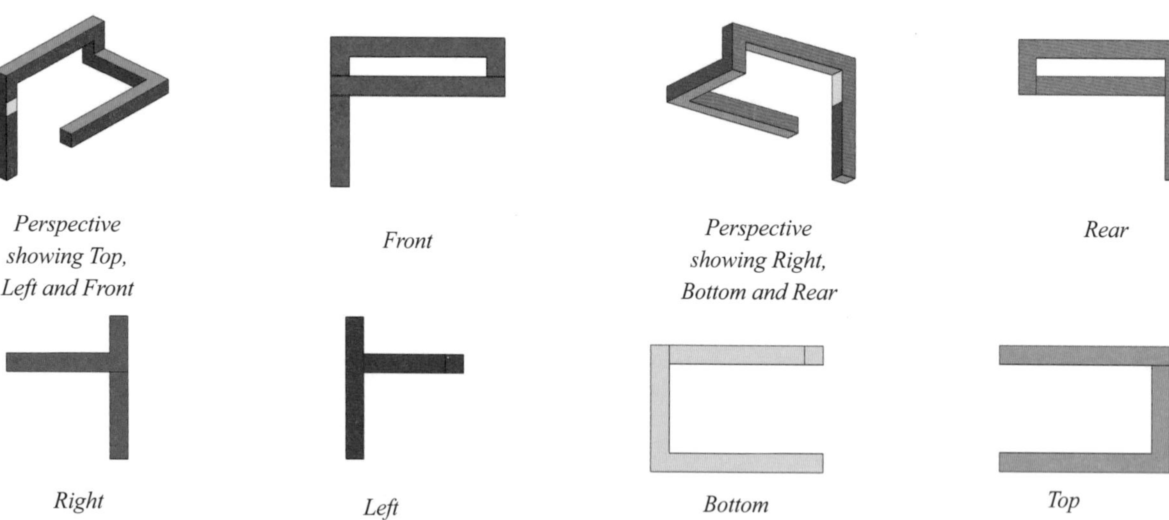

Perspective showing Top, Left and Front *Front* *Perspective showing Right, Bottom and Rear* *Rear*

Right *Left* *Bottom* *Top*

Second (Optional): *Focus on the outline of the 3D object.* You can also look at the outline of the perspective since it is composed of straight lines. Visually trace the continuous straight lines of the object to figure out its outline from different views. You may also try to draw the different views through this outline. At this point, you can spot **D** as the correct answer.

Question 4 B

First: *Determine or estimate the largest part (volume) of the 3D object.* This will aid you in figuring out the main component of the object. From this, associate the other details to the main component which are the smaller ones.

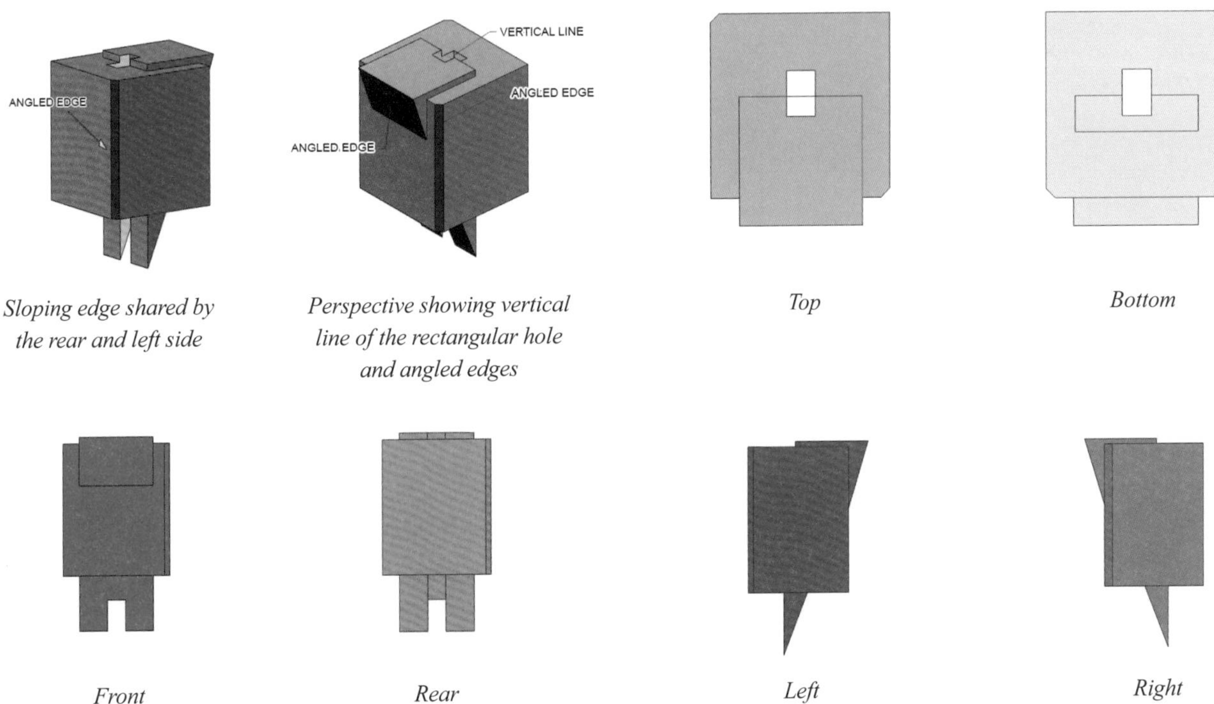

Sloping edge shared by the rear and left side

Perspective showing vertical line of the rectangular hole and angled edges

Top *Bottom*

Front *Rear* *Left* *Right*

Second: *Observe the details.* Do not think that smaller components are insignificant because these are most important. Notice that the main component has a total of six corners and two of them have small dimensions. Another detail appearing is the horizontal area between the two feet-like components at the bottom. Also, the box at the center passes all the way through the 3D object, so it should be reflected in the top and bottom view. The correct answer is **B**.

Question 5 A

First: *Look for slopes*. As observed, there are sloped and curved parts from the top to the rear. These areas should appear on both the rear and left views. It may not be obvious but you have to be observant of the other curve from top to the left side of the 3D object. Other slopes play insignificant roles since there are wider areas behind that cover them.

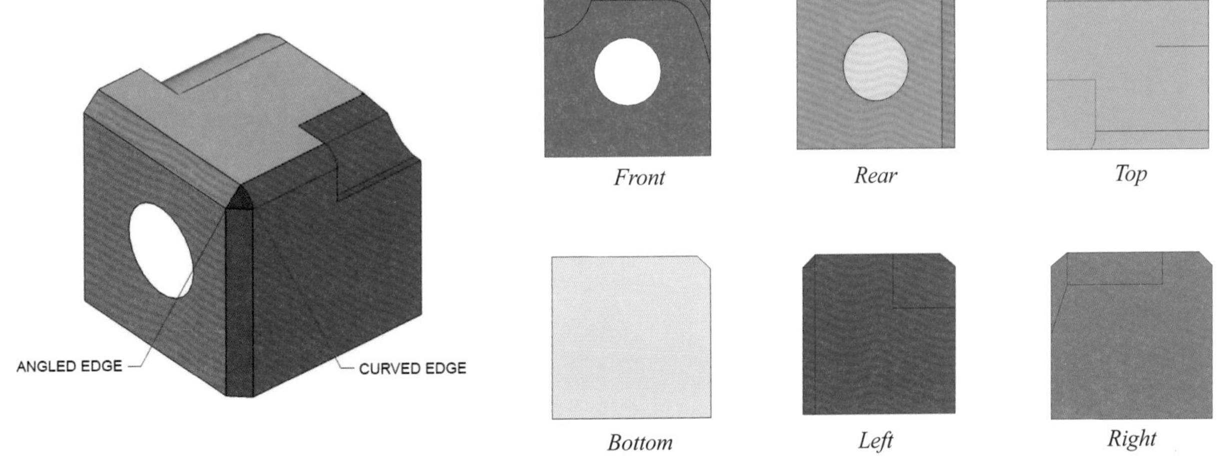

Front *Rear* *Top*

Bottom *Left* *Right*

Second: *Follow the outline of the whole 3D object.* Make sure to include the outline of the hole.

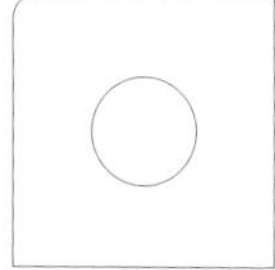
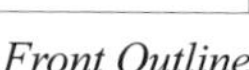
Front Outline

Rear Outline

Top Outline

Bottom Outline

Left Outline

Right Outline

Third: *Check the choices.* If you look at **A**, it has a hole in the center, which means it is either viewed from the front or rear. Be aware that the curve in **A** is located at the upper right, which is the same in the rear view and therefore, the correct answer

Question 6 E

First: *Scan the choices.* All of the choices have overlapping holes within; therefore, you can narrow down your standard views into two: the left and the right sides.

Second: *Sketch or imagine the standard sides.* Remember that if there are sloping edges in the front view, the angled plane should be seen on both the top and left sides or top and right sides. Furthermore, the edges of this shared area are straight when viewed on right and left.

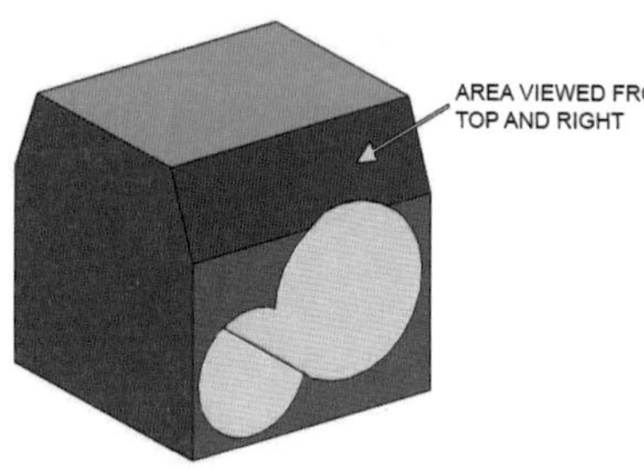

Perspective showing angled areas and hole

Right

Left

Third: *Compare with the choices.* Bear in mind that there are no angled edges on either the right or left side views, which makes Options **C** and **D** wrong. Next, consider the location of the hole with regard to the corners of the right and left views. You can instantly spot the correct match to the left side, which is **E**.

Question 7 B

First: *Focus on the outer outline of the 3D object.* You can start by counting the number of corners which is nine, and the number of sides which is eight. Notice that one of the edges is curved.

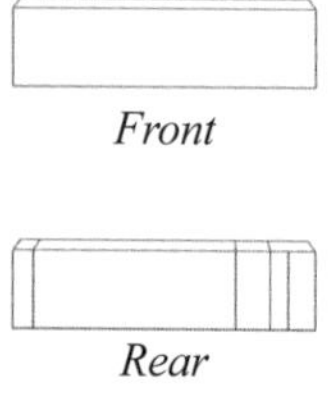
Front

Rear

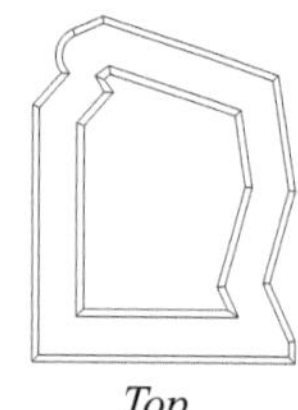
Top

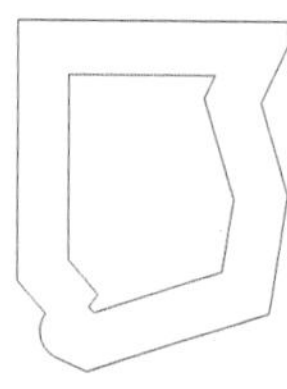

Bottom

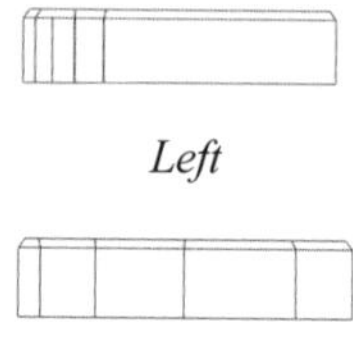
Left

Right

Second: *Compare with the choices.* Option **A** is obviously out since the curved edge does not appear. Option **C** is too thin when compared to the left, front, rear and right sides. Options **B** and **D** is quite similar except that the curved portion appears in Option **B**, which makes it the correct answer.

Question 8 D

First: *Be attentive to the holes of the 3D object.* There are two circles passing all the way through the right and left sides of the 3D object. The two rectangles, on the other hand, are passing through the front and the rear.

Second: *Study the sloping edges.* Three edges shaded in black are sloping which means that these areas are viewed from at least two standard sides.

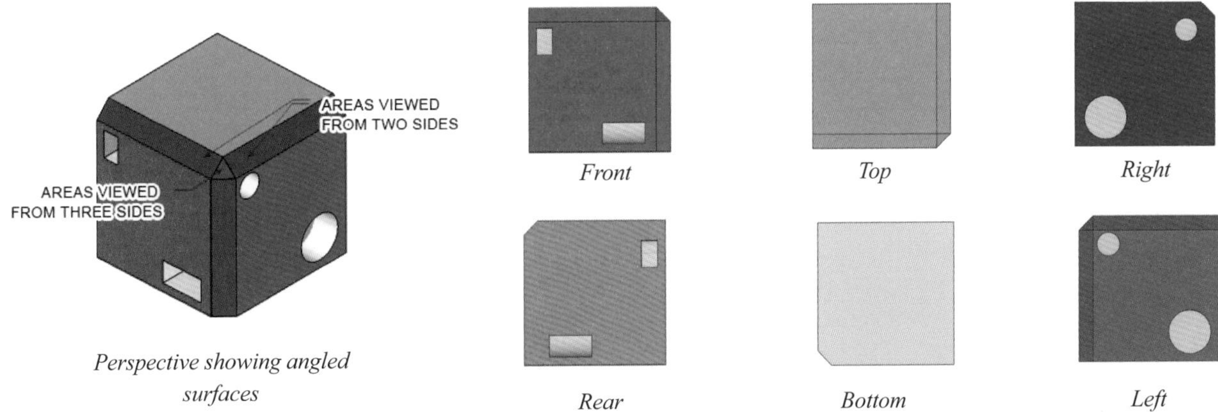

Perspective showing angled surfaces

Third: *Compare the standard views with the choices.* Focusing on the outlines of these different views, only one edge is angled in all six views. Associate this angled edge with the holes within the 3D object and notice its position. Option **D** is the correct answer because one of its sides is angled and the positions of the (sqaured) holes are correctly placed.

Question 9 C

First: *Sketch the six sides of the 3D object.* Be keen with the details such as the hole, slopes and curves within the object. Also, try to rotate the object that would fit the aperture.

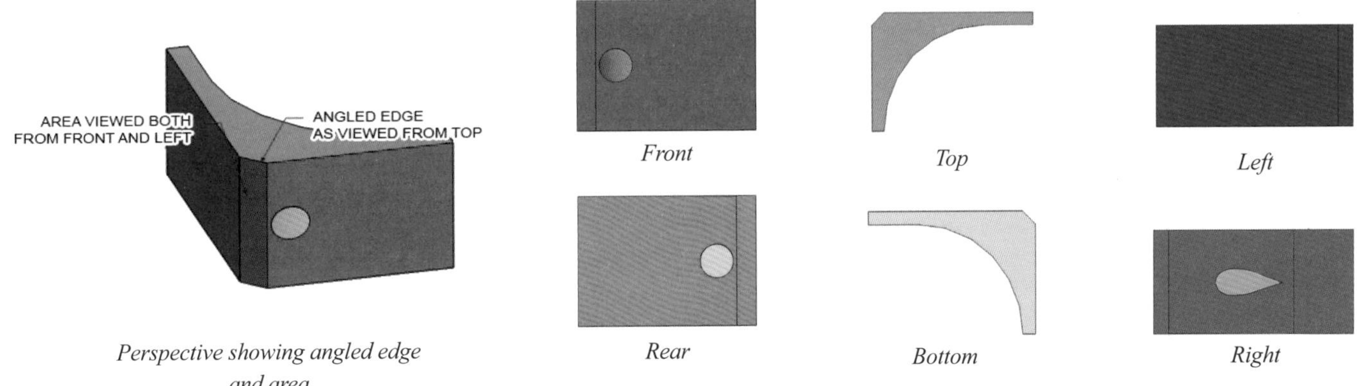

Perspective showing angled edge and area

Second: *Check the choices.* Option **A** is viewed from the top and is incorrect since the lower left should be angled and not curved. Option **B** is also incorrect because the hole is placed too near from the left edge. Remember that an angled edge showed from the top will still be shown both from the front and rear views. In Option **C**, there is enough space which is the angled area between the hole and the left edge. Therefore, **C** is the correct answer.

Question 10 A

First: *Concentrate on the largest surface of the 3D object.* Count the number of corners and determine the two smallest edges. Note that these two smallest edges are located alternately. The circular hole is located on the upper left from the front view and the rectangular hole is on the lower right when viewed from the front.

Second: *Sketch the six standard views.* This is important because the choices project any of the six sides of the 3D object.

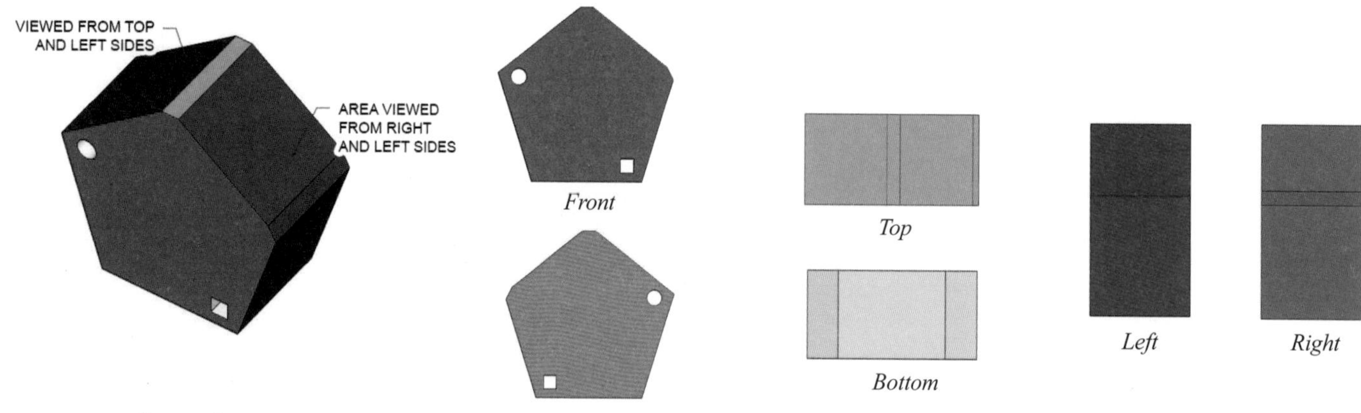

Perspective *Front* *Rear* *Top* *Bottom* *Left* *Right*

Third: *Check the choices.* You can instantly compare the rear standard view with Option **A** and thus, the correct answer.

Question 11 C

First: *Identify the holes.* From here, you can immediately get rid of choices **B** and **D** because both do not have square holes. Option **A** may also be tricky but if you look closely, the inner oval is positioned vertically which affects the distance from the square holes. This makes **A** an incorrect answer. There are also smaller elliptical holes through the sides of the 3D object.

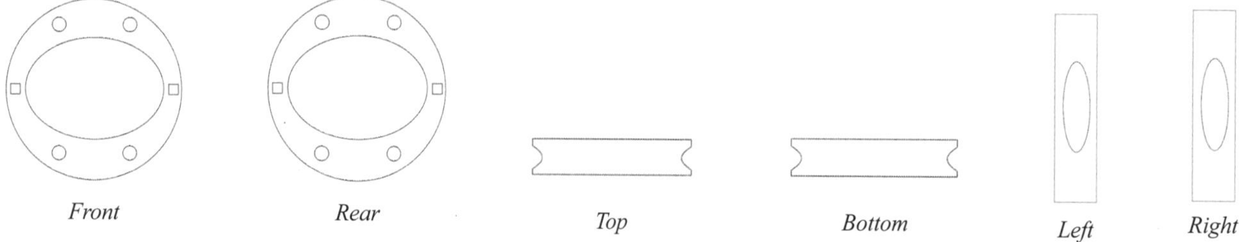

Front *Rear* *Top* *Bottom* *Left* *Right*

Second: *Check other options.* You can easily identify the correct answer, which is **C** for either the top or bottom view has the same outlines. Option **E** has straight edges but does not provide for the whole in the middle, which is incorrect.

Question 12 D

First: *Be observant on the number of the protruding components and the distances between them.* There are three triangles protruding and each does not cover up one another even when viewed from any standard sides.

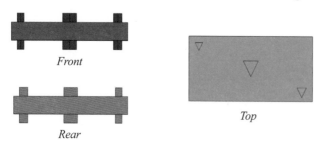

Front

Rear

Top

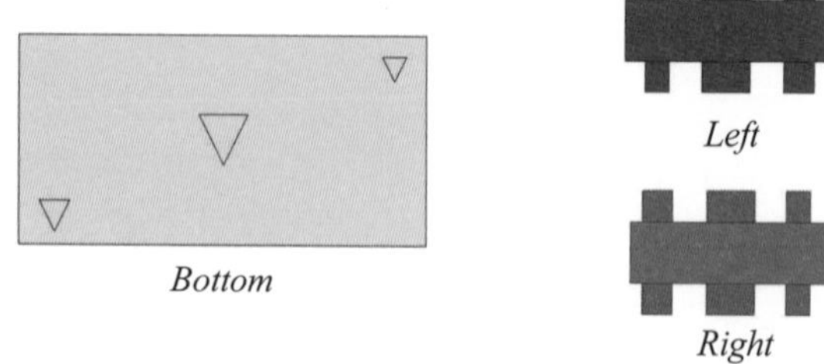

Bottom *Left* *Right*

Second: *Be keen on the sizes of the components.* Small discrepancy in sizes and distances make a big outcome on the aperture. In addition, the sizes of these triangles are different, the center being the biggest and the upper left triangle viewed on top being the smallest. By this, you can readily eradicate Options **A**, **B**, **C**, and **E**. The correct answer is **D**.

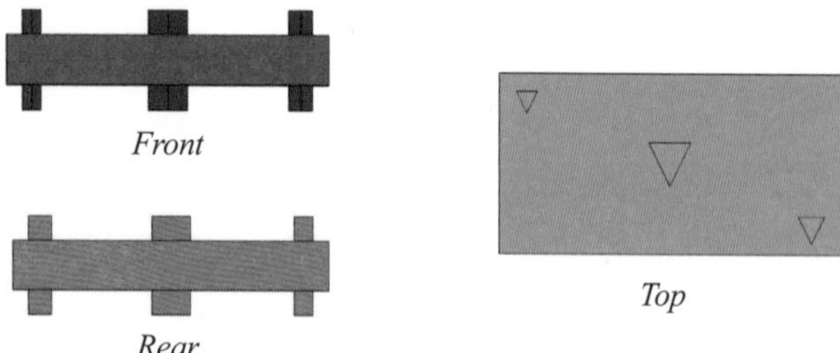

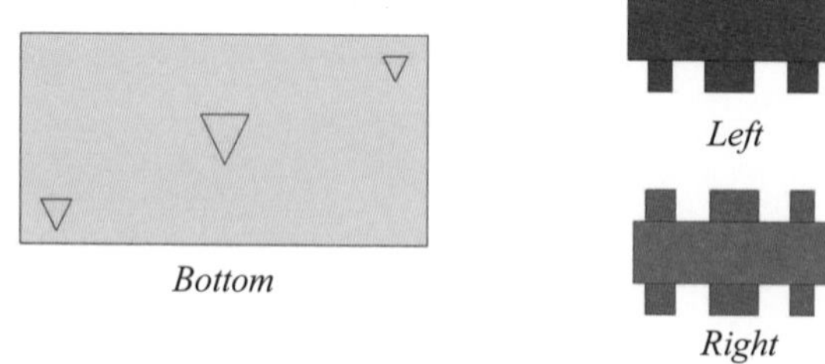

Question 13 B

First: *Scan the choices*. The options seem to be viewed from the different angles, so you may need to determine the six standard views.

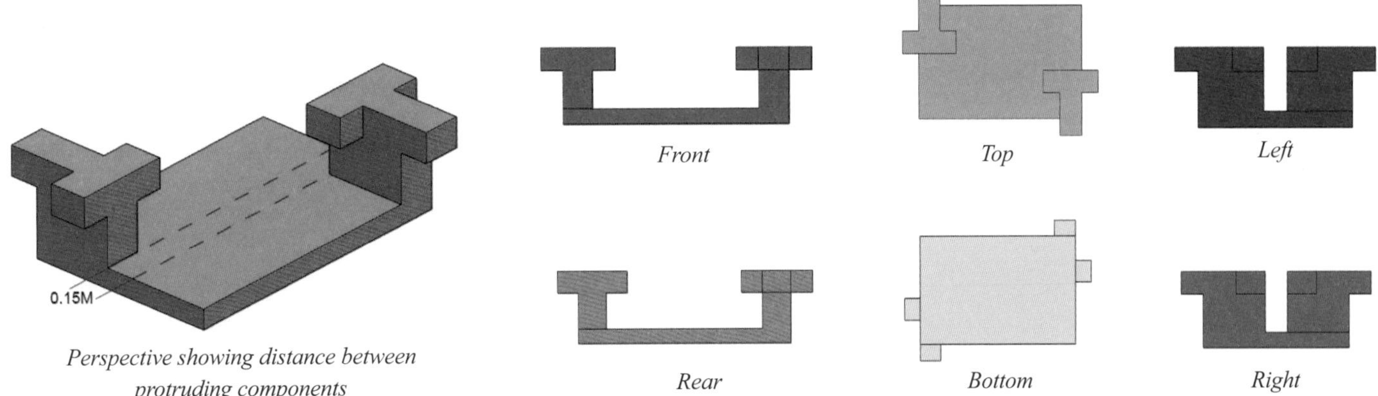

Perspective showing distance between protruding components

Second: *Focus on the protruding components of the 3D objects*. There are recognizable symbols in the 3D object. In this problem, there are two letter Ts protruding upwards. Two other Ts are seen from the front and rear views. Estimate the lengths and widths of the two protrusions. You can also map out and extend the lines of the base of Ts to further clarify the distance between the two protrusions.

Third: *Compare the choices*. Neither Option **A** nor **D** is correct because the other part of the T is not reflected on the front or rear or from the right or left view of the 3D object. Option **E** is also incorrect because another part of the T is not seen as compared to the top and bottom view. Option **C** is incorrect as well because of the circular hole in the center. Therefore, **B** is the only correct answer as viewed from the right or left side.

Question 14 A

First: *Focus on the largest part of the 3D object.* The largest part may not be always the one with the largest surface. In this case, it is the base of the 3D object. It is the bottom square with a circular hole in the center.

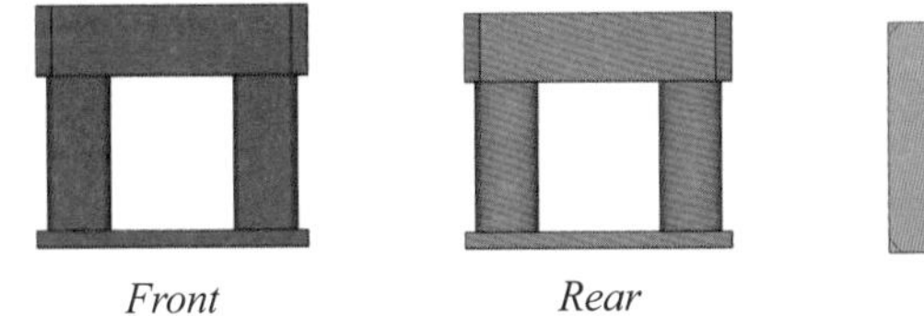

Front Rear Top Bottom Left Right

Second: *Compare the choices*. Take into account that the circular shape on the top portion passes all the way through it. Checking Option **A**, it really fits to the base of the 3D object and thus the correct answer.

Question 15 E

First: *Observe the characteristics of the 3D object.* The 3D object has a total of seven holes all over it. Now, focus on the largest flat surface of it and determine its outline.

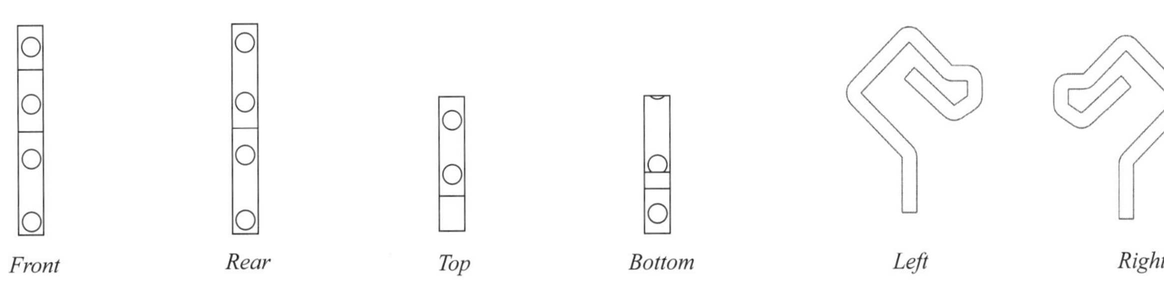

PART 2

Question 16 B

This is an easy question. All of the choices have similar shapes. The thing that matters within these options are the number of solid and dotted lines. Remember that the FRONT VIEW is directly along the TOP VIEW and so, they should have the same measurements and distances. Then, count the number of solid lines which are instantly seen from the TOP. Also, count the number of hidden lines which are represented by dotted lines as viewed from the TOP VIEW. By closely observing the FRONT VIEW, there are a total of eight solid lines and 2 dotted ones. The correct answer is **B**.

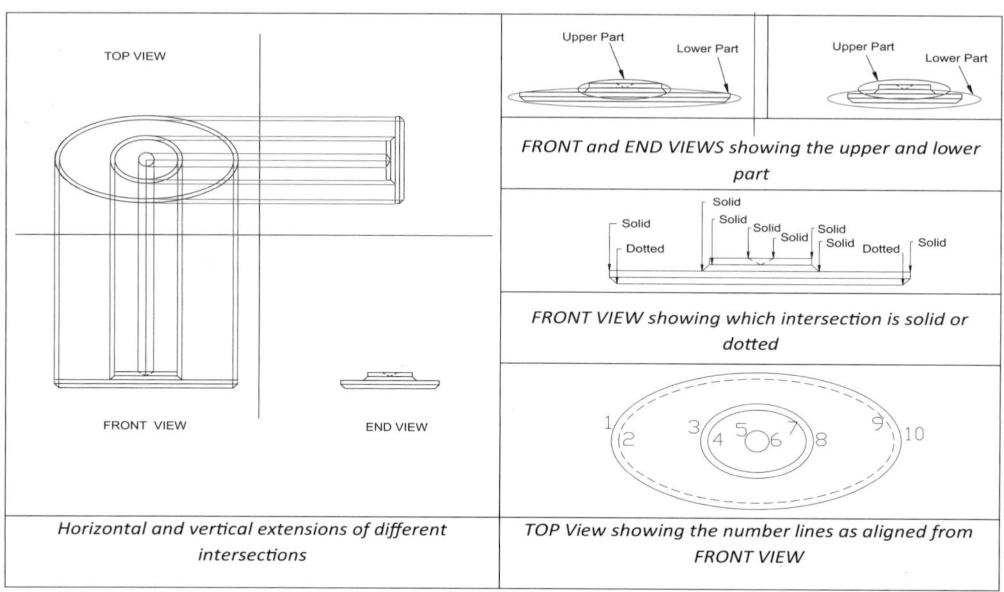

Horizontal and vertical extensions of different intersections

FRONT and END VIEWS showing the upper and lower part

FRONT VIEW showing which intersection is solid or dotted

TOP View showing the number lines as aligned from FRONT VIEW

Question 17 C

This is an average question. Similar with number 16, rotate the END VIEW 90 degrees counterclockwise and project all intersecting lines horizontally to the TOP VIEW area. Also extend lines vertically from the intersection on the FRONT VIEW to the area of the TOP VIEW. Mark the intersections and verify each line. Imagine this object to be a table with two trapezoidal feet. These feet are located below the table top and so, it should be hidden from the TOP VIEW. The right answer is **C**.

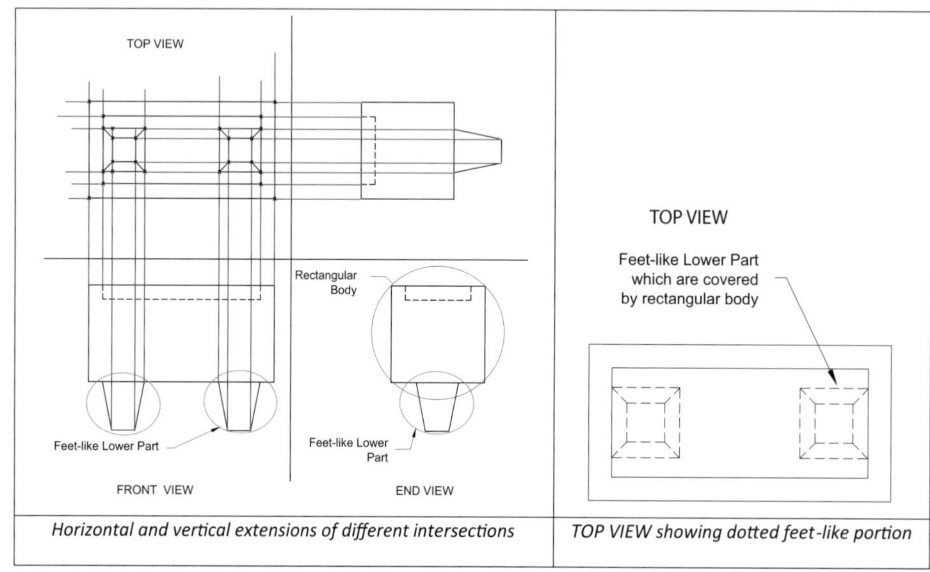

Horizontal and vertical extensions of different intersections

TOP VIEW showing dotted feet-like portion

Question 18 D

This poses as a difficult question. First, rotate the TOP VIEW 90 degrees clockwise. Then, draw vertical lines from each intersection of the rotated TOP VIEW towards the END VIEW area. Also, draw horizontal lines from intersections at the FRONT VIEW to the END VIEW. Next, mark its intersections and clarify which lines are solid and dotted ones. The correct answer here is **D**.

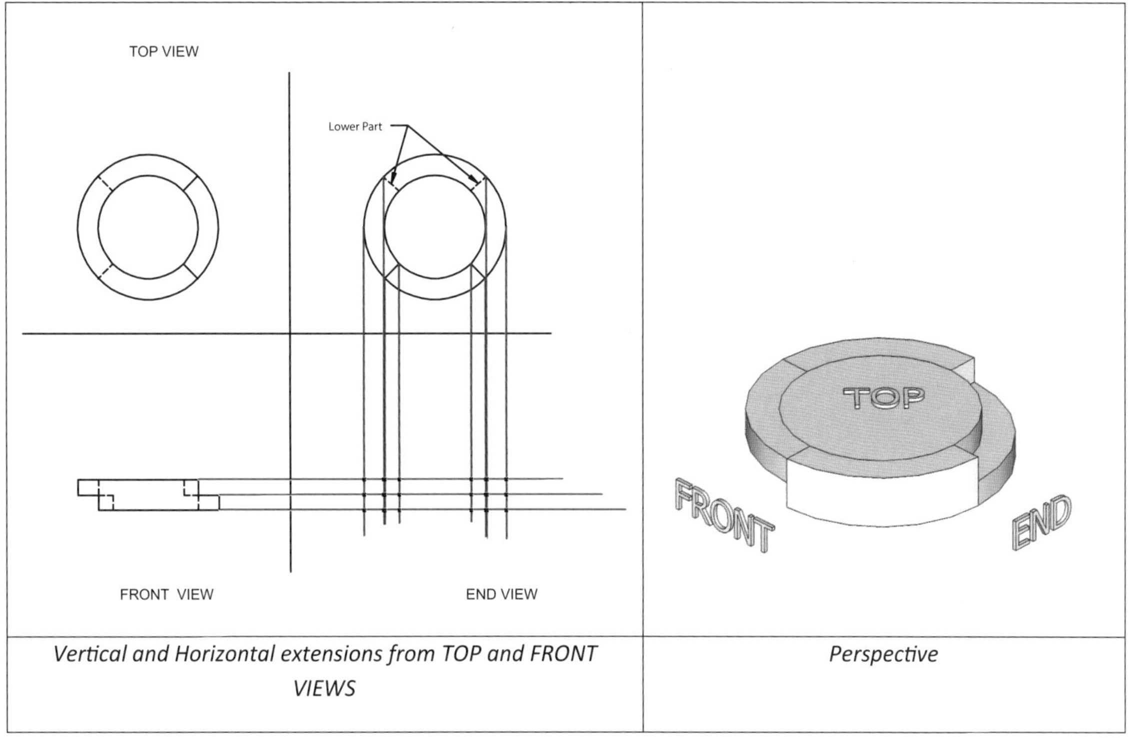

Vertical and Horizontal extensions from TOP and FRONT VIEWS | *Perspective*

Question 19 A

This question is easy. Similar to Question 18, rotate the top view 90 degrees clockwise. Then, create lines from all intersections at the TOP VIEW in a downward direction. Next, draw lines from each intersection at the FRONT VIEW and extend it horizontally until it reaches or intersects with the vertical ones. Mark each intersection but be aware that not all intersections are part of the END VIEW.

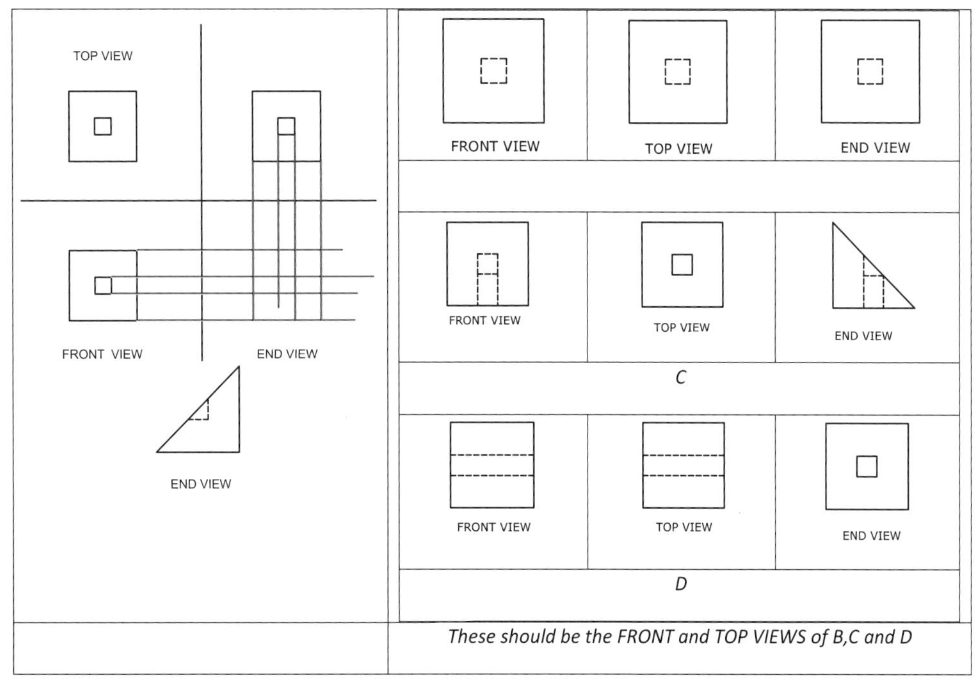

These should be the FRONT and TOP VIEWS of B,C and D

You can also check each of the choices. Option **A** is the right answer because the small inner square reflects to be solid lines in both TOP and FRONT views. Option **B**, on the other hand, is wrong since the dotted small square represents that it as a hole that passes all the way through the object. **C** is also incorrect because the dotted lines extends downwards to the edge of the square, which is not shown from the FRONT VIEW.

Question 20 B

This item is quite easy. You can start by instantly eliminating the wrong choice. One thing that is crucial to identify is the distance between the upper portion and its middle portion. Option **A** is incorrect because it is heavier on the right than the left side. **B**, on the other hand, has a heavier left part than the right one and so, it is the correct answer. Options **C** and **D** are both wrong because a circular shape viewed from the TOP and viewed not from the END should also not be circular from the FRONT.

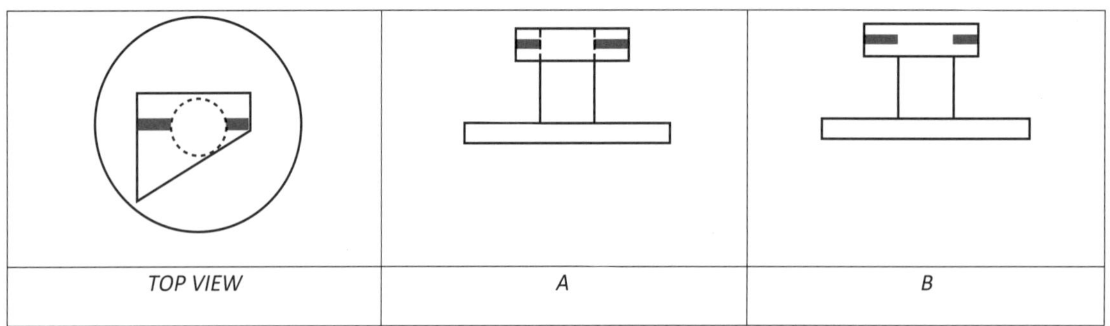

Question 21 C

This question has average difficulty. For a complicated looking object, you may want to go directly over the choices. It may be tricky because square and circle shapes from TOP both have straight edges from FRONT and END views. You can start by closely observing the solid and dotted lines at the END VIEW and especially at the FRONT VIEW since its lines are directly aligned with the TOP VIEW. Then count the number of solid and dotted lines and its sequence when viewed from the TOP. C is the right answer.

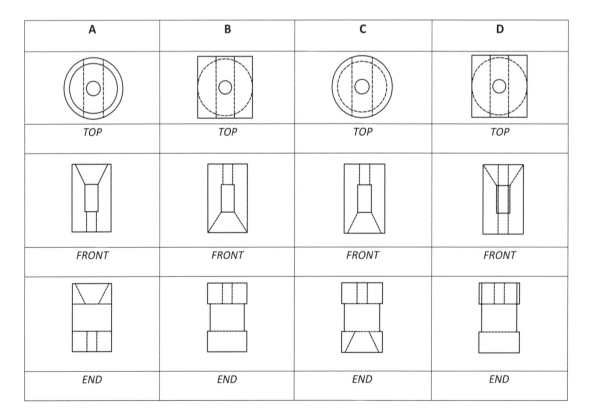

A	B	C	D
TOP	TOP	TOP	TOP
FRONT	FRONT	FRONT	FRONT
END	END	END	END

Question 22 C

To aid you in imagining the 3D object, you may need to label the different parts of it. The object seems like it has an upper and a lower plate with a cylindrical middle part. As obeserved in the END VIEW, the three circular holes pass all the way through the upper and lower plates of the object. The option that best reflects these characteristics is **C**. Option **D** is obviously wrong because its width is the same as that from the END VIEW. Option **A** is also wrong since the holes should be located more to the right than to the left of the plate. The cylindrical portion should be viewed in solid lines from the FRONT VIEW, which makes **B** – showing it in dashed lines (implying that it is hidden) is incorrect.

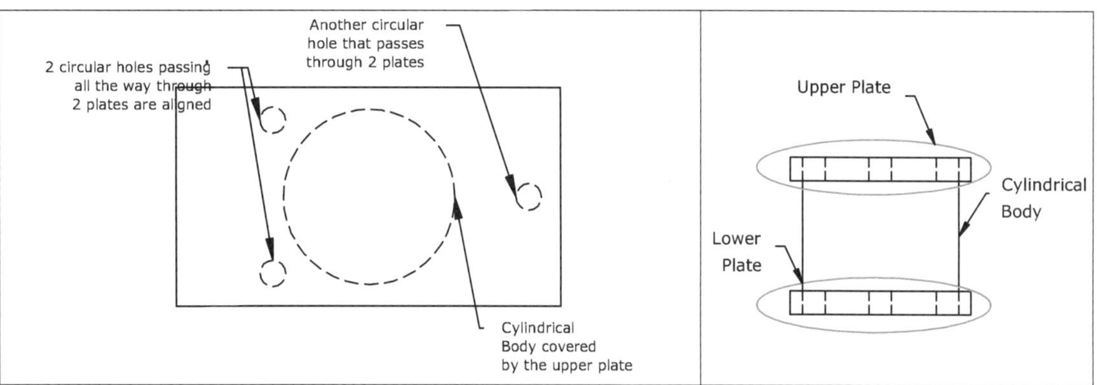

Question 23 D

This question is average in difficulty. Imagine that the object is like a computer monitor. It has a screen, a support, and a base. Now imagine if the monitor is viewed from top. You can start by rotating the END VIEW 90 degrees counterclockwise and leaving the FRONT VIEW as is. Then project horizontal lines from the intersections of the rotated END VIEW and vertical lines from intersections at the FRONT VIEW. Next, mark the created significant intersections.

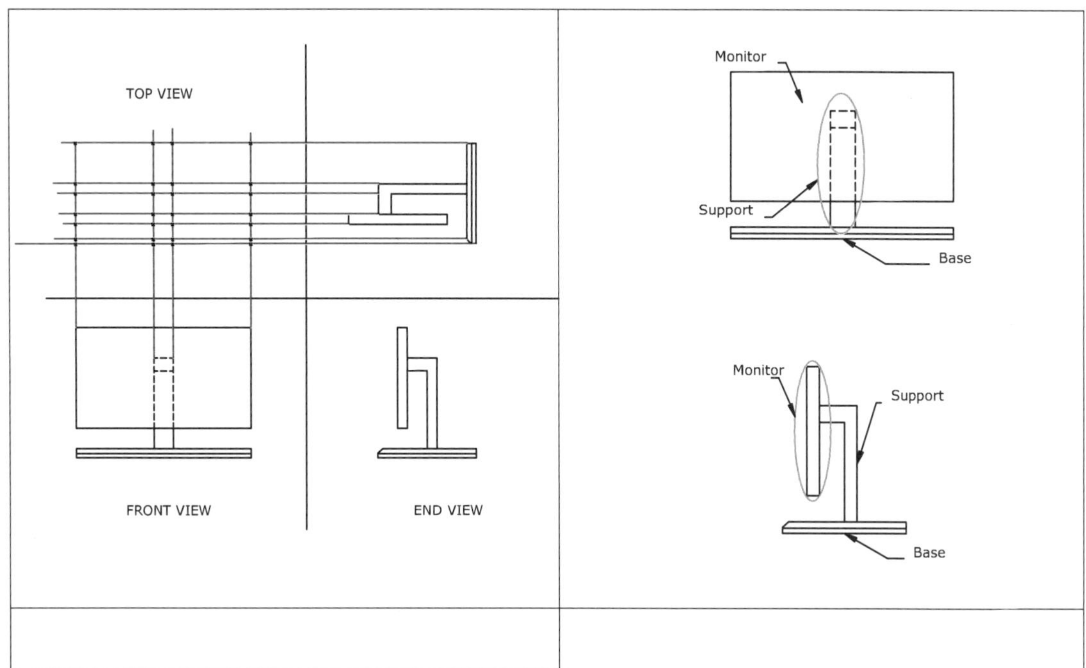

Also, take note of the sequence of the dotted and the solid lines. You can instantly delete **A** from the choices since the monitor is placed at the rear, which is incorrect. **B** is also incorrect because the slope on the base is not seen. **C** is wrong because the monitor seems to be outside the base, which is not true as seen from the END VIEW. **D** is the correct answer. Only the part of the suppport should be seen dotted from the TOP VIEW.

Question 24 A

This question may look complicated but it is actually easy. Keenly observe the characteristics of the object by verifying its form from the TOP to the FRONT VIEW, and vice versa. It is evident that there is a circular hole passing all the way through the 3D object. This "inner" hole should be seen dotted from the END VIEW. The only choice that best reflects this is **A**.

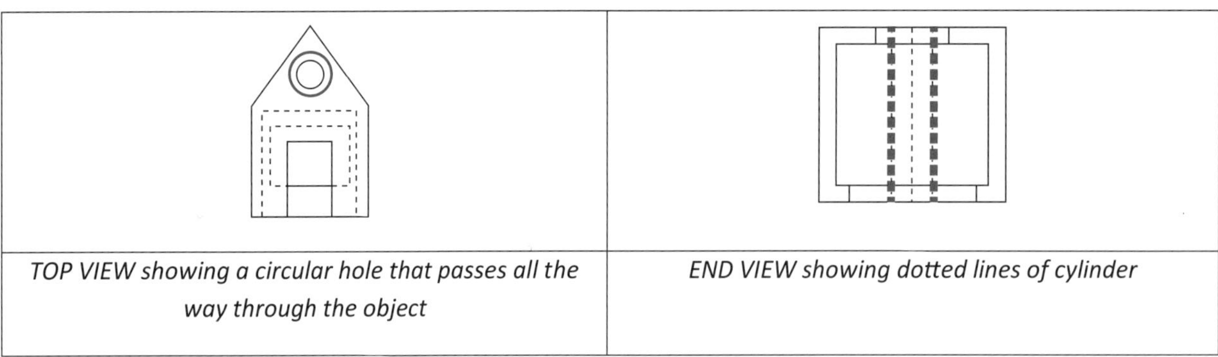

TOP VIEW showing a circular hole that passes all the way through the object

END VIEW showing dotted lines of cylinder

Question 25 D

Based on the choices, there are three equally sized circles within the 3D object. As observed from the END VIEW, the middle circle is dotted while the other two circles, which form as the cylinders are solid ones. Yet when viewed from the TOP, a rectangular piece or plate covers the other two holes of the cylinder, which are located at the front and rear. Therefore, the only solid circle should be the one at the center because it passes all the way through the two rectangular pieces while the top and bottom circles are located between two plates or rectangular pieces. The correct answer is **D**.

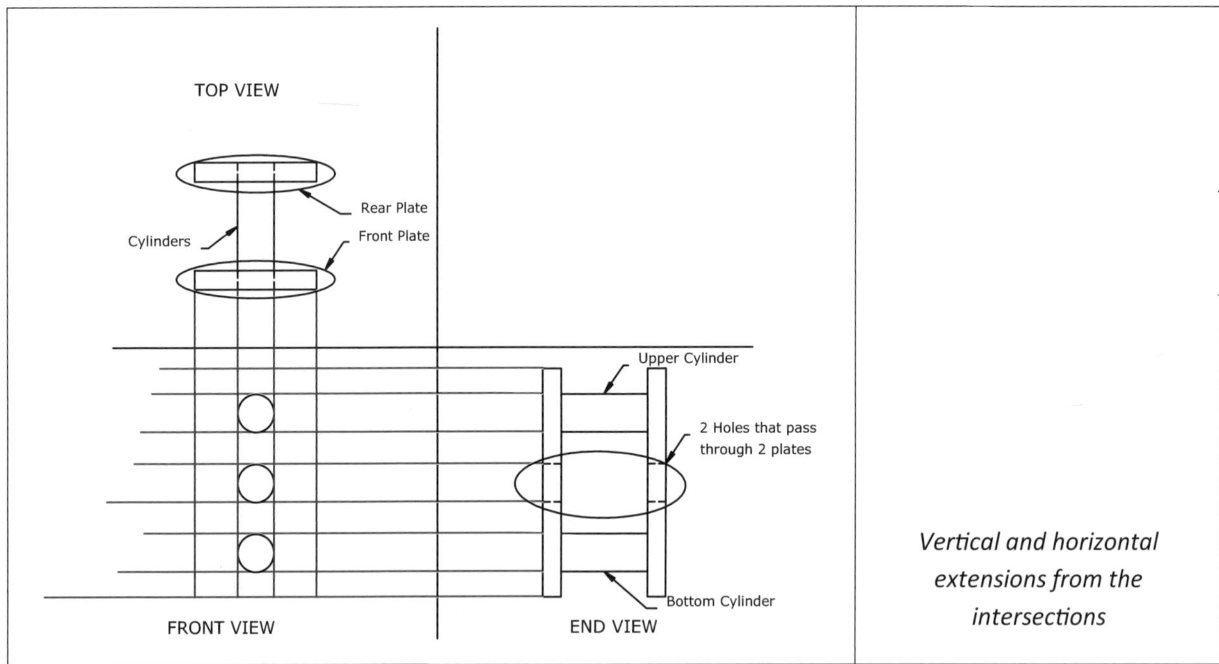

Vertical and horizontal extensions from the intersections

Question 26 B

This should be an easy one. If you rotate the TOP VIEW 90 degrees in a clockwise direction, you will realize that there is a rectangular portion at the left of the circle. Only **B** has a rectangular shape at its left part and so, it is absolutely the correct answer.

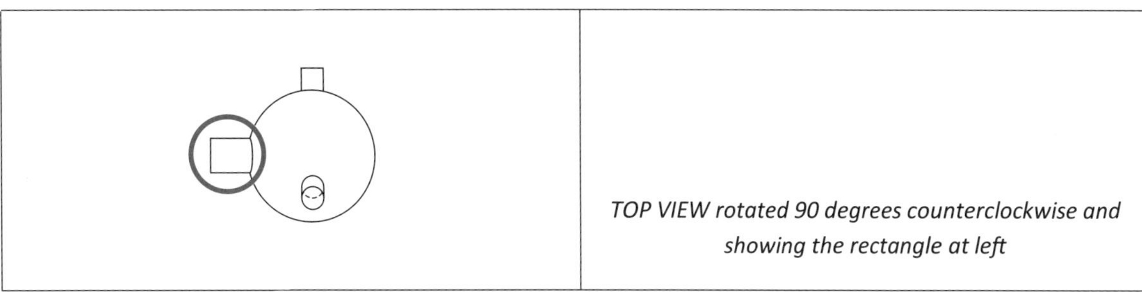

Question 27 B

If you think that the question poses difficuty because of the several intersections in the object's outline, you may directly go over the choices. **A** is wrong simply because it has a line or intersection at the center. Option **B** is the correct answer because it does not have a line at the center but rather, it is curved. **C** has several dotted lines, which are unnecessary. All lines should have been shown from the TOP VIEW. Lastly, **D** is incorrect since it only shows an outer line when it is obvious that there are angled lines viewed from front and end sides.

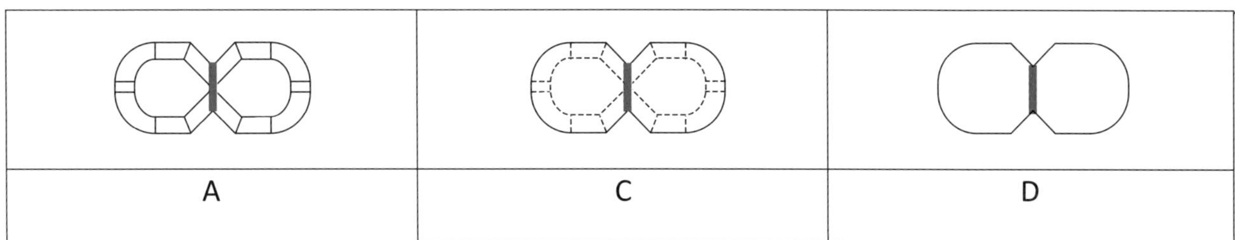

Question 28 A

Here, you can conclude instantly that there two intersecting cylindrical shapes within the 3D object. These cylinders pass all the way through it, which means that they should be hidden from view and therefore, represented by dotted lines. What you need to check are its sizes and position when viewed from the FRONT. Always remember that the TOP VIEW is always aligned with the FRONT VIEW. And so, the vertical cylinder should be bigger than the horizontal one. **A** is the correct answer.

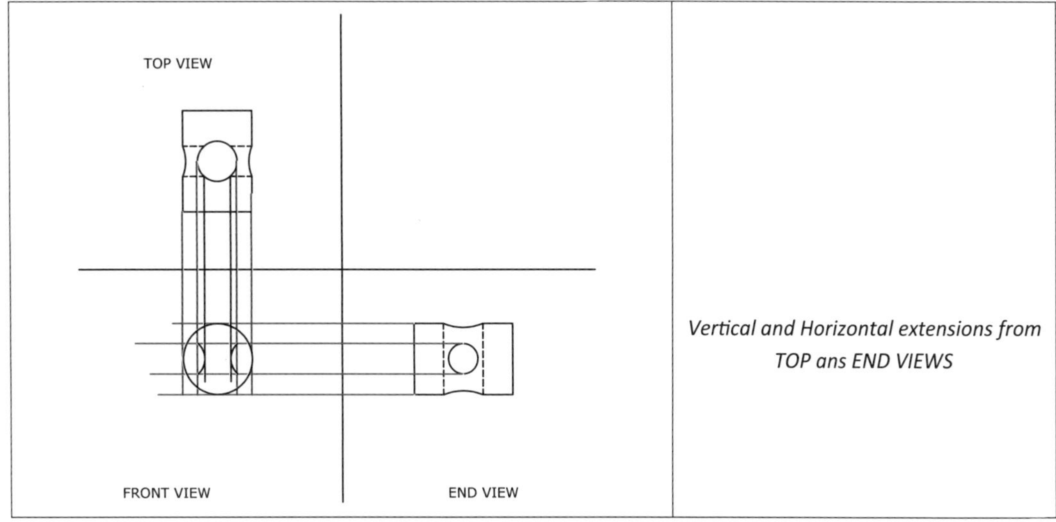

Question 29 A

At first glance, this may seem too hard but it is really not. This object is kind of symmetrical in a sense that it has four parts, which intersects at the center, so you need to take note of the shapes of each part. It is clear that one part is cylindrical as a circle is spotted from FRONT VIEW. Another obvious shape is the square from the END VIEW which creates a tube. The upper part is bigger than the rest. The bottom part is a smaller tube.

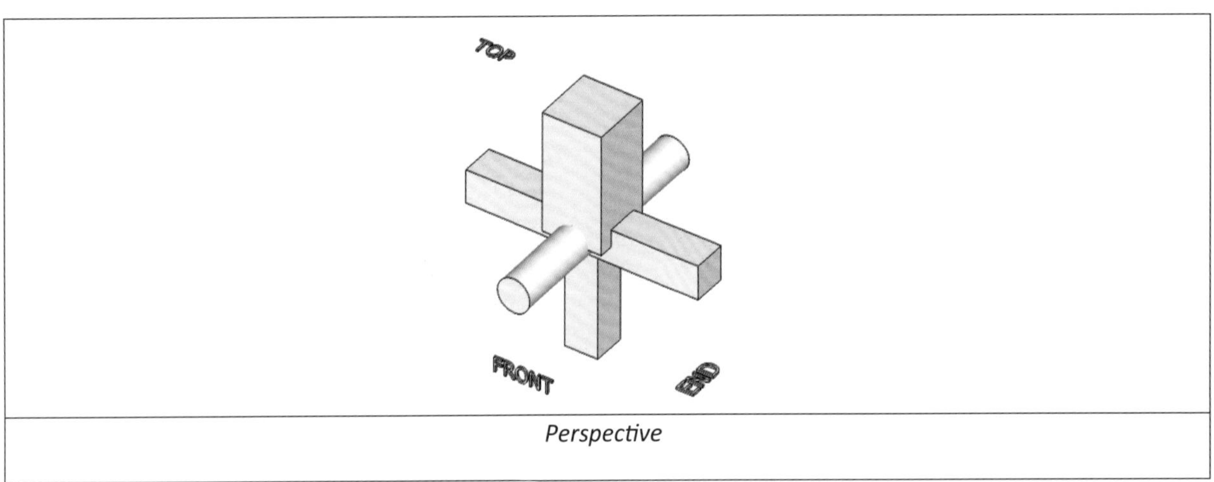

Perspective

With these noted characteristics, you can check each of the choices. **A** is the correct answer because the bottom tube, the bit parts of the cylinder, and the bigger tube should be dotted from the TOP VIEW. **B** and **C** are both incorrect becayse they show all solid lines. Option **D** is incorrect because its center is not the biggest part of the object.

Question 30 B

Rotate first the END VIEW 90 degrees counterclockwise and retain the FRONT VIEW. Then mark the intersections of the extended vertical and horizontal lines created from the two given views. The FRONT VIEW is similar with the END VIEW with three solid squares/cubes and three dotted ones; they only differ on the locations of the square/cubes. You will realize that the object is a large cube with small cubes as its corners. The dotted lines shown in the FRONT VIEW are cubes located at the rear or opposite face of the front. The dotted cubes seen in the END VIEW are located at its opposite face. The correct answer is **B**.

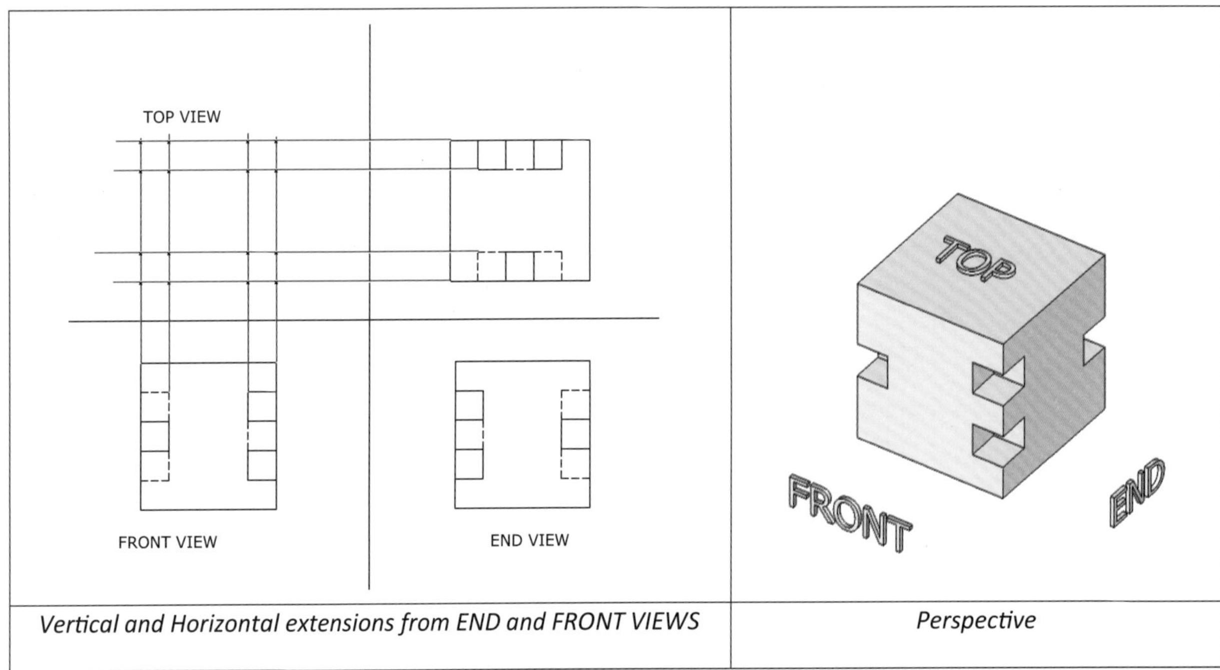

Vertical and Horizontal extensions from END and FRONT VIEWS

Perspective

PART 3

Question 31 D

This may be a very tricky question. The angles are directed in different ways, and you need to be very keen in observing the inner portion of each angle. Another crucial point is to find the smallest angle because some angles may differ for only a few degrees. At first glance, you can choose the one with the smallest angle. From here, compare the angle of your choice with the other options and check the given sequence if it fits. The correct answer is **D**.

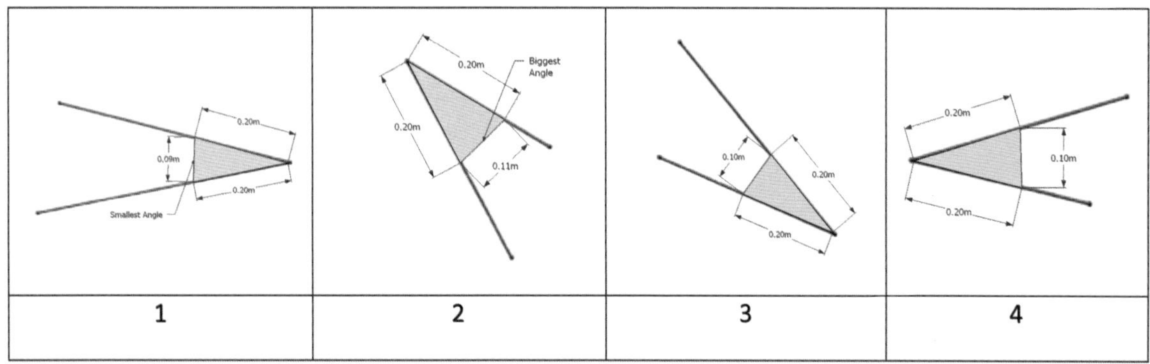

Question 32 C

Some angles are difficult to distinguish from others due the very small differences. 1, 2 and 3 may truly be confusing but you should realize that 4 has the smallest angle of all. Based on the choices, only **C** begins at 4 and so, it is the correct answer.

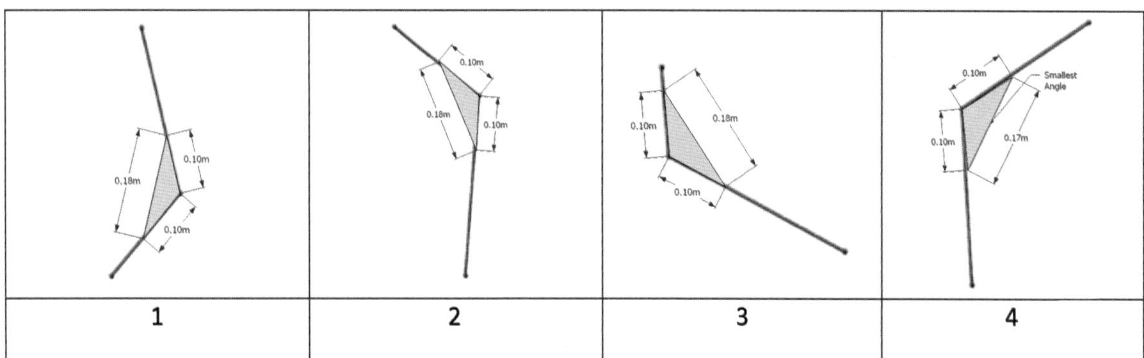

Question 33 B

Similar with Question 32, you need to identify first the option with the smallest angle. First, Keep on comparing each angle with one another until you can determine that 1 is the smallest one. The next bigger angles are no longer necessary once you distinguish the smallest because none in the given options repeats 1 as the first in the sequence.

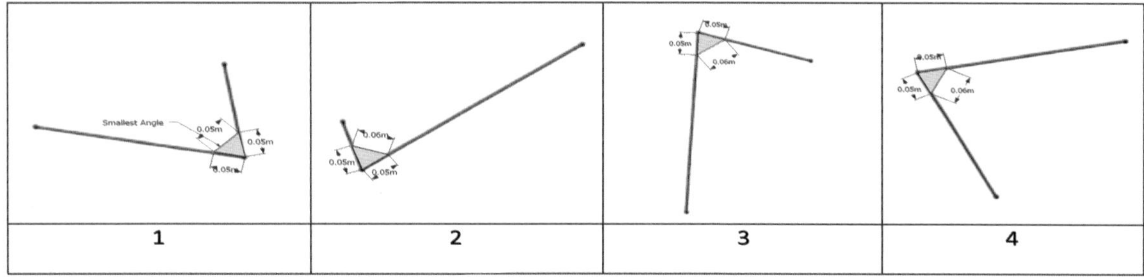

Question 34 C

For items that have very small angles, observe first the ones with the "darkest" angle. At first scan, the smallest may be 3 or 4. In this case, you can instantly eliminate options **A** and **B**. Next, closely compare 1 and 2 – 2 is slightly bigger than 1. The correct answer is **C**.

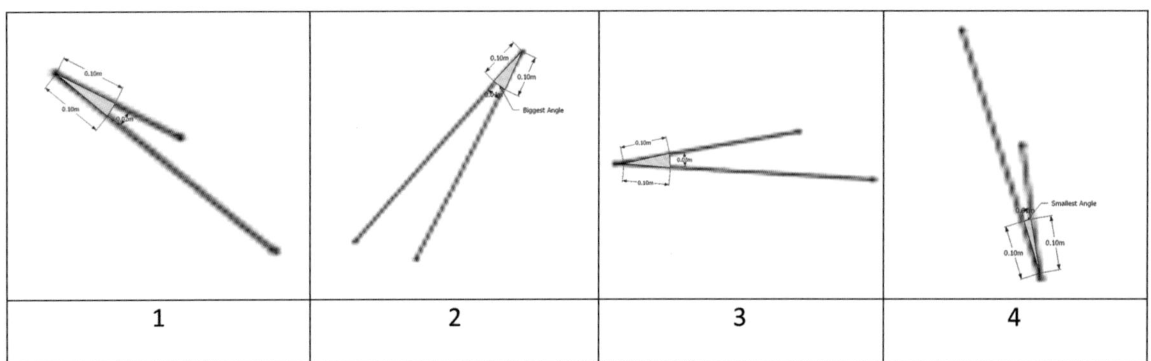

Question 35 A

All of the given angles resemble the letter L. It is easier if you compare the given angles to a letter L, which is a right angle. Determine first the smallest angle and observe that 1 is a bit smaller than 4. You may now delete **C** from your options. **A** here is the right answer because you already know that 4 is the next bigger angle to 1.

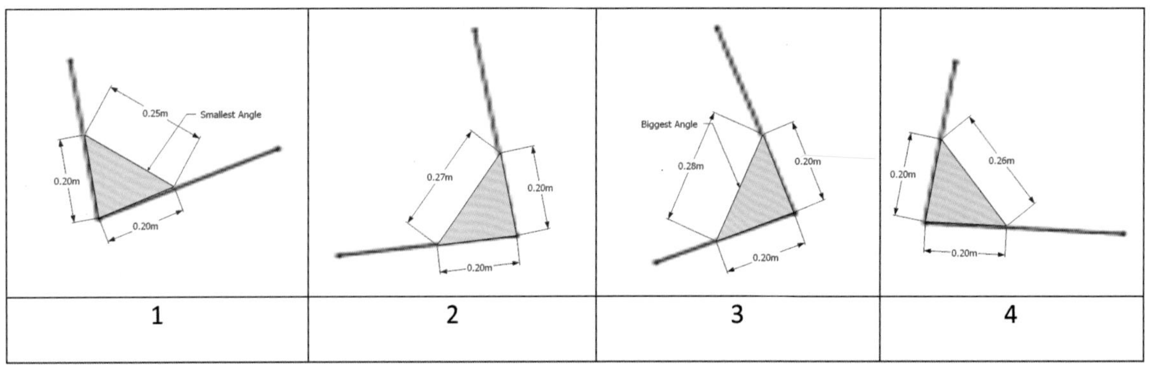

Question 36 D

Do not be deceived with the variations of the angle's rays in this question. Just focus on the bend of the angles. If you are unsure which angle is bigger, for example between 3 and 4, proceed to other angles to compare. The correct answer is **D**.

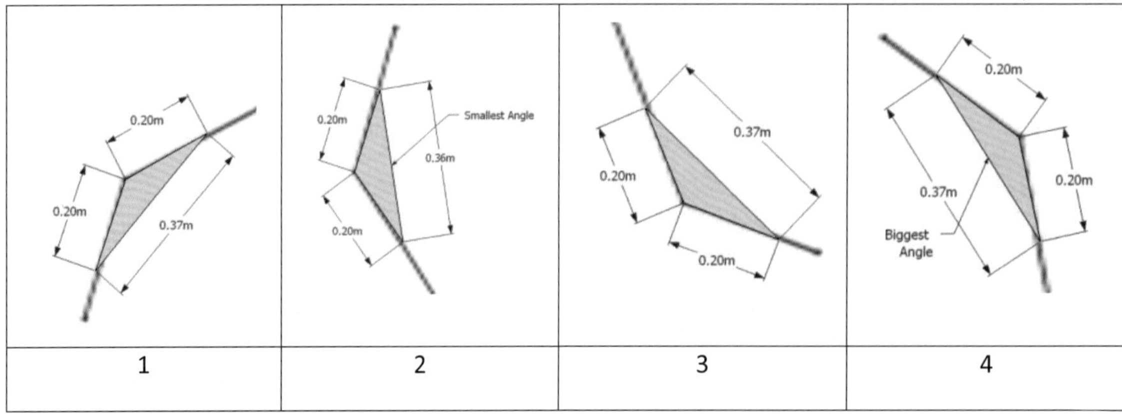

Question 37 B

First, compare the angles that are pointed in a similar direction. In this item, these are 2 and 3. Now notice that 2 is remarkably smaller than 3. Also, note that 1 and 4 have shorter rays than the others, and these are simply created to confuse you. The correct sequence should be 2-3-1-4, which is **B**.

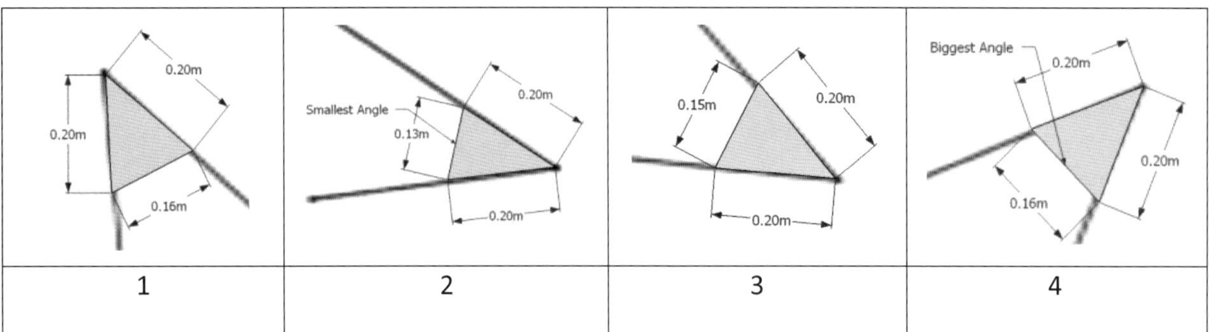

Question 38 A

Compare first 1 and 2 since they look similar. Between 1 and 2, 1 is smaller. On the other hand, between 3 and 4, it is 3 that is smaller. Next, compare 1 and 3, and see that 3 is smaller. Take note of the significant initial sequence and check it with the given choices. The correct answer is **A**.

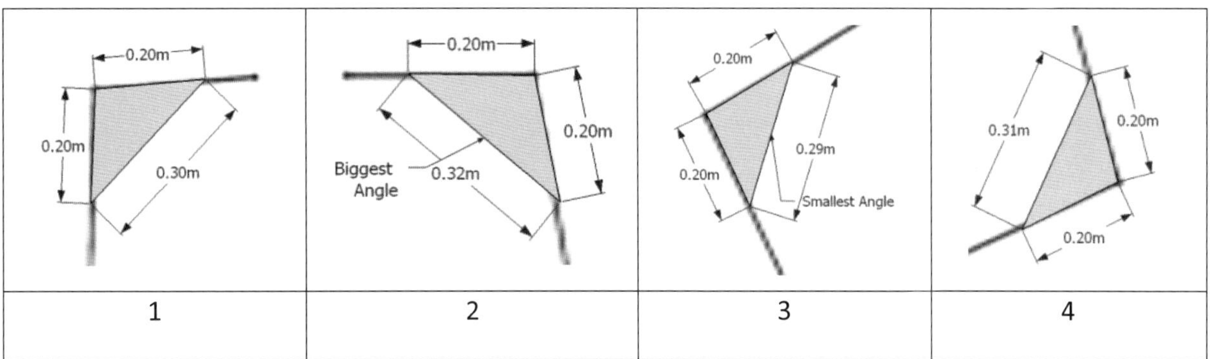

Question 39 D

For obtuse angles, the straighter the angle the bigger it is. Both 1 and 4 are bent to the right. Observe that 4 might look wide but it is 1 that is actually wider. Again, sizes of angles might deceive you and you need to be careful on that. 3 has the most bent leg and therefore, it is the smallest. The correct answer is **D**.

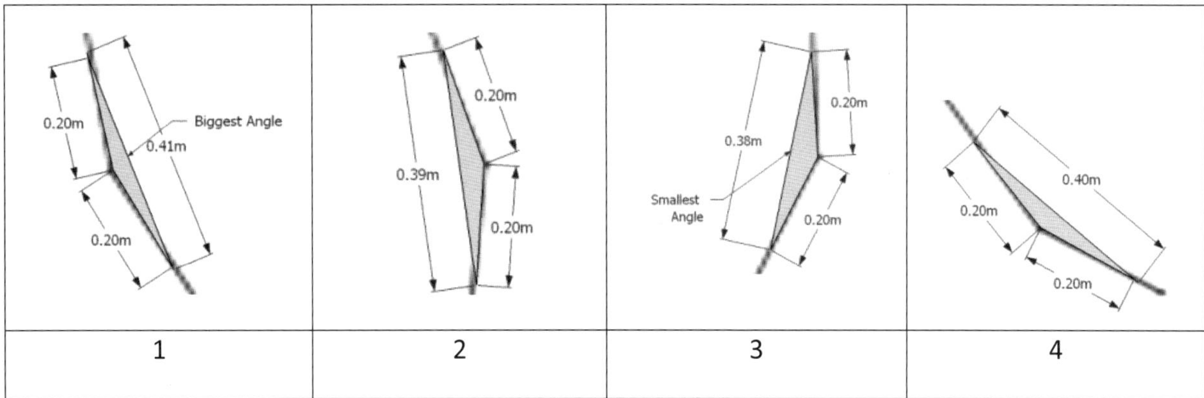

Question 40 C

At initial glance, 1 may be the smallest in size, but it is not the smallest angle. Next, proceed to compare 2 and 3 which seem to be alike. The most important thing is to determine the smallest angle, and it is 4. **C** is the correct answer.

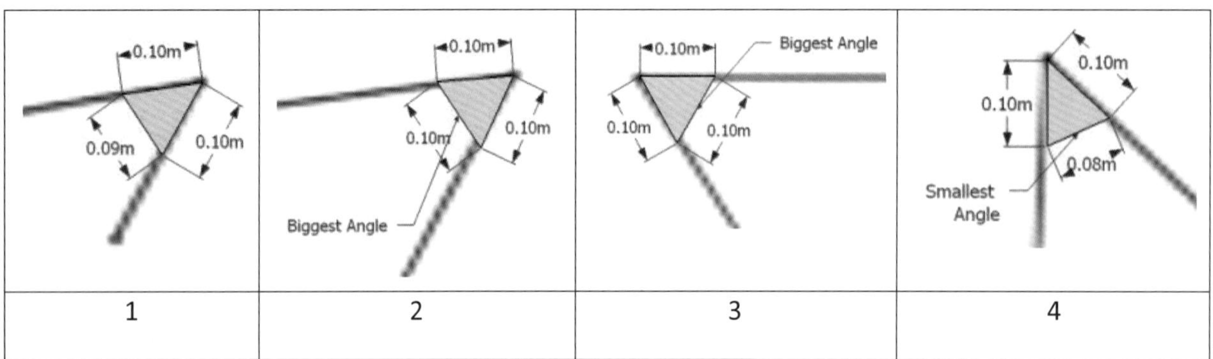

Question 41 B

Comparing 1 and 4 may be difficult since they are quite similar. However, you can observe that 1 is a bigger angle than 2 while 2 is a bit bigger than 3. The only sequence than can justify this is **B** which is 3-2-4-1.

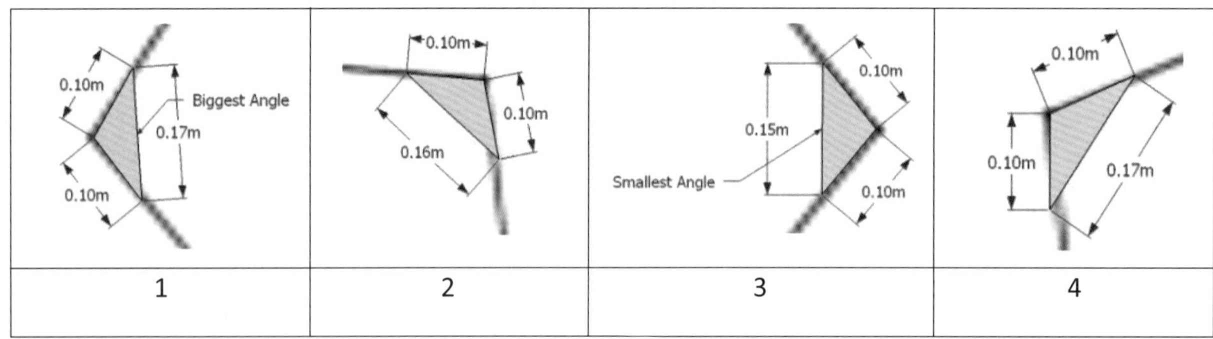

Question 42 C

Distinguishing smaller from bigger angles, which are closer to a line, is easy. In this item, 1 is the most bent among any other angles. 3 and 4 are closer to being straight lines. The correct answer is **C**.

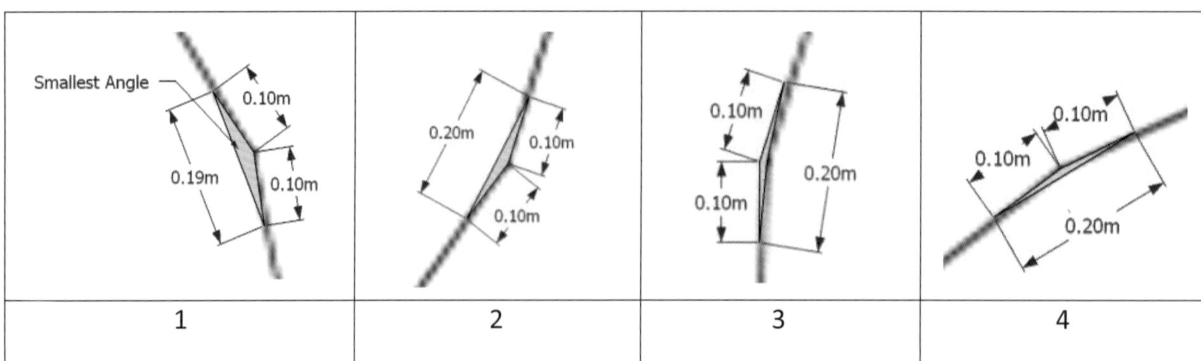

Question 43 A

In this question, you just have to try concentrating on each of the angle created by the same length of legs. This makes obvious that 4 is the smallest angle. Next, compare the angles between 1 and 2 and evidently, 1 is smaller. With at least 2 sequence determined which is 4-1, you can already choose the correct answer, and it is **A**.

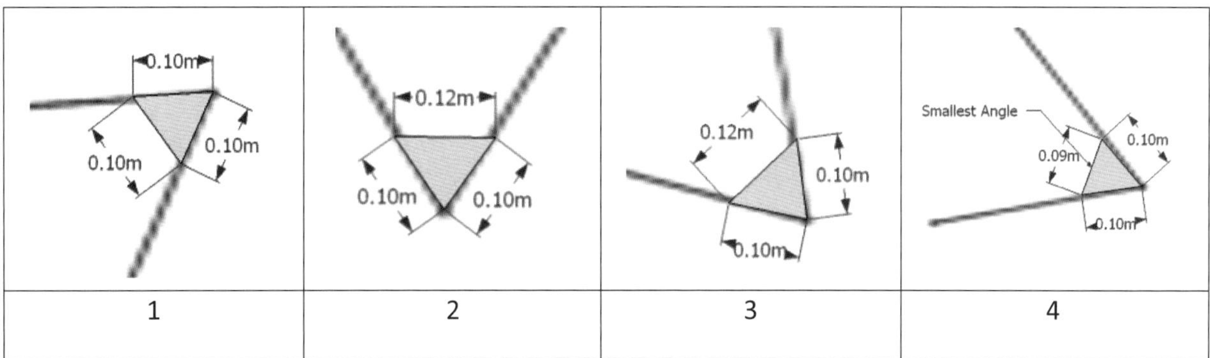

Question 44 B

Again, the angles in this question are like the letter L. The closer angle to be a letter L or a right angle is the smallest. 2 is best close to L and so, it should be the first on the sequence. Among the choices, only **B** starts with 2, therefore it is the correct answer.

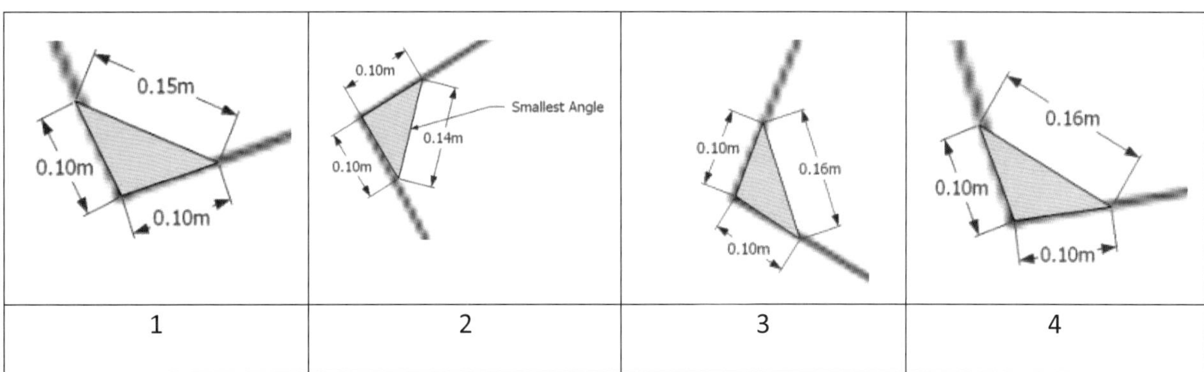

Question 45 A

This is an easy question. The most bent angle is 3 while, the one that is closest to being a line is 2. The correct sequence is 3-1-4-2. The correct answer is **A**.

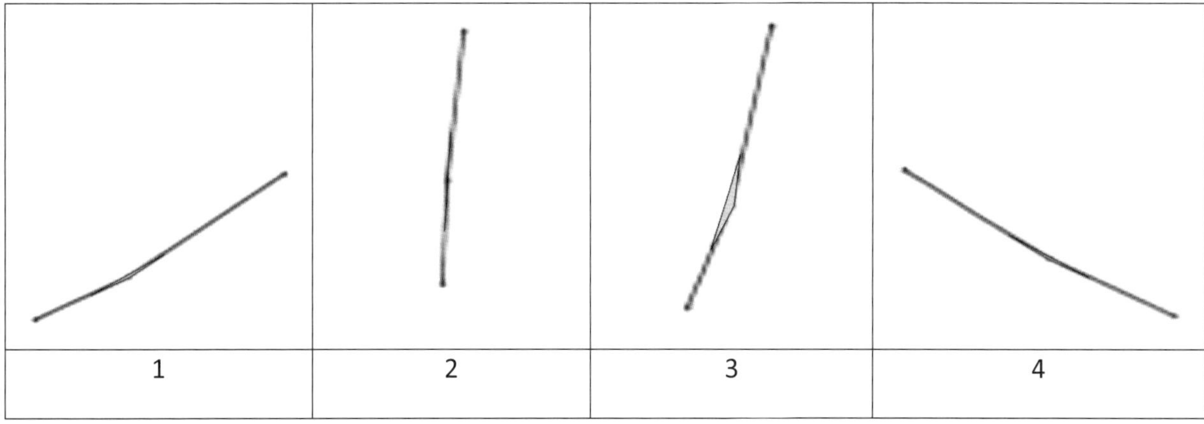

PART 4

Question 46 C

First: *study the foldings and count the number of layers of paper for each hole.* Start counting the layers of paper from Fold 1 then, count the layers on Fold 2. One hole is punched in 2 layers while the other is punched in 4 layers. The total number of holes should be 6.

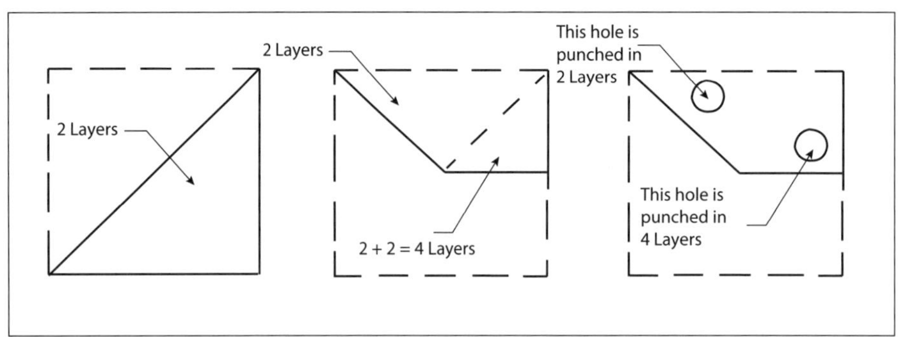

Second: *narrow down the choices.* Given that there should be 6 holes in total, the correct answer is **C**. It is the only option that has 6 holes.

Question 47 E

First: *study the number of layers in each of the holes.* You need to trace back the folding and determine how many folds there are for a hole. In total, there should be 5 punched holes.

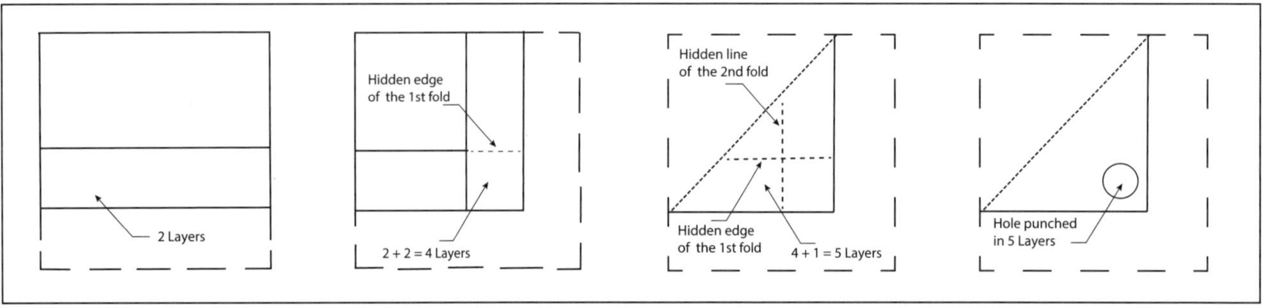

Question 48 B

Second: *narrow down the choices.* **A**, **B** and **C** are all obviously incorrect. Take note that the last fold, which is a single layer was taken from the first quadrant. Therefore, this part should only have 1 punched hole while the fourth quadrant should have 4 punched holes. The correct answer is **E**.

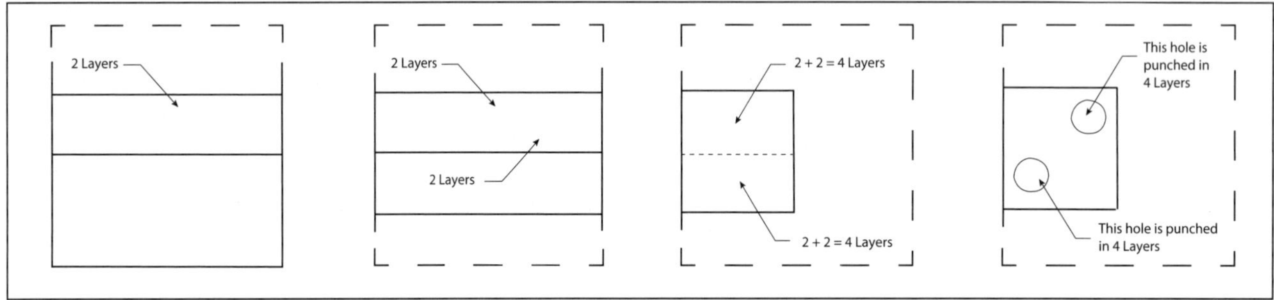

Second: *narrow down the choices.* Options **C**, **D** and **E** are all incorrect because they only have 6 to 7 holes. Be observant on the pattern of the fold. If the fold is symmetrical, then the punched holes should also be symmetrical. In this case, **B** is correct because the folding is symmetrical or a mirror image of the other. On the other hand, A has irregular placement of punched holes.

Question 49 D

First: *study the number of layers in each of the holes.* Carefully follow the folding and count the number of total layers where the hole was punched. The total number of layers is 8 and so should the number of the punched holes.

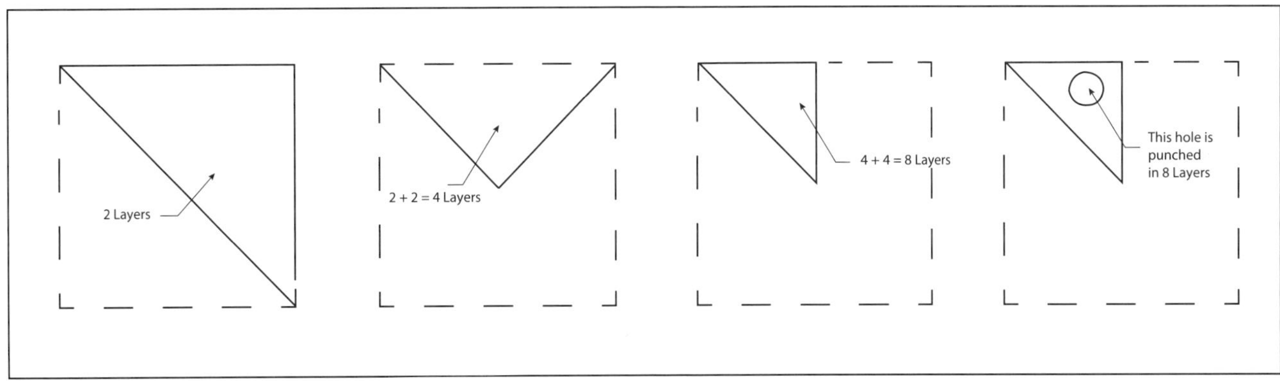

Second: *narrow down the choices.* **A** and **B** are both wrong because they have 6 holes. **E** has only 4, which is also incorrect. Narrowing down our choices to **C** and **D**, be keen on observing the location of the holes. You can start with the layer that was not moved. It is apparent that a mirror image pairing of holes should be present (similarly positioned at 1-2). Only option **D** has the 1-2 holes on each side. Therefore, it is correct.

Question 50 A

First: *study the number of layers in each of the holes.* One of the holes is punched in 4 layers and the other hole is punched in only 2 layers. Hence the total number of punched holes should be 6.

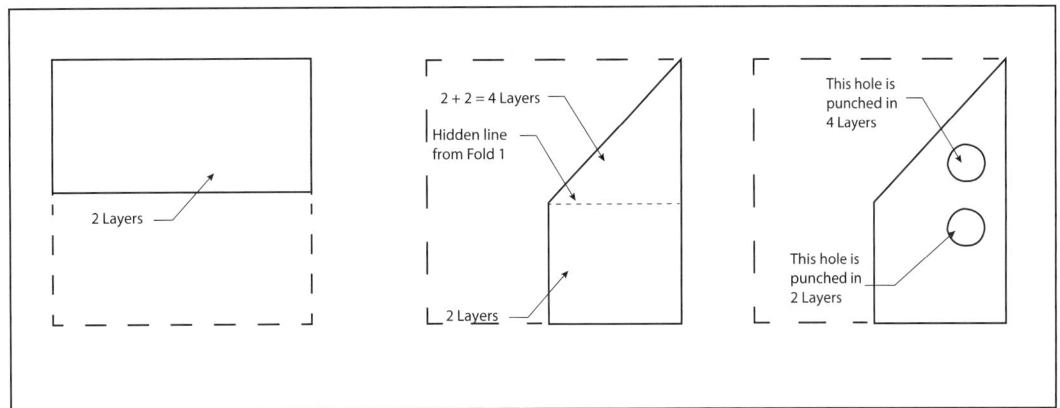

Second: *narrow down choices.* Options **B** and **E** are incorrect because they only have 4 holes. **C** is also wrong because it has 8 punched holes. Take note of the retained portion of the layer, which is the lower right half of the second quadrant. 2 holes should result from this fold: one on this side and another one on its opposite side (or the second hole from the upper left edge). In addition, please remember that the punched hole on the upper-right half ofthe paper was folded twice. 4 holes should result from this: 1 on the initial position of the punched hole, 1 on the third hole from the upper left edge, and 2 in the middle of the lower-most part of the paper. A is the right answer.

Question 51 B

First: *study the number of layers in each of the holes*. Be careful in excluding the layers that are not covered by the punched hole. Take note that the hole was punched on the inner center of the folded paper. This portion does not include the layer or the fold shown in the second quadrant. Therefore, the hole should result to only 4.

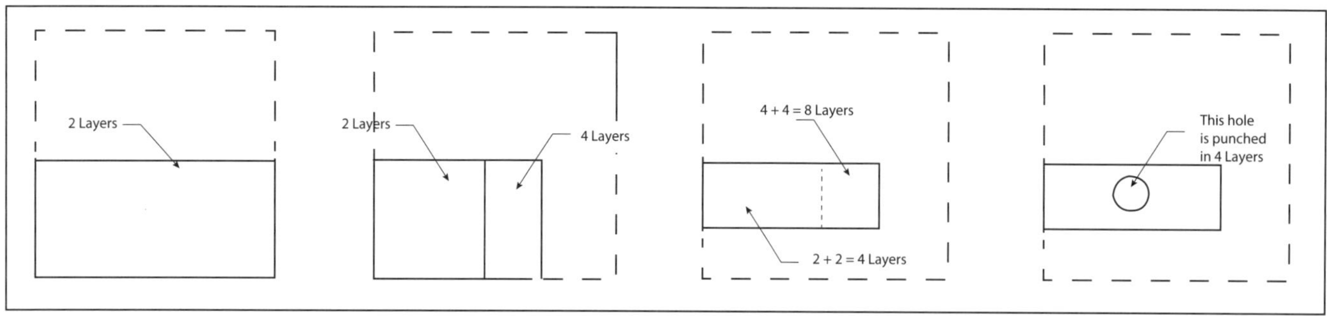

Second: *narrow down the choices*. You can easily eliminate **D** and **E** since they have 7 and 2 punched holes, respectively. The critical part here are the locations of the holes. You will determine this by mentally unfolding the layers one by one while taking note of the holes in the process. Finally, the holes are positioned vertically along the first and third quadrants. Here, **B** is the correct answer.

Question 52 C

First: *study the number of layers in each of the holes*. One by one, add each layer as they are folded to the next. Notice that one of the holes is punched in only 1 layer. Immediately, imagine this hole to be placed on the uppermost right corner of the paper when unfolded. Next, take note that the other hole is punched in 3 layers. So the total number of punched holes should be 4. You can now delete **A**, **B** and **D** from the choices.

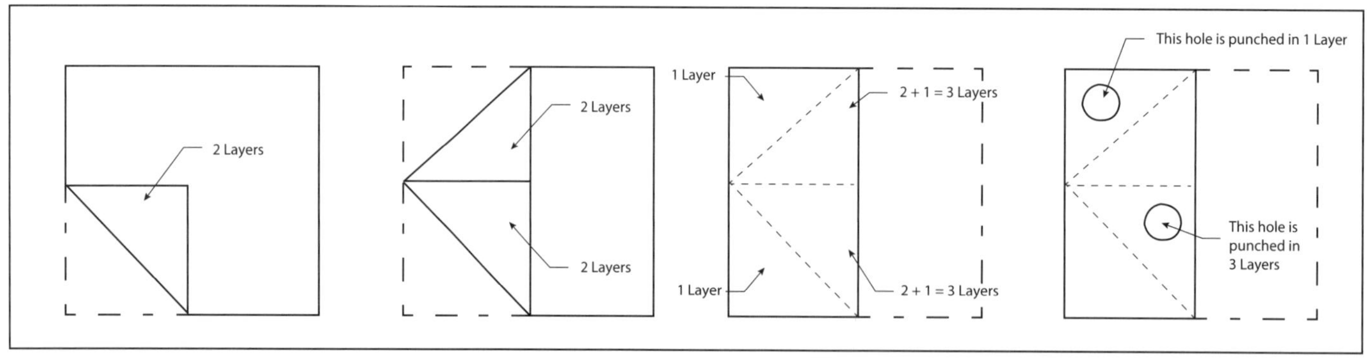

Second: *delete the correct placement of the holes*. Again, remember that the bottom hole is punched in 3 layers. If you unfold it, you will see that there should be a hole mirroring it (just beside it on the right). Next, look at the second quadrant to visualize where the fourth hole should go. It should be placed on the lowest left edge of the paper. Option **C** shows the correct answer.

Question 53 D

First: *study the number of layers in each of the holes*. This is an easy one since you can disregard the last fold. There is no punch hole in the last fold. Clearly, there should only be 2 punched holes.

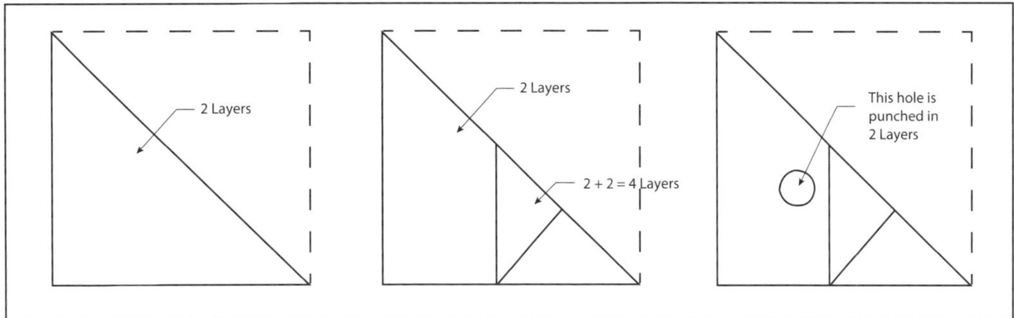

Second: *narrow down the choices*. You can effortlessly eradicate **A** from the choices. As observed, the third quadrant stays as is. With this information, further eliminate options **B** and **E**. Since the sheet is divided in two diagonally, the holes should be symmetrical showing the 3-2 and 2-3 positions. The correct answer is **D**.

Question 54 A

First: *study the number of layers in each of the holes*. Pay attention to the process of folding. You may even need to sketch out hidden edges and folds of the previous folding. The top and bottom holes are both punched in 2 layers while the middle one is punched in 4 layers. The total number punch holes should be 8.

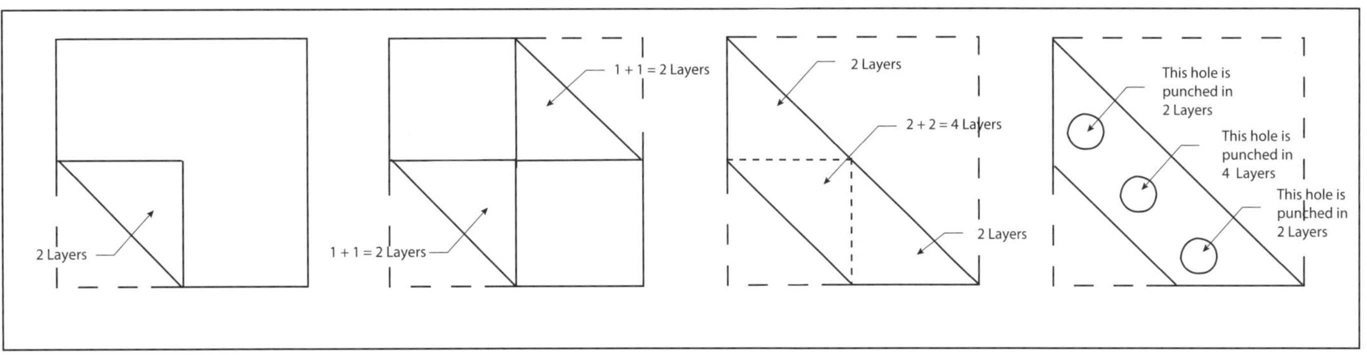

Second: *narrow down the choices.* **B** *and* **D** *are both incorrect because they only have 6 holes*. What you need to clarify now is the location of each hole. Through a representation of each hole with respect to its quadrant, it is easier to locate symmetrical holes. The bottom halves of quadrants 1 and 4 and the upper half of quadrant 3 are retained. Thereforc, there should have holes 1-3, 3-2, and 4-3. Given these 3 holes, you will realize that A is the correct answer.

Question 55 D

First: *study the number of layers in each of the holes*. Drawing the hidden edges behind the fold greatly helps in determining the number of punched holes. Do not forget that each portion of the sheet has a different number of layers. In this question, the upper hole is punched in 3 layers and the bottom one is punched in 2 layers. There should be a total of 5 punched holes.

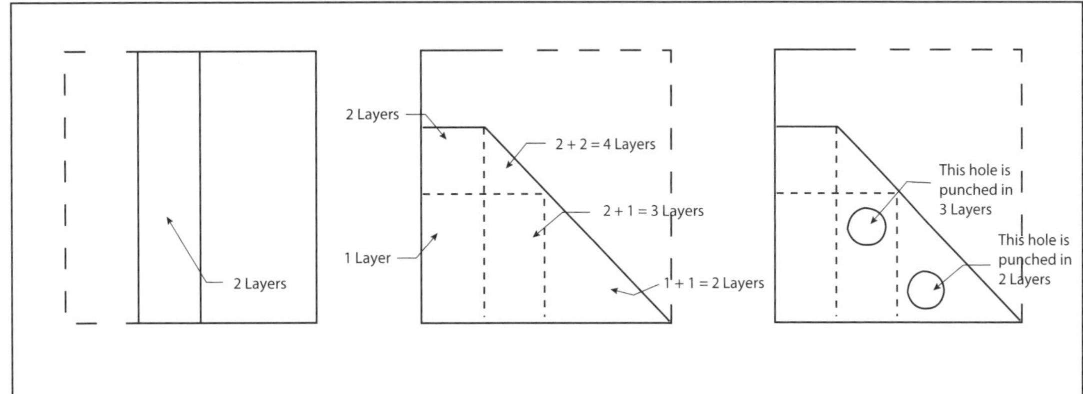

Second: *narrow down the choices*. Three of the choices which are **A**, **B** and **C** are readily eliminated. Subsequently, it is quite impossible to have hole 4-1 because diagonally, the opposite hole of 4-3 is 4-2. This makes **D** the correct answer.

Question 56 D

First: *study the number of layers in each of the holes*. The critical part here is Fold 2 in determining the number of layers where the holes are punched. There are 4 punch holes in total.

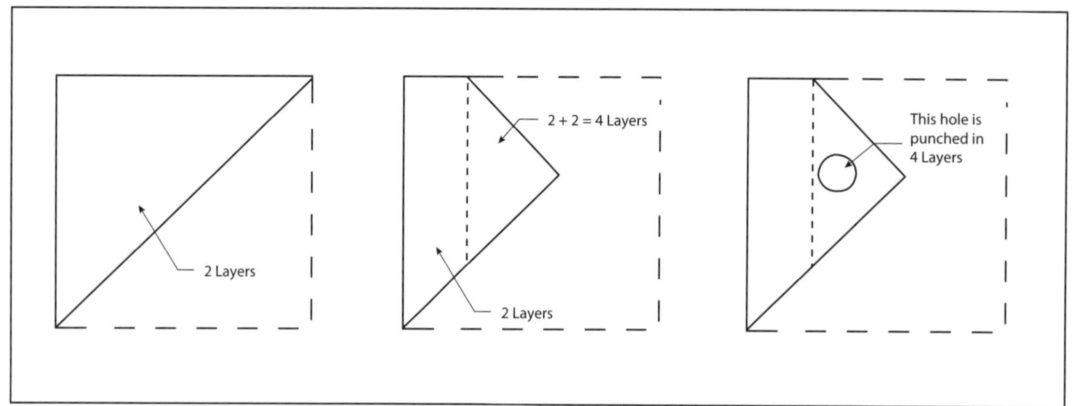

Second: *narrow down choices*. **B** has 6 and E has 3 holes, so these are both incorrect. Do not forget that if you unfold starting in Fold 2, the hidden line would be the upper edge of the plain square sheet. This means that there should be a hole in 2-2. Among the remaining choices, only **D** has the hole 2-2. Therefore, it is the correct answer.

Question 57 B

First: *study the number of layers in each of the holes*. Closely follow the folding in each step. The upper hole is punched in 6 layers while the lower hole is punched in 2 layers. Therefore, the total number of punched holes should be 8

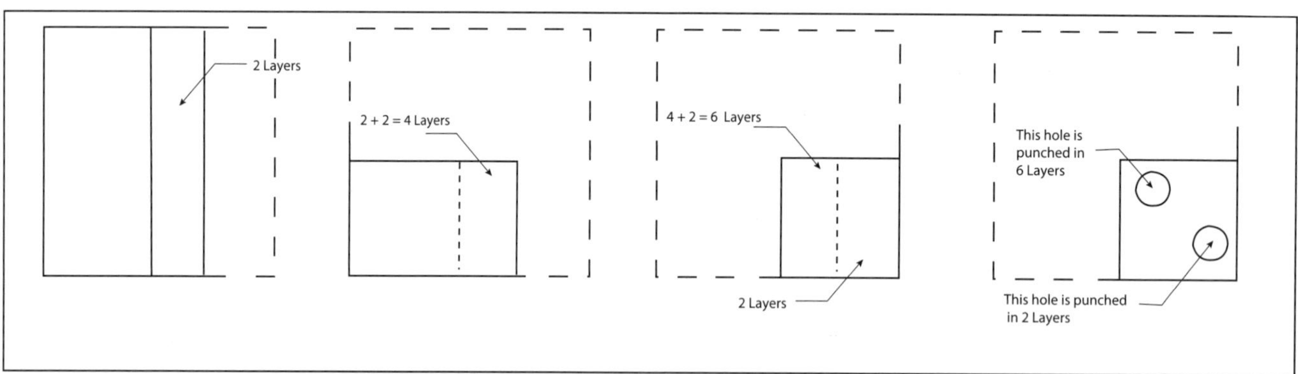

Second: *narrow down the choices*. Options **C**, **D** and **E** are all wrong. Next, notice that the only portion, which is not moved is the left half of the fourth quadrant. However, both **A** and **B** has hole 4-1. The next hole to study is the one which is punched in 2 layers. Through mentally unfolding the 2 layers, you will see that these holes are 3-3 and 1-1. Still **A** and **B** have 3-3 and 1-1. By critically observing the holes in 6 layers and unfolding the hidden parts, you will find that there should be holes 3-4 and 4-2. The option that has these holes is **B**, therefore, the right answer. Another quick way to determine the correct answer is recognizing that the second hole from the lowest right corner does not correspond to the postion of either of the two hole punches. Without visualizing the postion of the other punched holes,you can immediately choose **B** as the best option.

Question 58 E

First: *study the number of layers in each of the holes*. Imagine the folding process starting from Fold 1. If you have trouble picturing things out, try sketching the edges behind the fold and represent this with dashed lines. The upper hole is punched in 4 layers and the bottom hole is punched in 2 layers. Therefore, the total punched holes should be 6.

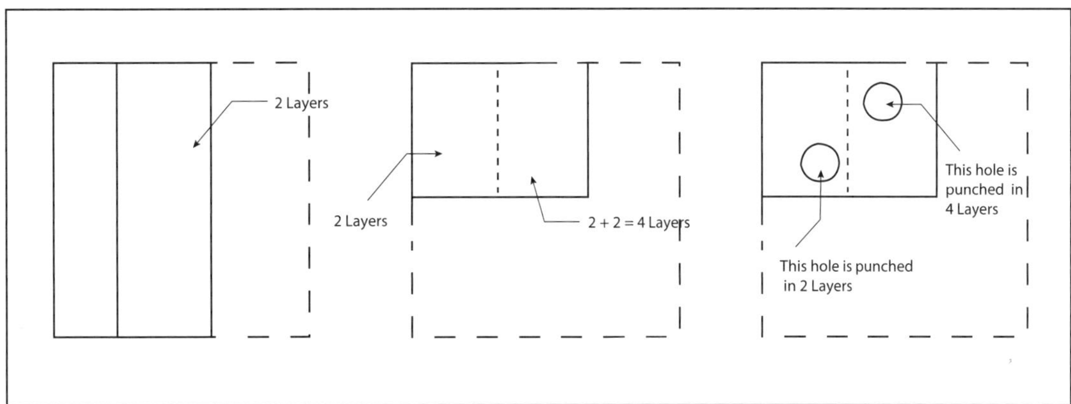

Second: *narrow down the choices*. Since there should be 6 punched holes, options **A**, **B** and **D** can now be eliminated. Both remaining options have holes 1-3 and 2-1. What you need to focus on are the holes punched in 4 layers. You would see that this hole is located on the upper right corner, which is hole 2-2. Option **C** does not have hole 2-2 and so, **E** is the right answer.

Question 59 C

First: *study the number of layers in each of the holes*. The unusual folding pattern shown in this question can be initially scary. However, this is, in fact, an easy question. You can draw the hidden edges and folds in order to avoid getting confused with the layers of the folds. These will serve as your clue in determining the exact location of the hole within the sheet: on the second column and second row from the left side of the paper. For this single punch, 1 hole is punched in 4 layers. This also results to 4 punched holes.

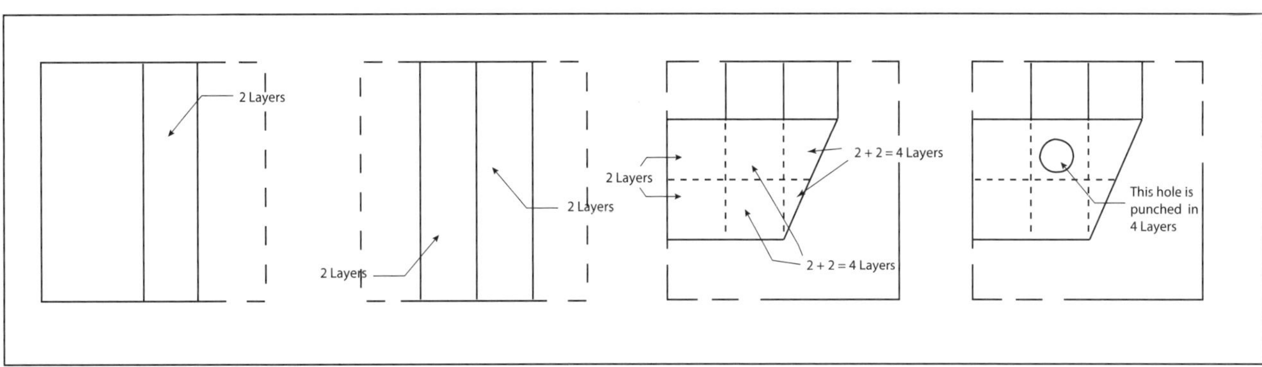

Second: *narrow down the choices*. Of the five options, only **B** does not have 4 holes. Now note that the right half of the first quadrant is not moved, so the position of the hole is 1-4. With this, **A** is automatically wrong. The next hole should be 4-1 since it is the opposite of 1-4 if you unfold Fold 3. This eliminates Option **D**. Finally, if you spread the remaining folds on both sides, holes 1-3 and 4-2 should be apparent, which are all positioned at the edge of the sheet. The correct answer is **C**.

Question 60 A

First: *study the number of layers in each of the holes*. The dashed lines will greatly help you in knowing the different areas of the fold. Knowing the number of layers of each part of the folding would greatly help as well. Through this, it would be clear that the 2 holes are both punched in 3 layers. Hence, the total number of punch holes is 6.

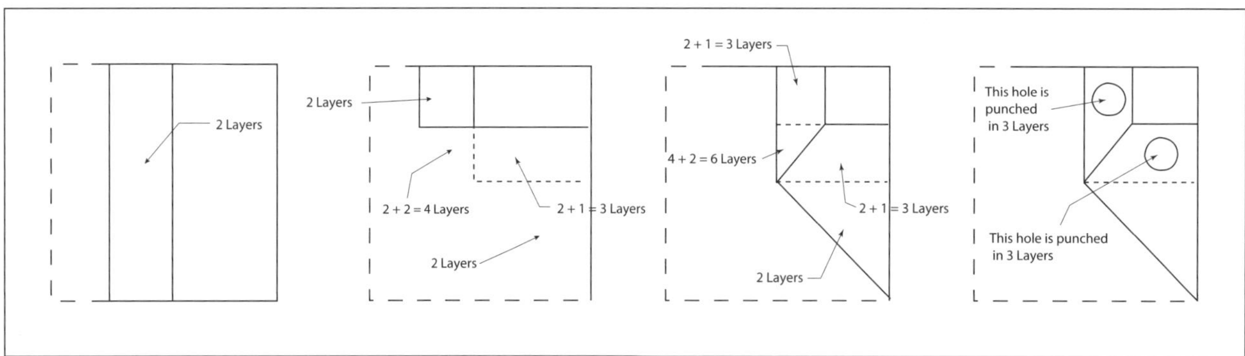

Second: *narrow down the choices*. You can now confidently exclude **B**, **C** and **D** as possible answers. The whole second quadrant remains and it should have holes 2-1 and 2-4. Both **A** and **E** have these holes so you need to proceed evaluating the other holes. The 3 layers where the upper hole is punched is folded from the left and because of that, there should be other holes in the first quadrant namely, 1-1 and 1-2. **A** is the correct answer.

PART 5

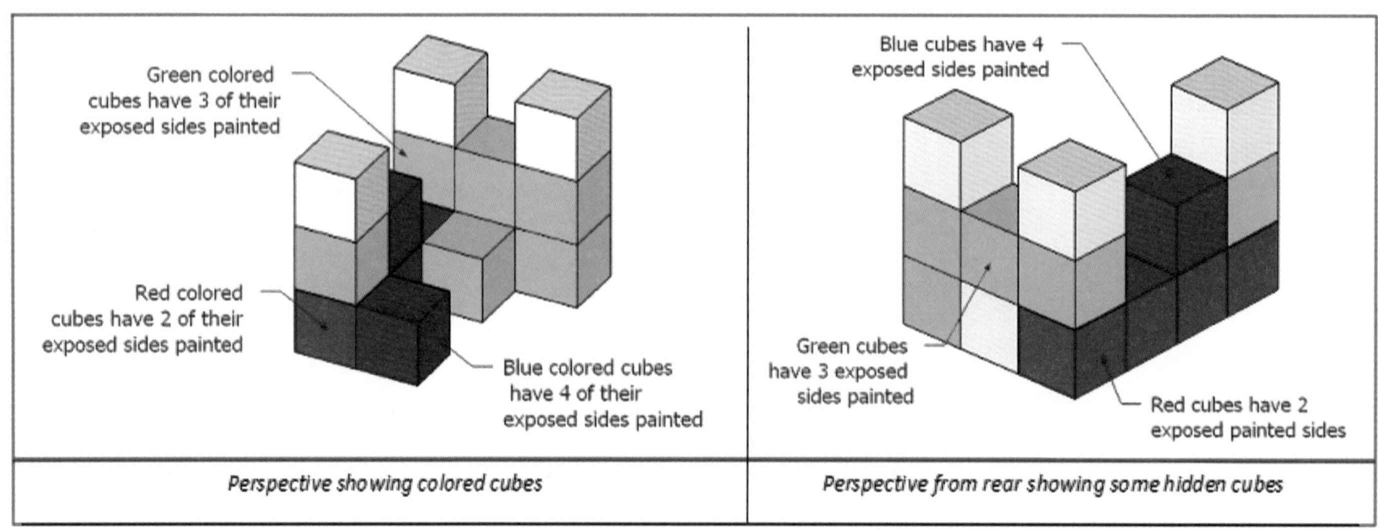

Perspective showing colored cubes | *Perspective from rear showing some hidden cubes*

Question 61 D

When a cube is attached to 3 other cubes excluding the base where it rests, the total number of exposed sides should be 2. The red colored cubes are the ones with 2 exposed sides painted. These cubes are usually located at the bottom or in the middle and often hidden by the other cubes. Hence, there are 4 cubes with 2 exposed sides painted. The answer is **D**.

Question 62 E

On the other hand, the green colored cubes represent those that have 2 other cubes attached to its sides. Remember that the base of the cube is always covered and thus not included in the count as an exposed side. This means that the exposed sides left should be 3. There are a total of 6 green cubes; therefore, the right answer is **E.**

Question 63 B

This question asks for the number of cubes with 4 exposed sides painted. In this case, there are 2 cubes which are connected to only 1 other cube. These are the blue-colored cubes. The correct answer is **B**.

You may also want to designate a number on each of the cube to prevent confusion. Then you can use the formula,which we have dicussed in the chapter lessons on cube counting: number of attached cubes + base of the cube itself = total number of hidden sides; 6 (total number of sides of a cube) – total number of hidden sides = number of exposed sides / painted

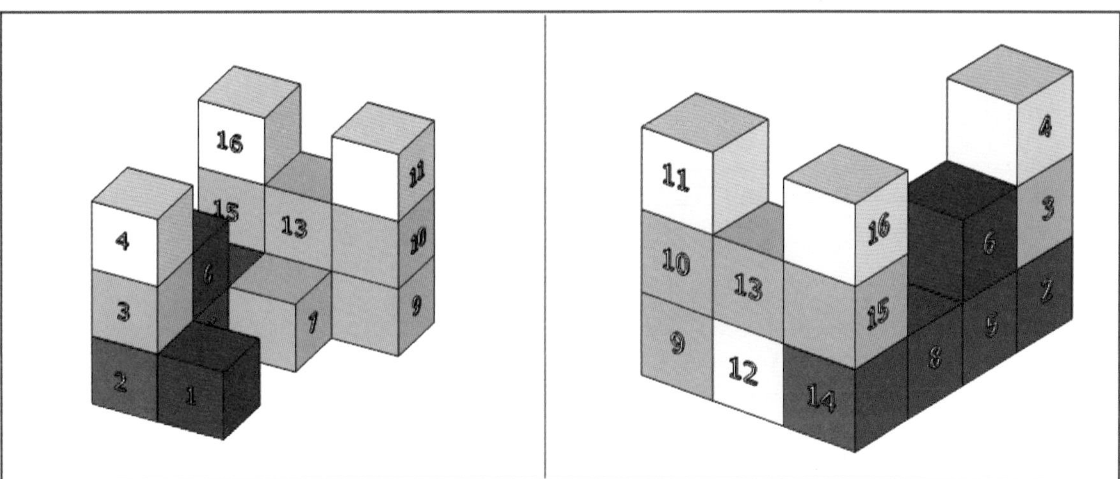

To answer Question 61, you need to look for cubes that have 3 other cubes attached to it. The attached cubes could be stacked to 3 of its sides, or 1 of them is on top of the cube. You do not consider those that are stacked under a cube because these merely serve as the base:

1. Cube 2 has 3 attached cubes, which are cubes 1 and 5 on its sides and cube 3 on its top. So, 3 + 1(base) = 4. Hence, 6 - 4 = 2 exposed sides painted.
2. Cube 5 has 3 attached cubes, which are cubes 2 and 8 on its sides and cube 6 on top. So, 3 + 1(base) = 4. Hence, 6 - 4 = 2 exposed sides painted.
3. Cube 8 has 3 cubes attached to its 3 sides, which are cubes 5, 7, and 14. So, 3 + 1(base) = 4. Hence, 6 - 4 = 2 exposed sides painted.
4. Cube 14 has 3 cubes attached to it, which are cubes 8 and 12 on its sides and cube 15 on its top. So, 3 + 1(base) = 4. Hence, 6 - 4 = 2 exposed sides painted.

In Question 62, since you are required to look for cubes that have 3 sides exposed, you will have to locate those that have 2 other cubes attached to it – either on 2 of its sides or 1 on its side and 1 on top. Again, discount the cube stacked under it because it simply serves as the base:

1. Cube 3 has 2 cubes attached to it, which are cube 4 on its top and cube 6 on one of its sides (cube 2 is not counted because it only serves as a base). So, 2 + 1(base, which is cube 2) = 3. Hence, 6 - 3 = 3 exposed sides painted.
2. Cube 7 has 2 cubes attached to 2 of its sides, which are cubes 8 and 12. So, 2 + 1(base) = 3. Hence, 6 - 3 = 3 exposed sides painted.
3. Cube 9 has 2 cubes attached to it, which are cube 10 on its top and cube 12 on one of its sides. So, 2 + 1(base) = 3. Hence, 6 - 3 = 3 exposed sides painted
4. Cube 10 has 2 cubes attached to it, which are cube 11 on top and cube 13 on one of its sides (cube 9 is not counted since it acts as the base). So, 2 + 1(basc, which is cube 9) = 3. Hence, 6 - 3 = 3 exposed sides painted.
5. Cube 13 has 2 cubes attached to its sides: cubes 10 and 15. So, 2 + 1 (base, which is cube 12) = 3. Hence, 6 - 3 = 3 exposed sides painted.
6. Cube 15 has 2 cubes attached to it, which are cube 13 on one of its sides and cube 16 on its top. So, 2 + 1 (base, which is cube 14) = 3. Hence, 6 - 3 = 3 exposed sides painted.

For Question 63, look for cubes that have 4 other cubes attached to it (except the one acting as base):

1. Cube 1 has only 1 cube attached to one of its sides, which is cube 2. So, 1 + 1(base) = 2. Hence, 6 - 2= 4 exposed sides painted.
2. Cube 6 has only 1 cube attached to one of its sides, which is cube 3. Cube 5 only serves as a base, so this should not be counted as an attachment. So, 1 + 1(base, which is cube 5) = 2. Hence, 6 - 2 = 4 exposed sides painted.

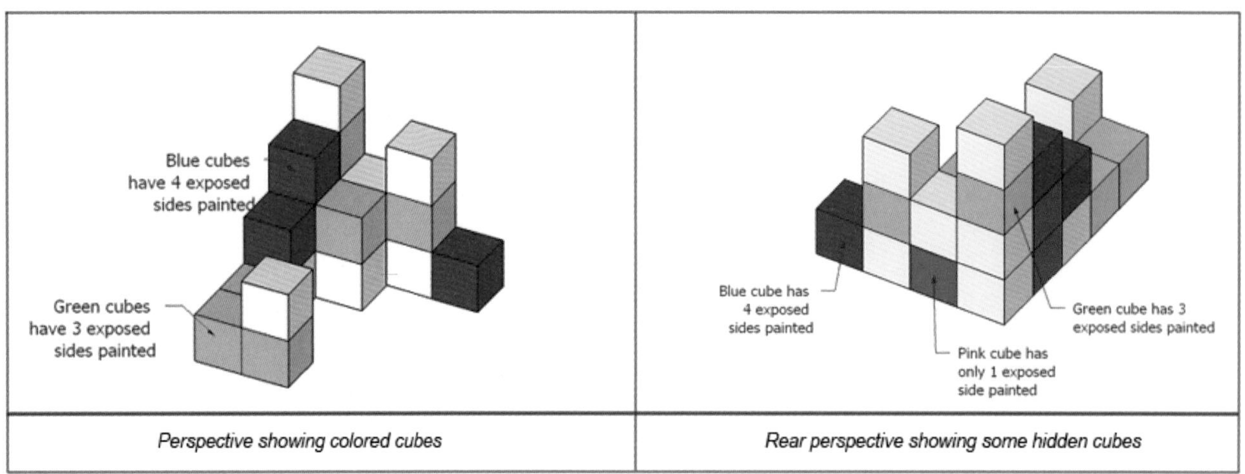

Perspective showing colored cubes | *Rear perspective showing some hidden cubes*

Question 64 C

A cube that has only 1 exposed side should have the most number of attached cubes. As illustrated, the pink colored cubes are surrounded with other cubes on 3 of its sides and 1 on top of it. As a result, only 1 side is seen. There are 3 pink-colored cubes. The correct answer is **C**.

Question 65 D

Since this question is looking for the number of cubes with 3 exposed sides, try locating cubes with 2 other cubes attached to it. Through a keen observation of each cube, you will find 6 cubes with 3 of its exposed sides painted. These are indicated as green cubes in the illustration. **D** is the correct answer.

Question 66 B

Lastly, the blue-colored cubes in the illustration are the ones with 4 of their sides exposed and painted. Always remember that only 1 should be attached to this kind of cube – a cube stacked under it is not counted because it serves as its base. These cubes are often located at the edge of the group. In this case, only 3 cubes in the diagram have 3 of their exposed sides painted. Hence, the correct answer is **B**.

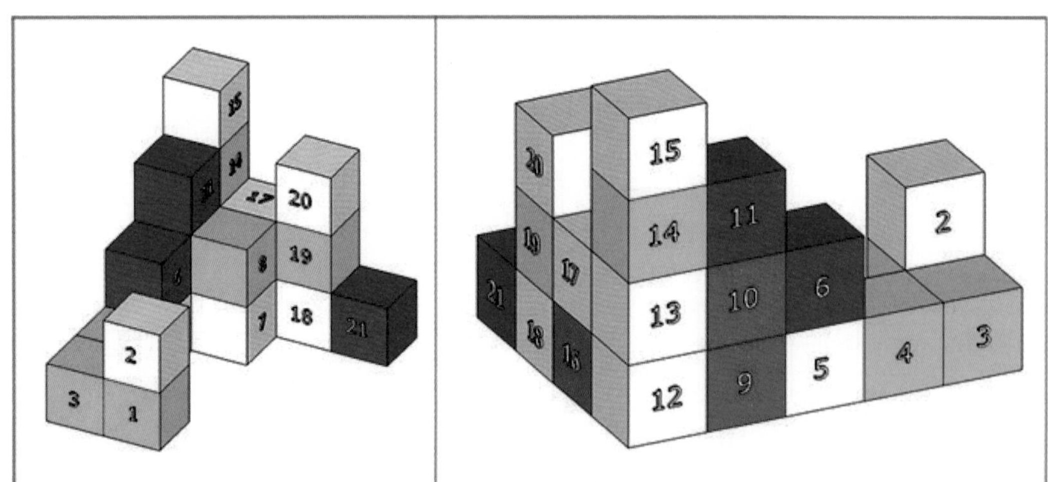

Again, if you are quick in math, you may want to focus on the number of attached cubes to each cube. You can simply subtract the number of cube/s attached to it to 5, which is the total number of sides exposed on each cube, excluding its base. With such information, in addition to assigning a number on each cube, you can note the number of exposed sides of each cube.

To answer Question 64, you need to look for cubes that has the most number of attached cubes (usually 4):

1. Cube 9 has 4 cubes attached to it, which are cubes 12, 5, 7 and 10. So, 4 + 1(base) = 5. Hence , 6 - 5 = 1 exposed side painted.

2. Cube 10 has 4 cubes attached to it, which are cubes 6, 13, 11 and 8. So, 4 + 1(base, which is cube 9)= 5. Hence , 6 - 5 = 1 exposed side painted.

3. Cube 16 has 4 cubes attached to it, which are cubes 7, 12, 18 and 17. So, 4 + 1(base)= 5. Hence , 6 - 5 = 1 exposed side painted.

For Question 65, remember that cubes with 2 other cubes attached to it have 3 of their exposed sides painted:

1. Cube 1 has 2 cubes attached to it, which are cubes 2 and 3. So, 2 + 1(base)= 3. Hence, 6 - 3 = 3 exposed sides painted.

2. Cube 3 has 2 cubes attached to it, which are cubes 1 and 4. So, 2 + 1(base) = 3. Hence , 6 - 3 = 3 exposed sides painted.

3. Cube 4 has 2 cubes attached to it, which are cubes 3 and 5. So, 2 + 1(base) = 3. Hence , 6 - 3 = 3 exposed sides painted.

4. Cube 8 has 2 cubes attached to it, which are cubes 17 and 10. So, 2 + 1(base) = 3. Hence , 6 - 3 = 3 exposed sides painted.

5. Cube 14 has 2 cubes attached to it, which are cubes 11 and 15. So, 2 + 1(base, which is 13) = 3. Hence , 6 - 3 = 3 exposed sides painted.

6. Cube 19 has 2 cubes attached to it which are cubes 17 and 20. So, 2 + 1(base which is 18) = 3. Hence, 6 - 3 = 3 exposed sides painted.

In Question 66, you need to look for cubes, which have only 1 cube attached to it on the side. Do not consider the cube that acts as a base. Start evaluating those that are located on the edges of the diagram:

1. Cube 6 has only cube 10 attached to it, so 1 + 1(base, which is cube 5) = 2. Hence , 6 - 2 = 4 exposed sides painted.

2. Cube 11 has only cube 14 attached to it , so 1 + 1(base which is cube 10) = 2. Hence , 6 - 2 = 4 exposed sides painted.

3. Cube 21 has only cube 18 attached to it, so 1 + 1(base) = 2. Hence , 6 - 2 = 4 exposed sides painted.

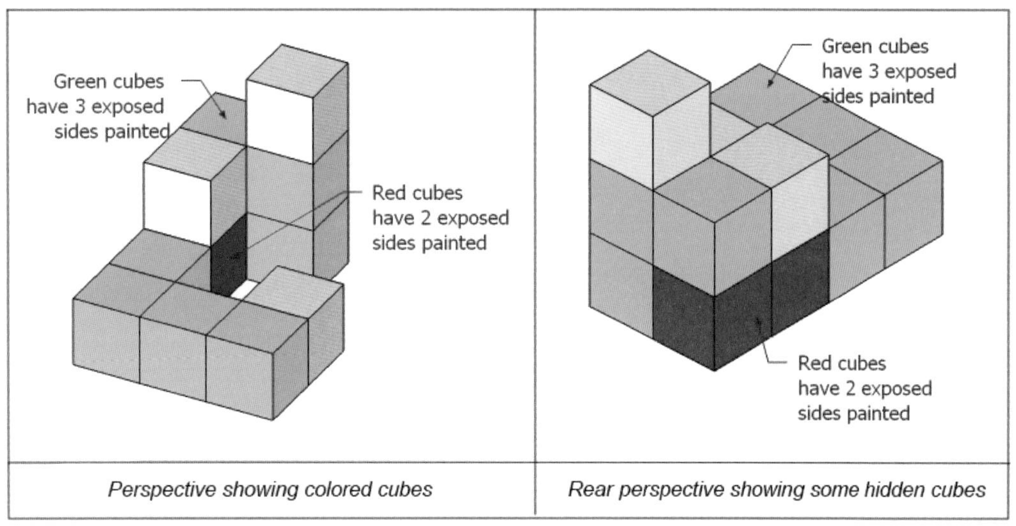

Perspective showing colored cubes | *Rear perspective showing some hidden cubes*

Question 67 A

For questions requiring you to look for for cubes with 2 of their exposed sides painted, you need to focus on the cubes located on the inner portion of the figure. These cubes are colored red in the illustration, and as observed, they are situated at the bottom. There are only 2, so the correct answer is **A**.

Question 68 E

Closely observe that cubes with 3 of their exposed sides painted are mostly seen at the edge of the figure and have 2 cubes attached to it (except those that serve as bases). The green-colored cubes in the illustration represent those with three exposed side. The correct answer is 7 – option **E**.

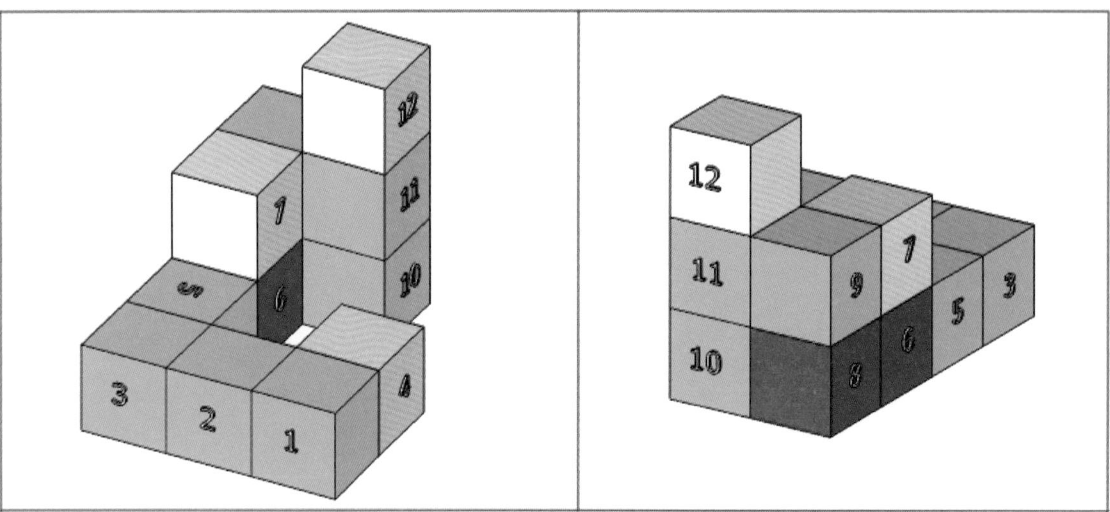

Alternative method: designating numbers or names on each cube, and then adding the number of attached cube/s to a constant 1 (which is the cube's base). The sum is subtracted to 6. The difference is the number of exposed side/s.

To answer Question 67, look for cubes that have 3 other cubes attached except that which acts as its base:

1. Cube 6 has 3 cubes attached to it – cubes 5, 7and 8. So, 3 + 1(base) = 4. Hence, 6 - 4 = 2 exposed sides painted.

2. Cube 8 has 3 cubes attached to it – cubes 6, 9 and 10. So, 3 + 1(base) = 4. Hence, 6 - 4 = 2 exposed sides painted.

In Question 68, your objective is to identify cubes that have 2 other cubes attached to it, except those that serve as their bases:

1. Cube 1 has 2 cubes attached to it – cubes 2 and 4. So, 2 + 1(base) = 3. Hence, 6 - 3 = 3 exposed sides painted.

2. Cube 2 has 2 cubes attached to it – cubes 1 and 3. So, 2 + 1(base) = 3. Hence , 6 - 3 = 3 exposed sides painted.

3. Cube 3 has 2 cubes attached to it – cubes 2 and 5. So, 2 + 1(base) = 3. Hence , 6 - 3 = 3 exposed sides painted.

4. Cube 5 has 2 cubes attached to it – cubes 3 and 6. So, 2 + 1(base) = 3. Hence , 6 - 3 = 3 exposed sides painted.

5. Cube 9 has 2 cubes attached to it – cubes 11 and 7. So, 2 + 1(base) = 3. Hence , 6 - 3 = 3 exposed sides painted.

6. Cube 10 has 2 cubes attached to it – cubes 8 and 11. So, 2 + 1(base) = 3. Hence , 6 - 3 = 3 exposed sides painted.

7. Cube 11 has 2 cubes attached to it – cubes 9 and 12. So, 2 + 1(base, which is cube 10) = 3. Hence , 6 - 3 = 3 exposed sides painted.

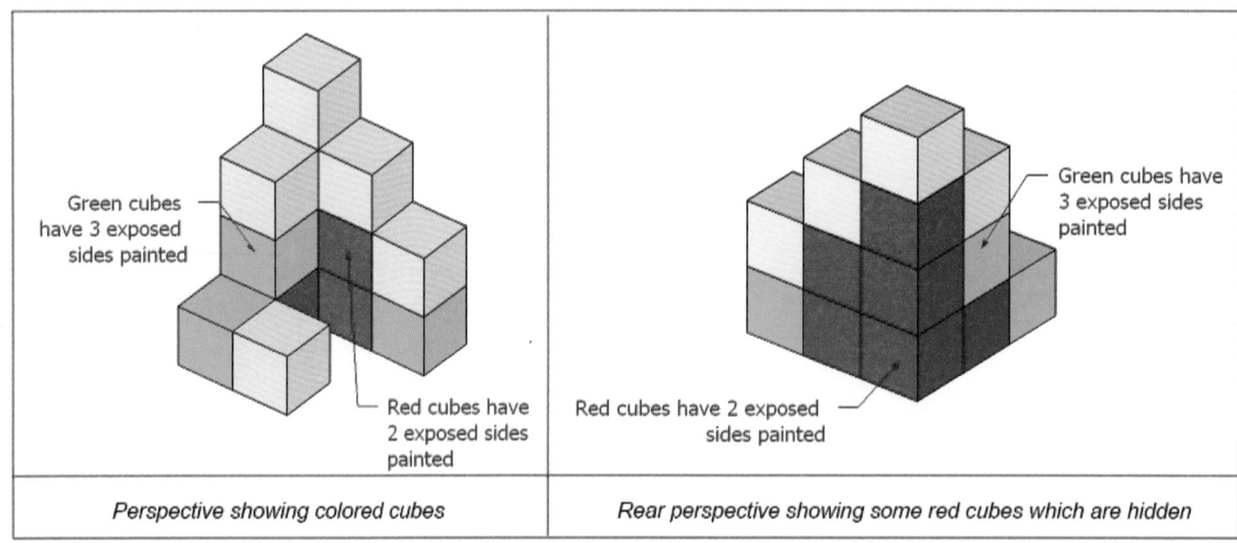

Perspective showing colored cubes	*Rear perspective showing some red cubes which are hidden*

Some cubes are hidden from view in the given perspective of the figure. Just keep in mind that for every cube visible on a second layer, a cube at the bottom of it, which may not be visible, serves as the support base.

Question 69 D

This question asks you to look for cubes with 2 of their sides exposed. These cubes are colored red in the illustration, and there are 6 of them. Thus, the correct answer is **D**.

Question 70 B

This question asks for cubes having 3 of their sides exposed and painted. To aid you in determining these, look for cubes at the corners and edges of the figure with only 1 layer. You will see that these three cubes are colored green in the illustration. The right answer is **B**.

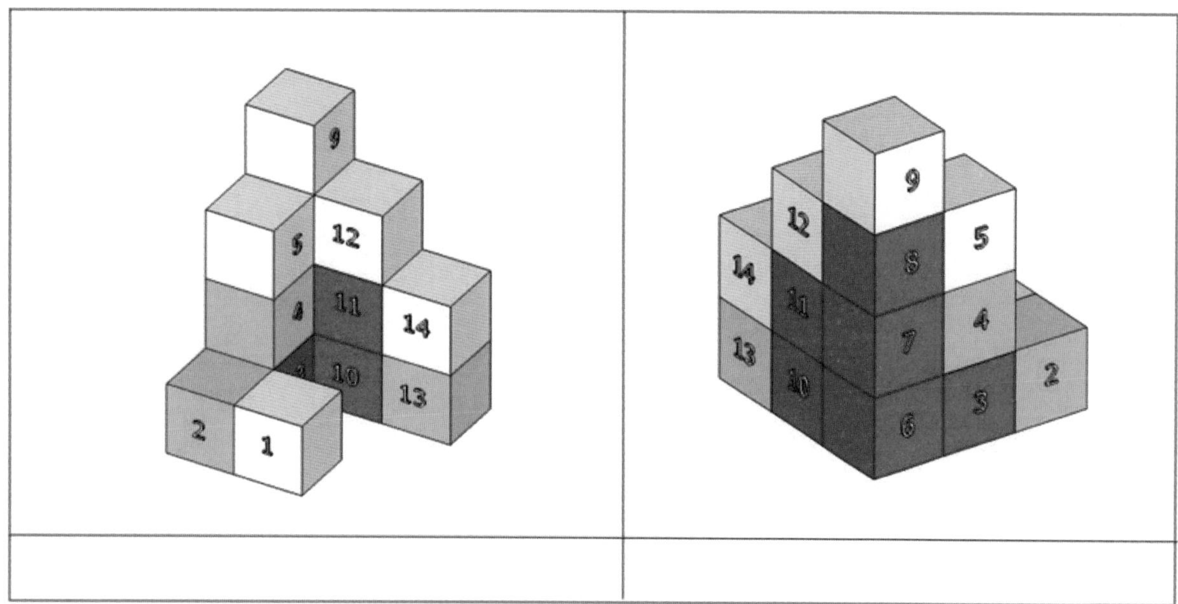

In Question 69, you are asked to determine how many cubes in the fugure would have 2 of its sides exposed. The tricky part in this question is understanding that the topmost cube (cube 9) represents another layer of hidden cubes stacked under it. Cubes of these types, whether placed on the corner or in between the stacks, have 3 other cubes attached to it (on its top and on 2 of its sides) :

1. Cube 3 has 3 cubes attached to it, which are cubes 2, 4 and 6. So, 3 + 1(base) = 4. Hence, 6 - 4 = 2 exposed sides painted.
2. Cube 6 has 3 cubes attached to it, which are cubes 3, 7 and 10. So, 3 + 1(base) = 4. Hence, 6 - 4 = 2 exposed sides painted.
3. Cube 7 has 3 cubes attached to it, which are cubes 4, 8 and 11. So, 3 + 1(base which is cube 6) = 4. Hence, 6 - 4 = 2 exposed sides painted.
4. Cube 8 has 3 cubes attached to it, which are cubes 5, 9 and 12. So, 3 + 1(base which is cube 7) = 4. Hence, 6 - 4 = 2 exposed sides painted.
5. Cube 10 has 3 cubes attached to it, which are cubes 6, 11and 13. So, 3 + 1(base) = 4. Then, 6 - 4 = 2 exposed sides painted.
6. Cube 11 has 3 cubes attached to it, which are cubes 7, 12 and 14. So, 3 + 1(base which is cube 10) = 4. Then, 6 - 4 = 2 exposed sides painted.

Question 70 asks you to count the number of cubes that have 3 sides exposed. These cubes are placed on the edges of the figure. Look for cubes that have 2 other cubes attached either 1 on top and another 1 on one of its sides or on any 2 of its sides:

1. Cube 2 has 2 cubes attached to it, which are cubes 1 and 3. So, 2 + 1(base) = 3. Hence, 6 - 3 = 3 exposed sides painted.
2. Cube 4 has 2 cubes attached to it, which are cubes 5 and 7. So, 2 + 1(base which is cube 3) = 3. Hence, 6 - 3 = 3 exposed sides painted.
3. Cube 13 has 2 cubes attached to it, which are cubes 10 and 14. So, 2 + 1(base) = 3. Hence, 6 - 3 = 3 exposed sides painted.

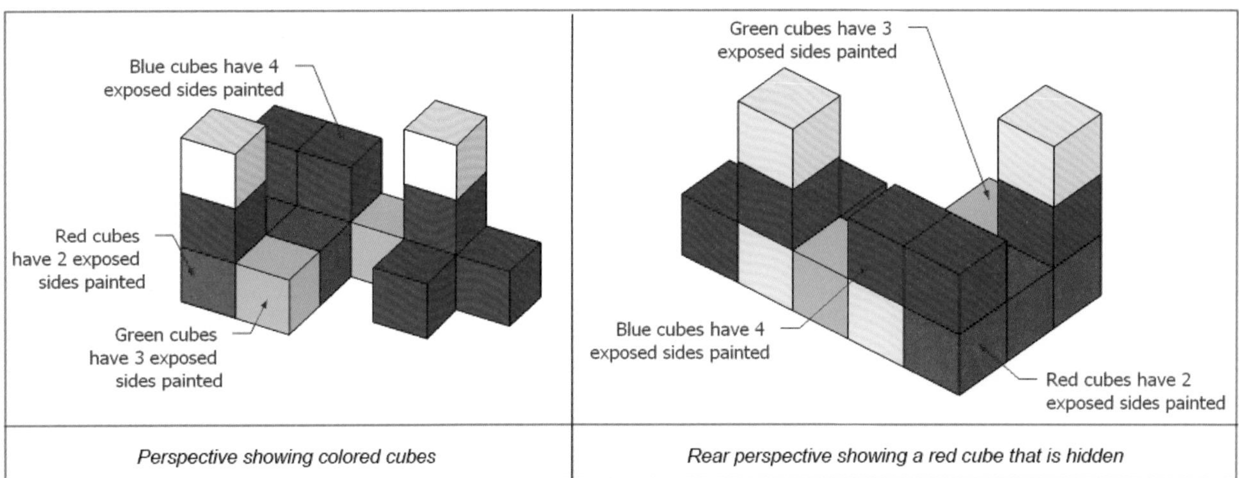

Perspective showing colored cubes | *Rear perspective showing a red cube that is hidden*

Question 71 C

To quickly determine cubes that have only 2 of its sides exposed, look at all corner and bottom cubes. Check whether 3 other cubes are attached on its sides or 2 other cubes are placed on its sides while another 1 is on top of it.

In the illustration, cubes that have 2 of their exposed sides are painted red. There are 3 other cubes attached to the red ones. It is as well evident that a corner cube below another cube has 2 of their exposed sides painted. There are a total of 4 red cubes and so, the right answer is **C**.

Question 72 B

The green-colored cubes in the illustration have 3 of their exposed sides painted. There are only 2 cubes that have this characteristic in the given figure. Hence, the correct answer is B.

Question 73 E

On the other hand, there are 6 cubes that have 4 of their exposed sides, and these are painted in blue in the illustration. The correct answer is **E**.

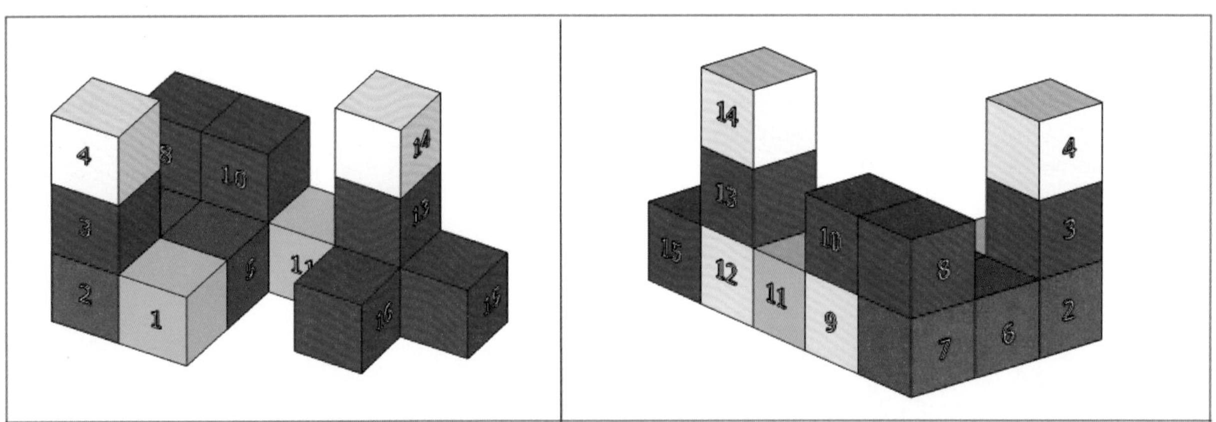

In Question 71, looking for cubes with 2 exposed sides would require you to consider those that have 3 other cubes attached to it:

1. Cube 2 has 3 cubes attached to it, which are cubes 1 and 6 on its sides and cube 3 on top. So, 3 + 1(base) = 4. Hence, 6 - 4 = 2 exposed sides painted.
2. Cube 5 has 3 cubes attached to 3 of its sides: cubes 1, 9 and 6. So, 3 + 1(base) = 4. Hence, 6 - 4 = 2 exposed sides painted.
3. Cube 6 has 3 cubes attached to it on 3 sides: cubes 5, 2 and 7. So, 3 + 1(base) = 4. Hence, 6 - 4 = 2 exposed sides painted.
4. Cube 7 has 2 cubes attached to its sides, which are cubes 6 and 9, and 1 on top, which is cube 8. So, 3 + 1(base) = 4. Hence, 6 - 4 = 2 exposed sides painted.

Question 72 requires you to look for cubes with 2 other cubes attached to it in order to determine those with 3 exposed sides:

1. Cube 1 has 2 cubes attached to its sides, which are cubes 2 and 5. So, 2 + 1(base) = 3. Hence, 6 - 3 = 3 exposed sides painted.
2. Cube 11 has 2 cubes attached to its sides, which are cubes 9 and 12. So, 2 + 1(base) = 3. Hence, 6 - 3 = 3 exposed sides painted.

In Question 73, you need to look for cubes that have only 1 cube attached to determine that these have 4 exposed sides:

1. Cube 3 has only 1 cube attached on its top, which is cube 4. So, 1 + 1(base, which is cube 2) = 2. Hence , 6 - 2 = 4 exposed sides painted.

2. Cube 8 has only 1 cube attached to it which is cube 10. So, 1 + 1(base, which is cube 7) = 2. Hence , 6 - 2 = 4 exposed sides painted.

3. Cube 10 has only 1 cube attached to it, which is cube 8. So, 1 + 1(base, which is cube 9) = 2. Hence , 6 - 2 = 4 exposed sides painted.

4. Cube 13 has only 1 cube attached on its top, which is cube 14. So, 1 + 1(base which is cube 12) = 2. Hence , 6 - 2 = 4 exposed sides painted.

5. Cube 15 has only 1 cube attached to it, which is cube 12. So, 1 + 1(base) = 2. Hence , 6 - 2 = 4 exposed sides painted.

6. Cube 16 has only 1 cube attached to it, which is also cube 12. So, 1 + 1(base) = 2. Hence , 6 - 2 = 4 exposed sides painted.

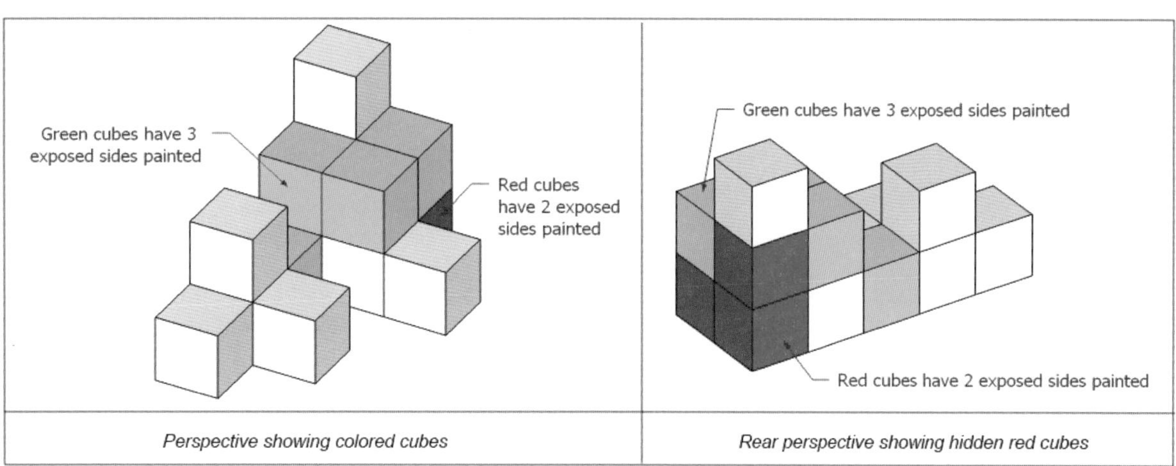

Perspective showing colored cubes | *Rear perspective showing hidden red cubes*

Question 74 C

Cubes that have 2 of their exposed sides painted are frequently seen at the bottom corner of a figure. These cubes are colored red in the illustration. There are a total of 3 red cubes. Thus, the correct answer is **C**.

Question 75 C

This question asks for the number of cubes that have 3 of their exposed sides painted. The green-colored cubes in the illustration are the ones with these characteristics. **C** is the correct answer because there should be 4 cubes with 3 exposed sides.

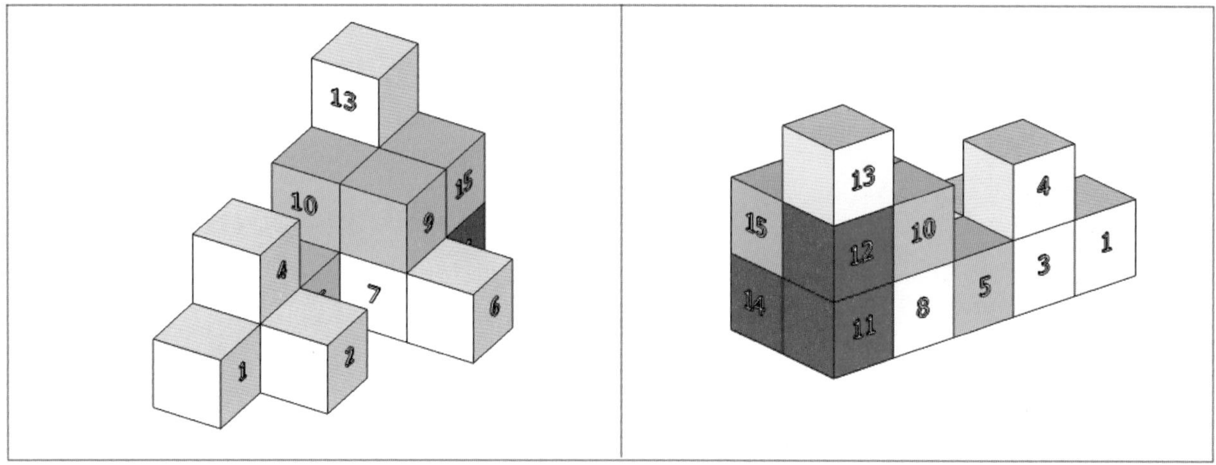

In Question 74, looking for cubes with 2 exposed sides would require you to calculate for those that have 3 other cubes attached to them:

1. Cube 11 has 3 cubes attached to it, which are cubes 14 and 8 on two of its sides and cube 12 on its top. So, 3 + 1(base) = 4. Hence, 6 - 4 = 2 exposed sides painted.

2. Cube 12 has 3 cubes attached to it, which are cubes 10 and 15 on two of its sides and cube 13 on its top. So, 3 + 1(base, which is cube 11) = 4. Hence, 6 - 4 = 2 exposed sides painted.

3. Cube 14 has 3 cubes attached to it, which are cubes 11 and 7 on two of its sides and cube 15 on its top. So, 3 + 1(base) = 4. Hence, 6 - 4 = 2 exposed sides painted.

In Question 75, you need to look for cubes that have 2 other cubes attached to it to confirm that these have 3 exposed sides:

1. Cube 5 has 2 cubes attached to it, which are cubes 8 and 3. So, 2 + 1(base) = 3. Hence, 6 - 3 = 3 exposed sides painted.

2. Cube 9 has 2 cubes attached to it, which are cubes 10 and 15. So, 2 + 1(base) = 3. Hence , 6 - 3 = 3 exposed sides painted.

3. Cube 10 has 2 cubes attached to it, which are cubes 9 and 12. So, 2 + 1(base,which is cube 8) = 3. Hence , 6 - 3 = 3 exposed sides painted.

4. Cube 15 has 2 cubes attached to it which are also cubes 9 and 12. So, 2 + 1(base, which is cube 14) = 3. Hence, 6 – 3 = 3 exposed sides painted.

PART 6

Question 76 B

First: *scan the choices.* This question is somewhat tricky because all the choices are angled in the same direction. However, what really matters here are the locations of the lines. Quite significantly, all options are pentagon-shaped.

Second: *establish the BASE.* Notice that only two parts of the figure are wider than the rest and both are pentagon-shaped. This means that one of them is the base and the corresponding shape is the top. What you need to focus now are the lines on each square (the smaller parts) as you fold the components.

Third: *rotate the folded figure.* You may need to flip the 3D object, making the base become the top portion. You can also put numbers in each component so you do not get confused. The correct answer is **B**.

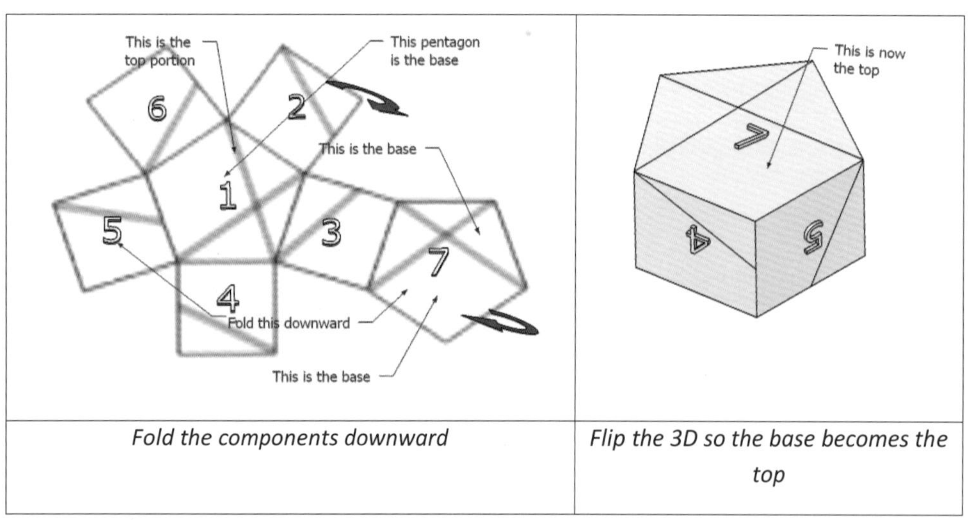

Fold the components downward	*Flip the 3D so the base becomes the top*

Question 77 C

In this question, the options are presented in different perspectives. The shapes of each component in every option varies.

First: *identify the essential features of the object.* Identify the geometric shapes of the object's components: squares and triangles. Notice that the squares are connected to the bigger/longer triangles on both ends and then the smaller triangles on one side each. There are 8 components in total. With these observations, you may be able to examine each option.

Second: *evaluate the options.* **A** is wrong because the smaller triangles are not visible. **B** is also wrong because it has a total of nine components. **C** has 8 components, and each shape from the unfolded figure is represented. **D** is wrong because although it also has 8 components, it shows the rectangle shape on two of its components. Thus, **C** is the correct answer.

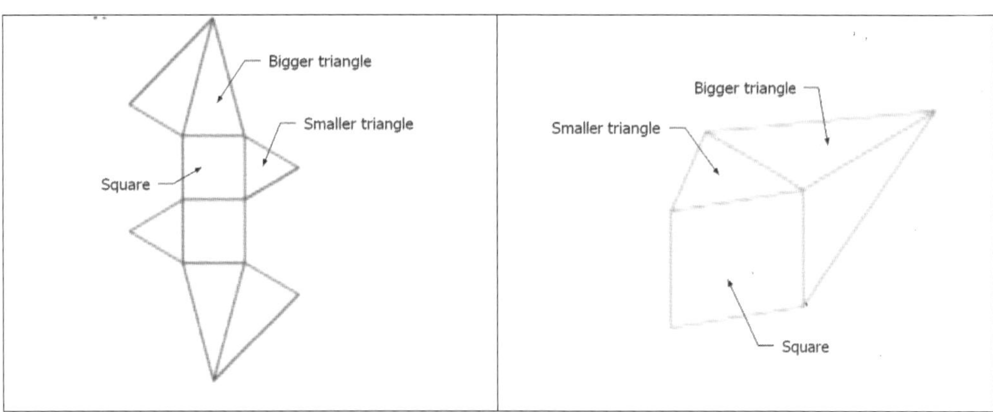

Question 78 D

The figure is just a simple cube. When figures have shadings or lines, you simply fold the components in a downward direction.

First: *compare each option.* Check the orientation of the shades in relation to each other. In option **A**, the position of the triangular obtuse shades should be sideways, not top and bottom, to the rectangular shade on the top face of the cube. In **B**, the positions of the rectangular shade on top and triangular shapes below it are correct. However, the horizontal rectangular shade on the center of the cube's right face should not be there. It should be on the other side and should be positioned in a vertical orientation. **C** has the correct orientation of the triangular and linear shades. However, a closer look at the triangular shades would reveal that their angles are neither obtuse nor equilateral. This leaves **D** as the correct answer.

Second: *visualize the folding process.* To double-check, simply visualize folding the figure continuously downward.

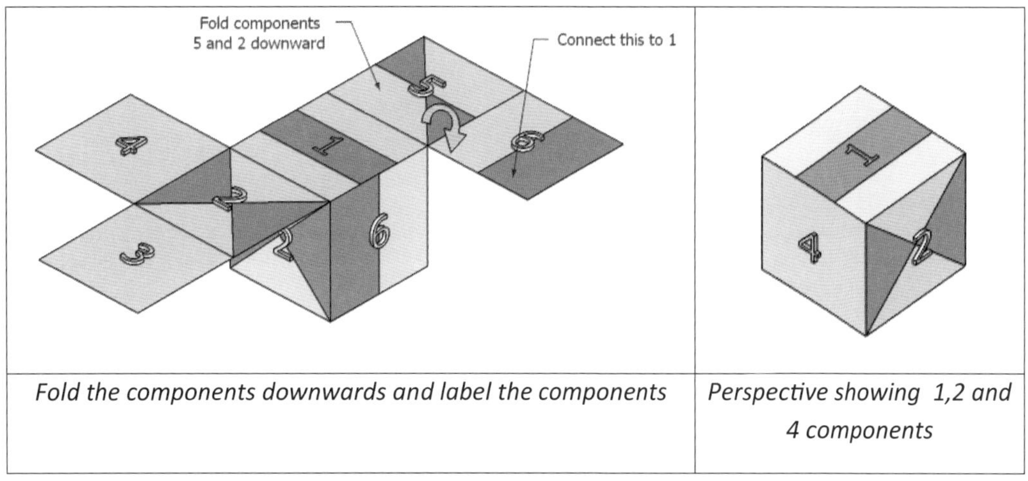

Fold the components downwards and label the components	*Perspective showing 1,2 and 4 components*

Question 79 B

First: *establish the BASE. At first glance, all the options are quite similar.* The tricky part is that they are all angled from different views. As seen in the unfolded figure, the biggest area has six sides and is located at the center portion. The rectangular components represent the depth or thickness of the object.

Second: *compare the options.* Immediately, you can eliminate **D** because its rectangular components are significantly wide. Between **A** and **B**, the sharply angled protrusion is longer in **A** than in the original figure. This is incorrect. Next, take note that the unfolded figure shows right angle corners on the opposite side of the nose-like protrusion. **C** has a right angle on one corner and a 1350 angle on the other corner. Option **B** is the correct answer since its base follows the same shape as the unfolded figure.

Question 80 B

First: *establish the BASE and count the components*. All of the options resemble a stair-like object. With this, you may choose the biggest area on the unfolded figure where many other components are connected. The dashed lines mean that the edges of some components are connected to it. Moreover, it is necessary to know that there are 13 components in total including the base.

Second. *Compare the options*. Option **A** is incorrect because there is a big rectangular piece on it and there are only 12 components. Options **C** and **D** are both wrong because **C** has only 10 components while **D** has 16. The correct answer is **B**.

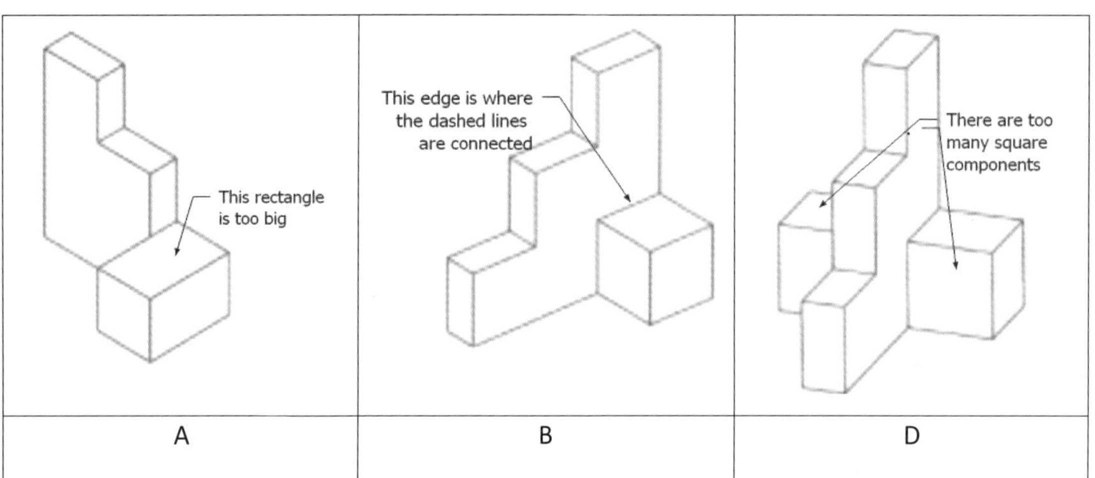

Question 81 C

First: *establish the BASE and then count the components*. For figures with a base that has a highly irregular shape, you have to take extra note of the details such as the number of slopes and the adjacency of the edges. In this case, the base has 2 sloping sides which are opposite to each other. The number of components totals 12.

Second: *compare the choices*. Keenly observe that there are 3 sloping sides on the base of option **A**, so this can be eliminated. **B** has only 8 components, which is wrong. Option **D** has a curved edge towards the top of the figure, which is also incorrect. This leaves **C** as the correct answer.

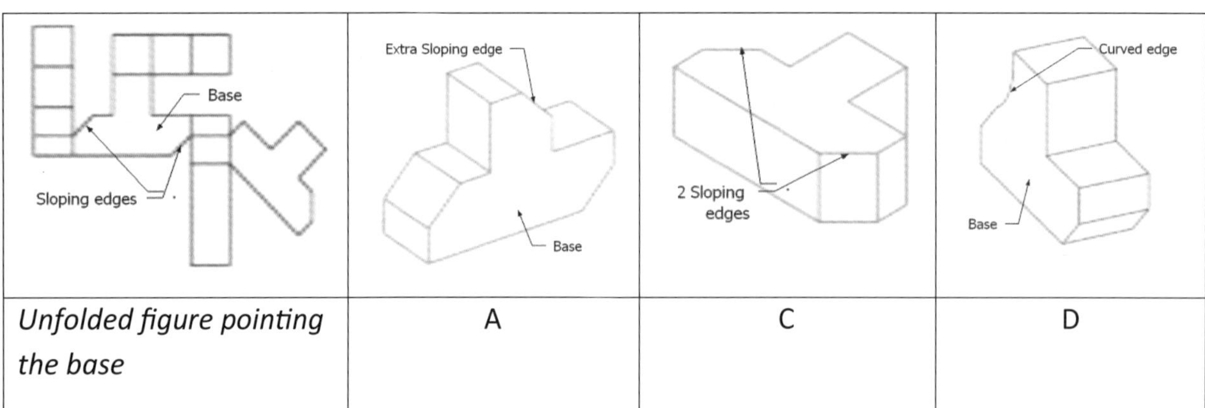

Question 82 A

First: *establish the BASE and count the components*. Assign numbers to each component as shown in the following illustration.

There are 9 components in the figure. Mentally fold the components surrounding the square base in a downward direction. You would realize that component 7 should be connected to components 1 and 3. By twisting the 3D figure, you will see that A is the correct answer.

Second: *compare the choices*. Keenly observe that components 8 and 7 are always connected to each other. Options **B** and **D** are both incorrect because the orientation of the shadings on component 8 and 7 do not correspond to the patterns shown on the unfolded figure. Option **C** is also incorrect since the shading of component 2 should be adjacent to that of component 4.

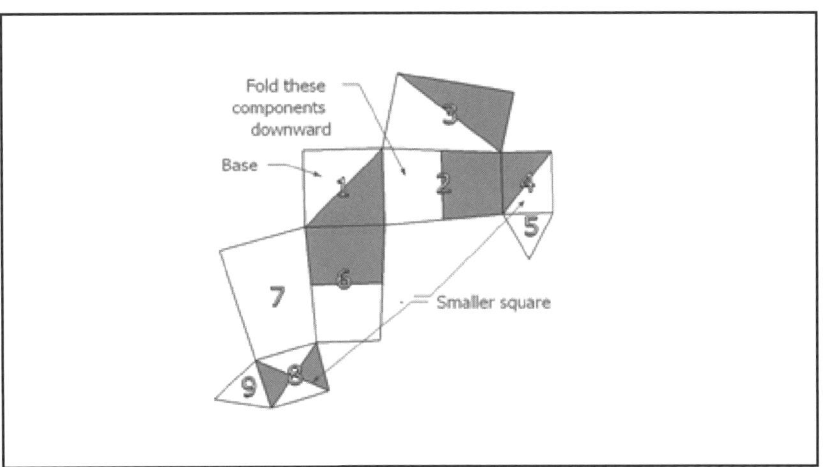

Question 83 D

This is another 3D figure, which is just a cube. Because a cube has a very basic, clean outline, you can directly go over each of the options and compare them with the patterns on the unfolded figure. Option **A** is obviously wrong because there is no way that the 3 unshaded sides would be directly adjacent to each other when attached. **B** is also incorrect because an unshaded side comes in between components 1 and 3, so they cannot be adjacent to each other either. **C** is wrong as well because the shaded part of component 6 should be inverted as shown on the unfolded figure. Therefore, **D** is the correct answer.

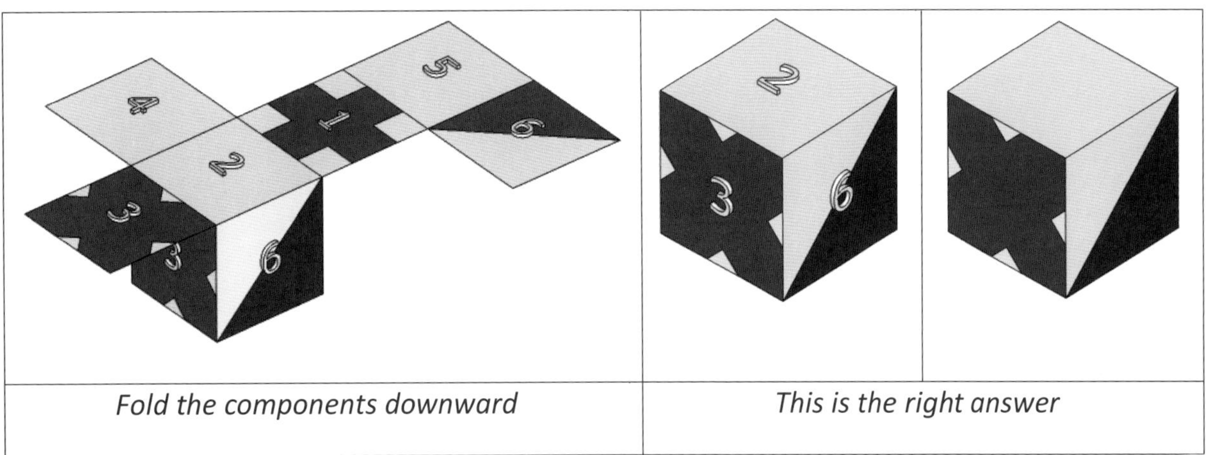

Fold the components downward	*This is the right answer*

Question 84 B

First: **establish the BASE**. All given choices look very similar in form, which is like a staircase. Counting the components will not work here because all options have 12. You must then carefully examine the base of the unfolded figure and focus on the differences in the dimensions of the components of the four options.

Second: evaluate each option. You can see that **A** has wider "steps" compared to the components of the unfolded figure. **B** has the most exact shapes and sizes of all the parts. Option C on the other hand, has square components which are obviously incorrect. Lastly, **D** is rectangular but they are narrower. This means **B** is the best answer.

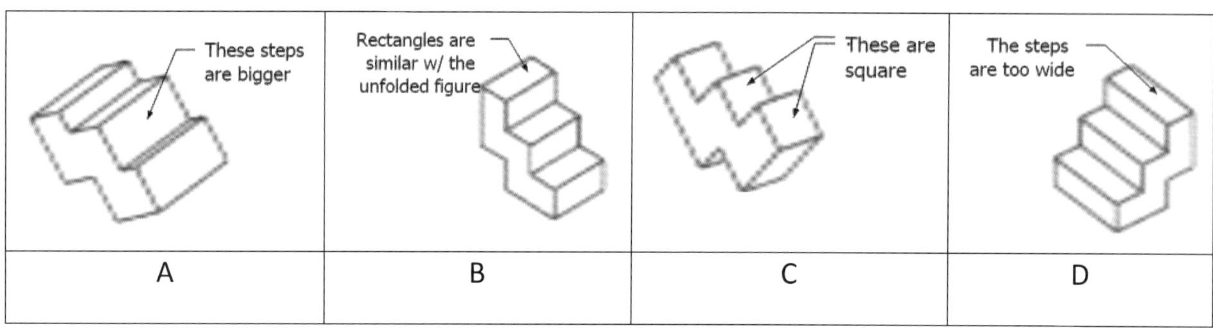

Question 85 D

First: *establish the BASE and count the components.* Again, choose the most unique and biggest component as the base. In this item, the base has 8 straight sides and 1 sloping side. In total, there are 11 components.

Second: *compare the choices.* If you twist option **A**, it has an "extra" 900 angled cut on its ledge, opposite the sloping side. Another wrong answer is **B** because it has 2 sloping sides instead of just 1. Next, observe that **C** has the widest surface for the base and lacks the inner angled cuts on the figure. This leaves **D** as the correct answer.

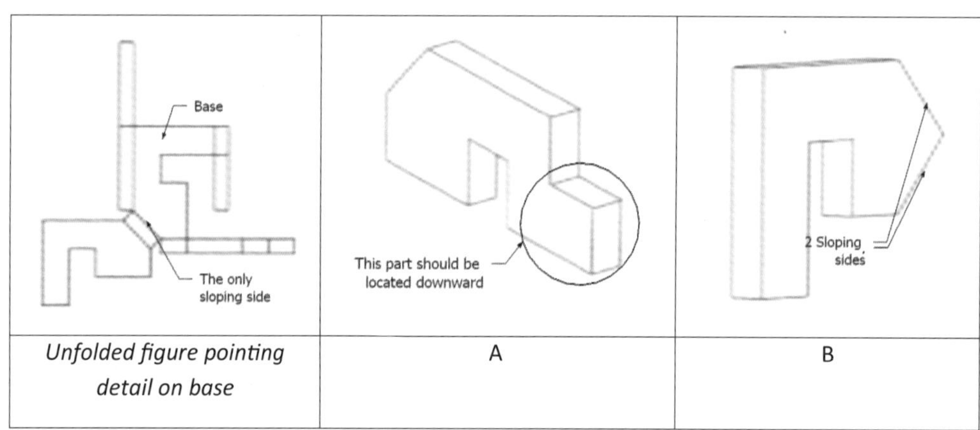

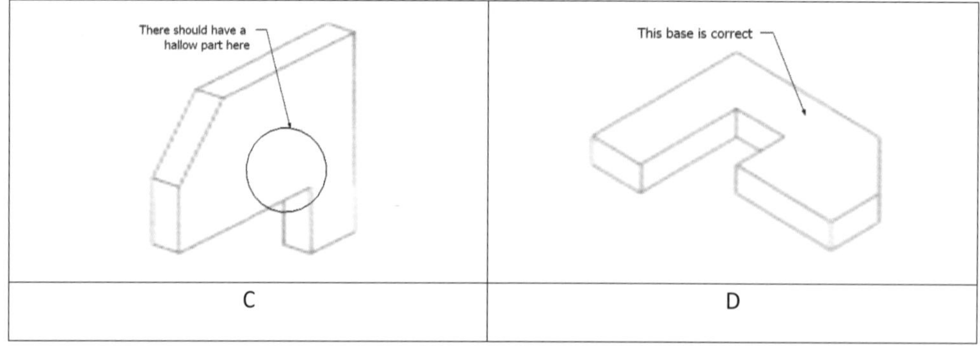

Question 86 C

First: *establish the BASE and count the components.* In this question, you have to keep in mind that the squares and the rectangles represent the thickness of the 3D object. Notice that the base has 4 straight sides, 1 sloping side, and 1 curved side.

Second: *compare the choices.* If you scan the options, **D** is clearly wrong because it is too thin and the square component is not present. Options **A** and **B** are also incorrect because they have 2 curved sides. The correct answer is **C**.

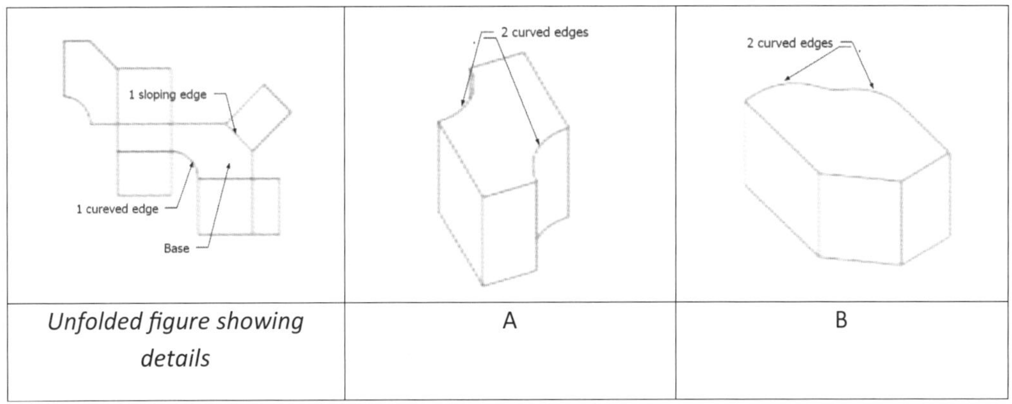

Unfolded figure showing details | A | B

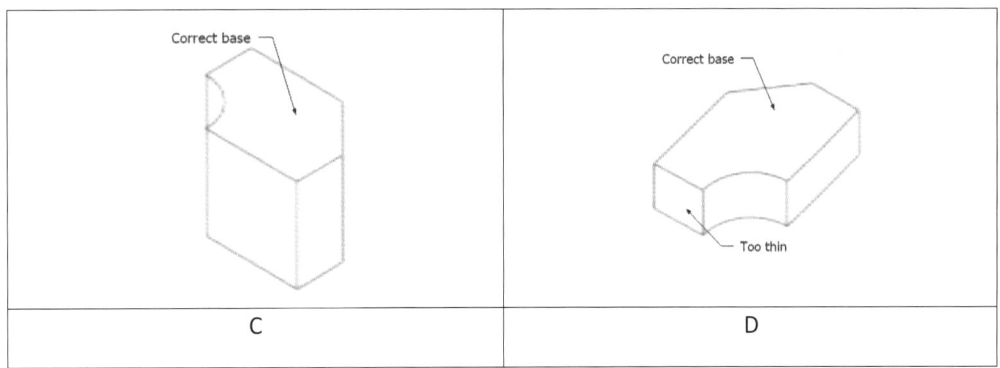

C | D

Question 87 A

This is an easy one. By simply comparing the largest surface and the thickness of the other rectangular components to each of the choices, you will realize that **A** is the correct answer. **B** has a thicker rectangular piece, which makes it a wrong choice. Options **C** and **D** have too different bases compared to the base of the unfolded figure. **A** is the best choice.

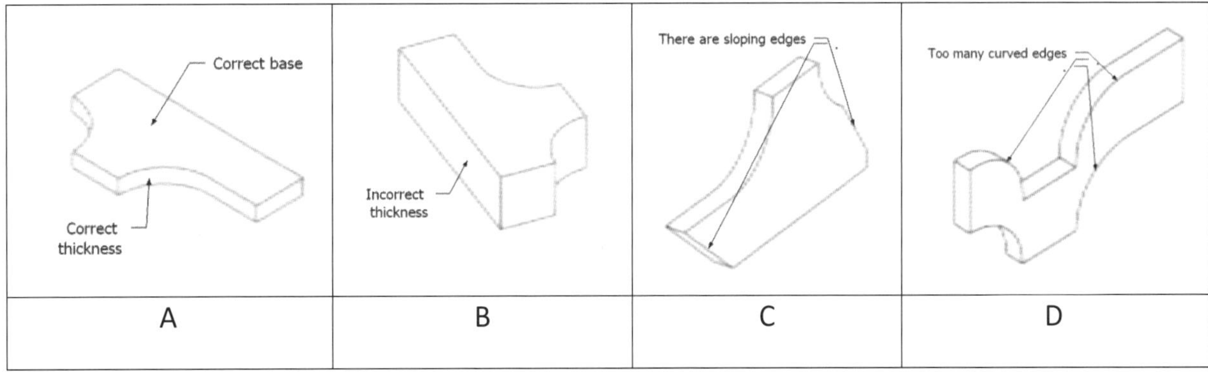

A | B | C | D

Question 88 C

First: *establish the base*. Choose the base where you can fold the other components around it. In this case, it is the pentagon shape with 2 triangular shades. Start folding the other components. A rough sketch will help here a lot. You can also put numbers on each side for easy distinction.

Second: *keenly compare the shading patterns in each option.*

Take careful note of the adjacent components and use your numbering. If nothing seems to match, try to visually twist or rotate the 3D figure. In Option **A**, the position of the 2 triangular shades on top (component 1) is reversed, therefore, incorrect. **B** has the correct orientation of the shadings in components 1, 2 and 3. However, component 4 should have the rectangular shade at the bottom. Option **B** shows a diagonal or triangular one, hence incorrect. **C** shows the shading orientation of components 7,6 and 2 to be correct. **D** shows the incorrect pattern of the shadings when the figure is folded.

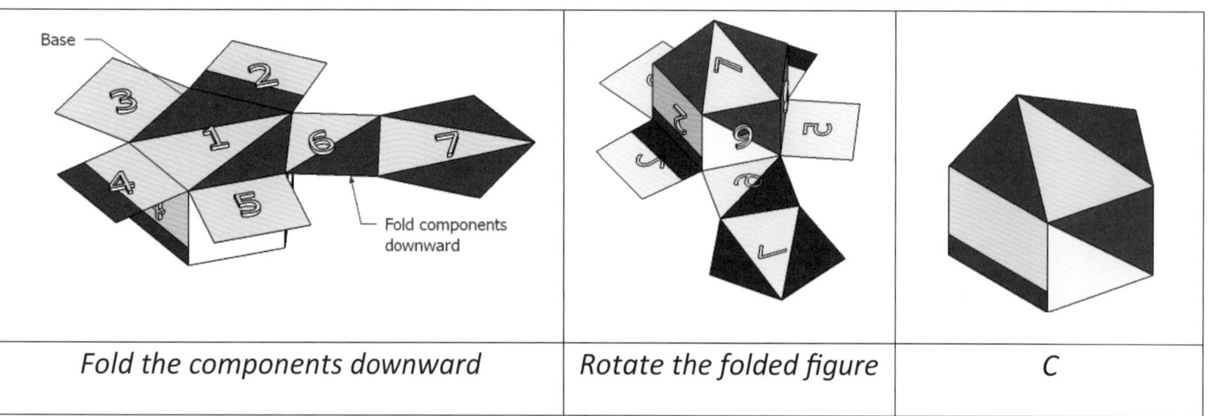

Fold the components downward	Rotate the folded figure	C

Question 89 A

First: *number each component.* Similar to Question 83, assigning a number on each side of the figure makes remembering the adjacent and attached sides easier. After folding the components in a downward direction, you can start comparing the different options.

Second: *evaluate the choice that shows the only different pattern.* Since options, **A**, **B**, and **C** all show the same orientation of the triangular shadings of 2 adjacent components, starting with **D** would be much easier. Components 2 and 3 would show two right triangles facing opposite each other and forming a white "V" in between as shown in **D**'s pattern. No other possible "combinations" seems to show the white "V" pattern. Now look at the possible third/adjacent face, which is component 4 and should be blank. **D** is definitely wrong.

Third: compare the choices with similar patterns. Next, consider the 3 options left. Look at the unfolded figure and imagine how the 4 components with the triangular shadings (2, 3, 5, and 6) show when "combined" once the figure is folded. You should visually twist and rotate the 3D figure.

A combination of components 3 and 6 would show a shaded "V" at the center (similar to the pattern shown on **A**, **B**, and **C**). Now look at the possible third component. An adjacent, third component would be 2. However, the resulting pattern would show an inverted shaded "V". None of the three options shows this pattern. Next, consider component 5. The resulting pattern is similar to option **A**.

To double-check, components 3 and 5 also show the pattern of a shaded "V." A third, adjacent face would be component 4, which has a blank face. None of **A**, **B**, or **C** shows this pattern.

No other combination or pattern seems possible. This confirms **A** as the correct answer.

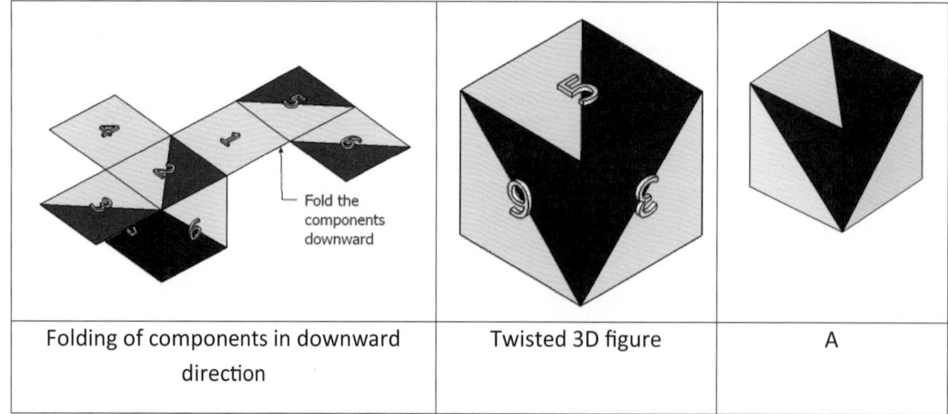

Folding of components in downward direction	Twisted 3D figure	A

Question 90 B

For this question, you need to count the number of components, which totals to 13. The unfolded figure does not have any unique component or part, so keep in mind that all geometric shapes must be equally important. The shapes that are found here are squares, trapezoids, and triangles. Take note that there should be smaller square components in the 3D figure. Only option **B** has this feature. Hence **B** is the correct answer.

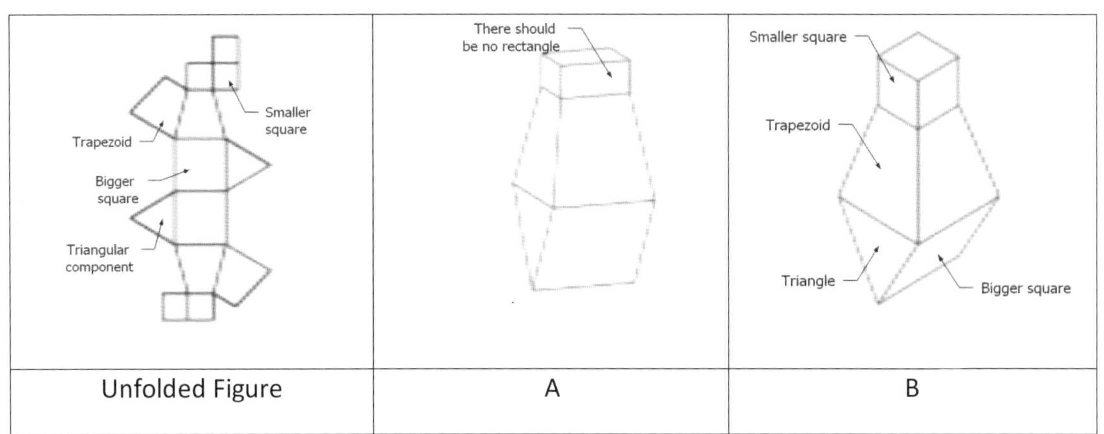

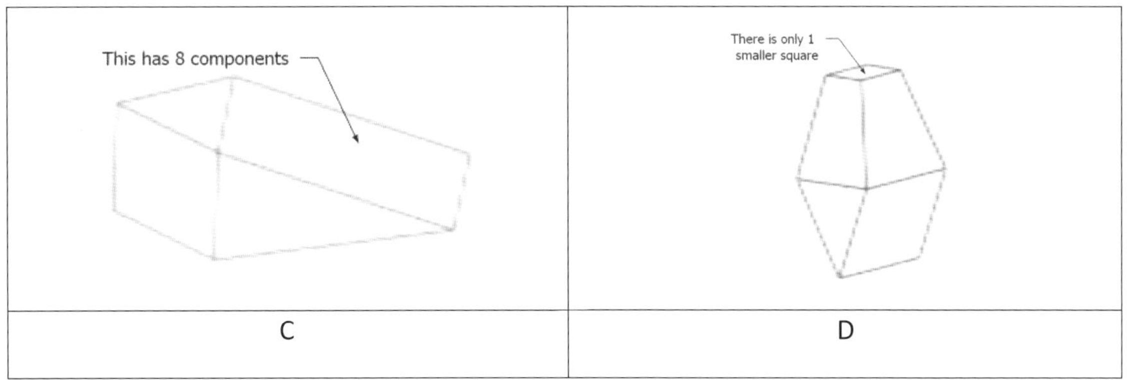

Question 1. C

Question Type: Recall

Strategy: SI; prior knowledge; P1 S3

This question can be somewhat tricky to a non-science candidate. The term "cosmic ray" is slightly mentioned in Paragraph 1 without any explicit reference to its meaning or scientific label. However, in Sentence 3, we can infer from the following line that "cosmic rays" pertain to the ionized atomic nuclei hitting the Earth's atmosphere: "ionized atomic nuclei hit the Earth's atmosphere continuously, with such 'cosmic rays' providing hints on energetic processes . . ."

The other answers are merely distractions. Option **A** is a typical decoy in the DAT RC, wherein one of the options is mentioned in one of the last two paragraphs. Indeed, the idea of "footprints of the air shower" is indicated in Paragraph 14. However, such elements are only one of the means to track cosmic rays. Paragraph 9 denotes the same idea pertaining to "short-lived particles." This makes **D** also incorrect.

The hypothesis that cosmic rays are gamma rays was put forward by Robert Millikan, but it is conclusively eliminated in Paragraph 13. **B** is thus incorrect. Finally, in Paragraph 12, some physicists suggested "the decay of magnetic monopoles" to generate cosmic rays – they are not cosmic rays themselves. This eliminates **E**.

Question 2 C

Question Type: Recall
Strategies: SaL, PoE; P2 S3 and S4

Question 3 E

Question Type: Recall
Strategies: SaL, attention to details; P2 S2 to S3
This question can be confusing because several names of scientists are mentioned within the passage. The main strategy here is to locate either the very first scientist who was named in the passage or the scientist whose work was associated to the earliest date. Fortunately, you only have to look for the one who was first mentioned in Paragraph 2:

"In 1910, a Jesuit priest named Theodor Wulf (1868 – 1946) went up the Eiffel Tower in Paris to measure radiation levels with an 'electroscope'."

The work of the other scientists came at later dates. Paragraph 4 identifies (A) Victor Hess as the physicist who made a series of ten balloon flights with an electroscope to investigate the phenomenon in 1911 to 1912. (B) Werner Kollhoerster is the German researcher who confirmed Hess' findings by conducting his own flights sometime in 1914. (C) Walter Boethe entered the picture only in 1929 when, together with Kollhoerster, he built a "coincidence counter" to study the real nature of cosmic rays (P6). Paragraph 7 would prove that (D) Arthur Holly Compton conducted his own studies in 1932.

E is the best answer.

Question 4 D

Question Types: Recall; Math-related
Strategies: SaL, attention to details; P4 S1 to S3
In 1911-1912, Victor Hess made a series of 10 balloon flights with an electroscope to investigate Wulf's suggestion that the radiation might be coming from the upper atmosphere or space. On the other hand, the German researcher named Werner Kollhoerster made 5 flights of his own, the last of which was on June 28, 1914 Thus, a total of 15 balloon flights were conducted manually.

Question 5 E

Question Type: Recall
Strategy: SI; P8, S4
Hess received the Nobel Prize for Physics in 1936 for discovering cosmic rays; although there was a widespread belief for a period of time that Robert Millikan discovered cosmic rays.

Question 6 B

Question Type: Recall
Strategy: SaL; P10, S1

Question 7 B

Question Type: Recall
Strategies: SaL, attention to details; P10, S2

Question 8 B

Question Type: Recall
Strategies: SaL or SI, attention to details in P11
This is a very easy question, although you need to make a careful reading of Paragraph 11 in order to weed out the other keywords and confirm "background noise" as the correct answer.

Question 9 B

Question Type: Recall
Strategies: SaL and SI
This question can only be confusing because of the other valid-sounding keywords. Also, option **B** is verbatim of the elements mentioned in Paragraph 12, which seems too easy and can make you suspicious if this is indeed the correct answer. Nevertheless, **B** is the best choice.

Question 10 E

Question Type: Recall
Strategies: SaL, PoE; P13, S1

Question 11 B

Question Type: Recall
Strategies: SI, attention to details; P5 S1, P9 S1 and last sentence
This question looks as though you would need to do a careful reading and then take note of specific dates from Paragraph 4 to Paragraph 7. However, the correct answer can be simply inferred from the last sentence of Paragraph 9:

"In the postwar period, up to the early 1950s, cosmic rays were investigated with balloons that carried stacks of photographic emulsions to high altitude to record the traces of these particles."

The postwar period is indicated in the passage to have begun in 1922 when Robert Millikan started conducting studies by launching automated balloons. This is stated in Sentence 1 of Paragraph 5. This confirms B (the period between 1922 and 1950) to be the best answer.

Question 12 D

Question Type: Evaluation Question (Implication)
Strategies: SI, PoE; P14, last sentence.
This question requires you to carefully understand and infer the relevance of the LOFAR telescope to the information discussed in Paragraph 14.

In the last sentence of Paragraph 14, it is mentioned that "the LOFAR low frequency radio telescope has been used for this purpose." As to the exact purpose, we can refer to the last part of Sentence 1 in the same paragraph where the detection of radio energy generated by the air shower is mentioned as the purpose for using LOFAR low-frequency radio telescope.

You may also opt to eliminate the other options by checking if any mention of the LOFAR telescope in relation to gamma rays, alpha particles, supernovas, or protons is mentioned.

Question 13 C

Question Type: Recall
Strategy: SaL; P13, S3

Question 14 D

Question Type: Recall
Strategy: Sal; P11, S1

Question 15 C

Question Type: True False Statements (Two Statements)
Strategies: SI; P14, S1
The first two measures of observing cosmic rays mentioned in Sentence 1 of Paragraph 14 prove the first statement to be true. On the other hand, the last sentence of the same paragraph indicates that the LOFAR low-frequency radio telescope is used to pick-up the radio energy generated by the air shower.

Question 16 D

Question Type:Exception/Negative Question; Evaluation Question
Strategies: SI, attention to details; P2, P4, P8

While this question asks you to select what is NOT a quality of ANN, the terms used in the different options are not verbatim of the descriptions used in the passage. Hence, identifying the best answer requires inferring from the relevant paragraph.

First, you need to locate the part of the passage that discusses the various functions of ANN, which is Paragraph 2. Next, evaluate the statements within the paragraph. Sentence 3 pertains to the functions specified in **A**, **B**, **E**. Sentence 5 pertains to **C**.

Alternatively, you can look at Paragraph 8 to infer that (A) analyzing data, (B) solving problems, (C) recognizing patterns, and (E) calculating unknown solutions can be performed by the ANN. This leaves **D** as the only option, which is not mentioned.

Paragraph 4 does denote that ANN cannot replicate exact biological systems behavior. Therefore, **D** is the correct answer.

Question 17 A

Question Type: True False Statements (Two Statements)
Strategy: SI; P8 last sentence, P9 S2
In the last sentence of Paragraph 8, the first statement is found to be true while the latter is supported by Sentence 2 in Paragraph 9.

Question 18 B

Question Type: Evaluation Question (Implication)
Strategies: SI, attention to details; P5, S1 to S2
This question tests your interpretation of the first two sentences of Paragraph 5:

"The neuron is the basic foundation from which the network systems are constructed for both Biological Neural Networks and Artificial Neural Networks. Every neuron is a system that handles signals out of inputs since it is a MIMO system (multiple-input, multiple-output)."

Question 19 D

Question Type: Recall
Strategies: SI, PoE; P3, P5
This is another question that requires you to recall and infer information at the same time on particular parts of the passage. You may combine the process of elimination and careful understanding of information to narrow down the best choice.

In Paragraph 3 Sentences 4 and 5, the passage is clear in eliminating the neural net as (A) linear, (B) causal or (E) cause-oriented, and (C) effects-oriented. To further confirm your answer, going over the discussions in Paragraph 3 Sentence 6 and Paragraph 5 Sentence 4 would support the idea that the neural net is layered. The correct answer is **D**.

Question 20 B

Question Type: Recall
Strategy: SaL; P5 last sentence

Question 21 C

Question Type: Recall
Strategy:SaL; P5, S2

Question 22 A

Question Type: True False Statements (Two Statements); Evaluation Question (Implication)
Strategies: SaL, SI; P8 S1
This question combines an assessment of your recall and inference skills. The first statement can be easily confirmed with Paragraph 8 Sentence 1.

On the other hand, the second statement is generally implied in the passage. Some clues can be found in Paragraph 1 (". . . is based on the neuron's interconnection in the human brain's nervous system"), in Paragraph 2 ("ANN strives to simulate the firing of synapses."), and in Paragraph 11("The first work regarding the activity pattern of the human brain was published by William

James." and "The Computer and the Brain . . . showcased propositions about several radical changes in the means, which researchers use to model the brain.")

Question 23 B

Question Type: Exception/Negative Question
Strategies: SaL, never lose sight of the question; P6 S4 to S5
(A) Electrical is stated in Paragraph 6 Sentence 4 while (C) digital, (D) analog and (E) hybrid are stated in Sentence 5 of the same paragraph. Although (B) temporal is also stated, this time in Sentence 6, it refers to the simulation of hybrid elements and not by the neurons. Therefore, the correct answer is **B**.

Question 24 D

Question Type: Recall
Strategies: SI, never lose sight of the question; P6 S6
Although this is a recall question, it also requires simple inference since the correct option does not use the exact same terms used in the passage. Moreover, the other choices tend to trick you with qualities that are associated with either the neurons or the ANN. Take note that the question asks for a characteristic of the hybrid PE (Processing Element).

From Paragraph 6 Sentence 6, "hybrid elements simulate both temporal and spatial movements." Temporal means time while spatial means space. **D** is thus the best option.

Question 25 A

Question Type: Recall
Strategy: SaL; P10 S2

Question 26 E

Question Type: Recall
Strategies: SI; P8 S5 to S7
This is another type of recall question that also compels you to do a little inference because of the way the question stem and the choices are reworded from the passage. The answer is a paraphrase from Paragraph 8 Sentences 5 to 7.

Question 27 C

Question Type: Evaluation Question (Main Idea)
Strategy: SI; P5 S1
This question measures your overall comprehension of the similarities and differences discussed between ANN and BNN. The best support for this question can be found in Sentence 1 of Paragraph 5. The best answer is **C**.

Question 28 B

Question Type: Recall
Strategy: SI; P11 (1986) S2
This question needs you to be quick in locating the required information within the passage. At the same time, you need to carefully understand the brief description in order to match the paraphrased options.

Paragraph 11 is the summarization of the historical view of ANN and BNN. Under the 1986 data in Sentence 2, the purpose of backpropagation is stated as minimizing error functions in neural nets.

Question 29 B

Question Type: Exception/Negative Question
Strategies: SaL, PoE, attention to details; P7 S4 to S5, P11 (1958)
This question mixes up two significant points in the development of the ANN research:

1. The 1958 data denotes that "Frank Rosenblatt created the Mark I Perceptron computer at Cornell University."

2. Reviewing Paragraph 7, Sentences 4 and 5 tell us that Papert and Minsky wrote a book entitled Perceptrons discrediting the ANN research.

This means that the statement in B, which says "Papert and Minsky created the Perceptron," is incorrect. They wrote and published Perceptrons, not the Perceptron. It was Frank Rosenblatt who created the Perceptron.

Indeed, you need to pay close attention to the subtle differences in the information as you eliminate each option in order to determine the best answer.

A is supported by Paragraph 11 in the 1951 history of the ANN: "The first Artificial Neural Network was made by Marvin Minsky while he was at Princeton."

C and **D** are also explicitly stated in Paragraph 11 in the 1949 and the 1943 data of the ANN history, respectively.

For option **E**, you can infer from the 1986 overview in Paragraph 11 that this statement is also correct.

The best answer to this question is, therefore, **B**.

Question 30 B

Question Type: Recall
Strategies: SaL, attention to details; P6 last sentence

Question 31 B

Question Type: Evaluation Question (Implication)
Strategies: SI, attention to details; P9, P10
In this question, you will need to use contextual clues in order

to determine the best option. Paragraph 9 repeatedly emphasizes a priori as unnecessary in the processing of data with artificial neural networks. This idea is expressed using different terms such as "little amount of underlying theory" and "assumptions characterized by patterns are not needed by the neural networks." The closest answer is **B**.

(A) "Inherent mental structures" is not really mentioned in Paragraph 9. (C) "Guided training and (D) "expert systems" are mentioned in Paragraph 8, but they are not associated with a priori assumptions. (E) "Overtraining" and "generalizations" are also mentioned in the immediately following paragraph, but they are two separate albeit contextually associated concepts.

Question 32 B

Question Type: Recall
Strategy: SI; P9 S1
The answer to this question is a paraphrase of the first sentence in Paragraph 9.

Question 33 D

Question Type: Recall
Strategy: SaL; P6 S6

Question 34 C

Question Type: Evaluation Question (Implication)
Strategies: SI, PoE; P8
This question requires your understanding of the concepts discussed in Paragraph 8 and distinguish them from the succeeding information presented in the succeeding paragraphs. While algorithmic solutions are used when there is enough information and underlying theory, expert systems are useful when there is not enough theoretical background and data. The difference in the use of the two systems clearly relies on the amount of available data that they have to process.

(A) Analysis, (B) training, and (D) generalization are tasks that can be performed by the ANN, based on the amount of data fed to the network. (E) Neurons form as the basic framework of the ANN. This confirms C as the correct answer.

Question 35 C

Question Type: Exception/Negative Question
Strategy:SI; P2 S1, S6 and S7, P8 last sentence
Sentence 1 of Paragraph 2 states that ANN is a non-linear type of system. The last sentence cites the capacity of neural networks to generalize and recognize (A) noise-corrupted patterns and (B) similarities among assorted inputs. In the last sentence of Paragraph 8, artificial neural networks are also known to generalize (D) random patterns and (E) complex distributions. These narrow down our option to C as the exception to ANN's generalization capabilities.

Question 36. Answer: B

Question Type: Application Question
Strategies: SI, attention to details; P6 S2
By just looking at the pattern of the musical scale given in this question, you will find the numbers 1, 2, 3, 5, 8, and 13 coinciding with the Fibonacci sequence of 0, 1, 1, 2, 3, 5, 8, 13 discussed in Paragraph 2. This makes **B** as the best answer.

A is wrong because, as Sentence 1 of Paragraph 2 indicates, the Greek octave has only 5 notes while the question specifies an octave of 8 notes. **C** is too general to be the best match for this question. Fractals, according to Paragraph 10, are visual patterns that show a replicating sequence, which could be based on the Fibonacci numbers or ANY OTHER system.

D sounds off: the question describes a musical scale, which does not equate a technique. On the other hand, **E** sounds like a probable option. However, you must remember that determining whether the golden section is observed or not in a musical composition requires looking at the ratio of the various rhythmic scales or melodic lines. You would not be able to tell if a golden section is present or not by taking just a single musical scale into account.

Question 37 D

Question Type: Exception/Negative Question
Strategies: SaL, prior knowledge, attention to details; P10 S7
The quickest way to answer this question is to consider which of the options would not have visible traits and patterns. Only the (D) wind has a gaseous property and therefore, difficult to visually observe any pattern. Moreover, it can exhibit erratic traits such as direction and speed to create any regular, self-replicating form.

In the second to the last sentence of Paragraph 7, the passage names the (C) circulatory system and (E) broccoli as examples of fractals in nature. From common knowledge, (A) snowflakes are known examples of fractals while (B) lightning does exhibit some sort of a repeating pattern.

Question 38 D

Question Type: Evaluation Question (Implication)
Strategies: SI, paraphrasing, attention to details; P3 S4
This question requires your ability to interpret the information given in Paragraph 3. Sentence 4 of this paragraph specifically states that the octave in a guitar "should be half the distance between the bridge at the lower end of the guitar and the nut where the strings cross over at the top of the guitar." This essentially implies the octave to be the middle point on a string in a guitar. The best answer is **D**.

The other answers are meant to mislead you to either draw from or assume that you need prior knowledge in music in order to answer this question.

Question 39 B

Question Type: Evaluation Question (Main Idea)
Strategies: SI, PoE; P6 S1
In Paragraph 6, the golden ratio is defined as two quantities having a ratio of the sum of to the larger quantity equaling the ratio of the larger quantity to the smaller one. This clearly eliminates **C**: no mention is made about the quantities being raised to an exponent.

A is a probable paraphrase except that it uses the term "sequentially" while the passage's definition implies equality. The same is the case in **D**: the golden section does not necessarily require an "expanding sequence" although this is usually a resulting pattern. The closest choice is **B** as the phrase "in the same way that" connotes an equal correspondence of the quantities.

Question 40 B

Question Type: Recall
Strategies: SaL, PoE; P12 S1

Question 41 C

Question Type: Evaluation Question (Main Idea)
Strategy: SI; P11, P12
This question requires your comprehension of Paragraph 11's main idea. Knowing the meaning of the word "paradox" would also help you determine the answer accurately.

"Paradox" means self-contradictory or contrary to common opinion. This is already indicated in Paragraph 11 Sentence 1: "One would expect that the construction of such complex shapes would require complex rules, but in reality, the algorithms (equations) that generate fractals are typically extraordinarily simple." Option C rephrases this idea.

Option **A**, although verbatim from Paragraph 11 as well, cannot be the correct answer. The statement that the algorithms of fractals involve loops is simply a confirmation – not a paradox – that the repeating equations ('loops"), albeit simple, can produce such visually-rich results. This is further confirmed in Paragraph 12 Sentence 5.

B, **D**, and **E** do not also state a paradox. Rather, these either describe or support the mechanics behind fractals.

Question 42 B

Question Type: Recall
Strategy: SaL; P8 S1

Question 43 A

Question Type: True False Statements (Two Statements)
Strategies: SaL; P2 S4, P7 S1

Question 44 A

Question Type: Application Question
Strategies: SI, attention to details; P4
In Sentence 1 of paragraph 4, musical notation in the Western system, "the frequency ratio 1:2 is generally identified as an octave." This means that the note an octave below 400Hz is 200Hz while the note above it is 800 Hz. The answer is A.

Question 45 D

Question Type: Recall
Strategies: SaL, SI, P10, S3

Question 46 D

Question Type: Evaluation Question (Main Idea)
Strategies: PoE, OA, SI; P1, P5, P14, P15
A quick way to deal with this question is to eliminate the most obvious wrong answers first. A is quite absolute in stating that math can be found in ALL music. Paragraph 14 notes, "Many algorithms that have no immediate musical relevance are used by composers as creative inspiration for their music." This means that mathematics is not really present in all music, but they merely serve as springboard for some – but not all – musicians.

C, on the other hand, is too specific. The passage does not solely discuss about the golden ratio or the Fibonacci numbers. **E** sounds somewhat possible. Still, nothing in the passage confirms the duplication of music and math in terms of content, at the very least. This leaves our possible choices between **B** and **D**.

The passage has indeed demonstrated that musical compositions and structures can be analyzed through the (B) use of mathematical patterns. However, this concept can also be included in the more encompassing statement found in option **D** – that is, "an intricate yet measurable relationship between music and math" has been observed and is being utilized by some composers through the use of math principles and algorithms. The best answer is **D**.

Question 47 A

Type of Question: Recall
Strategy: SaL; P13 S2

Question 48 C

Question Type: True False Statements (Statement and Reason)
Strategies: Sal and SI; P4
The first statement "The name of a note an octave above A is also A" is verbatim of Sentence 5 in Paragraph 4. However, the reason for this has to do with octave equivalency, which considers two notes an octave apart (for example, an octave above A) basically the same except in pitch. Hence, notes an octave apart are given the same note name (in the given example, also named A).

The reason given in the question, that the duplication in a note's name has to do with its combination with another note, is therefore, wrong.

Question 49 D

Question Type: Evaluation Question (Main Idea)
Strategies: PoE, OA, attention to details; P17
Similar to Question 46, the correct answer can be easily determined through a process of elimination. In addition, you have to note that the question specifically asks for the most possible closing statement for the last paragraph of the passage. This means that you also have to consider both the general idea of the passage AND the last few statements that will best connect to the given options.

The phrasing of Option **A** makes this choice wrong because it emphasizes math as the main subject of the passage. The passage, as well as the last paragraph, revolves around the relationship between math and music.

B is a true-sounding statement, but this is not mentioned anywhere in the passage or the last few paragraphs.

In Option **C**, the first half of the statement sounds applicable to the main idea of the passage. However, the second idea about mathematicians and musicians liking the other's discipline is not clearly suggested in the passage or the last paragraph.

This leaves **D** as the only best choice. Indeed, the last paragraph refers to certain mathematical applications or algorithms being employed to create beautiful music. This statement also applies to the idea of the passage in general.

Question 50 B

Type of Question: Recall
Strategy: SaL; P1 last sentence

Question 1 A

See: QR 3.2, 3.2.1, 8.2, 8.2.1
This is a rate problem with two initial values and two rates of growth. These can be combined into two expressions, one of Stephen's height and one of John's height. Let t be a variable for time in months:

Stephen: 4 ft + (.5 in/2 mo) t

John: 3 ft 10 in + (1 in/3 mo) t

Keeping track of units of measurement is very important in this kind of problem! Let's simplify these expressions by converting feet to inches. Remember, 12 inches to a foot. This gives:

Stephen: 48 in + t (1/4) in/mo

John: 46 in + t (1/3) in/mo

To find the time when their heights will be the same, simply set these expressions equal to each other and solve for t:

$$48 \text{ in} + t\,(1/4) \text{ in/mo} = 46 \text{ in} + t\,(1/3) \text{ in/mo}$$

$$2 \text{ in} = (t/12) \text{ in/mo}$$

$$t = 24 \text{ mo}$$

Finally, to find the height they will both be after 24 months, plug 24 back into the original expressions:

Stephen: 4 ft + (.5 in/2 mo) 24 = 4ft + 6in

John: 3ft 10 in + (1in/3 mo) 24 = 4ft + 6 in

Note: Evaluating both expressions is a quick way to check your work. If they aren't equal, something is wrong with your solution.

Question 2 E

See: QR 4.6, 4.6.1
First add 7 to both sides to set the quadratic equation equal to zero:

$$x^2 - 7x + 12 = 0 .$$

Next, check if you can factor the quadratic equation easily. In this case, you can:

$$(x-3)(x-4) = 0$$

$$(x-3) = 0 \text{ or } (x-4) = 0$$

$$x = 3 \text{ or } x = 4$$

Question 3 C

See: QR 7.2, 7.2.2
Remember, the "mean" is the average value of the set of numbers. Add the numbers together and divide by how many there are:

$$(7+7+8+10+13)/5 = 9 .$$

Question 4 A

See: QR 5.2, 5.2.2
Read the question carefully! It says this is an equilateral triangle, which means all of the sides are the same length and all of the angles are 60°.

Question 5 D

See: QR 7.1

First we need to find the probability that a single roll will turn up an even number. There are three possible even numbers (2, 4, and 6) out of six total possible outcomes. So the probability of rolling an even number once is:

$$p = 3/6 = 1/2.$$

Now to find the odds of rolling three even numbers in a row, multiply:

$$(p)(p)(p) = (1/2)(1/2)(1/2) = 1/8.$$

Question 6 C

See: QR 4.1, 4.1.4

We can treat $f(x) = 2f(x)$ as an algebraic equation with $f(x)$ as the variable. All we need to do is solve for $f(x)$. Subtracting $f(x)$ from both sides gives:

$$0 = f(x)$$

The function is equal to zero, no matter what x we put in. So $f(1) = 0$ is the solution.

Question 7 D

See: QR 2.4.3, 8.3

We are looking for the amount of berries produced over the course of two years. All we need to do is find the number produced in the first year and add it to the number produced in the second year. Let x be the number produced in year 1 and y be the number produced in year 2. Then:

$$x = .30\,(400) = 120$$

$$y = .85\,(400) = 340$$

$$\text{Total} = x + y = 120 + 340 = 460.$$

Question 8 D

See: QR 2.6

We are given the identity 2 km = 1.2 mi. We want to find an identity for 3.5 mi. If we divide both sides by 1.2, the right hand side will be 1 mi and we can then multiply by 3.5 to obtain:

$$(3.5/1.2)\ 2\text{ km} = 3.5\text{ mi}$$

The expression on the left is the solution we are looking for. Since the problem asks for an approximation, there are many ways we can approach it. Here is a simple one. Start with (3.5/1.2) 2 = 7/1.2. Now convert 1.2 to the fraction 6/5.

$$7/1.2 = 7/(6/5) = (7 \times 5)/6 = 35/6$$

All we need to do now is approximate 35/6. Notice:

$$35/6 = (36/6) - (1/6) = 6 - 1/6$$

But 1/6 is just a bit less than 1/5 = .2, so we can approximate the expression by:

$$6 - .2 = 5.8.$$

Question 9 D

See: QR 6.1, 6.1.4, 6.2, 6.2.1

Remember the definition of cotangent as cosine/sine. Also notice that $7\pi/6$ is in the lower left quadrant of the unit circle, where both cosine and sine are negative. These negatives will cancel and cotangent will be positive, the same as it is in the upper right quadrant. So:

$$\cot(7\pi/6) = \cot(\pi/6)$$

$$= \cos(\pi/6)/\sin(\pi/6)$$

$$= (\sqrt{3}/2)/(1/2)$$

$$= \sqrt{3}$$

Question 10 B

See: QR 5.1, 5.1.1, 5.2, 5.2.2, 6.1, 6.1.1

The key in this problem is to think of the line from the origin to the point (5 , 1) as the hypotenuse of a right triangle with legs of length 5 (along the x-axis) and 1. Then we can use the identity $\sin\theta$ = opposite/hypotenuse. The opposite leg has length 1. We can use the Pythagorean Theorem to find the length of the hypotenuse:

$$5^2 + 1^2 = c^2$$

$$c^2 = 26$$

$$c = \sqrt{26}$$

Therefore $\sin\theta = 1/\sqrt{26}$.

Question 11 C

See: QR 2.6, 3.2, 3.2.1

We are given the identity 1 cup = 360 g. We want to know how many cups are in 20 kg, so the first thing to do is convert grams to kilograms. Remember, 1 kg = 1000 g, so:

$$1\text{ cup} = (360/1000)\text{ kg} = 0.36\text{ kg}$$

Now set up the ratios, cross multiply, and solve for the unknown variable:

$$0.36\text{kg}/1\text{cup} = 20\text{kg}/x\text{ cups}$$

$$0.36x = 20$$

$$x = 20/0.36 = 2000/36 = 500/9$$

We can avoid finding the exact solution to this if we just notice that 500/9 is a little more than 500/10 = 50. The only solution close to 50 is 55.6.

Question 12 E

See: QR 2.5, 2.5.2

Since the solution options are all multiples of 1.5, we only need to figure out the order of magnitude. First consider the powers of 10:

$$(10^3 \times 10^8)/10^7 = 10^{11}/10^7 = 10^4$$

Now consider the multipliers. They approximately equal $(7 \times 4)/2 = 14$. So we have:

$$14 \times 10^4 = 1.4 \times 10^5$$

Therefore the correct answer is 1.5×10^5.

Question 13 C

See: QR 5.2, 5.2.2, 6.3, 6.3.3

The diagonal of a rectangle forms the hypotenuse of a right triangle. The legs are the sides of the triangle, in this case of length 3 and 5. To find the length of the diagonal, use the Pythagorean Theorem:

$$c^2 = 3^2 + 5^2 = 9 + 25 = 34$$

$$c = \sqrt{34}\,.$$

Question 14 E

See: QR 3.1, 3.1.1

We can convert the hours and the days to minutes separately, and add all of the resulting minutes together to get the total:

$$\text{Total} = 26\text{ min} + 14\text{ hr}\,(60\text{ min}/1\text{ hr}) + 3\text{ days}\,(24\text{ hr}/1\text{ day})(60\text{ min}/1\text{ hr})$$

$$= 26\text{ min} + 14\,(60\text{ min}) + 3\,(24)(60\text{ min})$$

$$= 26\text{ min} + 840\text{ min} + 4320\text{ min}$$

$$= 5186.$$

Question 15 B

See: QR 5.2, 5.2.3, 6.3, 6.3.3

The key in this problem is that the diagonal of a square inscribed in a circle is the diameter of the circle.

$$\text{Diameter} = 2 \times \text{radius} = 2 \times 3 = 6$$

The sides of any rectangle and its diagonal are related by the Pythagorean Theorem. Since all sides of a square are the same length a, we can use $b = a, c = 6$:

$$6^2 = a^2 + a^2$$

$$36 = 2a^2$$

$$18 = a^2$$

$$a = \sqrt{18} = 3\sqrt{2}\,.$$

Question 16 E

See: QR 2.4, 2.4.2

This problem translates to an equation with fractions on either side:

$$3x/6y = 5xy/Z$$

Z is the value we are looking for. We can reduce the fraction on the left, and then cross multiply:

$$x/2y = 5xy/Z$$

$$Zx = 10xy^2$$

$$Z = 10y^2\,.$$

Question 17 B

See: QR 4.1, 4.1.1, 4.3, 4.3.1

First we want to get rid of the parentheses by distributing the 2:

$$(3x + 2)2 - x = 6$$

$$6x + 4 - x = 6$$

Next, combine like terms:

$$5x + 4 = 6$$

Next isolate the x term on one side:

$$5x = 2$$

Finally we want a single x on the left, so divide both sides by 5:

$$x = 2/5\,.$$

Question 18 E

See: QR 6.1, 6.1.2

Use the trigonometric identity $\cos\theta$ = Adjacent / Hypotenuse. This gives:

$$\cos 30^\circ = S/4$$

$$\sqrt{3}/2 = S/4$$

$$S = 2\sqrt{3}\,.$$

Question 19 B

See: QR 6.1, 6.1.4, 6.2, 6.2.1
Since cosecant = 1/cosine, we know that:

$$1/(\cos x) = 2/\sqrt{3}$$

$$\cos x = \sqrt{3}/2$$

Whenever $\cos x$ is $\sqrt{3}/2$, $\sin x$ is either ½ or –½ depending on which quadrant of the unit circle x falls into. Since we are given that $\sqrt{3}/2 < x < 2\pi$ we know x is in the lower right quadrant. Therefore $x = 11\pi/6$ and $\sin x = -½$.

Question 20 E

See: QR 4.2, 4.2.2
Before we worry about the different options given, let's isolate the x terms on one side and the constants on the other:

$$(2/x) + 3 > 5 - (1/x) = (3/x) > 2 = (1/x) > (2/3)$$

Now be careful. It is tempting to multiply through by x to try and clear the denominator, but we don't know whether x is negative or positive. If it is negative, the direction of the inequality will change. We cannot tell whether (c) or (d) is the correct inequality. Therefore we can only say that (a) must be true.

Question 21 A

See: QR 5.3, 5.3.3
The surface area of a cylinder is:

A = (circumference of its base) × (height) + 2(area of base)

$$A = (2\pi r)(h) + 2(\pi r^2)$$

The radius of the base r = diameter x ½ = 3.

$$A = (6\pi \text{ cm})(10 \text{ cm}) + 18\pi \text{ cm}^2 = 78\pi \text{ cm}^2$$

To approximate this value, let $\pi = 3.1$

$$A = 78 \times 3.1 \text{ cm}^2 \approx 242$$

So the best approximation given is 245.

Question 22 B

See: QR 2.6
This is a ratio problem. You can think of it as asking, 65 miles is to 1 hour as 25 miles is to x hours. Mathematically, set it up like this:

$$65\text{mi}/1\text{hr} = 25\text{mi}/x$$

All we have to do now is cross multiply and solve for x.

$$65x = 25$$

$$x = 25/65 = 5/13 .$$

Question 23 B

See: QR 2.2, 2.2.3
Since this is an approximation problem, we can save time by rounding the given values to the nearest integer before doing any operations. \$39.99 becomes \$40 and \$15.75 becomes \$16. Then the total spent is approximately:

3(\$40) + 4(\$16) + 12(\$3)

= \$120 + \$64 + \$36

= \$220 .

Question 24 B

See: QR 2.4, 4.2
Convert 75% to a fraction, then multiply the two fractions together:

75% = 3/4

So 75% of 7/2 is:

$$(3/4)(7/2) = 21/8 .$$

Question 25 C

See: QR 2.5, 2.5.2
This question is asking the value of y in the equation:

$$(5.97 \times 10^{24})\, y = 1.90 \times 10^{27}$$

Since this is an approximation problem, it will make things easier if we round $5.97 \approx 6$ and $1.90 \approx 2$. Then:

$$y \approx (2 \times 10^{27})/(6 \times 10^{24})$$

$$= (1/3) \times (10^3) \approx .33 \times 10^3$$

$$= 3.3 \times 10^2$$

Our approximation is slightly different than the solution given due to different rounding, but clearly the correct answer is 3.2×10^2.

Question 26 E

See: QR 2.6
This is a ratio problem. We can write it in equation form like this:

$$2.2\text{lb}/1\text{kg} = x\text{ lb}/4.5\text{kg}$$

Now cross multiply and solve for x:

$$x = (2.2)(4.5) = 9.9 .$$

Question 27 C

See: QR 4.5, 4.5.2, 5.1, 5.1.1

We can use the properties of right triangles to solve this problem. Simply think of the line segment connecting the two points as the hypotenuse of a right triangle. Drawing a picture can help you visualize this. The lengths of two legs of the triangle are the horizontal and vertical distance between the points given:

$$x = 10 - (-2) = 12 \text{ and } y = 6 - 1 = 5$$

Now we can use the Pythagorean theorem to find the hypotenuse:

$$c^2 = 12^2 + 5^2 = 144 + 25 = 169$$

$$c = 13\,.$$

Note: this is a 5-12-13 triangle. If you memorize this relationship, you can save time by skipping the last calculation.

Question 28 A

See: QR 7.1, 7.1.2

First add the number of blue and yellow marbles to find the total, 20 marbles in the container. The probability of the first ball drawn being yellow is:

$$(\#\text{ yellow})/(\text{total }\#\text{ of marbles}) = 8/20 = 2/5$$

Since the problem specifies that there is no replacement the probability of the second ball being yellow is:

$$(\text{new }\#\text{ yellow})/(\text{new total }\#) = 7/19$$

The odds of both events happening is equal to the product of their individual probabilities:

$$P = (2/5)(7/19) = 14/95\,.$$

Question 29 E

See: QR 4.5, 4.5.4

To define a line we only need 2 points in a plane, so the problem gives more information than is necessary. We can pick 2 of the 3 points to use. To make calculations easier, choose any point with 0's or 1's first, then opt for points with integers closest to 0. In this case let's use (1 , 0) and (–1 , 3) to find an equation for the line in slope-intercept form:

$$y = (\text{slope})x + (y\text{–intercept})$$

Remember, slope = rise/run:

$$\text{slope} = (0-3)/[1-(-1)] = -(3/2)$$

$$y = -(3/2)x + b$$

To find b, plug a point into this equation (the point (1 , 0) will be easiest to use):

$$0 = -(3/2)1 + b$$

$$3/2 = b$$

So the final equation is:

$$y = -(3/2)x + (3/2)$$

But this doesn't appear as a solution option, so we need to try putting (c) (d) and (e) in slope-intercept form. It makes since to start with (e) since there are 2's and 3's as coefficients in it. When we rearrange, we see that (e) is in fact correct.

Question 30 C

See: QR 2.4, 2.4.2

First convert the integers to fractions with denominator 5, then combine:

$$[2 - (6/5)]\,/\,[1 + (2/5)]$$

$$= [10/5 - (6/5)]\,/\,[5/5 + (2/5)]$$

$$= (4/5)\,/\,(7/5)$$

$$= 4/7\,.$$

Question 31 E

See: QR 2.6

Since there are 7 men to every 4 women, 7 out of every 11 students are men. So 7/11 of the students are men. Multiplying this by the total number of students, we get:

$$(7/11)(143) = (7)(13) = 91\,.$$

Question 32 B

See: QR 2.4, 2.4.1

Options (c) (d) and (e) are easy to rule out since they are all greater than 1/2, whereas (b) is less than 1/2. The tricky one is (a). Here is a shortcut: using the fact that $\sqrt{3} < \sqrt{4} = 2$, we know that $1/\sqrt{3} > 1/2$. So the only solution less than 1/2 is 11/23.

Question 33 A

See: QR 2.4, 2.41, 2.4.2

First get rid of all decimals because the fractions are easier to work with. Multiply the left side by (100/100) and both sides by 10:

$$(60/270)(81/x) = 54$$

Now cancel common factors and solve:

$$(2/9)(81/x) = 54$$

$$(2)(9/x) = 54$$

$$1/x = 3$$

$$x = 1/3\,.$$

Question 34 D

See: QR 8.2, 8.2.3

This is essentially a compound interest problem. We have a present value of 4 meters, and a growth rate of 1.4 per year. So after three years:

$$\text{Future Height} = 4(1.40)3 = 10.976 \approx 11$$

But the problem is asking for the change in height, not the height itself. Therefore the solution is:

$$\text{Future Height} - \text{Present Height} = 11 - 4 = 7\,.$$

Question 35 B

See: QR 4.3, 4.3.1, 4.3.3

Notice that there are a lot of binomials hanging around this equation. First look for ways to cancel whole binomials, since that would simplify the equation quickly. Before we do that, though, we need to factor $(x^2 - x - 6)$. We need a two numbers whose sum is −1 and whose product is −6. −3 and 2 work. So:

$$(x^2 - x - 6) = (x - 3)(x + 2)$$

Multiplying the equation through by this factorization we get:

$$2(x - 3)/3 + 3(x + 2) = (5x - 1)$$

Distribute the coefficients and combine like terms, then solve for x:

$$(2x - 6)/3 + 3x + 6 = 5x - 1$$

$$(2x - 6)/3 = 2x - 7$$

$$2x - 6 = 6x - 21$$

$$15 = 4x$$

$$x = 15/4\,.$$

Question 36 C

See: QR 2.2, 2.2.1

Round 9.7 up to 10 and round 17.4 down to 17. Since we rounded one value up and the other down, at least a portion of the error will cancel itself out, but to be sure we are obtaining a close enough approximation (and assuming you have enough time) you can always multiply the original numbers for an exact solution.

$$10 \times 17 = 170.$$

Question 37 E

See: QR 3.1, 3.1.1, 8.2, 8.2.2

The total trip was 18 min + 12 min = 30 min long. Over these 30 minutes, the average speed was 28 mph. First find the total distance travelled, then divide by 2 to get the one-way distance from the house to the store:

$$(28 \text{ mph})(30 \text{ min}) = (28 \text{ mph})(1/2 \text{ hr}) = 14 \text{ miles}$$

$$14 \text{ miles} \div 2 = 7 \text{ miles}$$

Now we can solve for the value we are looking for. We know the distance (7 miles) and the amount of time it took to cover that distance (12 min):

$$x = (7 \text{ miles})/(12 \text{ min})$$

$$= (7 \text{ miles})/(1/5 \text{ hr})$$

$$= (7)(5) \text{ mph}$$

$$= 35 \text{ mph}\,.$$

Question 38 D

See: QR 7.1, 7.1.2

There are three events in this problem: the first green ball drawn, the second green ball drawn, and finally a red ball drawn. The probability of all three of them happening is equal to their individual probabilities multiplied together. Remember, the second and third events are dependent on the previous ones because the problem specifies that the balls are not replaced:

$$P(\text{1st ball is green}) = 3/9$$

$$P(\text{2nd ball is green, given the 1st was green}) = 2/8$$

$$P(\text{3rd ball is red, given the 1st and 2nd were green}) = 6/7$$

$$P(\text{all three}) = (3/9)(2/8)(6/7) = 1/14\,.$$

Question 39 A

See: QR 2.4.3, 8.3, 8.3.3

To find the percentage of juice in the mixture we need to find the weighted average of the ingredients:

$$[(0)2\text{cups} + (0.9)1\text{cup} + (0.6)3\text{cups}]/6 \text{ cups}$$

$$= 2.7/6$$

$$= 0.45 = 45\%\,.$$

Question 40 D

See: QR 7.2, 7.2.2

A good strategy for this problem is to convert all the fractions so they have the same least common denominator. In this case, 12:

4/12 got a 10

1/12 got a 9

3/12 got an 8

The rest = (12 – 8)/12 = 4/12 got a 7

Now we can think of the class as having 12 students total in it. Then the score breakdown is:

$$\{10, 10, 10, 10, 9, 8, 8, 8, 7, 7, 7, 7\}$$

To find the median, count 6 from either side and draw a line:

$$\{10, 10, 10, 10, 9, 8 \mid 8, 8, 7, 7, 7, 7\}$$

The median is the average of the two numbers on either side of the line, in this case 8 and 8. So the median is 8.